business essentials

FOURTEENTH EDITION

Ronald J. Ebert

Ricky W. Griffin

Please contact www.AskPearsonSupport.com with any queries on this content.
Please contact us with concerns about any potential bias at https://www.pearson.com/report-bias.html
You can learn more about Pearson's commitment to accessibility at https://www.pearson.com/us/accessibility.html

Cover Image by toozdesign/Shutterstock and Kuliperko/Shutterstock.

Library of Congress Control Number: 2024930209

1 2024

ISBN 10: 0-13-807244-2
ISBN 13: 978-0-13-807244-5

For Griffin, who is so curious about our world.
—R. W. G.

brief contents

Appendices

contents

preface

Wearing the Hats

There's an old adage about people wearing different "hats." This usually means that people have different roles to play in different settings. For example, your roles may include student, child, spouse, partner, employee, friend, and/or parent. Each of these roles needs a different hat—when you play the role of a student, for example, you wear one hat, but when you go to your part-time job, you put on a different hat. From the perspective of business, there are a variety of different hats that you might wear:

- ***The employee hat.*** One hat is as an employee working for a business. Many people wear this hat during the early stages of their career. To wear the hat successfully, you will need to understand your place in the organization—your job, how to work with others, and so on. You'll begin to see how to best wear this hat as you study organizing business enterprises in Chapter 6 and how organizations manage people in Chapter 10, as well as in several other places in this book.
- ***The employer or boss hat.*** It is also likely that one day other people will be working for you. You'll still have your own job responsibilities, of course. But you'll now also need to know how to manage other people—how to understand, lead, and motivate them and the social and legal parameters that affect how you deal with them. Chapters 3, 5, 8, and 9 provide information about how you can best wear this hat, although the manager's hat runs throughout the entire book.
- ***The consumer hat.*** Even if you don't work for a business, you will still wear the hat of a consumer. Whenever you fill your car at Shell, buy an airline ticket from Delta and charge it on Visa, order a new backpack from Amazon, buy clothes at H&M, or stream a movie on Netflix, you're consuming products created by business. To wear this hat effectively, you need to know how to assess the value of what you're buying, your rights as a consumer, and so on. We discuss how you can best wear this hat in Chapters 4, 7, 11, 12, and 13.
- ***The investor hat.*** The final business hat is that of an investor. You may buy a business or work for a company that lets you buy its stock. You may also invest in companies by buying their stock or shares of a mutual fund. For you to invest wisely, you must understand some basics, such as financial markets, business earnings, and the costs of investment. Chapters 4, 15, 16, and 17 and Appendix III will help you learn how to best wear this hat.

Many people wear more than one of these hats at the same time. Regardless of how many hats you wear or when you may be putting them on, it should be clear that you have in the past, do now, and will in the future interface with many businesses in different ways. Knowing how to best wear all these hats is what this book is all about.

New to This Edition

Chapter Updates

All facts, figures, and examples have been updated throughout the book to reflect the most current information available, such as the effects of the COVID-19 pandemic and advances in artificial intelligence. Similarly, all the end-of-chapter material has been revised and updated. Detailed chapter-by-chapter updates are summarized below.

Chapter 1

- Updated opening case about Harley Davidson
- New Finding a Better Way case about artificial intelligence
- Updated Entrepreneurship and New Ventures case about Brooklinen
- Updated Managing in Turbulent Times case about COVID-19
- Economic and financial data updated to the most current figures available

Chapter 2

- New opening case about Patagonia
- Updated Entrepreneurship and New Ventures case about Dan Price
- New Finding a Better Way case about Ally Financial
- Updated Managing in Turbulent Times case about the Honey Pot and Bea Dixon
- Economic and financial data updated to the most current figures available

Chapter 3

- New opening case about In-N-Out
- Updated Entrepreneurship and New Ventures case about InVenture
- Updated Finding a Better Way case about the gig economy
- Updated Managing in Turbulent Times case about Shake Shack
- Economic and financial data updated to the most current figures available

Chapter 4

- New opening case about Disney theme parks
- Updated Entrepreneurship and New Ventures case about women entrepreneurs
- Updated Finding a Better Way case about trade with Mexico
- New Managing in Turbulent Times case about the war in Ukraine
- New integrative case about Starbucks
- Economic and financial data updated to the most current figures available

Chapter 5

- Updated opening case about Alphabet
- Updated Entrepreneurship and New Ventures case about Kahn Academy
- New Finding a Better Way case about Airbnb
- Updated Managing in Turbulent Times case about crisis management
- Economic and financial data updated to the most current figures available

Chapter 6

- New opening case about REI
- Updated Entrepreneurship and New Ventures case about Valve Software
- New Finding a Better Way case about Spotify
- Updated Managing in Turbulent Times case about Illinois Tool Works
- Economic and financial data updated to the most current figures available

Chapter 7

- Updated opening case about the Cheesecake Factory
- New Entrepreneurship and New Ventures case about Breeco and Solo Stove
- New Finding a Better Way case about SSAB
- Updated Managing in Turbulent Times case about the airline industry
- Economic and financial data updated to the most current figures available
- New integrative case about Starbucks

Chapter 8

- Updated opening case about Hilton
- New Entrepreneurship and New Ventures case about Big Start Transit, LLC
- Updated Finding a Better Way case about Cirque de Soleil
- New Managing in Turbulent Times case about LGBTQIA+ rights in the workplace
- Economic and financial data updated to the most current figures available

Chapter 9

- New opening case about Rihanna
- Updated Entrepreneurship and New Ventures case about John DeJoria
- Updated Finding a Better Way case about Ruzwana Bashir
- New Managing in Turbulent Times case about controversy in the beer industry
- Economic and financial data updated to the most current figures available

Chapter 10

- Updated opening case about Wegmans
- New Entrepreneurship and New Ventures case about entrepreneurs in the C-Suite
- New Finding a Better Way case about Ping
- New Managing in Turbulent Times case about unionization
- Economic and financial data updated to the most current figures available
- New integrative case about Starbucks

Chapter 11

- Updated opening case about Ikea
- New Entrepreneurship and New Ventures case about Bloom Season
- New Finding a Better Way case about HERide
- Updated Managing in Turbulent Times case about Iconik
- Economic and financial data updated to the most current figures available

Chapter 12

- Updated opening case about Louis Vuitton
- Updated Entrepreneurship and New Ventures case about BedInABox
- New Finding a Better Way case about MyChart

- Updated Managing in Turbulent Times case about Uber
- Economic and financial data updated to the most current figures available

Chapter 13

- Revised opening case about Kiva Systems
- Updated Entrepreneurship and New Ventures case about Algramo
- Updated Finding a Better Way case about innovations in shopping
- New Managing in Turbulent Times case about Teton Trade Cloth
- Economic and financial data updated to the most current figures available
- New integrative case about Starbucks

Chapter 14

- New opening case about cybercrime
- New Entrepreneurship and New Ventures case about technology
- New Finding a Better Way case about artificial intelligence
- New Managing in Turbulent Times case about ransomware
- Economic and financial data updated to the most current figures available

Chapter 15

- New opening case about securities fraud
- Updated Entrepreneurship and New Ventures case about Collins Street Bakery
- New Finding a Better Way case about integrated financial statements
- Updated Managing in Turbulent Times case about IFRS
- Economic and financial data updated to the most current figures available
- New integrative case about Starbucks

Chapter 16

- New opening case about the Federal Reserve System
- Updated Entrepreneurship and New Ventures case about BlackRock
- New Finding a Better Way case about Bitcoin
- New Managing in Turbulent Times case about bank failures
- Economic and financial data updated to the most current figures available

Chapter 17

- Updated opening case about Fogo de Chão
- Updated Entrepreneurship and New Ventures case about microlending
- New Finding a Better Way case about angel investors
- New Managing in Turbulent Times case about WeWork
- Economic and financial data updated to the most current figures available
- New integrative case about Starbucks

Other Features

This edition further refines the Integrative Learning Portfolio introduced in the 13th edition, found at the end of each part. The three elements in each of these features are intended to help integrate various topics across different chapters, helping solve a common challenge faced by students in Introduction to Business. One element is called *Crafting a Business Plan*. This element focuses on the various stages in developing a business plan. The second element is an integrative case focusing on Starbucks. Over the course of all six parts of the book, this case illustrates all aspects of business as they relate to Starbucks. Finally, the third element is called *Finding Your Path*. This element looks at job market trends, starting salaries, and various career paths. In addition, each also has an employability component that examines how students can improve their prospects for finding an attractive job.

Cases

As described previously, all cases have been updated or replaced. Covering a wide variety of topics and organizations spanning numerous industries, including companies like Airbnb, Spotify, Netflix, and Uber, and growing topics like Artificial Intelligence (AI) and the gig economy, these real-world cases introduce relatable topics that draw students into the content of each chapter.

Steve Cho/Penta Press/Shutterstock

Transformational Leadership

Barbados-born Robyn Rihanna Fenty—better known as simply Rihanna—burst onto the music scene at age 17 and rocketed to fame with her song "Pon de Replay." Her debut single sold over 4 million copies and hit number two on the UK pop charts. She has since released seven more albums, has become one of the best-selling digital artists of all time, and is one of the youngest self-made female billionaires.

It may be surprising, then, to know that Rihanna made most of her money outside the studio as a multi-platform entrepreneur. Her makeup and skincare line, Fenty

Current Events

The author has added new coverage of the rapid growth of AI, the lingering impact of COVID-19, changing employment relationships, changing labor relations and demographics, inflation, and Environmental, Social, and Corporate Governance (ESG). He has also added coverage of emerging new employment relationships. All data and statistics have also been updated to the most current information available.

End-of-Chapter Activities

Five kinds of chapter-ending involvement activities—to reinforce and practice the use of chapter concepts—are included in this edition, and all have been updated for continued currency and relevance for students.

questions & exercises

QUESTIONS FOR REVIEW

4-1. What are the advantages and disadvantages of globalization? Give examples.

4-2. What are the three possible levels of involvement in international business? Give examples of each.

4-3. What are the elements of national competitive advantage? Give a current, real-world example of each condition.

4-4. Describe the five international organizational structures.

QUESTIONS FOR ANALYSIS

4-5. Make a list of five things you own, such as an item of furniture, a vehicle, electronics, and other consumer goods, making sure that each one was made in a different country. Develop a hypothesis about why each product was made in that particular country.

4-6. Assume your lumber company made a $1 million sale to a Japanese company on April 6, 2023, when the exchange rate was 131.56 yen to US$1. If the customer paid on April 28 when the exchange rate was 136.15 yen to US$1, how much did your company gain or lose on the transaction? (*Hint*: The invoice was for 131,560,000 yen. How much did your company receive on April 28?) During that time, did the dollar grow stronger against the yen or weaker?

4-7. Research and identify a protectionist tariff imposed by the United States. Do you support that tariff? If so, why?

4-8. Do you think that a firm operating internationally is better advised to adopt a single standard of ethical conduct or to adapt to local conditions? What are the advantages and disadvantages of adapting to local conditions?

APPLICATION EXERCISES

4-9. Identify a manufactured product (car, bike, computer, etc.) you think is made in the United States. Do some research and try to determine where the component parts are made. How much of your chosen product is actually made in the United States? List the parts and their countries of origin and identify the competitive advantage that you believe each place holds.

4-10. China is one of the fastest-growing markets in the world. Use Web or database research to uncover how to best describe China according to the five cultural dimensions. Cite the sources for your information.

Solving Teaching and Learning Challenges

Many students who take Introduction to Business courses have difficulty seeing the relevance of course topics to their lives and future careers and struggle to see how all of the elements of a business connect. This reduces the willingness of many students to prepare for class and to be engaged during class. We use the following resources to engage students with the content and to highlight how Introduction to Business is relevant and important for their employability and careers.

"What's in It for Me?"

Students sometimes question the value of a particular major, class, or textbook. We have worked tirelessly to make sure that you see the value of this class and book. To help with this, each chapter opens with a special feature we call "What's in It for Me?" This feature is intended to reinforce the notion of different roles, as described above. While each of the various roles—employee, employer, boss, consumer, and investor—are all important, this feature highlights some of the key implications for the different roles for each chapter.

Applied Learning Opportunities Throughout

Managing in Turbulent Times

- Students learn from disappointments, challenges, and opportunities real companies face.
- New features look at artificial intelligence, the virtual workplace, and changing demographics among consumers and employees.

managing in turbulent times

Ripple Effects in the Global Supply Chain

In February 2022, Russian forces invaded Ukraine in an escalation of the Russo-Ukraine war, which had been ongoing since 2014. The region had regained some stability in the intervening eight years, but infrastructure, shipping, and logistics were drastically weakened from dealing with continuing tensions and fighting, blocked aid, and infrastructure collapse, among the other massive challenges. With the full-scale invasion of the Russian military, Ukraine was unable to regain stability and saw dramatic impacts on its exports.

The strategic importance of Sevastopol, Crimea's largest city and a major port on the Black Sea, made it an important naval base and import/export point in the region. With the invasion of Russian troops and continuing armed conflicts, traffic at the port came to a standstill, and farmers were left with millions of tons of harvested grain and no way to get it out of the country.

Ukraine occupies a relatively small geographical area, but its exports have a big impact on the global economy. In 2021, Ukraine was the world's number-one exporter of sunflower oil, the second-largest exporter of barley, the third largest of wheat, and fourth largest of corn. At that time, 40 percent of the corn and wheat exported from Ukraine went to the Middle East and Africa. African nations, in particular, depended on Ukraine for grains, and aid agencies found they were unable to get desperately needed supplies to countries already grappling with severe food shortages.[14]

Russia produces about 25 percent of the world's nitrogen fertilizer, and the combined wheat exports of Ukraine and Russia make up nearly 30 percent of the exported global supply. Political sanctions against Russia, blocked ports in Ukraine, and direct conflict have combined to accelerate a world food shortage. Poor countries are unable to find alternative (and more expensive) suppliers, and world grain stores have begun to shrink.

annapasichnik/123RF

The global supply chain inextricably links seemingly unrelated regions and supplies. In the United States, the war had a direct impact on the import of materials needed to manufacture electronics, car batteries, and even medical equipment. Russia is a major exporter of these key metals, and without a steady supply, the United States and other producers passed along increased costs to consumers.[15]

The war also directly impacted Americans' grocery bills. Increased grain prices mean increased costs at every level of production, with the highest increases showing up on grocery store shelves. As consumer shopping habits moved back toward pre-pandemic spending, shoppers found that their budgets were stretched by staples, requiring them to cut back on other spending.

Global supply chains mean that events in faraway places have impacts on our lives. Bananas from Brazil, heavy metals from China, and even the grain that makes our favorite breakfast cereal—all of these conveniences are possible thanks to that global supply chain. That same interconnectedness, however, means that we also feel negative effects from distant conflicts and crises.

Finding a Better Way

- This boxed feature reveals examples of organizations that are "finding a better way" to meet business challenges and describes how they are doing it.

finding a better way

Car Wars: China Versus Mexico

In today's competitive global economy, businesses strive for every possible advantage. Many manufacturers, for example, locate their factories in countries that have an ample supply of low-cost skilled labor. During the 1980s and 1990s, the place to be was Mexico. Hundreds of factories were built just across the U.S.–Mexican border, and workers streamed to the region from other parts of Mexico for stable and well-paying jobs. But in the late 1990s, the world started to shift.

Mexican prosperity, fueled in part by its role as a center of manufacturing, led to increases in the cost of living, followed quickly by wage increases so workers could keep up. At about that same time, China began to emerge as an attractive manufacturing alternative. Wages in China were roughly one-third the wages in Mexico, and there was no shortage of workers eager to take steady jobs in factories making products for other countries. China's boom was Mexico's bust as one company after another reduced or eliminated manufacturing there and moved to Asia.

In more recent years, the situation started to tilt back in Mexico's favor. As China's economy flourished, its labor costs crept higher and higher, and when U.S. manufacturers factored in shipping costs, producing auto parts in Mexico once again became more cost effective. Time differences between the United States and China also make phone and video conferencing difficult. In addition, U.S. companies have taken flak for China's business practices. Companies are often heavily subsidized by the government, and low-paid workers are not offered the same benefits and protections as workers in the United States, causing what many deem to be an uneven playing field that takes jobs away from U.S. workers.

Vario Images GmbH & Co.KG/Alamy Stock Photo

Because of these socioeconomic shifts, Mexico made enormous gains in the automobile sector. Companies such as Nissan, Honda, Volkswagen, and Mazda invested billions of dollars in Mexican companies, and by 2022 the country as a whole was producing about 385,000 units a month, rivaling production by China, even as the U.S. auto market was still recovering from a slump resulting from reduced consumer spending and too much inventory. In 2023, the automotive industry made up nearly 20 percent of Mexico's overall manufacturing GDP. With the combined value of vehicles and related parts an estimated $68.7 billion USD, Mexico ranked as the fifth largest auto exporter in the world.[9] So, the battle for competitive advantage continues, and the back-and-forth nature of the industry and its resultant ups and downs will likely continue for the foreseeable future.

Entrepreneurship and New Ventures

- This updated boxed feature shows students entrepreneurs who have really made a difference, some in large firms, others in smaller start-up companies.

entrepreneurship and new ventures

Women Entrepreneurs Grow Global

In 2008, Laurel Delaney started writing a blog—*Women Entrepreneurs Grow Global*, or wegg®,—that focused on helping women entrepreneurs expand their businesses internationally. Delaney knew through personal experience that women-owned exporting businesses faced unique challenges. Inspired by an International Trade Centre report that "women-owned small and medium-sized enterprises (SMEs) that export tend to earn more, pay more, employ more people and be more productive than firms that only operate domestically," Delaney aimed to create a one-stop-shop resource where women could easily access educational resources.

In 2015, after observing that many of her clients were unaware of how to take their business global, Delaney incorporated as a 501(c)(3) to take advantage of grant and sponsorship funding from individuals, foundations, and corporations who wanted to support women entrepreneurs and business owners with their global growth expansion plans. She expanded her online reach with different educational platforms such as webinars and X (formally known as Twitter) by coming up with catchy program names like wegginar®, weggchat®, *and Club wegg®, which she trademarked,* and began to offer one-to-one peer mentoring. All wegg® programs feature successful professionals who provide participants with practical information to guide them through the many aspects of exporting, and provide concrete strategies for global entrepreneurship.

wegg® is the only USA nonprofit that consistently delivers global business educational offerings in a simple, engaging and affordable manner.

The mission of wegg® is "to educate, inspire, and nurture women business owners and entrepreneurs worldwide on how to go global so they can run healthier businesses and create a new future for themselves, their families and their community."

Laurel Delaney/WEGG

Laurel Delaney has helped over 1,800 women entrepreneurs expand into international markets.

By early 2023, wegg® had served over 40,000 women business owners and entrepreneurs.[17] Through its many affordable offerings, wegg® also now provides a VIP program for women business owners to access operational, legal, and strategic support; Club wegg® cohorts; and a monthly How She Went Global® podcast.

Beyond all the practical knowledge provided by wegg®, Delaney stays focused on her original goal: "I wanted to change the landscape for women from being risk-averse to having confidence to go for it—with the appropriate support."[18]

Integrative Learning Portfolio

The Integrative Learning Portfolio feature, found at the end of each part, is intended to help integrate various topics across different chapters, helping solve a common challenge faced by students in Introduction to Business. The Integrative Learning Portfolio is composed of three elements:

- Crafting a Business Plan: an assignment—which can be used across the semester—guiding students in developing a business plan.
- Integrative Case: an ongoing case featuring Starbucks which, throughout all six parts of the book, illustrates how all aspects of business relate to a single company.
- Finding Your Path: looks at job market trends, starting salaries, and various career paths related to the topics covered in each part.

part 3
Integrative Learning Portfolio

crafting a business plan

Goal of the Exercise

At this point, your business has an identity, and you've described the factors that will affect your business and how you will operate it. Part 3 of the business plan project asks you to think about your employees, the jobs they will be performing, and the ways in which you can lead and motivate them.

Exercise Background: Part 3 of the Business Plan

To complete this part of the plan, you need to refer back to the organizational chart that you created in Part 2. In this part of the business plan exercise, you'll take the different job titles you created in the organizational chart and give thought to the *skills* that employees will need to bring to the job *before* they begin. You'll also consider *training* you'll need to provide *after* they are hired as well as how you'll compensate your employees. Part 3 of the business plan also asks you to consider how you'll lead your employees and keep them happy and motivated.

conditions; and the tools, materials, equipment, and information used to perform it. Imagine your business on a typical day. Who is working and what are each person's responsibilities?

P3-4. Next, create a job specification for each job, listing the skills, other credentials, and qualifications needed to perform the job effectively.

Hint: As you write your job specifications, consider what you would write if you were composing an ad for the position. What would the new employee need to bring to the job to qualify for the position?

P3-5. What sort of training, if any, will your employees need once they are hired? How will you provide this training?

Hint: Refer to the discussion of training in this chapter. Will you offer your employees on-the-job training? Off-the-job training? Vestibule training?

Developing Skills for Your Career

For students to succeed in a rapidly changing job market, they should be aware of their career options and how to go about developing a variety of skills. In this book and MyLab Intro to Business, we focus on developing these skills in the following ways:

Communication: Communication is covered in several places throughout the book. For example, Chapter 5 discusses how leaders communicate the corporate culture, while Chapter 6 discusses how managers communicate the delegation process and how managers can use communication to offset errors in the grapevine.

Critical Thinking: Chapter 9 devotes specific attention to the decision-making process. Chapter 11 discusses the research process and research methods. Collaboration in teams and team-based methods of organizing are discussed in Chapters 6 and 8. At the end of each chapter, there is also a continuing team exercise.

Business Ethics and Social Responsibility: Chapter 2 is entirely devoted to ethics and social responsibility.

Information Technology Application and Computing Skills: Chapter 14 is devoted to information technology application and computing skills for business.

The Finding Your Path feature, part of the Integrative Learning Portfolio at the end of each part, looks at job market trends, starting salaries, and various career paths. In addition, each feature also has an employability component that examines how students can improve their prospects for finding an attractive job.

For more information and resources, visit **www.pearson.com**.

About MyLab Intro to Business

To improve student results, we recommend pairing the text content with **MyLab Intro to Business**, which is the teaching and learning platform that empowers you to reach every student. By combining trusted author content with digital tools and a flexible platform, MyLab personalizes the learning experience and will help your students learn and retain key course concepts while developing skills that future employers are seeking in their candidates. From **Mini Sims** to **Dynamic Study Modules**, MyLab Intro to Business helps you teach your course, your way. Learn more at https://mlm.pearson.com/northamerica/mybizlab/

Instructor Teaching Resources

Business Essentials 14e comes with the following teaching resources:

Supplements available to instructors at www.pearson.com	Features of the Supplement
Instructor's Manual authored by Joseph R. Cooke from Santa Fe Community College	• Chapter-by-chapter summaries • Teaching notes • Examples and activities • Teaching tips • Solutions to all questions and problems in the book
Test Bank authored by Susan Schanne	• Over 2,000 multiple-choice, true/false, and short answer/essay questions • Includes answer explanations • Aligned to Learning Objectives from the text • Classified according to difficulty level • AACSB learning standard identified (Written and oral communication, Ethical understanding and reasoning, Analytical thinking, Diverse and multicultural work environments, Reflective thinking, Application of knowledge, Interpersonal relations and teamwork, and Integration of real-world business experiences)
Computerized TestGen	TestGen allows instructors to: • Customize, save, and generate classroom tests • Edit, add, or delete questions from the Test Item Files • Analyze test results • Organize a database of tests and student results
PowerPoints authored by Jeffrey L. Anderson from Ohio University	Slides include all the graphs, tables, and equations in the textbook. PowerPoints meet accessibility standards for students with disabilities. Features include, but are not limited to: • Keyboard and Screen Reader access • Alternative text for images • High color contrast between background and foreground colors

Acknowledgments

This book bears the names of two authors. In reality, however, it reflects the combined efforts of many different people in what can only be called a team effort. First of all, we'd like to thank our reviewers and users of the 13th edition who provided valuable feedback on the current strengths of the book and how we could make it better.

Corinne Asher, Henry Ford College
Lynn Barbee, Ivy Tech Community College
Daniel Berndt, Central Carolina Community College
Gustavo Demoner, West Los Angeles College
Star Dutcher, Westminster Christian School
Gerald Goldstein, University of West Florida
Miriam Karanja, Arkansas Baptist College
Tammira Lucas, Harford Community College
Vershun L. McClain, Jackson State University
Gerald James Pierri, Villanova University
Muhammad Adnan Shahid, Richard Blank College of William & Mary
Evelyn Vargas, Houston Community College Northwest
Irene Wilder, Jefferson Community College

We are grateful to these reviewers as well as those who have chosen to remain anonymous. In addition, we would also like to thank the following individuals for their contributions to the MyLab course. We are truly appreciative of their hard work and important contributions.

Joe Cooke, Santa Fe Community College
Susan Leshnower, Midland College
Storm Russo, Valencia College
Susan Schanne, Eastern Michigan University
Susan Gall
Brad Wesner, Texas A&M University

I would also like to acknowledge the outstanding professionalism of the team at Pearson Education: Rebecca Caruso, Content Development Manager; Simon Jacobs, Commercial Product Manager; Bhanuprakash Sherla, Content Producer; Christina Verigan, Development Editor; and our Project Manager at Straive, Meghan DeMaio, have been instrumental in helping me continue to elevate the quality of my work and make this book even stronger.

I would also like to thank Joe Cooke for his contributions. Joe is a professor at Santa Fe Community College. Joe helped update or replace the boxes and cases throughout the book and revised and enhanced all of the end-of-chapter pedagogy. I would also like to acknowledge and express my gratitude to Ron Ebert. Ron and I worked on this book together for many years, and his imprint can still be found in many different places.

Finally, I would like to acknowledge my family. Their contributions to my work are far too extensive and personal to list. Suffice it to say that my wife, Glenda, and our children and grandchildren are the bedrock of my life. I am continually reminded by them of the fragility of life, the joy of being, and the importance of living every day to the fullest.

Ricky W. Griffin
2024

P.S. (from Ricky)

I would also like to take a few lines here to personally acknowledge and express my gratitude to Ron Ebert. Ron retired from the University of Missouri–Columbia a few years ago after a long and distinguished career but continued to work with me on revisions of this book. However, he has made the decision to retire from this work as well.

Ron was Chair of the Department of Management at Missouri when I completed my doctorate in 1978 and recruited me to join his department. Simply put, it was one of the best decisions of my life. I learned many lessons from Ron about scholarship, teaching, professionalism, and life and credit him for being one of my most significant mentors throughout my career. More importantly, though, he has been a wonderful friend. Ron, I miss working with you but will always treasure our friendship.

about the authors

Ronald J. Ebert is Emeritus Professor at the University of Missouri–Columbia. Professor Ebert's work has been based on more than thirty years of teaching experience at such schools as Sinclair College, University of Washington, University of Missouri, Lucian Blaga University of Sibiu (Romania), and Consortium International University (Italy). His consulting alliances have included such firms as Mobay Corporation, Kraft Foods, Oscar Mayer, Atlas Powder, and John Deere. He has designed and conducted management development programs for such diverse clients as the American Public Power Association, the U.S. Savings and Loan League, and the Central Missouri Manufacturing Training Consortium.

His experience as a practitioner fostered an advocacy for integrating concepts with best business practices in business education. The five business books he has coauthored have been translated into Spanish, Chinese (Simplified), Chinese (Traditional), Malaysian, Bahasa Indonesian, and Romanian languages. Professor Ebert has served as the Editor of the *Journal of Operations Management*. He is a Past President and Fellow of the Decision Sciences Institute. He has served as consultant and external evaluator for *Quantitative Reasoning for Business Studies*, an introduction-to-business project sponsored by the National Science Foundation. Professor Ebert retired from his role as co-author of this book after the publication of its 11th edition, but his imprint and myriad contributions can still be found in many different places throughout the text.

Ricky W. Griffin joined the faculty at Texas A&M University in 1981. During his career at Texas A&M, he has taught undergraduate and graduate courses in management, organizational behavior, human resource management, and international business. Professor Griffin's research interests include workplace aggression and violence, organizational security, workplace culture, and leadership. His work has been published in such journals as *Academy of Management Review, Academy of Management Journal, Administrative Science Quarterly,* and *Journal of Management*. He served as Associate Editor and then as Editor of *Journal of Management*.

Professor Griffin has led executive development programs and/or consulted with such firms as Halliburton, Concho, KBR, Ascend, Shell Oil Company, Six Flags, and WinCo. He has also delivered invited presentations in England, Italy, France, Switzerland, Poland, Saudi Arabia, South Africa, Hong Kong, and Australia. He has also served as a consulting expert in numerous legal cases involving workplace violence and bullying and general human resource and talent management practices.

In addition, Professor Griffin has authored or coauthored several leading textbooks and coedited three scholarly books. His books have been used at more than 500 colleges and universities on five continents and have been translated into Spanish, Russian, Polish, and Chinese. He has served the Academy of Management as Chair of the Organizational Behavior Division and as Program Chair of the Research Methods Division. He also has served as President of the Southwest Division of the Academy of Management and on the Board of Directors of the Southern Management Association. Professor Griffin is a Fellow of both the Academy of Management and the Southern Management Association. He has also won several awards for research and has been supported by more than $1,500,000 in external research funding. Professor Griffin has served as Director of the Center for Human Resource Management and Head of the Department of Management at Texas A&M University. He has also served as Executive Associate Dean and Interim Dean at the Mays Business School.

chapter 1

The U.S. Business Environment

Anna Sergeeva/ZUMA Press, Inc./Alamy Stock Photo

learning objectives

After reading this chapter, you should be able to:

1-1 Define the nature of U.S. business, describe the external environments of business, and discuss how these environments affect the success or failure of organizations.

1-2 Describe the different types of global economic systems according to the means by which they control the factors of production.

1-3 Show how markets, demand, and supply affect resource distribution in the United States; identify the elements of private enterprise; and explain the various degrees of competition in the U.S. economic system.

1-4 Explain the importance of the economic environment to business and identify the factors used to evaluate the performance of an economic system.

1-5 Learn about the skills you will gain through this text.

what's in it for me?

As you will see in our Opening Case, political, technological, cultural, and economic forces have created enormous challenges for Harley-Davidson, Inc., throughout the years. Even though the details change, these are the same general forces that will challenge you as you enter today's business world. All businesses are subject to the influences of economic forces. But these same economic forces also provide astute managers and entrepreneurs with opportunities for profits and growth. By understanding these economic forces and how they interact, you'll be better able to (1) appreciate how managers must contend with the challenges and opportunities resulting from economic forces from the standpoint of an employee and a manager or business owner and (2) understand why prices fluctuate from the perspective of a consumer. You should have a deeper appreciation of the environment in which managers work and a better understanding of why the prices you pay for goods and services go up and down.

In this chapter, we'll first introduce the concepts of profit and loss and then describe the external environments of businesses. As we will see, the domestic business environment, the global business environment, and the technological, political-legal, sociocultural, and economic environments are also important. Next, we'll look at some basic elements of economic systems and describe the economics of market systems. We'll also introduce and discuss several indicators that are used to gauge the vitality of our domestic economic system.

Take A Pix Media/Shutterstock

BCFC/Shutterstock

Reinventing an American Icon

In 1903, at about the same time Henry Ford was assembling his first factory-produced automobile in Detroit, Michigan, William S. Harley and Arthur Davidson were tinkering in a little wooden shed in Milwaukee, Wisconsin, with an idea that Harley had—to put a small gasoline engine on a bicycle. They had gathered some parts, but it took Arthur's brother, Walter, a machinist, to put it all together. However, much like Ford's first attempts to design a production automobile, the first Harley-Davidson motorcycle was a disappointment. The tiny 7-cubic-inch engine couldn't even make the bike go up a small hill. Still enamored with the idea of putting a motor on two wheels, the three men designed a bigger engine (almost 25 cubic inches), put it on a sturdier frame, and sold one bike that first year to a school friend.

In 1905, they produced a total of five bikes. They sold one through a dealership in Chicago and, taking a page from Ford's playbook, started racing their bikes against those of other budding manufacturers in physical as well as economic competition. In a 15-mile race in Chicago in 1905, their new design took first place, with an average speed of 47 miles per hour.

In 1907, with production at about 50 bikes per year, William Davidson, Arthur's brother, joined the company, and they incorporated as Harley-Davidson, Inc., splitting the stock four ways. Ownership of the company would stay in those families for the next 60 years.

Over the next few years, the company ramped up production and continued to innovate. In 1909, it introduced its first V-twin engine—a 39.5-cubic-inch monster that delivered all of 7 horsepower. Because of the rather awkward 45-degree angle of the two cylinders, the bike had a unique rumble.

World War I gave Harley a boost as the military bought over 20,000 bikes. By 1920, Harley-Davidson was the biggest motorcycle manufacturer in the world, with over 2,000 dealerships in 67 countries. By that time, the V-twin engine had grown to a respectable 45 cubic inches (almost 750 cubic centimeters).

Disaster struck in the form of the Great Depression. In 1929, Harley sales had reached 21,000 bikes but dropped to 3,703 by 1933. Because of its solid reputation, its prominence in the marketplace, and some astute diversification by management, Harley was one of only two American motorcycle manufacturers that survived the Great Depression. When World War II shifted motorcycle production back to military use, Harley was ready.

The other surviving motorcycle manufacturer, Indian, didn't fare as well. When it closed its doors in 1954, Harley-Davidson emerged as the only U.S. manufacturer. That same year, Harley introduced the first "Sportster," with its 55-cubic-inch engine and unique styling, and the returning soldiers who had been exposed to the bikes overseas created a huge domestic market. But the halcyon days wouldn't last.

Harley-Davidson had licensed the rights to build its motorcycles in Japan to Rikuo in the late thirties, before the war, a move that jump-started the Japanese motorcycle industry, and by the late sixties, Japanese bikes were flooding the marketplace. At the same time, Harley was suffering from aging and outdated equipment and high manufacturing costs. In an effort to stave off bankruptcy by generating cash from new investors, the majority shareholders of Harley (descendants of the founders) took the company public but retained 53 percent of the voting shares.

Meanwhile, the U.S. business environment was going through a phase of conglomeration—big companies like Bangor Punta were buying up smaller companies and often pillaging them for cash or wringing short-term profits from them and then leaving the empty shell.

It was Bangor Punta that tendered a generous offer for Harley shares in an attempt to buy up a controlling interest in the company. Harley President William Davidson urged stockholders not to sell, but Bangor kept sweetening the deal, and by December 1969, it owned over 16 percent of the outstanding shares and the hostile takeover looked imminent. Desperate to save the brand from being gutted, the majority shareholders swung a deal with a different corporate buyer they felt would better serve the firm's interests.

American Machine and Foundry (AMF) had started out about the same time as Ford and Harley, making cigarette-manufacturing machines, but over the years it had diversified into sailboats, bowling alleys, and other sports equipment. Unlike the struggling Harley-Davidson, AMF had cash to burn and was looking to buy up sports-related companies. AMF promised to breathe new life into the ailing motorcycle manufacturer and invest much-needed capital.

Unfortunately, after the takeover, AMF quickly broke its promise. Instead of investing capital, the firm focused on short-term profits by reducing quality, laying off workers, and cutting corners wherever possible. In 1981, with the company once again heading toward bankruptcy, 13 Harley-Davidson senior executives, led by William Davidson, rallied together and bought the company back from AMF for $80 million.

Shortly after regaining control of the company, Harley successfully lobbied President Ronald Reagan into imposing a 45 percent import tariff on bikes larger than 700 ccs, effectively eliminating any competition from abroad. But the writing was on the wall—the baby boomers who had been the bread-and-butter market for the big American bikes were already starting to age out, and Harley was struggling to find new markets. In what was seen as a bold move, Harley petitioned the International Trade Commission to drop the import tariff on big bikes, presumably to get younger people riding and increase overall ridership. Also, in 1986, Harley-Davidson, Inc., rejoined the New York Stock Exchange (NYSE: HOG) at $0.36 per share (retroactively adjusted for five 2:1 stock splits).

The 1990s saw ever-increasing competition from Japan, Europe, and even other American companies like Indian that had reemerged and gained a foothold in the market. In an effort to combat the changing marketplace, Harley pursued a new batch of innovations, such as the Softail and the sporty Buell. In fact, despite the intense competition, by 1998, demand for Harley-Davidson motorcycles exceeded supply, driving up prices, profits, and the stock price. In fact, on November 6, 2006, the stock price hit $73.77, but an aging demographic gradually began to take its toll. In 2015 the Board of Directors appointed Matt Levatich as CEO and he predicted a continuing slow-down in sales due to an aging demographic unless the Company took some dramatic steps. To create new markets and attract new riders, the Company introduced a novel line of sport bikes and other entry-level cruisers, along with the electric LiveWire and the Pan America adventure bike. Even so, in 2019, sales declined for the 5th year in a row, and in February 2020, with the stock price below $20, Levatich stepped down. His replacement, Jochen Zeitz, promptly reversed the company strategy to focus again on selling the high-margin bikes (Touring, Cruiser, and Trike) to older, wealthier customers, primarily in the United States and Europe. In 2020, Harley's full-year revenue sat at $4 billion. In 2021, full-year revenue for Harley products increased to $5.3 billion and climbed to $5.8 billion in 2022. More importantly, the company's net income (revenue minus expenses) increased dramatically. By early 2023, the stock price had climbed back up to nearly $40, and it may just be that focusing on the big bikes that made the company famous was the best strategy after all. (After studying the content in this chapter, you should be able to answer the set of discussion questions found at the end of the chapter.)

Business, Profit, and the External Environment

Learning Objective 1-1

Define the nature of U.S. business, describe the external environments of business, and discuss how these environments affect the success or failure of organizations.

What do you think of when you hear the word *business*? Does it conjure up images of large, successful corporations, such as Apple, Starbucks, and Amazon? Or of once-great but now struggling companies like Macy's, Kodak, and Yahoo!? Do you think of multinational giants such as Honda, General Electric, or Nestlé? Are you reminded of smaller firms down the street, such as your local supermarket or favorite chain restaurant? Or do you think of even smaller family-owned operations, such as your neighborhood pizzeria, the dry cleaner, or the florist around the corner?

Business and Profit

Business *organization that provides goods or services to earn profits*

Profits *difference between a business's revenues and its expenses*

All these organizations are **businesses**, organizations that provide goods or services that are then sold to earn profits. Indeed, the prospect of earning **profits**, the difference between a business's revenues and its expenses, is what encourages people to open and expand businesses. After all, profits are the rewards owners get for risking their money and time. The right to pursue profits distinguishes a business from those organizations—such as most state universities, hospitals, and government agencies—that run in much the same way but that generally don't seek profits.[1]

Consumer Choice and Demand In a capitalistic system, such as that in the United States, businesses exist to earn profits for owners; within certain broad constraints, an owner is free to set up a new business, grow that business, sell it, or even shut it down. But consumers also have freedom of choice. In choosing how to pursue profits, businesses must take into account what consumers want or need. No matter how efficient a business is, it won't survive if there is no demand for its goods or services. Neither a snowblower shop in Florida nor a beach umbrella store in Alaska is likely to do well.

Opportunity and Enterprise If enterprising businesspeople can spot a promising opportunity and then develop a good plan for capitalizing on it, they can succeed. For example, when large businesses such as Circuit City, Linens 'n Things, and Blockbuster Video close their doors, other firms profit from these closings by handling the inventory liquidations of these failed companies. And if oil prices decline, gasoline producers like ExxonMobil and BP will see their profits decline. However, food distributors like Sysco and DoorDash and delivery services such as FedEx may see their expenses drop due to lower fuel costs, and hence their profits will grow. In general, then, business opportunity involves goods or services that consumers need or want—especially if no one else is supplying them or if existing businesses are doing so inefficiently or incompletely.

The Benefits of Business So what are the benefits of businesses? Businesses produce most of the goods and services we consume, and they employ most working people. They create most innovations and provide a vast range of opportunities for new businesses, which serve as their suppliers. A healthy business climate also contributes to the quality of life and standard of living of people in a society.

Business profits enhance the personal incomes of millions of owners and stockholders, and business taxes help to support governments at all levels. Many businesses support charities and provide community leadership. However, some businesses also harm the earth's environment, and their decision makers sometimes resort to unacceptable practices for their own personal benefit.

We now turn our attention to the environment in which businesses operate. Understanding the environment provides a foundation for our subsequent discussions dealing with economic forces that play a major role in the success and failure of businesses everywhere.

The External Environments of Business

All businesses, regardless of their size, location, or mission, operate within a larger external environment. This **external environment** consists of everything outside an organization's boundaries that might affect it. (Businesses also have an *internal environment*, more commonly called *corporate culture*; we discuss this in Chapter 5.) Not surprisingly, the external environment plays a major role in determining the success or failure of any organization. Managers must, therefore, have a thorough and accurate understanding of their environment and then strive to operate and compete within it. Businesses can also influence their environments. Figure 1.1 shows the major dimensions and elements of the external environment as it affects businesses today. As you can see, these include the *domestic business environment*, the *global business environment*, the *technological environment*, the *political-legal environment*, the *sociocultural environment*, and the *economic environment*.

External Environment
everything outside an organization's boundaries that might affect it

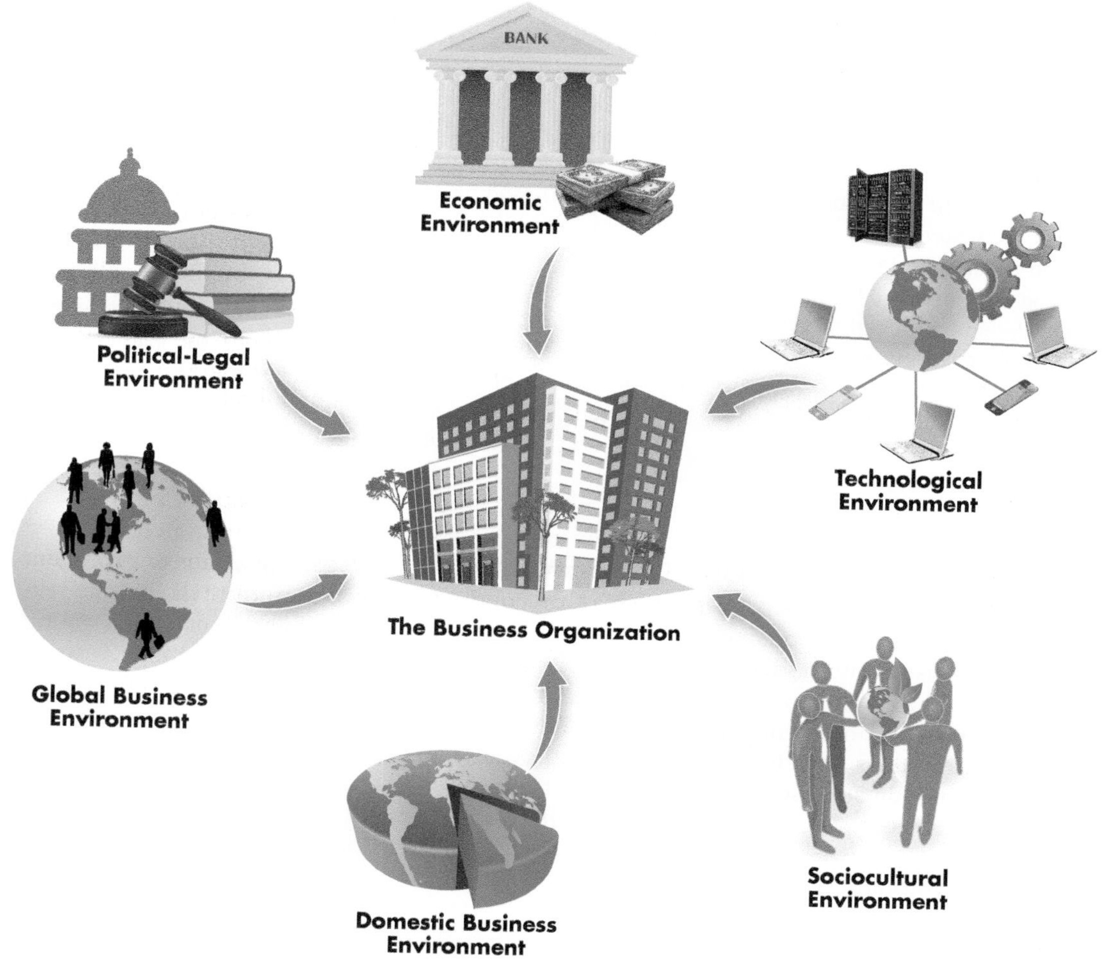

FIGURE 1.1 Dimensions of the External Environment

finding a better way

Artificial Intelligence: Changing the Way We Work

Markus Mainka/Shutterstock

Artificial intelligence, once the domain of science fiction, is now part of everyday life. ChatGPT, the natural language processing tool created by the U.S. company OpenAI, set records for the fastest-growing app in history, with over 100 million active users in the first two months after its launch.[2] ChatGPT (for generated pre-trained transformers) is a chatbot that can respond to prompts and questions from users, who simply enter information or requests into a box to start a conversation. The software searches for information on the Internet, scans it for suitability, and then paraphrases its results into an answer. OpenAI initially offered ChatGPT free of charge but has since updated its business model to a monthly subscription fee for ChatGPT's next iteration, GPT4.

ChatGPT can be used for a wide range of applications, from basic Google-type searches like "How can I safely introduce my dog to other dogs?" to computer coding problems and even poetry. Users can ask ChatGPT to create simple lists for packing or grocery shopping, or they can ask for a detailed description of works of art. ChatGPT can also assist with project management, offer tips to motivate you for your next big task, and some risk-taking students are even using it to do their homework.

In business, AI can be used to improve automation, from simple customer-service inquiries to full-scale production. Online retailers have used AI to transform shopping experiences by evaluating customers' past purchases and using that information to make enticing recommendations. Predictive analytics can help businesses spot trends and capitalize on them quickly. Banks use AI to detect fraudulent purchases and other activity, and even the smallest business owners can use AI to write marketing and social media copy.

One area where AI has proven particularly effective is supply chain management. AI performs highly detailed real-time analyses to forecast warehouse demand, improve shipping container loading, and even predict vehicle breakdowns and suggest changes to maintenance schedules.

Though AI has been hailed as a technological breakthrough of unprecedented proportions, it has also created ethical dilemmas. Teachers are grappling with how to address and regulate the use of AI in the classroom. Consumers and advocates have privacy and security concerns. Some experts believe that the way forward is firmly in the hands of AI, which will continue to learn from the activities and interactions of humans and computers. In contrast, in early 2023, Italy temporarily banned the use of ChatGPT over privacy concerns, and a group of researchers and technologists penned an open letter calling for a 6-month moratorium on the development of new artificial intelligence systems.[3]

Even so, AI is a natural consequence of consumer demand, and the free-market economy has proven itself to be a strong force for innovation and for meeting demand with products and services despite resistance from groups and even governments. Even commercial aircraft that we now take for granted were once considered questionable and even dangerous. AI is with us now, whether we choose to use it or not.

Domestic Business Environment *the environment in which a firm conducts its operations and derives its revenues*

Domestic Business Environment The **domestic business environment** refers to the environment in which a firm conducts its operations and derives its revenues. In general, businesses seek to be close to their customers, to establish strong relationships with their suppliers, and to distinguish themselves from their competitors. Take American Eagle, for example. The firm initially located its stores near urban college campuses and in shopping malls; it now locates stores in other, often more upscale, areas as well. The company also has a strong network of suppliers and is itself a wholesale supplier to other retailers through its Quite Logistics subsidiary. It has established a clear identity for itself within the domestic business environment that enables it to compete effectively with such competitors as Urban Outfitters and Abercrombie & Fitch.

Global Business Environment *the international forces that affect a business*

Global Business Environment The **global business environment** refers to the international forces that affect a business. Factors affecting the global environment at a general level include international trade agreements, international economic conditions, political unrest, and so forth. For example, as the effects of the 2020 COVID-19 pandemic in China began to spread, travel in that country plummeted. As a result, demand for fuel dropped in China, creating a surplus in other countries and leading to a fall in retail gasoline prices. Likewise, international air travel plunged as the virus spread around the globe. But as the pandemic waned, these trends were reversed. More recently, OPEC (discussed in Chapter 4) has taken a more proactive role in affecting the global supply and demand for oil. And in similar fashion, the war between Russia and Ukraine has disrupted supply and demand for various products and services—oil, wheat, and others—offered by these countries. Further, while some of the supply chain issues that arose during the pandemic have been addressed, there are still lingering effects of supply chain disruptions in some areas, such as automobile manufacturing.

At a more immediate level, any given business is likely to be affected by international market opportunities, suppliers, cultures, competitors, and currency values. For instance, American Eagle currently owns and operates hundreds of stores in North America but has other stores in 33 different countries operated under licensing agreements. And because it operates in so many different regions it has to contend with different languages, more diverse cultures, different forms of technology, different currencies, and many other factors. Complicating things further, many of its suppliers are foreign companies.

Technological Environment The **technological environment** generally includes all the ways by which firms create value for their constituents. Technology includes human knowledge, work methods, physical equipment, electronics and telecommunications, and various processing systems that are used to perform business activities. For instance, American Eagle relies on a sophisticated information system that tracks sales and inventory levels to be highly responsive to its customers. The firm also enjoys considerable success with its e-commerce websites.

Technological Environment *all the ways by which firms create value for their constituents*

Political-Legal Environment The **political-legal environment** reflects the relationship between business and government, usually in the form of government regulation of business. This environment is important for several reasons. First, the legal system defines in part what an organization can and cannot do. For instance, American Eagle is subject to a variety of political and legal forces, including product identification laws, employee hiring restrictions, and local zoning requirements. Likewise, various government agencies regulate important activities, such as advertising practices, safety and health considerations, and acceptable standards of business conduct. Abercrombie & Fitch has sued American Eagle three times, claiming copyright infringement, but in all three cases American Eagle won. Privacy is also becoming increasingly important as part of the political-legal area. The General Data Protection Regulation (GDPR), a regulation created by the European Union (EU), is intended to limit the transfer of personal information across national boundaries.

Political-Legal Environment *the relationship between business and government*

Sociocultural Environment The **sociocultural environment** includes the customs, mores, values, and demographic characteristics of the society in which an organization functions. Sociocultural processes also determine the goods and services, as well as the standards of business conduct, that a society is likely to value and accept. For example, American Eagle primarily targets high school and college-aged customers. However, the firm has also launched other brands such as aerie, Martin + Osa, 77kids, and Tailgate that focus on other demographic groups. Martin + Osa, for instance, targets men and women in the age group 28–40.

Sociocultural Environment *the customs, mores, values, and demographic characteristics of the society in which an organization functions*

Economic Environment The **economic environment** refers to relevant conditions that exist in the economic system in which a company operates. For example, if an economy is doing well enough that most people have jobs and wages are high, a growing company may find it necessary to pay even higher wages and offer more benefits to attract workers from other companies. But if many people in an economy

Economic Environment *relevant conditions that exist in the economic system in which a company operates*

American Eagle is affected by the external environment in many different ways. The domestic business environment, global business environment, technological environment, political-legal environment, sociocultural environment, and economic environment all interact to provide American Eagle with both opportunities and challenges.

are looking for jobs, a firm may be able to pay less and offer fewer benefits. Like many retailers, American Eagle experiences some financial pressures during recessionary conditions. In the post-pandemic era, more workers are demanding higher wages, also putting pressures on the firm. And, like many other brick-and-mortar retailers, American Eagle is also facing intense competition from online retailers like Amazon and Alibaba. The rest of this chapter is devoted to the economic environment; the other environments of business are covered throughout the rest of the book.

Learning Objective 1-2

Describe the different types of global economic systems according to the means by which they control the factors of production.

Economic Systems

A U.S. business operates differently from a business in France or the People's Republic of China, and businesses in those countries differ from those in Japan or Brazil. A key factor in these differences is the economic system of a firm's *home country*, the nation in which it does most of its business. An **economic system** is a nation's system for allocating its resources among its citizens, both individuals and organizations.

Economic System *a nation's system for allocating its resources among its citizens*

Factors of Production

A basic difference between economic systems is the way in which a system manages its **factors of production**, the resources that a country's businesses use to produce goods and services. Economists have long focused on four factors of production: *labor, capital, entrepreneurs*, and *physical resources*. In addition to these traditional four factors, many economists now include *information resources*. Note that the concept of factors of production can also be applied to the resources that an individual organization *manages* to produce tangible goods and intangible services.

Factors of Production *resources used in the production of goods and services—labor, capital, entrepreneurs, physical resources, and information resources*

Labor (Human Resources) *physical and mental capabilities of people as they contribute to economic production*

Labor People who work for businesses provide labor. **Labor**, sometimes called **human resources** or *human capital*, includes the physical and intellectual contributions people make while engaged in economic production. Starbucks, for example, employs over 380,000 people.[4] The firm's workforce includes the baristas who prepare coffees for customers, store managers, regional managers, coffee tasters, quality control experts, coffee buyers, marketing experts, financial specialists, and other specialized workers and managers.

Capital Obtaining and using labor and other resources requires **capital**, the financial resources needed to operate a business. You need capital to start a new business and then to keep it running and growing. For example, when Howard Schultz decided to buy the fledgling Starbucks coffee outfit back in 1987, he used personal savings and a loan to finance his acquisition. As Starbucks grew, he came to rely more on Starbucks's profits. Eventually, the firm sold stock to other investors to raise even more money. Starbucks continues to rely on a blend of current earnings and both short- and long-term debt to finance its operations and fuel its growth. Moreover, even when the firm decided to close 150 underperforming coffee shops a few years ago, it used capital to pay off leases and provide severance pay to employees who lost their jobs.

Capital *funds needed to create and operate a business enterprise*

Entrepreneurs An **entrepreneur** is a person who accepts the risks and opportunities entailed in creating and operating a new business. Three individuals founded Starbucks back in 1971 and planned to emphasize wholesale distribution of fresh coffee beans. However, they lacked the interest or the vision to see the retail potential for coffee. Schultz, however, was willing to accept the risks associated with retail growth, and after buying the company, he capitalized on the market opportunities for rapid growth. Had his original venture failed, Schultz would have lost most of his savings. Most economic systems encourage entrepreneurs, both to start new businesses and to make the decisions that allow them to create new jobs and make more profits for their owners.

Entrepreneur *businessperson or individual who accepts the risks and opportunities involved in creating and operating a new business venture*

Starbucks is the largest chain of coffee shops in the world. The company uses various factors of production, including (a) labor, such as these Starbucks baristas; (b) entrepreneurship, such as former CEO Howard Schultz; (c) physical resources, like these coffee beans; and (d) information like economic forecasts and coffee bean pricing data.

Physical Resources *tangible items that organizations use in the conduct of their businesses*

Physical Resources

Physical resources are the tangible things that organizations use to conduct their business. They include natural resources and raw materials, offices, storage and production facilities, parts and supplies, computers and peripherals, and a variety of other equipment. For example, Starbucks relies on coffee beans and other food products, the equipment it uses to make its coffee drinks, and paper products for packaging, as well as office equipment and storage facilities for running its business at the corporate level.

Information Resources *data and other information used by businesses*

Information Resources

The production of tangible goods once dominated most economic systems. Today, **information resources**, data and other information used by businesses, play a major role. Information resources that businesses rely on include market forecasts, the specialized knowledge of people, and economic data. In turn, much of what businesses do with the information results either in the creation of new information or the repackaging of existing information for new users. For example, Starbucks uses various economic statistics to decide where to open new outlets. It also uses sophisticated forecasting models to predict the future prices of coffee beans. And consumer taste tests help the firm decide when to introduce new products.

Types of Economic Systems

Different types of economic systems view these factors of production differently. In some systems, for example (and in theory), the ownership of both the factors of production and the actual businesses is private; that is, ownership is held by entrepreneurs, individual investors, and other businesses. As discussed next, these are market economies. In other systems, though (and also in theory), the factors of production and all businesses are owned or controlled by the government. These are called *planned economies*. Note that we described these kinds of systems as being "in theory." Why? Because in reality, most systems fall between these extremes.

Planned Economy *economy that relies on a centralized government to control all or most factors of production and to make all or most production and allocation decisions*

Market Economy *economy in which individuals control production and allocation decisions through supply and demand*

Communism *political system in which the government owns and operates all factors of production*

Economic systems also differ in the ways decisions are made about production and allocation. A **planned economy** relies on a centralized government to control all or most factors of production and to make all or most production and allocation decisions. In a **market economy**, individual producers and consumers control production and allocation by creating combinations of supply and demand. Let's look at each of these types of economic systems as well as mixed market economies in more detail.

Planned Economies

Planned economies take two basic forms: *communism* (discussed here) and *socialism* (discussed later as a form of mixed market economy). As envisioned by nineteenth-century German economist Karl Marx, **communism** is a system in which the government owns and operates all factors of production. Under such a system, the government would assign people to jobs; it would also own all business and control business decisions—what to make, how much to charge, and so forth. Marx proposed that individuals would contribute according to their abilities and receive benefits according to their needs. He also expected government ownership of production factors to be temporary; once society had matured, government would wither away, and workers would take direct ownership of the factors of production.

The former Soviet Union and many Eastern European countries embraced communism until the end of the twentieth century. In the early 1990s, however, one country after another renounced communism as both an economic and a political system. Today, North Korea, Vietnam, Laos, Cuba, and the People's Republic of China are the only nations remaining that are controlled by communist parties. However, China in particular now functions much more like a mixed market economy (discussed below) than a pure communist-based economy.

Market *mechanism for exchange between buyers and sellers of a particular good or service*

Market Economies

A **market** is a mechanism for exchange between the buyers and sellers of a particular good or service. (Like *capital*, the term *market* can have multiple meanings.) Market economies rely on capitalism and free enterprise to create an environment in which producers and consumers are free to sell and buy what they

entrepreneurship and new ventures

Luxury on a Budget

In 2014, Rich Fulop found himself "downsized" from his job as a finance manager, but he took that as an opportunity to go back to school at NYU's Stern School of Business, while his wife, Vicki, worked at a public relations firm. After a few years of long hours and hard work, they splurged on a much-needed vacation, where they were enthralled by the posh hotel's luxurious bed linens. When they came back home to New York, they went online looking for those same sheets. What they found instead was an opportunity. With a bit of paperwork, they created Brooklinen—an online retail outlet for quality sheets at an affordable price that would feature a satisfying shopping experience.

Using their combined business skills in finance and marketing, Rich and Vicki created a lean and profitable company in just a few years. By negotiating a manufacturing deal with a company in Israel, where the United States has free-trade agreements, they were able to cut costs by 22 percent, allowing them to sell high-quality sheets for between $100 and $200—expensive, but still a fraction of the price of Frette or Sferra sheets that sell for up to $1,000.

By 2017, Brooklinen had over 150,000 customers and was doing $50 million in sales, and expansion plans got a $10 million boost from a venture capitalist. But, as with any good idea, the Fulops weren't the only ones to see a need and fill it. At the same time they were launching their company, Ariel Kaye, tired of being just another face in a huge marketing firm, set out on her own, using Instagram to bring her Parachute home decor brand name to prominence.

Scott and Missy Tannen have a start-up story similar to that of the Fulops, but their concern was with ecoconscious sourcing, and so they started Boll & Branch to give consumers a pure, chemical-free, and socially responsible set of bed sheets. More recently, Rana Argenio left her job at Goldman Sachs to launch her own company, 10 Grove, which ties into her family's Texas-based linen factory, which in turn gets raw materials directly from a partner mill in Italy.

Igor Golovnov/Alamy Stock Photo

Brooklinen's response to increased competition has been to continue to tweak its model by adding complementary products and partnering with businesses like Floyd Inc., a maker of bed frames and bookshelves focusing on sustainability, and Newgate World, a boutique clock store. In 2018, the Fulops opened a "pop-up shop" with limited hours in Brooklyn near the East River to positive reviews and social media buzz.

All this competition drives prices down, which is good for customers and is a lynchpin of the capitalist system. It can be hard on the entrepreneur, though, as the market settles into an equilibrium state, in which profits dwindle until new companies lack motivation to provide more of the same product or service. As Brooklinen grows, it continues to develop new product lines related to sustainable comfort at home. For example, the company now sells its own exclusive loungewear, towels, candles, and home décor, and in 2023, it launched a new line of laundry-care products. In addition, customer tastes and preferences change over time. For companies like Brooklinen, the key to long-term success is to keep innovating and responding to the market.

choose (within certain limits). As a result, items produced and prices paid are largely determined by supply and demand. The underlying premise of a market economy is to create shared value—in theory, at least, effective businesses benefit because they earn profits on what they sell, and customers also benefit by getting what they want for the best price available.[5]

To understand how a market economy works, consider what happens when you go to a fruit market to buy apples. One vendor is selling apples for $1 per pound; another is charging $1.50. Both vendors are free to charge what they want, and you are free to buy what you choose. If both vendors' apples are of the same quality, you will buy the cheaper ones. If the $1.50 apples are fresher and healthier looking, you may buy them instead. In short, both buyers and sellers enjoy freedom of choice; that is, the vendors are free to charge whatever price they choose for their apples, and the customer is free to decide whether to buy the $1 apples, the $1.50 apples, someone else's apples, or no apples at all.

Taken to a more general level of discussion, individuals in a market system are free not only to buy what they want but also to work where they want and to invest, save, or spend their money in whatever manner they choose. Likewise, businesses are free to decide what products to make, where to sell them, and what prices to charge. This process contrasts markedly with that of a planned economy, in which individuals may be told where they can and cannot work, companies may be told what they can and cannot make, and consumers may have little or no choice in what they purchase or how much they pay. The political basis of market processes is called **capitalism**, which allows for the private ownership of the factors of production and encourages entrepreneurship by offering profits as an incentive. The economic basis of market processes is the operation of demand and supply, which we discuss in the next section.

Capitalism *system that sanctions the private ownership of the factors of production and encourages entrepreneurship by offering profits as an incentive*

Mixed Market Economy *economic system featuring characteristics of both planned and market economies*

Mixed Market Economies In reality, no "pure" planned or "pure" market economies really exist. Most countries rely on some form of **mixed market economy** that features characteristics of both planned and market economies. Even a market economy that strives to be as free and open as possible, such as the U.S. economy, restricts certain activities. Some products can't be sold legally, others can be sold only to people of a certain age, advertising must be truthful, and so forth. And the People's Republic of China, the world's most important planned economy, is increasingly allowing private ownership and entrepreneurship (although with stringent government oversight). Indeed, it is probably more accurate today to describe China as a mixed market economy in a country controlled by the communist party.

Privatization *process of converting government enterprises into privately owned companies*

When a government is making a change from a planned economy to a market economy, it usually begins to adopt market mechanisms through **privatization**, the process of converting government enterprises into privately owned companies. In Poland, for example, the national airline was sold to a group of private investors. In recent years, this practice has spread to many other countries as well. For example, the postal system in many countries is government owned and government managed. The Netherlands, however, privatized its TNT Post Group N.V. (now called Post NL), and it is among the world's most efficient post office operations. Canada has also privatized its air traffic control system. In each case, the new enterprise reduced its payroll, boosted efficiency and productivity, and quickly

Xinhua/Chen Sihan/Alamy Stock Photo

Many formerly planned economies have moved toward a more mixed economic model. For example, the People's Republic of China has used a planned economic model for decades but is now moving more toward a mixed market economy. These signs on a busy street, for instance, are promoting a variety of goods and services provided by merchants along the street and are very consistent with a mixed economic model.

became profitable. More recently, the government of Iran has privatized numerous oil refineries and petrochemical plants that were previously state owned (although they have not revealed their productivity data).

In the partially planned system called **socialism**, the government owns and operates selected major industries. In such mixed market economies, the government may control banking, transportation, or industries producing basic goods such as oil and steel. Smaller businesses, such as clothing stores and restaurants, though, are privately owned. Many Western European countries, including England and France, allow free market operations in most economic areas but keep government control of others, such as health care. In the United States, the debate over how best to handle health care is often tied to socialism, at least in the rhetoric of politicians. For instance, many opponents of universal or national health care characterize such measures as being socialist.

Socialism *planned economic system in which the government owns and operates only selected major sources of production*

The Economics of Market Systems

Learning Objective 1-3

Show how markets, demand, and supply affect resource distribution in the United States; identify the elements of private enterprise; and explain the various degrees of competition in the U.S. economic system.

Understanding the complex nature of the U.S. economic system is essential to understanding the environment in which U.S. businesses operate. In this section, we describe the workings of the U.S. market economy. Specifically, we examine the nature of *demand and supply, private enterprise*, and *degrees of competition*. We will then discuss private enterprise and forms of competition.

Demand and Supply in a Market Economy

A market economy consists of many different markets that function within that economy. As a consumer, for instance, the choices you have and the prices you pay for gas, food, clothing, and entertainment are all governed by different sets of market forces. Businesses also have many different choices about buying and selling their products. Dell Computer, for instance, can purchase keyboards from literally hundreds of different manufacturers. In addition to deciding where to buy supplies, its managers also have to decide what inventory levels should be, at what prices they should sell their goods, and how they will distribute these goods. Similarly, online retailers like Amazon can decide to use FedEx, UPS, or the U.S. Postal Service to deliver products bought by customers. Literally billions of exchanges take place every day between businesses and individuals; between businesses; and among individuals, businesses, and governments. Moreover, exchanges conducted in one area often affect exchanges elsewhere. For instance, when gas prices are high, this may also lead to prices going up for other products, ranging from food to clothing to delivery services. Why? Because each of these businesses relies heavily on gas to transport products.

The Laws of Demand and Supply On all economic levels, decisions about what to buy and what to sell are determined primarily by the forces of demand and supply.[6] **Demand** is the willingness and ability of buyers to purchase a product (a good or a service). **Supply** is the willingness and ability of producers to offer a good or service for sale. Generally speaking, demand and supply follow basic laws:

- The **law of demand**: Buyers will purchase (demand) *more* of a product as its price *drops* and *less* of a product as its price *increases*.
- The **law of supply**: Producers will offer (supply) *more* of a product for sale as its price *rises* and *less* of a product as its price *drops*.

Demand *the willingness and ability of buyers to purchase a good or service*

Supply *the willingness and ability of producers to offer a good or service for sale*

Law of Demand *principle that buyers will purchase (demand) more of a product as its price drops and less as its price increases*

Law of Supply *principle that producers will offer (supply) more of a product for sale as its price rises and less as its price drops*

The Demand and Supply Schedule To appreciate these laws in action, consider the market for pizza in your town (or neighborhood). If everyone is willing to pay $25 for a pizza (a relatively high price), the town's only pizzeria will produce a large supply. But if everyone is willing to pay only $5 (a relatively low price), it will make fewer pizzas. Through careful analysis, we can estimate how many pizzas will be sold at different

Demand and Supply Schedule *assessment of the relationships among different levels of demand and supply at different price levels*

Demand Curve *graph showing how many units of a product will be demanded (bought) at different prices*

Supply Curve *graph showing how many units of a product will be supplied (offered for sale) at different prices*

prices. These results, called a **demand and supply schedule**, are obtained from marketing research, historical data, and other studies of the market. Properly applied, they reveal the relationships among different levels of demand and supply at different price levels.

Demand and Supply Curves The demand and supply schedule can be used to construct demand and supply curves for pizza in your town. A **demand curve** shows how many products—in this case, pizzas—will be demanded (bought) at different prices. A **supply curve** shows how many pizzas will be supplied (baked or offered for sale) at different prices.

Figure 1.2 shows demand and supply curves for pizzas. As you can see, the quantity demanded increases as price decreases; the quantity supplied increases as price

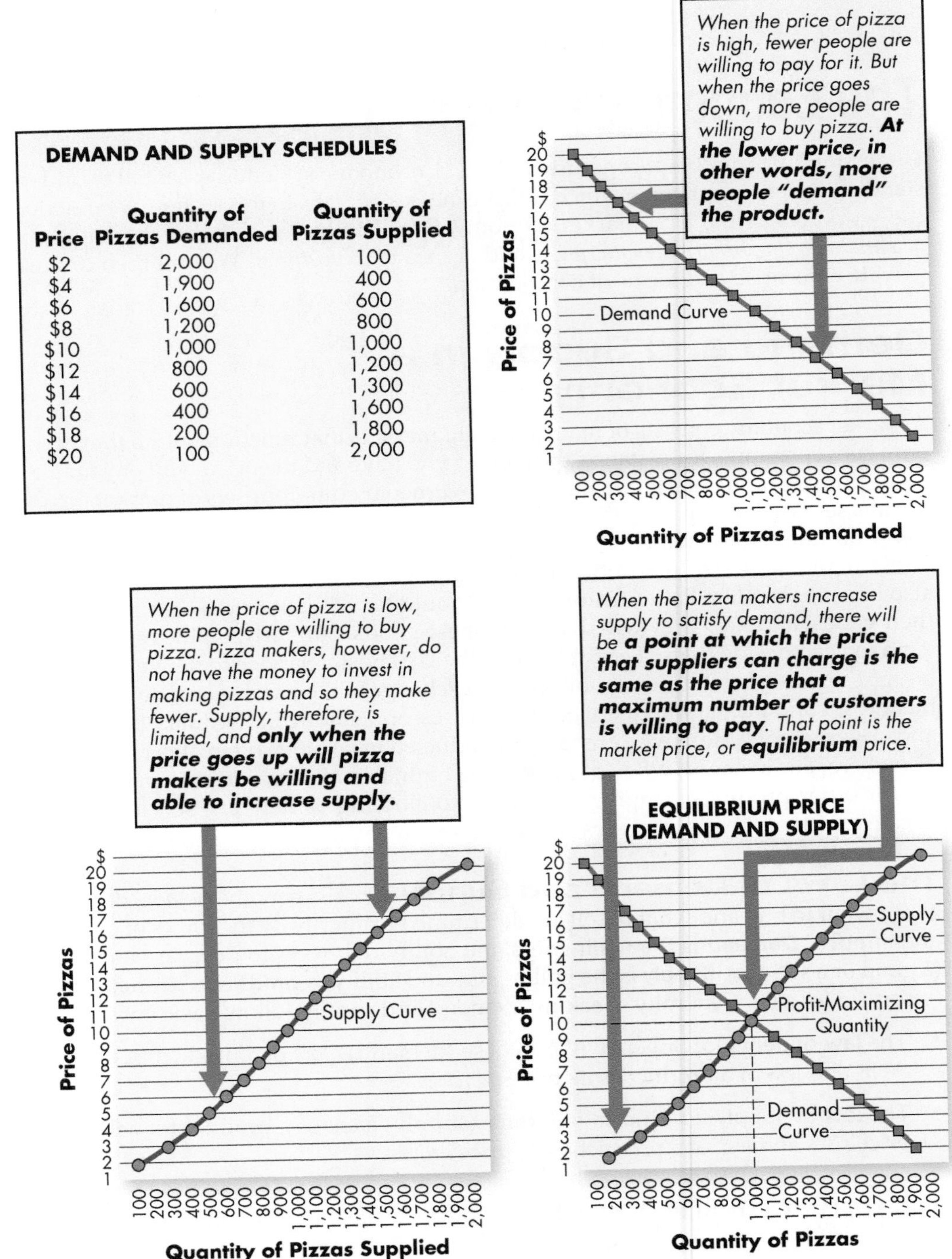

DEMAND AND SUPPLY SCHEDULES

Price	Quantity of Pizzas Demanded	Quantity of Pizzas Supplied
$2	2,000	100
$4	1,900	400
$6	1,600	600
$8	1,200	800
$10	1,000	1,000
$12	800	1,200
$14	600	1,300
$16	400	1,600
$18	200	1,800
$20	100	2,000

FIGURE 1.2 Demand and Supply

increases. When demand and supply curves are plotted on the same graph, the point at which they intersect is the **market price** (also called the **equilibrium price**), the price at which the quantity of goods demanded and the quantity of goods supplied are equal. In Figure 1.2, the equilibrium price for pizzas in our example is $10. At this point, the quantity of pizzas demanded and the quantity of pizzas supplied are the same: 1,000 pizzas per week.

Market Price (Equilibrium Price) *profit-maximizing price at which the quantity of goods demanded and the quantity of goods supplied are equal*

Surpluses and Shortages What if the pizzeria decides to make some other number of pizzas? For example, what would happen if the owner tried to increase profits by making *more* pizzas to sell? Or what if the owner wanted to lower overhead, cut back on store hours, and *reduce* the number of pizzas offered for sale? In either case, the result would be an inefficient use of resources and lower profits. For instance, if the pizzeria supplies 1,200 pizzas and tries to sell them for $10 each, 200 pizzas will not be bought. Our demand schedule shows that only 1,000 pizzas will be demanded at this price. The pizzeria will therefore have a **surplus**, a situation in which the quantity supplied exceeds the quantity demanded. It will lose the money that it spent making those extra 200 pizzas.

Surplus *situation in which quantity supplied exceeds quantity demanded*

Conversely, if the pizzeria supplies only 800 pizzas, a **shortage** will result, meaning the quantity demanded will be greater than the quantity supplied. The pizzeria will "lose" the extra profit that it could have made by producing 200 more pizzas. Even though consumers may pay more for pizzas because of the shortage, the pizzeria will still earn lower total profits than if it had made 1,000 pizzas. It will also risk angering customers who cannot buy pizzas and encourage other entrepreneurs to set up competing pizzerias to satisfy unmet demand. Businesses should seek the ideal combination of price charged and quantity supplied so as to maximize profits, maintain goodwill among customers, and discourage competition. This ideal combination is found at the equilibrium point.

Shortage *situation in which quantity demanded exceeds quantity supplied*

This simple example involves only one company, one product, and a few buyers. The U.S. economy—indeed, any market economy—is far more complex. Thousands of companies sell hundreds of thousands of products to millions of buyers every day. In the end, however, the result is much the same: Companies try to supply the quantity and selection of goods that will earn them the largest profits. For example, most families vacation during the summer months when children are out of school. As a result, airlines increase their capacity to popular travel destinations; and hotels, resorts, and car rental agencies at those destinations adjust their rates to account for the increased demand. But when September rolls around, airlines adjust their routes to other destinations and many summer resorts start to lower their rates. Adjustments then continue throughout the year to account for demand fluctuations during ski season, spring break, long weekends, and other times that people may decide to take vacations.

Private Enterprise and Competition in a Market Economy

Market economies rely on a **private enterprise** system—one that allows individuals to pursue their own interests with minimal government restriction. In turn, private enterprise requires the presence of four elements: private property rights, freedom of choice, profits, and competition.

Private Enterprise *economic system that allows individuals to pursue their own interests without undue governmental restriction*

1 ***Private property rights.*** Ownership of the resources used to create wealth is in the hands of individuals.
2 ***Freedom of choice.*** You can sell your labor to any employer you choose. You can also choose which products to buy, and producers can usually choose whom to hire and what to produce.
3 ***Profits.*** The attraction of profits (and freedom) leads some people to abandon the security of working for someone else and to assume the risks of

entrepreneurship. Anticipated profits also influence individuals' choices of which goods or services to produce.

4 *Competition.* If profits motivate individuals to start businesses, competition motivates them to operate those businesses efficiently. **Competition** occurs when two or more businesses vie for the same resources or customers. To gain an advantage over competitors, a business must produce its goods or services efficiently and be able to sell at a reasonable profit. To achieve these goals, it must convince customers that its products are either better or less expensive than those of its competitors. Competition, therefore, forces all businesses to make products better or cheaper or both. A company that produces inferior, expensive products is likely to fail.

Competition *vying among businesses for the same resources or customers*

Degrees of Competition Even in a free enterprise system, not all industries are equally competitive. Economists have identified four degrees of competition in a private enterprise system: *perfect competition, monopolistic competition, oligopoly,* and *monopoly*. Note that these are not always truly distinct categories but instead tend to fall along a continuum; perfect competition and monopoly anchor the ends of the continuum, with monopolistic competition and oligopoly falling in between. Table 1.1 summarizes the features of these four degrees of competition.

Perfect Competition *market or industry characterized by numerous small firms producing an identical product*

Perfect Competition For **perfect competition** to exist, two conditions must prevail: (1) all firms in an industry must be small, and (2) the number of firms in the industry must be large. Under these conditions, no single firm is powerful enough to influence the price of its product. Prices are, therefore, determined by such market forces as supply and demand.

In addition, these two conditions also reflect four principles:

1 The products of each firm are so similar that buyers view them as identical to those of other firms.
2 Both buyers and sellers know the prices that others are paying and receiving in the marketplace.
3 Because each firm is small, it is easy for firms to enter or leave the market.
4 Going prices are set exclusively by supply and demand and accepted by both sellers and buyers.

U.S. agriculture is a good example of perfect competition. The wheat produced on one farm is the same as that from another. Both producers and buyers are aware of

table 1.1 Degrees of Competition

Characteristic	Perfect Competition	Monopolistic Competition	Oligopoly	Monopoly
Example	Local farmer	Office supply store	Steel industry	Public utility
Number of competitors	Many	Many, but fewer than in perfect competition	Few	None
Ease of entry into industry	Relatively easy	Fairly easy	Difficult	Regulated by government
Similarity of goods or services offered by competing firms	Identical	Similar	Can be similar or different	No directly competing goods or services
Level of control over price by individual firms	None	Some	Some	Considerable

prevailing market prices. It is relatively easy to start producing wheat and relatively easy to stop when it's no longer profitable.

MONOPOLISTIC COMPETITION In **monopolistic competition**, numerous sellers are trying to make their products at least seem to be different from those of competitors. Although many sellers are involved in monopolistic competition, there tend to be fewer than in pure competition. Differentiating strategies include brand names (Tide versus Gain versus in-store house brands of detergent), design or styling (Levi's versus Wrangler versus Madewell jeans), and advertising (Coke versus Pepsi versus Dr Pepper). For example, in an effort to attract weight-conscious consumers, Kraft Foods promotes such differentiated products as low-fat Cool Whip, low-calorie Jell-O, and sugar-free Kool-Aid.

Monopolistic Competition *market or industry characterized by numerous buyers and relatively numerous sellers trying to differentiate their products from those of competitors*

Monopolistically competitive businesses may be large or small, but they can still enter or leave the market easily. For example, many local coffee shops and pizza parlors compete successfully with much larger firms like Starbucks and Pizza Hut. Likewise, many single-store clothing businesses in college towns compete by developing their own T-shirt and baseball cap designs with copyrighted slogans and logos.

Product differentiation also gives sellers some control over prices. For instance, even though Target shirts may have similar styling and other features, Ralph Lauren Polo shirts can be priced with little regard for lower Target prices. But the large number of buyers relative to sellers applies potential limits to prices; although Polo might be able to sell shirts for $20 more than a comparable Target shirt, it could not sell as many shirts if they were priced at $200 more.

OLIGOPOLY When an industry has only a handful of sellers, an **oligopoly** exists. As a general rule, these sellers are quite large. The entry of new competitors is hard because large capital investment is needed. Thus, oligopolistic industries (automobile, airline, and steel industries) tend to stay that way. Only two companies make large commercial aircraft: Boeing (a U.S. company) and Airbus (a European consortium). Furthermore, if the trend toward globalization continues, most experts believe that oligopolies will become increasingly prevalent.

Oligopoly *market or industry characterized by a handful of (generally large) sellers with the power to influence the prices of their products*

Oligopolists have more control over their strategies than do monopolistically competitive firms, but the actions of one firm can significantly affect the sales of every other firm in the industry. For example, when one firm cuts prices or offers incentives to increase sales, the others usually protect sales by doing the same. Likewise, when one firm raises prices, others generally follow suit. Therefore, the prices of comparable products are usually similar. When an airline announces new fare discounts, others adopt the same strategy almost immediately. Just as quickly, when discounts end for one airline, they usually end for everyone else.

MONOPOLY A **monopoly** exists when an industry or market has only one producer (or else is so dominated by one producer that other firms cannot compete with it). A sole producer enjoys complete control over the prices of its products. Its only constraint is a decrease in consumer demand as a result of increased prices. In the United States, laws such as the Sherman Antitrust Act (1890) and the Clayton Act (1914) forbid many monopolies and regulate prices charged by **natural monopolies**, industries in which one company can most efficiently supply all needed goods or services. Many electric companies are natural monopolies because they can supply all the power needed in a local area. Duplicate facilities—such as two power plants and two sets of power lines—would be wasteful.

Monopoly *market or industry in which there is only one producer that can therefore set the prices of its products*

Natural Monopoly *industry in which one company can most efficiently supply all needed goods or services*

Economic Indicators

Learning Objective 1-4

Explain the importance of the economic environment to business and identify the factors used to evaluate the performance of an economic system.

Because economic forces are so volatile and can be affected by so many things, the performance of a country's economic system varies over time. Sometimes it gains strength and brings new prosperity to its members (this describes the U.S. economy during the early years of the twenty-first century); other times, it weakens and damages fortunes (as was the case during 2009–2010). At still other times, it provides moderate growth, helping some members of society but not others (as is the case at present). Clearly, then, knowing how an economy is performing is useful for business owners and investors alike. Most experts look to various **economic indicators**—statistics that show whether an economic system is strengthening, weakening, or remaining stable—to help assess the performance of an economy.

Economic Indicators *statistics that help assess the performance of an economy*

Economic Growth, Aggregate Output, and Standard of Living

At one time, about half the U.S. population was involved in producing the food the country needed. Today, however, only about 1.4 percent of the U.S. population is involved in direct on-farm work.[7] But agricultural efficiency has actually improved because the industry has devised better ways of producing products with more efficient technology. We can therefore say that agricultural productivity has increased because we have been able to increase total output in the agricultural sector while decreasing the labor needed to produce that output.

We can apply the same concepts to a nation's economic system, although the computations are more complex. Fundamentally, how do we know whether an economic system is growing or not? Experts call the pattern of short-term ups and downs (or, better, expansions and contractions) in an economy the **business cycle**. The primary measure of growth in the business cycle is **aggregate output**, the total quantity of goods and services produced by an economic system during a given period.[8]

Business Cycle *short-term pattern of economic expansions and contractions*

Aggregate Output *the total quantity of goods and services produced by an economic system during a given period*

To put it simply, an increase in aggregate output is growth (or economic growth). When output grows more quickly than the population, two things usually follow:

1 Output per capita—the quantity of goods and services per person—goes up.
2 The system provides more of the goods and services that people want.

When these two things occur, people living in an economic system benefit from a higher **standard of living**, which refers to the total quantity and quality of goods and services that they can purchase with the currency used in their economic system. To know how much your standard of living is improving, you need to know how much your nation's economic system is growing (see Table 1.2).[9] For instance, although the U.S. economy reflects overall growth in most years, in 2009 the economy actually shrank by 2.6 percent due to the recession.

Standard of Living *the total quantity and quality of goods and services people can purchase with the currency used in their economic system*

Gross Domestic Product

Gross domestic product (GDP) refers to the total value of all goods and services produced within a given period by a national economy through domestic factors of production. GDP is a measure of aggregate output. Generally speaking, if GDP is going up, aggregate output is going up; if aggregate output is going up, the nation is experiencing *economic growth*.

Gross Domestic Product (GDP) *total value of all goods and services produced within a given period by a national economy through domestic factors of production*

Sometimes, economists also measure **gross national product (GNP)**, which refers to the total value of all goods and services produced by a national economy within a given period regardless of where the factors of production are located. What, precisely, is the difference between GDP and GNP? Consider a General Motors automobile plant in Brazil. The profits earned by the factory are included in U.S. GNP—but not in GDP—because its output is not produced domestically (that is, in the United States). Conversely, those profits are included in Brazil's GDP—but not GNP—because they are produced domestically (that is, in Brazil). Calculations quickly become complex because of different factors of production. The labor, for example, will be mostly

Gross National Product (GNP) *total value of all goods and services produced by a national economy within a given period regardless of where the factors of production are located*

table 1.2 U.S. GDP and GDP per Capita

2021 GDP ($ Trillion)	2021 GDP: Real Growth Rate (%)	2021 GDP per Capita: Purchasing Power Parity
$23	5.7%	$69.578

GDP (gross domestic product)

Brazilian but the capital mostly American. Thus, wages paid to Brazilian workers are part of Brazil's GNP even though profits are not.

Real Growth Rate GDP and GNP usually differ by less than 1 percent, but economists argue that GDP is a more accurate indicator of domestic economic performance because it focuses only on domestic factors of production. With that in mind, let's look at the middle column in Table 1.2. Here, we find that the real growth rate of U.S. GDP—the growth rate of GDP *adjusted for inflation and changes in the value of the country's currency*—was 5.7 percent in 2021. But what does this number actually mean? Remember that *growth depends on output increasing at a faster rate than population*. The U.S. population is growing at a rate of 0.60 percent per year.[10] The *real growth rate* of the U.S. economic system, therefore, has been modest since 2011.

GDP per Capita The number in the third column of Table 1.2 is a reflection of the standard of living: **GDP per capita** means GDP per individual person. We get this figure by dividing total GDP ($23 trillion) by total population, which happens to be around 332 million.[11] In a given period (usually calculated on an annual basis), the United States produces goods and services equal in value to $69,578 for every person in the country. Figure 1.3 shows both GDP and GDP per capita in the United States between 1950 and 2019. GDP per capita is a better measure than GDP itself of the economic well-being of the average person.

GDP Per Capita *gross domestic product divided by total population*

Real GDP **Real GDP** means that GDP has been adjusted to account for changes in currency values and price changes. To understand why adjustments are necessary, assume that pizza is the only product in a hypothetical economy. In 2021, a pizza cost $10; in 2021, a pizza cost $11. In both years, exactly 1,000 pizzas were produced. In 2020, the local GDP was $10,000($10 × 1,000); in 2021, the local GDP was $11,000($11 × 1,000). Has the economy grown? No. Because 1,000 pizzas were produced in both years, *aggregate output* remained the same. The point is to not be misled into believing that an economy is doing better than it is. If it is not adjusted, local GDP

Real GDP *GDP adjusted to account for changes in currency values and price changes*

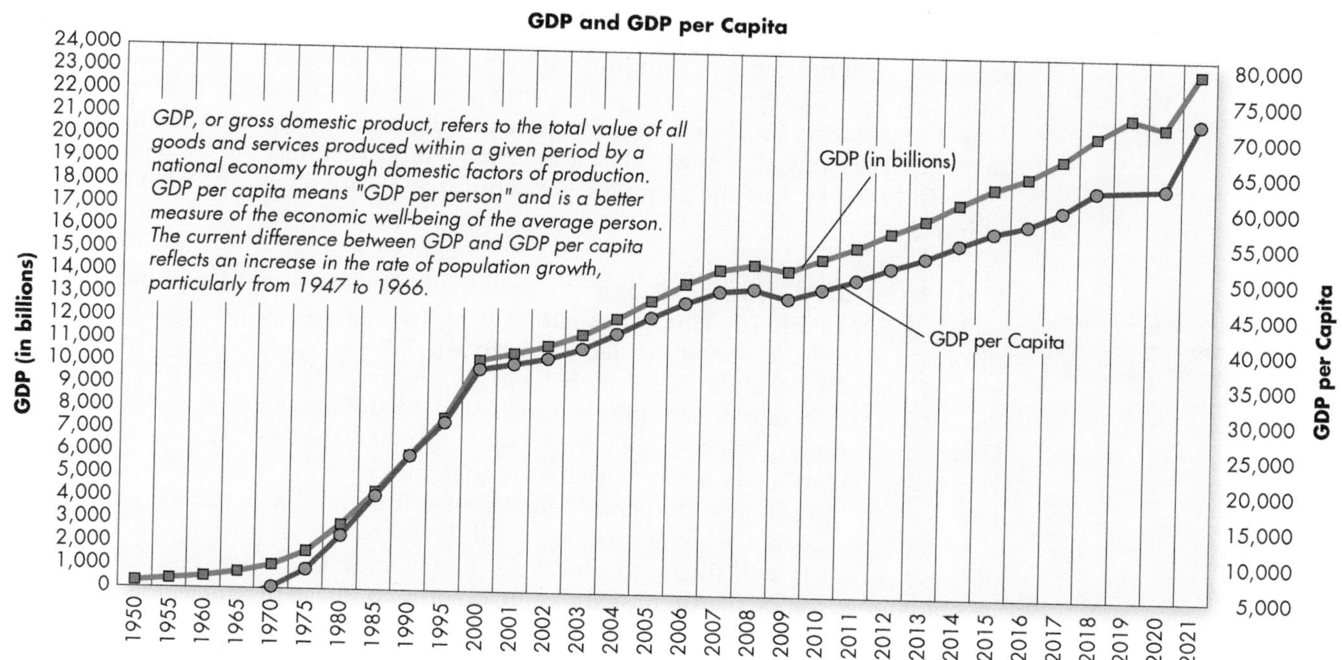

FIGURE 1.3 GDP and GDP per Capita
Source: Based on U.S. Bureau of Economic Analysis https://www.bea.gov/data/gdp and The World Bank. https://data.worldbank.org/indicator/NY.GDP.PCAP.CD?locations=US

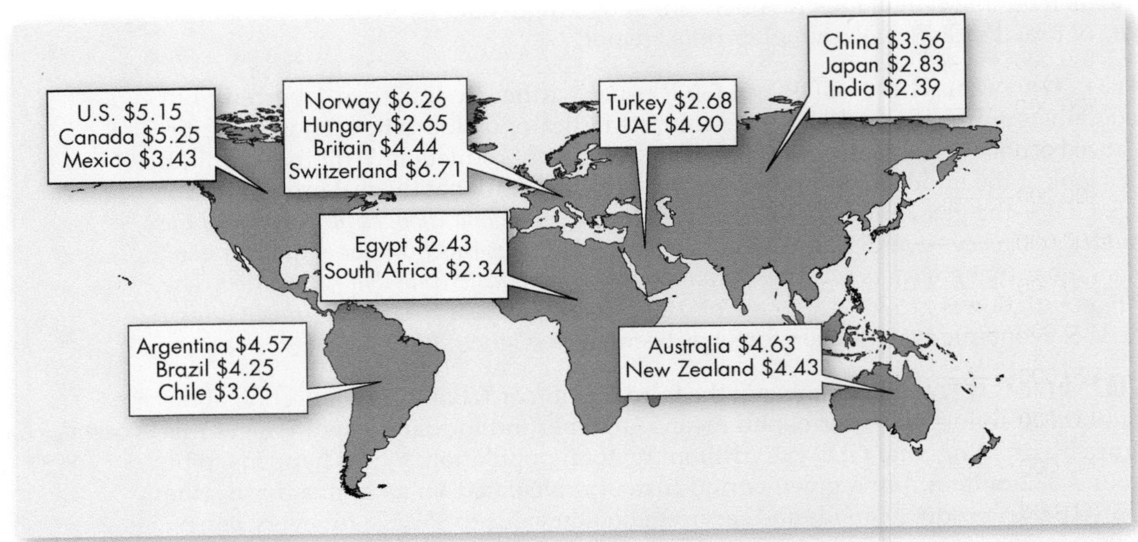

FIGURE 1.4 Price of a Big Mac in U.S. Currency in January 2020
Source: Based on The Big Mac Index. Published by the Economist website. https://www.economist.com/big-mac-index.

Nominal GDP *GDP measured in current dollars or with all components valued at current prices*

for 2022 is **nominal GDP**—GDP measured in current dollars or with all components valued at current prices.[12]

Purchasing Power Parity *the principle that exchange rates are set so that the prices of similar products in different countries are about the same*

Purchasing Power Parity In the example, *current prices* would be 2021 prices. In contrast, we calculate real GDP when we adjust GDP to account for changes in *currency values and price changes*. When we make this adjustment, we account for both GDP and **purchasing power parity**, the principle that exchange rates are set so that the prices of similar products in different countries are about the same. Purchasing power parity gives us a much better idea of *what people can actually buy with the financial resources allocated to them by their respective economic systems*. In other words, it gives us a better sense of standards of living across the globe. Figure 1.4 illustrates a popular approach to see how purchasing power parity works in relation to a Big Mac. For instance, the figure pegs the price of a Big Mac in the United States at $5.15. Based on currency exchange rates, a Big Mac would cost $6.71 in Switzerland and $6.26 in Norway. But the same burger would cost only $3.56 in China and $2.39 in India.

Productivity *a measure of economic growth that compares how much a system produces with the resources needed to produce it*

Productivity

A major factor in the growth of an economic system is **productivity,** which is a measure of economic performance that compares how much a system produces with the resources needed to produce it. Let's say that it takes 1 U.S. worker and 1 U.S. dollar to make 10 soccer balls in an 8-hour workday. Let's also say that it takes 1.2 German workers and the equivalent of 1.5 dollars in euros, the currency of Germany, to make 10 soccer balls in the same 8-hour workday. We can say that the U.S. soccer-ball industry is more productive than the German soccer-ball industry. The two factors of production in this extremely simple case are labor and capital.

If more products are being produced with fewer factors of production, the prices of these products will likely go down. As a consumer, therefore, you would need less of your currency to purchase the same quantity of these products. In short, your standard of living—at least with regard to these products—has improved. If your entire economic system increases its productivity, then your overall standard of living improves. In fact, standard of living improves *only* through increases in productivity.[13] Real growth in GDP reflects growth in productivity.

Productivity in the United States is generally increasing, and as a result, so are GDP and GDP per capita in most years (excluding the 2009 recession). Ultimately,

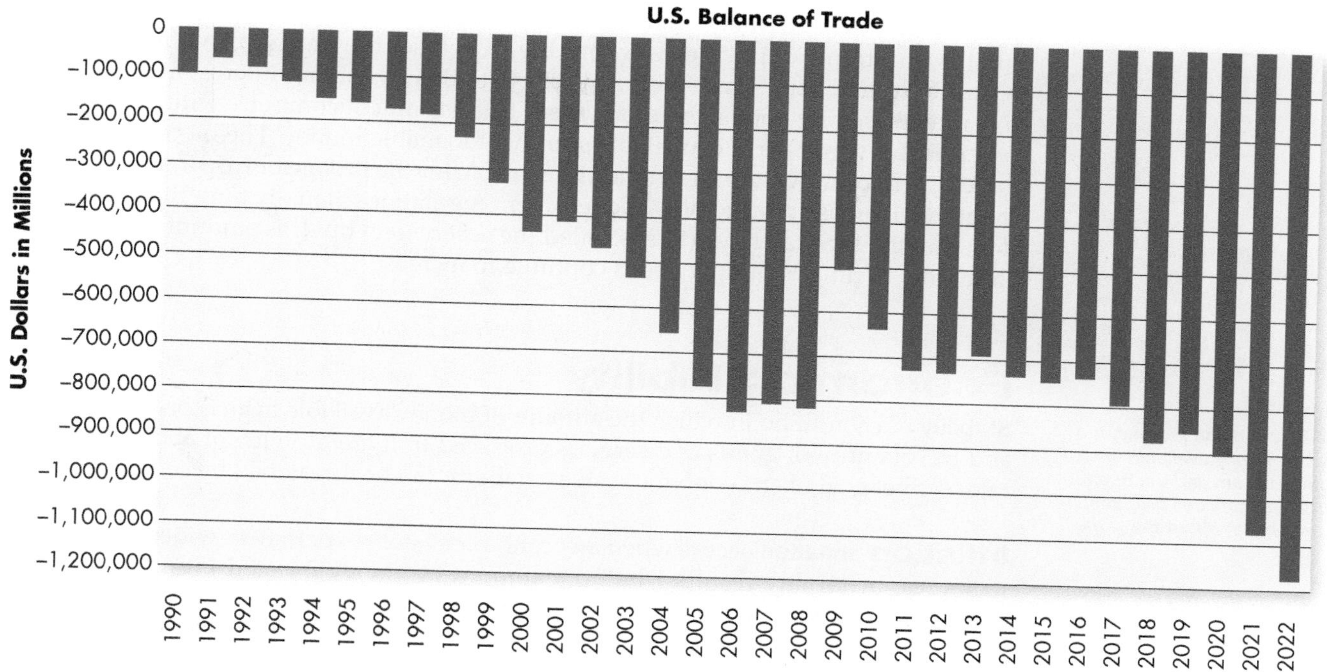

FIGURE 1.5 U.S. Balance of Trade
Source: U.S. Census Bureau. https://www.census.gov/foreign-trade/balance/c0004.html#2020

increases in these measures of growth mean an improvement in the standard of living. However, things don't always proceed so smoothly. Several factors can inhibit the growth of an economic system, including *balance of trade* and the *national debt*.

Balance of Trade A country's **balance of trade** is the economic value of all the products that it exports minus the economic value of its imported products. The principle here is quite simple:

Balance of Trade *economic value of all products a country exports minus the economic value of all products it imports*

- A *positive* balance of trade results when a country exports (sells to other countries) more than it imports (buys from other countries).
- A *negative* balance of trade results when a country imports more than it exports.

A negative balance of trade is commonly called a *trade deficit*. In 2022, the U.S. trade deficit was a little over $1 trillion. The United States is a *debtor nation* rather than a *creditor nation*. Recent trends in the U.S. balance of trade are shown in Figure 1.5.

Trade deficit affects economic growth because the amount of money spent on foreign products has not been paid in full. Therefore, it is, in effect, borrowed money, and borrowed money costs more in the form of interest. The money that flows out of the country to pay off the deficit can't be used to invest in productive enterprises, either at home or overseas.

National Debt Its **national debt** is the amount of money that the government owes its creditors. As of this writing, the U.S. national debt is around $31.2 trillion, or about $93,700 per U.S. citizen, and is increasing at a rate of around $2 billion per day. You can find out the national debt on any given day by going to any one of several Internet sources, including the U.S. National Debt Clock at https://www.pgpf.org/national-debt-clock.

National Debt *the amount of money the government owes its creditors*

How does the national debt affect economic growth? Although taxes are the most obvious way the government raises money, it also sells *bonds*—securities through which it promises to pay buyers certain amounts of money by specified future dates. (In a sense, a bond is an IOU with interest.[14]) These bonds are attractive investments because they are extremely safe: The U.S. government is not going to default on them (that is, fail to make payments when due). Even so, they must also offer a decent return on the buyer's investment, and they do this by paying interest at a competitive rate. By selling bonds, therefore, the U.S. government competes with every other potential borrower for the available supply of loanable money. The more money the government borrows, the less money is available for the private borrowing and investment that increase productivity. Government regulations actually limit the amount of debt that the U.S. can have (this is called the *debt ceiling*) but this amount is increased from time to time as budget needs continue to increase.

Economic Stability

Stability *condition in which the amount of money available in an economic system and the quantity of goods and services produced in it are growing at about the same rate*

Stability is a condition in which the amount of money available in an economic system and the quantity of goods and services produced in it are growing at about the same rate. A chief goal of an economic system, stability can be threatened by certain factors.

Inflation *occurs when widespread price increases occur throughout an economic system*

Inflation

Inflation occurs when an economic system experiences widespread price increases. Instability results when the amount of money injected into an economy exceeds the increase in actual output, so people have more money to spend but the same quantity of products available to buy. As supply and demand principles tell us, when people compete with one another to buy available products, prices go up. These high prices will eventually bring the amount of money in the economy back down. However, these processes are imperfect—the additional money will not be distributed proportionately to all people, and price increases often continue beyond what is really necessary. As a result, purchasing power for many people declines.

Consumer Price Index (CPI) *a measure of the prices of typical products purchased by consumers living in urban areas*

Keeping in mind that our definition of inflation is the occurrence of widespread price increases throughout an economic system, it stands to reason that we can measure inflation by measuring price increases. Price indexes such as the **consumer price index (CPI)** measure the prices of typical products purchased by consumers living in urban areas.[15] The CPI is expressed as a percentage of prices as compared to a base period. The current base period used to measure inflation is 1982–1984, which is set at 100 (indicating a percentage). For comparison purposes, the CPI index was 172.2 in 2000, 195.3 in 2005, 218.1 in 2010, 229.6 in 2012, 240.7 in 2016, and 256.6 in 2019. So, prices in 2010 reached more than double the level in the 1982–1984 base period. In 2022 inflation in the United States rose to around eight percent but slowed signs of slowing in 2023.

Although we tend to view inflation as bad, in most ways it is better than *deflation*, which happens when widespread price cuts occur. Whereas inflation creates instability, it also generally indicates the overall economy is growing (just in an erratic manner). But deflation generally means the overall economy is shrinking, a more serious problem from most perspectives.

Unemployment *the level of joblessness among people actively seeking work in an economic system*

Unemployment

Finally, we need to consider the effect of unemployment on economic stability. **Unemployment** is the level of joblessness among people actively seeking work in an economic system. When unemployment is low, there is a shortage of labor available for businesses to hire. As businesses compete with one another for the available supply of labor, they raise the wages they are willing to pay. Then, because higher labor costs reduce profit margins, they raise the prices of their products. Although consumers have more money to inject into the economy, this increase is soon undone by higher prices (inflation), so purchasing power declines.

At least two problems are related to unemployment:

1. If wage rates get too high, businesses will respond by hiring fewer workers and unemployment will go up.
2. Businesses could raise prices to counter increased labor costs, but they won't be able to sell as many of their products at higher prices. Because of reduced sales, they will cut back on hiring and, once again, unemployment will go up.

managing in turbulent times

Coronavirus: The Global Economic Impact of Disease

In 430 BC, Athenians were beaten as much by a plague as they were by the Spartans. In CE 165, the Roman army was devastated by smallpox. In CE 541, the bubonic plague killed half the population of Europe and millions of others across the globe, and in the 14th century, the plague altered the course of human history. As people became more mobile, rats and fleas carried the bubonic plague farther than ever before, decimating the population, depressing the global economy, and shifting the remaining workforce away from feudalism and labor-intensive crops toward capitalism and innovation.

In 1918, an avian-borne flu infected over a third of the world's population and took the lives of 50 million people. But unlike previously recorded pandemics that tended to target those with weaker immune systems, the "Spanish Flu" was most deadly for people between the ages of 20 and 40, which meant that it killed a large percentage of the world's workforce. In 1957, the world faced an outbreak of Asian flu, and by 1981, HIV/AIDS was ravaging a previously healthy population. Each of these public health crises, in addition to the horrific loss of human life, had both micro- and macroeconomic consequences.

More recently, the COVID-19 pandemic, which emerged in December 2019, sent a shock wave through the world markets as investors lost confidence in the economy. Longer term, the pandemic disrupted the workforce. Income falls when people don't work for several weeks or months. Under- or unemployed people curtail spending and the people who didn't receive that spending cut their own spending in turn, causing a downward spiral in GDP. In fact, second-quarter 2020 GDP plummeted by an unprecedented 29.9 percent. In addition, the decrease in the supply of some goods as factories ran at less than full capacity led to shortages, and that, in turn, led to high inflation in late 2022 and early 2023 as supply chain issues continued to plague manufacturing and retail across the board. It is important for the entrepreneur or manager of a business to keep these kinds of potential external calamities in mind and to work them into disaster contingency plans to avoid joining a long list of once strong companies like Revlon, Hertz, Brooks Brothers, and JC Penney who all filed for bankruptcy due to the pandemic.

What if the government tries to correct this situation by injecting more money into the economic system—say, by cutting taxes or spending more money? Prices in general may go up because of increased consumer demand. Again, purchasing power declines and inflation may set in.[16] In early 2020, unemployment was hovering around 3.5 percent.[17] By mid-2020, however, the impact of COVID-19 had pushed unemployment up to over 8 percent. By early 2023, though, unemployment had dropped to pre-pandemic levels.

Recessions and Depressions Unemployment is sometimes a symptom of a system-wide disorder in the economy. During a downturn in the business cycle, people in different sectors may lose their jobs at the same time. As a result, overall income and spending may drop. Feeling the pinch of reduced revenues, businesses may cut spending on the factors of production—including labor. Yet more people will be put out of work, and unemployment will only increase further. Unemployment that results from this trend is called *cyclical unemployment*.

If we look at the relationship between unemployment and economic stability, we are reminded that when prices get high enough, consumer demand for goods and services goes down. We are also reminded that when demand for products goes down, producers cut back on hiring and, not surprisingly, eventually start producing less. Consequently, aggregate output decreases. When we go through a period during which aggregate output declines, we have a recession. During a *recession*, producers need fewer employees—less labor—to produce products. Unemployment, therefore, goes up.

To determine whether an economy is going through a recession, we start by measuring aggregate output. Recall that this is the function of real GDP, which we find by making necessary adjustments to the total value of all goods and services produced within a given period by a national economy through domestic factors of production. A **recession** is more precisely defined as a period during which aggregate output, as measured by real GDP, declines. As noted previously, most economists agree that the

Recession *a period during which aggregate output, as measured by GDP, declines*

U.S. economy went into recession in 2008; most also agree that we were gradually emerging from that recession in 2011. A prolonged and deep recession is a **depression**. The last major depression in the United States started in 1929 and lasted more than 10 years. Most economists believe that the 2008–2011 recession, although the worst in decades, was not really a depression. However, it has come to be popularly known as the Great Recession, and we will use this phrase in this book.

Depression *a prolonged and deep recession*

Managing the U.S. Economy

The government acts to manage the U.S. economic system through two sets of policies: fiscal and monetary. It manages the collection and spending of its revenues through **fiscal policies**. Tax rates, for example, can play an important role in fiscal policies helping to manage the economy. One key element of President Obama's presidential platform was an overhaul of the U.S. tax system. Among other things, he proposed cutting taxes for the middle class, while simultaneously raising taxes for both higher-income people and businesses. During President Trump's presidency he initiated efforts to lower all taxes, although higher-income people and businesses saw the largest cuts. For a variety of reasons, however, little ever gets accomplished in the area of comprehensive tax reform. President Biden has proposed increasing rates for higher-income individuals, but this proposal was unlikely to succeed given strong Republican opposition.

Fiscal Policies *policies used by a government regarding how it collects and spends revenue*

Monetary policies focus on controlling the size of the nation's money supply. Working primarily through the Federal Reserve System (the nation's central bank, often referred to simply as "the Fed"), the government can influence the ability and willingness of banks throughout the country to lend money. For example, to help combat the Great Recession, the government injected more money into the economy through various stimulus packages. On the one hand, officials hoped that these funds would stimulate business growth and the creation of new jobs. On the other hand, though, some experts feared that increasing the money supply might also lead to inflation. In reality, inflation did go up but not by a large amount. A more recent example of the use of monetary policy took place during the 2020 COVID-19 pandemic. As economic activity ground to a halt, the Fed lowered interest rates to incentivize banks to continue to loan money. In 2022 and 2023 the Fed used interest rates to attempt to keep the economy from going into recession.

Monetary Policy *policy used by a government to control the size of its money supply*

Taken together, fiscal policy and monetary policy make up **stabilization policy**, government economic policy in which the goal is to smooth out fluctuations in output and unemployment and to stabilize prices. In effect, the Great Recession was a significant departure from stabilization as business valuations dropped and jobs were eliminated. The various government interventions, such as financial bailouts, represented strategies to restore economic stability.

Stabilization Policy *government economic policy intended to smooth out fluctuations in output and unemployment and to stabilize prices*

Learning Objective 1-5

Learn about the skills you will gain through this text.

Developing Skills in Your Career

If you haven't yet decided on a major, you may be thinking that this section isn't relevant to you. Let me assure you it is. Whether or not you plan on a career in business, the lessons you learn in this course will help you (in business or life or both). Moreover, it is only through the aggregate of your educational experience that you will have the opportunity to develop many of the skills that employers have identified as critical to success in the workplace. In this course and specifically in this text, you'll have the opportunity to develop and practice these skills in the following places:

- **Communication** Regardless of your job or level in an organization, being able to communicate effectively is extremely important. You need to be able to write clearly, tailor your message to the situation, and speak and listen well in order to succeed. Communication is covered in several places throughout the book. For example, Chapter 5 discusses how leaders communicate the corporate culture, while Chapter 6 discusses how managers communicate the delegation process and how managers can use communication to offset errors in the grapevine.

- **Critical Thinking** The ability to process information beyond a superficial level plays a vital role in organizations. It is relatively easy to read information, but critical thinking is necessary to understand patterns and relationships among that information. Chapter 9 devotes specific attention to the decision-making process. Chapter 11 discusses the research process and research methods.
- **Collaboration** More and more work today is being performed by people working together, either face-to-face or using Teams or Zoom. Consequently, it is important to know how to work with others effectively. Teams and team-based methods of organizing are discussed in Chapters 6 and 8. At the end of each chapter, there is also a continuing team exercise.
- **Business Ethics and Social Responsibility** Businesses and their leaders are coming under increased scrutiny to make sure that they are conducting themselves in an open and honest manner and are helping to address growing problems such as food shortages, climate change, and so forth. Chapter 2 is entirely devoted to ethics and social responsibility.
- **Information Technology Application and Computing Skills** Information technology is becoming ever more sophisticated and valuable to managers. New tools like advances in smartphones, AI, cloud computing, and collaborative software can all help managers make faster and better decisions. Chapter 14 is devoted to information technology application and computing skills for business.

summary of learning objectives

LEARNING OBJECTIVE 1-1

Define the nature of U.S. business, describe the external environments of business, and discuss how these environments affect the success or failure of organizations.

A *business* is an organization that sells goods or services to earn profits. The prospect of earning *profits*, the difference between a business's revenues and expenses, encourages people to open and expand businesses. Businesses produce most of the goods and services that Americans consume and employ most working people. A healthy business environment supports innovation and contributes to the quality of life and standard of living of people in a society.

The *external environment* of business refers to everything outside its boundaries that might affect it. Both the *domestic* and the *global business environment* affect virtually all businesses. The domestic business environment is the environment in which a business conducts its operations and derives its revenues. The global business environment also refers to the international forces that affect a business, for example, international trade agreements, economic conditions, and political unrest.

The *technological, political-legal, sociocultural,* and *economic environments* are also important. The technological environment includes all the ways by which firms create value for their constituents. Technology includes human knowledge, work methods, physical equipment, electronics, telecommunications, and various processing systems that are used to perform business functions. The political-legal environment reflects the relationship between business and government, usually in the form of government regulation of business. The sociocultural environment includes the customs, mores, values, and demographic characteristics of the society in which an organization functions. Sociocultural processes also determine the goods and services that a society is likely to value and accept. The economic environment refers to the relevant conditions that exist in the economic system in which an organization functions.

LEARNING OBJECTIVE 1-2

Describe the different types of global economic systems according to the means by which they control the factors of production.

Economic systems differ in the ways in which they manage the five *factors of production*: (1) *labor*, or *human resources*; (2) *capital*; (3) *entrepreneurship*; (4) *physical resources*; and (5) *information resources*. Labor, or human resources, includes the physical and intellectual contributions people make while engaged in business. Capital includes all financial resources needed to operate a business. Entrepreneurs are an essential factor of production. They are the people who accept the risks and opportunities associated with creating and operating businesses. Virtually every business will rely on physical resources, the tangible things organizations use to conduct their business. Physical resources include raw materials, storage and production facilities, computers, and equipment. Finally, information resources are essential to the success of a business enterprise. Information resources include data and other information used by business.

Economic systems can be differentiated based on the way they allocate the factors of production. A *planned economy* relies on a centralized government to control factors of production and make decisions. Under *communism*, the government owns and operates all sources of production. In a *market economy*, individuals—producers and consumers—control production and allocation decisions through supply and demand. A *market* is a mechanism for exchange between the buyers and sellers of a particular product or service. Sellers can charge what they want, and customers can buy what they choose. The political basis of market processes is *capitalism*, which fosters private ownership of the factors of production and encourages entrepreneurship by offering profits as an incentive. Most countries rely on some form of *mixed market economy*—a system featuring characteristics of both planned and market economies. *Socialism* may be considered a planned economy or a mixed economy, with government ownership of selected industries but considerable private ownership, especially among small businesses.

LEARNING OBJECTIVE 1-3

Show how markets, demand, and supply affect resource distribution in the United States; identify the elements of private enterprise; and explain the various degrees of competition in the U.S. economic system.

Decisions about what to buy and what to sell are determined by the forces of demand and supply. *Demand* is the willingness and ability of buyers to purchase a product or service. *Supply* is the willingness and ability of producers to offer a product or service for sale. A *demand and supply schedule* reveals the relationships among different levels of demand and supply at different price levels. The point at which the demand and supply curves intersect is called the *market or equilibrium price*. If a seller attempts to sell above the market price, they will have a surplus where the quantity supplied exceeds the demand at that price. Conversely, a shortage occurs when a product is sold below the equilibrium price and demand outstrips supply.

Market economies reflect the operation of a *private enterprise system*, a system that allows individuals to pursue their own interests without government restriction. Private enterprise requires the presence of four elements: (1) private property rights, (2) freedom of choice, (3) profits, and (4) competition. Economists have identified four degrees of competition in a private enterprise system: (1) *perfect competition*, (2) *monopolistic competition*, (3) *oligopoly*, and (4) *monopoly*. Perfect competition exists when all firms in an industry are small, there exist many of them, and no single firm is powerful enough to influence prices. In monopolistic competition, numerous sellers try to differentiate their product from that of the other firms.

An oligopoly exists when an industry has only a few sellers. It is usually quite difficult to enter the market in an oligopoly, and the firms tend to be large. A monopoly exists when there is only one seller in a market. A firm operating in a monopoly has complete control over the price of its products.

LEARNING OBJECTIVE 1-4

Explain the importance of the economic environment to business and identify the factors used to evaluate the performance of an economic system.

Economic indicators are statistics that show whether an economic system is strengthening, weakening, or remaining stable. The overall health of the economic environment—the economic system in which businesses operate—affects organizations. The two key goals of the U.S. system are *economic growth* and *economic stability*. Growth is assessed by *aggregate output*, the total quantity of goods and services produced by an economic system. Although gains in productivity can create growth, the *balance of trade* and the *national debt* can inhibit growth. While growth is an important goal, some countries may pursue economic stability. *Economic stability* means that the amount of money available in an economic system and the quantity of goods and services produced in it are growing at about the same rate. The two key threats to stability are *inflation* and *unemployment*. The government manages the economy through two sets of policies: *fiscal policies* (such as tax increases) and *monetary policies* that focus on controlling the size of the nation's money supply.

LEARNING OBJECTIVE 1-5

Learn about the skills you will gain through this text.

Individuals need a variety of skills to succeed in their careers. This book will help you develop and enhance your skills in the areas of communication, critical thinking, collaboration, business ethics and social responsibility, and information technology and computer applications.

key terms

questions & exercises

QUESTIONS FOR REVIEW

1-1. What are the benefits of a free market economy? What are the drawbacks?

1-2. What are the factors of production? Is one factor more important than the others? If so, which one? Why?

1-3. How are the demand and supply curves related?

1-4. Can business negatively affect society? Give an example of a negative effect.

QUESTIONS FOR ANALYSIS

1-5. Identify and describe at least three factors in the external environment that affect college enrollment. Explain how each trend affects colleges and universities. Explain how each factor may affect college and university enrollment, either by increasing or reducing it.

1-6. Give an example of a situation in which a surplus of a product led to decreased prices. Similarly, give an example of a situation in which a shortage led to increased prices. What eventually happened in each case? Why?

1-7. Explain how current economic indicators, such as inflation and unemployment, affect you personally. Explain how they may affect you as a manager.

1-8. How are the overall economic goals of stability and growth related? Can they be reconciled with each other? If so, how?

APPLICATION EXERCISES

1-9. Sarah and Olivia live on the outskirts of town. Since their car was in the shop, they took an Uber to an early morning medical appointment. The Uber cost $20. At about 8:30 AM, when searching for an Uber home, the app notified them that the ride home would be $80. Why do you think this happened? Do you think it is fair?

1-10. Pick a product or service that you buy infrequently, such as a car or a vacation. Pick a producer or provider, such as Jeep or Marriott, and determine: (1) how demand and supply affect this product or service, (2) what essential factors of production are most central to the supplier's operations, and (3) how fluctuations in economic indicators affect this business.

building a business: continuing team exercise

Build a team of three to five classmates. You will be working with this team throughout the semester to make decisions about the launch of a new product.

ASSIGNMENT

Meet with your team members and develop specific responses to the following:

1-11. Have each team member work individually to identify at least three trends in the external environment that will create business opportunities. Come together as a group and create a master list of trends.

1-12. Which trend does the group think creates the greatest opportunity for success? Why?

1-13. Identify a product, either a good or a service, that will take advantage of this opportunity. Although you will refine this throughout the semester, write a four- to six-sentence description of your product and how it will spark buyer interest.

1-14. Who is your competition for this product, either by direct competition or by substitute products? Is competition a good sign for your business?

team exercise

COMPETITION IN THE NEW MOBILE ECONOMY

Background Information

You are one of two owners of the Red Hot Coffee Pot. Your establishment is on a side street right off the main street through town. Your customer base is largely university students, artists, writers, and other locals who prefer your cozy atmosphere, with its overstuffed couches, fireplace, outdoor seating in the summer, shelves full of books to borrow and browse, locally roasted coffees, and, of course, free Wi-Fi. Within a five-block radius are at least three other coffeehouses with slightly less ambiance but otherwise similar perks, and prices are consistent for all the drinks and pastries across the range of competitors. However, you've become concerned because one of your competitors (the national chain store right around the corner) is promoting its new mobile app and customer loyalty program. Customers can order and pay online, pick up the drinks without having to wait in line, and earn points toward future purchases. Your profit margin is very narrow, and you are already seeing a slight decline in business, although you can't directly attribute that to the new app. Your partner is worried and has shown you a quick graph, drawn on a napkin during a lunch break, of the relationship between supply and demand, and has indicated that a reduction of price would theoretically increase quantity demanded and, therefore, according to your partner, market share and ultimately profits. You've decided to assemble a team to address this issue proactively.

Team Activity

Assemble a group of four or five people. Each group should develop a general strategy for responding to competitors' marketing strategies. Be sure to consider the following factors:

- How price changes affect the demand for your product and profits
- The number of competitors selling the same or a similar product
- The methods you can use—other than price—to attract new customers and retain current customers

FOLLOW-UP QUESTIONS

1-15. What form of competition best characterizes this market? What characteristics did you identify that led you to that conclusion?

1-16. Develop specific strategies based on each of the following situations:

- The average cup of coffee sells for $3 in your area. Right now you are selling 10,000 cups of coffee a month, and your fixed costs, including your own salary and that of your partner, are about $30,000 per month.
- The big chain store around the corner reduces its average sales price per cup to $2.80. As a result, your business falls off by 25 percent.

1-17. Discuss the role that various inducements other than price might play in affecting demand and supply in this market.

1-18. Is it always in a company's best interest to feature the lowest prices?

exercising your ethics

AI FOR INCREASED PROFITS

The Situation

You are a paralegal in an established law firm that has long been known for its attention to personal customer service. Though there are several partners and a large support staff, profits have been declining for three years and staff reports feeling overwhelmed with the volume of work, according to a recent culture survey. Paralegal staff spend a large portion of their time doing research and writing briefs for the partners.

The Dilemma

As part of the culture survey, the managing partners have asked staff to make suggestions to improve both working conditions and profitability. After some initial research and careful consideration, you bring a suggestion to the partners: use AI like ChatGPT to write the initial draft of legal briefs. Paralegals can then confirm details and edit before handing them off to partners. You propose a beta test where some briefs are drafted by AI and some by humans and the blinded drafts are put before a small group for feedback. You note that if the firm uses AI for initial drafts, it will relieve the workload pressure on paralegals, and the software may actually bring up issues that humans may not have considered.

The partners' decision about moving ahead with the plan is split about 50/50. One partner, an early adopter of tech, is a vocal proponent of AI and points out that all briefs will pass through several humans before they end up as part of a public record. Another partner, from a previous generation, is outraged at the suggestion, saying that it's tantamount to writing fiction.

QUESTIONS TO ADDRESS

1-19. What are the primary arguments both for and against using AI in this scenario?

1-20. What are the underlying ethical issues?

1-21. What would you do if you were faced with this situation, in both the paralegal and the managing partner roles?

cases

REINVENTING AN AMERICAN ICON

At the beginning of this chapter, you read about Harley-Davidson, Inc. Using the information presented in this chapter, you should now be able to answer these questions.

QUESTIONS FOR DISCUSSION

1-22. How do you think a recession would affect Harley-Davidson and why?

1-23. Do you think Harley made a mistake by shifting focus to smaller bikes as well as the Pan American and the LiveWire? If so, why? If not, why not?

1-24. What economic indicators would Harley management be most likely to watch, and why?

1-25. Do the turbulent rising and falling fortunes of business increase or decrease your confidence in a capitalistic system based on private enterprise?

1-26. What is your prediction for the future of Harley-Davidson? What is your rationale for your opinion based on what you have learned in this chapter?

COMPETITION IN THE ATHLETIC SHOE INDUSTRY

In 1839, Goodyear introduced a shoe with thick rubber soles melded to canvas fabric that was mainly for sailors, but the soft, non-slip "sneakers" (so named because they allowed the wearer to sneak around silently) were slow to take off with the general public. In 1892, the company adopted the brand name Keds after discovering the original brand name "Peds" was already trademarked. They began offering a lace-up design and focused marketing efforts on women, but it wasn't until 1936, when Gold Medal winner Jesse Owens wore a pair of Adidas at the Olympic Games, that people began to look at running and tennis shoes as a viable alternative to other kinds of casual footwear.

The athletic shoe industry continued to grow, supplying both professional athletes and the general public with comfortable, durable sports shoes. Then, in 1964, University of Oregon track-and-field coach Bill Bowerman and his former student Phil Knight founded Blue Ribbon Sports. They opened their first retail outlet in 1966 and launched a product line called Nike in 1972. They went public two years later as Nike, Inc. and launched the Air Jordan line of shoes in 1985.[18] With the success of the Air Jordan, Nike rocketed to name-brand familiarity and athletic shoes became more than just footwear—they became status symbols as well.

By the mid-'80s then, sneakers were common, and market demand continued to grow. A 2022 study predicted the global athletic footwear industry will reach USD 142.4 billion by 2026 as consumers increasingly realize the importance of using the appropriate type of shoes to prevent muscle injuries, leg injuries, knee pain, hip pain, and back pain.[19] The athletic footwear industry goes far beyond the sports-minded, however, with products designed for more than fitness. With spokespersons from Taylor Swift to Martha Stewart, athletic shoes have increased their footprint from an on-court presence to high fashion, artistic design, and runway-ready glamour.

QUESTIONS FOR DISCUSSION

1-27. Do some research to determine the top three to five athletic footwear manufacturers. How do the various manufacturers differentiate their products?

1-28. Which manufacturer's product do you think is superior? Give a short list of reasons for your opinion.

1-29. Do you think pricing strategies in the athletic footwear market are coordinated? If so, do you think the coordination is overt or a function of the market?

1-30. How hard would it be for a new company to get started in the athletic footwear industry today? What are the barriers to entry? What strategies would you suggest for someone with an idea for a new design of athletic footwear?

1-31. In terms of degrees of competition, how would you describe the market for athletic footwear? Justify your assertion.

1-32. Other than supply, what factors would affect the price that manufacturers and retail outlets are able to command for their products?

endnotes

[1] See Paul Heyne, Peter J. Boetke, and David L. Prychitko, *The Economic Way of Thinking*, 13th ed. (Upper Saddle River, NJ: Pearson, 2014), 172–176.

[2] Krystal Hu, "ChatGPT Sets Record for Fastest-Growing User Base—Analyst Note," Reuters, February 2, 2023, https://www.reuters.com/technology/chatgpt-sets-record-fastest-growing-user-base-analyst-note-2023-02-01/.

[3] Jeremy Kahn, "Musk and Wozniak among 1,100+ Signing Open Letter Calling for 6-Month Ban on Creating Powerful A.I.," *Fortune*, March 29, 2023, https://fortune.com/2023/03/29/elon-musk-apple-steve-wozniak-over-1100-sign-open-letter-6-month-ban-creating-powerful-ai/.

[4] *Hoover's Handbook of American Business 2022* (Austin, TX: Hoover's, 2022), 797–798.

[5] See Karl E. Case, Ray C. Fair, and Sharon Oster, *Principles of Economics*, 13th ed., updated (Upper Saddle River, NJ: Prentice Hall, 2017), 103–105.

[6] Michael Porter and Mark Kramer, "Creating Shared Value," *Harvard Business Review*, January–February 2011, 77.

[7] USDA, "Ag and Food Sectors and the Economy," last modified January 26, 2023, https://www.ers.usda.gov/data-products/ag-and-food-statistics-charting-the-essentials/ag-and-food-sectors-and-the-economy/

[8] Case, Fair, and Oster, *Principles of Economics*, 432–433.

[9] Central Intelligence Agency, *The World Factbook*, accessed March 1, 2023, https://www.cia.gov/library/publications/the-world-factbook/geos/us.html.

[10] United States Census Bureau, "Nevada and Idaho Are the Nation's Fastest-Growing States," accessed February 20, 2020, https://www.census.gov/newsroom/press-releases/2018/estimates-national-state.html.

[11] United States Census Bureau, "United States | 2022 Population Estimates," accessed March 1, 2023, https://www.census.gov/search-results.html?q=us+population+for+2022.

[12] See Olivier Blanchard, *Macroeconomics*, 8th ed. (Upper Saddle River, NJ: Pearson, 2020), 24–26.

[13] See Jay Heizer and Barry Render, *Operations Management*, 12th ed. (Upper Saddle River, NJ: Prentice Hall, 2018).

[14] Heyne, Boetke, and Prychitko, *The Economic Way of Thinking*, 491–493.

[15] Ronald M. Ayers and Robert A. Collinge, *Economics: Explore and Apply* (Upper Saddle River, NJ: Prentice Hall, 2004), 163–167.

[16] See Heyne, Boetke, and Prychitko, *The Economic Way of Thinking*, 403–409, 503–504.

[17] Department of Labor, Bureau of Labor Statistics, "The Employment Situation—March 2020," accessed February 20, 2020, https://www.bls.gov/news.release/pdf/empsit.pdf.

[18] Editors of Encyclopaedia Britannica, "Nike, Inc.," *Britannica*, last modified August 16, 2023, https://www.britannica.com/topic/Nike-Inc.

[19] "Sports Footwear Market Size Worth USD 142.40 Billion by 2026: Torsional Stability and Flexible Properties of Sports Shoes to Fuel Their Demand Worldwide, Says Fortune Business Insights™," *Business Insider*, February 21, 2020, https://markets.businessinsider.com/news/stocks/sports-footwear-market-size-worth-usd-142-40-billion-by-2026-torsional-stability-and-flexible-properties-of-sports-shoes-to-fuel-their-demand-worldwide-says-fortune-business-insights-1028926523.

chapter 2

Understanding Business Ethics and Social Responsibility

Docstockmedia/Shutterstock

learning objectives

After reading this chapter, you should be able to:

2-1 Explain how individuals develop their personal codes of ethics and why ethics are important in the workplace.

2-2 Distinguish social responsibility from ethics, identify organizational stakeholders, and characterize social consciousness today.

2-3 Show how the concept of social responsibility applies both to environmental issues and to a firm's relationships with customers, employees, and investors.

2-4 Identify four general approaches to social responsibility and note the role of social responsibility in small business.

2-5 Explain the role of government in social responsibility in terms of how governments and businesses influence each other.

2-6 Discuss how businesses manage social responsibility in terms of both formal and informal dimensions and how organizations can evaluate their social responsibility.

what's in it for me?

Business practices today are under more scrutiny than ever before. Business owners and managers are often torn between doing what makes sense for the bottom line (such as increasing profit) and doing what makes sense for general social welfare. By understanding the material in this chapter, you'll be better able to assess ethical and socially responsible issues facing you as an employee and as a boss or business owner and understand the ethical and socially responsible actions of businesses you deal with as a consumer and as an investor.

In this chapter, we'll look at ethics and social responsibility—what they mean and how they apply to environmental issues and to a firm's relationships with customers, employees, and investors. Along the way, we look at general approaches to social responsibility, the steps businesses must take to implement social responsibility programs, how issues of social responsibility and ethics affect small businesses, and how businesses attempt to manage social responsibility programs. But first, we begin this chapter by discussing ethics in the workplace—individual, business, and managerial.

Intellistudies/Shutterstock

Sundry Photography/Alamy Stock Photo

Earth as a Shareholder

Patagonia's founder and former CEO Yvon Chouinard claims, "I never wanted to be a businessman."[1] The billion-dollar company was born when Chouinard started selling climbing pitons he'd fashioned in a chicken coop turned blacksmith shop on his parents' property in Burbank, California. When his friends admired the pitons, he started selling them for $1.50, hoping it would keep him from having to find a job that would cut into his rock-climbing time.

Over 50 years later, Chouinard, enraged by a *Forbes* article that named him one of the world's richest men, made a radical decision not to take Patagonia public but rather to give it away. In a public statement in September 2022, Chouinard explained his decision, saying, "Instead of 'going public,' you could say we're 'going purpose.'" Patagonia's public statement explaining the shift opened with "Earth is now our only shareholder."

The Chouinard family transferred ownership of the definitive outdoor gear company to two organizations: the Patagonia Purpose Trust and the Holdfast Collective. Every dollar not reinvested in the company will be distributed to the Holdfast Collective to fight the global climate crisis. The family retains seats on the board of directors and guides the work of the collective.[2]

Chouinard's decision, though radical in the business world, is in keeping with his work as a self-described "existential dirtbag" whose mission has always been to make the world a better and fairer place.[3] As a Certified B Corp and a founding member of 1% For the Planet, Patagonia has a strong history of keeping social and environmental responsibility embedded in both the strategic plan and the daily workings of the business. The company seeks to center humans and the environment in its business, supporting everything from a relaxed dress code and flexible working hours to dedicating 1 percent of profits annually to grassroots climate activists.

The formation of Patagonia Purpose Trust is part of Chouinard's efforts not only to change the way outdoor gear is sold but to change the very nature of capitalism itself. In a public statement from Patagonia Works, the company stated: "The Patagonia Purpose Trust now owns all the voting stock of the company (two percent of the total stock) and exists to create a more permanent legal structure to enshrine Patagonia's purpose and values. It will help ensure that there is never deviation from the intent of the founder and to facilitate what the company continues to do best: demonstrate as a for-profit business that capitalism can work for the planet."

Patagonia's ownership structure is a unique and legally binding mechanism that prevents any person or group from recognizing financial gain from the company's profits and keeps the company's profits dedicated solely to its mission of caring for the planet. The Patagonia Purpose holds almost all the voting rights but none of the dividend rights. Those rights are held by the Holdfast Collective. This structure means that the trust cannot vote to maximize profits for shareholders, while the collective cannot influence the company's policies to maximize profits for charity.[4]

Chouinard has long been recognized for his groundbreaking steward ownership, and this new structure ensures that control of the company's policies and direction of investment remains firmly in the hands of the people most invested in its success—both financially and philanthropically. As of 2023, the Chouinard family's influence within both entities ensures the continuation of its founder and leader, Yvon.

Though the company has not addressed further succession plans, this move is in line with Chouinard's belief in business as an experiment. He is known more for direct action than deliberate planning, willing to take a step in any given direction and then assess the move for viability.

Patagonia CEO Ryan Gellert is another trailblazer who believes in passion over profit. He noted in an interview with Katie Couric, "The only consistent thing in my career is, I've always asked myself about the next opportunity in front of me: Does this look interesting? Is this tied to what I'm really passionate about?"[5] When he assumed direction of the company in 2020, one of the first things Chouinard discussed with him was transferring ownership and ensuring the continuation—and increase—of Patagonia's commitment to fighting the climate crisis.

Gellert acknowledges that as one of the world's largest retailers, Patagonia necessarily holds a large carbon footprint, but he is certain that can be balanced with conservation and restoration of the natural environment. "We have created the world's problems, and they're not solvable without businesses taking responsibility." (After studying the content in this chapter, you should be able to answer the set of discussion questions found at the end of the chapter.)

Ethics in the Workplace

Learning Objective 2-1

Explain how individuals develop their personal codes of ethics and why ethics are important in the workplace.

Just what is ethical behavior? **Ethics** are beliefs about what's right and wrong or good and bad. An individual's values and morals, plus the social context in which their behavior occurs, determine whether behavior is regarded as ethical or unethical. In other words, **ethical behavior** is behavior that conforms to individual beliefs and social norms about what's right and good. **Unethical behavior** is behavior that conforms to individual beliefs and social norms about what is defined as wrong and bad. **Business ethics** is a term often used to refer to ethical or unethical behaviors by employees and managers in the context of their jobs.

Ethics *beliefs about what is right and wrong or good and bad in actions that affect others*

Ethical Behavior *behavior conforming to generally accepted social norms concerning beneficial and harmful actions*

Unethical Behavior *behavior that does not conform to generally accepted social norms concerning beneficial and harmful actions*

Business Ethics *ethical or unethical behaviors by employees in the context of their jobs*

Individual Ethics

Because ethics are based on both individual beliefs and social context, they vary from person to person, from situation to situation, and from culture to culture. Social standards are broad enough to support differences in beliefs. Without violating general standards, people may develop personal codes of ethics reflecting a wide range of attitudes and beliefs.

Thus, ethical and unethical behaviors are determined partly by the individual and partly by the culture. For instance, virtually everyone would agree that if you see someone drop $20, the ethical thing to do would be to return it to the owner. But there'll be less agreement if you find $20 in an empty room but don't know who dropped it. Should you turn it in to the lost-and-found department? Or, because the rightful owner isn't likely to claim it, can you just keep it?

The Law and the Real World

Societies generally adopt formal laws that reflect prevailing ethical standards or social norms within that society. For example, because most people regard stealing as unethical, we have laws against stealing and ways of punishing those who steal. Those who write laws try to make them as clear and unambiguous as possible, but interpreting and applying them can still lead to ethical ambiguities. Real-world situations can often be interpreted in different ways, and it isn't always easy to apply statutory standards to real-life behavior. For instance, during the aftermath of natural disasters like hurricanes or earthquakes, desperate survivors sometimes break into grocery stores for food and water. These actions are, of course, illegal, but most law enforcement agencies will not press charges because of the circumstances.

Unfortunately, the epidemic of scandals that dominated business news over the past several years shows how willing people can be to take advantage of potentially ambiguous situations—and even create them. For example, Burger King, based in Florida, bought a Canadian fast-food chain and considered moving its corporate offices there simply to take advantage of lower Canadian taxes. Walgreens, headquartered in Illinois, bought a Swiss firm and could also have legally moved its corporate headquarters to Switzerland. However, in the face of adverse publicity and government pressure, both firms reversed course and decided not to relocate.[6] Similarly, in 2019 some drug manufacturers were criticized when they raised certain drug prices by several hundred percent. A few dropped some of those prices back to their previous levels, but others kept them at higher levels even in the wake of public outrage.[7] During the COVID-19 pandemic in 2020, reports surfaced that some wealthy individuals sought to "buy their way" to the front of the line for testing and for when a vaccine became available.[8]

Individual Values and Morals

How should we deal with business situations that are ambiguous in terms of both ethics and the law? No doubt we have to start with the values and morals of people in a business, its managers, employees, and other legal representatives. Each person's individual values and morals help determine a personal code of ethics. Values and morals, in turn, are determined by a combination of factors. As children, we start to form values and morals in response to our perceptions of the behavior of parents and other adults. Soon, we enter school, where we're influenced by peers, and as we grow into adulthood, experience shapes our lives and contributes to our ethical beliefs and our behavior. If you put financial gain at the top of your priority list, you may develop a code of ethics that supports the pursuit of material comfort. If you set family and friends as a priority, you'll no doubt adopt different standards.

Business and Managerial Ethics

Managerial Ethics *standards of behavior that guide individual managers in their work*

Managerial ethics are the standards of behavior that guide individual managers in their work.[9] Although your ethics can affect your work in any number of ways, it's helpful to classify them in terms of three broad categories.

Behavior Toward Employees This category of managerial ethics relates to such matters as hiring and firing, wages and working conditions, and privacy and respect. Ethical guidelines suggest and legal standards require that hiring and firing decisions should be based solely on a person's ability to perform a job. A manager who discriminates against people of color or women in hiring exhibits both unethical and illegal behavior. But what about the manager who hires a friend or relative who is qualified for the job when someone else might be equally qualified? Or slightly more qualified? Although such decisions may not be illegal, they may be questionable on ethical grounds.

Wages and working conditions, although regulated by law, are also areas for potential controversy. A manager may pay a worker less than they deserve, for example, because the manager knows that the employee can't afford to quit or risk losing the job by complaining. While it is hard to judge whether some cases are clearly ethical or unethical, others are fairly clear cut. Consider the behavior of Enron management toward company employees. Enron management encouraged employees to invest retirement funds in company stock and then, when financial problems began to surface, refused to permit them to sell the stock (even though top officials were allowed to sell). Ultimately, the firm's demise caused thousands of employees to lose their jobs and much of their pension savings.

Behavior Toward the Organization Ethical issues can also arise from employee behavior toward employers, especially in such areas as conflict of interest, confidentiality, and honesty. A *conflict of interest* occurs when an activity may benefit the individual, but to the detriment of their employer. Most companies have policies that forbid buyers from accepting gifts from suppliers, for instance, because such gifts might be construed as a bribe or an attempt to induce favoritism. Businesses in highly competitive industries—software and fashion apparel, for example—have safeguards against designers selling company secrets to competitors.

Relatively common problems in the general area of honesty include stealing supplies, padding expense accounts, calling in sick just to stay home and relax, and using other business resources for personal benefit.[10] Most employees are honest, but many organizations remain vigilant. Again, Enron is a good example of employees' unethical behavior toward an organization; top managers not only misused corporate assets but also often committed the company to risky ventures to further their own personal interests.

Behavior Toward Other Economic Agents Ethics also come into play in the relationship of a business and its employees with so-called *primary agents of interest*, mainly customers, competitors, stockholders, suppliers, dealers, and unions. In dealing with such agents, there is room for ethical ambiguity in just about every activity—advertising, financial disclosure, ordering and purchasing, bargaining and negotiation, and other business relationships. Bernard Madoff's investment scams cost hundreds of his clients their life savings. He led them to believe their money was safe and that they were earning large returns when in fact their money was being hidden and used to support his own extravagant lifestyle. He then used funds from new clients to pay returns to older clients (this is called a *Ponzi scheme*). Madoff's actions showed a blatant disregard for his investors.[11] But Madoff was not the end of the story. Unscrupulous people (and companies) still find ways to lure people into Ponzi schemes, usually by promising unusually high rates of return on investments. For example, in 2022 a total of 53 Ponzi schemes were identified that cost investors over $5.3 billion; many of these involved cryptocurrency.[12] In one scheme, owners of Trade Coin Club used new investments of Bitcoin to partially pay original investors, siphoning off $295 million for themselves. A relatively new area where people have been deceived involves non-fungible tokens (NFTs). An NFT is a cryptographic "token" associated with a unique digital asset. FTX is a virtual marketplace where investors bought and sold NFTs. In late 2022, FTX declared bankruptcy, and its founder, Sam Bankman-Fried, was found guilty of 7 counts of fraud in late 2023. He announces his intention to appeal, though, so no quick outcome is expected.[13]

Unethical behavior is not necessarily illegal. For example, businesses in the pharmaceutical industry are often criticized because of the rising prices of drugs. Critics argue that pharmaceutical companies reap huge profits at the expense of the average consumer. In its defense, the pharmaceutical industry argues that prices must be set high to cover the costs of research and development programs to develop new drugs. Similarly, oil companies are sometimes criticized for reaping big profits when gas supplies are low and prices are high. The solution to such problems seems obvious: Find the right balance between reasonable pricing and price gouging (responding to increased demand with overly steep price increases). But as with so many questions involving ethics, there arise significant differences of opinion about how to properly balance a business's financial interests with wider sustainability considerations.

Another problem is global variations in business practices. In many countries, bribes (sometimes called "expediting payments") are a normal part of doing business. U.S. law, however, forbids bribes, even if rivals from other countries are paying them. A U.S. power-generating company once lost a $320 million contract in the Middle East because it refused to pay bribes (although that word wasn't used, of course) that a Japanese firm used to get the job. Walmart's Mexico subsidiary has been charged with paying $24 million in bribes to local officials to sidestep regulations and obtain construction permits for new stores.[14] We'll discuss some of the ways in which social, cultural, and legal differences among nations affect international business in Chapter 4.

Assessing Ethical Behavior

What distinguishes ethical from unethical behavior is often subjective and subject to differences of opinion. So how can we decide whether a particular action or decision is ethical? The following three steps set a simplified course for applying ethical judgments to situations that may arise during the course of business activities:

1. Gather the relevant factual information.
2. Analyze the facts to determine the most appropriate moral values.
3. Make an ethical judgment based on the rightness or wrongness of the proposed activity or policy.

Unfortunately, the process doesn't always work as smoothly as these three steps suggest. What if the facts aren't clear cut? What if no moral values are agreed on? Nevertheless, you must make the judgment and decide how to go forward. Experts point out that judgments and decisions made in a moral and ethical manner lead to increased trust among all parties concerned. And trust is indispensable in any business transaction.

To fully assess the ethics of specific behavior, we need a more complex perspective. Consider a common dilemma faced by managers with expense accounts. Companies routinely provide managers with accounts to cover work-related expenses, hotel bills, meals, and rental cars or taxis when they're traveling on company business or entertaining clients for business purposes. They expect employees to claim only work-related expenses.

If a manager takes a client to dinner and spends $100, submitting a $100 reimbursement receipt for that dinner is accurate and appropriate. But suppose that this manager has a $100 dinner the next night with a good friend for purely social purposes. Submitting that receipt for reimbursement would be unethical, but some managers rationalize that it's okay to submit a receipt for dinner with a friend when they are on a business trip. Perhaps they tell themselves that they're underpaid and just "recovering" income due to them. (Most companies would allow reimbursement for the manager's meal, just not for the friend's meal.)

Ethical *norms* also come into play in a case like this. Consider four such norms and the issues they entail:[15]

1. ***Utility.*** Does a particular act optimize the benefits to those who are affected by it? (That is, do all relevant parties receive "fair" benefits?)
2. ***Rights.*** Does it respect the rights of all individuals involved?

eldar nurkovic/Shutterstock

This manager is traveling on business. While in Chicago, she invites an old college friend to join her for dinner. Assuming the dinner and conversation are social and not work-related, it would be unethical and illegal for her to charge her friend's meal to her expense account. Of course, it would be fine for her to charge her own meal to her company.

3 ***Justice.*** Is it consistent with what's fair?

4 ***Caring.*** Is it consistent with people's responsibilities to each other?

Figure 2.1 incorporates the consideration of these ethical norms into a model of ethical judgment making.

Now let's return to our case of the inflated expense account. Although the utility norm acknowledges that the manager benefits from a padded account, others, such as coworkers and owners, don't. Most experts would also agree that the act doesn't respect the rights of others (such as investors, who have to indirectly foot the bill). Moreover, it's clearly unfair and compromises the manager's responsibilities to other stakeholders by violating their trust. This particular act, then, appears to be clearly unethical.

Figure 2.1, however, also provides mechanisms for dealing with unique circumstances. Suppose, for example, that our manager loses the receipt for the legitimate

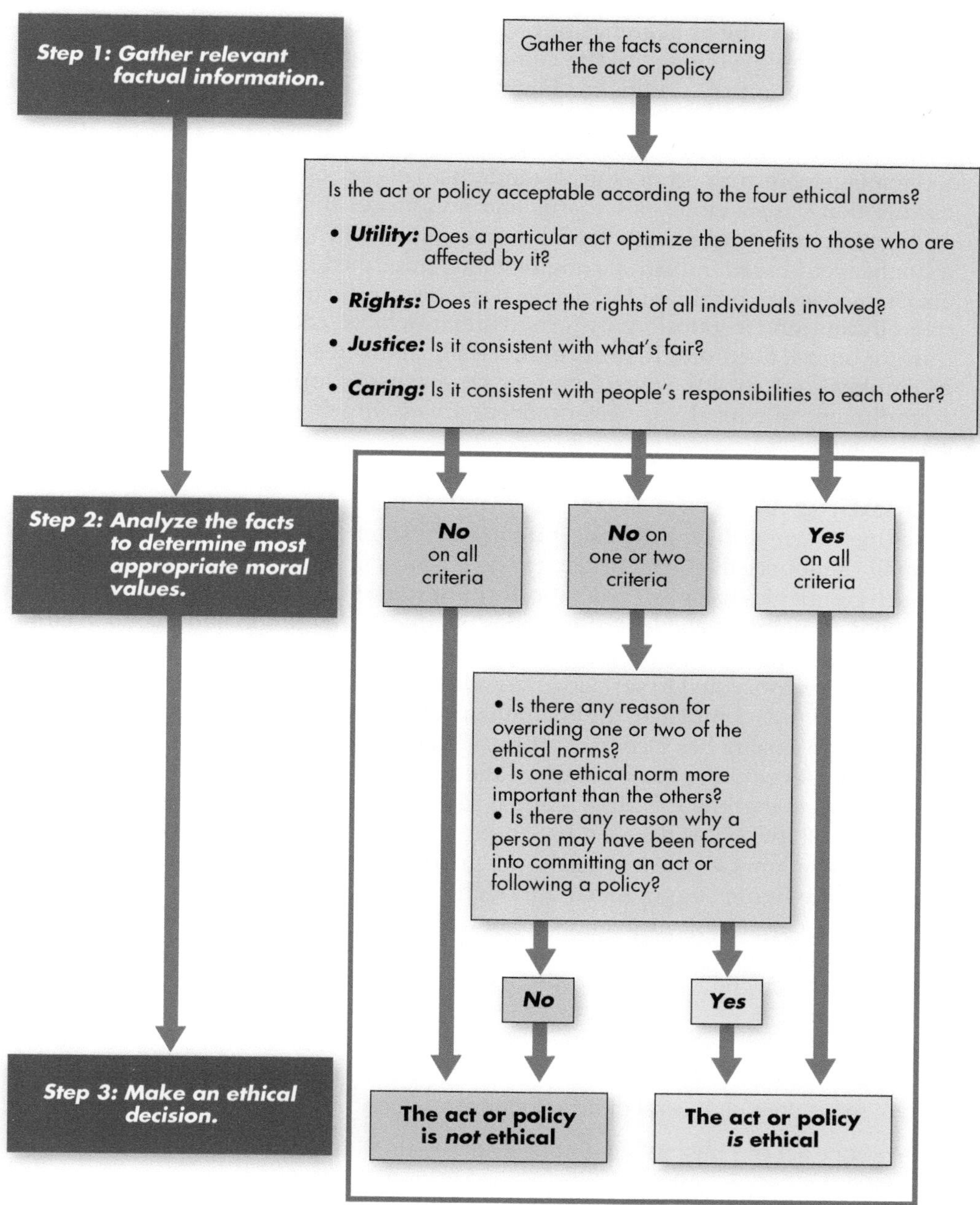

FIGURE 2.1 Model of Ethical Judgment Making

dinner but retains the receipt for the social dinner. Some people will now argue that it's okay to submit the illegitimate receipt because the manager is only doing so to get proper reimbursement. Others, however, will reply that submitting the alternative receipt is wrong under any circumstances. We won't pretend to arbitrate the case, and we will simply make the following point: Changes in most situations can make ethical issues either more or less clear cut.

Company Practices and Business Ethics

As unethical and even illegal activities by both managers and employees plague more companies, many firms have taken additional steps to encourage ethical behavior in the workplace. Many set up codes of conduct and develop clear ethical positions on how the firm and its employees will conduct business. An increasingly controversial area regarding business ethics and company practices involves the privacy of e-mail and other forms of communication that take place inside an organization. For instance, some companies monitor online searches conducted by their employees; the appearance of certain key words may trigger a closer review of how an employee is using the company's computer network. Although some companies argue they do this for business reasons, some employees claim that it violates their privacy.

Perhaps the single most effective step that a company can take is to demonstrate top management support of ethical standards. This policy contributes to a corporate culture that values ethical standards and announces that the firm is as concerned with good citizenship as with profits. For example, when United Technologies (UT), a Connecticut-based industrial conglomerate, published its 21-page code of ethics, it also named a vice president for business practices to ensure that UT conducted business ethically and responsibly. By formulating a detailed code of ethics and employing a senior official to enforce it, the firm sent a signal that it expects ethical conduct from its employees. Two of the most common approaches to formalizing top management commitment to ethical business practices are *adopting written codes* and *instituting ethics programs*.

Adopting Written Codes Like UT, many other businesses (Starbucks, Texas Instruments, Boeing, Apple, and Microsoft among them) have written codes that formally announce their commitment to do business in an ethical manner. The number of such companies has risen dramatically in the past three decades, and today almost all major corporations have written codes of ethics. Even Enron had a code of ethics, but managers must follow the code if it's going to work. On one occasion, Enron's board of directors voted to set aside the code to complete a deal that would violate it; after the deal was completed, the board then voted to reinstate the code! More recently, even though Boeing has a code of ethics, it was apparently violated more than once during the development and launch of the troubled 737 MAX.[16] Indeed, recent estimates indicate that the 737 MAX scandal cost Boeing more than $20 billion.[17]

Figure 2.2 illustrates the role that corporate ethics and values should play in corporate policy. You can use it to see how a good ethics statement might be structured. Basically, the figure suggests that although strategies and practices can change frequently and objectives can change occasionally, an organization's core principles and values should remain steadfast. Hewlett-Packard, for example, has had essentially the same written code of ethics, called *The HP Way*, since 1957. Its basic elements are the following:

- We have trust and respect for individuals.
- We focus on a high level of achievement and contribution.
- We conduct our business with uncompromising integrity.
- We achieve our common objectives through teamwork.
- We encourage flexibility and innovation.

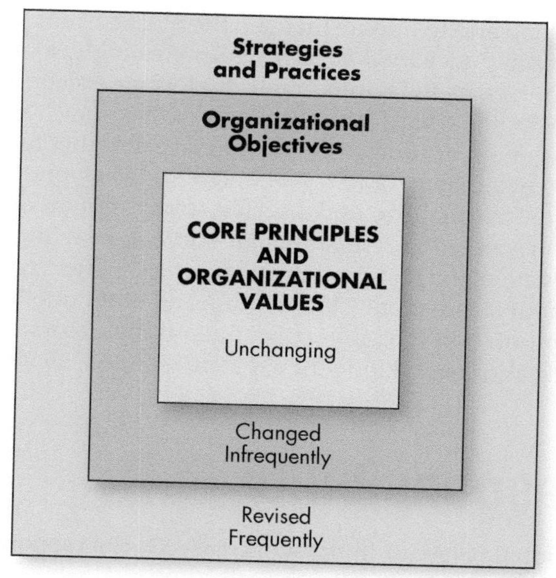

FIGURE 2.2 Core Principles and Organizational Values

Instituting Ethics Programs Many examples suggest that managers can learn ethical responses through experience. Businesses that sincerely stress the importance of ethical behavior and that consistently promote ethical cultures tend to have fewer ethical scandals than businesses that only pay lip service to ethics. But can business ethics be taught, either in the workplace or in schools? Not surprisingly, business schools have become important players in the debate about ethics education. Most analysts agree that even though business schools must address the issue of ethics in the workplace, companies must take the chief responsibility for educating employees. In fact, more and more firms are doing so.

For example, both ExxonMobil and Microsoft have major ethics programs. All managers must go through periodic ethics training to remind them of the importance of

Dimitrios Manis/ZUMA Press, Inc./Alamy Stock Photo

Wells Fargo has had a long-standing reputation for maintaining high ethical standards. However, this reputation was tarnished when a major scandal broke in 2016 and continued into 2018. Bankers at Wells Fargo were being incentivized to open multiple false accounts for the bank's current customers in order to build market share and make it look as though the bank's customer base was growing. In fact, the reported growth was mostly fictitious.

ethical decision making and to update them on the most current laws and regulations that might be particularly relevant to their firms. Interestingly, some of the more popular ethics training programs today are taught by former executives who have spent time in prison for their own ethical transgressions.[18] Others, such as Texas Instruments, have ethical hotlines, numbers that an employee can call, either to discuss the ethics of a particular problem or situation or to report unethical behavior or activities by others.

Businesses must also recognize how quickly strong reputations can be tarnished. For example, Silicon Valley Bank was a major success, providing financial services for numerous innovative and fast-growing companies. However, in 2023 allegations began to surface about fraud, money laundering, and other unethical problems at the bank. The bank's reputation took a beating, federal regulators stepped in and took over the ailing bank, and several top officials were indicted, all in a matter of months.

Learning Objective 2-2

Distinguish social responsibility from ethics, identify organizational stakeholders, and characterize social consciousness today.

Social Responsibility *the attempt of a business to balance its commitments to groups and individuals in its environment, including customers, other businesses, employees, investors, and local communities*

Organizational Stakeholders *those groups, individuals, and organizations that are directly affected by the practices of an organization and who therefore have a stake in its performance*

Social Responsibility

Ethics affect individual behavior in the workplace. **Social responsibility**, meanwhile, is a related concept that addresses the overall way in which a business attempts to balance its commitments to relevant groups and individuals in its environment. These groups and individuals are often called **organizational stakeholders**, who are groups, individuals, and other organizations that are directly affected by the practices of an organization and, therefore, have a stake in its performance. Major corporate stakeholders are identified in Figure 2.3.

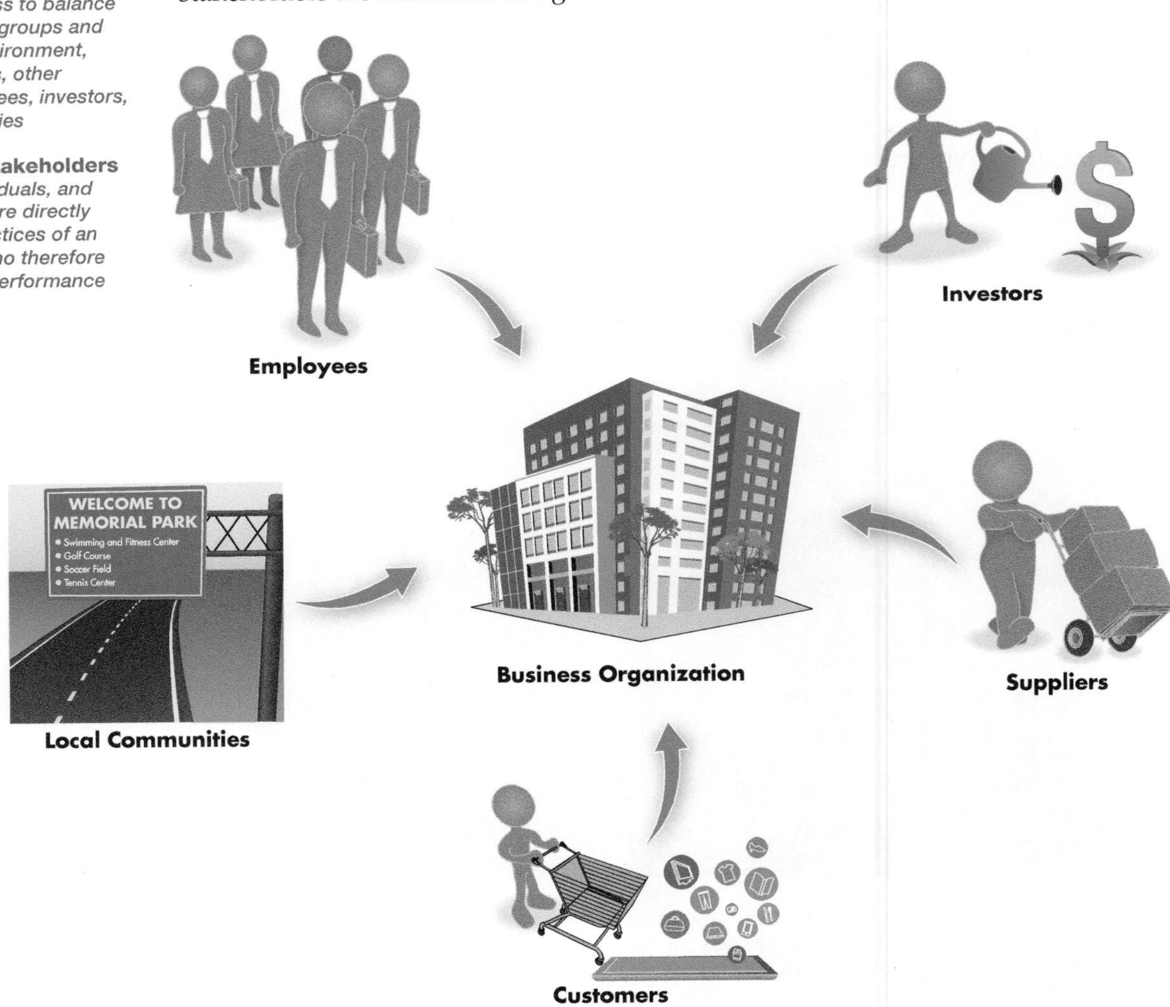

FIGURE 2.3 Major Corporate Stakeholders

The Stakeholder Model of Responsibility

Most companies that strive to be responsible to their stakeholders concentrate first and foremost on five main groups: (1) *customers*, (2) *employees*, (3) *investors*, (4) *suppliers*, and (5) the *local communities* where they do business. They may then select other stakeholders that are particularly relevant or important to the organization and try to address their needs and expectations as well.

Customers Businesses that are responsible to their customers strive to treat them fairly and honestly. They also seek to charge fair prices, honor warranties, meet delivery commitments, and stand behind the quality of the products they sell. L.L.Bean, Orvis, Starbucks, Google, and Trader Joe's are among those companies with excellent reputations in this area. In recent years, some regional banks have prospered by offering much stronger customer service than the large national banks (such as Wells Fargo and Bank of America). For instance, some offer their customers free coffee and childcare while they're in the bank conducting business. These smaller banks often simply seem to have a better sense of what customers want and often promote the fact that they are local, neighbors, and so forth. And as a result, in many cases their profits have grown at a faster rate than have the profits of larger national banks.

Together, these companies are combining social consciousness with venture capital and lending practices to lift communities out of poverty and make the world a better place.

Employees Businesses that are socially responsible in their dealings with employees treat workers fairly, make them a part of the team, and respect their dignity and basic human needs. Organizations such as The Container Store, Nucor Corporation, Starbucks, Microsoft, and American Express are committed to hiring, training, and promoting people of color. Each year, *Fortune* magazine publishes lists of the "Best Companies to Work for in America" and the "Best Workplaces for Diversity." These lists bring great publicity and also help attract more individuals who are eager to work for such highly regarded employers.

Investors To maintain a socially responsible stance toward investors, managers should follow proper accounting procedures, provide appropriate information to shareholders about financial performance, and manage the organization to protect

Michael G McKinne/Shutterstock

Some businesses have excellent reputations for treating their customers fairly and honestly. They charge fair prices, honor warranties, meet delivery commitments, and stand behind the quality of the products they sell. L.L.Bean, for example, has a very transparent and simple policy for returns.

entrepreneurship and new ventures

The Rise and Fall of Dan Price

Katherine Jones/Idaho Statesman/Tribune News Service/Getty Images

Dan Price grew up in Nampa, Idaho, listening to punk rock. As a teen, he learned to play bass, and by the age of 16 he'd been playing in bars and clubs, and his little band even had some limited national success. When the band broke up, Price made himself a job negotiating better credit card rates for the struggling nightclub owners he'd met.

Fast-forward a few years, and Price's fledgling business had grown to more than 200 clients and was netting up to $12,000 a month. In 2004, Price took his business model to Seattle and began processing credit card transactions himself using outsourced technology. By 2008 he'd built his company, Gravity Payments, into a viable enterprise with its own in-house credit card processing technology. By 2011, Price was making over $1 million a year, but something was bothering him. Chatting with one of his key employees who made only $35,000 a year, it struck him that most of his employees were struggling just to pay rent. As he thought about it and talked to people about a living wage in Seattle, he came upon a controversial idea: pay everyone, including himself, $70,000 a year.

He liquidated his investments, emptied his retirement accounts, and mortgaged his two properties—including a $1.2 million home with a view of Puget Sound—and poured the $3 million he raised into his company to fund his plan. On April 13, 2015, Price announced his decision to his staff, and the media lit up. Some called it a publicity stunt. Fox News attacked the idea, and multimillionaire radio host Rush Limbaugh called him a communist and predicted utter failure. Price's own brother, a cofounder of the firm, filed a lawsuit claiming mismanagement and asking the court to force Price to buy him out. Even some loyal customers accused him of making a political statement.

But the general public cheered him, and a BBC follow-up in 2020 reported that the number of employees had doubled in the intervening five years and the value of payments that the company processes annually had gone from $3.8 billion to $10.2 billion.

Price noted that employees had been able to pay off debt and buy their own homes in one of the most expensive cities in the United States and that the amount of money employees were voluntarily putting into their retirement plan had more than doubled.

Price was 19 and full of grand ambitions when he launched Gravity in 2004. At 38, Price had earned a reputation as a model corporate leader who put employees' interests ahead of his own, but this story doesn't have a happy ending.

In interviews with *The Seattle Times* in 2022, more than two dozen former Gravity employees said Price's carefully curated social media persona didn't line up with his real personality. These employees claimed Price cultivated a sense of fear among his employees and built a company that, as one former Gravity worker put it, was "just there to get Dan famous."[19]

In August 2022, following accusations of assault that resulted in two police investigations, Price resigned as CEO of the company he founded.[20] Still, the business goes on. The new CEO, Tammi Kroll, thanked Price for his time forming and leading Gravity, saying, "The company supports his decision to step aside. I am grateful to lead Gravity through this next chapter."[21]

shareholder rights and investments. Managers should also strive to be accurate and candid in assessing future growth and profitability, and they should avoid even the appearance of impropriety in such sensitive areas as insider trading, stock-price manipulation, and the withholding of financial data. Indeed, many of today's accounting scandals have stemmed from similarly questionable practices. For example, Theranos made false statements to investors regarding the company's new portable blood analyzer. In particular, the firm indicated that its new product could conduct comprehensive blood tests from finger drops of blood, revolutionizing the blood testing industry, but these claims were either overstated or false.[22] In 2022, the firm's founder, Elizabeth Holmes, was sentenced to 11 years in prison for fraudulent and unethical actions.[23]

Suppliers Businesses and managers should also manage with care their relations with suppliers. For example, it might be easy for a large corporation to take advantage of suppliers by imposing unrealistic delivery schedules and reducing profit margins by constantly pushing for lower prices. At one time, Walmart had a bad reputation for doing this. Many firms now recognize the importance of mutually beneficial partnership arrangements with suppliers. Thus, they keep suppliers informed about future plans, negotiate delivery schedules and prices that are acceptable to both firms, and so forth. Toyota and Amazon are among the firms acknowledged to have excellent relationships with their suppliers.

Local and International Communities Most businesses also try to be socially responsible to their local communities. They may contribute to local programs, such as Little League baseball; get actively involved in charitable programs, such as the United Way; and strive to simply be good corporate citizens by minimizing their negative impact on communities. Target, for example, donates a percentage of sales to the local communities where it does business. The company says it also gives over $4 million each week to neighborhoods, programs, and schools across the country.

The stakeholder model can also provide some helpful insights into the conduct of managers in international business. In particular, to the extent that an organization acknowledges its commitments to its stakeholders, it should also recognize that it has multiple sets of stakeholders in each country where it does business. Daimler-Benz (maker of Mercedes Benz automobiles), for example, has investors not only in Germany but also in the United States, Japan, and other countries where its shares are publicly traded. It also has suppliers, employees, and customers in multiple countries; its actions affect many different communities in dozens of different countries. Similarly, international businesses must also address their responsibilities in areas such as wages, working conditions, and environmental protection across different countries that have varying laws and norms regulating such responsibilities. ExxonMobil, for instance, has helped build hospitals and expand schools in the West African nation of Angola, where it has established a growing oil business. The firm also supports a local antimalaria program.

Contemporary Social Consciousness

Social consciousness and views toward social responsibility continue to evolve. Early American business leaders like John D. Rockefeller, J. P. Morgan, and Cornelius Vanderbilt created huge businesses and amassed large fortunes but also raised concerns about abuses of power. These concerns led to the nation's first laws regulating basic business practices. In the 1930s, many people blamed the Great Depression on a climate of business greed and lack of restraint. Out of this economic turmoil emerged new laws that dictated an expanded role for business in protecting and enhancing the general welfare of society. Hence, the concept of *accountability* was formalized. The new laws and regulations contributed to a sense of *laissez-faire* feelings about business during the growing economic prosperity of the late 1940s and 1950s.

In the 1960s and 1970s, however, business was again characterized as a negative social force. Some critics even charged that defense contractors had helped promote the Vietnam War to spur their own profits. Eventually, increased social activism prompted increased government regulation in a variety of areas. Health warnings were placed on cigarettes, for instance, and stricter environmental protection laws were enacted.

During the 1980s and 1990s, the general economic prosperity most sectors of the economy enjoyed led to another period of laissez-faire attitudes toward business. Although the occasional scandal or major business failure occurred, for the most part people seemed to view business as a positive force in society and one that was generally able to police itself through self-control and free-market forces. This view shifted again, though, during the Great Recession. Many observers faulted the mortgage lending practices of large banks for the crisis that started in 2008. Critics were also unhappy that the U.S. government bailed out both these same banks and other large businesses like General Motors and Chrysler. As we will describe in Chapter 16, there are also other kinds of bailouts that are somewhat more "routine," such as bank failures covered by the FDIC. Even then, though, there are situations where questions are raised. For example, the FDIC generally provides depositors with insurance coverage of up to $250,000 per account, but exceptions are sometimes made for wealthy clients.

Amid growing concerns about climate change and calls for more sustainable business practices, many businesses at least appear to have again moved toward a more responsible approach to doing business. Recycling programs are flourishing, for instance, within firms like Best Buy, Madewell, Patagonia, and General Motors. Many businesses also continue to operate in enlightened and socially responsible ways in other areas. For example, retailers such as Walmart and Target have policies against selling handguns and other weapons. GameStop refuses to sell mature-rated games to minors, and Anheuser-Busch promotes the concept of responsible drinking in some of its advertising.

Firms in numerous other industries have also integrated socially conscious thinking into their production plans and marketing efforts. The production of environmentally safe products has become a potential boom area, and many companies introduce products designed to be environmentally friendly. Electrolux, a Swedish appliance maker, has developed a line of water-efficient washing machines, a solar-powered lawn mower, and ozone-free refrigerators. Ford and General Motors are both aggressively studying and testing ways to develop and market low-pollution vehicles fueled by electricity, hydrogen, and other alternative energy sources, and Tesla's entire business model is based on electric-powered vehicles. The Company Store donates a comforter or blanket to a homeless child for every one it sells. Warby Parker sells sunglasses and glasses frames and donates half of the profits on each pair to nonprofit organizations.

Learning Objective 2-3

Show how the concept of social responsibility applies both to environmental issues and to a firm's relationships with customers, employees, and investors.

Areas of Social Responsibility

When defining its sense of social responsibility, a firm typically confronts four areas of concern: responsibilities toward the *environment*, its *customers*, its *employees*, and its *investors*.

Responsibility Toward the Environment

The topic of global climate has become a major issue for business and government alike. Although most experts agree that the Earth is warming, the causes, magnitude, and possible solutions are all subject to widespread debate. Further, while climate change has been occurring at a relatively mild pace, it seems to be accelerating. We are also increasing the likelihood of having troublesome weather around the globe—droughts, hurricanes, winter sieges, and so forth.[24] Indeed, 2021was the warmest year on Earth since records have been kept. The charges leveled against greenhouse emissions are disputed, but as one researcher puts it, "The only way to prove them for sure is to hang around 10, 20, or 30 more years, when the evidence would be overwhelming. But in the meantime, we're conducting a global experiment. And we're all in the test tube." The movie *The Day After Tomorrow* portrayed one possible scenario of rapid climate changes wrought by environmental damage, and 2011's *Contagion* and 2023's series *The Last of Us* illustrated the possible effects of a global pandemic caused by climate change.

Controlling *pollution*, the injection of harmful substances into the environment, is a significant challenge for contemporary business. Although noise pollution is now attracting increased concern, air, water, and land pollution remain the greatest problems in need of solutions from governments and businesses alike. In the following sections, we focus on the nature of the problems in these areas and on some of the current efforts to address them.

Air Pollution Air pollution results when several factors combine to lower air quality. Carbon monoxide emitted by cars contributes to air pollution, as do smoke and other chemicals produced by manufacturing plants. Air quality is usually worst in certain geographic locations, such as the Denver area and the Los Angeles basin, where pollutants tend to get trapped in the atmosphere. For this reason, the air around Mexico City and Beijing is generally considered to be among the most polluted in the world.

ttpang/Shutterstock

Air pollution is a major environmental concern today. Take Beijing, China, for example. As this photo illustrates, smog can greatly reduce visibility and poses a health risk for people living there.

Legislation has gone a long way toward controlling air pollution. Under current laws, many companies must use special equipment to limit the pollutants they expel into the air, but such efforts are costly. Air pollution is compounded by such problems as acid rain—which occurs when sulfur is pumped into the atmosphere and mixes with natural moisture, and falls to the ground as rain. Much of the damage to forests

finding a better way

A Strategic Approach

Consumers are increasingly demanding not only growth and profit but also social responsibility from businesses. Companies are turning to public statements and policies that they use in an effort to show they care about humans and the environment. Too often, however, those public-facing positions belie practices that play a part in or even increase problems like the continuing environmental crisis and persistent gender and racial inequity.

In December 2013, Ally Financial was ordered to pay $80 million in consumer monetary damages and $18 million in civil penalties after it was determined that 235,000 minority borrowers paid higher interest rates for auto loans because of the company's discriminatory pricing system. The higher rates resulted from the company's specific policy of allowing dealers to charge a "dealer markup" and then compensating dealers based on the markup. When the dust settled, Ally management decided to move "beyond giving programs that primarily focus on volunteering and philanthropy to a more strategic approach that supports social and business results. We're focusing on environmental, social, and governance (ESG) issues that differentiate us from our peers, provide a positive social impact and help our stakeholders understand what's important to us."[25]

In light of its new commitment to social issues and to honor the 50th anniversary of Title IX in 2022, Ally Financial made a commitment to spend advertising dollars equally

Karen Ambrose Hickey/SPP/Shutterstock

on men's and women's sports. Ally made a guaranteed financial commitment to the National Women's Soccer League's broadcast partners, which helped the league convince CBS to air the October championship game during primetime rather than the previous noon kickoff slot. The match became the most-watched game in league history, with viewership up 71 percent from the previous year and an average of 915,000 viewers. The increased viewership and resultant advertising dollars provided a boost for a league still reeling from revelations that it had ignored allegations of abuse for years.

and streams in the eastern United States and Canada has been attributed to acid rain originating in sulfur from manufacturing and power plants in the midwestern United States. The North American Free Trade Agreement (NAFTA), in both its original and revised versions, also includes provisions that call for tight controls on air pollution, especially targeting areas that affect more than one member nation.

Water Pollution Water becomes polluted primarily from chemical and waste dumping. For years, businesses and cities dumped waste into rivers, streams, and lakes with little regard for the consequences. Cleveland's Cuyahoga River was once so polluted that it literally burst into flames one hot summer day.

Thanks to new legislation and increased awareness, though, water quality in many areas of the United States is improving. The Cuyahoga River is now home to fish and used for recreation. Laws in New York and Florida forbidding dumping of phosphates (an ingredient found in many detergents) have helped to make Lake Erie and other major waters safe again for fishing and swimming. Both the Passaic River in New Jersey and the Hudson River in New York are much cleaner now than they were just a few years ago as a result of these new laws.

Land Pollution Two key issues characterize land pollution. The first is how to restore the quality of land that has already been damaged. Land and water damaged by toxic waste, for example, must be cleaned up for the simple reason that people still need to use them. The second problem is the prevention of future contamination. New forms of solid-waste disposal constitute one response to these problems. Combustible wastes can be separated and used as fuels in industrial boilers, and decomposition can be accelerated by exposing waste matter to certain microorganisms.

Toxic Waste Disposal An especially controversial problem in land pollution is toxic waste disposal. Toxic wastes are dangerous chemical or radioactive by-products of manufacturing processes. U.S. manufacturers produce between 40 and 60 million tons of such material each year. As a rule, toxic waste must be stored; it cannot be destroyed or processed into harmless material. Few people, however, want toxic waste storage sites in their backyards. A few years ago, American Airlines pled guilty—and became the first major airline to gain a criminal record—to a felony charge that it had mishandled some hazardous materials packed as cargo in passenger airplanes. Although fully acknowledging the firm's guilt, Anne McNamara, American's general counsel at the time, argued, "This is an incredibly complicated area with many layers of regulation. It's very easy to inadvertently step over the line."

Igor Jandric/Shutterstock

Water pollution is a serious problem in some locations, causing damage to rivers, streams, and public water supplies.

Recycling Recycling is another controversial area in land pollution. Recycling, the reconversion of waste materials into useful products, has become an issue not only for municipal and state governments but also for many companies engaged in high-waste activities. Certain products, such as aluminum cans and glass, can be efficiently recycled, whereas others are more troublesome. For example, brightly colored plastics, such as some detergent and juice bottles, must be recycled separately from clear plastics, such as milk jugs. Most plastic bottle caps, meanwhile, contain a vinyl lining that can spoil a normal recycling batch. Nevertheless, many local communities actively support various recycling programs, including curbside pickup of aluminum, plastics, glass, and pulp paper. Unfortunately, consumer awareness and interest in this area—and the policy priorities of businesses—are more acute at some times than at others.

One of today's more contentious business practices related to the natural environment is fracking. Fracking involves injecting water and chemical compounds into underground rock formations to break them apart. After this has been done, oil companies can then extract petroleum more easily and in areas where drilling was previously impossible. Fracking has led to a dramatic increase in the supply of oil and has resulted in lower energy prices. At the same time, though, environmentalists have expressed concerns that the chemical compounds used in fracking may be polluting underground water sources and causing instability in nearby towns and residential areas.[26]

Responsibility Toward Customers

A company that does not act responsibly toward its customers will ultimately lose their trust and business. To encourage responsibility, the Federal Trade Commission (FTC) regulates advertising and pricing practices, and the Food and Drug Administration (FDA) enforces labeling guidelines for food products. These government-regulating bodies can impose penalties against violators, who may also face civil litigation. For example, the FTC fined the social networking site Xanga $1 million for allowing children under the age of 13 to create accounts, in clear violation of the Children's Online Privacy Protection Act.[27] Similarly, the FTC has also fined Facebook and TikTok (several times) for various violations associated with individual privacy.

In recent years, some companies have also taken steps to develop and introduce more environmentally friendly products and services. And as they do this, they often begin to publicize their efforts in ways that are called "green marketing." The following list summarizes the central elements of "green marketing":

- *Production processes businesses,* such as Ford Motors and General Electric, modify their production processes to limit the consumption of valuable resources such as fossil fuels by increasing energy efficiency and reducing their output of waste and pollution by cutting greenhouse gas emissions.

Bonnie Cash/Bonnie Cash/UPI/Shutterstock

Shou Zi Chew is the CEO of Tik Tok. He recently was called to testify before a U.S. Congressional hearing about the popular social media's privacy policies.

- *Product modification products* can be modified to use more environmentally friendly materials, a practice S. C. Johnson encourages with its Greenlist of raw materials classified according to their impact on health and the environment. Committed to using only the safest materials on this list, S. C. Johnson eliminated 1.8 million pounds of volatile organic compounds from its glass cleaner Windex.[28]
- *Carbon offsets* are used by some companies that are committed to replenishing, repairing, or restoring those parts of the environment damaged by their operations, especially those that produce carbon dioxide (CO_2). One common method is for businesses to invest in reforestation programs to offset the CO_2 emissions of their products. Another is for a firm to adopt a clear and measurable goal for reducing its carbon footprint. For instance, United Airlines has pledged to be carbon-neutral by the year 2050.
- *Packaging reduction*, for example, reducing and reusing materials used in packaging products, is another important strategy of green marketing, which Starbucks has pioneered. Many businesses that ship goods directly to customers, such as Amazon and L.L.Bean, have introduced packaging that is easier to recycle; they have also created packaging that can be repurposed and used for other things.
- *Sustainability*, using renewable resources and managing limited resources responsibly and efficiently, is an important goal for any business pursuing a green policy. For example, Whole Foods Market is committed to buying food from farmers who use sustainable agriculture practices that protect the environment and agricultural resources, such as land and water.

Consumerism *form of social activism dedicated to protecting the rights of consumers in their dealings with businesses*

Consumer Rights Interest in business responsibility toward customers can be traced to the rise of **consumerism**, social activism dedicated to protecting the rights of consumers in their dealings with businesses. The first formal declaration of consumer rights protection came in the early 1960s, when President John F. Kennedy identified four basic consumer rights. Since then, general agreement on two additional rights has emerged; these rights are described in Figure 2.4. The Consumer Bill of Rights is backed by numerous federal and state laws.

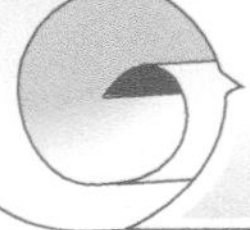

FIGURE 2.4 Consumer Bill of Rights

Johnson & Johnson has long been a respected consumer-products company. Many of its mainstays are products for babies, including shampoo, lotion, and powder. For decades the firm's baby powder used talc, a common ingredient in many powders. Talc itself is a mineral mined from earth deposits. However, many talc deposits also intermingle with asbestos, a known cancer-causing agent. Johnson & Johnson discovered this link and slowly began to replace talc in its powders with corn starch. However, the firm kept its awareness of the presence of asbestos in its powders secret and did not notify the proper government authorities. A number of lawsuits, though, forced the firm to acknowledge the presence of asbestos and, in 2023, the firm offered to settle these cases with $8.9 billion.[29]

Unfair Pricing Interfering with competition can take the form of illegal pricing practices. **Collusion** occurs when two or more firms collaborate on such wrongful acts as price fixing. Two European airlines, Virgin Atlantic and Lufthansa, admitted to colluding with rivals to raise the prices of fuel surcharges on passenger flights as much as 12 times the regular price during one 18-month period. British Airways and Korean Air were heavily fined for doing the same thing, but in exchange for turning them in, Virgin and Lufthansa were not penalized.[30] The U.S. Justice Department has charged Apple with price fixing and collusion related to its pricing of e-books.

Collusion *illegal agreement between two or more companies to commit a wrongful act*

Firms can also come under attack for *price gouging*, responding to increased demand with overly steep (and often unwarranted) price increases. For example, during threats of severe weather, people often stock up on bottled water and batteries. Unfortunately, some retailers take advantage of this pattern by marking up the prices of these items. Reports were widespread of gasoline retailers doubling or even tripling prices immediately after the events of September 11, 2001. Similar charges were made following the U.S. invasion of Iraq, after hurricanes Katrina and Rita damaged oil refineries along the Gulf Coast, and still again after the BP drilling accident shut down petroleum operations in that same area. And even more recently, a few retailers marked up prices for items such as hand sanitizers, home cleaning products, and toilet paper during the 2020 COVID-19 pandemic.[31]

Ethics in Advertising Attention is also often focused on ethics in advertising and product information. Some advertising may be misleading, promoting products for one price without acknowledging additional fees and other charges. Other examples include overstating a product features, stereotyping, and so forth. The IRS offers free tax services for low-income families. TurboTax promoted a product that would help taxpayers take advantage of this service without acknowledging that it charged a fee for this so-called "free" service. Similarly, HelloFresh has advertised free meals delivered to your home, but in reality the free meals were really just discount offsets if you bought a monthly subscription. And the makers of Airborne promoted a product that supposedly kept you from getting the flu or a cold when there was no evidence to support its claims.[32] Some critics also point to misleading labeling and advertising in the agricultural sector. Egg and chicken producers sometimes label their products "free range." That term connotes certain images, but in reality it only means that the chickens are not kept in cages; it says nothing about how densely they are packed into open pens.

Another issue concerns advertising that some consumers consider morally objectionable—for products such as underwear, condoms, alcohol, tobacco products, and firearms. Laws regulate some of this advertising (for instance, tobacco cannot be promoted in television commercials but can be featured in print ads in certain magazines), and many advertisers use common sense and discretion in their promotions. But some companies, such as Calvin Klein and Victoria's Secret, have come under fire for being overly explicit in their advertising. GoDaddy and Arby's also have reputations for the same thing.

Responsibility Toward Employees

In Chapter 10, we will show how a number of human resource management activities are essential to a smoothly functioning business. These activities—recruiting, hiring, training, promoting, and compensating—are also the basis for social responsibility toward employees.

Legal and Social Commitments By law, businesses cannot discriminate against people in any facet of the employment relationship for any reason not related to performance. For example, a company cannot refuse to hire someone because of ethnicity or pay someone a lower salary than someone else on the basis of gender. A company that provides its employees with equal opportunities without regard to race, sex, gender, or other irrelevant factors is meeting both its legal and its social responsibilities. Firms that ignore these responsibilities risk losing good employees and leave themselves open to lawsuits.

Most would also agree that an organization should strive to ensure that the workplace is physically and socially safe. Companies with a heightened awareness of social responsibility also recognize an obligation to provide opportunities to balance work and life pressures and preferences; help employees maintain job skills; and when terminations or layoffs are necessary, treat them with respect and compassion.

Ethical Commitments: The Special Case of Whistle-Blowers Respecting employees as people also means respecting their behavior as ethical individuals. Ideally, an employee who discovers that a business has been engaging in illegal, unethical, or socially irresponsible practices should be able to report the problem to higher-level management and feel confident that managers will stop the questionable practices. However, if no one in the organization will take action, the employee may inform a regulatory agency or the media and become what is known as a **whistle-blower**, an employee who discovers and tries to put an end to a company's unethical, illegal, or socially irresponsible actions by publicizing them.

Whistle-Blower *employee who detects and tries to put an end to a company's unethical, illegal, or socially irresponsible actions by publicizing them*

Unfortunately, whistle-blowers are sometimes demoted, fired, or, if they remain in their jobs, treated with mistrust, resentment, or hostility by coworkers. One study found that about half of all whistle-blowers eventually get fired, and about half of those who get fired subsequently lose their homes or families.[33] The law offers some recourse to employees who take action. The current whistle-blower law stems from the False Claims Act of 1863, which was designed to prevent contractors from selling defective supplies to the Union Army during the Civil War. With revisions to the law in 1986, the government can recover triple damages from fraudulent contractors. If the Justice Department does not intervene, a whistle-blower can proceed with a civil suit. In that case, the whistle-blower receives 25 to 30 percent of any money recovered. Bechtel Engineering is a large government contractor. A whistleblower recently reported that the firm was overcharging the government for labor costs. Bechtel was fined $57.75 million and the whistleblower received $13.75 million. Unfortunately, however, the prospect of large cash awards has generated a spate of false or questionable accusations.[34]

In the wake of the Madoff investment scams, news broke that a Boston fraud investigator had been trying to convince the Securities and Exchange Commission (SEC) for years that Madoff was engaging in illegal and unethical practices. His warnings, though, had been ignored. This embarrassing revelation led the SEC to announce that it was reviewing all of its procedures regarding whistle-blowing. The SEC chairman also pledged that new practices would be put into place to safeguard against future problems. Among these new procedures are a provision that the findings of any investigation are double-checked and verified by a different investigator.

Responsibility Toward Investors

Managers can abuse their responsibilities to investors in several ways. As a rule, irresponsible behavior toward shareholders means abuse of a firm's financial resources so that shareholder owners do not receive their due earnings or dividends. Companies can also act irresponsibly toward shareholder owners by misrepresenting company resources. Blatant financial mismanagement, such as paying excessive salaries to senior managers, sending them on extravagant "retreats" to exotic resorts, and providing frivolous perks, may be unethical but not necessarily illegal. In such situations, creditors and stockholders have few options for recourse. Forcing a management changeover is a difficult process that can drive down stock prices—a penalty that shareholders are usually unwilling to impose on themselves. However, insider trading and the misrepresentation of finances are clearly illegal as well as unethical.

Insider Trading **Insider trading** is using confidential information to gain from the purchase or sale of stocks. Suppose, for example, that a small firm's stock is currently trading at $50 a share (this means that $50 is the current price at which people are buying and selling the stock). If a larger firm is going to buy the smaller one, it might have to pay as much as $75 a share for a controlling interest. Individuals aware of the impending acquisition before it is publicly announced, such as managers of the two firms or the financial institution making the arrangements, could gain by buying the stock at $50 in anticipation of selling it for $75 after the proposed acquisition is announced.

Insider Trading *illegal practice of using special knowledge about a firm for profit or gain*

Informed executives can also avoid financial loss by selling stock that's about to drop in value. Legally, stock can be sold only on the basis of public information available to all investors. Potential violations of this regulation were at the heart of an insider trading scandal involving Martha Stewart. Sam Waksal, president of ImClone, learned that the company's stock was going to drop in value and hastily tried to sell his own stock. He also allegedly tipped off close friend Stewart, who subsequently sold her stock as well. Stewart, who argued that she never received Waksal's call and sold her stock only because she wanted to use the funds elsewhere, eventually pled guilty to other charges (lying to investigators) and served several months in prison. Waksal, meanwhile, received longer jail time (over seven years) and a larger fine (over $4 million) because his own attempts to dump his stock were clearly documented. More recently, former Congressman Stephen Buyer has been charged with insider trading based on inappropriate information he received in advance of the $26.5 billion merger between Sprint and T-Mobile. According to court documents he earned $350,000 on stock transactions related to the merger. He was found guilty in early 2023 but is appealing his conviction.[35]

Misrepresentation of Finances In maintaining and reporting its financial status, every corporation must conform to generally accepted accounting principles (GAAP; see Chapter 14). Unethical managers might project profits in excess of what they actually expect to earn, hide losses or expenses to boost paper profits, or slant financial reports to make the firm seem stronger than is really the case. In 2002, the U.S. Congress passed the *Sarbanes-Oxley Act*, which requires an organization's chief financial officer to personally guarantee the accuracy of all financial reporting (see Chapter 14).

Implementing Social Responsibility Programs

Learning Objective 2-4

Identify four general approaches to social responsibility and note the role of social responsibility in small business.

Opinions differ dramatically concerning social responsibility as a business goal. Although some oppose any business activity that threatens profits, others argue that social responsibility must take precedence. Some skeptics fear that businesses will gain too much control over the ways social projects are addressed by society as a whole or that they lack the expertise needed to address social issues. Still, many believe that corporations should help improve the lives of citizens because they are citizens themselves, often control vast resources, and may contribute to the problems that social programs address.

Approaches to Social Responsibility

Given these differences of opinion, it is little wonder that corporations have adopted a variety of approaches to social responsibility. As Figure 2.5 illustrates, the four stances that an organization can take concerning its obligations to society fall along a continuum ranging from the lowest to the highest degree of socially responsible practices.

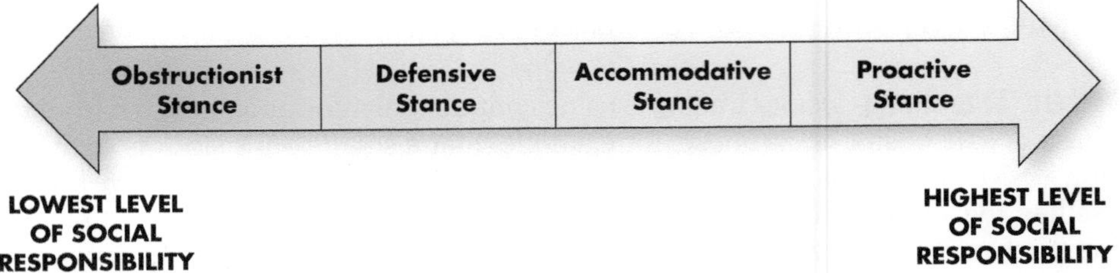

FIGURE 2.5 Spectrum of Approaches to Corporate Social Responsibility

Obstructionist Stance *approach to social responsibility that involves doing as little as possible and may involve attempts to deny or cover up violations*

Obstructionist Stance The few organizations that take an **obstructionist stance** to social responsibility usually do as little as possible to solve social or environmental problems, have little regard for ethical conduct, and will go to great lengths to deny or cover up wrongdoing. For example, IBP, a leading meat-processing firm, has a long record of breaking environmental protection, labor, and food-processing laws and then trying to cover up its offenses. Similarly, a Georgia peanut-processing plant owned by Peanut Corporation of America shipped products contaminated with salmonella. The firm's top manager allegedly knew that the products had failed safety tests but shipped them anyway to avoid losing money. The plant manager and three other officials subsequently served time in jail. Volkswagen was found guilty of knowingly and intentionally misreporting emissions data to make its automobiles look more environmentally friendly. In the wake of this scandal, VW paid billions of dollars in fines and suffered significant damage to its reputation.

Defensive Stance *approach to social responsibility by which a company meets only minimum legal requirements in its commitments to groups and individuals in its social environment*

Defensive Stance Organizations that take a **defensive stance** will do everything that is legally required, including admitting to mistakes and taking corrective actions, but nothing more. Defensive stance managers insist that their job is to generate profits and might, for example, install pollution-control equipment dictated by law but not higher-quality equipment to further limit pollution. Tobacco companies generally take this position in their marketing efforts. In the United States, they are legally required to include product warnings and to limit advertising to prescribed media. Domestically, they follow these rules to the letter of the law, but in some Asian and African countries, which don't have these rules, cigarettes are heavily promoted, contain higher levels of tar and nicotine, and carry few or no health warning labels.

Patti McConville/Alamy Stock Photo

Regulations governing advertising tobacco products vary from country-to-country. Adopting a defensive stance, most cigarette makers do what is legally required but nothing else.

Accommodative Stance A firm that adopts an **accommodative stance** meets and, in certain cases, exceeds its legal and ethical requirements. Such firms will agree to participate in social programs if solicitors convince them that given programs are worthy of their support. Both Shell and IBM, for example, will match contributions made by their employees to selected charitable causes.

Accommodative Stance *approach to social responsibility by which a company, if specifically asked to do so, exceeds legal minimums in its commitments to groups and individuals in its social environment*

Proactive Stance Firms with the highest degree of social responsibility exhibit the **proactive stance**: They take to heart the arguments in favor of social responsibility, view themselves as citizens in a society, indicate sincere commitment to improve the general social welfare, and surpass the accommodative stance by proactively seeking opportunities to contribute. The most common—and direct—way to implement this stance is to set up a foundation for providing direct financial support for various social programs. Table 2.1, using the most recent data, lists the top 30 corporate foundations.

Proactive Stance *approach to social responsibility by which a company actively seeks opportunities to contribute to the well-being of groups and individuals in its social environment*

An excellent example of a proactive stance is the McDonald's Corporation's Ronald McDonald House program. These houses, located close to major medical centers, can be used for minimal cost by families while their sick children are receiving medical treatment nearby. However, these categories are not sharply distinct; organizations do not always fit neatly into one category or another. The Ronald McDonald House program has been widely applauded, but McDonald's has also been accused of misleading consumers about the nutritional value of its food products.

Social Responsibility and the Small Business

As the owner of a garden supply store, how would you respond to a building inspector's suggestion that a cash payment will speed your application for a building permit? As the manager of a liquor store, would you call the police, refuse to sell, or

table 2.1 Top 22 Most Charitable Companies, 2022

Rank	Name/(State)
1	Novo Nordisk
2	The Goldman Sachs Group, Inc.
3	Microsoft Corporation
4	Wells Fargo & Company
5	Walmart
6	ExxonMobil Corporation
7	Gilead Sciences, Inc.
8	Starbucks Corporation
9	JPMorgan Chase & Co.
10	Chevron Corporation
11	The Walt Disney Company
12	Alphabet, Inc.
13	General Electric Company
14	Bank of America Corporation
15	Build-A-Bear Workshop, Inc.
16	OneHope
17	Cotopaxi
18	Two Blind Brothers
19	Patagonia, Inc.
20	BLQK Coffee
21	TOMS Shoes
22	Ben & Jerry's (owned by Unilever)

Source: Affan Mir "22 Most Charitable Companies in 2022" Yahoo.com https://www.yahoo.com/now/22-most-charitable-companies-2022-163953597.html?guccounter=1; and Mir, A. (2022, December 13). 5 Most charitable companies in 2022. Insider Monkey. https://www.insidermonkey.com/blog/5-most-charitable-companies-in-2022-1095390/

Rawpixel.com/Shutterstock

Many small business owners practice social responsibility, giving something of value back to their communities. This business owner is helping coach a youth sports team and is stressing the importance of unity and teamwork to his young players.

sell to a customer whose identification card looks forged? As the owner of a small laboratory, would you call the state board of health to make sure that it has licensed the company with whom you want to contract to dispose of medical waste? Who will really be harmed if a small firm pads its income statement to help it get a much-needed bank loan? Many of the examples in this chapter illustrate big business responses to ethical and social responsibility issues, but small businesses must answer many of the same questions. Differences between the two types of businesses are primarily differences of scale.

At the same time, the ethical issues are largely questions of *individual* ethics. What about questions of social responsibility? Can a small business, for example, afford a social agenda? Should it sponsor youth soccer teams, make donations to the United Way, and buy light bulbs from the Lion's Club service organization? Do joining the chamber of commerce and supporting the Better Business Bureau cost too much? Clearly, ethics and social responsibility are decisions faced by all managers in all organizations, regardless of rank or size. One key to business success is to decide in advance how to respond to the issues that underlie all questions of ethical and social responsibility.

The Government and Social Responsibility

Learning Objective 2-5

Explain the role of government in social responsibility in terms of how governments and businesses influence each other.

An especially important element of social responsibility is the relationship between business and government. In planned economies, for example, the government heavily regulates business activities, ostensibly to ensure that business supports some overarching set of social ideals. And even in market economies, considerable government control of business is still present, much of it directed at making sure that business interests do not damage social interests. Alternatively, businesses also attempt to influence the government by attempting to offset or reverse government restrictions. Businesses and the government use several methods in their attempts to influence each other.

How Governments Influence Business

The government (national, state, or local) attempts to shape social responsibility practices through both direct and indirect channels. Direct influence most frequently is manifested through *regulation*, whereas indirect influence can take a number of forms, most notably taxation policies.[36]

Direct Regulation The government most often directly influences organizations through **regulation**, the establishment of laws and rules that dictate what organizations can and cannot do. This regulation usually evolves from social beliefs about how businesses should conduct themselves. To implement legislation, the government generally creates special agencies to monitor and control certain aspects of business activity. For example, the Environmental Protection Agency handles environmental issues; the FTC and the FDA focus on consumer-related concerns; the Equal Employment Opportunity Commission, the National Labor Relations Board, and the Department of Labor help protect employees; and the SEC handles investor-related issues. These agencies have the power to levy fines or bring charges against organizations that violate regulations. During the COVID-19 pandemic, various regulators imposed a variety of travel and other restrictions to slow the spread of the disease.

Regulation *the establishment of laws and rules that dictate what organizations can and cannot do*

Another approach that governments can use to regulate business practices is through legislation. For instance, the U.S. Foreign Corrupt Practices Act provides for financial sanctions against businesses or business officials that engage in bribery. Siemens AG, a large German engineering firm, was investigated for practices that included routine bribery of foreign officials to win infrastructure construction projects. All told, the firm was alleged to have spent more than $1 billion in bribing officials in at least 10 different countries. Siemens agreed to pay the U.S. government a fine of $800 million. (The U.S. government had the authority to fine Siemens because the German firm has a class of stock listed on the New York Stock Exchange and was thus subject to the Foreign Corrupt Practices Act.[37]) Similarly, another German firm, Daimler-Benz AG, was charged with bribery in 22 countries, which helped the company earn more than $50 million in profit. The company was alleged to have given millions of dollars in bribes to foreign officials to win contracts supplying their governments with vehicles. Charges included conspiracy and falsifying records. Daimler agreed to pay $185 million in its settlement. An American entrepreneur named Joseph Sigelman launched a successful oilfield service company in the Colombian rainforest called PetroTiger but was charged with six counts of bribery, accepting kickbacks, and laundering money.[38] He eventually pled guilty to one charge, was sentenced to three years of probation, and was assessed a substantial fine. Ralph Lauren, Pfizer, Oracle, Tyco and Eli Lilly have all recently paid fines under this law.

Indirect Regulation Other forms of regulation are indirect. For example, the government can indirectly influence the social responsibility of organizations through its tax codes. In effect, the government can influence how organizations spend their social responsibility dollars by providing greater or lesser tax incentives. For instance, suppose that the government wanted organizations to spend more on training the chronically unemployed, people who lack most basic job skills and who routinely have trouble finding jobs. Congress could then pass laws that provided tax incentives to companies that opened new training facilities, and as a result of the tax break, more businesses would probably do so. Of course, some critics argue that regulation is already excessive. They maintain that a free market system would eventually accomplish the same goals as regulation, with lower costs to both organizations and the government.

How Business Influences Government

Just as governments can influence businesses, so, too, can businesses influence the government. Businesses have four main methods of addressing governmental pressures for more social responsibility: (1) personal contacts, (2) lobbying, (3) political

Clarence Thomas is a Justice serving on the U.S. Supreme Court. In 2023 there were several allegations raised that Justice Thomas and his wife took lavish vacations paid for by individuals and/or firms that had cases pending review by the Supreme Court.

action committees, and (4) favors. (During President Barack Obama's administration, he implemented several measures designed to restrict or regulate business influence on the government, especially through lobbying; however, during the administration of President Donald Trump, some of these measures were eliminated or reduced. President Joe Biden, in turn, reintroduced some of them.[39]) As a general example of business influence, Purdue Pharma, owned by the Sackler family, manufactured and promoted a pain medicine called OxyContin, cited as a major cause of the opioid crisis. The Sacklers allegedly gave large gifts to groups investigating opioids and advising government agencies on their impact.

Personal Contacts Because many corporate executives and political leaders travel in the same social circles, personal contacts and networks offer one method of influence. For instance, a business executive may be able to contact a politician directly and present their case regarding a piece of legislation being considered. The insider trading case involving Stephen Buyer discussed earlier included conversations that took place during a golf game. In addition, Supreme Court Justice Clarence Thomas has recently been questioned about lavish gifts he and his wife have received from a prominent real estate developer.

Lobbying *the use of persons or groups to formally represent an organization or group of organizations before political bodies*

Lobbying **Lobbying**, or the use of persons or groups to formally represent an organization or group of organizations before political bodies, is also an effective way to influence the government. The National Rifle Association (NRA), for example, has a staff of lobbyists in Washington with a substantial annual budget. These lobbyists work to represent the NRA's position on gun control and to potentially influence members of Congress when they vote on legislation that affects the firearms industry and the rights of gun owners. Presidents Obama and Biden have taken steps to control or limit lobbying. For instance, any discussion between a lobbyist and a member of Congress that goes beyond general conversation has to be written in the form of a letter and posted online. Some Republican leaders, though, claim that some of the lobbying restrictions were unnecessary and even punitive.

Political Action Committees (PACs) *special organizations created to solicit money and then distribute it to political candidates*

Political Action Committees Companies themselves cannot legally make direct donations to political campaigns, so they influence the government through *political action committees*. **Political action committees (PACs)** are special organizations created to solicit money and then distribute it to political candidates. Employees of a firm may be encouraged to make donations to a particular PAC because managers know that it will support candidates with political views similar to their own. PACs, in turn, make the contributions themselves, usually to a broad slate of state and national candidates.

dpa picture alliance/Alamy Stock Photo

Political action committees (PACs) solicit funds from donors and then pass those donations along to political candidates as a form of influence.

For example, FedEx's PAC is called FedExpac. FedExpac makes regular contributions to the campaign funds of political candidates who are most likely to work in the firm's best interests. As with lobbying, President Obama implemented measures to limit the influence of PACs. Presidents Trump and Biden have left these measures largely intact.

Favors Finally, organizations sometimes rely on favors and other influence tactics to gain support. Although these favors may be legal, they are still subject to criticism. A few years back, for example, two influential members of a House committee attending a fund-raising function in Miami were needed in Washington to finish work on a piece of legislation that FedEx wanted to see pass. The law being drafted would allow the company and its competitors to give their employees standby seats on airlines as a tax-free benefit. As a favor, FedEx provided one of its corporate jets to fly the committee members back to Washington. FedEx was eventually reimbursed for its expenses, so its assistance was not illegal, but some people argue that such actions are dangerous because of how they might be perceived.

Managing Social Responsibility

Learning Objective 2-6

Discuss how businesses manage social responsibility in terms of both formal and informal dimensions and how organizations can evaluate their social responsibility.

The demands for social responsibility placed on contemporary organizations by an increasingly sophisticated and educated public are stronger than ever. As we have seen, there are pitfalls for managers who fail to adhere to high ethical standards and for companies that try to circumvent their legal obligations. Organizations need to fashion an approach to social responsibility in the same way that they develop any other business strategy. In other words, they should view social responsibility as a major challenge that requires careful planning, decision making, consideration, and evaluation. They may accomplish this through both formal and informal dimensions of managing social responsibility.

Formal Organizational Dimensions

Some dimensions of managing social responsibility involve a formal and planned activity on the part of the organization. Indeed, some businesses are approaching social responsibility from a strategic perspective.[40] Formal organizational dimensions that can help manage social responsibility are (1) legal compliance, (2) ethical compliance, and (3) philanthropic giving.

Legal Compliance *the extent to which the organization conforms to local, state, federal, and international laws*

Legal Compliance

Legal compliance is the extent to which the organization conforms to local, state, federal, and international laws. The task of managing legal compliance is generally assigned to the appropriate functional managers. For example, the organization's top human resource executive is responsible for ensuring compliance with regulations concerning hiring, pay, and workplace safety and health. Likewise, the top financial executive generally oversees compliance with securities and banking regulations. The organization's legal department provides general oversight and answers queries from managers about the appropriate interpretation of laws and regulations. Unfortunately, though, legal compliance may not be enough; in some cases, for instance, perfectly legal accounting practices have still resulted in deception and other problems.[41]

Ethical Compliance *the extent to which the members of the organization follow basic ethical (and legal) standards of behavior*

Ethical Compliance

Ethical compliance is the extent to which the members of the organization follow basic ethical (and legal) standards of behavior. We noted previously that organizations have increased their efforts in this area by providing training in ethics and developing guidelines and codes of conduct. These activities serve as vehicles for enhancing ethical compliance. Many organizations also establish formal ethics committees. These committees might review proposals for new projects, help evaluate new hiring strategies, or assess a new environmental protection plan. They might also serve as a peer review panel to evaluate alleged ethical misconduct by an employee.[42]

Philanthropic Giving *the awarding of funds or gifts to charities or other worthy causes*

Philanthropic Giving

Finally, **philanthropic giving** is the awarding of funds or gifts to charities or other worthy causes. Target Corporation routinely gives 5 percent of its taxable income to charity and social programs. Kraft Heinz donates a meal's worth of money to food banks every time someone likes its Facebook page. For every $1 an employee contributes to charity, ExxonMobil gives $3. Omaha Steaks gives more than $100,000 per year to support the arts.[43] However, in the current climate of cutbacks, many corporations have also had to limit their charitable gifts over the past several years as they continue to trim their own budgets.[44] And many firms that continue to make contributions are increasingly targeting them to programs or areas where the firm will get something in return. For example, firms today are more likely to give money to job-training programs than to the arts. The logic is that they get more direct payoff from the former type of contribution—in this instance, a better-trained workforce from which to hire new employees.[45]

Informal Organizational Dimensions

In addition to these formal dimensions for managing social responsibility, there are also informal ones. Organization leadership and culture and how the organization responds to whistle-blowers all help shape and define people's perceptions of the organization's stance on social responsibility.

Organization Leadership and Culture

Leadership practices and organizational culture can go a long way toward defining the social responsibility stance an organization and its members will adopt.[46] Ethical leadership often sets the tone for the entire organization.

Whistle-Blowing

As we noted previously, whistle-blowing is the disclosure by an employee of illegal or unethical conduct on the part of others within the organization.[47] How an organization responds to this practice often illustrates its stance on social responsibility. Whistle-blowers may have to proceed through a number of channels to be heard, and they may even get fired for their efforts.[48] Many organizations, however, welcome their contributions. A person who observes questionable behavior typically first reports the incident to their boss. If nothing is done, the whistle-blower may then inform higher-level managers or an ethics committee, if one exists. Eventually, the person may have to go to a regulatory agency or even the media to be heard. Recent whistleblower cases have included Walgreens, Bank of America, and a number of hospitals and health care providers. Many of these cases involve overbilling for services and/or inducing customers to register for programs with hidden fees.[49]

Evaluating Social Responsibility

To make sure their efforts are producing the desired benefits, any business serious about social responsibility must apply the concept of control to social responsibility. Many organizations now require all employees to read their guidelines or code of ethics and then sign a statement agreeing to abide by it. A business should also evaluate how it responds to instances of questionable legal or ethical conduct. Does it follow up immediately? Does it punish those involved? Or does it use delay and cover-up tactics? Answers to these questions can help an organization form a picture of its approach to social responsibility.

More formally, an organization may sometimes actually evaluate the effectiveness of its social responsibility efforts. For example, when BP Amoco established a job-training program in Chicago, it allocated additional funds to evaluate how well the program was meeting its goals. In addition, some businesses occasionally conduct a **corporate social audit**, a formal and thorough analysis of the effectiveness of a firm's social performance. A task force of high-level managers from within the firm usually conducts the audit. It requires that the organization clearly define all of its social goals, analyze the resources it devotes to each goal, determine how well it is achieving the various goals, and make recommendations about which areas need additional attention. An estimated 90 percent of companies on the S&P 500 index published a corporate social responsibility report in 2022, compared to just 20 percent in 2015.

Corporate Social Audit *systematic analysis of a firm's success in using funds earmarked for meeting its social responsibility goals*

managing in turbulent times

A Higher Standard

The Honey Pot Company, founded by Beatrice Dixon in 2014, manufactures and distributes affordable, plant-based feminine care products sold at some of the heaviest of the heavyweight retailers, like Target and Walmart.

In 2020, Dixon, who is Black, suffered professional and personal racist attacks on social and other media after Target featured Dixon as part of a series of ads titled "Founders We Believe In." Support for Dixon and the Honey Pot Company led to not only a rebound in sales but a steady and sustained growth year over year since the company's inception. Since that social media recovery, Honey Pot has enjoyed increased support in the form of both sales and social media engagement.

In 2022, however, Dixon and the Honey Pot were thrust once again into the limelight when a false rumor surfaced on Twitter that Dixon was selling the company, specifically to white owners. A change in the formulation of the company's fan-favorite cleansing wash created a storm among consumers and social media followers who felt that they had been misled and that the change took the product away from "natural" and "plant-based." The change—the addition of a preservative—was partly in response to supply chain issues and partly to improve shelf stability.

Paras Griffin/Getty Images

The combination of the rumor (completely unfounded and since debunked multiple times on various platforms) and the change in formulation led Dixon to take to social media again in her defense. In a nearly 14-minute video posted to Instagram in May 2022, Dixon stated: "1. We have not sold. 2. The wash formulation has evolved for good reason. 3. We have and always will serve humans with vaginas best. Full stop."[50]

The backlash, which came from primarily Black women, highlighted a number of challenges that Dixon and other Black women–owned businesses face. The brand was built on the foundation of Black women's shared knowledge, experience, and community. Consumers felt a strong sense of ownership and representation and responded with swift and vehement outcry against both actual and perceived changes. In subsequent interviews and commentaries about the controversy, some media has brought attention to the standards that Black- and women-owned businesses are often held to.

In an interview with NPR, Dixon noted that Black-owned companies are often held to a higher standard by Black consumers because, historically, they have not been able to trust companies to do the research that has brought so many products and services to market, sometimes literally on the backs of Black people.

Dixon noted, "I completely understand because of all the things that we have been through as Black women, that when most things are not made for you and then you find a thing that you can align to and a founder that you can align to and a company that you know cares and that you know puts intention and love in—they look like you. They feel like you. They connect to you. I can understand how change with those type of circumstances can evoke that type of an emotion and reaction. And all that I would ask for is grace to understand from my point of view as well."[51]

summary of learning objectives

LEARNING OBJECTIVE 2-1

Explain how individuals develop their personal codes of ethics and why ethics are important in the workplace.

Ethics are beliefs about what's right and wrong or good and bad. *Ethical behavior* conforms to individual beliefs and social norms about what's right and good, and *unethical behavior* is behavior that individual beliefs and social norms define as wrong and bad. Though ethical behavior and the law are often the same, there can also be ambiguity. *Managerial ethics* are standards of behavior that guide managers. Managerial ethics can affect people's work in three broad categories: (1) *behavior toward employees*, (2) *behavior toward the organization*, and (3) *behavior toward other economic agents*.

One model for applying ethical judgments to business situations recommends the following three steps: (1) Gather relevant factual information, (2) analyze the facts to determine the most appropriate moral values, and (3) make an ethical judgment based on the rightness or wrongness of the proposed activity or policy. Perhaps the single most effective step that a company can take is to *demonstrate top management support*. In addition to promoting attitudes of honesty and openness, firms can also take specific steps to formalize their commitment: (1) *adopting written codes* and (2) *instituting ethics programs*.

LEARNING OBJECTIVE 2-2

Distinguish social responsibility from ethics, identify organizational stakeholders, and characterize social consciousness today.

Ethics affect individual behavior. *Social responsibility* is a related concept that refers to the way a firm attempts to balance its commitments to organizational stakeholders—those groups, individuals, and organizations that are directly affected by the practices of an organization and, therefore, have a stake in its performance. Many companies concentrate on five main groups: (1) *customers*, (2) *employees*, (3) *investors*, (4) *suppliers*, and (5) *local communities*.

Attitudes toward social responsibility have changed. The late nineteenth century, though characterized by the entrepreneurial spirit and the laissez-faire philosophy, also featured labor strife and predatory business practices. Concern about unbridled business activity was soon translated into laws regulating business practices. Out of the economic turmoil of the 1930s, when greed was blamed for business failures and the loss of jobs, came new laws protecting and enhancing social well-being. During the 1960s and 1970s, activism prompted increased government regulation in many areas of business. The economic prosperity of the 1980s and 1990s marked a return to the laissez-faire philosophy, but the recent epidemic of corporate scandals threatens to revive the 1930s call for more regulation and oversight.

LEARNING OBJECTIVE 2-3

Show how the concept of social responsibility applies both to environmental issues and to a firm's relationships with customers, employees, and investors.

A firm confronts four primary areas of concern when addressing social responsibility:

1. Responsibility toward the environment (including issues associated with climate change and air, water, and land pollution)
2. Responsibility toward customers (largely stemming from issues about consumer rights, unfair pricing, ethics in advertising, and green marketing)
3. Responsibility toward employees (including legal and social commitments and the special case of the whistle-blower)
4. Responsibility toward investors (including concerns about improper financial management, insider trading, and misrepresentation of finances)

LEARNING OBJECTIVE 2-4

Identify four general approaches to social responsibility and note the role of social responsibility in small business.

A business can take one of four stances concerning its social obligations to society: (1) *obstructionist stance*, (2) *defensive stance*, (3) *accommodative stance*, or (4) *proactive stance*. The few organizations that take an *obstructionist stance* to social responsibility usually do as little as possible to solve social or environmental problems, have little regard for ethical conduct, and will go to great lengths to deny or cover up wrongdoing. Organizations that take a *defensive stance* will do everything that is legally required, including admitting to mistakes and taking corrective actions, but nothing more. A firm that adopts an *accommodative stance* meets and, in certain cases exceeds, its legal and ethical requirements. Firms with the highest degree of social responsibility exhibit the *proactive stance*; they take to heart the arguments in favor of social responsibility, view themselves as citizens in a society, indicate sincere commitment to improve the general social welfare, and surpass the accommodative stance by proactively seeking opportunities to contribute.

For small business owners and managers, ethical issues are questions of individual ethics. But in questions of social responsibility, they must ask themselves if they can afford a social agenda. They should also realize that managers in *all* organizations face issues of ethics and social responsibility.

LEARNING OBJECTIVE 2-5

Explain the role of government in social responsibility in terms of how governments and businesses influence each other.

An especially important element of social responsibility is the relationship between business and government. The government (national, state, or local) attempts to shape social responsibility practices through direct and indirect channels. The government most often directly influences organizations through *regulation*, or the establishment of rules that dictate what organizations can and cannot do. To implement these rules and regulations, the government often creates special agencies to monitor and control certain aspects of business activity. Governments may also use legislation to forbid unethical practices such as bribery. Other forms of regulation are indirect, such as using tax codes that may encourage or discourage certain business decisions.

Businesses have four main methods of addressing governmental pressures for more social responsibility. Personal contacts and networks offer one method of influence. *Lobbying*, or the use of persons or groups to formally represent an organization or group of organizations before political bodies, is another. Companies themselves cannot legally make direct donations to political campaigns, so they influence the government through *political action committees (PACs)*, special organizations created to solicit money and then distribute it to political candidates. Finally, organizations sometimes rely on favors and other influence tactics to gain support.

LEARNING OBJECTIVE 2-6

Discuss how businesses manage social responsibility in terms of both formal and informal dimensions and how organizations can evaluate their social responsibility.

Organizations need to fashion an approach to social responsibility in the same way that they develop any other business strategy. Formal organizational dimensions that can help manage social responsibility are legal compliance, ethical compliance, and philanthropic giving. *Legal compliance* is the extent to which the organization conforms to local, state, federal, and international laws, and *ethical compliance* is the extent to which the members of the organization follow basic ethical (and legal) standards of behavior. Finally, *philanthropic giving* is the awarding of funds or gifts to charities or other worthy causes.

Informal methods of managing social responsibility include an organization's thoughts on leadership and culture and how organizations respond to whistle-blowers. Leadership practices and organization culture can go a long way toward defining the social responsibility stance an organization and its members will adopt. Ethical leadership often sets the tone for the entire organization. A key issue in social responsibility is how the organization handles whistle-blowers. Whistle-blowing is the disclosure by an employee of illegal or unethical conduct on the part of others within the organization. Although some organizations welcome the contributions of whistle-blowers, it is not uncommon for managers to ignore concerns.

To ascertain whether their efforts are producing the desired benefits, a business should evaluate how it responds to instances of questionable legal or ethical conduct. More formally, an organization may sometimes actually evaluate the effectiveness of its social responsibility efforts. A *corporate social audit* is a formal and thorough analysis of the effectiveness of a firm's social performance.

key terms

accommodative stance **(p. 57)**
business ethics **(p. 37)**
collusion **(p. 53)**
consumerism **(p. 52)**
corporate social audit **(p. 63)**
defensive stance **(p. 56)**
ethical behavior **(p. 37)**
ethical compliance **(p. 62)**
ethics **(p. 37)**
insider trading **(p. 55)**
legal compliance **(p. 62)**
lobbying **(p. 60)**
managerial ethics **(p. 38)**
obstructionist stance **(p. 56)**
organizational stakeholders **(p. 44)**
philanthropic giving **(p. 62)**
political action committees (PACs) **(p. 60)**
proactive stance **(p. 57)**
regulation **(p. 59)**
social responsibility **(p. 44)**
unethical behavior **(p. 37)**
whistle-blower **(p. 54)**

questions & exercises

QUESTIONS FOR REVIEW

2-1. What are three broad categories of ethical behavior in business?

2-2. When making decisions, who are the stakeholders that a business should consider, and what are those stakeholders' primary interests?

2-3. What are the major areas of social responsibility with which businesses should be concerned?

2-4. What are the four basic approaches to social responsibility?

2-5. What are two things top management can do to formalize ethical business practices?

QUESTIONS FOR ANALYSIS

2-6. Identify an area of your personal ethical code that seems at odds with general business practices or even capitalism in general. How do you reconcile the difference?

2-7. How does government influence the social responsibility of organizations? Should government be more or less involved in regulating social responsibility in business?

2-8. The Foreign Corrupt Practices Act makes it illegal for U.S. firms to bribe government officials in other countries. Is bribery universally considered unethical? What challenges could rules against bribery create for a U.S. company competing in the global marketplace?

APPLICATION EXERCISES

2-9. Describe your personal code of ethics. Be sure to include what you think is right and wrong, as well as your ethical framework for making decisions, and a statement describing how you have developed your ethical standards.

2-10. Identify four companies, each of which takes one of the four stances on social responsibility: obstructionist, defensive, accommodative, and proactive. For each company, highlight its actions that support your conclusion.

building a business: continuing team exercise

ASSIGNMENT

Meet with your team members and discuss your new business venture within the context of this chapter. Develop specific responses to the following:

2-11. Thinking about your business venture, identify at least three ethical issues that could potentially arise.

2-12. Should your venture have a formal statement of company practices and business ethics or simply rely on your own individual ethical standards? What are the pros and cons of each approach?

2-13. Who are the primary stakeholders in your new venture? Rank them in order of their relative importance.

2-14. Does it make sense for a new business to develop a formal social responsibility program? Why or why not?

team exercise

HOW FAR WOULD YOU GO?

Background Information

In 2023, Reuters released a report that Tesla vehicle camera images were circulated within the company on an internal messaging system.[52] Sensitive images of Tesla drivers, their garages and homes, and even their children were available to Tesla employees. Some Tesla drivers had agreed to share images to help Tesla develop and refine its self-driving capabilities. The customers were assured that identifying information would not be available to the company, but former and current employees reported that street signs, addresses, and other unique identifiers were clearly visible in the images and videos.

As part of the company's push for fully automated vehicles, thousands of images from vehicle cameras were provided to teams of human labelers to help teach the artificial intelligence system to recognize objects. The data labeling was first outsourced to a nonprofit organization with an office in Nairobi, Kenya, but has since been brought to an in-house team.

The data labeling team was tasked with helping Teslas recognize items in an effort to help Teslas that were having difficulty backing out of or into garages, so the team had access to images recorded within private residences. Ex-employees reported watching video footage of everything from laundry to children playing to intimate scenes.

Method

Working with a small group of other students, discuss how you would respond to this report, both internally and externally.

Considerations

- Data labeling is necessary to help further train AI.
- Ex-employees report that the images and video were only shared via an internal messaging system.
- Tesla drivers have agreed to share images and video specifically to assist in this training.
- Faces, house numbers, street signs, and other identifying information are not removed or blurred and are easily visible to the data labeling team.
- Recordings and images of minors are shared with the company.
- Among the images reportedly circulated was a video of the one-of-a-kind White Lotus sub from the 1977 James Bond film *The Spy Who Loved Me*. The owner of that sub is Elon Musk, Tesla's chief executive.

Discuss what policy changes you would suggest within the company and what accountability measures you would put in place. Externally, discuss with the team how Tesla should respond publicly to this report to restore consumer confidence.

When a difference of opinion arises among group members, try to determine the specific factors that influence different responses.

FOLLOW-UP QUESTIONS

2-15. What personal, social, and cultural factors do you think contribute to unethical behavior in the workplace?

2-16. Do you agree or disagree with the following statement: "The term *business ethics* is an oxymoron"? Support your answer with examples from your own work experience or that of someone you know.

2-17. If you were Tesla's director of human resources, how would you ensure compliance with your company's code of ethics?

2-18. If you were a Tesla employee and discovered that these images were being shared without knowledge or consent from customers, what would you do?

exercising your ethics

YOU CAN'T HAVE YOUR CAKE

The Situation

You are the frontline employee at a small combination bakery/flower shop/caterer that serves a wealthy clientele in a major city. Prices are high, but the shop is known for its quality and customer service, and the owner is well known in the community and rubs shoulders with the movers and the shakers. The job pays well and includes excellent benefits, the employment market is tight, and your cost of living is high. In addition, you and your wife have a baby on the way.

The Dilemma

Two young women entered the shop looking for a full-service wedding supplier for their upcoming ceremony. They both have dark complexions and black hair. They introduce themselves as Pushpa and Yalene. You help them choose the wedding flowers and a lovely three-tiered cake, along with an array of food for the reception. The cost is high, but they are willing to pay and put down a substantial deposit that will result in a $1,000 bonus for you.

The next day, the owner, after reviewing the contract, asks you to cancel the order and return the deposit. He does not give you a reason and, when pressed, becomes angry and tells you it is none of your business.

QUESTIONS TO ADDRESS

2-19. Describe the ethical issues. Be specific and clear.

2-20. What would you do in this situation? Explain your course of action.

2-21. Are the short-term consequences of your decision different from the long-term consequences? Describe the short- and long-term impacts.

cases

PATAGONIA: EARTH AS A SHAREHOLDER

Continued from page 37

At the beginning of this chapter, you read about Patagonia's unique B Corp structure. Using the information presented in this chapter, you should now be able to respond to these questions.

QUESTIONS FOR DISCUSSION

2-22. Do you think that the legal structure of Patagonia is a sustainable model that addresses social responsibility while still running a profitable business? Why or why not?

2-23. How would you describe Patagonia's approach to social responsibility?

2-24. Describe some of the informal dimensions of Patagonia's social responsibility.

2-25. Patagonia sells high-end outdoor equipment and clothing at a high price point within the market. Is it ethical for the company to price its goods so that they are out of reach for many people? How does Patagonia's pricing structure relate to its commitment to being socially responsible?

WHEN MOTHER NATURE STORMS IN

Why is social responsibility such a struggle? There's a dynamic at play between a business's profit motive and its responsibility to the greater good. Some classical economists claim that the profit motive should be the only driver of business, but the pure profit motive position does not take externalities into account. Externalities are costs (or benefits) imposed onto a third party that are not incorporated into the final cost. A classic example is a factory that pollutes the environment, creating a cost to society, but the fix for that is not part of the profit equation.

Business pursuing a more socially responsible agenda, then, must look beyond the traditional balance sheet and income statement when considering social impacts. For instance, social responsibility programs can boost employee morale in the workplace and lead to greater productivity, which has an impact on how profitable the company can be. Also, social responsibility programs can increase customer retention and loyalty.

According to a well-known consulting firm, Monitor Deloitte, "the term 'social impact' is used expansively to cover philanthropic and volunteering initiatives, sustainability efforts to mitigate social and environmental risk, and other core business activities that also deliver economic, social, and environmental benefits."[53]

In 2016, the firm identified six primary areas where a company's social impact efforts can drive business value:

- ***Brand differentiation.*** Social purpose has been shown to drive consumer purchasing decisions and enable companies to charge a price premium, leading to increased revenue.
- ***Talent attraction and retention.*** Alignment between company and employee values increases employee engagement, leading to improved profitability through higher productivity and cost reductions from lower turnover.
- ***Innovation.*** Efforts to improve the healthiness and/or environmental and social footprint of products can be an engine of innovation, spurring increased revenue from new products and new markets.
- ***Operational efficiency.*** Decreasing a company's footprint in packaging, water use, materials use, and waste production can yield significant cost savings.
- ***Risk mitigation.*** Failure to effectively address environmental and social risks can create serious financial and operational performance challenges. Social impact efforts can have important mitigation effects, resulting in avoided costs or lost revenues and higher valuations.

- ***Capital access and market valuation.*** Corporate social impact efforts are positively related to market valuation and cost of capital.[54]

QUESTIONS FOR DISCUSSION

2-26. Research a local business and determine what kinds of externalities might exist. What has the business done to mitigate those externalities?

2-27. Do you think that social responsibility is good for business? What would motivate a profit-seeking company to incur an additional expense to address social issues?

2-28. Research a large corporation and identify whether the company has a history of social responsibility. If the company has a plan, how does it square with the externalities of the business?

2-29. Do you think that U.S. businesses have a greater responsibility to create a profit for the shareholders or to focus on social impacts? Why?

2-30. What is the appropriate role of government in regulating social responsibility?

endnotes

[1] "Yvon Chouinard Donates Patagonia to Fight Climate Crisis," Patagonia Outdoor Clothing & Gear, accessed April 16, 2023, https://www.patagonia.com/ownership/.

[2] Patagonia, "Patagonia's Next Chapter: Earth Is Now Our Only Shareholder," Patagonia Works, September 14, 2022, https://www.patagoniaworks.com/press/2022/9/14/patagonias-next-chapter-earth-is-now-our-only-shareholder.

[3] "Yvon Chouinard—the 'Existential Dirtbag' Who Founded and Gifted Patagonia," *The Guardian*, Guardian News and Media, September 15, 2022, https://www.theguardian.com/global/2022/sep/15/yvon-chouinard-the-existential-dirtbag-who-founded-and-gifted-patagonia.

[4] Purpose, "The Patagonia Structure in the Context of Steward-Ownership," *Medium*, September 23, 2022, https://medium.com/@purpose_network/the-patagonia-structure-in-the-context-of-steward-ownership-e9db3d260dc6.

[5] Jennifer Liu, "2 Questions That Helped Patagonia's CEO Go from Packing Boxes for $6 an Hour to Leading a $3 Billion Brand," CNBC, March 18, 2023, https://www.cnbc.com/2023/03/18/patagonia-ceo-ryan-gellerts-best-career-advice-ask-these-2-questions.html.

[6] See "In Dixon, an Uproar over Walgreens Going Swiss," *USA Today*, July 30, 2014, 5B.

[7] Peter Loftus, "Drugmakers Raise Prices amid Shortages, Recalls," *Wall Street Journal*, January 20, 2018, accessed March 1, 2020, https://www.wsj.com/articles/drugmakers-raise-prices-amid-shortages-recalls-11547807400.

[8] Megan Twohey, Steve Eder, and Marc Stein, "Need a Coronavirus Test? Being Rich and Famous May Help," *New York Times*, March 18, 2020, https://www.nytimes.com/2020/03/18/us/coronavirus-testing-elite.html; Adam Harris, "It Pays to Be Rich During a Pandemic," *The Atlantic*, March 15, 2020, https://www.theatlantic.com/politics/archive/2020/03/coronavirus-testing-rich-people/608062/.

[9] This section follows the logic of Gerald F. Cavanaugh, *American Business Values: A Global Perspective*, 5th ed. (Upper Saddle River, NJ: Prentice Hall, 2006), Chapter 3.

[10] "CareerBuilder Releases Annual List of the Most Unusual Excuses for Calling in Sick, According to U.S. Employers," CareerBuilder.com, accessed January 8, 2017.

[11] "More Than 8,000 Investors Were Misled by This $1.2B Ponzi Scheme. Here's How to Spot a Fraud," CNBC.com, accessed March 3, 2020.

[12] Emily Dattilo, "Ponzi Schemes Surged in 2022. Many Involved Crypto," *Barron's*, February 10, 2023, https://www.barrons.com/articles/crypto-ponzi-schemes-2022-cbd3c63.

[13] "Desperate FTX Customers May Have Exploited NFT-Linked Loophole to Recover Funds Before Bankruptcy Filing," *Fortune*, November 11, 2022, fortune.com.

[14] "Walmart's Discounted Ethics," *Time*, May 7, 2012, 19.

[15] Manuel G. Velasquez, *Business Ethics: Concepts and Cases*, 6th ed. (Upper Saddle River, NJ: Prentice Hall, 2006), Chapter 2. See also John R. Boatright, *Ethics and the Conduct of Business*, 4th ed. (Upper Saddle River, NJ: Prentice Hall, 2003), 34–35, 57–59.

[16] David Schaper, "Boeing Safety Engineer Filed Ethics Complaint Last Year over 737 Max Safety Upgrades," NPR, October 2, 2019, https://www.npr.org/2019/10/02/766568896/boeing-safety-engineer-filed-ethics-complaint-last-year-over-737-max-safety-upgrades.

[17] Monica Miller, "737 Max: Boeing to Pay $200m over Charges It Misled Investors," BBC, September 23, 2022, https://www.bbc.com/news/business-63003632.

[18] Jeffrey S. Harrison and R. Edward Freeman, "Stakeholders, Social Responsibility, and Performance: Empirical Evidence and Theoretical Perspectives," *Academy of Management Journal*, 42, no. 5 (1999): 479–485. See also David P. Baron, *Business and Its Environment*, 5th ed. (Upper Saddle River, NJ: Prentice Hall, 2006), Chapter 18.

[19] Lauren Rosenblatt, "The Rise and Fall of Seattle Celebrity CEO Dan Price," *The Seattle Times*, December 25, 2022, https://www.seattletimes.com/business/seattle-celebrity-ceo-dan-prices-rise-and-fall-at-gravity-payments/.

[20] Gabrielle Bienasz, "Dan Price Is Stepping down amid Legal Troubles," *Entrepreneur*, August 18, 2022, https://www.entrepreneur.com/business-news/dan-price-is-stepping-down-amid-legal-troubles/433682.

[21] "Gravity Payments CEO Dan Price Resigns, Tammi Kroll to Take Over," FinTech Futures, August 22, 2022, https://www.fintechfutures.com/2022/08/gravity-payments-ceo-dan-price-resigns-tammi-kroll-to-take-over/.

[22] U.S. Securities and Exchange Commission, "Theranos, CEO Holmes, and Former President Balwani Charged with

Massive Fraud," March 14, 2018, https://www.sec.gov/news/press-release/2018-41.

23 Rohan Goswami, "Theranos Founder Elizabeth Holmes Sentenced to More Than 11 Years in Prison," November 18, 2022, https://www.cnbc.com/2022/11/18/former-theranos-ceo-elizabeth-holmes-sentenced-to-more-than-11-years-in-prison.html.

24 For a recent summary of these questions, see "Can Geoengineering Put the Freeze on Global Warming?" *USA Today*, February 25, 2011, 1B, 2B.

25 Ally, "A Relentless Ally for Social Good," Ally.com, accessed April 9, 2023, https://www.ally.com/about/social-impact/.

26 See "Frack Fluid Tracer," *Bloomberg Businessweek*, December 1–7, 2014, 37.

27 Bob Sullivan, "FTC Fines Xanga for Violating Kids' Privacy," MSNBC, September 7, 2006, http://www.msnbc.msn.com/id/14718350.

28 "10 Green Giants," CNN Money, accessed May 30, 2008, http://money.cnn.com/galleries/2007/fortune/0703/gallery.green_giants.fortune/7.html; http://www.scjohnson.com/environment/growing_1.asp.

29 Lisa Girion, "Johnson & Johnson Knew for Decades That Asbestos Lurked in Its Baby Powder," Reuters, December 14, 2018, https://www.reuters.com/investigates/special-report/johnsonandjohnson-cancer/.

30 Associated Press, "British Airways and Korean Air Lines Fined in Fuel Collusion," *New York Times*, August 2, 2007, http://www.nytimes.com/2007/08/02/business/worldbusiness/02air.html?scp=2&sq=british+airways+price+fixing&st=nyt.

31 Kate Gibson, "A $220 Bottle of Lysol? Coronavirus Leads to Price-Gouging," CBS News, March 8, 2020, https://www.cbsnews.com/news/coronavirus-amazon-lysol-price-gouging/.

32 MoneyWatch, "Intuit to Pay Customers $141 Million for Misleading TurboTax Ads," CBS News, May 4, 2022, https://www.msn.com/en-us/money/personalfinance/what-you-should-learn-from-turbotax-s-false-advertising-and-141-million-settlement/ar-AA1aTUxa.

33 Cora Daniels, "It's a Living Hell," *Fortune*, April 15, 2002, 367–368.

34 http://www.usdoj.gov/usao/iln/pr/chicago/2008/pr03_18_01.pdf, accessed May 30, 2008; Jacob Goldstein, "CVS to Pay $37.5 Million to Settle Pill Switching Case," *Wall Street Journal*, March 18, 2008, http://blogs.wsj.com/health/2008/03/18/cvs-to-pay-375-million-to-settle-pill-switching-case.

35 Larry Neumeister, "Ex-US Rep. Buyer Convicted of Illegal Stock Purchases," AP News, March 10, 2023, https://apnews.com/article/buyer-republican-congressman-indiana-f1b5acf3aed876518efd09f3c82e4971.

36 Nina Easton and Telis Demos, "The Business Guide to Congress," *Fortune*, May 11, 2012, 72–75.

37 "Siemens to Pay Huge Fine in Bribery Inquiry," *Wall Street Journal*, December 15, 2011, B1, B5.

38 "Felon or Mark?" *Bloomberg Businessweek*, January 19–25, 2015, 64–69.

39 Easton and Demos, "The Business Guide to Congress."

40 Peter A. Heslin and Jenna Ochoa, "Understanding and Developing Strategic Corporate Social Responsibility," *Organizational Dynamics* 37, no. 2 (2008): 125–144.

41 "Legal—but Lousy," *Fortune*, September 2, 2009, 192.

42 Lynn Sharp Paine, "Managing for Organizational Integrity," *Harvard Business Review*, March–April 2004, 106–115.

43 "To Give, or Not to Give," *Time*, May 11, 2012, 10.

44 "Battling 'Donor Dropsy,'" *Wall Street Journal*, July 19, 2010, B1, B4.

45 "A New Way of Giving," *Time*, July 24, 2010, 48–51. See also Michael Porter and Mark Kramer, "The Competitive Advantage of Corporate Philanthropy," *Harvard Business Review*, December 2009, 57–66.

46 David M. Messick and Max H. Bazerman, "Ethical Leadership and the Psychology of Decision Making," *Sloan Management Review*, Winter 1996, 9–22. See also Muel Kaptein, "Developing and Testing a Measure for the Ethical Culture of Organizations," *Journal of Organizational Behavior* 29 (2008): 923–947.

47 For a thorough review of the literature on whistle-blowing, see Janet P. Near and Marcia P. Miceli, "Whistle-Blowing: Myth and Reality," *Journal of Management* 22, no. 3 (1996): 507–526. See also Michael Gundlach, Scott Douglas, and Mark Martinko, "The Decision to Blow the Whistle: A Social Information Processing Framework," *Academy of Management Review* 28, no. 1 (2003): 107–123.

48 For instance, see "The Complex Goals and Unseen Costs of Whistle-Blowing," *Wall Street Journal*, November 25, 2012, A1, A10.

49 Rafi Mohammed, "It's Time to Ban Hidden Fees," *Harvard Business Review*, February 26, 2019, https://hbr.org/2019/02/its-time-to-ban-hidden-fees.

50 Company, The Honey Pot, "The Honey Pot Company on Instagram," Instagram, May 16, 2022, https://www.instagram.com/p/Cdocf69j-CW/?utm_source=ig_embed&ig_rid=a4b87ea1-9654-45e9-a5fe-c7feb732e7f5%2C+accessed+4%2F9%2F2023.

51 Ayesha Rascoe, "The Honey Pot's Beatrice Dixon Addresses Social Media Backlash," NPR, May 29, 2022, https://www.npr.org/2022/05/29/1101973253/the-honey-pots-beatrice-dixon-addresses-social-media-backlash.

52 Steve Stecklow, Aylong Cunningham, and Hyunjoo Jin, "Special Report: Tesla Workers Shared Sensitive Images Recorded by Customer Cars," Reuters, April 6, 2023, https://www.reuters.com/technology/tesla-workers-shared-sensitive-images-recorded-by-customer-cars-2023-04-06/.

53 Rhonda Evans and Tony Siesfeld, "Measuring the Business Value of Corporate Social Impact," Deloitte Insights, July 31, 2020, https://www2.deloitte.com/us/en/insights/topics/social-impact/business-value-of-improving-your-csr-scorecard.html/?id=us:2el:3lk:4di_gl:5eng:6di&ra nge=0/15/3/1/3/39/27/0:0,0/0/2/11/19/3/1/3/39/27/0:1.

54 Evans and Siesfeld, "Measuring the Business Value of Corporate Social Impact."

chapter 3

Entrepreneurship, New Ventures, and Business Ownership

Andreypopov/123RF

learning objectives

After reading this chapter, you should be able to:

3-1 Define *small business*, discuss its importance to the U.S. economy, and explain popular areas of small business.

3-2 Explain entrepreneurship and describe some key characteristics of entrepreneurial personalities and activities.

3-3 Describe distinctive competence, the business plan, and the start-up decisions made by small businesses and identify sources of financial aid available to such enterprises.

3-4 Discuss the trends in small business start-ups and identify the main reasons for success and failure among small businesses.

3-5 Explain sole proprietorships, partnerships, and cooperatives and discuss the advantages and disadvantages of each.

3-6 Describe corporations, discuss their advantages and disadvantages, and identify different kinds of corporations; explain the basic issues involved in managing a corporation and discuss special issues related to corporate ownership.

what's in it for me?

A recent Gallup poll suggests that almost two-thirds of the young people in the United States today are interested in entrepreneurship.[1] Even if you are not among that number, you will still be called on to interact with small businesses and entrepreneurs as a customer, as an investor, or as a client. You may also be trying to sell products or services to small businesses and entrepreneurs. One key to understanding entrepreneurship is to understand entrepreneurs themselves and what it takes for them to succeed. Lynsi Snyder displays many of the characteristics key to entrepreneurial success. Her tenure with In-N-Out Burger also highlights some of the problems inherent in converting a great business idea into a profitable enterprise. If you aspire to start and run your own business, you can learn valuable lessons from the experiences of business owners like Snyder who start small and build their businesses into something big. As an investor, you should also be better prepared to assess the market potential for new and up-and-coming businesses. This chapter will discuss these and additional issues important for starting and owning a business, including the business plan, the reasons for success and failure, and the advantages and disadvantages of different kinds of ownership. First, we'll start by defining a small business and identifying its importance in the U.S. economy.

andresr/123RF

Brunocoelho/Shutterstock

In-N-Out Is No Small Burger

Lynsi Snyder presents an atypical picture of a billionaire owner and president of an iconic national corporation. Now in her 40s, the heir to the wildly popular In-N-Out Burger sports Bible verse tattoos, competitively drag races, and openly discusses her battles with substance use. Though she generally avoids public appearances unless she is promoting Slave 2 Nothing, the foundation she started with her husband, Sean Ellingson (whom she publicly acknowledges she met on Tinder), Snyder has been vocal with the press about her intention to keep In-N-Out firmly in the family, with absolutely no intention of selling or going public.

In-N-Out was established in 1948 by Lynsi Snyder's grandparents, Harry and Esther Snyder. The first location in Baldwin Park, California, was a 10-foot-wide burger stand with no seating. Harry installed a two-way speaker system for placing orders that revolutionized how Americans ordered dinner. Early on, Harry stocked the kitchen through daily trips for local meat and produce. Esther did the books for the restaurant at their home, just around the corner from the stand. When it came time to expand the business, the Snyders doubled down on their commitment to fresh ingredients, lovingly prepared. They butchered their own meat, started a wholesale paper supply to source their packaging materials, and hired their own construction crews to build new restaurants.

At age 27, Lynsi Snyder took control of the company, which had grown to an estimated $550 million in sales at 251 locations. She had worked in various departments of In-N-Out as well as retail locations, taking part in the family business from a young age. She came to this position of ownership through a series of tragedies and personal struggles—including substance use and two divorces—that she says strengthened her. "The things that I've been through forced me to be stronger," she says. "When you persevere, you end up developing more strength."[2]

Lynsi's father, Guy Snyder, was the eldest son of Harry and Esther, but when Harry decided to retire, he passed the baton to Guy's younger brother, Rich. Guy battled opioid addiction and had occasional run-ins with the police as well as stints in rehab. In 1993, Rich died in a plane crash on his way to open the company's newest location, and Guy assumed leadership for six years as vice president to Esther, who was president, until he died of drug-related heart failure in 1999. Another family member, Mark Taylor, took the reins until 2010.

In-N-Out is an anomaly among fast-food restaurants. The retail locations are all company-owned, not franchised. Its menu has remained largely unchanged since its inception in the 1950s. Most of the chain's locations are in California, and the company has no plans to expand to all 50 states. All of its ingredients are fresh, never frozen, and delivered daily from one of the company-owned warehouses, all within driving distance of a chain location. In-N-Out locations are owned properties, not rented, and are usually situated carefully clear of urban core areas with higher property values and costs of living.

These cost-saving measures are passed along to the consumer. Though In-N-Out pricing has increased from its initial offering of a burger for a quarter prices have not risen commensurate with the market or even with inflation. The company prides itself on investing in its people, paying $13 an hour versus the industry average of $9.50 to entry-level employees. The typical manager has been with the company for almost 17 years and makes over $130,000. Not surprisingly, the company has an outstanding reputation as an employer, with a 2023 rating of 4.6 of five stars on Glassdoor, with Lynsi herself earning a 92 percent approval rating, numbers not regularly seen for fast-food restaurants.

Lynsi Snyder continues to hold fast to the family's vision of high-quality ingredients and a limited menu of basic offerings prepared well. The chain has a fervent following, including stars like Paris Hilton, Kylie Jenner, and chef Gordon Ramsay. She's also clear about holding the ownership of In-N-Out with no question. "It's not about the money for us," she says. "Unless God sends a lightning bolt down and changes my heart miraculously, I would not ever sell." (After studying this chapter, you should be able to respond to the set of discussion questions found at the end of the chapter.)

What Is a Small Business?

Learning Objective 3-1

Define *small business*, discuss its importance to the U.S. economy, and explain popular areas of small business.

The term *small business* is not easy to define. Locally owned and operated restaurants, dry cleaners, and hair salons are obviously small businesses, and giant corporations, such as Nike, Starbucks, Apple, Target, and Netflix, are clearly big businesses. Between these two extremes, though, fall thousands of companies that cannot be easily categorized.

The U.S. Department of Commerce has traditionally considered a business to be small if it has fewer than 500 employees. The U.S. **Small Business Administration (SBA)**, a government agency that assists small businesses, has different standards based on industry. For instance, a manufacturer is considered small if it has 1,500 or fewer employees. A wholesaling firm is small if it has between 100 and 500 employees. Other industries, though, such as services, retailing, and construction, are generally classified based on revenue rather than number of employees. Because strict numerical terms sometimes lead to ambiguous or confusing classifications, we will consider a **small business** as one that is independent (that is, not owned by or a unit of a larger business) and that has relatively little influence in its market. A small neighborhood grocer would be small, then, assuming it is not part of a chain and that market forces largely set the prices it pays to wholesalers and that it can charge its customers. Dell Computer was a small business when founded by Michael Dell in 1984, but today it's one of the world's largest computer companies and is not small in any sense of the term. Hence, it can negotiate from a position of strength with its suppliers and can set its prices with less consideration for what other computer firms are charging.

Small Business Administration (SBA) *government agency charged with assisting small businesses*

Small Business *independently owned business that has relatively little influence in its market*

The Importance of Small Business in the U.S. Economy

As Figure 3.1 shows, most U.S. businesses employ fewer than 100 people, and most U.S. workers are employed by small business. Moreover, this same pattern exists across most free market economies.

Figure 3.1(a) shows that 85.43 percent of all businesses employ 20 or fewer people. Another 12.13 percent employ between 20 and 99 people, and 2.18 percent employ between 100 and 499 people. Only about 0.10 of 1 percent employ 1,000 or more people. Figure 3.1(b) shows that 23.52 percent of all workers are employed by firms with fewer than 20 people, and 29.62 percent are employed by firms with between 20 and 99 people. Another 25.29 percent are employed by firms with between 100 and 499 people. We can measure the impact of small business on the U.S. economy in terms of its impact on *job creation* and *innovation*, as well as its *contributions to big business*.

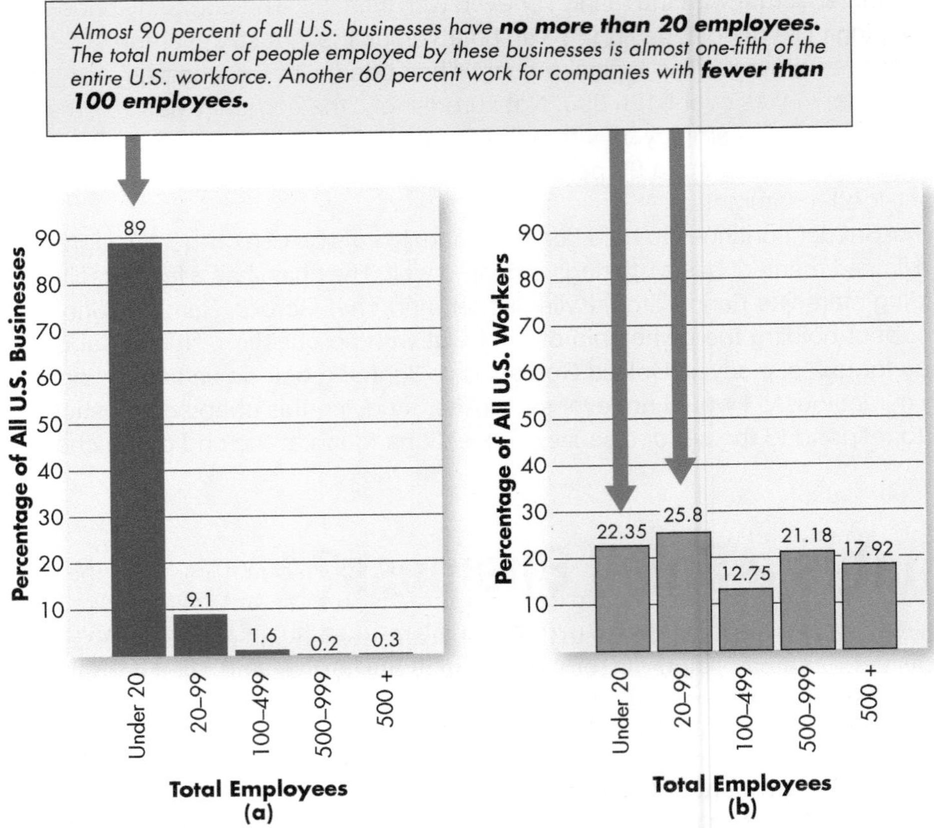

FIGURE 3.1 The Pervasiveness of Small Business in the United States
Source: Data from U.S. Census Bureau. www.census.gov/. Totals do not equal 100% due to rounding.

Job Creation Small businesses—especially in certain industries—are an important source of new (and often well-paid) jobs. Small businesses have accounted for two-thirds of all new jobs created in the past 25 years.[3] Of course, jobs are created by companies of all sizes, all of which hire and lay off workers. Although small firms often hire at a faster rate, they also tend to cut jobs at a higher rate. They are generally the first to hire in times of economic recovery, and big firms are generally the last to lay off workers during downswings. Many small businesses were rocked by the pandemic, but by the first quarter of 2022, most of those lost jobs had been recovered.[4]

However, relative job growth among businesses of different sizes is not easy to determine. For one thing, when a successful small business starts adding employees at a rapid clip, it may quickly cease being small. For example, Dell Computer had exactly one employee in 1984 (Michael Dell himself). But the payroll grew to around 100 employees in 1986, over 2,000 in 1992, more than 39,000 in 2004, 94,300 in 2010, and 133,000 in 2022. Although there was no precise point at which Dell turned from "small" into "large," some of the jobs it created would have been counted in the small business sector and some in the large.

Innovation History reminds us that major innovations are as likely to come from small businesses (or individuals) as from big ones. Small firms and individuals invented the PC, the stainless-steel razor blade, the photocopier, and the jet engine and launched Apple, Facebook, Amazon, Starbucks, Instagram, and eBay. Innovations are not always new products, though. Michael Dell didn't invent the PC; he developed an innovative way to build it (buying finished components and then assembling them) and an innovative way to sell it (directly to consumers, first by telephone and now online). Similarly, Reed Hastings, founder of Netflix, invented neither the DVD nor the DVD rental business, but he did introduce revolutionary new payment and delivery models. In general, small businesses produce 16 times as many patents per employee as large patenting firms.[5]

Contributions to Big Business Most of the products made by big businesses are sold to consumers by small ones. For example, most dealerships that sell Chevrolets, Toyotas, and Hondas are independently operated. Even as more shoppers turn to online shopping, smaller businesses still play critical roles. For instance, most larger traditional retailers with an online presence actually outsource the management of this part of their business and the distribution of their products to other firms, many of them small or regional companies. Smaller businesses also provide data storage services for larger businesses. Moreover, small businesses provide big ones with many of their services and raw materials. Microsoft, for instance, relies on hundreds of small firms for most of its routine code-writing functions.

Popular Areas of Small Business Enterprise

Small businesses play a major role in services, retailing, construction, wholesaling, finance and insurance, manufacturing, and transportation. Generally, the more resources that are required, the harder a business is to start and the less likely it is that small firms dominate an industry. Remember, too, that *small* is a relative term. The criteria (number of employees and total annual sales) differ among industries and are often meaningful only when compared with truly large businesses. Figure 3.2 shows the distribution of all U.S. businesses employing fewer than 20 people across industry groups.

Services About 56.2 percent of businesses with fewer than 20 employees are involved in the service industry, which ranges from marriage counseling to computer software, from management consulting to professional dog walking. Partly because they require few resources (and hence don't cost as much to start), service providers constitute a large segment of small business.

Retailing Retailers, which sell products made by other firms directly to consumers, account for about 13.69 percent of small businesses. Usually, people who start small retail businesses favor specialty shops, such as big men's clothing or gourmet coffees that let the owners focus limited resources on narrow or small market segments.

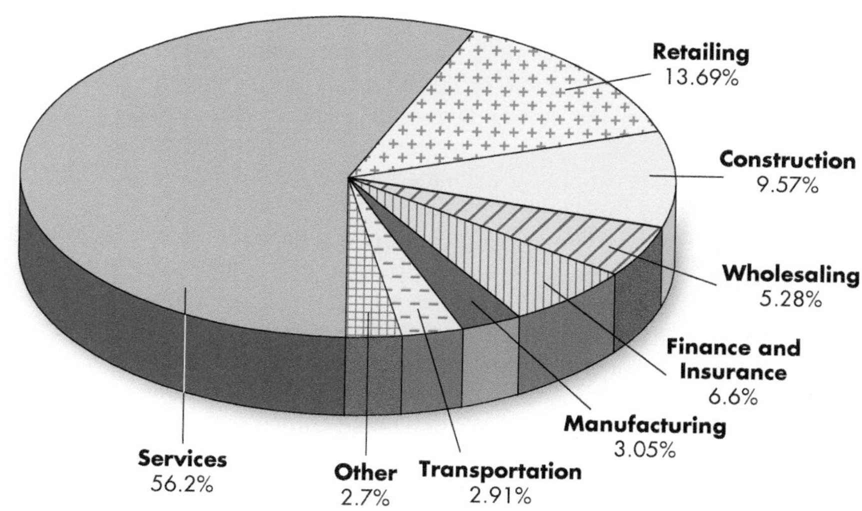

FIGURE 3.2 Small Business by Industry
Source: U.S. Census Bureau. www.census.gov/

Construction About 9.57 percent of all U.S. businesses are involved in construction. Because many construction jobs are small local projects, such as a homeowner adding a garage or remodeling a room, local contractors are often best suited to handle them.

Wholesaling Small business owners often do well in wholesaling, which accounts for about 5.28 percent of businesses with fewer than 20 employees. Wholesalers buy products in bulk from manufacturers or other producers and store them in quantities and locations convenient for selling them to retailers.

Finance and Insurance Financial and insurance firms account for about 6.6 percent of small businesses. Most of these businesses, such as local State Farm Insurance offices, are affiliates of or agents for larger national firms. Small locally owned banks are also common in smaller communities and rural areas.

Manufacturing More than any other industry, manufacturing lends itself to big business, but it still accounts for about 3.05 percent of firms with fewer than

finding a better way

The Rise of the Gig Economy

Manufacturing was once the dominant technology in the United States. During the 1970s, though, manufacturing entered a long period of decline, primarily due to a wave of globalization. International competitors came onto the scene with better equipment, much higher levels of efficiency, and employees willing to work for lower wages. Faced with a battle for survival, some U.S. companies disappeared, but many others underwent a long and difficult period of change by eliminating waste and transforming themselves into leaner, more efficient, and more responsive entities and, of course, by taking advantage of global supply chains.

As the U.S. manufacturing sector continues to contract due to globalization, a tremendous growth in the service sector, often fueled by visionary entrepreneurs, has kept the overall U.S. economy from declining at the same rate. A service organization is one that transforms resources into an intangible output and creates time or place utility for its customers. For example, Netflix provides online streaming. Facebook offers its members a venue for networking and interacting with others, and your local hairdresser cuts your hair. In 1947, the service sector was responsible for less than half of the U.S. gross national product (GNP). By 1975, however, this figure was nearly 65 percent, and by 2016, it had reached approximately 80 percent. In fact, by 2022, four out of five American workers in the private sector were employed in the service economy.[6]

Moreover, employment in service occupations is expected to continue to represent a larger share of employment in the U.S. economy. The Bureau of Labor Statistics' list of the fastest-growing occupations between 2012 and 2022 indicated almost all of these occupations were in the service sector, largely in the areas of professional and business services and health care and social assistance.

Gemenacom/Shutterstock

Another rapidly growing sector of the U.S. economy is the gig economy. Composed of freelancers and contractors who work on a temporary basis, often outside set hours, this sector relies heavily on technology, using laptops and mobile devices or online tools to provide services. In 2023, there were over 70 million people freelancing, and that number is estimated to reach 79.6 million by 2025 and 90.1 million by 2028.[7]

As more people choose gigs over or in addition to full-time jobs as employees, big businesses face new challenges. Accustomed to the independence and flexibility of owning a business, gig workers may chafe at the traditional supervision structures and constraints of full-time employment. With a growing number of workers choosing the gig economy, the United States may see a continued decline in manufacturing jobs and come to rely more heavily on the service and gig sectors for the health of its overall economy.

Dotshock/Shutterstock

New businesses often get started in response to emerging opportunities.

20 employees. Indeed, small manufacturers sometimes outperform big ones in such innovation-driven industries as electronics, equipment and machine parts, and computer software.

Transportation About 2.91 percent of small companies are in transportation and related businesses, including many taxi and limousine companies, charter airplane services, and tour operators.

Other The remaining 2.7 percent or so of small businesses are in other industries, such as small research-and-development laboratories and independent media companies—start-up web channels, small-town newspapers, and radio broadcasters.

Entrepreneurship

Learning Objective 3-2

Explain entrepreneurship and describe some key characteristics of entrepreneurial personalities and activities.

We noted previously that Dell Computer started as a one-person operation and grew into a giant corporation. Dell's growth was spurred by the imagination and skill of Michael Dell, the entrepreneur who founded the company. **Entrepreneurs** are people, like Dell, who assume the risk of business ownership.[8] **Entrepreneurship** is the process of seeking business opportunities under conditions of risk. However, not all entrepreneurs have the same goals.

Entrepreneur *businessperson or individual who accepts the risks and opportunities involved in creating and operating a new business venture*

Entrepreneurship *the process of seeking business opportunities under conditions of risk*

Entrepreneurship Goals

People may decide to pursue entrepreneurship for a variety of reasons. Many entrepreneurs seek to launch a new business with the goal of independence—independence from working for someone else, coupled with some reasonable degree of financial security. Such entrepreneurs want to achieve a safe and secure financial future for themselves and their families but do not necessarily aspire to grow their business beyond their capacity to run it. Consider Jack Matz, a former corporate executive in Houston who lost his job when his firm merged with another. Rather than look for another management position, Matz opened a photocopying and custom printing business near a local university. His goal was to earn enough money to lead a comfortable life until he retires in 10 years. The term *small business* is most closely associated with these kinds of enterprises.

Other entrepreneurs, however, launch new businesses with the goal of growth and expansion—that is, to transform their venture into a large business. This was Dell's vision when he started his business; likewise, when Howard Schultz took over

Starbucks, he also had plans to grow and develop the fledgling coffee company into a much larger enterprise. Terms such as *new ventures* and *start-ups* are often used to refer to these kinds of businesses.

In still other cases, the goals of an entrepreneur may not always be clear in the early stages of business development. For instance, one entrepreneur might launch a business with little or no expectation that it will have huge growth potential but then find that it can grow dramatically. Mark Zuckerberg, for example, had no idea that his Facebook firm would grow to its present size. Another entrepreneur might start out with ambitious growth plans but find that expected opportunities cannot be realized: Perhaps there is no large market or another firm established dominance over that market first.

Entrepreneurial Characteristics

Regardless of their goals, many successful entrepreneurs share certain characteristics. Among these characteristics are resourcefulness and a concern for good, often personal, customer relations. Most of them also have a strong desire to be their own bosses. Many express a need to "gain control over my life" or "build for the family" and believe that building successful businesses will help them do it. They can also deal with uncertainty and risk.

Yesterday's entrepreneur was often stereotyped as "the boss"—self-reliant, male, and able to make quick, firm decisions. Today's entrepreneur is seen more often as an open-minded leader who relies on networks, business plans, and consensus. Past and present entrepreneurs also have different views on such topics as how to succeed, how to automate business, and when to rely on experience in the trade or on basic business acumen.[9]

Consider Julie Wainwright. She had served as CEO of several small businesses before making the decision to start her own business when she was in her 50s. After doing some intensive marketing research and setting some clear goals for her new venture she launched The RealReal. Her vision was to create a virtual marketplace where people could buy and sell secondhand luxury good such as Louis Vuitton bags, Chanel gowns, and so forth. Her start-up did $10 million in sales the first year and today is worth over $1 billion.[10]

Among other things, Wainwright's story illustrates what is almost always a key element in entrepreneurship: risk. Interestingly, most successful entrepreneurs seldom see what they do as risky. Whereas others may focus on possibilities for failure and balk at gambling everything on a new venture, most entrepreneurs are so passionate about their ideas and plans that they see little or no likelihood of failure. Wainwright started her venture in her home with two employees. She picked up items from sellers and delivered them to buyers using a rented U-Haul truck and personally answered most customer emails.

Starting and Operating a New Business

Learning Objective 3-3

Describe distinctive competence, the business plan, and the start-up decisions made by small businesses and identify sources of financial aid available to such enterprises.

First the Internet and more recently social media have dramatically changed the rules for starting and operating a small business. Setting up is easier and faster than ever, more potential opportunities are available than at any other time, and the ability to gather and assess information is at an all-time high. Today, for example, many one-person retailers do most of their business—both buying and selling—on Internet auction sites, such as eBay.

Even so, would-be entrepreneurs must make the right start-up decisions. For instance, they need to have a clear vision of why their business will succeed. They must also decide how to get into business—should they buy an existing business or build from the ground up? They must know when to seek expert advice and where to find sources of financing. If, for example, a new firm needs financial backing from investors or a line of credit from vendors or distributors, the entrepreneur must have in place a comprehensive, well-crafted business plan. Creating a business plan, in turn, begins with understanding the potential firm's distinctive competencies.

Understanding Distinctive Competencies

An organization's distinctive competencies are the aspects of business that the firm performs better than its competitors. The distinctive competencies of small business usually fall into three areas: (1) the ability to identify new niches in established markets, (2) the ability to identify new markets, and (3) the ability to move quickly to take advantage of new opportunities.

Identifying Niches in Established Markets An **established market** is one in which many firms compete according to relatively well-defined criteria. For example, the video rental market was well established when Hastings decided to launch Netflix. Blockbuster was the dominant firm, but many independent video rental firms were also prospering. Retail outlets kept an inventory of video products available for rent. Customers drove or walked to the stores, paid a fee, and took a video home. They kept it for a defined period of time and then returned it to the store (with a late fee, if they kept it too long). A **niche** is simply a segment of a market that is not currently being exploited. In general, small entrepreneurial businesses are better at discovering these niches than are larger organizations. Large organizations usually have so many resources committed to older, established business practices that they may be unaware of new opportunities. Entrepreneurs can see these opportunities and move quickly to take advantage of them. Reed Hastings's decision to rent DVDs by mail allowed Netflix to develop and exploit a niche.

Established Market *one in which many firms compete according to relatively well-defined criteria*

Niche *a segment of a market that is not currently being exploited*

Entrepreneurs Dave Gilboa and Neil Blumenthal founded Warby Parker, a business that sells prescription eyewear through the mail. The entrepreneurs realized that most consumers disliked the experience of going to an optical shop to try on glasses and then were irritated at the price of those glasses. So Warby Parker offers lower-priced glasses with contemporary designs and a money-back guarantee. Astute marketing then allowed them to get a quick start with their niche business, selling more than 50,000 pairs of glasses and generating profits after only a single year of operation.[11] Warby Parker has now established itself as a leading eyewear retailer.

Identifying New Markets Successful entrepreneurs also excel at discovering whole new markets. Discovery can happen in at least two ways. First, an entrepreneur can transfer a product or service that is well established in one geographic market to a second market. This is what Marcel Bich did with ballpoint pens, which occupied a well-established market in Europe before Bich introduced them in the United States more than 60 years ago. Bich's company, Société Bic, eventually came to dominate the U.S. market.

Second, entrepreneurs can sometimes create entire industries. Entrepreneurial inventions of the dry paper copying process and the semiconductor have created vast new industries. Not only were the first companies to enter these markets successful (Xerox and National Semiconductor, respectively), but their entrepreneurial activity also spawned the development of hundreds of other companies and hundreds of thousands of jobs. Again, because entrepreneurs are not encumbered with a history of doing business in a particular way, they are usually better at discovering new markets than are larger, more mature organizations.

First-Mover Advantages A **first-mover advantage** is any advantage that comes to a firm because it exploits an opportunity before any other firm does. Sometimes large firms discover niches within existing markets or new markets at just about the same time as small entrepreneurial firms, but they cannot move as quickly as small companies to take advantage of these opportunities. Many app developers for

First-Mover Advantage *any advantage that comes to a firm because it exploits an opportunity before any other firm does*

smartphones and other forms of digital commerce exploit first-mover advantage. For instance, SPINX Digital is a small firm that started out designing websites for customers. Today, SPINX has been recognized as one of the best app designers in the world.[12]

Numerous reasons account for the difference. For example, many large organizations make decisions slowly because each of their many layers of hierarchy has to approve an action before it can be implemented. Also, large organizations may sometimes put a great deal of their assets at risk when they take advantage of new opportunities. Every time Boeing decides to build a new model of a commercial jet, it is making a decision that could literally bankrupt the company if it does not turn out well. The size of the risk may make large organizations cautious. The dollar value of the assets at risk in a small organization, in contrast, is quite small. Managers may be willing to "bet the company" when the value of the company is only $100,000. They might be unwilling to "bet the company" when the value of the company is $1 billion.

Crafting a Business Plan

Business Plan *document in which the entrepreneur summarizes the business strategy for the proposed new venture and how that strategy will be implemented*

After the would-be entrepreneur has defined a potential distinctive competence and made the decision to proceed, the next step is formulating a **business plan** in which the entrepreneur describes a business strategy for the new venture and demonstrates how it will be implemented.[13] A real benefit of a business plan is the fact that in the act of preparing it, the would-be entrepreneur is forced to develop the business idea on paper and firm up their thinking about how to launch it before investing time and money in it. The idea of the business plan isn't new. What is new is the use of specialized business plans, mostly because creditors and investors demand them as tools for deciding whether to finance or invest.

Setting Goals and Objectives A business plan describes the match between the entrepreneur's abilities and experiences and the requirements for producing or marketing a particular product. It also defines strategies for production and marketing, legal elements and organization, and accounting and finance. In particular, a business plan should answer three questions: (1) What are the entrepreneur's goals and objectives? (2) What strategies will be used to obtain them? (3) How will these strategies be implemented?

Sales Forecasting Although a key element of any business plan is sales forecasts, plans must carefully build an argument for likely business success based on sound logic and research. Entrepreneurs, for example, can't forecast sales revenues without first researching markets. Simply asserting that the new venture will sell 100,000 units per month is not credible; the entrepreneur must demonstrate an understanding of the current market, of the strengths and weaknesses of existing firms, and of the means by which the new venture will compete. Without the sales forecast, no one can estimate the required size of a plant, store, or office or decide how much inventory to carry and how many employees to hire.

Financial Planning Financial planning refers to the entrepreneur's plan for turning all other activities into dollars. It generally includes a cash budget, an income statement, balance sheets, and a breakeven chart. The cash budget shows how much money you need before you open for business and how much you need to keep the business going before it starts earning a profit. Most small businesses struggled and many failed during the 2020 COVID-19 pandemic, in part because they lacked sufficient financial reserves to survive during the period of mandated closures and the effects of social distancing.[14]

Starting the Small Business

A Chinese proverb says that a journey of a thousand miles begins with a single step. This is also true of a new business. The first step is the individual's commitment to becoming a business owner. In preparing a business plan, the entrepreneur must choose the industry and market in which they plan to compete. This choice means assessing not only industry conditions and trends but also one's own abilities and interests. Like big business managers, small business owners must understand the nature of the enterprises in which they are engaged.

Buying an Existing Business After an entrepreneur has forecasted sales and completed the financial planning, they must decide whether to buy an existing business or start from scratch. Many experts recommend the first approach because, quite simply, the odds are better: If it's successful, an existing business has already proven its ability to attract customers and generate profit. It has also established relationships with lenders, suppliers, and other stakeholders. Moreover, an existing track record gives potential buyers a much clearer picture of what to expect than any estimate of a start-up's prospects.

Ray Kroc bought McDonald's as an existing business, added entrepreneurial vision and business insight, and produced a multinational giant. Both Southwest Airlines and Starbucks were small but struggling operations when entrepreneurs took over and grew them into large businesses. About 35 percent of all new businesses that were started in the past decade were bought from someone else.

Franchising Most McDonald's, Subway, 7-Eleven, RE/MAX, Holiday Inn, and Dunkin' (formerly Dunkin' Donuts) Donuts outlets are franchises operating under licenses issued by parent companies to local owners. A **franchise** agreement involves two parties, a *franchisee* (the local owner) and a *franchiser* (the parent company).[15]

Franchise *arrangement in which a buyer (franchisee) purchases the right to sell the good or service of the seller (franchiser)*

Franchisees benefit from the parent corporation's experience and expertise, and the franchiser may even supply financing. It may pick the store location, negotiate the lease, design the store, and purchase equipment. It may train the first set of employees and managers and issue standard policies and procedures. Once the business is open, the franchiser may offer savings by allowing the franchisee to purchase from a central location. Marketing strategy (especially advertising) may also be handled by the franchiser. In short, franchisees receive—that is, invest in—not only their own ready-made businesses but also expert help in running them.

Franchises have advantages for both sellers and buyers. Franchises can grow rapidly by using the investment money provided by franchisees. The franchisee gets to own a business and has access to big-business management skills. The franchisee does not have to build a business step by step, and because each franchise outlet is probably similar to other outlets, failure is less likely. Recent statistics show that franchising is on the upswing. For instance, franchise businesses added 312,478 jobs in 2022 and generated economic output of almost $1 trillion. The franchise sector contributed an estimated 3.78 percent of the U.S. GDP in 2022.[16]

Perhaps the most significant disadvantage in owning a franchise is the start-up cost. Franchise prices vary widely. The fee and investment requirements for a Firehouse Subs shop ranges from $131,150 to $928,405; to open a Wendy's the total outlay ranges from $330,000 to $3,700,000. At the other extreme, a Playball Kids franchise runs from $6000 to $8000. Most franchising contracts require that the franchisee pay an upfront fee plus the cost of building a facility. The fee quoted for Wendy's, for example, is a fee of $330,000 to buy an existing franchise but doesn't include the price paid to the existing franchisee, while the higher range includes construction costs for a new location. And professional sports teams (which are also franchises) can cost several hundred million dollars. Franchisees may also be obligated to contribute a percentage of sales to parent corporations. From the perspective of the parent company, some firms choose not to franchise to retain more control over quality and earn more profits for themselves. Starbucks, for instance, does not franchise its coffee shops. (Starbucks does have licensing agreements where other firms operate Starbucks kiosks and other niche outlets; it does not, though, franchise individual free-standing coffee shops to individuals.)

Starting from Scratch Despite the odds, some people seek the satisfaction that comes from planting an idea and growing it into a healthy business. Starting from scratch also has practical reasons. A new business doesn't suffer the ill effects of a prior owner's errors, and the start-up owner is free to choose lenders, equipment, inventories, locations, suppliers, and workers. Of all new businesses begun in the past decade, about 62 percent were started from scratch. Tesla, Walmart, Microsoft, Amazon, and Twitter are among today's successful businesses that were started from scratch by an entrepreneur.

But as we have already noted, the risks of starting a business from scratch are greater than those of buying an existing firm. New business founders can only make projections about their prospects. Success or failure depends on identifying a genuine opportunity, such as a product for which many customers will pay well but which is currently unavailable. To find openings, entrepreneurs must study markets and answer the following questions:

- Who and where are my customers?
- How much will those customers pay for my product?
- How much of my product can I expect to sell?
- Who are my competitors?
- Why will customers buy my product rather than the product of my competitors?

Financing the Small Business

Although the choice of how to start a business is obviously important, it's meaningless unless you can get the money to finance your ideas. Among the more common sources for funding are family and friends, personal savings, lending institutions, investors, and governmental agencies. Lending institutions are more likely to help finance the purchase of an existing business because the risks are better understood. Individuals starting new businesses will probably have to rely on personal resources. One of the many causes of the 2008–2011 recession was a sharp reduction in the availability of credit, including funds to help start new businesses. This credit crunch, in turn, limited both new start-up funding and funding for existing businesses wanting to make new investments. During the 2020 COVID-19 pandemic, however, federal lending policies were implemented to encourage banks to extend credit to small businesses to help them remain afloat.

According to the National Federation of Independent Business, personal resources, not loans, are the most important sources of money. Including money borrowed from friends and relatives, personal resources account for more than two-thirds of all money invested in new small businesses, and one-half of that is used to purchase existing businesses. Getting money from banks, independent investors, and government loans requires extra effort. At a minimum, banks and private investors will want to review business plans, and government loans have strict eligibility guidelines.

Venture Capital Company *group of small investors who invest money in companies with rapid growth potential*

Venture capital companies are groups of small investors seeking to make profits on companies with rapid growth potential. Most of these firms do not lend money. They invest it, supplying capital in return for partial ownership (like stocks, discussed later in this chapter). They may also demand representation on boards of directors. In some cases, managers need approval from the venture capital company before making major decisions. In most cases, venture capitalists do not provide money to start a new business; instead, once a business has been successfully launched and its growth potential established, they provide the funds to fuel expansion. Of all venture capital currently committed in the United States, about 28 percent comes from true venture capital firms. Steve Case, cofounder of AOL, operates a successful venture capital company. He looks to invest in new start-ups that have a great business idea, a passionate entrepreneur, and a solid and well-crafted business plan.[17]

Small Business Investment Company (SBIC) *government-regulated investment company that borrows money from the SBA to invest in or lend to a small business*

Small business investment companies (SBICs) also invest in companies with potential for rapid growth. They are federally licensed to borrow money from the SBA and to invest it in or lend it to small businesses, and they are themselves investments for their shareholders. Past beneficiaries of SBIC capital include Apple, Intel, and FedEx. The government also sponsors *minority enterprise small business investment companies (MESBICs)*. As the name suggests, MESBICs target minority-owned businesses.

SBA Financial Programs Since its founding in 1953, the SBA has sponsored financing programs for small businesses that meet standards in size and independence. Eligible firms must be unable to get private financing at reasonable terms. The most common form of SBA financing, its *7(a) loans programs*, allows small businesses to borrow from commercial lenders and guarantees to repay up to 85 percent of loans of up to $150,000 and 75 percent of loans of more than $150,000.[18] The SBA's *special purpose loans* target businesses with specific needs, such as meeting international demands or implementing pollution-control measures. For loans under $50,000, the SBA offers the *micro loan program*. The *Certified Development Company (504) program* offers fixed interest rates on loans from nonprofit community-based lenders to boost local economies.[19]

The SBA also helps entrepreneurs improve their management skills. The Service Corps of Retired Executives (SCORE) is made up of retired executives who volunteer to help entrepreneurs start new businesses. The **Small Business Development Center (SBDC)** program consolidates information from various disciplines and institutions for use by new and existing small businesses.

Small Business Development Center (SBDC) *SBA program designed to consolidate information from various disciplines and make it available to small businesses*

Other Sources of Financing Some entrepreneurs find financing from overseas investors. James Buck developed a new implantable heart device to treat certain heart conditions but could not find adequate funding in the United States to start his business. He ended up looking to investors in Asia and obtained $5 million from the government of Malaysia.[20] There are also a growing number of online financing options. For instance, Kabbage.com is an online company that provides cash advances to small business.[21]

Trends, Successes, and Failures in New Ventures

Learning Objective 3-4

Discuss the trends in small business start-ups and identify the main reasons for success and failure among small businesses.

For every Sam Walton, Mark Zuckerberg, Mary Kay Ash, or Bill Gates—entrepreneurs who transformed small businesses into big ones—there are many entrepreneurs who fail. In 2019, prior to the pandemic, 1.04 million new businesses were launched in the United States; another 928,000 failed.[22] Historically, between 650,000 and 900,000 businesses have been started and between 600,000 and 850,000 have failed each year. In this section, we look first at a few key trends in small business start-ups. Then we examine some of the reasons for success and failure in small business undertakings.

Trends in Small Business Start-Ups

As noted previously, thousands of new businesses are started in the United States every year. Several factors account for this trend, and in this section, we focus on five of them.

Emergence of E-Commerce The most significant trend is the rapid emergence of e-commerce and other online points of entry. Because the Internet provides fundamentally new ways of doing business, savvy entrepreneurs have created and expanded new businesses faster and easier than ever before. Such leading-edge firms as Google, Amazon, and eBay owe their existence to the Internet. Figure 3.3 underscores this point by summarizing the growth in e-commerce retail sales from 2000 through 2021.

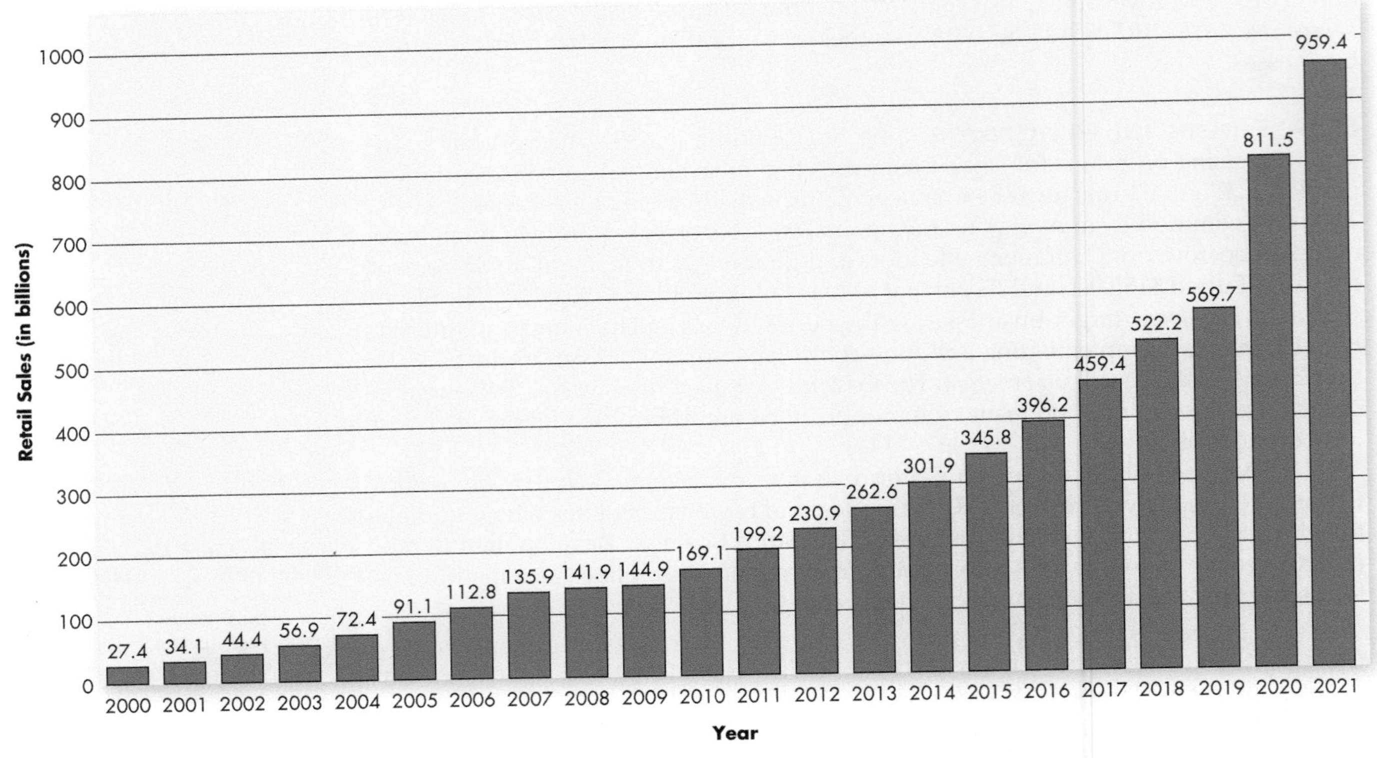

FIGURE 3.3 E-Commerce Retail Sales
Source: Data from U.S. Census Bureau. https://www.census.gov/retail/mrts/www/data/excel/tsadjustedsales.xls

Crossovers from Big Business More businesses are being started by people who have opted to leave big corporations and put their experience to work for themselves. In some cases, they see great new ideas that they want to develop. Others get burned out in the corporate world. Some have lost their jobs, only to discover that working for themselves was a better idea anyway. John Chambers spent several years working at IBM and Wang Laboratories/GLOBAL before he decided to try his hand at entrepreneurship. After resigning from Wang in 1991, he signed on to help Cisco, then a small and struggling firm. Under his leadership and entrepreneurial guidance, Cisco has become one of the largest and most important technology companies in the world.

Opportunities for People of Color and Women More small businesses are also being started by people of color and women.[23] The number of businesses owned by African Americans increased by 60 percent during the most recent 5-year period for which data are available and now is about 2 million. The number of businesses owned by Hispanic people has grown 44 percent and now is about 2.25 million. Ownership among Asian American people has increased 41 percent and among Pacific Islanders 35 percent.[24]

There are roughly 12 million businesses owned by women, and they generate a combined $1.8 trillion in revenue a year and employ about 10.1 million workers.[25] Figure 3.4 shows some of the reasons women cite for starting their own businesses. Anne Beiler bought a small Amish-owned pretzel stand to support her family when her husband decided to become a no-fee marriage counselor. She worked long hours and continued to tinker with both her menu and pretzel recipes until things began to take off. She grew her business into a national chain called Auntie Anne's Soft Pretzels before selling to another company. And as we noted in the previous chapter, Beatrice Dixon's multimillion-dollar company, the Honey Pot, manufactures and distributes affordable, plant-based feminine care products, and she is one of the first 40 women of color to raise over $1 million in venture capital.

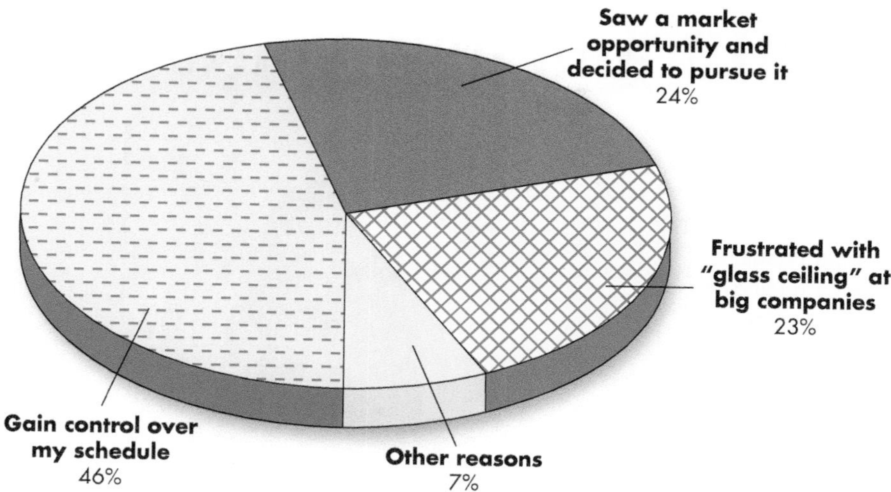

FIGURE 3.4 Reasons Women Give for Starting Businesses

Global Opportunities Many entrepreneurs are also finding new opportunities in international markets. Doug Mellinger founded PRT Group, a software development company. One of Mellinger's biggest problems was finding trained programmers. There aren't enough U.S.-based programmers to go around, and international-born programmers face strict immigration quotas. So Mellinger set up shop on Barbados, a Caribbean island where the government helped him attract international programmers and did everything it could to make things easier. Today, PRT (now enherent Corp.) has customers and suppliers from dozens of nations.

Better Survival Rates More people are encouraged to test their skills as entrepreneurs because the small business failure rate has declined. During the 1960s and 1970s, fewer than half of all new start-ups survived more than 18 months; only one in five lasted 10 years. Now, however, over half can expect to survive for at least 4 years and a third survive for 10 years or longer.[26]

Reasons for Failure

Unfortunately, even though survival rates have improved, almost half of all new businesses still will not enjoy long-term success. Why do some succeed and others fail? Although no set pattern has been established, four general factors contribute to failure:

1. ***Managerial incompetence or inexperience.*** Some entrepreneurs put too much faith in common sense, overestimate their own managerial skills, or believe that hard work alone ensures success. If managers don't have a sound business plan, don't know how to make basic business decisions, or don't understand basic management concepts and principles, they aren't likely to succeed in the long run.
2. ***Neglect.*** Some entrepreneurs try to launch ventures in their spare time, and others devote only limited time to new businesses. But starting a small business demands an overwhelming time commitment. If you aren't willing to put in the time and effort that a business requires, you aren't likely to survive.
3. ***Weak control systems.*** Effective control systems keep a business on track and alert managers to potential trouble. If your control systems don't signal impending problems, you may be in serious trouble before you spot more obvious difficulties. For instance, some businesses fail because they do a poor job of managing their credit collection policies. Anxious to grow, they may be too liberal in extending credit to their customers and then end up not being able to collect all the money that is owed to them.

entrepreneurship and new ventures

Small Investment, Big Payoff

Alison Buck/Getty Images

When well-established individuals or businesses need a loan, they generally head to the bank. What happens, though, when someone lacks a credit history or wants to start a business in a region where banks are not a reliable source of funding?

Enter the business of microlending—very small loans made to individuals to start a new business. The need for this service is particularly pronounced in developing nations, where budding entrepreneurs require just $100 or $200 to get their business off the ground. Lenders still need some kind of data, however, to determine who is the best candidate for even the smallest of loans.

As a researcher for an investment bank, Shivani Siroya became aware of microfinance and the challenges that both borrowers and lenders faced. Microfinance became her passion, and she went back to school to study health economics and econometrics at Columbia University. From there she dived fully into the issues as a UN researcher working in Africa, where she determined that the real problem was simply lack of data. In April 2011, she founded InVenture, now called Tala, a tech company that leverages mobile technology to create credit scores for unbanked individuals.

To collect data that could be used for credit decisions on microloans, Tala developed a mobile app that monitors the length of users' phone calls and tracks their financial transactions. With a proprietary algorithm, Tala evaluates over 10,000 indicators of responsibility. For example, applicants whose average phone calls were longer than 4 minutes were thought to have stronger relationships, making them a better credit risk. Using this and other more complex data, Tala approved half of its applicants, making small loans, often between $20 and $100, and charging just 5 percent interest, resulting in an impressive repayment rate of 85 percent in the company's first year of operation.

By 2022, Tala had grown to provide services on three continents and in four countries, with expansion plans in the works. Its app had garnered over a million five-star reviews, and it had served over 6 million customers. With $2.7 billion disbursed, Tala has clearly demonstrated the existing and growing need for this type of lending.

4 ***Insufficient capital.*** Some entrepreneurs are overly optimistic about how soon they'll start earning profits. In most cases, it takes months or even years. Amazon didn't earn a profit for 10 years but obviously still required capital to pay employees and to cover other expenses. Experts say you need enough capital to operate at least 6 months without earning a profit; some recommend enough to last a year.[27] Many small businesses struggled or closed in 2020 and 2021 because they lacked sufficient capital to survive the effects of the pandemic.

Reasons for Success

Four basic factors are also typically cited to explain small business success:

1 ***Hard work, drive, and dedication.*** Small business owners must be committed to succeeding and willing to spend the time and effort to make it happen. Tai Lee wanted to open a restaurant in College Station, Texas, but did not have sufficient capital. He partnered with a local investor and opened Veritas Wine and Bistro in 2009. In the early days, he typically spent 14 hours a day managing the restaurant, handling the cooking, and greeting customers. His

wife also worked beside him, waiting on customers and taking reservations. This schedule persisted for over three years. Eventually, though, Veritas took off and became a big success. Today, Tai owns four restaurants and a lucrative catering business and has a gourmet food truck that has received national acclaim.

2 ***Market demand for the products or services being provided.*** Careful analysis of market conditions can help small business owners assess the probable reception of their products. Attempts to expand restaurants specializing in baked potatoes, muffins, and gelato often struggle, but hamburger and pizza chains continue to expand. In the case of Veritas, College Station had relatively few fine dining options and that segment of the market was clearly underserved.

3 ***Managerial competence.*** Successful owners may acquire competence through training or experience or by drawing on the expertise of others. Few, however, succeed alone or straight out of college. Most spend time in successful companies or partner with others to bring expertise to a new business. Tai Lee studied both business and culinary arts before opening Veritas. He also sought advice from other successful entrepreneurs.

4 ***Luck.*** After Alan McKim started Clean Harbors, an environmental cleanup firm in New England, he struggled to keep his business afloat and was running low on capital. Before his funding was exhausted, though, the U.S. government committed $1.6 billion to toxic waste cleanup—McKim's specialty. He quickly landed several large government contracts and put his business on solid financial footing. Had the government fund not been created at just the right time, McKim might well have failed. Similarly, Netflix might not have succeeded if it had not started just as customers were shifting away from videocassettes to DVDs.

Noncorporate Business Ownership

Learning Objective 3-5

Explain sole proprietorships, partnerships, and cooperatives and discuss the advantages and disadvantages of each.

Whether they intend to launch a small local business or a new venture projected to grow rapidly, all entrepreneurs must decide which form of legal ownership best suits their goals: *sole proprietorship, partnership,* or *corporation.* Because this choice affects a host of managerial and financial issues, few decisions are more critical. Entrepreneurs must consider their own preferences, their immediate and long-range needs, and the advantages and disadvantages of each form. Table 3.1 compares the most important differences among the three major ownership forms.

table 3.1 Comparative Summary: Three Forms of Business Ownership

Business Form	Liability	Continuity	Management	Sources of Investment
Proprietorship	Personal, unlimited	Ends with death or decision of owner	Personal, unrestricted	Personal
General Partnership	Personal, unlimited	Ends with death or decision of any partner	Unrestricted or depends on partnership agreement	Personal by partner(s)
Corporation	Capital invested	As stated in charter, perpetual or for specified period of years	Under control of board of directors, which is selected by stockholders	Purchase of stock

Sole Proprietorships

Sole Proprietorship *business owned and usually operated by one person who is responsible for all of its debts*

The **sole proprietorship** is owned and usually operated by one person. About 72 percent of all U.S. businesses are sole proprietorships; however, they account for only about 4 percent of total business revenues. Though usually small, they may be as large as stand-alone steel mills, small factories, or department stores.

Advantages of Sole Proprietorships Freedom may be the most important benefit of sole proprietorships. Because they own their businesses, sole proprietors answer to no one but themselves. Sole proprietorships are also easy to form. Sometimes, you can go into business simply by putting a sign on the door. The simplicity of legal setup procedures makes this form appealing to self-starters and independent spirits, as do low start-up costs.

Another attractive feature is the tax benefits extended to businesses that are likely to suffer losses in their early stages. Tax laws permit owners to treat sales revenues and operating expenses as part of their personal finances, paying taxes based on their personal tax rate. They can cut taxes by deducting business losses from income earned from personal sources other than the business.

Unlimited Liability *legal principle holding owners responsible for paying off all debts of a business*

Disadvantages of Sole Proprietorships A major drawback is **unlimited liability**; a sole proprietor is personally liable for all debts incurred by the business. If the company fails to generate enough cash, bills must be paid out of the owner's pocket. Another disadvantage is lack of continuity; a sole proprietorship legally dissolves when the owner dies. Although the business can be reorganized by a successor, executors or heirs must otherwise sell its assets.

Finally, a sole proprietorship depends on the resources of one person whose managerial and financial limitations may constrain the business. Sole proprietors often find it hard to borrow money to start their business or to expand it. Many bankers fear that they won't be able to recover loans if owners become disabled or insolvent.

Partnerships

General Partnership *business with two or more owners who share in both the operation of the firm and the financial responsibility for its debts*

The most common type of partnership, the **general partnership**, is similar to a sole proprietorship but is owned by more than one person. Partners may invest equal or unequal sums of money. In most cases, partners share the profits equally or in proportion to their investment. In certain cases, though, the distribution of profits may be based on other things. A locally prominent athlete, for instance, may lend their name to the partnership and earn profits without actually investing funds. And sometimes one partner invests all or most of the funds needed for the business but plays no role in its management. This person is usually called a *silent partner*. Another partner might invest little or nothing but provide all the labor. In this case, the financial investor likely owns all or most of the entire business, and the labor partner owns less. But over time and as specified in a contract, the labor partner gradually gains a growing ownership stake in the business (usually called *sweat equity*).

Advantages of Partnerships The most striking advantage of general partnerships is the ability to grow by adding new talent and money. Because banks prefer to make loans to enterprises that are not dependent on single individuals, partnerships find it easier to borrow money when compared to sole proprietorships. They can also invite new partners to join by investing money.

Like a sole proprietorship, a partnership can be organized by meeting only a few legal requirements. Even so, all partnerships must begin with an agreement of some kind. In all but two states, the Revised Uniform Limited Partnership Act requires the filing of specific information about the business and its partners. Partners may also agree to bind themselves in ways not specified by law. In any case, an agreement should answer questions such as the following:

- Who invested what sums?
- Who will receive what share of the profits?
- Who does what, and who reports to whom?
- How may the partnership be dissolved? In the event of dissolution, how will assets be distributed?
- How will surviving partners be protected from claims made by a deceased partner's heirs?

The partnership agreement is strictly a private document. No laws require partners to file agreements with any government agency. Nor are partnerships regarded as legal entities. In the eyes of the law, a partnership is just two or more people working together. Because partnerships have no independent legal standing, the Internal Revenue Service (IRS) taxes partners as individuals.

Disadvantages of Partnerships For general partnerships as for sole proprietorships, unlimited liability is the greatest drawback. Each partner may be liable for all debts incurred by the partnership. If any partner incurs a business debt, all partners may be liable, even if some of them did not know about or agree to the new debt.

Partnerships also share with sole proprietorships the potential lack of continuity. When one partner dies or leaves, the original partnership dissolves, even if one or more of the other partners want it to continue. But dissolution need not mean a loss of sales revenues. Survivors may form a new partnership to retain the old firm's business.

A related disadvantage is difficulty in transferring ownership. No partner may sell out without the consent of the others. A partner who wants to retire or to transfer interest to a son or daughter must have the other partners' consent.

Alternatives to General Partnerships Because of these disadvantages, general partnerships are among the least popular forms of business. Roughly 3.8 million U.S. partnerships generate only about 15 percent of total sales revenues.[28] To resolve some of the problems inherent in general partnerships, especially unlimited liability, some partners have tried alternative agreements. The **limited partnership** allows for **limited partners** who invest money but are liable for debts only to the extent of their investments. They cannot, however, take active roles in business operations. A limited partnership must have at least one **general (or active) partner**, mostly for liability purposes. This is usually the person who runs the business and is responsible for its survival and growth.

Under a **master limited partnership**, an organization sells shares (partnership interests) to investors on public markets such as the New York Stock Exchange. Investors are paid back from profits. The master partner retains at least 50 percent ownership and runs the business, and minority partners have no management voice. (The master partner differs from a general partner, who has no such ownership restriction.) The master partner must regularly provide minority partners with detailed operating and financial reports.

Limited Partnership *type of partnership consisting of limited partners and a general (or managing) partner*

Limited Partner *partner who does not share in a firm's management and is liable for its debts only to the limits of said partner's investment*

General (or **Active**) **Partner** *partner who actively manages a firm and who has unlimited liability for its debts*

Master Limited Partnership *form of ownership that sells shares to investors who receive profits and that pays taxes on income from profits*

Cooperatives

Sometimes, groups of sole proprietorships or partnerships agree to work together for their common benefit by forming cooperatives. **Cooperatives** combine the freedom of sole proprietorships with the financial power of corporations. They give members greater production power, greater marketing power, or both. However, they are limited to serving the specific needs of their members. Although cooperatives make up only a minor segment of the U.S. economy, their role is still important in agriculture. Ocean Spray, the Florida Citrus Growers, Riceland, and Cabot Cheese are among the best-known cooperatives.

Cooperatives *form of ownership in which a group of sole proprietorships or partnerships agree to work together for common benefits*

Learning Objective 3-6

Describe corporations, discuss their advantages and disadvantages, and identify different kinds of corporations; explain the basic issues involved in managing a corporation and discuss special issues related to corporate ownership.

Corporations

There are about 6 million corporations in the United States. As you can see from Figure 3.5, they account for about 17 percent of all U.S. businesses but generate about 81 percent of all sales revenues.[29] Almost all large businesses use this form, and corporations dominate global business. As we will see, corporations need not be large; many small businesses also elect to operate as corporations.

According to recent data, Walmart, one of the world's largest corporations, posted annual revenue of over $573 billion, with total profits of almost $14 billion. Even "smaller" large corporations post huge sales figures. The New York Times Company, though 500th in size among U.S. corporations, posted a profit of $219 million on revenues of $3 billion. Given the size and influence of this form of ownership, we devote a great deal of attention to various aspects of corporations.

The Corporate Entity

When you think of corporations, you probably think of giant operations such as Walmart, Google, or Apple. The very word *corporation* inspires images of size and power. In reality, however, your corner newsstand has as much right to incorporate as a giant automaker. Moreover, the newsstand and Apple would share the characteristics of all **corporations**: legal status as separate entities, property rights and obligations, and indefinite life spans.

Corporation *business that is legally considered an entity separate from its owners and is liable for its own debts; owners' liability extends to the limits of their investments*

In 1819, the U.S. Supreme Court defined a corporation as "an artificial being, invisible, intangible, and existing only in contemplation of the law." The court defined the corporation as a legal person. Corporations may, therefore, perform the following activities:

- Sue and be sued
- Buy, hold, and sell property
- Make and sell products
- Commit crimes and be tried and punished for them

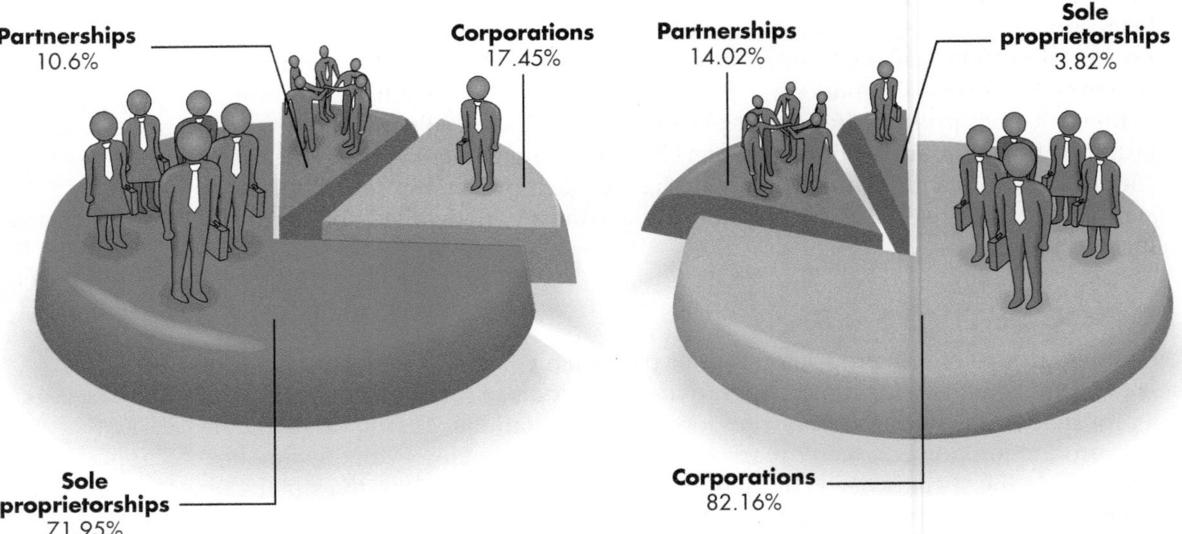

FIGURE 3.5 Proportions of U.S. Firms in Terms of Organization Type and Sales Revenue
Source: U.S. Census Bureau. www.census.gov/

Advantages of Incorporation The biggest advantage of corporations is **limited liability**; investor liability is limited to personal investment (through stock ownership, covered later) in the corporation. In the event of failure, the courts may seize and sell a corporation's assets but cannot touch the investors' personal possessions. If, for example, you invest $1,000 in stock in a corporation that ends up failing, you may lose your $1,000, but no more. In other words, your liability is limited to the $1,000 you invested.

Limited Liability *legal principle holding investors liable for a firm's debts only to the limits of their personal investments in it*

Another advantage is continuity. Because it has a legal life independent of founders and owners, a corporation can, at least in theory, continue forever. For example, the distiller Jim Beam was founded in 1795. Shares of stock may be sold or passed on to heirs, and most corporations also benefit from the continuity provided by professional management. Finally, corporations have advantages in raising money. By selling stock, they expand the number of investors and the amount of available funds. Continuity and legal status tend to make lenders more willing to grant loans.

Disadvantages of Incorporation Although a chief attraction is ease of transferring ownership, this same feature can create complications. For example, using a legal process called a **tender offer**, an offer to buy shares made by a prospective buyer directly to a corporation's shareholders, a corporation can be taken over against the will of its managers. Another disadvantage is start-up cost. Corporations are heavily regulated, and incorporation entails meeting the complex legal requirements of the state in which the firm is chartered.

Tender Offer *offer to buy shares made by a prospective buyer directly to a target corporation's shareholders, who then make individual decisions about whether to sell*

The biggest disadvantage of incorporation, however, is **double taxation**. In addition to income taxes on company profits, stockholders also pay taxes on income returned by their investments in the corporation. Thus, the profits earned by corporations are taxed twice—once at the corporate level and then again at the ownership level. Because profits are treated as owners' personal income, sole proprietorships and partnerships are taxed only once.

Double Taxation *situation in which taxes may be payable both by a corporation on its profits and by shareholders on dividend incomes*

The advantages and disadvantages of corporate ownership have inspired laws establishing different kinds of corporations. Most are intended to help businesses take advantage of the benefits of the corporate model without assuming all the disadvantages. We discuss these corporate forms next.

Types of Corporations

We can classify corporations as either *public* or *private*. But within these broad categories, we can identify several specific types of corporations, some of which are summarized in Table 3.2.

- The most common form of U.S. corporation is the **closely held (or private) corporation**. Stock is held by only a few people and is not available for sale to the public. The controlling group of stockholders may be a family, a management group, or even the firm's employees. Most smaller corporations fit this profile.

Closely Held (or Private) Corporation *corporation whose stock is held by only a few people and is not available for sale to the general public*

- When shares are publicly issued, the firm becomes a **publicly held (or public) corporation**. Stock is widely held and available for sale to the public. Many large businesses are of this type.

Publicly Held (or Public) Corporation *corporation whose stock is widely held and available for sale to the general public*

- The **S corporation** (more fully called the *Subchapter S corporation*) is a hybrid of a closely held corporation and a partnership. It is organized and operates like a corporation, but it is treated like a partnership for tax purposes. To qualify, firms must meet stringent legal conditions. For instance, stockholders must be individual U.S. citizens.

S Corporation *hybrid of a closely held corporation and a partnership, organized and operated like a corporation but treated as a partnership for tax purposes*

- Another hybrid is the **limited liability corporation (LLC)**. Owners are taxed like partners, each paying personal taxes only. However, they also enjoy the benefits of limited liability accorded to publicly held corporations. LLCs have grown in popularity in recent years, partially because of IRS rulings that allow corporations, partnerships, and international investors to be partial owners.

Limited Liability Corporation (LLC) *hybrid of a publicly held corporation and a partnership in which owners are taxed as partners but enjoy the benefits of limited liability*

table 3.2 Types of Corporations

Type	Distinguishing Features	Examples
Closely Held	Stock held by only a few people Subject to corporate taxation	Hobby Lobby MasterCard PrimeStar
Publicly Held	Stock widely held among many investors Subject to corporate taxation	Apple Starbucks Texas Instruments
Subchapter S	Organized much like a closely held corporation Subject to additional regulation Subject to partnership taxation	Minglewood Associates EnTech Pest Systems Frontier Bank
Limited Liability	Organized much like a publicly held corporation Subject to additional regulation Subject to partnership taxation	Nike Global Ground Support Ritz-Carlton
Professional	Subject to partnership taxation Limited business liability Unlimited professional liability	Norman Hui, DDS & Associates B & H Engineering Anderson, McCoy & Orta
Multinational	Spans national boundaries Subject to regulation in multiple countries	Toyota Nestlé General Electric

Professional Corporation *form of ownership allowing professionals to take advantage of corporate benefits while granting them limited business liability and unlimited professional liability*

Multinational (or Transnational) Corporation *form of corporation spanning national boundaries*

- **Professional corporations** are most likely composed of doctors, lawyers, accountants, or other professionals. Although the corporate structure means protection from unlimited financial liability, members are not immune from unlimited liability. Professional negligence by a member can entail personal liability on an individual's part.
- As the term implies, the **multinational (or transnational) corporation** spans national boundaries. Stock may be traded on the exchanges of several countries, and managers are likely to be of different nationalities.

Managing a Corporation

Corporate Governance *roles of shareholders, directors, and other managers in corporate decision making and accountability*

Creating any type of corporation can be complicated because of the various legal conditions that must be met. In addition, once the corporate entity comes into existence, it must be managed by people who understand the principles of **corporate governance**, the roles of shareholders, directors, and other managers in corporate decision making and accountability. In this section, we discuss the principles of *stock ownership* and *stockholders' rights* and describe the role of *boards of directors*. We then examine some special issues related to corporate ownership.

Stockholder (or Shareholder) *owner of shares of stock in a corporation*

Corporate governance is established by the firm's bylaws and usually involves three distinct bodies. **Stockholders (or shareholders)** are the owners of a corporation, investors who buy ownership shares in the form of stock. The *board of directors* is a group elected by stockholders to oversee corporate management. Corporate *officers* are top managers hired by the board to run the corporation on a day-to-day basis.

Stock Ownership and Stockholders' Rights Corporations sell shares, called *stock*, to investors who then become stockholders, or shareholders. Profits are distributed among stockholders in the form of *dividends*, and corporate managers serve at stockholders' discretion. In a closely held corporation, only a few people own stock. Shares of publicly held corporations are widely held.

Board of Directors *governing body of a corporation that reports to its shareholders and delegates power to run its day-to-day operations while remaining responsible for sustaining its assets*

Boards of Directors The governing body of a corporation is its **board of directors.** Boards communicate with stockholders and other stakeholders through such channels as an annual report, a summary of a firm's financial health. They also

managing in turbulent times

The Changing Winds of Fortune

In 2001, restaurateur Danny Meyer opened a hot dog cart in New York City's Madison Square Park as part of a citywide effort to rehabilitate the area. Three years later, the city started taking bids for a more permanent kiosk-style facility. Meyer submitted an idea and, based on his success with his first little venture, got the chance to create his version of a roadside burger stand, right in the heart of Manhattan.

Success for Shake Shack didn't come overnight, but Meyer's dedication and hard work eventually paid off. As the customer base grew, he realized he'd hit upon something, and he and his team started opening new locations, one by one, with a lot of care and deliberation as they created a business model they could duplicate. Once he had the system solidified, Meyer went to venture capitalists for expansion funds. Three initial investors took an equity interest in the company in exchange for cash and the possibility that the company would go public in the future, giving them a market for their stock holdings and the possibility of a large return on investment.

By 2015, when Meyer took the company public, Shake Shack was operating 13 locations in four countries. By offering 5 million new shares of stock for sale at a price of $21 per share, the company raised $105 million in just a few days. By May 2016, Shake Shack stock had almost reached $100 a share, making Meyer's 21 percent ownership interest worth almost $1 billion. However, the stock market can be fickle, and the price of shares dropped quickly back to $40 and stayed there for several years until recovering in 2018 and 2019 to its

MrWinn/Shutterstock

previous high as the company's expansion efforts and branding finally began to pay off. Unfortunately, in the latter months of 2019, the company announced that its exclusive delivery agreement with Grubhub might affect earnings, and stockholders sold off shares, dropping the price almost overnight from $100 to $60. Then, in March 2020, as the market plunged overall due to the global economic effects of the COVID-19 pandemic, the stock dropped again. Meyer's careful planning and strategic thinking kept the chain afloat, though, and by April 2023, Shake Shack had established over 400 locations in cities from Seattle to London to Istanbul, adapting along the way with menu items specific to local cultures, such as a cherry blossom shake in Japan, a shake made with the tropical plant pandan in Singapore, and a red bean shake in South Korea.[30]

set policy on dividends, major spending, and executive compensation. They are legally responsible and accountable for corporate actions and are increasingly being held personally liable for them.

Officers Although board members oversee operations, most do not participate in day-to-day management. Rather, they hire a team of managers to run the firm. This team, called **officers**, is usually headed by the firm's **chief executive officer (CEO)**, who is responsible for overall performance. Other officers typically include a *president*, who is responsible for internal management, and *vice presidents*, who oversee various functional areas such as marketing and operations. In some larger companies, top managers both lead the company and serve on the board of directors. In such instances those individuals are called *inside directors*, whereas independent directors who do not hold positions in the firm are called *outside directors*.

Officers *top management team of a corporation*

Chief Executive Officer (CEO) *the top manager of an organization*

Special Issues in Corporate Ownership

In recent years, several issues have grown in importance in the area of corporate ownership, including *joint ventures and strategic alliances*, *employee stock ownership plans*, and *institutional ownership*. Other important issues in contemporary corporate ownership involve *mergers*, *acquisitions*, *divestitures*, and *spin-offs*.

Strategic Alliance *strategy in which two or more organizations collaborate on a project for mutual gain*

Joint Venture *strategic alliance in which the collaboration involves joint ownership of the new venture*

Joint Ventures and Strategic Alliances In a **strategic alliance**, two or more organizations collaborate on a project for mutual gain. When partners share ownership of what is essentially a new enterprise, it is called a **joint venture**. The number of strategic alliances has increased rapidly in recent years on both domestic and international fronts. For example, General Motors and Ford have a new strategic alliance to jointly develop 10-speed transmissions for automobiles.[31] Ford also has a research-and-development joint venture with Volkswagen that is focused on electric and autonomous vehicles.

Employee Stock Ownership Plan (ESOP) *arrangement in which a corporation holds its own stock in trust for its employees, who gradually receive ownership of the stock and control its voting rights*

Employee Stock Ownership Plans An **employee stock ownership plan (ESOP)** allows employees to own a significant share of the corporation through trusts established on their behalf. Current estimates count about 6,500 ESOPs in the United States. The number of ESOPs has declined a bit in recent years, but they still are an important part of corporate ownership patterns in the United States.

Institutional Investor *large investor, such as a mutual fund or a pension fund, that purchases large blocks of corporate stock*

Institutional Ownership Most individual investors don't own enough stock to exert influence on corporate managers. In recent years, however, more stock has been purchased by **institutional investors**. Because they control enormous resources, these investors—especially mutual and pension funds—can buy huge blocks of stock. The national teachers' retirement system (TIAA CREF) has assets of more than $505 billion, much of it invested in stocks. Institutional investors own almost 80 percent of all stock in the S&P 500 in the United States.

Mergers, Acquisitions, Divestitures, and Spin-Offs Another important set of issues includes mergers, acquisitions, divestitures, and spin-offs. Mergers and acquisitions involve the legal joining of two or more corporations. A divestiture occurs when a corporation sells a business operation to another corporation; with a spin-off, it creates a new operation.

Merger *the union of two corporations to form a new corporation*

Mergers and Acquisitions (M&As) A **merger** occurs when two firms combine to create a new company. For example, Delta and Northwest Airlines merged to form one large company under the Delta name. Their logic was that by becoming a single entity they could operate more efficiently. Seeing the benefits that Delta was earning from its larger size, United Airlines and Continental soon followed suit. Only a few years later, American Airlines and US Airways also merged. In each case, it took about four years to achieve a full integration of the merged companies.

Acquisition *the purchase of one company by another*

In an **acquisition**, one firm buys another outright. Many deals that are loosely called mergers are really acquisitions. Why? Because one of the two firms will usually control the newly combined ownership. In general, when the two firms are roughly the same size, the combination is usually called a merger even if one firm is taking control of the other. When the acquiring firm is substantially larger than the acquired firm, the deal is really an acquisition. So-called M&As are an important form of corporate strategy. They let firms increase product lines, expand operations, go international, and create new enterprises. Halliburton Corporation routinely buys other smaller firms as a way to both increase its revenues and enter new markets.

Divestiture *strategy whereby a firm sells one or more of its business units*

Spin-Off *strategy of setting up one or more corporate units as new, independent corporations*

Divestitures and Spin-Offs Sometimes, a corporation decides to sell a part of its existing business operations or set it up as a new and independent corporation. Several reasons may account for such a step. A firm might decide, for example, that it should focus more specifically on its core businesses, and thus it will sell off unrelated or underperforming businesses. Such a sale is called a **divestiture**. When a firm sells part of itself to raise capital, the strategy is known as a **spin-off**. A spin-off may also mean that a firm deems a business unit more valuable as a separate company.

summary of learning objectives

LEARNING OBJECTIVE 3-1

Define *small business*, discuss its importance to the U.S. economy, and explain popular areas of small business.

A *small business* is independently owned and managed and has relatively little influence in its market. Most U.S. businesses are small businesses and employ fewer than 20 people. Small businesses are vitally important to the economy because of (1) *job creation*, (2) *innovation*, and (3) *contributions to big business*. The most common types of small businesses are firms engaged in (1) *services*, (2) *retailing*, and (3) *construction*. Services make up the largest sector, in part because most service businesses require relatively little capital to start. In contrast, relatively fewer small businesses manufacture products because the start-up costs are often high.

LEARNING OBJECTIVE 3-2

Explain entrepreneurship and describe some key characteristics of entrepreneurial personalities and activities.

Entrepreneurs are people who assume the risk of business ownership. Some entrepreneurs have a goal of independence and financial security, and others want to launch a new venture that can be grown into a large business. Most successful entrepreneurs are resourceful and concerned for customer relations. They have a strong desire to be their own bosses and can handle ambiguity and surprises. Today's entrepreneur is often an open-minded leader who relies on networks, business plans, and consensus, and is just as likely to be of any gender. Finally, although successful entrepreneurs understand the role of risk, they do not necessarily regard what they do as being risky.

LEARNING OBJECTIVE 3-3

Describe distinctive competence, the business plan, and the start-up decisions made by small businesses and identify sources of financial aid available to such enterprises.

A new business must first understand its potential distinctive competence, such as the ability to identify a niche (or unmet need) in an established market. Another distinctive competence is the ability to serve a new unexploited market. Still another is the ability to move quickly to take advantage of new opportunities, often called "first-mover advantage."

After identifying a potential distinctive competence, the next step in entrepreneurship is developing a business plan. A *business plan* summarizes business strategy for the new venture and shows how it will be implemented. The key elements of a business plan are setting goals and objectives, sales forecasting, and financial planning. Business plans are increasingly important because creditors and investors demand them as tools for deciding whether to finance or invest.

Entrepreneurs must also decide whether to buy an existing business, operate a franchise, or start from scratch. Entrepreneurs who choose to buy an existing business have better chances for success compared to those who start from scratch because of existing relationships with vendors and customers. Franchises provide considerable support in setup and operation, but franchise costs can be high and severely cut into profits. Starting a business from scratch can be the riskiest yet most rewarding way to start a new business.

To start a new business, it is essential to have money to finance the operation. Common funding sources include personal funds, family and friends, savings, lenders, investors, and governmental agencies. Lending institutions are more likely to finance an existing business than a new business because the risks are better understood. *Venture capital companies* are groups of small investors seeking to make profits on companies with rapid growth potential. Most of these firms do not lend money but rather invest it, supplying capital in return for partial ownership. New businesses may also seek funding from small business investment companies (SBICs) as well as through Small Business Administration (SBA) programs.

LEARNING OBJECTIVE 3-4

Discuss the trends in small business start-ups and identify the main reasons for success and failure among small businesses.

Five trends have helped facilitate the growth in new businesses started in the United States every year. These trends are: (1) *the emergence of e-commerce*, (2) *crossovers from big business*, (3) *increased opportunities for minorities and women*, (4) *new opportunities in global enterprise*, and (5) *improved rates of survival among small businesses*.

However, more than half of all small businesses fail. Four basic factors contribute to most small business failure: (1) *managerial incompetence or inexperience*, (2) *neglect*, (3) *weak control systems*, and (4) *insufficient capital*. Likewise, four basic factors explain most small business success: (1) *hard work, drive, and dedication*; (2) *market demand for the products or services being provided*; (3) *managerial competence*; and (4) *luck*.

LEARNING OBJECTIVE 3-5

Explain sole proprietorships, partnerships, and cooperatives and discuss the advantages and disadvantages of each.

A *sole proprietorship* is a business owned by one person. The most significant advantage to organizing as a sole proprietorship is the freedom to make decisions. In addition, it is relatively easy to form and operate a sole proprietorship. There are tax benefits for new businesses likely to suffer losses in early stages because these losses can offset income from another business or job on the tax return of a sole proprietor. A major drawback is *unlimited liability*, which is the legal concept that makes the owners of a sole proprietorship personally responsible for all its debts. Another disadvantage is that a sole proprietorship lacks continuity; when the owner dies or leaves the business, it does not continue to exist. Finally, a sole proprietorship depends on the resources of a single individual.

A *general partnership* is a sole proprietorship multiplied by the number of partner owners. The biggest advantage is its ability to grow by adding new talent and money. Partners report their share of the partnership's income, and it is taxed on their individual tax return. Like a sole proprietorship, *unlimited liability* is a drawback. Partnerships may lack continuity, and transferring ownership may be hard. No partner may sell out without the consent of the others. There are also special forms of partnerships, most notably limited partnerships and master limited partnerships.

Cooperatives combine the freedom of sole proprietorships with the financial power of corporations. A cooperative is a group of sole proprietorships or partnerships working together to gain greater production or marketing power.

LEARNING OBJECTIVE 3-6

Describe corporations, discuss their advantages and disadvantages, and identify different kinds of corporations; explain the basic issues involved in managing a corporation and discuss special issues related to corporate ownership.

All *corporations* share certain characteristics: legal status as separate entities, property rights and obligations, and indefinite life spans. They may sue and be sued; buy, hold, and sell property; make and sell products; and commit crimes and be tried and punished for them. The biggest advantage of incorporation is *limited liability*: Investor liability is limited to one's personal investments in the corporation. Another advantage is continuity; a corporation can last indefinitely and does not end with the death or withdrawal of an owner. Finally, corporations have advantages in raising money. By selling stock, they expand the number of investors and the amount of available funds. Continuity and the ability to sell stock tend to make lenders more willing to grant loans.

One disadvantage is that a corporation can be taken over against the will of its managers. Another disadvantage is start-up cost. Corporations are heavily regulated and must meet complex legal requirements in the states in which they're chartered. The greatest potential drawback to incorporation is *double taxation* of profits. Profits are taxed first at the level of the corporation and then taxed as dividends when distributed to the stockholders. Corporations may be either private or public. A private, or closely held, corporation has only a small number of owners, and shares of stock are not available to the general public. Public corporations are able to sell their stock on the stock exchanges and have the ability to raise large amounts of capital. Special forms of ownership, such as S corporations, LLCs, and professional corporations, combine the limited liability of a corporation with the tax treatment of partnerships.

Corporations sell shares, called *stock*, to investors who then become *stockholders* (or shareholders) and the real owners. Profits are distributed among stockholders in the form of *dividends*, and managers serve at their discretion. The governing body of a corporation is its *board of directors*. Most board members do not participate in day-to-day management but rather hire a team of managers. This team, called *officers*, is usually headed by a *chief executive officer (CEO)* who is responsible for overall performance.

Several issues have grown in importance in the area of corporate ownership. In a *strategic alliance*, two or more organizations collaborate on a project for mutual gain. When partners share ownership of a new enterprise, the arrangement is called a *joint venture*. An *employee stock ownership plan (ESOP)* allows employees to own a significant share of the corporation through trusts established on their behalf. More stock is now being purchased by *institutional investors*. A *merger* occurs when two firms combine to create a new company, and in an *acquisition*, one firm buys another outright. A *divestiture* occurs when a corporation sells a part of its existing business operations or sets it up as a new and independent corporation. When a firm sells part of itself to raise capital, the strategy is known as a *spin-off*.

key terms

acquisition **(p. 96)**
board of directors **(p. 94)**
business plan **(p. 82)**
chief executive officer (CEO) **(p. 95)**
closely held (or private) corporation **(p. 93)**
cooperatives **(p. 91)**
corporate governance **(p. 94)**
corporation **(p. 92)**
divestiture **(p. 96)**
double taxation **(p. 93)**
employee stock ownership plan (ESOP) **(p. 96)**
entrepreneur **(p. 79)**
entrepreneurship **(p. 79)**
established market **(p. 81)**
first-mover advantage **(p. 81)**
franchise **(p. 83)**
general (or active) partner **(p. 91)**
general partnership **(p. 90)**
institutional investor **(p. 96)**
joint venture **(p. 96)**
limited liability **(p. 93)**
limited liability corporation (LLC) **(p. 93)**
limited partner **(p. 91)**
limited partnership **(p. 91)**
master limited partnership **(p. 91)**
merger **(p. 96)**
multinational (or transnational) corporation **(p. 94)**
niche **(p. 81)**
officers **(p. 95)**
professional corporation **(p. 94)**
publicly held (or public) corporation **(p. 93)**
S corporation **(p. 93)**
small business **(p. 75)**
Small Business Administration (SBA) **(p. 75)**
Small Business Development Center (SBDC) **(p. 85)**
small business investment company (SBIC) **(p. 84)**
sole proprietorship **(p. 90)**
spin-off **(p. 96)**
stockholder (or shareholder) **(p. 94)**
strategic alliance **(p. 96)**
tender offer **(p. 93)**
unlimited liability **(p. 90)**
venture capital company **(p. 84)**

questions & exercises

QUESTIONS FOR REVIEW

3-1. Why are small businesses important to the U.S. economy?

3-2. Which industries are easiest for a small business to enter? Which are hardest? Why?

3-3. What are the primary reasons for new business failure and success?

3-4. What are the basic forms of business ownership? What are the key advantages and disadvantages of each?

QUESTIONS FOR ANALYSIS

3-5. After considering the characteristics of entrepreneurs, do you think that you would be a good candidate to start your own business? Why or why not?

3-6. Choose a company in a highly competitive industry. How does that company stay competitive? Do you think it is gaining market share or losing, and why?

3-7. Identify three sources of funding for new businesses. What are the advantages and disadvantages of each?

3-8. Why might a closely held corporation choose to remain private? Why might it choose to be publicly traded?

APPLICATION EXERCISES

3-9. Identify a publicly traded company. Research its original form of business and detail its transition from small, privately held company to its initial public offering.

3-10. Although more than half of all small businesses don't survive five years, franchises have a much better track record. However, it can be difficult to buy a franchise. Research a popular food industry franchise, such as Panera Bread, Sonic, Five Guys, or Subway, and detail the requirements for net worth and liquid cash for the franchisee as well as up-front and annual fees.

building a business: continuing team exercise

ASSIGNMENT

Meet with your team members and discuss your new business venture within the context of this chapter. Develop specific responses to the following:

3-11. Have each member identify individual entrepreneurial strengths and weaknesses. Where are the gaps?

3-12. For the specific business you are starting (in this exercise), does it make more sense to start from scratch, to buy an existing business, or to buy a franchise? Why?

3-13. How will you most likely finance your new venture?

3-14. What factors will most likely contribute to your success? What factors might cause your business to fail? Is there a way to minimize or eliminate these risk factors?

3-15. What form of ownership will your group use? What are the advantages and disadvantages of this approach?

team exercise

A TASTY IDEA

Background Information

Suppose that you and three friends from college would like to open a new restaurant. Collectively, you have almost 20 years of experience in the restaurant industry, and with lots of new houses in the area, you think that there's an opportunity to make a lot of money if you can offer interesting food at good prices. You've identified an existing vacant restaurant for rent, but you realize that even though the space is ready to go, it's still going to take a significant amount of funding to get this business off the ground. As recent college graduates, you don't have a lot of money, so you're looking for the best source of funding. Realistically, you realize that you're going to need at least $100,000 in working capital to sustain operations until your business starts to return a profit.

Team Activity

STEP 1

Individually or in a group of two or three students, brainstorm a list of options for financing.

STEP 2

For each of the funding options, develop a list of pros and cons. Be sure to consider all the implications of each form of financing, including interest rates, repayment options, and eligibility requirements.

FOLLOW-UP QUESTIONS

3-16. Before getting financing, what will be expected of you and your business partners?

3-17. Which source of financing would be best for you and your partners? Why?

3-18. What form of business ownership would be most appropriate for your new restaurant, and why?

exercising your ethics

FLAT ROOF FUNDING FIASCO

The Situation

You have recently come across a business idea for a new form of flat roofing that could revolutionize the construction industry by making flat roofs more cost-effective, durable, energy efficient. You spent five months gathering information and building a business plan for a manufacturing plant in Portland, Oregon. There is no way to start small because of necessary economies of scale; the main customers will be commercial construction jobs such as malls, warehouses, and big box stores. In order to create the product, you require an initial investment of $5 million, but your projected profits after five years are projected to be robust, giving investors an extraordinary rate of return, but you need to get started right away before a competitor enters the market.

The Dilemma

You took your business plan to a group of investors, and they were suitably impressed, so much so that they took your business plan, created and funded a corporation, and hired a management team to execute the plan, leaving you completely out of the picture. The business turned out to be a huge success but you got nothing for all your hard work.

QUESTIONS TO ADDRESS

3-19. What do you think your rights are to a business idea?

3-20. What could you have done to protect your business idea?

3-21. Is it fair and ethical for a group of investors to adopt a business plan and execute it without compensating the person who came up with the idea? Support your opinion with a reasoned argument.

cases

IN-N-OUT IS NO SMALL BURGER

Continued from page 75

At the beginning of this chapter, you read about the inception and growth of In-N-Out Burger. Using the information presented in this chapter, you should now be able to answer the following questions.

3-22. What are some of the primary reasons for In-N-Out's success?

3-23. Why do you think the company is so firmly opposed to selling or going public? What do you think are the advantages and disadvantages of private versus public ownership?

3-24. Can you think of other examples of small businesses with a cult-like following? How have they gained popularity? How has increased visibility on social media impacted the ability of businesses to get new customers?

3-25. Consider In-N-Out's journey from a small business to the company it is today. What advice would you give to a small business startup that aspires to that level of success?

ICE CREAM HEADACHE

If you have ever visited a Cold Stone Creamery, you are familiar with the seemingly endless list of ice creams and toppings as well as prepared cakes and other confections. You may not be aware, however, that Cold Stone is a franchise sold by Kahala Brands (a subsidiary of MTY Foods), whose other franchisee opportunities include Baja Fresh, Taco Time, and Blimpie Restaurants.[32]

In case you are considering opening your own Cold Stone, you might be interested in the conditions of ownership. Those who wish to purchase a Cold Stone franchise must show that they are financially sound, with at least $125,000 of cash available and a $250,000 net worth. The total investment estimate for a Cold Stone Creamery franchise ranges from $53,200 to $602,775. Once in operation, franchisees will pay a royalty fee of 6 percent of gross sales and an advertising fee of 3 percent of gross sales.[33]

Kahala Brands provides support in site selection, lease terms, and equipment selection. It provides 11 days of training at the company's headquarters and 3 additional days of training at the franchisee's location. Once the business is up and running, it provides continued support through newsletters and annual meetings, cooperative advertising arrangements, and a toll-free hotline.

QUESTIONS FOR DISCUSSION

3-26. What would be the advantages of buying a Cold Stone Creamery franchise as opposed to starting an ice cream shop from scratch?

3-27. What are the disadvantages of buying a Cold Stone Creamery franchise?

3-28. While franchise owners must have at least $125,000 of cash available, start-up costs can be more than four times this amount. What are the most likely sources of funding for a franchise?

3-29. In addition to the company website or marketing materials, gather the information you think you would need in deciding whether to invest in a Cold Stone Creamery franchise. What kind of information did you gather, and what were your sources?

3-30. On the basis of your research, do you think that you would be interested in owning a Cold Stone Creamery franchise? Why or why not?

endnotes

[1] Bernhard Schroeder, "According to a Recent Study, About 54% of Gen Z Indicated They Want to Start Their Own Company," *Forbes*, February 18, 2020, https://www.forbes.com/sites/bernhardschroeder/2020/02/18/a-majority-of-gen-z-aspires-to-be-entrepreneurs-and-perhaps-delay-or-skip-college-why-that-might-be-a-good-idea/?sh=655296175a45; "Oh, to Be Young, and an Entrepreneur," *USA Today*, February 8, 2013, 8B; "Two-Thirds of Teens Said They Were 'Likely' to Consider Starting a Business," Junior Achievement USA, accessed August 28, 2023, https://jausa.ja.org/news/press-releases/survey-the-new-normal-hasn-t-dampened-teens-interest-in-becoming-entrepreneurs.

[2] Chloe Sorvino, "Exclusive: In-N-Out Billionaire Lynsi Snyder Opens Up About Her Troubled Past and the Burger Chain's Future," *Forbes*, February 21, 2019, https://www.forbes.com/sites/chloesorvino/2018/10/10/exclusive-in-n-out-billionaire-lynsi-snyder-opens-up-about-her-troubled-past-and-the-burger-chains-future/?sh=4ec4f2404b9c.

[3] Daniel Wilmoth, "Small Business Job Creation Fact Sheet," Small Business Association, April 2022, https://advocacy.sba.gov/wp-content/uploads/2022/04/Small-Business-Job-Creation-Fact-Sheet-Apr2022.pdf.

[4] Wilmoth, "Small Business Job Creation Fact Sheet."

[5] See U.S. Small Business Administration, "About SBA," accessed March 1, 2020, http://www.sba.gov/aboutsba.

[6] Mitchell Barnes, Lauren Bauer, and Wendy Edelberg, "Nine Facts About the Service Sector in the United States," Brookings, September 29, 2022, https://www.brookings.edu/research/nine-facts-about-the-service-sector-in-the-united-states/.

[7] Plamen Tsekov, "Council Post: How to Properly Navigate the Gig Economy and the Large Pool of It Experts," *Forbes*, March 21, 2023, https://www.forbes.com/sites/forbestechcouncil/2023/03/20/how-to-properly-navigate-the-gig-economy-and-the-large-pool-of-it-experts/?sh=7d652d336794.

[8] John Byrne, "The 12 Greatest Entrepreneurs of Our Time," *Fortune*, April 9, 2012, 68–86.

[9] "A New Generation Rewrites the Rules," *Wall Street Journal*, May 22, 2002, R4. See also Mark Henricks, "Up to the Challenge," *Entrepreneur*, February 2006, 64–67.

[10] Noah Kagan, "3 Billionaire Entrepreneurs Who Started in Their 50s," OkDork, May 6, 2022, https://okdork.com/successful-entrepreneurs-who-started-in-their-50s/.

[11] "A Startup's New Prescription for Eyewear," *Businessweek*, July 4–10, 2011, 49–51.

[12] 10 Best Design, "10 Best App Developers," March 6, 2023, https://www.10bestdesign.com/firms/app/.

[13] See Thomas Zimmerer and Norman Scarborough, *Essentials of Entrepreneurship and Small Business Management*, 6th ed. (Upper Saddle River, NJ: Prentice Hall, 2018).

[14] "'I Can't Keep Doing This:' Small Business Owners Are Giving Up," *New York Times*, July 13, 2020; Alexander Burke, "The Impact of COVID-19 on Small Business Outcomes and Expectations," *Proceedings of the National Academy of Sciences*, July 9, 2020; "Living Day to Day: Small Business Owners Fight for Survival After COVID-19 Restriction," Euronews, July 21, 2020.

[15] James Combs, David Ketchen, Christopher Shook, and Jeremy Short, "Antecedents and Consequences of Franchising: Past Accomplishments and Future Challenges," *Journal of Management* (January 2011): 99–126.

[16] Statista Research Department, "Franchising in the U.S.—Statistics & Facts," Statista, November 18, 2022, https://www.statista.com/topics/5048/franchising-zin-the-us/#topicOverview.

[17] "Case Looks for Passion in Start-Ups," *USA Today*, March 26, 2013, 3B.

[18] See U.S. Small Business Administration, "Loans," accessed February 28, 2020, https://www.sba.gov/content/7a-loan-amounts-fees-interest-rates.

[19] United States Census Bureau, accessed February 28, 2020, http://www.census.gov/ces/dataproducts/bds/data_firm.html.

[20] "To Fund a Startup, Go to Kuala Lumpur," *Bloomberg Businessweek*, February 25–March 3, 2012.

[21] "Small Businesses Go Alternative for Loans," *USA Today*, November 14, 2012, 1B. See also "Alternative Online Lenders Fill Funding Needs for Small Businesses," *Forbes*, September 23, 2014.

[22] United States Census Bureau, accessed March 1, 2023, http://www.census.gov/ces/dataproducts/bds/data_firm.html.

[23] United States Census Bureau, "2021 Economic Census Surveys of Minority and Women Owned Business Enterprises," accessed, https://www.census.gov/.

[24] Peter Hoy, "Minority and Women Owned Businesses Skyrocket," *Inc.*, May 1, 2006, 20–24.

[25] Zimmerer and Scarborough, *Essentials of Entrepreneurship and Small Business Management*, 20. See also National Association of Women Business Owners, accessed June 15, 2023, https://www.nawbo.org/.

[26] See U.S. Small Business Administration, "Frequently Asked Questions," accessed February 15, 2020, http://app1.sba.gov/faqs/faqIndexAll.cfm?areaid=24. See also U.S. Small Business Administration, "Frequently Asked Questions," accessed February 15, 2020, https://www.sba.gov/sites/default/files/FAQ_March_2014_0.pdf.

[27] Tala, "Tala Raises over $30 Million in New Financing Led by IVP," news release, accessed February 24, 2017, http://tala.co/press releases.

[28] U.S. Small Business Administration, accessed March 3, 2020, http://www.sba.gov.

[29] U.S. Small Business Administration, http://www.sba.gov.

[30] Danielle Wiener-Bronner, "Inside Shake Shack's Unusual Global Strategy | CNN Business," CNN, June 18, 2019, https://www.cnn.com/2019/06/18/business/shake-shack-mexico-city/index.html.

[31] "GM, Ford Team to Develop 10-Speed Transmissions," *USA Today*, April 16, 2013, 2B.

[32] "Brands," Kahala Brands—Restaurant Franchising, accessed April 15, 2023, https://www.kahalamgmt.com/brands/.

[33] "Cold Stone Creamery FAQs," Cold Stone Creamery Franchise, accessed April 15, 2023, https://coldstonecreameryfranchise.com/research/cold-stone-creamery-faqs/.

chapter 4

Understanding the Global Context of Business

oneinchpunch/123RF

learning objectives

After reading this chapter, you should be able to:

4-1 Discuss the rise of international business and describe the major world marketplaces, trade agreements, and alliances.

4-2 Explain how differences in import–export balances, exchange rates, and foreign competition determine the ways in which countries and businesses respond to the international environment.

4-3 Discuss the factors involved in deciding to do business internationally and in selecting the appropriate levels of international involvement and international organizational structure.

4-4 Explain the role and importance of the cultural environment in international business.

4-5 Describe some of the ways in which economic, legal, and political differences among nations affect international business.

what's in it for me?

As we will see in this chapter, global forces—business as well as political—affect each and every one of us on a daily basis. As you begin your business career, regardless of whether you see yourself living abroad, working for a big company, or starting your own business, the global economy will affect you in a variety of ways. Exchange rates for different currencies and global markets for buying and selling are all of major importance to everyone, regardless of their role or perspective. As a result, this chapter will better enable you to (1) understand how global forces affect you as a customer, (2) understand how globalization affects you as an employee, and (3) assess how global opportunities and challenges can affect you as a business owner and an investor. You will also gain insights into how wages and working conditions in different regions are linked to what we buy and the prices we pay.

This chapter explores the global context of business. We begin with an exploration of the major world marketplaces and trade agreements that affect international business. Next, we examine several factors that help determine how countries and businesses respond to international opportunities and challenges. We then direct our attention to some of the decisions managers must make if they intend to compete in international markets. Finally, we conclude with a discussion of some of the social, cultural, economic, legal, and political factors that affect international business.

Carlos E. Santa Maria/Shutterstock

Yoshio Tsunoda/AFLO/Shutterstock

The Magic Kingdom Goes Global

The myth is that Walt Disney arrived in Hollywood with only $40 in his pocket, and although that's hard to validate, it is verifiable that he and his brother had started several businesses that had failed before they found some limited success with Disney Studios making short cartoons. Eventually, they created "Steamboat Willy," the first cartoon featuring the now iconic Mickey Mouse. Not long after, in 1937, Disney Studios was the first U.S. studio to release a full-length animated movie, *Snow White and the Seven Dwarfs*.

The revenue from *Snow White*'s success opened new possibilities for the Disney brothers and their company. Never one to ignore a dream, Walt had an idea to create a theme park that was family friendly, clean, and based on his popular movies. In the early 1950s, he promoted the idea to investors, gathered $17 million, and created Disneyland, opening it to the public in 1955.

Walt died in December 1966, but his legacy lived on, and Walt Disney World opened near Orlando, Florida, in 1971. By that time, Walt Disney Studios was a booming, publicly traded company with a life of its own, and as of December 2022, in addition to the two domestic resorts, the company was operating four Disney destination resorts across the globe, in Shanghai, Paris, Hong Kong, and Tokyo, bringing in billions of dollars a year. In fact, for the quarter that ended December 31, 2022, revenues for that division of the company, Disney Parks, Experiences, and Products, were $8.7 billion and segment operating income was $3.1 billion.[1]

With two highly successful U.S. resorts as a model and a healthy balance sheet, Disney had a good foothold for global expansion. Disney's parks all have themed areas and most have a broad avenue, Main Street U.S.A., leading up to a central fairy-tale castle. However, the Imagineers who created the various parks had to take into account local customs and preferences as they developed themed areas in new countries. For instance, when designing Hong Kong Disneyland, Imagineers consulted with a feng shui expert who advised on placement of the major rides and activities to promote balance and harmony. In Shanghai Disneyland, Main Street U.S.A. was replaced with a large garden featuring Disney versions of Chinese zodiac animals. The design also included larger seating areas at restaurants because a study indicated that Chinese guests linger longer over meals. Disney is also not the only game in town in China. As of March 31, 2021, AECOMM, a multinational infrastructure firm, counted up to 156 theme parks in China with another 80 parks forecast over the next five years.[2]

At Tokyo DisneySea, the Tower of Terror ride was reenvisioned because it was based on *The Twilight Zone* television series, which had never aired in Japan. Instead, Tokyo DisneySea's version is centered on the story of an American socialite, explorer, and hotelier who stole an African artifact, an act that left him and his hotel cursed.

Disney's Imagineers also considered cultural changes at Disneyland Paris. Because a majority of the nonlocal visitors to Disneyland Paris come from Britain, the Imagineers built a major Alice in Wonderland area and, for the French, an area devoted to the Oscar-winning Disney movie *Ratatouille*. In addition, Discovery Land in Paris is informed by the novels of French author Jules Verne and is heavily influenced by his Victorian vision of the future. Geography plays a part in design as well. In California, the Pirates of the Caribbean ride that inspired the blockbuster movie franchise drops into a cavern, but in Paris, the water table was too high to allow underground tunneling, so the entire attraction was built above ground, necessitating that the boats be winched up to the opening.

Although Disney has not announced any plans for new theme parks, it continues to expand globally. In 2022, The Walt Disney Company created a new segment called International Content and Operations to manage the direct-to-consumer business around the world and to expand local and regional content for its streaming services. While some companies struggle to adapt to the challenges of globalization, Disney continues to double down on global expansion.[3] (After studying this chapter, you should be able to respond to the set of discussion questions found at the end of the chapter.)

The Contemporary Global Economy

Learning Objective 4-1

Discuss the rise of international business and describe the major world marketplaces, trade agreements, and alliances.

The total volume of world trade is immense—more than $23.2 trillion in merchandise is traded each year. Foreign investment in the United States exceeds $275 billion, and U.S. investment abroad is more than $400 billion.[4] As more firms engage in international business, the world economy is fast becoming an interdependent system through a process called **globalization**.

Globalization *process by which the world economy is becoming a single interdependent system*

We often take for granted the diversity of products we can buy as a result of international trade. Your television, your shoes, your smartphone, and even your morning coffee or juice are probably **imports**, products made or grown abroad and sold domestically in the United States. At the same time, the success of many U.S. firms depends on **exports**, products made or grown here, such as machinery, electronic equipment, and grains, and shipped for sale abroad.

Import *product made or grown abroad but sold domestically*

Export *product made or grown domestically but shipped and sold abroad*

Firms such as McDonald's, Microsoft, Apple, and Starbucks have found international markets to be a fruitful area for growth. But firms sometime stumble when they try to expand abroad. Both Nordstrom and Target failed in Canada because they underestimated the power of existing Canadian retailers and the loyalty they had built among Canadian shoppers. Forever 21 recently announced it was closing its operations in China. And Walmart failed in its effort to dominate retailing in Germany.[5] Home Depot first opened and then closed dozens of stores in China, for example, because labor costs are so low there that few homeowners are interested in "do-it-yourself" projects. Similarly, Best Buy also closed its stores in China because consumers there tend to buy their electronics goods at lower prices from local or online merchants.[6] When Disney first opened a theme park in Hong Kong, it performed poorly because Disney managers made the park too "American" and bungled the park's initial advertising campaign.

The impact of globalization doesn't stop with firms looking to open locations abroad or having to close locations that fail. Small firms with no international operations (for example, an independent coffee shop) may still buy from international suppliers, and even individual contractors or self-employed individuals can be affected by fluctuations in exchange rates.

Indeed, international trade is becoming increasingly important to most nations and their businesses. Many countries that once followed strict policies to protect domestic business now encourage trade just as aggressively. They are opening borders to foreign businesses, offering incentives for domestic businesses to expand internationally, and making it easier for foreign firms to partner with local firms. Likewise, as more industries and markets become global, so, too, are the firms that compete in them.

Several forces have combined to spark and sustain globalization. For one thing, governments and businesses are more aware of the benefits of globalization

Islemount Images/Alamy Stock Photo

Some globalization protestors, like this man, fear that multinational companies will wipe out small domestic businesses like family farms.

to businesses and shareholders. These benefits include the potential for higher standards of living and improved business profitability. New technologies have made international travel, communication, and commerce faster and cheaper than ever before. Finally, there are competitive pressures: Sometimes a firm must expand into foreign markets simply to keep up with competitors.

Globalization is not without its detractors. Some critics charge that globalization allows businesses to exploit workers in less developed countries and bypass domestic environmental and tax regulations. For example, businesses pay workers in Vietnam and Indonesia lower wages than their counterparts in the United States. Factories in China are not subject to the same environmental protection laws as are firms in Europe. And businesses that headquarter their corporate offices in the Cayman Islands pay lower taxes. Critics also charge that globalization leads to the loss of cultural heritages and often benefits people with wealth more than people with fewer resources. For instance, as the English language becomes increasingly widespread throughout the world, some local languages are simply disappearing. Similarly, local residents in Africa receive relatively few economic benefits when oil or precious minerals are discovered on their land; prosperous investors buy the rights from landowners, who often don't realize the value of these resources. As a result, many international gatherings of global economic leaders are marked by protests and demonstrations.

The Major World Marketplaces

Managers involved with international businesses need a solid understanding of the global economy, including the major world marketplaces. This section examines some fundamental economic distinctions among countries based on wealth and then looks at some of the world's major international marketplaces.

Distinctions Based on Wealth The World Bank, an agency of the United Nations, uses per capita income, average income per person, to make distinctions among countries. Its current classification method consists of four different categories of countries:[7]

1. *High-income countries:* Those with annual per capita income greater than $12,695
2. *Upper-middle-income countries:* Those with annual per capita income between $4,096 and $12,695

3 *Lower-middle-income countries:* Those with annual per capita income between $4,095 and $1,046
4 *Low-income countries* (sometimes called *developing countries*)*:* Those with annual per capita income less than $1,046

Geographic Clusters The world economy generally revolves around three major marketplaces: North America, Europe, and Pacific Asia. In general, these clusters include relatively more of the upper-middle- and high-income nations but relatively fewer low- and lower-middle-income countries.

North America As the world's largest marketplace and most stable economy, the United States dominates the North American market. Canada also plays a major role in the international economy, and the United States and Canada are among each other's largest trading partners.

Mexico has been a major manufacturing center, especially along the U.S. border, where labor and transportation costs are relatively low. This has encouraged many firms from the United States and other countries to build factories. However, Mexico's role as a low-cost manufacturing center is in flux. Just a few years ago, many experts believed that the emergence of China as a low-cost manufacturing center would lead companies to begin to shift their production from Mexico to China.[8] (Drug-related violence, especially along the northern Mexican border, also contributed to this shift.)

Europe Europe is often regarded as two regions—Western and Eastern. Western Europe, dominated by Germany, the United Kingdom, and France, has long been a mature but fragmented marketplace. The transformation of this region via the European Union (discussed later in this chapter) into an integrated economic system has further increased its importance. Digital commerce and technology have also become increasingly important in this region. Online start-ups have surged in southeastern England, the Netherlands, and the Scandinavian countries; Ireland is now one of the world's largest exporters of software; Strasbourg, France, is a major center for biotech start-ups; Barcelona, Spain, has many flourishing software and online companies; and the Frankfurt region of Germany is dotted with software and biotech start-ups.

Eastern Europe has also gained in importance, both as a marketplace and as a producer. Such multinational corporations as Daewoo, Nestlé, General Motors, and ABB Asea Brown Boveri have all set up operations in Poland. Ford, General Motors, Suzuki, and Volkswagen all have new factories in Hungary. In contrast, governmental instability, corruption, and uncertainty have hampered development in parts of Russia, Bulgaria, Albania, Romania, and other countries.

Pacific Asia Pacific Asia is generally agreed to consist of Japan, China, Thailand, Malaysia, Singapore, Indonesia, South Korea, Taiwan, Vietnam, the Philippines, and Australia. Fueled by strong entries in the automobile, electronics, and banking industries, the economies of these countries grew rapidly in the 1970s and 1980s. Since then, they have continued to grow in global importance. However, the COVID-19 pandemic also dealt many of these countries major blows. China was especially hit hard. (Its Wuhan province was apparently the original source of the virus.) Still, large firms in this region such as Toyota, Toshiba, and Nippon Steel (Japan); Samsung and Hyundai (South Korea); and Chinese Petroleum (Taiwan) are major players in the global economy. Vietnam has emerged as a major manufacturing center, and Hong Kong is a major financial center.

China, one of the world's most densely populated countries, has also emerged as an important consumer market and now boasts one of the world's largest economies. Although its per capita income remains low, the sheer number of potential consumers makes it an important market. India, though not part of Pacific Asia, is also rapidly emerging as one of the globe's most important economies. As in North America and Europe, technology promises to play an increasingly important role in the future of this region. In some parts of Asia, however, poorly developed electronic infrastructures, slower adoption of computers and information technology, and a higher percentage of lower-income consumers hamper the emergence of technology firms.

finding a better way

Car Wars: China Versus Mexico

Vario images GmbH & Co.KG/Alamy Stock Photo

In today's competitive global economy, businesses strive for every possible advantage. Many manufacturers, for example, locate their factories in countries that have an ample supply of low-cost skilled labor. During the 1980s and 1990s, the place to be was Mexico. Hundreds of factories were built just across the U.S.–Mexican border, and workers streamed to the region from other parts of Mexico for stable and well-paying jobs. But in the late 1990s, the world started to shift.

Mexican prosperity, fueled in part by its role as a center of manufacturing, led to increases in the cost of living, followed quickly by wage increases so workers could keep up. At about that same time, China began to emerge as an attractive manufacturing alternative. Wages in China were roughly one-third the wages in Mexico, and there was no shortage of workers eager to take steady jobs in factories making products for other countries. China's boom was Mexico's bust as one company after another reduced or eliminated manufacturing there and moved to Asia.

In more recent years, the situation started to tilt back in Mexico's favor. As China's economy flourished, its labor costs crept higher and higher, and when U.S. manufacturers factored in shipping costs, producing auto parts in Mexico once again became more cost effective. Time differences between the United States and China also make phone and video conferencing difficult. In addition, U.S. companies have taken flak for China's business practices. Companies are often heavily subsidized by the government, and low-paid workers are not offered the same benefits and protections as workers in the United States, causing what many deem to be an uneven playing field that takes jobs away from U.S. workers.

Because of these socioeconomic shifts, Mexico made enormous gains in the automobile sector. Companies such as Nissan, Honda, Volkswagen, and Mazda invested billions of dollars in Mexican companies, and by 2022 the country as a whole was producing about 385,000 units a month, rivaling production by China, even as the U.S. auto market was still recovering from a slump resulting from reduced consumer spending and too much inventory. In 2023, the automotive industry made up nearly 20 percent of Mexico's overall manufacturing GDP. With the combined value of vehicles and related parts an estimated $68.7 billion USD, Mexico ranked as the fifth largest auto exporter in the world.[9] So, the battle for competitive advantage continues, and the back-and-forth nature of the industry and its resultant ups and downs will likely continue for the foreseeable future.

Trade Agreements and Alliances

Various legal agreements have sparked international trade and shaped the global business environment. Virtually every nation has formal trade treaties with other nations. A *treaty* is a legal agreement that specifies areas in which nations will cooperate with one another. Among the most significant treaties is the *North American Free Trade Agreement*. The *European Union*, the *Association of Southeast Asian Nations*, and the *World Trade Organization*, all governed by treaties, are also instrumental in promoting international business activity.

North American Free Trade Agreement (NAFTA) *agreement to gradually eliminate tariffs and other trade barriers among the United States, Canada, and Mexico*

North American Free Trade Agreement/United States–Mexico–Canada Agreement

The **North American Free Trade Agreement (NAFTA)**, signed in 1994, removed most tariffs and other trade barriers among the United States, Canada, and Mexico; it also included agreements on environmental issues and labor abuses.

Many experts agreed that NAFTA at least partially achieved its basic purpose—to create a more active and unified North American market. It created several hundred thousand new jobs, although this number was smaller than NAFTA proponents had originally hoped. Critics, however, argued that NAFTA did not do enough to help the United States achieve a better trade balance with its partners.

As a result, President Donald Trump pushed to replace NAFTA with the **United States–Mexico–Canada Agreement (USMCA)**, which was signed by the three partner countries in 2018 and took effect on July 1, 2020. From the standpoint of the United States, a primary goal of the renegotiated treaty is to increase exports from the United States to Mexico (primarily) and Canada. The USMCA will eventually replace NAFTA altogether, but contracts signed on or before June 30, 2020, will continue to be governed by NAFTA.

United States–Mexico–Canada Agreement (USMCA) *trade agreement signed by Canada, Mexico, and the United States in 2018 intended to promote trade among the three nations*

The European Union The **European Union (EU)** includes most European nations, as shown in Figure 4.1. These nations have eliminated most quotas and set uniform tariff levels on products imported and exported within their group. In 1992, virtually all internal trade barriers went down, making the EU the largest free marketplace in the world. The adoption of a common currency, the *euro*, by most member nations further solidified the EU's position in the world economy. In 2016 the citizens of the United Kingdom, one of the most important members of the EU, voted to withdraw from the Union. The withdrawal process was formally initiated by the government of the United Kingdom in March 2017 and was completed in early 2020. In 2022, though, Britain was facing its gravest economic crisis in a generation, and many people blamed the crisis on Britain's departure from the EU. In one major poll, only 32 percent of British citizens affirmed that leaving the EU was a good idea; 56 percent thought it was a mistake.[10]

European Union (EU) *agreement among major European nations to eliminate or make uniform most trade barriers affecting group members*

FIGURE 4.1 The Nations of the European Union
Source: Adapted from European Union, http://europa.eu/eurpean-union/index_en, accessed May 1, 2020.

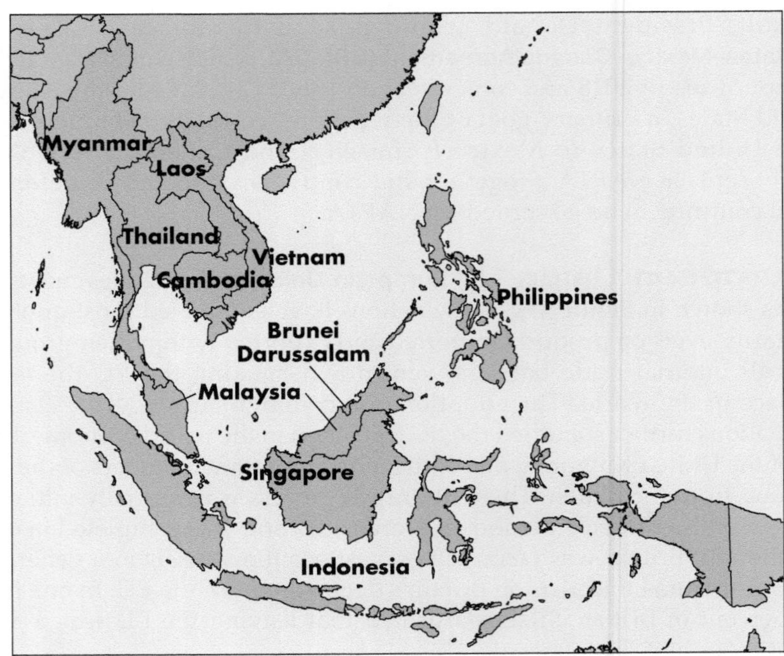

FIGURE 4.2 The Nations of the Association of Southeast Asian Nations (ASEAN)

Association of Southeast Asian Nations (ASEAN) *organization for economic, political, social, and cultural cooperation among Southeast Asian nations*

The Association of Southeast Asian Nations

The **Association of Southeast Asian Nations (ASEAN)** was founded in 1967 as an organization for economic, political, social, and cultural cooperation. In 1995, Vietnam became the group's first communist member. Figure 4.2 shows a map of the ASEAN countries. Because of its relative size, the ASEAN does not have the same global economic significance as NAFTA and the EU.

General Agreement on Tariffs and Trade (GATT) *international trade agreement to encourage the multilateral reduction or elimination of trade barriers*

World Trade Organization (WTO) *organization through which member nations negotiate trading agreements and resolve disputes about trade policies and practices*

The World Trade Organization

The **General Agreement on Tariffs and Trade (GATT)** was signed in 1947. Its purpose was to reduce or eliminate trade barriers, such as tariffs and quotas. It did so by encouraging nations to protect domestic industries within agreed-on limits and to engage in multilateral negotiations. The GATT proved to be relatively successful. So, to further promote globalization, most of the world's countries joined to create the **World Trade Organization (WTO)**, which began on January 1, 1995. (The GATT is the actual treaty that governs the WTO.) The 164 member countries (and an additional 23 observer countries) are required to open markets to international trade, and the WTO is empowered to pursue three goals:[11]

1 Promote trade by encouraging members to adopt fair-trade practices.
2 Reduce trade barriers by promoting multilateral negotiations.
3 Establish fair procedures for resolving disputes among members.

Learning Objective 4-2

Explain how differences in import–export balances, exchange rates, and foreign competition determine the ways in which countries and businesses respond to the international environment.

International Trade

The global economy is essentially defined by international trade. International trade occurs when an exchange involving goods, services, and/or currency takes place across national boundaries. Although international trade has many advantages, it can also pose problems if a country's imports and exports don't maintain an acceptable balance. Table 4.1 lists the United States' 15 largest trading partners. However, the United States also does business with many more countries. For instance, in 2022, the United States exported $5.3 billion to Egypt, $3.9 billion to Kuwait, $3.7 billion to Poland, and $183 million to Zambia; imports from those same countries were

table 4.1 Major Trading Partners of the United States (in Billions)

Rank	Country	Exports	Imports	Total Trade	Percent of Total Trade
	Total, Top 15 Countries	**1,200.5**	**2117.7**	**3,318.3**	**74.4%**
1	Canada	298.5	371.0	669.5	15.0%
2	Mexico	273.9	382.1	655.9	14.7%
3	China	124.5	462.6	587.0	13.2%
4	Japan	67.5	122.6	190.1	4.3%
5	Germany	60.8	119.0	179.8	4.0%
6	South Korea	60.0	95.6	155.6	3.5%
7	Vietnam	9.7	109.6	119.4	2.7%
8	United Kingdom	62.9	52.2	115.2	2.6%
9	India	39.7	73.5	113.1	2.5%
10	Taiwan	35.9	77.0	112.9	2.5%
11	Netherlands	60.1	28.6	88.7	2.0%
12	France	38.1	47.8	85.9	1.9%
13	Switzerland	32.2	51.2	83.4	1.9%
14	Ireland	13.4	68.0	81.5	1.8%
15	Italy	23.3	57.0	80.3	1.8%

Source: U.S. Census Bureau

$2.3 billion, $2.8 billion, $4.3 billion, and $179 million, respectively. In deciding whether an overall balance exists between imports and exports, economists use two measures: *balance of trade* and *balance of payments*.

Balance of Trade

A country's **balance of trade** is the total economic value of all the products that it exports minus the economic value of all the products that it imports. A *positive balance of trade* results when a country exports (sells to other countries) more than it imports (buys from other countries). A *negative balance of trade* results when a country imports more than it exports.

Balance of Trade *economic value of all products a country exports minus the economic value of all products it imports*

Relatively small trade imbalances are common and are unimportant. Large imbalances, however, are another matter. The biggest concern about trade balances involves the flow of currency. When U.S. consumers and businesses buy foreign products, dollars flow from the United States to other countries; when U.S. businesses are selling to foreign consumers and businesses, dollars flow back into the United States. A large negative balance of trade means that many dollars are controlled by interests outside the United States.

A **trade deficit** occurs when a country's imports exceed its exports, when it has a negative balance of trade. When exports exceed imports, the nation enjoys a **trade surplus**. Several factors, such as general economic conditions and the effect of trade agreements, influence trade deficits and surpluses. For example, higher domestic costs, greater international competition, and continuing economic problems among some of its regional trading partners have slowed the tremendous growth in exports that Japan once enjoyed. But rising prosperity in China and India has led to strong increases in both exports from and imports to those countries.

Trade Deficit *situation in which a country's imports exceed its exports, creating a negative balance of trade*

Trade Surplus *situation in which a country's exports exceed its imports, creating a positive balance of trade*

Figures 4.3 and 4.4 highlight two series of events: (1) recent trends in U.S. exports and imports and (2) the resulting trade deficit. As Figure 4.3 shows, both U.S. imports and U.S. exports, with minor variations, have been generally increasing—a trend that's projected to continue.

Trade deficits between 2006 and 2022 are shown in Figure 4.4. A deficit occurred in each of these years because more money flowed out to pay for foreign imports than flowed in to pay for U.S. exports. For example, in 2022, the United States exported around $1.7 trillion in goods and services and imported around $2.7 trillion in goods

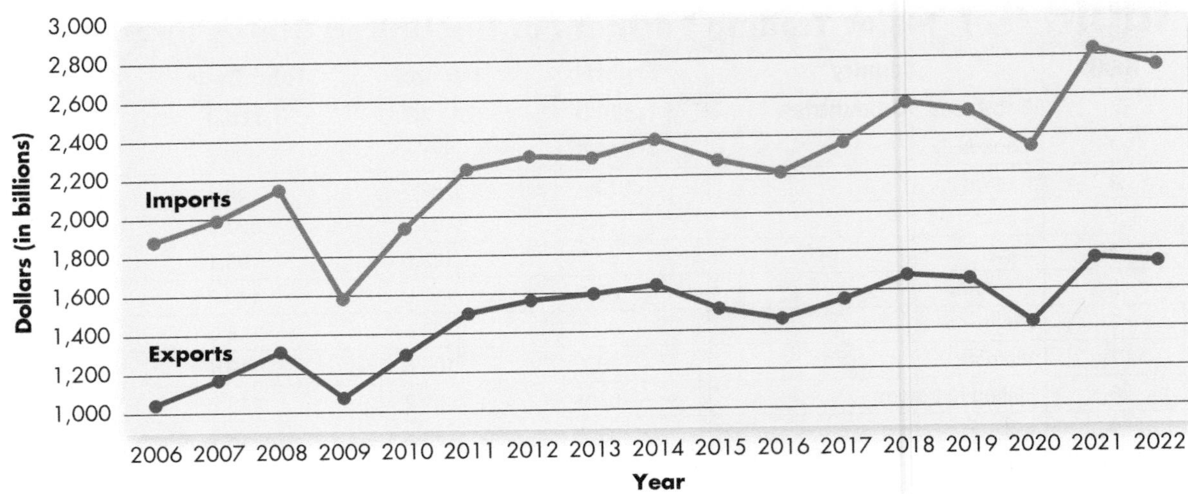

FIGURE 4.3 U.S. Imports and Exports
Source: U.S. Census Bureau

and services. Because imports exceeded exports, the United States had a *trade deficit* of approximately $1 trillion (the difference between exports and imports). Note also that both exports and imports declined in 2009 from the previous year. This was a result of the global economic slowdown during that period. There was also a small decrease from 2021 to 2022, mostly attributable to the COVID-19 pandemic.

Balance of Payments

Balance of Payments *flow of all money into or out of a country*

The **balance of payments** refers to the flow of *money* into or out of a country. The money that a country pays for imports and receives for exports, its balance of trade, accounts for much of its balance of payments. Other financial exchanges are also factors. Money spent by tourists in a country, money spent by a country on foreign-aid programs, and money exchanged by buying and selling currency on international money markets affects the balance of payments.

For instance, suppose that the United States has a negative balance of trade of $1 million. Now, suppose that this year, U.S. citizens travel abroad as tourists and spend a total of $200,000 in other countries. This amount gets added to the balance of trade to form the balance of payments, which is now a negative $1.2 million. Now, further suppose that tourists from other countries come to the United States and spend the equivalent of $300,000 while they are here. This has the effect of reducing the negative balance of payments to $900,000. Then, further suppose that the United States then sends $600,000 in aid to help the victims of a tsunami-ravaged country in Asia. Because this represents additional dollars leaving the United States, the balance of payments is now a negative $1.5 million. For many years last century the United States enjoyed a positive balance of payments. Recently, however, the overall balance has become negative.

Exchange Rates

Exchange Rate *rate at which the currency of one nation can be exchanged for the currency of another nation*

The balance of imports and exports between two countries is affected by the rate of exchange between their currencies. An **exchange rate** is the rate at which the currency of one nation can be exchanged for that of another. Suppose, for example, that the exchange rate between the U.S. dollar and the British pound was $2 to £1. This means that it costs £1 to "buy" $2 or $1 to "buy" £0.5. Stated differently, £1 and $2 have the same purchasing power, or £1 = $2.

At the end of World War II, the major nations of the world agreed to set *fixed exchange rates*. The value of any country's currency relative to that of another would remain constant. The goal was to allow the global economy to stabilize. Today, however, *floating exchange rates* are the norm, and the value of one country's currency

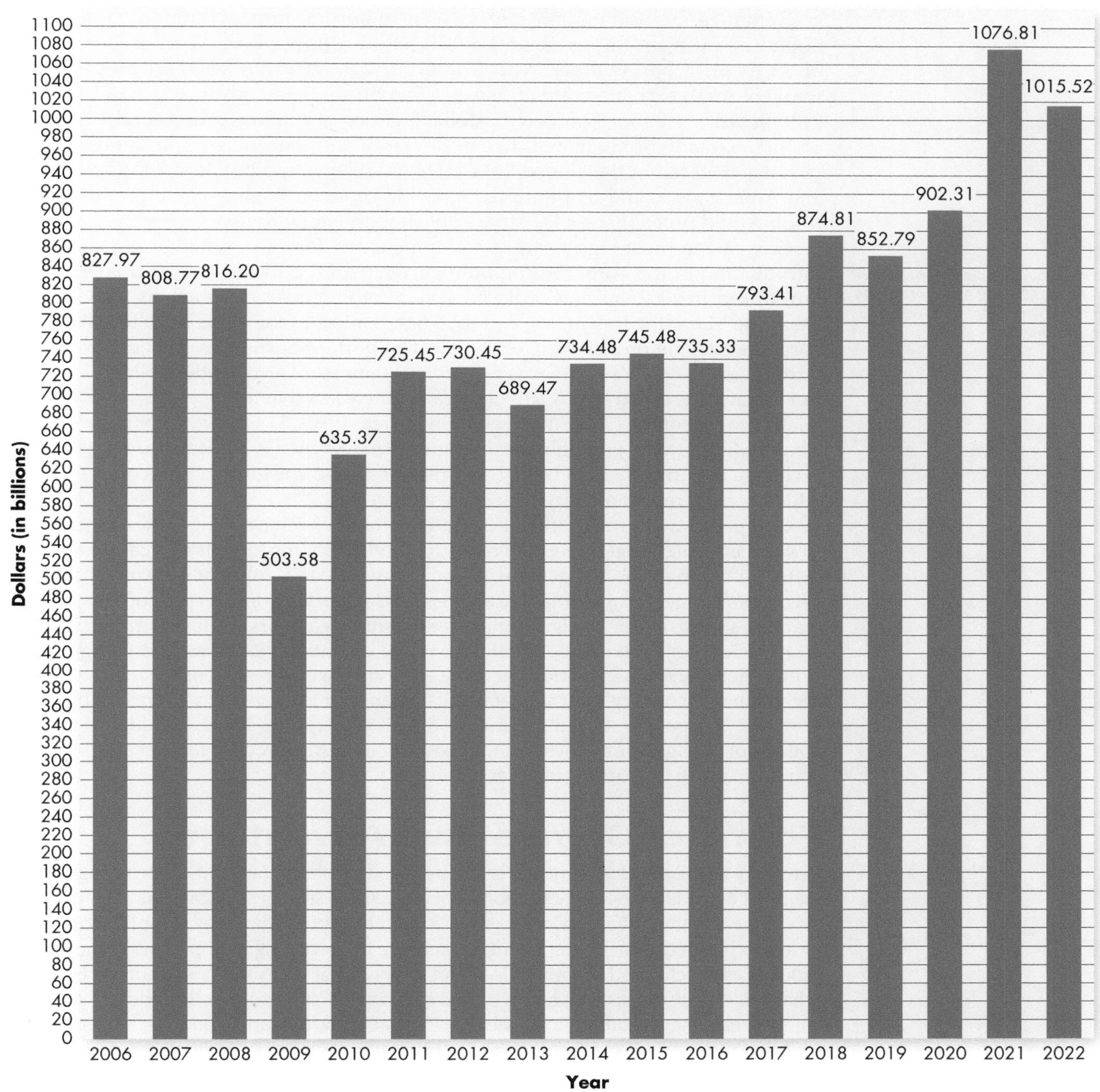

FIGURE 4.4 U.S. Trade Deficit
Source: U.S. Census Bureau

relative to that of another varies with market conditions. For example, when many British citizens want to spend pounds to buy U.S. dollars (or goods), the value of the dollar relative to the pound increases. Demand for the dollar is high, and a currency is strong when demand for it is high. It's also strong when there's high demand for the goods manufactured with that currency. On a daily basis, exchange rates fluctuate very little. Significant variations usually occur over longer time spans. Highly regulated economic systems such as that in China are among the few that still use fixed exchange rates. The Chinese government regulates the flow of currency—its own as well as all others—into and out of China and determines the precise rate of exchange within its borders.

Exchange-rate fluctuation can have an important impact on balance of trade. Suppose you want to buy some English tea for £10 per box. At an exchange rate of \$2 to £1, a box will cost you \$20(£10 × 2 = 20). But what if the pound is weaker? At an exchange rate of, say, \$1.25 to £1, the same box would cost you only \$12.50(£10 × 1.25 = 12.50). If the dollar is strong in relation to the pound, the prices of all U.S.-made products will rise in England, and the prices of all English-made products will fall in the United States. The English would buy fewer U.S. products, and Americans would be prompted to spend more on English-made products. The result would probably be a U.S. trade deficit with England.

Euro a common currency shared among most of the members of the EU (excluding Denmark, Sweden, and the United Kingdom)

One of the most significant developments in foreign exchange has been the introduction of the **euro**, the common currency of the EU. The euro was officially introduced in 2002 and has replaced several other currencies, such as the German Deutsche Mark, the Italian lira, and the French franc. In the years since its debut, the euro has become one of the world's most important currencies. When it was first introduced, the euro's value was pegged as being equivalent to the dollar: €1 = \$1. But because the dollar was relatively weak in the years that followed, its value eroded relative to that of the euro. At one point in the late 1990s, \$1 was worth only about half a euro. More recently, though, the dollar has strengthened relative to the euro and the exchange rate in early 2023 was \$1 = €.94. Of course, the global effects of COVID-19 added considerable volatility to exchange rates.

Companies with international operations must watch exchange-rate fluctuations closely because changes affect overseas demand for their products and can be a major factor in competition. In general, when the value of a country's currency rises—becomes stronger—companies based there find it harder to export products to foreign markets and easier for foreign companies to enter local markets. It also makes it more cost efficient for domestic companies to move operations to lower-cost foreign sites. When the value of a currency declines—becomes weaker—the opposite occurs. As the value of a country's currency falls, its balance of trade usually improves because domestic companies should experience a boost in exports. There should also be less reason for foreign companies to ship products into the domestic market and less reason to establish operations in other countries.

Forms of Competitive Advantage

Before we discuss the fundamental issues involved in international business management, we must consider one last factor: forms of *competitive advantage*. Because no country can produce everything that it needs, countries tend to export what they can produce better or less expensively than other countries and use the proceeds to import what they can't produce as effectively. This principle doesn't fully explain why nations export and import what they do. Such decisions hinge partly on the advantages that a particular country enjoys regarding its abilities to create or sell certain products and resources.[12] Economists traditionally focused on absolute and comparative advantage to explain international trade. But because this approach focuses narrowly on such factors as natural resources and labor costs, a more contemporary view of national competitive advantage has emerged.

Absolute Advantage the ability to produce something more efficiently than any other country can

Absolute Advantage

An **absolute advantage** exists when a country can produce something that is cheaper or of higher quality than any other country. Saudi Arabian oil, Brazilian coffee beans, and Canadian timber come close (because these countries have such abundant supplies of these resources), but examples of true absolute advantage are rare. For example, many experts say that the vineyards of France produce the world's finest wines. But the burgeoning wine business in California demonstrates that producers there can also make good wines—wines that rival those from France but come in more varieties and at lower prices.

Comparative Advantage the ability to produce some products more efficiently than others

Comparative Advantage

A country has a **comparative advantage** in goods that it can produce more efficiently or better than other nations. If businesses in a given country can make computers more efficiently than they can make automobiles, then that nation has a comparative advantage in computer manufacturing.

In general, both absolute and comparative advantages translate into competitive advantage. Brazil, for instance, can produce and market coffee beans knowing full well that few other countries have the right mix of climate, terrain, and altitude to enter the coffee bean market. The United States has comparative advantages in the computer industry (because of technological sophistication) and in farming (because of large amounts of fertile land and a temperate climate). South Korea has a comparative advantage in electronics manufacturing because of efficient operations and cheap labor. As a result of each country's comparative advantage, U.S. firms export computers and grain to South Korea and import smartphones from South Korea. South Korea can produce food, and the United States can build smartphones, but each nation imports certain products because the other holds a comparative advantage in the relevant industry.

National Competitive Advantage In recent years, a theory of national competitive advantage has become a widely accepted model of why nations engage

managing in turbulent times

Ripple Effects in the Global Supply Chain

In February 2022, Russian forces invaded Ukraine in an escalation of the Russo-Ukraine war, which had been ongoing since 2014. The region had regained some stability in the intervening eight years, but infrastructure, shipping, and logistics were drastically weakened from dealing with continuing tensions and fighting, blocked aid, and infrastructure collapse, among the other massive challenges. With the full-scale invasion of the Russian military, Ukraine was unable to regain stability and saw dramatic impacts on its exports.

The strategic importance of Sevastopol, Crimea's largest city and a major port on the Black Sea, made it an important naval base and import/export point in the region. With the invasion of Russian troops and continuing armed conflicts, traffic at the port came to a standstill, and farmers were left with millions of tons of harvested grain and no way to get it out of the country.

Ukraine occupies a relatively small geographical area, but its exports have a big impact on the global economy. In 2021, Ukraine was the world's number-one exporter of sunflower oil, the second-largest exporter of barley, the third largest of wheat, and fourth largest of corn. At that time, 40 percent of the corn and wheat exported from Ukraine went to the Middle East and Africa. African nations, in particular, depended on Ukraine for grains, and aid agencies found they were unable to get desperately needed supplies to countries already grappling with severe food shortages.[14]

Russia produces about 25 percent of the world's nitrogen fertilizer, and the combined wheat exports of Ukraine and Russia make up nearly 30 percent of the exported global supply. Political sanctions against Russia, blocked ports in Ukraine, and direct conflict have combined to accelerate a world food shortage. Poor countries are unable to find alternative (and more expensive) suppliers, and world grain stores have begun to shrink.

annapasichnik/123RF

The global supply chain inextricably links seemingly unrelated regions and supplies. In the United States, the war had a direct impact on the import of materials needed to manufacture electronics, car batteries, and even medical equipment. Russia is a major exporter of these key metals, and without a steady supply, the United States and other producers passed along increased costs to consumers.[15]

The war also directly impacted Americans' grocery bills. Increased grain prices mean increased costs at every level of production, with the highest increases showing up on grocery store shelves. As consumer shopping habits moved back toward pre-pandemic spending, shoppers found that their budgets were stretched by staples, requiring them to cut back on other spending.

Global supply chains mean that events in faraway places have impacts on our lives. Bananas from Brazil, heavy metals from China, and even the grain that makes our favorite breakfast cereal—all of these conveniences are possible thanks to that global supply chain. That same interconnectedness, however, means that we also feel negative effects from distant conflicts and crises.

National Competitive Advantage *international competitive advantage stemming from a combination of factor conditions, demand conditions, related and supporting industries, and firm strategies, structures, and rivalries*

in international trade.[13] **National competitive advantage** derives from four conditions:

1 *Factor conditions* are the factors of production we discussed in Chapter 1—*labor, capital, entrepreneurs, physical resources*, and *information resources*.

2 *Demand conditions* reflect a large domestic consumer base that promotes strong demand for innovative products.

3 *Related and supporting industries* include strong local or regional suppliers or industrial customers.

4 *Strategies, structures, and rivalries* refer to firms and industries that stress cost reduction, product quality, higher productivity, and innovative products.

When several attributes of national competitive advantage exist, a nation is likely to be heavily involved in international business. Japan, for instance, has strong domestic demand for automobiles. Its carmakers have well-oiled supplier networks, and domestic firms have competed intensely with one another for decades. The country also has a strong network of suppliers that puts a premium on quality, efficiency, and innovation. These circumstances help explain why Japanese car companies such as Toyota and Honda are successful in foreign markets.

Learning Objective 4-3

Discuss the factors involved in deciding to do business internationally and in selecting the appropriate levels of international involvement and international organizational structure.

International Business Management

Regardless of where a firm is located, its success depends largely on how well it's managed. International business is so challenging because basic management tasks—planning, organizing, directing, and controlling—are much more difficult when a firm operates in markets scattered around the globe.

Managing means making decisions. In this section, we examine the three basic decisions that a company must make when considering globalization. The first decision is whether to go international. Once that decision has been made, managers must decide on the level of international involvement and on the organizational structure that will best meet the firm's global needs.

Going International

As the world economy becomes increasingly globalized, more and more firms are expanding their international operations. U.S. firms are aggressively expanding abroad, and foreign companies such as BP and Nestlé continue to expand into foreign markets as well, including the U.S. market. This route, however, isn't appropriate for every company. If you buy and sell fresh fish, you'll probably find it more profitable to confine your activities to limited geographic areas because storage and transport costs may be too high to make international operations worthwhile. As Figure 4.5 shows, several factors affect the decision to go international.

Gauging International Demand In considering international expansion, a company must determine whether its products are in demand abroad. Products that are successful in one country may be useless in another. Even when there is demand, advertising and promotion may still need to be adjusted. For example, bicycles are largely used for recreation in the United States but are seen as basic transportation in China. Hence, a bicycle maker would need to use different marketing strategies in each of these countries. Market research or the prior market entry of competitors may indicate whether there's an international demand for a firm's products.

Adapting to Customer Needs If its product is in demand, a firm must decide whether and how to adapt it to meet the special demands of foreign customers. For example, to satisfy local tastes, McDonald's sells wine in France, beer in Germany, gazpacho in Spain, and some vegetarian sandwiches in India. Likewise, consumer

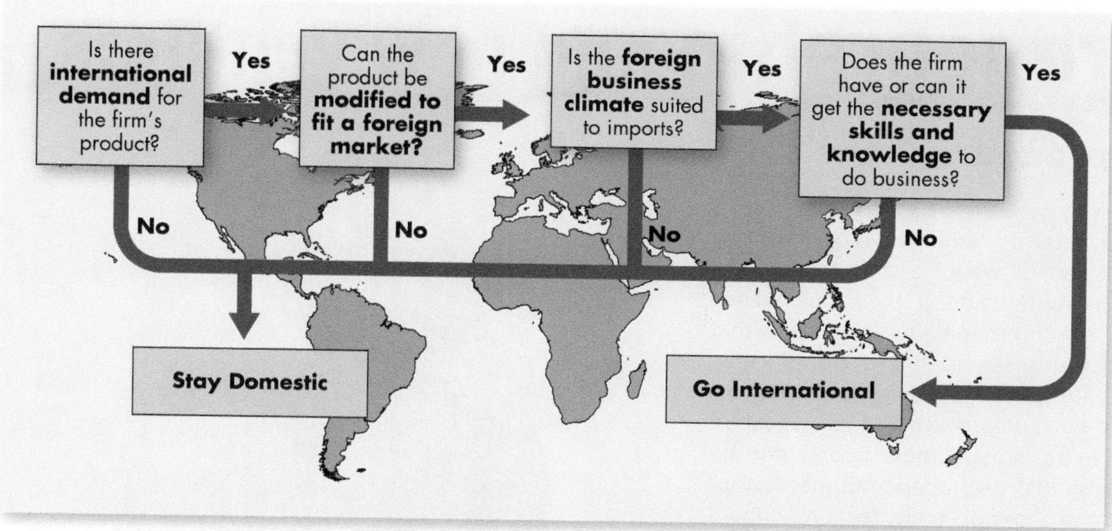

FIGURE 4.5 Going International

electronics companies have to be aware that different countries use different kinds of electric sockets and different levels of electric power. Therefore, regardless of demand, customer needs must still be considered.

Outsourcing and Offshoring

Outsourcing, the practice of paying suppliers and distributors to perform certain business processes or to provide needed materials or services, has become a popular option for going international. It has become so popular because (1) it helps firms focus on their core activities and avoid getting sidetracked on secondary activities and (2) it reduces costs by locating certain business functions in areas where relevant costs are low.[16]

Outsourcing *the practice of paying suppliers and distributors to perform business processes or to provide needed materials or services*

The practice of outsourcing to foreign countries is more specifically referred to as **offshoring**. Many companies today contract their manufacturing to low-cost factories in Asia. Similarly, many service call centers today are outsourced to businesses located in India. DirecTV, Chase Bank Credit Card Services, and several home mortgage support businesses have established call centers in India and have enjoyed considerable success. In contrast, FTD's network of florists opened a call center in India but subsequently closed it. As it turns out, many people who call to order flowers need more personal assistance—advice on types of flowers, colors of arrangements, and so forth—than can be provided by someone from a different culture on the other side of the world.

Offshoring *the practice of outsourcing to foreign countries*

Levels of International Involvement

After deciding to go international, a firm must determine the level of its involvement. Several levels are possible: A firm may act as an exporter or importer, organize as an international firm, or (like most of the world's largest industrial firms) operate as a multinational firm.

Exporters and Importers

An **exporter** makes products in one country to distribute and sell in others. An **importer** buys products in foreign markets and brings them home for resale. Both conduct most of their business in their home nations. Both entail the lowest level of involvement in international operations, and both are good ways to learn the fine points of global business. Many large firms entered international business as exporters. General Electric and Coca-Cola, among others, exported to Europe for several years before setting up production sites there. It is also useful to remember that most import–export transactions involve both activities. A bottle of French wine sold in New York, for instance, was exported by the French winery but simultaneously imported by a U.S. wine distributor.

Exporter *firm that distributes and sells products to one or more foreign countries*

Importer *firm that buys products in foreign markets and then imports them for resale in its home country*

entrepreneurship and new ventures

Women Entrepreneurs Grow Global

In 2008, Laurel Delaney started writing a blog—*Women Entrepreneurs Grow Global*, or wegg®,—that focused on helping women entrepreneurs expand their businesses internationally. Delaney knew through personal experience that women-owned exporting businesses faced unique challenges. Inspired by an International Trade Centre report that "women-owned small and medium-sized enterprises (SMEs) that export tend to earn more, pay more, employ more people and be more productive than firms that only operate domestically," Delaney aimed to create a one-stop-shop resource where women could easily access educational resources.

In 2015, after observing that many of her clients were unaware of how to take their business global, Delaney incorporated as a 501(c)(3) to take advantage of grant and sponsorship funding from individuals, foundations, and corporations who wanted to support women entrepreneurs and business owners with their global growth expansion plans. She expanded her online reach with different educational platforms such as webinars and X (formally known as Twitter) by coming up with catchy program names like wegginar®, weggchat®, *and Club wegg®, which she trademarked*, and began to offer one-to-one peer mentoring. All wegg® programs feature successful professionals who provide participants with practical information to guide them through the many aspects of exporting, and provide concrete strategies for global entrepreneurship.

wegg® is the only USA nonprofit that consistently delivers global business educational offerings in a simple, engaging and affordable manner.

The mission of wegg® is "to educate, inspire, and nurture women business owners and entrepreneurs worldwide on how to go global so they can run healthier businesses and create a new future for themselves, their families and their community."

Laurel Delaney/WEGG

Laurel Delaney has helped over 1,800 women entrepreneurs expand into international markets.

By early 2023, wegg® had served over 40,000 women business owners and entrepreneurs.[17] Through its many affordable offerings, wegg® also now provides a VIP program for women business owners to access operational, legal, and strategic support; Club wegg® cohorts; and a monthly How She Went Global® podcast.

Beyond all the practical knowledge provided by wegg®, Delaney stays focused on her original goal: "I wanted to change the landscape for women from being risk-averse to having confidence to go for it—with the appropriate support."[18]

International Firm *firm that conducts a significant portion of its business in foreign countries*

International Firms As exporters and importers gain experience and grow, many move to the next level of involvement. **International firms** conduct a meaningful amount of their business abroad and may even maintain overseas manufacturing facilities. An international firm may be large, but it's still basically a domestic company with international operations. Folgers, for instance, sells more ground coffee in the United States than any other business. It buys coffee from suppliers in several foreign countries, processes the beans in U.S. facilities, and sells Folgers products only in North America. So the firm buys and sells across national boundaries but also generates most of its revenues from its domestic market.

Multinational Firm *firm that designs, produces, and markets products in many nations*

Multinational Firms Most **multinational firms**, firms that design, produce, and market products in many nations, such as ExxonMobil, Nestlé, Honda, and Unilever, don't think of themselves as having domestic and international divisions. Headquarters locations are almost irrelevant, and planning and decision making are geared to international markets. The world's largest non-U.S. multinationals in 2016 based on sales, profits, and employees are shown in Table 4.2.

table 4.2 The World's Largest Non-U.S. Companies by Sales, Profits, and Number of Employees (2022)

Company	Sales ($ millions)	Profits ($ billions)	Number of Employees
State Grid	460,616.9		
China National Petroleum	411,692.9		
Sinopec Group	401,313.5		
Saudi Aramco	400,399.1		
Volkswagen	295,819.8		
Saudi Aramco		105.4	
Industrial and Commercial Bank of China		54.0	
China Construction Bank		46.9	
Agricultural Bank of China		37.4	
Tencent Holdings		34.9	
China National Petroleum			1,090,345
State Grid			871,145
Hon Hai Precision Industry			826,608
China Post Group			748,920
Volkswagen			672,789

Source: Fortune Global 500 rankings 2022, https://fortune.com/ranking/global500/.

We can't underestimate the economic impact of multinational firms. Consider just the impact of the 500 largest multinationals: In 2019, these 500 firms generated $29.4 trillion in revenues and $1.65 trillion in owner profits.[19] They employed tens of millions of people, bought materials and equipment from literally thousands of other firms, and paid billions in taxes. Moreover, their products affected the lives of hundreds of millions of consumers, competitors, investors, and even protestors.

International Organization Structures

Different levels of international involvement entail different kinds of organizational structures. A structure that would help coordinate an exporter's activities would be inadequate for those of a multinational. In this section, we consider the spectrum of organizational strategies, including *independent agents, licensing arrangements, branch offices, strategic alliances*, and *foreign direct investment*.

Independent Agents

An **independent agent** is an individual or organization that represents an exporter in foreign markets. Independent agents often act as sales representatives: They sell the exporter's products, collect payment, and make sure that customers are satisfied. They often represent several firms at once and usually don't specialize in a particular product or market. Peter So operates an import–export office in Hong Kong. He and his staff of three handle imports from about 15 foreign companies into Hong Kong and about 10 Hong Kong firms that export products abroad.

Independent Agent *individual or organization that agrees to represent an exporter's interests*

Licensing Arrangements

Companies seeking more involvement may opt for licensing arrangements. A **licensing arrangement** is a contract under which one firm allows another to use its brand name, operating procedures, or proprietary technology. Firms give individuals or companies exclusive rights (called *licensing agreements*) to manufacture or market their products in that market. In return, the exporter receives a fee plus ongoing payments (royalties) that are calculated as a percentage of the license holder's sales. Franchising is a popular form of licensing. For example, McDonald's, Pizza Hut, and Hertz Car Rental have franchises around the world.

Licensing Arrangement *arrangement in which firms choose individuals or organizations to manufacture or market their products in another country*

Branch Office *foreign office set up by an international or multinational firm*

Branch Offices Instead of developing relationships with foreign agents or licensing companies, a firm may send its own managers to overseas branch offices, where the firm has more direct control than it does over agents or license holders. **Branch offices** also furnish a more visible public presence in foreign countries, and foreign customers tend to feel more secure when a local branch office is present. Halliburton, a Houston-based oil field supply and services company, opened a branch office in Dubai to more effectively establish relationships with customers in the Middle East. Turkish Airlines has branch offices in most cities where it flies.

Strategic Alliance *arrangement (also called joint venture) in which a company finds a foreign partner to contribute approximately half of the resources needed to establish and operate a new business in the partner's country*

Strategic Alliances In a **strategic alliance**, a company finds a partner in the country in which it wants to do business. Each party agrees to invest resources and capital into a new business or to cooperate in some mutually beneficial way. This new business, the alliance, is owned by the partners, who divide its profits. Such alliances are sometimes called *joint ventures*, but the term *strategic alliance* has arisen because such partnerships are playing increasingly important roles in the strategies of major companies. Nestlé (a Swiss company) and General Mills (a U.S. company) have a global joint venture called Cereal Partners Worldwide, or CPW. When the new venture was launched in 1991, General Mills provided brand recognition and proprietary cereal processing techniques, and Nestlé provided global distribution channels and marketing expertise. Today CPW markets cereals and other breakfast foods in over 130 countries. In many countries, such as Mexico, India, and China, laws make alliances virtually the only way to do international business. Mexico, for example, requires that all foreign firms investing there have local partners. Likewise, local interests own the majority of both Disney theme parks in China; Disney is the minority owner but also collects management and licensing fees.

In addition to easing the way into new markets, alliances give firms greater control over foreign activities than agents and licensees. Alliances also allow firms to benefit from the knowledge and expertise of foreign partners. Microsoft, for example, relies heavily on alliances when it expands into new international markets. This approach has helped the firm learn the intricacies of doing business in China and India, two of the hardest emerging markets to crack.

Foreign Direct Investment (FDI) *arrangement in which a firm buys or establishes tangible assets in another country*

Foreign Direct Investment **Foreign direct investment (FDI)** involves buying or establishing tangible assets in another country. Dell Computer, for example, has built assembly plants in Europe and China. Volkswagen has built a factory in Brazil, and Coca-Cola has built bottling plants in dozens of different countries. FedEx has a major distribution center in Paris. Each of these activities represents FDI by a firm in another country.

Understanding the Cultural Environment

Learning Objective 4-4

Explain the role and importance of the cultural environment in international business.

A major factor in the success—or failure—of international business activity is having a deep understanding of the cultural environment and how it affects business. As mentioned earlier, Disney's Hong Kong theme park struggled after it first opened, in large part because Disney made the mistake of minimizing all elements of Chinese culture in the park—essentially making it a generic miniature reproduction of the original Disneyland in California. Disney also confused potential visitors with ads showing a father, mother, and two children walking hand-in-hand toward the theme park, overlooking China's laws at that time that restricted many families to a single child. Only after a refurbishment to make the park more Chinese and a revised ad campaign did attendance begin to improve.[20] A country's culture includes all the values, symbols, beliefs, and language that guide behavior.

Values, Symbols, Beliefs, and Language

Cultural values and beliefs are often unspoken; they may even be taken for granted by those who live in a particular country. Cultural factors do not necessarily cause problems for managers when the cultures of two countries are similar. Difficulties can arise, however, when there is little overlap between the home culture of a manager and the culture of the country in which business is to be conducted. For example, most U.S. managers find the culture and traditions of England relatively familiar. The people of both countries speak the same language and share strong historical roots, and the two countries have a strong history of commerce between them. When U.S. managers begin operations in China or the Middle East, however, many of those commonalities disappear.

In Japanese, the word *hai* (pronounced "hi") means "yes." In conversation, however, this word is used much like people in the United States use "uh-huh"; it moves a conversation along or shows the person with whom you are talking that you are paying attention. So when does *hai* mean "yes" and when does it mean "uh-huh"? This turns out to be a relatively difficult question to answer. If a U.S. manager asks a Japanese manager if he agrees to some trade arrangement, the Japanese manager is likely to say, "Hai"—but this may mean "Yes, I agree," "Yes, I understand," or "Yes, I am listening." Some U.S. managers become frustrated in negotiations with their Japanese counterparts, who continue to raise issues that Americans believe have already been settled (because the Japanese managers said "Yes"). Many of these managers fail to recognize that "yes" does not always mean "yes" in Japan.

Cultural differences between countries can have a direct impact on business practice. For example, the religion of Islam teaches that people should not make a living by exploiting the misfortune of others; as a result, charging interest payments as is done in many parts of the world is seen as immoral. There are Sharia-compliant practices that do allow charging interest, but only under certain circumstances. Banks, for example, can lend money for people to buy homes but the interest received by the bank on these mortgages and the risks associated with each mortgage must be shared between the lender and the buyer.

Some cultural differences between countries can be even subtler and yet have a major impact on business activities. For example, in the United States, most managers clearly agree about the value of time. Most U.S. managers schedule their activities tightly and then try to adhere to their schedules. Other cultures do not put such a premium on time. In the Middle East, managers do not like to set appointments, and they rarely keep appointments set too far into the future. U.S. managers interacting with managers from the Middle East might misinterpret the late arrival of a potential business partner as a negotiation ploy or an insult, when it is rather a simple reflection of different views of time and how people can best use it.[21]

Language itself can be an important factor. Beyond the obvious and clear barriers posed by people who speak different languages, subtle differences in meaning can also play a major role. For example, Imperial Oil of Canada markets gasoline under the brand name Esso. When the firm tried to sell its gasoline in Japan, it learned that *esso* means "stalled car" in Japanese. Likewise, when Chevrolet first introduced a U.S. model called the Nova in Latin America, General Motors executives could not understand why the car sold poorly. They eventually learned, though, that, in Spanish, *no va* means "It doesn't go." The color green is used extensively in Muslim countries, but it signifies death in some other countries.

Employee Behavior Across Cultures

Managers in international business also have to understand that there are differences in what motivates people in different cultures. Although it's impossible to predict exactly how people from different cultures will react in the workplace, some insights have been developed from research on individual behaviors and attitudes across different cultures. This research, conducted by Geert Hofstede, identifies five important dimensions along which people seem to differ across cultures.[22] These dimensions are illustrated in Figure 4.6.

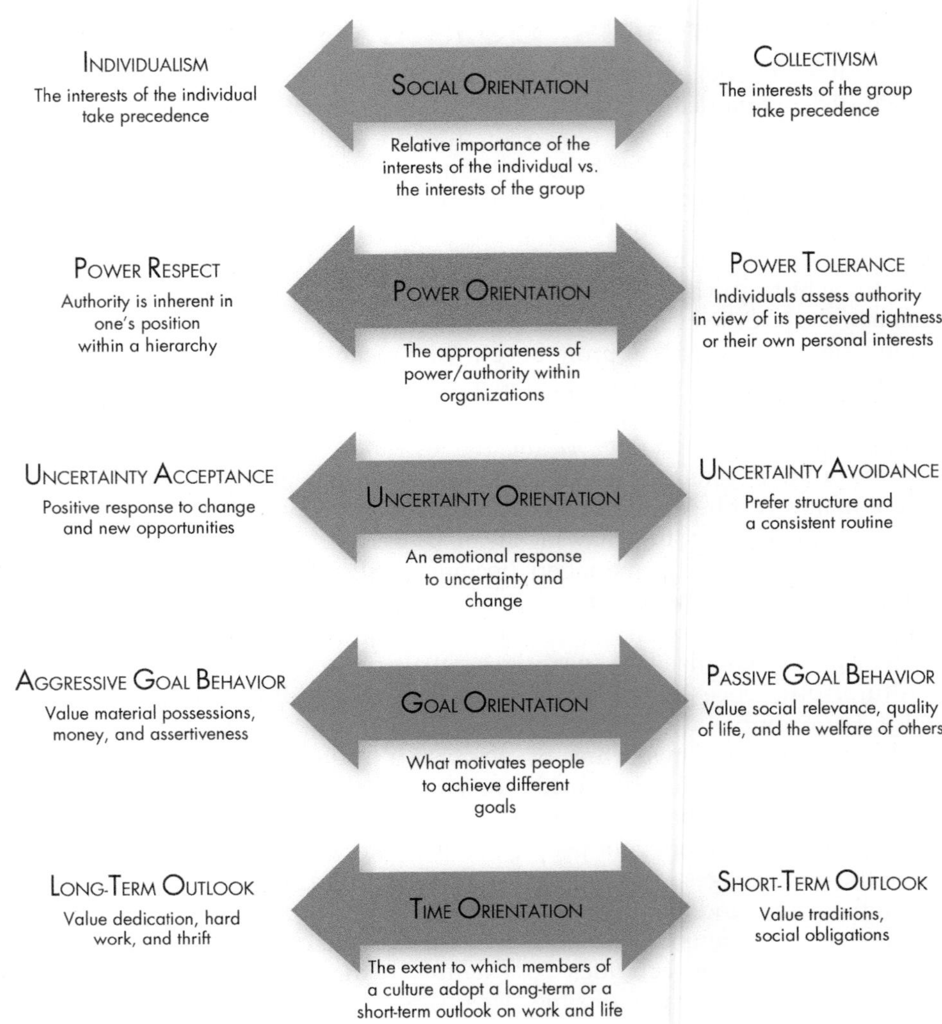

FIGURE 4.6 Hofstede's Five Dimensions of National Culture

Social Orientation *a person's beliefs about the relative importance of the individual versus groups to which that person belongs*

The first dimension is **social orientation**. Social orientation is a person's beliefs about the relative importance of the individual versus groups to which that person belongs. The two extremes of social orientation are individualism and collectivism. *Individualism* is the cultural belief that the person comes first. Research suggests that people in the United States, the United Kingdom, Australia, Canada, New Zealand, and the Netherlands tend to be relatively individualistic. *Collectivism* is the belief that the group comes first. Research has found that people from Mexico, Greece, Hong Kong, Taiwan, Peru, Singapore, Colombia, and Pakistan tend to be relatively collectivistic in their values. In countries with higher levels of individualism, many workers may prefer reward systems that link pay with the performance of individual employees. In a more collectivistic culture, such a reward system may in fact be counterproductive because singling out an individual employee for recognition may cause embarrassment.

Power Orientation *the beliefs that people in a culture hold about the appropriateness of power and authority differences in hierarchies such as business organizations*

A second important dimension is **power orientation**, the beliefs that people in a culture hold about the appropriateness of power and authority differences in hierarchies such as business organizations. Some cultures are characterized by *power respect*. This means that people tend to accept the power and authority of their superiors simply on the basis of their position in the hierarchy and to respect their right to hold that power. Research has found that people in France, Spain, Mexico, Japan, Brazil, Indonesia, and Singapore are relatively power accepting. In contrast, people in cultures with a *power tolerance* orientation attach much less significance to a person's position in the hierarchy. These individuals are more willing to question a decision or mandate from someone at a higher level or perhaps even refuse to accept it. Research suggests that people in the United States, Israel, Austria, Denmark, Ireland, Norway, Germany, and New Zealand tend to be more power tolerant.

The third basic dimension of individual differences is *uncertainty orientation*. **Uncertainty orientation** is the feeling individuals have regarding uncertain and ambiguous situations. People in cultures with *uncertainty acceptance* are stimulated by change and thrive on new opportunities. The research suggests that many people in the United States, Denmark, Sweden, Canada, Singapore, Hong Kong, and Australia are among those in this category. In contrast, people with *uncertainty avoidance* tendencies dislike and will avoid ambiguity whenever possible. The research found that many people in Israel, Austria, Japan, Italy, Colombia, France, Peru, and Germany tend to avoid uncertainty whenever possible.

Uncertainty Orientation *the feeling individuals have regarding uncertain and ambiguous situations*

The fourth dimension of cultural values is goal orientation. In this context, **goal orientation** is the manner in which people are motivated to work toward different kinds of goals. One extreme on the goal orientation continuum is *aggressive goal behavior*. People who exhibit aggressive goal behaviors tend to place a high premium on material possessions, money, and assertiveness. In contrast, people who adopt *passive goal behavior* place a higher value on social relationships, quality of life, and concern for others. According to the research, many people in Japan tend to exhibit relatively aggressive goal behaviors, whereas many people in Germany, Mexico, Italy, and the United States reflect moderately aggressive goal behaviors. People from the Netherlands and the Scandinavian countries of Norway, Sweden, Denmark, and Finland all tend to exhibit relatively passive goal behaviors.[23]

Goal Orientation *the manner in which people are motivated to work toward different kinds of goals*

A fifth dimension is called time orientation. **Time orientation** is the extent to which members of a culture adopt a long-term versus a short-term outlook on work, life, and other elements of society. Some cultures, such as those of Japan, Hong Kong, Taiwan, and South Korea, have a longer-term orientation. One implication of this orientation is that people from these cultures are willing to accept that they may have to work hard for many years before achieving their goals. Other cultures, such as those of Pakistan and West Africa, are more likely to have a short-term orientation. As a result, people from these cultures may prefer jobs that provide more immediate rewards. Research suggests that people in the United States and Germany tend to have an intermediate time orientation.[24]

Time Orientation *the extent to which members of a culture adopt a long-term versus a short-term outlook on work, life, and other elements of society*

Barriers to International Trade

Learning Objective 4-5

Describe some of the ways in which economic, legal, and political differences among nations affect international business.

Whether a business is truly multinational or sells to only a few foreign markets, several factors will affect its international operations. Success in foreign markets will largely depend on the ways a business responds to *social and cultural forces* (as described previously) and *economic, legal, and political barriers* to international trade.

Economic Differences

Although cultural differences are often subtle, economic differences can be fairly pronounced. As we discussed in Chapter 1, in dealing with mixed-market economies like those of France and Sweden, firms must know when—and to what extent—the government is involved in a given industry. The French government, for instance, is heavily involved in all aspects of airplane design and manufacturing. The impact of economic differences can be even greater in planned economies such as those of China and Vietnam, where the government owns and operates many factors of production.

Legal and Political Differences

Governments can affect international business in many ways. They can set conditions for doing business within their borders and even prohibit doing business altogether. For example, businesses that want to establish operations in China must have a local partner that owns at least half of the new enterprise. Governments can also control the flow of capital and use tax legislation to discourage or encourage activity in a given industry. They can even confiscate the property of foreign-owned companies. In this section, we discuss some of the more common legal and political issues in international business: *quotas, tariffs,* and *subsidies; local content laws;* and *business practice laws.*

Quota *restriction on the number of products of a certain type that can be imported into a country*

Embargo *government order banning exportation or importation of a particular product or all products from a particular country*

Tariff *tax levied on imported products*

Subsidy *government payment to help a domestic business compete with foreign firms*

Quotas, Tariffs, and Subsidies Even free market economies, such as that of the United States, have some quotas or tariffs, both of which affect prices and quantities of foreign-made products. A **quota** restricts the number of products of a certain type that can be imported and, by reducing supply, raises the prices of those imports. The United States has imposed quotas on ice cream and timber: Belgian ice-cream makers are limited in the amount of their product they can ship to the United States each year, and Canada can ship only specified amounts of timber per year. Quotas are often determined by treaties. Better terms are often given to friendly trading partners, and quotas are typically adjusted to protect domestic producers.

The ultimate quota is an **embargo**, a government order forbidding exportation or importation of a particular product—or even all products—from a specific country. Many nations control bacteria and disease by banning certain agricultural products. Since the days of the Cold War in the 1950s, the United States had an embargo against Cuba, and it wasn't until 2015 that this embargo was loosened in some areas. The United States also has embargoes against trade with Libya, Iran, and North Korea. When the United States imposes an embargo, it means that U.S. firms can't invest in these countries, and their products can't legally be sold in U.S. markets. Numerous other temporary embargos were initiated during the COVID-19 pandemic due to concerns about spreading the disease. And in 2022 both the United States and the EU imposed embargos on certain goods and services exported by Russia as a form of pressure on that country for its war against Ukraine.

Tariffs are taxes on imported products. They raise the prices of imports by making consumers pay not only for the products but also for tariff fees. Tariffs take two forms: revenue and protectionist. Revenue tariffs are imposed to raise money for governments, but most tariffs, called *protectionist tariffs*, are meant to discourage particular imports. For example, firms that import ironing-board covers into the United States pay a 7 percent tariff on the price of the product. Firms that import women's athletic shoes pay a flat rate of $0.90 per pair plus 20 percent of the product price. Chinese manufactured paper clips exported to the United States carry a 127 percent tariff. Such figures are determined through a complicated process designed to put foreign and domestic firms on competitive footing (that is, to make the foreign goods cost about the same as the domestic goods).

Quotas and tariffs are imposed for numerous reasons. The U.S. government aids domestic automakers by restricting the number of Japanese cars imported into this country. Because of national security concerns, we limit the export of technology (for example, computer and nuclear technology to China). The United States isn't the only country that uses tariffs and quotas. To protect domestic firms, Italy imposes high tariffs on electronic goods. As a result, Asian-made televisions are very expensive in Italy.

A **subsidy** is a government payment to help a domestic business compete with foreign firms. They're actually indirect tariffs that lower the prices of domestic goods rather than raise the prices of foreign goods. For example, many European governments subsidize farmers to help them compete against U.S. grain imports.

Protectionism *practice of protecting domestic business against foreign competition*

The Protectionism Debate In the United States, **protectionism**, the practice of protecting domestic business at the expense of free market competition, is controversial. Supporters argue that tariffs and quotas protect domestic firms and jobs as well as shelter new industries until they're able to compete internationally. They contend that we need such measures to counter steps taken by other nations. During the 2012 London Olympics, critics were outraged when it was discovered that Ralph Lauren, provider of official U.S. team uniforms, had outsourced the production of those uniforms to firms in China. These critics charged that the jobs of making the uniforms should have gone to U.S. workers. However, Ralph Lauren pointed out that the uniforms would have cost a lot more if they had been made in the United States. Other advocates justify protectionism in the name of national security. A nation, they argue, must be able to produce efficiently the goods needed for survival in case of war.

Critics cite protectionism as a source of friction between nations. They also charge that it drives up prices by reducing competition. They maintain that although jobs in some industries would be lost as a result of free trade, jobs in other industries (for example, electronics and automobiles) would be created if all nations abandoned protectionist tactics.

Protectionism sometimes takes on almost comic proportions. Neither Europe nor the United States grows bananas, but both European and U.S. firms buy and sell bananas in foreign markets. Problems arose a few years ago when the EU put a quota on bananas imported from Latin America, a market dominated by two U.S. firms, Chiquita and Dole, to help firms based in current and former European colonies in the Caribbean. To retaliate, the United States imposed a 100 percent tariff on certain luxury products imported from Europe, including Louis Vuitton handbags, Scottish cashmere sweaters, and Parma ham.

Local Content Laws Many countries, including the United States, have **local content laws**, requirements that products sold in a country be at least partly made there. Firms seeking to do business in a country must either invest there directly or take on a domestic partner. In this way, some of the profits from doing business in a foreign country stay there rather than flow out to another nation. For instance, foreign-made automobiles imported into the United States are required to have a minimum percentage of their components manufactured by U.S. suppliers. Both China and India currently require that when a foreign firm enters into a joint venture with a local firm, the local partner must have the controlling ownership stake.

Local Content Law *law requiring that products sold in a particular country be at least partly made there*

Business Practice Laws Some businesses entering new markets encounter problems in complying with stringent regulations and bureaucratic obstacles. Such practices are affected by the **business practice laws** by which host countries govern business practices within their jurisdictions. As part of its entry strategy in Germany several years ago, Walmart had to buy existing retailers rather than open brand-new stores because, at the time, the German government was not issuing new licenses to sell food products. Walmart also was not allowed to follow its normal practice of refunding price differences on items sold for less by other stores because the practice is illegal in Germany. In addition, Walmart had to comply with business-hour restrictions: Stores can't open before 7:00 A.M., must close by 8:00 P.M. on weeknights and 4:00 P.M. on Saturday, and must remain closed on Sunday. After a few years, Walmart eventually decided its meager profits in Germany didn't warrant the effort it required to generate them and closed all of its stores there.[25]

Business Practice Law *law or regulation governing business practices in given countries*

Sometimes, a legal—even an accepted—practice in one country is illegal in another. In some South American countries, for example, it is sometimes legal to bribe business and government officials. These bribes are generally called "expediting fees" or something similar. The existence of **cartels**, associations of producers that control supply and prices, also gives tremendous power to some nations, such as those belonging to the Organization of Petroleum Exporting Countries (OPEC). U.S. law forbids both bribery and cartels.

Cartel *association of producers whose purpose is to control supply and prices*

Finally, many (but not all) countries forbid **dumping**, selling a product abroad for less than the cost of production at home. U.S. antidumping legislation sets two conditions for determining whether dumping is being practiced:

Dumping *practice of selling a product abroad for less than the cost of production*

1. Products are being priced at "less than fair value."
2. The result unfairly harms domestic industry.

The United States charged Japan and Brazil with dumping steel at prices 70 percent below normal value. To protect local manufacturers, the U.S. government imposed a significant tariff on steel imported from those countries.[26]

summary of learning objectives

LEARNING OBJECTIVE 4-1

Discuss the rise of international business and describe the major world marketplaces, trade agreements, and alliances.

Importing and exporting products from one country to another greatly increases the variety of products available to consumers and businesses. Several forces have combined to spark and sustain globalization. Governments and businesses have become aware of the potential for higher standards of living and increased profits. New technologies make international travel, communication, and commerce faster and less expensive. In addition, some companies expand into foreign markets just to keep up with their competitors.

North America, Europe, and Pacific Asia represent three geographic clusters that are the major marketplaces for international business activity. These major marketplaces include relatively more of the upper-middle-income and high-income nations but relatively few low-income and low-middle-income countries.

Trade treaties are legal agreements that specify how countries will work together to support international trade. The most significant treaties are (1) the *North American Free Trade Agreement (NAFTA)*, being supplanted by the United States–Mexico–Canada Agreement (USMCA); (2) the *European Union (EU)*; (3) the *Association of Southeast Asian Nations (ASEAN)*; and (4) the *General Agreement on Tariffs and Trade (GATT)*.

LEARNING OBJECTIVE 4-2

Explain how differences in import–export balances, exchange rates, and foreign competition determine the ways in which countries and businesses respond to the international environment.

Economists use two measures to assess the balance between imports and exports. A nation's *balance of trade* is the total economic value of all products that it exports minus the total economic value of all products that it imports. When a country's imports exceed its exports, it has a *negative balance of trade* and it suffers a *trade deficit*. A *positive balance of trade* occurs when exports exceed imports, resulting in a *trade surplus*.

The *balance of payments* refers to the flow of money into or out of a country. Payments for imports and exports, money spent by tourists, funding from foreign-aid programs, and proceeds from currency transactions all contribute to the balance of payments.

Exchange rates, the rates at which one nation's currency can be exchanged for that of another, are a major influence on international trade. Most countries use *floating exchange rates*, in which the value of one currency relative to that of another varies with market conditions.

Countries *export* what they can produce better or less expensively than other countries and use the proceeds to *import* what they can't produce as effectively. Economists once focused on two forms of advantage to explain international trade: *absolute advantage* and *comparative advantage*. Today, the theory of *national competitive advantage* is a widely accepted model of why nations engage in international trade. According to this theory, comparative advantage derives from four conditions: (1) factor of production conditions; (2) demand conditions; (3) related and supporting industries; and (4) strategies, structures, and rivalries.

LEARNING OBJECTIVE 4-3

Discuss the factors involved in deciding to do business internationally and in selecting the appropriate levels of international involvement and international organizational structure.

Several factors enter into the decision to go international. A company wishing to sell products in foreign markets should consider the following questions: (1) Is there a *demand* for its products abroad? (2) If so, must it *adapt* those products for international consumption? Companies may also go international through outsourcing and offshoring.

After deciding to go international, a firm must decide on its level of involvement. Several levels are possible: (1) *exporters and importers*, (2) *international firms*, and (3) *multinational firms*. Different levels of involvement require different kinds of organizational structure. The spectrum of international organizational strategies includes the following: (1) *independent agents*, (2) *licensing arrangements*, (3) *branch offices*, (4) *strategic alliances* (or *joint ventures*), and (5) *foreign direct investment (FDI)*. Independent agents are foreign individuals or organizations that represent an exporter in foreign markets. Another option, licensing arrangements, represents a contract under which one firm allows another to use its brand name, operating procedures, or proprietary technology. Companies may also consider establishing a branch office by sending managers overseas to set up a physical presence. A strategic alliance occurs when a company seeking international expansion finds a partner in the country in which it wishes to do business. Finally, FDI is the practice of buying or establishing tangible assets in another country.

LEARNING OBJECTIVE 4-4

Explain the role and importance of the cultural environment in international business.

A country's culture includes all the values, symbols, beliefs, and language that guide behavior. Cultural values and beliefs are often unspoken; they may even be taken for granted by those who live in a particular country. Cultural factors do not necessarily cause problems for managers when the cultures of two countries are similar. Difficulties can arise, however, when there is little overlap between the home culture of a manager and the culture of the country in which business is to be conducted. Cultural differences between countries can have a direct impact on business practice. Some cultural differences between countries, such as the meaning of time, can be even subtler and yet have a major impact on business activities. Language itself can be an important factor. Beyond the obvious and clear barriers posed by people who speak different languages, subtle differences in meaning can also play a major role.

Managers in international business also have to understand that there are differences in what motivates people in different cultures. *Social orientation* is a person's beliefs about the relative importance of the individual versus groups to which that person belongs. A second important dimension is *power orientation*, the beliefs that people in a culture hold about the appropriateness of power and authority differences in hierarchies, such as business organizations. *Uncertainty orientation* is the feeling individuals have regarding uncertain and ambiguous situations. *Goal orientation* is the manner in which people are motivated to work toward different kinds of goals. *Time orientation* is the extent to which members of a culture adopt a long-term versus a short-term outlook on work, life, and other elements of society.

LEARNING OBJECTIVE 4-5

Describe some of the ways in which economic, legal, and political differences among nations affect international business.

Economic differences among nations can be fairly pronounced and can affect businesses in a variety of ways. Common legal and political issues in international business include *quotas, tariffs, subsidies, local content laws*, and *business practice laws*. Quotas restrict the number of certain products that can be imported into a country, and a tariff is a tax that a country imposes on imported products. Subsidies are government payments to domestic companies to help them better compete with international companies. Another legal strategy to support a nation's businesses is implementing local content laws that require products sold in a country to be at least partially made there. Business practice laws control business activities within their jurisdiction and create obstacles for businesses trying to enter new markets.

The term *protectionism* describes the practice of protecting domestic businesses at the expense of free market competition. Although some economists argue that legal strategies such as quotas, tariffs, and subsidies are necessary to protect domestic firms, others argue that protectionism ultimately hurts consumers because of the resulting higher prices.

A final obstacle to international business is that business practices legal in one country may not be legal in another. Bribery, the formation of cartels, and dumping are forbidden in the United States, but legal in other countries, which is challenging for U.S. companies trying to enter some foreign markets.

key terms

absolute advantage (p. 116)
Association of Southeast Asian Nations (ASEAN) (p. 112)
balance of payments (p. 114)
balance of trade (p. 113)
branch office (p. 122)
business practice law (p. 127)
cartel (p. 127)
comparative advantage (p. 116)
dumping (p. 127)
embargo (p. 126)
euro (p. 116)
European Union (EU) (p. 111)
exchange rate (p. 114)
export (p. 107)
exporter (p. 119)
foreign direct investment (FDI) (p. 122)
General Agreement on Tariffs and Trade (GATT) (p. 112)
globalization (p. 107)
goal orientation (p. 125)
import (p. 107)
importer (p. 119)
independent agent (p. 121)
international firm (p. 120)
licensing arrangement (p. 121)
local content law (p. 127)
multinational firm (p. 120)
national competitive advantage (p. 118)
North American Free Trade Agreement (NAFTA) (p. 110)
offshoring (p. 119)
outsourcing (p. 119)
power orientation (p. 124)
protectionism (p. 126)
quota (p. 126)
social orientation (p. 124)
strategic alliance (p. 122)
subsidy (p. 126)
tariff (p. 126)
time orientation (p. 125)
trade deficit (p. 113)
trade surplus (p. 113)
uncertainty orientation (p. 125)
United States–Mexico–Canada Agreement (USMCA) (p. 111)
World Trade Organization (WTO) (p. 112)

questions & exercises

QUESTIONS FOR REVIEW

4-1. What are the advantages and disadvantages of globalization? Give examples.

4-2. What are the three possible levels of involvement in international business? Give examples of each.

4-3. What are the elements of national competitive advantage? Give a current, real-world example of each condition.

4-4. Describe the five international organizational structures.

QUESTIONS FOR ANALYSIS

4-5. Make a list of five things you own, such as an item of furniture, a vehicle, electronics, and other consumer goods, making sure that each one was made in a different country. Develop a hypothesis about why each product was made in that particular country.

4-6. Assume your lumber company made a $1 million sale to a Japanese company on April 6, 2023, when the exchange rate was 131.56 yen to US$1. If the customer paid on April 28 when the exchange rate was 136.15 yen to US$1, how much did your company gain or lose on the transaction? (*Hint*: The invoice was for 131,560,000 yen. How much did your company receive on April 28?) During that time, did the dollar grow stronger against the yen or weaker?

4-7. Research and identify a protectionist tariff imposed by the United States. Do you support that tariff? If so, why?

4-8. Do you think that a firm operating internationally is better advised to adopt a single standard of ethical conduct or to adapt to local conditions? What are the advantages and disadvantages of adapting to local conditions?

APPLICATION EXERCISES

4-9. Identify a manufactured product (car, bike, computer, etc.) you think is made in the United States. Do some research and try to determine where the component parts are made. How much of your chosen product is actually made in the United States? List the parts and their countries of origin and identify the competitive advantage that you believe each place holds.

4-10. China is one of the fastest-growing markets in the world. Use Web or database research to uncover how to best describe China according to the five cultural dimensions. Cite the sources for your information.

building a business: continuing team exercise

ASSIGNMENT

Meet with your team members and discuss your new business venture within the context of this chapter. Develop specific responses to the following:

4-11. Are you likely to acquire any of your materials, products, or services from abroad? Why or why not?

4-12. Are there likely to be any export opportunities for your products or services? Why or why not? If you are able to export your product, will it need to be adapted to sell in foreign markets?

4-13. To what extent, if any, will your new venture be affected by social and cultural differences, economic differences, and/or legal and political differences across cultures?

team exercise

WEIGHING THE TRADE-OFFS

The Situation

Able Systems is a software company specializing in technology solutions for the food industry, including supermarkets and restaurants. All of your customers are located in the United States and operate nearly 24 hours a day. You provide excellent phone support for customers who have an issue, but your expenses are increasing and you're looking for ways to contain costs.

The Dilemma

Able Systems has tried to stem escalating phone support costs by limiting the number of specialists working on each shift, but long wait times have angered customers. Because of the technical and problem-solving skills needed to provide remote support, hiring less-qualified employees is just not an option. You're looking at your competitors and you've noticed that many have offshored their operations—hiring employees in other countries to provide support. Because of a large number of English speakers and an adequate supply of applicants with the education needed for a support position, you are considering setting up a phone support center in Jamaica.

This solution is not without concerns. If you offshore your support operation, you will have to lay off most of the U.S. support employees. You're willing to provide outplacement services to make sure that they can find new jobs, but you're still concerned about the impact of layoffs on your remaining employees. A group of programmers who caught wind of this proposal have begun to wonder if their jobs are next. In addition, local elected officials are concerned about the impact of layoffs on the local economy. Your boss is pressuring you for a recommendation and you're weighing the pros and cons of both options.

Team Activity

4-14. Have each member of the team create a list of the pros and cons of offshoring the phone support. As you develop your list, be sure to consider all of the stakeholders in this decision—the company's executives, employees, customers, and community.

4-15. Gather your group together and reveal, in turn, each member's lists of pros. Narrow the list to the three or four most commonly cited and important advantages of offshoring phone support.

4-16. In similar fashion, have each member of the team read their list of disadvantages. Identify the most significant disadvantages based on your team's assessment.

4-17. Considering the interests of all stakeholders, what is the best option in this situation?

exercising your ethics

PAYING HEED TO FOREIGN PRACTICES

The Situation

Assume that you're an up-and-coming manager at a medium-sized manufacturing company. Your company is one of only a few making certain components for radiant floor-heating systems. The primary advantage of these systems is that they are energy efficient and can result in lower heating costs. Although radiant floor heating is just catching on in the United States, there is a lot of potential in foreign markets where energy is expensive. You've been assigned to head up your company's new operations in a Latin American country. Because two of your competitors are also trying to enter this same market, your boss wants you to move as quickly as possible. You also sense that your success in this assignment will determine your future with the company.

You need to build a production facility and have just completed meetings with local government officials. However, you're pessimistic about your ability to get things moving quickly. You've learned, for example, that it will take 10 months to get a building permit for the facility. Moreover, once the building's up, it will take another six months to get utilities. Finally, the phone company says that it may take up to two years to install the phone lines that you need for high-speed Internet access.

The Dilemma

Various officials have indicated that time frames could be considerably shortened if you were willing to pay special "fees." These expediting fees seem largely legitimate but you are not sure. You suspect that a small part of the fees are bribes, and you're aware that the practice of paying bribes is both unethical and illegal in the United States. In this foreign country, however, it's not illegal and not even considered unethical. Moreover, if you don't pay and one of your competitors does, you'll be at a major competitive disadvantage. In any case, your boss isn't likely to understand the long lead times necessary to get the operation running. Fortunately, you have access to a source of funds that you could spend without the knowledge of anyone in the home office.

QUESTIONS TO ADDRESS

4-18. What are the key ethical issues in this situation?

4-19. What do you think most managers would do in this situation?

4-20. What would you do?

cases

THE MAGIC KINGDOM GOES GLOBAL

Continued from page 107

At the beginning of this chapter, you read about the challenges and opportunities faced by Disney as it expanded its theme parks across the globe. Using the information presented in this chapter, you should now be able to respond to these questions.

QUESTIONS FOR DISCUSSION

4-21. Do you think small business owners and entrepreneurs face the same global challenges and opportunities that a large corporation like Disney faces? What are the major challenges and opportunities for small businesses going global?

4-22. Disney's recent acquisition of 20th Century Fox for $71 billion makes Disney one of the largest communications and entertainment companies in the world. Do you think this kind of global expansion is good for consumers?

4-23. What role does local culture play in doing business in foreign countries? Do you think companies should adapt to local customs or be faithful to the brand and expect local consumers to embrace the changes that come with global expansionism?

GENERAL MOTORS OUTSOURCING TO MEXICO

As the social and political winds shift, so do the terms of trade between countries. In 1866, as Canada moved toward independence, the country tightened its borders and created roadblocks to free trade. The Canadian Conservative Party managed to keep protectionist policies in place for decades. Even so, by 1935, the economic argument for globalization was winning out over the anti-American rhetoric, and the United States and Canada entered into industry-specific but disconnected bilateral trade agreements, such as the Auto Pact, to reduce tariffs on both sides of the border.

Prior to the Auto Pact, only 3 percent of vehicles sold in Canada were made in the United States, but most auto parts for Canadian cars were manufactured in the United States, and overall, Canada was experiencing a large trade deficit with the United States in the automobile sector. By 1968, 60 percent of Canadian-manufactured cars were being sold in the United States, and 40 percent of cars purchased in Canada were made in the United States. Automobile and parts production soon surpassed pulp and paper to become Canada's largest industry, and attention turned to the question of a broader free-trade agreement between the two countries. During the next two decades, economists argued that Canadian real GDP would be significantly increased if both U.S. and Canadian tariffs and other trade barriers were removed and Canadian industry could consequently produce on a larger, more efficient scale. However, the protectionism mindset persisted until 1988, when U.S. President Ronald Reagan and Canadian Prime Minister Brian Mulroney ushered in the era of the Canada–United States Free Trade Agreement. Shortly afterward, Mexico joined the ongoing negotiations, and the North American Free Trade Agreement (NAFTA) was born (ratified on January 1, 1994), creating one of the largest trade blocs in the world, as measured by gross domestic product.

Still, trade agreements don't solve all problems, especially in light of societal changes. For instance, in December 2018, Mary Barra, the CEO of General Motors (NYSE: GM), faced a firestorm of criticism and bad publicity over an announcement that GM would be shutting down domestic plants and laying off up to 15,000 workers. GM insisted it was not looking to shift production to other countries but instead was being forced to drop several models because of a shift in the demand curve away from smaller cars built in the United States and toward sports utility vehicles (SUVs) like the Chevrolet Blazer. Tooling up for the Blazer took years and millions of dollars, and the cost to move manufacturing of that model back to the United States would be prohibitive. In addition, in the United States, the average GM assembly employee earns about $30 per hour before tax. By contrast, an assembly worker in Silao, Mexico, with 10 years of experience earns about $4.50 per hour before tax. Despite the bad press and political pressure to keep U.S. factories open, Barra executed the layoffs in 2019 and closed five plants in the United States and Canada.

Changing times require a changing legal landscape, so on July 1, 2020, the United States, Mexico, and Canada replaced NAFTA with the United States–Mexico–Canada Agreement (USMCA). The ultimate effects of this new agreement are yet to be seen, and as the political, economic, and cultural climates continue to change, factors of production will shift as well. New leadership will pursue new goals, the COVID-19 outbreak forever changed the way we work and travel, trade disputes still persist between the United States and China, and the war in Ukraine precipitated global supply chain issues. The very products we demand and consume continue to change as well. For instance, the last internal-combustion car produced at GM's Detroit-Hamtramck Assembly plant, a Chevy Impala, rolled off the production line on February 20, 2020, as the company started retooling for electric vehicles.

QUESTIONS FOR DISCUSSION

4-24. What effect will the United States–Mexico–Canada Agreement (USMCA) have on GM's short- and long-term plans to shift manufacturing to Mexico and to Canada?

4-25. Is "offshoring" good for the consumer? Is it good for the nation as a whole? What competitive advantage do Mexico and Canada have over the United States that would cause GM to shift operations to those countries?

4-26. How does competition drive companies like GM to move manufacturing out of the United States? What other economic factors are at play in that decision?

4-27. What role does the current cultural environment in the United States play in corporate decisions to manufacture goods in other countries? Is the culture in the United States static or dynamic?

4-28. Describe the interplay between the economic, legal, and political environments in the three countries of USMCA. Does the treaty address these issues? If so, how?

endnotes

[1] The Walt Disney Company, "The Walt Disney Company Reports First Quarter Earnings for Fiscal 2023," February 8, 2023, https://thewaltdisneycompany.com/the-walt-disney-company-reports-first-quarter-earnings-for-fiscal-2023/.

[2] Michael Switow, "Chinese Theme Park Industry Continues to Grow Despite Pandemic," IAAPA, March 31, 2021, https://www.iaapa.org/news/funworld/chinese-theme-park-industry-continues-grow-despite-pandemic.

[3] The Walt Disney Company, "The Walt Disney Company Creates International Content Group to Expand Pipeline of Local Content and Continue to Grow Its Global Direct-to-Consumer Business," January 1, 2022, https://thewaltdisneycompany.com/the-walt-disney-company-creates-international-content-group-to-expand-pipeline-of-local-content-and-continue-to-grow-its-global-direct-to-consumer-business/.

[4] See United States Department of Commerce, Bureau of Economic Analysis, "International Investment Position," accessed April 10, 2023, http://www.bea.gov/newsreleases/international/intinv/intinvnewsrelease.htm.

[5] See Thomas Lee, "U.S. Retailers Often Fail in a Key International Market—at Big Cost to Holders," TheStreet, March 9, 2023, https://www.thestreet.com/retail/the-primary-reason-why-u-s-retailers-fail-in-canada; Tianwei Zhang, "Forever 21 to Exit China Market," *Women's Wear Daily*, April 26, 2019, https://wwd.com/business-news/retail/forever-21-to-exit-china-market-1203118534/; Leo Saini, "Why Walmart Failed in Germany," Better Marketing, November 22, 2019, https://bettermarketing.pub/why-walmart-failed-in-germany-3fdcc6469b89.

[6] "Best Buy, Home Depot Find China Market a Tough Sell," *USA Today*, February 23, 2011, 5B.

[7] See World Bank Data Team, "New Country Classifications by Income Level, 2022–2023," *World Bank Blogs*, accessed April 10, 2023, http://blogs.worldbank.org/opendata/new-country-classifications-2022. See also Ricky W. Griffin and Michael W. Pustay, *International Business: A Managerial Perspective*, 9th ed. (Upper Saddle River, NJ: Prentice Hall, 2020).

[8] Thomas Friedman, *The World Is Flat* (New York: Farrar, Straus, and Giroux, 2005).

[9] Ricardo Rascon, "Overview of Mexico's Automotive Manufacturing Industry," News & Insights for Manufacturing in Mexico, accessed April 30, 2023, https://insights.tetakawi.com/automotive-manufacturing-industry-in-mexico.

[10] Mark Landler, "Buffeted by Economic Woes, U.K. Stats to Look at Brexit with 'Bregret,'" *New York Times*, November 22, 2022, https://www.nytimes.com/2022/11/22/world/europe/uk-brexit-regret.html.

[11] World Trade Organization, "Members and Observers," accessed April 12, 2023, http://www.wto.org/English/thewto_e/whatis_e/tif_e/org6_e.htm.

[12] Griffin and Pustay, *International Business: A Managerial Perspective*. See also Steven Husted and Michael Melvin, *International Economics*, 8th ed. (Boston: Addison Wesley Longman, 2019), 54–61; and Karl E. Case and Ray C. Fair, *Principles of Economics*, 10th ed. (Upper Saddle River, NJ: Prentice Hall, 2017).

[13] Michael Porter, *The Competitive Advantage of Nations* (Boston: Addison Wesley Longman, 2001), 54–61. See also Case and Fair, *Principles of Economics*.

[14] Karen Braun, "Column: Ukraine's Rising Role in Grain Exports Complicates Impact of Crisis," Reuters, January 26, 2022, https://www.reuters.com/markets/us/ukraines-rising-role-grain-exports-complicates-impact-crisis-2022-01-26/.

[15] Eric Hamilton, "The Global Supply Chain Consequences of the Russia-Ukraine War," University of Florida News, February 21, 2023, https://news.ufl.edu/2023/02/russia-ukraine-global-supply-chain/.

[16] Lee J. Krajewski, Manoj Malhotra, and Larry P. Ritzman, *Operations Management: Processes and Value Chains*, 10th ed. (Upper Saddle River, NJ: Prentice Hall, 2017), 401–403.

[17] Our impact. Women Entrepreneurs Grow Global. (2023, September 15). https://womenentrepreneursgrow-global.org/our-impact/

[18] Laurel Delaney, "The Secret Sauce to Getting More Women to Export," Thrive Global, accessed March 25, 2020, https://thriveglobal.com/stories/the-secret-sauce-to-getting-more-women-to-export/.

[19] "Global 500," CNN Money, accessed March 20, 2020, http://money.cnn.com/magazines/fortune/global500/2012/full_list/index.html.

[20] "Main Street, H.K.—Disney Localizes Mickey to Boost Its Hong Kong Theme Park," *Wall Street Journal*, January 23, 2008, B1, B2.

[21] See Erin Meyer, "How Late Is Late?," The Conversation, January 17, 2017, https://theconversation.com/how-late-is-late-70976; "What If There Weren't Any Clocks to Watch?" *Newsweek*, June 30, 1997, 14.

[22] Charlotte Nickerson, "Hofstede's Cultural Dimensions Theory & Examples," Simply Psychology, accessed on June 17, 2023, https://www.simplypsychology.org/hofstedes-cultural-dimensions-theory.html.

[23] Geert Hofstede, "The Business of International Business Is Culture," *International Business Review* 3, no. 1 (1994): 1–14.

[24] Geert Hofstede, *Culture's Consequences: International Differences in Work-Related Values* (Beverly Hills, CA: Sage, 1980); Geert Hofstede, "The Business of International Business Is Culture," *International Business Review* 3, no. 1 (1994): 1–14.

[25] Ecomclips, "Why Walmart Failed in Germany and Europe: The Main Reasons," March 11, 2023, https://ecomclips.com/blog/why-walmart-failed-in-europe-what-went-wrong-in-germany/.

[26] Reuters Staff, "U.S. Imposes Duties on Structural Steel from China, Mexico," Reuters, September 4, 2019, https://www.reuters.com/article/us-usa-trade-steel/us-imposes-duties-on-structural-steel-from-china-mexico-idUSKCN1VP2R7.

[27] Nina Zipkin, "10 Inspiring Quotes from Howard Schultz on Great Leadership and Business Success," Entrepreneur, June 5, 2018, https://www.entrepreneur.com/business-news/10-inspiring-quotes-from-howard-schultz-on-great-leadership/314514.

[28] "Starbucks Reports Q1 Fiscal 2023 Results," Starbucks Corporation—Starbucks Reports Q1 Fiscal 2023 Results, accessed April 30, 2023, https://investor.starbucks.com/press-releases/financial-releases/press-release-details/2023/Starbucks-Reports-Q1-Fiscal-2023-Results/default.aspx.

[29] Kathleen Elk, "When a Competitor Tried to Buy Starbucks, Howard Schultz Was Rescued by Bill Gates Sr.," CNBC, October 4, 2017, https://www.cnbc.com/2017/10/04/bill-gates-sr-helped-howard-schultz-buy-starbucks.html.

part 1

Integrative Learning Portfolio

crafting a business plan

Goal of the Exercise

In Chapter 3, we discussed how the starting point for virtually every new business is a *business plan*. Business plans describe the business strategy for any new business and demonstrate how that strategy will be implemented. One benefit of a business plan is that in preparing it, would-be entrepreneurs must develop their idea on paper and firm up their thinking about how to launch their business before investing time and money in it. In this exercise, you'll get started on creating your own business plan.

Exercise Background: Part 1 of the Business Plan

The starting point for any business plan is coming up with a "great idea." This might be a business that you've already considered setting up. If you don't have ideas for a business already, look around. What are some businesses with which you come into contact on a regular basis? Restaurants, childcare services, and specialty stores are a few examples you might consider. You may also wish to create a business that is connected with a talent or interest you have, such as crafts, cooking, or car repair. It's important that you create a company from "scratch" rather than use a company that already exists. You'll learn more if you use your own ideas.

Once you have your business idea, your next step is to create an "identity" for your business. This includes determining a name for your business and an idea of what your business will do. It also includes identifying the type of ownership your business will take, topics we discussed in Chapter 3. The first part of the plan also briefly looks at who your ideal customers are as well as how your business will stand out from the crowd. Part 1 of the plan also looks at how the business will interact with the community and demonstrate social responsibility, topics we discussed in Chapter 2. Finally, almost all business plans today include a perspective on the impact of global business.

Your Assignment

STEP 1

To complete this assignment, you first need to download the *Business Plan Student Template* file from the book's companion website at www.pearsonhighered.com/ebert. This is a Microsoft Word file you can use to complete your business plan. For this assignment, you will fill in "Part 1" of the plan.

STEP 2

Once you have the *Business Plan Student Template* file, you can begin to answer the following questions in "Part 1: The Contemporary Business Environment."

P1-1. What is the name of your business?

Hint: When you think of the name of your business, make sure that it captures the spirit of the business you're creating.

P1-2. What will your business do?

Hint: Imagine that you are explaining your idea to a family member or a friend. Keep your description to 30 words or fewer.

P1-3. What form of business ownership (sole proprietorship, partnership, or corporation) will your business take? Why did you choose this form?

Hint: For more information on types of business ownership, refer to the discussion in Chapter 3.

P1-4. Briefly describe your ideal customer. What would he or she be like in terms of age, income level, and so on?

Hint: You don't have to give too much detail in this part of the plan; you'll provide more details about customers and marketing in later parts of the plan.

P1-5. Why will customers choose to buy from your business instead of your competition?

Hint: In this section, describe what will be unique about your business. For example, is the product special or will you offer the product at a lower price?

P1-6. All businesses have to deal with ethical issues. One way to address these issues is to create a code of ethics. List three core principles your business will follow.

Hint: To help you consider the ethical issues that your business might face, refer to the discussion in Chapter 2.

P1-7. A business shows social responsibility by respecting all of its stakeholders. What steps will you take to create a socially responsible business?

Hint: Refer to the discussion of social responsibility in Chapter 2. What steps can you take to be a "good citizen" in the community? Consider also how you may need to be socially responsible toward your customers and, if applicable, investors, employees, and suppliers.

P1-8. Will you sell your product in another country? If so, what countries and why? What challenges will you face?

Hint: To help you consider issues of global business, refer to this chapter. Consider how you will expand internationally (e.g., independent agent, licensing). Do you expect global competition for your product? What advantages will foreign competitors have?

Note: Once you have answered the questions, save your Word document. You'll be answering additional questions in later chapters.

case PART 1 STARBUCKS 1970–1987

The entrepreneurial journey is not for everyone. Yes, the highs are high and the rewards can be thrilling. But the lows can break your heart. Entrepreneurs must love what they do to such a degree that doing it is worth sacrifice and, at times, pain. But doing anything else, we think, would be unimaginable.[27]

—Howard Schultz

james anderson/Alamy Stock Photo

On February 2, 2023, Starbucks announced a record $8.7 billion in sales for the fiscal quarter ending January 1, 2023, from 36,170 stores across the globe. Interim CEO Howard Schultz reported, "Starbucks performance in Q1 demonstrates the strength and resilience of our business and accelerating demand for Starbucks Coffee all around the world. We posted today's strong results despite challenging global consumer and inflationary environments, a soft quarter for retail overall, and the unprecedented, COVID-related headwinds that unfolded in China in Q1."[28] The market cap (capitalization) for Starbucks on that date was over $130 billion. Market cap is determined by the number of shares outstanding times the price per share and is a measure of the overall value of a company. To get an idea of how much a billion dollars is, if you put 4,000 asterisks on a single sheet of 8½ by 11 paper and stacked up 500 of those pages, you'd have a stack about two inches tall representing 2 million dots. It would take 500 of those stacks to make a billion, and that would be a stack of paper over 83 feet high. That's with 4,000 dots per page. Now imagine 130 of those 83-foot stacks. It's no wonder that Starbucks is such a household name today.

The Founders' Story

The ubiquitous Starbucks logo that we see today in airports, on city streets, and in grocery stores around the world started with an idea that arose in 1970 as three friends sat drinking diner coffee in a little café in Seattle, Washington. The three entrepreneurs looking for an idea were Jerry Baldwin, Zev Siegl, and Gordon Bowker.

Bowker grew up in Seattle, his mother's hometown. As a student at the University of San Francisco, he became roommates with San Francisco native Jerry Baldwin. They met Siegl on a cross-country road trip in 1962 and became friends. The three went their separate ways but reunited again in Seattle in the late 1960s. Baldwin, just out of the army, had recently started working at Boeing; Siegl was working as a history teacher; and Bowker was writing for *Seattle* magazine. One thing all three men had in common was their entrepreneurial spirit, and they decided to start a business together.

The question was: What business?

Starbucks's Start

They made a stab at writing screenplays for a local television station and then switched to radio broadcasts and making documentary films. These short-lived enterprises went nowhere, but the three were not dissuaded, and so, meeting over breakfast, drinking weak restaurant coffee, and brainstorming ideas, Bowker flashed the coffee idea. He'd been driving to Vancouver, British Columbia, on a regular basis to get good coffee beans, and he had started collecting orders and delivering beans to others in the Seattle area. Baldwin and Siegl liked the idea enough to start researching the potential and found a gourmet coffee shop in Berkeley called Peet's, run by Alfred Peet. Peet had grown up in the Netherlands working in the family coffee business. Peet agreed to supply the three men with fresh-roasted coffee beans once they got their business off the ground.

They found a small corner storefront near Pike Place Market and gathered a few thousand dollars of working capital to launch their newest venture. All they needed now was a logo and a name. The three settled on a character name from *Moby Dick*—Starbuck—and Bowker's former colleague came up with the now-iconic mermaid, which has such a fan following that new iterations of the logo are as eagerly anticipated as movie releases. With all the pieces in place, on March 30, 1971, they opened the doors to the first Starbucks store, focusing on coffee beans and teas along with a selection of brewing devices and grinders. The beverages they served were free coffee samples to customers. In those early days, Bowker was the publicist, Baldwin did the bookkeeping, and Siegl was the buyer. It was a good mix of talents, skills, and interests.

Growing Pains

The next few years saw the fledgling business grow, adding locations in University Village and Edmonds and expanding offerings but still not actually serving coffee. Then, in 1975, the surgeon general announced that coffee might increase the risk of cancer. Then an unexpected freeze in Brazil decimated the coffee crop, causing coffee prices to soar. Struggling to stay afloat, the group found out the building in which they leased their flagship store was being torn down. They moved a few blocks north to 1912 Pike Place, which is still in operation and is widely considered the "original" Starbucks by tourists.

The team limped along into the late 1970s, expanding slowly. Siegl had ideas on ways to expand and diversify the business, but the other two partners wanted to stay focused on roasting coffee beans and selling commercial and home-use machines. In May 1980, Bowker and Baldwin bought Siegl out. For the 1980–81 fiscal year, sales reached $4.4 million, an increase over the prior year of almost 50 percent.

Howard Schultz Comes Aboard

In early 1982, Starbucks opened a store in the University District—the first location to sell brewed coffee, and in September, it hired an enthusiastic young executive named Howard Schultz.

Schultz had been working for a Swedish company called Hammarplast, selling kitchen equipment and housewares, and he'd noticed that Starbucks continually placed large orders for drip coffee makers. Curious, he'd flown from New York to Seattle to see what was happening and immediately fell in love with Starbucks. With his background in sales and marketing, he had some ideas on how to expand the business rapidly and was eager to share them. Bowker and Baldwin were reluctant and almost didn't hire him, but Schultz made another impassioned pitch and joined the team as the marketing director.

In 1983, the company sent Schultz to a trade show in Italy where he had his first latte and noted that there were over 1,500 small coffee shops in Milan alone, places where friends came to meet and catch up. The coffee stores there were community gathering places, not just a place to get a lovely espresso.

Schultz returned with a new wave of enthusiasm for selling not just brewed coffee but all the European-style drinks, from espresso to lattes, but Baldwin and Bowker still insisted on focusing on beans. They didn't see any potential in sit-down coffeehouses. Schultz, on the other hand, was convinced that these little coffeehouses would catch on like wildfire.

Dissatisfied, Schultz left Starbucks in early 1986 to start his own company, Il Giornali, the success of which proved his point. Meanwhile, Starbucks struggled as Bowker's entrepreneurial start-ups spread him too thin. He had started Red Hook Brewing, a real estate development company, and a company to produce Olympic ski films. He sold his shares in the struggling Starbucks, leaving Baldwin as the only remaining founding member. Baldwin started looking for a way out.

Starbucks had bought Peet's in 1984 for $3.8 million, and even though sales for both companies were over $10 million, Starbucks was strapped for cash.[29] Baldwin decided he wanted to put his energy into Peet's, so he put the Starbucks brand and assets up for sale.

Schultz gathered a group of investors and, in August 1987, bought the name, the roasting plant, and six stores of Starbucks from Baldwin for $3.8 million. He was a man on a mission with a vision. His idea was to create a "third place" between work and home built on unique coffee drinks and a social experience like the ones he'd seen in Italy. With Schultz at the helm now, the Starbucks ship was leaving the dock, but there were still rough waters ahead and miles to go before it would be the leviathan it is today.

QUESTIONS FOR DISCUSSION

P1-9. Think of an entrepreneur currently in the news or someone you admire. What qualities and traits does that person demonstrate that make them entrepreneurial? Are those traits different today than they were in the 1970s and '80s when Bowker and his team started Starbucks?

P1-10. How are the current economic, political, and social environments of today different from those of 45 years ago? How are they similar? How about 10 years ago? How about five?

P1-11. Do you think that Bowker and his friends were unique in some way, or were they just in the right place at the right time with the right idea?

P1-12. What is the corporate form of ownership? What are the economic, social, and ethical benefits and drawbacks of running a business as a corporation?

P1-13. Does demand have to precede supply, or can a company create demand by creating supply? What do you think were the significant events that created demand for gourmet coffee back in the 1980s?

P1-14. What kind of ethical concerns arise when a group of people get together to start a business?

finding your path

CAREERS IN BUSINESS

Most experts agree that the people with the most successful careers are those who make an effort to plan them. And just as a career is a lifelong progression, you should not think about career planning as just being a search for your first job. Indeed, over the course of your working life you will likely change jobs several times and work for multiple employers. You will also discover new interests and may need to revisit your career path as those interests change and as the nature of jobs and organizations evolves. At the end of each part of this book you will find a section like this that focuses specifically on careers and career-related issues, ideas, and suggestions.

MAKING YOURSELF EMPLOYABLE

One big part of a successful career is having options. Ideally, you want to try to avoid being in a situation in which you have limited job opportunities and feel compelled to take a job that does not interest you or meet your needs. To the contrary, you should try to always keep yourself in a position such that if you want or need a new job you will have multiple options from which to choose and you will be able to accept a job that will be interesting, fulfilling, and rewarding. To give yourself the best opportunity for this, you need to remember that learning and skill development are not passive—once you start your first full-time career position, you should not just sit back and stop thinking about the future. Instead, you should focus on continuing to learn, to develop and enhance your skills, and to think about where you might go next. Essentially, your goal should be to try to make yourself a valuable asset to the point that employers will actively want you to join them. In Chapter 5, we will introduce and discuss a set of key managerial skills, and in future "Finding Your Path" features, we will revisit those skills as they relate to the various concepts and topics discussed in each section. For this first discussion, though, our focus will be a bit more general. We start by reminding you of key knowledge-based concepts you need to know and be able to discuss.

"Big Picture" Economic Issues

One thing you need to keep abreast of are "big picture" economic issues. Suppose you are in a job interview and make a comment about how interest rates are rising, unemployment rates are falling, or the economy is growing. Assuming that you are correct in your comments, this can help reinforce the image that you are knowledgeable and informed; however, if you are wrong, then you may appear to be less informed. It is unlikely that anyone would expect you to know the exact prime lending rate from three months ago, but you still need to know basic trends. If you haven't taken any economics courses yet you will most likely do so as part of your degree program. These courses will help you strengthen your understanding of economic issues and what they mean for business.

Ethics and Social Responsibility

Ethics and social responsibility are very important in today's business world. As you begin your career, you need to do a candid self-assessment of your values, ethical standards, and stance on social responsibility and then be able to articulate them. You also need to be aware of how others see you in this context. For instance, you should be careful posting on social media. Some employers actually scan social media platforms about potential employees. No one will object to you having fun and sharing details with your friends. However, posting images of yourself engaged in questionable activities might harm your chances for the job. If you want to further develop your understanding of ethics many philosophy departments offer courses related to ethics and values. Perhaps you need to take an elective and such a course might both satisfy this requirement while also helping you better understand how ethics are formed and used in decision making.

New Ventures and Entrepreneurship

You may also start your career with a smaller firm and/or intend to launch your own business in the future. Therefore, you also need to be informed about how new and small businesses get started, how they grow, and why they succeed or fail. New ventures and entrepreneurship courses are becoming increasingly common (and popular), and some schools even offer a major (or minor) in entrepreneurship.

Global Issues

As we discussed in this chapter, the global context of business is more important today than ever before. Just as it is important to understand broad economic issues, so, too, is it important to be knowledgeable about the global economy as well as economic issues like the balance of payments and its impact on business. More specifically, if you are interviewing for a position in a company that has international operations, you should make sure you are familiar with those as well. While it is very unlikely that your first job will involve an international assignment, it is certainly possible that this will happen in the future. Many degree programs today require one or more courses in international or global business. Such courses can help you further develop your skills and understanding as they relate to global issues. In addition, you might also consider taking one (or more) foreign language courses as part of your education. Spanish and Chinese are especially popular—and important—today.

chapter 5

Managing the Business

Kzenon/Shutterstock

learning objectives

After reading this chapter, you should be able to:

5-1 **Describe** the nature of management and identify the four basic functions that constitute the management process.

5-2 **Identify** different types of managers likely to be found in an organization by level and area.

5-3 **Describe** the basic roles and skills required of managers.

5-4 **Explain** the importance of strategic management and effective goal setting in organizational success.

5-5 **Discuss** contingency planning and crisis management in today's business world.

5-6 **Describe** the development and explain the importance of corporate culture.

what's in it for me?

Sergey Brin and Larry Page, cofounders of Google, clearly are effective managers, and they understand what it takes to build a business and then keep it at the forefront of its industry. A manager is someone whose primary responsibility is to carry out the management process. In particular, a manager is someone who plans and makes decisions, organizes, leads, and controls human, financial, physical, and information resources. Today's managers face a variety of interesting and challenging situations. The average executive works more than 60 hours a week, has enormous demands placed on their time, and faces increased complexities posed by globalization, domestic competition, government regulation, shareholder pressure, and rapidly changing technologies. The job is complicated even more by rapid changes (such as recessions, financial crises, or the COVID-19 pandemic in 2020), other unexpected disruptions, exciting new opportunities, and both minor and major crises. The manager's job is unpredictable and fraught with challenges, but it is also filled with opportunities to make a difference. Good managers can propel an organization into unprecedented realms of success, whereas poor managers can devastate even the strongest of organizations.[1] After reading this chapter, you'll be better positioned to carry out various management responsibilities yourself. And from the perspective of a consumer or investor, you'll be able to more effectively assess and appreciate the quality of management in various companies.

In this chapter, we explore the importance of strategic management and effective goal setting to organizational success. We also examine the functions that constitute the management process and identify different types of managers likely to be found in an organization by level and area. Along the way, we look at basic management skills and roles and explain the importance of corporate culture.

pkchai/Shutterstock

Donisl/Alamy Stock Photo

Alphabet Soup

Sergey Brin and Larry Page met at Stanford University in 1995, where they were graduate students in computer science. Page was working on a software development project designed to create an index of websites by scouring for keywords and other linkages. Brin joined him on the project, and when they were satisfied that they'd developed something with commercial value, they tried to license the technology to other search companies. They couldn't find a buyer and instead focused on procuring enough investment capital to keep refining and testing their product, eventually building their idea, Google, into the world's largest search engine. In August 2015, the company was renamed Alphabet, Inc., and made Google a subsidiary. The name holds a dual meaning, both as a collection of letters that represent language and as a reference to the investment term *alpha* (returns above a benchmark). The strategy behind Alphabet as a parent was to allow the company to more easily and logically expand into domains outside Internet search and advertising, a division they called "Other Bets." Shortly after the reorganization, Brin and Page turned the helm of the Google subsidiary over to an up-and-coming star manager named Sundar Pichai.

Pichai grew up in a two-room apartment and earned his engineering degree in India before moving to the United States to attend Stanford University and then the Wharton School of Business, where he got his master of business administration (MBA) degree. He joined Google in 2004, where he led the product management and innovation efforts for Google Chrome. He went on to oversee the development of other applications, such as Gmail and Google Maps, and the Chromebook. In 2013, Brin and Page put him in charge of the Android operating system project. In each position, Sundar showed the ability to grow the product, reach new users, and maintain a focus on both quality and revenue to help drive Google's largest growth engine. While coworkers describe his style as low key, his technical skills and vision put him at the head of the line for promotions at Google. Even though his move into the CEO position represented a major leap, Pichai had been running many aspects of Google since October 2014.

Although Google is the company's big moneymaker, Brin and Page focus significant resources on research and development in other areas (Other Bets). Alphabet's semisecret research facility "X," also known as the "moonshot factory," focuses on innovative projects that may or may not pan out. The goal is simply to provide resources and freedom to some of the best and brightest dreamers in the world and to let their ideas develop into the reality of the future.

When projects reach a certain scale, they "graduate" from X to become stand-alone companies. Most, like the self-driving car project Waymo, join Alphabet's Other Bets. A few have been acquired by Google or spun out independently. Upon graduation, project leaders become executives, and employees are given a stake in the company. However, the transition is not always easy. Since Alphabetization, the original leaders of several X projects have either left or been replaced. The person who comes up with an idea and nurtures it through its infancy often isn't the right person to take it to the next level.

With Pichai leading the major moneymaker for Alphabet (still listed on the NASDAQ as GOOG), shares bumped the $800 mark at the end of 2016, making Alphabet worth over $578 billion (as measured by market cap, which is the price of the stock times the total number of shares outstanding). In late 2019, Brin and Page turned the entire organization over to Pichai, and they stepped down to pursue other interests. By December 2019, shares were trading at $1,339.39 and the market cap was just shy of a trillion dollars, making it one of the most valuable companies in the world. On July 18, 2022, the company split its stock 20:1, bringing the market price per share down to $112.76 from its pre-split price of $2255.34. Still, with nearly 13 billion shares outstanding, the market cap was nearly $1.5 trillion. A $1,000 investment back in 2004 when the company went public would have been worth almost $40,000 in May of 2023.

Brin and Page were remarkably successful at building a team of talented and creative employees, like Pichai, and providing them with a work environment and culture that foster the kind of productivity and innovation for which they were hired. But maybe the most important legacy the founders left was a strong guiding vision. As they wrote in the 2015 annual report:

> At Google, our innovations in search and advertising have made our website widely used and our brand one of the most recognized in the world. We generate revenues primarily by delivering online advertising that consumers find relevant and that advertisers find cost-effective. Google's core products such as Search, Android, Maps, Chrome, YouTube, Google Play and Gmail each have over one billion monthly active users. And we believe we are just beginning to scratch the surface. Google's vision is to remain a place of incredible creativity and innovation that uses our technical expertise to tackle big problems. Our Other Bets are also making important strides in their industries, and our goal is for them to become thriving, successful businesses in the long term.[2]

But Pichai doesn't have smooth sailing ahead. The company has been facing criticism over how it manages hate speech and extremist content spread online and how it deals with children's privacy on its YouTube video service. Recently, its employees have organized to protest what some claimed was a lack of action on sexual harassment by executives as well as Google's claims of political bias and intrusive data collection. More recently, in the midst of laying off 12,000 workers, Pichai's compensation package was $226 million, causing dissent in the ranks. (After studying this chapter, you should be able to answer a set of discussion questions found at the end of this chapter.)

The Management Process

Learning Objective 5-1

Describe the nature of management and identify the four basic functions that constitute the management process.

All corporations depend on effective management. Whether they run a multibillion-dollar business, such as Google or Apple, or a small local fashion boutique or corner taco stand, **managers** perform many of the same functions and have many of the same responsibilities. These include analyzing their competitive environments and planning, organizing, directing, and controlling the day-to-day operations of their business. Ultimately, they are also responsible for the performance and effectiveness of the teams, divisions, or companies that they head.

Manager *someone whose primary work responsibilities are a part of the management process*

Although we focus on managers in business settings, remember also that the principles of management apply to other kinds of organizations as well. Charitable enterprises, churches, the military, educational institutions, and government agencies all need to be managed and therefore need managers. The prime minister of Canada, curators at New York's Museum of Modern Art, the dean of your college, and the chief administrator of your local hospital are all managers (although they may have different titles, of course). Remember, too, that managers bring to small organizations much the same kinds of skills—the ability to make decisions and respond to a variety of challenges—that they bring to large ones. Regardless of the nature and size of an organization, managers are among its most important resources.

Basic Management Functions

Management *process of planning, organizing, leading, and controlling an organization's resources to achieve its goals*

Management itself is the process of planning, organizing, leading, and controlling an organization's financial, physical, human, and information resources to achieve its goals. Managers oversee the use of all these resources in their respective firms. All aspects of a manager's job are interrelated. Any given manager is likely to be engaged in each of these activities during the course of any given day. Consider the management process at Alphabet and Google. Sergey Brin and Larry Page founded Google shortly after graduating from Stanford and still control the company today through their majority ownership of its stock. To run the company to the owners' satisfaction, CEO Sundar Pichai must first create goals and plans that articulate what they want the company to accomplish. Then he relies on effective organization to help make those goals and plans reality. Pichai also must pay close attention to the people who work for the company, and keep a close eye on how well the company is performing. Each of these activities represents one of the four basic managerial functions: (1) setting goals is part of planning, (2) setting up the organization is part of organizing, (3) managing people is part of leading, and (4) monitoring performance is part of controlling (see Figure 5.1).

Planning *management process of determining what an organization needs to do and how best to get it done*

Planning

Determining what the organization needs to do and how best to get it done requires *planning*. **Planning** has three main components. It begins when managers determine the firm's goals. Next, they develop a comprehensive *strategy* for achieving those goals. After a strategy is developed, they design *tactical and operational plans* for implementing the strategy. We discuss these three components in more detail later in this chapter. Laxman Narasimhan is the newest CEO of Starbucks. He is responsible for developing strategies and strategic plans to keep Starbucks growing while simultaneously maintaining quality. He must also ensure that the firm's strategic, tactical, and operational planning efforts are all integrated and consistent with one another.

Organizing *management process of determining how best to arrange an organization's resources and activities into a coherent structure*

Organizing

Managers must also organize people and resources. For example, some businesses prepare charts that diagram the various jobs within the company and how those jobs relate to one another. These *organization charts* help everyone understand roles and reporting relationships, key parts of the **organizing** function. Some businesses go so far as to post their organization chart on an office wall. But in most larger businesses, roles and reporting relationships, although important, may be too complex to draw as a simple box-and-line diagram. Starbucks has over 32,000 coffee shops in more than 80 countries. In addition, the firm also owns the Evolution Fresh fruit and vegetable juice company, Ethos Water, and Teavana (tea-related products) and has myriad licensing

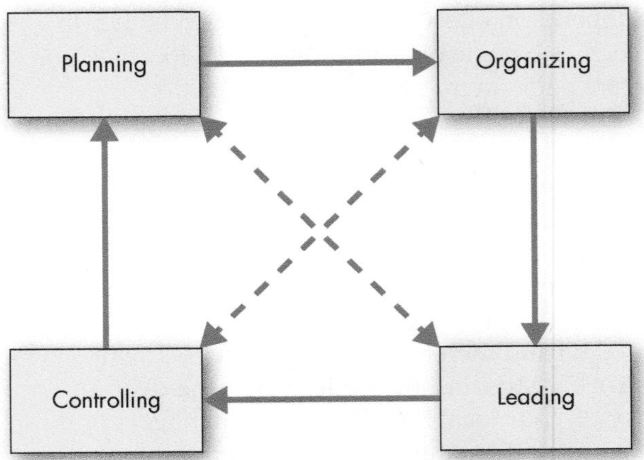

FIGURE 5.1 The Management Process

Marvin Ellison (CEO of Lowe's), Mary Barra (CEO of General Motors), and Tim Cook (CEO of Apple) are all senior managers responsible for overseeing the planning, organizing, leading, and controlling functions in their businesses.

and joint venture agreements with PepsiCo, Beam, and other companies. Narasimhan is responsible for creating and managing an organization structure for Starbucks to facilitate coordination across these various products and divisions and promote faster decision making. We explore organizing in more detail in Chapter 6.

Leading Managers have the power to give orders and demand results. Leading, however, involves more complex activities. When **leading**, a manager works to guide and motivate employees to meet the firm's objectives. Legendary management figures such as Walt Disney, Sam Walton (of Walmart), and Herb Kelleher (of Southwest Airlines) had the capacity to unite their employees in a clear and targeted manner and motivate them to work in the best interests of their employer. Their employees respected them, trusted them, and believed that by working together, both the firm and they as individuals would benefit. Laxman Narasimhan and his predecessor (and founder) Howard Schultz have both been very effective leaders at Starbucks. Starbucks was the first privately owned business to offer stock options to its employees, and among the first to provide benefits to part-time employees. The company has an excellent reputation for communicating with all of its employees, and those employees, in turn, generally hold Narasimhan in high regard. (Schultz was also widely admired when he was running the company.) Leading involves a number of different processes and activities, which are discussed in Chapter 9.

Leading *management process of guiding and motivating employees to meet an organization's objectives*

Controlling **Controlling** is the process of monitoring a firm's performance to make sure that it is meeting its goals. All CEOs must pay close attention to costs and performance. Managers at United Airlines, for example, focus on numerous indicators of performance they can constantly measure and adjust. Everything from on-time arrivals to baggage-handling errors to the number of empty seats on an airplane to surveys of employee and customer satisfaction are regularly and routinely monitored. If on-time arrivals start to slip, managers focus on the problem and get it fixed. If customers complain too much about the food, catering managers figure out how to improve it. As a result, no single element of the firm's performance can slip too far before it's noticed and fixed. At Starbucks, new products are generally tested in a limited number of coffee shops before they are rolled out on a large scale. But if products don't meet expectations and forecasts, the company is also willing to drop them.

Controlling *management process of monitoring an organization's performance to ensure that it is meeting its goals*

Figure 5.2 illustrates the control process that begins when management establishes standards, often for financial performance. If, for example, a company sets a goal of increasing its sales by 20 percent over the next 10 years, an appropriate standard to assess progress toward the 20-percent goal might be an increase of about 2 percent a year.

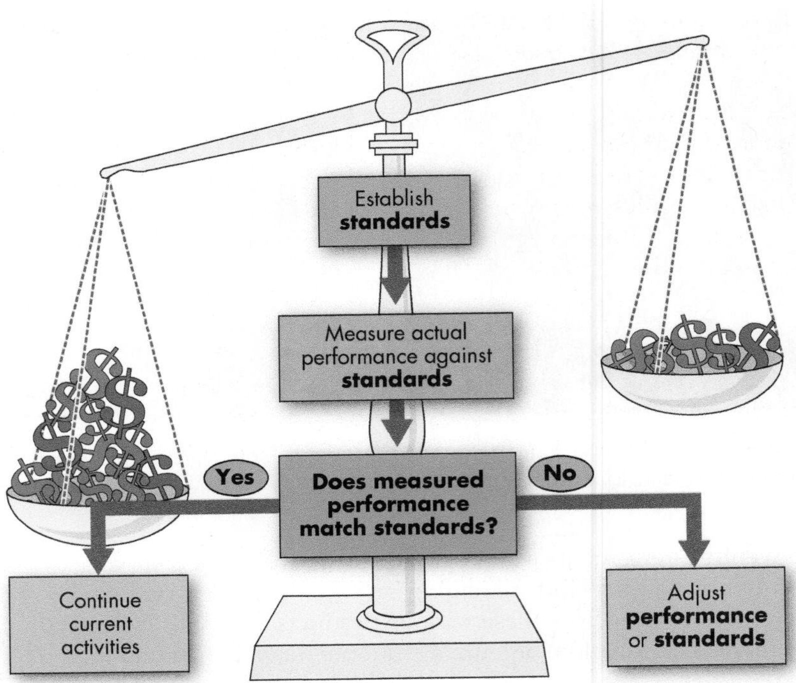

FIGURE 5.2 The Control Process

Managers then measure actual performance each year against standards. If the two amounts agree, the organization continues along its present course. If they vary significantly, however, one or the other needs adjustment. If sales have increased 2.1 percent by the end of the first year, things are probably fine. If sales have dropped 1 percent, some revision in plans may be needed. For example, managers can decide to lower the original goal or spend more money on advertising.

The Science and the Art of Management

Given the complexity inherent in the manager's job, one may ask whether management is more of a science or an art. In fact, effective management is a blend of both science and art. And successful executives recognize the importance of combining both the science and the art of management as they practice their craft.[3]

The Science of Management Many management problems and issues can be approached in ways that are rational, logical, objective, and systematic. Managers can gather data, facts, and objective information. They can use quantitative models and decision-making techniques to determine what seem to be the best course of action. They need to take such a scientific approach to solving problems whenever possible, especially when they are dealing with relatively routine and straightforward issues. When Starbucks considers entering a new market, its managers look closely at a wide variety of objective details as they formulate their plans. Technical, diagnostic, and decision-making skills (which we will discuss later in the chapter) are especially important when approaching a management task or problem from a scientific perspective.

The Art of Management Even though managers may try to be scientific as often as possible, they must frequently make decisions and solve problems on the basis of intuition, experience, instinct, and personal insights. Relying heavily on conceptual, communication, interpersonal, and time management skills, for example, a manager may have to decide among multiple courses of action that look equally attractive. During the 2020 COVID-19 pandemic, for example, many managers had to make decisions about closures and changes to operating procedures based on their intuition, and they relied heavily on personal judgment. And even "objective facts" may prove wrong. When Starbucks was planning its first store in New York City, market research clearly showed that New Yorkers preferred drip coffee to more exotic espresso-style coffees. After first installing more drip coffeemakers and fewer espresso makers than in their other stores, managers had to backtrack when New Yorkers lined up clamoring for espresso. Starbucks now introduces a standard menu and layout in all its stores, regardless of presumed market differences, and then makes necessary adjustments later. Thus, managers must blend an element of intuition and personal insight with hard data and objective facts.[4]

Becoming a Manager

How does one acquire the skills necessary to blend the science and art of management and become a successful manager? Although there are as many variations as there are managers, the most common path involves a combination of education and experience.[5]

The Role of Education Many of you reading this text right now are doing so because you are enrolled in a management course at a college or university. You are already acquiring management skills in an educational setting. When you complete the course (and this book), you will have a foundation for developing your management skills in more advanced courses. A college degree has become almost a requirement for career advancement in business, and virtually all CEOs in the United States have a college degree. MBA degrees are also common among successful executives today. In addition, most foreign universities offer academic programs in management.

Even after obtaining a degree, most prospective managers have not seen the end of their management education. Many middle and top managers periodically return to campus to participate in executive or management development programs, ranging in duration from a few days to several weeks. First-line managers also take advantage of extension and continuing education programs offered by institutions of higher education or through online media. A recent innovation in extended management education is the executive MBA program offered by many top business schools, in which middle and top managers with several years of experience complete an accelerated program of study on weekends.[6] Finally, many large companies have in-house training programs for furthering managers' education. Indeed, some firms have even created what are essentially corporate universities to provide the specialized education they believe is required for their managers to remain successful.[7] McDonald's, General Electric, and Shell Oil are among the leaders in in-house courses. Occurring alongside formal education routes is also a distinct trend toward online educational development for managers.[8]

Africa Studio/Shutterstock

Education plays a vital role in becoming a manager. Prospective managers usually complete at least one degree in business, taking courses in finance, marketing, accounting, management, and other areas.

The primary advantage of education as a source of management skills is that, as a student, a person can follow a well-developed program of study, becoming familiar with current research and thinking on management. Many college students can devote full-time energy and attention to learning. On the negative side, management education is often general and meets the needs of a wide variety of students; specific know-how may be hard to obtain. Further, although many aspects of the manager's job can be discussed in a book, it is hard to appreciate and understand them until you have experienced them.

The Role of Experience This book will help provide a solid foundation for enhancing management skills. Even if you were to memorize every word in every management book ever written, however, you could not then step into a top management position and immediately be effective. Why not? Management skills must also be learned through experience. Most managers advanced to their present positions from other jobs. Only by experiencing the day-to-day pressures a manager faces and by meeting a variety of managerial challenges can an individual develop insights into the real nature and character of managerial work.

For this reason, most large companies, and many smaller ones as well, have developed management-training programs for their prospective managers. People are hired from college campuses, from other organizations, or from the ranks of the organization's first-line managers and operating employees. These people are systematically assigned to a variety of jobs. Over time, the individual is exposed to most, if not all, of the major aspects of the organization. In this way, the manager learns by experience. The training programs at some companies, such as Procter & Gamble, General Mills, and Shell Oil, are so good that other companies try to hire people who have graduated from them.[9] Even without formal training programs, managers can achieve success as they profit from varied experiences. For example, Herb Kelleher was a practicing attorney before he took over at Southwest Airlines and led it to become one of the most successful and admired businesses in the United States. Of course, natural ability, drive, and self-motivation also play roles in acquiring experience and developing management skills.

The majority of effective managers learn their skills through a combination of education and experience. Some type of college degree, even if not in business administration, usually provides a foundation for a management career. The individual then gets a first job and subsequently progresses through a variety of management situations. During the manager's rise in the organization, occasional education "updates," such as management-development programs, may supplement on-the-job experience. Increasingly, managers also need to acquire international expertise as part of their personal development. As with general managerial skills, international expertise can be acquired through a combination of education and experience.[10]

Learning Objective 5-2

Identify different types of managers likely to be found in an organization by level and area.

Types of Managers

Although all managers plan, organize, lead, and control, not all managers have the same degree of responsibility for these activities. It is helpful to classify managers according to levels and areas of responsibility.

Levels of Management

The three basic levels of management are *top, middle,* and *first-line* management. As summarized in Table 5.1, most firms have more middle managers than top managers and more first-line managers than middle managers. Both the power of managers and the complexity of their duties increase as they move up the ladder.

Top Manager *manager responsible for a firm's overall performance and effectiveness*

Top Managers Like Laxman Narasimhan (Starbucks), Sundar Pichai (Alphabet), Bob Iger (Disney) and Jane Fraser (Citi), the fairly small number of executives who get the chance to guide the fortunes of most companies are top managers. Common titles for top managers include *president, vice president, treasurer, chief executive officer* (CEO), and *chief financial officer (CFO).* **Top managers** are responsible for the overall performance

table 5.1 The Three Levels of Management

Level	Examples	Responsibilities
Top managers	President, vice president, treasurer, CEO, chief financial officer (CFO)	• Responsible for the overall performance and effectiveness of the firm • Set general policies, formulate strategies, and approve all significant decisions • Represent the company in dealings with other firms and with government bodies
Middle managers	Plant manager, operations manager, division manager, regional sales manager	• Responsible for implementing the strategies and working toward the goals set by top managers
First-line managers	Supervisor, office manager, project manager, group leader, sales manager	• Responsible for supervising the work of employees who report to them • Ensure employees understand and are properly trained in company policies and procedures

and effectiveness of the firm. They set general policies, formulate strategies, approve all significant decisions, and represent the company in dealings with other firms and with government bodies. Mary Barra, chairman (the official title of the position of head of the firm's board of directors) and CEO of General Motors, is a top manager.

Middle Managers Just below the ranks of top managers is another group of managers who also occupy positions of considerable autonomy and importance and who are called *middle managers*. Titles such as *plant manager, operations manager*, and *division manager* designate middle-management slots. In general, **middle managers** are responsible for implementing the strategies and working toward the goals set by top managers.[11] For example, if top management decides to introduce a new product in 12 months or to cut costs by 5 percent in the next quarter, middle managers are primarily responsible for determining how to meet these goals. The manager of a Merck research lab or a regional sales manager of General Motors will likely be a middle manager.

Middle Manager *manager responsible for implementing the strategies and working toward the goals set by top managers*

First-Line Managers Those who hold such titles as *supervisor, office manager, project manager*, and *group leader* are **first-line managers**. Although they spend most of their time working with and supervising the employees who report to them, first-line managers' activities are not limited to that arena. At a building site, for example, the project manager not only ensures that workers are carrying out construction as specified by the architect but also interacts extensively with materials suppliers, community officials, and middle- and upper-level managers at the home office. The supervisor of lab technicians at a Merck research facility and the supervisor of a production line at a General Motors factory would be considered first-line managers.

First-Line Manager *manager responsible for supervising the work of employees*

Areas of Management

In any large company, top, middle, and first-line managers work in a variety of areas, including human resources, operations, marketing, information, and finance. For the most part, these areas correspond to the types of basic management skills described later in this chapter and to the wide range of business principles and activities discussed in the rest of this book.

Human Resource Managers Most companies have *human resource managers* who hire and train employees, evaluate performance, and determine compensation. At large firms, separate departments deal with recruiting and hiring, wage and salary levels, and labor relations. A smaller firm may have a single department—or even a single person—responsible for all human resource activities. (We discuss the key issues in human resource management in Chapter 10.)

Operations Managers As we will see in Chapter 7, the term *operations* refers to the systems by which a firm produces goods and services. Among other duties, *operations managers* are responsible for production, inventory, and quality control. Manufacturing companies such as General Electric, General Motors, and Caterpillar have a strong need for operations managers at many levels. Such firms typically have a *vice president for operations* (top manager), *plant managers* (middle managers), and *production supervisors* (first-line managers). In recent years, sound operations management practices have become increasingly important to a variety of service organizations.

Marketing Managers As we will see in Chapter 11, marketing encompasses the development, pricing, promotion, and distribution of goods and services. *Marketing managers* are responsible for getting products from producers to consumers. Marketing is especially important for firms that manufacture or sell consumer products, such as Under Armour, Frito-Lay, and Apple. Such firms often have large numbers of marketing managers at several levels. For example, a large consumer products firm is likely to have a *vice president for marketing* (top manager), several *regional marketing managers* (middle managers), and several *district sales managers* (first-line managers).

entrepreneurship and new ventures

Innovations in Management

In 2004, Sal Khan made a series of rudimentary instructional videos to help his cousin, Nadia, with some math problems. By the end of 2019, the Khan Academy website was drawing over 18 million unique visitors every month and had evolved into an international adaptive learning system providing free education to anyone with web access. When the COVID-19 pandemic closed classrooms in 2020, Khan Academy became a major resource for educating millions of students who had been asked to stay home. Going into 2020, the organization had partnered with 280 school districts, focusing on math, science, and SAT prep education.[12]

The platform's mission is to provide free, world-class education to anyone, anywhere. With 12.8 billion learning minutes logged by Khan Academy users in 2020, the platform saw a 300 percent increase from the previous year. Khan Academy consistently ranks among the highest-used and most-trusted resources by teachers, students, and parents, and it continues to develop new tools and offerings to support students where they need it most. In 2023, Khan Academy launched Khanmigo, an AI-based teaching assistant, partnering with classroom teachers to fine-tune the tool and its interface.[13]

In an interview with Stephen Meyer of *Forbes* magazine, Khan identified his three core management strategies:

1 ***Motivate managers by linking talent development to their compensation.*** Even though as a not-for-profit Khan Academy can't offer big bonuses and stock options, Khan pays well—commensurate with the upper quartile of Silicon Valley. He's a firm believer in rewarding good work with adequate pay, and the productivity of his team proves his point.

Jose Luis Cereijido/EPA-EFE/Shutterstock

2 ***Make it easier for managers by giving them tools.*** One of his goals is to create a library of internal videos that capture the Khan approach to every imaginable challenge, from how to read a financial statement to delegation, stating, "It would be very hypocritical if we're out there trying to make tools and resources for the rest of the world to learn, but we weren't doing that with our own people."

3 ***Set an example.*** Khan is just discovering management for himself. He'd rather be making videos and coding, but as the organization has grown, so has his role, and he's begun to develop a whole new generation of managers, leading and teaching by example.

Khan's perspective is that the role of management is mentoring rather than motivating. "It's an eighteenth- or nineteenth-century phenomenon to say the role of a manager is to get someone to do work," he explains. "That's wrong. The role of a modern manager is, 'How do I develop my people?'"[14]

Information Managers Occupying a fairly new managerial position in many firms, *information managers* design and implement systems to gather, organize, and distribute information. Huge increases in both the sheer volume of information and the ability to manage it have led to the emergence of this important function. Although still relatively few in number, the ranks of information managers are growing at all levels. Some firms have a top-management position for a *chief information officer* (CIO). Middle managers help design information systems for divisions or plants. Computer systems managers within smaller businesses are usually first-line managers. We'll discuss information management in more detail in Chapter 13.

Financial Managers Nearly every company has *financial managers* to plan and oversee its accounting functions and financial resources. Levels of financial management may include *CFO* or *vice president for finance* (top), a *division controller* (middle), and an *accounting supervisor* (first-line manager). Some financial institutions, such as Wells Fargo and State Farm Insurance, have even made effective financial management the company's reason for being. We'll discuss financial management in more detail in Chapters 14 and 15.

Other Managers Some firms also employ other specialized managers. Many companies, for example, have public relations managers. Chemical, pharmaceutical, and technology companies such as Dow Chemical, Merck, and HP have research and development managers. The range of possibilities is wide, and the areas of management are limited only by the needs and imagination of the firm.

Management Roles and Skills

Learning Objective 5-3

Describe the basic roles and skills required of managers.

Regardless of their levels or areas within an organization, all managers must play certain roles and exhibit certain skills if they are to be successful. The concept of a role, in this sense, is similar to the role an actor plays in a theatrical production. A person does certain things, meets certain needs, and has certain responsibilities in the organization. In the sections that follow, first we highlight the basic roles managers play and then discuss the skills they need to be effective.

Managerial Roles

Research offers a number of interesting insights into the nature of managerial roles.[15] Based on detailed observations of what executives do, it appears that many of their activities fall into 10 different roles. These roles, summarized in Table 5.2, fall into three basic categories: interpersonal, informational, and decisional.

table 5.2 Basic Managerial Roles

Category	Role	Sample Activities
Interpersonal	Figurehead Leader Liaison	Attending ribbon-cutting ceremony for new plant Encouraging employees to improve productivity Coordinating activities of two project groups
Informational	Monitor Disseminator Spokesperson	Scanning industry reports to stay abreast of developments Sending memos outlining new organizational initiatives Making a speech to discuss growth plans
Decisional	Entrepreneur Disturbance handler Resource allocator Negotiator	Developing new ideas and fostering innovation Resolving conflict between two subordinates Reviewing and revising budget requests Reaching agreement with a key supplier or labor union

Interpersonal Roles *a category of managerial roles, including figurehead, leader, and liaison*

Interpersonal Roles Three **interpersonal roles** are inherent in the manager's job. First, the manager is often expected to serve as a *figurehead*—taking visitors to dinner, attending ribbon-cutting ceremonies, and the like. These activities are typically more ceremonial and symbolic than substantive. The manager is also expected to serve as a *leader*—hiring, training, and motivating employees. A manager who formally or informally shows subordinates how to do things and how to perform under pressure is leading. Finally, managers can have a *liaison* role. This role often involves serving as a coordinator or link among people, groups, or organizations. For example, companies in the computer industry may use liaisons to keep other companies informed about their plans. This enables Microsoft, for example, to create software for interfacing with new Canon printers at the same time those printers are being developed. And managers at Canon can simultaneously incorporate new Microsoft features into the printers they introduce.

Informational Roles *a category of managerial roles, including monitor, disseminator, and spokesperson*

Informational Roles The three **informational roles** flow naturally from the interpersonal roles just discussed. The process of carrying out the interpersonal roles places the manager at a strategic point to gather and disseminate information. The first informational role is that of *monitor*, one who actively seeks information that may be of value. The manager questions subordinates, is receptive to unsolicited information, and attempts to be as well informed as possible. The manager is also a *disseminator* of information, transmitting relevant information back to others in the workplace. When the roles of monitor and disseminator are viewed together, the manager emerges as a vital link in the organization's chain of communication. The third informational role focuses on external communication. The *spokesperson* formally relays information to people outside the unit or outside the organization. For example, a plant manager at Dow Chemical may transmit information to top-level managers so that they will be better informed about the plant's activities. The manager may also represent the organization before a chamber of commerce or consumer group. Although the roles of spokesperson and figurehead are similar, one basic difference exists between them. When a manager acts as a figurehead, the manager's presence as a symbol of the organization is what is of interest. In the spokesperson role, however, the manager carries information and communicates it to others in a formal sense.

Decisional Roles *a category of managerial roles, including entrepreneur, disturbance handler, resource allocator, and negotiator*

Decisional Roles The manager's informational roles typically lead to the **decisional roles**. The information acquired by the manager as a result of performing the informational roles has a major bearing on important decisions that they makes. There are four decisional roles. First, the manager has the role of *entrepreneur*, the voluntary initiator of change. A manager at 3M Company developed the idea for the Post-it Note but had to "sell" it to other skeptical managers inside the company. A second decisional role is initiated not by the manager but by some other individual or group. The manager responds to the role of *disturbance handler* by handling such problems as strikes, copyright infringements, or problems in public relations or corporate image.

The third decisional role is that of *resource allocator*. As resource allocator, the manager decides how resources are distributed and with whom they will work most closely. For example, a manager typically allocates the funds in the unit's operating budget among the unit's members and projects. A fourth decisional role is that of *negotiator*. In this role, the manager enters into negotiations with other groups or organizations as a representative of the company. For example, managers may negotiate a union contract, an agreement with a consultant, or a long-term relationship with a supplier. Negotiations may also be internal to the organization. The manager may, for instance, mediate a dispute between two subordinates or negotiate with another department for additional support.

Ryan Miller/Getty Images

Managers play a variety of important roles. One key interpersonal role is that of figurehead. These managers, for example, are cutting a ribbon symbolizing the opening of a new business.

Basic Management Skills

In addition to fulfilling numerous roles, managers also need a number of specific skills if they are to succeed. The most fundamental management skills are *technical, interpersonal, conceptual, diagnostic, communication, decision-making*, and *time management* skills.[16] Global and technology skills are also becoming increasingly important.

Technical Skills

The skills needed to perform specialized tasks are called **technical skills**. A programmer's ability to write code, an animator's ability to draw, and an accountant's ability to audit a company's records are all examples of technical skills. People develop technical skills through a combination of education and experience. Technical skills are especially important for first-line managers. Many of these managers spend considerable time helping employees solve work-related problems, training them in more efficient procedures, and monitoring performance.

Technical Skills *skills needed to perform specialized tasks*

Human Relations Skills

Effective managers also generally have good **human relations skills**, skills that enable them to understand and get along with other people. A manager with poor human relations skills may have trouble getting along with subordinates, cause valuable employees to quit or transfer, and contribute to poor morale. Although human relations skills are important at all levels, they are probably most important for middle managers, who must often act as bridges between top managers, first-line managers, and managers from other areas of the organization. Managers should possess good communication skills. Many managers have found that being able both to understand others and to get others to understand them can go a long way toward maintaining good relations in an organization.

Human Relations Skills *skills in understanding and getting along with people*

Conceptual Skills

Conceptual skills refer to a person's ability to think in the abstract, to diagnose and analyze different situations, and to see beyond the present situation. Conceptual skills help managers recognize new market opportunities and threats. They can also help managers analyze the probable outcomes of their decisions. The need for conceptual skills differs at various management levels. Top managers depend most on conceptual skills, first-line managers least. Although the purposes and everyday needs of various jobs differ, conceptual skills are required in almost any job-related activity. In many ways, conceptual skills may be the most important

Conceptual Skills *abilities to think in the abstract, diagnose and analyze different situations, and see beyond the present situation*

ingredient in the success of executives in e-commerce businesses. For example, the ability to foresee how a particular business application will be affected by or can be translated to the Internet is clearly conceptual in nature.

Decision-Making Skills *skills in defining problems and selecting the best courses of action*

Decision-Making Skills **Decision-making skills** include the ability to effectively define a problem and to select the best course of action. These skills involve gathering facts, identifying solutions, evaluating alternatives, and implementing the chosen alternative. Periodically following up and evaluating the effectiveness of the choice are also part of the decision-making process. These skills allow some managers to identify effective strategies for their firm, such as Michael Dell's commitment to direct marketing as the firm's primary distribution model. But poor decision-making skills can also lead to failure and ruin. Indeed, poor decision making played a major role in the demise of such once major U.S. businesses as Montgomery Ward, American Motors, Lehman Brothers, Circuit City, and Enron and the decline of firms like Bed Bath & Beyond and Kodak. We'll discuss decision making more fully in Chapter 9.

Time Management Skills *skills associated with the productive use of time*

Time Management Skills **Time management skills** involve the productive use of time by managers. Suppose, for example, that a CEO is paid $2 million in base salary (this is not an especially large CEO salary, by the way!). Assuming that she works 50 hours a week and takes 2 weeks of vacation, our CEO earns $800 an hour—a little more than $13 per minute. Any amount of time that she wastes clearly represents a large cost to the firm and its stockholders. Most middle- and lower-level managers receive much smaller salaries than this, of course, but their time is still valuable, and poor use of it still translates into costs and wasted productivity.

To manage time effectively, managers must address four leading causes of wasted time:

1. ***Paperwork (both hardcopy and digital).*** Some managers spend too much time deciding what to do with letters and reports. Most documents of this sort are routine and can be handled quickly. Managers must learn to recognize those documents that require more attention.
2. ***Telephone calls.*** Experts estimate that managers get interrupted by their landline or cell phone every 5 minutes. To manage this time more effectively, they suggest having an assistant screen all calls and setting aside a certain block of time each day to return the important ones.
3. ***Meetings.*** Many managers spend as much as 4 hours a day in meetings. To help keep this time productive, the person handling the meeting should specify a clear agenda, start on time, keep everyone focused on the agenda, and end on time.
4. ***E-mail and SMS.*** Increasingly, managers are relying heavily on e-mail, SMS (short message service, or texts), and other forms of digital communication. Time is wasted when managers have to sort through spam and a variety of electronic folders, inboxes, and archives.

Global Management Skills Tomorrow's managers must equip themselves with the special tools, techniques, and skills required to compete in a global environment—in other words, they need *global management skills*. They will have to understand foreign markets, cultural differences, and the motives and practices of foreign rivals. They also must gain an understanding of how to collaborate with others around the world on a real-time basis.

On a more practical level, businesses will require more managers who are capable of understanding international operations. In the past, most U.S. businesses hired local managers to run their operations in the various countries in which they operated. More recently, however, the trend has been to transfer U.S. managers to foreign locations. This practice helps firms transfer their corporate cultures to foreign operations. In addition, foreign assignments help managers become better prepared for international

Shutterstock

Delegating tasks to competent, knowledgeable employees is a key skill managers must develop to protect their time for high-level decision making and strategic work.

competition as they advance within the organization. The top management teams of large corporations today are also likely to include directors from other countries.

Management and Technology Skills Another significant issue facing tomorrow's managers is technology, especially as it relates to communication. Managers have always had to deal with information. In today's world, however, the amount of information has reached staggering proportions. In the United States alone, people exchange hundreds of millions of e-mail messages every day; texting is also becoming increasingly prevalent.[17] Further, new forms of technology have added to a manager's ability to process information while simultaneously making it even more important to organize and interpret an ever increasing wealth of input and to develop effective *technology skills*.

Technology has also begun to change the way the interaction of managers shapes corporate structures. Elaborate networks control the flow of a firm's lifeblood—information. This information no longer flows strictly up and down through hierarchies. It now flows to everyone simultaneously. As a result, decisions are made quicker, and more people are directly involved. With e-mail, videoconferencing, and other forms of communication, neither time nor distance—nor such corporate boundaries as departments and divisions—can prevent people from working more closely together. More than ever, bureaucracies are breaking down, and planning, decision making, and other activities are beginning to benefit from group building and teamwork. We discuss the effects technology has on business in more detail in Chapter 13.

Strategic Management: Setting Goals and Formulating Strategy

Learning Objective 5-4

Explain the importance of strategic management and effective goal setting in organizational success.

As we noted previously, planning is a critical part of the manager's job. Managers today are increasingly being called on to think and act strategically. **Strategic management** is the process of helping an organization maintain an effective alignment with its environment. For instance, if a firm's business environment is heading toward fiercer competition, the business may need to start cutting its costs and developing more products and services before the competition really starts to heat up. Likewise, if an industry is globalizing, a firm's managers may need to start entering new markets and developing international partnerships during the early stages of globalization rather than waiting for its full effects.

Strategic Management *process of helping an organization maintain an effective alignment with its environment*

Goal *objective that a business hopes and plans to achieve*

Strategy *broad set of organizational plans for implementing the decisions made for achieving organizational goals*

The starting point in effective strategic management is setting **goals**—objectives that a business hopes and plans to achieve. Every business needs goals. Remember, however, that deciding what it intends to do is only the first step for an organization. Managers must also make decisions about what actions will and will not achieve company goals. Decisions cannot be made on a problem-by-problem basis or merely to meet needs as they arise. In most companies, a broad program underlies those decisions. That program is called a **strategy**, which is a broad set of organizational plans for implementing the decisions made for achieving organizational goals. Let's begin by examining business goals more closely.

Setting Business Goals

Goals are performance targets, the means by which organizations and their managers measure success or failure at every level. Different organizations, of course, pursue different goals, and the goals of any given organization change over time. At Lowe's, CEO Marvin Ellison is currently focusing on revenue growth, the firm's stock price, and new breakthroughs in the interface between retailers and customers. At General Motors, CEO Mary Barra's goals include keeping abreast of new developments in the areas of alternative fuels for motor vehicles and breakthroughs in autonomous driving technologies. And CEO Scott Kirby's goals at United Airlines are to continue to improve operational efficiency, revenues, and profits while also overcoming some of the negative imagery created by the firm's past lapses in customer service. Kirby is also focused on how to meet growing demand for air travel in the post-pandemic era.

Purposes of Goal Setting

An organization functions systematically when it sets goals and plans accordingly. An organization commits its resources on all levels to achieve its goals. Specifically, we can identify four main purposes in organizational goal setting:

1. ***Goal setting provides direction and guidance for managers at all levels.*** If managers know precisely where the company is headed, there is less potential for error in the different units of the company. Starbucks, for example, has a goal of increasing capital spending by 10 percent, with all additional expenditures devoted to opening new stores. This goal clearly informs everyone in the firm that expansion into new territories is a high priority for the firm.
2. ***Goal setting helps firms allocate resources.*** Areas that are expected to grow will get first priority. The company allocates more resources to new projects with large sales potential than it allocates to mature products with established but stagnant sales potential. Thus, Starbucks continues to invest in new store expansion but also is investing heavily in new technologies (such as automated brewing stations) and faster ways to get its products to customers (such as delivery-only locations), and its online initiatives are currently given a lower priority.
3. ***Goal setting helps to define corporate culture.*** For years, the goal at General Electric has been to push each of its divisions to first or second in its industry. The result is a competitive (and often stressful) environment and a corporate culture that rewards success and has little tolerance for failure. At the same time, however, GE's appliance business, medical technology, aircraft engine unit, and financial services business are each among the best in their respective industries. Eventually, the firm's CEO set an even higher company-wide standard: to make the firm the most valuable one in the world.
4. ***Goal setting helps managers assess performance.*** If a unit sets a goal of increasing sales by 10 percent in a given year, managers in that unit who attain or exceed the goal can be rewarded. Units failing to reach the goal will also be compensated accordingly. GE has a long-standing reputation for evaluating managerial performance, richly rewarding those who excel—and getting rid of those who do not.

Managers' performance is evaluated by their ability to set and then meet important goals. To understand their departments' effectiveness, managers closely track their actual results against goals and objectives.

Kinds of Goals Goals differ from company to company, depending on the firm's purpose and mission. Every enterprise has a purpose, or a reason for being. Businesses seek profits, universities seek to discover and transmit new knowledge, and government agencies seek to set and enforce public policy. Many enterprises also have missions and **mission statements**, statements of how they will achieve their purposes in the environments in which they conduct their businesses.

Mission Statement *organization's statement of how it will achieve its purpose in the environment in which it conducts its business*

A company's mission is usually easy to identify, at least at a basic level. Starbucks' new CEO Laxman Narasimhan recently reframed the firm's mission: "With every cup, with every conversation, with every community—we nurture the limitless possibilities of human connection."[18] But businesses sometimes have to rethink their strategies and mission as the competitive environment changes. As noted earlier, for instance, while Starbucks was once focused almost completely on traditional coffee shops it has shifted its focus a bit toward delivery and digital connectivity. The demands of change force many companies to rethink their missions and revise their statements of what they are and what they do.

In addition to its mission, every firm also has *long-term, intermediate*, and *short-term goals*:

- **Long-term goals** relate to extended periods, typically 5 years or more. For example, American Express might set a long-term goal of doubling the number of participating merchants during the next 10 years. Netflix might adopt a long-term goal of increasing its subscriber base by 10 percent during the next eight years.

Long-Term Goal *goal set for an extended time, typically 5 years or more into the future*

- **Intermediate goals** are set for a period of one to five years. Companies usually set intermediate goals in several areas. For example, the marketing department's goal might be to increase sales by 3 percent in two years. The production department might want to reduce expenses by 6 percent in four years. Human resources might seek to cut turnover by 10 percent in two years. Finance might aim for a 3 percent increase in return on investment in three years.

Intermediate Goal *goal set for a period of 1 to 5 years into the future*

- **Short-term goals** are set for perhaps 1 year and are developed for several different areas. Increasing sales by 2 percent this year, cutting costs by 1 percent next quarter, and reducing turnover by 4 percent over the next six months are examples of short-term goals.

Short-Term Goal *goal set for the near future*

After a firm has set its goals, it then focuses attention on strategies to accomplish them.

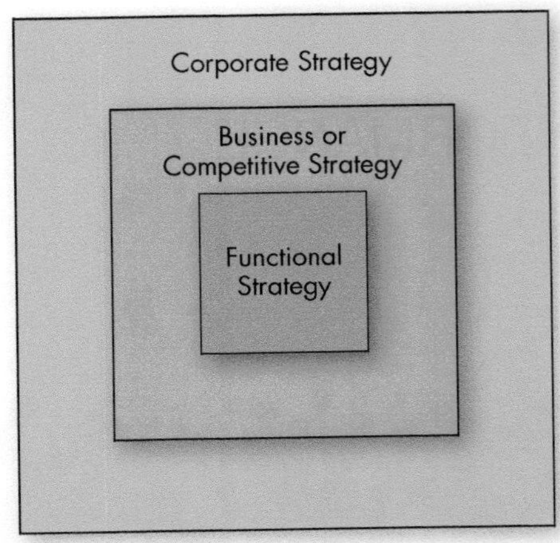

FIGURE 5.3 Hierarchy of Strategy
Source: Based on Thomas L. Wheelen and J. David Hunger, *Strategic Management and Business Policy*, 8th ed. (Upper Saddle River, NJ: Prentice Hall, 2002), 14.

Types of Strategy

As shown in Figure 5.3, the three types of strategy usually considered by a company are *corporate strategy, business* (or *competitive*) *strategy*, and *functional strategy*.

Corporate Strategy *strategy for determining the firm's overall attitude toward growth and the way it will manage its businesses or product lines*

Corporate Strategy

The purpose of **corporate strategy** is to determine what business or businesses a company will own and operate. Some corporations own and operate only a single business. The makers of WD-40, for example, concentrate almost exclusively on that brand. Other corporations own and operate many businesses. A company may decide to *grow* by increasing its activities or investment or to *retrench* by reducing them.

Sometimes a corporation buys and operates multiple businesses in compatible industries as part of its corporate strategy. For example, the restaurant chains operated by YUM! (KFC, Pizza Hut, and Taco Bell) are clearly related to one another. This strategy is called *related diversification*. However, if the businesses are not similar, the strategy is called *unrelated diversification*. Samsung, which owns electronics, construction, chemicals, catering, and hotel businesses, is following this approach. Pfizer's corporate strategy calls for maintaining a core of top-selling medical products while also investing in the search for new breakthroughs. One method Pfizer uses to develop new breakthroughs is buying shares of small companies that may be on the verge of discovering a new medical breakthrough.

Business (or Competitive) Strategy *strategy, at the business-unit or product-line level, focusing on improving a firm's competitive position*

Business (or Competitive) Strategy

When a corporation owns and operates multiple businesses, it must develop strategies for each one. **Business (or competitive) strategy**, then, takes place at the level of the business unit or product line and focuses on improving the company's competitive position. For example, at this level, General Motors makes decisions about how best to compete in an industry that includes Ford, Toyota, Volkswagen, and other automobile companies. In this respect, the company has committed heavily to expanding its product offerings and serving customers through new technology. The firm's Chevrolet division, for example, focuses on entry-level products that appeal to a broad array of customers, whereas the Cadillac division focuses more on luxury vehicles that appeal to more affluent customers. At the same time, GM is also investing heavily in technologies related to autonomous vehicles, electric vehicles, and how best to compete with newer entrants like Tesla and Rivian.

finding a better way

Frontline CEO

REUTERS/Alamy Stock Photo

In 2020, the COVID-19 pandemic turned offices into ghost towns and radically altered not only the way most companies conducted business but also the way they managed people. Gone were the days of weekly in-person meetings, conversations around the watercooler, and team lunches. Instead, workers were on digital platforms from their home offices, living rooms, and bedrooms. In April 2022, Airbnb CEO Brian Chesky sent out a company-wide memo outlining the company's new policy, *Live and Work Anywhere*.[19] In the memo, Chesky reported that in spite of the challenges of restructuring business and work-from-home policies, the company had experienced the most productive two-year period in its history: "In the last two years, we navigated the pandemic, rebuilt the company from the ground up, went public, upgraded our entire service, and reported record earnings, all while working remotely. It's clear that flexibility works for Airbnb." Chesky discussed the challenges of redesigning the company this way but said, "I trust you, and flexibility only works when you trust the people on your team."

Chesky went on to say that if Airbnb's mission was to hire and retain the "best people in the world," the company would need to look outside of a 50-mile radius from its headquarters in San Francisco. To further this mission, Chesky announced that the new policy regarding remote work would center around five main points:

1 You can work from home or the office.
2 You can move anywhere in the country you work in, and your compensation won't change.
3 You have the flexibility to travel and work around the world.
4 We'll meet up regularly for gatherings.
5 We'll continue to work in a highly coordinated way.

The policy, Chesky noted, did not mean that employees would only connect digitally. The company created a new division—Ground Control—whose responsibility was intentionally and thoughtfully bringing teams together for in-person meetings and events. As a general rule, employees would come together for a week at a time each quarter, and not always at company headquarters.[20]

The CEO of Airbnb did more than offer this flexibility to his employees—he embraced it himself, living in and working from a variety of Airbnbs for six months. Chesky found himself personally living the experiences of many of his customers, including exorbitant cleaning fees that only appeared after bookings, long lists of chores, and concerns about security. The result of his experiment was the launch of more than 50 upgrades, new features, and improvements in May 2023.

The experiment of the Live and Work Anywhere policy seems to have been successful as well. NPR reported in April 2023 that in the year after implementing its policy, Airbnb added 900,000 hosts, with 6.6 million hosts worldwide. Revenue has risen, and attrition is at an all-time low. The company also credits the policy for its boost in hiring women and underrepresented minorities, saying that the flexibility of the policy allows it to offer diverse benefits to a diverse workforce.[21]

Airbnb's chief is not the only one who has committed to being a "frontline CEO." According to a Harvard Business School study that reported only 3 percent of an average CEO's time is spent with customers, "Spending time with the rank and file and with savvy external frontline constituencies is an indispensable way to gain reliable information on what is really going on in the company and in the industry."[22] In an age of dramatic corporate culture shifts, Brian Chesky looked for inspiration from the people most directly impacted by his company's policies and actions.

Functional Strategy At the level of **functional strategy**, managers in specific areas such as marketing, finance, and operations decide how best to achieve corporate goals by performing their functional activities most effectively. At Apple, for example, each business unit has considerable autonomy in deciding how to use the single website at which the company has located its entire range of services. General Motors, meanwhile, develops functional strategies for marketing its vehicles and operations strategies for distributing them. The real challenges—and opportunities—lie in successfully creating these strategies. Therefore, we now turn our attention to the basic steps in strategy formulation.

Functional Strategy *strategy by which managers in specific areas decide how best to achieve corporate goals through productivity*

Formulating Strategy

Planning is often concerned with the nuts and bolts of setting goals, choosing tactics, and establishing schedules. In contrast, *strategy* tends to have a wider scope. By definition, it is a broad concept that describes an organization's intentions. Further, a strategy outlines how the business intends to meet its goals and includes the organization's responsiveness to new challenges and new needs. Because a well-formulated strategy is so vital to a business's success, most top managers devote substantial attention and creativity to this process. **Strategy formulation** involves the three basic steps summarized in Figure 5.4 and discussed next.

Strategy Formulation *creation of a broad program for defining and meeting an organization's goals*

Strategic Goal *goal derived directly from a firm's mission statement*

Step 1: *Setting Strategic Goals*—**Strategic goals** are derived directly from a firm's mission statement. For example, Disney continually focuses on expanding its dominance of the family entertainment industry. The company continues to invest in its existing properties (expanding its theme parks in Orlando with new rides and attractions, for example, in 2022 and 2023) and opening new theme parks (Shanghai in 2016, for instance). In addition, Disney has also made a number of strategic acquisitions in recent years, including Pixar, Marvel, Lucasfilm, and 21st Century Fox Entertainment. Each of these initiatives has allowed the firm to add to its revenue base and increase its profit.

Step 2: *Analyzing the Organization and the Environment: SWOT Analysis*—After strategic goals have been established, managers usually attempt to assess both their organization and its environment. A common framework for this assessment is called a **SWOT analysis**. This process involves assessing organizational strengths and weaknesses (the S and W) and environmental opportunities and threats (the O and T). In formulating strategy, managers attempt to capitalize on organizational strengths and take advantage of environmental opportunities. During this same process, they may seek ways to overcome or offset organizational weaknesses and avoid or counter environmental threats. Scanning the business environment for threats and opportunities is often called **environmental analysis**. Changing consumer tastes and hostile takeover offers are threats, as are new government regulations that will limit a firm's opportunities. Even more important threats come from new products and new competitors. For example, online music services such as Apple Music dramatically reduced consumer demand for CDs and CD players. Now, however, other streaming music services like Spotify and Pandora have emerged as threats to Apple Music. Likewise, the emergence of digital photography has dramatically weakened companies tied to print photography. Opportunities, meanwhile, are areas in which the

SWOT Analysis *identification and analysis of organizational strengths and weaknesses and environmental opportunities and threats as part of strategy formulation*

Environmental Analysis *process of scanning the business environment for threats and opportunities*

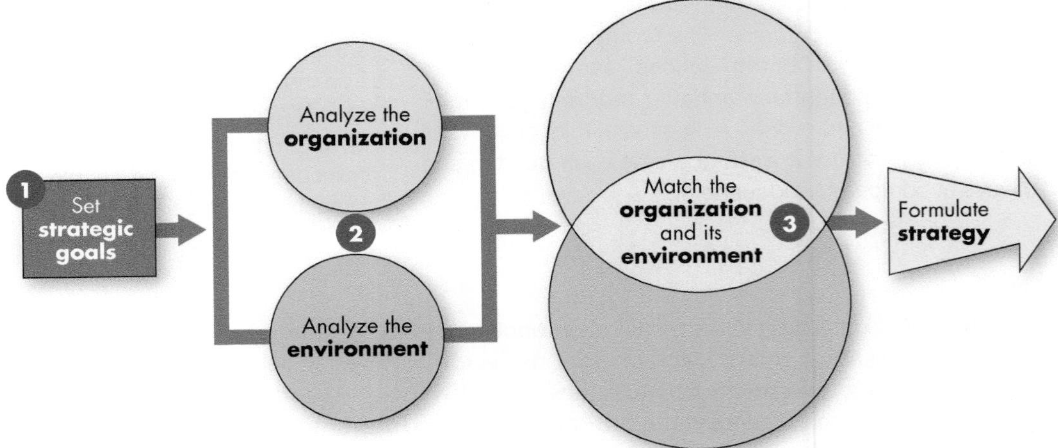

FIGURE 5.4 Strategy Formulation
Source: Adapted from Stephen P. Robbins and Mary Coulter, *Management*, 12th ed. (Upper Saddle River, NJ: Prentice Hall, 2014), 242.

firm can potentially expand, grow, or take advantage of existing strengths. For example, when Pepsi managers recognized the growing market potential for bottled water, they moved quickly to launch their Aquafina brand and to position it for rapid growth.

In addition to analyzing external factors by performing an environmental analysis, managers must also examine internal factors. The purpose of such an **organizational analysis** is to better understand a company's strengths and weaknesses. Strengths might include surplus cash, a dedicated workforce, an ample supply of managerial talent, technical expertise, or weak competition. For example, Apple's strength in new product innovation has helped facilitate the firm's consistent ability to both systematically introduce new products and modify and update existing ones. A cash shortage, aging factories, a heavily unionized workforce, and a poor public image can all be important weaknesses for any firm.

Organizational Analysis *process of analyzing a firm's strengths and weaknesses*

Step 3: *Matching the Organization and Its Environment*—The final step in strategy formulation is matching environmental threats and opportunities against corporate strengths and weaknesses. This matching process is at the heart of strategy formulation. That is, a firm should attempt to leverage its strengths so as to capitalize on opportunities and counteract threats. It should also attempt to shield its weaknesses, or at least not allow them to derail other activities. For instance, knowing how to distribute consumer products and pharmaceuticals (a strength) allows Pfizer to add new businesses and extend existing ones that use the same distribution models. But a firm that lacked a strong understanding of consumer product distribution would be foolish to add new products whose success relied heavily on efficient distribution.

Understanding strengths and weaknesses may also determine whether a firm typically takes risks or behaves more conservatively. Either approach can be successful. For example, Google's reputation as an innovator, its cadre of creative product designers and engineers, and strong cash reserves all allow the firm to constantly look for new product ideas and quickly test them in the market. In contrast, Apple has many of the same strengths, but because its products require longer design and manufacturing cycles, and in most cases more financial investment, the firm is more deliberate and systematic in rolling out new products.

A Hierarchy of Plans

After strategy has been formulated, it needs to then be translated into more operational language. This process generally involves the creation of actual plans. Plans can be viewed on three levels: *strategic*, *tactical*, and *operational*. Managerial responsibilities are defined at each level. The levels constitute a hierarchy because implementing plans is practical only when there is a logical flow from one level to the next (see Figure 5.5).

- **Strategic plans** reflect decisions about resource allocations, company priorities, and the steps needed to meet strategic goals. They are usually created by the firm's top management team but, as noted previously, often rely on input from others in the organization. So, the fundamental outcome of the strategic planning process is the creation of a strategic plan. General Electric's decision that viable businesses must rank first or second within their respective markets is a matter of strategic planning.

Strategic Plan *plan reflecting decisions about resource allocations, company priorities, and steps needed to meet strategic goals*

- **Tactical plans** are shorter-term plans for implementing specific aspects of the company's strategic plans. That is, after a strategic plan has been created, managers then develop shorter-term plans to guide decisions so they are consistent with the strategic plan. They typically involve upper and middle management. Dell's effort to extend its distribution expertise into the markets for televisions and other home electronics is an example of tactical planning.

Tactical Plan *generally short-term plan concerned with implementing specific aspects of a company's strategic plans*

- **Operational plans**, which are developed by mid-level and lower-level managers, set short-term targets for daily, weekly, or monthly performance. Starbucks, for instance, has operational plans dealing with how its stores must buy, store, and brew coffee.

Operational Plan *plan setting short-term targets for daily, weekly, or monthly performance*

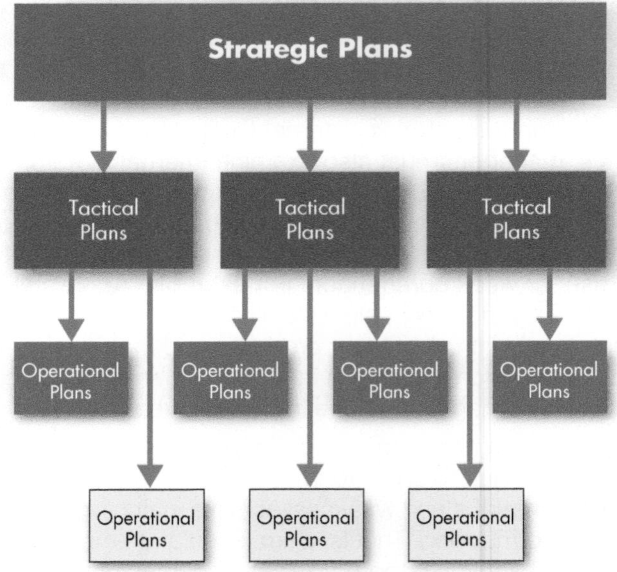

FIGURE 5.5 The Hierarchy of Plans

Learning Objective 5-5

Discuss contingency planning and crisis management in today's business world.

Contingency Planning and Crisis Management

Because business environments are often difficult to predict and because the unexpected can create major problems, most managers recognize that even the best-laid plans sometimes simply do not work out. For instance, security workers at Heathrow Airport in London (one of the world's busiest airports) announced dates to strike during the heaviest travel periods during the summer of 2023. Their strikes primarily targeted British Airways, the airline that dominates Terminals 3 and 5 at Heathrow. The issue was low wages. Because managers know such things can happen, they often develop alternative plans in case things go awry. Two common methods of dealing with the unknown and unforeseen are *contingency planning* and *crisis management*.

Contingency Planning

Contingency Planning
identifying aspects of a business or its environment that might entail changes in strategy

Contingency planning seeks to identify in advance important aspects of a business or its market that might change. It also identifies the ways in which a company will respond to changes. Suppose, for example, that a company develops a plan to create a new division. It expects sales to increase at an annual rate of 10 percent for the next 5 years, and it develops a marketing strategy for maintaining that level. But suppose that sales have increased by only 5 percent by the end of the first year. Does the firm (1) abandon the venture, (2) invest more in advertising, or (3) wait to see what happens in the second year? Whichever choice the firm makes, its efforts will be more efficient if managers decide in advance what to do in case sales fall below planned levels.

Contingency planning helps them do exactly that. To help cope with the 2023 summer strikes at Heathrow, British Airways redeployed 1,000 other employees, hired temporary workers, and re-routed some flights to Gatwick, London's other airport.

Disney also does a reasonably good job of contingency planning. Its theme park operations in central Florida, for example, have occasionally been forced to shut down temporarily in anticipation of hurricanes. When the COVID-19 pandemic hit in 2020, Disney was able to utilize many components of its existing weather-based contingency plans to systematically first close its theme parks and then its adjacent resorts.

Similarly, Disney was also able to then begin to plan for how and under what circumstances its resorts and theme parks would reopen.[23] And when the company decided to close a *Star Wars*–themed hotel near its Hollywood Studios theme park, announcements were made months in advance and reservations were halted to minimize the inconvenience for guests wishing to book a stay there.

Crisis Management

A crisis is an unexpected emergency requiring immediate response. **Crisis management** involves an organization's methods for dealing with emergencies. Seeing the consequences of poor crisis management after the California wildfires in 2020 and 2021, the Canadian fires of 2023, the impact of Hurricane Ida in 2021, and the Maui wildfires in 2023, many firms indicated their intent to create new and better crisis management plans and procedures. These plans focus on such things as terrorist threats, mass shootings, cybersecurity breaches, climate-driven disasters, and so forth.

Crisis Management *organization's methods for dealing with emergencies*

For example, both Reliant Energy and Duke Energy rely on computer trading centers where trading managers actively buy and sell energy-related commodities. If a terrorist attack or natural disaster were to strike their trading centers, they would

managing in turbulent times

When Data Disaster Strikes

A good strategic plan includes both contingency and crisis management planning that enables a company to recover from all kinds of external disasters like fire, flood, pandemic, computer or network failure, and data loss. While most businesses never see a fire outside their door, and even crises like the 2019 Australian wildfires or the 2020 pandemic, although catastrophic, are fairly rare, network failure and data loss are fairly common.

In September 2017, Equifax announced a data breach that exposed the personal information of 147 million people. The company agreed to a global settlement of $425 million to help people affected by the data breach and then extended the class-action lawsuit filing period to include losses incurred by consumers through 2023. That same year, in a supply-chain attack, hackers spread destructive malware in part by compromising the update mechanism for a legitimate Ukrainian accounting application. In May 2019, hackers stole photos of travelers and license plates from a surveillance contractor for U.S. Customs and Border Protection and posted the stolen data to the dark web. Criminals continue to target organizations with ransomware that encrypts a system's data and then demand a ransom to decrypt it—swindling victims of billions of dollars a year in the process.

A destructive strain called LockerGoga targeted industrial and manufacturing firms—at times forcing production plants to switch to manual control or inflicting long-term damage to systems that control physical equipment. American Medical Collection Agency (AMCA), a massive health care–related debt collector, suffered a data breach that spanned over 6 months from late 2018 through March 2019. The compromised information included first and last names, dates of birth, phone numbers, addresses, dates of medical services, health care providers, and data on balances due. Costs associated with the breach forced the company into Chapter 11 bankruptcy.

matejmo/iStock/Getty Images

The list of data breaches, infiltrations, and attacks goes on, and the costs are astronomical.

Not all data security incidents are breaches. Sometimes data are improperly stored and publicly accessible—they may not have been stolen, but they were still exposed. First American, the massive real estate and title insurance firm, exposed 885 million sensitive customer financial records, accidentally making the information accessible to anyone on First American's website. The data included Social Security numbers, driver's license images, bank account numbers and statements, mortgage and tax documents, and wire transaction receipts. Even the federal government is not immune to data breaches. In April 2023, an Air National Guardsman was arrested for sharing national secrets in a Discord chat.[25]

Security experts have long warned that the increasing number of devices connected to the Internet—the so-called Internet of Things—would present an enormous security issue, and as more and more people work from remote locations while accessing company networks, the risks are going nowhere but up.

essentially be out of business. Consequently, Reliant and Duke have created secondary trading centers at other locations. In the event of a shutdown at their main trading centers, these firms can quickly transfer virtually all their core trading activities to their secondary centers within 30 minutes or less.[24] However, many firms still do not have comprehensive crisis management strategies. For example, as the COVID-19 pandemic swept around the world in 2020, a survey found that only about 57 percent of U.S. businesses had plans in place to deal with such a viral or bacterial pandemic. As a result, many businesses had to make decisions on the fly and respond to events with a much greater sense of urgency than might have been the case had they had better plans in place.

Learning Objective 5-6

Describe the development and explain the importance of corporate culture.

Management and the Corporate Culture

Corporate Culture *the shared experiences, stories, beliefs, and norms that characterize an organization*

Every organization—big or small, more successful or less successful—has an unmistakable "feel" to it. Just as every individual has a unique personality, every company has a unique identity, or a **corporate culture**, the shared experiences, stories, beliefs, and norms that characterize an organization. This culture helps define the work and business climate that exists in an organization.

A strong corporate culture serves several purposes. For one thing, it directs employees' efforts and helps everyone work toward the same goals. Some cultures, for example, stress financial success to the extreme, whereas others focus more on quality of life. In addition, corporate culture helps newcomers learn accepted behaviors. If financial success is the key to a culture, newcomers quickly learn that they are expected to work long, hard hours, and that the "winner" is the one who brings in the most revenue. But if quality of life is more fundamental, newcomers learn that it's more acceptable to spend less time at work and that balancing work and nonwork is encouraged.

Building and Communicating Culture

Where does a business's culture come from? In some cases, it emanates from the days of an organization's founder. Firms such as Disney, Walmart, and Starbucks, for example, still bear the imprint of their founders. In other cases, an organization's culture is forged over a long period by a constant and focused business strategy. Pepsi, for example, has an achievement-oriented culture tied to its long-standing goal of "beating" its biggest competitor, Coca-Cola. Similarly, Google has a sort of "work hard, play hard" culture stemming from its constant emphasis on innovation and growth coupled with lavish benefits and high pay.

Corporate culture influences management philosophy, style, and behavior. Managers, therefore, must carefully consider the kind of culture they want for their organizations and then work to nourish that culture by communicating with everyone who works there.

To use a firm's culture to its advantage, managers must accomplish several tasks, all of which hinge on effective communication. First, managers themselves must have a clear understanding of the culture. Second, they must transmit the culture to others in the organization. Thus, training and orientation for newcomers in an organization often include information about the firm's culture. A clear and meaningful statement of the organization's mission is also a valuable communication tool. Finally, managers can maintain the culture by rewarding and promoting those who understand it and work toward maintaining it.

Changing Culture

Organizations must sometimes change their cultures. In such cases, they must also communicate the nature of the change to both employees and customers. According to the CEOs of several companies that have undergone radical change in the last decade or so, the process usually goes through three stages:

1. ***At the highest level, analysis of the company's environment highlights extensive change as the most effective response to its problems.*** This period is typically characterized by conflict and resistance.

Danita Delimont/Alamy Stock Photo

Sam Walton honed his craft as a retailer at Walton's Five and Dime. He then used his experience to create a unique corporate culture when he founded Walmart.

2 ***Top management begins to formulate a vision of a new company.*** Whatever that vision, it must include renewed focus on the activities of competitors and the needs of customers.

3 ***The firm sets up new systems for appraising and compensating employees who enforce the firm's new values.*** The purpose is to give the new culture solid shape from within the firm.

After Continental and United Airlines merged into a single, much larger airline, top managers developed a plan for creating one new unified corporate culture, drawing from the best of the cultures at the two individual airlines. The entire process took more than three years, although some employees say that the cultures have still not been completely integrated.[26] Similar problems and challenges arose during Tesla's acquisition of Twitter and Kroger's merger with Albertson's.

summary of learning objectives

LEARNING OBJECTIVE 5-1

Describe the nature of management and identify the four basic functions that constitute the management process.

Management is the process of planning, organizing, leading, and controlling a firm's resources to achieve its goals. *Planning* is determining what the organization needs to do and how best to get it done. The process of arranging resources and activities into a coherent structure is called *organizing*. When *leading*, a manager guides and motivates employees to meet the firm's objectives. *Controlling* is the process of monitoring performance to make sure that a firm is meeting its goals.

Effective management is a blend of both science and art. Many management problems and issues can be approached in ways that are rational, logical, objective, and systematic. Managers can gather data, facts, and objective information and use quantitative models and decision-making techniques to arrive at "correct" decisions. But even though managers may try to be scientific as often as possible, they must frequently make decisions and solve problems on the basis of intuition, experience, instinct, and personal insights.

The most common path to becoming a successful manager involves a combination of education and experience. A college degree has become almost a requirement for career advancement in business, and virtually all CEOs in the United States have a college degree. Management skills must also be learned through experience. Most managers advanced to their present positions from other jobs. Only by experiencing the day-to-day pressures a manager faces and by meeting a variety of managerial challenges can an individual develop insights into the real nature and character of managerial work.

LEARNING OBJECTIVE 5-2

Identify different types of managers likely to be found in an organization by level and area.

The three levels of management are top, middle, and first-line. The few executives who are responsible for the overall performance of large companies are *top managers*. Just below top managers are *middle managers*, including plant, operations, and division managers, who implement strategies, policies, and decisions made by top managers. Supervisors and office managers are the *first-line managers* who work with and supervise the employees who report to them.

In any large company, most managers work in one of five areas. *Human resource managers* hire and train employees, evaluate performance, and determine compensation. *Operations managers* are responsible for production, inventory, and quality control. *Marketing managers* are responsible for getting products from producers to consumers. *Information managers* design and implement systems to gather, organize, and distribute information. Finally, *financial managers*, including the chief financial officer (top), division controllers (middle), and accounting supervisors (first-line), oversee accounting functions and financial resources.

LEARNING OBJECTIVE 5-3

Describe the basic roles and skills required of managers.

Most managerial activities fall into 10 different roles. These roles fall into three basic categories: interpersonal, informational, and decisional. Three interpersonal roles inherent in the manager's job are *figurehead, leader*, and *liaison*. The three informational roles are *monitor, disseminator*, and *spokesperson*. The four decisional roles are *entrepreneur, disturbance handler, resource allocator*, and *negotiator*.

Effective managers must develop a number of important skills. Traditionally, five managerial skills have been identified: technical skills, human relations skills, conceptual skills, decision-making skills, and time management skills. *Technical skills* are skills needed to perform specialized tasks, including a programmer's ability to write code or an animator's ability to draw. *Human relations skills* are skills in understanding and getting along with other people. *Conceptual skills* refer to the ability to think abstractly, diagnose and analyze different situations, and see beyond the present. *Decision-making skills* include the ability to define a problem and select the best course of action. *Time management skills* refer to the productive use of time, including managing e-mail, telephone calls, and meetings. In the 21st century, several new skills have become increasingly important to managers. *Global management skills* include understanding foreign markets, cultural differences, and the motives and practices of foreign rivals. *Technology management skills* include the ability to process, organize, and interpret an ever increasing amount of information.

LEARNING OBJECTIVE 5-4

Explain the importance of strategic management and effective goal setting in organizational success.

Strategic management is the process of helping an organization maintain an effective alignment with its environment. It starts with setting *goals*, objectives that a business hopes (and plans) to achieve. Goal setting is vital to the organization for several reasons. Goal setting provides direction and guidance for managers at all levels. Goal setting also helps firms to allocate resources and define corporate culture. Finally, goal setting is essential to managers who wish to assess performance. Most companies will create mission statements and long-term, intermediate, and short-term goals.

Strategy refers to a broad set of organizational plans for achieving organizational goals. The three types of strategy usually considered by a company are *corporate strategy, business* (or *competitive*) *strategy*, and *functional strategy*. Formulating strategy involves setting strategic goals, analyzing the organization and its environment, and then matching the organization to its environment. Most organizations have a hierarchy of strategic, tactical, and operational plans.

LEARNING OBJECTIVE 5-5

Discuss contingency planning and crisis management in today's business world.

Companies often develop alternative plans in case things go awry. Two common methods of dealing with the unforeseen are *contingency planning* and *crisis management*. Contingency planning is planning for change. It seeks to identify in advance important aspects of a business or its market that might change. It also identifies the ways in which a company will respond to changes. Crisis management involves an organization's methods for dealing with emergencies.

LEARNING OBJECTIVE 5-6

Describe the development and explain the importance of corporate culture.

Every company has a unique identity called *corporate culture*: its shared experiences, stories, beliefs, and norms. It helps define the work and business climate of an organization. A strong corporate culture directs efforts and helps everyone work toward the same goals. Corporate culture can also help new employees learn acceptable behaviors. Managers must carefully consider the kind of culture they want for their organizations and then work to nourish that culture by communicating it with everyone who works there. If an organization must change its culture, it must communicate the nature of the change to both employees and customers.

key terms

business (or competitive) strategy **(p. 158)**
conceptual skills **(p. 153)**
contingency planning **(p. 162)**
controlling **(p. 145)**
corporate culture **(p. 164)**
corporate strategy **(p. 158)**
crisis management **(p. 163)**
decisional roles **(p. 152)**
decision-making skills **(p. 154)**
environmental analysis **(p. 160)**
first-line manager **(p. 149)**
functional strategy **(p. 159)**
goal **(p. 156)**
human relations skills **(p. 153)**
informational roles **(p. 152)**
intermediate goal **(p. 157)**
interpersonal roles **(p. 152)**
leading **(p. 145)**
long-term goal **(p. 157)**
management **(p. 144)**
manager **(p. 143)**
middle manager **(p. 149)**
mission statement **(p. 157)**
operational plan **(p. 161)**
organizational analysis **(p. 161)**
organizing **(p. 144)**
planning **(p. 144)**
short-term goal **(p. 157)**
strategic goal **(p. 160)**
strategic management **(p. 155)**
strategic plan **(p. 161)**
strategy **(p. 156)**
strategy formulation **(p. 160)**
SWOT analysis **(p. 160)**
tactical plan **(p. 161)**
technical skills **(p. 153)**
time management skills **(p. 154)**
top manager **(p. 148)**

questions & exercises

QUESTIONS FOR REVIEW

5-1. What are the roles and responsibilities of top, middle, and first-line managers?

5-2. What are the four basic functions of management? Briefly describe each one.

5-3. What are the three basic steps in strategy formulation?

5-4. What is corporate culture? How is it formed? How is it sustained? How does it relate to the corporate mission and vision?

QUESTIONS FOR ANALYSIS

5-5. Relate the five basic management skills (technical, human relations, conceptual, decision-making, and time management) to the four activities in the management process (planning, organizing, leading, and controlling). For example, which skills are most important in leading a company to success?

5-6. What are the differences between leadership and management? Give an example of each.

5-7. What contingencies would a major retailer of home improvement supplies need to consider in planning? How do you think the organization would address those risks?

5-8. Some business people claim that "culture trumps mission." What do you think that statement means and how would that affect the corporate strategy?

APPLICATION EXERCISES

5-9. Research a high-level manager of a well-known company by reading interviews or biographies. What are the strategies and skill sets that make that manager successful? How are that manager's background, education, and experience relevant to the job?

5-10. Critique three mission statements from various companies. Describe how the mission relates to vision, values, strategies, and culture. How effective do you think the mission statements are? How useful? How clearly do they reflect the identity of the company?

building a business: continuing team exercise

ASSIGNMENT

Meet with your team members and discuss your new business venture within the context of this chapter. Develop specific responses to the following:

5-11. What areas of management will be most important in your business? Will these change over time?

5-12. What basic management skills will be most important to your business? Will these change over time?

5-13. What are the specific business goals of your new venture?

5-14. For your venture, is there a difference between your corporate and business strategies?

5-15. Does your management team need to develop any contingency plans? Why or why not?

5-16. What sort of corporate culture do you want to create for your venture? What steps will you take to do so?

team exercise

DREAMS CAN COME TRUE

The Situation

Arturo Juarez has years of experience in the travel industry as a manager at a high-end hotel as well as sales director at a large travel agency. He is ready to start his own business, Dream Vacations, offering travel-planning services for individuals and families. His company will research destinations, hotels, and activities and help its customers make travel memories by providing top-notch service and creative solutions. To achieve this goal, Arturo is working to develop contracts with resorts in the Caribbean, South America, and the Mediterranean to get better pricing for his customers. He hopes that his business will grow at least 10 percent per year over the first five years through advertising and referrals. Initially, Arturo plans to operate out of office space in Atlanta, but his goal is to have offices in South Carolina, Alabama, and Tennessee within two years.

Team Activity

Arturo has asked for a team of students to provide him with assistance in getting his company going. Form a group of three to five students to provide guidance to Arturo.

ACTION STEPS

5-17. Working with your group and based on the information in the scenario, develop a draft mission statement for Dream Vacations. Why is developing a mission statement important?

5-18. Considering the mission statement of Dream Vacations and the information provided in the case, what are the company's long-term goals? How should Arturo measure these goals?

5-19. What intermediate goals will help Dream Vacations meet its long-term goals and realize its mission? What types of corrective action should Arturo take if the company fails to meet these goals?

5-20. Identify the short-term goals of Dream Vacations. Are short-term goals more or less important than long-term goals?

exercising your ethics

PEOPLE PROBLEMS

The Situation

You are the controller at a manufacturing company that sells refrigeration and food packaging equipment worldwide. Your company recently hired a temporary worker, Kelly, to help put a new international sales tax tracking system in place. She's well qualified, a hard worker, a team player, and highly effective at her job. You want to bring her on full time, so you have jumped through all the hoops and created a middle-management job for her that would put her on equal footing with her current boss, the accounting manager, Elizabeth (who reports to you). You are going to finish the process as soon as you get back from a week of vacation.

The Dilemma

While you were gone, Elizabeth obtained Kelly's résumé from the temp agency. She noticed some holes in the timeline and met with Kelly in a closed meeting. After the meeting, she had security escort Kelly out of the building and warned her not to return. She wrote a memo to you stating that in the interview, as she probed some of the discrepancies in the résumé and job application, Kelly revealed that she had struggled with alcohol issues when she was younger, but now she was 15 years clean and sober. Despite this, Elizabeth felt that Kelly's past made her unqualified for the job, and felt so strongly about it that she, Elizabeth, would resign if Kelly was brought back in any capacity. Elizabeth has been with the company for 20 years and runs the accounting department like a tight ship. In fact, it's one of the best departments in the company and always makes you look good in the management meetings.

QUESTIONS TO ADDRESS

5-21. What areas of management functions are involved in this scenario?

5-22. What are the ethical issues in this situation?

5-23. What is the logical, business-based approach for a manager to take in this situation? Explain your position.

5-24. What would you do and why?

5-25. How would you describe the culture of this company, based on the limited information in the scenario?

Cases

ALPHABET SOUP

Continued from page 143

At the beginning of this chapter, you read about how Alphabet's founders manage their employees and plan for the future. Using the information presented in this chapter, you should now be able to answer the following questions:

QUESTIONS FOR DISCUSSION

5-26. Describe examples of each of the management functions illustrated in this case.

5-27. Which management skills seem to be most exemplified in Sergey Brin and Larry Page?

5-28. What role have goals and strategy played in the success of Alphabet?

5-29. How do you feel about Sundar Pichai's $229 million salary? Explain why you feel the way you do and how you would address your concerns if you worked at Alphabet.

TEAM RED WHITE & BLUE

In high school, Mike Erwin was an athlete and student leader. That continued in college, where Erwin secured a nomination and enrolled at the U.S. Military Academy (USMA) at West Point. He thrived in the highly regimented program offered by the school. After graduating in 2002 with a degree in economics, he served three combat tours with the First Cavalry Division and 3rd Special Forces Group. He hoped to get his MBA after he came home from his third tour in Iraq and Afghanistan, but the military had other ideas and sent him to study psychology at the University of Michigan.

There, Erwin grew interested in the theory of positive psychology, a relatively novel discipline that involves studying the behaviors that lead people to report greater happiness, along with lives of purpose and meaning.

As a military man, Erwin had a realization. While there were many great nonprofit organizations set up to serve returning veterans, he couldn't point to one that sought to help modern veterans improve their lives according to the principles he was studying.

People were eager to "support the troops" who were returning from war by helping with career, financial, and health issues, but Erwin believed there was a deeper need. So he decided to try to fill the void. In the summer of 2010, Erwin started an organization he called Team Red White & Blue as an emotional gesture "to enrich the lives of America's veterans by connecting them to their community through physical and social activity." Rather than offering veterans a specific solution to a short-term problem, like helping them find jobs or lobbying the government for more generous veterans benefits, Team RWB created loosely organized communities to give veterans a sense of belonging, purpose, and physical achievement—one of the things that many veterans say they miss after leaving the armed forces.

It was actually a much simpler idea than it sounds. For Erwin, an avid runner, the natural first step was to organize communities of veterans to run in road races. "In 2011, it was just running," Erwin later recounted in a 2013 *Inc.* interview. "In 2012, it was running and triathlons and CrossFit. Now, it's running, rock climbing, swimming. Anything that increases your heart rate, we're there." By then, Team RWB had 24,000 members.

Erwin's enthusiasm and the organization's simple mission to enrich veterans' lives attracted media attention disproportionate to its size. With the acclaim, other veterans joined in to form new chapters and Fortune 500 companies kicked in sponsorship money. In short order, despite being resource constrained and having no paid employees, the organization grew beyond anything that Erwin had envisioned. Without any intention to do so, Erwin accidentally became an entrepreneur and the de facto Executive Director of the organization.

In 2013, one of the world's top consulting firms helped Team RWB develop a professional business and strategic plan. During that process, Erwin found himself ruminating on his place in the organization. He recognized that Team RWB needed to be professionalized in order to scale, and so, in early 2013, he stepped down as the ED and turned the reins over to his deputy director and longtime friend JJ Pinter, who was also a West Point graduate. Erwin continued to chair the board of directors until 2016 when he took some time off to teach, spend time with his family, and pursue other endeavors.

Fate called Erwin back to the directorship in 2019, when Pinter stepped down as the ED due to a family health crisis, and the board of directors asked Mike Erwin to return.[27] Under his leadership, by 2023, Team RWB had over 200,000 members and had reached almost 200 locations across the country.

QUESTIONS FOR DISCUSSION

5-30. As executive director (ED), how deeply do you think Erwin is involved in each of the four management functions? Briefly describe the types of decisions that he might make as they relate to each of the four functions.

5-31. The text describes a variety of skills that are essential to management. Which skills do you think are most important for Erwin as his organization grows?

5-32. How do you think leading and managing a not-for-profit organization (NPO) is different than leading and managing a for-profit organization?

5-33. What do you think were the critical elements that have led Team RWB to such success?

5-34. What role do you think the board of directors of Team RWB (see https://www.teamrwb.org/about-us/leadership/) play in leading and managing the organization? How is an NPO board of directors different than that of a for-profit company? How do you think the NPO board and the ED should interact?

endnotes

1 See Ricky W. Griffin, *Management*, 14th ed. (Boston: Cengage Learning, 2024).

2 Alphabet, *Annual Report 2015*, accessed April 1, 2020, https://abc.xyz/investor/static/pdf/2015_alphabet_annual_report.pdf.

3 Gary Hamel and C. K. Prahalad, "Competing for the Future," *Harvard Business Review*, July–August 1994, 122–128. See also Joseph M. Hall and M. Eric Johnson, "When Should a Process Be Art, Not Science?" *Harvard Business Review*, March 2009, 58–65.

4 James Waldroop and Timothy Butler, "The Executive as Coach," *Harvard Business Review*, November–December 1996, 111–117.

5 See Steven J. Armstrong and Anis Mahmud, "Experiential Learning and the Acquisition of Managerial Tacit Knowledge," *Academy of Management Learning & Education* 7, no. 2 (2008): 189–208.

6 "The Executive MBA Your Way," *Businessweek*, October 18, 1999, 88–92.

7 "Despite Cutbacks, Firms Invest in Developing Leaders," *Wall Street Journal*, February 9, 2009, B4.

8 "Turning B-School into E-School," *Businessweek*, October 18, 1999, 94.

9 See "Reunion at P&G University," *Wall Street Journal*, June 7, 2000, B1, B4, for a discussion of Procter & Gamble's training programs.

10 For an interesting discussion of these issues, see Rakesh Khurana, "The Curse of the Superstar CEO," *Harvard Business Review*, September 2002, 60–70.

11 Anneloes Raes, Marielle Heijltjes, Ursula Glunk, and Robert Row, "The Interface of the Top Management Team and Middle Managers: A Process Model," *Academy of Management Review*, January 2011, 102–126.

12 Khan Academy, "More Than 280 School Districts Enroll in Khan Academy, NWEA Mastery-Based Learning Offerings," Khan Academy Blog, December 8, 2021, https://blog.khanacademy.org/more-than-280-school-districts-enroll-in-khan-academy-nwea-mastery-based-learning-offerings/.

13 Khan Academy, "How Real-World Teacher Feedback Enhances and Improves Khanmigo, an AI-Powered Teaching Assistant," Khan Academy Blog, June 23, 2023, https://blog.khanacademy.org/how-real-world-teacher-feedback-enhances-and-improves-khanmigo-an-ai-powered-teaching-assistant/.

14 Stephen J. Meyer, "Salman Khan: The World's Best-Known Teacher Is Learning to Lead," *Forbes*, December 3, 2014; Web, December 16, 2016.

15 Henry Mintzberg, *The Nature of Managerial Work* (New York: Harper & Row, 1973).

16 See Robert L. Katz, "The Skills of an Effective Administrator," *Harvard Business Review*, September–October 1974, 90–102, for a classic discussion of several of these skills. For a recent perspective, see J. Brian Atwater, Vijay R. Kannan, and Alan A. Stephens, "Cultivating Systemic Thinking in the Next Generation of Business Leaders," *Academy of Management Learning & Education* 7, no. 1 (2008): 9–25.

[17] Stephanie Burns, "9 Clever Ways to Use Text Messaging in Your Business," *Forbes*, September 6, 2019, https://www.forbes.com/sites/stephanieburns/2019/09/06/9-clever-ways-to-use-text-messaging-in-your-business/#2d8a43ef2951.

[18] Heidi Peiper, "A New Mission for Starbucks," Starbucks Stories & News, April 24. 2023, https://stories.starbucks.com/stories/2023/a-new-mission-for-starbucks/.

[19] Airbnb, "Airbnb's Design for Employees to Live and Work Anywhere," February 7, 2023, https://news.tifrbnb.com/airbnbs-design-to-live-and-work-anywhere/.

[20] Rina Torchinsky, "Airbnb Will Let Its Employees Live and Work Anywhere," NPR, April 30, 2022, https://www.npr.org/2022/04/30/1095756450/airbnb-will-let-its-employees-live-and-work-anywhere.

[21] Andrea Hsu, "Airbnb Let Its Workers Live and Work Anywhere. Spoiler: They're Loving It," NPR, April 28, 2023, https://www.npr.org/2023/04/28/1172213330/airbnb-hybrid-remote-work-from-home-office-digital-nomad.

[22] Trey Williams, "What Airbnb's CEO Learned About Leadership After Living in Rentals for 6 Months," *Fortune*, May 4, 2023, https://fortune.com/2023/05/04/airbnb-ceo-brian-chesky-lessons-rentals/.

[23] "Disney Operations Shut Down; Focus Now on When (and How) to Re-open," WDW News Today, accessed March 18, 2020, https://wdwnt.com/.

[24] Del Jones, "Next Time," *USA Today*, October 4, 2005, 1B, 2B.

[25] Aric Toler, Malachy Browne, and Julian E. Barnes, "Airman Shared Sensitive Intelligence More Widely and for Longer Than Previously Known," *The New York Times*, April 21, 2023, https://www.nytimes.com/2023/04/21/us/politics/jack-teixeira-leaks-russia-ukraine.html.

[26] "Marriage at 30,000 Feet," *Bloomberg Businessweek*, February 6–February 12, 2012, 36–40.

[27] Bill Murphy Jr., "A Veteran Brings New Meaning to Coming Home," *Inc.*, November 12, 2013, https://www.inc.com/bill-murphy-jr/team-rwbs-goal-help-veterans-find-the-one-thing-they-want-most.html; Team Red White & Blue, "Founder and Former Chairman Returns to Lead Service Organization," November 5, 2019, https://www.teamrwb.org/team-red-white-blue-announces-mike-erwin-as-executive-director/; Character & Leadership Center, "About Mike Erwin," accessed September 10, 2020, http://characterleadership.center/about/.

chapter 6

Organizing the Business

NicoElNino/Shutterstock

learning objectives

After reading this chapter, you should be able to:

6-1 Discuss the factors that influence a firm's organizational structure.

6-2 Explain specialization and departmentalization as two of the building blocks of organizational structure.

6-3 Describe centralization and decentralization, delegation, and authority as the key ingredients in establishing the decision-making hierarchy.

6-4 Explain the differences among functional, divisional, matrix, and international organizational structures and describe the most popular new forms of organizational design.

6-5 Describe the informal organization and discuss intrapreneuring.

what's in it for me?

All managers need the assistance of others to succeed and so must trust the members of their team to do their jobs and carry out their responsibilities. The team members themselves need the support of their boss and a clear understanding of their role in the organization. The working relationship between managers and the people who report to them is one of the most critical elements of an organization. As you will see in this chapter, managing the basic frameworks that organizations use to get their work done, *structure*, is a fundamental part of the management process.

Imagine asking a child to build a castle with a set of Legos. She selects a few small pieces and other larger ones. She uses some red ones, some green ones, and some blue ones. When she finishes, she has her own castle, unlike any other. Another child, presented with the same task, constructs a different castle. He selects size pieces, for example, and combines them in different ways. The children's activities, choosing certain combinations of Lego pieces and then putting them together in unique ways, are in many ways analogous to the manager's job of organizing. Managers at similar companies competing in the same industries may create structures that are nearly identical to one another, completely different from one another, or somewhere in between.

Organizing is deciding how best to group organizational elements. Just as children select different kinds of Lego blocks, managers can choose a variety of structural possibilities. And just as the children can assemble the pieces in any number of ways, so, too, can managers put the organization together in many different ways. Understanding the nature of these building blocks and the different ways in which they can be configured can have a powerful impact on a firm's competitiveness.

By understanding the material in this chapter, you'll also be prepared to understand your "place" in the organization that employs you. Similarly, as a boss or owner, you'll be better equipped to create the optimal structure for your own organization. This chapter examines factors that influence a firm's organizational structure. We discuss the building blocks of organizational structure as well as the differences in decision making found among different types of organizations. Along the way, we look at a variety of organizational structures and describe the most popular new forms of organizational design.

Ground Picture/Shutterstock

Joshua Rainey/Alamy Stock Photo

Focus on Mission

In 1935, outdoor enthusiasts Mary and Lloyd Anderson were shopping for an ice axe in Seattle, and they could only find one at a ski shop for $20. Keep in mind that $20 in 1935 was the equivalent of about $440 in 2023. Mary decided to go directly to the Austrian source and procured the same axe for $3.50 (about $74 in 2023), including shipping. Word got out that the Andersons could get outdoor equipment at a reasonable price, and soon they had orders for more—and not just ice axes, but all kinds of hard-to-find outdoor equipment. In 1938 they got together with 21 of their friends and formed Recreational Equipment, Inc. (REI) to import and sell outdoor equipment using an unusual form of business called a cooperative, or co-op, where the business is actually owned by the customers.

With a $30 no-interest loan from the Andersons, the co-op set up at a local grocery store, using the Andersons' attic to store inventory. As sales and membership grew, Lloyd penned the co-op's mission, effective November 30, 1938:

> *Intent of the founders of this organization was to secure sufficient membership to make group buying possible; to distribute the goods with as little overheads expense as possible, using membership cooperation with the work as much as possible; to gradually build up a reserve for purchasing stock; to have the membership fee ($1.00) so that everyone interested will be financially able to join.*

Over the next eight decades, the company grew from an idea and a single shelf in a grocery store to 181 locations in 42 states and the District of Columbia. In 2022, REI paid $323 million in dividends to its 23 million members and reported $3.85 billion in sales. Despite its expansion from humble beginnings to an American icon, REI retains much of the spirit of the founders. It invested $6.9 million in 503 nonprofits and achieved climate neutrality by offsetting the equivalent of 320,300 metric tons of carbon dioxide.[1] And in 2023, you could get a membership for $20 and a quality ice axe for around $100.

Despite its size and unconventional ownership structure, the internal management structure is strikingly ordinary yet effective. Highly hierarchical, REI developed a divisional structure that allows regions to adapt by decentralizing the decision making to regional managers. Even so, REI's business units are also organized by function. These horizontal functions include things like marketing, finance, and human resources. For some companies, vertical hierarchies and decentralized decision making can dilute the mission of the company. Still, REI is a mission-driven organization with a focus on involvement in mission culture at all levels, from the CEO to the frontline employees. This helps the company keep the informal organization aligned with the formal organizational goals.

As the business grew, the mission statement evolved. In 2009, an employee bulletin reported that "REI's core purpose is to ' . . . inspire, educate and outfit for a lifetime of outdoor adventure and stewardship.' As a cooperative, everyone in the company and customers, producers, and suppliers, are invited into the mission of REI and asked to play a part in creating the unique REI experience."[2]

In 2023, the mission evolved: "We believe that it's in the wild, untamed and natural places that we find our best selves, so our purpose is to awaken a lifelong love of the outdoors, for all."[3]

Former CEO Jerry Stritzke said of the mission culture of REI: "It's a compelling competitive advantage, and as we look to the future, I think that idea of having a community organized around a shared passion—in this case, a love of a life lived outside—is really important."[4] As of 2023, REI has appeared on *Fortune* magazine's "100 Best Companies to Work for in America" every year since the list debuted in 1998. Employee benefits include an Employee Discount Program, Yay Days (paid time off to connect with the outdoors), Challenge Grants (funds toward personal recreation goals), professional growth and development, and tuition reimbursement, emphasizing the value upper management places on the employees and the outdoors and reinforcing the mission culture that still reflects the values of the founding members.

Both founders lived long enough to see their idea become a living legacy of their passion for the outdoors and for giving back to the community. Lloyd Anderson passed away in 2000 at age 98, and Mary Anderson died in 2017 at the age of 107. (After studying this chapter, you should be able to answer the set of questions found at the end of the chapter.)

What Is Organizational Structure?

Learning Objective 6-1

Discuss the factors that influence a firm's organizational structure.

One key decision that business owners and managers must address is how best to structure their organization. Stated differently, they must decide on an appropriate organizational structure. We can define **organizational structure** as the specification of the jobs to be done within an organization and the ways in which those jobs relate to one another.[5] Perhaps the easiest way to understand structure is in terms of an *organization chart*.

Organizational Structure *specification of the jobs to be done within an organization and the ways in which they relate to one another*

Organization Charts

Most small businesses create an **organization chart** to clarify structure and to show employees where they fit into a firm's operations. Figure 6.1 is an organization chart for Contemporary Landscape and Lawn Services, a small but growing business in a small Texas community. Each box in the chart represents a specific job. The solid lines define the *chain of command*. The **chain of command**, in turn, refers to *reporting relationships* within the company. In theory, such reporting relationships follow a "chain" from the highest level in the organization to the lowest. For example, the retail shop, nursery, and landscape operations managers all report to the owner and

Organization Chart *diagram depicting a company's structure and showing employees where they fit into its operations*

Chain of Command *reporting relationships within a company*

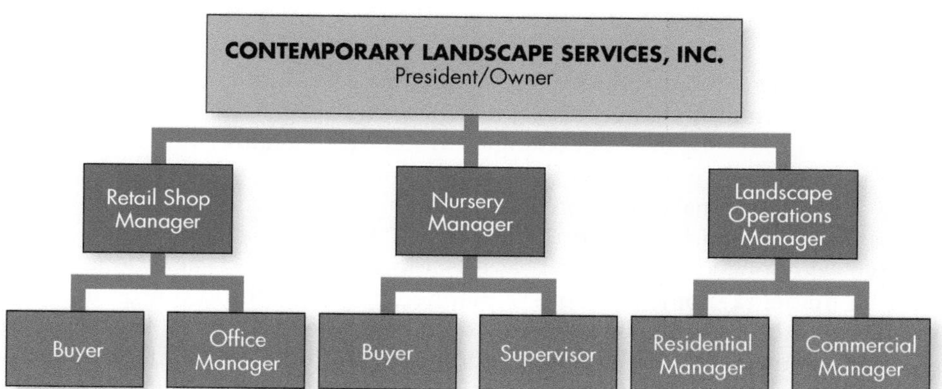

FIGURE 6.1 The Organization Chart

president. Within the landscape operation is one manager for residential accounts and another for commercial accounts. Similarly, other managers oversee the retail shop and the nursery.

The organization charts of large firms are far more complex and include individuals at many more levels than those shown in Figure 6.1. Size prevents many large firms from even having charts that include all their managers. Typically, they create one organization chart showing overall corporate structure, separate charts for each division, and even more charts for individual departments or units.

Recall our definition of organizational structure: the specification of the jobs to be done within an organization and the ways in which those jobs relate to one another. The boxes in the organization chart represent the jobs, and the lines connecting the boxes show how the jobs are related. As we will see, however, even though organizational structure can be broken down into a series of boxes and lines, virtually no two organizations will have the same structure. Further, as the nature of jobs continues to change, it becomes increasingly difficult to compartmentalize individual jobs. What works for Microsoft will not work for Google, JetBlue, ExxonMobil, Amazon, or the U.S. Department of Commerce. Likewise, the structure of the American Red Cross will probably not work for Urban Outfitters, Target, Starbucks, or the University of Nebraska. And organizations that make extensive use of teams may even have to use teams or groups rather than individual jobs as the basic building block of their structure.

Determinants of Organizational Structure

How is an organization's structure determined? Ideally, managers carefully assess a variety of important factors as they plan for and then create an organizational structure that will allow their organization to function most efficiently and effectively.

Many factors play a part in determining an organization's optimal structure. Chief among them are the organization's *mission* and *strategy*. A dynamic and rapidly growing business, for example, needs an organizational structure that allows it to be flexible, to respond quickly to changes in its environment and strategy, and to grow. A stable organization with only modest growth goals and a more conservative strategy will most likely function best with a different organizational structure, perhaps one less flexible and more focused on current business activities.

Size of the company and elements of the organization's environment also affect organizational structure. As we saw in Chapter 5, organizing is a key part of the management process. As such, it must be conducted with an equal awareness of both a firm's external and internal environments. A large services provider or manufacturer operating in a strongly competitive environment, such as American Airlines or HP (formerly Hewlett-Packard), requires a different organizational structure than a local hair salon or clothing boutique. Even after an organizational structure has been created, it is rarely free from tinkering—or even outright re-creation. Most organizations change their structures on an almost continuous basis. These changes are driven by decisions to achieve a better fit with the organization's shifting environment, changes in corporate and business strategies, actions taken by competitors, new technologies, and myriad other reasons.

Since it was first incorporated over a hundred years ago Ford Motor Company has undergone literally dozens of major structural changes, hundreds of moderate changes, and thousands of minor changes. In 1995, for instance, the firm announced a major restructuring plan called Ford 2000, which was intended to integrate all of Ford's vast international operations into a single, unified structure by the year 2000. By 1998, however, midway through implementation of the grand plan, top Ford executives announced major modifications, indicating that: (1) additional changes would be made, (2) some previously planned changes would not be made, and (3) some recently realigned operations would be changed again. In 1999, managers announced another set of changes intended to eliminate corporate bureaucracy, speed decision making, and improve communication and working relationships among people at different levels of the organization. Early in 2001, Ford announced yet more sweeping changes intended to boost the firm's flagging bottom line and stem a decline in product quality. More significant changes followed in both 2003 and 2004, and in 2006, the firm announced several plant closings, resulting in even more changes. Not surprisingly, yet another major reorganization was announced in 2010 as the firm sought to deal with a global recession and a major slump in automobile sales. In 2019, Ford indicated its intention to cease production of traditional sedans and focus more on energy-efficient and self-driving vehicles. These shifts in strategy will be accompanied by even more structural changes. Most recently, in 2022, Ford announced that it was going to structure itself into two basic units, one focused on gasoline-powered vehicles and the other focused on electric-powered vehicles.[6]

entrepreneurship and new ventures

Sometimes Flatter Is Better

In smaller entrepreneurial organizations, simple, flat organizational structures with very few top managers usually work well. Unlike more complex companies, a start-up entrepreneurial organization is often relatively unstructured and informal. The advantage of this structure is that decisions can be made quickly and the structure is flexible enough to adapt to a rapidly changing market. One drawback of a flatter structure, however, is that with very few top managers, decision making can quickly overwhelm day-to-day operations.

Perhaps one of the most iconic examples of a simple entrepreneurial structure is Valve Software, the company that created the *Half-Life*, *Counter-Strike*, and *Portal* video games series. Although Valve has over 800 employees, they have no designated managers. During the development of their iconic PC-based video game, *Half-Life*, the company created cross-discipline teams called "cabals" to design the final product and bring it to market.

Valve's structure has recently come under fire. In January 2023, gaming-news YouTube channel People Make Games interviewed current and former employees as part of an investigative report and compared the company's culture to *Lord of the Flies*.[7]

Valve's personnel are predominantly white males in a white male–dominated industry notorious for its lack of diversity. Since the teams themselves are responsible for hiring, it's not surprising that most of the new hires are also white males. Former employees and other critics note that the company's diversification has decreased over the course of its operation. These same teams are responsible for conducting employee evaluations and determining pay, and the report notes that the lack of accountability or clear management leads to vague merit systems and unfair pay divisions.

Valve continues to dominate the online gaming industry. In the same month as the People Make Games report was published, Steam, Valve's game distribution platform, broke records with over 10 million concurrent active in-game

Patrick Pleul/picture-alliance/dpa/AP Images

players and 32 million concurrent online users.[8] Valve is a privately owned company, famously secretive about its development and releases, with no obligation to be open to public scrutiny. It remains to be seen if the company's flat organizational structure will be able to effectively change its culture.

In an interview with *Bloomberg Businessweek*, Valve cofounder Gabe Newell explained it this way:

> When we started Valve [in 1996], we thought about what the company needed to be good at. We realized that here, our job was to create things that hadn't existed before. Managers are good at institutionalizing procedures, but in our line of work that's not always good. Sometimes the skills in one generation of product are irrelevant to the skills in another generation. Our industry is in such technological, design, and artistic flux that we need somebody who can recognize that. It's pretty rare for someone to be in a lead role on two consecutive projects.[9]

Even though the company has grown from a small entrepreneurial venture to a company with billions of dollars in revenue, it's still privately held and the organizational structure is still flat, and Newell hasn't expressed any intention to change that.

The Building Blocks of Organizational Structure

Learning Objective 6-2

Explain specialization and departmentalization as two of the building blocks of organizational structure.

The first steps in developing the structure of any business, large or small, involve three activities:

1. *Specialization.* Determining who will do what
2. *Departmentalization.* Determining how people performing certain tasks can best be grouped together
3. *Establishment of a decision-making hierarchy.* Deciding who will be empowered to make which decisions and who will have authority over others

These three activities are the building blocks of all business organizations. In this section, we discuss specialization and departmentalization. Because the decision-making hierarchy actually includes several elements, we cover it in more detail in the next section.

Job Specialization

Job Specialization *the process of identifying the specific jobs that need to be done and designating the people who will perform them*

The process of identifying the specific jobs that need to be done and designating the people who will perform them leads to **job specialization**. In a sense, all organizations have only one major job, such as making cars (Tesla), selling finished goods to consumers (Samsung), or providing telecommunications services (Verizon). Usually, that job is very complex in nature. For example, the "job" of Nucor Corporation is converting scrap steel (such as wrecked automobiles) into finished steel products (such as beams and reinforcement bars). Similarly, the "job" of American Airlines is to transport passengers and their luggage from one airport to another.

To perform this one overall job, managers actually break it down, or specialize it, into several smaller jobs. Thus, some workers at Nucor transport the scrap steel to the company's mills. Others operate shredding equipment before turning raw materials over to the workers, who then melt them into liquid form. Other specialists oversee the flow of the liquid into molding equipment, where it is transformed into new products. Finally, other workers are responsible for moving finished products to a holding area before they are shipped out to customers. At American, some specialists schedule flights, others book passengers, others fly the planes, and still others deal with passenger luggage and other cargo. When the overall job of the organization is broken down like this, workers can develop real expertise in their jobs, and employees can better coordinate their work with that done by others.

In a small organization, the owner may perform every job. As the firm grows, however, so does the need to add and specialize jobs so that others can perform them. To see how specialization can evolve in an organization, consider the case of The Walt Disney Company. When Walt Disney first opened his animation studio, he and his brother Roy were involved in everything. For example, when Walt Disney Studios created, *Steamboat Willie* the first cartoon the company distributed, they were the only coproducers. Walt cowrote the story and voiced Mickey Mouse. Both Disney brothers oversaw the animation, filming, music, and sound synchronization and then tackled the business of selling the cartoon to theater operators.

Today, however, a Disney animated feature is made possible only through the efforts of thousands of people. The job of one computer animator may be to create the face of a single character throughout an entire feature. Another specialist may be charged with coloring background images in certain scenes. People other than artists are responsible for the subsequent operations that turn individual computer-generated images into a moving picture or for the marketing of the finished product.

Job specialization is a natural part of organizational growth. It also has certain advantages. For example, specialized jobs are learned more easily and can be performed more efficiently than nonspecialized jobs, and it is also easier to replace people who leave an organization if they have highly specialized jobs. However, jobs

Some products can be made through either job specialization on mass production assembly lines or by skilled craftspeople doing intensive work. The bicycle maker on the left, for instance, is hand-crafting an expensive, custom bike while the workers on the right are using specialized jobs to mass produce less expensive bikes.

at lower levels of the organization are especially susceptible to overspecialization. If such jobs become too narrowly defined, employees may become bored and careless, derive less satisfaction from their jobs, and lose sight of their roles in the organization. These conditions, in turn, may prompt people to look for more interesting jobs elsewhere.

Departmentalization

After jobs are specialized, they are then grouped into logical units, a process known as **departmentalization**. Departmentalized companies benefit from this division of activities; control and coordination are narrowed and made easier, and top managers can see more easily how various units are performing. In larger firms, departments are usually called *divisions*.

Departmentalization *process of grouping jobs into logical units*

Departmentalization allows the firm to treat each department as a **profit center**, a separate company unit responsible for its own costs and profits. Thus, Macy's can calculate the profits it generates from the children's department, the home furnishings department, the luggage department, and every other department within a given store separately. Managers can then use this information in making decisions about advertising and promotional events, space allocation adjustments, budgeting, and so forth.

Profit Center *separate company unit responsible for its own costs and profits*

Managers do not departmentalize jobs randomly, of course. They group them logically, according to some common thread or purpose. In general, departmentalization occurs along *functional, product, process, customer*, or *geographic* lines (or any combination of these).

Functional Departmentalization

Many service and manufacturing companies, especially smaller ones just getting started, use **functional departmentalization** to create departments according to a group's functions or activities. Most new start-up firms, for instance, use functional departmentalization. Such firms typically have production, marketing and sales, human resources, and accounting and finance departments. Departments may also be further subdivided. For example, the marketing department might be divided into separate groups for market research, advertising, sales promotions, and social media.

Functional Departmentalization *dividing an organization according to groups' functions or activities*

Product Departmentalization

Both manufacturers and service providers often opt for **product departmentalization**, dividing an organization according to the specific product or service being created. This becomes especially true when a firm grows and starts to offer multiple products or services. The Kraft Heinz Company uses this approach to divide departments. For example, the Oscar Mayer division focuses on hot dogs and lunch meats, the Kraft Cheese division focuses on cheese

Product Departmentalization *dividing an organization according to specific products or services being created*

products, and the Maxwell House and Planters divisions focus on coffee and packaged nuts, respectively.[10] Because each division represents a defined group of products or services, managers at Kraft Heinz are able—in theory—to focus on *specific* product lines in a clear and defined way.

Process Departmentalization *dividing an organization according to production processes used to create a good or service*

Process Departmentalization Other manufacturers favor **process departmentalization,** in which the organization is divided according to production processes used to create a good or service. This principle is logical for Vlasic, which has three separate departments to transform cucumbers into either fresh-packed pickles, pickles cured in brine, or relishes. Cucumbers destined to become fresh-packed pickles must be packed into jars immediately, covered with a solution of water and vinegar, and prepared for sale. Those slated to be brined pickles must be aged in brine solution before packing. Relish cucumbers must be minced and combined with a host of other ingredients. Each process requires different equipment and worker skills, and different

finding a better way

The Evolving Structure of Spotify

When Daniel Ek and Martin Lorentzon launched Spotify on October 7, 2008, they knew they would have to go big and go fast, and to do that, the Stockholm partners would have to also go global. At the same time, the pair wanted to maintain the culture and mindset that had made the company successful so far.

By 2013, the company had 15 million subscribers, the staff had grown to 30 teams—each with 10 members—and they had already started to experiment with nontraditional ways of working together based on knowledge rather than strict accountability. Ek and Lorentzon started an agile process review—the same kind of process they would use to develop an app. The agile process incorporates elements of iterative development and continuous feedback. Rules and practices are kept to a minimum, and developers are empowered to collaborate and make decisions together as a group quickly and effectively.

The company was working from a heterarchy rather than a hierarchy. In a heterarchy, employees are unranked, but they can be organized and grouped using a variety of different characteristics.[11] The resulting organizational framework first grouped employees into small units, each with a clear mission, a set of principles, and a senior leader. Within each of these "mission groups" were smaller squads and chapters. Squads were mini start-ups that encouraged creativity and included cross-functional roles. Chapters shared the same manager and were meant to focus on personal growth and skills development by discussing shared challenges. Bridging these groups was a "guild" made up of employees with similar skills and interests who shared their coding experiences and knowledge.[12]

Andrew Testa/Shutterstock

As Spotify matured into a massive music marketplace, the groups and clusters developed into an N-form organizational structure with an emphasis on sharing knowledge across business activities. The N stands for "network" and denotes an organizational structure in which units representing different stages in the production process establish informal links with one another rather than joining together in a more traditional vertical integration. This organizational structure works well for the rapid development of new products and services by networking experts from across the organization. It also allows managers and executives to be highly involved in the development process. This organizational structure arises out of Spotify's corporate mission and vision, enabling a wide variety of employees to work together to continuously improve the quality of the music streaming service. In addition, Spotify's business model, generic competitive strategy, and intensive growth strategies drive the evolution of the company's structure.[13]

departments were created for each. Some service providers also use this approach as well. For instance, an automobile insurance company might use one department to receive claims from policy holders, another to review coverage, and another to issue payments.

Customer Departmentalization Larger multiproduct retail stores like Macy's and Walmart actually derive their generic name, department stores, from the manner in which they are structured—a men's department, a women's department, a luggage department, a lawn and garden department, and so on. Each department targets a specific customer category (men, women, people who want to buy luggage, people who want to buy a lawn mower) by using **customer departmentalization** to create departments that offer products and meet the needs of identifiable customer groups. Thus, a customer shopping for a baby's crib at Walmart can bypass lawn and garden supplies and head straight for children's furniture. In general, the store is more efficient, and customers get better service because salespeople tend to specialize and gain expertise in their departments. Another illustration of customer departmentalization is reflected in most banks. An individual wanting a consumer loan goes to the retail banking office, whereas a small business owner goes to the commercial banking office and a farmer goes to the agricultural loan department.

Customer Departmentalization *dividing an organization to offer products and meet needs for identifiable customer groups*

Geographic Departmentalization **Geographic departmentalization** divides firms according to the areas of the country or the world that they serve. Levi Strauss, for instance, has one division for North and South America; one for Europe, the Middle East, and North Africa; and one for the Asia Pacific region.[14] Within the United States, geographic departmentalization is common among utilities. For example, Southern Company organizes its power subsidiaries into four geographic departments—Alabama, Georgia, Gulf, and Mississippi Power.

Geographic Departmentalization *dividing an organization according to the areas of the country or the world served by a business*

Multiple Forms of Departmentalization Because different forms of departmentalization have different advantages, as firms grow in size they tend to adopt different types of departmentalization for various levels. The company illustrated in Figure 6.2 uses functional departmentalization at the top level. At the middle level, production is divided along geographic lines. At a lower level, marketing is departmentalized by product group. Larger firms are virtually certain to use all of these different forms of departmentalization in various areas.

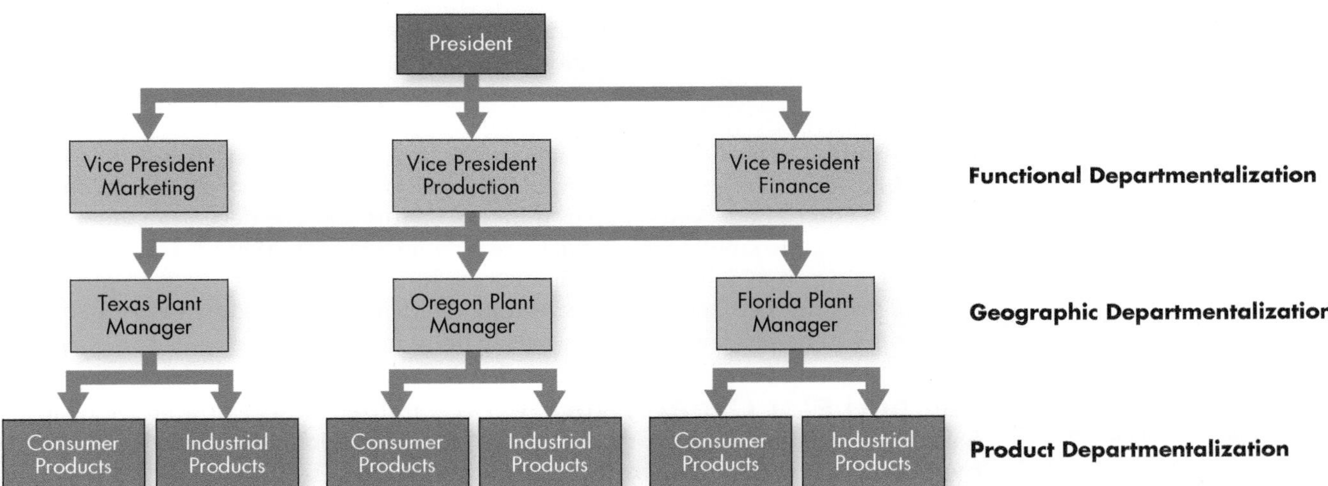

FIGURE 6.2 Multiple Forms of Departmentalization

Establishing the Decision-Making Hierarchy

Learning Objective 6-3

Describe centralization and decentralization, delegation, and authority as the key ingredients in establishing the decision-making hierarchy.

The third major building block of organizational structure is the establishment of a decision-making hierarchy. This is usually done by formalizing reporting relationships. When the focus is on the reporting relationships among individual managers and the people who report to them, it is most commonly referred to as *delegation*. However, when the focus is on the overall organization, it becomes a question of decentralization versus *centralization*.

Distributing Authority: Centralization and Decentralization

Some managers make the conscious decision to retain as much decision-making authority as possible at the higher levels of the organizational structure; others decide to push authority as far down the hierarchy as possible. Although we can think of these two extremes as anchoring a continuum, most companies fall somewhere between the middle of such a continuum and one end point or the other.

Centralized Organization
organization in which most decision-making authority is held by upper-level management

Centralized Organizations In a **centralized organization**, most decision-making authority is held by upper-level managers.[15] McDonald's practices centralization as a way to maintain standardization. All restaurants must follow precise steps in buying products and making and packaging menu items. Most advertising is handled at the corporate level, and any local advertising must be approved by a regional manager. Restaurants even have to follow prescribed schedules for facilities' maintenance and upgrades such as floor polishing and parking lot cleaning. Centralized authority is most commonly found in companies that face relatively stable and predictable environments and is also typical of small businesses. During times of uncertainty, businesses have a tendency to move toward greater degrees of centralization. As the COVID-19 pandemic spread around the globe in 2020, many businesses moved all their major decision-making authority to their corporate headquarters.

Decentralized Organization
organization in which a great deal of decision-making authority is delegated to levels of management at points below the top

Decentralized Organizations As a company gets larger and more decisions must be made, the company tends to adopt **decentralized organization**, in which much decision-making authority is delegated to levels of management at various points below the top. Decentralization is typical in firms that have complex and dynamic environmental conditions. It is also common in businesses that specialize in customer services. Decentralization makes a company more responsive by allowing managers increased discretion to make quick decisions in their areas of responsibility. For example, Urban Outfitters practices relative decentralization in that it allows individual store managers considerable discretion over merchandising and product displays. Whole Foods Market takes things even further in its decentralization. Stores are broken up into small teams, which are responsible for making decisions on issues such as voting on which new staff members to hire and which products to carry based on local preferences. This practice taps into the idea that the people who will be most affected by decisions should be the ones making them.[16]

Flat Organizational Structure
characteristic of decentralized companies with relatively few layers of management

Tall Organizational Structure
characteristic of centralized companies with multiple layers of management

Tall and Flat Organizations Decentralized firms tend to have relatively fewer layers of management, resulting in a **flat organizational structure** like that of the hypothetical law firm shown in Figure 6.3(a). Centralized firms typically require multiple layers of management and thus have **tall organizational structures**, as in the U.S. Army example in Figure 6.3(b). Because information, whether upward or downward bound, must pass through so many organizational layers, tall structures are prone to delays in information flow.

As organizations grow in size, it is both normal and necessary for them to become at least somewhat taller. For instance, a small firm with only an owner-manager and a few employees is likely to have two layers: the owner-manager and the employees who report to that person. As the firm grows, more layers will be needed. In general, managers should ensure that they have only the number of layers the firm needs. Too few layers can create chaos and inefficiency, whereas too many layers can create rigidity and bureaucracy. Many governmental organizations have relatively tall structures. Quicken Loans, in contrast, works consistently to keep its structure flat so that decisions can be made based on local needs and situations.

Span of Control As you can see in Figure 6.3, the distribution of authority in an organization also affects the number of people who work for any individual manager. In a flat organizational structure, the number of people directly managed by one supervisor, the manager's **span of control**, is usually wide. In tall organizations, span of control tends to be narrower. Employees' abilities and the supervisor's managerial skills influence how wide or narrow the span of control should be, as do the similarity and simplicity of tasks and the extent to which they are interrelated.

Span of Control *number of people supervised by one manager*

If lower-level managers are given more decision-making authority, their supervisors will have fewer responsibilities and may then be able to take on a widened span of control. Similarly, when several employees perform either the same simple task or a group of interrelated tasks, a wide span of control is possible and often desirable. For instance, because of the routine and interdependent nature of jobs on an assembly line, one supervisor may well control the entire line.

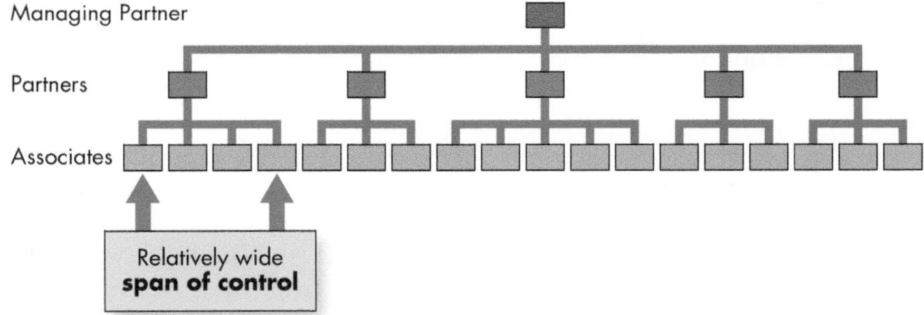

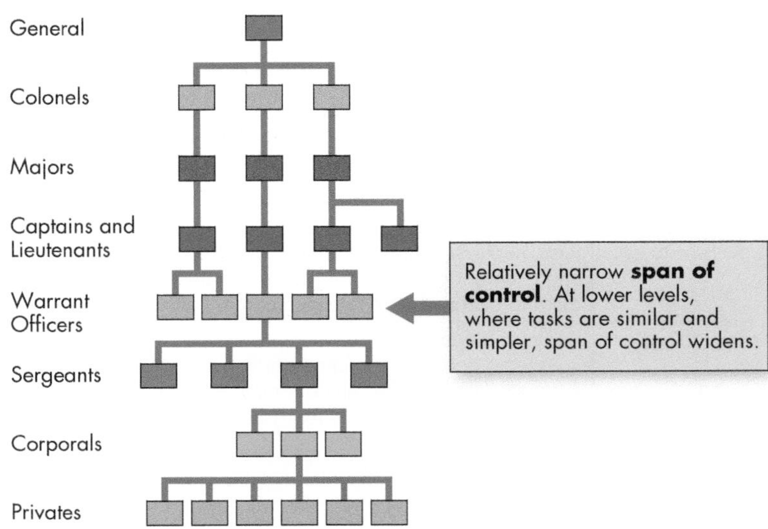

FIGURE 6.3 Organizational Structures and Span of Control

In contrast, when jobs are more diversified or prone to change, a narrow span of control is preferable. Consider how Electronic Arts develops video games. Design, art, audio, and software development teams have specialized jobs whose products must come together in the end to create a coherent game. Although related, the complexities involved with and the advanced skills required by each job mean that one manager can oversee only a small number of employees.

The Delegation Process

Delegation *process through which a manager allocates work to subordinates*

Responsibility *duty to perform an assigned task*

Authority *power to make the decisions necessary to complete a task*

Accountability *obligation employees have to their manager for the successful completion of an assigned task*

Delegation is the process through which a manager allocates work to subordinates. In general, the delegation process involves the following:

1. Assigning **responsibility**, the duty to perform an assigned task.
2. Granting **authority**, or the power to make the decisions necessary to complete the task.
3. Creating **accountability**, the obligation employees have for the successful completion of the task.

For the delegation process to work smoothly, responsibility and authority must be equivalent. Table 6.1 lists some common obstacles that hinder the delegation process, along with strategies for overcoming them.

Three Forms of Authority

As individuals are delegated responsibility and authority, a complex web of interactions develops in the forms of *line, staff,* and *committee and team* authorities.

Line Authority *organizational structure in which authority flows in a direct chain of command from the top of the company to the bottom*

Line Department *department directly linked to the production and sales of a specific product*

Line Authority The type of authority that flows up and down the chain of command is **line authority**. Most companies rely heavily on **line departments** linked directly to the production and sales of specific products. For example, in the division of Clark Equipment that produces forklifts and small earthmovers, line departments include purchasing, materials handling, fabrication, painting, and assembly (all of which are directly linked to production) along with sales and distribution (both of which are directly linked to sales).

As the doers and producers, each line department is essential to an organization's ability to sell and deliver finished goods. A bad decision by the manager in one department can hold up production for an entire plant. For example, suppose the painting department manager at Clark Equipment changes a paint application on a batch of forklifts, which then show signs of peeling paint. The batch will have to be repainted (and perhaps partially reassembled) before the machines can be shipped.

table 6.1 Learning to Delegate Effectively

I'm afraid to delegate because . . .	Solution
My team doesn't know how to get the job done.	If members of your team are exhibiting opportunities for improved performance, offer them the training necessary for them to become more effective at their jobs.
I like controlling as many things as possible.	Recognize that trying to accomplish everything yourself while your team does nothing only sets you up for burnout and failure. As you begin to relinquish control, you will come to trust your team more as you watch your team members succeed.
I don't want anyone on my team outperforming me.	High-performing team members are a reflection of your success as a manager. Encourage them to excel, praise them for it, and share the success of your team with the rest of the organization.
I don't know how to delegate tasks effectively.	Consider taking a management training course or reading some books on the topic of delegating effectively.

managing in turbulent times

Keeping the Organizational Tools Sharp

Kristoffer Tripplaar/Alamy Stock Photo

There's been quite a bit of news about the death of manufacturing jobs in the United States, but Illinois Tool Works (NYSE:ITW), headquartered in Glenview, Illinois, is out to prove the critics wrong. Established in 1912 to manufacture metal-cutting tools, the company has grown over the past century to more than 48,000 employees around the globe. Beginning in 1980, ITW grew through the acquisition of hundreds of smaller companies, acquiring their product lines and distinctive competencies. Today, the company is organized into seven operating divisions: Automotive OEM; Test & Measurement and Electronics; Food Equipment; Polymers & Fluids; Welding; Construction Products; and Specialty Products. Its products and services are quite diverse—in ITW's Automotive OEM division, the company produces plastic and metal components for automobiles and light trucks, while its Polymers and Fluids division produces industrial adhesives, cleaning and lubrication fluids, and polymers and fillers for automotive repairs and maintenance.

ITW's structure is built around a highly decentralized philosophy. Each of the seven operating divisions is designed to operate as a smaller, more flexible, entrepreneurial organization, maintaining its own revenue and cost centers. Decision making is highly decentralized, with most decisions about strategy made within the divisions. The company believes that this ITW business model not only responds effectively to customer needs but also maximizes economic performance.

Another key to the success of Illinois Tool Works is its proprietary 80/20 Front-to-Back Business Process which is an operating philosophy that states that 80 percent of its revenues and profits should come from just 20 percent of its customers. In a company where innovation is the key, this philosophy has helped ITW to focus its energies on product lines that will create the most synergy. ITW also emphasizes *customer back innovation*, a term it uses to describe that innovation is customer centered and focuses on the key needs of its most important constituents.

Illinois Tool Works has a strong global presence, operating in 51 countries, with major operations in Australia, Belgium, Brazil, Canada, China, the Czech Republic, Denmark, France, Germany, Ireland, Italy, the Netherlands, Spain, Switzerland, and the United Kingdom. Though the United States is its biggest market, nearly a quarter of its revenues are generated in Europe, the Middle East, and Africa, and more than 20 percent in Asia Pacific and other global markets. This geographic diversification helps to mitigate the risk associated with a downturn in any regional economy.

Despite the unpredictability of the economy, sticking with these winning strategies for over 30 years has paid off for Illinois Tool Works. With over 19,000 granted and pending patents, a proprietary business model, and commitment to the health of the manufacturing sector, Illinois Tool Works seems to have found a winning combination. Its 2022 total revenue hit $15.9 billion, and its 2023 growth projections are up to 4 percent. The company expresses to its employees, shareholders, and customers that the reason for this continued success is its decentralized, entrepreneurial culture.[17]

Staff Authority Some companies also rely on **staff authority**, which is based on special expertise and usually involves advising line managers in areas such as law, accounting, and human resources. A corporate attorney, for example, may advise the marketing department as it prepares a new contract with the firm's advertising agency, but it will not typically make decisions that affect how the marketing department does its job. **Staff members** help line departments make decisions but do not usually have the authority to make final decisions.

Staff Authority *authority based on expertise that usually involves counseling and advising line managers*

Staff Members *advisers and counselors who help line departments in making decisions but who do not have the authority to make final decisions*

Typically, the separation between line authority and staff responsibility is clearly delineated and is usually indicated in organization charts by solid lines (line authority) and dotted lines (staff responsibility), as shown in Figure 6.4. It may help to understand this separation by remembering that whereas *staff managers* generally provide services to management, *line managers* are directly involved in producing the firm's products.

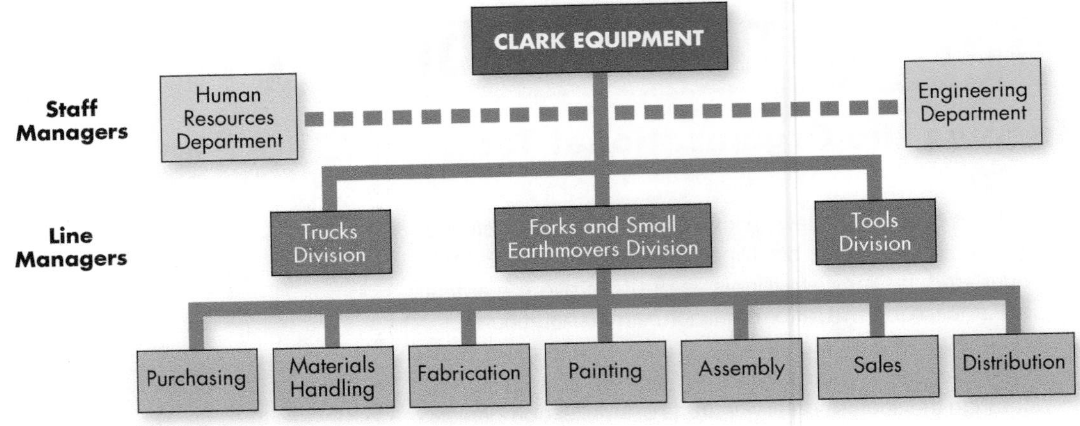

FIGURE 6.4 Line and Staff Organization

Committee and Team Authority *authority granted to committees or teams involved in a firm's daily operations*

Work Team *groups of operating employees who are empowered to plan and organize their own work and to perform that work with a minimum of supervision*

Committee and Team Authority Some organizations have recently started to grant *committee and team authority* to groups that play central roles in daily operations. A committee, for example, may consist of top managers from several major areas. If the work of the committee is especially important and if the committee members will be working together for an extended time, the organization may grant it **committee and team authority**, special authority as a decision-making body beyond the individual authority possessed by each of its members.

At the operating level, many firms today also use **work teams** that are empowered to plan, organize, and perform their work with minimal oversight and often with special authority as well. Most U.S. companies today use teams in at least some areas; some make widespread use of teams throughout every area of their operations.

Basic Forms of Organizational Structure

Learning Objective 6-4

Explain the differences among functional, divisional, matrix, and international organizational structures and describe the most popular new forms of organizational design.

Organizations can structure themselves in an almost infinite number of ways; according to specialization, for example, or departmentalization or the decision-making hierarchy. Nevertheless, it is possible to identify four basic forms of organizational structure that reflect the general trends followed by most firms: (1) *functional*, (2) *divisional*, (3) *matrix*, and (4) *international*.

Functional Structure

Functional Structure *organization structure in which authority is determined by the relationships between group functions and activities*

Under a **functional structure**, relationships between group functions and activities determine authority. Functional structure is used by most small- to medium-sized firms, which are usually structured around basic business functions: a marketing department, an operations department, and a finance department. The benefits of this approach include specialization within functional areas and smoother coordination among them.

In large firms, coordination across functional departments becomes more complicated. Functional structure also fosters centralization (which can be desirable but is usually counter to the goals of larger businesses) and makes accountability more difficult. As organizations grow, they tend to shed this form and move toward one of the other three structures. Figure 6.5 illustrates a functional structure.

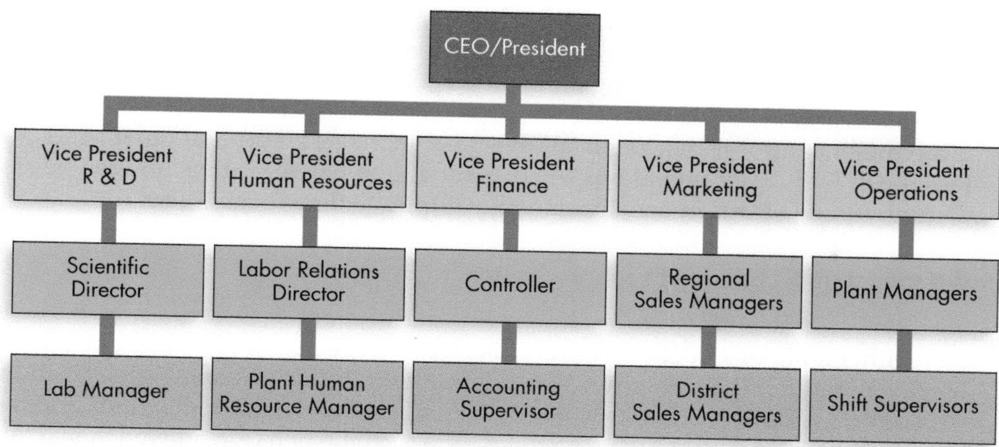

FIGURE 6.5 Functional Structure

Divisional Structure

A **divisional structure** relies on product departmentalization. Organizations using this approach are typically structured around several product-based **divisions** that resemble separate businesses in that they produce and market their own products. The head of each division may be a corporate vice president or, if the organization is large enough, a divisional president. In addition, each division usually has its own identity and operates as a relatively autonomous business under the larger corporate umbrella. Figure 6.6 illustrates a divisional structure.

Divisional Structure *organizational structure in which corporate divisions operate as autonomous businesses under the larger corporate umbrella*

Division *department that resembles a separate business in that it produces and markets its own products*

Johnson & Johnson, one of the most recognizable names in health care products, organizes its company into three major divisions: consumer health care products, medical devices and diagnostics, and pharmaceuticals. Each major division is then broken down further. The consumer health care products division relies on product departmentalization to separate baby care, skin and hair care, topical health care, oral health care, women's health, over-the-counter medicines, and nutritionals. These divisions reflect the company's diversification, which can help shield it from revenue loss during downturns such as economic damage that accompanied the 2020 COVID-19 pandemic. Because they are separate, the other divisions may be insulated from downturns that affect only some segments of the economy.

Consider also that Johnson & Johnson's over-the-counter pain management medicines are essentially competition for their pain management pharmaceuticals. For instance, if the FDA decides that a specific prescription medication can now be sold over the counter without a prescription, revenue from prescriptions will almost

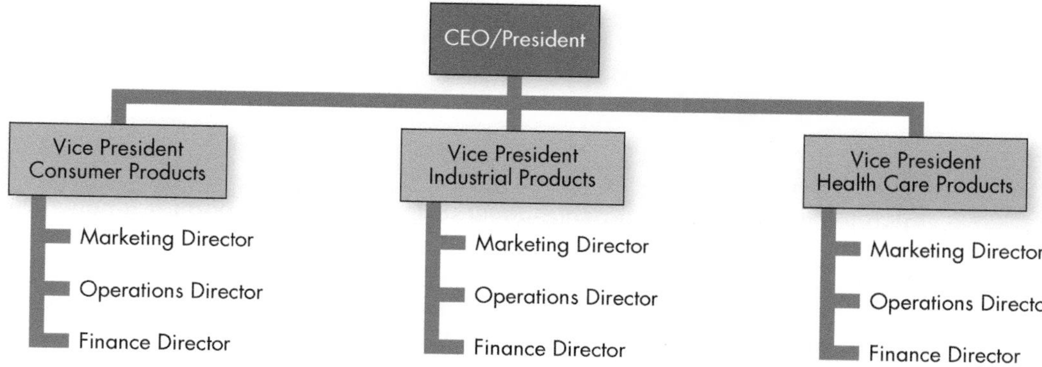

FIGURE 6.6 Divisional Structure

certainly decline while more revenue can be gained from over-the-counter sales. Divisions can maintain healthy competition among themselves by sponsoring separate advertising campaigns, fostering different corporate identities, and so forth. They can also share certain corporate-level resources (such as market research data). However, if too much control is delegated to divisional managers, corporate managers may lose touch with daily operations. Also, competition between divisions can become disruptive, and efforts in one division may duplicate those of another.[18]

Matrix Structure

Matrix Structure *organizational structure created by superimposing one form of structure onto another*

Sometimes a **matrix structure**, a combination of two separate structures, works better than either simpler structure alone. This structure gets its matrix-like appearance, when shown in a diagram, by using one underlying "permanent" organizational structure (say, the divisional structure flowing up and down in the diagram), and then superimposing a different organizing framework on top of it (e.g., the functional form flowing side to side in the diagram). This highly flexible and readily adaptable structure was pioneered by National Aeronautics and Space Administration (NASA) for use in developing specific space programs.

Suppose a company using a functional structure wants to develop a new product as a one-time special project. A team might be created and given responsibility for that product. The project team may draw members from existing functional departments, such as finance and marketing, so that all viewpoints are represented as the new product is being developed; the marketing member may provide ongoing information about product packaging and pricing issues, for instance, and the finance member may have useful information about when funds will be available.

In some companies, the matrix organization is a temporary measure installed to complete a specific project and affecting only one part of the firm. In these firms, the end of the project usually means the end of the matrix—either a breakup of the team or a restructuring to fit it into the company's existing line-and-staff structure. Ford, for example, uses a matrix organization to design new models, such as the 2020 Mustang. A design team composed of people with engineering, marketing, operations, and finance expertise was created to design the newest version of the iconic sports car. After the team's work was done, the team members moved back to their permanent functional jobs.[19]

In other settings, the matrix organization is a semipermanent fixture. Figure 6.7 shows how Martha Stewart Living Omnimedia has created a permanent matrix organization for its lifestyle business. As you can see, the company is organized broadly into media and merchandising groups, each of which has specific products and product groups. For instance, an Internet group is housed within the media group. Layered on top of this structure are teams of lifestyle experts led by area specialists organized into groups, such as cooking, entertainment, weddings, crafts, and so forth. Although each group targets specific customer needs, they all work, as necessary, across all product groups. An area specialist in weddings, for example, might contribute to an article on wedding planning for an Omnimedia magazine, contribute a story idea for an Omnimedia cable television program, and supply content for an Omnimedia site. This same individual might also help select fabrics suitable for wedding gowns that are to be retailed.

International Structure

International Organizational Structures *approaches to organizational structure developed in response to the need to manufacture, purchase, and sell in global markets*

Several different **international organizational structures** are also common among firms that actively manufacture, purchase, and sell in global markets. These structures also evolve over time as a firm becomes more globalized. For example, when Walmart opened its first store outside the United States in 1992, it set up a special projects team. In the mid-1990s, the firm created a small international department to handle overseas expansion. Several years later, international sales and expansion had become such a major part of operations that a separate international division headed up by a senior vice president was created. International operations have now become so

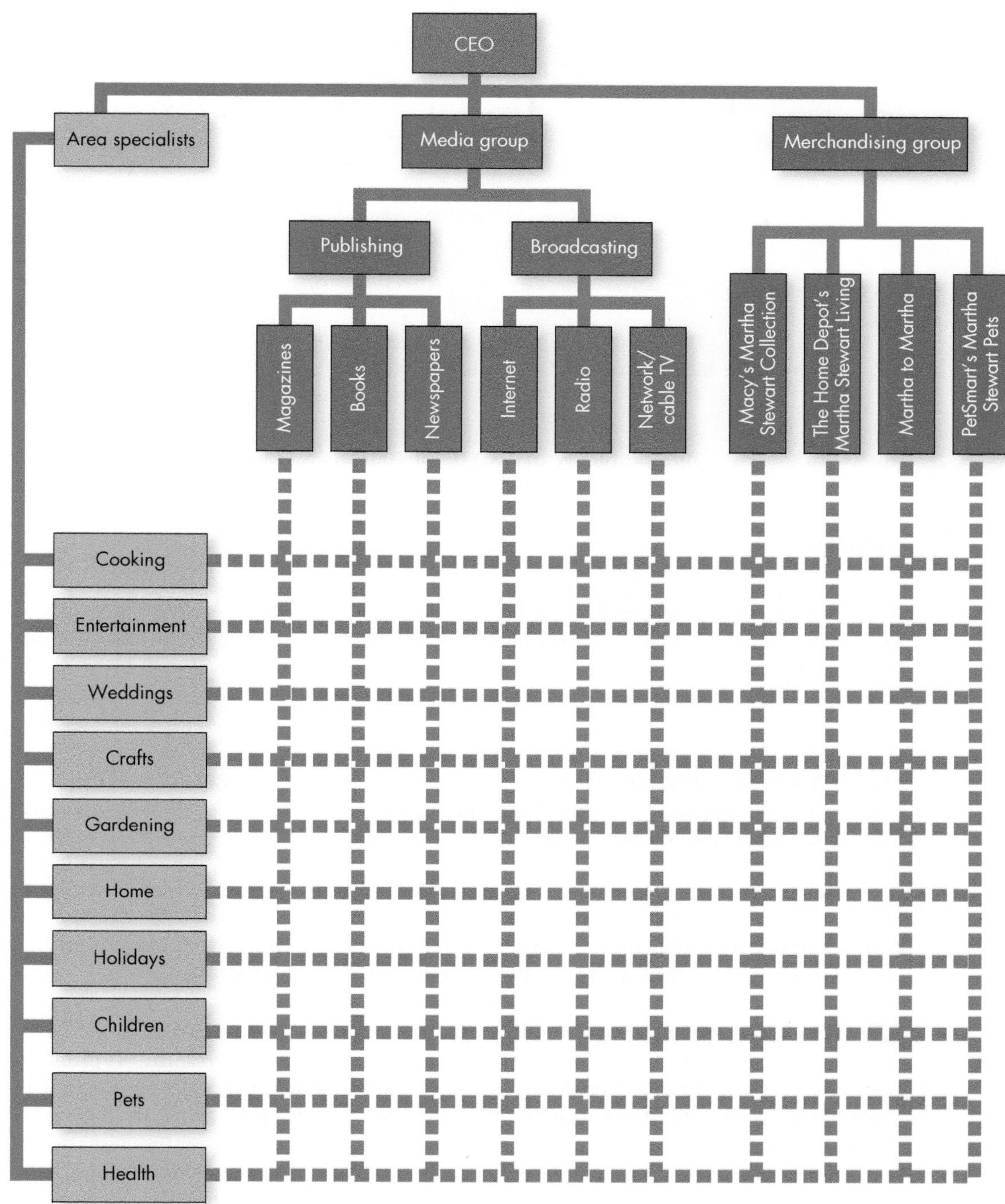

FIGURE 6.7 Matrix Organization of Martha Stewart Living Omnimedia

important to Walmart that the international division has been further divided into geographic areas, such as Mexico and Europe. And as the firm expands into more foreign markets, such as Africa and India, new units have been created to oversee those operations.

Some companies adopt a truly global structure in which they acquire resources (including capital), produce goods and services, engage in research and development, and sell products in whatever local market is appropriate, without consideration of national boundaries. Until a few years ago, General Electric (GE) kept its international business operations as separate divisions, as illustrated in Figure 6.8. Now, however, the company functions as one integrated global organization. GE businesses around

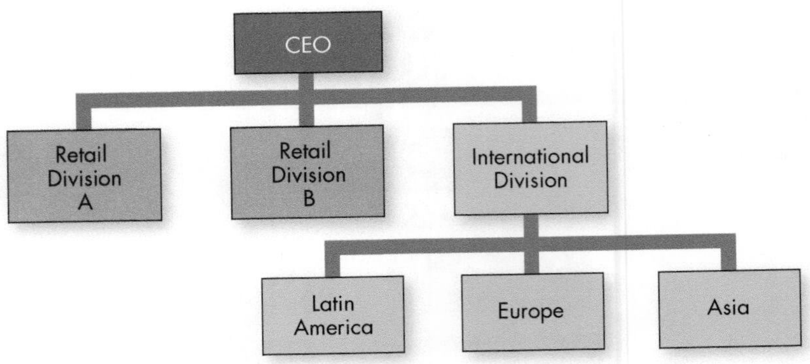

FIGURE 6.8 International Division Structure

the world connect and interact with each other constantly, and managers freely move back and forth among them. This integration is also reflected in GE's executive team, which includes executives from the United States, Spain, China, Sweden, France, and England.

New Forms of Organizational Structure

As the world grows increasingly complex and fast-paced, organizations also continue to seek new forms of organization that permit them to compete effectively. Among the most popular of these new forms are the *team organization*, the *virtual organization*, and the *learning organization*.

Team Organization *Team organization* relies almost exclusively on project-type teams, with little or no underlying functional hierarchy. People rotate from project to project as dictated by their skills and the demands of those projects. In some cases employees may be a part of multiple teams at the same time. At Texas Instruments, for example, most managers are assigned to one "priority" team to which they devote more than half their time and two or three "secondary" teams, each of which gets a smaller amount of their time. As the term suggests, team authority is the underlying foundation of organizations that adopt this organizational structure.

Virtual Organization Another increasingly common type of structure is the *virtual organization*. A virtual organization has little or no formal structure. Typically, it has only a handful of permanent employees, a small staff, and a modest administrative facility. As the needs of the organization change, its managers bring in temporary workers, lease facilities, and outsource basic support services to meet the demands of each unique situation. As the situation changes, the temporary workforce changes in parallel, with some people leaving the organization and others entering. Facilities and the subcontracted services also change. In other words, the virtual organization exists only in response to its own needs and requirements. This structure would be applicable to research or consulting firms that hire consultants based on the specific content knowledge required by each unique project. As the projects change, so, too, does the composition of the organization. Figure 6.9 illustrates a hypothetical virtual organization.

Learning Organization The so-called *learning organization* works to integrate continuous improvement with continuous employee learning and development. Specifically, a learning organization works to facilitate the lifelong learning and personal development of all of its employees while continually transforming itself to respond to changing demands and needs.

Although managers might approach the concept of a learning organization from a variety of perspectives, the most frequent goals are superior quality, continuous

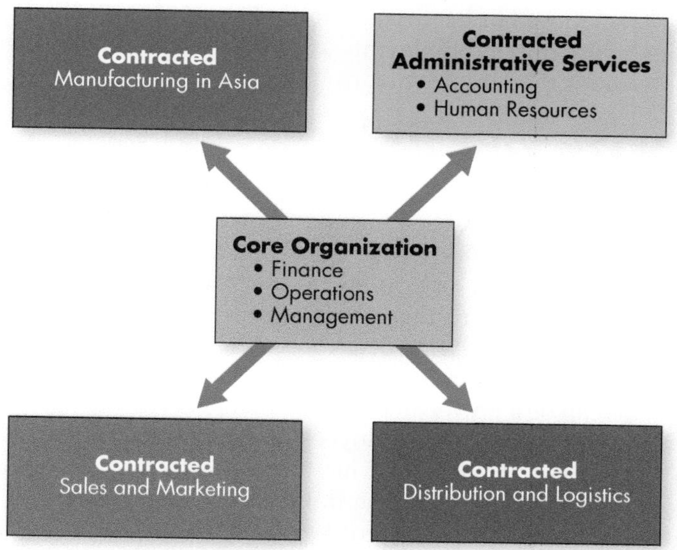

FIGURE 6.9 The Virtual Organization

improvement, and ongoing performance measurement. The idea is that the most consistent and logical strategy for achieving continuous improvement is to constantly upgrade employee talent, skill, and knowledge. For example, if each employee in an organization learns one new thing each day and can translate that knowledge into work-related practice, continuous improvement will logically follow. Indeed, organizations that wholeheartedly embrace this approach believe that only through constant employee learning can continuous improvement really occur. Shell Oil's Shell Learning Center boasts state-of-the-art classrooms and instructional technology, lodging facilities, a restaurant, and recreational amenities. Line managers rotate through the center to fulfill teaching assignments, and Shell employees routinely attend training programs, seminars, and related activities.

Informal Organization

Learning Objective 6-5

Describe the informal organization and discuss intrapreneuring.

Informal Organization *network, unrelated to the firm's formal authority structure, of everyday social interactions among company employees*

The structure of a company, however, is by no means limited to the *formal organization* as represented by the organization chart and the formal assignment of authority. Frequently, the **informal organization**, everyday social interactions among employees that transcend formal jobs and job interrelationships, effectively alters a company's formal structure.[20] This level of organization is sometimes just as powerful as—if not more powerful than—the formal structure. In February 2020, Bob Iger, long-serving and highly successful CEO of the Walt Disney Company, stepped down and was replaced by his hand-picked successor Bob Chapek. Over the next two years, Chapek made some high-profile errors and came under fire from many Disney employees. In a surprise move in late 2022, Disney's board of directors fired Chapek and announced that Iger, who was the chairman of the board, was returning to run the company. Much of the discussion that led to the surprising events of 2022 took place outside formal structural arrangements in the organization. Members of the board of directors and other executives, for example, held secret meetings and reached confidential agreements among themselves before Chapek's future with the company was addressed in a formal manner.[21] In most cases, however, their very nature makes it hard to document these kinds of secret meetings and backroom deals.

On the negative side, the informal organization can reinforce office politics that put the interests of individuals ahead of those of the firm and can disseminate distorted or inaccurate information. For example, if the informal organization is highlighting false information about impending layoffs, valuable employees may act quickly (and unnecessarily) to seek other employment.

Informal Groups

Informal groups are simply groups of people who decide to interact among themselves. They may be people who work together in a formal sense or who just get together for lunch, during breaks, or after work. They may talk about business, the boss, or non–work-related topics such as families, movies, or sports. Their impact on the organization may be positive (if they work together to support the organization), negative (if they work together in ways that run counter to the organization's interests), or irrelevant (if what they do is unrelated to the organization).

Informal groups can be a powerful force that managers cannot ignore.[22] One classic study described how a group of employees at a furniture factory subverted their boss's efforts to increase production. They tacitly agreed to produce a reasonable amount of work but not to work too hard. One man kept a stockpile of completed work hidden as a backup in case he got too far behind. In another example, auto workers described how they left out gaskets and seals and put soft-drink bottles inside car doors to cause customer complaints.[23] Their purpose was to "hurt" their employer by lowering product quality.

Of course, informal groups can also be a positive force, as when people work together to help out a colleague who has suffered a personal tragedy. For example, several instances of this behavior were reported in the wake of Hurricane Harvey that devastated parts of Houston in 2017. Numerous accounts have also surfaced of people banding together to help coworkers and neighbors during the 2020 COVID-19 pandemic. And even more recently, a police officer in a small Texas town was killed by a criminal he was trying to apprehend. The officer left behind a wife and two small children. Law enforcement officers from across the area and friends from the local community all joined together informally to help the family deal with its loss.[24]

In recent years, various online platforms have served as a catalyst for the emergence of more and different kinds of informal or interest groups. As one example, Chevron uses its internal network to facilitate a wide array of interest groups that bring together people with common interests. And increasingly, workers who lose their jobs as a result of layoffs band together digitally to offer moral support to one another and to facilitate networking as they all look for new jobs.[25] Indeed, social media plays a major role in informal groups today.

Organizational Grapevine

Grapevine *informal communication network that runs through an organization*

The **grapevine** is an informal communication network that can permeate an entire organization. Grapevines are found in all organizations except the smallest, but they do not always follow the same patterns as nor do they necessarily coincide with formal channels of authority and communication. Research has identified two kinds of grapevines.[26] One such grapevine, the gossip chain, occurs when one person spreads the message to many other people. Each one, in turn, may either keep the information confidential or pass it on to others. The gossip chain is likely to carry personal information. The other common grapevine is the cluster chain, in which one person passes the information to a few selected individuals. Some of the receivers pass the information to a few other individuals; the rest keep it to themselves.

There is some disagreement about how accurate the information carried by the grapevine is, but research is increasingly finding it to be fairly accurate, especially when the information is based on fact rather than speculation. One study found that the grapevine may be between 75 percent and 95 percent accurate.[27] That same study also found that informal communication is increasing in many organizations for several basic reasons. One contributing factor is the continued growth in merger, acquisition, and takeover activity. Because such activity can greatly affect the people within an organization, it follows that they may spend more time talking about it.[28] A second contributing factor is that as more and more corporations move facilities regularly and have more but smaller administrative centers, employees tend to talk less and less to others outside the organization and more and more to one another. Yet another contributing factor is simply the widespread availability of information technology that makes it easier than ever before for people to communicate quickly and easily. Much like in informal groups, social media plays a growing role in the grapevine.

More recently, another study looked at the effects of economic fluctuations and large-scale job losses on informal communication. More than half of the survey participants reported a sharp increase in gossip and rumors in their organizations. The same survey also reported an increase in the amount of eavesdropping in most businesses.[29] Further, in another recent survey, 32 percent of people claimed to use their work e-mail inappropriately, and 48 percent admitted gossiping with other employees through their e-mail.[30] One poll a few years ago found that 47 percent of those responding indicated that they gossiped at work and 18 agreed that no topics were "off-limits." And yet another study reported a third of working professionals have been asked by their supervisors about what people were gossiping about; this same study also found that 29 percent of working professionals indicated that gossip is their primary source of information about what is happening inside the organization.[31]

We should also note that much of our understanding of grapevine communication pre-dates some of the more widespread communication methods people use today, such as texting, social media, and so forth. Logically, it would seem that the incidence of informal communication might be much greater today simply because people don't have to physically be together to exchange information. They may also be a bit more careful, too, since their messages may be seen by others outside their own networks. Clearly, more research is needed to help clarify these and other issues.

Attempts to eliminate the grapevine are fruitless, but fortunately managers do have some control over it. By maintaining open channels of communication and responding vigorously to inaccurate information, managers can minimize the damage the grapevine can do. The grapevine can actually be an asset. By learning who the key people in the grapevine are, for example, managers can partially control the information they receive and use the grapevine to sound out employee reactions to new ideas, such as a change in human resource policies or benefit packages. Managers can also get valuable information from the grapevine and use it to improve decision making.[32]

Intrapreneuring

Good managers recognize that the informal organization exists whether they want it or not and can use it not only to reinforce the formal organization but also to harness its energy to improve productivity.

Many firms, including Rubbermaid, DreamWorks Animation, 3M, and Xerox, encourage and support **intrapreneuring**, creating and maintaining the innovation and flexibility of a small-business environment within a large, bureaucratic structure. Historically, most innovations have come from individuals in small businesses. As businesses increase in size, however, innovation and creativity tend to become casualties in the battle for more sales and profits. In some large companies, new ideas are even discouraged, and champions of innovation have been stalled in midcareer. At Lockheed Martin, the Advanced Development Programs (ADP) encourages intrapreneurship in the tradition of Skunk Works, a legendary team developed in 1943 as engineer Kelly Johnson's response to Lockheed's need for a powerful jet fighter. Johnson's innovative organization approach broke all the rules, and not only did it work, but it also taught Lockheed the value of encouraging that kind of thinking.[33] Alphabet clumps smaller units and start-ups together so that creative thinking can be reinforced across the organization.

Intrapreneuring *process of creating and maintaining the innovation and flexibility of a small-business environment within the confines of a large organization*

Three intrapreneurial roles exist in large organizations.[34] To successfully use intrapreneurship to encourage creativity and innovation, the organization must find one or more individuals to perform these roles. The *inventor* is the person who actually conceives of and develops the new idea, product, or service by means of the creative process. Because the inventor may lack the expertise or motivation to oversee the transformation of the product or service from an idea into a marketable entity, however, a second role comes into play. A *product champion* is usually a middle manager who learns about the project and becomes committed to it. They help overcome organizational resistance and convinces others to take the innovation seriously. The product champion may have only limited understanding of the technological aspects of the innovation. Nevertheless, product champions are skilled at knowing how the organization works, whose support is needed to push the project forward, and where to go to secure the resources necessary for successful development. A *sponsor* is a top-level manager who approves of and supports a project. This person may fight for the budget needed to develop an idea, overcome arguments against a project, and use organizational politics to ensure the project's survival. With a sponsor in place, the inventor's idea has a much better chance of being successfully developed.

summary of learning objectives

LEARNING OBJECTIVE 6-1

Discuss the factors that influence a firm's organizational structure.

Each organization must develop an appropriate *organizational structure*—the specification of the jobs to be done and the ways in which those jobs relate to one another. Most organizations change structures almost continuously. Firms prepare *organization charts* to clarify structure and to show employees where they fit into a firm's operations. Each box represents a job, and solid lines define the *chain of command*, or *reporting relationships*. The charts of large firms are complex and include individuals at many levels. Because size prevents them from charting every manager, they may create single organization charts for overall corporate structure and separate charts for divisions. An organization's structure is determined by a variety of factors, including the organization's mission and strategy, size, environment, and history. Structure is not static but is changed and modified frequently.

LEARNING OBJECTIVE 6-2

Explain specialization and departmentalization as two of the building blocks of organizational structure.

The process of identifying specific jobs and designating people to perform them leads to *job specialization*. After they're specialized, jobs are grouped into logical units—the process of *departmentalization*. Departmentalization follows one (or any combination) of five forms:

1. *Functional departmentalization* based on functions or activities
2. *Product departmentalization* based on products or services offered
3. *Process departmentalization* based on production processes used to create goods and services
4. *Customer departmentalization* based on customer types or customer groups
5. *Geographic departmentalization* based on geographic areas

Larger companies may take advantage of different types of departmentalization for various levels.

LEARNING OBJECTIVE 6-3

Describe centralization and decentralization, delegation, and authority as the key ingredients in establishing the decision-making hierarchy.

After jobs have been specialized and departmentalized, firms establish decision-making hierarchies. One major issue addressed through the creation of the decision-making hierarchy involves whether the firm will be relatively *centralized* or relatively *decentralized*. In a centralized organization, decision-making authority is retained at the top levels of the organization. Centralized authority systems typically require multiple layers of management and thus *tall organizational structures*. Conversely, in a decentralized organization, most decision-making authority is delegated to lower levels of management. A related concept is *span of control*, which refers to the number of people who report to a manager. Tall, centralized organizations tend to have a narrow span of control, whereas flat, centralized organizations tend to have wider spans of control.

Decentralized firms tend to have relatively fewer layers of management, resulting in a *flat organizational structure. Delegation* is the process through which a manager allocates work to subordinates. In general, the delegation process involves three steps:

1 The assignment of *responsibility*

2 The granting of *authority*

3 The creation of *accountability*

As individuals are delegated responsibility and authority in a firm, a complex web of interactions develops.

These interactions may take one of three forms of authority: line, staff, or committee and team. Line authority follows the chain of command, and staff authority relies on expertise in areas such as law, accounting, and human resources.

LEARNING OBJECTIVE 6-4

Explain the differences among functional, divisional, matrix, and international organizational structures and describe the most popular new forms of organizational design.

Most firms rely on one of four basic forms of organizational structure: (1) *functional*, (2) *divisional*, (3) *matrix*, or (4) *international*. A functional structure is based on organizational functions, such as marketing, finance, or operations. A divisional structure, in contrast, groups activities in terms of distinct product or service groups. A matrix structure, a combination of two structures, imposes one type of structure on top of another. Several different international organizational structures have emerged in response to the need to manufacture, purchase, and sell in global markets. A company may start with a small international department that may grow into an international division. As global competition becomes more complex, companies may experiment with ways to respond. Some adopt truly global structures, acquiring resources and producing and selling products in local markets without consideration of national boundaries.

Organizations also continue to seek new forms of organization that permit them to compete effectively. The most popular new forms include the following:

1 *Team organizations*, which rely almost exclusively on project-type teams with little or no underlying functional hierarchy

2 *Virtual organizations*, which have little or no formal structure and just a handful of employees

3 *Learning organizations*, which work to integrate continuous improvement with ongoing employee learning and development

LEARNING OBJECTIVE 6-5

Describe the informal organization and discuss intrapreneuring.

The *formal organization* is the part that can be represented in chart form. The *informal organization*, everyday social interactions among employees that transcend formal jobs and job interrelationships, may alter formal structure. Two important elements are found in most informal organizations. *Informal groups* consist of people who decide to interact among themselves. Their impact on a firm may be positive, negative, or irrelevant. The *grapevine* is an informal communication network that can run through an entire organization. Because it can be harnessed to improve productivity, some organizations encourage the informal organization. Many firms also support *intrapreneuring*—creating and maintaining the innovation and flexibility of a small business within the confines of a large, bureaucratic structure. In large organizations, intrapreneurship requires the participation of individuals who will serve roles as inventors, product champions, and sponsors.

key terms

accountability **(p. 184)**
authority **(p. 184)**
centralized organization **(p. 182)**
chain of command **(p. 175)**
committee and team authority **(p. 186)**
customer departmentalization **(p. 181)**
decentralized organization **(p. 182)**
delegation **(p. 184)**
departmentalization **(p. 179)**
division **(p. 187)**
divisional structure **(p. 187)**
flat organizational structure **(p. 182)**
functional departmentalization **(p. 179)**
functional structure **(p. 186)**
geographic departmentalization **(p. 181)**
grapevine **(p. 192)**
informal organization **(p. 191)**
international organizational structures **(p. 188)**
intrapreneuring **(p. 193)**
job specialization **(p. 178)**
line authority **(p. 184)**
line department **(p. 184)**
matrix structure **(p. 188)**
organization chart **(p. 175)**
organizational structure **(p. 175)**
process departmentalization **(p. 180)**
product departmentalization **(p. 179)**
profit center **(p. 179)**
responsibility **(p. 184)**
span of control **(p. 183)**
staff authority **(p. 185)**
staff members **(p. 185)**
tall organizational structure **(p. 182)**
work team **(p. 186)**

questions & exercises

QUESTIONS FOR REVIEW

6-1. Describe the five basic forms of departmentalization. Give examples of each.

6-2. What are the advantages and disadvantages of a decentralized organizational structure?

6-3. What is the difference between responsibility and authority?

6-4. Why do some managers have difficulties in delegating authority? Of these reasons, which do you think would be the most significant issue for you?

6-5. Why is a company's informal organization important?

QUESTIONS FOR ANALYSIS

6-6. Why does the structure of an organization matter?

6-7. Create a hypothetical organizational structure for a start-up Internet shopping site. How might this structure change as the business grows?

6-8. Do you think that you would want to work in a matrix organization where you were assigned simultaneously to multiple units or groups? Why or why not?

APPLICATION EXERCISES

6-9. Draw a high-level organization chart for your college or university. How would you describe it in terms of the organizational structures identified in this chapter?

6-10. Select a company where you would like to work one day. Using online research, determine if the company has a functional, divisional, matrix, international, team, virtual, or learning organization. Explain how you arrived at this conclusion. Do you believe that this organizational structure is consistent with the organization's mission? Do you think that organizational structure is well suited to your working style and preferences?

building a business: continuing team exercise

ASSIGNMENT

Meet with your team members and discuss your new business venture within the context of this chapter. Develop specific responses to the following:

6-11. Thinking ahead one year, how many employees do you expect to have in your business? How did you come to this conclusion?

6-12. Draw a sample organization chart for your business in 1 year. Although you won't know the names of all your employees, your organization chart should include job titles.

6-13. Will decision making in your business be centralized or decentralized? Be sure to support your conclusion.

6-14. How do you think that your organizational structure will change over time? Will it be the same in 10 years?

team exercise

GETTING WITH THE PROGRAM

Background Information

You are the founder of a small but growing high-tech company that develops new iPhone apps. With your current workload and new contracts in the pipeline, your business is thriving, except for one problem: You cannot find computer programmers for product development. Worse yet, current staff members are being lured away by other high-tech firms. After suffering a particularly discouraging personnel raid in which competitors captured three of your most valued employees, you hire a consultant to help design organizational changes designed to encourage worker loyalty. You already pay top dollar, but the continuing exodus tells you that programmers are looking for something more.

Method

Working with three or four classmates, identify some ways in which specific organizational changes might improve the working environment and encourage employee loyalty. As you analyze the following factors, ask yourself the obvious question: If I were a programmer, what organizational structures would encourage me to stay?

- ***Level of job specialization.*** With many programmers describing their jobs as tedious because of the focus on detail in a narrow work area, what changes, if any, would you make in job specialization? Right now, for instance, few of your programmers have any say in product design.
- ***Decision-making hierarchy.*** What decision-making authority would encourage people to stay? Is expanding employee authority likely to work better in a centralized or decentralized organization?
- ***Team authority.*** Can team empowerment make a difference? Taking the point of view of the worker, describe the ideal team.
- ***Intrapreneuring.*** What can your company do to encourage and reward innovation?

FOLLOW-UP QUESTIONS

6-15. With the average computer programmer earning nearly $80,000 a year and with all competitive firms paying top dollar, why might organizational issues be critical in determining employee loyalty?

6-16. If you were a programmer, what organizational factors would make a difference to you? Why?

6-17. As the company founder, how willing would you be to make major organizational changes in light of the shortage of qualified programmers?

exercising your ethics

HEARD IT THROUGH THE GRAPEVINE

The Situation

Assume that you are a divisional manager at a large high-tech company. The company has just lost a large contract, and the human resources director has advised company executives that they must cut the workforce by 10 percent within three months to preserve their financial position. You are distressed at the prospect of losing long-time employees, especially those nearing retirement or with young families.

The Dilemma

As you ponder the situation, another regional member has brought up a potential solution that will spare you from actually laying off employees. "The grapevine has worked against us in the past, so let's make it work for us this time. If we leak word that the company is planning to cut pay by 15 percent for most of the workforce as a result of the loss of this contract, people will get scared. They'll start looking for jobs or reevaluating retirement and the layoff will take care of itself. Once we've reached the desired level of resignations, we will reassure the remaining employees that their jobs are secure."

QUESTIONS TO ADDRESS

6-18. What are the ethical issues in this situation?

6-19. What do you think most people would do in this situation?

6-20. What would you do in this situation?

Cases

FOCUS ON MISSION

Continued from page 175

At the beginning of this chapter, you read about REI's mission-driven organizational structure, both internal and external. Using the information presented in this chapter, you should now be able to answer the following questions.

QUESTIONS FOR DISCUSSION

6-21. Chose a business you are familiar with, such as a place you have worked. What was the organizational structure? Do you think a different model would work better? Why or why not?

6-22. How do you think a formal organizational structure relates to or is informed by the environment of the business? How is organizational structure related to the product or service of the business?

6-23. Do some research to determine REI's major competitors. Choose one and determine its organizational structure. Is it the same as REI's? How are the two organizational structures different, and what do they have in common?

A MORE NIMBLE STRUCTURE

In 2005, a trio of friends—Rob Kalin, Chris Maguire, and Haim Shoppick—formed a company designed to be an online marketplace for handmade goods. Within two years, Etsy had nearly half a million sellers, its one-millionth sale, and venture capital investments of over $3 million. The company continued expanding rapidly, acquiring more funding and purchasing smaller competitors along the way. In March 2015, with the previous year's sales hitting nearly $2 billion, the company announced that it would be going public. The IPO and subsequent management transitions were sometimes rocky, and first-quarter financial reports in 2023 indicated a 4.6 percent decline in sales over the previous year but a growth in active buyers, who numbered 89.9 million.[35]

With the 2015 advent of Amazon Handmade, the competition for customers and sellers increased dramatically. The company rolled out Etsy Studio in early 2017, billing it as a one-stop shop for craft enthusiasts, marketing specifically to Etsy sellers, and offering a curated shopping experience for people who want to recreate the things they'd seen on Etsy.[36]

In spite of its new offering, the company struggled. Josh Silverman assumed the role of CEO in 2017, the day after the company announced a layoff of 80 employees—its first staff reduction ever—and its former CEO, Chad Dickerson, was fired by the board. Shortly thereafter, Silverman oversaw further restructuring, resulting in the loss of 140 more jobs at the company.[37] Silverman explained in a press release that the layoffs would create a "more nimble structure."[38]

In a 2021 interview with the podcast 20VC, Silverman described the company as "agile" in everything from team structure to software development, noting that tracking metrics and acting on them quickly enabled the company to capitalize on growth and trends. He also explained that the company's organizational structure and culture allowed for failure: "Setting up a system where failure is affordable and picking when you can fail are two important things. If you will embrace failure, you gotta have those two things in place."[39]

QUESTIONS FOR DISCUSSION

6-24. In your workplace or college, how "agile" do you think the organization is?

6-25. Do you think the practice of "safe failure" is a good idea for a workplace? Can you think of a time in your career (either as an employee or student) when a failure resulted in growth or progress?

6-26. Do you think it is possible to sustain an atmosphere of innovation and experimentation in a public company where stakeholders have an interest in proven profitability?

6-27. Etsy's mission is "Keep Commerce Human." Do you think this is a viable mission for a public company with almost 90 billion buyers? Why or why not?

endnotes

1 "REI Releases 2022 Impact Report and Financials, Distributes $323 Million Back to Co-Op Community," REI, April 26, 2023, https://www.rei.com/newsroom/article/rei-releases-2022-impact-report-financials-distributes-323-million-back-to-community.

2 "REI—Working Together for a Better World," accessed May 7, 2023, https://www.rei.com/pdf/jobs/2009-Best-Company-for-25-Years-REI-for-REI.pdf.

3 "Who We Are & What We Offer: REI Co-Op," REI, accessed May 7, 2023, https://www.rei.com/about-rei/business.

4 Elswright, "REI: A Land Before Technology," October 29, 2017, https://elswrightmba.wordpress.com/2017/10/23/rei-a-land-before-technology/.

5 See Richard Daft, *Organization Theory & Design*, 14th ed. (Cengage, 2024).

6 Beth Baumann, "Ford's Restructuring Plan Is Sure to Have a Devastating Impact in Michigan," Townhall, May 20, 2019, https://townhall.com/tipsheet/bethbaumann/2019/05/20/yikes-fords-restructuring-plan-will-axe-a-number-of-white-collar-jobs-n2546619; Camila Domonoske, "Ford Announces a Historic Restructuring as It Pivots to an Electric Future," NPR, March 2, 2022, https://www.npr.org/2022/03/02/1083913314/ford-modele-split-unitselectric-gas; Ford, "Ford Accelerating Transformation: Forming Distinct Auto Units to Scale EVs, Strengthen Operations,

Unlock Value," March 2, 2022, https://media.ford.com/content/fordmedia/fna/us/en/news/2022/03/02/ford-accelerating-transformation.html.

[7] Jody Macgregor, "Valve's Unusual Corporate Structure Causes Its Problems, Report Suggests," *PC Gamer*, January 27, 2023. https://www.pcgamer.com/valves-unusual-corporate-structure-causes-its-problems-report-suggests/; Chris Bratt and Anni Sayers, "Working at Valve: 'A Fearless Adventure' or 'Lord of the Flies'?" People Make Games, January 25, 2023, https://www.youtube.com/watch?v=s9aCwCKgkLo.

[8] Jess Weatherbed, "Steam Hits 10 Million Concurrent In-Game Players in Record-Breaking Weekend," The Verge, January 9, 2023, https://www.theverge.com/2023/1/9/23546139/steam-10-million-concurrent-players-record-breaking-valve-gaming.

[9] David Burkus, *Under New Management: How Leading Organizations Are Upending Business as Usual* (Boston: Houghton Mifflin Harcourt, 2016), 177–178.

[10] "Brands People Love," Kraft Heinz, accessed March 29, 2020, https://www.kraftheinzcompany.com/brands.html.

[11] Gunnar Hedlund, "Strategy: Search for New Paradigms," Special Issue, *Strategic Management Journal* 15 (Summer 1994): 73–90.

[12] Darja Smite, Nils Brede Moe, Georgiana Levinta, and Marcin Floryan, "Spotify Guilds: How to Succeed With Knowledge Sharing in Large-Scale Agile Organizations," *IEEE Software* 36, no. 2 (February 21, 2019): 51–57, https://doi.org/10.1109/MS.2018.2886178.

[13] Jennifer Riggins, "How Spotify Adopted and Outsourced Its Platform Mindset," *The New Stack*, March 3, 2023. https://thenewstack.io/how-spotlify-adopted-platform-engineering-culture/.

[14] See Levi Strauss & Co., accessed March 20, 2020, http://www.levistrauss.com/Company/WorldwideRegions.aspx.

[15] Michael E. Raynor and Joseph L. Bower, "Lead from the Center," *Harvard Business Review*, May 2001, 93–102.

[16] Gary Hamel, "What Google, Whole Foods Do Best," *Fortune*, September 27, 2007, 59.

[17] "Discover ITW," ITW, accessed May 7, 2023, https://www.itw.com/about-itw/discover-itw/.

[18] *Hoover's Handbook of American Business 2023* (Austin, TX: Hoover's Business Press, 2023), 74–76; Brian Dumaine, "How I Delivered the Goods," *Fortune Small Business*, October 2002, 78–81; Charles Haddad, "FedEx: Gaining on the Ground," *Businessweek*, December 16, 2002, 126–128; Claudia H. Deutsch, "FedEx Has Hit the Ground Running, but Will Its Legs Tire?" *New York Times*, October 13, 2002, BU7; Forbes, February 16, 2006, http://www.forbes.com/finance; PBS.org, "Who Made America," June 19, 2008, http://www.pbs.org/wgbh/theymadeamerica/whomade/fsmith_hi.html.

[19] S. Deng, J. Xu, and Y. Han, "A Proprietary Component Manufacturer's Global Supply Chain Design: The Impacts of Tax and Organizational Structure," *Omega* 115 (2023): 102777.

[20] "The Office Chart That Really Counts," *Businessweek*, February 27, 2006, 48–49.

[21] Joe Flint, Robbie Whelan, Erich Schwartzel, Emily Glazer, and Jessica Toonkel, "Bob Iger vs. Bob Chapek: Inside the Disney Coup," *Wall Street Journal*, December 17, 2022, https://www.wsj.com/articles/bob-iger-bob-chapek-disney-coup-11671236928.

[22] Rob Cross, Nitin Nohria, and Andrew Parker, "Six Myths About Informal Networks—and How to Overcome Them," *Sloan Management Review*, Spring 2002, 67–77.

[23] Robert Schrank, *Ten Thousand Working Days* (Cambridge, MA: MIT Press, 1978); Bill Watson, "Counter Planning on the Shop Floor," in Peter Frost, Vance Mitchell, and Walter Nord, eds., *Organizational Reality*, 2nd ed. (Glenview, IL: Scott, Foresman, 1982), 286–294.

[24] Abigail Jones, "Texas Law Enforcement Entities Show Support After Cameron Police Officer Killed on Duty," KXAN.com, May 11, 2023, https://www.kxan.com/news/texas/texas-law-enforcement-entities-show-support-after-cameron-police-officer-killed-on-duty/.

[25] "After Layoffs, More Workers Band Together," *Wall Street Journal*, February 26, 2002, B1.

[26] Keith Davis, "Management Communication and the Grapevine," *Harvard Business Review*, September–October 1953, 43–49.

[27] "Spread the Word: Gossip Is Good," *Wall Street Journal*, October 4, 1988, B1.

[28] See David M. Schweiger and Angelo S. DeNisi, "Communication with Employees Following a Merger: A Longitudinal Field Experiment," *Academy of Management Journal*, March 1991, 110–135.

[29] "Job Fears Make Offices All Fears," *Wall Street Journal*, January 20, 2009, B7.

[30] Institute of Leadership and Management, "32% of People Making Inappropriate Use of Work Emails," April 20, 2011, accessed April 12, 2013.

[31] The Human Capital Hub, "Workplace Gossip: Everything You Need to Know," accessed April 28, 2023, https://www.thehumancapitalhub.com/articles/workplace-gossip-everything-you-need-to-know.

[32] Nancy B. Kurland and Lisa Hope Pelled, "Passing the Word: Toward a Model of Gossip and Power in the Workplace," *Academy of Management Review* 25, no. 2 (2000): 428–438.

[33] Lockheed Martin, "Skunk Works," June 19, 2008, http://www.lockheedmartin.com/aeronautics/skunkworks/index.html.

[34] See Gifford Pinchot III, *Intrapreneuring* (New York: Harper & Row, 1985).

[35] Etsy, Inc. "First Quarter 2023 Results," April 2023, https://s22.q4cdn.com/941741262/files/doc_financials/2023/q1/Exhibit-99-1-Q1-2023.pdf.

[36] Anthony Ha, "Etsy Studio Is a New Marketplace for Craft Supplies," TechCrunch, February 14, 2017, https://techcrunch.com/2017/02/14/etsy-studio/.

[37] Catherine Shu, "Etsy Will Cut 15 Percent of Its Workforce in a New Round of Layoffs," TechCrunch, June 22, 2017, https://techcrunch.com/2017/06/21/etsy-will-cut-15-percent-of-its-workforce-in-a-new-round-of-layoffs/.

[38] Shu, "Etsy Will Cut 15 Percent of Its Workforce in a New Round of Layoffs."

[39] *20VC:* with Harry Stebbings, "Etsy CEO, Josh Silverman," January 18, 2021, https://www.thetwentyminutevc.com/josh-silverman/.

chapter 7

Operations, Quality, and Supply Chain Management

Katharine Andriotis/Alamy Stock Photo

learning objectives

After reading this chapter, you should be able to:

7-1 **Explain** the meaning of *operations* and discuss the growth in the services and goods sectors of the U.S. economy.

7-2 **Identify** the three kinds of utility created by operations and the characteristics that distinguish service operations from goods production.

7-3 **Explain** how companies with different business strategies are best served by having different operations capabilities.

7-4 **Identify** the major factors that are considered in operations planning.

7-5 **Discuss** the information contained in four kinds of operations schedules—the master operations schedule, detailed schedule, staff schedule, and project schedule.

7-6 **Discuss** the two key activities required for operations control.

7-7 **Identify** the activities and underlying objectives involved in total quality management.

7-8 **Explain** how a supply chain strategy differs from traditional strategies for coordinating operations among firms.

what's in it for me?

Perhaps you have been pleasantly surprised by a new product you purchased or smiled at excellent service. In either case, you'll find it easy to relate to the topics in this chapter. We'll explore the numerous ways companies align their operations processes with their business plans, and we will discuss how these decisions contribute to a firm's ability to create a high-quality product. Gaining an appreciation for the many steps it takes to bring high-quality goods and services to market will help make you a smarter consumer and more effective employee. And if you're a manager, understanding that production activities are pliable and should be reoriented to better support new business strategies will help you redefine your company and its marketplace over time.

michaeljung/Shutterstock

Made from Scratch

LMWH/Shutterstock

The Cheesecake Factory's processing technology started with a pizza oven, a small freezer room, and one woman's commitment to quality.

In 1972, Evelyn and Oscar Overton took the last of their savings and moved from their home in Detroit, Michigan, to Los Angeles, California, to try their hand, one last time, at entrepreneurship. Evelyn had been selling cheesecakes from a small setup in her basement for almost 30 years, but she dreamed of something bigger. However, it was their son David who finally made that dream come true when he opened a little shop in Beverly Hills in 1978 that showcased his mom's product. On opening day, confident that the store would be a huge success, he decided to open after the lunch crowd. A line formed at the door at 2 o'clock, and business has grown ever since. By 2023, The Cheesecake Factory had expanded to nearly 350 restaurants, including 30 international locations.

The Cheesecake Factory's lunch and dinner menus include seafood, pasta, burgers, and more, designed to appeal to a broad clientele, and most of the food is made from scratch. The only thing not made on demand, ironically, is the cheesecake. The iconic dessert comes from the company's bakery division, which operates two bakery production facilities—one in Calabasas Hills, California, and one in Rocky Mount, North Carolina—producing quality cheesecakes and other baked products for its restaurants, international licensees, and third-party bakery customers.

One of the core values of The Cheesecake Factory is to provide a product that looks, tastes, and feels homemade. Despite the incredible volume of desserts, the company resists a great deal of automation in its operations. That's not to say that the operations of the bakery for the world-famous restaurant chain are in any way antiquated; rather, the company has learned to be very selective in where, how, and why it applies new technologies. For instance, production managers use state-of-the-art inventory systems to label and track all items, from raw materials to finished products, and the company has automated processes that make sense to automate, like mixing, baking, and freezing. But finishing is still done by hand.

In the restaurants themselves, kitchens are organized as a production line. Orders, with the recipes, appear on computer monitors above the food prep stations, where the prep cooks chop veggies, meat, and seasonings while a timer counts down. The cook assembles the final product, and it is quality checked by the head cook before going out to the customer. The system is streamlined, efficient, and highly replicable. Every Cheesecake Factory follows the same formula and uses the same system, ensuring both quality of food and quality of service. In addition, the company uses data analytics to forecast not only how many guests to expect on a given night but also what they will likely order. The model allows each restaurant to order the right kinds and the right amount of ingredients, and to have just the right number of staff on board.

In 2012, Atul Gawande wrote a piece for the *New Yorker* in which he praised the operations management of The Cheesecake Factory and mused about why his own industry, health care, couldn't seem to integrate some of the obvious operational efficiencies that the restaurant chain had implemented to combine both profit and service.

In addition to quality control, Gawande noticed that "the managers monitored the pace, too—scanning the screens for a station stacking up red flags, indicating orders past the target time, and deciding whether to give the cooks at the station a nudge or an extra pair of hands. They watched for waste—wasted food, wasted time, wasted effort. The formula was Business 101: Use the right amount of goods and labor to deliver what customers want and no more. Anything more is waste, and waste is lost profit."

Despite his commitment to process, David Overton claims that people are his greatest asset, and his employees back him up on that. In fact, in 2022, *Fortune* magazine named The Cheesecake Factory one of "100 Best Companies to Work For®" for the ninth year in a row.[1] (After studying this chapter, you should be able to answer the set of questions found at the end of the chapter.)

What Does *Operations* Mean Today?

Learning Objective 7-1

Explain the meaning of *operations* and discuss the growth in the services and goods sectors of the U.S. economy.

Although you may not always think about it, you are constantly involved in business activities that provide goods and services to customers. You wake up to the sound of your favorite digital music, and on your bus ride to work or school, you message on a smartphone. Your instructors, the bus driver, the messaging provider, and the music provider all work in **service operations (or service production)**. They provide intangible and tangible service products, such as entertainment, transportation, education, and communications services. Firms that make only tangible products—smartphones, coffee, clothing, buses, textbooks—are engaged in activities for **goods operations (or goods production)**.

The term **operations (or production)** refers to all the activities involved in making products—goods and services—for customers. In developed countries, much of what we need or want, from health care to fast food, is produced by service operations. In general, managers in the service sector give more consideration to the human element in operations (as opposed to the equipment or technology involved) because success or failure often depends on provider–customer contact. As we will see, a key difference between goods and services operations is the customer's involvement in service operations.

Service Operations (or Service Production) *activities producing intangible and tangible products, such as entertainment, transportation, and education*

Goods Operations (or Goods Production) *activities producing tangible products, such as smartphones, coffee, clothing, buses, and textbooks*

Operations (or Production) *activities involved in making products—goods and services—for customers*

Jasen Wright/Shutterstock

Zave Smith/Getty Images

Some businesses focus on service operations and others on goods operations. The auto factory on the left is producing goods (i.e., cars and trucks), while the hair salon on the right is providing services.

Although companies are typically classified as either goods producers or service providers, the distinction is often blurred. Consider General Motors (GM). When you think of GM, you may first think of cars and trucks, tangible goods the company makes and sells. However, GM is not just a goods producer. In addition to manufacturing various kinds of vehicles, GM also provides financing to purchasers through GM Financial, a service operation.

Growth in the Services and Goods Sectors

Historically, agriculture was the dominant economic sector in the early years of the United States. Eventually, though, manufacturing began to grow in importance and became the economic core of the U.S. economy from the nineteenth century into the mid-twentieth century. Services then began a rapid climb in economic importance in terms of both number of employees and percentage of gross domestic product (GDP)—the value of all goods and services produced by the economy, excluding foreign income. The outsourcing of U.S. manufacturing to other countries became a major concern in recent decades, so that by the year 2000, employment in the goods-producing sector (mining, construction, and manufacturing) was only about 20 percent of private-sector employment versus 80 percent in services. Still, the United States remains the world's second largest exporter of manufactured goods, trailing only China and ahead of both Germany and Japan.[2]

Of course, both goods and service industries are important, but as you can see from Figure 7.1, employment has risen significantly in the service sector and has leveled off at just 11 to 12 percent in goods-producing industries for years 2004 through 2022. Much of this growth comes from e-commerce, business services, health care, amusement and recreation, and education.

By 2022, the service sector's growth generated about 68 percent of private-sector national income. As Figure 7.2 shows, the service sector's greater percentage of GDP has hovered above 50 percent in recent years. At the same time, the smaller 11 percent of the workforce in goods-producing jobs produced almost half of national income.

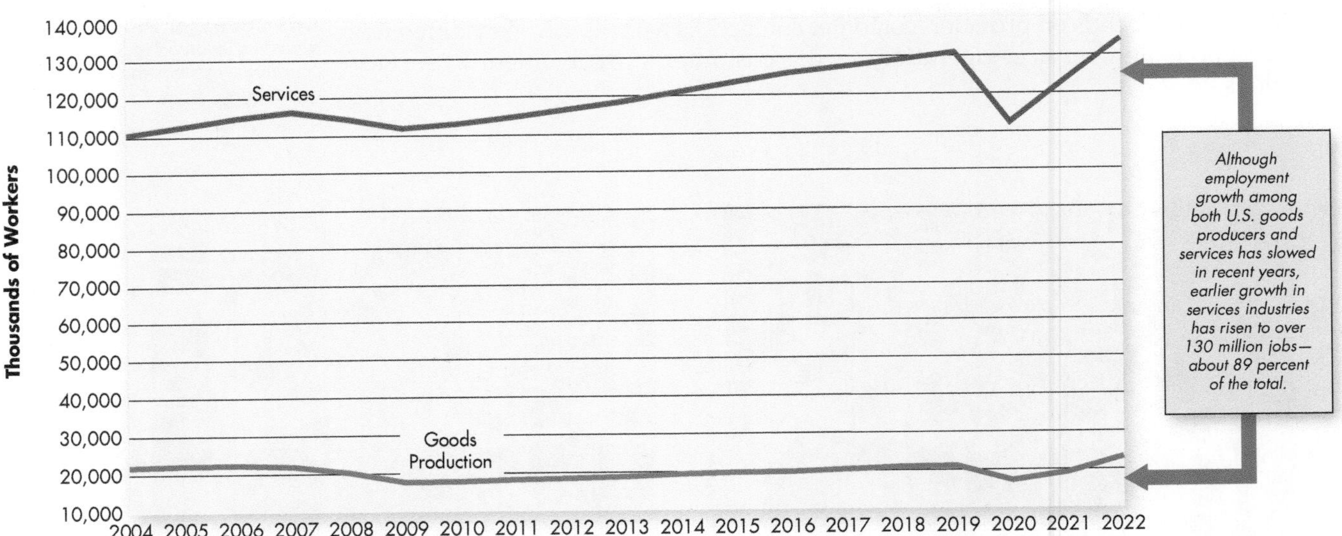

FIGURE 7.1 Employment in Goods and Services Sectors
As you can see, employment in both the goods and services sectors of the U.S. economy has grown steadily this century. There was a brief downturn in 2009 (the Great Recession) and a sharper one in 2020–2021 (COVID), but these were only temporary. Service sector jobs have consistently provided around 89 percent of the overall total.
Sources: Services: U.S. BUREAU OF LABOR STATISTICS. https://data.bls.gov/timeseries/CES0700000001?data_tool=Xgtable and Goods: U.S. BUREAU OF LABOR STATISTICS. https://data.bls.gov/pdq/SurveyOutputServlet. Accessed April 25, 2023.

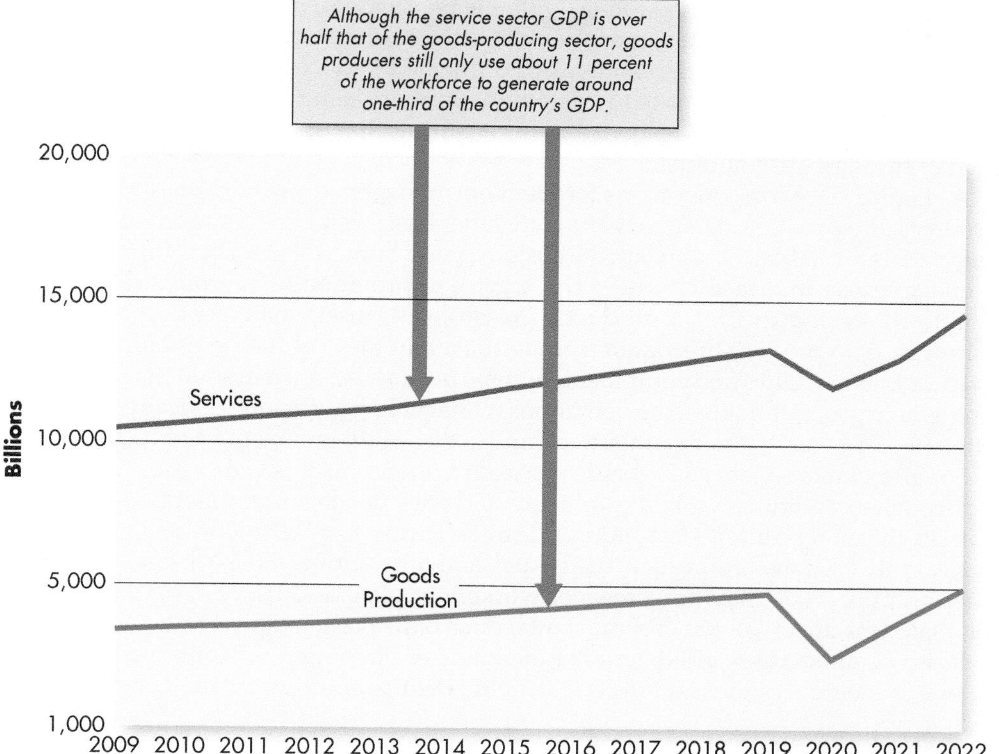

FIGURE 7.2 GDP from Goods and Services
Source: U.S. Bureau of Economic Analysis. https://apps.bea.gov/iTable/iTable.cfm?reqid=19&step=3&isuri=1&nipa_table_list=6&categories=survey; accessed April 25, 2023.

Globally, though, U.S. manufacturing faces intense competition from other nations. A recent international survey of industrial executives ranks China as the most competitive manufacturing country, followed by the United States (second), Germany (third), Japan (fourth), and Canada (ninth).[3] The fact that Chinese workers must work for low wages is a major reason for that country's competitiveness.

Creating Value Through Operations

Learning Objective 7-2

Identify the three kinds of utility created by operations and the characteristics that distinguish service operations from goods production.

To understand a firm's production processes, we need to know what kinds of benefits its production provides, both for itself and for its customers. Production provides businesses with economic results: profits, wages, and goods purchased from other companies. At the same time, it adds customer value by providing **utility**—the ability of a product to satisfy a want or need—in terms of form, time, and place:

Utility *product's ability to satisfy a human want or need*

- ***Form utility.*** Production makes products available: By converting raw materials and human skills into finished goods and services, production creates *form utility*, as when Cinemark combines building materials, theater seats, and projection equipment to create an entertainment venue.
- ***Time utility.*** When a theater offers midday, afternoon, and evening shows seven days a week, it creates *time utility*; that is, it adds customer value by making products available when different consumers want them.
- ***Place utility.*** When a theater offers a choice of 15 movies, all under one roof, at a popular location, it creates *place utility*: It makes products available where they are convenient for consumers.

Operations (Production) Management *systematic direction and control of the activities that transform resources into finished products that create value for and provide benefits to customers*

Operations (Production) Managers *managers responsible for ensuring that operations activities create value and provide benefits to customers*

Creating a product that customers value is no accident; it results from organized effort. **Operations (production) management** is the systematic direction and control of the activities that transform resources into finished services and goods that create value for and provide benefits to customers. In overseeing production, operations (production) managers are responsible for ensuring that operations activities create what customers want and need.

As Figure 7.3 shows, **operations (production) managers** draw up plans to transform resources into products. First, they bring together basic resources: knowledge, physical materials, information, equipment, the customer, and human skills. Then, they put them to effective use in a facility where the service is provided or the physical good is produced. As demand for a product increases, operations managers schedule and control work to produce the required amount. Finally, they control costs, quality levels, inventory, and facilities and equipment. In some businesses, often in small start-up firms such as sole proprietorships, the operations manager is one person. Typically, however, different employees work together to complete these different responsibilities.

Some operations managers work in service "factories," such as FedEx package-sorting depots, whereas others work in production factories making smartphones; still others work in offices, restaurants, hospitals, and stores. Farmers are operations managers who create utility by transforming soil, seeds, fuel, and other inputs into soybeans, milk, and other outputs. They may hire crews of workers to plant and harvest, opt instead for automated machinery, or prefer some combination of workers and machinery. These types of decisions affect costs and determine the kinds of buildings and equipment farmers include in their operations and the quality and quantity of the goods they produce.

Differences Between Service and Goods Manufacturing Operations

Both service and manufacturing operations transform raw materials into finished products. In service operations, however, the raw materials, or inputs, are not things like glass or steel. These service inputs are people who have either unsatisfied needs or possessions needing care or alteration. In service operations, finished products or outputs are people with needs met and possessions serviced.

There are several obvious differences between service and manufacturing operations. Four aspects of service operations can make service production more

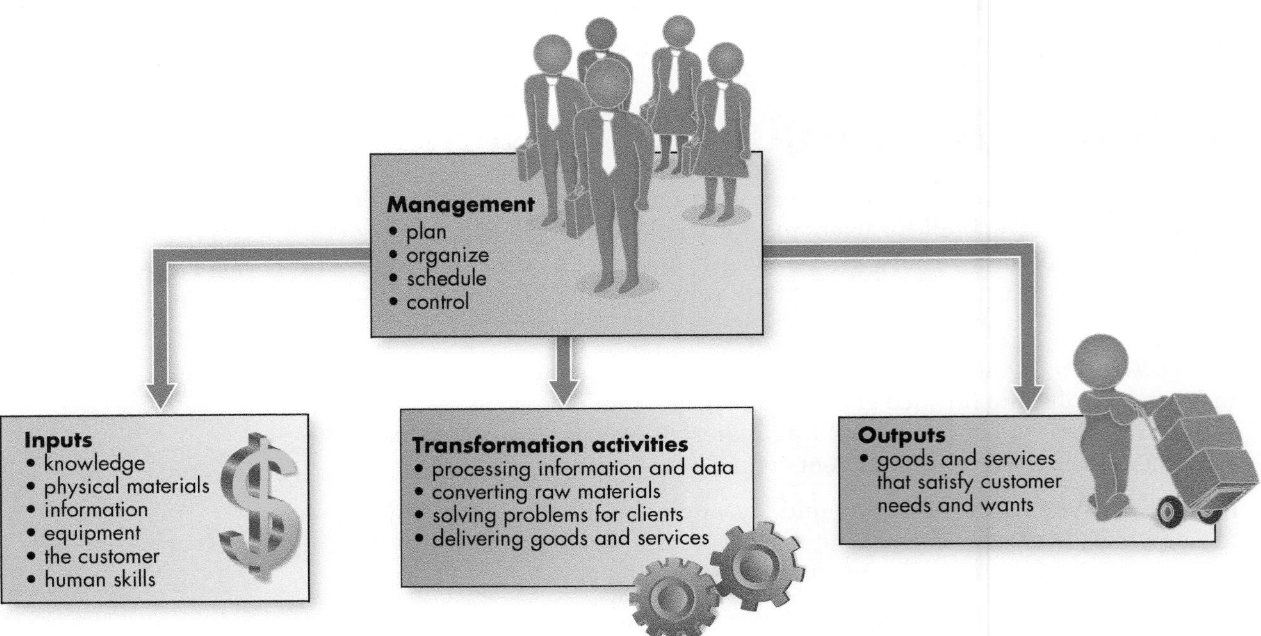

FIGURE 7.3 The Resource Transformation Process

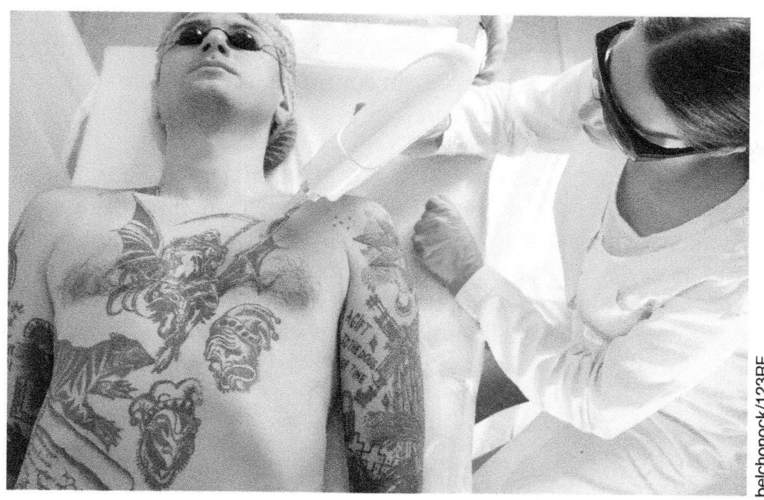

belchonock/123RF

Because service operations transform customers or their possessions, the customer is often present in the operations process. For example, customers who want a tattoo must go to a tattoo parlor and "be present" in order to achieve the desired outcome.

complicated than simple goods production: (1) interacting with customers, (2) the intangible and unstorable nature of some services, (3) the customer's presence in the process, and (4) service quality considerations.

Interacting with Customers Manufacturing operations emphasize outcomes in terms of physical goods, like a new jacket or backpack. But the products of most *service* operations are really combinations of goods and services—both making a pizza *and* delivering (serving) it. Service workers need different skills. For example, gas company employees may need strong interpersonal skills to calm frightened customers who have reported gas leaks. In contrast, the same skills are somewhat less important for factory workers who install gas pipes in manufactured homes.

Services Can Be Intangible and Unstorable Two prominent characteristics—*intangibility* and *unstorability*—set services apart from physical goods:

- ***Intangibility.*** Services often can't be touched, tasted, smelled, or seen, but they're still there. An important satisfier for customers, therefore, is the *intangible* value they receive in the form of pleasure, gratification, or a feeling of safety. For example, if you hire an attorney to handle a legal matter, you purchase not only the intangible quality of legal expertise but also the equally intangible reassurance that someone is helping you.
- ***Unstorability.*** Many services, such as trash collection, transportation, child care, and house cleaning, can't be produced ahead of time and then stored for high-demand periods. If a service isn't used when available, it's usually wasted. Services, then, are typically characterized by a high degree of *unstorability*.

Customers' Presence in the Operations Process Because service operations transform customers or their possessions, the customer is often present in the operations process. To get a haircut, for example, most of us have to go to a hair salon. As participants in the operations process, customers can affect it. As a customer, you expect the salon to be conveniently located (place utility), to be open for business at convenient times (time utility), to provide safe and comfortable facilities, and to offer high-quality grooming (form utility) at reasonable prices (value for money spent). Accordingly, the manager sets hours of operation, available services, and an appropriate number of employees to meet customer requirements. But what happens if a customer, scheduled for only a haircut, also asks for additional services, such as color highlights or a shave, when they arrive? In this case, the service provider must quickly adjust the service activities to provide customer satisfaction. High customer contact has the potential to affect the process significantly. The manufacturers who produce the salon's scissors or shampoo, in contrast, don't have to worry if a customer makes a last-minute change in demands.

Intangibles Count for Service Quality Consumers use different measures to judge services and goods because services include intangibles, not just physical objects. Most service managers know that quality of work and quality of service are not necessarily the same thing. Your car, for example, may have been flawlessly repaired (quality of work), but you'll probably be unhappy with the service if you're forced to pick it up days later than promised because the work wasn't finished on time (quality of service).

Operations Processes

Operations Process *set of methods and technologies used to produce a good or a service*

To better understand the diverse kinds of production in various firms and industries, it is helpful to classify production according to differences in operations processes. An **operations process** is a set of methods and technologies used to produce a good or a service. Banks, for example, use two processes—document shredding and data encryption—to protect confidential information. Automakers use precision painting methods (equipment and materials) to produce a high-quality paint finish.

We can classify goods production into broad groupings by asking whether its operations process has a "make-to-order" or a "make-to-stock" emphasis. We can classify services according to the extent of customer contact required.

Make-to-Order Operations *activities for one-of-a-kind or custom-made production*

Make-to-Stock Operations *activities for producing standardized products for mass consumption*

Goods Production Processes: Make-to-Order Versus Make-to-Stock Processes Clothing, such as evening gowns and suits, is available either off-the-shelf in department stores or custom-made at a designer or tailor shop. The designer or tailor's **make-to-order operations** respond to one-of-a-kind gown or suit requirements, including unique patterns, materials, sizes, and shapes, depending on customers' characteristics. **Make-to-stock operations**, in contrast, produce standard gowns in large quantities to be stocked on store shelves or in displays for mass consumption. The production processes are quite different for the two settings, including procedures for designing gowns and suits; planning for materials purchases; equipment and work methods for cutting, sewing, and assembling gowns and suits; and employee skills for production.

Service Production Processes: Extent of Customer Contact In classifying services, we may also ask whether we can provide a service without the customers' presence in the production system. In answering this question, we classify services according to *extent of customer contact*.

Low-Contact System *level of customer contact in which the customer need not be part of the system to receive the service*

Low-Contact Systems Gas and electric companies, auto repair shops, and lawn-care services are examples of **low-contact systems**: Customers are not in contact with the post office while the service is performed. Consider the postal delivery operations at your local U.S. post office. Postal employees gather mail from mailboxes, sort it, and send it on its delivery journey to addressees. Customers can receive the service—mail sent and mail received—without setting foot in the processing center or interacting with a mail carrier. A coal-shipping firm is also a low-contact system. As such, it does not need to be highly focused about the appearance of its trains, since no paying passengers are riding on them.

High-Contact System *level of customer contact in which the customer is part of the system during service delivery*

High-Contact Systems Think about your local public transit system. The service is transportation; when you purchase transportation, you board a bus or train. For example, the Bay Area Rapid Transit (BART) system, which connects San Francisco with outlying suburbs, is, like all public transit systems, a **high-contact system**: To receive the service, the customer must be part of the system. Thus, managers must worry about the cleanliness of trains, safety of passengers, and the usability of its ticket kiosks. Other examples of high-contact systems include: hair salons, dental and medical offices, law offices, and consulting firms.

Business Strategy as the Driver of Operations

Learning Objective 7-3

Explain how companies with different business strategies are best served by having different operations capabilities.

There is no one standard way for doing production, either for services or for goods. Rather, it is a flexible activity that can be molded into many shapes to give quite different operations capabilities for different purposes. How, then, do companies go about selecting the kind of production that is best for them? They aim to adopt the kind of production that achieves the firm's larger business strategy in the most efficient way possible.

The Many Faces of Production Operations

Consider the four firms listed in Table 7.1. Two are in goods production (Toyota and 3M), and the other two (Save-a-Lot and FedEx) are in services. These successful companies have contrasting business strategies, and as we shall see, they have chosen different operations capabilities. Each company has identified a business strategy that it uses for attracting customers in its industry. More than 40 years ago, Toyota chose *quality* as the strategy for competing in selling autos. Save-A-Lot grocery stores, in contrast to others in the grocery industry, offer customers *lower prices*. The *flexibility* strategy at 3M emphasizes new product development in an ever-changing line of products for home and office. FedEx competes in the overnight delivery market by emphasizing delivery *dependability*.

Business Strategy Determines Operations Capabilities

Successful firms design their operations to support the company's business strategy.[4] In other words, managers adjust production operations to support the firms' target markets. Because our four firms use different business strategies, we should expect to see differences in their operations, too. The top-priority **operations capability (production capability)**—the special ability that production does especially well to outperform the competition—is listed for each firm in Table 7.2 along with key operations characteristics for implementing that capability. Each company's operations capability matches up with its business strategy so that the firm's activities—from top to bottom—are focused in a particular direction.

Operations Capability (Production Capability) *special ability that production does especially well to outperform the competition*

For example, because Toyota's top priority focuses on quality, its operations, the resource inputs for production, the transformation activities, and the outputs from production are devoted first and foremost to that characteristic. Its car designs and production processes emphasize appearance, reliable performance, and desirable features at a reasonable price. All production processes, equipment, and training are designed to build better cars. The entire culture supports a quality emphasis among employees, suppliers, and dealerships. Had Toyota instead chosen to compete as the low-price car in the industry, as some successful car companies do, then a cost-minimization focus

table 7.1 Business Strategies That Win Customers for Four Companies

Company	Strategy for Attracting Customers	What the Company Does to Implement Its Strategy
Toyota	Quality	Cars perform reliably, have an appealing fit and finish, and consistently meet or exceed customer expectations at a competitive price.
Save-A-Lot	Low price	Foods and everyday items are offered at savings up to 40 percent less than conventional food chains.
3M	Flexibility	Innovation is vital, with more than 55,000 products in a constantly changing line of convenience items for home and office.
FedEx	Dependability	Every delivery is fast and on time, as promised.

table 7.2 Operations Capabilities and Characteristics for Four Companies

Operations Capability	Key Operations Characteristics
Quality (Toyota)	• High-quality standards for materials suppliers • Just-in-time materials flow for lean manufacturing • Specialized, automated equipment for consistent product buildup • Operations personnel are experts on continuous improvement of product, work methods, and materials
Low cost (Save-A-Lot)	• Avoids excessive overhead and costly inventory (no floral departments, sushi bars, or banks that drive up costs) • Limited assortment of products (staples), in one size only for low-cost restocking, lower inventories, and less paperwork • Many locations; small stores—less than half the size of conventional grocery stores—for low construction and maintenance costs • Reduces labor and shelving costs by receiving and selling merchandise out of custom shipping cartons
Flexibility (3M)	• Maintains some excess (expensive) production capacity available for fast start-up on new products • Adaptable equipment and facilities for production changeovers from old to new products • Hires operations personnel who thrive on change • Many medium- to small-sized manufacturing facilities in diverse locations, which enhances creativity
Dependability (FedEx)	• Customer automation: uses electronic and online communications tools with customers to shorten shipping time • Wireless information system for package scanning by courier, updating of package movement, and package tracking by customer • Maintains a company air force, global weather forecasting center, and ground transportation for pickup and delivery, with backup vehicles for emergencies • The 25 automated regional distribution hubs process 3.5 million packages per day for next-day deliveries

would have been appropriate, giving Toyota's operations an altogether different form. Toyota's operations support its chosen business strategy. Several years ago, however, the firm tried to change elements of its operations processes, with the unfortunate side effect that quality slipped. When managers realized what was happening, their commitment to quality was reestablished. By 2014, Toyota had regained its position as the world's top-selling automaker.

Expanding into Additional Capabilities Finally, it should be noted that excellent firms learn, over time, how to achieve more than just one competence. The firms in Table 7.1 eventually became excellent in several capabilities. Aside from dependability, FedEx is also noted for world-class service quality and cost containment. To reduce costs, the company eliminates jobs that become unnecessary with advances in technology, sells off its older inefficient airplanes, and reduces the number of flights required by its planes by rerouting its air and ground fleets.

Learning Objective 7-4

Identify the major factors that are considered in operations planning.

Operations Planning

Let's turn now to a discussion of production activities and resources that are considered in every business organization. Like all good managers, we start with planning. Managers from many departments contribute to decisions about operations. As Figure 7.4 shows, however, no matter how many decision makers are involved, the process is a logical sequence of decisions.

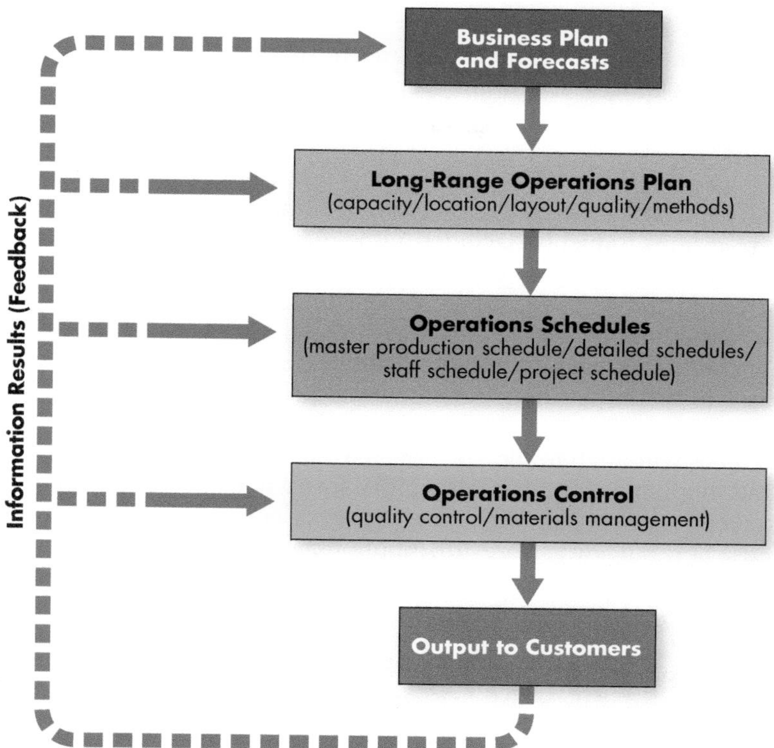

FIGURE 7.4 Operations Planning and Control

The business plan and forecasts developed by top managers provide guidance for long-term operations plans. Covering a two- to five-year period, the operations plan anticipates the number of plants or service facilities and the amount of labor, equipment, transportation, and storage needed to meet future demand for new and existing products. The planning activities fall into five categories: *capacity, location, layout, quality,* and *methods planning*.

Capacity Planning

The amount of a product that a company can produce under normal conditions is its **capacity**. A firm's capacity depends on how many people the firm employs and the number and size of its facilities. A supermarket's capacity for processing payments from customers, for instance, depends on its number of point-of-sale (checkout) stations. A typical store has excess capacity—more stations than it needs—on an average Tuesday, but on Saturday morning or during the three days before Thanksgiving, they'll all be running at full capacity. Of course, employees may not be working at the stations during times of low demand, but the store nevertheless has the physical stations in place for when they are needed.

Capacity *amount of a product that a company can produce under normal conditions*

Long-range capacity planning considers both current and future requirements. If capacity is too small for demand, the company must turn away customers, a situation that cuts into profits and alienates both customers and salespeople. If capacity greatly exceeds demand, the firm is wasting money by maintaining facilities that are too large, keeping excess machinery online, or employing too many workers.

The stakes are high in capacity decisions: While expanding fast enough to meet future demand and to protect market share from competitors, managers must also consider the costs of expanding. When markets are growing, greater capacity is desirable. In troubled times, however, existing capacity may be too large and too expensive to maintain, requiring a reduction in size.

Location Planning

Because location affects production costs and flexibility, sound location planning is crucial for factories, offices, and stores. Depending on its site, a company may be able to produce low-cost products, or it may find itself at a cost disadvantage relative to its competitors.

Consider the reasons why Slovakia has been known as "Detroit East" for several years. Several major automobile manufacturers, including Volkswagen, Peugeot, Jaguar, and Kia, have major production facilities in the region. Indeed, the Central European country is an ideal place to produce cars. It has a good railroad system and nearby access to the Danube River, meaning economical transportation for incoming materials and outgoing cars after they are manufactured. The area also has skilled, hard-working laborers, and prevailing wages are lower than those in surrounding countries.[5]

In contrast to manufacturing, consumer services concentrate on being located near customers. Thus, fast-food restaurants, such as Taco Bell and McDonald's, are located near areas with high traffic, such as busy highways, college campuses, hospital cafeterias, and shopping malls. At retail giant Walmart, managers of the company's huge distribution centers regard Walmart outlets as their customers. To ensure that truckloads of merchandise flow quickly to stores, distribution centers are located near the hundreds of Walmart stores that they supply, not near the companies that supply them.

entrepreneurship and new ventures

In Pursuit of the Smokeless Fire

In 2011, Amos Stoltzfus and Jonathon Miller launched Breeo, a manufacturer of smokeless fire pits based on the idea of a campfire but self-contained and easily added to any outdoor living space. Breeo's firepits also have cooking surfaces around the outside, and customers can buy additional accessories to cook over the flame. Operating from a small base in Ohio, Breeo marketed the fire pits as a fun and easy way to cook outdoors.

Three years later, the pair formed Breeo Industries and expanded the product line to three models. In 2015, the company moved its headquarters to Pennsylvania, where it partnered with PennEagle Manufacturing. A year later, Breeo employed seven people and shipped 1,270 fire pits, and a year after that, Breeo and PennEagle merged to create Breeo, LLC. In 2020, the firm rebranded its products to focus on cooking as a skill. It also launched the Firemaster Club, which is a customer rewards program, and started publishing videos and blogs to promote outdoor cooking as a blend of ruggedness and finesse.

Like most manufacturing companies, Breeo uses a process layout for its operations, starting with laser cutting the parts, then punching and rolling them into shapes, followed by welding, finishing, and quality control, which also packages the products for shipping.[6] The process may not be radically innovative, but it gets the product out the door.

In addition to a focus on operations, there is a strong emphasis on culture at Breeo. All Breeo products are manufactured in the United States, and the company takes pride in Lancaster, Pennsylvania, where its headquarters is located, deep in the heart of Amish Country. The company has deliberately hired a large number of Amish team members, which reinforces its ties to Lancaster and welcomes the cultural elements of hard work and high ethical standards. The company's website notes, "At Breeo, we value continuous improvement and developing others. In action this looks like innovation, having the right people in the right seats, sharing our success, supporting community and mission outreach."[7] The company believes in a strong commitment to collaboration and teamwork. It has kept its operations small—in 2023, there were only 26 full-time employees—it says, in part, to ensure quality and customer service.[8]

JaysonPhotography/Shutterstock

In comparison, the company's main U.S. competitor, Solo Stove, has over 200 employees in the United States and nearly as many in Mexico. Solo Stove is part of a publicly owned company and sources its materials internationally. Breeo capitalizes on these differences in its marketing strategy, noting that its smaller size promotes a culture of innovation and collaboration and proudly stating that its materials and manufacturing are all American made.

Layout Planning

Layout is the physical location or floor plan for service centers, machinery, equipment, customers, and supplies. It determines whether a company can respond efficiently to demand for more and different products or whether it finds itself unable to match competitors' speed and convenience. Among the many layout possibilities, three well-known alternatives—(1) *process layouts (or custom-product layouts)*, (2) *product layouts (or same-steps layouts)*, and (3) *fixed-position layouts*—are presented here to illustrate how different layouts serve different purposes for operations.

Process Layouts In a **process layout** (also called **custom-product layout**), which is well suited to *make-to-order shops* (or *job shops*) specializing in custom work, equipment and people are grouped according to function. FedEx Office stores, for example, use custom-products layouts to accommodate a variety of custom jobs. Specific activities or processes, such as photocopying, faxing, computing, binding, and laminating, are performed in separate, specialized areas of the store. Walk-in customers—both individuals and small-business clients—move from area to area performing the self-service tasks they need to do.

Process Layout (Custom-Product Layout) *physical arrangement of production activities that groups equipment and people according to function*

The main advantage of process layouts is flexibility—at any time, the shop can process individual customer orders, each requiring different kinds of work. Depending on its work requirements, a client being served or a job being processed may flow through three activity areas, another through just one area, and still others through four or more work zones. Figure 7.5 shows the process layout of a service provider—a medical clinic. The path taken through the facility reflects the unique treatments for one patient's visit. Goods producers such as machine shops, woodworking and print shops, and dry-cleaning stores, as well as health clinics and physical fitness studios, are among the many facilities using custom-product layouts.

Product Layouts A **product layout** (also called a **same-steps layout** or **assembly line layout**) is set up to provide one type of service or make one type of product in a fixed sequence of production steps. All units go through the same set of steps. It is efficient for large-volume make-to-stock operations that mass-produce many units of a product quickly: A partially finished product moves step by step through

Product Layout (Same-Steps Layout) *physical arrangement of production steps designed to make one type of product in a fixed sequence of activities according to its production requirements*

Assembly Line Layout *a same-steps layout in which a product moves step by step through a plant on conveyor belts or other equipment until it is completed*

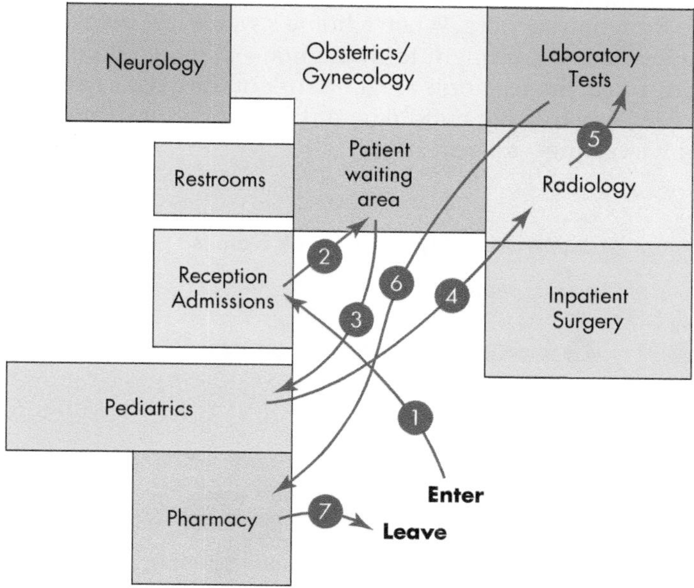

FIGURE 7.5 Process Layout for a Service Provider—a Medical Clinic

FIGURE 7.6 Product Layout for a Service—Automated Car Wash

the plant on conveyor belts or other equipment, often in a straight line, as it passes through each stage until the product is completed. Automobile, food-processing, and television-assembly plants use same-steps layouts, as do mail-processing facilities, such as UPS or the U.S. Postal Service.

Figure 7.6 shows a product layout at a service provider—an automatic car wash. Figure 7.7 is a goods-producer assembling parts needed to make storm windows. Same-steps layouts are efficient because the work skill is built into the equipment, allowing unskilled labor to perform simple tasks. But they are often inflexible, especially where they use specialized equipment that's hard to rearrange for new applications. During the 2020 COVID-19 pandemic, some large manufacturers, such as General Motors and Ford, retooled some of their manufacturing facilities to help produce vital medical equipment such as ventilators. This retooling was expensive, in part because it had to be done quickly.

Fixed-Position Layout *labor, equipment, materials, and other resources are brought to the geographic location where all production work is done*

Fixed-Position Layouts A **fixed-position layout** is often used when size, shape, or other factors make it difficult to move the service to another production facility. In fixed-position layouts, the product or client remains at one location; equipment, materials, and human skills are moved to that location, as needed, to perform the service or to build the product. While a patient is recovering at home from a knee replacement, for example, physical rehabilitation specialists come to the patient's home for rehab services. When a home's water line breaks or the roof starts leaking, repair services are brought to that home—at its fixed position—where the services are performed. Such layouts are used for building cruise and cargo ships that can't be moved, for constructing buildings, and for agricultural operations—plowing, fertilizing, and harvesting—at farm sites.

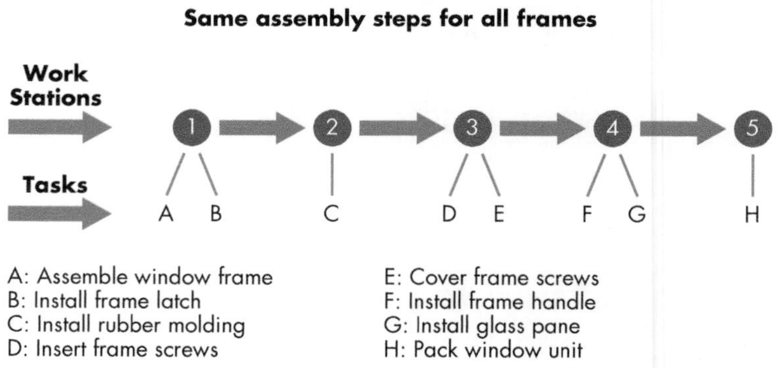

Same assembly steps for all frames

Work Stations → 1 → 2 → 3 → 4 → 5

Tasks → A B (1), C (2), D E (3), F G (4), H (5)

A: Assemble window frame
B: Install frame latch
C: Install rubber molding
D: Insert frame screws
E: Cover frame screws
F: Install frame handle
G: Install glass pane
H: Pack window unit

FIGURE 7.7 Product Layout for Goods Production—Storm Window Assembly

Quality Planning

Every operations plan includes activities for ensuring that products meet the firm's and customers' quality standards. The American Society for Quality defines **quality** as a subjective term, the combination of "characteristics of a product or service that bear on its ability to satisfy stated or implied needs."[9] Such characteristics may include a reasonable price and dependability in delivering the benefits it promises.

Quality *combination of "characteristics of a product or service that bear on its ability to satisfy stated or implied needs"*

Planning for quality begins when products are being designed. As we will see later, product design is a marketing responsibility, but it involves operations managers, too. Early in the process, goals are established for both performance and consistency. **Performance** refers to how well the product does what it is supposed to do. For loyal buyers of Godiva premium chocolates, performance includes such sensory delights as aroma, flavor, color, and texture. "Truly fine chocolates," observes master chocolatier Thierry Muret, "are always fresh, contain high-quality ingredients like cocoa beans and butter . . . and feature unusual textures and natural flavors." The recipe was designed to provide these features. Superior performance helps Godiva remain one of the world's top brands.[10]

Performance *dimension of quality that refers to how well a product does what it is supposed to do*

In addition to performance, quality also includes **consistency**, the sameness of product quality from unit to unit. Business travelers using Courtyard by Marriott, for example, enjoy high consistency with each overnight stay, which is one reason Courtyard by Marriott is among the best-selling brands in the lodging industry. Courtyard by Marriott achieved this status by offering guests the same amenities across all of its Courtyard hotels, which number more than 1,200 in over 60 countries and territories. Designed for business travelers, most guest rooms include a Courtyard Suite with high-speed Internet access; meeting space; access to an exercise room, restaurant and lounge, and swimming pool; and 24-hour access to food. The layout of the suites is identical at many locations, the rooms are always clean, and check-in/checkout procedures are identical so that lodgers know what to expect with each overnight stay. This consistency is achieved by monitoring for uniformity of materials and supplies, encouraging conscientious work, training employees, and maintaining equipment.

Consistency *dimension of quality that refers to sameness of product quality from unit to unit*

In addition to product design, quality planning includes employees deciding what constitutes a high-quality product—for both goods and services—and determining how to measure these quality characteristics.

Methods Planning

In designing operations systems, managers must identify each production step and the specific methods for performing it. They can then reduce waste and inefficiency by examining procedures on a step-by-step basis by using an approach called *methods improvement*.

Improving Process Flows Improvements for operations begin by documenting current production practices. A detailed description, often using a diagram called a *process flowchart*, is helpful in organizing and recording information. The flowchart identifies the sequence of production activities, movements of materials, and work performed at each stage of the process. It can then be analyzed to isolate wasteful activities, sources of delay, and other inefficiencies in both goods and services operations. The final step is implementing improvements.

Improving Customer Service Consider, for example, the traditional checkout method at hotels. The process flowchart in Figure 7.8 shows five stages of customer activities. Hotel checkout can be time consuming for customers standing in line to pay. They become impatient and annoyed, especially during peak checkout times when lines are long. Other hotel tasks are disrupted, too, as managers are forced to reassign employees to the front desk to assist with surging checkout lines. Hotel managers developed an improved checkout method that avoids wasting time in line for customers and reduces interruptions of other staff duties as well. It saves

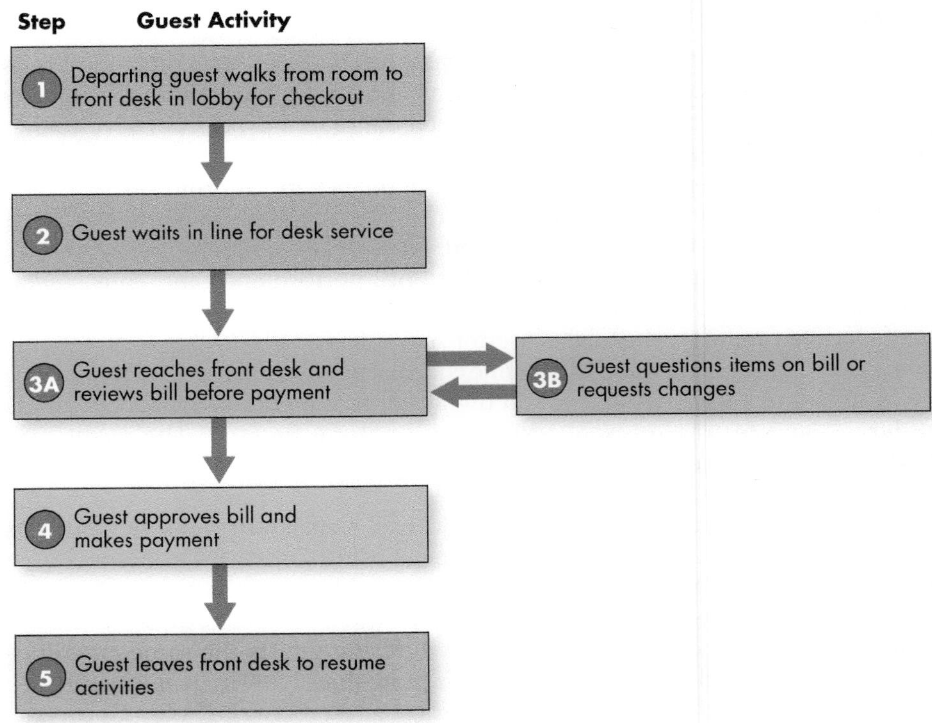

FIGURE 7.8 Flowchart of Traditional Guest Checkout

time by eliminating steps 1, 2, 3A, and 5. On the morning of departure, some hotels deliver final room bills under departing guests' room doors. Or, customers can review e-mailed bills and invoices using their smartphones anytime before departure. If the bill is correct, no further checkout is required, and the hotel submits the charges against the credit card that the customer provided during check-in.

Learning Objective 7-5

Discuss the information contained in four kinds of operations schedules—the master operations schedule, detailed schedule, staff schedule, and project schedule.

Operations Scheduling

Continuing with the flow of activities in Figure 7.4, once managers and their teams have determined the operations plans, they then develop timetables for implementing the plans. This aspect of operations, called *operations scheduling*, identifies times when specific activities will occur. In this section we consider four general kinds of schedules. (1) The *master schedule* is "the game plan" for deciding the volume of upcoming activities for months ahead. (2) *Detailed schedules* show day-to-day activities that will occur in production. (3) *Staff schedules* identify which and how many employees will be working and when. (4) Finally, *project schedules* provide coordination for completing large-scale projects.

The Master Operations Schedule

Master Operations Schedule *schedule showing which products will be produced and when in upcoming time periods*

Scheduling of operations occurs at different levels. First, a top-level **master operations schedule** shows which services or products will be produced and when, in upcoming time periods. Logan Aluminum, for example, makes coils of aluminum that it supplies to customer companies that use it to make beverage cans. Logan's master schedule, with a format like the partial schedule shown in Figure 7.9, covers production for 60 weeks in which more than 300,000 tons will be produced. For various types of coils (products), the master schedule specifies how many tons will be produced each week, helping managers determine the kinds of materials, equipment, and other resources that will be needed for each upcoming week.

Coil # (Product)	8/4/25	8/11/25	8/18/25	...	11/3/25	11/10/25
TC016	1,500	2,500			2,100	600
TC032	900		2,700		3,000	
TR020	300		2,600			1,600

FIGURE 7.9 Example of Partial Master Operations Schedule

The master schedule for a service provider, such as a regional food retailer, may begin with the planned number of retail stores to be operating in each quarter of the coming 2 years. Then, key resources needed in each quarter to provide customer services for all stores are identified (estimated). Figure 7.10 shows an example of such a partial master schedule. It provides information for planning on how many people the company will have to hire and train, planning for purchases of food products and the financing needed for those purchases, and planning for construction requirements of new stores.

Detailed Schedules

Although the master production schedule is the backbone for overall scheduling, additional information comes from **detailed schedules**, schedules showing daily work assignments with start and stop times for assigned jobs at each work station. Logan's production employees need to know the locations of all coils in the plant and their various stages of completion. Managers must assign start and stop times, and employees need scheduled work assignments daily, not just weekly. Detailed short-term schedules allow managers to use customer orders and information about equipment status to update sizes and the variety of coils to be made each day.

Detailed Schedule *schedule showing daily work assignments with start and stop times for assigned jobs*

KEY RESOURCES	Quarter/Year							
	1/2025	**2/2025**	**3/2025**	**4/2025**	**1/2026**	**2/2026**	**3/2026**	**4/2026**
Number of Stores	17	17	18	19	20	20	21	22
Staffing Level (no. of Employees)	1,360	1,360	1,530	1,615	1,700	1,700	1,653	1,827
Fresh Vegetables (tons)	204	204	192	228	240	240	230	260
Canned Goods (case loads)	73,950	77,350	80,100	80,100	83,000	84,500	88,600	90,200
Fresh Meats Etc.	–	–	–	–	–	–	–	–
– – –								

FIGURE 7.10 Food Retailer's Partial Operations Schedule

Staff Schedules and Computer-Based Scheduling

Staff Schedule *assigned working times in upcoming days for each employee on each work shift*

Scheduling is useful for employee staffing in service companies, too, including restaurants, hotels, and transportation and landscaping companies. **Staff schedules**, in general, specify assigned working times in upcoming days—perhaps for as many as 30 days or more—for each employee on each work shift. Staff schedules consider employees' needs and the company's efficiency and costs, including the ebbs and flows of demand for production.

Computer-based scheduling, using tools such as the *ABS Visual Staff Scheduler® PRO* (VSS Pro) software, can easily handle multishift activities for many employees—both part time and full time. It accommodates vacation times, holiday adjustments, and daily adjustments in staffing for unplanned absences and changes in production schedules.

Project Scheduling

Special projects, such as new business construction or redesigning a product, require close coordination and precise timing among many activities. In these cases, project management is facilitated by project scheduling tools, including Gantt charts and PERT.

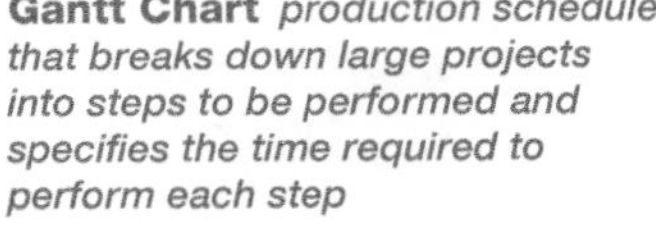

Gantt Chart *production schedule that breaks down large projects into steps to be performed and specifies the time required to perform each step*

The Gantt Graphical Method Named after its developer, Henry Gantt, a **Gantt chart** breaks down large projects into steps to be performed and specifies the time required to perform each one. The project manager lists all activities needed to complete the work, estimates the time required for each step, records the progress on the chart, and checks the progress against the time scale on the chart to keep the project moving on schedule. If work is ahead of schedule, some employees may be shifted to another project. If it's behind schedule, workers may be added or completion delayed.

Figure 7.11 shows a Gantt chart for the renovation of a college classroom. It shows progress to date and schedules for remaining work and that some steps can be performed at the same time (e.g., step D can be performed during the same time as steps C and E), but others cannot (e.g., step A must be completed before any of the others can begin). Step E is behind schedule; it should have been completed before the current date.

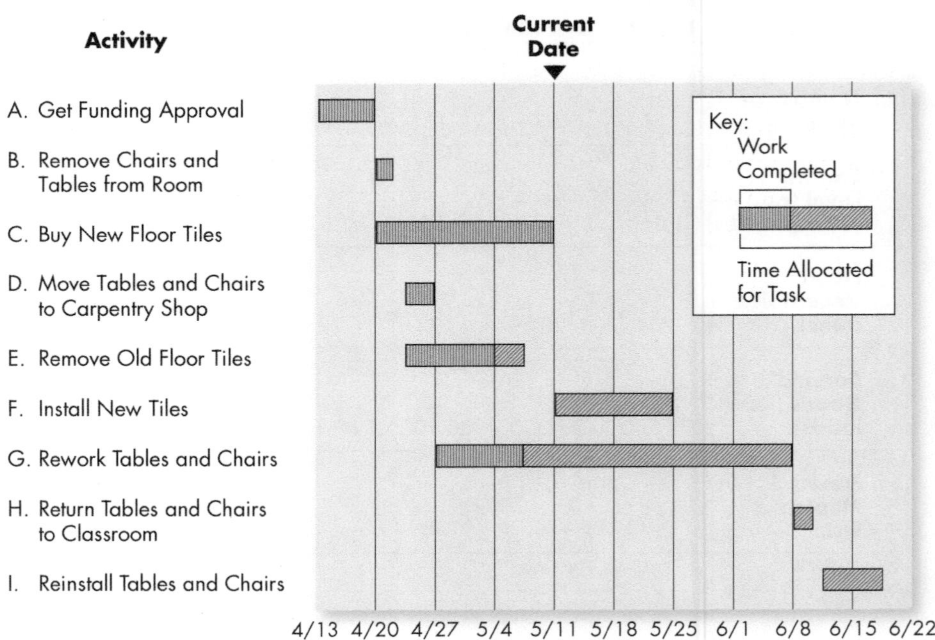

FIGURE 7.11 Gantt Chart

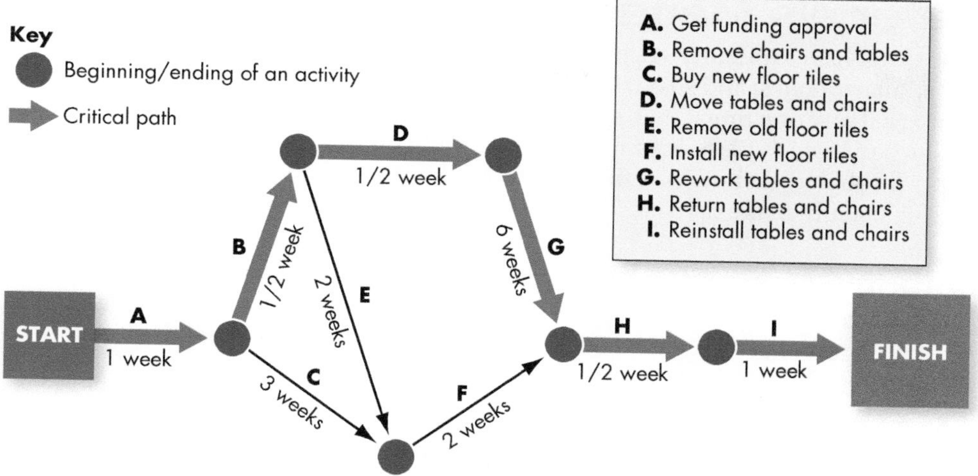

FIGURE 7.12 PERT Chart

Project Scheduling with PERT Charts The *Program Evaluation and Review Technique (PERT)* provides even more information for controlling the progress of large projects. Along with times required to perform the activities, the layout of the **PERT chart** uses arrows to show the necessary *sequence* among activities, from start to finish, for completing the project. It also identifies the *critical path*, the most time-consuming set of activities, for completing the project.

PERT Chart *production schedule specifying the sequence of activities, time requirements, and critical path for performing the steps in a project*

Figure 7.12 shows a PERT chart for renovating the college classroom. The project's nine activities and the times required to complete them are identified. Each activity is represented by an arrow. The arrows are positioned to show the required sequence for performing the activities. For example, chairs and tables can't be returned to the classroom (H) until after they've been reworked (G) and after new floor tiles are installed (F). Accordingly, the diagram shows arrows for G and F coming before activity H. Similarly, funding approval (A) has to occur before anything else can get started.

The critical path is informative because it reveals the most time-consuming path for project completion, and for most projects, speed of completion is vital. The critical path for classroom renovation consists of activities A, B, D, G, H, and I, requiring 9.5 weeks. It's critical because a delay in completing any of those activities will cause corresponding lateness beyond the planned completion time (9.5 weeks after start-up). Project managers will watch those activities and, if potential delays arise, take special action—by reassigning workers and equipment—to speed up late activities and stay on schedule.

Operations Control

Learning Objective 7-6

Discuss the two key activities required for operations control.

Once long-range plans have been put into action and schedules have been drawn up, **operations control** requires managers to monitor performance by comparing results with detailed plans and schedules. If employees do not meet schedules or quality standards, managers can take corrective action. **Follow-up**, checking to ensure that production decisions are being implemented, is a key and ongoing facet of operations.

Operations Control *process of monitoring production performance by comparing results with plans and taking corrective action when needed*

Follow-Up *operations control activity for ensuring that production decisions are being implemented*

Operations control includes *materials management* and *quality control*. Both activities ensure that schedules are met and products delivered, both in quantity and in quality.

Materials Management

Materials Management *process of planning, organizing, and controlling the flow of materials from sources of supply through distribution of finished goods*

Some of us have difficulty keeping track of personal items now and then—clothes, books, smartphones, and so on. Imagine keeping track of thousands, or even millions, of things at any one time. That's the challenge in **materials management**, the process by which managers plan, organize, and control the flow of materials from sources of supply through distribution of finished goods. For manufacturing firms, basic materials costs usually make up 50 to 75 percent of total product costs.

Materials Management Activities for Physical Goods Once a product has been designed, successful materials flows depend on five activities. From selecting suppliers on through the distribution of finished goods, materials managers engage in the following areas that compose materials management:

Supplier Selection *process of finding and choosing suppliers from whom to buy*

Purchasing *acquisition of the materials and services that a firm needs to produce its products*

Transportation *activities in transporting resources to the producer and finished goods to customers*

Warehousing *physical distribution operation concerned with the storage of goods*

Inventory Control *process of receiving, storing, handling, and counting of all raw materials, partly finished goods, and finished goods*

- **Supplier selection** is the process of finding and choosing suppliers of services and materials. This step includes evaluating potential suppliers, negotiating terms of service, and maintaining positive buyer–seller relationships.
- **Purchasing** (sometimes called *procurement*) is the acquisition of all the raw materials and services that a company needs to produce its products. Most large firms have purchasing departments to buy proper services and materials in the amounts needed.
- **Transportation** is the means of transporting resources to the producer and finished goods to customers.
- **Warehousing** is the storage of both incoming materials for production and finished goods for distribution to customers.
- **Inventory control** includes the receiving, storing, handling, and counting of all raw materials, partly finished goods, and finished goods. It ensures that enough materials inventories are available to meet production schedules, while at the same time avoiding expensive excess inventories.

Lean Production System *production system designed for smooth production flows that avoid inefficiencies, eliminate unnecessary inventories, and continuously improve production processes*

Just-In-Time (JIT) Production *type of lean production system that brings together all materials at the precise time they are required at each production stage*

Lean Production Systems Managers must take timing into consideration when managing materials as well. Pioneered by Toyota, **lean production systems** are designed for smooth production flows that avoid inefficiencies, eliminate unnecessary inventories, and continuously improve production processes. **Just-in-time (JIT) production**, a type of lean system, brings together all needed materials at the precise moment they are required for each production stage, not before, thus creating fast and efficient responses to customer orders. All resources flow continuously—from arrival as raw materials to final assembly and shipment of finished products.

JIT production reduces the number of goods in process (goods not yet finished) to practically nothing. It minimizes inventory costs, reduces storage space requirements for inventories, and saves money by replacing stop-and-go production with smooth movement. Once smooth flow is the norm, disruptions are more visible and employees can resolve them more quickly. Finding and eliminating disruptions by the continuous improvement of production is a major objective of JIT production.

Inventory Management Is Crucial for Producing Services For many service firms, too, the materials stakes are high. UPS delivers 25.2 million packages every day and promises that all of them will arrive on schedule. It keeps this promise by tracking the locations, schedules, and on-time performance of 582 aircraft and over 123,000 vehicles. However, the most important "inventory" used for many high-contact services is not physical goods but exists in the form of information about service product offerings, clients, their interests, needs, activities, and even their plans for interactions with other clients.

Consider, as an example, the *inventories of information* at Collette Vacations, where the *management of information* is a vital activity. Collette offers five product lines—Classic Tours, Exploration Tours (for smaller groups), Spotlight Tours, River Cruises, and Private Tours—that collectively offer more than 172 escorted tours on all seven continents including more than 65 countries. Each tour (the product), designed by a professional tour planner, includes a complete itinerary, duration, advanced arrangements for accommodations, and pricing. Vacationers select from among land tours, river cruises, and rail journeys that include sightseeing, meals, entertainment, and accommodations to experience new places, people, history, and culture.

As a tour begins, one of the company's more than 200 professional tour managers interacts face-to-face with clients as friend and guide for the entire duration, often 8 to 14 days, while handling all day-to-day details—confirming meal availabilities, ensuring hotel room accommodations, arranging local transportation, helping with sightseeing selections, providing knowledge of local culture, assisting each tourist with any questions or problems, and handling emergencies.

As you can see, these many activities create vast amounts of information—the *inventory of information*—that must be accurate and accessible for success with current tours and clients and for all the thousands of clients booked on hundreds of future tours. It is also vital for contacting many thousands of potential customers with advance information about tours that will be offered a year or two in the future.[11]

Quality Control

Quality control is taking action to ensure that operations produce goods or services that meet specific quality standards. Consider, for example, service operations in which customer satisfaction depends largely on the employees who provide the service. By monitoring services, managers and other employees can detect mistakes and make corrections. First, however, managers or other personnel must establish specific standards and measurements. At a bank, for example, quality control for teller services might require supervisors to observe employees periodically and evaluate their work according to a checklist. Managers would review the results with employees and either confirm proper performance or indicate changes for bringing performance up to standards.

Quality Control *action of ensuring that operations produce products that meet specific quality standards*

The high quality of customer–employee interactions is no accident in firms that monitor customer encounters and provide training for employee skills development. Many managers realize that without employees trained in customer-relationship skills, quality suffers, and businesses, such as airlines and hotels, can lose customers to better-prepared competitors.

Seventyfour74/123RF

Quality control means taking action to ensure that operations produce products that meet specific quality standards. This quality control inspector is checking finished products before shipment to make sure they meet or surpass the standards set by their customers.

Quality Improvement and Total Quality Management

Learning Objective 7-7

Identify the activities and underlying objectives involved in total quality management.

It is not enough to *control* quality by inspecting products and monitoring service operations as they occur, as when a supervisor listens in on a catalog sales service representative's customer calls. Businesses must also consider *building* quality into goods and services in the first place. Hospitals, such as Saint Luke's Hospital of Kansas City, use employee teams to design quality-assured treatment programs and patient-care procedures. Learning from past staff and patient problems, teams continuously redesign treatments, work methods, and procedures to eliminate the sources of quality problems. Whether it's administering a treatment, changing bed linens, restocking supplies, or filling out paperwork, they insist that every job be done correctly without error ("do it right the first time") rather than relying on inspection to catch mistakes and make corrections after they occur. To compete on a global scale, U.S. companies continue to emphasize a quality orientation. All employees, not just managers, participate in quality efforts, and firms have embraced new methods to measure progress and to identify areas for improvement. In many organizations, quality improvement has become a way of life.

The airline industry is both consolidated and highly competitive, and airlines have found that, in general, it's not possible for them to clearly differentiate on price and schedule alone. As a result, many airlines tend to focus a lot on the major determinants of customer satisfaction. For example, just about everyone who flies wants the plane to take off and land on time and the luggage to arrive when they do. So, airlines concentrate on on-time performance and baggage handling. In addition, many business travelers also want better and more spacious seating on their plane and access to a relaxing lounge before departure.

The Quality–Productivity Connection

It's no secret that *quality* and *productivity* are watchwords in today's competitive environment. Companies are not only measuring productivity and insisting on improvements; they also are requiring that quality brings greater satisfaction to customers, improves sales, and boosts profits.

Productivity *the amount of output produced compared with the amount of resources used to produce that output*

Productivity is a measure of economic performance: It compares how much we produce with the resources we use to produce it. The formula is fairly simple. The more services and goods we can produce while using fewer resources, the more productivity grows and the more everyone—the economy, businesses, and workers—benefits. At the national level, the most common measure is called *labor productivity* because it uses the amount of labor worked as the resource to compare against the benefits, the country's GDP, resulting from using that resource:

$$\text{Labor productivity of a country} = \frac{\text{GDP for the year}}{\text{Total number of labor hours worked for the year}}$$

This equation illustrates the general idea of productivity. We prefer the focus on labor, rather than on other resources (such as capital or energy), because most countries keep accurate records on employment and hours worked. Thus, national labor productivity can be used for measuring year-to-year changes and for comparing productivities with other countries. For 2021, for example, U.S. labor productivity was $74.78 of output per hour worked by the nation's labor force. By comparison, Norway was $84.46, Ireland was $128.21, and Belgium was $73.61. In contrast, Colombia was $24.02, lowest among the 46 measured countries.[12]

Managing for Quality

Total Quality Management (TQM) *all activities involved in getting high-quality goods and services into the marketplace*

Total quality management (TQM) includes all the activities necessary for getting high-quality goods and services into the marketplace. TQM begins with leadership and a desire for continuously improving both processes and products. It must consider

managing in turbulent times

Fasten Your Seat Belts, Please

Historically, airlines operate on a very thin margin of profitability even in a good year, so when oil prices soar and demand for travel drops, the industry suffers.

Economic uncertainty following the global financial crisis led airlines to cut services and adopt surcharges for things that had once been included in the price of the ticket, such as checked bags and on-board meals. Many airlines also made operational improvements to enhance efficiency and customer experience, including chip-enabled baggage control and more fuel-efficient planes. By the end of 2019, according to the International Air Transport Association (IATA), the world's airline industry had achieved a 10-year profit streak, even though those profits were increasingly concentrated among the sector's largest intercontinental airlines. Smaller and less efficient carriers had taken the brunt of adverse geopolitical and economic events, such as unfavorable exchange rates, turmoil in Latin and Central America, increased tariffs (and the resulting decrease in cargo movement), and a spate of air tragedies, most notably due to the ill-fated Boeing 737 MAX. Amid all this turbulence, passenger demand was strong, and it looked like a bit of smooth sailing might be on the horizon until the COVID-19 outbreak all but grounded the industry, leaving the future of even the strongest airlines in doubt.

Ton koene/Alamy Stock Photo

In 2023, with air travel once again reaching pre-pandemic levels, the Department of Transportation issued the largest fines in its history, facilitating refunds of over $1 billion to consumers in two years. Secretary of Transportation Pete Buttigieg called for the creation of an Airline Customer Service Dashboard with mandated airline reporting. The department issues the Air Travel Consumer Report, allowing consumers transparent and current monthly data to make informed decisions. The department believes the combination of required reporting and fines for violations will bring a greater level of accountability to the industry.[13]

all aspects of a business, including customers, suppliers, and employees. To marshal the interests of all these stakeholders, TQM first evaluates the costs of poor quality. TQM then identifies the sources causing unsatisfactory quality, assigns responsibility for corrections, and ensures that those who are responsible take steps for improving quality.

The Cost of Poor Quality As we noted earlier, several years ago Toyota inadvertently allowed its product quality to slip. As a result, the firm was forced to recall more than 24 million cars between 2009 and 2013, costing the world's then-number-one automaker billions of dollars and a severe blemish to its high-quality image. Problems ranging from sticking gas pedals to stalling engines and malfunctioning fuel pumps were dangerous and costly not only to Toyota but also to many consumers.

As with goods producers, service providers and customers suffer financial distress from poor-quality service products. The banking industry is a good example. As a backbone of the U.S. financial system, banks and their customers are still suffering because of bad financial products, most notably home mortgage loans during 2008 and 2009. Lenders during "good times" began relaxing (or even ignoring altogether) traditional lending standards for determining whether borrowers were creditworthy. Lenders in some cases intentionally overstated property values so customers could borrow more money than the property justified. Borrowers were sometimes encouraged to overstate (falsify) their incomes and were not required to present evidence of income or even employment. Some borrowers, unaware of the terms of their loan agreements, were surprised after an initial time lapse when a much higher interest rate (and monthly payment) suddenly kicked in. Unable to meet their payments, borrowers had to abandon their homes. Meanwhile, banks were left holding foreclosed properties, unpaid (defaulted) loans, and no cash. With shortages of bank funds threatening to shut down the nation's financial system, the entire country felt the widespread costs of poor quality—loss of equity by homeowners from foreclosures, a weakened economy, high unemployment, and loss of retirement funds in peoples' savings accounts. More recently, Silicon Valley Bank, Signature Bank, and First Republic Bank all failed in 2023 due to poor financial products and weak controls despite oversight by the Federal Reserve.

Quality Ownership: Taking Responsibility for Quality To ensure high-quality goods and services, many firms assign responsibility for some aspects of TQM to specific departments or positions. These specialists and experts may be called in to assist with quality-related problems in any department, and they keep everyone informed about the latest developments in quality-related equipment and methods. They also monitor quality-control activities to identify areas for improvement.

The backbone of TQM, however, and its biggest challenge, is motivating all employees and the company's suppliers to achieve quality goals. Leaders of the quality movement use various methods and resources to foster a quality focus, such as training, verbal encouragement, teamwork, and tying compensation to work quality. When those efforts succeed, employees and suppliers will ultimately accept **quality ownership**, the idea that quality belongs to each person who creates it while performing a job.

Quality Ownership *principle of total quality management that holds that quality belongs to each person who creates it while performing a job*

With TQM, everyone—purchasers, engineers, janitors, marketers, machinists, suppliers, and others—must focus on quality. At Saint Luke's Hospital of Kansas City, for example, every employee receives the hospital's "balanced scorecard" showing whether the hospital is meeting its goals: fast patient recovery for specific illnesses, 94 percent or better patient-satisfaction rating, every room cleaned when a patient has gone to the X-ray department, and the hospital's return on investment being sufficient to earn a good bond rating in the financial markets. Quarterly scores show the achievement level reached for each goal. Every employee can recite where the hospital is excelling and where it needs improvement. In recognition of its employees' dedication to quality performance, Saint Luke's received the Malcolm Baldrige National Quality Award, the prestigious U.S. award for excellence in quality, and is a five-time winner of the Missouri Quality Award.[14]

Tools for Total Quality Management

Hundreds of tools have proven useful for quality improvement, ranging from statistical analysis of product data, to satisfaction surveys of customers, to **competitive product analysis**, a process by which a company analyzes a competitor's products to identify desirable improvements. Using competitive analysis, for example, Bose might take apart a set of Beats headphones and test each component. The results would help managers decide which Bose product features are satisfactory, which features should be upgraded, and which operations processes need improvement. In this section, we describe five of the most commonly used tools for TQM: (1) *value-added analysis*, (2) *quality improvement teams*, (3) *getting closer to the customer*, (4) *the ISO series*, and (5) *business process reengineering*.

Competitive Product Analysis *process by which a company analyzes a competitor's products to identify desirable improvements*

Value-Added Analysis **Value-added analysis** refers to the evaluation of all work activities, materials flows, and paperwork to determine the value that they add for customers. It often reveals wasteful or unnecessary activities that can be eliminated without jeopardizing customer service. The basic tenet is so important that Tootsie Roll Industries, the venerable candy company, employs it as a corporate principle: "We run a trim operation and continually strive to eliminate waste, minimize cost, and implement performance improvements."[15]

Value-Added Analysis *process of evaluating all work activities, materials flows, and paperwork to determine the value that they add for customers*

Quality Improvement Teams Companies throughout the world have adopted **quality improvement teams**, which are patterned after the successful Japanese concept of *quality circles*, collaborative groups of employees from various work areas who meet regularly to define, analyze, and solve common production problems. The teams' goal is to improve both their own work methods and the products they make. Quality improvement teams organize their own work, select leaders, and address problems in the workplace. For years, Motorola sponsored company-wide team competitions to emphasize the value of the team approach, to recognize outstanding team performance, and to reaffirm the team's role in the company's continuous-improvement culture. Many firms today use variations on this concept, although they often use different names for these teams.

Quality Improvement Team *total quality management tool in which collaborative groups of employees from various work areas work together to improve quality by solving common shared production problems*

Getting Closer to the Customer Successful businesses take steps to know what their customers want in the products they consume. Struggling companies, however, have often lost sight of customers as the driving force behind all business activity. Such companies waste resources by designing products that customers do not want. Sometimes, they ignore customer reactions to existing products. For instance, some airlines seem to disregard customer complaints about poor service. Or companies fail to keep up with changing customer preferences. BlackBerry mobile devices, for example, fell behind competing products because they did not offer customers the features that Samsung, Motorola, and Apple provided.

Successful firms take steps to know what their customers want in the products they consume. The financial services department of Caterpillar (CAT), for example, was one of the first recipients of a Malcolm Baldrige National Quality Award for high ratings by its customers (that is, dealers and buyers of Caterpillar equipment). Buying and financing equipment from Cat Financial became easier as CAT moved its services increasingly online. Customers now have 24/7 access to information on how much they owe on equipment costing anywhere from $30,000 to $2 million, and they can make payments around the clock, too. In the past, the 60,000 customers had to phone a CAT representative, who was often unavailable, resulting in delays and wasted time. The improved online system is testimony to Cat Financial's dedication in knowing what customers want and then providing it.[16] Recent Baldrige award winners have included AARP, Midway USA, and GBMC Health Care.

Identifying Customers—Internal and External Improvement projects are undertaken for both external and internal customers. Internal suppliers and internal customers exist wherever one employee or activity relies on others. For example, marketing managers rely on internal accounting information—costs for materials, supplies, and wages—to plan marketing activities for coming months. The marketing manager is a customer of the firm's accountants; the information user relies on the information supplier. Accountants in a TQM environment recognize this supplier–customer connection and take steps to improve information for marketing.

The ISO Series Perhaps you've driven past companies proudly displaying large banners that announce "This Facility Is ISO Certified." The ISO (pronounced ICE-oh) label is a mark of quality achievement respected throughout the world, and in some countries it's a requirement for doing business. ISO has several levels of certification, but the two most relevant to TQM are ISO 9000 and ISO 14000.[17]

ISO 9000 **ISO 9000** is a certification program attesting that a factory, a laboratory, or an office has met the rigorous quality management requirements set by the International Organization for Standardization (ISO). Today, more than 170 countries have adopted ISO 9000 as a national standard. Over 1 million certificates have been issued worldwide to organizations meeting the ISO standards.

ISO 9000 *program certifying that a factory, laboratory, or office has met the quality management standards set by the International Organization for Standardization*

The standards of *ISO 9000* require firms to show that they follow documented procedures for testing products, training workers, keeping records, and fixing defects. It allows international companies to determine (or be assured of) quality of product (or the business) when shipping for, from, and to suppliers across borders. To become certified, companies must document the procedures followed by workers during every stage of production. The purpose is to ensure that a company's processes can create products exactly the same today as they did yesterday and as they will tomorrow.

ISO 14000 *certification program attesting to the fact that a factory, laboratory, or office has improved its environmental performance*

ISO 14000 The **ISO 14000** program certifies improvements in environmental performance by requiring a firm to develop an *environmental management system*: a plan documenting how the company has acted to improve its performance in using resources (such as raw materials) and in managing pollution. A company not only must identify hazardous wastes that it expects to create but also must stipulate plans for treatment and disposal.

Business Process Reengineering Every business consists of processes, activities that it performs regularly and routinely in conducting business, such as receiving and storing materials from suppliers, billing patients for medical treatment, filing insurance claims for auto accidents, and filling customer orders from Internet sales. Any business process can increase customer satisfaction by performing it well. By the same token, any business process can disappoint customers when it's poorly managed.

Business Process Reengineering *rethinking and radical redesign of business processes to improve performance, quality, and productivity*

Business process reengineering focuses on improving a business process—rethinking each of its steps by starting from scratch. *Reengineering* is the fundamental rethinking and radical redesign of business processes to achieve dramatic improvements as measured by cost, quality, service, and speed. The discussion of CAT's changeover to an online system for customers is an example. CAT reengineered the whole payments and financing process by improving equipment, retraining employees, and connecting customers to CAT's databases. As the example illustrates, redesign is guided by a desire to improve operations and thereby provide higher-value services for customers.

Learning Objective 7-8

Explain how a supply chain strategy differs from traditional strategies for coordinating operations among firms.

Adding Value Through Supply Chains

Supply Chain (or Value Chain) *flow of information, materials, and services that starts with raw-materials suppliers and continues adding value through other stages in the network of firms until the product reaches the end customer*

The term *supply chain* refers to the group of companies and stream of activities that work together to create a product. A **supply chain (or value chain)** for any product is the flow of information, materials, and services that starts with raw-materials suppliers and continues adding value through other stages in the network of firms until the product reaches the end customer.

Figure 7.13 shows the chain of activities for supplying baked goods to consumers. Each stage adds value for the final customer. This bakery example begins with raw materials (grain harvested from the farm). It also includes storage and transportation activities, factory operations for baking and wrapping, and distribution to retailers. Each stage depends on the others for success in getting freshly baked goods to consumers. However, a failure by any link can create problems for the entire chain. Indeed, many of the food and cleaning products shortages experienced during the COVID-19 pandemic were due to breakdowns in supply chains. Suppose, for example, that a particular company routinely orders and receives various chemicals that are then combined to manufacture hand sanitizer. The finished product is poured into containers and labels are applied to the containers. The bottles are then packed into cardboard boxes. Next, a shipping company picks up boxes of the product from the manufacturer and transports them to a distribution center, where they are stored and then picked up again to be delivered to a retailer that has placed an order (and this is actually a very simple supply chain example). Now, further suppose the company that provides the cardboard boxes was located in an area that was greatly affected by the COVID-19 and closed its doors for several weeks. In reality, there was plenty of hand sanitizer, shipping companies willing to transport it, and retailers wanting to sell

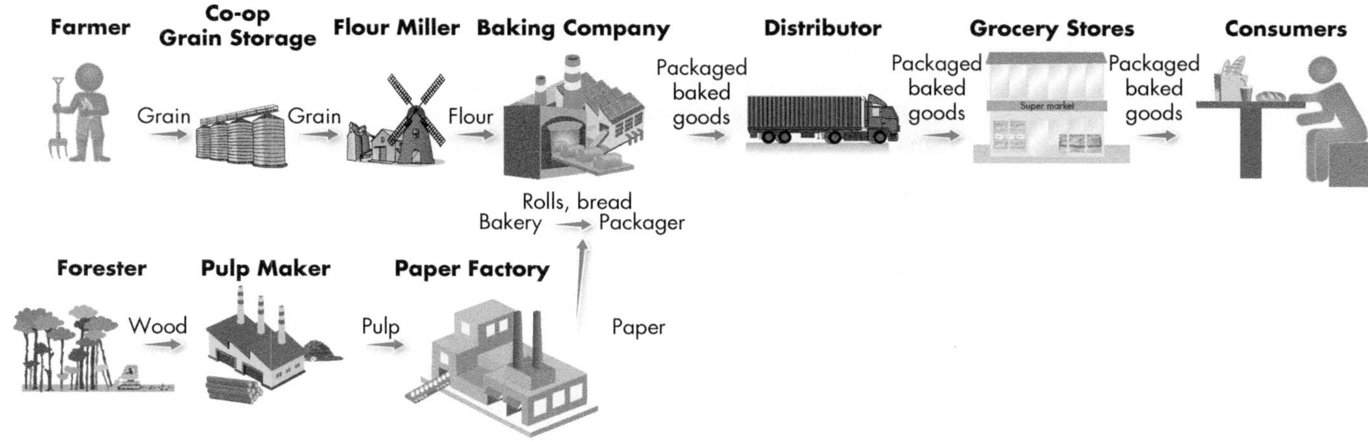

FIGURE 7.13 Supply Chain for Baked Goods

it. However, because no boxes were available near the beginning of the supply chain, customers at the end of the supply chain would not be able to purchase it. Supply chain disruptions attributable to the pandemic continued to plague some products and regions for several years.

The Supply Chain Strategy

Traditional strategies assume that companies are managed as individual firms rather than as members of a coordinated supply system. Supply chain strategy is based on the idea that members of the chain will gain competitive advantage by working as a coordinated unit. Although each company looks out for its own interests, it works closely with suppliers and customers throughout the chain. Everyone focuses on the entire chain of relationships rather than on just the next stage in the chain.

A traditionally managed bakery, for example, would focus simply on getting production inputs from flour millers and paper suppliers, and then on supplying baked goods to distributors. Unfortunately, this approach limits the chain's performance and doesn't allow for possible improvements when activities are more carefully coordinated. Proper management and better coordination among supply chain activities can provide fresher baked goods at lower prices.

Supply Chain Management **Supply chain management (SCM)** looks at the chain as a whole to improve the overall flow through a system composed of companies working together. Because customers ultimately get better value, supply chain management gains competitive advantage for each of the chain's members.

Supply Chain Management (SCM) *principle of looking at the supply chain as a whole to improve the overall flow through the system*

An innovative supply chain strategy was the heart of Michael Dell's vision when he established Dell Inc. Dell's concept improves performance by sharing information among chain members. Dell's long-term production plans and up-to-the-minute sales data are available to suppliers online. The process starts when customers' orders are automatically translated into updated production schedules in the factory. These schedules are used not only by operations managers at Dell but also by such parts suppliers as chip-maker Intel, which adjust their own production and shipping activities to better meet Dell's production needs. In turn, parts suppliers' updated schedules are transmitted to their materials suppliers, and so on up the chain. As Dell's requirements change, suppliers up and down the chain synchronize their schedules to produce only the right materials and parts. As a result, Dell's prices are low, and turnaround time for shipping PCs to customers is reduced to a matter of hours instead of days.

Reengineering Supply Chains for Better Results Process improvements and reengineering often are applied in supply chains to lower costs, speed up service, and coordinate flows of information and material. Because the smoother flow of accurate information along the chain reduces unwanted inventories and transportation, avoids delays, and cuts supply times, materials move faster to business customers and individual consumers. SCM offers faster deliveries and lower costs than customers could get if each member acted only according to its own operations requirements.

Outsourcing and Global Supply Chains

Outsourcing *the practice of paying suppliers and distributors to perform business processes or to provide needed materials or services*

Outsourcing is the strategy of paying suppliers and distributors to perform certain business processes or to provide needed materials or services. The decision to outsource expands supply chains. Of course, this served to further disrupt supply chains during the 2020 COVID-19 pandemic. For instance, many companies around the globe use parts and components manufactured in China. As you will recall, China was the first country to be hit by the virus and was one of the hardest hit. To better control the spread of the virus, the Chinese government ordered most businesses, including factories, to shut down for several weeks. This shutdown, in turn, led to shortages of parts that companies in other countries had come to depend on.

finding a better way

Social Responsibility in the Supply Chain

Archaeologists have found evidence that blacksmiths were making steel as far back as the thirteenth century BC. Most likely, the discovery of steel resulted from iron being left too long in coal furnaces that contained high levels of carbon. The carbon made the iron stronger, harder, and more durable. Today, steel is a crucial industry for developed nations, but it is also one of the most energy-intensive; every ton of steel produced in a traditional blast furnace results in over 1.5 tons of carbon dioxide.

Enter Swedish steel maker SSAB, which is on a mission to reduce its carbon footprint. Already a leader in recycling steel, SSAB has refined its manufacturing process to fuel its blast furnaces with hydrogen instead of coke (a form of coal). Instead of releasing carbon dioxide as a by-product, the blast furnaces produce water, which is used to source more hydrogen, resulting in a natural, closed cycle. No polluted water is discharged, and no carbon dioxide is emitted; SSAB describes this as a fossil-free process.

Changing operations to this degree is not an easy task. SSAB's old production facilities needed to be drastically redesigned and couldn't be repurposed without missing production quotas.

As SSAB continues to develop its "fossil-free" HYBRIT technology, it aims to be the first steel company to provide fossil-free steel to market, a goal it expects to reach by 2026. By 2030, it plans to eliminate nearly all carbon dioxide emissions from its operations. As SSAB describes, the company "aims to create a fossil-free value chain, from the mine to the end-product."[18]

Roland Magnusson/Shutterstock

As SSAB goes green, its efforts will reverberate across other industries that use its steel. In 2021, Volvo Group unveiled the world's first vehicle made of fossil-free steel from SSAB. A move toward green steel is an important step for Volvo Group, as well as for the transport and infrastructure industries as a whole, particularly considering that around 70 percent of a truck's weight comes from steel and cast iron.

Martin Lindqvist, president and CEO at SSAB, reports, "Our collaboration with Volvo Group shows that green transition is possible and brings results. Together, we will continue reducing climate impact all the way to the end customer while ensuring that our customers get high-quality steel."[19]

The movement of manufacturing and service operations from the United States to countries such as China, Mexico, and India has reduced U.S. employment in traditional jobs. It has also created new operations jobs for SCM. Maytag, for example, had to develop its own internal global operations expertise before it could decide to open a new refrigerator factory in Mexico, import refrigerators from South Korea's Daewoo, and get laundry appliances from South Korea's Samsung Electronics. In departing from a long-standing practice of domestic production, Maytag adopted new supply chain skills for evaluating prospective outsourcing partners.

Skills for coordinating Maytag's domestic activities with those of its cross-border partners didn't end with the initial decision to get appliances from Mexico and Korea. Maytag personnel in their Newton, Iowa, headquarters have near-constant interaction with their partners on a host of continuing new operations issues. Product redesigns are transferred from the United States and used at remote manufacturing sites. Arrangements for cross-border materials flows require compliance with each country's commerce regulations. Production and global transportation scheduling are coordinated with U.S. market demand so that outsourced products arrive in the right amounts and on time without tarnishing Maytag's reputation for high quality. Although manufacturing operations are located remotely, they are closely integrated with the firm's home-base activities. That tightness of integration demands on-site operations expertise on both sides of the outsourcing equation. Global communication technologies are essential. The result for outsourcers is a greater need of operations skills for integration among dispersed facilities.

summary of learning objectives

LEARNING OBJECTIVE 7-1

Explain the meaning of *operations* and discuss the growth in the services and goods sectors of the U.S. economy.

Operations (or *production*) refers to all the activities involved in making products—goods and services—for customers. In modern societies, much of what we need or want is produced by service operations, where success or failure depends on provider-customer contact. Many companies, such as General Electric, provide both goods and services. Employment has risen significantly in the service sector over the past 10 years. However, the 11 percent of the U.S. workforce employed in producing goods generate 32 percent of national income.

Production, or operations, adds customer value by providing *utility*—the ability of a product to satisfy a want or need—in terms of form, time, and place: (1) *form utility*: by turning raw materials and human skills into finished goods and services, production adds customer value by making products available; (2) *time utility*: production provides customer value by making products available when customers want them; and (3) *place utility*: production adds customer value by making products available where they are convenient for customers.

Operations management is the systematic direction and control of the activities that transform resources into finished goods and services that create value for and provide benefits to customers. Through their operations processes—using resources that include knowledge, physical materials, information, equipment, the customer, and human skills—firms provide benefits for themselves and for their customers.

LEARNING OBJECTIVE 7-2

Identify the three kinds of utility created by operations and the characteristics that distinguish service operations from goods production.

Although the creation of both goods and services involves resources, transformations, and finished products, service operations differ from goods manufacturing in several important ways. In service production, the raw materials are not things such as glass or steel, but rather people who choose among sellers because they have unsatisfied needs or possessions in need of care or alteration. Therefore, whereas services are typically performed, goods are physically produced. In addition, services are largely *intangible* and more *unstorable* than most physical goods. As an example, it is difficult to store a supply (an inventory) of childcare services. If the services are not consumed when available, they are lost forever.

Service businesses, therefore, focus explicitly on the intangibility and unstorable nature of their products. Because services are intangible, for instance, providers work to ensure that customers receive value in the form of pleasure, satisfaction, or a feeling of safety. Often they also focus on both the transformation process and the final product (such as making the loan interview a pleasant experience as well as providing the loan itself). As part of the transformation process, service providers typically focus on *customer–provider contact*. This requires service workers who, because they interact with customers, possess different skills than workers producing physical goods.

An *operations process* is a set of methods and technologies used to produce a good or service. Goods production can be classified as *make-to-order* or *make-to-stock*. Make-to-order operations respond to specific customer specifications, and make-to-stock operations produce standardized goods for mass consumption.

Service operations can be classified according to the extent of customer contact. In a *low-contact system*, customers have a limited presence as the service is performed. Low-contact systems include mail and package delivery, auto repair, lawn care services, and gas and electric providers. In contrast, in a *high-contact system*, the customer is present as the service is delivered. Examples of high-contact systems include airlines and hair salons.

LEARNING OBJECTIVE 7-3

Explain how companies with different business strategies are best served by having different operations capabilities.

Production is a flexible activity that can be molded into many shapes to give different operations capabilities (production capabilities) for different purposes. Its design is best driven from above by the firm's larger business strategy. When firms adopt different strategies for winning customers in specific target markets, they should also adjust their *operations capabilities*—what production must do especially well—to match the chosen strategy. That is, different target markets have different desires or expectations for the products—services and goods—that they seek. Accordingly, operations managers must clarify and understand their target market's most preferred product characteristic from among the following: Do they want low-cost products? The highest-quality products? Dependability of product performance? A wide variety of offerings rather than just a few? To meet any chosen strategy, then, operations managers adopt an operations capability that is geared toward meeting the target customers' needs. The operations capability that is appropriate for a low-cost strategy, for example, is different from the kind of competence that is best for a dependability strategy. Accordingly, the operations characteristics, such as number and size of production facilities, employee skills, kinds of equipment, and operations activities, will be different, resulting in different operations capabilities to better support their different purposes.

LEARNING OBJECTIVE 7-4

Identify the major factors that are considered in operations planning.

Operations planning includes five major considerations: (1) *Capacity planning* considers current and future capacity requirements for meeting anticipated customer demand. The amount of a product that a company can produce under normal conditions is its *capacity*, and it depends on how many people it employs and the number and sizes of its facilities. (2) *Location planning* is crucial because a firm's location affects costs of production, ease of transportation, access to skilled workers, and convenient accessibility for customers. (3) *Layout planning* determines the physical location of service teams, machinery, equipment, and facilities and affects how efficiently a company can respond to customer demand. A *process (custom-products) layout* is effective for make-to-order production specializing in custom-designed services or goods. A *product (same-steps) layout*, such as an assembly line, is often used for large-volume, make-to-stock production of services or goods. A *fixed-position layout* is necessary when, because of size, shape, or any other reason, the service to be provided cannot be moved to another facility. Instead, the product or client remains at one location; equipment, materials, and human skills are moved to that location, as needed, to perform the service or to build the product. (4) *Quality planning* begins when products are being designed and extends into production operations for ensuring that the desired performance and consistency are built into products. Quality is defined as the combination of "characteristics of a product or service that bear on its ability to satisfy stated or implied needs." Quality planning involves setting goals for both *performance* and *consistency*. (5) *Methods planning* considers each production step and the specific methods for performing it to produce services and goods. The purpose is to reduce waste and inefficiency by methods improvement procedures.

LEARNING OBJECTIVE 7-5

Discuss the information contained in four kinds of operations schedules—the master operations schedule, detailed schedule, staff schedule, and project schedule.

Operations scheduling identifies times when specific operations activities will occur. The *master schedule*, the top-level schedule for upcoming production, shows how many of which products (services or goods) will be produced in each time period, in weeks or months ahead, to meet upcoming customer demand. Thereafter, the schedule shows how many units of each major resource—materials, employees, equipment—will be required. By identifying these future resource requirements, managers can develop plans for acquiring the resources on time for upcoming time periods.

Detailed schedules take a shorter-range perspective by specifying daily work assignments with start and stop times for assigned jobs at each workstation. Detailed schedules allow managers and other employees to make last-minute adjustments so that resources are available and matched to meet immediate customer service requirements.

Staff schedules identify who and how many employees will be working and their assigned working times on each work shift for the upcoming month or months. Staff scheduling considers the needs of employees as well as the company's goals of maximizing efficiency and controlling costs.

Finally, *project schedules* provide information for completing large-scale projects using project scheduling tools, such as *Gantt* and *PERT charts*. A Gantt chart breaks down special large projects into the sequence of steps to be performed and specifies the time required to perform each. Gantt charts help managers to assess if work is ahead or behind schedule so that adjustments can be made. PERT charts show the necessary sequence among activities and identify the critical path—the most time-consuming set of activities for completing the project.

LEARNING OBJECTIVE 7-6

Discuss the two key activities required for operations control.

Materials management and quality control are two key activities of operations control. Once plans and schedules have been drawn up, operations control requires managers to monitor performance by comparing results against those plans and schedules. If schedules or quality standards are not met, managers take corrective action. Follow-up—checking to ensure that decisions are being implemented—is an essential facet of operations control. Materials management—including supplier selection, purchasing, transportation, warehousing, and inventory control—facilitates the flow of materials. Materials management is the process by which managers plan, organize, and control the flow of materials and services from sources of supply through distribution of finished products to customers. For producing and delivering physical goods, it may use lean production systems, such as just-in-time operations, for smooth production flows that avoid inefficiencies, comply with schedules, eliminate unnecessary inventories, and continuously improve production processes. For high-contact services, such as tourism and vacation services, inventory exists in the forms of information about service offerings, facilities arrangements, clients, client interests, activities schedules, and plans for interactions among and with clients. Quality control means taking action to ensure that operations produce goods and services that meet specific quality standards. By monitoring products and services, managers and other employees can detect mistakes, identify potential quality failures, and make corrections to avoid poor quality. Both materials management and quality control are essential to ensure that schedules are met and products delivered, both in quality and quantity.

LEARNING OBJECTIVE 7-7

Identify the activities and underlying objectives involved in total quality management.

Successful companies focus on productivity, which measures both the quantity and quality of the products produced or delivered. Productivity compares the level of production with the amount of resources used to produce it. *Total quality management* (*TQM*) is a customer-driven culture for offering products with characteristics that customers want. It includes all the activities necessary for getting customer-satisfying goods and services into the marketplace and, internally, getting every job to give better service to internal customers (other departments) within the organization. TQM begins with leadership and a desire for continuously improving both processes and products. It considers all aspects of a business, including customers, suppliers, and employees. The TQM culture fosters an attitude of *quality ownership* among employees and suppliers, the idea that quality belongs to each person who creates it while performing a job, so that quality improvement becomes a continuous way of life. It identifies the *costs of poor quality*, including all forms of financial distress resulting from poor-quality products, and uses cost-of-poor-quality information as a guide for process improvement to prevent such costs in the future.

Numerous quality improvement tools can then be used to gain those improvements and reduce those costs. Some process improvement tools of TQM include competitive product analysis, value-added analysis, the use of quality improvement teams, business process reengineering, and "getting closer to the customer" to gain valid information about what customers really want, so that improved products more closely meet customer desires.

ISO 9000 is a certification program attesting that a factory, laboratory, or office has met the rigorous quality management requirements set by the International Organization for Standardization. Similarly, *ISO 14000* certifies improvements in environmental performance. Finally, business process reengineering focuses on the radical redesign of business processes to achieve improvements in cost, quality, service, and speed.

LEARNING OBJECTIVE 7-8

Explain how a supply chain strategy differs from traditional strategies for coordinating operations among firms.

The supply chain strategy is based on the idea that members of the *supply chain*, the stream of all activities and companies that add value in creating a product, will gain competitive advantage by working together as a coordinated unit. The supply chain for any product, be it a service or a physical good, is the flow of information, materials, and services that starts with raw-materials suppliers and continues adding value through other stages in the network of firms until the product reaches the end customer. In contrast, traditional strategies assume that companies are managed as individual firms, each acting in its own interest. By managing the chain as a whole—using *supply chain management*—companies can more closely coordinate activities throughout the chain. Because accurate information is shared between companies along the chain, they can reduce unwanted materials and transportation, avoid delays in deliveries to cut supply times, quickly add service centers to meet upsurges in demand, and move materials faster through the chain. By sharing information across all stages in the chain, overall costs and inventories can be reduced, quality can be improved, and overall flow through the system can be improved, thus providing customers higher value from faster deliveries and lower costs.

Outsourcing, the strategy of paying suppliers and distributors to perform certain business processes or to provide needed materials or services, expands supply chains. The prevalence of outsourcing has created new operations jobs in supply chain management.

key terms

assembly line layout **(p. 213)**
business process reengineering **(p. 226)**
capacity **(p. 211)**
competitive product analysis **(p. 224)**
consistency **(p. 215)**
detailed schedule **(p. 217)**
fixed-position layout **(p. 214)**
follow-up **(p. 219)**
Gantt chart **(p. 218)**
goods operations (or goods production) **(p. 203)**
high-contact system **(p. 208)**
inventory control **(p. 220)**
ISO 9000 **(p. 225)**
ISO 14000 **(p. 226)**
just-in-time (JIT) production **(p. 220)**
lean production system **(p. 220)**
low-contact system **(p. 208)**
make-to-order operations **(p. 208)**
make-to-stock operations **(p. 208)**
master operations schedule **(p. 216)**
materials management **(p. 220)**
operations capability (production capability) **(p. 209)**
operations control **(p. 219)**
operations process **(p. 208)**
operations (or production) **(p. 203)**
operations (production) management **(p. 206)**
operations (production) managers **(p. 206)**
outsourcing **(p. 228)**
performance **(p. 215)**
PERT chart **(p. 219)**
process layout (custom-product layout) **(p. 213)**
product layout (same-steps layout) **(p. 213)**
productivity **(p. 222)**
purchasing **(p. 220)**
quality **(p. 215)**
quality control **(p. 221)**
quality improvement team **(p. 225)**
quality ownership **(p. 224)**
service operations (or service production) **(p. 203)**
staff schedule **(p. 218)**
supplier selection **(p. 220)**
supply chain management (SCM) **(p. 227)**
supply chain (value chain) **(p. 226)**
total quality management (TQM) **(p. 222)**
transportation **(p. 220)**
utility **(p. 205)**
value-added analysis **(p. 224)**
warehousing **(p. 220)**

questions & exercises

QUESTIONS FOR REVIEW

7-1. Describe, in your own words, the meaning and significance of business operations. What do we mean when we talk about operations? What does it encompass? What does it exclude?

7-2. What are the major differences between goods-production operations and service operations?

7-3. What are the major differences between high-contact and low-contact service systems? Give an example of each, comparing and contrasting them.

7-4. What are the three kinds of utility (give examples of each)?

QUESTIONS FOR ANALYSIS

7-5. How would you describe the five major operations planning activities to an administrator of your college or to a local business owner? Use specific examples as they apply to your chosen organization.

7-6. List three products you have had trouble finding at some point in your life due to supply chain disruptions. Where in the chain do you think things broke down and why?

7-7. Choose three different businesses that you frequent and rate the quality of their service or product on a scale of 1–5, with 1 being poor quality and 5 being high quality. How do you think their production operations affect quality? What might they do differently to improve quality?

7-8. If you were a member of a quality improvement team at your college or a local business of your choice, what would be four to five specific high-impact operations recommendations? Describe which two would be the most important, and briefly explain what strategies you might employ as a manager to implement those two recommendations.

APPLICATION EXERCISES

7-9. Map out the process for enrolling in classes at your school by drawing a process flowchart that shows the stages in the activity, and then tell how you would use that flowchart as part of a methods improvement approach to operations planning.

7-10. Create a short memo to a struggling manufacturing business explaining the benefits of formal operating planning schedules.

building a business: continuing team exercise

ASSIGNMENT

Meet with your team members to consider your new business venture and how it relates to the operations management and quality topics in this chapter. Develop specific responses to the following:

7-11. In what ways is your business connected with service operations? Identify the ways it is connected with goods production. Which of these, service operations or goods production, is more important to your business? Why?

7-12. Explain what must be done to ensure that your operations capabilities are consistent with your business strategy. How does your mission statement support operations? What kinds of quality control measures should you consider?

7-13. Discuss how your team is going to identify the key operations characteristics that best provide support for accomplishing your business strategy. Based on the discussion, what are the key characteristics that seem to be most prominent at this stage of development of your business?

7-14. Analyze the planned production activities for your business to determine the operations processes for which total quality management will be important.

7-15. In what ways, if any, will supply chains be of concern for your business? Explain.

team exercise

CALCULATING THE COST OF COMPETITION

The Situation

You are part of the operations management team for Safety Solutions, Inc., a Houston, Texas, company that recently went public. The main product line is a video surveillance system that is integrated with inside and outside sensors and a 24/7 call center that responds to any disturbances by calling both 911 and selected members of the leadership and crisis response team. Until it went public, Safety Solutions was a family-owned company built on the "Made in America" theme. Unfortunately, the company's success has spawned copycat businesses that are providing similar products and services at a lower cost, and so the company's bottom line is suffering.

The Dilemma

The CEO, Beth Meyer, who is new to the company, has asked your team to come up with several alternatives to increase operating efficiency and thereby decrease costs, in order to increase profits. She has already put pressure on the sales and marketing teams to increase sales, but even if sales increase over time, she still expects you to boost operating efficiencies. She is especially interested in the idea of "offshoring" production to a company in Mexico that is manufacturing the sensors and video equipment for most of your competitors as well as outsourcing the call center to a company in India that manages this service for other security firms. The long-term lease for the combined call center and factory is up for renewal soon, so this would be a good time to make this kind of move and would save the company millions of dollars a month in costs, including the lease, insurance, and the wages and benefits of about a thousand laid-off, nonunion employees.

FOLLOW-UP QUESTIONS

7-16. If you were a customer, what would you hope the company would do? Would your answer be different if you were an investor or stockholder? What would you want the company to do if you were an employee?

7-17. What are the pros and cons of moving both manufacturing and the call center to other countries?

7-18. What other options are available?

7-19. What course of action does your team advise, and why? What are both the short- and long-term ramifications of your recommendation?

exercising your ethics

PROMISES, PROMISES

The Situation

You are an operations manager for a factory that makes replacement car mufflers and tailpipes. Your products are distributed throughout the country to muffler-repair shops that install them on used vehicles. After several years of modest but steady growth, your company recently suffered a downturn and shut down 5 percent of the factory's production capacity. Two supervisors and 70 production workers were laid off.

The Dilemma

After returning from lunch, you get a phone call from the general manager of King Kong Mufflers, one of the nation's top three muffler-repair chains, who says the following:

> *I suppose you know that we're about to sign a contract for your firm to supply us with replacement parts in large volumes, beginning two months from now. Your sales manager assures me that you can reliably meet my needs, and I just want to confirm that promise with you before I sign the contract.*

This is the first you've heard about this contract. While your potential customer is talking, you realize that meeting his needs will require a 20 percent increase in your current production capacity. Two months, however, isn't enough time to add more equipment, acquire tools, hire and train workers, and contract for supplies. An increase this large might even require a bigger building (which would take considerably more than two months to arrange). However, you also know how much your firm needs the business. The caller waits in silence while you gather your thoughts.

QUESTIONS TO ADDRESS

7-20. What are the underlying ethical issues in this situation?

7-21. From an ethical standpoint, what is an appropriate response to the customer's question? What steps should you take in responding to it? Explain.

7-22. What would you say on the phone at this time to this customer?

Cases

MADE FROM SCRATCH

Continued from page 203

At the beginning of this chapter, you read about the operational philosophy of The Cheesecake Factory. Using the information presented in this chapter, you should now be able to answer these questions.

QUESTIONS FOR DISCUSSION

7-23. How would you define *quality*, and how is quality measured in the restaurant industry? Are some measurements more useful than others? Explain.

7-24. Would you categorize The Cheesecake Factory as a service provider or a provider of goods or both? How would your classification affect your quality control decisions? How would it affect the way you approach operations?

7-25. Describe how *process flowcharts* may be helpful for methods improvement in restaurant operations. What kinds of information would you hope to gain from the flowcharts?

7-26. Identify a major U.S. restaurant chain that has recently received *poor quality ratings*. Who are its customers, and what are the basic causes that led to declining quality?

7-27. U.S. restaurants must comply with local health regulations. The results of periodic inspections have to be posted or published, or both. What actions would you recommend be considered by restaurants to overcome negative perceptions from a less-than-satisfactory rating?

SUPPLY CHAIN TRANSPARENCY

The candy manufacturing giant Hershey announced in 2017 that it would move toward greater transparency and accountability by using Sourcemap, an open-source, interactive platform that maps elements within a supply chain. With its suppliers mapped on Sourcemap, consumers could see where the ingredients for their favorite confections came from and how long it took for raw materials to reach manufacturing. The company also linked photos, videos, and stories to the map to showcase farmers and growers and to educate consumers about the ingredients in their products.[20]

Hershey had already adopted SmartLabel in 2015, a service that allows consumers to scan the barcode on their favorite candy bar and get more information about it, including a complete ingredient list, allergens, claims information, religious certifications, and more.[21]

In 2018, the company announced plans to completely eliminate "commodity-driven deforestation" from its supply chain by 2030. Hershey chocolate is grown in various places around the globe, but the company specifies a list of locations on its website: Brazil, Cameroon, Côte d'Ivoire, Colombia, Dominican Republic, Ecuador, Ghana, Indonesia, Nigeria, Papua New Guinea, and Peru. According to the National Wildlife Federation, cacao farming can devastate rain forests in the tropical areas where it is grown and "deforestation in nearly every country where it is produced, as rain forests are cut down to make way for cocoa monoculture." Hershey notes its commitment to removing sources from its supply chain that contribute to this deforestation.[22]

Using Sourcemap, companies and consumers can drill down into the details of each supply chain element mapped on the site. Consumers can make conscious buying decisions with more information than they've ever had before. Clicking on each location on the map brings up information about the growing, harvesting, and shipping of each ingredient, from cacao beans and sugar to milk and vanilla.

Hershey and other chocolate manufacturers are also using Sourcemap and other platforms to increase their human rights records. The global cacao market exists in poor countries with dismal child labor and worker protections. Cacao harvest is a labor-intensive hands-on process, from hand-picking the cacao beans and splitting them open with a machete to sun-drying the beans for the right amount of time. Hershey's use of Sourcemap enables consumers to hold the company accountable for finding fair-trade farmers and sources that uphold its commitment to human rights.[23]

QUESTIONS FOR DISCUSSION

7-28. Sourcemap is open-source, meaning it is free for anyone to use. Users upload information themselves, meaning the Hershey Company is responsible for the information found on its map. How transparent do you think its Sourcemap is, and how much should consumers rely on the information provided?

7-29. Do you think consumers will be more likely to purchase products from companies that provide transparency and traceability in their supply chain? Why or why not?

7-30. If you worked for a company that manufactured goods, would you advocate for the use of a transparency tool like Sourcemap, or would you recommend an outside service that tracks information on your company's behalf? Provide reasons for your recommendation.

7-31. Consider businesses such as grocery stores, auto dealers, hardware stores, or others that provide products to consumers. Could you identify ways in which these companies could use Sourcemap or another traceability tool to inform customers about supply chain issues? Do you think it would have a positive impact?

7-32. Given that providing information about the supply chain requires additional expenditures for a company (personnel hours to provide the information, media representation, potential outside services), do you think it's a worthwhile investment?

endnotes

1 Atul Gawande, "Big Med: Restaurant Chains Have Managed to Combine Quality Control, Cost Control, and Innovation. Can Health Care?" *New Yorker*, August 13, 2012, http://www.newyorker.com/magazine/2012/08/13/big-med.

2 World Trade Organization, "International Trade and Market Access Data," accessed March 30, 2020, https://www.wto.org.

3 Deloitte, "Analysis: 2016 Global Manufacturing Competitiveness Index," accessed January 25, 2017, http://www2.deloitte.com/global/en/pages/manufacturing/articles/global-manufacturing-competitiveness-index.html.

4 Alex Hill and Terry Hill, *Manufacturing Operations Strategy*, 6th ed. (Basingstoke, UK: Palgrave Macmillan, 2017); James A. Fitzsimmons and Mona J. Fitzsimmons, *Service Management: Operations Strategy, Information Technology*, 9th ed. (Boston: Irwin McGraw-Hill, 2017).

5 Joel Stein, "Outsourcing Home Cooking," *Time* 171, no. 6 (2019): 61, Business Source Premier, EBSCOhost.

6 "How to Build a Breeo Fire Pit," YouTube, April 16, 2019, https://youtu.be/8MbaLbuYL6g.

7 Breeo, "The Original Smokeless Fire Pit," accessed May 13, 2023, https://breeo.co/pages/our-story.

8 Kona Equity, "Breeo LLC," accessed May 13, 2023, https://www.konaequity.com/company/breeo-llc-4391243842/.

9 American Society for Quality, "ASQ Glossary of Terms," accessed May 2, 2023, http://asq.org/glossary/q.html.

10 Godiva, "How We Make Chocolate," accessed March 20, 2020, http://www.godiva.com/experience-godiva/HowWeMakeChocolate_RichArticle,default,pg.html.

[11] Collette Vacations, "About Collette" and "Ways to Tour," accessed May 1, 2023, http://www.collettevacations.com.

[12] Organisation for Economic Co-operation and Development, "GDP per Hour Worked," accessed May 1, 2023, https://data.oecd.org/lprdty/gdp-per-hour-worked.htm#indicator-chart.

[13] U.S. Department of Transportation, "Air Travel Consumer Report: January 2023 Numbers," accessed May 13, 2023, https://www.transportation.gov/briefing-room/air-travel-consumer-report-january-2023-numbers.

[14] "Missouri Quality Award: Fifth Win for Saint Luke's, Second Time as a Health System," November 2010, https://www.saintlukeshealthsystem.org/article/missouri-quality-award; Del Jones, "Baldrige Award Honors Record 7 Quality Winners," *USA Today*, November 26, 2003, 6B.

[15] Tootsie Roll Industries, Inc., *Annual Report 2021* (Chicago: 2011), 1.

[16] Del Jones, "Baldrige Award Honors Record 7 Quality Winners."

[17] ISO, "ISO 9000:2015: Quality Management Systems—Fundamentals and Vocabulary," accessed April 1, 2020, https://www.iso.org/standard/45481.html; ISO, "ISO 14000 Family: Environmental Management," accessed April 1, 2020, https://www.iso.org/iso-14001-environmental-management.html.

[18] SSAB, "Hybrit. A New Revolutionary Steelmaking Technology," accessed May 7, 2023, https://www.ssab.com/en/fossil-free-steel/insights/hybrit-a-new-revolutionary-steelmaking-technology.

[19] Volvo Construction Equipment, "Volvo Launches World's First Vehicle Using Fossil-Free Steel,". https://www.volvoce.com/global/en/news-and-events/press-releases/2021/volvo-launches-worlds-first-vehicle-using-fossil-free-steel/.

[20] Open Sourcemap—Development Environment, "Hershey's Supply Chain Map," accessed May 13, 2023, https://open.sourcemap.com/maps/59bc0c4f18612b0f7a20af11.

[21] The Hershey Company, "About Our Ingredients," accessed May 13, 2023, https://www.thehersheycompany.com/en_us/home/ingredients/about-our-ingredients.html.

[22] The Hershey Company, "Deforestation," accessed May 13, 2023, https://www.thehersheycompany.com/en_us/home/sustainability/sustainability-focus-areas/environment/deforestation.html.

[23] "The Hershey Company's Bittersweet Success," accessed May 13, 2023, https://dev.harbert.auburn.edu/binaries/documents/center-for-ethical-organizational-cultures/cases/hershey.pdf.

[24] Schultz, Howard, and Dori Jones Yang, *Pour Your Heart Into It: How Starbucks Built a Company One Cup at a Time.* New York, NY: Hachette, 2014. Kindle Edition page 80.

part 2
Integrative Learning Portfolio

crafting a business plan

Goal of the Exercise

In Part 1 of the business plan project, you formulated a basic identity for your business. Part 2 of the business plan project asks you to think about the goals of your business, some internal and external factors affecting the business, and the organizational structure of the business.

Exercise Background: Part 2 of the Business Plan

As you learned in Chapter 5, every business sets goals. In this part of the plan, you'll define some of the goals for your business.

Part 2 of the business plan also asks you to perform a basic SWOT analysis. As you'll recall from Chapter 5, a SWOT analysis looks at the business's *strengths, weaknesses, opportunities,* and *threats*. The strengths and weaknesses are internal factors—things that the business can control. The opportunities and threats are generally external factors that affect the business:

Sociocultural forces	Will changes in population or culture help your business or hurt it?
Economic forces	Will changes in the economy help your business or hurt it?
Technological forces	Will changes in technology help your business or hurt it?
Competitive forces	Does your business face much competition or very little?
Political-legal forces	Will changes in laws help your business or hurt it?

Each of these forces will affect different businesses in different ways, and some of these may not apply to your business at all.

Part 2 of the business plan also asks you to determine how the business is to be run. Part of this will require you to create an organizational chart to get you thinking about the different tasks needed for a successful business. You'll also examine various factors relating to operating your business.

Your Assignment

STEP 1

Open the saved *Business Plan* file you began working on in Part 1. You will continue to work from the same file you started working on in Part 1.

STEP 2

For the purposes of this assignment, you will answer the questions in "Part 2: The Business of Managing":

P2-1. Provide a brief mission statement for your business.

Hint: Refer to the discussion of mission statements in Chapter 5. Be sure to include the name of your business, how you will stand out from your competition, and why a customer will buy from you.

P2-2. Consider the goals for your business. What are three of your business goals for the first year? What are two intermediate to long-term goals?

Hint: Refer to the discussion of goal setting in Chapter 5. Be as specific and realistic as possible with the goals you set. For example, if you plan to sell a service, how many customers do you want by the end of the first year, and how much do you want each customer to spend?

P2-3. Perform a basic SWOT analysis for your business, listing its main strengths, weaknesses, opportunities, and threats.

Hint: We explained previously what factors you should consider in your basic SWOT analysis. Look around at your world, talk to classmates, or talk to your instructor for other ideas in performing your SWOT analysis.

P2-4. Who will manage the business?

Hint: Refer to the discussion of managers in Chapter 5. Think about how many *levels* of management as well as what *kinds* of managers your business needs.

P2-5. Show how the "team" fits together by creating a simple organizational chart for your business. Your chart should indicate who will work for each manager as well as each person's job title.

Hint: As you create your organizational chart, consider the different tasks involved in the business. To whom will each person report? Refer to the discussion of organizational structure in Chapter 6 for information to get you started.

P2-6. Create a floor plan of the business. What does it look like when you walk through the door?

Hint: When sketching your floor plan, consider where equipment, supplies, and furniture will be located.

P2-7. Explain what types of raw materials and supplies you will need to run your business. How will you produce your good or service? What equipment do you need? What hours will you operate?

Hint: Refer to the discussion of operations in this chapter for information to get you started.

P2-8. What steps will you take to ensure that the quality of the product or service stays at a high level? Who will be responsible for maintaining quality standards?

Hint: Refer to the discussion of quality improvement and TQM in this chapter for information to get you started. *Note*: Once you have answered the questions, save your Word document. You'll be answering additional questions in later chapters.

case PART 2 STARBUCKS, 1987–1990

"I never once believed, *not ever*, that my plan was not going to work."[i]

—Howard Schultz

Starbucks served its first official cup of coffee in April 1984. It had been about a year since Schultz, still just a marketing director at that time, had taken his fateful trip to Milan, where he'd been inspired by the multitude of little neighborhood coffee shops serving dark, rich espresso and other coffee drinks we now take for granted but that were relatively rare in the United States.

Within a few months, the first experiment on the corner of Fourth and Spring in downtown Seattle was blossoming. Still, Starbucks identified itself as a seller of whole beans that could be ground to order rather than a gathering place. But on August 18, 1987, as the new owner and CEO of the company, Schultz set out to change that. As he explained to his investors, he was on a mission to reinvent the world of coffee the way Nike was reinventing athletic shoes.

As Schultz worked to merge Starbucks into Il Giornali, keeping the Starbucks name and logo, he faced two significant challenges: (1) morale was at an all-time low, and (2) as he'd noted in the business plan that he used to gather funding, there was a lack of experienced management, especially in light of his plans to open 125 stores in the next five years and to eventually take Starbucks public and even longer term to take it global (although Starbucks already had a store in Vancouver, BC, so technically it was already a global company).

Schultz knew that if he were going to succeed, he'd need to hire good people with management experience. So he turned to Lawrence Maltz, who had 20 years of experience in business management with a profitable public beverage company. Maltz took on the helm as vice president of Operations, Finance, and Human Resources, while Schultz maintained his duties handling expansion, design, marketing, and investor relations.

Even before Schultz took over, he had a toehold in Chicago, where he'd already put the wheels in motion to open an Il Giornali. He hoped both the Chicago and Vancouver stores would show investors and management that the tiny idea germinating in Seattle was portable and could be replicated at a profit. The problem was an operating one. Chicago was 2,000 miles from Seattle headquarters and the warehouse where the beans were roasted, leaving Schultz to worry about quality control.

It turned out Chicago was slow to warm up to specialty coffee, so in 1989, Schultz scrambled for additional funding, but operating losses and slower-than-expected expansion hindered his efforts. Two things happened to turn Chicago around: (1) hiring experienced managers and (2) time. In 1990, the stores in the Windy City began to turn a profit as the customer base hit a critical mass. Word of mouth was still Starbucks's most valuable marketing tool.

In addition to the rapid expansion of stores serving coffee and selling whole beans, Starbucks was developing a robust mail-order business. Again, though, quality was a concern. Shipping roasted beans across the country meant the possibility of stale product. To the rescue came foil-lined FlavorLock vacuum packaging. Selling to a broader customer base meant more demand for stores that helped fuel growth. It also solved the problem of getting fresh beans to new markets. Even a simple thing like the FlavorLock bags meant the company could expand and serve fresh coffee without having to build a roasting plant in every city.

Alexandra Buxbaum/Shutterstock

Expansion didn't mean profits. In fact, the company was experiencing just the opposite. Starbucks was still losing money, with Schultz constantly reminding the board of directors that it was all part of the plan and the goal was to stay ahead of the curve until the company reached a critical mass, saying, "We're going to keep losing money until we can do three things. We have to attract a management team well beyond our expansion needs. We have to build a world-class roasting facility. And we need a computer information system sophisticated enough to keep track of sales in hundreds and hundreds of stores."[ii]

It was during this decade of expansion that Schultz began to ask himself what the real allure was of Starbucks. Certainly, the coffee was good, but he began to realize that the experience—even more than the coffee—resonated with more and more people. Schultz saw coffee as an affordable luxury, a taste of romance and the exotic. This epiphany led the board to finally explore the idea of Starbucks as "the third place," a place other than work and home where people could grab a taste of Colombia, chat with a friend, or just hang out around other people, even if not interacting. In short, Starbucks was creating in America what Schultz had seen in Milan.

QUESTIONS FOR DISCUSSION

P2-9. How important was the role of operations in Schultz plan to expand? Explain your answer.

P2-10. Schultz wrote, "As a parent, or as an entrepreneur, you begin imprinting your beliefs from Day One, whether you realize it or not. Once the children, or the people of the company, absorb those values, you can't suddenly change their worldview with a lecture on ethics." [24] How do you think Starbucks' corporate culture affects the customer experience? Do you think the culture is different today than it was in the late eighties? How and why?

P2-11. What aspects of the customer experience in a particular store are related to operations?

P2-12. How do you think Starbucks was structured in the early years? Based on your research, how do you think the structure has changed since then, if at all, and why?

P2-13. What are the pros and cons of expanding a business nationally and globally? What challenges does Starbucks faces as it expands across the world?

P2-14. What type of manager was Schultz in the early years?

[i] Howard Schultz and Dori Jones Yang, *Pour Your Heart into It: How Starbucks Built a Company One Cup at a Time* (New York: Hachette, 2014), Kindle Edition page 73.

[ii] Schultz and Yang, *Pour Your Heart into It*, Kindle Edition page 141.

finding your path

CAREERS IN BUSINESS

Demand for prospective employees with business degrees continues to grow. The U.S. Bureau of Labor Statistics, for example, forecasts that job growth prospects for business majors will increase by around 7 percent from 2021 to 2031. While many other fields of study also reflect growing demand, well-prepared business graduates are almost always in demand. Of course, this demand may drop temporarily during an economic downturn, but it has consistently rebounded when the economy started to grow again. There is also variation based on structural factors. During the economic downturn associated with the COVID-19 pandemic in 2020, for example, demand for managers in energy-related businesses dropped but grew in fields associated with logistics and supply chain management.

Some people want to have careers in general management, whereas others look at more specialized areas of management, such as operations or supply chain management. Demand for general management graduates is projected to grow by 8 percent from 2021 to 2031, while demand for operations and supply chain graduates is expected to grow by around 20 percent. The starting salary for general management graduates is currently about $58,800, while operations and supply chain graduates have an average starting salary of approximately $57,000.

MAKING YOURSELF EMPLOYABLE

In Chapter 5, we discussed the importance of seven core management skills: technical, human relations, conceptual, decision-making, time management, global management, and management and technology skills. Most managerial positions require the proficient application of all these skills, although there is some variability in their importance for different kinds of jobs. For example, a job that involves substantial statistical analyses requires especially strong technical skills, whereas a job focused primarily on creating and developing work teams may need very strong human relations skills.

As you move forward with your education, it is a good idea to start (if you haven't already done so) keeping a log or record of what activities you engage in that can help you both develop these skills and provide evidence that you have done so. For example, let's suppose that you have been elected or chosen to lead a club or professional association comprising students majoring in a certain field. As you move into this role, you learn that two other officers have been disagreeing over something to the point that there is open conflict between them. First of all, you should see this as an opportunity to develop your human relations skills. You might want to meet with each of them to develop insights into why the conflict developed and how it might be resolved. You can also gather additional insights by talking to others in the club, the club's faculty advisor, and/or other experienced professionals, such as your professor or successful manager. Once you have resolved the conflict, reflect on what you did right (and, perhaps, wrong) and record this experience in your log. Later, when you are applying for jobs or developing your professional résumé, you can note both the role you played and details about what you accomplished. For example, instead of just listing your position, you can embellish the activity with all of your accomplishments, like this:

- **2021–22:** President, Management Club
  - Managed an annual budget of $4500.00
  - Increased club membership by 10 percent
  - Resolved long-standing internal disagreement over club strategy
  - Led the development of a unified new strategic plan

What do these entries show? A prospective employer looking at this résumé entry will see that you (1) know how to manage within a budget (technical skill), (2) can create interest, as shown by the growth in membership numbers (leadership), (3) can resolve conflict (interpersonal skill), and (4) demonstrate strategic vision (conceptual skill). This entry alone might be sufficient to garner preliminary interest from employers. Hopefully, however, during your educational time you will have other experiences and so can add more entries like this one to your résumé. In addition, don't forget that your first job will likely not be your last. Indeed, there is a strong probability that you will seek other jobs during your career. Therefore, continue to keep a log or record of your activities, especially those that illustrate skill development and performance recognition.

A word of warning, though. There can be a fine line between documenting events to present yourself in a favorable—and accurate—manner and exaggerating your accomplishments in ways that suggest questionable ethics. For instance, suppose you are a member of a team (but not the leader) that achieves a new product breakthrough. It's great to indicate this on your résumé. However, you should not attribute the breakthrough just to your own efforts. So say this:

- Was a member of a team that achieved a new product breakthrough that resulted in substantial revenue growth

It's not okay, however, to say this:

- Led a team that achieved a new product breakthrough that resulted in substantial revenue growth.

PART 3 | PEOPLE IN ORGANIZATIONS

chapter 8

Employee Behavior and Motivation

Vadimgozhda/123RF

learning objectives

After reading this chapter, you should be able to:

8-1 Identify and discuss the basic forms of behaviors that employees exhibit in organizations.

8-2 Describe the nature and importance of individual differences among employees.

8-3 Explain the meaning and importance of psychological contracts and the person–job fit in the workplace.

8-4 Identify and summarize the most important models and concepts of employee motivation.

8-5 Describe some of the strategies and techniques used by organizations to improve employee motivation.

what's in it for me?

Think about people as jigsaw puzzles. Puzzles consist of various pieces that fit together in precise ways. And, of course, no two puzzles are exactly alike. They have different numbers of pieces, the pieces are of different sizes and shapes, and they fit together in different ways. The same can be said of people, their behaviors, and the causes of those behaviors. Each of us is a whole picture, like a fully assembled jigsaw puzzle, but the puzzle pieces that define us and the way those pieces fit together are unique. Every person in an organization is fundamentally different from everyone else. To be successful, managers must recognize that these differences exist, attempt to understand them, and then see if they can harness them in ways that are beneficial to both the individuals themselves and the organization.

They also need to understand why people work. People obviously work for a wide variety of different reasons. Some people want money; others want a challenge. Some want prestige, some want security, and still others want power. What people in an organization want from work and how they think they can achieve it plays an instrumental role in determining their motivation to work. As we see in this chapter, motivation is vital to all organizations. Indeed, the difference between highly effective organizations and less effective ones often lies in the motivations of their members.

Successful managers usually have at least a fundamental understanding of what accounts for employee behavior and motivation in organizations. Thus, managers need to understand the nature of individual motivation, especially as it applies to work situations. By understanding the basic elements of this chapter, you'll be better able to (1) understand your own feelings toward your work from the perspective of an employee and (2) understand the feelings of others toward their work from the perspective of a manager or owner. To start developing your understanding, let's begin by describing the different forms of behaviors that employees exhibit at work. We'll then examine many of the ways that people differ from one another. Later in the chapter, we'll look at some important models and concepts of employee motivation, as well as some strategies and techniques used by organizations to improve employee motivation.

Flashon Studio/Shutterstock

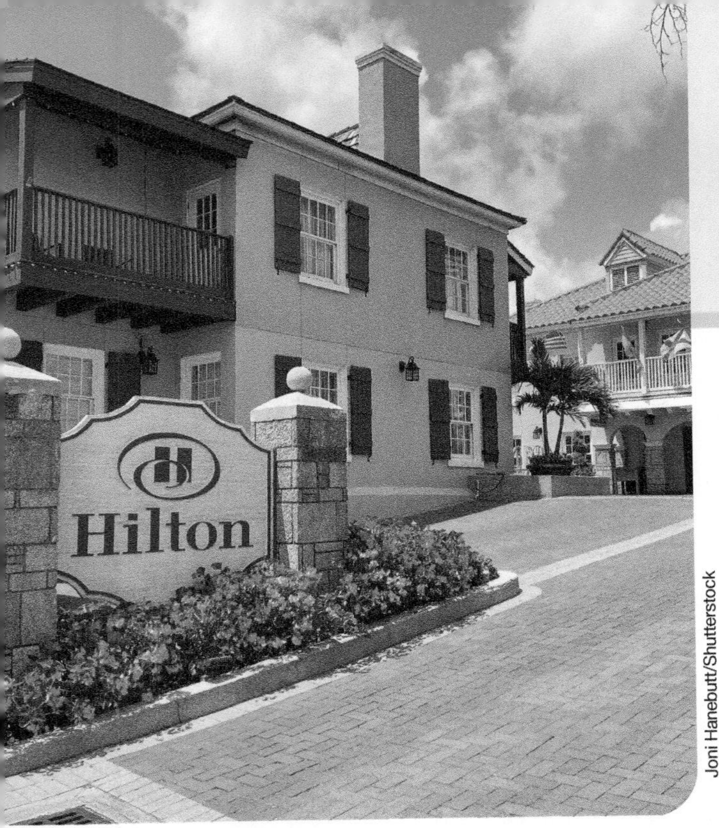

Joni Hanebutt/Shutterstock

Hilton has been recognized as one of the best places to work in America.

Building a Culture of Hospitality

At the end of World War I, a young man named Conrad Hilton came home to Cisco, Texas, with money he'd saved up while serving in the U.S. Army Quartermaster Corps. Even though it was a meager $5,000 (roughly equivalent to $70,000 in 2023), he was impatient to invest it rather than spend it, so when he saw the old Mobley Hotel for sale, he bought it. In 1925, Conrad opened the first Hilton Hotel in Dallas, and in 1927 in Waco, Texas, the first hotel with air-conditioning. In 1947, he opened the first hotel in the world with a television in every room.

The corporate mission for Hilton Hotels still reflects the founder's original vision, and it is central to Hilton's recruitment efforts, including its recent "Every Job Makes the Stay" campaign, which aims to spotlight employees in frontline and hourly positions. It applies its focus on "creating the best, most inclusive home away from home" to its employees as well as its customers. As Laura Fuentes, Hilton's chief human resources officer, says: "As a business of people serving people, we built this campaign as we always do—with our Team Members at the core. This campaign was inspired by our Team Members and mirrors how they talk about their jobs. At Hilton, we are guided by our purpose to fill the earth with the light and warmth of hospitality by dreaming big and spreading hope at our hotels and in our communities."[1]

While many companies lovingly attend to the working conditions of white-collar employees—with treadmill desks, soothing quiet rooms, hybrid remote-work schedules, and whimsical common areas—the needs of service workers are all but ignored. Hilton Hotels is attempting to rectify this imbalance with an ambitious program to spruce up employee spaces in hopes that doing so will improve employees' experience and, in turn, reduce turnover, improve customer service, and drive profitability.

The initiatives began after Hilton's initial public offering in 2013 (Hilton was owned by private equity firm Blackstone from 2007 to 2013), under the guidance of CEO Christopher Nassetta. "I put on a housekeeper's jacket and I'm like, Wow, this is heavy," the Hilton CEO told *Fortune* recently. "It didn't feel very comfortable or flexible, and I'm thinking, We got this wrong—we're not giving them the right clothing to wear." Nassetta and his team decided that changes were in order; in early 2018 the company launched a partnership with Under Armour to have the sports apparel giant redesign lighter, more comfortable workwear.

That's just one of several employee-focused changes that led *Fortune* magazine to crown the 100-year-old company as one of the World's Best Workplaces 2022, awarding the global chain second place overall. The only hospitality company on *Fortune*'s list, Hilton has held its position in the top 25 since 2016. It has also received similar praise from ranking organizations in many countries, including the United States, Austria, China, Ireland, Peru, Turkey, and Uruguay, including the number-one spot for women in the United States and Turkey.[2] It's a sweet validation for Nassetta, who, upon taking the reins at Hilton in 2007, found an organization that "had lost our way a bit," he said. "We forgot that we are a business of people serving people, and the corporate environment got very disconnected from the front line."[3]

Hilton's commitment to making sure the frontline workers reflect the mission of the company hearkens back to corporate ideals that developed in the late 1920s, when Western Electric, in Hawthorne, Illinois, hired Elton Mayo, a sociologist, to conduct experiments on worker productivity. Mayo increased the lighting and saw worker output improve. But when he lowered the lighting, the productivity continued to increase. Ultimately, Mayo concluded that it wasn't the actual changes that made a difference but that workers were responding to the attention they were receiving from management. Hilton continues to constantly observe and refine working conditions for its employees, which leaders credit as one of the reasons Hilton has some of the lowest turnover rates in the industry.

Although hotels and resorts across the globe were forced to suspend services in the United States due to the COVID-19 pandemic, Hilton—with approximately 60,000 direct employees in its corporate offices and hotels in the United States, and 200,000 more through franchise hotels—made the decision to furlough workers as opposed to laying them off. Furloughed Hilton employees in the United States were given direct access to an online resource center and expedited hiring processes for temporary jobs at leading companies, including Amazon, CVS, Lidl, Albertsons, Plastics Industry Association, and Sunrise Senior Living.

Fuentes put it this way: "To me, it boils down to creating not a work experience or an employee experience but a human experience that makes people feel like they are seen, they are welcome, they are heard, they will be taken care of, and they can take care of their families and loved ones, and that they belong to something greater than themselves."[4]

(After studying the content of this chapter, you should be able to answer the set of discussion questions found at the end of the chapter.)

Forms of Employee Behavior

Learning Objective 8-1

Identify and discuss the basic forms of behaviors that employees exhibit in organizations.

We explained back in Chapter 1 that economic systems use various factors of production and that labor is one of these factors. For any given organization, then, labor consists of the people who work for that organization—managers, operating employees, people in support roles, and so forth. The behaviors and motivation of these individuals go a long way in determining an organization's success. In this chapter, we will examine both the causes and effects of employee behaviors and work motivation from a variety of perspectives.

Employee behavior is the pattern of actions by the members of an organization that directly or indirectly influences the organization's effectiveness. Some employee behaviors, called *performance behaviors*, directly contribute to productivity and performance. Other behaviors, referred to as *organizational citizenship*, provide positive benefits to the organization but in more indirect ways. *Counterproductive behaviors* detract from performance and actually cost the organization. Let's look at each type of behavior in a bit more detail.

Employee Behavior *the pattern of actions by the members of an organization that directly or indirectly influences the organization's effectiveness*

Performance Behaviors

Performance behaviors are the total set of work-related behaviors that the organization expects employees to display. Essentially, these behaviors are directly targeted at performing a job. For some jobs, performance behaviors can be narrowly defined and easily measured. For example, an assembly-line worker who sits or stands by a moving conveyor and attaches parts to a product as it passes by has relatively few performance behaviors. The worker is expected to remain at the workstation for a predetermined number of hours and correctly attach the parts. Such performance can often be assessed quantitatively by measuring the percentage of parts correctly attached. Similarly, sales representatives are expected to promote

Performance Behaviors *the total set of work-related behaviors that the organization expects employees to display*

the firm's products and services, find new customers, and keep existing customers satisfied. Sales revenue, customer retention, and sales growth, then, are common performance indicators for sales jobs.

For some jobs, however, performance behaviors are more diverse and difficult to assess. For example, consider the case of a research-and-development scientist at Merck & Co. The scientist works in a lab trying to find new scientific breakthroughs that have commercial potential. The scientist must apply knowledge and experience gained from previous research. Intuition and creativity are also important. But even with all the scientist's abilities and effort, a new breakthrough may take months or even years to accomplish and validate, and even longer to start generating revenue and profit.

Organizational Citizenship

Organizational Citizenship *positive behaviors that do not directly contribute to the bottom line*

Employees can also engage in positive behaviors that do not directly contribute to the bottom line. Such behaviors are often called **organizational citizenship**.[5] Organizational citizenship refers to the behavior of individuals who make a positive overall contribution to the organization. Consider, for example, an employee who does work that is highly acceptable in terms of both quantity and quality. However, they refuse to work overtime, won't help newcomers learn the ropes, and are generally unwilling to make any contribution beyond the strict performance requirements of their job. This person may be seen as a good performer, but they are not likely to be seen as a good organizational citizen. Another employee, though, may exhibit a comparable level of performance, but they always work late when the boss asks them to, they take time to help newcomers learn their way around, and they are perceived as being helpful and committed to the organization's success. They are likely to be seen as a better organizational citizen.

A number of factors, including individual, social, and organizational variables, play roles in promoting or minimizing organizational citizenship behaviors. For example, the personality, attitudes, and needs of the individual may cause some people to be more helpful than others. Similarly, the individual's work group may encourage or discourage such behaviors. And the organization itself, especially its corporate culture, may or may not promote, recognize, and reward these types of behaviors. During the 2020 COVID-19 pandemic, many individuals, especially those in the health care industry and first responders, stepped forward and worked beyond the normal scope of their jobs.

Fizkes/Shutterstock

Organizational citizenship is the behavior of individuals who make a positive contribution to the organization above and beyond strict job performance. This manager, for example, is helping her colleagues better understand important organizational processes and customer expectations.

Counterproductive Behaviors

Still other work-related behaviors are actually counterproductive. **Counterproductive behaviors** are those that detract from, rather than contribute to, organizational performance. **Absenteeism** occurs when an employee does not show up for work. Some absenteeism, of course, has a legitimate cause, such as illness, jury duty, or death or illness in the family. Other times, the employee may report a feigned legitimate explanation that's actually just an excuse to stay home. When employees are absent, legitimately or not, their work may not get done at all, substitutes may need to be hired to do it, or others in the organization must pick up the slack. In any event, though, absenteeism results in direct costs to a business.

Counterproductive Behaviors *behaviors that detract from organizational performance*

Absenteeism *when an employee does not show up for work*

Turnover occurs when people quit their jobs. An organization usually incurs costs in replacing workers who have quit, and loses productivity while seeking a replacement and training someone new, and so on. Turnover results from a number of factors,

Turnover *annual percentage of an organization's workforce that leaves and must be replaced*

managing in turbulent times

Extending Protections Beyond the Legal Minimum

In the first five months of 2023, over 400 anti-trans bills were introduced around the country. In fact, by May 2023, anti-trans legislation had been introduced in nearly every state in America. These bills ranged from a proposed law that would allow sports coaches to confirm gender identity in youth sports to legislation that would rezone public libraries as adult venues if they hosted drag queen story hours.[6] Though sexual orientation and gender identity are both protected classes under federal law, states increasingly have attempted to override that power with specific state-level laws.

The 2023 state legislation continued a trend that began in 2018, following a movement aimed to redefine sex discrimination to exclude transgender and nonbinary people. That year, 56 major companies—from Apple and PepsiCo to Deutsche Bank and The Dow Chemical Company—issued a joint statement publicly committing to extending protections to their transgender and nonbinary employees. The statement begins: "We, the undersigned businesses, stand with the millions of people in America who identify as transgender, gender non-binary, or intersex, and call for all such people to be treated with the respect and dignity everyone deserves."[7]

The statement goes on to say that "diversity and inclusion are good for business" and notes that over 80 percent of Fortune 500 companies have protections in place and inclusive benefits for transgender, nonbinary gender, and intersex employees. The statement closes with a "call for respect and transparency in policymaking, and for equality under the law for transgender people."[8]

Ropes & Gray Law Firm supported the 2018 statement without hesitation, and its support for the LGBTQ community has been steadfast. With CEO Julie Jones at the helm, Ropes & Gray has long practiced diversity and inclusion as part of its foundation. Its commitment to diversity recognizes employees'

Sundry Photography/Shutterstock

need for affiliation. Its explicit diversity actions include not only a Diversity Committee but three separate named standing organizations, including the Ropes Multicultural Forum, which hosts educational offerings, conversations, and other events showcasing employees of diverse cultural backgrounds and offering them an opportunity to belong to a supportive affinity group. The LGBTQ+ Forum does the same for members of that community. The firm proudly reports that nearly 50 percent of its lawyers are female and maintains a supportive forum for females as well. Each of the forums also focuses its efforts on raising awareness of and education about the legal issues surrounding these communities and strives to inform other lawyers in the firm and the wider legal community.[9]

In 2022, Ropes & Gray continued to honor individual differences and served as a global sponsor of the LGBTQ+ business network Out Leadership's international summit OutQUORUM. There, Ropes & Gray partner Peter Erichsen said, "At Ropes & Gray, our collective hats are off to Todd Sears and Out Leadership for their groundbreaking research, their tactical efforts to advance LGBTQ+ equality, and for convening all of us to work together with common purpose. We are proud to stand alongside all of you in your efforts to make the business world, and the world at large, more inclusive, equitable, and vibrant."[10]

including aspects of the job, the organization, the individual, the labor market, and family influences. In general, a poor person–job fit (which we'll discuss later in the chapter) is also a likely cause of turnover. There are some employees whose turnover doesn't hurt the business, but when productive employees leave an organization, it does reflect counterproductive behavior.

Other forms of counterproductive behavior may be even more costly for an organization. *Theft and sabotage*, for example, result in direct financial costs for an organization. *Sexual and racial harassment* also cost an organization, both indirectly (by lowering morale, producing fear, and driving off valuable employees) and directly (through financial liability if the organization responds inappropriately). *Workplace aggression and violence* are also a concern in some organizations, as is *bullying*.

Individual Differences Among Employees

Learning Objective 8-2

Describe the nature and importance of individual differences among employees.

Individual Differences *personal attributes that vary from one person to another*

What causes some employees to be more productive than others, to be better citizens than others, or to be more counterproductive than others? As we already noted, every individual is unique. **Individual differences** are personal attributes that vary from one person to another. Individual differences may be physical, psychological, and emotional. The individual differences that characterize a specific person make that person unique. As we see in the sections that follow, basic categories of individual differences include *personality* and *attitudes*.[11]

Personality at Work

Personality *the relatively stable set of psychological attributes that distinguish one person from another*

Personality is the relatively stable set of psychological attributes that distinguish one person from another. In recent years, researchers have identified five fundamental traits that are especially relevant to organizations. These are commonly called the *"big five" personality traits. Emotional intelligence*, although not part of the "big five," also plays a large role in employee personality.

"Big Five" Personality Traits *five fundamental personality traits especially relevant to organizations*

The "Big Five" Personality Traits The **"big five" personality traits** are shown in Figure 8.1 and can be summarized as follows.

- *Agreeableness* is a person's ability to get along with others. A person with a *high* level of agreeableness is gentle, cooperative, forgiving, understanding, and good natured in dealings with others. A person with a *low* level of agreeableness is often irritable, short tempered, uncooperative, and generally antagonistic toward other people. Highly agreeable people are better at developing good working relationships with coworkers, whereas less agreeable people are not likely to have particularly good working relationships.
- *Conscientiousness* in this context refers to the individual's persistence, dependableness, and orderliness. *Highly conscientious* people tend to focus on relatively few tasks at one time; as a result, they are likely to be organized, systematic, careful, thorough, responsible, and self-disciplined. *Less conscientious* people tend to pursue a wider array of tasks; as a result, they are often more disorganized and irresponsible, as well as less thorough and self-disciplined. Highly conscientious people tend to be relatively higher performers in a variety of different jobs.
- *Emotionality* refers to the degree to which people tend to be positive or negative in their outlook and behaviors toward others. People with *positive* emotionality are relatively poised, calm, resilient, and secure; people with negative emotionality are more excitable, insecure, reactive, and subject to mood swings. People with positive emotionality might be expected to better handle job stress, pressure, and

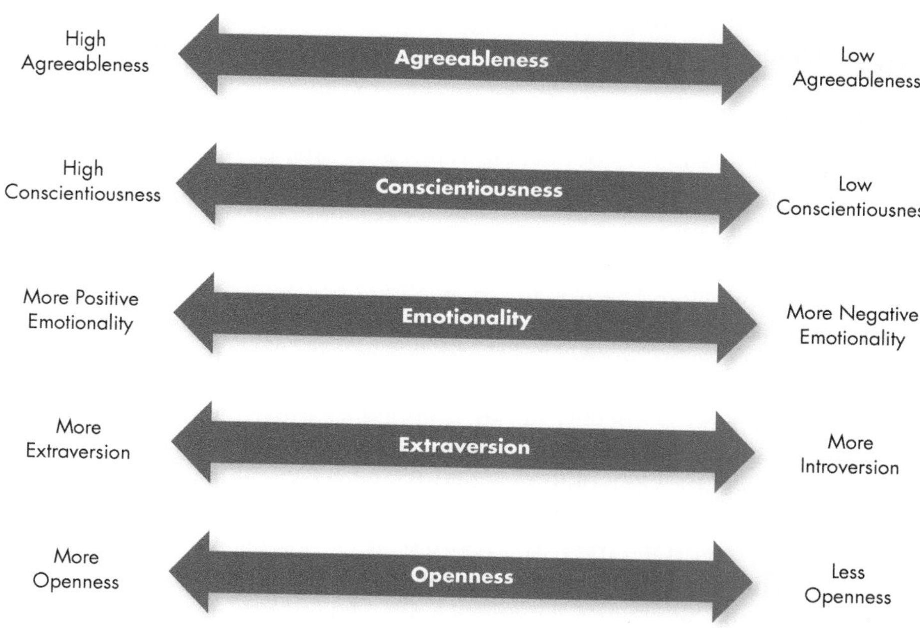

FIGURE 8.1 The "Big Five" Personality Traits

tension. Their stability might also lead them to be seen as being more reliable than their less stable counterparts.

- *Extraversion* refers to a person's comfort level with relationships. *Extraverts* are sociable, talkative, assertive, and open to establishing new relationships. *Introverts* are much less sociable, talkative, and assertive, and more reluctant to begin new relationships. Extraverts tend to be higher overall job performers than introverts and are more likely to be attracted to jobs based on personal relationships, such as sales and marketing positions.
- *Openness* reflects how open or rigid a person is in terms of their beliefs. People with *high* levels of openness are curious and willing to listen to new ideas and to change their own ideas, beliefs, and attitudes in response to new information. People with *low* levels of openness tend to be less receptive to new ideas and less willing to change their minds. People with more openness are often better performers because of their flexibility and the likelihood that they will be better accepted by others in the organization.

The practical value of the "big five" framework is that it encompasses an integrated set of traits that research suggests are valid predictors of individual behaviors in many work situations. Thus, managers who can both understand the framework and assess these traits in their employees are in a good position to understand how and why the employees behave as they do.

The Myers-Briggs Framework Another interesting approach to understanding personalities in organizations is the Myers-Briggs framework. This framework, based on the classical work of Carl Jung, differentiates people in terms of four general dimensions. These are defined as follows.

- ***Extraversion (E) versus introversion (I).*** Extraverts get their energy from being around other people, whereas introverts are worn out by others and need solitude to recharge their energy.
- ***Sensing (S) versus intuition (N).*** Sensing types prefer concrete things, whereas intuitives prefer abstract concepts.

- ***Thinking (T) versus feeling (F).*** Thinking individuals base their decisions more on logic and reason, whereas feeling individuals base their decisions more on feelings and emotions.
- ***Judging (J) versus perceiving (P).*** People who are the judging type enjoy completion or being finished, whereas perceiving types enjoy the process and open-ended situations.

To use this framework, people complete a questionnaire designed to measure their personality on each dimension. Higher or lower scores in each of the dimensions are used to classify people into 1 of 16 different personality categories. The **Myers-Briggs Type Indicator (MBTI)** is a popular questionnaire that some individuals and organizations use to assess personality types. It is among the most popular selection instruments used today, with as many as 1.5 million people completing it each year. Research suggests that the MBTI is a useful method for determining some aspects of communication styles and interaction preferences. In terms of personality attributes, however, questions exist about both the validity and the stability of the MBTI.

Myers-Briggs Type Indicator (MBTI) *a popular questionnaire that some organizations use to assess personality types*

Emotional Intelligence The concept of emotional intelligence has been identified in recent years and also provides some interesting insights into personality. **Emotional intelligence, or emotional quotient (EQ)**, refers to the extent to which people are self-aware, can manage their emotions, can motivate themselves, express empathy for others, and possess social skills.[12] These various dimensions can be described as follows:

Emotional Intelligence (Emotional Quotient, EQ) *the extent to which people are self-aware, can manage their emotions, can motivate themselves, express empathy for others, and possess social skills*

- *Self-awareness* refers to a person's capacity for being aware of how they are being perceived by others. In general, more self-awareness allows people to more effectively guide their own lives and behaviors.
- *Managing emotions* refers to a person's capacities to balance anxiety, fear, and anger so that these feelings do not overly interfere with getting things accomplished.
- *Motivating oneself* is a person's ability to remain optimistic and to continue striving in the face of setbacks, barriers, and failure.
- *Empathy* is a person's ability to understand how others are feeling even without being explicitly told.
- *Social skills* help people get along with others and establish positive relationships.

Research suggests that people with high EQs may perform better than others, especially in jobs that require a high degree of interpersonal interaction (such as a public relations specialist) or that involve influencing or directing the work of others (such as a project manager). Moreover, EQ appears to be something that isn't biologically based but that can be developed.

Other Personality Traits at Work Besides these complex models of personality, several other specific personality traits are also likely to influence behavior in organizations. Among the most important are locus of control, self-efficacy, authoritarianism, Machiavellianism, self-esteem, and risk propensity.

Locus of control is the extent to which people believe their behavior has a real effect on what happens to them.[13] Some people, for example, believe that if they work hard they will succeed. They may also believe that people who fail do so because they lack ability or motivation. People who believe that individuals are in control of their lives are said to have an internal locus of control. Other people think that fate, chance, luck, or other people's behavior determines what happens to them. For example, an employee who fails to get a promotion may attribute that failure to a politically motivated boss or just bad luck, rather than to a personal lack of skills or poor performance record. People who think that forces beyond their control dictate what happens to them are said to have an external locus of control.

Locus of Control *the extent to which people believe that their behavior has a real effect on what happens to them*

Self-efficacy is a related but subtly different personality characteristic. A person's **self-efficacy** is that person's belief about their capabilities to perform a task. People with high self-efficacy believe that they can perform well on a specific task, whereas

Self-Efficacy *a person's belief about their capabilities to perform a task*

people with low self-efficacy tend to doubt their ability to perform a specific task. Coupled with the individual's personality, self-assessments of ability contribute to self-efficacy. Some people simply have more self-confidence than others. This belief in their ability to perform a task effectively results in their being more self-assured and better able to focus their attention on performance.[14]

Another important personality characteristic is **authoritarianism**, the extent to which a person believes that power and status differences are appropriate within hierarchical social systems such as organizations.[15] For example, a person who is highly authoritarian may accept directives or orders from someone with more authority purely because the other person is "the boss." In contrast, a person who is not highly authoritarian, although still carrying out reasonable directives from the boss, is more likely to question things, express disagreement with the boss, and even refuse to carry out orders if they are for some reason objectionable. A highly authoritarian manager may be relatively autocratic and demanding, and highly authoritarian subordinates are more likely to accept this behavior from their leader. A less authoritarian manager, however, may allow subordinates a bigger role in making decisions, and less authoritarian subordinates might respond more positively to this behavior.

Authoritarianism *the extent to which a person believes that power and status differences are appropriate within hierarchical social systems such as organizations*

Machiavellianism is another important personality trait. This concept is named after Niccolò Machiavelli, a sixteenth-century author. In his book *The Prince*, Machiavelli explained how the nobility could more easily gain and use power. The term **Machiavellianism** is now used to describe behavior directed at gaining power and controlling the behavior of others. Research suggests that the degree of Machiavellianism varies from person to person. More Machiavellian individuals tend to be rational and nonemotional, may be willing to lie to attain their personal goals, put little emphasis on loyalty and friendship, and enjoy manipulating others' behavior. Less Machiavellian individuals are more emotional, less willing to lie to succeed, value loyalty and friendship highly, and get little personal pleasure from manipulating others.

Machiavellianism *used to describe behavior directed at gaining power and controlling the behavior of others*

Self-esteem is the extent to which a person believes that they are a worthwhile and deserving individual. A person with high self-esteem is more likely to seek higher-status jobs, be more confident in the ability to achieve higher levels of performance, and derive greater intrinsic satisfaction from accomplishments. In contrast, a person with less self-esteem may be more content to remain in a lower-level job, be less confident of ability, and focus more on extrinsic rewards (extrinsic rewards are tangible and observable rewards such as a paycheck, job promotion, and so forth). Among the major personality dimensions, self-esteem is the one that has been most widely studied in other countries.

Self-Esteem *the extent to which a person believes that they is a worthwhile and deserving individual*

GaudiLab/Shutterstock

Authoritarianism refers to how people assess the legitimacy of directives given to them by people in authority. This executive is assigning new tasks and responsibilities to the managers on her team. Assuming they see the new assignments as being appropriate, they will be motivated to work toward completing them as expected.

Although more research is clearly needed, the published evidence suggests that self-esteem as a personality trait does indeed exist in a variety of countries and that its role in organizations is reasonably important across different cultures.

Risk Propensity *the degree to which a person is willing to take chances and make risky decisions*

Risk propensity is the degree to which a person is willing to take chances and make risky decisions. A manager with a high risk propensity, for example, might be more willing to experiment with new ideas and gamble on new products. Such a manager might also lead the organization in new and different directions. This manager might be a catalyst for innovation or, if the risky decisions prove to be bad ones, might jeopardize the continued well-being of the organization. A manager with low risk propensity might lead an organization to stagnation and excessive conservatism or might help the organization successfully weather turbulent and unpredictable times by maintaining stability and calm. Thus, the potential consequences of a manager's risk propensity depend heavily on the organization's environment.

Attitudes at Work

Attitudes *a person's beliefs and feelings about specific ideas, situations, or people*

People's attitudes also affect their behavior in organizations. **Attitudes** reflect our beliefs and feelings about specific ideas, situations, or other people. Attitudes are important because they are the mechanism through which we express our feelings. An employee's comment that they feel underpaid reflects their feelings about their pay. Similarly, when a manager says that they like the new advertising campaign, they are expressing their feelings about the organization's marketing efforts.

How Attitudes Are Formed Attitudes are formed by a variety of forces, including our personal values, our experiences, and our personalities. For example, if we value honesty and integrity, we may form especially favorable attitudes toward a manager whom we believe to be honest and moral. Similarly, if we have had negative and unpleasant experiences with a particular coworker, we may form an unfavorable attitude toward that person. Any of the "big five" or individual personality traits may also influence our attitudes. Understanding the basic structure of an attitude helps us see how attitudes are formed and can be changed.

Attitude Structure Attitudes are usually viewed as stable dispositions to behave toward objects in a certain way. For any number of reasons, a person might decide that they does not like a particular political figure or a certain restaurant (a disposition). We would expect that person to express consistently negative opinions of the candidate or restaurant and to maintain the consistent, predictable intention of not voting for the political candidate or not eating at the restaurant. In this view, attitudes contain three components: (1) cognition, (2) affect, and (3) intention.

Cognition *the knowledge a person presumes to have about something*

Cognition is the knowledge a person presumes to have about something. You may believe you like a class because the textbook is excellent, the class meets at your favorite time, the instructor is outstanding, and the workload is light. This "knowledge" may be true, partially true, or totally false. For example, you may intend to vote for a particular candidate because you think you know where the candidate stands on several issues. In reality, depending on the candidate's honesty and your understanding of their statements, the candidate's thinking on the issues may be exactly the same as yours, partly the same, or totally different. Cognitions are based on perceptions of truth and reality, and, as we note later, perceptions do not always agree with reality.

Affect *a person's feelings toward something*

A person's **affect** is that person's feelings toward something. In many ways, affect is similar to emotion; it is something over which we have little or no conscious control. For example, most people react to words such as *love, hate, sex*, and *war* in a manner that reflects their feelings about what those words convey. Similarly, you may like one of your classes, dislike another, and be indifferent toward a third. If the class you dislike is an elective, you may not be particularly concerned about your participation or final grade. But if it is the first course in your chosen major, your affective reaction may cause you considerable anxiety.

Intention guides a person's behavior. If you like your instructor, you may intend to take another class from them next semester. Intentions are not always translated into actual behavior, however. If the instructor's course next semester is scheduled for 8 AM and you don't like getting started that early, you may decide that another instructor is just as good. Some attitudes and their corresponding intentions are much more central and significant to an individual than others. You may intend to do one thing (take a particular class) but later alter your intentions because of a more significant and central attitude (fondness for sleeping late).

Intention *part of an attitude that guides a person's behavior*

Cognitive Dissonance When two sets of cognitions or perceptions are contradictory or incongruent, a person experiences a level of conflict and anxiety called **cognitive dissonance**. Cognitive dissonance also occurs when people behave in a fashion that is inconsistent with their attitudes. For example, a person may realize that smoking and overeating are dangerous yet continue to do both. Because the attitudes and behaviors are inconsistent with each other, the person probably will experience a certain amount of tension and discomfort and may try to reduce these feelings by changing the attitude, altering the behavior, or perceptually distorting the circumstances. For example, the dissonance associated with overeating might be resolved by continually deciding to go on a diet "next week." Cognitive dissonance affects people in a variety of ways. We frequently encounter situations in which our attitudes conflict with each other or with our behaviors. Dissonance reduction is the way we deal with these feelings of discomfort and tension. In organizational settings, people who contemplate leaving the organization may wonder why they continue to stay and work hard. As a result of this dissonance, they may conclude that the company is not so bad after all, that they have no immediate options elsewhere, or that they will leave "soon."

Cognitive Dissonance *when two sets of cognitions or perceptions are contradictory or incongruent*

Key Work-Related Attitudes People in an organization form attitudes about many different things. Employees are likely to have attitudes about their salary, their promotion possibilities, their boss, employee benefits, and so on. Especially important attitudes are *job satisfaction* and *organizational commitment*.

- **Job satisfaction** reflects the extent to which people have positive attitudes toward their jobs. (Some people use the word *morale* instead of *job satisfaction*.) Satisfied employees tend to be absent less often, to be good organizational citizens, and to stay with the organization. Dissatisfied employees may be absent more often, may experience stress that disrupts coworkers, and may be continually looking for another job. Contrary to "common sense" and what a lot of managers believe, however, high levels of job satisfaction do not necessarily lead to higher levels of productivity.

Job Satisfaction *degree of enjoyment that people derive from performing their jobs*

- **Organizational commitment**, sometimes called *job commitment*, reflects an individual's identification with the organization and its mission. Highly committed people will probably view themselves as true members of the firm (for example, referring to the organization in personal terms, such as "we make high-quality products"), overlook minor sources of dissatisfaction, and see themselves remaining members of the organization. Less committed individuals are more likely to see themselves as outsiders (e.g., referring to the organization in less personal terms, such as "they don't pay their employees very well"), to express more dissatisfaction about things, and to not see themselves as long-term members of the organization.

Organizational Commitment *an individual's identification with the organization and its mission*

Managers can promote satisfaction and commitment by taking a few critical steps. To start, if the organization treats its employees fairly and provides reasonable rewards and job security, its employees are more likely to be satisfied and committed. Allowing employees to have a say in how things are done can also promote these attitudes. Designing jobs so that they are stimulating can enhance both satisfaction and commitment. Another key element is understanding and respecting what experts call *psychological contracts*, which we will discuss in the next section.

Learning Objective 8-3

Explain the meaning and importance of psychological contracts and the person–job fit in the workplace.

Matching People and Jobs

Given the array of individual differences found in people and the many different forms of employee behaviors that can occur in organizations, it stands to reason that managers would like to have a good match between people and the jobs they are performing. Two key methods for helping to understand this match are *psychological contracts* and the *person–job fit.*

Psychological Contracts

Psychological Contract *set of expectations held by an employee concerning what they will contribute to an organization (referred to as contributions) and what the organization will in return provide the employee (referred to as inducements)*

A **psychological contract** is the overall set of expectations held by employees and the organization regarding what employees will contribute to the organization and what the organization will provide in return. Unlike a formal business contract, a psychological contract is not written on paper, nor are all of its terms explicitly negotiated.[16]

Figure 8.2 illustrates the essential nature of a psychological contract. The individual makes a variety of *contributions* to the organization, such as effort, ability, loyalty, skills, and time. These contributions satisfy the individual's obligation under the contract. For example, Jill Henderson, a branch manager for Charles Schwab and Co., uses her knowledge of financial markets and investment opportunities to help her clients make profitable investments. Her MBA in finance, coupled with hard work and motivation, has led her to become one of the firm's most promising young managers. The firm believed she had these attributes when it hired her and expected that she would do well.

In return for these contributions, the organization provides *inducements* to the individual. These inducements satisfy the organization's contract obligation. Some inducements, such as pay and career opportunities, are tangible rewards. Others, such as job security and status, are more intangible. Henderson started at Schwab at a competitive salary and has received a salary increase each of the six years she has been with the firm. She has also been promoted twice and expects another promotion in the near future.

In this instance, both Henderson and Schwab apparently perceive the psychological contract to be fair and equitable. Both will be satisfied with the relationship and will do what they can to continue it. Henderson is likely to continue to work hard and effectively, and Schwab is likely to continue to increase her salary and give her promotions. In other situations, however, things might not work out as well. If either party sees an inequity in the contract, that party may initiate a change. The employee might ask for a pay raise or promotion, put forth less effort, or look for a better job elsewhere. The organization can also initiate change by training the worker to improve skills, transferring the worker to another job, or firing the worker.

All organizations face the basic challenge of managing psychological contracts. They want value from their employees, and they need to give employees the right inducements. For instance, underpaid employees may perform poorly or leave for better jobs elsewhere. Similarly, employees may even occasionally start to steal from their employer as an unethical and illegal way to balance the psychological contract.

FIGURE 8.2 The Psychological Contract

Sergey Smirnov/Alamy Stock Photo

Person–job fit is an important consideration when hiring people to perform specific jobs. For instance, some people might thrive working in extreme weather conditions, performing risky jobs, or traveling most of the time. Other people, in contrast, would balk at any of these opportunities and instead only want to work under mild weather conditions, performing low-risk tasks, or never traveling. Consider, for example, the job of cleaning external windows on high-rise buildings like the person shown here. Some people can handle jobs like this easily, while others might be terrified!

When an organization starts to downsize or impose cutbacks, the process of managing psychological contracts may become more complicated. For example, many organizations used to offer at least reasonable assurances of job permanence as a fundamental inducement to employees. Now, however, job permanence is less likely, so alternative inducements may be needed. Among the new forms of inducements provided by some companies are additional training opportunities and increased flexibility in working schedules.

The Person–Job Fit

The **person–job fit** refers to the extent to which a person's contributions and the organization's inducements match one another. A good person–job fit is one in which the employee's contributions match the inducements the organization offers. In theory, each employee has a specific set of needs they want fulfilled and a set of job-related behaviors and abilities to contribute. If the organization can take perfect advantage of those behaviors and abilities and exactly fulfill those needs, it will have achieved a perfect person–job fit. Good person–job fit, in turn, can result in higher performance and more positive attitudes. A poor person–job fit, though, can have just the opposite effects.

Person–Job Fit *the extent to which a person's contributions and the organization's inducements match one another*

Basic Motivation Concepts and Theories

Learning Objective 8-4

Identify and summarize the most important models and concepts of employee motivation.

Broadly defined, **motivation** is the set of forces that cause people to behave in certain ways. One worker may be motivated to work hard to produce as much as possible, whereas another may be motivated to do just enough to survive. Managers must understand these differences in behavior and the reasons for them.

Motivation *the set of forces that cause people to behave in certain ways*

Over the years, a steady progression of theories and studies have attempted to address these issues. In this section, we survey the major studies and theories of employee motivation. In particular, we focus on three approaches to human relations in the workplace that reflect a basic chronology of thinking in the area: (1) *classical theory* and *scientific management*, (2) *early behavioral theory*, and (3) *contemporary motivational theories*.

Classical Theory

Classical Theory of Motivation *theory holding that workers are motivated solely by money*

According to the **classical theory of motivation**, workers are motivated solely by money. In his 1911 book *The Principles of Scientific Management*, industrial engineer Frederick Taylor proposed a way for both companies and workers to benefit from this widely accepted view of life in the workplace. If workers are motivated by money, Taylor reasoned, paying them more should prompt them to produce more. Meanwhile, the firm that analyzed jobs and found better ways to perform them would be able to produce goods more cheaply, make higher profits, and pay and motivate workers better than its competitors.

Taylor's approach was known as *scientific management*. His ideas captured the imagination of many managers in the early twentieth century. Soon, manufacturing plants across the United States were hiring experts to perform time-and-motion studies: Industrial engineering techniques were applied to each facet of a job to determine how to perform it most efficiently. These studies were the first scientific attempts to break down jobs into easily repeated components and to devise more efficient tools and machines for performing them.[17] Two of Taylor's colleagues, Frank and Lillian Gilbreth, were featured in a popular book *Cheaper by the Dozen*, explaining how they applied scientific management to their large family. The book was later made into a movie.

Early Behavioral Theory

In 1925, a group of Harvard researchers began a study at the Hawthorne Works of Western Electric outside Chicago. With an eye to increasing productivity, they wanted to examine the relationship between changes in the physical environment and worker output.

The results of the experiment were unexpected, even confusing. For example, increased lighting levels improved productivity. For some reason, however, so did lower lighting levels. Moreover, against all expectations, increased pay failed to increase productivity. Gradually, the researchers pieced together the puzzle. The explanation lay in the workers' response to the attention they were receiving. The researchers concluded that productivity rose in response to almost any management action that workers interpreted as special attention. This finding, known today as the **Hawthorne effect**, had a major influence on human relations theory, although in many cases it amounted simply to convincing managers that they should pay more attention to employees.

Hawthorne Effect *tendency for productivity to increase when workers believe they are receiving special attention from management*

Dmytro Zinkevych/Shutterstock

Treating employees with respect and recognizing that they are valuable members of the organization can go a long way toward motivating employees to perform at their highest levels. This manager is explaining to one of her workers how to perform tasks more efficiently. She is doing so in a way that will motivate the employee to follow the new procedures.

Following the Hawthorne studies, managers and researchers alike focused more attention on the importance of good human relations in motivating employee performance. Stressing the factors that cause, focus, and sustain workers' behavior, most motivation theorists became concerned with the ways in which management thinks about and treats employees. The major motivation theories include the *human resources model*, the *hierarchy of needs model*, and the *two-factor theory*.

Human Resources Model: Theories X and Y In one historically important book, behavioral scientist Douglas McGregor concluded that managers tended to have radically different beliefs about how best to use the human resources employed by a firm. He classified these beliefs into sets of assumptions that he labeled "Theory X" and "Theory Y." The basic differences between these two theories are shown in Table 8.1.

Managers who subscribe to the **Theory X** perspective tend to believe that people are naturally lazy and uncooperative and must be either punished or rewarded to be made productive. Managers who are inclined to accept Theory Y tend to believe that people are naturally energetic, growth-oriented, self-motivated, and interested in being productive.

Theory X *theory of motivation holding that people are naturally lazy and uncooperative*

McGregor argued that **Theory Y** managers are more likely to have satisfied and motivated employees. Theory X and Y distinctions are somewhat simplistic and offer little concrete basis for action, however. Their value lies primarily in their ability to highlight and classify the behavior of managers in light of their attitudes toward employees.

Theory Y *theory of motivation holding that people are naturally energetic, growth-oriented, self-motivated, and interested in being productive*

Maslow's Hierarchy of Needs Model Psychologist Abraham Maslow's **hierarchy of human needs model** proposed that people have several different needs they attempt to satisfy in their work. Maslow classified these needs into five basic types and suggested they be arranged in the hierarchy of importance, as shown in Figure 8.3. According to Maslow, needs are hierarchical because lower-level needs must be met before a person will try to satisfy higher-level needs.

Hierarchy of Human Needs Model *theory of motivation describing five levels of human needs and arguing that basic needs must be fulfilled before people work to satisfy higher-level needs*

Once a set of needs has been satisfied, it ceases to motivate behavior. For example, if you feel secure in your job (that is, your security needs have been met), additional opportunities to achieve even more security, such as being assigned to a long-term project, will probably be less important to you than the chance to fulfill social or esteem needs, such as working with a mentor or becoming the member of an advisory board.

If, however, a lower-level need suddenly becomes unfulfilled, most people immediately refocus on that lower level. Suppose, for example, you are seeking to meet your self-esteem needs by working as a divisional manager at a major company. If you learn that your division and, consequently, your job may be eliminated, you might well find the promise of job security at a new firm as motivating as a promotion once would have been at your old company.

The period spanning 2018 and 2019 was excellent for business and for individuals wanting to work—many jobs were available and unemployment was very low. As a result, many workers were focusing on social and esteem needs. But when the 2020

table 8.1 Theory X and Theory Y

Theory X	Theory Y
People are lazy.	People are energetic.
People lack ambition and dislike responsibility.	People are ambitious and seek responsibility.
People are self-centered.	People can be selfless.
People resist change.	People want to contribute to business growth and change.
People are gullible and not bright.	People are intelligent.

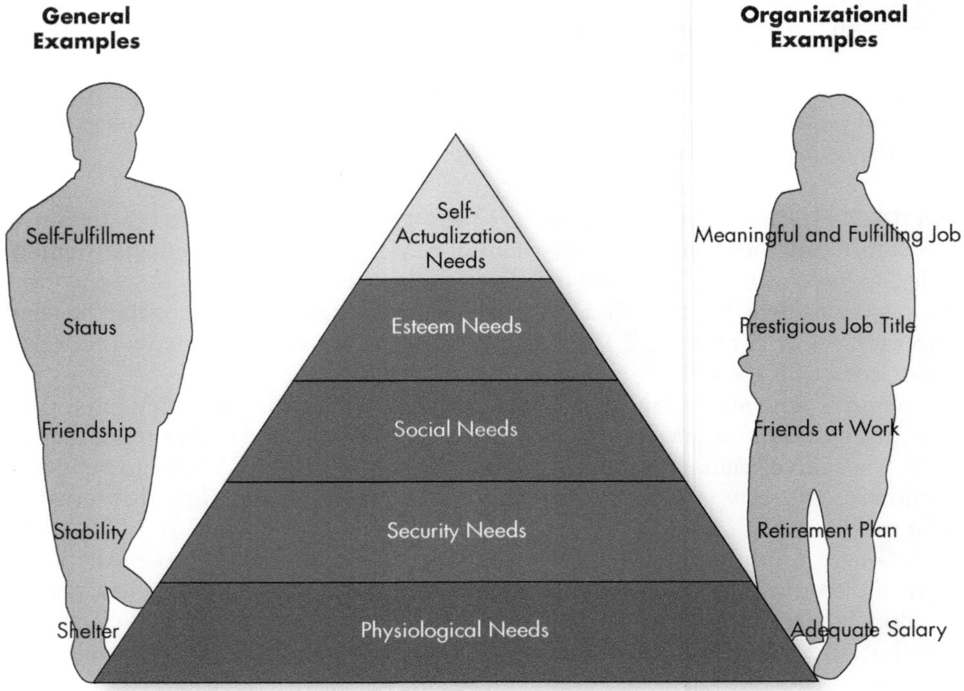

FIGURE 8.3 Maslow's Hierarchy of Human Needs
Source: Maslow, Abraham H.; Frager, Robert D.; Fadiman, James, *Motivation and Personality*, 3rd Ed., © 1987. Adapted and Electronically reproduced by permission of Pearson Education, Inc., Upper Saddle River, NJ.

COVID-19 pandemic swept the globe, many people lost or feared losing their jobs. During this period, physiological and security needs became much more important to these individuals.

Two-Factor Theory After studying a group of accountants and engineers, psychologist Frederick Herzberg concluded that job satisfaction and dissatisfaction depend on two factors: *hygiene factors*, such as working conditions, and *motivation factors*, such as recognition for a job well done.

Two-Factor Theory *theory of motivation holding that job satisfaction depends on two factors, hygiene and motivation*

According to Herzberg's **two-factor theory**, hygiene factors affect motivation and satisfaction only if they are absent or fail to meet expectations. For example, workers will be dissatisfied if they believe they have poor working conditions. If working conditions are improved, however, they will not necessarily become satisfied; they will simply not be dissatisfied. If workers receive no recognition for successful work, they may be neither dissatisfied nor satisfied. If recognition is provided, they will likely become more satisfied. During the 2020 COVID-19 pandemic some workers at Amazon walked off their jobs because they felt the firm wasn't doing enough to protect their health.

Figure 8.4 illustrates the two-factor theory. Note that motivation factors lie along a continuum from satisfaction to no satisfaction. Hygiene factors, in contrast, are likely to produce feelings that lie on a continuum from dissatisfaction to no dissatisfaction. Whereas motivation factors are directly related to the work that employees actually perform, hygiene factors refer to the environment in which they work.

This theory suggests that managers should follow a two-step approach to enhancing motivation. First, they must ensure that hygiene factors, such as working conditions or clearly stated policies, are acceptable. This practice will result in an absence of dissatisfaction. Then they must offer motivation factors, such as recognition or added responsibility, as a way to improve satisfaction and motivation.

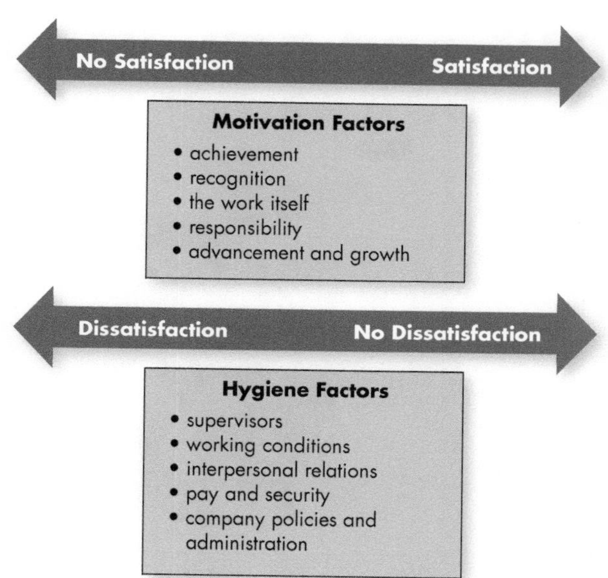

FIGURE 8.4 Two-Factor Theory of Motivation

Other Important Needs Each theory discussed so far describes interrelated sets of important individual needs within specific frameworks. David McClelland, a Harvard professor, described three other needs he suggested that people may learn and develop as they grow up. These "acquired" needs are the needs for achievement, affiliation, and power. Most people, however, are more familiar with the three needs as stand-alone concepts rather than as part of the original theory itself.

Need for Achievement *an individual's desire to accomplish a goal or task as effectively as possible*

The **need for achievement** arises from an individual's desire to accomplish a goal or task as effectively as possible.[18] Individuals who have a high need for achievement tend to set moderately difficult goals and to make moderately risky decisions. High-need achievers also want immediate, specific feedback on their performance. They want to know how well they did something as quickly after finishing it as possible. For this reason, high-need achievers frequently take jobs in sales, where they get almost immediate feedback from customers, and avoid jobs in areas such as research and development, where tangible progress is slower and feedback comes at longer intervals. Preoccupation with work is another characteristic of high-need achievers. They think about it on their way to the workplace, during lunch, and at home. They find it difficult to put their work aside, and they become frustrated when they must stop working on a partly completed project. Finally, high-need achievers tend to assume personal responsibility for getting things done. They often volunteer for extra duties and find it difficult to delegate part of a job to someone else. Accordingly, they derive a feeling of accomplishment when they have done more work than their peers without the assistance of others.

Need for Affiliation *an individual's desire for human companionship*

Many individuals also experience the **need for affiliation**—the need for human companionship.[22] Researchers recognize several ways that people with a high need for affiliation differ from those with a lower need. Individuals with a high need tend to want reassurance and approval from others and usually are genuinely concerned about others' feelings. They are likely to act and think as they believe others want them to, especially those with whom they strongly identify and desire friendship. As we might expect, people with a strong need for affiliation most often work in jobs with a lot of interpersonal contact, such as sales and teaching positions. While no research data support this, it seems likely that when people were practicing social distancing and being advised to stay at home during the 2020 COVID-19 pandemic, those with high needs for affiliation may have been more affected than those with lower needs for affiliation.

entrepreneurship and new ventures

The Uber of Nonemergency Medical Transportation

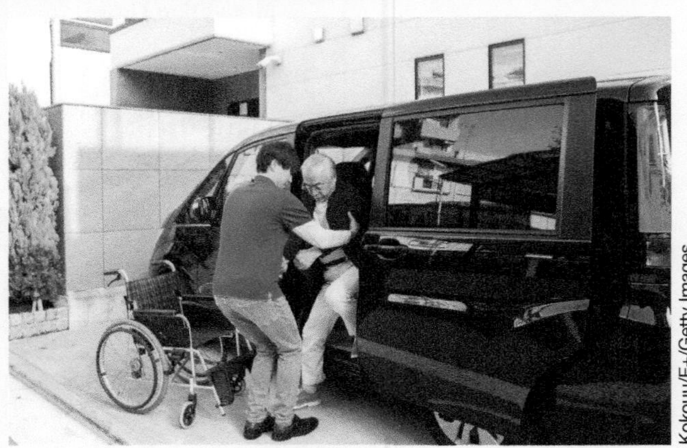
Kokouu/E+/Getty Images

When there is an emergency almost anywhere in the United States, a person can dial 911 and expect a quick response, complete with on-scene stabilization and rescue efforts and transportation to a medical facility (usually a hospital). What happens, though, when someone needs transportation to and from medical care that isn't an emergency, such as dialysis or a regular exam? If a person doesn't or can't drive or if they don't have a friend or family member's support, what can they do?

Enter Big Start Transit, LLC, in Dallas, Texas. Founder Tanya Biggers decided on an innovative approach to nonemergency medical transportation (NEMT) and paratransit—transportation services that supplement public transport routes. Drawing on the success of Uber and other ride-sharing companies, she decided to create a similar model for medically vulnerable riders and people with disabilities.

Every driver for Big Star Transit is an owner-operator, meaning they own a small business and contract with Big Star Transit to provide service. Big Star Transit provides a robust onboarding, training, and support structure to ensure the safety of its riders and drivers and to set up owner-operators for success.

The support system at Big Star Transit includes safety inspections of vehicles, pre-screening of passengers, business education and resources, and even a vehicle lease program that isn't dependent on personal credit. The company provides the education and training necessary to acquire the qualifications and earn certification to perform these services. It has a dedicated app for passengers and one for drivers, much like other ride-share platforms.

The company's website provides some insight into its philosophy:

> "We don't subscribe to 'the way we've always done it' because we know there's a better way. Our team incorporates women and minority leadership roles, diversity of backgrounds, genders, and ethnicities, and legions of professional, entrepreneurial Operators. Our network takes pride in giving us their 'boots on the ground' insights that just keep making us better. We audaciously believe we can evolve the traditional models, and we do so for the benefit of our passengers, our Operators, and the industry at large."[19]

This model and philosophy led to Big Star Transit's inclusion on Ernst & Young's finalist list for Entrepreneur of the Year in 2023, after winning for the Southwest region.[20] Ernst & Young has been recognizing innovation and entrepreneurship for almost 40 years. Finalists are selected based on criteria including financial performance, growth, impact, and entrepreneurial spirit. The national winner represents the United States at the World Entrepreneur of the Year conference.[21] Big Star Transit is one of only a handful of female-led organizations on the list.

Need for Power *the desire to control one's environment, including financial, material, informational, and human resources*

A third major individual need is the **need for power**—the desire to control one's environment, including financial, material, informational, and human resources.[23] People vary greatly along this dimension. Some individuals spend much time and energy seeking power; others avoid power if at all possible. People with a high need for power can be successful managers if three conditions are met. First, they must seek power for the betterment of the organization rather than for their own interests. Second, they must have a fairly low need for affiliation because fulfilling a personal need for power may well alienate others in the workplace. Third, they need plenty of self-control to curb their desire for power when it threatens to interfere with effective organizational or interpersonal relationships.[24]

Contemporary Motivation Theory

More complex and sophisticated models of employee behavior and motivation have been developed in recent years.[25] Two of the more interesting and useful ones are *expectancy theory* and *equity theory*.

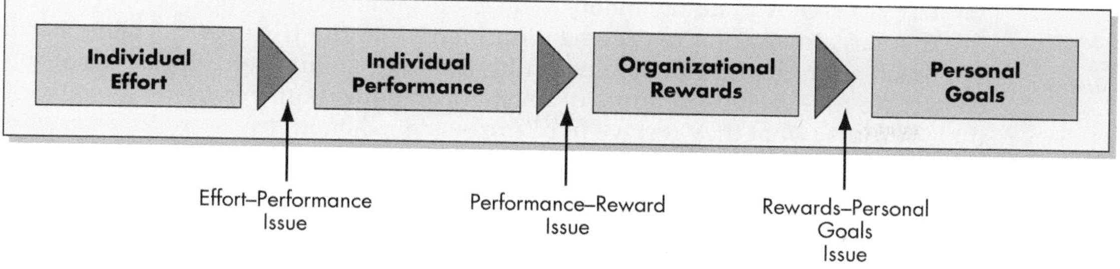

FIGURE 8.5 Expectancy Theory Model

Expectancy Theory *theory of motivation holding that people are motivated to work toward rewards that they want and that they believe they have a reasonable chance of obtaining*

Expectancy Theory

Expectancy theory suggests that people are motivated to work toward rewards that they want *and* that they believe they have a reasonable chance—or expectancy—of obtaining. A reward that seems out of reach is not likely to be motivating even if it is intrinsically positive. Figure 8.5 illustrates expectancy theory in terms of issues that are likely to be considered by an individual employee.

Consider the case of an assistant department manager who learns that their firm needs to replace a retiring division manager three levels above them in the organization. Even though the assistant department manager might want the job, they do not apply because they doubt they will be selected. In this case, they consider the performance–reward issue: They believe that their performance will not get them the position because it would be such a large promotion. They also learn that the firm is looking for a production manager on the night shift. They think they could get this job but choose not to apply because the overnight work hours are not desirable (the rewards–personal goals issue). Finally, they learn of a department manager opening one level higher than their current position in their own division. They may apply for this job because they want it and think they have a good chance of getting it. In this case, their consideration of all the issues has led to an expectancy that they can reach a goal.

Expectancy theory helps explain why some people do not work as hard as they can when their salaries are based purely on seniority. Paying employees the same whether they work hard or do just enough to get by removes the financial incentive for them to work harder. In other words, they ask themselves, "If I work harder, will I get a pay raise?" (the performance–reward issue) and conclude that the answer is "no." Similarly, if hard work will result in one or more undesirable outcomes, such as a transfer to another location or a promotion to a job that requires excessive travel and longer work hours (the rewards–personal goals issue), employees may not be motivated to work hard.

LightField Studios/Shutterstock

Different people want different things from their work. Some people like to travel, for example, while others do not. This manager, checking in for his flight, seems to be pleased with his upcoming business trip.

Equity Theory *theory of motivation holding that people evaluate their treatment by the organization relative to the treatment of others*

Equity Theory **Equity theory** focuses on social comparisons, people evaluating their treatment by the organization relative to the treatment of others. This approach suggests that people begin by thinking about their inputs (what they contribute to their jobs in terms of time, effort, education, experience) relative to their outputs (what they receive in return—salary, benefits, recognition, security). At this point, the comparison is similar to the psychological contract discussed earlier. As viewed by equity theory, though, the result is a ratio of contribution to return. When they compare their own ratios with those of other employees, they ask whether their ratios are comparable to, greater than, or less than those of the people with whom they are comparing themselves. Depending on their assessments, they experience feelings of equity or inequity. Figure 8.6 illustrates the three possible results of such an assessment.

For example, suppose a new college graduate gets a starting job at a large manufacturing firm. Their starting salary is $65,000 a year, they get an inexpensive company car, and they share an assistant with another new employee. If they

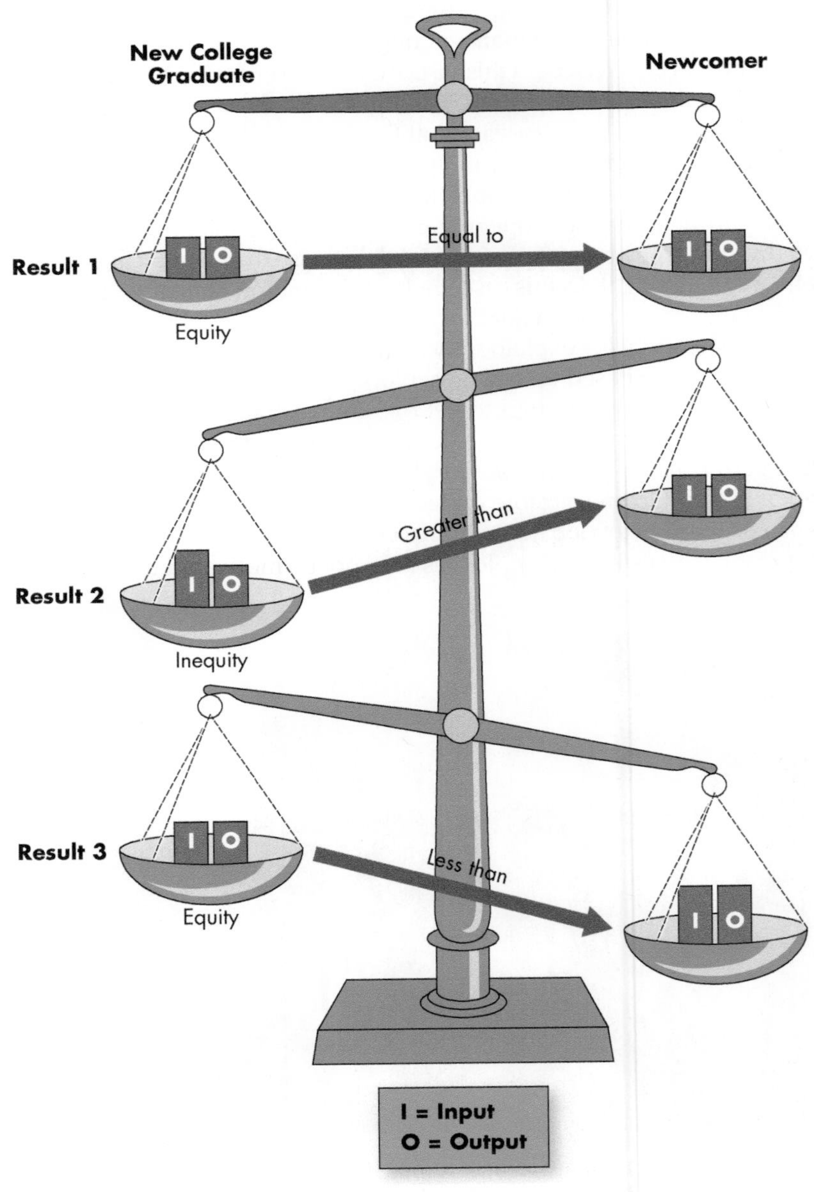

FIGURE 8.6 Equity Theory: Possible Assessments

later learn that another new employee has received the same salary, car, and staff arrangement, they will feel equitably treated (result 1 in Figure 8.6). However, if the other newcomer has received $75,000, a more expensive company car, and their own personal assistant, they may feel inequitably treated (result 2 in Figure 8.6).

Note, however, that for an individual to feel equitably treated, the two ratios do not have to be identical, only equitable. Assume, for instance, that our new employee has a bachelor's degree and two years of work experience. Perhaps they learn subsequently that the other new employee has an advanced degree and 10 years of experience. After first feeling inequity, the new employee may conclude that the person with whom they compared themselves is actually contributing more to the organization (more education and experience). That employee is perhaps equitably entitled, therefore, to receive more in return (result 3 in Figure 8.6).

When people feel they are being inequitably treated, they may act in various constructive and some not so constructive ways to restore fairness. For example, they may speak to their boss about the perceived inequity. Or (less constructively) they may demand a raise, reduce their efforts, work shorter hours, or just complain to their coworkers. They may also rationalize, find different people with whom to compare themselves, or leave their jobs.

Strategies and Techniques for Enhancing Motivation

Learning Objective 8-5

Describe some of the strategies and techniques used by organizations to improve employee motivation.

Understanding what motivates workers is only one part of the manager's job. The other part is applying that knowledge. Experts have suggested—and many companies have implemented—a range of programs designed to make jobs more interesting and rewarding, to make the work environment more pleasant, and to motivate employees to work harder.

Reinforcement/Behavior Modification

Some managers try to influence workers' behavior through systematic rewards and punishments for specific behaviors. Such managers first try to define the specific behaviors they want their employees to exhibit (working hard, being courteous to

Joerg Boethling/Alamy Stock Photo

John Deere uses positive reinforcement to help sustain motivation in its factories. Workers get pay increases and other rewards when they master new skills and perform at a high level.

customers, stressing quality) and the specific behaviors they want to eliminate (wasting time, being rude to customers, ignoring quality). Then they try to shape employee behavior by linking positive reinforcement with desired behaviors and punishment with undesired behaviors.

Positive Reinforcement *reward that follows desired behaviors*

Positive reinforcement is used when a company or manager provides a reward when employees exhibit desired behaviors, such as working hard, helping others, and so forth. When rewards are tied directly to performance, they serve as positive reinforcement. For example, paying large cash bonuses to salespeople who exceed quotas prompts them to work even harder during the next selling period. John Deere uses a reward system based on positive reinforcement. Among other things, the company gives its workers pay increases when they complete college courses and demonstrate mastery of new job skills.

Punishment *unpleasant consequences of an undesirable behavior*

Punishment is designed to change behavior by presenting people with unpleasant consequences if they exhibit undesired behaviors. Employees who are repeatedly late for work, for example, may be suspended or have their pay docked. Similarly, when the National Football League or Major League Baseball fines or suspends players found guilty of steroid abuse or sports betting, the organization is seeking to change players' behavior by punishing them.

Social Learning *learning that occurs when people observe the behaviors of others, recognize their consequences, and alter their own behavior as a result*

Social learning occurs when people observe the behaviors of others, recognize their consequences, and alter their own behavior as a result. A person can learn to do a new job by observing others or by watching videos. Or an employee may learn to avoid being late by seeing the boss chew out fellow workers. Social learning theory, then, suggests that individual behavior is determined by a person's cognitions and social environment. More specifically, people are presumed to learn behaviors and attitudes at least partly in response to what others expect of them.

Using Goals to Motivate Behavior

Management by Objectives (MBO) *set of procedures involving both managers and subordinates in setting goals and evaluating progress*

Performance goals are also commonly used to direct and motivate behavior. The most frequent method for setting performance goals is called **management by objectives (MBO)**, which is a system of collaborative goal setting that extends from the top of an organization to the bottom. MBO involves managers and subordinates in setting goals and evaluating progress. When the cycle starts (perhaps at the beginning of the year), the organization develops and communicates its overall goals and plans. Managers then collaborate with each of their subordinates to set individual goals that will best contribute to the organization's goals. Managers meet periodically to review progress toward individual goals, and then, usually on an annual basis, they evaluate goal achievement and use the results as a basis for starting the cycle over again.

According to many experts, motivational impact is the biggest advantage of MBO. When employees sit down with managers to set upcoming goals, they learn more about company-wide objectives, feel they are an important part of a team, and see how they can improve company-wide performance by reaching their own goals. If an MBO system is used properly, employees should leave meetings not only with an understanding of the value of their contributions but also with fair rewards for their performances. They should also accept and be committed to the moderately difficult and specific goals they have helped set for themselves.[26]

Participative Management and Empowerment

Participative Management and Empowerment *method of increasing job satisfaction by giving employees a voice in the management of their jobs and the company*

When a firm uses **participative management and empowerment**, it gives its employees a voice in how they do their jobs and in how the company is managed; the employees become empowered to take greater responsibility for their own performance. Not surprisingly, participation and empowerment often make employees feel more committed to organizational goals they have helped to shape.

finding a better way

It's an Actual Circus Out There

Imaginechina Limited/Alamy Stock Photo

What can big business learn from the circus? Guy Laliberté dropped out of college in 1978 and traveled Europe with the circus before joining a troupe of performers who needed some public relations help. After gaining a $1 million grant to build a big-tent show, Guy gathered his best performers together and created Cirque du Soleil. Although he sold most of his share in the company in 2015 for $1.5 billion, his innovative vision and passion for performance live on, as does his equally innovative commitment to his performers.

As a company that depends on teamwork, Cirque du Soleil has taken a radical approach to the way it manages people. Harnessing the power of energy and engagement, the company has steered away from traditional methods of employee motivation and shifted toward more open and honest conversations, asking for constant feedback and promoting shared responsibilities among all members of the company.

Knowing that the performers and support personnel on the ground are the ones who create a unique and thrilling customer experience, Cirque made it a goal to create an employee experience that supported the overall vision of the company. And research has shown that although financial rewards and gifts create immediate happiness, true loyalty and commitment come from shared experiences and human connection. To that end, Cirque du Soleil created programs like Cirque Jams, encouraging employees to get together to practice their favorite sports and outside activities, and Parade and Panache, peer recognition programs that allow employees to celebrate their accomplishments.

Instead of traditional performance management systems with ratings and criteria, every four months, employees meet with their managers for an open discussion. In addition to these open forums, a five-minute survey is sent out to every employee three or four times a year that asks questions pertaining to what it's like to work at Cirque and what the employee cares about most. After this information is collected, each leader is given a personal dashboard so they can see the results, determine what needs to be changed, and commit to actions that will make it happen. Imagine how successful a company could be if all the teams were as effective and dependable as those of Cirque du Soleil.

In 2022, Cirque de Soleil successfully restructured following bankruptcy that resulted in layoffs of nearly 95 percent of its staff and performers in 2020 as a result of the COVID-19 pandemic. Industry experts say that, prior to the pandemic, the creative company took some big risks that had mixed results. The closure of all of its shows for over a year due to the pandemic was almost the death of the 40-year-old company. As the Cirque troupes returned to performance venues worldwide, leadership looked again to employees to drive innovation. Acting CEO Stéphane Lefebvre put it this way: "At the Cirque, we need to be more creative than we've ever been. I was talking to our employees and the creative production team recently about innovation. Innovation doesn't just mean technology—it's this idea of coming up with new experiences."[27]

Participation and empowerment can be used in large firms or small firms, both with managers and operating employees. For example, managers at General Electric who once needed higher-level approval for any expenditure more than $5,000 now have the autonomy to make their own expense decisions up to as much as $50,000. At Adam Hats Company, a small firm that makes men's dress, military, and cowboy hats, workers who previously had to report all product defects to supervisors now have the freedom to correct problems themselves or even return products to the workers who are responsible for them. Google allows employees to devote 20 percent of their work time to experimenting with new ideas apart from their normal job duties; 3M provides the same option to its employees for 15 percent of the individual's work time. And Netflix allows its employees to take unlimited vacation time so long as they meet their work obligations and perform at a consistently high level.

Although some employees thrive in participative programs, such programs are not for everyone. People may be frustrated by responsibilities they are not equipped to handle. Moreover, participative programs may actually result in dissatisfied employees if workers see the invitation to participate as more symbolic than substantive or if managers never act on their suggestions or ideas. One key, say most experts, is to invite participation only to the extent that employees want to have input and only if participation will have real value for an organization.

Work Teams and Team Structures

We have already noted the increased use of teams in organizations. Yet another benefit that some companies get from using teams is increased motivation and enhanced job satisfaction among those employees working in teams. Although teams are often less effective in traditional and rigidly structured bureaucratic organizations, they frequently help smaller, more flexible organizations make decisions more quickly and effectively, enhance company-wide communication, and encourage organizational members to feel more like a part of an organization. In turn, these attitudes usually lead to higher levels of both employee motivation and job satisfaction.[28]

But managers should remember that teams are not for everyone. Levi Strauss, for example, encountered major problems when it tried to use teams. Individual workers previously performed repetitive, highly specialized tasks, such as sewing zippers into jeans, and were paid according to the number of jobs they completed each day. In an attempt to boost productivity, company management reorganized everyone into teams of 10 to 35 workers and assigned tasks to the entire group. Each team member's pay was determined by the team's level of productivity. In practice, however, faster workers became resentful of slower workers because they reduced the group's total output. Slower workers, meanwhile, resented the pressure put on them by faster-working coworkers. As a result, motivation, satisfaction, and morale all dropped, and Levi Strauss eventually abandoned the teamwork plan altogether.

Job Enrichment and Job Redesign

Whereas goal setting and MBO programs and empowerment can work in a variety of settings, *job enrichment* and *job redesign* programs are generally used to increase satisfaction in jobs significantly lacking in motivational properties.

Job Enrichment *method of increasing job satisfaction by adding one or more motivating factors to job activities*

Job Enrichment Programs

Job enrichment is intended to add one or more motivating factors to job activities. For example, job rotation programs expand growth opportunities by rotating employees through various positions in the same firm. Workers gain not only new skills but also a broader overview of their work and their organization. Other programs focus on increasing responsibility or recognition. At United Airlines, for example, flight attendants now have more control over their own scheduling. The jobs of flight service managers were enriched when they were given more responsibility and authority for assigning tasks to flight crew members.

Job Redesign *method of increasing job satisfaction by designing a more satisfactory fit between workers and their jobs*

Job Redesign Programs

Job redesign acknowledges that different people want different things from their jobs. By restructuring work to achieve a more satisfactory fit between workers and their jobs, job redesign can motivate individuals with strong needs for career growth or achievement. Job redesign is usually implemented in one of three ways: through *combining tasks, forming natural work groups*, or *establishing client relationships*.

COMBINING TASKS The job of combining tasks involves enlarging jobs and increasing their variety to make employees feel that their work is more meaningful. In turn, employees become more motivated. For example, the job done by a programmer who maintains computer systems might be redesigned to include some system design and system development work. While developing additional skills, the programmer also gets involved in the overall process of system development.

Forming Natural Work Groups People who do different jobs on the same projects are candidates for natural work groups. These groups are formed to help employees see the place and importance of their jobs in the total structure of the firm. The groups are valuable to management because the people working on a project are usually the most knowledgeable about it and the most capable problem solvers.

Establishing Client Relationships Establishing client relationships means letting employees interact with customers. This approach increases job variety. It gives workers both a greater sense of control and more feedback about performance than they get when their jobs are not highly interactive. For example, software writers at Microsoft watch test users work with programs and discuss problems with them directly rather than receiving feedback from third-party researchers.

Modified Work Schedules and Alternative Workplaces

As another way of increasing job satisfaction, many companies also use *modified work schedules*, different approaches to working hours and the workweek. Two common forms of modified scheduling are *work-share programs* and *flextime programs*. A related approach is the alternative workplace strategy.[29]

Work-Share Programs

At Steelcase, the country's largest maker of office furnishings, two talented people in the marketing division both wanted to work only part time but the company needed a full-time employee. They arrived at a solution: They now share a single full-time job. With each working 2.5 days a week, both got their wish and the job gets done—and done well. The practice, known as **work sharing (or job sharing)**, has "brought sanity back to our lives," according to at least one Steelcase employee.

Work Sharing (or Job Sharing) *method of increasing job satisfaction by allowing two or more people to share a single full-time job*

Job sharing usually benefits both employees and employers. Employees, for instance, tend to appreciate the organization's attention to their personal needs. At the same time, the company can reduce turnover and save on the cost of benefits. On the negative side, job-share employees generally receive fewer benefits than their full-time counterparts and may be the first to be laid off when cutbacks are necessary.

Flextime Programs

Flextime programs allow people to choose their working hours by adjusting a standard work schedule on a daily or weekly basis. That is, employees are allowed to choose when they work as long as they meet certain requirements. In some cases, businesses allow their employees almost total discretion over when they work as long as their jobs get done. At the other extreme, employees may be allowed some options but also have some required work hours. Steelcase, for instance, uses flextime for all of its employees but requires them to work certain core hours. This practice allows everyone to reach coworkers at a specified time of day. Employees can then decide whether to make up the rest of the standard 8-hour day by coming in and leaving early (by working 6:00 AM to 2:00 PM or 7:00 AM to 3:00 PM) or late (9:00 AM to 5:00 PM or 10:00 AM to 6:00 PM).

Flextime Programs *method of increasing job satisfaction by allowing workers to adjust work schedules on a daily or weekly basis*

In another variation, companies may also allow employees to choose four, five, or six days on which to work each week. Some, for instance, may choose Monday through Thursday, others Tuesday through Friday. By working 10 hours in four work-days, employees still complete 40-hour weeks.

Alternative Workplaces

A rapidly growing number of U.S. workers do a significant portion of their work via **telecommuting (or teleworking)**, performing some or all of a job away from traditional office settings. Working from a connected home office, telecommuters can keep abreast of everything going on at the company. Almost 80 percent of white-collar and other professional workers in the United States perform at least some of their work from a location other than their office. Experts also estimate that more than 5 percent of those workers work exclusively from home

Telecommuting (or Teleworking) *form of flextime that allows people to perform some or all of a job away from standard office settings*

or other remote settings. Of course, these numbers changed dramatically during the 2020 COVID-19 pandemic, as many workers who had never worked from home were required to do so. It remains to be seen how the use of alternative workplaces will change after the health crisis has passed—if it will revert to previous levels, remain at higher levels, or somewhere in between.

Many businesses still struggle with this question today, but others have been experimenting with versions of what are called *hybrid* work arrangements. These arrangements allow workers to spend part of their time working remotely but also require (or suggest) that they also spend some time at the traditional work site. Halliburton, for instance, requires employees at its Houston headquarters facility to spend 10 days per month in the office but allows them to work remotely the rest of the time.

Advantages and Disadvantages of Modified Schedules and Alternative Workplaces Flextime and alternative workplaces give employees more freedom in their professional and personal lives. These options allow workers to plan around the work schedules of spouses and the school schedules of young children. Studies show that the increased sense of freedom and control may reduce stress and improve individual productivity (under normal conditions, at least).

Companies also benefit in other ways. In urban areas, for example, such programs can reduce traffic congestion and similar problems that contribute to stress and lost work time. Furthermore, employers benefit from higher levels of commitment and job satisfaction. John Hancock Insurance, Shell, and MetLife are among the major U.S. corporations that have successfully adopted some form of flextime.

Conversely, flextime sometimes complicates coordination because people are working different schedules. In addition, if workers are paid by the hour, flextime may make it difficult for employers to keep accurate records of when employees are actually working.

As for telecommuting, it may not be for everyone. For instance, some people may be attracted to telecommuting because they envision not having to shave or put on makeup and relish the idea of spending the day in their pajamas. But not everyone has the necessary self-discipline to work from home without supervision and others come to miss the social interaction of the workplace. One study has shown that even though telecommuters may be producing results, those with strong advancement ambitions may miss networking and "rubbing elbows" with management on a day-to-day basis.

Girts Ragelis/Shutterstock

Businesses have often allowed employees to work remotely, usually from a home office, as part of their overall motivational strategy. This manager, for example, is attending a virtual meeting from her home office. The COVID-19 pandemic pushed many more businesses to adopt this practice, but since then many companies have been requiring on-site work at least part of the time.

Another obstacle to establishing a telecommuting program is convincing management that it can be beneficial for all involved. Telecommuters may have to fight the perception from both bosses and coworkers that if they are not being supervised, they are not working. Managers, admits one experienced consultant, "usually have to be dragged kicking and screaming into this. They always ask 'How can I tell if someone is working when I can't see them?'" By the same token, he adds, "that's based on the erroneous assumption that if you can see them, they are working." Most experts agree that reeducation and constant communication are requirements of a successful telecommuting arrangement. Both managers and employees must determine expectations in advance.

As we have illustrated in this chapter, employee behavior and motivation are important concepts for managers to understand. They are also complex processes that require careful consideration by managers. For example, a clumsy attempt to motivate employees to work harder without fully considering all factors can actually have just the opposite effect. But managers who do take the time to understand the people with whom they work can better appreciate their efforts. Another important factor that affects employee behavior is *leadership*, the subject of our next chapter.

summary of learning objectives

LEARNING OBJECTIVE 8-1

Identify and discuss the basic forms of behaviors that employees exhibit in organizations.

Employee behavior is the pattern of actions by the members of an organization that directly or indirectly influences the organization's effectiveness. *Performance behaviors* are the total set of work-related behaviors that the organization expects employees to display. They directly contribute to productivity and performance. *Organizational citizenship*, in contrast, refers to the behavior of individuals who make a positive overall contribution to the organization, although not directly contributing to the bottom line. A number of factors, including individual and organizational variables, play roles in promoting or minimizing organizational citizenship behaviors. *Counterproductive behaviors* are those that detract from, rather than contribute to, organizational performance. Counterproductive behaviors include absenteeism, turnover, theft and sabotage, sexual and racial harassment, and workplace aggression and violence.

LEARNING OBJECTIVE 8-2

Describe the nature and importance of individual differences among employees.

Individual differences are personal attributes that vary from one person to another, such as personality and attitudes. *Personality* is the relatively stable set of psychological attributes that distinguish one person from another. The *"big five" personality traits* are *agreeableness, conscientiousness, emotionality, extraversion*, and *openness. Agreeableness* is a person's ability to get along with others. *Conscientiousness*, another of the "big five" traits, refers to the individual's persistence, dependableness, and orderliness. *Emotionality* refers to the degree to which people tend to be positive or negative in their outlook and behaviors toward others. *Extraversion* refers to a person's comfort level with relationships. Extraverts are sociable, talkative, assertive, and open to new relationships and tend to be higher performers. Finally, *openness* is how open or rigid a person is in terms of their beliefs. People with a high level of openness are curious and willing to listen to new ideas and are, therefore, often higher performers. The potential value of this framework is that it encompasses an integrated set of traits that appear to be valid predictors of certain behaviors in certain situations. Thus, managers who can both understand the framework and assess these traits in their employees are in a good position to understand how and why they behave as they do.

The Myers-Briggs framework differentiates people in terms of four general dimensions: sensing, intuiting, judging, and perceiving. Higher and lower positions in each of the dimensions are used to classify people into 1 of 16 different personality categories. Research suggests that the Myers-Briggs Type Indicator is a useful method for determining communication styles and interaction preferences.

Emotional intelligence, or *emotional quotient (EQ)*, refers to the extent to which people are self-aware, can manage their emotions, can motivate themselves, can express empathy for others, and possess social skills. Preliminary research suggests that people with high EQs perform better than others. Just as important, it appears that emotional intelligence is not biologically based but can be learned.

Other important personality traits are locus of control, self-efficacy, authoritarianism, Machiavellianism, self-esteem, and risk propensity. *Locus of control* is the extent to which people believe their behavior has a real effect on what happens to them. People with an internal locus of control believe that they will succeed if they work hard, whereas those with an external locus of control believe that fate, chance, luck, or the behavior of others determines their own success. A similar concept is *self-efficacy*. A person's self-efficacy is their belief about the ability to perform a task. *Authoritarianism* is the extent to which a person believes that power and status differences are acceptable within an organization. A person who is highly authoritarian is more likely to accept direction and orders from a supervisor. *Machiavellianism* is a personality trait related to an individual's desire to gain power and control the behavior of others. *Self-esteem* is a personality trait that refers to the extent to which a person believes that their is worthwhile and deserving. Individuals with high self-esteem are more likely to seek higher-status jobs and are more confident in their performance. Finally, *risk propensity* refers to the degree to which a person is willing to take chances and make risky decisions. This characteristic can be a major influence on a manager's decision-making behavior.

Attitudes reflect our beliefs and feelings about specific ideas, situations, or other people. Attitudes are important because they are the mechanism through which we express our feelings. Attitudes are formed by a variety of forces, including our personal values, our experiences, and our personalities. Attitudes are usually viewed as stable dispositions to behave toward objects in a certain way and contain three components: cognition, affect, and intention. *Cognition* is the knowledge a person presumes to have about something. A person's *affect* is their feelings toward something, and *intention* guides a person's behavior. When two sets of cognitions or perceptions are contradictory or incongruent, a person experiences a level of conflict and anxiety called *cognitive dissonance*. Especially important work-related attitudes are *job satisfaction* and *organizational commitment*. Job satisfaction, also known as *morale*, is the extent to which people have positive attitudes toward their jobs. Organizational commitment, in contrast, reflects an individual's identification with the organization and its mission.

LEARNING OBJECTIVE 8-3

Explain the meaning and importance of psychological contracts and the person–job fit in the workplace.

A *psychological contract* is the overall set of expectations held by employees and the organization regarding what employees will contribute to the organization and what the organization will provide in return. An individual makes a variety of contributions to the organization, such as effort, ability, loyalty, skills, and time. In return, the organization provides inducements such as pay, career opportunities, job security, and status. All organizations must manage psychological contracts, providing the right inducements to retain employees.

A good *person–job fit* is achieved when the employee's contributions match the inducements the organization offers. Having a good match between people and their jobs can help enhance performance, job satisfaction, and motivation.

LEARNING OBJECTIVE 8-4

Identify and summarize the most important models and concepts of employee motivation.

Motivation is the set of forces that cause people to behave in certain ways. Early approaches to motivation assumed that workers are motivated solely by money. Managers applied this theory through *scientific management* by paying workers for productivity and finding more efficient ways of getting things done. However, the results of a study at Western Electric revealed that worker productivity improves in response to special attention, a phenomenon known as the *Hawthorne effect*.

As a result, researchers focused more on the effect of human relations on employee performance. Abraham Maslow's *hierarchy of human needs* model holds that people at work try to satisfy one or more of five different needs: physiological, security, social, esteem, and self-actualization. According to this theory, people are motivated by their lowest level of unsatisfied need.

Frederick Herzberg's *two-factor theory* argues that satisfaction and dissatisfaction depend on *hygiene factors*, such as working conditions, and *motivation factors*, such as recognition for a job well done. Herzberg suggests that the absence of hygiene factors causes dissatisfaction, but the presence of these same factors does not cause motivation. Employees are motivated by the presence of one or more motivation factors.

McClelland's acquired needs theory hypothesized that workers may have three types of needs: the needs for achievement, affiliation, and power. These needs are shaped over time and influence behavior. Those with high achievement needs are motivated by challenging tasks, whereas those with high affiliation needs desire to develop personal connections with other workers. Employees with high power needs have a desire to control their environment.

Douglas McGregor proposed the human resources model. He described two types of managers. Theory X managers believe that workers are naturally lazy and unmotivated, and Theory Y managers believe that people are naturally self-motivated and interested in being productive.

Expectancy theory suggests that people are motivated to work toward rewards they have a reasonable expectancy of obtaining. *Equity theory* focuses on social comparisons—people evaluating their treatment by the organization relative to its treatment of others.

LEARNING OBJECTIVE 8-5

Describe some of the strategies and techniques used by organizations to improve employee motivation.

Several major strategies and techniques are often used to make jobs more interesting and rewarding. *Positive reinforcement* is used when a company or manager provides a reward when employees exhibit desired behaviors, whereas *punishment* is designed to change behavior by presenting employees with unpleasant consequences if they exhibit undesired behaviors. *Social learning* occurs when people observe the behaviors of others and recognize their consequences, altering their own behavior as a result.

Management by objectives (MBO) is a system of collaborative goal setting that extends from the top of an organization to the bottom. Managers periodically meet with subordinates to review progress toward goals, increasing satisfaction and commitment. In *participative management and empowerment*, employees are given a voice in how they do their jobs and in how the company is managed. Participative management tends to increase employee commitment to organizational goals.

Using *teams* is another strategy to increase motivation. Job enrichment and job redesign are generally used to increase satisfaction in jobs significantly lacking motivating factors. *Job enrichment* adds motivating factors to job activities. *Job redesign* is a method of increasing job satisfaction by designing a more satisfactory fit between workers and their jobs through combining tasks, forming natural workgroups, or establishing client relationships. Some companies also use *modified work schedules*—different approaches to working hours and the workweek. Common options include *work sharing (job sharing)*, *flextime programs*, and *telecommuting*.

key terms

absenteeism **(p. 247)**
affect **(p. 252)**
attitudes **(p. 252)**
authoritarianism **(p. 251)**
"big five" personality traits **(p. 248)**
classical theory of motivation **(p. 256)**
cognition **(p. 252)**
cognitive dissonance **(p. 253)**
counterproductive behaviors **(p. 247)**
emotional intelligence (emotional quotient, EQ) **(p. 250)**
employee behavior **(p. 245)**
equity theory **(p. 262)**
expectancy theory **(p. 261)**
flextime programs **(p. 267)**
Hawthorne effect **(p. 256)**
hierarchy of human needs model **(p. 257)**

individual differences **(p. 248)**
intention **(p. 253)**
job enrichment **(p. 266)**
job redesign **(p. 266)**
job satisfaction **(p. 253)**
locus of control **(p. 250)**
Machiavellianism **(p. 251)**
management by objectives (MBO) **(p. 264)**
motivation **(p. 255)**
Myers-Briggs Type Indicator (MBTI) **(p. 250)**
need for achievement **(p. 259)**
need for affiliation **(p. 259)**
need for power **(p. 260)**
organizational citizenship **(p. 246)**
organizational commitment **(p. 253)**
participative management and empowerment **(p. 264)**
performance behaviors **(p. 245)**
personality **(p. 248)**
person–job fit **(p. 255)**
positive reinforcement **(p. 264)**
psychological contract **(p. 254)**
punishment **(p. 264)**
risk propensity **(p. 252)**
self-efficacy **(p. 250)**
self-esteem **(p. 251)**
social learning **(p. 264)**
telecommuting (or teleworking) **(p. 267)**
Theory X **(p. 257)**
Theory Y **(p. 257)**
turnover **(p. 247)**
two-factor theory **(p. 258)**
work sharing (or job sharing) **(p. 267)**

questions & exercises

QUESTIONS FOR REVIEW

8-1. What are the "big five" personality traits and how do they contribute to employee performance?

8-2. What are the three structural components of an attitude? Be sure to describe each.

8-3. What are the strategies and techniques for enhancing employee motivation? Give examples of each.

8-4. What are the pros and cons of participative management?

QUESTIONS FOR ANALYSIS

8-5. What is a psychological contract? Describe the psychological contract you currently have or have had in the past with an employer, or describe the psychological contract that you have with the instructor in this class.

8-6. Do you think that most people are relatively satisfied or dissatisfied with their work? What factors do you think most contribute to satisfaction or dissatisfaction?

8-7. What was your most recent job experience in terms of your contributions and the organization's inducements?

8-8. What would you tell a worker performing a simple and routine job who wants more challenge and enjoyment from work?

APPLICATION EXERCISES

8-9. Assume you are about to start your own business. What would you do from the beginning to ensure that your employees will be satisfied and motivated?

8-10. Ask an employer what they believe motivates their employees. Identify one or more theories of motivation that seem consistent with this manager's approach.

building a business: continuing team exercise

ASSIGNMENT

Meet with your team members and discuss your new business venture within the context of this chapter. Develop specific responses to the following:

8-11. Thinking about your new business venture, choose two dramatically different positions in the company and define performance behaviors for each position. What counterproductive behaviors would be most detrimental to your business?

8-12. If you were able to measure the emotional intelligence of prospective employees, which dimension or dimensions will be most important to you?

8-13. There are many theories of motivation. If you believe that Maslow's needs hierarchy best explains motivation in the workplace, how will you motivate your employees to work hard?

8-14. Another popular theory of motivation is Herzberg's two-factor theory. How could you apply this theory to your new business venture?

8-15. In your new company, will employees be able to work from home or work flexible hours? Why or why not?

team exercise

TOO MUCH OF A GOOD THING

The Situation

Brandy Littlefoot runs an online business supplying authentic Native American foods to local restaurants. She runs a tight ship, the way her father did when he ran the company. Employees work from 8 AM to 5 PM and have one week of paid time off during their first five years with the company. Those who have been with the company for over five years have two weeks of paid time off. Littlefoot's company also offers a small retirement plan and decent health benefits. She pays market wages with cost-of-living increases annually to keep up with inflation. Since the pandemic, however, Brandy has seen a severe drop in sales and therefore profits, which she expected to turn around once the food service industry recovered. Instead, she experienced high employee turnover and continued declines in sales despite an increase in demand from her local customers. With a minimum staff, she can't keep up with the orders. Her solution is to push her employees harder, saying, "They should be grateful for the overtime."

Method

In groups of four, step into the role of management consultants. Start by analyzing Brandy's workforce issues from the following perspectives and then develop a set of recommendations to help her manage her workforce more effectively.

8-16. ***Job satisfaction and morale.*** As part of a 77-year-old, family-owned business, Brandy's employees were generally happy and loyal before the downturn. What opportunities do you think Brandy has to improve job satisfaction and morale in order to hire and retain good employees?

8-17. ***Theory X versus Theory Y.*** Does Brandy seem to reflect more of a Theory X or Theory Y philosophy of management? What advice would you give her to increase retention and employee motivation?

8-18. ***Two-factor theory.*** Analyze the various ways in which improving such motivational factors as recognition, added responsibility, advancement, and growth might reduce the importance of hygiene factors, including pay and security.

8-19. ***Expectancy theory.*** Analyze the effect on productivity of redesigning the company's compensation structure—namely, by paying lower base salaries while offering greater earnings potential through a quota-based incentive system. Why would linking performance with increased pay that is achievable through hard work motivate employees?

8-20. What is your group's most important recommendation? Why do you think it is likely to succeed?

exercising your ethics

DOUBLE DIPPING

The Situation

In 2022, Equifax (EFX) used a program called The Work Number to ascertain that 24 of its employees were holding second or even third full-time jobs. These employees were terminated because their employment contracts with Equifax stipulated that they would work exclusively for Equifax. CEO Mark Begor reminded staff in an email, "We expect our team to be fully dedicated to EFX and have one role . . . their job at EFX."[30]

Employees had grown used to doing remote work and reporting virtually. Equifax used additional information like chats with managers and VPN usage to confirm that its workers were indeed holding other jobs. The Work Number company is owned by Equifax, and the company has additional products like Talent Report Employment monitoring that will scan government records and other public information about employees.

The Dilemma

You are the human resource manager for a midsize corporation, and the CEO has expressed interest in using similar products to check the employment status of all full-time workers. Employees had been ordered back to the office following company-wide remote work, but the pushback was so strong that the CEO reconsidered that decision. She is concerned that some employees are "double dipping," taking advantage of remote work policies to work second jobs on the clock. You know that the company has had record sales and productivity numbers for the past three years, and you know there are a number of employees who have sought additional employment. There is no specific exclusivity policy, but the CEO wants you to include the consideration of outside work in employee evaluations and pay rates. You're concerned about the way this news might be perceived as punitive and that it has the potential to negatively impact employee motivation.

QUESTIONS TO ADDRESS

8-21. What are the ethical issues in this case?

8-22. What do you think most managers would do in this situation?

8-23. What would you do? Justify your answer.

cases

BUILDING A CULTURE OF HOSPITALITY

Continued from page 245

At the beginning of this chapter, you read about Hilton's commitment to frontline employees. Using the information presented in this chapter, you should now be able to answer these questions.

QUESTIONS FOR DISCUSSION

8-24. Do you think that higher pay is the best way to increase employee engagement and commitment? What leads you to this conclusion?

8-25. What factors motivate you personally?

8-26. Explain Hilton's employee support programs in light of the classical theory of motivation.

8-27. How could Maslow's hierarchy of needs help to explain the relationship between pay and productivity?

8-28. Use equity theory, expectancy theory, or two-factor theory to explain Hilton's employee engagement programs.

8-29. Do you believe that companies have greater social responsibility to pay higher wages or to provide a supportive workplace? Support your claim.

WORK–LIFE BALANCE

During the COVID-19 pandemic, a huge portion of the workforce switched to remote work, whether they wanted to or not. As the world shifted to a new normal, many employers found that their worker productivity had not been harmed by remote or hybrid work policies and that productivity had actually *increased*. Employees—especially moms—found that they could complete their assignments, meet with colleagues, and complete projects while juggling childcare, school pick-ups, and family care more easily if they worked from home. As employers began exploring shifting their workforce back to in-person, traditional business hours, they often found strong resistance from staff, sometimes leading to larger conversations about workers' rights or unionization. In a 2023 survey of U.S. CEOs, the Conference Board found that only about 3 percent of 1,100 CEOs were planning to scale back on remote work options in 2023.

As employees are increasingly recognizing their bargaining power, companies are taking a close look at day-to-day operations and finding ways to increase employee attraction and retention. Madeleine Niebauer, CEO and founder of Chief, thinks she has found at least part of the solution: a 32-hour work week.

When Niebauer founded her company, she thought about how to incorporate a different set of values from the very beginning. She strove to set an example by creating a company that really cares about a work–life balance. Payroll hours are capped at 32 per week, with each person choosing their day off, as long as it's communicated to their team. She credits the policy with high employee retention and with attracting qualified and overqualified candidates for open positions. Other companies have moved to a 32-hour work week but then cut employee pay by 20 percent. Niebauer's tactic was instead to offer full-time pay and benefits but to position salaries in the middle of industry pay ranges.

"I really believe that people shouldn't live their lives for work," Niebauer says. "I think people should live their lives for the people and the passion in their lives. I think, for the majority of us, that consists of things outside of work."[31]

Research by Peakon, a human resources platform, indicates that women-led companies are more likely to adopt such policies. In a study of over 60,000 employees, respondents indicated that female leadership was stronger in five specific areas: strategy, mission, belief, communication, and autonomy.[32] In addition, *Forbes* magazine specifically notes: "Employees at women-led companies seem to enjoy more autonomy and are specifically more satisfied with work-from-home policies when compared to male-led companies."[33]

QUESTIONS FOR DISCUSSION

8-30. How do you feel about remote work? Would you rather have a job in which you have set office hours, or would you rather work from home? Do you think that working from home would cause you to be more productive or less productive? Why?

8-31. Consider businesses such as grocery stores, auto dealers, hardware stores, or others that provide products to consumers. Could you identify ways in which these companies could provide goods and services with remote workers?

8-32. How do you think companies can balance flexible schedules with accountability?

endnotes

[1] Hilton Careers, "Why Every Job Makes the Stay: Q&A with Laura Fuentes, Chief Human Resources Officer," Hilton.com, May 8, 2023, https://jobs.hilton.com/us/en/blogarticle/why-every-job-makes-the-stay-qa-with-laura-fuentes-chief-human-resources-officer?_gl=1*1cire7r*_gcl_au*NDIxNTQxNDYuMTY4ODU4MDg4MQ.

[2] "Hilton Ranked #2 Workplace in the World." Stories From Hilton, October 13, 2022. https://stories.hilton.com/releases/hilton-ranked-2-workplace-in-the-world.

[3] "100 Best Companies to Work For," *Fortune*, 2019, https://fortune.com/best-companies/2019/hilton-worldwide-holdings/.

[4] "We've All Heard Of IQ and EQ. But What Is Your CQ—Your 'Crisis Quotient?,'" Executive Mentors, Leadership Training, August 22, 2022, https://www.excoleadership.com/articles/weve-all-heard-of-iq-and-eq-but-what-is-your-cq-your-crisis-quotient/.

[5] Dennis W. Organ, Philip M. Podsakoff, and Nathan P. Podsakoff, "Expanding the Criterion Domain

to Include Organizational Citizenship Behavior: Implications for Employee Selection," in *Handbook of Industrial and Organizational Psychology*, ed. Sheldon Zedeck (Washington, DC: American Psychological Association, 2010).

[6] "2023 Anti-Trans Bills: Trans Legislation Tracker," accessed May 17, 2023, https://translegislation.com/.

[7] National LGBTQ Task Force, "56 Major Companies Respond to Alarming Effort to Erase Transgender People from Legal Protections," press release, November 1, 2018, https://www.thetaskforce.org/news/56-major-companies-respond-to-alarming-effort-to-erase-transgender-people-from-legal-protections/.

[8] National LGBTQ Task Force, "56 Major Companies Respond to Alarming Effort to Erase Transgender People from Legal Protections."

[9] Ropes & Gray, "Diversity," accessed May 17, 2023, https://www.ropesgray.com/en/firm/diversity.

[10] Ropes & Gray, "Ropes & Gray Sponsors Out Leadership's Global Summit on LGBTQ+ Diversity in the Boardroom," accessed May 17, 2023, https://www.ropesgray.com/en/newsroom/news/2022/March/Ropes-Gray-Sponsors-Out-Leaderships-Global-Summit-on-LGBTQ-Diversity-in-the-Boardroom.

[11] Oleksandr S. Chernyshenko, Stephen Stark, and Fritz Drasgow, "Individual Differences: Their Measurement and Validity," in *Handbook of Industrial and Organizational Psychology*, ed. Sheldon Zedeck. See also Ricky W. Griffin and Jean M. Phillips, *Organizational Behavior*, 13th ed. (Boston: Cengage, 2020).

[12] See Daniel Goleman, *Emotional Intelligence: Why It Can Matter More Than IQ* (New York: Bantam Books, 1995). See also Kenneth Law, Chi-Sum Wong, and Lynda Song, "The Construct and Criterion Validity of Emotional Intelligence and Its Potential Utility for Management Studies," *Journal of Applied Psychology* 89, no. 3 (2004): 483–596.

[13] J. B. Rotter, "Generalized Expectancies for Internal vs. External Control of Reinforcement," *Psychological Monographs* 80 (1966): 1–28.

[14] See Jeffrey Vancouver, Kristen More, and Ryan Yoder, "Self-Efficacy and Resource Allocation: Support for a Nonmonotic, Discontinuous Model," *Journal of Applied Psychology* 93, no. 1 (2008): 35–47.

[15] T. W. Adorno, E. Frenkel-Brunswik, D. J. Levinson, and R. N. Sanford, *The Authoritarian Personality* (New York: Harper & Row, 1950).

[16] Denise M. Rousseau, "The Individual-Organization Relationship: The Psychological Contract," in *Handbook of Industrial and Organizational Psychology*, ed. Sheldon Zedeck. See also Griffin and Phillips, *Organizational Behavior*.

[17] See Daniel Wren, *The History of Management Thought*, 6th ed. (New York: John Wiley & Sons), 2008.

[18] David McClelland, *The Achieving Society* (Princeton, NJ: Nostrand, 1961). See also David C. McClelland, *Human Motivation* (Cambridge, UK: Cambridge University Press, 1988).

[19] Big Star Transit, LLC, "Services," accessed May 17, 2023, https://bigstartransit.com/services/.

[20] EY Americas, "EY Announces Winners for the Entrepreneur Of The Year® 2023 Southwest Award," press release, June 26, 2023, https://www.ey.com/en_us/news/2023/06/ey-announces-winners-for-the-eoy-2023-southwest-award.

[21] EY, "EY Entrepreneur of the Year® US Program," accessed May 17, 2023, https://www.ey.com/en_us/entrepreneur-of-the-year-us.

[22] Stanley Schachter, *The Psychology of Affiliation* (Palo Alto, CA: Stanford University Press, 1959).

[23] David McClelland and David H. Burnham, "Power Is the Great Motivator," *Harvard Business Review*, March–April 1976, 100–110.

[24] Yasuhiro Yamakawa, Mike W. Peng, and David L. Deeds, "Rising from the Ashes: Cognitive Determinants of Venture Growth After Entrepreneurial Failure," *Entrepreneurship: Theory & Practice* 39, no. 2 (2015): 209–235.

[25] Lyman Porter, Gregory Bigley, and Richard Steers, *Motivation and Work Behavior*, 8th ed. (New York: McGraw-Hill), 2008.

[26] Gary P. Latham, "The Importance of Understanding and Changing Employee Outcome Expectancies for Gaining Commitment to an Organizational Goal," *Personnel Psychology* 54 (2001): 707–720.

[27] Brendan Kelly, "What Will Cirque du Soleil Look Like as It Recovers from Near-Death Experience?," *Montreal Gazette*, May 6, 2022, https://montrealgazette.com/entertainment/local-arts/what-will-cirque-du-soleil-look-like-as-it-recovers-from-near-death-experience.

[28] Adam M. Grant, Yitzhak Fried, and Tina Juillerat, "Work Matters: Job Design in Classic and Contemporary Perspectives," *Handbook of Industrial and Organizational Psychology*, ed. Sheldon Zedeck. See also Bradley Kirkman and T. Brad Harris, *3D Team Leadership: A New Approach for Complex Teams* (Palo Alto, CA: Stanford University Press, 2017). See also Griffin and Phillips, *Organizational Behavior*.

[29] Stephanie Armour, "Working 9-to-5 No Longer," *USA Today*, December 6, 2004, 1B, 2B. See also Griffin and Phillips, *Organizational Behavior*.

[30] Gabrielle Bienasz, "Equifax Used Its Own Technology to Find—and Fire—24 Workers with Secret Second Jobs," *Entrepreneur*, October 14, 2022, https://www.entrepreneur.com/business-news/equifax-fires-24-workers-with-secret-second-jobs/437263.

[31] Grace Mayer, "4 Day Work Week Benefits Parents Self Care Side Hustles," *Business Insider*, May 7, 2023. https://www.businessinsider.com/4-day-work-week-benefits-parents-self-care-side-hustles-2023-5.

[32] Gleb Tsipursky, "The Return to the Office Once Seemed Inevitable. A New Study Shows Companies Are Already Reversing Course," *Fortune*, March 9, 2023, https://fortune.com/2023/03/09/return-to-office-seemed-inevitable-new-study-shows-companies-already-reversing-course-careers-remote-work-gleb-tsipursky/.

[33] Caroline Castrillon, "Why Women-Led Companies Are Better for Employees," *Forbes*, March 26, 2019, https://www.forbes.com/sites/carolinecastrillon/2019/03/24/why-women-led-companies-are-better-for-employees/?sh=40dcf1283264.

Chapter 9

Leadership and Decision Making

Stockbroker/123RF

learning objectives

After reading this chapter, you should be able to:

9-1 Define *leadership* and distinguish it from management.

9-2 Summarize early approaches to the study of leadership.

9-3 Discuss the concept of situational approaches to leadership.

9-4 Describe transformational and charismatic perspectives on leadership.

9-5 Identify and discuss leadership substitutes and neutralizers.

9-6 Discuss leaders as coaches and examine gender and cross-cultural issues in leadership.

9-7 Describe strategic leadership, ethical leadership, and virtual leadership.

9-8 Relate leadership to decision making and discuss both rational and behavioral perspectives on decision making.

what's in it for me?

Is your boss a manager? A leader? What does this person do to inspire you to work harder? Do you aspire to be a manager or a leader? When you have a leadership position, what will you do to inspire your employees to work harder? Do you think management and leadership are the same thing? These are some of the issues we'll explore in this chapter. In Chapter 8, we described the primary determinants of employee behavior and noted that managers can influence the behavior and enhance the motivation of employees. Now it's time to examine in detail how leaders go about influencing employee behavior and motivating employee performance. We will place these strategies and tactics in the context of various approaches to leadership through the years, including the situational perspective accepted today. Understanding these concepts will help you function more effectively as a leader and give you more insight into how your manager or boss strives to motivate you through their own leadership.

We start this chapter by taking a look at the nature of leadership. We then describe early approaches to leadership, as well as the situational perspective accepted today. Next, we examine leadership through the eyes of followers as well as alternatives to leadership. The changing nature of leadership and emerging issues in leadership are discussed next. Finally, we describe the important related concept of decision making.

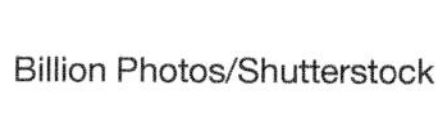
Billion Photos/Shutterstock

Steve Cho/Penta Press/Shutterstock

Transformational Leadership

Barbados-born Robyn Rihanna Fenty—better known as simply Rihanna—burst onto the music scene at age 17 and rocketed to fame with her song "Pon de Replay." Her debut single sold over 4 million copies and hit number two on the UK pop charts. She has since released seven more albums, has become one of the best-selling digital artists of all time, and is one of the youngest self-made female billionaires.

It may be surprising, then, to know that Rihanna made most of her money outside the studio as a multi-platform entrepreneur. Her makeup and skincare line, Fenty Beauty by Rihanna; her fashion line, Savage X Fenty; and her latest venture, Fenty Maison, have all played roles in cementing Rihanna's place in fashion, skincare, and pop culture, and she continues to invest in and create money-making ventures. At the heart of all of these ventures, however, are Rihanna's personal beliefs and values.

In addition to following a key investment strategy—diversification of her portfolio—Rihanna has become a symbol of transformational leadership and inclusion. She operates from a belief that she can't know everything, so she approaches her ventures carefully and with humility, seeking advice and learning from the successes and failures of other people. She prides herself on being a "smart control freak" and seeking out both new talent and experienced designers for her brands. "I can't just think I know everything," she says, calling Fenty house a "hub" for talent.[1]

Inclusivity from the ground up is a hallmark of Rihanna's ventures. While Fenty Beauty was not the first brand to produce an extended line of foundation shades, Rihanna's line certainly set the standard for other producers to consider a wide range of skin tones and representation. Her fashion lines have always included extended sizing and celebration of nonbinary individuals, with accessible styles for multiple body types and fashion expressions.

Rihanna employs a charismatic leadership style to engage her fans—the Rihanna Navy—in social justice discourse. She uses her wildly popular, painstakingly cultivated Instagram feed not only to showcase her brands, herself, and her family but to spark discussions about larger global issues that are important to her. She has posted about the Israeli-Palestinian conflict, the Black Lives Matter movement, and anti-trans legislation, among other hot-button topics. She uses her platform to amplify voices and issues that might otherwise go unnoticed by her Navy.

In both her recording career and her other business ventures, Rihanna has embraced her own individualism and modeled it for the public. In the recording industry, Rihanna is known for producing hit after hit in her own distinctive and versatile style. She brings a different energy to the runway than she does to the boardroom, embracing situational leadership as she adapts to each business challenge, engaging other people as team players.

Her collaborations extend beyond the studio as well. As a barrier-breaking woman of color, Rihanna does not squander the opportunities her power affords her. She created the Clara Lionel Foundation in honor of her grandmother to further climate-resilience initiatives in the Caribbean and the United States, helping nations and communities prepare for and withstand climate-related disasters. The foundation has amassed partners to create a coalition of organizations working together.

There are obvious pitfalls in looking to pop culture for examples of positive leadership, but looking at her rise to fame, the way she manages challenges and mistakes, her commitment to inclusivity, and her collaborative skills, it's easy to see the multiple ways Rihanna exemplifies the transformational leadership style. She is out to disrupt industries, bring new players to public attention, and leverage her power and influence for good. (After studying the content of this chapter, you should be able to answer the set of discussion questions found at the end of the chapter.)

The Nature of Leadership

Learning Objective 9-1

Define *leadership* and distinguish it from management.

In Chapter 8, we discussed the factors that affect employee behavior and motivation in organizations. Another important element that has an impact on behavior and motivation is leadership. For instance, the leader's own personality or attitudes will influence how they behave and see other people. Similarly, the leader is often in the best position to affect the behaviors of others and to motivate them to be more productive.

Because *leadership* is a term often used in everyday conversation, you might assume that it has a common and accepted meaning. In reality, though, the word *leadership* is often misused or used in ways too general to be of any value. We define **leadership** as the processes and behaviors used by someone, such as a manager, to motivate, inspire, and influence the behaviors of others.

Leadership *the processes and behaviors used by someone, such as a manager, to motivate, inspire, and influence the behaviors of others*

Leadership and Management

One of the most common mistakes managers make is assuming that leadership and management mean the same thing, when they are really different concepts. A person can be a manager, a leader, both, or neither.[2] Some of the basic distinctions between the two are summarized in Figure 9.1. As illustrated in the circle on the left, management (as discussed in Chapter 5) focuses primarily on the activities of planning, organizing, leading, and controlling. Leadership, in contrast, is much more closely related to activities such as setting agendas, aligning activities, inspiring people, and monitoring outcomes. As also illustrated in the figure, management and leadership may occasionally overlap but each is also a discrete and separate set of activities. Hence, a person in an organization may be a manager (but not a leader), a leader (but not a manager), or both a manager and a leader.

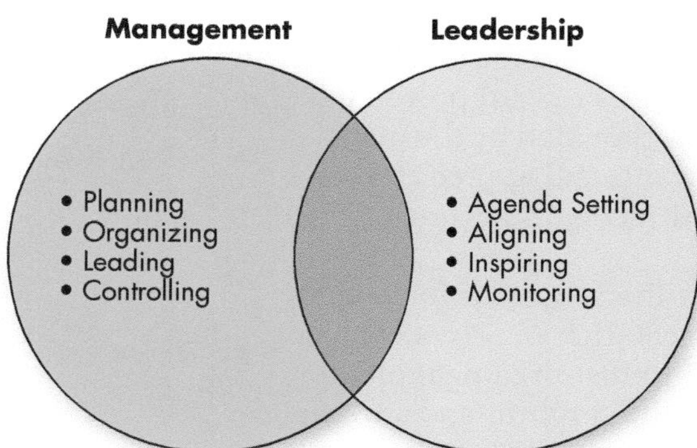

FIGURE 9.1 Distinctions Between Management and Leadership

Consider the various roles of managers and leaders in a hospital setting. The chief of staff (chief physician) of a large hospital is clearly a manager by virtue of their position. However, a particular chief of staff may not be respected or trusted by others and may have to rely solely on the authority vested in the position to get people to do things. In contrast, a nurse in the emergency department at the same hospital with no formal authority may be quite effective at taking charge of chaotic situations and directing others in dealing with specific patient problems. This chief of staff is a manager but not really a leader, whereas this nurse is a leader but not really a manager.

Finally, the head of pediatrics in the hospital, supervising a staff of 20 other doctors, nurses, and attendants, may also enjoy the staff's complete respect, confidence, and trust. They readily take advice from the head of pediatrics, follow directives without question, and often go far beyond what is necessary to help carry out the unit's mission. Thus, the head of pediatrics is both a manager (by virtue of the position they occupy) and a leader (by virtue of the respect they command from others and their willingness to follow direction).

Organizations need both management and leadership if they are to be effective. Management in conjunction with leadership can help achieve planned orderly change, and leadership in conjunction with management can keep the organization properly aligned with its environment.

Leadership and Power

Power *the ability to affect the behavior of others*

To fully understand leadership, it is necessary to first understand *power*. **Power** is the ability to affect the behavior of others. Of course, an individual can have power without actually using it. For example, a football coach has the power to bench a player who is not performing up to par. The coach seldom has to use this power because players recognize that the power exists and they work hard to keep their starting positions. In organizational settings, usually five kinds of power can be identified: legitimate, reward, coercive, referent, and expert power.[3]

Legitimate Power *power granted through the organizational hierarchy*

Legitimate power is power granted through the organizational hierarchy; it is the power defined by the organization to be accorded to people occupying a particular position. A manager can assign tasks to a subordinate, and a subordinate who refuses to do them can be reprimanded or even fired. Such outcomes stem from the manager's legitimate power as defined and vested in that manager by the organization. Legitimate power, then, is essentially the same as authority. Virtually all managers have legitimate power over their subordinates. The mere possession of legitimate power, however, does not by itself make someone a leader. Some subordinates follow only orders that are strictly within the letter of organizational rules and policies. If asked to do something not in their job descriptions, they refuse or choose to do a poor job. The manager of such employees is exercising authority but not leadership.

Reward Power *the power to give or withhold rewards*

Reward power is the power to give or withhold rewards. Rewards that a manager may control include salary increases, bonuses, promotion recommendations, praise, recognition, and interesting job assignments. In general, the greater the number of rewards a manager controls and the more important the rewards are to subordinates, the greater is the manager's reward power. If the subordinate values only the formal organizational rewards provided by the manager, then the manager is not a leader. If the subordinate also wants and appreciates the manager's informal rewards, such as praise, gratitude, and recognition, however, then the manager is also exercising leadership.

Coercive Power *the power to force compliance by means of psychological, emotional, or physical threat*

Coercive power is the power to force compliance by means of psychological, emotional, or physical threat. Physical coercion in organizations was once relatively common. In most organizations today, however, coercion is limited to verbal reprimands, written reprimands, disciplinary layoffs, fines, demotion, and termination. Some managers occasionally go so far as to use verbal abuse, humiliation, and psychological coercion in an attempt to manipulate subordinates. (Of course, most people agree that these are not appropriate managerial behaviors.) Prison guards sometimes feel as though they have to resort to the use of coercive power. Charlie Ergen, cofounder and chairman of the board of Dish Network, has a reputation for yelling at employees, belittling managers in front of their peers, and imposing harsh penalties on those who disagree with him.[4] The more punitive the elements under a manager's control and the more important they are to subordinates, the more coercive power the manager possesses. The more a manager uses coercive power, however, the more likely that manager is to provoke resentment and hostility and the less likely they are to be seen as a leader.[5]

Compared with legitimate, reward, and coercive power, which are relatively concrete and grounded in objective facets of organizational life, **referent power** is more abstract. It is based on identification, imitation, loyalty, or charisma. Followers may react favorably because they identify in some way with a leader, who may be like them in personality, background, or attitudes. In other situations, followers might choose to imitate a leader with referent power by wearing the same kind of clothes, working the same hours, or espousing the same management philosophy. Referent power may also take the form of charisma, an intangible attribute of the leader that inspires loyalty and enthusiasm. Thus, while a manager might have referent power, it is more likely to be associated with leadership. In 2020 during the COVID-19 pandemic, referent power came into play as people closely observed the extent to which government leaders practiced the same kinds of preventive steps being advocated for everyone, such as social distancing and wearing face masks.

Referent Power *power based on identification, imitation, loyalty, or charisma*

Expert power is derived from information or expertise. A manager who knows how to interact with an eccentric but important customer, a scientist who is capable of achieving an important technical breakthrough that no other company has dreamed of, and an administrative assistant who knows how to unravel bureaucratic red tape all have expert power over anyone who needs that information. The more important the information and the fewer the people who have access to it, the greater is the degree of expert power possessed by any one individual. In general, people who are both leaders and managers tend to have a great deal of expert power.

Expert Power *power derived from information or expertise*

Early Approaches to Leadership

Learning Objective 9-2

Summarize early approaches to the study of leadership.

Although leaders and leadership have profoundly influenced history, careful scientific study of them began only about a century ago. Early studies focused on the *traits*, or personal characteristics, of leaders. Later research shifted to examine actual leader *behaviors*.

Trait Approaches to Leadership

Early researchers believed that notable leaders had some unique set of qualities or traits that distinguished them from their peers and endured throughout history. This **trait approach to leadership** led researchers to focus on identifying the essential leadership traits, including intelligence, dominance, self-confidence, energy, activity (versus passivity), and knowledge about the job. Unfortunately, the list of potential leadership traits quickly became so long that it lost any practical value. In addition, the results of many studies were inconsistent. For example, one argument stated that the most effective leaders were tall, like Abraham Lincoln. But critics were quick to point out that neither Napoleon Bonaparte nor Adolf Hitler was tall, but both were effective leaders in their own way.

Trait Approach to Leadership *focused on identifying the essential traits that distinguished leaders*

Although the trait approach was all but abandoned several decades ago, in recent years, it has resurfaced. For example, some researchers have again started to focus on

Pictorial Press Ltd/Alamy Stock Photo

MPVHistory/Alamy Stock Photo

GL Archive/Alamy Stock Photo

Dinodia Photos/Alamy Stock Photo

When asked to identify important leaders, people often mention influential historical figures such as Winston Churchill, Abraham Lincoln, Martin Luther King Jr., and Mother Teresa.

a limited set of traits. These traits include emotional intelligence, mental intelligence, drive, motivation, honesty and integrity, self-confidence, knowledge of the business, and charisma. The initial research findings from this work show promise but are far from being definitive.

Behavioral Approaches to Leadership

After early trait research failed to shed much light on leadership, most researchers began to shift away from the trait approach and to look at leadership as a set of actual behaviors. The goal of the **behavioral approach to leadership** was to determine what actual *behaviors* were employed by effective leaders. These researchers assumed that the behaviors of effective leaders differed somehow from the behaviors of less effective leaders, and that the behaviors of effective leaders would be the same across all situations.

Behavioral Approach to Leadership *focused on determining what behaviors are employed by leaders*

This research led to the identification of two basic forms of leader behavior. Although different researchers applied different names, these are the basic leader behaviors identified during this period:

Task-Focused Leader Behavior *leader behavior focusing on how tasks should be performed to meet certain goals and to achieve certain performance standards*

Employee-Focused Leader Behavior *leader behavior focusing on satisfaction, motivation, and well-being of employees*

- **Task-focused leader behavior:** Task-focused leader behavior occurs when a leader focuses on how tasks should be performed to meet certain goals and to achieve certain performance standards.
- **Employee-focused leader behavior:** Employee-focused leader behavior occurs when a leader focuses on the satisfaction, motivation, and well-being of employees.

During this period, people believed that leaders should always try to engage in a healthy dose of both behaviors, one to increase performance and the other to increase job satisfaction and motivation. Experts also began to realize that they could train managers to engage in these behaviors in a systematic manner. But they also discovered that other leader behaviors needed to be considered, and that, in some circumstances, different combinations of leader behaviors might be more effective than other combinations.

For instance, suppose a new manager takes over a work site that is plagued by low productivity and whose workers, although perhaps satisfied, are not motivated to work hard. The leader should most likely emphasize task-focused behaviors to improve lagging productivity. But suppose the situation is different—productivity is high, but workers are stressed out about their jobs and have low levels of job satisfaction. In this instance, the manager should most likely concentrate on employee-focused behaviors to help improve job satisfaction. This line of thinking led to the development of *situational theories*.

The Situational Approach to Leadership

Learning Objective 9-3

Discuss the concept of situational approaches to leadership.

Situational Approach to Leadership *assumes that appropriate leader behavior varies from one situation to another*

The **situational approach to leadership** assumes that appropriate leader behavior varies from one situation to another, as shown in Figure 9.2. The early trait and behavioral approaches to leadership were both universal in nature. They attempted to prescribe leader behaviors that would lead to a set of universal outcomes and consequences. For instance, proponents of these universal perspectives might argue that tall and intelligent people or people who are consistently employee focused will always be good leaders. In reality, though, research has found this simply is not true. So, the situational approach to leadership attempts to identify various forms of leader behavior that result in contingent outcomes and consequences. By contingent, we mean that they depend on elements of the situation and characteristics of both the leader and followers.

Consider, for example, how Edward Bastian, CEO of Delta Airlines, has to vary his leadership style when he is interacting with different kinds of people. When he is dealing with investors, he has to convey an impression of confidence about the company's financial picture and future. When he interacts with union officials, he generally needs to take a firm stand on cost control combined with collaboration. When interacting with other Delta executives and managers, he often stresses the importance of diversity and inclusion. Bastian also often speaks to leaders at other airlines and has to balance their mutual interests against Delta's own competitive situation. And when dealing with customers, he has to be interpersonally engaging and respectful.

Leadership characteristics include the manager's value system, confidence in subordinates, personal inclinations, feelings of security, and actual behaviors. Subordinate characteristics include the subordinates' need for independence, readiness to assume responsibility, tolerance for ambiguity, interest in the problem, understanding of goals, knowledge, experience, and expectations. Situational characteristics that affect decision making include the type of organization, group effectiveness, the problem itself, and time pressures. Three important situational approaches to leadership are (1) the *path–goal theory*, (2) the *decision tree approach*, and (3) the *leader–member exchange model*.

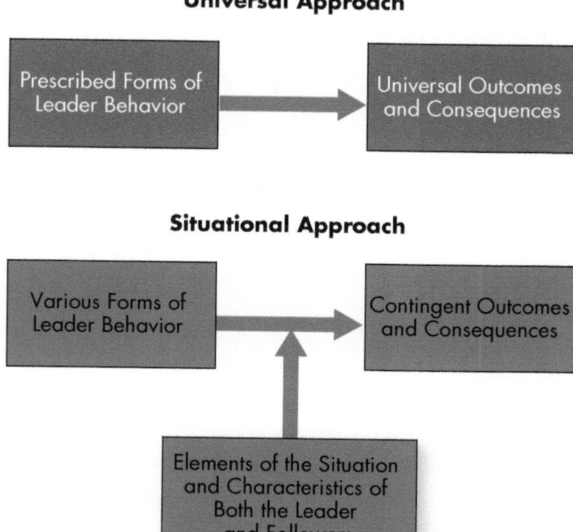

FIGURE 9.2 The Situational Approach to Leadership

Path–Goal Theory *theory of leadership that is a direct extension of the expectancy theory of motivation*

The **path–goal theory** of leadership is a direct extension of the expectancy theory of motivation discussed in Chapter 8.[6] Recall that the primary components of expectancy theory include the likelihood of attaining various outcomes and the value associated with those outcomes. The path–goal theory of leadership suggests that the primary functions of a leader are to make valued or desired rewards available in the workplace and to clarify for the subordinate the kinds of behavior that will lead to goal accomplishment and valued rewards. So, more specifically, the leader should clarify for subordinates their paths to personal goal attainment.

Path–goal theory identifies four kinds of behaviors that leaders can use, depending on the situation. *Directive leader behavior* lets subordinates know what is expected of them, gives guidance and direction, and schedules work. *Supportive leader behavior* is being friendly and approachable, showing concern for subordinates' welfare, and treating members as equals. *Participative leader behavior* includes consulting with subordinates, soliciting suggestions, and allowing participation in decision making. *Achievement-oriented leader behavior* sets challenging goals, expects subordinates to perform at high levels, encourages subordinates, and shows confidence in subordinates' abilities.

Decision Tree Approach *approach to leadership that provides decision rules for deciding how much participation to allow*

Another major contemporary approach to leadership is the **decision tree approach**. Like the path–goal theory, this approach attempts to prescribe a leadership style appropriate to a given situation. It also assumes that the same leader may display different leadership styles. But the decision tree approach concerns itself with only a single aspect of leader behavior: subordinate participation in decision making. The decision tree approach assumes that the degree to which subordinates should be encouraged to participate in decision making depends on the characteristics of the situation. In other words, no one decision-making process is best for all situations. After evaluating a variety of problem attributes (characteristics of the problem or decision), the leader determines an appropriate decision style that specifies the amount of subordinate participation.

Leader–Member Exchange (LMX) Model *approach to leadership that stresses the importance of variable relationships between supervisors and each of their subordinates*

The **leader–member exchange (LMX) model** stresses the importance of variable relationships between supervisors and each of their subordinates.[7] Each superior–subordinate pair represents a "vertical dyad." The model differs from previous approaches in that it focuses on the differential relationship leaders often establish with different subordinates. This model suggests that supervisors establish a special relationship with a small number of trusted subordinates, referred to as "the in-group." The in-group usually receives special duties requiring responsibility and autonomy; they may also receive special privileges. Subordinates who are not a part of this group are called "the out-group," and they receive less of the supervisor's time and attention. However, the key element of this theory is the concept of individual vertical dyads and how leaders have different relationships with each of their subordinates.

Leadership Through the Eyes of Followers

Learning Objective 9-4

Describe transformational and charismatic perspectives on leadership.

Another recent perspective that has been adopted by some leadership experts focuses on how leaders are seen through the eyes of their followers. The two primary approaches to leadership through the eyes of followers are *transformational leadership* and *charismatic leadership*. Donald Trump's successful bid for the U.S. presidency in 2016 was fueled in part by many people's perceptions that he was both a transformational and charismatic leader. Indeed, during his campaign, he frequently talked about the need to change the way the United States addressed issues such as health care, immigration, and foreign policy. Many people were attracted to him because of his personal charisma as well.

Transformational Leadership

Transformational leadership focuses on the importance of leading for change (as opposed to leading during a period of stability). According to this view, much of what a leader does involves carrying out what might be thought of as basic management "transactions," such as assigning work, evaluating performance, and making decisions. Occasionally, however, the leader has to engage in transformational leadership to initiate and manage major change, such as managing a merger, creating a new work team, or redefining the organization's culture.

Thus, **transformational leadership** is the set of abilities that allows a leader to recognize the need for change, to create a vision to guide that change, and to execute the change effectively. Some experts believe that change is such a vital organizational function that even successful firms need to change regularly to avoid becoming complacent and stagnant. In contrast, **transactional leadership** is very similar to basic management in that it involves routine, regimented activities. Only a leader with real abilities to influence people can hope to perform both functions successfully. Accordingly, leadership for change is extremely important.

Transformational Leadership *the set of abilities that allows a leader to recognize the need for change, to create a vision to guide that change, and to execute the change effectively*

Transactional Leadership *comparable to management, it involves routine, regimented activities*

Some leaders are able to adopt either transformational or transactional perspectives, depending on their circumstances. For instance, when Jeff Bezos started Amazon, his strategy was to simply sell books through an online store. When Amazon developed sustainable revenues, he used transactional leadership to slowly grow the business and build cash reserves. Bezos then adopted a transformational style as he led the company to become a major online "retailer" of thousands of different products. He next reverted to a transactional approach to again let the business entrench itself. More recently, Bezos has again been using transformational leadership as Amazon develops new methods for product distribution, explores new product lines and extensions, and positions itself as a more direct competitor for Apple and Google.[8]

Charismatic Leadership

Charismatic leadership is a type of influence based on the leader's charisma, a form of interpersonal attraction that inspires support and acceptance. Charismatic leaders are likely to have a lot of confidence in their beliefs and ideals and a strong need to influence people. They also tend to communicate high expectations about follower performance and to express confidence in their followers. Many of the most influential leaders in history have been extremely charismatic, including entrepreneurs Mary Kay Ash, Steve Jobs, and Elon Musk; civil rights leader Martin Luther King Jr.; and Pope John Paul II. Unfortunately, charisma can also empower leaders in other directions. Adolf Hitler, for instance, had strong charismatic qualities.

Charismatic Leadership *type of influence based on the leader's personal charisma*

Most experts today acknowledge three crucial elements of charismatic leadership:[9]

1. Charismatic leaders envision likely future trends and patterns, set high expectations for themselves and for others, and behave in ways that meet or exceed those expectations.
2. Charismatic leaders energize others by demonstrating personal excitement, personal confidence, and consistent patterns of success.
3. Charismatic leaders enable others by supporting them, empathizing with them, and expressing confidence in them.

Charismatic leadership ideas are quite popular among managers today and are the subject of numerous books and articles.[10] Unfortunately, few studies have specifically attempted to test the meaning and impact of charismatic leadership. Lingering ethical concerns about charismatic leadership also trouble some people. They stem from the fact that some charismatic leaders inspire such blind faith in their followers that these followers may engage in inappropriate, unethical, or even illegal behaviors just because the leader instructed them to do so. This tendency likely played a role in the unwinding of both Enron and Arthur Andersen because people followed orders from their charismatic leaders to illegally hide information, shred documents, and mislead investigators.

entrepreneurship and new ventures

Charisma and Message

In 1980, John DeJoria had lost his housing and was living in an old Rolls-Royce in Los Angeles. He had just invested all of his savings—amounting to just $700—in a little venture with his Scottish American hairstylist, Paul Mitchell. With a bare-bones budget, they sold their self-branded hair care products to salons by going door-to-door. Although the first two years were difficult, they had almost $1 million in annual sales in their third year of operation. Today, Paul Mitchell products are sold in more than 150,000 beauty salons in 87 countries, and annual sales exceed $1 billion.

DeJoria is a serial entrepreneur, having started more than a dozen businesses, including House of Blues, DeJoria Diamonds, and Patrón Spirits. In each of his businesses, DeJoria makes high-quality products and prioritizes sustainability. In an interview with *Fortune* magazine, he explains, "A lot of people make things to sell. But when the product is old, the consumer tosses it out and buys something else. If you make things with the highest quality, you'll be in the reorder business, which keeps the sales growing." Sustainability is particularly important in the Paul Mitchell product line. Paul Mitchell was the first beauty products company to reject animal testing and labels itself "Cruelty-Free since 1980."

While much of DeJoria's success can be attributed to hard work, his charisma and message inspire others. One of his mottos is "Success unshared is failure." He is committed to giving back through organizations such as Habitat for Humanity and Food4Africa, and Paul Mitchell Schools raised over $24 million for charity in since 2004. He is also the founder of Grow Appalachia, an organization that helps those in rural areas overcome food insecurity by growing their own food. Not surprisingly, DeJoria signed The Giving Pledge, founded by Warren Buffett and Bill Gates, through which the world's wealthiest citizens commit to giving most of their wealth to philanthropy.[11]

In 2011, DeJoria and his wife, Eloise, created the Peace Love and Happiness Foundation, an organization that is funded by the family and directs interested parties to donate directly to its partners. Two of these partner organizations are nonprofits founded by DeJoria and his family: Mobile Loaves & Fishes, which helps people struggling with homelessness like DeJoria once did, and Grow Appalachia, which, as mentioned above, is dedicated to providing sustainable solutions to poverty in the Appalachia region.[12]

Taking over a leadership role from someone with substantial personal charisma is also a challenge. This stems from the fact that people tend to compare new leaders to previous leaders in the same positions. For instance, the immediate successors to successful and charismatic athletic coaches such as Vince Lombardi (Green Bay Packers) and Phil Jackson (Chicago Bulls) each failed to measure up to their predecessors' legacies and were subsequently fired. And when Disney's Bob Iger stepped down after years of unparalleled success as CEO, his successor, Bob Chapek, lasted only two years before he was fired and the board of directors brought Iger back to run the company again.

Learning Objective 9-5

Identify and discuss leadership substitutes and neutralizers.

Special Issues in Leadership

Another interesting perspective on leadership focuses on *alternatives* to leadership. In some cases, certain factors may actually *substitute* for leadership, making actual leadership unnecessary or irrelevant. In other cases, factors may exist that *neutralize* or negate the influence of a leader even when that individual is attempting to exercise leadership.

Leadership Substitutes

Leadership substitutes are individual, task, and organizational characteristics that tend to outweigh the need for a leader to initiate or direct employee performance. In other words, if certain factors are present, the employee will perform their job capably, even without the direction of a leader. Table 9.1 identifies several basic leadership substitutes.

Leadership Substitutes *individual, task, and organizational characteristics that tend to outweigh the need for a leader to initiate or direct employee performance*

Consider, for example, what happens when an ambulance with a critically injured victim screeches to the door of a hospital emergency department. Do the emergency department employees stand around waiting for someone to take control and instruct them on what to do? The answer is no: They are highly trained, well-prepared professionals who know how to respond and work together as a team without someone playing the role of leader. When a US Airways flight crashed into the Hudson River in 2009, all members of the flight crew knew exactly what to do, without waiting for orders. As a result of their effective and prompt actions, a disaster was averted, and all passengers on the plane were quickly rescued. (This event was dramatized in the 2015 movie *Sully*, starring Tom Hanks.)

Leadership Neutralizers

In other situations, even if a leader is present and attempts to engage in various leadership behaviors, those behaviors may be rendered ineffective—or neutralized—by various factors that can be called **leadership neutralizers**. Suppose, for example, that a relatively new and inexperienced leader is assigned to a work group composed of experienced employees with long-standing performance norms and a high level of group cohesiveness. The norms and cohesiveness of the group may be so strong that there is little the new leader can do to change things.

Leadership Neutralizers *factors that may render leader behaviors ineffective*

In addition to group factors, elements of the job itself may also limit a leader's ability to "make a difference." Consider, for example, employees working on a moving assembly line. Employees may only be able to work at the pace of the moving line, so performance quantity and quality are constrained by the speed of the line and the simplicity of each individual task.

Finally, organizational factors can also neutralize at least some forms of leader behavior. Suppose a new leader is accustomed to using merit pay increases as a way to motivate people. But in a new job, pay increases may be dictated by union contracts and based solely on employee seniority and cost of living. The leader's previous approach to motivating people would be neutralized, and new approaches would have to be identified.

table 9.1 Leadership Substitutes and Neutralizers

Individual factors	• Individual professionalism • Individual ability, knowledge, and motivation • Individual experience and training • Indifference to rewards
Job factors	• Structured/automated • Highly controlled • Intrinsically satisfying • Embedded feedback
Organization factors	• Explicit plans and goals • Rigid rules and procedures • Rigid reward system not tied to performance • Physical distance between supervisor and subordinate
Group factors	• Group performance norms • High level of group cohesiveness • Group interdependence

Learning Objective 9-6

Discuss leaders as coaches and examine gender and cross-cultural issues in leadership.

The Changing Nature of Leadership

Various alternatives to leadership aside, many settings still call for at least some degree of leadership, although the nature of that leadership continues to evolve. Among the recent changes in leadership that managers should recognize are the increasing role of *leaders as coaches* as well as *gender* and *cross-cultural patterns* of leader behavior.

Leaders as Coaches

We noted in Chapter 6 and again in Chapter 8 that many organizations today are using teams. Many other organizations are attempting to become less hierarchical by eliminating the old-fashioned command-and-control mentality often inherent in bureaucratic organizations and instead motivating and empowering individuals to work independently. In each case, the role of leaders is also changing. Whereas leaders were once expected to control situations, direct work, supervise people, closely monitor performance, make decisions, and structure activities, many leaders today are instead being asked to change how they manage people. Perhaps the best description of this new role is for the leader to become more of a *coach* than an *overseer*.[13]

From the standpoint of a business leader, a coaching perspective would call for the leader to help select and train team members and other new employees, to provide some general direction, and to help the team get the information and other resources it needs. Coaches from different teams may play important roles in linking the activities and functions of their respective teams. Some leaders may function as *mentors*, helping less experienced employees learn the ropes and better preparing them to advance within the organization; they may also help resolve conflicts among team members and mediate other disputes that arise. But beyond these activities, the leader keeps a low profile and lets the group get its work done with little or no direct oversight, just as during a game, an athletic coach trusts their players to execute the plays successfully.

Jeff Bezos, founder and CEO of Amazon, often plays the role of coach. He likes to focus on long-term, strategic issues and leave the daily management of Amazon to senior managers. But their decisions must also be consistent with his vision for the firm. As a result, he works with them on a regular basis to help them develop their decision-making skills and to equip them with the information they need to help lead the firm in the directions he has set.

Gender and Leadership

Given that most leadership theories and research studies traditionally focused on male leaders, developing a better understanding of how or whether gender plays a role in leadership is an obvious and important next step. Research suggests that a leader's gender is not a good indicator of their leadership style and performance; however, it does influence what stakeholders and the public expect from them. Research consistently shows that strong and authoritative women are often penalized for a perceived lack of warmth and compassion, while men are not.[14] Related research shows suggests that when leaders deviate from gender stereotypes, they lose support.[15] Despite this, most people believe that gender is not a factor in a leader's effectiveness.[16]

Much more work needs to be done to better understand the dynamics of gender and leadership, in terms of both how they are related and how they are perceived. One thing that is clear, however, is that gender is not an indicator of leadership success or failure. High-profile and successful female leaders, such as Mary Barra (CEO of General Motors), Sarah London (CEO of Centene), and Angela Merkel (former chancellor of Germany), continue to demonstrate the effectiveness with which women can be exceptional leaders. And since 2020, several CEOs have come out as transgender, including Caroline Farberger (CEO of Swedish Insurance company ICA), Wynne Nowland (CEO of insurance brokerage

finding a better way

Women Leading the Way

In the small Pakistani community where Ruzwana Bashir was born and raised, women were expected to aspire to marriage and children, not college and entrepreneurship. Bashir, however, was encouraged by teachers who urged her to pursue higher education. She broke through those gender and culture barriers and continues to work against them as the founder and CEO of the travel site Peek.

As she began her career in the financial services industry, Bashir felt pressure to act like her male counterparts. At the Forbes Under 30 summit, she explains, "In that environment as a woman, you can feel crowd-forced to conform." While earning her MBA at Harvard's Business School as a Fulbright Scholar, she realized that traditionally feminine attributes can be an advantage. "Those 'female' traits of empathy and compassion—of being collaborative—are true business strengths."

At Oxford, she became president of the Oxford Union, a debating society known for hosting speakers as famous as Senator John McCain and fashion designer Tom Ford. She was only the second female Asian president of that prestigious society, following in the footsteps of former Pakistani president Benazir Bhutto, who became the union's leader in 1977. It was at Oxford that Bashir first wore Western clothing, and although she excelled in school, she always felt different in race, gender, and class. It was in 2012, after spending over 20 frustrating hours trying to arrange a getaway with friends to Turkey, that she and cofounder Oskar Bruening launched Peek.com, adding yet another benchmark to her already impressive social résumé—that of a woman-founded tech company. Although several travel websites already exist, Peek occupies a unique space in the market. Peek helps travelers plan the perfect trip, including itineraries for a "Perfect Day" at the chosen destination.

At Peek, the company has maintained a staffing mix of 50 percent men and 50 percent women, with considerable ethnic diversity. Bashir encourages female employees and introduces them to mentors. She also practices what she preaches—allowing herself to show vulnerability rather than presenting the traditionally male decisive and authoritative style.

Nils Jorgensen/Shutterstock

Ruzwana Bashir, cofounder of travel site Peek

In addition, she is an outspoken advocate for women's rights worldwide. In 2014, she wrote a groundbreaking essay that drew attention to the abuse of women in the United Kingdom's Asian communities. "Growing up the way I did gave me empathy and understanding for different walks of life," Bashir says. "It inspired me to choose the kind of company I wanted to build."[17]

Ruzwana Bashir is committed to an ethical leadership style, considering the impact of her actions on not just the bottom line but on the people involved with and dependent on her company. When the travel industry was brought to its knees during the COVID-19 pandemic, Bashir worked to mitigate the impact not only for her employees but for customers as well. "We knew as a company that thousands of businesses relied on us, so we needed to make sure we could make it through," Bashir noted in an interview with *Avenue* magazine. Peek worked to establish contactless check-ins, sought PPP loans for their vendors, and pivoted to highlight local activities as travelers stayed closer to home.[18]

Bradley & Parker), and Martine Aliana Rothblatt (founder of Sirius XM and CEO of United Therapeutics), which could pave the way for more inclusivity among the C-suite. Indeed, in 2000 only two Fortune 500 companies were led by women and there were no openly LGBTQ+ CEOs. Today among the Fortune 500, 41 have women CEOs and four have LGBTQ CEOs.[19]

Cross-Cultural Leadership

Another changing perspective on leadership relates to cross-cultural issues. In this context, *culture* is used as a broad concept to encompass both international differences and diversity-based differences within one culture. For instance, Japan is generally characterized by *collectivism* (group before individual), whereas the United States is based more on *individualism* (individual before group). So when a Japanese firm sends an executive to head up the firm's operation in the United States, that person will likely find it necessary to acknowledge the importance of individual contributions, recognition, and rewards and the differences in individual and group roles that exist in Japanese and U.S. businesses.

In Europe, leaders must often be aggressive, and meetings are frequently characterized by loud verbal exchanges and arguments. In Japan, though, more emphasis is put on consensus building and polite exchanges of dialogue. Similarly, cross-cultural factors also play a growing role in organizations as their workforces become more diverse. As people with diverse backgrounds, histories, and experiences achieve more leadership positions, it will be necessary to reassess how applicable current theories and models of leadership are when applied to this increasingly diverse pool of leaders.

Learning Objective 9-7

Describe strategic leadership, ethical leadership, and virtual leadership.

Emerging Issues in Leadership

Finally, three emerging issues in leadership warrant discussion. These issues are *strategic leadership, ethical leadership*, and *virtual leadership.*

Strategic Leadership

Strategic Leadership *leader's ability to understand the complexities of both the organization and its environment and to lead change in the organization so as to enhance its competitiveness*

Strategic leadership is a somewhat new concept that explicitly relates leadership to the role of top management. **Strategic leadership** is a leader's ability to understand the complexities of both the organization and its environment and to lead change in the organization so as to enhance its competitiveness. Howard Schultz, former CEO and executive chairman of Starbucks, was recognized as a strong strategic leader. Not content to continue functioning as "simply" a coffee retailer, Schultz was always on the lookout for new opportunities and how Starbucks could effectively exploit those opportunities. Both Jeff Bezos (Amazon) and Mary Barra (General Motors) are also considered very effective strategic leaders.

To be successful as a strategic leader, a manager needs to have a thorough and complete understanding of the organization—its history, its culture, its strengths, and its weaknesses. In addition, the leader needs a firm grasp of the organization's external environment. This understanding has to include current business and economic conditions and circumstances as well as significant trends and issues on the horizon. The strategic leader also must recognize the firm's current strategic advantages and shortcomings.

Ethical Leadership

Most people have long assumed that business leaders are ethical people. But in the wake of recent corporate scandals at firms such as Silicon Valley Bank, Boeing, Wells Fargo, Volkswagen, Toshiba, and Walmart, faith in business leaders is not as strong as it perhaps once was. As a result, now more than ever, high standards of ethical conduct are being held up as a prerequisite for effective leadership. More specifically, business leaders are being called on to maintain high ethical standards for their own conduct, to unfailingly exhibit ethical behavior, and to hold others in their organizations to the same standards—in short, to practice **ethical leadership.**

Ethical Leadership *leader behaviors that reflect high ethical standards*

The behaviors of top leaders are being scrutinized more than ever, and those responsible for hiring new leaders for a business are looking more closely at the backgrounds of those being considered. The emerging pressures for stronger corporate governance models are likely to further increase the commitment to select only those individuals with high ethical standards for leadership positions in business and to hold them more accountable than in the past for both their actions and the consequences of those actions.

Virtual Leadership

Finally, **virtual leadership** is also emerging as an important issue for organizations. Leaders and their employees traditionally worked together in the same physical location and engaged in face-to-face interactions on a regular basis. But in today's world, both leaders and their employees may work in locations that are far from one another. Such arrangements might include people working remotely from a home office on a hybrid schedule or people actually living and working far from company headquarters. While hybrid work was already increasing, it surged during the 2020 COVID-19 pandemic as people were either encouraged or required to work remotely. Indeed, some firms, like Microsoft and Amazon, felt that remote work during this period was so effective that they announced it would become a permanent practice for some specific jobs. As a result of the overall increase in remote work, though, many leaders, previously unaccustomed to being responsible for people working remotely, had to quickly develop and use new virtual leadership capabilities.

Virtual Leadership *leadership in settings where leaders and followers interact electronically rather than in face-to-face settings*

Increasingly, then, communication between leaders and their subordinates happens largely by telephone, e-mail, social media, and online platforms like Teams and Zoom. One implication may be that leaders in these situations must work harder at creating and maintaining relationships with their employees that go beyond words on a digital screen. Although nonverbal communication, such as smiles and handshakes, may not be possible online, managers can instead make a point of adding a few personal words in an e-mail or text message (whenever appropriate) to convey appreciation, reinforcement, or constructive feedback.

managing in turbulent times

A Sudsy Dust-up

In March 2023, beverage giant Anheuser-Busch engaged Dylan Mulvaney, a transgender TikTok star with a whopping 12.5 million followers, to promote a contest. In the short video, Mulvaney jokes about March Madness while dressed up in Audrey Hepburn style. Within days, there was a vicious, transphobic, and loud backlash, perhaps best personified by Kid Rock's video of himself wearing a MAGA hat backward and cursing Anheuser-Busch before shooting up cases of Bud Light with an AR-15. Within days, the backlash had grown to a movement including Fox News personalities, other celebrities, and even lawmakers. Sales of Bud Light dropped over 20 percent as these vocal opponents gained followers of their own.[20]

In many of these videos, people swore off drinking Bud Light in favor of other beers, not realizing the reach of Anheuser-Busch and its over 500 owned brands. Those drinkers who switched to Coors Light did so without realizing Coors' support of the LGBTQIA+ community for over 20 years, including workplace protections for employees and partnership with Denver Pride. Meanwhile, some lawmakers, led by Texan Republican Ted Cruz, have gone so far as to open a literal Congressional investigation into Anheuser-Busch's partnership with Mulvaney.[21]

The advertising mind behind this very small partnership, which involved sending Mulvaney a can with her image on it and sponsoring her single video, was Alissa Heinerscheid, who received attention from far-right news media outlets. She received hate mail and death threats, and Anheuser-Busch placed her and Daniel Blake, the Group VP responsible for greenlighting the partnership, on a leave of absence.

In a statement following the personnel actions, Anheuser-Busch's CEO Brendan Whitworth said, "We never intended to be part of a discussion that divides people," in a press release titled "Our Responsibility to America." "We are in the business of bringing people together over a beer." The company then immediately released its future advertising plans, which include a focus on patriotism, country music, and sports.[22]

Anheuser-Busch isn't the only beermaker to have riled stereotypical beer drinkers. Miller Lite released a commercial during Women's History Month highlighting women's contributions to beermaking over the centuries and essentially apologizing for its use of sexualized images of women to sell beer. Sofia Colucci, chief marketing officer of Molson-Coors, received so much harassment—including death threats—that

(continued)

she deleted several social media accounts to protect herself and her family.[23] In contrast to its competitor's statement, Molson-Coors issued a much more forceful missive in which its chief communications and corporate affairs officer, Adam Collins, said, "People can take issue with our ads or our brands, but we won't stand by as people personally attack our employees—especially given that these are company decisions, and are never made by one single person."

Mulvaney herself went silent for several weeks following the eruption of the controversy. She has since responded by saying, "What I'm struggling to understand is the need to dehumanize and to be cruel." She hopes to get back to "making people laugh" and to continue to share her life on social media.[24]

As the buying power of the LGBTQIA+ community continues to rise (according to research by LGBT Capital, their annual purchasing power in the United States is roughly $1.1 trillion),[25] companies will continue to grapple with marketing to an increasingly divisive and divided public when it comes to sexuality, gender, and gender expression.[26] These companies will be challenged to examine the cross-cultural values of their various consumers and to decide what ethical leadership looks like in the face of controversy.

Barry King/Alamy Stock Photo

PJiiiJane/Alamy Stock Photo

Leadership, Management, and Decision Making

Learning Objective 9-8

Relate leadership to decision making and discuss both rational and behavioral perspectives on decision making.

We noted previously the differences and similarities between managing and leading. *Decision making* is another important related concept. Indeed, decision making is a fundamental component of both leadership and management—managers and leaders must frequently make decisions.

The Nature of Decision Making

Decision Making *choosing one alternative from among several options*

Decision-Making Process *recognizing and defining the nature of a decision situation, identifying alternatives, choosing the "best" alternative, and putting it into practice*

Decision making can refer to either a specific act or a general process. **Decision making** is the act of choosing one alternative from among a set of alternatives. The decision-making process, however, is much more than this. One step of the process, for example, is that the person making the decision must both recognize that a decision is necessary and identify the set of feasible alternatives before selecting one. Hence, the **decision-making process** includes recognizing and defining the nature of a decision situation, identifying alternatives, choosing the "best" alternative, and putting it into practice.[27]

The word *best* implies effectiveness. Effective decision making requires that the decision maker understand the situation driving the decision. Most people would consider an effective decision to be one that optimizes some set of factors, such as profits, sales, employee welfare, and market share. In some situations, though, an effective decision may be one that minimizes losses, expenses, or employee turnover. It may even mean selecting the best method for going out of business, laying off employees, or terminating a strategic alliance. For instance, during the COVID-19 pandemic in 2020, many businesses and their leaders had to cope with dramatic drops in revenue and subsequently had to decide how to cut costs, modify their business models, and so forth.

We should also note that managers make decisions about both problems and opportunities. For example, making decisions about how to cut costs by 10 percent reflects a problem—an undesirable situation that requires a solution. But decisions are also necessary in situations of opportunity. Learning that the firm is earning higher-than-projected profits, for example, also requires a subsequent decision. Should the extra funds be used to increase shareholder dividends, reinvest in current operations, or expand into new markets? Of course, it may take a long time before a manager can know if the right decision was made.

Types of Decisions Managers must make many different types of decisions. In general, however, most decisions fall into one of two categories: *programmed* and *nonprogrammed*.[28] A **programmed decision** is one that is relatively structured or recurs with some frequency (or both). Starbucks uses programmed decisions to purchase new supplies of coffee beans, cups, and napkins, and Starbucks employees are trained in exact procedures for brewing coffee. Likewise, a small-town Ford dealer may make a decision to sponsor a local youth soccer team each year. Thus, when the soccer club president calls, the dealer already knows what they will do. Many decisions regarding basic operating systems and procedures and standard organizational transactions are of this variety and can therefore be programmed.[29]

Programmed Decision *decision that is relatively structured or recurs with some frequency (or both)*

Nonprogrammed decisions, in contrast, are relatively unstructured and occur much less often. Disney's decision to buy the *Stars Wars* properties from George Lucas was a nonprogrammed decision. Managers faced with such decisions must treat each one as unique, investing enormous amounts of time, energy, and resources into exploring the situation from all perspectives. Intuition and experience are major factors in nonprogrammed decisions. Most decisions made by top managers involving strategy (including mergers, acquisitions, and takeovers) and organization design are nonprogrammed. Nonprogrammed decisions also include those concerning new facilities, new products, labor contracts, and legal issues.

Nonprogrammed Decision *decision that is relatively unstructured and that occurs with low frequency*

Decision-Making Conditions Just as decisions are of different kinds, the conditions in which decisions must be made also are different. Managers sometimes have an almost perfect understanding of conditions surrounding a decision, but at other times they have few clues about those conditions. In general, the circumstances that exist for the decision maker are conditions of certainty, risk, or uncertainty.[30]

CERTAINTY When the decision maker knows with reasonable certainty what the alternatives are and what conditions are associated with each alternative, a **state of certainty** exists. Suppose, for example, that managers at Singapore Airlines make a decision to buy five new planes to fly international routes. Their next decision is from whom to buy them. Because only two companies in the world make these kinds of planes, Boeing and Airbus, Singapore Airlines knows its options with relative certainty. Each has proven products and can guarantee prices and delivery dates. The airline thus knows the alternative conditions associated with each. There is little ambiguity and relatively little chance of making a bad decision.

State of Certainty *when the decision maker knows with reasonable certainty what the alternatives are and what conditions are associated with each alternative*

Few organizational decisions, however, are made under conditions of true certainty. The complexity and turbulence of the contemporary business world make such situations rare. Even the airplane purchase decision we just considered has less certainty than it appears. The aircraft companies may not be able to guarantee delivery dates, so they may write cost-increase or inflation clauses into contracts. Thus, the airline may be only partially certain of the conditions surrounding each alternative.

RISK A more common decision-making condition is a state of risk. Under a **state of risk**, the availability of each alternative and its potential payoffs and costs are all associated with probability estimates.[31] Suppose, for example, that a labor contract negotiator for a company receives a "final" offer from the union right before a strike deadline. The negotiator has two alternatives: to accept or to reject the offer. The risk centers on whether the union representatives are bluffing. If the company negotiator accepts the offer, they avoid a strike but commit to a relatively costlier labor contract.

State of Risk *when the availability of each alternative and its potential payoffs and costs are all associated with probability estimates*

If the company negotiator rejects the contract, they may get a more favorable contract if the union is bluffing but may provoke a strike if it is not.

On the basis of past experience, relevant information, the advice of others, and personal judgment, the company negotiator may conclude there is about a 75 percent chance that union representatives are bluffing and about a 25 percent chance that they will back up their threats. Thus, the company negotiator can base a calculated decision on the two alternatives (accept or reject the contract demands) and the probable consequences of each. When making decisions under a state of risk, managers must reasonably estimate the probabilities associated with each alternative. For example, if the union negotiators are committed to a strike if their demands are not met, and the company negotiator rejects their demands because they guess the workers will not strike, the miscalculation will prove costly. Decision making under conditions of risk is accompanied by moderate ambiguity and chances of a bad decision.

State of Uncertainty *when the decision maker does not know all the alternatives, the risks associated with each, or the likely consequences of each alternative*

Uncertainty Most major decision making in contemporary organizations is done under a **state of uncertainty**. The decision maker does not know all the alternatives, the risks associated with each, or the likely consequences of each alternative. This uncertainty stems from the complexity and dynamism of contemporary organizations and their environments. The emergence of various forms of online commerce as a significant force in today's competitive environment has served to increase both revenue potential and uncertainty for most managers. Most major decisions made during the early stages of the 2020 COVID-19 pandemic were of this nature because managers were unsure of how quickly and how far the virus would spread, how long the pandemic would last, and how to most effectively respond to it from both public health and economic perspectives. More recently, in 2023 business leaders were facing the uncertainties of inflation and possible recession.

To make effective decisions in these circumstances, managers must acquire as much relevant information as possible and approach the situation from a logical and rational perspective. Intuition, judgment, and experience always play major roles in the decision-making process under conditions of uncertainty. Even so, uncertainty is the most ambiguous condition for managers and the one most prone to error.[32]

Rational Decision Making

Managers and leaders should strive to be rational in making decisions. Figure 9.3 shows the steps in the rational decision-making process.

Recognizing and Defining the Decision Situation

The first step in rational decision making is recognizing that a decision is necessary; some stimulus or spark must initiate the process. The stimulus for a decision may be either positive or negative. Managers who must decide how to invest surplus funds, for example, face a positive decision situation. A negative financial stimulus could involve having to trim budgets because of cost overruns.

Inherent in making such a decision is the need to precisely define the problem. Consider the situation faced by Walmart during its growth and entry into international markets. As the discount retailer was establishing itself as a dominant retailer in the United States, marketing managers decided they needed to start thinking about expanding to other countries.

Identifying Alternatives

Once the decision situation has been recognized and defined, the second step is to identify alternative courses of effective action. Developing both obvious, standard alternatives and creative, innovative alternatives is useful. In general, the more important the decision, the more attention is directed to developing alternatives. Although managers should seek creative solutions, they must also recognize that various constraints often limit their alternatives. Common constraints include legal restrictions, moral and ethical norms, and constraints imposed by the power and authority of the manager, available technology, economic considerations, and unofficial social norms. After making the decision to enter foreign markets, Walmart leaders identified several possible options.

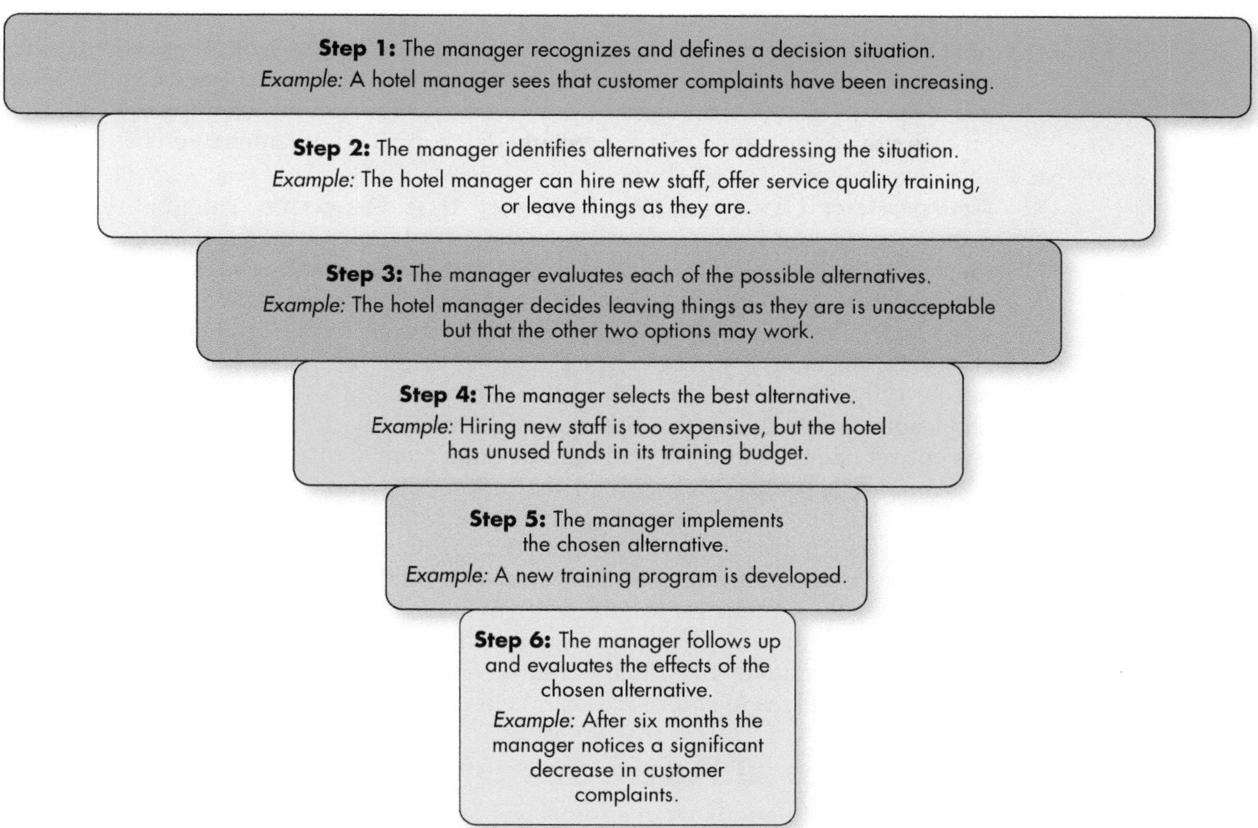

FIGURE 9.3 Steps in the Rational Decision-Making Process
Source: Based on Griffin, *Management*, 8e. © 2005 South-Western, a part of Cengage Learning, Inc. www.cengage.com/permissions.

Evaluating Alternatives The third step in the decision-making process is evaluating each of the alternatives. Some alternatives may not be feasible because of legal or financial barriers. Limited human, material, and information resources may make other alternatives impractical. Managers must thoroughly evaluate all the alternatives to increase the chances that the alternative finally chosen will be successful. Walmart leaders performed preliminary analyses on each foreign market under consideration, immediately rejecting some (such as Pakistan) but identifying others to keep under consideration.

Selecting the Best Alternative Choosing the best available alternative is the real crux of decision making. Even though many situations do not lend themselves to objective, mathematical analysis, managers and leaders can often develop subjective estimates and weights for choosing an alternative. Decision makers should also remember that finding multiple acceptable alternatives may be possible; selecting just one alternative and rejecting all the others might not be necessary. Walmart chose to initially focus on Mexico, China, Russia, Germany, and Argentina.

Implementing the Chosen Alternative After an alternative has been selected, managers and leaders must put it into effect. Walmart opened offices in each country it wanted to enter. Managers in those offices, in turn, began learning about local market details, governmental requirements for market entry, potential suppliers, and so forth. Managers must also consider people's resistance to change when implementing decisions. The reasons for such resistance include insecurity, inconvenience, and fear of the unknown. Managers should anticipate potential resistance at various stages of the implementation process. However, even when all alternatives have been evaluated as precisely as possible and the consequences of each alternative have been weighed, unanticipated consequences are still likely. Employees may resist or protest change; they may even quit rather than agree to it. Other factors, such as unexpected cost increases, a less-than-perfect fit with existing organizational subsystems, or unpredicted effects on cash flow or operating expenses, could develop after implementation has begun.

Following Up and Evaluating the Results The final step in the decision-making process requires that managers and leaders evaluate the effectiveness of their decision. They should make sure that the chosen alternative has served its original purpose. If an implemented alternative appears not to be working, they can respond in several ways. Another previously identified alternative (the original second or third choice, for instance) could be adopted. Or they might recognize that the situation was not correctly defined to begin with and start the process all over again. Finally, managers and leaders might decide that the original alternative is, in fact, appropriate but either has not yet had time to work or should be implemented in a different way.

Walmart managers determined that entry into Mexico and Argentina, among others, would be relatively easy and that the company would be allowed to set up wholly owned subsidiaries to operate there. Entry into China would be more difficult but could be done through joint ventures with local partners. This was also the case for several other countries. Russia, though, looked to be more challenging. Walmart concluded that the only viable way to enter the market there would be to buy one or more existing retailers. Eventually, after several potential deals fell through, Walmart abandoned its plans to enter Russia and closed its office in that country.

Behavioral Aspects of Decision Making

If all decision situations were approached as logically as described in the previous section, more decisions would prove successful. Yet decisions are often made with little consideration for logic and rationality. Some experts have estimated that U.S. companies use rational decision-making techniques less than 20 percent of the time. Of course, as noted in Chapter 5, even when organizations try to be logical, they sometimes fail. For example, when Starbucks opened its first coffee shops in New York, it relied on scientific marketing research, taste tests, and rational deliberation in making a decision to emphasize drip over espresso coffee. However, that decision proved wrong because it became clear that New Yorkers strongly preferred the same espresso-style coffees that were Starbucks mainstays in the West. Hence, the firm had to reconfigure its stores hastily to meet customer preferences.

In contrast, sometimes a decision made with little regard for logic can still turn out to be correct.[33] Important ingredients in how these forces work are behavioral aspects of decision making. These include *political forces, intuition, escalation of commitment*, and *risk propensity*.

Coalition *an informal alliance of individuals or groups formed to achieve a common goal*

Political Forces in Decision Making Political forces contribute to the behavioral nature of decision making. One major element of politics, *coalitions*, is especially relevant to decision making. A **coalition** is an informal alliance of individuals or groups formed to achieve a common goal. This common goal is often a preferred decision alternative. For example, coalitions of stockholders frequently band together to force a board of directors to make a certain decision.

When these coalitions enter the political arena and attempt to persuade lawmakers to make decisions favorable to their interests, they are called *lobbyists*. Lobbyists may also donate money to help elect a candidate who is more likely to pursue their agendas. A recurring theme in U.S. politics is the damaging influence these special interest groups have on politicians, who may feel unduly obligated to favor campaign donors when making decisions. Political forces clearly influenced many decisions made during the 2020 COVID-19 pandemic.

Intuition *an innate belief about something, often without conscious consideration*

Intuition **Intuition** is an innate belief about something, often without conscious consideration. Managers sometimes decide to do something because it "feels right" or they have a hunch. This feeling is usually not arbitrary, however. Rather, it is based on years of experience and practice in making decisions in similar situations. Such an inner sense may help managers make an occasional decision without going through a full-blown rational sequence of steps. That said, all managers, but most especially inexperienced ones, should be careful not to rely too heavily on intuition. If rationality and logic are continually flouted for "what feels right," the odds are that disaster will strike one day.

Escalation of Commitment Another important behavioral process that influences decision making is **escalation of commitment** to a chosen course of action. In particular, decision makers sometimes make decisions and then become so committed to the course of action suggested by that decision that they stay with it, even when it appears to have been wrong.[34] For example, when people buy stock in a company, they sometimes refuse to sell it even after repeated drops in price. They choose a course of action, buying the stock in anticipation of making a profit, and then stay with it even in the face of increasing losses. Moreover, after the value drops, they may rationalize that they can't sell at such a low price because they will lose money.

Escalation of Commitment *condition in which a decision maker becomes so committed to a course of action that they stay with it even when it appears to have been wrong*

For years Sears and Kmart were dominant forces in the U.S. retailing sector. Sears was an anchor store in most shopping centers and was the nation's largest retailer. Its Christmas catalogs were widely anticipated each year, and its stores were known for "one-stop-shopping" destinations that carried everything from tools to toys. Kmart, meanwhile, was the country's largest discount retailer and was known as *the* place to shop for low prices. However, Sears essentially ignored the growth of such competitive threats like online shopping and specialized big-box stores like Home Depot, Best Buy, and even general merchandiser Target. Kmart, for its part, didn't see Walmart as a threat and was slow to adopt the leading-edge technologies that were fueling Walmart's growth. Consequently, both Sears and Kmart lost most of their market share, and were acquired by Transformco Properties, which is primarily a real estate company that has struggled to manage the once-mighty retailers.

Risk Propensity and Decision Making The behavioral element of **risk propensity** is the extent to which a decision maker is willing to gamble when making a decision. Some managers are cautious about every decision they make. They try to adhere to the rational model and are extremely conservative in what they do. Such managers are more likely to avoid mistakes, and they infrequently make decisions that lead to big losses. Others are extremely aggressive in making decisions and willing to take risks.[35] They rely heavily on intuition, reach decisions quickly, and often risk big investments on their decisions. As in gambling, these managers are more likely than their conservative counterparts to achieve big successes with their decisions; they are also more likely to incur greater losses.[36] The organization's culture is a prime ingredient in fostering different levels of risk propensity.

Risk Propensity *extent to which a decision maker is willing to gamble when making a decision*

summary of learning objectives

LEARNING OBJECTIVE 9-1

Define *leadership* and distinguish it from management.

Leadership refers to the processes and behaviors used by someone to motivate, inspire, and influence the behaviors of others. Although leadership and management are often related, they are not the same. Leadership involves such things as developing a vision, communicating that vision, and directing change. Management, meanwhile, focuses more on outlining procedures, monitoring results, and working toward outcomes.

Power is the ability to affect the behavior of others. In organizational settings, there are usually five kinds of power: (1) legitimate, (2) reward, (3) coercive, (4) referent, and (5) expert power. *Legitimate power* is power granted through the organizational hierarchy; it is the power defined by the organization to be accorded to people occupying a particular position. *Reward power* is the power to give or withhold rewards. *Coercive power* is the power to force compliance by means of psychological, emotional, or physical threat. *Referent power* is based on identification, imitation, loyalty, or charisma. *Expert power* is derived from information or expertise.

LEARNING OBJECTIVE 9-2

Summarize early approaches to the study of leadership.

The *trait approach to leadership* focused on identifying the traits of successful leaders. The earliest researchers believed that important leadership traits included intelligence, dominance, self-confidence, energy, activity (versus passivity), and knowledge about the job. However, this research did not produce conclusive results. More recent researchers have started to focus on traits such as emotional and mental intelligence, drive, motivation, honesty and integrity, self-confidence, knowledge of the business, and charisma.

The *behavioral approach* to leadership sought to determine what behaviors were employed by effective leaders. Research identified two basic and common leader behaviors: *task-focused* and *employee-focused* leader behaviors. It is thought that leaders should engage in both behaviors to increase performance and motivation.

LEARNING OBJECTIVE 9-3

Discuss the concept of situational approaches to leadership.

The *situational approach to leadership* proposes that there is no single best approach to leadership. Instead, situational factors influence the approach to leadership that is most effective. This approach was proposed as a continuum of leadership behavior, ranging from having the leader make decisions alone to having employees make decisions with minimal guidance from the leader. Each point on the continuum is influenced by *characteristics of the leader, their subordinates*, and the *situation*.

The path–goal theory of leadership is a direct extension of the expectancy theory of motivation. It suggests that the primary functions of a leader are to make valued or desired rewards available in the workplace and to clarify for the subordinate the kinds of behavior that will lead to goal accomplishment and valued rewards. The leader should clarify the paths to goal attainment. Path–goal theory identifies four kinds of behaviors that leaders can use, depending on the situation: (1) *directive leader behavior*, (2) *supportive leader behavior*, (3) *participative leader behavior*, and (4) *achievement-oriented leader behavior*.

The decision tree approach attempts to prescribe a leadership style appropriate to a given situation. The decision tree approach assumes that the degree to which subordinates should be encouraged to participate in decision making depends on the characteristics of the situation. After evaluating a variety of problem attributes (characteristics of the problem or decision), the leader determines an appropriate decision style that specifies the amount of subordinate participation.

The *leader-member exchange (LMX) model of leadership* stresses the importance of variable relationships between supervisors and each of their subordinates. Each superior–subordinate pair represents a "vertical dyad." The model differs from previous approaches in that it focuses on the differential relationship leaders often establish with different subordinates.

LEARNING OBJECTIVE 9-4

Describe transformational and charismatic perspectives on leadership.

Transformational leadership (as distinguished from *transactional leadership*) focuses on the set of abilities that allows a leader to recognize the need for change, to create a vision to guide that change, and to execute the change effectively. *Charismatic leadership* is influence based on the leader's personal charisma. The basic concept of charisma suggests that charismatic leaders are likely to have self-confidence, confidence in their beliefs and ideals, and a need to influence people. They also tend to communicate high expectations about follower performance and to express confidence in their followers.

LEARNING OBJECTIVE 9-5

Identify and discuss leadership substitutes and neutralizers.

Leadership substitutes are individual, task, and organizational factors that tend to outweigh the need for a leader to initiate or direct employee performance. In other words, if certain factors are present, the employee will perform their job without the direction of a leader. Examples of leadership substitutes include individual professionalism, highly structured jobs, explicit plans and goals, and group performance norms. Even if a leader attempts to engage in leadership behaviors, *leadership neutralizers* may render the leader's efforts ineffective. Such neutralizers include group cohesiveness as well as elements of the job itself.

LEARNING OBJECTIVE 9-6

Discuss leaders as coaches and examine gender and cross-cultural issues in leadership.

Many organizations expect their leaders to play the role of *coach*—to select team members, provide direction, train, and develop—but otherwise allow the group to function autonomously. Some leaders may function as mentors, helping less experienced employees learn the ropes and better preparing them to advance in an organization.

Another factor altering the face of leadership is the number of women advancing to higher levels. Although there appear to be few differences between men and women leaders, the growing number of women leaders suggests a need for more study. Some evidence indicates that women are more democratic in decision making and have the potential to be excellent leaders, as shown by a number of high-profile, successful female leaders.

Another changing perspective on leadership relates to cross-cultural issues. In this context, *culture* encompasses international differences and diversity-based differences within one culture. For example, the level of collectivism or individualism can affect a manager's leadership style.

LEARNING OBJECTIVE 9-7

Describe strategic leadership, ethical leadership, and virtual leadership.

Strategic leadership is the leader's ability to lead change in the organization so as to enhance its competitiveness. To be effective as a strategic leader, a manager needs to have a thorough and complete understanding of the organization's history, culture, strengths, and weaknesses. Business leaders are also being called on to practice *ethical leadership*—that is, to maintain high ethical standards for their own conduct, and to hold others in their organizations to the same standards. As more leaders and employees work in different settings, a better understanding of *virtual leadership* is also becoming more important.

LEARNING OBJECTIVE 9-8

Relate leadership to decision making and discuss both rational and behavioral perspectives on decision making.

Decision making—choosing one alternative from among several options—is a critical management and leadership skill. Decision making can refer to either a specific act or a general process. Most decisions fall into one of two categories: programmed and nonprogrammed. A programmed decision is one that is relatively structured or recurs with some frequency (or both). Nonprogrammed decisions are relatively unstructured and occur much less often. There are three different conditions in which decisions must be made. These are conditions of certainty, risk, or uncertainty. When the decision maker knows what the alternatives are and the likely outcomes, a *state of certainty* exists. Under a *state of risk*, the availability of each alternative and its payoffs and costs are not clear. Finally, in a *state of uncertainty*, the decision maker does not know all the alternatives, risks, or consequences.

The *rational perspective* prescribes a logical process for making decisions. It involves six steps: (1) recognizing and defining the decision situation, (2) identifying alternatives, (3) evaluating alternatives, (4) selecting the best alternative, (5) implementing the chosen alternative, and (6) following up and evaluating the results. The *behavioral perspective* acknowledges that things such as *political forces, intuition, escalation of commitment*, and *risk propensity* are also important aspects of decision making.

key terms

behavioral approach to leadership (p. 282)
charismatic leadership (p. 285)
coalition (p. 296)
coercive power (p. 280)
decision making (p. 292)
decision-making process (p. 292)
decision tree approach (p. 284)
employee-focused leader behavior (p. 282)
escalation of commitment (p. 297)
ethical leadership (p. 290)
expert power (p. 281)
intuition (p. 296)
leader–member exchange (LMX) model (p. 284)
leadership (p. 279)
leadership neutralizers (p. 287)
leadership substitutes (p. 287)
legitimate power (p. 280)
nonprogrammed decision (p. 293)
path–goal theory (p. 284)
power (p. 280)
programmed decision (p. 293)
referent power (p. 281)
reward power (p. 280)
risk propensity (p. 297)
situational approach to leadership (p. 283)
state of certainty (p. 293)
state of risk (p. 293)
state of uncertainty (p. 294)
strategic leadership (p. 290)
task-focused leader behavior (p. 282)
trait approach to leadership (p. 281)
transactional leadership (p. 285)
transformational leadership (p. 285)
virtual leadership (p. 291)

questions & exercises

QUESTIONS FOR REVIEW

9-1. What are the basic differences between management and leadership?

9-2. What are the basic premises underlying the trait approach to leadership?

9-3. What are leadership substitutes and neutralizers?

9-4. What are the steps in rational decision making?

QUESTIONS FOR ANALYSIS

9-5. Which type or types of leadership power does your current supervisor exercise?

9-6. When is task-focused leader behavior most important? When is it more important for a leader to exhibit employee-focused behavior?

9-7. Give a current example of a virtual leader. As a potential "follower," what issues would be of most concern to you? What would the issues be from the perspective of the "leader" role in such a situation?

9-8. Identify a leader who you believe exhibits charismatic leadership. What are the behaviors that support your choice?

APPLICATION EXERCISES

9-9. Overwhelmingly, the CEOs of the largest companies in the United States are white males, but women and people of color are making inroads. Identify one or more leaders who are not white, middle-aged males, and describe the challenges they face as well as strategies or traits that makes them successful.

9-10. Sir Richard Branson is one of the wealthiest citizens of the United Kingdom. According to *Forbes*, in 2023, he had an estimated net worth of about $3 billion and has owned 400 companies under his Virgin conglomerate. Based on a bit of research, how would you classify Branson's leadership style? What are the pros and cons of his leadership style? Would you want to work for Branson as part of his management team? Why or why not?

building a business: continuing team exercise

ASSIGNMENT

Meet with your team members to consider your new business venture and how it relates to the leadership topics in this chapter. Develop specific responses to the following:

9-11. How will you select a leader for your organization? What traits or characteristics will be most important to you when selecting a leader?

9-12. Which types of power will be most important to the leader of your business venture?

9-13. What leadership substitutes could support your business venture as you get started?

9-14. Are there any leadership neutralizers that could derail your new effort?

9-15. As your business venture gets off the ground, you will have to make many important decisions. Will you rely more heavily on rational decision making or intuition? Why?

team exercise

MANAGING CHANGES IN STRATEGIC DIRECTION

The Situation

CW Services provides professional cleaning services for clinics, grocery stores, and other customers who need a high level of sanitation. CW is a lean operation, with a flat organizational structure and a small number of managers. Although recent economic events have caused drastic reductions to be made in both workforce and pay, the company is considered essential and so is still operational. However, employees are disgruntled and are mostly staying on because they are afraid to lose their jobs. Consequently, customer complaints are on the rise, and the company has lost some key clients, causing a further decline in revenues and more layoffs. The company has asked your team to come in as consultants to conduct leadership workshops for the management team. Your job is to develop a set of concrete recommendations about how to coach employees through these turbulent times, increase quality and employee engagement, and ultimately save the company.

Team Activity

Assemble teams of four students and assign each group member one of the following approaches to leadership:

- Leader–member exchange (LMX) model
- Path–goal theory
- Task-focused leader
- Employee-focused leader

ACTION STEPS

9-16. Working individually, develop at least one motivational strategy based on your assigned approach to leadership that you believe would be most likely to achieve the best results in the shortest amount of time.

9-17. Assemble your team and share your assignment perspectives. Make sure you define each approach, outline the strategy, and tie it back to the facts of the case.

9-18. As a group, develop a list of advantages and disadvantages for each approach.

9-19. As a group, select the most appropriate leadership style and change management strategy and develop a justification for that decision.

exercising your ethics

PAINTED INTO A CORNER

The Situation

You are the relatively new chief executive officer (CEO) for Progressive Paints and Coatings, Inc. (PPC), a leading manufacturer of paints and stains in the United States. You were hired for your mission-driven leadership style and your commitment to balancing profits with customer service. The company's CFO, Jeff Johnson, has been with the company for 20 years, and you and Jeff have become close friends. You and Jeff just completed an optimistic quarterly call with Wall Street analysts. The stock price increased 5 percent, reflecting the positive earnings reports that have exceeded expectations. So far, during your short tenure as CEO, earnings have risen steadily every quarter, and there was a recent article in *Forbes* that attributed the company's earnings growth to your leadership. In addition, both you and Jeff have been rewarded generously with stock bonuses that are even more valuable because of the increase in stock price. The board is happy, and so are the stockholders.

PPC's mission is as follows:

- Act with integrity at all times.
- Deliver consistent sales and earnings growth.
- Develop innovative products to meet future needs.
- Work safely, protect the environment, and support the communities where we operate.
- Achieve superior shareholder returns.

The Dilemma

A few days after the quarterly earnings call, you get a message through the internal reporting system from the controller, who reports to the CFO, indicating she believes that there were at least $5.4 million of expenses that should have been reported in the last quarter (accrued) and that revenues had been overinflated to meet expectations. In addition, she reported that the CFO had failed to disclose that Lowe's, Inc., had decided to discontinue carrying your products in favor of a competitor.

QUESTIONS TO ADDRESS

9-20. What are the ethical issues in this case?

9-21. How would you address this situation?

9-22. How would you reconcile your strategy with the mission statement?

cases

TRANSFORMATIONAL LEADERSHIP

Continued from page 279

At the beginning of this chapter, you read about Rihanna's rise to fame and her entrepreneurial spirit, as well as her transformational leadership style. Using the information presented in this chapter, you should now be able to respond to these questions.

QUESTIONS FOR DISCUSSION

9-23. What personal traits does Rihanna possess that identify her as a leader?

9-24. Do you think anyone could adopt Rihanna's leadership style and be as successful? Why or why not?

9-25. Do you believe that Rihanna's gender played a part in her success? Why or why not?

9-26. What are three important lessons from Rihanna's rise to fame?

THE MAN BEHIND THE GENIUS

Without doubt, Steve Jobs, cofounder of Apple, was a one-of-a-kind leader. In many ways, Jobs was defined by his passion for innovation and willingness to take risks. As the leader of a company that created the iMac, iPhone, iPod, and iPad, Jobs demonstrated that he could see beyond the present and motivate his employees by sharing his vision clearly and compellingly. According to Apple's current CEO, Tim Cook, "Even though he was running a large company, he kept making bold moves that I don't think that anyone else would have done."[37]

The challenge, however, for Jobs and Apple was this same vision and passion. A visionary and charismatic leader's strength is an ability to mobilize their employees to work toward a goal at super-human speed. Yet, when the vision is flawed, the employees demonstrate the same commitment and move quickly, and even dangerously, in the wrong direction.[38] Often, these visionary leaders effectively screen out negative chatter, but this is not always positive, particularly when employees discover a fatal flaw.

Jobs had a unique managerial style. According to Joe Nocera of the *New York Times*, he "violated every rule of management. He was not a consensus builder but a dictator who listened mainly to his own intuition. He was a maniacal micromanager. He had an astonishing aesthetic sense, which businesspeople almost always lack . . . . He never mellowed, never let up on Apple employees, never stopped relying on his singular instincts in making decisions about how Apple products should look and how they should work."[39]

Although inspiring thousands of employees and millions of customers, Jobs could be brutal when dealing with employees who failed to successfully implement his vision. Despite many successes, Apple had its failures. One of the most notable was the MobileMe e-mail system. Jobs was so disappointed by flaws in the system that he fired the employee leading the MobileMe effort in front of a crowd of employees.

Jobs's passion was at the core of his being. When Jobs had a liver transplant in 2009, he found himself in the hospital with an oxygen mask. He pulled off the mask and, though barely able to speak, told the pulmonologist that he was unwilling to suffer through the poor design. Ultimately, Jobs succumbed to pancreatic cancer in 2011, but he left an indelible mark on the world.

QUESTIONS FOR DISCUSSION

9-27. Do you think Steve Jobs was a charismatic leader? What leads you to this conclusion?

9-28. Jobs enjoyed almost cultlike loyalty among his employees. Why do you think people clamored to work for Apple under Jobs's leadership?

9-29. What challenges face employees working for a leader such as Jobs?

9-30. Describe Jobs with respect to intuition, escalation of commitment, and risk propensity.

9-31. Do you think that you would have enjoyed working for Apple during Jobs's leadership? Why or why not?

9-32. How does a leader differ from a manager? Describe the situational approach to leadership and three major theories within this category. How would the path–goal theory help you identify the most appropriate leadership style in a situation?

endnotes

[1] Derrick Bryson Taylor, "Rihanna on How to Be a Boss (in Business and in Life)," *The New York Times*, May 20, 2019, https://www.nytimes.com/2019/05/20/t-magazine/entertainment/rihanna-business-tips.html.

[2] See John Kotter, "What Leaders Really Do," *Harvard Business Review*, December 2001, 85–94. See also Ricky W. Griffin and Jean M. Phillips, *Organizational Behavior*, 14th ed. (Boston: Cengage, 2024).

[3] John R. P. French and Bertram Raven, "The Bases of Social Power," in *Studies in Social Power*, ed. Dorwin Cartwright (Ann Arbor, MI: University of Michigan Press, 1959), 150–167.

[4] "Management Secrets from the Meanest Company in America," *Bloomberg Businessweek*, January 2, 2013, 46–51. See also "Intuit—27 Year Stock Price History | INTU," Macrotrends, accessed April 3, 2020, https://www.macrotrends.net/stocks/charts/INTU/intuit/stock-price-history.

[5] "Bad Bosses Can Be Bad for Your Health," *USA Today*, August 8, 2012, 5B; Bennett J. Tepper, "Abusive Supervision in

Work Organizations: Review, Synthesis, and Research Agenda," *Journal of Management* 33, no. 3 (2007): 261–289; R. W. Griffin, A. Hanna, T. Smith, and B. L. Kirkman, "How Bad Leaders Impact Organizational Behavior," in *Overcoming Bad Leadership in Organizations* (New York: Oxford University Press, 2022), 224–250.

[6] Martin G. Evans, "The Effects of Supervisory Behavior on the Path–Goal Relationship," *Organizational Behavior and Human Performance* 5, no. 3 (1970): 277–298; Robert J. House and Terence R. Mitchell, "Path-Goal Theory of Leadership," *Journal of Contemporary Business* 3 (Autumn 1974): 81–98. See also Gary Yukl, *Leadership in Organizations*, 9th ed. (Upper Saddle River, NJ: Prentice Hall, 2019); Griffin and Phillips, *Organizational Behavior*.

[7] George Graen and J. F. Cashman, "A Role-Making Model of Leadership in Formal Organizations: A Developmental Approach," in *Leadership Frontiers*, ed. J. G. Hunt and L. L. Larson (Kent, OH: Kent State University Press, 1975), 143–165; Fred Dansereau, George Graen, and W. J. Haga, "A Vertical Dyad Linkage Approach to Leadership Within Formal Organizations: A Longitudinal Investigation of the Role-Making Process," *Organizational Behavior and Human Performance* 15 (1975): 46–78.

[8] Rodrigo Salvaterra, "Who Is Winning: Google, Amazon, Facebook, or Apple?," Towards Data Science, accessed April 4, 2020, https://towardsdatascience.com/who-is-winning-google-amazon-facebook-or-apple-45728660473.

[9] David A. Waldman and Francis J. Yammarino, "CEO Charismatic Leadership: Levels-of-Management and Levels-of-Analysis Effects," *Academy of Management Review* 24, no. 2 (1999): 266–285. See also Griffin and Phillips, *Organizational Behavior*.

[10] Jane Howell and Boas Shamir, "The Role of Followers in the Charismatic Leadership Process: Relationships and Their Consequences," *Academy of Management Review* 30, no. 1 (2005): 96–112.

[11] Emily Canal, "FORBES 400: Meet The American Billionaires Attending The Forbes Under 30 Summit," Forbes.Com 1, Business Source Premier, EBSCOhost, 2014, accessed February 3, 2017; Dinah Eng, "Adventures of a Serial Entrepreneur," *Fortune* 165, no. 6 (2012): 23–26; Business Source Premier, EBSCOhost, accessed February 3, 2017; Chase Peterson-Withorn, "After Building Two Billion-Dollar Brands, John Paul DeJoria Shares His Success," Forbes.com 1, Business Source Premier, EBSCOhost, 2014, accessed May 13, 2015.

[12] Peace Love & Happiness Family Foundation, "Partners," accessed June 23, 2023. https://www.peacelovehappinessfoundation.org/partners.

[13] J. Richard Hackman and Ruth Wageman, "A Theory of Team Coaching," *Academy of Management Review* 30, no. 2 (2005): 269–287.

[14] https://www.pewresearch.org/social-trends/2015/01/14/chapter-2-what-makes-a-good-leader-and-does-gender-matter/.

[15] https://www.cambridge.org/core/journals/political-science-research-and-methods/article/abs/do-voters-prefer-gender-stereotypic-candidates-evidence-from-a-conjoint-survey-experiment-in-japan/52469B655EAEA141116CC00CFF2F8A64.

[16] https://www.pewresearch.org/social-trends/2015/01/14/chapter-3-obstacles-to-female-leadership/.

[17] Leena Rao, "How Ruzwana Bashir Became Silicon Valley's Favorite British Import," *Fortune*, November 2, 2016, accessed March 22, 2017, http://fortune.com/2016/11/02/ruzwana-bashir-peek-silicon-valley/.

[18] Alexis Schwartz, "Can Travel Experience Startup Peek Hit Unicorn Status amid the Delta Outbreak?," Avenue Magazine, October 4, 2021, https://avenuemagazine.com/ruzwana-bashir-peek-travel-experiences-startup/.

[19] https://fortune.com/2023/06/06/lgbtq-ceo-fortune-500-pride/.

[20] Samantha Riedel and Abby Monteil, "The Dylan Mulvaney and Bud Light Fiasco: Everything You Need to Know." Them, May 19, 2023, https://www.them.us/story/dylan-mulvaney-bud-light-drama-explained#intcid=_them-bottom-recirc_f8e914c6-6664-4a4c-8d14-5c3daf459dc5_similar2-3.

[21] "Ted Cruz Says He's Opening an Investigation into Bud Light." MSNBC, May 19, 2023, https://www.msnbc.com/rachel-maddow-show/maddowblog/ted-cruz-says-s-opening-investigation-bud-light-rcna85237.

[22] Anheuser-Busch, "Our Responsibility to America," press release, April 14, 2023, https://www.anheuser-busch.com/newsroom/our-responsibility-to-america.

[23] "Women Drinking Beer Clothed: Why Are Rightwingers Melting Down over Miller Lite?," *The Guardian*, May 17, 2023, https://www.theguardian.com/media/2023/may/17/miller-lite-ads-women-clothing-misogyny.

[24] "Dylan Mulvaney on TikTok," TikTok, accessed May 29, 2023, https://www.tiktok.com/@dylanmulvaney/video/7226873048345939242.

[25] LGBT Capital, "Estimated LGBT Purchasing Power: LGBT-GDP," 2020, http://www.lgbt-capital.com/docs/Estimated_LGBT-GDP_(table)_-_2020.pdf.

[26] Amanda Holpuch, "Behind the Backlash Against Bud Light's Transgender Influencer," *The New York Times*, April 14, 2023, https://www.nytimes.com/article/bud-light-boycott.html.

[27] For a review of decision making, see E. Frank Harrison, *The Managerial Decision Making Process*, 5th ed. (Boston: Houghton Mifflin, 1999). See also Elke U. Weber and Eric J. Johnson, "Mindful Judgment and Decision Making," in *Annual Review of Psychology 2009*, ed. Susan T. Fiske, Daniel L. Schacter, and Robert Sternberg (Palo Alto, CA: Annual Reviews, 2009), 53–86; Gerd Gigerenzer and Wolfgang Gaissmaier, "Heuristic Decision Making," in *Annual Review of Psychology 2011*, ed. Susan T. Fiske, Daniel L. Schacter, and Shelley Taylor (Palo Alto, CA: Annual Reviews, 2011), 451–482. See also Griffin and Phillips, *Organizational Behavior*.

[28] George P. Huber, *Managerial Decision Making* (Glenview, IL: Scott, Foresman, 1980).

[29] For an example, see Paul D. Collins, Lori V. Ryan, and Sharon F. Matusik, "Programmable Automation and the Locus of Decision-Making Power," *Journal of Management* 25 (1999): 29–53.

[30] George Huber, *Managerial Decision Making*. See also David W. Miller and Martin K. Starr, *The Structure of Human Decisions* (Englewood Cliffs, NJ: Prentice Hall, 1976);

Alvar Elbing, *Behavioral Decisions in Organizations*, 2nd ed. (Glenview, IL: Scott, Foresman, 1978).

[31] Rene M. Stulz, "Six Ways Companies Mismanage Risk," *Harvard Business Review*, March 2009, 86–94.

[32] Gerard P. Hodgkinson, Nicola J. Bown, A. John Maule, Keith W. Glaister, and Alan D. Pearman, "Breaking the Frame: An Analysis of Strategic Cognition and Decision Making Under Uncertainty," *Strategic Management Journal* 20 (1999): 977–985.

[33] "Making Decisions in Real Time," *Fortune*, June 26, 2000, 332–334; see also Malcolm Gladwell, *Blink* (New York: Little, Brown, 2005).

[34] Barry M. Staw and Jerry Ross, "Good Money After Bad," *Psychology Today*, February 1988, 30–33; D. Ramona Bobocel and John Meyer, "Escalating Commitment to a Failing Course of Action: Separating the Roles of Choice and Justification," *Journal of Applied Psychology* 79 (1994): 360–363.

[35] Gerry McNamara and Philip Bromiley, "Risk and Return in Organizational Decision Making," *Academy of Management Journal* 42 (1999): 330–339.

[36] See Brian O'Reilly, "What It Takes to Start a Startup," *Fortune*, June 7, 1999, 135–140, for an example.

[37] Brian Caulfield, "Steve Jobs Bio: Neither Insane nor Great," *Forbes*, October 26, 2011, accessed June 28, 2013, http://www.forbes.com/sites/briancaulfield/2011/10/26/steve-jobs-bio-neither-insane-nor-great/.

[38] Erik Sherman, "The Problem with Charismatic Leaders," Inc.com, accessed April 2, 2020, http://www.inc.com/erik-sherman/the-problem-with-charismatic-leaders.html.

[39] Frederick E. Allen, "Steve Jobs Broke Every Leadership Rule. Don't Try It Yourself," *Forbes*, August 27, 2011, accessed May 26, 2020, http://www.forbes.com/sites/frederickallen/2011/08/27/steve-jobs-broke-every-leadership-rule-dont-try-that-yourself/.

chapter 10

Human Resource Management and Labor Relations

Fizkes/Shutterstock

learning objectives

After reading this chapter, you should be able to:

10-1 **Define** *human resource management*, discuss its strategic significance, and explain how managers plan for their organization's human resource needs.

10-2 **Discuss** the legal context of human resource management and identify contemporary legal issues.

10-3 **Identify** the steps in staffing a company and discuss ways in which organizations recruit and select new employees.

10-4 **Describe** the main components of a compensation and benefits system.

10-5 **Describe** how managers develop the workforce in their organization through training and performance appraisal.

10-6 **Discuss** workforce diversity, the management of knowledge workers, and the use of a contingent workforce as important changes in the contemporary workplace.

10-7 **Explain** why workers organize into labor unions and describe the collective bargaining process.

what's in it for me?

Do you—or will you in the future—work for someone else as an employee? Do you—or will you in the future—own a business and have employees who work for you? In either case, human resource management is a critical activity for you to understand. Effectively managing human resources is the lifeblood of organizations. A firm that takes this activity seriously and approaches it from a strategic perspective has a much better chance for success than does a firm that simply goes through the motions. By understanding the material in this chapter, you'll be better able to understand (1) the importance of properly managing human resources in a unit or business you own or manage and (2) why and how your employer provides the working arrangements that most directly affect you.

We start this chapter by explaining how managers plan for their organization's human resource needs. We'll also discuss ways in which organizations select, develop, and assess employee performance and examine the main components of a compensation system. Along the way, we'll look at some key legal issues involved in hiring, compensating, and managing workers in today's workplace and discuss workforce diversity. Finally, we'll explain why workers organize into labor unions and describe the collective bargaining process. Let's get started with some basic concepts of human resource management.

Micchaelpuche/123RF

Patti McConville/Alamy Stock Photo

Putting Employees First

Wegmans Food Markets, a family-owned East Coast chain with more than 100 stores in eight states and the District of Columbia, prides itself on its commitment to customers, and it shows. But commitment to customers is only half of Wegmans's overall strategy, which calls for reaching its customers through its employees, a strategy that has garnered the company a place on the 100 Best Companies to Work For for all 25 consecutive years that *Fortune* has been compiling that list, ranking number 4 in 2022.[1]

Wegmans, which has remained in family hands since its founding in 1915, has an advantage in the ability to be as generous with its resources as its family of top executives wants to be. It doesn't have to do everything with quarterly profits in mind, and the firm likes to point out that taking care of its employees is a long-standing priority. Profit sharing and fully funded medical coverage incentive programs were introduced shortly after World War II as a way to attract and retain qualified workers during the days of salary and wage freezes because those benefits weren't counted as wages. Today, health benefits are a standard for full-time workers, but Wegmans extends that coverage to part-timers as well, who make up about two-thirds of the company's workforce of over 52,000. In part, the strategy of extending benefits to this large segment of the labor force is intended to make sure that stores have enough good workers for crucial peak periods, but there's no denying that the costs of employee-friendly policies can mount up. The minimum starting pay rate of $15 per hour is more than double the 2023 federal minimum wage. At 15 to 17 percent of sales, Wegmans's labor costs are well above the 12 percent industry average for the supermarket industry. But according to one company human resources (HR) executive, holding down labor costs isn't necessarily a strategic priority: "We would have stopped offering free health insurance [to part-timers] a long time ago," she admits, "if we tried to justify the costs."

Even today, the company goes above and beyond the minimum benefits offered by most companies. For instance, under the company's Employee Scholarship Program, full-time workers can receive up to $4,000 a year for four years and part-timers up to $2,000. Since its inception in 1984, the program has handed out more than 42,000 scholarships totaling $130 million.[2] Like most Wegmans policies, this one combines employee outreach with long-term corporate strategy: "This program has made a real difference in the lives of many young people," says President and CEO Colleen Wegman, who adds that it's also "one of the reasons we've been able to attract the best and the brightest to work at Wegmans." In addition to its health care and scholarship programs, Wegmans offers perks such as fitness center discounts, compressed workweeks, telecommuting, and domestic-partner benefits that extend to same-sex partners. Wegmans is also committed to embracing all aspects of diversity and inclusion and has numerous programs in place to offer employment and advancement opportunities to people from underrepresented groups.

In an industry where total turnover hovers around 19 percent (and can approach 100 percent for part-timers) and related costs have been known to outstrip total annual profits by 40 percent, Wegmans employee turnover is about 6 percent. In fact, almost 20 percent of Wegmans employees have been with the company for at least

10 years, and many have logged at least a quarter of a century. Employee longevity benefits the company by sustaining a more knowledgeable staff, and it reflects a positive working environment.

Despite its employee-centric approach to management, the company still has to balance profits, convenience, and technology with its labor costs, ethical beliefs, politics, and human resources management, which isn't easy. For instance, Wegmans scrapped its SCAN scan-and-go checkout option in September 2022 after experiencing a high volume of losses due to shoplifting. It has since rolled out "smart carts" that allow customers to see a running total of items as they are placed into and removed from these carts. This rollout is much more modest, however, with the chain introducing the carts in only two stores in 2023 as a test market.[3]

Wegmans remains a customer and employee darling in 2023, reporting some of the highest satisfaction rates in the industry, which explains its low turnover. Wegmans has also developed a cultlike following of customers who prefer to shop there over even the boutique-style experiences offered by some of its competitors.[4] (After studying the content of this chapter, you should be able to answer the set of discussion questions found at the end of the chapter.)

The Foundations of Human Resource Management

Learning Objective 10-1

Define *human resource management*, discuss its strategic significance, and explain how managers plan for their organization's human resource needs.

Human resource management (HRM) is the set of organizational activities directed at attracting, developing, and maintaining an effective workforce. In recent years, experts have come to appreciate the strategic importance of HRM as well as the need for systematic human resource planning.

The Strategic Importance of HRM

Human Resource Management (HRM) *set of organizational activities directed at attracting, developing, and maintaining an effective workforce*

Human Resources (HR) *the people comprising an organization's workforce*

Human resources (HR) are the people comprising an organization's workforce. Human resources are critical for effective organizational functioning. HRM (or "personnel," as it is sometimes called) was once relegated to second-class status in many organizations, but its importance has grown dramatically in recent years. Its growing importance stems from increased legal complexities, the recognition that people are a valuable resource for improving productivity, and an increased awareness of the costs associated with poor HRM.[5] For example, during the past several years, Microsoft has announced a number of different layoffs (including one affecting 5,000 and another 14,000 employees), mostly individuals working in software development. At the same time, though, the firm has continued to expand and hire thousands of other highly talented people for jobs related to online search, network integration, and artificial intelligence (AI), important growth areas for the company. This careful and systematic approach to talent management, reducing employees in areas where they are no longer needed and adding new talent to key growth areas, reflects a strategic approach to HRM.

Indeed, most managers understand that the effectiveness of their HR function has a substantial impact on the bottom-line performance of their firm. Poor HR planning can result in spurts of inefficient hiring followed by costly layoffs, which are expensive in terms of unemployment compensation payments, training, public relations, and employee morale. Haphazard compensation systems do not attract, keep, and motivate good employees, and outmoded recruitment practices can expose the firm to expensive and embarrassing discrimination lawsuits. Consequently, the chief HR executive of most large businesses is a vice president directly accountable to the CEO, and many firms develop sophisticated strategic HR plans and integrate those plans with other strategic planning activities.

Even organizations with as few as 200 employees usually have an HR manager and an HR department charged with overseeing these activities. Responsibility for HR activities, however, is often shared between the HR department and line managers. The HR department may recruit and initially screen prospective new employees, for instance, but the final hiring decisions are usually made by managers in the department where the new employees will work. Similarly, although the HR department may establish performance appraisal policies and procedures, the actual evaluation and coaching of employees are generally done by their immediate superiors.

Human Capital *reflects the organization's investment in attracting, retaining, and motivating an effective workforce*

Talent Management *the view that the people in an organization represent a portfolio of valuable talents that can be effectively managed and tapped in ways best targeted to organizational success*

The growing awareness of the strategic significance of HRM has even led to new terminology to reflect a firm's commitment to people. **Human capital** reflects the organization's investment in attracting, retaining, and motivating an effective workforce. Hence, just as the phrase *financial capital* is an indicator of a firm's financial resources and reserves, so, too, does *human capital* serve as a tangible indicator of the value of the people who make up an organization.[6] Similarly, some managers today think in terms of talent management. **Talent management** reflects the view that the people in an organization represent a portfolio of valuable talents and skills that can be effectively managed and tapped in ways best targeted to organizational success.

HR Planning

As you can see in Figure 10.1, the starting point in attracting qualified new employees is planning. Specifically, HR planning involves job analysis and forecasting the demand for and supply of labor.

Job Analysis *systematic analysis of jobs within an organization*

Job Description *description of the duties and responsibilities of a job; its working conditions; and the tools, materials, equipment, and information used to perform it*

Job Specification *description of the skills, abilities, and other credentials and qualifications required by a job*

Job Analysis

Job analysis is a systematic analysis of jobs within an organization; most firms have trained experts who handle these analyses. A job analysis results in two things:

- The **job description** lists the duties and responsibilities of a job; its working conditions; and the tools, materials, equipment, and information used to perform it.
- The **job specification** lists the skills, abilities, and other credentials and qualifications needed to perform the job effectively.

Job analysis information is used in many HRM activities. For instance, knowing about job content and job requirements is necessary to develop appropriate selection methods, create job-relevant performance appraisal systems, and set equitable compensation rates.

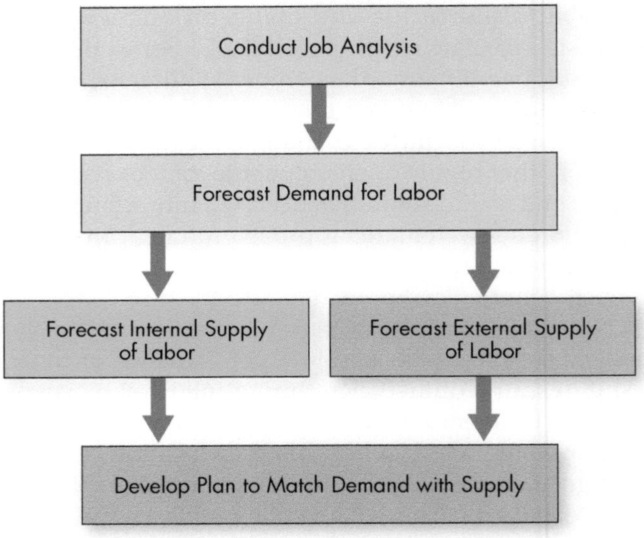

FIGURE 10.1 The HR Planning Process

Forecasting HR Demand and Supply After managers fully understand the jobs to be performed within an organization, they can start planning for the organization's future HR needs. Managers start by assessing trends in past HR usage, future organizational plans, and general economic trends.

Forecasting the supply of labor is really two tasks:

1. Forecasting *internal supply*, the number and type of employees who will be in the firm at some future date
2. Forecasting *external supply*, the number and type of people who will be available for hiring from the labor market at large

Replacement Charts At higher levels of an organization, managers also plan for specific people and positions. The technique most commonly used is the **replacement chart**, which lists each important managerial position, who occupies it, how long that person will probably stay in it before moving on (either to another position or to retirement), and who is now qualified or soon will be qualified to move into it. (In most firms today, of course, this information is now digital.) This technique allows ample time to plan developmental experiences for people identified as potential successors for critical managerial jobs. Halliburton, for instance, has a detailed replacement system that the firm calls its Executive Succession System (ESS). When a manager's performance is reviewed each year, notations are placed in the system about the person's readiness for promotion, potential positions for promotion, and what development activities are needed to prepare the individual for promotion. Other managers throughout the firm can access the system whenever they have positions available.

Replacement Chart *list of each management position, who occupies it, how long that person will likely stay in the job, and who is qualified as a replacement*

Skills Inventories To facilitate both planning and identifying people for transfer or promotion, some organizations also have **employee information systems (skills inventories)** that contain information on each employee's education, skills, work experience, and career aspirations. Such a system can quickly locate every employee who is qualified to fill a position. Again, although these systems were once handled with hardcopy charts and files, they are almost always in digital form today.

Employee Information System (Skills Inventory) *computerized system containing information on each employee's education, skills, work experiences, and career aspirations*

Forecasting the external supply of labor is a different problem altogether. Planners must rely on information from outside sources, such as state employment commissions, government reports, and figures supplied by colleges on the numbers of students in major fields.

Matching HR Supply and Demand After comparing future demand and internal supply, managers can make plans to manage predicted shortfalls or overstaffing. If a shortfall is predicted, new employees can be hired, current employees can be retrained and transferred into understaffed areas, individuals approaching retirement can be enticed to stay on, or labor-saving or productivity-enhancing systems can be installed. If overstaffing is expected to be a problem, the main options are transferring the extra employees, not replacing individuals who quit, encouraging early retirement, and laying off workers. During the Great Recession of 2008–2011, many firms found it necessary to reduce the size of their workforces through layoffs. Others responded to the economic downturn by reducing the number of hours their employees worked, by imposing pay cuts on their employees, or by some combination of all these approaches. The same issues arose during the COVID-19 pandemic in 2020 but in both directions. Many firms, such as traditional retailers and restaurants like Macy's and Olive Garden, were hurt by various "shelter in place" requirements and laid off hundreds of thousands of people. In contrast, as demand for such products as toilet tissue and cleaning supplies surged, companies like Procter & Gamble and Clorox hired new employees to help meet this demand, and as fewer people ventured out to shop, online retailing skyrocketed and companies like Amazon went into aggressive hiring mode.

Learning Objective 10-2

Discuss the legal context of human resource management and identify contemporary legal issues.

The Legal Context of HRM

A number of laws regulate various aspects of employee–employer relations, especially in the areas of equal employment opportunity, compensation and benefits, labor relations, and occupational safety and health. Several of the most significant ones are summarized in Table 10.1.

Equal Employment Opportunity

Title VII of the Civil Rights Act of 1964 *forbids discrimination in all areas of the employment relationship*

Title VII of the Civil Rights Act of 1964 forbids discrimination in all areas of the employment relationship, such as hiring, opportunities for advancement, compensation increases, layoffs, and terminations, against members of certain protected classes based on factors such as race, color, gender, religious beliefs, or national origin. Prior to the passage of this law organizations could openly discriminate against people of color and women, for example. The intent of Title VII is to ensure that employment decisions are made on the basis of an individual's qualifications rather than on the basis of personal biases. The law has reduced direct forms of discrimination (e.g., refusing to promote people of color into management, failing to hire men as flight attendants, refusing to hire women as construction workers) as well as indirect forms of discrimination (using employment tests that white applicants pass at a higher rate than do Black applicants, for instance). Note, however, that organizations are free to base employment decisions on such job-related factors as qualifications, performance, seniority, and so forth. For example, an organization can certainly hire a male job applicant instead of a female applicant if he is more qualified (i.e., has more education and/or experience related to the job). However, he cannot be hired simply because of his sex or gender expression.

table 10.1 Major Laws and Regulations Affecting Human Resource Management

Major Laws and Regulations Affecting Human Resource Management
Equal Employment Opportunity
Title VII of the Civil Rights Act of 1964 (as amended by the Equal Employment Opportunity Act of 1972). Forbids discrimination on the basis of race, color, sex, religious beliefs, or national origin in all areas of the employment relationship.
Age Discrimination in Employment Act. Outlaws discrimination against people older than 40 years.
Various executive orders, especially Executive Order 11246 in 1965. Requires employers with government contracts to engage in affirmative action.
Pregnancy Discrimination Act. Specifically outlaws discrimination on the basis of pregnancy.
Vietnam Era Veterans' Readjustment Assistance Act. Extends affirmative action mandate to military veterans who served during the Vietnam War.
Americans with Disabilities Act. Specifically outlaws discrimination against disabled persons.
Civil Rights Act of 1991. Makes it easier for employees to sue an organization for discrimination but also limits punitive damage awards if they win.
Compensation and Benefits
Fair Labor Standards Act. Establishes minimum wage and mandated overtime pay for work in excess of 40 hours per week.
Equal Pay Act of 1963. Requires that men and women be paid the same amount for doing the same job.
Employee Retirement Income Security Act (ERISA) of 1974. Regulates how organizations manage their pension funds.
Family and Medical Leave Act (FMLA) of 1993. Requires employers to provide up to 12 weeks of unpaid leave for family and medical emergencies.
Labor Relations
National Labor Relations Act. Spells out procedures by which employees can establish labor unions and requires organizations to bargain collectively with legally formed unions; also known as the *Wagner Act*.
Labor-Management Relations Act. Limits union power and specifies management rights during a union-organizing campaign; also known as the *Taft-Hartley Act*.
Health and Safety
Occupational Safety and Health Act (OSHA) of 1970. Mandates the provision of safe working conditions.

Employment requirements such as test scores and other qualifications are legally defined as having an adverse impact on people of color and women when such individuals meet or pass the requirement at a rate less than 80 percent of the rate of non-Hispanic white, male group members. Criteria that have an **adverse impact** on protected groups can be used only when there is clear evidence that they effectively identify individuals who are better able than others to do the job. The **Equal Employment Opportunity Commission (EEOC)** is charged with enforcing Title VII as well as several other employment-related laws.

Adverse Impact *when people of color and women meet or pass the requirement for a job at a rate less than 80 percent of the rate of non-Hispanic, white, male group members (in the United States)*

Equal Employment Opportunity Commission (EEOC) *federal agency enforcing several discrimination-related laws*

The **Age Discrimination in Employment Act**, passed in 1967, amended in 1978 and again in 1986, is an attempt to prevent organizations from discriminating against older workers. In its current form, it outlaws discrimination against people older than 40 years. Both the Age Discrimination in Employment Act and Title VII require passive nondiscrimination, or **equal employment opportunity**. Employers are not required to seek out and hire people of color, but they must treat all who apply fairly.

Age Discrimination in Employment Act *outlaws discrimination against people older than 40 years*

Equal Employment Opportunity *legally mandated nondiscrimination in employment on the basis of race, creed, sex, or national origin*

Several executive orders, however, require that employers holding government contracts engage in **affirmative action**, actively and intentionally seeking and hiring employees from groups that are underrepresented in the organization. These organizations must have a written **affirmative action plan** that spells out employment goals for underused groups and how those goals will be met. These employers are also required to act affirmatively in hiring Vietnam-era veterans (as a result of the Vietnam Era Veterans' Readjustment Assistance Act) and qualified disabled individuals. Finally, the Pregnancy Discrimination Act forbids discrimination against pregnant people.

Affirmative Action *intentionally seeking and hiring employees from groups that are underrepresented in the organization*

Affirmative Action Plan *written statement of how the organization intends to actively recruit, hire, and develop members of relevant protected classes*

In 1990, Congress passed the **Americans with Disabilities Act**, which forbids discrimination on the basis of disabilities and requires employers to provide reasonable accommodations for disabled employees.

Americans with Disabilities Act *forbids discrimination on the basis of disabilities and requires employers to provide reasonable accommodations for disabled employees*

More recently, the **Civil Rights Act of 1991** amended the original Civil Rights Act as well as other related laws by making it easier to bring discrimination lawsuits while simultaneously limiting the amount of punitive damages that can be awarded against employers in those lawsuits.

Civil Rights Act of 1991 *amended the original Civil Rights Act*

Compensation and Benefits

Laws also regulate compensation and benefits. The **Fair Labor Standards Act**, passed in 1938 and amended frequently since then, sets a minimum wage and requires the payment of overtime rates for work in excess of 40 hours per week. Salaried professional, executive, and administrative employees are exempt from the minimum hourly wage and overtime provisions. The **Equal Pay Act of 1963** requires that people be paid the same amount for doing the same job, regardless of their sex. Attempts to circumvent the law by having different job titles and pay rates for men and women who perform the same work are also illegal. Basing an employee's pay on seniority or performance is legal, however, even if it means that a man and woman are paid different amounts for doing the same job.

Fair Labor Standards Act *sets a minimum wage and requires the payment of overtime rates for work in excess of 40 hours per week*

Equal Pay Act of 1963 *requires that men and women be paid the same amount for doing the same job*

The provision of benefits is also regulated in some ways by state and federal laws. Certain benefits are mandatory, such as workers' compensation insurance for employees who are injured on the job. Employers who provide a pension plan for their employees are regulated by the **Employee Retirement Income Security Act (ERISA) of 1974**. The purpose of this act is to help ensure the financial security of pension funds by regulating how they can be invested. The **Family and Medical Leave Act (FMLA) of 1993** requires employers to provide up to 12 weeks of unpaid leave for family and medical emergencies.

Employee Retirement Income Security Act (ERISA) of 1974 *ensures the financial security of pension funds by regulating how they can be invested*

Family and Medical Leave Act (FMLA) of 1993 *requires employers to provide up to 12 weeks of unpaid leave for family and medical emergencies*

Labor Relations

Union activities and management's behavior toward unions constitute another heavily regulated area. The **National Labor Relations Act** (also known as the **Wagner Act**), passed in 1935, established procedures for employees to vote on whether to be represented by a union. If they vote to be represented by a union, management is required to bargain collectively with that union. The **National Labor Relations Board (NLRB)** was established by the Wagner Act to enforce its provisions. Following a series

National Labor Relations Act ***(also known as the* Wagner Act)** *sets up a procedure for employees to vote on whether to have a union*

National Labor Relations Board (NLRB) *established by the Wagner Act to enforce its provisions*

Labor-Management Relations Act (*also known as the* Taft-Hartley Act) *passed to limit union power*

of severe strikes in 1946, the **Labor-Management Relations Act** (also known as the **Taft-Hartley Act**) was passed in 1947 to limit union power. The law increases management's rights during an organizing campaign. The Taft-Hartley Act also contains the National Emergency Strike provision, which allows the president of the United States to prevent or end a strike that endangers national security. Taken together, these laws balance union and management power. Employees can be represented by a legally created and managed union, but the business can make non-employee-related business decisions without interference.

Health and Safety

Occupational Safety and Health Act (OSHA) of 1970 *federal law setting and enforcing guidelines for protecting workers from unsafe conditions and potential health hazards in the workplace*

The **Occupational Safety and Health Act (OSHA) of 1970** directly mandates the provision of safe working conditions. It requires that employers (1) provide a place of employment that is free from hazards that may cause death or serious physical harm and (2) obey the safety and health standards established by the Department of Labor. Safety standards are intended to prevent accidents, whereas occupational health standards are concerned with preventing occupational disease. For example, standards limit the concentration of cotton dust in the air because this contaminant has been associated with lung disease in textile workers. The standards are enforced by OSHA inspections, which are conducted when an employee files a complaint about unsafe conditions or when a serious work-related accident occurs.

Spot inspections of plants in especially hazardous industries such as mining and chemicals are also made. Employers who fail to meet OSHA standards may be fined. For instance, in December 2018, a construction worker in New York died after a roof collapsed where he was installing solar panels. An OSHA investigation concluded that the worker's employer, Northridge Construction, failed to provide fall protection devices and protective helmets, did not insure the structural integrity of the roof, and misused a ladder. The firm was fined $224,620. Similarly, Donghee Alabama LLC, an automobile parts manufacturer, was charged with numerous violations leading to the death of one of its employees. This firm was fined $145,438.[7] Dollar General, a large national retailer, has been fined over $15 million since 2017 for a wide variety of infractions. In recent years, most OSHA violations involved workers repairing or replacing roofs, working in trenches, or operating machinery and equipment without proper safety equipment.

Other Legal Issues

In addition to these established areas of HR legal regulation, several other legal issues are also noteworthy.

Sexual Harassment *making unwelcome sexual advances in the workplace*

Sexual Harassment

Sexual harassment is defined by the EEOC as unwelcome sexual advances in the work environment. If the conduct is unwelcome and occurs with sufficient frequency to create an abusive work environment, the employer is responsible for changing the environment by warning, reprimanding, or firing the harasser. The courts have defined two types of sexual harassment:

Quid Pro Quo Harassment *form of sexual harassment in which sexual favors are requested in return for job-related benefits*

1 In cases of **quid pro quo harassment**, the harasser offers to exchange something of value for sexual favors. A supervisor, for example, might tell or suggest to a subordinate that they will be recommended for a promotion or a raise in exchange for sexual favors.

Hostile Work Environment *form of sexual harassment deriving from off-color jokes, lewd comments, and so forth*

2 The creation of a **hostile work environment** is a more subtle form of sexual harassment. A group of employees who continually make offensive jokes and lewd comments and perhaps decorate the work environment with inappropriate photographs may create a hostile work environment for other colleagues.

In recent years, the concept of harassment has been expanded to encompass unwelcome or inappropriate behaviors regarding ethnicity, religion, and age. For example, courts have ruled that bullying employees due to their religion constitutes discrimination and must be addressed by employers.

Andreypopov/123RF

Workplace harassment and bullying are concerns for all managers but often fall to human resource managers for solutions. This manager appears to be bullying his assistant using verbal abuse. Their organization should have policies and procedures in place for her to report his behavior and detailing how the organization will address the problem.

Employment at Will The concept of **employment at will** holds that both employer and employee have the mutual right to terminate an employment relationship at any time for any reason, with or without advance notice to the other. Over the past two decades, however, terminated employees have challenged the employment-at-will doctrine by filing lawsuits against former employers on the grounds of wrongful discharge.

Employment at Will *principle, increasingly modified by legislation and judicial decision, that organizations should be able to retain or dismiss employees at their discretion*

In the past several years, such suits have put limits on employment-at-will provisions in certain circumstances. In the past, for example, organizations were guilty of firing employees who filed workers' compensation claims or took "excessive" time off to serve on jury duty. More recently, however, the courts have ruled that employees may not be fired for exercising rights protected by law.

The Patriot Act In response to the terrorist attacks of September 11, 2001, the U.S. government passed legislation that increases its powers to investigate and prosecute suspected terrorists. This legislation, known as the **Patriot Act**, has several key implications for HRM. For instance, certain "restricted" individuals (including ex-convicts and aliens from countries deemed by the State Department to have "repeatedly provided support for acts of international terrorism") are ineligible to work with potentially dangerous biological agents. More controversial are sections granting government investigators access to previously confidential personal and financial records.

Patriot Act *legislation that increased U.S. government's power to investigate and prosecute suspected terrorists*

In addition to these areas of legal regulation, other issues also continue to emerge. For instance, in recent years, gender identity, sexual orientation, country of origin, and immigration have all taken on renewed social significance in ways that have implications for human resource management. In response, many organizations have taken clearer and more emphatic measures to communicate that they will not tolerate discrimination of any form based on, for instance, gender identity or immigration status.

Staffing the Organization

Learning Objective 10-3

Identify the steps in staffing a company and discuss ways in which organizations recruit and select new employees.

When managers have determined that new employees are needed and understand the legal context in which they operate, they can then turn their attention to recruiting and hiring the right mix of people. This involves two processes: (1) acquiring new employees from outside the company and (2) promoting current employees from within. Both external and internal staffing, however, start with effective *recruiting*.

Recruiting Employees

Recruiting *process of attracting qualified persons to apply for jobs an organization is seeking to fill*

Recruiting is the process of attracting qualified persons to apply for the jobs that are open.

Internal Recruiting *considering present employees as candidates for openings*

Internal Recruiting

Internal recruiting means considering present employees as candidates for openings. Promotion from within can help build morale and keep high-quality employees from leaving. For higher-level positions, a digital skills inventory system (as discussed earlier) may be used to identify internal candidates, or managers may be asked to recommend individuals to be considered. Of course, internal promotions also create new openings that then have to be filled.

External Recruiting *attracting persons outside the organization to apply for jobs*

External Recruiting

External recruiting involves attracting people outside the organization to apply for jobs. External recruiting methods include posting jobs on the company website or other online job sites, such as Monster.com and LinkedIn; holding campus interviews for potential college recruits; using employment agencies or executive search firms to scout for potential talent; seeking referrals by present employees; advertising in traditional print publications; and hiring so-called walk-ins (unsolicited applicants).

The organization must also keep in mind that recruiting decisions often go both ways—the organization is recruiting an employee, but the prospective employee is also selecting a job. For instance, when unemployment is low (meaning fewer people are seeking work), businesses may have to work harder to attract new employees. But when unemployment is higher (meaning more people are looking for work), organizations may find it easier to recruit prospective employees without having to resort to expensive hiring incentives. But even if a firm can take its pick of the best potential employees, it still should treat all applicants with dignity and respect and strive for a good person–job fit. Hiring the wrong employee can cost the company about half of a low-skilled worker's annual wages or three to five times upper-level employees' annual wages. Therefore, hiring the "wrong" employee for $50,000 per year could cost the company at least $25,000. These costs stem from training, counseling, low productivity, termination, and recruiting and hiring a replacement.

Realistic Job Preview (RJP) *providing the applicant with a real picture of what it would be like performing the job the organization is trying to fill*

One generally successful method for facilitating a good person–job fit is what is called a **realistic job preview (RJP)**. As the term suggests, the RJP involves providing the applicant with a real picture of what performing the job that the organization is trying to fill would be like.[8] For example, it would not make sense for a firm to tell an applicant that the job is exciting and challenging when in fact it is known to be routine and straightforward, yet some managers do this to hire the best people. The likely outcome is a dissatisfied employee who will quickly start looking for a better job. If the company is more realistic about a job, though, the person hired will be more likely to remain in the job for a longer period of time. Of course, a manager might not want to describe a job as boring and monotonous, even if that is in fact accurate. An effective solution to this dilemma may be to allow job applicants to observe people performing the job or perhaps watch a short video of the job and then allow the applicants to make their own assessments of how well the job aligns with their interests.

Selecting Employees

Once the recruiting process has attracted a pool of applicants, the next step is to select whom to hire. The intent of the selection process is to gather from applicants the information that will predict job success and then to hire the candidate(s) likely to be most successful.

Application Forms

The first step in selection is usually asking the candidate to fill out an application. An application form is an efficient method of gathering information about the applicant's previous work history, educational background, and other job-related demographic data. Application forms are seldom used for upper-level jobs; candidates for such positions usually provide the same information on their résumé. Most applications are now prepared and submitted online, although some firms still use traditional paper forms.

Tests Employers sometimes ask candidates to take tests during the selection process. Tests of ability, skill, aptitude, or knowledge relevant to a particular job are usually the best predictors of job success, although tests of general intelligence or personality are occasionally useful as well. Some companies use a test of the "Big Five" personality dimensions (or other personality measures) discussed in Chapter 8 to predict success.

Interviews Interviews are a popular selection device, although they are actually often a poor predictor of job success. For example, biases inherent in the way people perceive and judge others when they first meet affect subsequent evaluations. Interview validity can be improved by training interviewers to be aware of potential unconscious biases and by tightening the structure of the interview. In a structured interview, questions are written in advance, and all interviewers follow the same question list with each candidate. Structured interviews tend to be used for jobs that are relatively routine, such as some administrative assistant positions, data entry jobs, and college admissions processing positions. For interviewing managerial or professional candidates, a somewhat less structured approach can be used. Although question areas and information-gathering objectives are still planned in advance, specific questions vary with the candidates' backgrounds. Sometimes, companies are looking for especially creative employees and may try to learn more about the individual's creativity during an interview.

Other Techniques Organizations also use other selection techniques that vary with circumstances. Polygraph tests, once popular, are declining in popularity. However, organizations occasionally require applicants to take physical exams (being careful that their practices are consistent with the Americans with Disabilities Act). Many organizations are using drug tests, especially in situations in which drug-related performance problems could create serious safety hazards. For example, potential employees who may be handling hazardous chemicals or medical waste or engaging in public transportation activities like driving buses are likely to be drug tested. In many situations, these techniques are applied after an offer has been extended but with that offer being dependent on a successful follow-up test. For instance, an offer might specify something like "This offer is contingent upon your successfully passing a drug screening test." Many organizations also run background checks on prospective employees. Reference checks with previous employers are also used, but they have been shown to have limited value because individuals are likely to provide only the names of references that will give them positive recommendations. Even worse, some applicants have been known to literally make up references.

Compensation and Benefits

Learning Objective 10-4

Describe the main components of a compensation and benefits system.

People who work for a business expect to be paid, of course, and most workers today also expect certain benefits from their employers. Indeed, a major factor in retaining talented employees is a company's **compensation system**, the total package of rewards that it offers employees in return for their contributions to the organization's mission. Creating an effective compensation system requires finding the right balance between offering sufficient inducements to attract and retain employees while also keeping labor costs in line with revenues and competing employers.

Compensation System *total package of rewards that organizations provide to individuals in return for their labor*

Wages and Salaries

Wages and salaries are the dollar amounts paid to employees for their labor. **Wages**, on the one hand, are paid for time worked. For example, if your job pays you $15 an hour, that is your wage. A **salary**, on the other hand, is paid for performing a job. A salaried executive earning $100,000 per year is paid to achieve results even if that

Wages *compensation in the form of money paid for time worked*

Salary *compensation in the form of money paid for discharging the responsibilities of a job*

means working 5 hours one day and 15 the next. Salaries are usually expressed as an amount paid per month or year.

In setting wage and salary levels, a company may start by looking at its competitors. Firms must also decide how their internal wage and salary levels will compare for different jobs. Some organizations pay everyone doing the same job the same amount. In other organizations, though, an employee with more experience or who consistently performs at a higher level may earn more than another employee doing the same job. This practice is legal and can be motivational so long as the reasons for the pay differential are job related and not based on bias or favoritism.

Incentive Programs

Incentive Program *special compensation program designed to motivate high performance*

Bonus *individual performance incentive in the form of a special payment made over and above the employee's salary*

Merit Salary System *individual incentive linking compensation to performance in nonsales jobs*

Studies have shown that beyond a certain point, more money will not necessarily result in better performance. Money motivates employees only if it is tied directly to performance. The most common method of establishing this link is the use of **incentive programs**, special pay programs designed to motivate high performance. Some programs are available to individuals, whereas others are distributed on a company-wide basis.

A sales bonus is a typical incentive. Employees receive **bonuses**, special payments above their salaries, when they sell a certain number or certain dollar amount of goods for a designated period, such as a week, month, quarter, or year. Employees who fail to reach this goal earn no bonuses. **Merit salary systems** link pay raises to performance levels in nonsales jobs.

Executives commonly receive stock options as incentives. Apple CEO Tim Cook, for example, can buy several thousand shares of company stock each year at a predetermined price. If his managerial talent leads to higher profits and stock prices, he can buy the stock at a price lower than the market value for which, in theory, he is partially responsible. He is then free to sell the stock at market price at a specified future date, keeping the profits for himself, or to retain the stock for as long as he wants.

Pay for Performance (or **Variable Pay)** *individual incentive that rewards a manager for especially productive output*

Another popular incentive plan is called **pay for performance** (or **variable pay**). In essence, managers are rewarded for especially productive output with earnings that significantly exceed the cost of bonuses. The number of variable pay programs in the United States has been growing consistently for the last decade, and most experts predict that they will continue to grow in popularity. Many firms say that variable pay is a better motivator than merit raises because the range between generous and modest merit raises is usually quite small.

Profit-Sharing Plan *incentive plan for distributing bonuses to employees when company profits rise above a certain level*

Gainsharing Plan *incentive plan that rewards groups for productivity improvements*

Pay-for-Knowledge Plan *incentive plan to encourage employees to learn new skills or become proficient at different jobs*

Company-Wide Incentives Some incentive programs apply to all the employees in a firm. Under **profit-sharing plans**, for example, profits earned above a certain level are distributed to employees. Also, **gainsharing plans** distribute bonuses to employees when a company's costs are reduced through greater work efficiency. **Pay-for-knowledge plans** pay workers to learn new skills and to become proficient at different jobs.

Benefits Programs

Benefits *compensation other than wages and salaries*

Workers' Compensation Insurance *legally required insurance for compensating workers injured on the job*

Benefits, compensation other than wages and salaries and other incentives offered by a firm to its workers, account for a substantial percentage of most compensation budgets. Most companies are required by law to pay a tax for Social Security retirement benefits and provide **workers' compensation insurance**, insurance for compensating workers injured on the job. Most businesses also provide some level of health, life, and disability insurance for their full-time employees, as well as paid time off for vacations and holidays. A few, such as Starbucks and The Container Store, also provide similar benefits, but at a reduced level, to their part-time employees. Some also allow employees to use payroll deductions to buy stock at discounted prices. Counseling services for employees with alcohol, drug, or emotional problems are also provided

finding a better way

Getting Your Hands Dirty

Jeppe Gustafsson/Shutterstock

When John A. Solheim was 13, he began making golf putters with his father, Karsten Solheim, in the family's garage. Karsten was an engineer with General Electric and a golfer who didn't like the state of putters in 1959, so he used his engineering knowledge to design a putter with the shaft attached at the blade's center instead of the heel. He named his design Ping because of the distinctive sound the club made as it contacted the ball. A new company was born.

While John was still in high school, he assumed an active leadership role at Ping. Karsten focused on new ideas and innovation, while John managed production. With a bit of luck and a lot of hard work, Ping grew into one of the premier golf equipment companies in the world. As the company expanded, John took over managing relationships with the USGA, the R&A, and the PGA Tour and maintained direct involvement with the manufacturing processes. One employee reported, "If we are behind on orders and need help keeping up, you will see him out there on the production line."[10] The Solheim family remained at the center of the business, and they promoted Ping employees who would be able to maintain the company's culture and quality. Doug Hawken was one of those people. Hawken worked his way up from assistant to production manager to president and chief operating officer, spanning a 45-year career at Ping.

In 2017, John Karsten Solheim, Karsten's grandson and John A.'s oldest son, was named president of Ping, succeeding Doug Hawken. Throughout these changes, the company culture stayed strong.

Like his father, John K. could often be seen working on the production line. John K. says he is trained on "about five or six" roles on the line and he finds the work therapeutic compared to his role as president. "Everybody rotates . . . I was using the cut saw early this morning, and now I'm screwing in the back weight," John K. recently shared after a particularly long shift. "But I've done lofts and lies. I've done the ferrule grinding. I've installed Arccos sensors."[11]

Even though he's the company's president, John K. values his connection to the employees. For example, one employee recalled, "I had a medical situation a while back that I took some time off to take care of, and when I returned, the CEO walked right up and asked me how I was doing. That's a big deal."[12]

by some large employers, as are on-site childcare centers. Some companies even provide reduced membership fees at gyms and health clubs, as well as insurance or other protection for identity theft.[9]

Retirement Plans Retirement plans (or pension plans) constitute another important—and sometimes controversial—benefit that is available to many employees. Company-sponsored retirement plans were historically set up to pay pensions to workers when they retire (these are referred to as *defined benefit plans*). In some cases, the company contributed all the money to the pension fund. In others, both the company and employees made contributions. In some cases, though, some companies have run into problems because they have not set aside enough money to cover the retirement funds they have agreed to provide.

Many companies today are transitioning to what are called defined contributions plans, also known as 401(k) plans. Under these plans, contributions from the employee, sometimes matched by the employer, are invested in various options like stock and/or bond funds, money markets, government treasury bills, and so forth. The individual's retirement account is subject to greater risk (as well as potentially greater returns) while the employer incurs less risk. Both FedEx and Goodyear have recently made this shift for all their employees. Other employers who have also made this transition include Anheuser-Busch, Wells Fargo, General Motors, AT&T, General Electric, and Walmart.

Containing the Costs of Benefits As the range of benefits has increased, so has concern about containing the costs of these benefits. Many companies are experimenting with cost-cutting plans while still attracting and retaining valuable employees. One approach is the **cafeteria benefits plan**. A certain dollar amount of benefits per employee is set aside so that each employee can choose from a variety of alternatives.

Cafeteria Benefits Plan *benefit plan that sets limits on benefits per employee, each of whom may choose from a variety of alternative benefits*

Another area of increasing concern is health care costs. Medical expenses have increased insurance premiums, which, in turn, have increased the cost to employers of maintaining benefits plans. Many employers are looking for new ways to cut those costs. One increasingly popular approach is for organizations to create their own networks of health care providers. These providers agree to charge lower fees for services rendered to employees of member organizations. In return, they enjoy established relationships with large employers and, thus, more clients and patients. Insurers also charge less to cover the employees of network members because they make lower reimbursement payments.

Learning Objective 10-5

Describe how managers develop the workforce in their organization through training and performance appraisal.

Developing the Workforce

After a company has hired new employees, it must acquaint them with the firm and their new jobs. Managers also take steps to train and develop employees and to further develop necessary job skills. In addition, every firm has some system for performance appraisal and feedback.

Training and Development

Training *usually refers to teaching operational or technical employees how to do the job for which they were hired*

Development *usually refers to teaching managers and professionals the skills needed for both present and future jobs*

In HRM, **training** usually refers to teaching operational or technical employees how to do the job for which they were hired. It also refers to technical areas such as new software and technology. **Development** refers to teaching managers and professionals the skills needed for both present and future jobs and includes improved decision making, strategic leadership, and so forth.[13] Most organizations provide regular training and development programs for managers and employees. For example, IBM spends more than $574 million annually on programs and has a vice president in charge of employee education. IBM employees log more than 28.6 million hours per year on training and education.[14] U.S. businesses typically spend more than $101 billion annually on training and development programs away from the workplace. Over $370 billion is spent annually worldwide. And these figures do not include wages, salaries, and benefits paid to employees while they are participating in such programs.

Assessing Training Needs The first step in developing a training plan is to determine what needs exist. For example, if employees do not know how to operate the equipment necessary to do their job, a training program on how to operate the equipment is clearly needed. In contrast, when a group of office workers is performing poorly, training may or may not be the answer. The problem could be motivation, aging technology, poor supervision, inefficient work design, or a deficiency of skills and knowledge. Only the last problem could be remedied by training. As training programs are being developed, the manager should set specific and measurable goals specifying what participants are to learn. Managers should also develop procedures to evaluate the training program after employees complete it.

Common Training Methods Many different training and development methods are available. Selection of methods depends on many considerations, but perhaps the most important is training content. When the training content is factual

Pressmaster/Shutterstock

Many businesses invest in their employees by providing access to training and development opportunities. These managers are in a training program designed to help them refine and enhance their conceptual and strategic thinking skills.

material (such as company rules or explanations of how to fill out forms), assigned reading, programmed learning, and lecture methods work well. When the content is interpersonal relations or group decision making, however, firms need to use a method that allows interpersonal contact, such as role playing or case discussion groups. When employees must learn a physical skill, methods allowing practice and the actual use of tools and materials are needed, as in **on-the-job training** or **vestibule training**. (Vestibule training enables participants to focus on safety, learning, and feedback rather than on productivity.)

On-the-Job Training *training, sometimes informal, conducted while an employee is at work*

Vestibule Training *off-the-job training conducted in a simulated environment*

Web-based and other digital media–based training are especially popular today. Such methods allow a mix of training content, are relatively easy to update and revise, let participants use a variable schedule, and lower travel costs.[15] However, they are limited in their capacity to simulate real activities and facilitate face-to-face interaction. Xerox, Massachusetts Mutual Life Insurance, and Ford have all reported tremendous success with these methods. In addition, most training programs rely on a mix of methods. Schneider Electric, for example, has dedicated in-person and online academies for managers and early-career employees in a range of topics and skills. They also offer in-person, extended reality, and online resources related to energy efficiency, electrical safety, sustainability, and data centers.[16]

Finally, some larger businesses have their own self-contained training facilities, often called *corporate universities*. McDonald's was among the first to start this practice with its so-called Hamburger University in Illinois. All management trainees for the firm attend training programs there to learn exactly how long to grill a burger, how to maintain good customer service, and so on. The popular hamburger chain In-N-Out Burger also has a similar training venue it calls In-N-Out University. Other firms that use this approach include Shell Oil and General Electric.[17]

Evaluation of Training Finally, the effectiveness of training and development programs should always be evaluated. Typical evaluation approaches include measuring one or more relevant criteria (such as attitudes or performance) before and after the training, and determining whether the criteria changed as a result of the training and development. Evaluation measures collected at the end of training are easy to get, but actual performance measures collected when the trainee is on the job are more important. Trainees may say that they enjoyed the training and learned a lot, but the true test is whether their job performance improves after their training.

Performance Appraisal

Performance Appraisal *evaluation of an employee's job performance to determine the degree to which the employee is performing effectively*

Once employees are trained and settled into their jobs, one of management's next concerns is performance appraisal.[18] **Performance appraisal** is a formal assessment of how well employees are doing their jobs. Employees' performance should be evaluated regularly for many reasons. One reason is that performance appraisal may be necessary for validating selection devices or assessing the impact of training programs. A second, administrative reason is to aid in making decisions about pay raises, promotions, and training. Still another reason is to provide feedback to employees to help them improve their current performance and plan their future careers.[19]

Because performance evaluations often help determine wages and promotions, they must be fair and nondiscriminatory. In the case of appraisals, managers use content validation to show that the appraisal system accurately measures performance on important job elements and does not measure traits or behaviors that are irrelevant to job performance.

Common Appraisal Methods Two basic categories of appraisal methods commonly used in some organizations are objective methods and judgmental methods. Objective measures of performance include actual output (number of units produced), scrap rate, dollar volume of sales, and number of claims processed. Objective performance measures may be contaminated by "opportunity bias" if some persons have a better chance to perform than others. For example, a sales representative selling snowblowers in Michigan has a greater opportunity to generate revenue than does a colleague selling the same product in Alabama. Fortunately, adjusting raw performance figures for the effect of opportunity bias and thereby arriving at figures that accurately represent each individual's performance is often possible.

Judgmental methods, including ranking and rating techniques, are the most common way to measure performance. Ranking compares employees directly with one another and orders them from best to worst. Ranking has a number of drawbacks. Ranking is difficult for large groups because the individuals in the middle of the distribution may be hard to distinguish from one another accurately. Comparisons of people in different work groups are also difficult. For example, an employee ranked third in a high-performing group may be more valuable and performing at a higher level than an employee ranked first in a lower-performing group. Another criticism of ranking is that the manager must rank people on the basis of overall performance, even though each person likely has both strengths and weaknesses. Furthermore, rankings do not provide useful information for feedback. To be told that one is ranked third is not nearly as helpful as to be told that the quality of one's work is outstanding, its quantity is satisfactory, one's punctuality could use improvement, or one's interpersonal skills are excellent.

Rating differs from ranking in that it compares each employee with a fixed standard rather than with other employees. A rating scale provides the standard. Figure 10.2 gives examples of graphic rating scales for a bank teller. Each consists of a performance dimension to be rated (punctuality, congeniality, and accuracy), followed by a scale on which to make the rating. In constructing graphic rating scales, performance dimensions that are relevant to job performance must be selected. In particular, they should focus on job behaviors and results rather than on personality traits or attitudes.

Errors in Performance Appraisal Errors or biases can occur in any kind of rating or ranking system.[20] One common problem is *recency error*, the tendency to base judgments on the subordinate's most recent performance because it is most easily recalled. Often a rating or ranking is intended to evaluate performance over an entire time period, such as 6 months or a year, so the recency error does introduce error into the judgment. Other errors include overuse of one part of the scale—being too lenient, being too severe, or giving everyone a rating of "average."

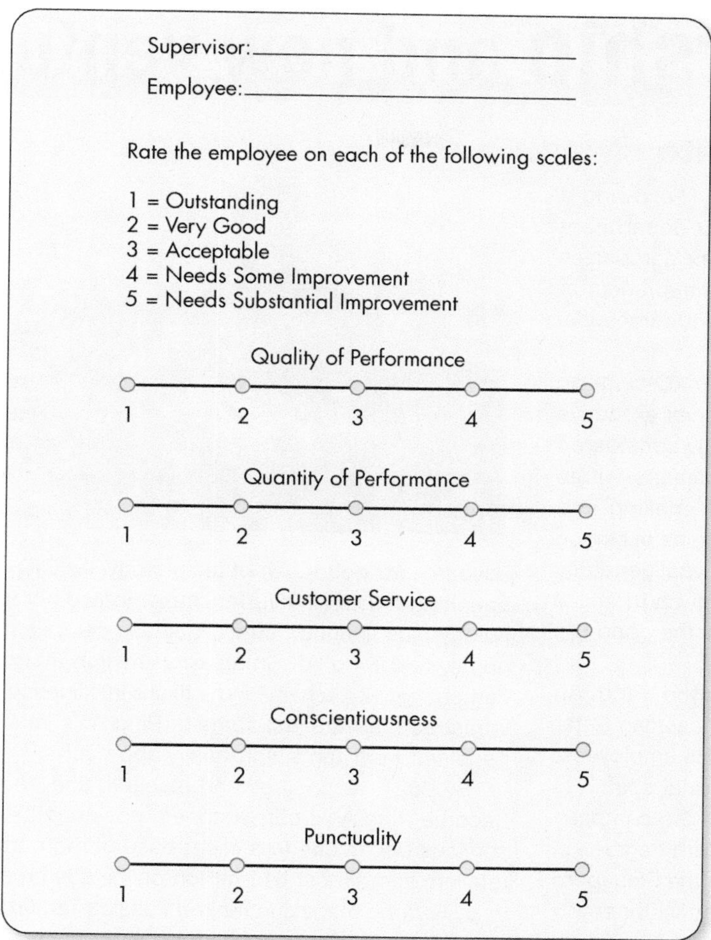
Supervisor:______________________

Employee:______________________

Rate the employee on each of the following scales:

1 = Outstanding
2 = Very Good
3 = Acceptable
4 = Needs Some Improvement
5 = Needs Substantial Improvement

Quality of Performance

1 2 3 4 5

Quantity of Performance

1 2 3 4 5

Customer Service

1 2 3 4 5

Conscientiousness

1 2 3 4 5

Punctuality

1 2 3 4 5

FIGURE 10.2 Sample Performance Evaluation Form

Halo error is allowing the assessment of an employee on one dimension to "spread" to ratings of that employee on other dimensions. For instance, if an employee is outstanding on quality of output, a rater might tend to give that employee higher marks than deserved on other dimensions. Errors can also occur because of race, sex, or age discrimination, intentionally or unintentionally. The best way to offset these errors is to ensure that a valid rating system is developed at the outset and then to train managers in how to use it.

One interesting approach to performance appraisal used in some organizations today is called **360-degree feedback**, in which managers are evaluated by everyone around them—their boss, their peers, and their subordinates. Such a complete and thorough approach provides people with a far richer array of information about their performance than does a conventional appraisal given by just the boss. Of course, such a system also takes considerable time and must be handled so as not to breed fear and mistrust in the workplace.[21]

360-Degree Feedback *performance appraisal technique in which managers are evaluated by everyone around them—their boss, their peers, and their subordinates*

Performance Feedback The last step in most performance appraisal systems is giving feedback to subordinates about their performances. This is usually done in a private meeting between the person being evaluated and their boss. The discussion should generally be focused on the facts: the assessed level of performance, how and why that assessment was made, and how it can be improved in the future. Feedback interviews are not easy to conduct, however. Many managers are uncomfortable with providing candid feedback, especially if the feedback is negative and subordinates are disappointed by what they hear. Properly training managers, however, can help them conduct more effective feedback interviews.[25]

entrepreneurship and new ventures

Entrepreneurs in the C-Suite

In a 2023 *Forbes* article, Tonika Bruce wrote, "Following a traditional structure where innovation or R&D department heads report to a vice president isn't enough for companies seeking reinvention and innovation. Hiring an entrepreneur at the C-suite level can bring in a needed dose of entrepreneurial leadership."[22]

Historically, businesspeople use the term *C-suite* to describe high-ranking executives such as the chief executive officer (CEO) and chief financial officer (CFO), considered among the most powerful and influential positions within an organization, at the vanguard of decision making and strategizing. For many years, there was a certain type of person who occupied those positions. The profile was generally middle-aged men with advanced degrees who had familial or fraternal connections. In other words, it was the good old boys' club.

However, as founder and chairman of the Ping An Insurance Company of China, Shenzhen businessman Peter Ma Mingzhe wasn't looking for traditional C-suite employees. He wanted to find people with an entrepreneurial spirit. He saw a need for innovation in the organization if the company was to continue to thrive. Enter Jessica Tan. With degrees in electrical engineering and economics from MIT, the Singapore native joined the international consulting firm McKinsey & Company in 2000. There, she worked with clients from all over the world to increase the use of cutting-edge technology in their operations. One of those clients was Ping An.

Ping An rose from an entrepreneurial idea when Peter Ma founded the company in 1988 as China's first joint-stock insurance company. The name Ping An translates as *safety*, but the company's exponential growth was anything but safe. By 1992, the company had become a national insurance company, and in 1994, it expanded into life insurance and became the first Chinese financial institution to allow foreign investors. In 2003, the company acquired Fujian Asia Bank and then in 2006 the Shenzhen Commercial Bank. In 2012, the company established Lufax, a wealth management platform, and it hired Tan in 2013.

Tan's journey with the company began with the role of Ping An's chief information officer (CIO), a position she used to advocate for better use of technology. As CIO and later chief operating officer (COO), Tan implemented her vision of "technology plus finance." Lufax, Chinese car sales website Autohome, and Ping An Smart City—which incorporates cloud computing, blockchain, and artificial intelligence into traditional infrastructure—are just some of Ping An's ventures that have benefited from Tan's tech-heavy approach.

Southworks/Shutterstock

By 2021, technology and research and development had become Ping An's cornerstones, powering its retail financial services operations to a client base of more than 220 million retailers and almost 611 million online customers. That same year, *Fortune* magazine ranked Jessica Tan sixth on its list of the World's 50 Greatest Leaders.

Jessica Tan brings more than just technological innovation to her role. In a country where the gender pay gap is increasing rather than shrinking and in an industry infamous for excluding women, Tan spearheaded Ping An's Life's Talent Program as a gateway for high-potential women to enter the insurance industry. Ping An's Mother's Needlework charity, which encourages women from the Yi ethnic group to create and sell handcrafted goods, has recently been extended from China into Cambodia. By 2023, almost 50 percent of Ping An's employees were women, and more than three-quarters of Ping An Life's senior business directors were women.[23]

Tan attributes Ping An's success to its entrepreneurial culture: "The whole company is very aggressive, very innovative, always thinking about what's next to ensure that we continue to grow."[24]

Because traditional performance appraisal methods and approaches to performance feedback are often criticized and are subject to numerous flaws and shortcomings, managers have started looking for alternative methods for assessing performance. One of the most promising newer methods is what is known as the "check-in" approach. Rather than conducting formal reviews on an annual basis and using a very structured methodology, which is the traditional method, the check-in method involves managers and their direct reports having regularly scheduled "conversations" in which the primary goal is to provide feedback on both how the subordinate is doing and what she or he may need to do to improve. These conversations occur as often as monthly but at least once per quarter. The outcomes are also documented for future reference.

New Challenges in the Changing Workplace

Learning Objective 10-6

Discuss workforce diversity, the management of knowledge workers, and the use of a contingent workforce as important changes in the contemporary workplace.

In addition to the challenges we have already considered, HR managers face several new challenges reflecting the changing economic and social environments of business.

Managing Workforce Diversity

One extremely important set of HR challenges centers on **workforce diversity**, the range of workers' attitudes, values, beliefs, and behaviors that differ by sex and gender, race, age, ethnicity, physical ability, and other relevant characteristics. In the past, organizations tended to work toward homogenizing their workforces, getting everyone to think and behave in similar ways. Partly as a result of affirmative action efforts, however, many U.S. organizations are now creating more diverse workforces than ever before.

Workforce Diversity *the range of workers' attitudes, values, beliefs, and behaviors that differ by gender, race, age, ethnicity, physical ability, and other relevant characteristics*

Figure 10.3 shows recent trends in age and ethnic composition of the U.S. workforce. The picture is clearly one of increasing diversity. The number of white Americans as a percentage of the total workforce is declining steadily, offset by increases in every other racial group. Most striking are the growing numbers of people of Hispanic origin (who may be members of any racial group). The U.S. Department of Labor estimates that by 2050 nearly a quarter of the workforce will be Hispanic.

Today, organizations are recognizing that diversity can be a competitive advantage. For example, by hiring the best people available from every single group rather than hiring from just one or a few groups, a firm can develop a higher-quality labor force. Similarly, a diverse workforce can bring a wider array of information to bear on problems and can provide insights on marketing products to a wider range of consumers.

Managing Knowledge Workers

Traditionally, employees added value to organizations because of what they did or because of their experience. In the information age, however, employees who add value because of what they know are usually called **knowledge workers**. Knowledge workers, which include computer scientists, engineers, physical scientists, game developers, and software application designers, typically require extensive and highly specialized training. Once they are on the job, retraining and training updates are critical to prevent their skills from becoming obsolete. It has been suggested, for example, that the half-life of a technical education in engineering is about three years.

Knowledge Workers *employees who are of value because of the knowledge they possess*

A firm's failure to update the skills of its knowledge workers not only results in the loss of competitive advantage but also increases the likelihood that those workers will go to other firms that are more committed to updating their skills. Hence, HR managers must ensure that the proper training is prepared to enable knowledge workers to stay current while also making sure they are compensated at market rates.

A major part of this challenge is recruiting new knowledge workers on a regular basis. Given both the high demand for knowledge workers and their relative short supply, firms often resort to extreme measures to recruit the best and brightest. For example, Google, Facebook, and Zynga often compete head-to-head for programmers and software engineers. To help recruit knowledge workers, these firms offer such lavish perks as free massages, laundry services, gourmet meals and snacks, and premium coffee beverages.[26]

Contingent and Temporary Workers

A final contemporary HR issue of note involves the growing use of contingent and temporary workers. Many employers use contingent and temporary workers to increase their flexibility and, in most cases, lower their costs.

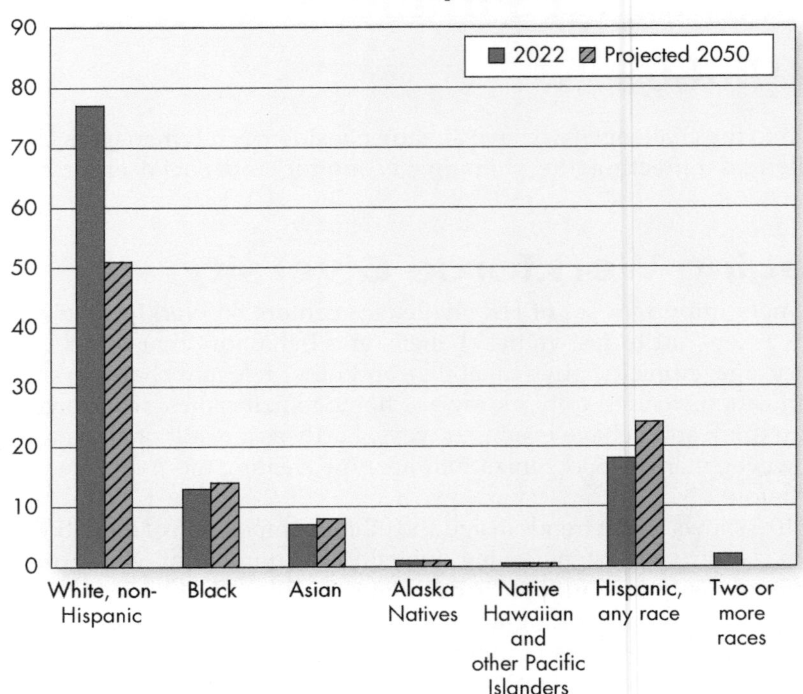

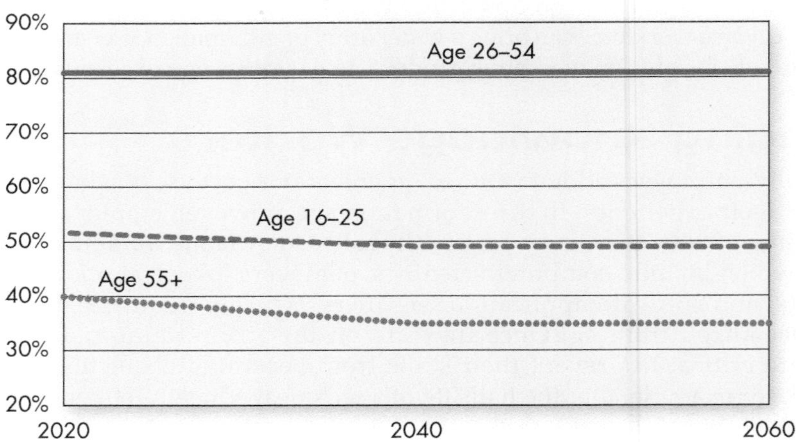

FIGURE 10.3 Changing Composition of the U.S. Labor Force by Ethnicity and Age

Notes: Percentages do not equal 100 percent because respondents may identify as more than one category; projected 2050 data for two or more races unavailable.

Sources: Bureau of Labor Statistics, https://www.bls.gov/opub/reports/race-and-ethnicity/2021/home.htm and https://www.bls.gov/web/empsit/cpseea08b.htm (accessed May 15, 2023); Diversity Resources. https://www.diversityresources.com/projected-composition-of-the-american-workforce/ https://www.bls.gov/cps/cpsaat18.htm (accessed May 15, 2023); Bureau of Labor Statistics. https://www.bls.gov/cps/cpsaat18.htm (accessed May 15, 2023).

Contingent Worker *employee hired on something other than a full-time basis to supplement an organization's permanent workforce*

Trends in Contingent and Temporary Employment A **contingent worker** is a person who works for an organization on something other than a permanent or full-time basis. Categories of contingent workers include independent contractors, on-call workers, temporary employees (usually hired through outside agencies), and contract and leased employees. Another category is part-time workers. In recent years, there has been an explosion in the use of such workers by organizations.

For instance, in 2022, around 41 percent of employed U.S. workers fell into one of these categories, up from 20 percent in 2017.

Managing Contingent and Temporary Workers One key to managing contingent workers effectively is careful planning and analysis. Rather than having to call in workers sporadically, and with no prior notice, organizations try to bring in specified numbers of workers for well-defined periods of time. For instance, most retailers hire temporary seasonal employees for the Christmas holiday shopping period. On the basis of their past experience, they generally know how many people they need to hire and when they need to hire them. Firms should also be able to document the labor-cost savings of using contingent workers.

A second key is recognizing what can and cannot be achieved by using contingent and temporary workers. For instance, these workers may lack the firm-specific knowledge to perform as effectively as a permanent employee would perform.

managing in turbulent times

Union Busting

Employees at an Augusta, Maine, Chipotle Mexican Grill had been complaining to management about understaffing for some time before they walked off the job and locked the restaurant doors in June 2022. Their concerns were not just about compensation; understaffing led to serious safety concerns not only for employees who were working with potentially dangerous equipment but also for customers who were being served food that had been out on steam tables too long or prepared in a kitchen that hadn't been cleaned properly. Employees were regularly opening and closing the restaurant and completing prep work at roughly 30 percent of required staffing levels.

In a letter sent to Chipotle management and signed by 10 employees of the location, workers asked for immediate attention to address the expectations of management, which they claimed were "not only unreasonable demands, but they put the crew and the community at risk."[27] The group of employees noted that training was incomplete or entirely missing, employees were expected to routinely work 60 hours per week, and the continuing strain on staff resulted in high turnover and poor morale.

Workers returned to their jobs within a couple of days but continued efforts to unionize, filing a petition that same month. They hoped that a collective bargaining agreement would bring some accountability to ensure adequate staffing, competitive pay, and safe working conditions. Less than a month later, however, that Chipotle location was shuttered, closing for good. The company cited "staffing issues" but publicly supported its employees' legal right to unionize.

In March 2023, following a decision by the National Labor Relations Board, Chipotle Mexican Grill paid out $240,000 to workers from that location. The NLRB ruled that the closure was retaliation for unionization efforts and that, further, the company blacklisted specific employees, preventing them from obtaining work at any other Chipotle location. Chipotle denies any wrongdoing. As of mid-2023, only one Chipotle restaurant nationwide had successfully unionized.

Chipotle is not the only national chain in hot water with the NLRB. Amazon and Starbucks have both been found breaking anti-labor unionization laws. Though their actions were clearly illegal, the NLRB found that the coffee and retail industry giants had done things like send anti-union text messages to personal phones, remove publicly posted union information and notices, and fire pro-union employees without cause.[28]

Traditional career trajectories and benefits have changed dramatically in the past 50 years, with a greater share of workers holding part-time or retail positions rather than long-term manufacturing or white-collar jobs with union protection and guaranteed retirement benefits. Workers have sought the protection of unions for wages, safety, hours, and other working conditions that have long been ignored, especially for lower-wage workers and people of color.

The Bureau of Labor Statistics reports that between October 2021 and September 2022, the NLRB saw a 53 percent increase in union petitions, and data suggests that over 60 million workers wanted to start a job in that same time frame but couldn't. As the job market continues to polarize, the increasing disparity in pay and working conditions between CEOs and direct service workers drives a renewed interest in union membership.[29]

Meanwhile, laws that protect corporations and their revenue generation have resulted in a nearly toothless agency with little power to hold them accountable. Funding has remained the same at the National Labor Relations Board for nearly 10 years. Adjustments for inflation mean over a 25 percent funding cut and critical staff shortages—overall staffing levels have decreased by 25 percent, and field staffing has dropped by 50 percent.[30]

Companies—especially those under increased public scrutiny—will continue to grapple with the balance of maximizing profit and attracting and retaining an adequate workforce.

They are also less committed to the organization and less likely to engage in organizational citizenship behaviors.

Finally, managers must make decisions about how to integrate contingent workers into the organization. These decisions may be as simple as whether to invite contingent workers to the holiday party, or they may be more complicated, such as whether to grant contingent workers access to such employee benefits as counseling services and child care.

Learning Objective 10-7

Explain why workers organize into labor unions and describe the collective bargaining process.

Dealing with Organized Labor

A **labor union** is a group of individuals working together to achieve shared job-related goals, such as higher pay, shorter working hours, more job security, better benefits, or improved working conditions. **Labor relations** refers to the process of dealing with a group of employees who are represented by a union.

Labor Union *group of individuals working together to achieve shared job-related goals, such as higher pay, shorter working hours, more job security, greater benefits, or better working conditions*

Labor Relations *process of dealing with employees who are represented by a union*

Unionism Today

In the years immediately following World War II and continuing through the mid-1960s, most unions routinely won certification elections. In recent years, however, labor unions have been winning certification only about half the time.[31] As a result, although millions of workers still belong to unions, union membership as a percentage of the total workforce has steadily declined. In 2007, only 12.1 percent of U.S. workers belonged to a labor union, down from 20.1 percent in 1983, when the U.S. Department of Labor first began compiling data.[32] In general, membership tends to increase when workers worry about job security due to industry downturns, recessions, and so forth. In 2021, union membership was 10.31 percent. These trends are shown in Figure 10.4.

The Future of Unions Even though several of its members withdrew from the parent organization in 2005, the American Federation of Labor and Congress of Industrial Organizations (AFL-CIO), as well as independent major unions such as the Teamsters and the National Education Association (NEA), still play a major role in U.S. business. Unions in the traditional strongholds of goods-producing industries continue to wield considerable power as well. The United Auto Workers (UAW) was for decades one of the largest unions in the United States. But it, too, seems to be entering a period of decline. The traumas experienced by the U.S. auto industry in 2008–2009, for instance, required the UAW to make many major concessions to help Ford, DaimlerChrysler (now Daimler AG), and General Motors survive. In addition, auto plant closures will dramatically reduce the number of auto jobs in the years to come.

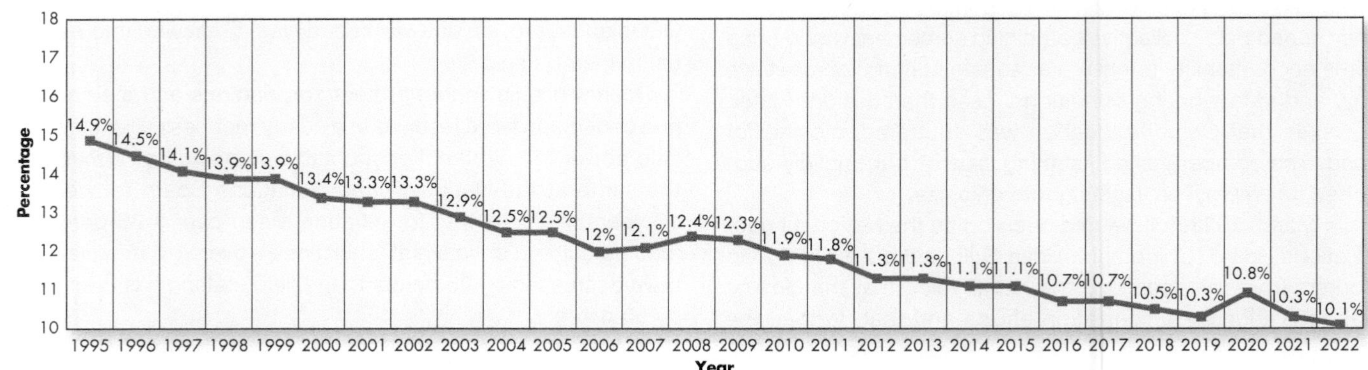

FIGURE 10.4 Percentage of Workers Who Belong to Unions: 1995–2021

Sources: U.S. Bureau of Labor Statistics, https://www.bls.gov/news.release/union2.htm, 2023; https://www.bls.gov/opub/ted/2019/union-membership-rate-10-point-5-percent-in-2018-down-from-20-point-1-percent-in-1983.htm?view_full; https://www.bls.gov/news.release/pdf/union2.pdf

Another issue affecting the future of unionism is the geographic shift in the U.S. economy. For the most part, unionism in the United States started in the Northeast and Midwest regions and in cities such as New York, Detroit, Pittsburgh, Cleveland, St. Louis, and Chicago. But over the past several decades, a pronounced shift has occurred as businesses have moved their operations to the South and Southwest, areas that do not have a strong union heritage. For instance, Nucor Corporation, the largest steel producer in the United States, locates its facilities in smaller communities in the southern United States in part because it knows these workers are not prone to unionization.

Collective Bargaining

The power of unions comes from collective action, forcing management to listen to the demands of all workers rather than to just the few who speak out. **Collective bargaining** is the process by which labor and management negotiate conditions of employment for union-represented workers and draft a labor contract.

Collective Bargaining *process by which labor and management negotiate conditions of employment for union-represented workers*

Reaching Agreement on Contract Terms The collective bargaining process begins when the union is recognized as the exclusive negotiator for its members and union leaders meet with management representatives to agree on a labor contract. By law, both parties must sit down at the bargaining table and negotiate in good faith. Figure 10.5 shows what is called the "bargaining zone." For instance, in theory, employers want to pay as little as possible; they will generally pay more than the minimum, but there is also some upper limit beyond which they will not pay. Likewise, unions want the highest pay possible but expect to get less. But they, too, have a limit beyond which they will not go.

For example, suppose the bargaining issue is pay increases. The employer may initially propose a pay increase of 2 percent but (secretly) be willing to offer up to 6 percent. However, under no circumstances can it afford to pay more than 8 percent. The union, meanwhile, may initially demand a 10 percent increase but (secretly) be willing to accept as little as 4 percent. Assuming each party negotiates in good faith and is willing to make concessions to the other, the real bargaining zone falls between the union minimum (4 percent) and the employer maximum (6 percent). The real outcome will then depend on such things as other items being negotiated and the skills of the respective negotiators.

Sometimes, this process goes quite smoothly. At other times, the two sides cannot agree. For instance, the preceding example should result in an agreement because the union minimum and the employer maximum provide a bargaining zone. But if the union demands no less than 8 percent and the employer is unwilling to give more

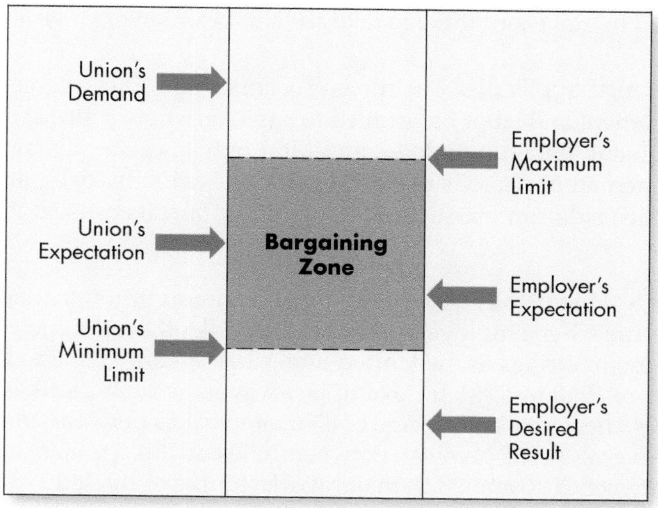

Union's Demand
Employer's Maximum Limit
Union's Expectation
Bargaining Zone
Employer's Expectation
Union's Minimum Limit
Employer's Desired Result

FIGURE 10.5 The Bargaining Zone

than a 4 percent increase, there is no bargaining zone. Resolving the impasse depends in part on the nature of the contract issues, the willingness of each side to use certain tactics, such as strikes, and the prospects for mediation or arbitration.

Contract Issues The labor contract itself can address an array of different issues. Issues that are typically most important to union negotiators include *compensation, benefits*, and *job security*. Certain management rights, such as control over hiring policies and work assignments, are also negotiated in most bargaining agreements. Other possible issues might include such specific details as working hours, overtime policies, rest period arrangements, differential pay plans for shift employees, the use of temporary workers, grievance procedures, and allowable union activities (dues collection, union bulletin boards, and so forth).

Cost-of-Living Adjustment (COLA) *labor contract clause tying future raises to changes in consumer purchasing power*

Wage Reopener Clause *clause allowing wage rates to be renegotiated during the life of the contract*

COMPENSATION Compensation includes both current and future wages. One common tool for securing wage increases is a **cost-of-living adjustment (COLA)**. Most COLA clauses tie future raises to the *consumer price index (CPI)*, a government statistic that reflects changes in consumer purchasing power. Almost half of all labor contracts today include COLA clauses.

A union might be uncomfortable with a long-term contract based solely on COLA wage increases. One solution is a **wage reopener clause**, which allows wage rates to be renegotiated at preset times during the life of the contract.

BENEFITS Employee benefits are also an important component in most labor contracts. Unions typically want employers to pay all or most of the costs of insurance for employees. Other benefits commonly addressed during negotiations include retirement benefits, paid holidays, and working conditions. Because of surging health care costs, employee health insurance premiums have become a major point of contention in recent years. For example, many employees have much larger co-pays today when they visit their doctor than was the case a few years ago. (A *co-pay* is the dollar amount a patient pays to the doctor; insurance then pays the remainder.) Some companies reserve the right to deny coverage of an employer's spouse if that person has access to health insurance through their own employer.

JOB SECURITY Job security also remains an important agenda item in many bargaining sessions today. Unions have historically fought for the use of seniority to determine who is retained in the event that job cuts are necessary. Employers, meanwhile, may object to this position because newer workers generally earn lower wages.

Unions have also focused their efforts on preserving jobs for workers in the United States in the face of business efforts to outsource production in some sectors to countries where labor costs are cheaper. For example, the AFL-CIO has been an outspoken opponent of efforts to normalize trade relations with China, fearing that more businesses might be tempted to move jobs there to take advantage of lower wage levels.

When Bargaining Fails An impasse occurs when, after a series of bargaining sessions, management and labor have failed to agree on a new contract or a contract to replace an agreement that is about to expire. Although it is generally agreed that both parties suffer when an impasse is reached and some action by one party against the other is taken, each side can use several tactics to support its cause until the impasse is resolved.

Strike *labor action in which employees temporarily walk off the job and refuse to work*

UNION TACTICS Historically, one of the most common union tactics has been the **strike**, which occurs when employees temporarily walk off the job and refuse to work. The number of major strikes in the United States has steadily declined over the past few decades. From 1960 to 1980, for example, an average of 281 strikes occurred per year. In the 1980s, there was an average of 83 major strikes per year; in the 1990s, this figure fell to an average of 35 per year. Between 2000 and 2010, major strikes averaged 20 per year.[33] Between 2010 and 2021, major work stoppages totaled 178, an average of 15 per year. In 2019, the United Auto Workers (UAW) went on strike against General

Jim West/Alamy Stock Photo

Unions sometimes resort to strikes as leverage as a way to extract better pay and benefits from employers. These UPS workers, represented by the Teamsters union, are picketing in order to publicize their stance during contract negotiations.

Motors for several weeks. The UAW's goals for the strike included increased job security and a clearer path for temporary workers to transition to permanent status. In 2023, the Writers Guild of America went on strike against the Alliance of Motion Picture and Television Producers. The major issue in this strike was residual income for writers from streaming revenues. And also in 2023 the United Auto Workers struck all three major U.S. automakers demanding higher wages and a shortened work week, among several other things.

To support a strike, a union faced with an impasse has recourse to additional legal activities:

- In **picketing**, workers march in front of the employer's facility with signs explaining their reasons for striking.
- A **boycott** occurs when union members agree not to buy the products of a targeted employer. Workers may also urge consumers to boycott the firm's products.
- Another alternative to striking is a **work slowdown**. Instead of striking, workers perform their jobs at a much slower pace than normal. A variation is the *sickout*, during which large numbers of workers call in sick.

Picketing *labor action in which workers publicize their grievances at the entrance to an employer's facility*

Boycott *labor action in which workers refuse to buy the products of a targeted employer*

Work Slowdown *labor action in which workers perform jobs at a slower than normal pace*

Management Tactics Like workers, management can respond forcefully to an impasse with the following:

- **Lockouts** occur when employers deny employees access to the workplace. Lockouts are illegal if they are used as offensive weapons to give management a bargaining advantage. However, they are legal if management has a legitimate business need (for instance, avoiding a buildup of perishable inventory). When Major League Baseball failed to reach a new contract agreement with its players association in 2022, the league owners imposed a lockout until an agreement was reached. In 2023, nurses at Ascension Seton Medical Center in Austin, Texas, returned to work after a one-day strike to discover they had been locked out of the facility as negotiations continued.
- A firm can also hire temporary or permanent replacements called **strikebreakers**. However, the law forbids the permanent replacement of workers who strike because of unfair practices. In some cases, an employer can obtain legal injunctions that either prohibit workers from striking or prohibit a union from interfering with its efforts to use replacement workers.

Lockout *management tactic whereby workers are denied access to the employer's workplace*

Strikebreaker *worker hired as a permanent or temporary replacement for a striking employee*

Mediation and Arbitration Rather than wield these often unpleasant weapons against one another, labor and management can agree to call in a third party to help resolve the dispute.

Mediation *method of resolving a labor dispute in which a third party suggests but does not impose a settlement*

Arbitration *method of resolving a labor dispute in which both parties agree to submit to the judgment of a neutral party*

In **mediation**, the neutral third party (the mediator) can suggest but cannot impose a settlement on the other parties.

In **arbitration**, the neutral third party (the arbitrator) dictates a settlement between the two sides, which have agreed to submit to outside judgment. In some disputes, such as those between the government and public employees, arbitration is compulsory, or required by law.

Managing an organization's HR is both a complex and an important undertaking. Most businesses can buy the same equipment and use the same technology as their competitors. But differences in employee talent and motivation are not easily copied. Consequently, most well-managed companies today recognize the value provided by their employees and strive to ensure that the HR function is managed as efficiently and effectively as possible.

summary of learning objectives

LEARNING OBJECTIVE 10-1

Define *human resource management*, discuss its strategic significance, and explain how managers plan for their organization's human resource needs.

Human resource management (*HRM*) is the set of organizational activities directed at attracting, developing, and maintaining an effective workforce. *Human resources (HR)* are critical for effective organizational functioning. HRM was once relegated to second-class status in many organizations, but its importance has grown dramatically in the past two decades. Its new importance stems from increased legal complexities, the recognition that human resources are a valuable means for improving productivity, and the awareness today of the costs associated with poor HRM. *Human capital* reflects the organization's investment in attracting, retaining, and motivating an effective workforce. Hence, just as the phrase *financial capital* is an indicator of a firm's financial resources and reserves, so, too, does human capital serve as a tangible indicator of the value of the people who compose an organization.

Job analysis is a systematic analysis of jobs within an organization, resulting in two things: a *job description* and a *job specification*. A job description lists the duties and responsibilities of a job, whereas a job specification identifies the skills, abilities, and qualifications needed to perform the job. Managers must plan for future HR needs by assessing past trends, future plans, and general economic trends. Forecasting labor supply is really two tasks: (1) *forecasting internal supply* and (2) *forecasting external supply*. To analyze internal supply, HR managers often develop *employee information systems* (or skills inventories). The next step in HR planning is matching HR supply and demand.

LEARNING OBJECTIVE 10-2

Discuss the legal context of human resource management and identify contemporary legal issues.

A number of laws regulate various aspects of employee–employer relations, especially in the areas of equal employment opportunity, compensation and benefits, labor relations, and occupational safety and health. *Title VII of the Civil Rights Act of 1964* forbids discrimination in all areas of the employment relationship, such as hiring, opportunities for advancement, compensation increases, layoffs, and terminations, against members of certain protected classes based on factors such as race, color, gender, religious beliefs, or national origin. In addition to enforcing rules against overt discrimination, the *Equal Employment Opportunity Commission (EEOC)* is also charged with evaluating employment requirements that have *adverse impact*.

Several other laws have expanded the scope of antidiscrimination law. The *Age Discrimination in Employment Act*, passed in 1967, amended in 1978, and amended again in 1986, is an attempt to prevent organizations from discriminating against older workers. The *Pregnancy Discrimination Act* forbids discrimination against women who are pregnant. The *Americans with Disabilities Act* forbids discrimination on the basis of disabilities and requires employers to provide reasonable accommodations for disabled employees. The *Civil Rights Act of 1991* amended the original Civil Rights Act as well as other related laws by both making it easier to bring discrimination lawsuits and simultaneously limiting the amount of punitive damages that can be awarded in those lawsuits.

Affirmative action was created through executive order and requires government contractors to make proactive attempts to recruit, hire, and promote employees from groups that are underrepresented in the organization.

The *Fair Labor Standards Act*, passed in 1938 and amended frequently since then, sets a minimum wage and requires the payment of overtime rates for work in excess of 40 hours per week. The *Equal Pay Act of 1963* requires that men and women be paid the same amount for doing the same job. Employers who provide a pension plan for their employees are regulated by the *Employee Retirement Income Security Act (ERISA) of 1974*. The *Family and Medical Leave Act (FMLA) of 1993* requires employers to provide up to 12 weeks of unpaid leave for family and medical emergencies.

The *National Labor Relations Act* (also known as the Wagner Act), passed in 1935, sets up a procedure for employees to vote on whether to have a union. The *Labor-Management Relations Act* (also known as the Taft-Hartley Act) was passed in 1947 to limit union power. Taken together, these laws balance union and management power. Employees can be represented by a legally created and managed union, but the business can make non-employee-related business decisions without interference.

The *Occupational Safety and Health Act (OSHA) of 1970* directly mandates the provision of safe working conditions. Under the Americans with Disabilities Act of 1990, AIDS is considered a disability, and employers cannot require an HIV test or any other medical examination as a condition of employment. Sexual harassment, both quid pro quo harassment and a hostile work environment, is forbidden under antidiscrimination law as well.

In general, employees work under the legal concept of *employment at will*, which gives both the employee and the employer the right to terminate an employment relationship at any time. However, this concept has been tested in the courts and limited in scope by a variety of legislative provisions.

LEARNING OBJECTIVE 10-3

Identify the steps in staffing a company and discuss ways in which organizations recruit and select new employees.

Staffing an organization means recruiting and hiring the right mix of people. *Recruiting* is the process of attracting qualified persons to apply for open jobs, either from within the organization or from outside the organization. To help prospective employees understand the job, some employers offer a *realistic job preview (RJP)*.

The next step is the *selection process*, gathering information that will predict applicants' job success and then hiring candidates. Common selection techniques include application forms; tests of ability, aptitude, or knowledge; and interviews.

LEARNING OBJECTIVE 10-4

Describe the main components of a compensation and benefits system.

A company's *compensation system* is the financial rewards given by the organization to its employees in exchange for their work. *Wages* are the hourly compensation paid to operating employees. *Salary* refers to compensation paid for total contributions, as opposed to pay based on hours worked. A good compensation system can help attract qualified applicants, retain present employees, and stimulate high performance at a cost reasonable for one's industry and geographic area.

Companies may also try to link compensation to performance through *incentive programs*. Individual incentive programs include *bonuses*, *merit salary systems*, and *variable pay*. Company-wide incentives include *profit sharing*, *gainsharing*, and *pay-for-knowledge plans*.

Benefits are things of value other than wages that the organization provides to its workers. Most employers are required to pay into Social Security on behalf of employees and to maintain workers' compensation insurance, protecting employees injured on the job. Many companies also provide health, life, and disability insurance. Other types of benefits include employee stock ownership plans, counseling services, on-site child care, and reduced-fee memberships at gyms and health clubs. Many companies provide retirement plans for their employees, although many are funded entirely by employee contributions. Companies that offer *cafeteria benefit plans* set aside a certain dollar amount per employee for benefits, allowing the employee to select the benefits most important to their individual situation.

LEARNING OBJECTIVE 10-5

Describe how managers develop the workforce in their organization through training and performance appraisal.

In HRM, *training* usually refers to teaching operational or technical employees how to do the job for which they were hired. *Development* refers to teaching managers and professionals the skills needed for both present and future jobs. Most organizations provide regular training and development programs for managers and employees. The first step in developing a training plan is to determine what needs exist. Many different training and development methods are available—assigned reading, programmed learning, lecture, role playing, case discussion groups, on-the-job training, vestibule training, web-based training, and other electronic media-based training. Training and development programs should always be evaluated for effectiveness.

Once employees are trained and settled into their jobs, one of management's next concerns is performance appraisal. *Performance appraisal* is a formal assessment of how well employees are doing their jobs. Because performance evaluations often help determine wages and promotions, they must be fair and nondiscriminatory. Two basic categories of appraisal methods commonly used in organizations are objective methods and judgmental methods. Objective measures of performance include actual output (number of units produced), scrap rate, dollar volume of sales, and number of claims processed. Judgmental methods, including ranking and rating techniques, are the most common way to measure performance. Ranking compares employees directly with one another and orders them from best to worst. Rating differs from ranking in that it compares each employee with a fixed standard rather than with other employees, with a rating scale providing the standard. Errors or biases can occur in any kind of rating or ranking system. One common problem is recency error—the tendency to base judgments on the subordinate's most recent performance because it is most easily recalled. Halo error is allowing the assessment of an employee on one dimension to "spread" to ratings of that employee on other dimensions. The last step in most performance appraisal systems is giving feedback to subordinates about their performance, usually done in a private meeting between the person being evaluated and their boss.

LEARNING OBJECTIVE 10-6

Discuss workforce diversity, the management of knowledge workers, and the use of a contingent workforce as important changes in the contemporary workplace.

Workforce diversity refers to the range of workers' attitudes, values, beliefs, and behaviors that differ by gender, race, age, ethnicity, physical ability, and other relevant characteristics. In the past, organizations tended to work toward homogenizing their workforces; however, many organizations are now realizing that diversity can be a competitive advantage.

Employees who add value because of what they know are usually called *knowledge workers*, and managing them skillfully helps determine which firms will be successful in the future. *Contingent workers*, including independent contractors, on-call workers, temporary employees, contract and leased employees, and part-time employees, work for organizations on something other than a permanent or full-time basis. Organizations must understand when it is appropriate to use contingent workers and how to integrate them into the organization.

LEARNING OBJECTIVE 10-7

Explain why workers organize into labor unions and describe the collective bargaining process.

Labor relations is the process of dealing with employees who are represented by a union. A *labor union* is a group of individuals working together to achieve shared job-related goals, such as higher pay, shorter working hours, more job security, greater benefits, or better working conditions. At one time, almost a third of the entire U.S. labor force belonged to a labor union, with the largest membership following World War II into the mid-1960s. Union membership fell from 20.1 percent of the workforce in 1983 to only 10.31 percent of the workforce in 2021.

The intent of *collective bargaining* is to agree on a labor contract between management and the union that is satisfactory to both parties. The contract contains agreements about such issues as wages, work hours, job security, promotion, layoffs, discipline, benefits, methods of allocating overtime, vacations, rest periods, and the grievance procedure. Sometimes, the process of collective bargaining goes quite smoothly, and management and the union agree to the terms of a new contract. However, when bargaining fails, the union has the option to go on *strike*, *picket* the organization, organize a *boycott*, or implement a *work slowdown*. Management has options as well; it may *lock out* employees until an agreement has been reached or hire *strikebreakers*. Rather than wielding these weapons, labor and management can agree to call in a third party, either a *mediator* or *arbitrator*, to help resolve the dispute.

key terms

questions & exercises

QUESTIONS FOR REVIEW

10-1. What are some of the strategic considerations in human resource management?

10-2. Why is the formal training of workers so important to most employers? Why don't employers simply let people learn about their jobs as they perform them?

10-3. What benefits do firms typically use to attract and keep productive workers? What are some of the less traditional benefits that firms are using?

10-4. What is a knowledge worker? What strategies do companies use to retain knowledge workers?

QUESTIONS FOR ANALYSIS

10-5. What are some significant legal issues with regard to recruiting, hiring, and managing employees?

10-6. What are your views and feelings about collective bargaining? What reasons can you give for your opinions?

10-7. What are the advantages and challenges of recruiting a diverse workforce?

10-8. How much will benefit considerations affect your choice of an employer after graduation? What types of benefits would be most and least appealing to you, and why?

APPLICATION EXERCISES

10-9. Go online and search for at least three companies that are considered great places to work. Describe the compensation, benefits, and perks at each of these companies. Of the three companies you chose, which is most appealing to you, and why? Which is the least appealing, and why?

10-10. Interview someone familiar with a company's current hiring processes. Briefly outline how the company recruits employees to apply for jobs, the steps in the selection process, and the orientation program for new employees. Relate your notes back to the topics and learning objectives in this chapter.

building a business: continuing team exercise

ASSIGNMENT

Meet with your team members to consider your new business venture and how it relates to the concepts of HRM discussed in this chapter. Develop specific responses to the following:

10-11. As your new venture grows, you will need to hire employees. How will you recruit people to apply for jobs within your organization?

10-12. Ideally, you will be able to select from many applicants for jobs within your company. How will you select the best employee from the pool of applicants?

10-13. How will employees be compensated in your company? How do you think that this compensation system will reflect your company's mission and goals?

10-14. What types of benefits will you offer to employees? In view of the high cost of benefits, how have you selected these benefits?

10-15. Describe your system for performance appraisal and training. How will you reward good employees? When you have weak employees, how will you change their behavior?

team exercise

THE DOWNSIDE OF DOWNSIZING

The Situation

A moderate-sized consulting company is going through tough times after losing a major contract. As a result, the leadership team is asking managers to make two budget cut proposals for their departments: a 15 percent budget cut that will likely be implemented and a 30 percent cut that may be implemented depending on the big picture. One of the managers has come to you for advice. She is new to her position and has little experience to draw from. However, it is obvious to her that 90 percent of her budget is personnel and the other 10 percent is overhead and other fixed costs that really can't be cut in the short term. To achieve a 15 percent cut she will need to lay off one employee; to achieve 30 percent 2 employees will be laid-off. The members of her team are as follows:

- Tony Jones: white male; 10 years with the company; has been turning in above-average performance ratings from his annual reviews for the past two years, even though his actual performance has been suffering due to a divorce and other personal issues, including showing up late for work and calling in sick several times a month.
- Amanda Wiggens: white female; ambitious; three years with the company; above-average performer; puts in extra time at work; some of her subordinates have complained

about her directness and lack of tact and have even reported angry outbursts; you have informally counseled her in interpersonal communications skills.

- Jorge Gonzalez: Hispanic male; two years with the company; speaks fluent Spanish, has great connections in the Latino business community, and has brought in several new clients during the past year; you have rated his work as average due to lack of English communication skills and tardiness.
- Taylor Henderson: white female, 25 years with the company; average performer; filed a sexual harassment complaint against a different member of the leadership team last year, which is now in mediation; she is a friend of the company president and is the first person most people talk to when they call the company; she has an immense amount of institutional knowledge and memory, but she comes across as a bit curt on the phone.
- Wanda Jackson: African American female; eight years with the company; during formal performance reviews, you have rated her as outstanding for the past three years; Taylor Henderson mentioned on promise of anonymity that Jackson was looking for another job and had in fact applied for one with a competing firm; Wanda often works late, even though she is a salaried employee and does not get overtime pay.
- Jerry Loudder: white male; single parent; five years with the company; gets his work done but has not brought in any new clients and goes home right at five; Jerry has a lot of experience and even though he does not work late, he always hits the deadlines and his work quality is excellent; he often mentors the younger members of the group.
- Martha Strawser: white female; one year with the company; she is putting her husband through college and appears to have much promise—in fact, some members of the leadership team have mentioned that she may be vice presidential material once she gains some experience; she holds an MBA and is outgoing and well connected in the business community.

Team Activity

Assemble a group of four students. Your group has agreed to provide the manager with a recommendation.

ACTION STEPS

10-16. As a group, discuss the underlying legal and ethical issues in this situation. What laws must be considered before making this decision?

10-17. Working individually, prioritize the layoff list. Make notes about your reasoning for each potential layoff.

10-18. Have all team members discuss their recommendation with the group, justifying their decision on the basis of both ethical and legal considerations.

10-19. Develop a group recommendation for both the 15 percent scenario and the 30 percent scenario.

10-20. Now that you have decided which employee to lay off first, develop a set of recommendations on how layoffs should be handled. Be sure to consider how to communicate your decision to the employee being laid off as well as those who remain.

exercising your ethics

OPERATING TACTICALLY

The Situation

Assume that you work as a manager for a medium-sized company that is facing a serious union-organizing campaign. Your boss, who is determined to keep the union out of the workplace, has just given you a list of things to do to thwart the efforts of the organizers. For example, he has suggested each of the following tactics:

- Whenever you learn about a scheduled union meeting, you should schedule a "worker appreciation" event at the same time. He wants you to offer free pizza and to give cash prizes that winners must be present to receive.
- He wants you to look at the most recent performance evaluations of the key union organizers and supporters and to terminate the one with the lowest overall evaluation based on the "need to lower costs."
- He wants you to announce that the firm is seriously considering such new benefits as on-site childcare, flexible work schedules, telecommuting options, and exercise facilities. Although you know that the firm is indeed looking into these benefits, you also know that, ultimately, your boss will provide far less lavish benefits than he wants you to suggest.

The Dilemma

When you questioned the ethics—and even the legality—of these tactics, your boss explained that he was seriously concerned that a union victory might actually shut down the company's domestic operations altogether, forcing it to move all production capacities to lower-cost foreign plants. He concluded by saying that he was really looking out for the employees, even if he had to play hardball to help them.

QUESTIONS TO ADDRESS

10-21. What are the ethical issues in this situation?

10-22. What are the basic arguments for and against extreme measures to fight unionization efforts?

10-23. What do you think most managers would do in this situation? What would you do?

cases

A UNIQUE PARTNERSHIP DRIVES WEGMANS

Continued from page 309

At the beginning of this chapter, you read about Wegmans and its approach to human resource management. Using the information presented in this chapter, you should now be able to respond to these questions.

QUESTIONS FOR DISCUSSION

10-24. If you were an HR executive at Wegmans, would you focus more on *internal recruiting* or on *external recruiting*? Would your strategy for higher-level positions differ from your strategy for lower-level positions? How would current economic conditions influence your strategy?

10-25. As an HR executive at Wegmans, you need to hire a group of new employees as part of your management-trainee program—people who will be put on a track leading, ultimately, to positions as store managers. Briefly outline your program for developing these employees.

10-26. If you were an employee at Wegmans, how would you expect your annual performance appraisal to be conducted? Given the company's customer-relations strategy, which appraisal methods do you think would be most appropriate?

FINDING THE WORK–LIFE BALANCE

SAS Institute is a private tech company headquartered in Cary, North Carolina, that has more than 6,000 employees in the United States and twice that many worldwide. Like most great companies, SAS pays its employees well. This is important—as a company that helps businesses turn raw data into useful information, their employees are at the core of their success. However, SAS also places a very high value on work–life balance. SAS has a company-wide standard that employees don't work more than 37.5 hours per week. Of course, at times employees need to put in extra hours, but they are encouraged to take time off soon afterward to recharge. Each employee has a private office (no cubicles or shared workspaces) and is able to take advantage of the on-site subsidized hair and nail salons, shoe and jewelry repair shops, and dry-cleaning and tailoring services. Many services are provided for free on-site, such as tax preparation and a health clinic and pharmacy. The company even offers a seasonal farmers market right at Cary headquarters.

SAS Institute is an ideal employer for those with families. Employees' children are welcomed at work, both at the subsidized on-site daycare center and in the cafeteria, which includes kid-friendly items such as octopus-shaped hot dogs on the menu. Employees with school-aged children are encouraged to bring their kids to work with them on the occasional teacher workdays, making the balancing act of parenting and working a little easier. In a recent survey, one employee put it this way: "SAS has provisions to support you at whatever stage of life you are in—child care for your newborn to preschooler, resources for dealing with your teenager and college planning, help with your elderly parent. More importantly, a real sense of community is built when people work together for so long."

Founder and CEO Jim Goodnight believes that it's essential for employees to feel trusted and valued. By almost every metric, this has paid off. In the software industry, turnover tends to be about 20 percent per year, as employees hop from one job to the next in hopes of higher pay or better working conditions. This is not the case at SAS, where turnover is 5 to 8 percent. In a recent survey, more than 95 percent of employees rated SAS as an employer with great challenges, great atmosphere, great rewards, and even great bosses.

QUESTIONS FOR DISCUSSION

10-27. After reading about SAS Institute, what would appeal to you most about working there?

10-28. What trade-offs is SAS making to offer the benefits and culture described?

10-29. What types of policies and benefits do you believe are most supportive of work–life balance?

10-30. What challenges might you face as a manager working in this environment? How could you overcome these challenges?

endnotes

1 "Fortune Media and Great Place to Work® Name Wegmans to 2023 Fortune 100 Best Companies to Work For®, Ranking #4," Wegmans, April 4, 2023, https://www.wegmans.com/news-media/press-releases/fortune-media-and-great-place-to-work-name-wegmans-to-2023-fortune-100-best-companies-to-work-for/.

2 "Building a Future with the Help of the Wegmans Scholarship Program," Wegmans Careers, accessed June 7, 2023, https://jobs.wegmans.com/scholarships.

3 Nathaniel Meyersohn, "Wegmans Ends Self-Checkout App After Too Much Shoplifting | CNN Business," CNN, September 16, 2022, https://www.cnn.com/2022/09/16/business-food/wegmans-scan-and-go-app-shoplifting/index.html.

4 Great Place to Work, "Working at Wegmans Food Markets, Inc.," Great Place to Work®, accessed June 7, 2023, https://www.greatplacetowork.com/certified-company/1000459.

5 Caitlin Ray et al., "Human Capital Resources: Reviewing the First Decade and Establishing a Foundation for Future Research," *Journal of Management* 49, no. 1, May 2, 2022, https://doi.org/10.1177/01492063221085912. See also Mark Allen, "The Real Costs of Bad Management—and What You Can Do About It," *Graziadio Business Review*

22, no. 1 (2019), https://gbr.pepperdine.edu/2019/03/the-real-costs-of-bad-management-and-what-you-can-do-about-it/; Lisa Frye, "The Cost of a Bad Hire Can Be Astronomical," SHRM, May 9, 2017, https://www.shrm.org/resourcesandtools/hr-topics/employee-relations/pages/cost-of-bad-hires.aspx.

[6] Christopher M. Barnes et al., "Human Sustainability and Work: A Meta-Synthesis and New Theoretical Framework," *Journal of Management* 49, no. 6, October 31, 2022, https://journals.sagepub.com/doi/abs/10.1177/01492063221131541. See also Monique Danao and Kelly Main, "What Is Human Capital Management (HCM)?" Forbes.com, December 22, 2022, https://www.forbes.com/advisor/business/what-is-human-capital-management/.

[7] "Recent OSHA Enforcement Cases," *Industrial Safety & Hygiene News*, December 2022, https://www.ishn.com/articles/111241-recent-osha-enforcement-cases.

[8] Lin Grensing-Pophal, "Providing Realistic Job Previews Through 360-Degree Video," SHRM, March 30, 2018, https://www.shrm.org/resourcesandtools/hr-topics/talent-acquisition/pages/realistic-job-previews-360-degree-video.aspx?_ga=2.33189948.325382201.1689127354-421056115.1689127354.

[9] Hang Nguyen, "Why These Companies Offer Identity Theft Protection as a Benefit," *The San Diego Union-Tribune*, November 21, 2021, https://www.sandiegouniontribune.com/top-workplaces/story/2021-11-21/why-these-companies-offer-identity-theft-protection-as-a-benefit.

[10] Chris Benguhe and RaeAnne Marsh, "Frontline CEOs—Who Aren't Afraid to Get Their Hands Dirty," *International Business Times*, July 7, 2021, https://www.ibtimes.com/frontline-ceos-who-arent-afraid-get-their-hands-dirty-3240070.

[11] Benguhe and Marsh, "Frontline CEOs."

[12] Benguhe and Marsh, "Frontline CEOs."

[13] Kenneth B. Brown and Traci Sitzmann, "Training and Employee Development for Improved Performance," in *Handbook of Industrial and Organizational Psychology*, vol. 2: *Selecting and Developing Members for the Organization*, ed. Sheldon Zedeck (Washington, DC: American Psychological Association), 469–504.

[14] https://www.ibm.com/ibm/history/ibm100/us/en/icons/employeeedu/#:~:text=Today%20IBM%20spends%20over%20US,traditional%20and%20non%2Dtraditional%20learning, accessed May 17, 2023. https://www.ibm.com/ibm/history/ibm100/us/en/icons/employeeedu/#:~:text=Today%20IBM%20spends%20over%20US,traditional%20and%20non%2Dtraditional%20learning, accessed May 17, 2023.

[15] Roger Trapp, "Why Companies Need to Change Their Approach to Learning," *Forbes*, June 28, 2023. See also Michael Gullan. "How e-Learning Can Help Burnt-Out Employees," *Independent Online*, July 13, 2023, https://www.iol.co.za/business-report/careers/how-e-learning-can-help-burnt-out-employees-755de2f1-796a-4e23-abfc-d9b7b672b21a.

[16] Isabel Thottam, "8 Companies with Awesome Training and Development Programs," Monster, n.d., https://www.monster.com/career-advice/article/companies-with-awesome-training-development-programs. See also "Why Schneider Electric," SE.com, n.d., https://www.se.com/us/en/about-us/careers/overview.jsp.

[17] "The Secret Sauce at In-N-Out Burger," Bloomberg.com, accessed on April 15, 2020; "Despite Cutbacks, Firms Invest in Developing Leaders," wsj.com, accessed April 15, 2020.

[18] Jessica L. Wildman, Wendy L. Bedwell, Eduardo Salas, and Kimberly A. Smith-Jentsch, "Performance Measurement at Work: A Multilevel Perspective," in *Handbook of Industrial and Organizational Psychology*, Vol. 1: *Building and Developing the Organization*, ed. Sheldon Zedeck (Washington, DC: American Psychological Association, 2010), 303–341.

[19] See Thomas W. H. Ng et al., "Employer-Sponsored Career Development Practices and Employee Performance and Turnover: A Meta-Analysis," *Journal of Management*, September 19, 2022, https://doi.org/10.1177/01492063221125143. See also Paul Levy and Jane Williams, "The Social Context of Performance Appraisal: A Review and Framework for the Future," *Journal of Management* 30, no. 6 (2004): 881–905.

[20] See Michael Hammer, "The 7 Deadly Sins of Performance Measurement (and How to Avoid Them)," *MIT Sloan Management Review*, Spring 2007, 19–30.

[21] See Angelo S. DeNisi and Avraham N. Kluger, "Feedback Effectiveness: Can 360-Degree Appraisals Be Improved?" *Academy of Management Executive* 14, no. 1 (2000): 129–139.

[22] YEC Council Post, "Hiring Entrepreneurs in the C-Suite Can Boost Business Productivity," *Forbes*, April 10, 2023. https://www.forbes.com/sites/theyec/2023/04/07/hiring-entrepreneurs-in-the-c-suite-can-boost-business-productivity/?sh=507755315b5c.

[23] Michael Wayne, "How Ping An Group's Jessica Tan Became a Global Business Figure," *The CEO Magazine*, October 18, 2021, https://www.theceomagazine.com/business/coverstory/jessica-tan-ping-an-insurance/.

[24] "Jessica Tan's Interview with IMD," Ping An, accessed June 7, 2023, https://group.pingan.com/media/perspectives/Jessica-Tan-s-Interview-with-IMD.html.

[25] See M. Tagliabue, S. S. Sigurjonsdottir, and I. Sandaker, "The Effects of Performance Feedback on Organizational Citizenship Behaviour: A Systematic Review and Meta-Analysis," *European Journal of Work and Organizational Psychology* 29, no. 6 (2020): 841–861, https://doi.org/10.1080/1359432X.2020.1796647. See also Barry R. Nathan, Allan Mohrman, and John Milliman, "Interpersonal Relations as a Context for the Effects of Appraisal Interviews on Performance and Satisfaction: A Longitudinal Study," *Academy of Management Journal*, June 1991, 352–369.

[26] "Welcome to Silicon Valley: Perksville, USA," *USA Today*, July 5, 2012, 1A, usatoday.com.

[27] Keith Edwards, "Augusta Chipotle Workers Walk Out, Claim Unsafe Conditions due to Understaffing," *Kennebec Journal and Morning Sentinel*, June 17, 2022, https://www.centralmaine.com/2022/06/16/augusta-chipotle-workers-walk-out-claim-unsafe-conditions-due-to-understaffing/.

[28] Noam Scheiber, "Judge Finds Amazon Broke Labor Law in Anti-Union Effort," *The New York Times*, January 31, 2023,

https://www.nytimes.com/2023/01/31/business/economy/amazon-union-staten-island-nlrb.html.

[29] Heidi Shierholz, "Unionization Increased by 200,000 in 2022: Tens of Millions More Wanted to Join a Union, but Couldn't," Economic Policy Institute, accessed June 7, 2023, https://www.epi.org/publication/unionization-2022/.

[30] "Union Election Petitions Increase 57% in First Half of Fiscal Year 2022," National Labor Relations Board, April 6, 2022, https://www.nlrb.gov/news-outreach/news-story/union-election-petitions-increase-57-in-first-half-of-fiscal-year-2022.

[31] http://www.bls.gov/opub/cwc/cb20100628ar01p1.htm.

[32] U.S. Department of Labor, Bureau of Labor Statistics, "Union Members Summary," accessed April 15, 2020, http://www.bls.gov/news.release/union2.nr0.htm.

[33] U.S. Department of Labor, Bureau of Labor Statistics, "Major Work Stoppages in 2019," accessed April 15, 2020, http://www.bls.gov/news.release/pdf/wkstp.pdf.

part 3
Integrative Learning Portfolio

crafting a business plan

Goal of the Exercise

At this point, your business has an identity, and you've described the factors that will affect your business and how you will operate it. Part 3 of the business plan project asks you to think about your employees, the jobs they will be performing, and the ways in which you can lead and motivate them.

Exercise Background: Part 3 of the Business Plan

To complete this part of the plan, you need to refer back to the organizational chart that you created in Part 2. In this part of the business plan exercise, you'll take the different job titles you created in the organizational chart and give thought to the *skills* that employees will need to bring to the job *before* they begin. You'll also consider *training* you'll need to provide *after* they are hired as well as how you'll compensate your employees. Part 3 of the business plan also asks you to consider how you'll lead your employees and keep them happy and motivated.

Your Assignment

STEP 1

Open the *Business Plan* file you began working on in Parts 1 and 2.

STEP 2

For the purposes of this assignment, you will answer the questions in "Part 3: People in Organizations":

P3-1. What do you see as the "corporate culture" of your business? What types of employee behaviors, such as organizational citizenship, will you expect?

Hint: Will your business demand a casual environment or a more professional environment? Refer to the discussion on employee behavior in Chapter 8 for information on organizational citizenship and other employee behaviors.

P3-2. What is your philosophy on leadership? How will you manage your employees day to day?

Hint: Refer to the discussion on leadership in Chapter 9 to help you formulate your thoughts.

P3-3. Looking back at your organizational chart in Part 2, briefly create a job description for each team member.

Hint: As you learned in this chapter, a job description lists the duties and responsibilities of a job; its working conditions; and the tools, materials, equipment, and information used to perform it. Imagine your business on a typical day. Who is working and what are each person's responsibilities?

P3-4. Next, create a job specification for each job, listing the skills, other credentials, and qualifications needed to perform the job effectively.

Hint: As you write your job specifications, consider what you would write if you were composing an ad for the position. What would the new employee need to bring to the job to qualify for the position?

P3-5. What sort of training, if any, will your employees need once they are hired? How will you provide this training?

Hint: Refer to the discussion of training in this chapter. Will you offer your employees on-the-job training? Off-the-job training? Vestibule training?

P3-6. A major factor in retaining skilled workers is a company's compensation system—the total package of rewards it offers employees in return for their labor. Part of this compensation system includes wages or salaries. What wages or salaries will you offer for each job? Why did you decide on that pay rate?

Hint: Refer to the discussion in this chapter for more information on forms of compensation. You may also want to check out sites such as www.salary.com, which includes a salary wizard you can use to determine how much people with different job titles are making in your area and across the United States.

P3-7. As you learned in this chapter, incentive programs are special programs designed to motivate high performance. What incentives will you use to motivate your workforce?

Hint: Be creative and look beyond a simple answer, such as giving pay increases. Ask yourself: Who are my employees and what is important to them? Refer to the discussion in this chapter for more information on the types of incentives you may want to consider.

Note: Once you have answered the questions, save your Word document. You'll be answering additional questions in later chapters.

case PART 3 STARBUCKS, 1990–1991

Labor is not fighting for a larger slice of the national pie. Labor is fighting for a larger pie.

Walter Reuther

—Writing in *The New Republic*, Vol. 114 (1946)

John Ferguson/Alamy Stock Photo

Howard Schultz grew up in the Bayview Projects in Brooklyn, New York. His father worked off and on for various companies, but the Schultz family never had much money. Howard was the first member of the family to go to college when he landed a football scholarship. Even though the scouts singled him out, he never actually played, but he did take some business classes. Those classes landed him his job with Hammarplast selling coffee makers, which led him to Starbucks. Schultz's father had no medical insurance, and he struggled with health issues that kept him from working. This left an indelible impression on Schultz, who was determined to create a company that supported all workers.

By 1990, working on infusions of equity financing, Starbucks had established stores in Chicago, Los Angeles, San Francisco, Vancouver, and, of course, Seattle. Schultz wasn't focused solely on expansion, though. He wanted to build the kind of company that valued its people. "I wanted people to feel proud of working at Starbucks, to believe in their hearts that management trusted them and treated them with respect," Schultz has said. But despite the company's success, Schultz found that employee morale was often low and that employees distrusted management.

Starbucks had purchased Peet's Coffee's five San Francisco stores in 1984 and had gone heavily into debt. In addition, managing the purchase and the remote stores took a toll on management, leaving many employees feeling discouraged. A group of employees from the roasting plant voted to unionize. By 1987, however, employees didn't feel the union was doing them any good and voted to decertify. Schultz considered this a win for his management style and his respect for frontline workers.

Intent on honoring the workers who represented Starbucks most directly, Schultz gathered his management team and drafted the company's first mission statement: "To establish Starbucks as the premier purveyor of the finest coffee in the world while maintaining our uncompromising principles as we grow." In addition, one of the guiding principles that came out of that retreat was "to provide a great work environment and treat each other with respect and dignity."

Drafting the mission statement took three months and involved over 50 employees, but Schultz wanted to make sure the mission wasn't just wall decoration, so he implemented a mission review system. Employees were encouraged to make suggestions and report situations and behaviors that were contrary to the company's mission.

In October of 1990, Starbucks finally turned a profit, and Schultz wanted to reward his employees somehow. He wanted to give the frontline workers, most of whom were part-time, incentives to help the company grow, even if it was just by providing outstanding customer service. One of his most controversial ideas was "bean stock," providing employees with stock in the company. Stockholders who had paid hard cash for their shares were skeptical, but Schultz assured them that employees who held a tiny bit of ownership would be more loyal to the company and the growth in share price would more than make up for the dilution resulting from the additional shares being disbursed to employees. The board of directors approved the plan in May 1991, but Schultz wasn't done. In addition to granting stock options to employees, the company instituted a generous healthcare plan and other employee benefits and began calling employees "partners."

The first "bean stock" shares given out in 1991 were valued at $6 per share; partners were awarded 12 percent of their salary in stock. For example, an employee earning $20,000 per year received $2,400 in stock, which equated to

400 shares. After five years and two stock splits, the original 400 shares had multiplied to be 1,600 shares worth $33 each, for a total value of $52,800. If that employee had held onto those original 1991 shares, the stock would have split four more times, and their total value in 2023 would be nearly $100 per share. The $2,400 investment would have grown to over $2.5 million.

QUESTIONS FOR DISCUSSION

P3-8. Starbucks was one of the first privately held companies to offer stock as compensation. At the time, do you think it motivated employees to provide better service? Why or why not?

P3-9. What are the differences between unions today and the unions of the 1920s and 1930s? How are they the same? What is your personal opinion on unionization?

P3-10. Do you think Howard Schultz's leadership style was the driving force behind his success? If so, what traits contributed to his success? If not, what do you think was the driving force behind his success?

P3-11. How do you think compensation and benefits have changed over the past 30 years?

P3-12. How do you think employee motivation has changed over the past 30 years, and why?

P3-13. How would you describe Schultz's leadership style? Do you know of a manager or leader who shares some of those same traits, and if so, how effective is that leader or manager, in your opinion? How about objectively—how is that manager's or leader's organization or department performing?

P3-14. Do you think workers today are happier than they were 30 years ago? Why or why not?

finding your path

CAREERS IN BUSINESS

When someone asks you what you want in a job, never say, "I want to work with people." This response is actually very common. So what's wrong with it? Basically, it doesn't really convey any information. Perhaps it's easier to understand this if, instead of that response, you were to say, "I do not want to work with people." How much do you think that response will help? Not at all, of course, and it may keep you from getting a job. Every hiring manager assumes that you want to work with people, so to tell them that trivializes both your interests and your capabilities. So what should you say? First of all, you need to be honest. But also make sure your answer has substance and says something meaningful about yourself and your interests. It is almost certain that at some point you will be asked the question, so have an answer ready. Consider these options, for instance:

- "I want a job in which I can continue to learn and develop my skills."
- "I want to work with interesting, motivated, and bright people."
- "I want to help all those around me realize their full potential and how they can better contribute to the organization and to society in general."

Part 3 of our book focused on two general areas, motivation and leadership and the specific field of human resource management. Students who graduate with a degree in human resource management generally have an average starting salary of $58,500 and can project a 7 percent increase in the number of jobs in this field between now and 2028.

MAKING YOURSELF EMPLOYABLE

You will, of course, be working with people for your entire career. To better prepare for this, it is important to develop your own human relations skills (these are sometimes referred to as interpersonal skills).

DEVELOPING YOUR HUMAN RELATIONS SKILLS

To start developing human relations skills, you first need to assess your current skill level. In general, do you get along with other people? If not, ask yourself why. Are you closed minded? Do you listen to others? Are you willing to take criticism and constructive feedback? Are you both willing to follow the lead of others and also able to step forward into a leadership role? These are all useful indicators of your human relations skills. Of course, you may also be deceiving yourself, so try this: Identify someone you both trust and that you know will be totally honest with you. This can be your best friend, your life partner, a parent, or a religious leader. Ask this person the questions above about yourself: "Am I open or closed minded?" "Do I listen well?" and so forth. But here is a key takeaway: If you get defensive and want to debate the person's assessment, take that as a warning sign. If someone is willing to give you candid feedback about yourself, consider that a gift. And the only thing to say when someone gives you a gift is "Thank you!"

HUMAN RESOURCE MANAGEMENT

As discussed previously and in Chapter 10, human resource management (HRM) is a growing field. And, indeed, individuals who want to "work with people" may be attracted to HRM as a profession. If this is you, great. However, be sure that you are thinking about HRM for the right reasons. As an HRM professional, you will not be sitting around all day simply talking to people. HRM is just as serious a field as any other. And you will be a manager—a manager who helps your organization attract, develop, and retain talent. And sometimes the work is especially challenging—you may play a role in deciding whose jobs get eliminated during a workforce reduction and then delivering that news to the individuals who are losing their jobs. Some people are also attracted to HRM because they don't think they are good at statistics and other quantitative methods and assume that HRM doesn't rely on those tools. Don't be fooled by this, though. HR managers rely heavily on statistical analysis for many elements of their job. So, if you want to work in the field of HRM, understand the details of what is involved, the legal context of employment, and both current and emerging trends involving new approaches to compensation, alternative work arrangements, performance management, and so forth. And if you expect to work in an area with a strong union presence, make sure you know the essentials of labor relations.

PART 4 | PRINCIPLES OF MARKETING: BUILDING RELATIONSHIPS WITH CUSTOMERS FOR COMPETITIVE ADVANTAGE

chapter 11

Marketing Processes and Consumer Behavior

AS photostudio/Shutterstock

learning objectives

After reading this chapter, you should be able to:

11-1 **Explain** the concept of marketing and identify the five forces that constitute the external marketing environment.

11-2 **Explain** the purpose of a marketing plan and identify its main components.

11-3 **Explain** market segmentation and how it is used in target marketing.

11-4 **Discuss** the purpose of marketing research and compare the four marketing research methods.

11-5 **Describe** the consumer buying process and the key factors that influence that process.

11-6 **Discuss** the four categories of organizational markets and the characteristics of business-to-business (B2B) buying behavior.

11-7 **Discuss** the marketing mix as it applies to small business.

what's in it for me?

Businesses adapt to their environments in many different ways. One common approach is to use marketing basics in innovative ways to appeal to the forces of the external marketing environment. This chapter discusses these basics along with the marketing plan and components of the marketing mix, as well as target marketing and market segmentation. It also explores key factors that influence consumer and organizational buying processes. By understanding the marketing methods and ideas in this chapter, you will better appreciate the function of marketing professionals in business and also become a more informed consumer.

Daily Travel Photos/Shutterstock

Suwan Waenlor/Shutterstock

More Than Just Meatballs

The first thing that comes to mind when you think of IKEA is probably hard-to-pronounce furniture names and a DIY challenge. Or perhaps you imagine a Sunday afternoon spent meandering through the store's giant warehouse, envisioning a new look for every room in your house, or maybe your first thought is those delicious Swedish meatballs.

IKEA is the world's largest furniture and home appliance manufacturer and retailer. Founded over seven decades ago in Småland, Sweden, by then 17-year-old Ingvar Kamprad, in 2023, the IKEA Group had 460 IKEA stores in more than 60 markets, employed about 225,000 people globally and boasted an inventory of more than 9,500 products. It reported 775 million store visits and 5 billion visits to the website.[1] The company's continually evolving marketing strategy is a large part of that success.

The brands that everyone knows are the ones that have a very clear identity. IKEA is one of those brands. Its message of ease, value, and maximizing your space is clear in everything it does. IKEA is well known for clean advertising with a few bold colors (blue, yellow, and orange, which are the brand's colors) and images showing immaculate homes with modern, clean decor. When you see a picture of an IKEA bedroom, you know it's an IKEA bedroom. Additionally, IKEA has built a reputation for sustainability, heavily promoting actions like its use of bio-friendly glue and including sustainability metrics in its annual reports.

IKEA constantly adds new products to its offerings. Any time IKEA changes things up, it gives current customers a further incentive to come and check things out and creates new opportunities to catch the interest of would-be customers.

In addition to the shift from print to online catalogs in 2018, IKEA has continued to focus on a multifaceted viral marketing program. From Instagram Reels showcasing products in real life to the Square Metre Challenge promoted on YouTube, IKEA links all of its social media programs on its website. Cross-platform marketing encourages visitors to add IKEA-specific hashtags to show off IKEA products in their personal living spaces and professional offices.[2]

"Our communication reflects IKEA values both visually and in tone of voice, so marketing and communications coworkers include art directors and copywriters, interior designers and project leaders. Together they work with the IKEA catalog, IKEA websites, publications, brochures, advertising, internal communication and public relations."[3]

IKEA's marketing strategy clearly focuses on product and price elements of the marketing mix. Even so, the company doesn't ignore place and promotion. Product campaigns contain engaging images, videos, and text and items are placed mise-en-scène—deliberately placed in situations where it almost feels as though the customer is stumbling upon them organically rather than seeing them in a promotion. In addition to a strong social media presence, the company is embedded in pop culture. You can see IKEA products in movies such as *Fight Club* and *500 Days of Summer* and TV programs such as *30 Rock*, *Being Human*, and *Ghost Town*.

None of this is random. IKEA's marketing plan is closely tied to and informed by the overall business idea and company vision, prominently published on the website. "'To create a better everyday life for the many people,' this is the IKEA vision. Our business idea is 'to offer a wide range of well-designed, functional home furnishing products at prices so low that as many people as possible will be able to afford them.' Our vision also goes beyond home furnishing. We want to create a better everyday for all people impacted by our business."[4] (After studying the content in this chapter, you should be able to answer a set of discussion questions found at the end of the chapter.)

What Is Marketing?

Learning Objective 11-1

Explain the concept of marketing and identify the five forces that constitute the external marketing environment.

As consumers, we are influenced by the marketing activities of businesses like IKEA, Procter & Gamble, Apple, AT&T, Toyota, and Domino's that want us to buy their products rather than those of their competitors. Being consumers makes us the essential ingredients in the marketing process. Every day, we express needs for such necessities as food, clothing, and shelter and wants for such nonessentials as entertainment and leisure activities. Our needs and wants are major forces that drive marketing.

What comes to mind when you think of marketing? Most of us think of marketing as advertisements for products like fast foods, movies, soft drinks, and cars. Marketing, however, actually encompasses a much wider range of activities. The American Marketing Association defines **marketing** as "activities, a set of institutions, and processes for creating, communicating, delivering, and exchanging offerings that have value for customers, clients, partners, and society at large."[5] To see this definition in action, we'll continue this chapter by looking at some marketing basics, including the ways marketers build relationships with customers. We'll then examine forces that constitute the external marketing environment, followed by marketing strategy, the marketing plan, and the components of the marketing mix. We'll then discuss market segmentation and how it is used in target marketing. Next, we'll examine marketing research, followed by a look at key factors that influence the buying processes of consumers and industrial buyers. Finally, we'll consider the marketing mix for small business and then go beyond domestic borders to explore the international marketing mix.

Marketing *activities, a set of institutions, and processes for creating, communicating, delivering, and exchanging offerings that have value for customers, clients, partners, and society at large*

Delivering Value

What causes buyers to purchase one product instead of another? Although our desires for the wide variety of available goods and services may be almost limitless, in most cases our financial resources are not, and so we have to be selective in what we choose to buy. Accordingly, customers usually try to buy products that offer the best value when it comes to meeting their needs and wants.

Value and Benefits The **value** of a product refers to its comparative benefits versus costs. Benefits, in turn, include not only the functions of the product but also the emotional satisfaction associated with owning, experiencing, or possessing it. For instance, a pair of $40 basketball shoes from Walmart may be perfectly adequate for most recreational players, but many people still spend much more for the latest version of shoes endorsed by Jordan, LeBron, Durant, or Kyrie because of their style or cachet. But every product also has costs, including the sales price, the buyer's time finding the product, and even the emotional costs of making a purchase decision (such as deciding which pair of basketball shoes to buy). A satisfied customer perceives the benefits derived from the purchase to be greater than its costs. Thus, the simple but important ratio for value is derived as follows:

Value *relative comparison of a product's benefits versus its costs*

$$\text{Value} = \frac{\text{Benefits}}{\text{Costs}}$$

The marketing strategies of leading firms focus on increasing value for customers. Marketing resources are deployed to add benefits and/or decrease costs of products to provide greater value. To satisfy customers, a company may do the following:

- Develop an entirely new product that performs better (provides greater performance benefits) than existing products.
- Keep a retail store open longer hours during a busy season (adding the benefit of greater shopping convenience).
- Offer price reductions (the benefit of lower costs).
- Offer information that explains how a product can be used in new ways (the benefit of new uses at no added cost).

Value and Utility To understand how marketing creates value for customers, we need to know the kind of benefits that buyers get from a firm's goods or services. As we discussed in Chapter 7, those benefits provide customers with **utility**, the ability of a product to satisfy a person's wants or needs. Think about the competitive marketing efforts for Microsoft's Xbox series and those for Sony's competing PlayStation game consoles. In both companies, marketing strives to provide four kinds of utility in the following ways:

Utility *product's ability to satisfy a human want or need*

Form Utility *providing products with features that customers want*

Time Utility *providing products when customers will want them*

Place Utility *providing products where customers will want them*

Possession Utility *transferring product ownership to customers by setting selling prices, setting terms for customer credit payments, and providing ownership documents*

1. **Form utility**. Marketing has a voice in designing products with features that customers want. Microsoft's Xbox One X features Cortana artificial intelligence (AI) technology (voice-controlled console software) and can share highlights of your game on social media. Sony's newest PlayStation 5 (PS5) provides enhanced higher resolution (up to 1440p) and Remote Play, which allows players to stream PlayStation games from their PS5 to phones, tablets, and other consoles..
2. **Time utility**. Marketing creates a time utility by providing products *when* customers will want them. Both Sony and Microsoft create Internet buzz and rumors among gamers by hinting at upcoming release dates without mentioning specifics. For example, both Microsoft and Sony are hinting at a late 2020 release date for their newest consoles. The initial offering of PlayStation 5 sold out entirely on its initial launch day (November 12, 2020).
3. **Place utility**. Marketing creates a place utility by making products easily accessible—by making products available *where* customers will want them. Xbox One X and PS5 are available online at Amazon.com and at many brick-and-mortar retailers such as GameStop, Best Buy and Target. Both also offer online networks as well.
4. **Possession utility**. Marketing creates a possession utility by transferring product ownership to customers by setting selling prices; setting terms for customer credit payments, if needed; and providing ownership documents. Both Xbox One X and PS5 sell for around $499.

As you can imagine, marketing responsibilities at Microsoft and Sony are extremely challenging in such a competitive arena, and the stakes are very high. Because they determine product features, and the timing, place, and terms of sale that provide utility and add value for customers, marketers must anticipate customers' wants and needs well in advance of actual product launches. And in today's rapidly changing environment, businesses must also be prepared to quickly adapt to fads and shifting wants and needs. Marketing methods for creating utility are described in this and the following two chapters.

Goods, Services, and Ideas

As consumers, we encounter the marketing of tangible goods virtually everywhere we look—on social media and other online sites, on television, in magazines, along the highways and roadsides, on store fronts, in sports arenas, and in our mailboxes.

Marketing actually applies to two types of customers: those who buy consumer goods and those who buy industrial goods. In a department store, a salesperson may ask if you'd like to try a new cologne. On your social media account, a popup ad may promote a new sports drink or local restaurant. A television ad from a pharmaceutical company may proclaim the virtues of its new cold medicine. Your local auto dealer may offer an economy car at a discounted price. These products are all **consumer goods**, tangible goods that you, the consumer, may buy for personal use. Firms that sell goods to consumers for personal consumption are engaged in consumer marketing, also known as business-to-consumer (B2C) marketing.

Consumer Goods *physical products purchased by consumers for personal use*

Marketing also applies to **industrial goods**, physical items used by companies to produce other products. Surgical instruments and bulldozers are industrial goods, as are machine components and parts and raw materials such as integrated circuits, steel beams, coffee beans, and plastic tubing. Firms that sell goods to other companies are engaged in industrial marketing, also known as business-to-business (B2B) marketing. We should also note, though, that some goods can be both consumer and industrial goods. For instance, coffee beans can be marketed to individual consumers who want to grind their own coffee at home as well as coffee shops who buy the same beans for in-store use.

Industrial Goods *physical products purchased by companies to produce other products*

Marketing techniques are also applied to **services**, products with intangible (nonphysical) features, such as professional advice, timely information for decisions, or vacation packaging. Service marketing, the application of marketing for services, continues to be a major growth area in the United States. Insurance companies, airlines, public accountants, and health clinics all engage in service marketing, both to individuals (consumer markets) and to other companies (industrial markets). Thus, the terms *consumer marketing* and *industrial marketing* include services as well as goods.

Services *products having nonphysical features, such as information, expertise, or an activity that can be purchased*

Finally, marketers also promote ideas, such as "inspirational values" as seen in "Encouragement, Pass It On," on YouTube and in popular television commercials. Ads in theaters warn us against copyright infringement and piracy. Other marketing campaigns may stress the advantages of avoiding fast foods or abstaining from texting while driving, or the importance of smoking cessation, or they may promote a political party or candidate. During the COVID-19 pandemic in 2020, some firms like AT&T and General Motors launched ads emphasizing their willingness to help people during difficult times by deferring payments and offering large discounts. While they were promoting their products, of course, they were doing so in a low-key manner that would presumably cause potential customers to see them as being sympathetic and focusing on their concerns for consumers.

Relationship Marketing and Customer Relationship Management

Although marketing often focuses on single transactions for products, services, or ideas, marketers also take a longer-term perspective. Thus, **relationship marketing** is a type of marketing that emphasizes building lasting relationships with customers and suppliers. Stronger relationships, including stronger economic and social ties, can result in greater long-term satisfaction, customer loyalty, and customer retention.[6] IKEA has used relationship marketing very successfully. Similarly, Starbucks's Rewards attracts return customers with free coffee refills and other extras. Likewise, commercial banks offer economic incentives to encourage longer-lasting relationships. Longtime customers who use a certain number of the bank's products (for example, checking accounts, savings accounts, and loans) accumulate credits toward free or reduced-price products or services, such as free investment advice or reduced checking account fees. Airline frequent flyer programs similarly build stronger ties between air travelers and airlines.

Relationship Marketing *marketing strategy that emphasizes building lasting relationships with customers and suppliers*

Like many other marketing areas, the ways that marketers go about building relationships with customers have changed dramatically. **Customer relationship management (CRM)** is an organized method that a firm uses to build better information connections with clients, so that managers can develop stronger company–client relationships.

Customer Relationship Management (CRM) *organized methods that a firm uses to build better information connections with clients, so that stronger company–client relationships are developed*

The power of online communications coupled with the ability to gather and assemble information on customer preferences allows marketers to better predict what clients will want and buy. Viking Cruises, for instance, communicates with people who have booked future cruises months in advance of departures with e-mails containing onboard restaurant menus and food recipes from countries that vacationers will be visiting. Viking also encourages social networking among booked passengers to establish pre-voyage friendships, which can lead to faster face-to-face acquaintanceships once they board Viking ships.

Data Warehousing *the collection, storage, and retrieval of data in electronic files*

Data Mining *the application of electronic technologies for searching, sifting, and reorganizing pools of data to uncover useful information*

Compiling and storing customers' data, known as **data warehousing**, provides the "raw materials" from which marketers can extract information that enables them to find new clients and identify their best customers. Marketers can then inform these priority clients about upcoming new products and postpurchase service reminders. **Data mining** automates the massive analysis of data by using computer software to sift, sort, and search for previously undiscovered clues about what customers look at and react to and how they might be influenced. Marketers use these tools to get a clearer picture about how knowing a client's preferences can satisfy those particular needs, thereby building closer, stronger relationships with those customers.[7]

Toronto-based Fairmont Resort Hotels, for example, first used data mining to rebuild its customer-relations package by finding out what kinds of vacations their customers prefer and then placing ads where they were more likely to reach those customers. When data mining revealed the worldwide destinations of Fairmont customers, it helped determine Fairmont's decision to buy their customers' number one preference, the Savoy in London.[8] Fairmont's enhanced CRM has attracted new guests and strengthened relationships and loyalty among existing clients through web-based promotions and incentives. Using profiles of guest information, Fairmont identifies target traveler segments and supplies travelers with personalized price discounts and special hotel services.[9] We'll discuss data warehousing and data mining in more detail in Chapter 14.

The Marketing Environment

Marketing plans and strategies are not determined unilaterally by any business—rather, they are strongly influenced by powerful outside forces. As you see in Figure 11.1, every marketing program must recognize the factors in a company's *external environment*, which is everything outside an organization's boundaries that might affect it. In this section, we'll discuss how these external forces affect the marketing environment in particular.

FIGURE 11.1 The External Marketing Environment

Political–Legal Environment The **political–legal environment**, both global and domestic, has profound effects on marketing. For example, environmental legislation has determined the destinies of entire industries. The political push for alternative energy sources is creating new markets and products for relatively new companies such as India's Suzlon Energy Limited (large wind turbines), wind-powered electric generators by Germany's Nordex Group, and wind farms and power plants by Spain's Siemens Gamesa Corporation. Marketing managers try to maintain favorable political and legal environments in several ways. To gain public support for products and activities, marketers use ad campaigns to raise public awareness of important issues. Companies contribute to political candidates and frequently support the activities of political action committees (PACs) maintained by their respective industries.

Political–Legal Environment *the relationship between business and government*

Sociocultural Environment The **sociocultural environment** also affects marketing. Changing social values force companies to develop and promote new products, such as poultry and meat without antibiotics and growth hormones, for both individual consumers and industrial customers. Just a few years ago, organic foods were available only in specialty food stores such as Whole Foods. Today, in response to a growing demand for healthy foods, Target's Good & Gather product line brings affordable organic food to a much larger audience. Grocers like Kroger and H-E-B also have set aside large areas in their stores where consumers can find organic and/or natural products. In addition, new industrial products reflect changing social values: A growing number of wellness programs are available to companies for improving employees' health. Quest Diagnostics, for example, a B2B company, supplies a "Blueprint for Wellness" service that assesses employee health care risks in client companies and recommends programs for reducing those risks. This and other trends reflect the values, beliefs, and ideas that shape society. In similar fashion, businesses strive to distance themselves from people and products that are potentially offensive. For example, in 2018, Nike faced backlash after featuring NFL quarterback Colin Kaepernick in its "Just Do It" ad campaign. Kaepernick had become controversial for protesting racial injustice by kneeling during the national anthem before football games. While some consumers supported Kaepernick's message, others were outraged and boycotted Nike. In 2022, music star and designer Kanye West publicly made antisemitic remarks and other controversial comments. As a result, several of his sponsors, including Balenciaga, Adidas, Gap, and Vogue, quickly canceled their partnerships with West.

Sociocultural Environment *the customs, mores, values, and demographic characteristics of the society in which an organization functions*

Technological Environment The **technological environment** creates new goods and services. New products make existing products obsolete, and many products change our values and lifestyles. In turn, lifestyle changes often stimulate new products not directly related to the new technologies themselves. Mobile devices, the availability of a vast array of apps, and social media, for example, facilitate business communication, just as prepackaged meals provide convenience for busy household cooks. Both kinds of products also free up time for recreation and leisure.

Technological Environment *all the ways by which firms create value for their constituents*

Economic Environment Because economic conditions determine spending patterns by consumers, businesses, and governments, the **economic environment** influences marketing plans for product offerings, pricing, and promotional strategies. Marketers are concerned with such economic variables as inflation, interest rates, and recession. Thus, they monitor the general business cycle and specific economic patterns and projections to anticipate trends in consumer and business spending. During the 2020 COVID-19 pandemic, many businesses had to adjust their marketing activities to account for shifts in consumer and industrial demand, decreased spending patterns, high unemployment, and so forth. As life and business returned to normal, businesses considered pent-up demand and changes in consumer habits as they developed post-COVID marketing plans.

Economic Environment *relevant conditions that exist in the economic system in which a company operates*

Jasmin Merdan/Alamy Stock Photo

The technological environment has had major influences on how products and services are marketed. For instance, apps can now show people how their home would look with new furniture, new paint, or other changes. Furniture retailers and decorating supply companies can use this technology to better promote their products and services.

Competitive Environment *the competitive system in which businesses compete*

Competitive Environment In a **competitive environment**, marketers try to convince buyers that they should purchase their company's products rather than another's. Because both consumers and commercial buyers have limited resources, every dollar spent on one product means one dollar less available for other purchases. Each marketing program, therefore, seeks to make its product the most attractive. Expressed in business terms, a failed program loses the buyer's dollar forever (or at least until it is time for the next purchase decision).

To promote products effectively, marketers must first understand which of three types of competition they face:

Substitute Product *product that is dissimilar from those of competitors but that can fulfill the same need*

1 **Substitute products** may not look alike or they may seem different from one another, but they can fulfill the same need. For example, an individual's cholesterol level may be controlled with either of two competing products: a physical fitness program or a drug regimen. The fitness program and the drugs compete as substitute products. Similarly, online video streaming services like Netflix provide substitute products for conventional television programming, movie theaters, and conventional DVDs. A Royal Caribbean cruise, a Colorado ski resort, and a Disney theme park offer substitute products for a family looking for a spring break vacation.

Brand Competition *competitive marketing that appeals to consumer perceptions of benefits of products offered by particular companies*

2 **Brand competition** occurs between similar products and is based on buyers' perceptions of the benefits of products offered by particular companies. For digital communication, do you use email (such as Google's Gmail platform), texting (through providers like AT&T or Verizon), or messaging (through Facebook or WhatsApp)? Brand competition is based on users' perceptions of the benefits offered by each product.

International Competition *competitive marketing of domestic products against foreign products*

3 **International competition** matches the products of domestic marketers against those of foreign competitors. As we saw back in Chapter 4, many businesses today compete in global markets. Ford and General Motors (U.S. firms) compete with BMW and Volkswagen (German firms) and Toyota and Nissan (Japanese firms) in every global automobile market. Apple (a U.S. company) competes with Samsung (a Korean company). Sony (a Japanese company) competes with LG (a Korean company). And in each case, these businesses compete in their home countries, the home countries of their international competitors, and many neutral countries as well. Take Coca-Cola, for example. In the United States, Coke clearly promotes itself as a traditional, mainstream American product. In other countries, Coke is also recognized as an American icon. But the company presents itself as more of a global brand than an American brand. Indeed, Coca-Cola sponsors more than 100 different national Olympic teams around the world.

Developing the Marketing Plan

Learning Objective 11-2

Explain the purpose of a marketing plan and identify its main components.

Once marketing managers have a basic understanding of their role and the nature of their competition, their next step is to develop their marketing plan. A marketing manager at a major home appliance manufacturing company explains the concept of *developing the marketing plan* by using the following analogy of planning a trip:

- "First, you decide where you want to go and what you want to happen when you get there. Why take this trip and not others, instead?"
  [Identify the *objective* or *goal* to be achieved.]
- "At some stage, you decide when the trip will happen and how you'll get to the destination."
  [*Plan* for *when* it will happen, and for the *paths* (or *routes*) that will be taken to get there.]

managing in turbulent times

A Santa Fe Icon

Founded in 2013, Iconik, like many start-up coffee shops, was struggling to stay open by 2016. Although Santa Fe, New Mexico, is a tourist favorite, the local demographic is an eclectic mix of artists, cowboys, state workers, retirees, and just plain folk, like Sean Ham, an independent systems analyst and computer software designer who liked working in the coffee bars around town. Even so, the city's claim to coffee fame up to that point was putting butter in an otherwise good cup and calling it healthy.

By coffeehouse standards, at 2,000 square feet, the Lena Street Iconik is sprawling, with an embellished-warehouse ambiance that includes exposed overhead heating and ventilation ducts and general openness. It's nestled into a cozy business development at the end of a dead-end street, surrounded by design and yoga studios, professional offices, a hair salon, artist studios, dance and fitness studios, physical therapists, architects, and a martial arts center.

In 2016, Ham got word that Iconik was about to shut down, so he and some local investors bought it. Rather than trying to appeal to the masses, Ham focused on serving the prototypical Iconik customer who appreciates the quality food, excellent service, ambiance, and, of course, the classically roasted coffee. Patrons range from hippies to hipsters, cowpunchers to scriptwriters writing about cowpunchers, office workers to students. The baristas and other wait staff are as diverse as the rest of the place: aspiring fashion designers, visual artists, and assorted would-be writers. Iconik roasts coffees from Latin America, Indonesia, and Africa on a 1927 Otto Swadlo coffee roaster. The main area features a 14-seat community table forged from a slab of wood found in an Albuquerque junkyard. It's the kind of place where people gather for the camaraderie as much as for the coffee.

Ironically enough, while the coffee at Iconik is notoriously some of the most expensive in town ($2.75 per 10 ounces

ZUMA Press Inc/Alamy Stock Photo

for drip), the grilled cheese made with brie, jack, and berry compote plus a side salad with housemade vinaigrette goes for $8.75; the generously portioned, slightly spicy kale-kohlrabi salad with puffed rice and fish sauce for $8; and the local lamb sliders with tzatziki for $9.50.

During the COVID-19 pandemic of 2020, when most restaurants and coffee shops were forced to close down, Iconik shifted its marketing mix to include eggs, milk, flour, and a few other staples that were hard to get at the grocery store and was one of the first non-drive-up food service companies to enact curbside delivery to better serve loyal customers and ride out the governor's restricted-movement orders. In 2023, as restrictions relaxed and business started to resume to normal, Ham opened a third location, Iconik Red, in what was once a Discount Tire store on the going-to-work-downtown side of the street, but he didn't include a drive-through window. Ham doesn't see his café as a place to pick up a cup of coffee on the way to the office. "This is a place to come and hang out," Ham says, choosing to differentiate his store from dozens of competitors.[10]

- "Every trip requires resources, so you identify those resource requirements and compare them against resources that are available."
  [*Evaluate resource* requirements and availabilities.]
- "If available resources are too expensive, then you adjust the trip so it becomes affordable."
  [*Adjust plans* as needed to become *realistic* and *feasible*.]
- "During and after the trip, you assess the successes (what went right) and the drawbacks (what went wrong) and remember them so you can make the next trip even better."
  [Keep notes and data about what happened because *learning* from this experience increases the chances for *greater success on the next*.]

Marketing Plan *detailed strategy for focusing marketing efforts on consumers' needs and wants*

As you will see, our discussion of the marketing plan contains many of these elements. The **marketing plan** identifies the marketing objectives, stating what marketing will accomplish in the future. It also includes a strategy that identifies the specific activities and resources that will be used to meet the needs and desires of customers in the firm's chosen target markets, so as to accomplish the marketing objectives.

Marketing Objectives *the things marketing intends to accomplish in its marketing plan*

First and foremost, marketing plans are future oriented, showing what will be happening with marketing's upcoming activities. Every well-developed marketing plan, as shown in Figure 11.2, begins with objectives or goals that set the stage for everything that follows. **Marketing objectives**, the goals the marketing plan intends to accomplish, are the foundation that guides all the detailed activities in the plan. The marketing objectives themselves, however, exist solely to support the company's overall business mission (at the top in Figure 11.2) and typically focus on maintaining or enhancing the organization's future competitive position in its chosen markets. Suppose, for example, that Starbucks's overall business mission is to be the world's

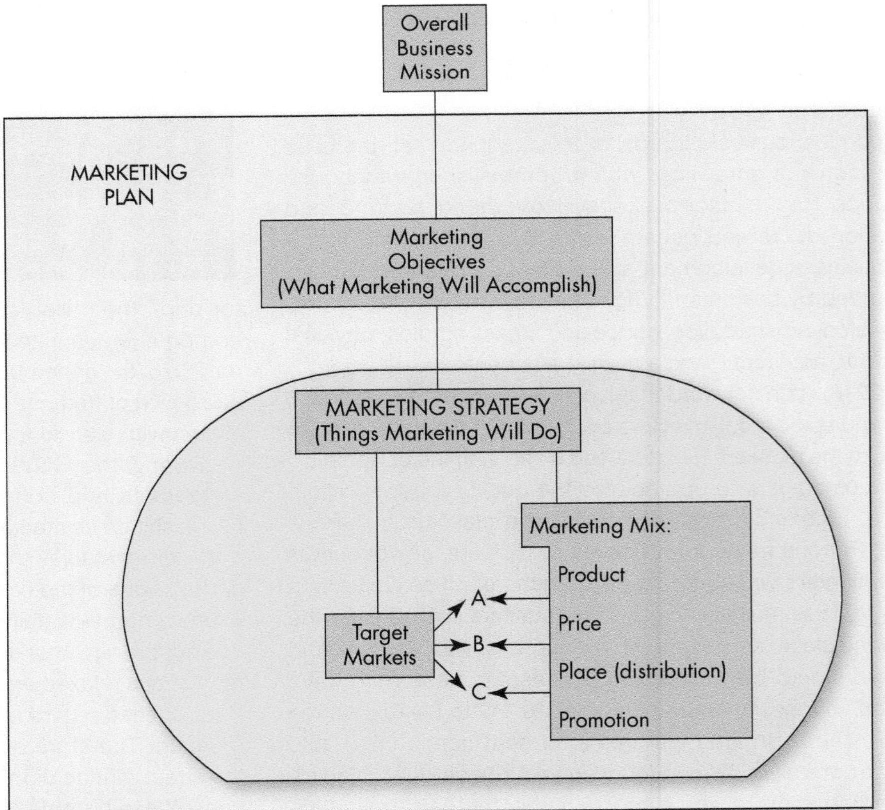

FIGURE 11.2 Components of the Marketing Plan

leading retailer of specialty coffee. Two supporting marketing objectives, then, could be (1) a 5 percent increase in its worldwide market share by, say, 2027 and (2) to be the leading retailer (in dollar sales) of specialty coffee in China by 2029.

Marketing Strategy: Planning the Marketing Mix

The marketing team can develop a strategy once it has clarified the marketing objectives. Specifically, **marketing strategy** identifies the planned marketing programs, all the marketing activities that a business will use to achieve its marketing goals, and when those activities will occur. If planned activities are not affordable or feasible, then marketers may need to adjust the activities or goals until realistic plans emerge. Finally, because marketing planning is an ongoing process—not just a one-time activity—it can be improved through experience by learning from past successes and mistakes.

Marketing Strategy *all the marketing programs and activities that will be used to achieve the marketing goals*

Marketing managers are the people responsible for planning, organizing, leading, and controlling the organization's marketing resources toward supporting and accomplishing the organization's overall mission. To meet these responsibilities, marketing managers rely on mapping out a clear strategy for planning and implementing all the activities that result in the transfer of goods or services to customers. As you can see in Figure 11.2, the marketing strategy focuses on the needs and wants of customers in the company's chosen target markets. Marketing strategy also includes four basic components (often called the *Four Ps*) of the **marketing mix**—*product, pricing, place,* and *promotion*—that marketing managers use to attract customers in target markets. The specific activities for each of the Four Ps are designed differently to best meet the needs of each target market.

Marketing Manager *manager who plans and implements the marketing activities that result in the transfer of products from producer to consumer*

Marketing Mix *combination of product, pricing, promotion, and place (distribution) strategies used to market products*

Product Marketing begins with a **product**, a good, a service, or an idea designed to fill a customer's need or want. Producers often promote particular features of products to distinguish them in the marketplace. **Product differentiation** is the creation of a feature or image that makes a product differ enough from existing products to attract customers. For example, in the years since Apple introduced the first iPhone, a succession of newer models evolved with faster, more powerful, and increasingly consumer-friendlier innovations. The iPhone's industry-leading features have attracted an enormous customer following that contributes substantially to Apple's sustained financial success. The design for the newest iPhone, for example, offers more new features than previous models to keep on top in the increasingly competitive smartphone market. The phone is thinner and lighter, and it has a new Retina HD display, an improved three-lens camera, new night mode features, and a faster operating system.

Product *good, service, or idea that is marketed to fill consumers' needs and wants*

Product Differentiation *creation of a product feature or product image that differs enough from existing products to attract customers*

Meanwhile, Samsung surged onto the scene with its competitive Galaxy series. Like Apple, Samsung has introduced several versions of the Galaxy over the years. Popular features have included more powerful and removable batteries, faster download and upload speeds, the popular Android operating system, and numerous additional features. The phone is also dustproof and water resistant.

Samsung's Galaxy currently has the largest global market share of the smartphone market, while Apple is number two. In the U.S. market, however, Apple has a larger share than Samsung. We discuss product development more fully in Chapter 12.

Pricing The **pricing** of a product, selecting the best price at which to sell it, is often a balancing act. On the one hand, prices must be high enough to cover both direct costs (such as the costs of actually manufacturing the product) and indirect costs (such as operating, administrative, research, and marketing costs). On the other hand, prices can't be so high that customers routinely turn to lower-priced competitors. Successful pricing means finding a profitable middle ground between these two extremes.

Pricing *process of determining the best price at which to sell a product*

Both low- and high-price strategies can be effective in different situations. Lower prices, for example, generally lead to more units being sold but lower profits on each unit. Higher prices usually limit the number of units being sold but increase profits per unit. In some cases, though, higher prices may also actually attract customers by signaling that a product is of high quality. We also discuss pricing in more detail in Chapter 12.

Place (Distribution) *part of the marketing mix concerned with getting products from producers to consumers*

Place (Distribution) In the marketing mix, **place** (or **distribution**) refers to *where* and *how* customers get access to the products they buy. When products are created, they must then be made available to customers at some *location* (*place*) such as a retail store, on a digital device, or by direct delivery to the customer. *Distribution* is the set of activities that moves products from producers to customers. Placing a product in the proper outlet, like a retail store, requires decisions about several activities, all of which are concerned with getting the product from the producer to the consumer. Decisions about warehousing and inventory control are distribution decisions, as are decisions about transportation options.

Firms must also make decisions about the *channels* through which they distribute products. Many manufacturers, for example, sell goods to other companies that, in turn, distribute them to retailers. Others sell directly to major retailers, such as Target and Kroger. Still others sell directly to final consumers. We explain distribution decisions further in Chapter 13.

Promotion *aspect of the marketing mix concerned with the most effective techniques for communicating information about and selling a product*

Promotion The most visible component of the marketing mix is no doubt **promotion**, which is a set of techniques for communicating information about products. The most important promotional tools include advertising, personal selling, sales promotions, publicity/public relations, and direct or interactive marketing. Promotion decisions are discussed further in Chapter 13, but we will briefly describe four of the most important promotional tools here.

Advertising *any form of paid nonpersonal communication used by an identified sponsor to persuade or inform potential buyers about a product*

Advertising **Advertising** is any form of paid nonpersonal communication used by an identified sponsor to persuade or inform potential buyers about a product. For example, financial advisory companies that provide investment and securities products reach their customer audience by advertising in *Fortune* magazine and on the Bloomberg television network.

Personal Selling *person-to person sales*

Personal Selling Many products (such as insurance, custom-designed clothing, and real estate) are best promoted through **personal selling**, person-to-person sales. Industrial goods and services rely significantly on personal selling. When companies

pio3/Shutterstock

Rolex has had sustained success as a result of its well-conceived marketing mix. The Swiss company focuses exclusively on high-quality watches (product), sells them for thousands of dollars (price), uses an exclusive network of high-quality retailers (distribution), and advertises them in interesting ways (promotion).

Michael Nagle/Bloomberg/Getty Images

Urban Outfitters is a successful—but sometimes controversial—retailer. The company offers low-priced and unique products targeted at young, urban-oriented consumers. But the firm has also had some public relations problems due in part to some products that crossed the line from snarky or ironic to offensive.

buy from other companies, purchasing agents and others who need technical and detailed information are often referred to the selling company's sales representatives.

SALES PROMOTIONS Historically, relatively inexpensive items have often been marketed through **sales promotions**, which involve one-time direct inducements to buyers. Premiums (usually free gifts), coupons, and package inserts are all sales promotions meant to tempt consumers to buy products. More recently, however, these promotions have expanded into B2B sales and to sales of larger items to consumers through online deals at sources such as Groupon.

Sales Promotion *direct inducements such as premiums, coupons, and package inserts to tempt consumers to buy products*

PUBLIC RELATIONS **Public relations** includes all communication efforts directed at building goodwill. It seeks to build favorable attitudes in the minds of the public toward the organization and its products. The Ronald McDonald House Charities, and its association with McDonald's Corporation, is a well-known example of public relations. During the 2020 COVID-19 pandemic, YouTube sponsored several online concerts, shows, and other activities as part of its efforts to enhance its image with a "captive" target market sheltering in place.

Public Relations *communication efforts directed at building goodwill and favorable attitudes in the minds of the public toward the organization and its products*

Blending It All Together: Integrated Strategy

An **integrated marketing strategy** ensures that the Four Ps blend together so that they are compatible with one another and with the company's nonmarketing activities. As an example, consider the case of Toyota, the world's largest automaker. Its 30-year auto superiority, even with its massive product recalls a few years ago, stems from a coherent marketing mix that is tightly integrated with its production strategy. Offering a relatively small number of different models, Toyota targets auto customers who want high quality, excellent performance reliability, and moderate prices (a good value for the price). With a smaller number of different models than offered by U.S. automakers, fewer components and parts are needed, purchasing costs are lower, and less factory space is required for inventory and assembly in Toyota's lean production system. Lean production's assembly simplicity yields higher quality, the factory's cost savings lead to lower product prices, and speedy production gives shorter delivery times in Toyota's distribution system. Taken together, this integrated strategy is completed when Toyota's advertising communicates its message of consistent industry-high customer satisfaction.

Integrated Marketing Strategy *strategy that blends together the Four Ps of marketing to ensure their compatibility with one another and with the company's nonmarketing activities*

Marketing Strategy: Target Marketing and Market Segmentation

Learning Objective 11-3

Explain market segmentation and how it is used in target marketing.

Target Market *the particular group of people or organizations on which a firm's marketing efforts are focused*

Market Segmentation *process of dividing a market into categories of customer types, or "segments," having similar wants and needs and who can be expected to show interest in the same products*

Marketers have long known that products cannot be all things to all people. The emergence of the marketing concept and the recognition of customers' needs and wants led marketers to think in terms of **target markets**—the particular groups of people or organizations on which a firm's marketing efforts are focused. Selecting target markets is usually the first step in the marketing strategy.

Target marketing requires **market segmentation**, dividing a market into categories of customer types, or "segments," having similar wants and needs and who can be expected to show interest in the same products. Once they have identified segments, companies may adopt a variety of strategies. Some firms market products by targeting more than one segment. Not that many years ago General Motors tried to offer automobiles for virtually every segment of the market. Its brands included Chevrolet, Buick, Oldsmobile, Pontiac, and Cadillac, as well as specialty products like Saturn, Saab, and Hummer plus assorted SUVs and pickup trucks. The financial crisis of 2008–2011, though, pushed GM to the brink of financial ruin and caused the company to have to accept a bailout from the U.S. government. To deal with the crisis, GM sold some of its product lines and shut down several others. Today the firm is a much leaner company, targeting fewer marketing segments and earning much higher profits.

Product Positioning *process of fixing, adapting, and communicating the nature of a product*

In contrast, some businesses have always focused on a narrower range of products, such as Ferrari's high-priced sports cars, aiming at just one segment. Note that segmentation is a strategy for analyzing consumers, not products. Once marketers identify a target segment, they can begin marketing products for that segment. The process of fixing, adapting, and communicating the nature of the product itself is called **product positioning**.

Identifying Market Segments

By definition, members of a market segment must share some common traits that affect their purchasing decisions. In identifying consumer segments, researchers look at several different influences on consumer behavior. We discuss five of the most important variables next.

Geographic Segmentation

Geographic Variables *geographic units that may be considered in developing a segmentation strategy*

Geographic Segmentation *geographic units, from countries to neighborhoods, that may be considered in identifying different market segments in a segmentation strategy*

Many buying decisions are affected by the places people call home. Urban residents don't need agricultural equipment, and sailboats sell better near large bodies of water than in the mountains. **Geographic variables** are the geographic units, from countries to neighborhoods, that researchers consider in a strategy of **geographic segmentation**. McDonald's restaurants in Germany, in contrast to those in the United States, offer beer on the menu. Pharmacies in Jackson Hole, Wyoming, sell firearms that are forbidden in Chicago. Starbucks has been focusing on the growing geographic segment in China. One method Starbucks is using is offering many more tea options, since tea is a preferred beverage among Chinese consumers.

Demographic Segmentation

Demographic Segmentation *a segmentation strategy that uses demographic characteristics to identify different market segments*

Demographic Variables *characteristics of populations that may be considered in developing a segmentation strategy*

Demographic segmentation is a strategy used to separate consumers by demographic variables. **Demographic variables** describe populations by identifying traits, such as age, income, gender, ethnic background, marital status, race, religion, and social class, as detailed in Table 11.1. Depending on the marketer's purpose, a demographic segment can be a single classification (for example, ages 20–34) or a combination of categories (ages 20–34, married without children, earning \$25,000–\$44,999 a year).

For example, Hot Topic started as a California-based chain specializing in clothes, accessories, and jewelry designed to appeal to Generation Y and Millennials, a demographic consisting of U.S. consumers born between the 1980s and 1990s. The theme was pop culture music because it was the biggest influence on the target demographic group's fashion tastes. More recently, Hot Topic has become a national retail chain for clothing, accessories, and entertainment products relating to today's pop culture.

table 11.1 Examples of Demographic Variables

Age	Under 5, 5–11, 12–19, 20–34, 35–49, 50–64, 65+
Education	Grade school or less, some high school, graduated from high school, some college, college degree, advanced degree
Family life cycle	Young single, young married without children, young married with children, older married with children under 18, older married without children under 18, older single, other
Family size	1, 2–3, 4–5, 6+
Income	Less than $15,000, $15,000–$24,999, $25,000–$50,000, $50,000–$100,000, $100,000–$200,000, more than $200,000
Regional	African, American, Asian, British, Eastern European, French, German, Irish, Italian, Latin American, Middle Eastern, Scandinavian
Race	American Indian, Asian, Black, White
Religion	Buddhist, Catholic, Hindu, Jewish, Muslim, Protestant
Gender	Man, woman, nonbinary

Geo-Demographic Segmentation

As the name implies, **geo-demographic segmentation** is a combination strategy. **Geo-demographic variables** are a combination of geographic and demographic traits and are becoming the most common segmentation tools. An example would be young urban professional women, well-educated, 25- to 54-year-olds with high-paying professional jobs living in the "downtown" zip codes of major cities. Chico's targets many women in this segment, offering stylish travel clothing well suited to the needs of this subset in the larger population. Segmentation is more effective because the greater number of variables defines the market more precisely.

Geo-Demographic Segmentation *using a combination of geographic and demographic traits for identifying different market segments in a segmentation strategy*

Geo-Demographic Variables *combination of geographic and demographic traits used in developing a segmentation strategy*

Psychographic Segmentation

Markets can also be separated into a **psychographic segmentation** according to such **psychographic variables** as lifestyles, interests, personalities, and attitudes. For example, Burberry, traditionally promoted as "The Iconic British Luxury Brand" whose raincoats have been a symbol of British tradition since 1856, has in recent years repositioned itself as a global luxury brand like Gucci and Louis Vuitton. The strategy calls for attracting a different type of customer—the top-of-the-line, fashion-conscious individual—who enjoys the prestige of shopping at stores like Neiman Marcus, Bergdorf Goodman, and Harrod's. Psychographics are particularly important to marketers because, unlike demographics and geographics, they can be changed by marketing efforts. With the onset of global interdependence and open communications, marketing today is changing some traditional lifestyles and attitudes in nations around the globe. Polish companies, for example, have overcome consumer resistance by promoting the safety and desirability of using credit cards rather than depending on solely using cash.[11] Indeed, businesses in many different countries have used a variety of different payment options to make it easier for consumers to buy their products. Some countries, such as Sweden, have become almost cashless. India has also moved aggressively toward a cashless economy, originally intended to reduce illegal transactions but also having a tremendous impact on consumers.[12]

Psychographic Segmentation *a segmentation strategy that uses psychographic characteristics to identify different market segments*

Psychographic Variables *consumer characteristics, such as lifestyles, opinions, interests, and attitudes, that may be considered in developing a segmentation strategy*

Behavioral Segmentation

Behavioral segmentation uses **behavioral variables** to market items based on how customers actually behave. These behaviors, in turn, may be caused by a variety of factors. One example is heavy users (customers who buy in bulk, the key to success for Sam's and Costco). Another is what might be called situation buyers. (Halloween, for example, is now the second-largest U.S. "holiday" in terms of spending.) A final example is specific purpose. (All Free Clear is a detergent for people who have skin reactions to additives in other detergents.)

Behavioral Segmentation *a segmentation strategy that uses behavioral variables to identify different market segments*

Behavioral Variables *behavioral patterns displayed by groups of consumers and that are used in developing a segmentation strategy*

Learning Objective 11-4

Discuss the purpose of marketing research and compare the four marketing research methods.

Marketing Research

Marketing Research *the study of what customers need and want and how best to meet those needs and wants*

Unfortunately, no matter how logically or rationally marketing managers approach their work, their decisions and plans may still be less than perfect, but the consequences of their decisions and plans about marketing mix and segmentation strategy can be long-lasting. To make the best decisions and develop the most effective plans possible, marketers try to be customer focused and base their actions on timely information about marketplace trends. **Marketing research**, the study of what customers need and want and how best to meet those needs and wants, is a powerful tool for gaining decision-making information.

The relationship of research to the overall marketing process is shown in Figure 11.3. Ultimately, its role is to increase competitiveness by clarifying the interactions among a firm's stakeholders (including customers), marketing variables, environmental factors, and marketing decisions. Researchers use several methods to obtain, interpret, and apply information about customers. They determine the kinds of information needed for decisions on marketing strategy, goal setting, and target-market selection. In doing so, they may conduct studies about customer responses to proposed changes in the marketing mix. One researcher, for example, might study response to an experimental paint formula (new product). Another might explore the response to a price reduction (new price) on condominiums. Still a third might check responses to a proposed advertising campaign (new promotion). Marketers also try to learn whether customers will more likely purchase a product in a specialty shop or online (new place).

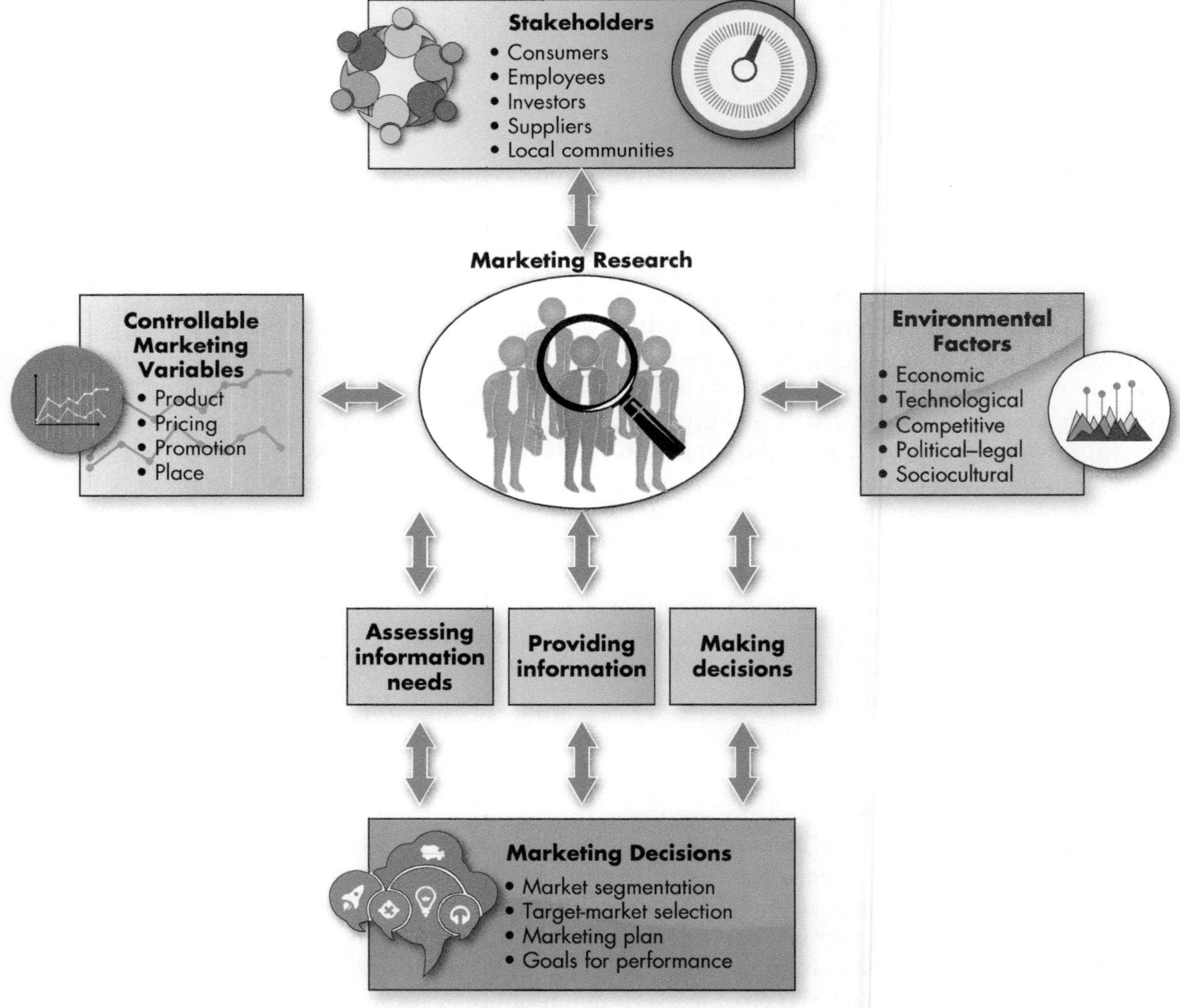

FIGURE 11.3 Market Research and the Marketing Process

The importance of selling products in international markets has expanded the role of marketing research. For example, when a company decides to sell goods or services globally, it must decide whether to standardize products across all markets or to specialize by offering different versions for each market. Accordingly, market research's orientation has become increasingly globalized.

The Research Process

Market research can occur at almost any point in a product's life cycle. Typically, then, it's used in developing new products or altering existing products. When Marriott decided to launch its Fairfield Inn & Suites brand, it sent teams of managers to spend time in other economy hotels across the country to test everything from the thickness of towels to the firmness of mattresses to the size of the rooms. It also conducted numerous focus group interviews with economy-minded travelers to find out what was more and less important to them. After three years of research, the Fairfield brand was successfully launched. Universal routinely sends employees to rival theme parks "undercover" to see how guests are enjoying new rides, new restaurants, and new merchandise.

Marketing research usually follows five basic steps. But even very effective companies can stumble if their research process is flawed. Consider the classic example of Coca-Cola that we will use to illustrate the five steps in the marketing research process.

1. ***Study the current situation.*** What is the need and what is being done to meet it? In the mid-1980s, marketing managers at Coca-Cola became concerned by its declining market share. The company decided to undertake a now famous (or infamous) marketing study to identify ways to reverse this decline.
2. ***Select a research method.*** In choosing from a wide range of methods, marketers must consider the effectiveness and costs of different options. Coca-Cola's preliminary information suggested that the taste of Coke was the main source of the problem. In particular, Coca-Cola was losing market share to Pepsi-Cola because customers found that Pepsi tasted sweeter. Researchers decided to use taste tests for consumer opinions on a "New Coke" formula that was sweeter than original Coke.
3. ***Collect data.*** Most research data can be classified into one of two categories. **Secondary data** are already available from previous research. Several different U.S. government agencies, including the Census Bureau and the Department of Labor, for instance, provide online data collected by the government on geographic and demographic variables. Using secondary data can save time, effort, and money. However, when secondary sources are unavailable or inadequate, researchers must obtain **primary data**, new data from newly performed research. In Coca-Cola's study, primary data were collected from some 200,000 consumer "tasters" who compared the New Coke versus the taste of the original Coke and Pepsi.

Secondary Data *data that are already available from previous research*

Primary Data *new data that are collected from newly performed research*

4. ***Analyze the data.*** Once data are collected they must be analyzed and organized into meaningful information. Analysis of data in the Coke research found that more than one-half of the consumer tasters rated New Coke to be tastier than original Coke and Pepsi.
5. ***Prepare a report.*** This report should describe the study's methodology and findings. It should also identify solutions and, where appropriate, make recommendations on a course of action. Coca-Cola's resulting recommendation—to replace original Coke with the New Coke—was implemented. As it turned out, the decision was a costly disaster that eventually resulted in restoring original Coke under a new name—Coca-Cola Classic—and then withdrawing New Coke from the market. As it turned out, research flaws had biased the results: (1) Taste testers were not told that if New Coke was launched, then original Coke would no longer be available, and (2) consumers' long-standing attachment to the original Coke brand would be lost when the product was withdrawn from the market.[13]

Most companies undertake marketing research before launching new products. But even strong marketing research may prove inaccurate. For instance, when Google launched Google Glass in 2014, it anticipated huge demand. But slow sales caused the firm to stop distribution in early 2015.

This Coca-Cola example was a costly learning experience, illustrating that even the most successful companies encounter occasional marketing mistakes. Although Coke's market research ultimately led them down the wrong path, many others, including Marriott Hotels and Resorts, Samsung Electronics, and Procter & Gamble personal care products, have conducted market research campaigns that led to increased market share and a better understanding of their markets.

Research Methods

The success of a research study often depends on the method a research team uses. Consider the following four basic methods of market research:

Observation *research method that obtains data by watching and recording consumer behavior*

Survey *research method of collecting consumer data using questionnaires, telephone calls, and face-to-face interviews*

Focus Group *research method using a group of people from a larger population who are asked their attitudes, opinions, and beliefs about a product in an open discussion*

Experimentation *research method using a sample of potential consumers to obtain reactions to test versions of new products or variations of existing products*

1. **Observation** involves watching and recording consumer behavior. Today, information technology systems, including live camera feeds and computer recordings, allow marketers to observe consumer preferences rapidly and with great accuracy. Electronic scanners and data files at brick-and-mortar stores, along with data storage of television viewing, phone transactions, and website activity, allow marketers to see each consumer's purchasing history—what products and brands that person prefers over a set period of time.
2. Sometimes, marketers must go a step further and ask questions. One way to get valuable information is by using **surveys**, a method of collecting data in which the researcher interacts with people to gather facts, attitudes, or opinions, either by mailing or e-mailing questionnaires, by telephone calls, or by conducting face-to-face interviews. United Parcel Service (UPS) surveyed customers to find out how to improve service. Clients wanted more interaction with drivers because they can offer practical advice on shipping. As a result, UPS added extra drivers, providing them with more time with customers. Most surveys today are conducted online.
3. In a **focus group**, participants are gathered in one place (either in person or in online group sessions), presented with an issue or situation, and then asked to discuss it. The researcher takes notes and makes video recordings but provides only a minimal amount of structure. This technique allows researchers to explore issues too complex for questionnaires and can produce creative solutions.
4. **Experimentation** compares the responses of the same or similar people under different circumstances. For example, a firm trying to decide whether to include

finding a better way

A Safer Ride

Though over 99 percent of Lyft rides and nearly that same percentage of Uber rides ended without incident in 2020 and 2021, that's little consolation to the almost 5,000 reported victims of assaults during ride-shares those same years or the families of the 30 riders who lost their lives. The overwhelming majority of those victims were women. The second-highest category of victims was LGBTQIA+ riders. For these riders, the ride-share platforms create guides to rider safety, including tips like waiting for your ride inside at night, communicating your ride intentions to a trusted friend or family member, and telling the driver that you've done so.[14]

Kiersten Harris was alarmed by those numbers and wanted to create a platform that made the experience of unsafe rides a thing of the past. She wanted a platform that would provide a safety net for which the passenger didn't have to take full responsibility. She imagined an app that would give riders a sense of safety while actively combating human trafficking, domestic violence, and stalking.

As a driver for Uber, Jillian Anderson heard horror stories from some of her passengers about harassment and assaults during rides. Female-presenting and LGBTQIA+ people would specifically request a ride with her because they felt safe in her car. When Harris presented the opportunity to create a new platform, Anderson was thrilled to bring her computer science engineering skills on board.

Harris and Anderson imagined an entire company of trusted, vetted, reputable, and safe drivers. They imagined that a victim of crime might be able to escape from a dangerous situation with the click of a button on a smartphone. And so, in 2020, HERide was born. Available only in select cities and centered in and around Atlanta, Georgia, the company takes an everyday convenience—hailing a ride at any time—and gives it a unique twist. Riders familiar with Lyft and Uber will find the same concepts and structure in HERide. They simply open the app, enter their destination, and select a ride.

fotostorm/Getty Images

Harris didn't want to create a whole new ride-share industry—just a new experience within it. "Starting in an already established industry doesn't mean you have to recreate the wheel," Harris said. "We wanted to improve the rideshare system for women, so we looked for ways to do that." The company promotes a rigorous vetting process for its drivers, in-ride security features, and higher pay for drivers. Harris works to differentiate HERide in a market dominated by two household names. So far, customers have shown fierce brand loyalty, and social media followers have lauded and promoted the company—drivers and riders alike.[15]

walnuts in a new candy bar probably wouldn't learn much by asking people what they thought of the idea. However, the company could ask a random sample of people to try the new candy with walnuts and then provide their opinions and a different random sample to try the candy without walnuts and provide their opinions. If the two groups offer different opinions, the company will have valuable information about whether or not to include walnuts in its new candy.

Understanding Consumer Behavior

Learning Objective 11-5

Describe the consumer buying process and the key factors that influence that process.

Although marketing managers can tell us what features people generally want in a new refrigerator, even if they conduct "perfect" marketing research about refrigerators, they cannot always tell us why people buy particular refrigerators. What preferences are consumers fulfilling? Is there a psychological or sociological explanation for why they purchase one product and not another? These questions and many others are addressed in the study of **consumer behavior**, the decision process by which people buy and consume products.

Consumer Behavior *study of the decision process by which people buy and consume products*

Influences on Consumer Behavior

To understand consumer behavior, marketers draw heavily on such fields as psychology and sociology. The result is a focus on four major influences on consumer behavior: (1) *psychological*, (2) *personal*, (3) *social*, and (4) *cultural*. By identifying which influences are most active in certain circumstances, marketers try to explain consumer choices and predict future buying behavior.

Psychological influences include an individual's motivations, perceptions, ability to learn, and attitudes.

Personal influences include lifestyle, personality, and economic status.

Social influences include family, opinion leaders and influencers (people whose opinions are valued by others), and such reference groups as friends, coworkers, and professional associates.

Cultural influences include culture (the way of living that distinguishes one large group from another), subculture (smaller groups with shared values), and social class (the cultural ranking of groups according to such criteria as background, occupation, and income).

Although these factors can have a strong impact on a consumer's choices, their effect on actual purchases is sometimes weak or negligible. Some consumers, for example, exhibit high **brand loyalty**; they regularly purchase products, such as McDonald's foods or Starbucks coffee, because they are satisfied with their performance. Such people, though, are less subject to influence and stick with preferred brands. In contrast, the clothes you wear, the social network you choose, and the way you decorate your room often reflect social and psychological influences on your consumer behavior.

Psychological Influences *include an individual's motivations, perceptions, ability to learn, and attitudes that marketers use to study buying behavior*

Personal Influences *include lifestyle, personality, and economic status that marketers use to study buying behavior*

Social Influences *include family, opinion leaders (people whose opinions are sought by others), and such reference groups as friends, coworkers, and professional associates that marketers use to study buying behavior*

Cultural Influences *include culture, subculture, and social class influences that marketers use to study buying behavior*

Brand Loyalty *pattern of repeated consumer purchasing based on satisfaction with a product's performance*

The Consumer Buying Process

Students of consumer behavior have constructed various models to help show how consumers decide to buy products. Figure 11.4 presents one such model. At the core of this and similar models is an awareness of the many influences that lead to consumption. Ultimately, marketers use this information to develop marketing plans.

Problem or Need Recognition This process begins when the consumer recognizes a problem or need. Need recognition also occurs when you have a chance

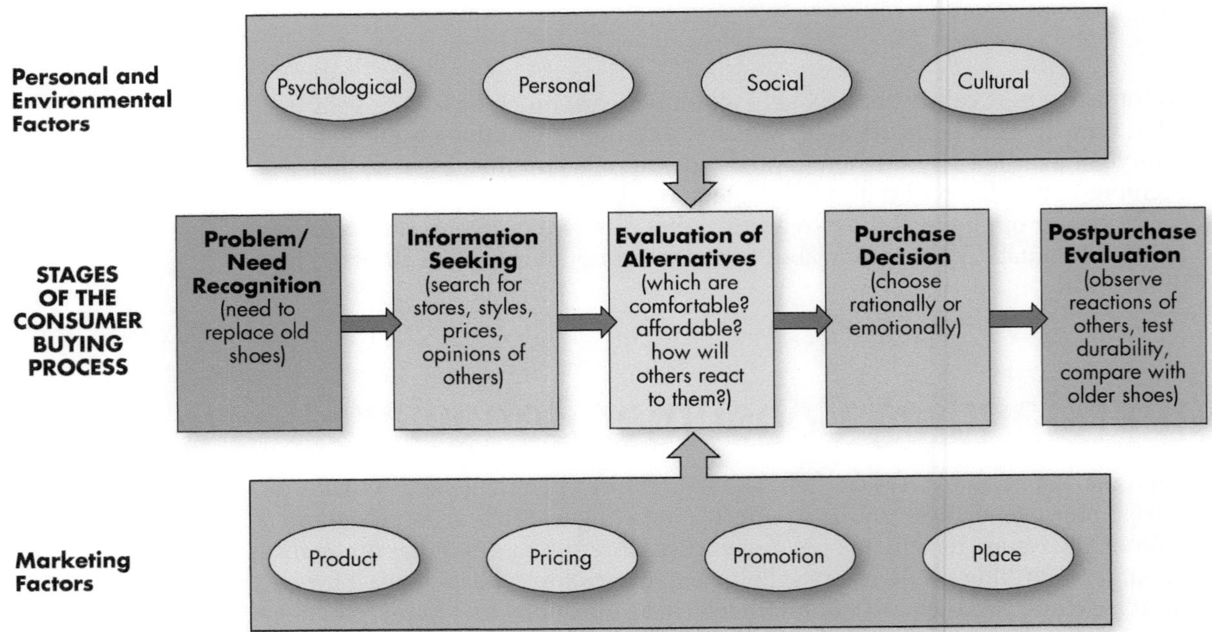

FIGURE 11.4 The Consumer Buying Process

to change your buying habits. When you obtain your first job after graduation, for example, your new income may enable you to buy things that were once too expensive for you. You may find that you need professional clothing, apartment furnishings, and a car. Bank of America and Citibank cater to such shifts in needs when they market credit cards to college students.

Information Seeking Having recognized a need, consumers then tend to seek information. The search is not always extensive, but before making major purchases, most people seek at least some information from personal sources, public sources, and experiences. Before joining a gym, you may read about your area gyms on yelp.com or you may visit a few gyms in your neighborhood. From this information search, consumers develop an **evoked set** (or **consideration set**), which is the group of products they will consider buying.

Evoked Set (or **Consideration Set**) *group of products consumers will consider buying as a result of information search*

Evaluation of Alternatives If someone is in the market for skis, they probably have some idea of who makes skis and how they differ. By analyzing product attributes (price, prestige, quality) of the consideration set, consumers compare products before deciding which one best meets their needs.

Purchase Decision Ultimately, in most cases consumers make purchase decisions. "Buy" decisions are based on rational motives, emotional motives, or a combination of the two. **Rational motives** involve the logical evaluation of product attributes: cost, quality, and usefulness. **Emotional motives** involve nonobjective factors and include sociability, imitation of others, and aesthetics. For example, you might buy the same brand of jeans as your friends to feel accepted in a certain group, not because your friends happen to have the "good sense" to prefer durable, reasonably priced jeans.

Rational Motives *reasons for purchasing a product that are based on a logical evaluation of product attributes*

Emotional Motives *reasons for purchasing a product that are based on nonobjective factors*

Postpurchase Evaluation Interestingly, marketing does not stop with the sale of a product; what happens after the sale is also important. Marketers want consumers to be happy after buying products so that they are more likely to buy them again. Because consumers do not want to go through a complex decision process for every purchase, they often repurchase products they have used and liked. Not all consumers are satisfied with their purchases, of course. These buyers are not likely to purchase the same product(s) again and are much more apt to broadcast their poor experiences than are satisfied customers. This is why some companies work so hard to correct problems reported by disgruntled customers.

Organizational Marketing and Buying Behavior

Learning Objective 11-6

Discuss the four categories of organizational markets and the characteristics of business-to-business (B2B) buying behavior.

In the consumer market, buying and selling transactions are visible to the public. Equally important, though far less visible, are organizational (or commercial) markets. Marketing to organizations that buy goods and services used in creating and delivering consumer products or public services involves various kinds of markets and buying behaviors different from those in consumer markets.

Business Marketing

Business marketing involves organizational or commercial markets that fall into four B2B categories: (1) services companies, (2) industrial, (3) reseller, and (4) government and institutional markets. Taken together, the B2B markets do more than $25 trillion in business annually—more than double the amount of business conducted in the U.S. consumer market.[16]

Services Companies Market *firms engaged in the business of providing services to the purchasing public*

Services Market The **services companies market** encompasses the many firms that provide services to the purchasing public. Imagine, for example, the materials and supplies Disney World needs to provide exceptional experiences for visitors. Similar needs exist to operate United Airlines, Netflix, and the accounting firm PwC. Everything from veterinary clinics to hospitality services providers to health care centers and nursery schools buy materials needed to provide services to customers.

Industrial Market *organizational market consisting of firms that buy goods that are either converted into products or used during production*

Industrial Market The **industrial market** includes businesses that buy goods to be converted into other products or that are used up during production. It includes farmers, manufacturers, and some retailers. For example, piano manufacturer Steinway buys wood, wood stain, metal, and other materials from other companies to make grand pianos. The company also buys office supplies, tools, and factory equipment—items never seen by piano buyers—that are used at its production facilities in New York and Germany.

Reseller Market *organizational market consisting of intermediaries that buy and resell finished goods*

Reseller Market Before products reach consumers, they pass through a **reseller market** consisting of intermediaries, including wholesalers and retailers, that buy and resell finished goods. For example, as a leading distributor of parts and accessories for the pleasure boat market, Coast Distribution System buys lights, steering wheels, and propellers and resells them to marinas and boat-repair shops.

Institutional Market *organizational market consisting of such nongovernmental buyers of goods and services as hospitals, churches, museums, and charitable organizations*

Government and Institutional Market In addition to federal and state governments, there are over 89,000 local governments in the United States. In 2020, state and local governments spent $4.2 trillion for durable goods, nondurables, services, and construction. The **institutional market** consists of nongovernmental organizations, such as hospitals, churches, museums, and charities, that also use supplies and equipment as well as legal, accounting, and transportation services.

B2B Buying Behavior

In some respects, organizational buying behavior bears little resemblance to consumer buying practices. The primary differences include the buyers' purchasing skills and an emphasis on buyer–seller relationships.

Differences in Buyers Unlike most consumers, organizational buyers purchase in large quantities and are professional, specialized, and well informed. These characteristics of B2B buyers include the following:

- Industrial buyers usually *buy in bulk or large quantities*. Because of this fact, and with so much money at stake, buyers are often experts about the products they buy. On a regular basis, B2B buyers study competing products and alternative suppliers by attending trade shows, by networking with others electronically, by reading trade literature, and by holding technical discussions with sellers' representatives.
- As professionals, B2B buyers *are trained in methods for negotiating purchase terms*. Once buyer–seller agreements have been reached, they also sign formal legal contracts.
- As a rule, industrial buyers *are company specialists in a line of items and are often experts about the products they buy*. As one of several buyers for a large bakery, for example, you may specialize in food ingredients. Another buyer may specialize in baking equipment, while a third may buy office equipment and supplies.

Differences in the Buyer–Seller Relationship Consumer–seller relationships are often impersonal, short-lived, one-time interactions. In contrast, B2B situations often *involve frequent and long-term buyer–seller relationships*. The development of a long-term relationship provides each party with access to the technical strengths of the other as well as the security of knowing what future business activities to expect. Thus, a buyer and a supplier may, for instance, form a design team to create products to benefit both parties. Accordingly, industrial sellers emphasize personal selling by trained representatives who understand the needs of each customer.

Social Media and Marketing

Social networking as used by marketers today refers to communications that flow among people and organizations interacting through an online platform that facilitates building social relations among its users. From a marketing perspective, **social networking media** are the websites or access channels, such as Facebook, Instagram, Twitter, LinkedIn, TikTok, Threads, and YouTube, to which millions of consumers go for information and discussions before making their purchase decisions.

Social Networking *network of communications that flow among people and organizations interacting through an online platform*

Social Networking Media *websites or access channels, such as Facebook, Twitter, LinkedIn, and YouTube, to which consumers go for information and discussions*

Viral Marketing and Social Networking **Viral marketing** is a form of marketing that relies on social networking and the Internet to spread information like a "virus" from person to person. The marketing purpose may be to increase brand awareness, to promote new product ideas, or to foster excitement for stimulating sales. Messages about new cars, sports events, movies, and many other goods and services flow via networks among potential customers who pass the information on to others. Using various social network formats—games, contests, chat rooms, blogs, and bulletin boards—marketers encourage potential customers to try out products and tell other people about them. For example, as Disney plans to launch new movies featuring characters from the *Star Wars* mythology and the Marvel universe, it often releases brief sample footage months—or even years—in advance. The hope is that viewers will like what they see and help build anticipation for the new movie well before it actually opens in theaters. Marketers, including such giants as Bank of America, McDonald's, eBay, and Cisco, use **corporate blogs** increasingly for public relations, branding, and otherwise spreading messages that stimulate chat about products in target markets.[17]

Viral Marketing *type of marketing that relies on the Internet to spread information like a "virus" from person to person about products and ideas*

Corporate Blogs *comments and opinions published on the web by or for an organization to promote its activities*

Web-Driven Revenue with Social Networking Although many major consumer companies have their own Facebook pages, small businesses also use social media channels to increase revenues by networking with customers in target markets. Luna Shark Productions, for example, is a small podcasting company in South Carolina. One of its most recent podcasts was the ninth most listened to on Spotify in March 2023. The firm attributes its success to extensive social networking across various social media channels.

How effective can social networking be? Viral marketing and social networking can lead to consumer awareness faster and with wider reach than traditional media messages—and at a lower cost. It works for two reasons. First, people rely on online media for information that they used to get from newspapers, magazines, and television. Equally important, however, is the interactive element—people become participants in the process of spreading the word by forwarding information to and seeking information from other users.

The continuing growth of social media is changing marketing practices of businesses and consumer behavior, too. Facebook has become the Internet's most-used social media site, with about 2.9 billion active users each month and more than 1.97 billion users each day. Although Facebook is the leader, X (formerly Twitter), Instagram, and numerous other fast-growing networks are collectively having a major impact. These growth profiles reflect not only the huge size of the social media industry but also the enormous population of participants who influence and persuade one another to explore new ideas and products, thus becoming both consumers and sellers. The industry's growth is attributed especially to (1) increasing numbers of mobile device users, (2) more participants in the older-than-55 demographic who are using X, and (3) greater global reach to more potential users. As companies gain experience, they are using social media in new ways. In addition to advertising promotions, Kellogg Company uses social media for consumer research and to get new product ideas.

Procter & Gamble has learned that viral exposure on Facebook can generate more sales than can TV advertising. And eBay finds that its sellers and buyers use social media to guide other buyers and sellers to eBay's website. For students of marketing, the social media trend has two clear implications: (1) As consumers using social media, you will receive a growing number of tempting product exposures; and (2) as a user of social media who becomes familiar with its applications and technical operations, you will find a growing number of career opportunities in social media positions.

The International Marketing Mix

Marketing internationally means mounting a strategy to support global business operations. Foreign customers differ from domestic buyers in language, customs, business practices, and consumer behavior. If they go global, marketers must reconsider each element of the marketing mix: product, pricing, place, and promotion.

International Products Some products can be sold abroad with virtually no changes. Coca-Cola and Marlboro are the same in Peoria, Illinois, and Paris, France. In other cases, U.S. firms have had to create products with built-in flexibility, like an electric shaver that is adaptable to either 110- or 220-volt outlets so travelers can use it in both U.S. and European electrical outlets. Frequently, however, domestic products require a major redesign for buyers in foreign markets. To sell computers in Japan, for example, Apple had to develop a Japanese-language operating system.

International Pricing When pricing for international markets, marketers must consider the higher costs of transporting and selling products abroad. For example, because of the higher costs of buildings, rent, equipment, and imported meat as well as differences in exchange rates, a McDonald's Big Mac that costs $5.15 in the United States has a price tag of $6.26 in Norway.

International Distribution In some industries, including consumer products and industrial equipment, delays in starting new international distribution networks can be costly, so companies with existing distribution systems often enjoy an advantage. Many companies have avoided time delays by buying existing businesses

Images of Africa Photobank/Alamy Stock Photo

Before creating an international ad like this Kenyan advertisement for Coca-Cola, it is crucial to research what disparities, such as meaning of words, traditions, and taboos, exist between different societies. For example, German manufacturers of backpacks label them as "body bags," not terribly enticing to the U.S. consumer. Can you guess why Gerber baby food is not sold in France? The French translation of Gerber is "to vomit"! Effective marketing does not just involve knowledge of culture abroad but also requires a general sensitivity to social trends and language.

with already-established distribution and marketing networks. Procter & Gamble, for example, bought Revlon's Max Factor and Betrix cosmetics, both of which have distribution and marketing networks in foreign markets. Distribution methods used in the United States, though, don't always fit in international markets. For example, in Europe, Breathe Right nasal strips are identified as "medicinal" and must be sold in pharmacies.

International Promotion Occasionally, a good ad campaign is a good campaign just about anywhere. Quite often, however, U.S. promotional tactics do not succeed in other countries. Many Europeans believe that a product must be inherently shoddy if a company resorts to any advertising, particularly the U.S. hard-sell variety.

International marketers are ever more aware of cultural differences that can cause negative reactions to improperly advertised products. Some Europeans, for example, are offended by TV commercials that show weapons or violence. However, some European advertising is more provocative and sexually explicit than would be accepted in some countries. Meanwhile, cigarette commercials that are banned from U.S. television thrive in many Asian and some European markets. Managers must carefully match product promotions to local customs and cultural values to successfully promote sales and avoid offending customers.

entrepreneurship and new ventures

A Place to Bloom

There is a striking dearth of literature about business owners and entrepreneurs who are BIPOC (Black, Indigenous, people of color) or LGBTQIA+. The Intuit-owned company Mailchimp, long a staple of marketing for businesses, aims to change that with the publication of *Bloom Season*, an online magazine featuring "historically excluded" (not just underrepresented) entrepreneurs.

In its inaugural edition in 2022, Bloom Season used its platform to collaborate and showcase Black creators and entrepreneurs. In its second season, the spotlight turned to the LGBTQIA+ community. The website features a collection of stories, advice, and articles to support entrepreneurs from the ideation stage through the creation of business, marketing, and scaling. Information is written by and for historically excluded people. Articles range from the benefits of managing mental health, to hiring queer leaders, to how to celebrate Pride all year.

Bloom Season seeks to do more than reinforce existing silos, where Black and LGBTQIA+ business owners are marketed to. The website shares thoughtfully crafted content to address the specific challenges of each group while creating a space for conversation and collaboration. Using the considerable market voice of both Inuit and Mailchimp, the project draws attention to the immense potential for diverse entrepreneurs.

For this venture, Intuit and Mailchimp partnered with the impact innovation company Kin. Their website opens with this statement: "Kin is a creative company designed to advance social change through culture. We partner with brands, organizations, and innovators to create bold, transformative, and purposeful work." Co-founded by Sophie Ozoux and Kwame Taylor-Hayford, Kin has won international acclaim for its creative and groundbreaking work.

nicolasmenijes/123RF

With partners like Delta Air Lines, Uber, Ben & Jerry's and Chobani, Kin has harnessed the power of intimately understanding nuances between communities, crafting messages for vastly underrepresented and untapped markets like BIPOC and LGBTQIA+ customers and their allies who are eager to do business with companies whose values align with and support them.

As companies continue to look for ways to balance politically and socially divided markets, Kin and its clients are tipping that balance to a more deliberately slanted message, using their marketing efforts to drive lasting social change.

Because of the need to adjust the marketing mix, success in international markets is hard won. But whether a firm markets in domestic or international markets, the basic principles of marketing still apply—only their implementation changes.

Learning Objective 11-7

Discuss the marketing mix as it applies to small business.

Small Business and the Marketing Mix

Many of today's largest firms were once small businesses. Behind the success of many small firms, in turn, lies a skillful application of the marketing concept and an understanding of each element in the marketing mix.

Small-Business Products

Some new products and firms are doomed at the start because few customers want or need what they have to offer. Many fail to estimate realistic market potential, and some offer new products before they have clear pictures of their target segments. In contrast, a thorough understanding of what customers want has paid off for many small firms. Take, for example, the case of Little Earth Productions, Inc., a company that makes fashion accessories, such as handbags. Originally, the company merely considered how consumers would use its handbags. But after examining shopping habits, Little Earth Productions redesigned for better in-store display. Because stores can give handbags better visibility by hanging them instead of placing them on floors or low countertops, Little Earth Productions added small handles specifically for that purpose, resulting in increased sales. More recently, Little Earth has been concentrating on accessories for sports fans, such as logoed purses, headbands, wallets, and hair accessories.

Small-Business Pricing

Haphazard pricing can sink a firm with a good product. Small-business pricing errors usually result from a failure to estimate operating expenses accurately. The founder of Nomie Baby, makers of spill-proof removable car seat covers for infants, started by setting prices too low. Considering only manufacturing and materials costs, other costs—shipping, storage, designing—were mistakenly ignored and not covered by the original selling price. Thereafter, when start-up prices were increased to cover all costs, sales (fortunately) remained strong. New business owners, afraid to set prices too high, often tend to underprice. Underpricing, in turn, then leads to financial crisis. Failing business owners have often been heard to say, "I didn't realize how much it costs to run a business!" Sometimes, however, firms discover their prices are too low, even when they cover all costs. A computer error at Headsets.com once caused cost-only prices rather than retail prices to be posted for the company's products on the Internet. The CEO was surprised that the erroneous low prices did not create a surge in sales. Instead, steady consumer response indicated that the firm's products were not as price sensitive as believed, so the company raised original prices once, by 8 percent. Revenue rose as sales continued with little or no change from previous levels.[18] When small businesses set prices by carefully assessing costs and understanding their competitive market, many earn satisfactory profits.

Small-Business Distribution

The ability of many small businesses to attract and retain customers depends partly on the choice of location, especially for new service businesses.

In distribution, as in other aspects of the marketing mix, however, smaller companies may have advantages over larger competitors. A smaller company may be able to address customers' needs more quickly and efficiently with an added personal touch. During the COVID-19 pandemic in 2020, many small businesses were quick to start manufacturing and distributing face masks and expand local delivery services for food and other products.

Small-Business Promotion

Successful small businesses plan for promotional expenses as part of start-up costs. Some hold down costs by using less expensive promotional methods, like publicity in local newspapers and online messaging and other forms of social media. Other small businesses identify themselves and their products with associated groups, organizations, and events. Thus, a crafts gallery might partner with a local art league to organize public showings of their combined products.

summary of learning objectives

LEARNING OBJECTIVE 11-1

Explain the concept of marketing and identify the five forces that constitute the external marketing environment.

Marketing is responsible for creating, communicating, and delivering value and satisfaction to customers. With limited financial resources, customers buy products that offer the best value, measured by the relationship between benefits and costs. Marketers must understand customers' wants and needs because they determine product features and the timing, place, and terms of sale that provide utility and add value for customers. A product may be a tangible good, a service, or even an idea. Products may be classified as either consumer products or industrial products when they are marketed to businesses or nonprofit organizations. Although marketing often focuses on single transactions for products, services, or ideas, marketers also take a longer-term perspective by managing customer relationships to benefit the organization and its stakeholders. *Customer relationship marketing* emphasizes building lasting relationships with customers and suppliers. Stronger relationships, including stronger economic and social ties, can result in greater long-term satisfaction, customer loyalty, and customer retention.

Five outside factors make up a company's external environment and influence its marketing programs: (1) The *political and legal environment* includes laws and regulations that may define or constrain business activities; (2) the *sociocultural environment* involves people's values, beliefs, and ideas that affect marketing decisions; (3) the *technological environment* includes new technologies that affect existing and new products; (4) the *economic environment* consists of conditions such as inflation, recession, and interest rates that influence organizational and individual spending patterns; and (5) the *competitive environment* is that in which marketers must persuade buyers to purchase their products rather than their competitors'.

LEARNING OBJECTIVE 11-2

Explain the purpose of a marketing plan and identify its main components.

A *marketing plan* is a statement of all the future marketing activities and resources that will be used to meet the desires and needs of customers so that the firm's overall business mission will be accomplished. It begins with objectives or goals setting the stage for everything that follows. *Marketing objectives*—the things marketing intends to accomplish—are the foundation that guides all of the detailed activities in the marketing plan. The marketing objectives focus on maintaining or enhancing the organization's future competitive position in its chosen markets. A marketing strategy can be developed once the marketing objectives have been clarified. *Marketing strategy* identifies the planned marketing programs, including all the marketing activities that will be used for achieving the marketing goals, when those activities will occur, and the contents of its programs. If planned activities are not affordable—requiring more resources than are available—then activities, programs, or goals are adjusted until realistic plans emerge.

Marketing strategy includes four basic components (often called the "Four Ps") of the *marketing mix*—product, pricing, place (distribution), and promotion—that marketing managers use to satisfy customers in target markets. The specific activities for each of the Four Ps are designed differently to best meet the needs of each target market. Marketing begins with a *product*, a good, service, or idea designed to fill a customer's need or want. Conceiving and developing new products is a constant challenge for marketers, who must always consider changing technology, consumer wants and needs, and economic conditions. Producers often promote particular features of products to distinguish them in the marketplace. *Product differentiation* is the creation of a feature or image that makes a product differ enough from existing products to attract consumers. The *pricing* of a product is often a balancing act. Prices must be high enough to support a variety of operating, administrative, research, and marketing costs, but low enough that consumers don't turn to competitors. In the marketing mix, *place* (or distribution) refers to where and how consumers get access to the products they buy. The most visible component of the marketing mix is *promotion*, a set of techniques for communicating information about products. The most important promotional tools include advertising, personal selling, sales promotions, publicity/public relations, and direct or interactive marketing.

LEARNING OBJECTIVE 11-3

Explain market segmentation and how it is used in target marketing.

Marketers think in terms of *target markets*—particular groups of people or organizations on which a firm's marketing efforts are focused. Target marketing requires *market segmentation*—dividing a market into categories of customer types or "segments," such as age, geographic location, or level of income. Members of a market segment have similar wants and needs and share some common traits that influence purchasing decisions. Once they identify segments, companies adopt a variety of strategies for attracting customers in one or more of the chosen target segments. Five variables are often used for segmentation: (1) *Geographic variables* are the geographic units that may be considered in developing a segmentation strategy. (2) *Demographic variables* describe populations by identifying such traits as age, income, gender, ethnic background, and marital status. (3) *Geo-demographic variables* combine demographic variables with geographic variables, such as an age category coupled with urban areas. (4) *Psychographic variables* include lifestyles, interests, and attitudes. (5) *Behavioral variables* include categories of behavioral patterns such as online consumers or large-volume buyers. Marketers search for segments showing promise for generating new sales if marketing efforts by other companies have overlooked or misjudged the segment's market potential. Such competitive weaknesses present marketing opportunities for other companies to enter into those segments. Desirable segments with market potential then become candidate target markets and, once chosen, they become part of the marketing strategy where the companion marketing mix is developed.

LEARNING OBJECTIVE 11-4

Discuss the purpose of marketing research and compare the four marketing research methods.

Effective marketing decisions should be customer based and focused on timely information about trends in the marketplace. *Marketing research* is a tool for gaining such information; it is the study of what customers want and how best to meet those needs. Researchers use several methods to obtain, interpret, and apply information about customers. They determine the kinds of information needed for marketing strategy, goal setting, target-market selection, and developing new or altered products for specific market segments. Marketing research's orientation has become increasingly globalized because of the increasing importance of selling products internationally.

Research success depends on which of four basic research methods is used: (1) *Observation* means watching and recording consumer preferences and behavior. By using live camera feeds, computer tracking, and other electronic technologies, marketers observe and record consumer preferences rapidly and with great accuracy. (2) The heart of any *survey* is a questionnaire on which participants record responses. Surveys can get responses to specific questions quickly and at relatively lower cost. (3) In a *focus group*, people are gathered in one place, presented with an issue or topic, and asked to discuss it. The researcher takes notes, makes video recordings, and encourages open discussion by providing only a minimal amount of structure for the group's discussion. This technique allows researchers to explore issues too complex for questionnaires; it can produce creative ideas and solutions. (4) *Experimentation* compares the responses and behaviors of the same or similar people under different conditions that are of interest to the researcher. Experimentation can be relatively expensive because of the costs of obtaining the experimental setting, securing participants, paying participants, and paying those who administer the experiment.

LEARNING OBJECTIVE 11-5

Describe the consumer buying process and the key factors that influence that process.

In the study of *consumer behavior*, marketers evaluate the decision process by which people buy and consume products. There are four major influences on consumer behavior: (1) *Psychological influences* include an individual's motivations, perceptions, ability to learn, and attitudes. (2) *Personal influences* include lifestyle, personality, and economic status. (3) *Social influences* include family, opinion leaders, and reference groups such as friends, coworkers, and professional associates. (4) *Cultural influences* include culture, subculture, and social class. At times, these influences have a significant impact on buying decisions, although consumers demonstrate high *brand loyalty* at times, regularly purchasing the same products.

Observers of consumer behavior have constructed various models to help marketers understand how consumers decide to purchase products. One model considers five influences that lead to consumption: (1) *Problem or need recognition*: The buying process begins when the consumer recognizes a problem or need. (2) *Information seeking*: Having recognized a need, consumers seek information. The information search leads to an evoked set (or consideration set)—a group of products they will consider buying. (3) *Evaluation of alternatives*: By analyzing product attributes (price, prestige, quality) of the consideration set, consumers compare products to decide which product best meets their needs. (4) *Purchase decision*: "Buy" decisions are based on rational motives, emotional motives, or both. *Rational motives* involve the logical evaluation of product attributes, such as cost, quality, and usefulness. *Emotional motives* involve nonobjective factors and include sociability, imitation of others, and aesthetics. (5) *Postpurchase evaluations*: Consumers continue to form opinions after their purchase. Marketers want consumers to be happy after the consumption of products so that they are more likely to buy them again.

LEARNING OBJECTIVE 11-6

Discuss the four categories of organizational markets and the characteristics of business-to-business (B2B) buying behavior.

The various organizational markets exhibit different buying behaviors from those in consumer markets. Business marketing involves organizational or commercial markets that fall into four B2B categories. (1) The *services companies market* encompasses the many firms that provide services to the purchasing public. Every service company, from pet care to hospitality services to health care and nursery schools, airlines, and more, buys resources needed to provide services to customers. (2) The *industrial market* consists of businesses that buy goods to be converted into other products or that are used during production. It includes farmers, manufacturers, and some retailers. (3) Before some products reach consumers, they pass through a *reseller market* consisting of intermediaries—wholesalers and retailers—that buy finished goods and resell them. (4) The *government and institutional market* includes federal, state, and local governments and nongovernmental buyers—hospitals, churches, museums, and charities—that purchase goods and services needed for serving their clients. Taken together, these four organizational markets do more than two times the business annually as the U.S. consumer markets.

Unlike most consumers, organizational buyers purchase in large quantities and are professional, specialized, and well informed. As professionals, they are trained in methods for negotiating purchase terms. Once buyer–seller agreements have been reached, they also arrange formal contracts. In contrast with consumer–seller relationships that are often one-time interactions, B2B situations involve frequent and enduring buyer–seller relationships that provide each party, buyer and seller, with access to the technical strengths of the other. Thus, a buyer and a supplier may form a design team to create products to benefit both parties. Accordingly, industrial sellers emphasize personal selling by trained representatives who understand the needs of each customer.

LEARNING OBJECTIVE 11-7

Discuss the marketing mix as it applies to small business.

Each element in the marketing mix can determine success or failure for any *small business*. Many *products* are failures because consumers don't need what they have to offer. A realistic market potential requires getting a clearer picture of what target segments want. Small-business *pricing* errors usually result from a failure to estimate start-up costs and operating expenses accurately. In addition to facilities construction or rental costs, shipping, storage, wages, taxes, utilities, and materials costs also must be considered. By carefully assessing costs, and by learning what customers are willing to pay, prices can be set to earn satisfactory profits. Perhaps the most crucial aspect of *place*, or distribution, is location, especially for services businesses, because locational convenience determines the ability to attract customers. Although *promotion* can be expensive and is essential for small businesses, costs can be reduced by using less expensive promotional methods. Local newspaper articles, online messaging, and television programming cover business events, thus providing free public exposure.

key terms

advertising **(p. 358)**
behavioral segmentation **(p. 361)**
behavioral variables **(p. 361)**
brand competition **(p. 354)**
brand loyalty **(p. 366)**
competitive environment **(p. 354)**
consumer behavior **(p. 365)**
consumer goods **(p. 351)**
corporate blogs **(p. 369)**
cultural influences **(p. 366)**
customer relationship management (CRM) **(p. 351)**
data mining **(p. 352)**
data warehousing **(p. 352)**
demographic segmentation **(p. 360)**
demographic variables **(p. 360)**
economic environment **(p. 353)**
emotional motives **(p. 367)**
evoked set (or consideration set) **(p. 367)**
experimentation **(p. 364)**
focus group **(p. 364)**
form utility **(p. 350)**
geographic segmentation **(p. 360)**
geographic variables **(p. 360)**
geo-demographic segmentation **(p. 361)**
geo-demographic variables **(p. 361)**
industrial goods **(p. 351)**
industrial market **(p. 368)**
institutional market **(p. 368)**
integrated marketing strategy **(p. 359)**
international competition **(p. 354)**
market segmentation **(p. 360)**
marketing **(p. 349)**
marketing manager **(p. 357)**
marketing mix **(p. 357)**
marketing objectives **(p. 356)**
marketing plan **(p. 356)**
marketing research **(p. 362)**
marketing strategy **(p. 357)**
observation **(p. 364)**
personal influences **(p. 366)**
personal selling **(p. 358)**
place (distribution) **(p. 358)**
place utility **(p. 350)**
political–legal environment **(p. 353)**
possession utility **(p. 350)**
pricing **(p. 357)**
primary data **(p. 363)**
product **(p. 357)**
product differentiation **(p. 357)**
product positioning **(p. 360)**
promotion **(p. 358)**
psychographic segmentation **(p. 361)**
psychographic variables **(p. 361)**
psychological influences **(p. 366)**
public relations **(p. 359)**
rational motives **(p. 367)**
relationship marketing **(p. 351)**
reseller market **(p. 368)**
sales promotions **(p. 359)**
secondary data **(p. 363)**
services **(p. 351)**
services companies market **(p. 368)**
social influences **(p. 366)**
social networking **(p. 369)**
social networking media **(p. 369)**
sociocultural environment **(p. 353)**
substitute product **(p. 354)**
survey **(p. 364)**
technological environment **(p. 353)**
time utility **(p. 350)**
target market **(p. 360)**
utility **(p. 350)**
value **(p. 349)**
viral marketing **(p. 369)**

questions & exercises

QUESTIONS FOR REVIEW

11-1. What are the five forces in the external marketing environment?

11-2. What is the difference between value and utility?

11-3. What is market segmentation, and how is it used in target marketing?

11-4. What are four ways that companies conduct market research?

QUESTIONS FOR ANALYSIS

11-5. Select three everyday products (personal fitness training, vacuum cleaners, dog food, cell phones, coffee, or shoes, for example). How are these different products aimed toward different market segments? How does the marketing mix differ for each segment?

11-6. Imagine being the marketing manager for a local chain of family dining restaurants. How would you adapt the marketing mix to an economic downturn? How would you adapt it to an economic boom?

11-7. Select a well-known company. After doing a bit of research on the company website and in the news, how would you summarize the company's marketing plan? For instance: What are the target demographics? What products or services does the company offer? Are there different strategies for each product line?

11-8. Assume two companies make similar wooden picture frames. One company is a small business producing the frames mostly by hand, and the other is a very large business that mass produces frames using an automated assembly line. What are the advantages and disadvantages for each? How would you market these—similarly or differently?

APPLICATION EXERCISES

11-9. Describe how the consumer buying process applied to a recent purchase. Address the factors that influenced your purchase as well as the steps in your purchase and how the company's marketing mix affected your decision.

11-10. Choose an existing product that is not widely known. Once you have identified the product, describe how you would use what you have learned about marketing to increase demand for the product.

building a business: continuing team exercise

ASSIGNMENT

Meet with your team members to consider your new business venture and how it relates to the marketing processes and consumer behavior topics in this chapter. Develop specific responses to the following:

11-11. Develop a "Statement of Marketing Objectives" for your company. Justify those marketing objectives by explaining how they contribute to the overall business mission of the company.

11-12. Identify the target market(s) for your business. Who are your customers? Describe the characteristics of customers in your target market(s).

11-13. Discuss how your team is going to identify the existing competitors in your chosen market. Based on the discussion, what are the key elements of your marketing plans that will give you a competitive edge over those competitors?

11-14. Consider, again, the customers in your target market(s). Are they individual consumers, organizations, or a mix of both consumers and organizations? Describe in detail the buying process(es) you expect them to use for purchasing your product(s). Discuss whether the customer buying process should or should not be a concern for your company.

11-15. Develop a preliminary design of the marketing mix for your target market(s). In addition, identify the ways in which you will conduct market research. Retain this information for carryover and refinement in the following chapters.

team exercise

FINDING THE SILVER LINING

Oliver Douglas recently recovered from a relatively rare blood disorder called acute myeloid leukemia. During treatment and recovery, he realized that he could have used more help tracking medications and appointments, researching treatments and symptoms, and communicating with his care team as well as connecting up with other people dealing with the same or similar conditions. During treatment, he had a lot of time to think, and now that he's feeling better, he has developed an idea for an app for Android and iPhones that will coordinate care and connect users with resources. He has developed a business plan that includes both technical aspects of the app, which he calls Silver Lining, and a rough draft of the financial plan, but he has no idea how to approach the marketing portion of the plan. He has come to your team for advice.

Team Activity

11-16. As a group, describe the characteristics, wants, and needs of the potential target market(s).

11-17. Discuss how broad or narrow the market should be, as well as the pros and cons of each approach.

11-18. Address each element of the marketing mix and describe how it might appeal to the target market.

11-19. Assign one team member to each of the four marketing research options. Have each group member identify the pros and cons of the type of research they have been assigned.

11-20. Discuss marketing strategies and the main components of a marketing plan.

11-21. As a group, draft a marketing plan for Douglas's Silver Lining app.

exercising your ethics

THE $480 MILLION QUESTION

The Situation

You work for Titan Burgers, a national restaurant chain, and you are part of a management team that includes finance, HR, you (marketing), product development, legal, and investor relations managers. Your industry sector is suffering right now, but the government is offering zero-interest loans that will likely not need to be paid back. The legislative intent was to support small businesses, but the law was vague, and so legal and finance applied for $480 million and got it, as did many of the other big restaurant chains that had legal and finance departments. Subsequently, the fund ran out of money while many small, local hometown restaurants were shuttering for good.

The Dilemma

The CEO has convened your management advisory group to make a recommendation about what to do with the money.

The finance manager admits that your company has a $3 billion cash reserve, which should be enough to weather the economic downturn, but that it would be fiscally imprudent to turn down a legitimate loan/gift of $480 million.

Legal counsel says that the loan application was totally in order and that it was up to the government to decide who would get the loan and who would not. The investor relations manager agrees with finance and legal counsel and adds that the money would have just ended up with a large competitor anyway.

Some employees are reporting that they are hearing complaints from some customers about corporate greed and that pickets are congregating at outlets across the country. A poll of the employees indicates that a majority are in favor of sending the money back.

The product development manager is adamant that the company should give the money back so that it can be available to actual small businesses, and is looking across the table at you to back her up. She doesn't have a valid business argument; she just feels it's the right thing to do.

You note that sales are down and there is quite a bit of buzz in the media and on social media deriding the big chains for taking money that was meant for local businesses.

QUESTIONS TO ADDRESS

11-22. What are the ethical issues in this situation?

11-23. From an ethical standpoint, what are your obligations as the marketing manager in this situation?

11-24. As the marketing manager, what recommendation would you argue for in this situation, and how would you attempt to persuade your peers?

cases

MORE THAN JUST MEATBALLS

Continued from page 349

At the beginning of this chapter, you read about IKEA and its continually evolving marketing plan. Using the information presented in this chapter, you should now be able to answer the following questions.

QUESTIONS FOR DISCUSSION

11-25. What forces in the external environment have created opportunities or challenges for IKEA? Explain.

11-26. How would you describe IKEA's marketing philosophy in terms of its value package, marketing mix, and overall approach?

11-27. Describe the consumer buying process for someone purchasing furniture. How would the buying process for an IKEA customer be similar to and different from the buying process for someone purchasing furniture from a more traditional local store?

11-28. Search IKEA on social media. On the basis of what you find, how would you describe its target audience?

SHAVING OFF THE PROFITS

There aren't many consumer products segments Procter & Gamble (P&G) has dominated as thoroughly as shaving. King C. Gillette patented the first safety razor more than 100 years ago. It was the official razor of World War I, thanks to a government contract that put 3.5 million of them into the hands of American soldiers, and then, for decades, Gillette was mostly alone, with just its lackluster drugstore aisle competitor Schick for company. When the high-end mall brand the Art of Shaving posed the briefest of threats in the late '90s, Procter & Gamble just bought it. But then came the budget subscription service Dollar Shave Club. Launched with the help of a viral YouTube commercial in 2011, it raised a total of $163.5 million by the end of 2015 and was acquired by P&G archrival Unilever for $1 billion in 2016.

And then along came Harry's, an affordable direct-to-consumer brand started by Andy Katz-Mayfield and Jeff Raider in 2013. In January 2018, Harry's raised $375 million and was valued at $1 billion. Supply, funded through a series of six-digit Kickstarter campaigns, promises to bring back the perfect single-blade safety razor. Walker & Company's Bevel collected $33 million in venture capital to bring out a single-blade safety razor designed specifically for people of color with coarser and curlier facial hair. Billie, a women-focused brand, garnered $6 million in venture capital funding, and the British start-up Cornerstone now sells subscription boxes containing razor replacements, toothpaste, and face wash, thanks to an initial seed funding of $10 million.

In addition to increased competition from brands that appeal to younger people, Gillette's core market segment, the baby boomers, are aging out. Older people just don't shave as often. And the younger crowd, in general, is becoming more relaxed about facial hair.

In response to this pressure, the company cut product prices in 2017 by an average of 12 percent, probably contributing to the decline in 2018 sales revenue. If P&G was hoping to offset the price decrease with increased volume, it didn't happen. The 2019 earnings report showed the Gillette-led grooming segment was the worst-performing unit, with a sales decline of 5 percent. In fact, Procter & Gamble as a whole saw drastic declines in total net income in both 2018 and 2019 and wrote down the market value of the investment by a whopping $8 billion. The company saw some recovery in the early 2020s, partly thanks to embracing a more comprehensive array of grooming products aimed at hair styling rather than removal.

QUESTIONS FOR DISCUSSION

11-29. How would you best describe P&G's marketing strategy for Gillette?

11-30. What elements of P&G's external marketing environment, if any, are influencing the company's marketing strategy? Explain your reasoning.

11-31. Why do you suppose lowering the prices of Gillette products didn't increase sales?

11-32. Explain the roles of target marketing and market segmentation as they apply in this case.

11-33. In what ways are the components of P&G's marketing mix being affected by the situation described in this case? Give examples to illustrate.

endnotes

[1] "About Us," IKEA.com, February 15, 2023, https://about.ikea.com/en/about-us.

[2] Berfin Cezim, "IKEA's Digital Marketing Strategy: Top Things to Know About the Company's Success," Digital Agency Network, March 31, 2023, https://digitalagencynetwork.com/ikea-digital-marketing-strategy/.

[3] "Work with Us," IKEA, accessed April 24, 2020, https://www.ikea.com/ms/en_US/the_ikea_story/working_at_ikea/work_areas_marketing_communications.html.

[4] "IKEA Vision, Culture and Values," IKEA, accessed April 24, 2020, https://ikea.jobs.cz/en/vision-culture-and-values/.

[5] American Marketing Association, "Definition of Marketing," accessed May 28, 2023, https://www.ama.org/AboutAMA/Pages/Definition-of-Marketing.aspx.

[6] Philip Kotler and Gary Armstrong, *Principles of Marketing*, 18th ed. (Upper Saddle River, NJ: Prentice Hall, 2021), 7.

[7] "CRM (Customer Relationship Management)," TechTarget.com, accessed May 29, 2023, http://searchcrm.techtarget.com/definition/CRM; "Customer Relationship Management," Wikipedia, accessed May 29, 2023, http://en.wikipedia.org/wiki/Customer_relationship_management.

[8] Poonam Khanna, "Hotel Chain Gets Personal with Customers," *Computing Canada*, April 8, 2005, 18.

[9] "Fairmont Hotels & Resorts: Website Development and Enhanced CRM," Accenture, accessed May 29, 2023, http://www.accenture.com.

[10] Teya Vitutvitu@sfnewmexican.com, "Iconik Coffee Roasters Expanding to Former Discount Tire Store," Santa Fe New Mexican, February 9, 2023, https://www.santafenewmexican.com/news/local_news/iconik-coffee-roasters-expanding-to-former-discount-tire-store/article_c1263a52-a3df-11ed-964a-abc24ee680d9.html.

[11] "Financial Cards in Poland," Euromonitor International (May 2008), http://www.euromonitor.com.

[12] https://sweden.se/life/society/a-cashless-society; http://www.cashlessindia.gov.in.

[13] Scott Smith, "Coca-Cola Lost Millions Because of This Market Research Mistake," *Qualtrics* (blog), January 21, 2013, http://www.qualtrics.com/blog/coca-cola-market-research/.

[14] "Uber US Safety Report 2019 2020, Powered by Box," Uber US Safety Report, accessed June 24, 2023, https://uber.app.box.com/s/vkx4zgwy6sxx2t2618520xt35rix022h?uclick_id=a52b5186-9ed3-4524-b802-fa36e4bb15ae.; "Lyft's Community Safety Report," Lyft Blog, accessed June 24, 2023, https://www.lyft.com/blog/posts/lyfts-community-safety-report]

[15] Lily Jackson, "Black Woman-Owned Rideshare App Launches in Atlanta to Offer Female, LGBTQ Safety," Reckon, October 7, 2020, https://www.reckon.news/news/2020/10/black-woman-owned-rideshare-app-launches-in-atlanta-to-offer-female-lgbtq-safety.html.

[16] U.S. Census Bureau, U.S. Department of Commerce, "Lists and Structure of Governments," accessed May 29, 2023, http://www.census.gov.

[17] Judy Strauss, Adel El-Ansary, and Raymond Frost, *E-Marketing*, 5th ed. (Upper Saddle River, NJ: Prentice Hall, 2007); "Ten Corporate Blogs Worth Reading," February 19, 2009, http://www.blogtrepreneuer.com.

[18] Eilene Zimmerman, "Real-Life Lessons in the Delicate Art of Setting Prices," *New York Times*, April 20, 2011, http://www.nytimes.com/2011/04/21/business/smallbusiness/21sbiz.html?pagewanted=all&_r=0.

chapter 12

Developing and Pricing Products

Alex Segre/Alamy Stock Photo

learning objectives

After reading this chapter, you should be able to:

12-1 **Explain** the definition of a product as a value package and how to classify goods and services.

12-2 **Describe** the new product development process.

12-3 **Describe** the stages of the product life cycle (PLC) and methods for extending a product's life.

12-4 **Identify** the various pricing objectives that govern pricing decisions and describe the price-setting tools used in making these decisions.

12-5 **Discuss** pricing strategies that can be used for different competitive situations and identify the pricing tactics that can be used for setting prices.

what's in it for me?

Becoming a leading business in any market takes a solid understanding of how to develop an attractive product and how best to set prices to achieve profit and market share objectives. This chapter describes what constitutes a good product, identifies important classifications of products, and discusses the activities involved in developing new products. We will also see that any product's marketing success depends on setting prices that appeal to each target audience. By understanding this chapter's methods for pricing, you'll have a clearer picture of how to select pricing that is appropriate for meeting different business objectives, recognize and apply various price-setting tools, and revise pricing strategies and tactics as products move through their life cycles. You'll also be prepared to evaluate a company's product and pricing activities as they relate to its marketing programs and competitive potential.

For example, think about the next product you may decide to purchase. It may be a new purse, a backpack, a baseball cap, or new clothes. Any one of these items is likely to be available in a range of styles and at an array of different prices. Let's suppose that it is actually a business case to carry your laptop computer and assorted materials you need for your new job. If you have some discretionary funds, are joining a company where image seems important, and want to make the best impression possible, you may lean toward buying a more expensive case. However, if you have limited funds and the firm seems to put little emphasis on image or style, you might instead look for a lower-priced case.

As we saw in Chapter 11, managers are responsible for developing marketing plans and strategies for meeting customers' needs and wants. We also saw that marketing strategy focuses on the four components (the Four Ps) of the marketing mix: product, price, place, and promotion. Most managers understand, however, that in making strategic marketing decisions it is virtually impossible to focus on one element of the marketing mix (such as product design) without considering the other elements (such as product price) at the same time. In this chapter, we'll look at two of the Four Ps in more detail. We'll start by looking at *product* development and how a company decides what products it will offer to its customers. Next, we'll look at the concept of *pricing* and the price-setting tools used in making pricing decisions. In our next chapter, we'll consider the remaining two elements in the marketing mix: *place* (distribution) and *promotion*.

Ashwin/123RF

Kristina Bumphrey/Starpix/Shutterstock

Some celebrities and other high-income consumers are willing to pay thousands of dollars for designer products like Louis Vuitton purses and handbags.

The Thirty-Thousand-Dollar Handbag

In 1837, as steam-powered trains and ships were making travel more accessible, 16-year-old Louis Vuitton walked 292 miles to Paris to work as a trunk maker's apprentice. In 1858, he debuted his new trunk design that was rectangular, unlike its dome-shaped predecessors, making it easy to stack. The cotton canvas fabric was lightweight, durable, and waterproof, ideal for travel. The company benefited from the travel boom, and in 1896, Louis's son Georges created the iconic Louis Vuitton monogram, a floral pattern with an interlocking L and V, in honor of his father, who had passed away a few years earlier. Since then, Louis Vuitton purses have become one of the most coveted and pricey fashion accessories in the world, in the same class as jewelry and elegant automobiles.

Curiously (and tellingly), the Louis Vuitton USA website doesn't even have an option to sort by price, but a quick scan of its simple leather purses reveals a broad selection of handbags priced around $3,000, whereas the same search on Walmart suggests $50 for a similar tote.

So how do you price a purse? Functionally, a purse is fairly standard in size, shape, and use. It's a bag, usually with pockets, often with handles. In a straightforward sense, the purse's value package is similar to a backpack or even a briefcase. However, purses are unusual in that they can range from $30 or less to $30,000 or more. At first blush, it might seem logical that the cost of manufacturing a $30,000 purse could be a thousand times more than the cost of producing a $30 purse, forcing the price upward, and that those high-cost materials could make the higher-priced purse a thousand times more functional, but with some consideration, those hypotheses seem unlikely.

Certainly, one reason Louis Vuitton products are so expensive is the high manufacturing cost. For example, the luxury brand shies away from outsourcing manufacturing to cheaper locations. Its collections are handmade by experienced craftspeople using expensive materials, and the most advanced machinery touching its products is the humble sewing machine.

But the real key to Louis Vuitton's value package seems to be two factors: (1) controlling supply and (2) reputation.

Often when brands produce too much of a product, they offload the extras by holding sales or selling them at discount shopping outlets. Louis Vuitton suspends production of a product once it hits its sales target and claims to be the only brand in the world that never holds sales or discounts its wares. In addition, limited supply means that when you buy a Louis Vuitton purse and show up at the Oscars ceremony, you are likely to be the only one with that purse. So a large part of the LV value package is status. Your Louis Vuitton accessory tells the world that you are important and unique. Your Walmart bag serves the same function—it holds your keys and your phone—but doesn't send the same message.

Compare purses to gas for your car. With supply far outstripping demand, gas prices dropped below $2 per gallon for a moment in early 2020 as suppliers and dealers frantically reduced prices to bring the market back into equilibrium.

Although dropping the price increased quantity demanded, the entire demand curve had shifted to the left, meaning that demand overall was reduced, drastically in this case. At one point, the price of oil dropped below zero (theoretically), meaning that the supply was so far in excess of demand that there was virtually no market for a barrel of oil. It used to be a given that demand for oil was inelastic, meaning that within a relevant and fairly broad range of price changes, quantity demanded would not be significantly affected. However, when worldwide demand drops, price drops as well. So the price of gas at the pumps, somewhat like the price of a Louis Vuitton purse, is completely determined by consumer demand, showing that when it comes right down to it, price is established by what a willing buyer will pay a willing seller. (After studying the content in this chapter, you should be able to answer a set of discussion questions found at the end of the chapter.)

What Is a Product?

Learning Objective 12-1

Explain the definition of a product as a value package and how to classify goods and services.

In developing the marketing mix for any product, whether goods or services, marketers must consider what customers really want when they purchase products. Only then can these marketers plan strategies effectively. We begin this section where product strategy begins: by understanding that every product is a *value package* that provides benefits to satisfy the needs and wants of customers. Next, we describe the major *classifications of products,* both for consumers and for organizations. Finally, we discuss one of the most important decisions faced by any business: its *product mix*.

The Value Package

Whether a product is a physical good, a service, or some combination of the two, customers get value from the various benefits, features, and rewards associated with that product. **Product features** are the qualities, tangible and intangible, that a company builds into its products, such as an electric motor on a lawnmower (or the taste and health benefits of a nutrition bar, the styling of a shirt, or the low-price guarantees of a travel website). However, as we discussed previously, to attract buyers, features must also provide benefits; the lawnmower must also be easy to use and cut grass efficiently and effectively. The owner's "pleasure" in knowing that the mower is nearby and ready to use when needed is an intangible reward.

Product Features *tangible and intangible qualities that a company builds into its products*

Today's customer regards a product as a bundle of attributes, benefits, and features, which, taken together, marketers call the **value package**. Increasingly, buyers expect to receive products with greater value—with more benefits and features at reasonable costs—so firms must compete on the basis of enhanced value packages. Consider, for example, the possible attributes in a laptop computer value package:

Value Package *a product that is marketed as a bundle of value-adding attributes, including reasonable cost*

- Easy access to understandable prepurchase information
- Features such as wireless capabilities
- Attractive color and design
- Useful software packages
- Attractive prices
- Fast, simple online ordering
- Secure credit card purchasing
- Assurance of speedy delivery
- Warranties
- Easy access to follow-up technical support

finding a better way

Keeping Ahead of Demand

Judy Faulkner was 36 years old in 1979 when she launched Human Services Computing in her Wisconsin basement after borrowing $70,000 from friends and family. Her background and degrees were in mathematics and computer science, but her father and mother were both in the health care field, so she focused her early efforts on the health care industry. Faulkner's company was in the vanguard of digitizing patient records, but it wasn't until 1983 that it released its first product, Cadence Enterprise Scheduling, and not until 1987 that it released Resolute Professional Billing. In 1990, the company changed its name to Epic Systems, and in 1992, it released EpicCare, a Windows-based electronic health records (EHR) system. In 1997, the company earned net income of $6.6 million on sales of almost $31 million. By 2002, sales had increased to $105 million, and the company had 805 employees. In 2003, Faulkner predicted that the company's products would help move the industry toward EHR as a standard of practice and secured a $1.8 billion deal with Kaiser Permanente for the Epic system and the related patient portal called MyChart.[1] By 2010, the Centers for Medicare & Medicaid Services, a part of the U.S. government, launched a program to incentivize the use of EHR,[2] and by 2021, all health systems were required to give patients access to their EHR in an electronic format.[3]

Epic had begun developing the original iteration of MyChart in the early 2000s, and more and more data has become available to patients over the years. "It became a little harder for patients to navigate and know what the most important things were to deal with at any moment," said Sean Bina, vice president of access and patient experience. In 2018, the company began planning for a major redesign. Overall, the redesign "started with what we were hearing from patients directly, and we did a lot of rapid iterations and getting patient feedback: seeing what worked well and what didn't," says Trevor Berceau, product development lead.[4] By the time the redesign rolled out in 2020, annual sales had reached $3.3 billion, and the company boasted 60,000 square feet of office space housing over 12,000 people.

auremar/Shutterstock

Although the company keeps its main focus on Epic and MyChart, developers are constantly working to make the products better. "One of things our customer executives tell us all the time is that they want to stand on each other's shoulders," Faulkner says. "They want to know what others are doing so they can do it, too. And so we call that imitate to innovate. And what we're saying is that it's good to have a Chief Innovation Officer, but you really also need a Chief Imitation Officer to watch what others are doing and share."[5]

By 2023, there were over 300 million patient charts in Epic.[6] Faulkner that year reported net worth of $7.3 billion, up from $5.5 billion in 2020, and her *Forbes* ranking of the world's top billionaires improved from 836 to 312 in that same amount of time.[7]

Despite suggestions to take the company public, Faulkner has kept it privately held, saying, "If you are publicly traded, then your legal fiduciary duty is to increase shareholder value. We think our duty is to keep patients healthy, keep healthcare organizations strong, and keep clinicians happy."[8]

Although the laptop includes physical *features*—processing devices and other hardware—many items in the value package are services or intangibles that, collectively, add value by providing *benefits* that increase the customer's satisfaction. Reliable data processing is certainly a benefit, but so, too, are speedy delivery and easy access to technical support. Today, more and more firms compete on the basis of enhanced value packages. Top-performing companies find that the addition of a simple new service often pleases customers far beyond the cost of providing it. Just making the purchase transaction faster and more convenient, for example, adds value by sparing customers long waits and cumbersome paperwork. Visitors to Walt Disney World can now download and activate a mobile app before they leave home. Upon arrival in Florida, they can then use this app to open their resort room door, enter theme parks, help schedule times to visit major attractions without long lines, order food from quick-service restaurants, and charge good at points of sale. Hence, the app serves to increase the value package for visitors by making it easier to plan daily activities.

Classifying Goods and Services

For marketers, it is generally useful to classify products according to expected buyers. These fall into two groups: (1) buyers of consumer products and (2) buyers of organizational products. As we saw previously in Chapter 11, the **consumer** and **industrial buying** processes differ significantly. Similarly, marketing products to consumers is very different from marketing products to businesses and other organizations.

Consumer *person who purchases products for personal use*

Industrial Buyer *a company or other organization that buys products for use in producing other products (goods or services)*

Classifying Consumer Products Consumer products are commonly divided into three categories that differ in terms of typical buyer behavior. These categories are outlined in Table 12.1.

1 **Convenience goods** (such as milk and bottled water) and **convenience services** (such as those offered by fast-food restaurants) are consumed rapidly and regularly. They are inexpensive and are purchased often and with little exertion of time and effort.
2 **Shopping goods** (such as appliances and mobile devices) and **shopping services** (such as hotel or airline reservations) are more expensive and are purchased less often than convenience products. Consumers often compare brands, sometimes in different stores and via online searches. They may also evaluate alternatives in terms of style, performance, color, price, and other criteria.
3 **Specialty goods** (such as wedding gowns and tuxedoes) and **specialty services** (such as catering for wedding receptions or health care insurance) are extremely important and expensive purchases. Consumers usually decide precisely what they want and are not likely to accept substitutes. They often go from source to source, sometimes spending a great deal of money and time to get exactly what they want.

Convenience Goods *inexpensive physical goods that are consumed rapidly and regularly*

Convenience Services *inexpensive services that are consumed rapidly and regularly*

Shopping Goods *moderately expensive, infrequently purchased physical goods*

Shopping Services *moderately expensive, infrequently purchased services*

Specialty Goods *expensive, rarely purchased physical goods*

Specialty Services *expensive, rarely purchased services*

Classifying Organizational Products Depending on how much they cost and how they will be used, industrial products can also be divided into three categories. These are summarized in Table 12.2.

- **Production items** are goods or services that are used directly in the conversion (production) process, such as petroleum that is converted into gasoline, and passenger demand information that is converted into bus or train services. Most consumer products, including food, clothing, housing, and entertainment services, are created from production items.

Production Items *goods or services that are used in the conversion (production) process to make other products*

table 12.1 Categories of Consumer Products

Category	Description	Examples
Convenience goods and services	• Consumed rapidly and regularly • Inexpensive • Purchased often and with little input of time and effort	• Milk • Bottled water • Fast food
Shopping goods and services	• Purchased less often • More expensive • Consumers may shop around and compare products based on style, performance, color, price, and other criteria.	• Television • Tires • Hotel reservation
Specialty goods and services	• Purchased infrequently • Expensive • Consumer decides on a precise product and will not accept substitutions and spends a good deal of time choosing the "perfect" item.	• Luxury jewelry • Wedding dress • Health care insurance

table 12.2 Organizational Products

Category	Description	Examples
Production items	• Goods or services used directly in the production process	• Loads of tea processed into tea bags • Information processing for real-time production • Jet fuel used by airline services
Expense items	• Goods or services that are consumed within a year by firms producing other goods or supplying other services	• Oil and electricity for machines • Building maintenance • Legal services
Capital items	• Permanent (expensive and long-lasting) goods and services • Life expectancy of more than a year • Purchased infrequently, so transactions often involve decisions by high-level managers	• Buildings (offices, factories) • Fixed equipment (water towers, baking ovens) • Accessory equipment (information systems, computers, airplanes) • Financial advisory services

Expense Items *industrial products purchased and consumed within a year by firms producing other products*

- **Expense items** are goods and services that are consumed within a year by organizations producing other goods or supplying other services. The term *expense items* stems from the standard practice of accounting in which expenditures are classified as either (1) expense items or (2) capital items, depending on how quickly they are consumed. Thus, paper used in printers and building maintenance services are expense items if they are expected to be consumed within a year.

Capital Items *expensive, long-lasting, infrequently purchased industrial products, such as a building, or industrial services, such as a long-term agreement for data warehousing services*

- **Capital items** are longer-lasting (expensive and sometimes permanent) goods and services. They have expected lives of more than a year and typically last several years. Buildings (offices, factories), fixed equipment (water storage towers, baking ovens), and accessory equipment (information systems, computers, airplanes) are all capital goods. Capital services are those for which long-term commitments are made, such as long-term insurance services, architectural services, and financial advisory services. Because capital items are expensive and long-lasting, they often involve decisions by high-level managers.

The Product Mix

Product Mix *the group of products that a firm makes available for sale*

The group of products that a company makes available for sale, whether consumer, industrial, or both, is its **product mix**. E*TRADE, for example, offers online financial investing and trading services, retirement planning, and educational resources. Black & Decker makes toasters, food blenders, electric drills, and a variety of other appliances and tools. 3M makes everything from Post-it Notes to optical systems and more than 1,000 tape and adhesive products.

Many companies begin with a single product, such as simple brewed coffee. Over time, they find that the initial product fails to suit every customer shopping for the product type. To meet market demand, they begin to introduce similar products, such as flavored coffees and various coffee bean roasts, designed to reach more customers. For example, Starbucks stores expanded their line of coffees by adding different Italian-style espresso beverages that include mochas, cappuccinos, lattes, and flavored blended crèmes, followed by lighter roasts, different sizes, iced coffees, and so forth. A group of products that are closely related because they function in a similar manner (e.g., flavored coffees) or are sold to the same customer group (e.g., stop-in coffee drinkers) who will use them in similar ways is a **product line**.

Product Line *group of products that are closely related because they function in a similar manner or are sold to the same customer group who will use them in similar ways*

Companies sometimes extend their horizons and identify opportunities outside existing product lines. The result, *multiple* (or *diversified*) *product lines*, is evident at ServiceMaster, which was among the first successful home services companies that offered mothproofing and carpet cleaning. The company then expanded its product line by adding other closely related services for homeowners: lawn care (TruGreen), pest control (Terminix), and cleaning (Merry Maids). After years of serving *residential customers*, ServiceMaster then added another product line of *business and industry services*, including landscaping and janitorial services, education services (management of support services for schools and institutions, including physical facilities and financial and personnel resources), and health care services (management of support services—plant operations, asset management, laundry/linen supply—for long-term care facilities). Multiple product lines increase the chances that a firm can grow rapidly and can help offset the consequences of declining revenues or increased competition in any one product line.

Developing New Products

Learning Objective 12-2

Describe the new product development process.

To expand or diversify product lines—in fact, just to survive—firms must develop and introduce streams of new products. Faced with competition and shifting customer preferences, no firm can count on a single successful product to carry it forever. Even products that have been popular for decades need frequent renewal to keep up with changing technologies and shifting consumer tastes.

Consider one of the best-known brands in the United States, Levi's jeans. Its riveted denim styles were once market leaders, but the company failed to keep pace with changing tastes, fell behind new products from competitors, and lost market share among 14- to 19-year-old males during the 1990s. One industry analyst commented that Levi's "hasn't had a successful new product in years." Things changed in 2003, on the 130th anniversary of the company's invention of jeans, when Levi's introduced the then-new Signature Brand of casual clothing to mass-channel shoppers, originally available in Walmart stores in the United States. The Signature Brand continues to have a popular following, with convenient shopping access online at Google and the websites of Walmart, Amazon, and Meijer. More recently, Levi's expanded again to accommodate different body types and styles with numerous options available on its website (levi.com) to customize jeans and shorts by fabric, fit, and design.

The New Product Development Process

For many years, the growing demand for improved health care has stimulated the development of new dietary supplements, heart medicines, and other pharmaceuticals, along with new equipment for diagnosing ailments, surgical procedures, and monitoring patient recovery. However, companies that develop and sell these products face a big challenge. Developing new products can cost well over $100 million, sometimes even more than $1 billion, and it can take as long as 8 to 10 years, sometimes longer, to get a new product through the approval process at the U.S. Food and Drug Administration (FDA).

Testing first for FDA approval and then for market acceptance can be the most time-consuming stage of development. For example, for years Merck & Co. invested heavily to develop an experimental heart drug called anacetrapib to raise levels of good cholesterol, thereby reducing the risk of heart attack. Merck & Co. spent years on laboratory research and a lengthy test study, using 1,600 patients, and the results of that study then have to withstand further analysis. If successful, Merck estimated that it could cash in on the growth of the cholesterol-lowering drug market, with industry estimates of peak sales potential ranging from $3 billion to $10 billion per year. Unfortunately, the drug failed to meet the required standards for FDA approval and so Merck stopped research on anacetrapib and moved on to other potential new drugs. However, getting that far through development requires a great deal of time, patience, money, and risk of failure.[9]

Product development is a long and expensive process, and like Merck & Co., many firms have research and development (R&D) departments for exploring new

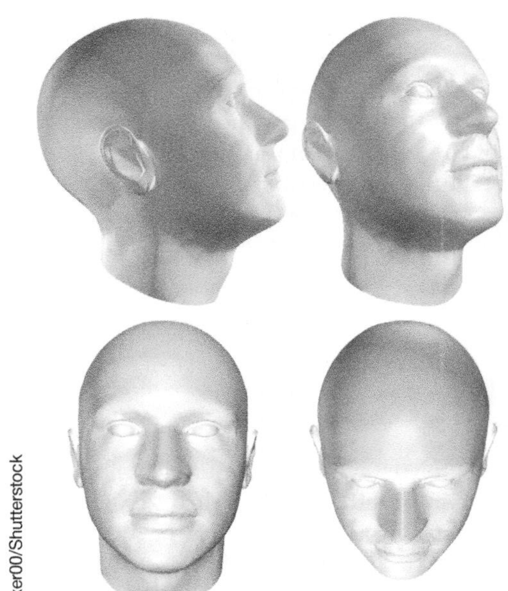

Fixer00/Shutterstock

Designers used to create products, such as this head for a human-like toy, by sculpting models out of clay. Now they use "rapid prototyping," a technology that allows several employees to work simultaneously on three-dimensional (3D) digital/visual "models" that can be e-mailed to clients for instant review. It now takes just hours, instead of weeks, to make an initial sculpture.

entrepreneurship and new ventures

Can Beds Come in Boxes?

Bill Bradley was working in his machine shop in Johnson City, Tennessee, in 2004 when a couple of friends asked him if he could design a machine that could compress a queen-size foam mattress into a package small enough to ship to someone's home. It took him about 18 months to perfect the process, and it wasn't until 2007 that he shipped the first mattress from his start-up, BedInABox, providing a quality product at a lower price than consumers could get in a mattress or furniture store.

As it turns out, it doesn't take much to design a mattress and a marketing campaign, put up a website, and have a big mattress manufacturing company fulfill the orders. Because of this, by 2019 more than 175 bed-in-a-box companies were in operation, including big players like Purple, Casper, Nectar, Leesa, and Tuft & Needle.

The ease of forming an online mattress company creates an environment of monopolistic competition in which a large number of firms offer a functionally similar product, and so companies strive to differentiate themselves based on value or quality rather than price. For instance, BedInABox touts its 20-year warranty, which includes a 120-day, zero-risk sleep guarantee that provides for a full refund on returned mattresses, as well as the claim that they are "Made in America" and one of the only companies that actually manufactures its own product.

Demand is elastic, so if a company like BedInABox raises prices, consumers are likely to gravitate to an alternative. In addition, because the industry is so easy to get into, profits are hard to come by. Although most of the home-delivery mattress companies are private, Casper went public in February 2020 and published financial statements for the years ended December 31, 2017, 2018, and 2019, showing losses of nearly $100 million each year. As you would expect, the company cited narrow margins on sales (the difference between the price and the cost of the mattresses) and high marketing costs as ongoing concerns. Lowering prices might increase volume, but overall sales revenue would probably decrease, and raising prices would probably drive customers to the competitors. In November 2021, Casper announced that it would be acquired by Durational Capital Management. The transaction was completed in January 2022, and Casper's stock was delisted from the New York Stock Exchange. Still, there are dozens if not hundreds of choices in online mattresses, and a survey by the International Sleep Products Association reported that 54 percent of mattresses were purchased online in 2023, up from 5 percent in 2017.[10]

prostooleh/123RF

In the meantime, BedInABox barely makes the radar screen in the online mattress industry that it practically invented.

product possibilities. Why do they devote so many resources to exploring product possibilities, rejecting many seemingly good ideas along the way? First, high *mortality rates* for new ideas mean that only a few new products reach the market. Second, for many companies, *speed to market* with a product is as important as care in developing it. During the 2020 COVID-19 pandemic, many pharmaceutical companies quickly shifted R&D funds to seek treatments and vaccines for the virus.

Product Mortality Rates

Some experts suggest that it takes 50 new product ideas to generate one product that finally reaches the market. Even then, only a few of these survivors become successful products. Many seemingly great ideas have failed as products. Creating a successful new product has become increasingly difficult—even for the most experienced marketers. Why? The number of new products hitting the market each year has increased dramatically; in 2022 alone, there were approximately 213,000 new brand extensions and over 10,000 totally new brand launches. In most years, the U.S. consumer packaged goods industry alone launches between 20,000 and 40,000 products (foods, beverages, school supplies, and other nonfood products).[11] At any given time, however, the average North American supermarket carries a total of only about 44,000 different items. Clearly, then, new products have to battle to take shelf space away from existing products. Indeed, about 9 out of 10 new products fail each year because of lack of space or weak customer demand. Those with the best chances are innovative and deliver unique benefits. The single greatest factor in product failure is the lack of significant difference (i.e., the new product is very much like or imitates an existing product). Some prominent examples of this are Pibb Xtra (formerly Mr. Pibb) versus Dr Pepper, which although still on the market is a relatively minor competitor, and Burger King's Big King, its answer to the Big Mac.

The more rapidly a product moves from the laboratory to the marketplace, the more likely it is to survive. By introducing new products ahead of competitors, companies establish market leadership. They become entrenched in the market before being challenged by newer competitors. For example, sales of Apple's first iPad surged after its introduction in early 2010, and estimates are that more than 13 million units were sold by year end, for a 75 percent share of the world's tablet PC sales. While nearly every other company in the industry has tried to come out with competing products since 2011, iPad continues to be a global market leader. How important is **speed to market** (or **time compression**) to a firm's success in responding rapidly to customer demand or market changes? One study reports that a product that is only three months late to market (three months behind the leader) loses 12 percent of its lifetime profit potential. After a six-month delay, it will lose 33 percent.

Speed to Market *strategy of introducing new products to respond quickly to customer or market changes*

The Seven-Step Development Process

To increase their chances of developing a successful new product, many firms adopt some version of a seven-step process for developing physical goods. (We will discuss the process for services next.)

1. ***Product ideas.*** Product development begins with a search for ideas for new products. Ideas typically come from consumers, the sales force, R&D departments, suppliers, or engineering personnel. For the product development example discussed previously in this chapter, Merck & Co.'s research scientists were convinced by 2003 that a pill could be developed to prevent heart attacks.
2. ***Screening.*** This stage is designed to eliminate ideas that do not mesh with the firm's abilities or objectives. Representatives from marketing, engineering, operations, and finance provide input at this stage. Collaboration among Merck's scientific, marketing, and finance personnel concluded that the protein inhibitor called anacetrapib had reasonable prospects for commercial development.

3 ***Concept testing.*** Once ideas have been screened, companies use market research to get consumers' input about benefits and prices. Early test results for similar products by other companies indicated that Merck's product concept offered acceptable scientific chances for possible commercialization.

4 ***Business analysis.*** After gathering consumer opinions, marketers compare production costs and benefits to see whether the product meets minimum profitability goals. Merck's development team concluded that the product could become profitable, with a market potential of up to $10 billion, but revenues would be offset with projected high multiyear development costs.

5 ***Prototype development.*** Once the firm has determined the potential profitability of a product, engineering, R&D, or design groups produce a prototype. This can be extremely expensive, often requiring the use of three-dimensional computer models followed with expensive equipment to produce the first physical product. Initial development of Merck's anacetrapib required three to five years of laboratory-based chemical and biological science.

6 ***Product testing and test marketing.*** Applying lessons from the prototype, the company goes into limited production. It then tests the product to see if it meets performance requirements. If it does, it may be sold on a trial basis in limited areas to test consumer reaction. In 2016, Merck entered Phase III of the testing that began in 2011, with some 20,000 patients, and it completed testing in March 2017.

7 ***Commercialization.*** If test marketing proves positive, the company begins full-scale production and marketing. Because promotional and distribution channels must be established, this stage can be quite expensive. Gradual commercialization, with the firm providing the product to more and more areas over time, prevents undue strain on initial production capabilities. However, delays in commercialization give other firms the opportunity to bring out competing products. Unfortunately for Merck, test results for its new drug were not encouraging, and so the firm decided to not proceed further.

Variations in the Process for Services

The development of services involves many of the same stages. Basically, Steps 2, 3, 4, 6, and 7 are the same. There are, however, important differences in Steps 1 and 5:

1 ***Service ideas.*** The search for service ideas includes defining the *service value package*, identifying the tangible and intangible features that characterize the service, and stating service specifications. For example, a firm that wants to offer year-end cleaning services to office buildings might commit itself to the following specifications: The building interior will be cleaned with no interference in customer service by midnight on January 5, including carpets swept free of all dust and debris and washbowls and lavatory equipment polished.

5 ***Service process design.*** Instead of prototype development, services require a three-part *service process design*. (1) *Process selection* identifies each step in the service, including sequence and timing. *Example (partial) process identification:* Office cleanings will be performed December 26–January 5, beginning at 8 PM through 5 AM. Steps: (i) furniture removal from office to hallway; (ii) dust, wash, and dry office walls and fixtures; (iii) power vacuum carpets; (iv) power wet-wash carpets; (v) blow-dry carpets; (vi) return furniture to office; and (vii) final removal of cleaning equipment from the client facility begins on January 5, to be completed by midnight. (2) *Worker requirements* state employee behaviors, skills, capabilities, and interactions with customers during the service encounter. *Example (partial) requirements:* One supervisor and 22 workers on 9-hour shifts (1-hour rest break) for 11½ days. Crew supervisor (accessible 24/7) and two lead workers (during work hours) will interact with

RossHelen editorial/Alamy Stock Photo

Large hotels have detailed process designs for functions such as housekeeping. The designs specify when and how rooms will be cleaned, for example, and include quality indicators that can be used to assess the performance of each housekeeper or housekeeping team.

the customer as needed. Workers will (i) be prebriefed on furniture-moving requirements, carpet characteristics, and safety requirements; (ii) be skilled in operation of any and all cleaning equipment; and (iii) respond courteously in encounters with the client, referring questions to the supervisor or lead workers. (3) *Facility requirements* designate all the equipment that supports service delivery. *Example equipment requirements (partial):* (i) eight power-dolly transports for moving furniture; (ii) 50 heavy covers for protecting furniture; (iii) 10 industrial Class II power wet-washers for carpets; (iv) 12 industrial-power carpet vacuums; (v) forty 5-gallon containers Get-it-All scrubbing/sanitizing cleanser; and (vi) large-haul-capacity truck to transport materials, supplies, and equipment to and from client facility.

During the 2020 COVID-19 pandemic, many organizations quickly developed and adopted new ways of delivering services to customers. For instance, car dealerships enhanced their online sales and marketing efforts, set up online financing services, and provided home delivery of new vehicles. Restaurants that had previously been dine-in only offered curbside pickup and/or home delivery. And some banks and other financial services businesses allowed customers to skip a loan payment. As the pandemic waned in 2023, some of these services remained popular, and others disappeared.

Product Life Cycle

Learning Objective 12-3

Describe the stages of the product life cycle (PLC) and methods for extending a product's life.

When a product reaches the market, it begins the **product life cycle (PLC)**, a series of stages through which it passes during its commercial life. Depending on the product's ability to attract and keep customers, its PLC may be a matter of months, years, or decades. Strong, mature products (such as Tide laundry detergent and H&R Block tax preparation) have had long, productive lives. Some, like Coca-Cola, just seem to go on and on, while others, like VCRs and portable cassette players, progress through all four stages fairly quickly, are replaced by products based on newer technologies, and then disappear.

Product Life Cycle (PLC) *series of stages in a product's commercial life*

Stages in the PLC

The life cycle for both goods and services is a natural process in which products are born, grow in stature, mature, and finally decline and (potentially) die. Look at the two graphics in Figure 12.1. In Figure 12.1(a), the four phases of the PLC are applied to several products with which you may be familiar:

Introduction. This stage begins when the product reaches the marketplace. Marketers focus on making potential customers aware of the product and its benefits. Extensive development, production, and sales costs generally offset any profits during this first stage.

Growth. If the new product attracts enough customers, sales start to climb rapidly. Marketers may lower price slightly and continue promotional efforts to increase sales. The product starts to earn profits as revenues surpass costs. During this phase other firms may also move rapidly to introduce their own versions of the successful new product.

Maturity. This is typically the longest stage in the PLC for many products, and may last years or even decades. Sales growth peaks, plateaus, and then may start to slowly decline. Although the product earns its highest profit level early in this stage, increased competition eventually forces price cutting, increasing the costs of advertising and promotional expenditures, and lowering profits. Toward the end of the stage, sales start to fall.

Decline. Sales and profits continue to fall as new products in the introduction stage take away sales. Firms end or reduce promotional support (ads and salespeople) but may let the product linger to provide some profits.

Figure 12.1(b) plots the relationship of the PLC to a product's typical profits (in black) or losses (in red). Although the early stages of the PLC often show financial losses, increased sales for successful products recover previous losses and continue to generate profits until the decline stage. As a result of loss of profits and declining market share, for example, Kodak quit marketing traditional film cameras in the United States in 2004. In 2012, the company announced it would stop making its newer line of digital cameras, too, because of declining profits. Today there is only a very small market for film cameras. For many products, profitable life spans are short. That's why some firms, such as 3M (producer of Post-it Notes and thousands of other products), rely on innovation for constant replenishment of product lines.

Extending Product Life: An Alternative to New Products

Companies try to keep products in the maturity stage as long as they can. At year-end 2012, after 80 years in publication, *Newsweek* magazine mailed its final print issue. At the same time, *Newsweek*'s life was extended by launching a new online version. Sales of televisions also have been revitalized through the years by such feature changes as color, portability, stereo capability, enlarged flat screens, home theater features, streaming capabilities, and other new smart TV features. In fact, companies can extend product life through a number of creative means. Foreign markets, for example, offer three approaches to extending life cycles:

Product Extension *marketing an existing product globally instead of just domestically*

Product Adaptation *modifying an existing product for greater appeal in different countries*

1. In **product extension**, an existing product is marketed globally instead of just domestically. Coca-Cola, Pizza Hut, and Levi's jeans are examples of product extensions.
2. With **product adaptation**, the product is modified for greater appeal in different countries. In Germany, a McDonald's meal includes beer, and Jeep puts the steering wheel on the right side for sales in South Africa and Japan. Because it involves product changes, this approach is usually more costly than product extension.

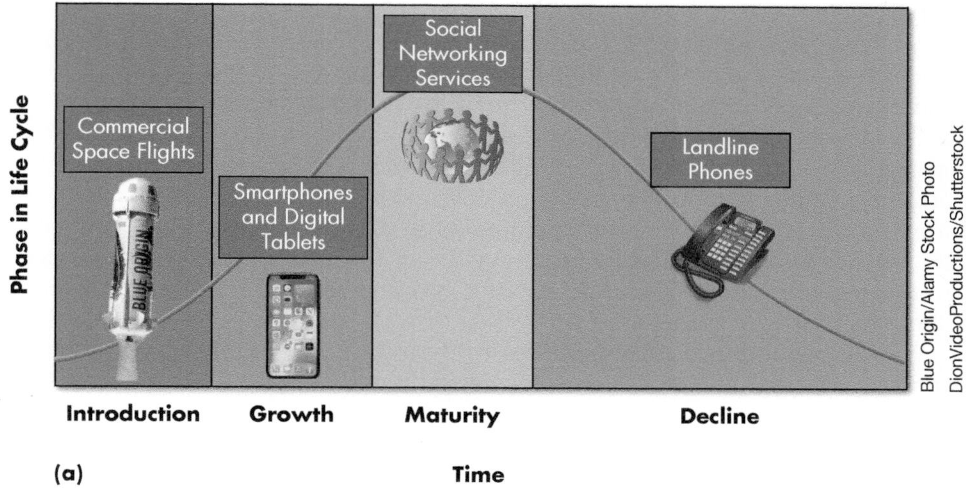

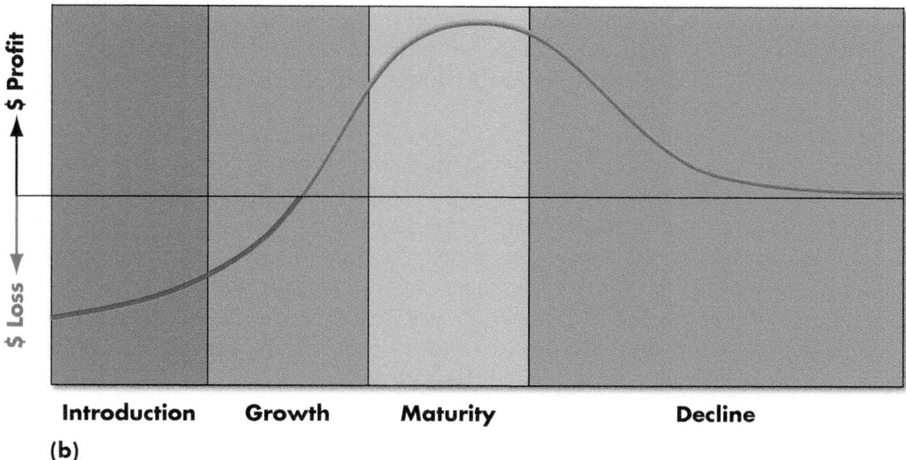

FIGURE 12.1 Products in the Life Cycle: (a) Phases and (b) Profit (or Loss)

3 **Reintroduction** means reviving, for new markets, products that are becoming obsolete in older ones. NCR (originally National Cash Register), for instance, reintroduced manually operated cash registers in Latin America. Boeing sells older models of its aircraft in developing countries. Kent & Curwen, a renowned English clothier founded in 1926, has only one store remaining in Britain but opened dozens of stores in China. In addition to China, today the retailer has outlets in Japan, Taiwan, and Macau.[12]

Reintroduction *reviving obsolete or older products for new markets*

Identifying Products

As we noted previously, developing a product's features is only part of a marketer's job. Marketers must also identify products so that consumers recognize them. Two important tools for this task are *branding* and *packaging*.

Branding Products Coca-Cola is one of the best-known brands in the world. Some Coke executives claim that if all the company's other assets were obliterated, they could go to lenders and borrow $100 billion on the strength of the brand name alone. Indeed, Interbrand, a global brand-ranking firm, says the Coke brand in 2022 was worth $57.5 billion in terms of revenue generation from its ability to create demand for the product.

Branding *process of using symbols to communicate the qualities of a product made by a particular producer*

Industry observers regard brands as a company's most valuable asset.[13] **Branding** is a process of using names and symbols, like Coca-Cola, the Mercedes tri-star logo, Nike's "swoosh," Apple's apple silhouette with the bite missing, or McDonald's golden arches, to communicate the qualities of a particular product made by a particular producer. Brands are designed to signal uniform quality—customers who try and like a product can return to it by remembering its name or its logo. Burger King recently changed its logo to a simpler shape that evokes images of a hamburger. Similarly, the energy services firm Schlumberger has changed both its name (to SLB) and logo to symbolize a strategic move away from fossil-fuel based services to alternative energy services. And Twitter has changed its logo from a blue bird silhouette to simply the letter X.

Brand Awareness *extent to which a brand name comes to mind when a consumer considers a particular product category*

Several benefits result from successful branding, including brand loyalty and **brand awareness**, the brand name that first comes to mind when you consider a particular product category. What company, for example, comes to mind when you need to ship a document a long way on short notice? For many people, UPS has the necessary brand awareness, while for others it may be FedEx.

Table 12.3 shows the 2022 rankings of the top global brands based on estimates of each brand's dollar value. It reflects the earnings boost that each brand delivers—an index of a brand's power to increase sales and earnings, both present and future—and shows how much those future earnings are worth today. Only global brands, those with sales of at least 20 percent outside the home country, are included.

Gaining Brand Awareness The expensive, sometimes fierce, struggle for brand recognition is perhaps nowhere more evident than in branding battles among online businesses. Collectively, the top four digital brands—Google (ranked 2nd), Amazon (3rd), Facebook (14th), and eBay (44th)—spend billions of dollars a year on brand development. Moreover, the mounting costs of establishing a brand identity mean that many more would-be online businesses do and will probably fail.

With its growing importance in nearly every industry, marketers are finding more effective, less expensive ways to gain brand awareness. In addition to using viral marketing and social networking, recent successes have been found with *product placements*.

Product Placement *promotional tactic for brand exposure in which characters in television, film, music, magazines, or video games use a real product with its brand visible to viewers*

Product Placements Although a commercial break during a television program usually means a trip to the kitchen, entertainment programming still gets our full attention. And that's when marketers are turning up the promotional juice with **product placement**, a promotional tactic for brand exposure in which characters in television, film, music, magazines, or video games use a real product with a brand visible to viewers.

table 12.3 World's 10 Most Valuable Brands (2022)

Rank	Brand	2022 Brand Value ($ billions)
1	Apple	$482.215
2	Microsoft	$278.288
3	Amazon	$274.819
4	Google	$251.751
5	Samsung	$87.689
6	Toyota	$59.757
7	Coca-Cola	$57.535
8	Mercedes-Benz	$56.103
9	Disney	$50.325
10	Nike	$50.289

Source: Interbrand, "Interbrand Releases 19th Annual Best Global Brands Report," accessed February 3, 2023, https://www.interbrand.com/best-brands/best-global-brands/2022/ranking/.

Michael Kemp/Alamy Stock Photo

Coca-Cola has one of the strongest and most recognized brands in the world. Its distinctive lettering is immediately recognized regardless of country or language. From Afghanistan to Zimbabwe, Coca-Cola is a brand that has universal recognition and enormous value.

Product placements are effective because the message is delivered in an unobtrusive manner that holds the customer's interest. When used in successful films and TV shows, the brand's association with famous performers is an implied celebrity endorsement. The idea is to legitimize the brand in the minds of target customers. In all, more than $11.4 billion is spent annually on product placements, especially in television, and major companies often have dedicated marketers or hire external experts to assist in product placements. One of the first major success stories was the use of Reese's Pieces in Steven Spielberg's blockbuster movie *E.T. the Extra-Terrestrial*. For years, BMW used James Bond movies to introduce new models of exotic cars. In the Tom Hanks movie *Sully*, characters made a point of staying in Marriott hotels. IKEA shows up in *Deadpool*, and Audi is used in *The Avengers* and *Captain America*. In print placements, HP computers appear in the photo layouts in the IKEA catalog. Television placements are also widespread, including Hyundai in the series *Leverage* and *Burn Notice*, and Junior Mints played a star role when one was dropped into a surgical incision on *Seinfeld*. Chevrolets are often seen in *Transformer* movies.

Product placements are especially effective for TV because of the popularity of streaming services. Viewers watching recorded programming can use their DVRs to skip commercial breaks, but product placements within the programs are unavoidable.

Ideal product placements show the product in a positive or neutral (or passive) manner, but seldom, if ever, in a negative light. For instance, in a dramatic fictional story about a plane crash caused by poor maintenance or pilot error, the airline will almost always also be fictional—no airline would pay to have its brand portrayed in this manner and most would sue if it were. Further, the product placement will usually be aimed at the same demographic as the target audience of the media where the product is shown. For instance, product placements in *Avengers: Age of Ultron* included Beats earphones, Adidas sneakers, Under Armour workout gear, and Levi's jeans.

Types of Brand Names Just about every product has a brand name. Generally, different types of brand names—*national, licensed,* or *private*—increase buyers' awareness of the nature and quality of competing products. When customers are satisfied with a product, marketers try to build brand loyalty among the largest possible segment of repeat buyers.

National Brands *brand-name product produced by, widely distributed by, and carrying the name of a manufacturer*

National Brands **National brands** are produced by, widely distributed by, and carry the name of the manufacturer. These brands (for example, Netflix, Progressive Insurance, Scotch Tape, and Scope mouthwash) are often widely recognized by customers because of consistent national advertising, and they are, therefore, valuable assets. Because the costs of developing a national brand are high, some companies use a national brand on several related products. Procter & Gamble markets Ivory Shampoo, capitalizing on the name of its bar soap and dishwashing liquid. Mars markets several different versions of its Snickers candy bars. Although cost efficient, doing this can sometimes dilute the original brand name's effectiveness. Coors Light Beer now outsells original Coors Beer.

Licensed Brands *brand-name product for whose name the seller has purchased the right from an organization or individual*

Licensed Brands We have become used to companies (and even personalities) selling the rights to put their names on products. These are called **licensed brands.** For example, the popularity of auto racing generates millions of dollars in revenues for the NASCAR brand, which licenses its name on car accessories, apparel, headsets, and myriad other items with the names of popular drivers such as Martin, Gordon, Johnson, Stewart, and Edwards. Harley-Davidson's famous logo, emblazoned on boots, eyewear, gloves, purses, lighters, and watches, brings the motorcycle maker more than $50 million annually. Along with brands such as Coors and Ferrari, licensing for character-based brands, such as Tinker Bell, Mickey Mouse, and other Disney characters, is equally lucrative. Marketers exploit brands because of their public appeal due to the image and status that customers hope to gain by being associated with them.

Private Brand (or Private Label) *brand-name product that a wholesaler or retailer has commissioned from a manufacturer*

Private Brands When a wholesaler or retailer develops a brand name and has a manufacturer put it on a product, the resulting name is a **private brand** (or **private label**). Macy's, for instance, has sold many different products under private brand labels, including Hudson Park, Aqua, Maison Jules, Alfani, Charter Club, Club Room, Home Design, and Studio Silver. Many supermarkets also sell private brand versions of milk, bread, and other food staples.

Packaging *physical container in which a product is sold, advertised, or protected*

Packaging Products

With a few exceptions, products need some form of **packaging** to reduce the risk of damage, breakage, or spoilage, and to increase the difficulty of stealing small products. A package also serves as an in-store advertisement that makes the product attractive, displays the brand name, and identifies features and benefits. Amazon's corporate logo, printed on the boxes it uses to ship goods to consumers, has helped build its brand awareness. Also, packaging features, such as laundry pods for Tide detergent, add utility for consumers.

Learning Objective 12-4

Identify the various pricing objectives that govern pricing decisions and describe the price-setting tools used in making these decisions.

Determining Prices

Pricing *process of determining what a company will receive in exchange for its products*

The second major component of the marketing mix is **pricing**, determining what the customer pays and the seller receives in exchange for a product. Setting prices involves understanding how they contribute to achieving the firm's sales objectives. To learn more about how prices are determined, we will begin by discussing the objectives that influence a firm's pricing decisions. Then we describe the major tools that companies use to meet those objectives.

Pricing to Meet Business Objectives

Pricing Objectives *the goals that sellers hope to achieve in pricing products for sale*

Pricing objectives are the goals that sellers hope to achieve in pricing products for sale. Some companies have *profit-maximizing pricing objectives*, others have *market share pricing objectives*, and still others are concerned with pricing for *e-business objectives*. Pricing decisions are also influenced by the need to compete in the marketplace, by social and ethical concerns, and even by corporate image. In recent years, we've also seen how prices of financial products, loans, and other borrowing are determined by the government's persuasion and its control of interest rates in times of economic crisis.

Profit-Maximizing Objectives The seller's pricing decision is critical for determining the firm's revenue, which is the result of the selling price times the number of units sold.

$$\text{Revenue} = \text{Selling price} \times \text{Units sold}$$

Companies that set prices to maximize profits want to set the selling price to sell the number of units that will generate the highest possible total profits. If a company sets prices too low, it will probably sell more units but may miss out on additional profits on each unit (and may even lose money on each exchange). If a company sets prices too high, it will make a large profit on each item but will sell fewer units. Again, the firm may lose money, and it may also be left with excess inventory because of fewer units sold.

In calculating projected profits, managers weigh sales revenues against costs for materials and labor, as well as capital resources (plant and equipment) and marketing costs (such as maintaining a large sales staff). To use these resources efficiently, many firms set prices to cover costs and achieve a targeted level of return for owners.

Market Share (Market Penetration) Objectives In the long run, a business must make a profit to survive. Because they are often willing to accept minimal profits, or even losses, in the short run to get buyers to try products, companies may initially set low prices for new products to establish **market share** (or **market penetration**), a company's percentage of the total industry sales for a specific product type. Even with established products, market share leadership may outweigh profit as a pricing objective. For brands such as Philadelphia Cream Cheese and Starbucks coffee, dominating a market means that consumers are more likely to buy something with which they are familiar. Market domination means continuous sales of more units and higher profits, even at lower unit prices.

Market Share (or Market Penetration) *company's percentage of the total industry sales for a specific product type*

Pricing for E-Business Objectives When pricing for online sales, marketers must consider different kinds of costs and different forms of consumer awareness. Many e-businesses reduce both costs and prices because of the Internet's unique marketing capabilities. Because the web provides a more direct link between producer and customer, buyers often avoid the added costs of wholesalers and retailers.

Another factor is the ease of comparison shopping—obviously, point-and-click shopping can be much more efficient than driving from store to store in search of the best price. Moreover, both consumers and business buyers can get lower prices by joining online for greater purchasing power. Consumers, doctors, and benefits managers can now more easily compare prices of generic and name-brand drugs. This can save consumers' money and it also reduces the costs to employers who provide a prescription discount program. Companies like GoodRX, ScriptSave WellRX, and the Simple Savings Card all provide pricing transparency and consumer discounts.

Price-Setting Tools

Whatever a company's objectives, managers like to measure the potential impact before deciding on final prices. Two tools used for this purpose are *cost-oriented pricing* and *breakeven analysis*. Although each can be used alone, both are often used because they provide different kinds of information for determining prices that will allow the company to reach its objectives.

Cost-Oriented Pricing **Cost-oriented pricing** considers a firm's desire to make a profit and its need to cover operating costs.

$$\text{Selling price} = \text{Seller's costs} + \text{Profit}$$

Cost-Oriented Pricing *pricing that considers the firm's desire to make a profit and its need to cover operating costs*

A T-shirt store manager would price shirts by calculating the cost of making them available to shoppers. Thus, price would include the costs of store rent, employee wages, utilities, product displays, insurance, and the shirt manufacturer's price.

If the manufacturer's price is $8 per shirt and the store sells shirts for $8, the store won't make any profit. Nor will it make a profit if it sells shirts for $8.50 each, or even $10 or $11. To be profitable, the company must charge enough to cover both product and other costs. Together, these factors determine the **markup**, the amount added to an item's purchase cost to sell it at a profit. In this case, a reasonable markup of $7 more than the purchase cost means a $15 selling price. The following equation calculates the markup percentage and determines what percent of every dollar of revenue is gross profit:

Markup *amount added to an item's purchase cost to sell it at a profit*

$$\text{Markup percentage} = \frac{\text{Markup}}{\text{Sales price}} \times 100\%$$

For our shirt retailer, the markup percentage is 46.7:

$$\text{Markup percentage} = \frac{\$7}{\$15} \times 100\% = 46.7\%$$

Out of every $1.00 taken in, $0.467 will be gross profit. Out of gross profit, of course, the store must still pay rent, utilities, insurance, and all other costs.

For experienced price setters, an even simpler method uses a standard cost-of-goods percentage to determine the markup amount. Many retailers, for example, use 100 percent of cost-of-goods as the standard markup. If the manufacturer's price is $8 per shirt, the markup (100 percent) is also $8, so the selling price is $16.

Breakeven Analysis: Cost-Volume-Profit Relationships

Variable Cost *cost that changes with the quantity of a product produced and sold*

Fixed Cost *cost that is incurred regardless of the quantity of a product produced and sold*

Using cost-oriented pricing, a firm will cover **variable costs**, costs that change with the number of units of a product produced and sold, such as raw materials, sales commissions, and shipping. Firms also need to pay **fixed costs**, such as rent, insurance, and utilities, that must be paid *regardless of the number of units produced and sold.*

Breakeven Analysis *identifies the sales volume where total costs equal total revenues by assessing costs versus revenues at various sales volumes and showing, at any particular selling price, the amount of loss or profit for each volume of sales*

Costs, selling price, and the number of units sold determine how many units a company must sell before all costs, both variable and fixed, are covered, and it begins to make a profit. **Breakeven analysis** identifies the sales volume where total costs equal total revenues by assessing costs versus revenues for various sales volumes and showing, at any particular selling price, the amount of loss or profit for each volume of sales.

If you were the manager of a T-shirt store, how would you determine how many shirts you needed to sell to break even? We know that the *variable cost* of buying each shirt from the manufacturer is $8. This means that the store's annual variable costs depend on how many shirts are sold—the number of shirts sold times the $8 cost for each shirt. Say that *fixed costs* for keeping the store open for 1 year are $100,000 (no matter how many shirts are sold). At a selling price of $15 each, how many shirts must be sold *so that total revenues exactly cover both* fixed and variable costs? The answer is the **breakeven point**, which is 14,286 shirts:

Breakeven Point *sales volume at which the seller's total revenue from sales equals total costs (variable and fixed) with neither profit nor loss*

$$\text{Breakeven point (in units)} = \frac{\text{Total fixed cost}}{\text{Price} - \text{Variable cost}}$$

$$= \frac{\$100{,}000}{\$15 - \$8} = 14{,}286 \text{ shirts}$$

The breakeven analysis for this example is shown in Figure 12.2. If the store sells fewer than 14,286 shirts, it loses money for the year. If sales go higher than 14,286, profits grow by $7 for each additional shirt. If the store sells exactly 14,286 shirts, it will cover all its costs but earn zero profit. This sales number, then is the breakeven point.

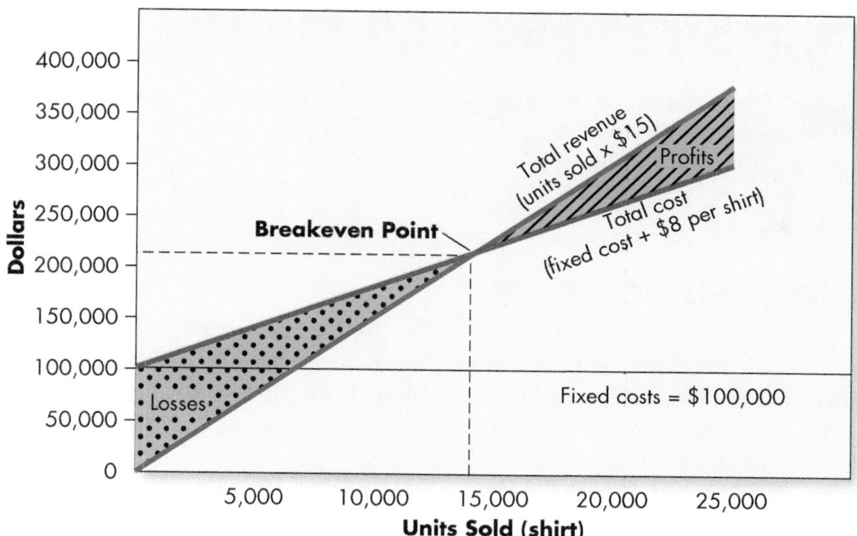

FIGURE 12.2 Breakeven Analysis

vanit Janthra/Alamy Stock Photo

Amazon has become a low-price leader for most products. The firm operates a network of warehouses and distribution centers and can package and deliver most products cheaper and faster than its competitors.

Zero profitability at the breakeven point can also be seen by using the profit equation:

$$\text{Profit} = \begin{matrix}\text{Total}\\ \text{Revenue}\end{matrix} - \left(\begin{matrix}\text{Total}\\ \text{Fixed}\\ \text{Cost}\end{matrix} + \begin{matrix}\text{Total}\\ \text{Variable}\\ \text{Cost}\end{matrix}\right)$$

$$= (14{,}286\,\text{shirts} \times \$15) - (\$100{,}000\,\text{Fixed Cost} + [14{,}286\,\text{shirts} \times \$8\,\text{Variable Cost}])$$

$$\$0 = (\$214{,}290) - (\$100{,}000 + \$114{,}288)$$

(rounded to the nearest whole shirt)

Learning Objective 12-5

Discuss pricing strategies that can be used for different competitive situations and identify the pricing tactics that can be used for setting prices.

Pricing Strategies and Tactics

The pricing tools discussed in the previous section help managers set prices on specific goods. They do not, however, help them decide on pricing philosophies for diverse competitive situations. In this section, we discuss pricing *strategy* (pricing as a planning activity) and some basic pricing *tactics* (ways in which managers implement a firm's pricing strategies).

Pricing Strategies

Pricing is an extremely important element in the marketing mix as well as a flexible marketing tool; it is certainly easier to change prices than to change products or distribution channels. This section will look at how pricing strategies can result in widely differing prices for similar products.

Pricing Existing Products A firm has three options for pricing existing products:

1 Pricing above prevailing market prices for similar products to take advantage of the common assumption that higher price means higher quality
2 Pricing below market prices while offering a product of comparable quality to higher-priced competitors
3 Pricing at or near market prices

Godiva chocolates and Patek Philippe watches price high by promoting prestige and quality images, while Hershey's chocolates and Timex watches are priced much lower. For these products, consumers most likely recognize differences in the products and know what they are buying. Both Budget and Dollar car-rental companies promote themselves as low-priced alternatives to Hertz and Enterprise. Since all four companies rent the same kinds of cars, Hertz and Enterprise generally stress that their customers get greater convenience and better customer service. Pricing below prevailing market price works if a firm offers a product of acceptable quality while keeping costs below those of higher-priced competitors.

Price Skimming *setting an initially high price to cover new product costs and generate a profit*

Penetration Pricing *setting an initially low price to establish a new product in the market*

Pricing New Products When introducing new products, companies can often choose between higher prices or lower prices. **Price skimming**, setting an initial higher price to cover development and introduction costs and generate a large profit on each item sold, works only if marketers can convince customers that a new product is truly different from existing products and there is no foreseeable major competition on the horizon. Apple's introduction of its MP3 player, the iPod, is a good example. With no strong competitors entering the market for several years, Apple was able to maintain a high retail price with little discounting, even at Walmart ($399 during its first year). However, as competitors introduced new products and as the iPhone also became a common music storage device, demand for the iPod declined and Apple had to reduce its prices. Apple discontinued the iPod in 2022 but continued to sell backstock from existing inventory for as little as $100. In contrast, **penetration pricing**, setting an initial low price to establish a new product in the market, seeks to create customer interest and stimulate trial purchases. Penetration strategy is the best strategy when introducing a product that has or expects to have competitors quickly. Gillette uses this strategy on nearly all of its new shaving systems to make sure they receive a high early adoption rate.

Start-up firms often use one-price, fixed pricing for launching new products. Carbonite started its online backup service with its strategy of "one-flat-low price," no matter how much space you needed to back up your computer files.[14] Although its pricing strategy changed as the company grew, to date the company has backed up more than 500 billion computer files. When new blockbuster movies are released, most movie theaters charge one price for all showings. After a few weeks, though, when the initial demand has subsided, they may start offering discounted tickets to showings at off-peak times.

Fixed Versus Dynamic Pricing for Online Business The digital marketplace has introduced a highly variable pricing system as an alternative to conventional fixed pricing for both consumer and business-to-business (B2B) products. At present, fixed pricing is still the most common option for cybershoppers, as well as most traditional brick-and-mortar retailers. In contrast, dynamic pricing, like eBay's auction bidding, uses flexibility between buyers and sellers to determine prices. Similarly, most major airlines use dynamic pricing. For instance, as a particular flight gets booked and there are fewer seats available the prices for those seats tend to increase.

Another kind of dynamic pricing, the reverse auction, allows sellers to alter prices privately on an individual basis. At Priceline.com, for example, consumers set a price (below the published fixed price) they are willing to pay for airfare (or a rental car or a hotel room). Then an airline can complete the sale by accepting the bid price. For B2B purchases, MediaBids.com uses reverse advertising auctions to sell ad space. A company will notify MediaBids that it is going to spend $1,000 for advertising. Publications then use their ad space as currency to place bids for the advertising dollars. The company can then accept the bid that offers the most ad exposure in the best publication.[15] Budget-conscious companies seeking legal advice are increasingly turning to reverse auctions for lower-cost contracts with law firms as well. Competing law firms, bidding downward in online chat rooms, enter price bids to provide a client company's legal services. Law firms, however, are concerned with reports that about 40 percent of the legal market is being decided in reverse auctions, and the auctions are cutting as much as 15 to 40 percent from traditional legal fees.[16]

managing in turbulent times

The High Cost of Price Wars

Stuck in Paris in 2008 with no cab in sight, serial entrepreneurs Travis Kalanick and Garrett Camp started brainstorming. As they joked around, they came up with the idea of a mobile app that could call a nearby car in a short amount of time at a reasonable rate, matching buyers (who need to get from point A to point B) with sellers (who have a car and are willing to transport buyers). At home in San Francisco, they developed the idea into a company and called it UberCab, later dropping the "cab" because of complaints from the city.

Uber developed its variable-price model after observing consumer demand and driver behavior in Boston in early 2012. Many drivers "clocked off" the system at 1 AM, just as people were rolling out of bars and restaurants and looking for rides home. Rather than having people wait a long time for a ride because of a limited supply of drivers, Uber decided to reward drivers for staying on the clock after 1 AM by providing premium fares. Supply quickly matched demand, and Uber expanded its market and its business based on its dynamic pricing model.

The company states on the website: "When you go to request a ride on a Saturday night, you might find that the price is different than the cost of the same trip a few days earlier. That's because of our dynamic pricing algorithm, which adjusts rates based on a number of variables, such as time and distance of your route, traffic and the current rider-to-driver demand. Sometimes, this can mean a temporary increase in price during particularly busy periods.

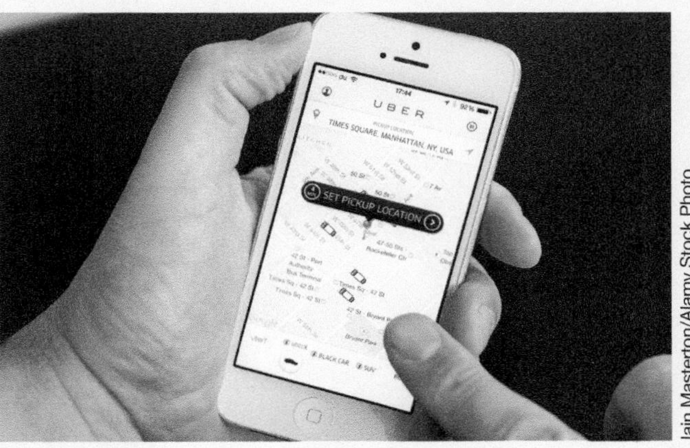

Iain Masterton/Alamy Stock Photo

"When demand increases, Uber uses variable costs to encourage more drivers to get on the road and help deal with number of rider requests. When we notify you of an Uber fare increase, we notify drivers as well. If you decide to go ahead and request your ride, you'll get an alert on the app to make sure you know that the rates have changed."[17]

Uber and Lyft have completely disrupted the ride-for-hire industry, creating new cost-effective options for consumers. However, profitability and longevity aren't just a function of being the lowest-cost provider. In fact, the price wars have hurt both companies as well as the traditional taxi services.

Bundling Strategy *grouping several products together to be sold as a single unit at a reduced price, rather than individually*

Bundling A **bundling strategy** groups several products together to be sold as a single unit rather than individually. Suppose you have two insurance policies with different companies, one for life insurance and another for auto insurance. You may benefit from bundling—that is, buying both policies as a "package" from just one company. First, your total premium payments may be reduced. In addition, you gain the convenience of communicating with and making payments to just one instead of two companies. The bundling company gains, too, with additional sales of two instead of just one product. CenturyLink, for example, offers a bundle of home phone, Internet, cloud storage, and DirecTV services that is priced below the combined individual prices for the four services.

Pricing Tactics

Price Lining *setting a limited number of prices for certain categories of products*

Regardless of its pricing strategy, a company may adopt one or more *pricing tactics*. Companies selling multiple items in a product category often use **price lining**, offering all items in certain categories at a limited number of prices. A department store, for example, might predetermine $175, $250, and $500 as the *price points* for men's suits, so all men's suits would be set at one of these three prices. This practice allows the store to have a suit for all of the different customer segments it hopes to attract. Grocery stores use this strategy as well; for example, in canned goods, they will usually carry a national brand, a store brand, and a generic brand.

Psychological Pricing *pricing tactic that takes advantage of the fact that consumers do not always respond rationally to stated prices*

Odd-Even Pricing *psychological pricing tactic based on the premise that customers prefer prices not stated in even dollar amounts*

Psychological pricing takes advantage of the fact that customers are not completely rational when making buying decisions. One type, **odd-even pricing**, is based on the theory that customers prefer prices that are not stated in even dollar amounts. Thus, customers often regard prices of $1,000, $100, $50, and $10 as significantly higher than $999.95, $99.95, $49.95, and $9.95, respectively. Of course, the price set for a product is not always the price for which it sells. Sellers must often resort to price reductions,

Firms often use psychological pricing tactics to entice customers to buy their products. For instance, this candy store is promoting various products that are priced at one cent below the next dollar amount. The idea is that people may see a price of $4.99 to be meaningfully lower than a price of $5.

or discounts, to stimulate sales. Auto dealers, vacation resorts, airlines, and hotels offer **discount** prices to stimulate demand during off-peak seasons. Hyatt Hotels, like many others, offers commercial room discounts for frequent business users and for large-scale events such as conventions, trade shows, and special events. During the 2020 COVID-19 pandemic, many hotels offered large discounts on rooms for future stays in order to lock in future revenue and maintain cash flow.

Discount *price reduction offered as an incentive to purchase*

International Pricing

When Procter & Gamble (P&G) reviewed its prospects for marketing products in new overseas markets, it encountered an unsettling fact. Because it typically priced products to cover hefty R&D costs, profitably priced items were out of reach for too many global consumers. The solution was, in effect, to reverse the process. Now P&G conducts research to find out what foreign buyers can afford and then develops products that those markets can buy. P&G penetrates markets with lower-priced items and encourages customers to trade up as they become able to afford higher-quality products.

Another strategy calls for increasing foreign market share by pricing products below cost. As a result, a given product is priced lower in a foreign market than in its own country. As we saw in Chapter 4, this practice is called *dumping*, which is illegal in the United States. The Coalition of Gulf Shrimp Industries once petitioned the U.S. International Trade Commission (ITC) to impose special tariffs on seven countries—China, Ecuador, India, Indonesia, Malaysia, Thailand, and Vietnam—accused of using government subsidies enabling unfair price reductions, or dumping, against the U.S. shrimp industry. If allegations of dumping are proven, international law allows the country whose businesses are affected to impose penalties called *countervailing duties* on products coming from those countries found guilty of dumping, as a remedy to balance prices.[18]

summary of learning objectives

LEARNING OBJECTIVE 12-1

Explain the definition of a product as a value package and how to classify goods and services.

Customers buy products to receive value that satisfies a want or a need. Thus, a successful product is a *value package*, a bundle of attributes that, taken together, provides the right features and offers the right benefits that satisfy customers' wants and needs. *Features* are the qualities, tangible and intangible, that are included with the product. To be satisfying, features must provide *benefits* that allow customers to achieve the end results they want. The value package has services and features that add value by providing benefits that increase the customer's satisfaction.

Products (both goods and services) can be classified according to expected buyers as either *consumer products* or *organizational products*. *Convenience products* are inexpensive consumer goods and services that are consumed rapidly and regularly. *Shopping products* are more expensive and are purchased less often than convenience products. *Specialty products* are extremely important and expensive goods and services. *Organizational products* are classified as either *production items, expense items*, or *capital items*. Production items are goods and services used directly in the production process. *Expense items* are goods or services consumed within a year to produce other products. *Capital items* are expensive and long-lasting goods and services that have expected lives of several years.

The group of products that a company makes available for sale is referred to as its *product mix*. Although many companies start with a single product, they tend to expand into product lines, a group of products that are closely related in function or target market. Companies may develop multiple product lines to serve different types of customers or to meet the needs of existing customers in new ways. Multiple product lines allow a company to grow and can help offset the consequences of slow sales in any one product line.

LEARNING OBJECTIVE 12-2

Describe the new product development process.

To expand and diversify product lines, new products must be developed and introduced. Many firms have research and development (R&D) departments and services development teams for exploring new product possibilities by adopting a basic seven-step process: (1) *Product ideas*: searching for ideas for new products. (2) *Screening*: eliminating all product ideas that do not mesh with the firm's abilities or objectives. (3) *Concept testing*: using market research to get consumers' input about product benefits and prices. (4) *Business analysis*: comparing production costs and benefits to see whether a product meets minimum profitability goals. (5) *Prototype development*: producing a preliminary version of a product. (6) *Product testing and test marketing*: going into limited production, testing the product to see if it meets performance requirements, and, if so, selling it on a limited basis. (7) *Commercialization*: beginning full-scale production and marketing.

For the development of services, there are two important differences in the seven-step model: (1) *Service ideas*: The search for service ideas includes defining the service value package, thus identifying the tangible and intangible features that characterize the service, and stating service specifications. (2) *Service process design*: Instead of prototype development, services require a service process design that identifies each step in the service. The design also identifies worker requirements—employee behaviors, skills, capabilities, and interactions with customers during the service encounter—and facility requirements.

LEARNING OBJECTIVE 12-3

Describe the stages of the product life cycle (PLC) and methods for extending a product's life.

The product life cycle (PLC) for a good or a service product is a series of four stages or phases characterizing the product's profit-producing life. (1) *Introduction*: This stage begins when the product reaches the marketplace. Marketers focus on consumers aware of the product and its benefits. Extensive development, production, and sales costs erase all profits. (2) *Growth*: Sales begin to climb and the product begins to show a profit as marketers decrease prices slightly and continue promotional expenditures. Profits begin as revenues surpass costs. (3) *Maturity*: Typically the longest stage in the PLC, sales growth peaks and then starts to slow. The product's profits are highest early in this stage. As increased competition forces price cutting, along with more advertising and promotional expenses, profits begin to diminish. (4) *Decline*: Sales and profits continue to fall as new products take away sales. Firms end or reduce promotional support (ads or salespeople are reduced), but modest support allows the product to linger with minimal profits. Eventually the product dies.

Three prominent methods are used for extending the lives of declining or even recently deceased products. (1) In *product extension*, an existing product is marketed globally instead of just domestically. A product that is in the maturity stage or even declining domestically may provide value to customers in other countries. (2) With *product adaptation*, the product is modified to contain changed features that appeal to new customers in different countries. (3) *Reintroduction* means reviving, for new markets, products that are becoming obsolete or have died in older ones.

Marketers must also identify products so that consumers recognize them. Branding is the process of using names and symbols to communicate the qualities of a particular product made by a particular producer. Branding can create brand awareness, in which buyers are aware of a brand, and brand loyalty, in which buyers demonstrate consistent buying behavior.

Marketers can use product placement to increase brand awareness and brand loyalty. Product placement occurs when a brand is featured in television, film, magazines, or video games. There are three different kinds of brand names. *National brands* are produced by, widely distributed by, and carry the brand name of the manufacturer. When a company allows another company to use its brand name, that is a *licensed brand*. The final kind of brand name is a *private brand*, which is given to a product by the wholesaler or retailer rather than the manufacturer.

LEARNING OBJECTIVE 12-4

Identify the various pricing objectives that govern pricing decisions and describe the price-setting tools used in making these decisions.

In pricing, managers decide what the company will get in exchange for its products. Pricing objectives refer to the goals that producers hope to attain as a result of pricing decisions. Two major pricing objectives are (1) *Pricing to maximize profits*: Set the price to sell the number of units that will generate the highest possible total profits. With prices set too low, the seller misses the chance to make additional profits on each of the many units sold. With prices set too high, a larger profit will be made on each unit, but fewer units will be sold. (2) *Market share objectives*: Pricing is used for establishing market share. The seller is willing to accept minimal profits, even losses, to get buyers to try products. The seller may use pricing to establish market share—a company's percentage of the total market sales for a specific product type.

Managers often prefer to measure the potential impact before deciding on final prices. For this purpose, two basic tools are used: (1) *Cost-oriented pricing* begins by determining total costs for making products available to buyers, including wages, rent, materials, and insurance. Added to those costs is a *markup* for profit to arrive at a selling price. (2) *Breakeven analysis* is used to calculate the breakeven point, the number of sales units that must be sold for total revenue to equal total costs (which results in neither a profit nor a loss). To calculate the breakeven point, the company must identify all fixed and variable costs associated with the product. The formula for the breakeven point is the total fixed costs divided by the difference between the sales price and the unit variable cost.

LEARNING OBJECTIVE 12-5

Discuss pricing strategies that can be used for different competitive situations and identify the pricing tactics that can be used for setting prices.

Pricing for existing products can be set above, at, or below market prices for similar products. High pricing is often interpreted as meaning higher quality and prestige, and low pricing may attract greater sales volume by keeping costs below those of higher-priced competitors. Pricing strategies for new products include *price skimming*—setting an initially high price to cover costs and generate a profit—that may allow a firm to earn a large profit on each item sold; marketers must convince customers that a product is truly different from existing products. *Penetration pricing*—setting an initially low price to establish a new product in the market—seeks to generate customer interest and stimulate trial purchases. Strategies for e-businesses include dynamic versus fixed pricing. *Dynamic pricing* establishes individual prices by real-time interaction between the seller and each customer on the Internet. *Fixed pricing* is the traditional one-price-for-all arrangement.

Regardless of its pricing strategy, a company can then adopt any of three tactics for setting prices: (1) With *price lining*, any product category (such as women's shoes) will be set at three or four price levels, and all shoes will be priced at one of those levels. (2) *Psychological pricing* acknowledges that customers are not completely rational when making buying decisions, as with *odd-even pricing* in which customers regard prices such as $10 as being significantly higher than $9.95. (3) *Discount pricing* uses price reductions to stimulate sales.

key terms

brand awareness **(p. 394)**
branding **(p. 394)**
breakeven analysis **(p. 398)**
breakeven point **(p. 398)**
bundling strategy **(p. 402)**
capital items **(p. 386)**
consumer **(p. 385)**
convenience goods **(p. 385)**
convenience services **(p. 385)**
cost-oriented pricing **(p. 397)**
discount **(p. 403)**
expense items **(p. 386)**
fixed cost **(p. 398)**
industrial buyer **(p. 385)**
licensed brands **(p. 396)**
market share (or market penetration) **(p. 397)**
markup **(p. 398)**
national brands **(p. 396)**
odd-even pricing **(p. 402)**
packaging **(p. 396)**
penetration pricing **(p. 400)**
price lining **(p. 402)**
price skimming **(p. 400)**
pricing **(p. 396)**
pricing objectives **(p. 396)**
private brand (or private label) **(p. 396)**
product adaptation **(p. 392)**
product extension **(p. 392)**
product features **(p. 383)**
product life cycle (PLC) **(p. 391)**
product line **(p. 386)**
product mix **(p. 386)**
product placement **(p. 394)**
production items **(p. 385)**
psychological pricing **(p. 402)**
reintroduction **(p. 393)**
shopping goods **(p. 385)**
shopping services **(p. 385)**
specialty goods **(p. 385)**
specialty services **(p. 385)**
speed to market (or time compression) **(p. 389)**
value package **(p. 383)**
variable cost **(p. 398)**

questions & exercises

QUESTIONS FOR REVIEW

12-1. What is a value package?

12-2. How would you explain the product development process?

12-3. What are the various classifications of consumer and industrial products? Give an example of a good and a service for each category other than those discussed in the text.

12-4. What pricing strategies can companies use for different competitive situations?

QUESTIONS FOR ANALYSIS

12-5. Describe the four stages of the product life cycle and the marketing mix that is used in each. Provide at least one example of a product in each stage other than those provided in the text.

12-6. Some companies have very narrow product mixes, producing just one or two products, while others have many different products. What are the advantages of each approach?

12-7. Suppose that a small publisher selling to book distributors has fixed operating costs of $600,000 each year and variable costs of $3.00 per book. How many books must the firm sell to break even if the selling price is $6.00?

12-8. Describe price skimming and penetration pricing. What types of new products would be best suited to price skimming? What types of products will be most successful with penetration pricing?

APPLICATION EXERCISES

12-9. For this exercise, select a car or truck or other vehicle, something you wouldn't ordinarily buy, and identify the target market. Once you've identified the target market, describe the features of the vehicle that appeal specifically to the target market.

12-10. Select a product and analyze pricing objectives for it. What information would you want to gather if you were to adopt a profit-maximizing objective? What information would you want to gather if you were to adopt a market share objective?

building a business: continuing team exercise

ASSIGNMENT

Meet with your team members to consider your new business venture and how it relates to the product and pricing topics in this chapter. Develop specific responses to the following:

12-11. Consider the customers in your target market or markets. Are they individual consumers, organizations, or a combination of both? For each of your target markets, identify what customers will expect in the product features and in the value-package features.

12-12. Identify your business's product mix, including its product line or lines, if any. How do you justify this product mix rather than others you might have chosen?

12-13. Will your product or products require new product development or modifications of existing products, or are they fully developed and ready to go? How quickly do you anticipate your products will be developed and ready for market? How long a life span do you expect for your products?

12-14. Consider various pricing objectives and strategies to use when your products first go to market. Which pricing objective or objectives seem most appropriate for your entry into the markets? Identify the pricing strategy or strategies that seem best suited for your business. Explain.

12-15. Various pricing tactics, too, are available for planning your business. Describe the pricing tactics you expect to use on opening the business. Explain your choice or choices. Might you resort to different pricing tactics as your products move through various stages in the life cycles? Explain your reasoning.

team exercise

THE PRICE IS RIGHT

You are a member of a team of business students who have organized for the purpose of starting a small business selling mobile phone cases. You have recently established a business relationship with an Indonesian manufacturer that can provide durable and attractive cases at a low cost, and you have secured a kiosk at a local mall that you believe is an excellent location for selling the cases. However, you must decide on a pricing strategy for the phone cases. You have been provided with the following information:

- Your monthly expenses will be rent on the mall kiosk ($2,500) and hourly pay for your four employees. The kiosk will be open 300 hours per month and the hourly cost of an employee (including benefits) is $15/hour. In addition, you have hired a business manager who will handle ordering the inventory, maintaining the accounting records, and scheduling employees. The business manager's monthly salary is $6,000 per month.
- The Indonesian manufacturer of the phone cases has committed to delivering a variety of cases at a cost of $5 per case for the next year in return for a promise that you will order only from this supplier. There are no other vendors selling these cases within 100 miles, and they are expected to be popular.

Team Activity

12-16. Assemble a group of four students and assign each group member to one of the following pricing philosophies:

- Because the future is uncertain, the primary objective of this business venture is to maximize immediate profits.
- The amount of competition in the market is considerable, so the business wishes to price at a level that will give it a large share of the market.
- The business wishes to establish a premium image for its phone cases.
- The business believes that repeat business is the key to success, so it wishes to use penetration pricing.

Have each group member describe the pricing strategy that they think the business should use for phone cases, based on the assigned philosophy. Be sure to list the benefits of each approach.

12-17. As a group, develop a consensus about the best pricing philosophy and a rationale for why you have selected this approach.

12-18. Using the information provided in the case, identify the fixed and variable costs.

12-19. Using the amounts calculated in Step 2, calculate the breakeven point at a sales price of $15, $20, $25, and $30. On the basis of these answers as well as your assessment of likely monthly sales, decide on the best price for the phone cases.

12-20. What other pricing tactics might you employ at the phone case kiosk to increase sales?

exercising your ethics

DRIVING A LEGITIMATE BARGAIN

The Situation

In buying his first new car, Matt visited showrooms and websites for every make of SUV. After weeks of reading and test driving, he settled on a brand-new, well-known Japanese-made vehicle with a manufacturer's suggested retail price of $37,500. The price included accessories and options that Matt considered essential. Because he planned to own the car for at least five years, he was willing to wait for just the right package rather than accept a lesser-equipped car already on the lot. Negotiations with Gary, the sales representative, continued for two weeks. Finally, a sales contract was signed for $33,500, with delivery due no more than two or three months later if the vehicle had to be special ordered from the factory and earlier if Gary found the exact car when he searched other dealers around the country. On August 30, to secure the terms of the agreement, Matt wrote a check for $1,000 to the dealer.

The Dilemma

Matt received a call on September 14 from Angela, Gary's sales manager: "We couldn't get the model you ordered," she reported, "because the new models just came out, but we've got your car, just as you ordered. We've discounted it by the same amount, so it's $35,500 to you instead of the MSRP of $39,500." After some argument, he told Angela to send him back everything he had signed plus his $1,000 deposit, claiming that the deal was off.

QUESTIONS TO ADDRESS

12-21. How would you characterize the particular ethical issues in this situation?

12-22. From an ethical standpoint, what are the obligations of the sales representative and the sales manager regarding the pricing of the product in this situation?

12-23. If you were Angela, the sales manager, how would you defend your actions?

12-24. If you were responsible for maintaining good customer relations at the dealership, how would you handle this matter, considering the interests of both the consumer and the business?

cases

THE THIRTY-THOUSAND-DOLLAR HANDBAG

Continued from page 383

At the beginning of this chapter, you read about pricing strategies in the handbag industry. Using the information presented in this chapter, you should now be able to answer the following questions:

12-25. How would you describe the value package of the Louis Vuitton purse?

12-26. What is Louis Vuitton's target market? Do you think it is evolving or is it static?

12-27. If you were starting a small boutique store that carried handbags, what kinds of bags would you stock and why?

12-28. Pick a small business in your community. In a paragraph or two, describe the products or services provided by the company and the target market(s). Taking those two things into consideration, how do you think the company sets its prices?

12-29. Do you think the economic downturn of 2008 affected the price of Louis Vuitton handbags? Do you think the economic crisis of 2020 affected the price of Louis Vuitton and other luxury handbags? Why or why not?

A PLANNED OBSOLESCENCE

Arlo Technologies recognizes the product life cycle and even informs customers that it will stop supporting products that have become obsolete. Arlo started out as a brand of security cameras marketed by Netgear. In early 2018, the board of directors of Netgear voted to spin off Arlo as its own company, but Netgear retained control of the new company by keeping a majority of the voting stock. According to the company's website, by mid-2023, it had shipped 28.5 million devices representing 7.5 million registered accounts and 2 million paid accounts.[19]

In early 2023, the company announced that it would stop supporting Arlo Gen 3 and Arlo Pro wireless home security camera systems in April 2023, meaning those devices lost access to functions, including free cloud storage, firmware updates, and security patches. The cameras were initially produced and marketed between 2014 and 2019.[20]

The decision was based on the company's end-of-life policy that states, "The Arlo Products may reach the end of their product life cycle for a number of reasons, including changing market demands, technology innovation, development of alternate and more efficient software platforms, and/or improvements in product and cloud security."[21]

QUESTIONS FOR DISCUSSION

12-30. Do you think it is ethical for Arlo to refuse to support older products? Why or why not?

12-31. Do you think there should be laws governing planned obsolescence? Why or why not?

12-32. What other options would Arlo have in lieu of discontinuing support?

12-33. If you were the CEO of Arlo, how would you justify planned obsolescence to your employees?

endnotes

[1] Zippia, "Epic Systems History: Founding, Timeline, and Milestones," September 9, 2022, https://www.zippia.com/epic-systems-careers-22677/history/.

[2] https://www.cms.gov/newsroom/fact-sheets/cms-finalizes-requirements-medicaid-electronic-health-records-ehr-incentive-program.

[3] https://blog.petrieflom.law.harvard.edu/2021/07/12/new-rule-puts-medical-data-in-patients-hands/.

[4] "Epic on MyChart Redesign: 'A More Personalized Experience for Patients,'" Healthcare IT News, December 17, 2020, https://www.healthcareitnews.com/news/epic-mychart-redesign-more-personalized-experience-patients.

[5] Steve Forbes, "Building Company Culture and Innovating the Future with Judy Faulkner," *Forbes*, August 23, 2021, https://www.forbes.com/sites/steveforbes/2020/11/06/building-company-culture-and-innovating-the-future-with-judy-faulkner/?sh=485e7f5e5303.

[6] MyChart, "About MyChart," accessed June 24, 2023, https://www.mychart.org/About.

[7] "Judy Faulkner," *Forbes*, accessed June 24, 2023, https://www.forbes.com/profile/judy-faulkner/?sh=1c10685933b8.

[8] "An Epic Viewpoint: An Interview with Judy Faulkner, CEO of Epic Systems," accessed June 24, 2023, https://www.liebertpub.com/doi/10.1089/heat.2016.29026.jfa.

[9] Ron Winslow, "Cholesterol Drug Advances," *Wall Street Journal*, November 18, 2010, B1–B2; "Anacetrapib for the Treatment of Dyslipidemia," *Issues in Emerging Health Technologies: Canadian Agency for Drugs and Technologies in Health,* March 2013, http://www.cadth.ca/media/pdf/EH0007-000Anacetrapib_e.pdf; John Carroll, "Anacetrapib," *FierceBiotech*, October 8, 2012, http://www.fiercebiotech.com/special-reports/anacetrapib.

[10] "39 Official Mattress Industry Statistics 2023—The Roundup," accessed June 24, 2023, https://theroundup.org/mattress-industry-statistics/.

[11] United States Department of Agriculture: Economic Research Service, "New Products," accessed April 19, 2020, http://www.ers.usda.gov/topics/food-markets-prices/processing-marketing/new-products.aspx#UV2FtzemFcI; "Food Marketing System in the U.S.: New Product Introductions," *USDA Economic Research Service*, May 21, 2023, http://www.ers.usda.gov.

[12] Kelvin Chan, "Tired Western Brands Find New Life in Asia," Yahoo! News, September 8, 2022, http://news.yahoo.com/tired-western-brands-life-asia-070448945.html.

[13] Interbrand, "Interbrand Releases 22th Annual Best Global Brands Report," accessed May 22, 2023, http://www.interbrand.com/en/best-global-brands/2022/downloads.aspx.

[14] Carbonite, "About Carbonite," accessed September 19, 2023, https://www.carbonite.com.

[15] "Reverse Auction," *Encyclopedia of Management, 2009*, Encyclopedia.com, January 16, 2011, http://www.encyclopedia.com/doc/1G2-3273100254.html; MediaBids.com, accessed September 19, 2023, http://www.mediabids.com/.

[16] Patrick G. Lee, "Pricing Tactic Spooks Lawyers," *Wall Street Journal*, August 2, 2011, B5.

[17] Jessica Phillips, "How Uber's Dynamic Pricing Model Works," Uber Blog, January 11, 2022, https://www.uber.com/en-gb/blog/uber-dynamic-pricing/.

[18] "Hearing Set in U.S. on Dumping Charges," SeafoodSource.com, January 4, 2023, http://www.seafoodsource.com/newsarticledetail.aspx?id=19025.

[19] Arlo, "Investor Relations," accessed June 23, 2023, https://investor.arlo.com/ir-home/default.aspx.

[20] Danny Palmer, "Arlo Will End Support for These Older Cameras in April. Here's What You Need to Know," ZDNET, January 3, 2023, https://www.zdnet.com/home-and-office/smart-home/arlo-will-end-support-for-these-older-cameras-in-april-heres-what-you-need-to-know/.

[21] "Arlo End-of-Life Policy," accessed June 23, 2023, https://downloads.arlo.com/images/PDFs/EOL_Policy/Arlo_End-of-Life-Policy-2022.pdf?cid=gw.

chapter 13

Distributing and Promoting Products

quiggyt4/Shutterstock

learning objectives

After reading this chapter, you should be able to:

13-1 **Explain** the meaning of *distribution mix* and identify the different channels of distribution.

13-2 **Describe** the role of wholesalers and the functions performed by e-intermediaries.

13-3 **Describe** the different types of retailing and explain how online retailers add value for consumers on the Internet.

13-4 **Define** *physical distribution* and describe the major activities in the physical distribution process.

13-5 **Identify** the objectives of promotion and the considerations in selecting a promotional mix and discuss the various kinds of advertising promotions.

13-6 **Outline** the tasks involved in personal selling and describe the various types of sales promotions.

what's in it for me?

To become a successful retailer in any market takes a solid understanding of how best to distribute and promote products to customers. This chapter describes different types of wholesalers, retailers, and intermediaries as well as how the online marketplace has changed the nature of how companies do business. By understanding this chapter's methods for distributing and promoting products, you'll have a clearer picture of how to sort out and identify the different kinds of people who are targeted by various companies, products, and advertising campaigns. As an informed consumer, you'll have a better self-awareness of when you are being targeted with promotional activities by businesses. You'll also be prepared to evaluate a company's distribution methods, advertising programs, and competitive potential.

As we saw in Chapter 12, marketing managers are concerned with deciding what products a company will offer to its customers and determining prices for those products. In this chapter, we'll look at the other two of the Four Ps of the marketing mix. We'll start by looking at the concept of *place*, the *distribution mix*, and the different channels and methods of distribution. We'll then look at *promotion* and discuss the factors to consider in selecting a promotional mix. Finally, we'll discuss the tasks involved in personal selling and various types of sales promotions.

ximagination/123RF

vanit Janthra/Alamy Stock Photo

Chaos Theory at Work

In the early days of U.S. commerce, people waited with anticipation for the Sears catalog and then, with even more anticipation, for the Wells Fargo wagon to bring their orders. In 1897, the Sears catalog was almost 800 pages and even had a section offering homes for sale. Pre-cut lumber, doors, windows, and roofing were shipped by rail for the buyer to self-assemble. (Some of these homes are still standing today.) The order could take weeks or even months to reach a neatly organized Sears warehouse, where workers processed the paperwork, packed the items, and shipped them to the customer. But even this slow process was a radical improvement over the pre-railroad system of carts and wagons that would supply local stores with a limited array of goods.

Today, we expect to go to a store like Walmart to find just about anything we need in large supply, but even more importantly, we expect to be able to order online and receive our shipment within days, if not hours. You might think that tight organization and complex algorithms to collect and collate individual and marketplace buying patterns and personal shopping preferences would be at the heart of this rapid delivery system we enjoy. That's certainly part of it, but you might be surprised at what actually enables Amazon to ship so quickly. The secret lies in transportation and warehouse management. Transportation affects delivery time for obvious reasons. If you have a warehouse in Seattle, moving an order to a customer in Boston takes quite a bit of time and logistics.

Central to Amazon's fast service are the giant fulfillment centers scattered across the globe. But it's more than just the size and number of warehouses; it's how they are organized that makes them so effective.

The standard stock management wisdom is to divide the warehouse and its shelves into sections and put away items accordingly, but Amazon fulfillment centers are radically different. These centers have no consumer electronics section or kitchen appliances section. When a shipment of batteries comes in, an associate doesn't find the batteries section on a warehouse map and then walk over to that section. Instead, when goods come into a fulfillment center, associates place them wherever space is available. There is no organization. Placement is completely random, and so, for a traditionalist, the warehouse will look entirely chaotic and disorganized. But there is logic in this random chaos.

For a business-to-business supplier, it would make sense to keep 50 packages of something—say, D-cell batteries—packaged in bulk. However, since Amazon mostly serves consumers who want just one or two small packages of batteries per order, it makes sense to break down the bulk items in advance. Then, rather than crossing the entire warehouse (Amazon's largest warehouse in 2023 was 4.1 million square feet, almost twice as big as the tallest skyscraper in Los Angeles—the 73-story Wilshire Grand Hotel[1]) to put items on a predetermined shelf, associates just put items in the first open spot, scanning the barcodes on the shelf and on the product. The system can instantly identify where those batteries are placed, and there may be batteries all over the warehouse, scattered here and there. But if the warehouse stores batteries in 50 separate locations, there's a much better chance that a pack is close to the person filling your order. There's also a greater chance that the other items in your order are also nearby.

Still, searching around for the items to fill an order, with over 12 million different items in stock, could be daunting. Enter Kiva Systems. In 2012, Amazon bought the robotics company, and now people don't go searching for the shelves. The shelves come to the people. Little Kiva robots pick up the shelves with the items and bring them to the packaging area and then take them away again once the item has been picked and added to the order. From the outside, the random placement of items on shelves—and the shelves themselves moving to and fro in a never-ending dance—can look like chaos. But it's a meticulously choreographed production and the key to getting batteries on Christmas Eve when you only ordered them that morning.

Kiva robots outnumber humans in Amazon's massive warehouse by about an 8-to-1 ratio. In 2022, Amazon added Proteus robots with additional safety features and integrations to its warehouse logistics. The next big breakthrough is likely something we haven't even imagined yet. The business students of today will definitely have a hand in creating the shopping experience of the future. (After studying the content in this chapter, you should be able to answer a set of discussion questions found at the end of the chapter.)

The Distribution Mix

Learning Objective 13-1

Explain the meaning of *distribution mix* and identify the different channels of distribution.

In addition to a good product mix and effective pricing, the success of any product also depends on its **distribution mix**, the combination of distribution channels by which a firm gets products to end users. In this section, we look at intermediaries and different kinds of distribution channels. Then we discuss some benefits consumers reap from services provided by intermediaries.

Distribution Mix *combination of distribution channels by which a firm gets its products to end users*

Intermediaries and Distribution Channels

Once called *middlemen*, **intermediaries** help to distribute goods, either by moving them or by providing information that stimulates their movement from sellers to customers. **Wholesalers**, like C&S Wholesale, are intermediaries who sell products to other businesses for resale to final consumers. **Retailers**, such as Walmart and Amazon, sell products directly to consumers.

Intermediary *individual or firm that helps to distribute a product*

Wholesaler *intermediary who sells products to other businesses for resale to final consumers*

Retailer *intermediary who sells products directly to consumers*

Distribution of Goods and Services A **distribution channel** is the path a product follows from producer to end user. Figure 13.1 shows how four popular distribution channels can be identified according to the channel members involved in getting products to buyers.

Distribution Channel *network of interdependent companies through which a product passes from producer to end user*

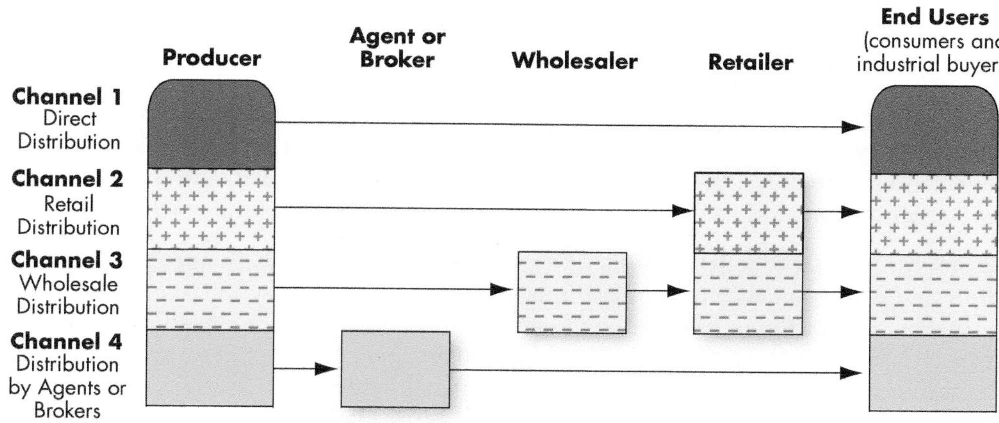

FIGURE 13.1 Channels of Distribution

Keith Dannemiller/Alamy Stock Photo

At this plant of an electrical components supplier, this employee assembles electrical systems according to a process that meets the requirements for its industrial customers. The finished assemblies are shipped from the plant to customers' facilities, illustrating a direct (producer to customer) channel of distribution.

Direct Channel *distribution channel in which a product travels from producer to consumer without intermediaries*

Channel 1: Direct Distribution In a **direct channel**, the product travels from the producer to the consumer or other buyer without intermediaries. Avon, Dell, GEICO, and Tupperware, as well as many online companies, use this type of channel. Most business goods, especially those bought in large quantities, are sold directly by the manufacturer to the industrial buyer.

Channel 2: Retail Distribution In Channel 2, producers distribute consumer products through retailers. Goodyear, for example, maintains its own network of retail outlets. Levi's has its own outlets but also produces jeans for other retailers. Large outlets, such as Walmart, buy merchandise directly from producers and then resell to customers online and at Walmart retail stores. Consumers can also go online to buy popular products such as book, movie, and music downloads from online retailers. Many industrial buyers, such as businesses buying office supplies from Staples, also rely on this channel.

Channel 3: Wholesale Distribution Once the most widely used method of nondirect distribution, traditional brick-and-mortar Channel 2 distribution requires a large and costly amount of floor space for storing and displaying merchandise. Wholesalers relieve this space problem by storing merchandise and restocking retailer store displays frequently. With approximately 90 percent of its space used to display merchandise and only 10 percent needed for storage and office facilities, the combination convenience store and gas station's use of wholesalers is an example of Channel 3.

Sales Agent *independent intermediary who generally deals in the related product lines of a few producers and forms long-term relationships to represent those producers and meet the needs of many customers*

Broker *independent intermediary who matches numerous sellers and buyers as needed, often without knowing in advance who they will be*

Channel 4: Distribution by Agents or Brokers Sales agents or brokers represent producers and receive commissions on the goods they sell to consumers or industrial users. **Sales agents**, such as online travel agents, generally deal in the related product lines of a few producers, such as tour companies, to meet the needs of many customers. In industries like real estate and stock exchanges, **brokers** match numerous sellers and buyers as needed to sell properties, often without knowing in advance who they will be.

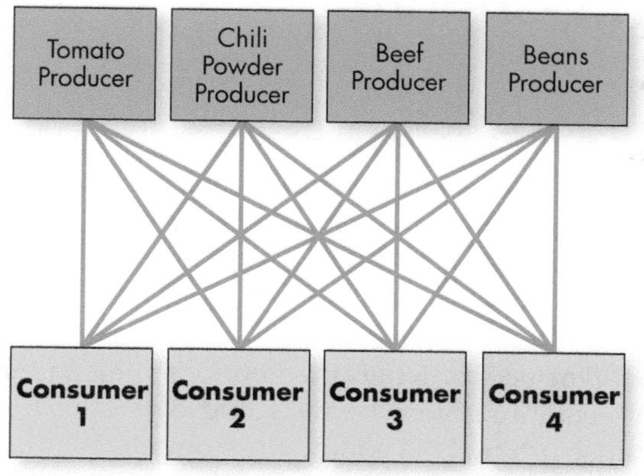

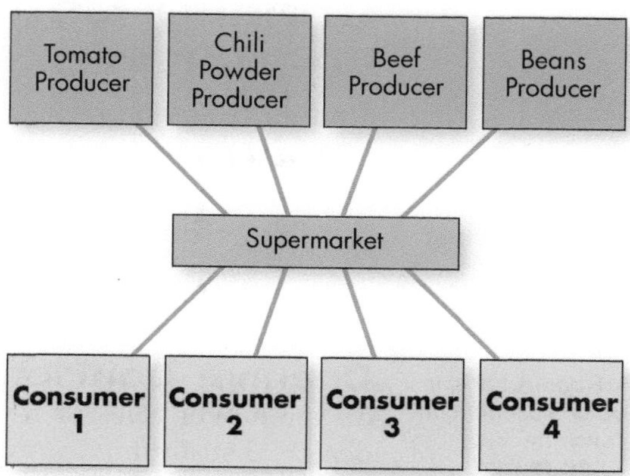

FIGURE 13.2 The Value-Adding Intermediary

The Pros and Cons of Nondirect Distribution One downfall of nondirect distribution is higher prices—the more "stations" in the channel, the more intermediaries there are that need to make a profit by charging a markup or commission, and the higher the final price. Intermediaries, however, can offer *added value* by providing time-saving information and making the right quantities of products available where and when consumers need them. Figure 13.2 illustrates the problem of making chili without the benefit of a common intermediary, the supermarket. As a consumer, you would obviously spend a lot more time, money, and energy if you tried to gather all the ingredients from separate producers. In short, intermediaries exist because they provide necessary services that move products efficiently from producers to users.

Distribution Strategies

Selecting an appropriate distribution network is a strategic decision; it determines both the amount and cost of *market coverage* that a product gets, or how many of any kind of intermediary will be used. Generally, strategy depends on the type of product and the degree of market coverage that is most effective in getting it to the greatest number of customers. Marketers strive to make a product accessible in just enough locations to satisfy customers' needs. You can buy milk and bottled water, for instance, in many different retail outlets, but there are very few outlets for buying a new Ferrari. Three strategies, (1) *intensive*, (2) *exclusive*, and (3) *selective distribution*, provide different degrees of market coverage.

- **Intensive distribution** means distributing through as many channels and channel members as possible (both wholesalers and retailers). It is normally used for low-cost consumer goods with widespread appeal, such as candy and magazines. M&M's candies enter the market through many different retail outlets—supermarkets, vending machines, drugstores, online, and so forth.

Intensive Distribution *strategy by which a product is distributed through as many channels as possible*

- With **exclusive distribution**, a manufacturer grants the exclusive right to distribute or sell a product to a limited number of wholesalers or retailers, usually in a given geographic area. Such agreements are most common for high-cost prestige products. Rolex watches are sold only by "Official Rolex Jewelers."

Exclusive Distribution *strategy by which a manufacturer grants exclusive rights to distribute or sell a product to a limited number of wholesalers or retailers in a given geographic area*

- Using **selective distribution**, a producer selects only wholesalers and retailers that will give a product special attention in sales effort, display and promotion advantage, and so forth. Selective distribution is used most often for consumer products such as furniture and appliances. Frigidaire and Whirlpool use selective distribution for appliances to cement relationships with wholesalers who will then market Frigidaire and Whirlpool over other brands.

Selective Distribution *strategy by which a company uses only wholesalers and retailers who give special attention to specific products in its sales efforts*

Channel Conflict and Channel Leadership

Manufacturers and services providers (such as Nike, LG Electronics, and Allied Insurance) may distribute through more than one channel, and many retailers (such as Walgreens) are free to strike agreements with as many producers (like the makers of Tylenol, Advil, and Aleve) as capacity permits. In such cases, *channel conflict* may arise. Conflicts are resolved through better coordination, and a key factor in coordinating the activities of organizations is *channel leadership*.

Channel Conflict *conflict arising when the members of a distribution channel disagree over the roles they should play or the rewards they should receive*

Channel Conflict

Channel conflict occurs when members of the channel disagree over roles or rewards. John Deere and State Farm would object to their dealers distributing tractors and insurance products of competing brands. Likewise, a manufacturer-owned outlet store runs the risk of alienating other retailers of its products when it discounts the company's products. Conflict may arise if one channel member has more power or is perceived as getting preferential treatment. Before Apple started opening its own retail stores, it distributed its products through many non-Apple retail stores. By opening its own retail outlets, channel conflict was created because the Apple stores substantially reduced sales at stores formerly used to distribute and sell Apple products. Such conflicts, of course, can defeat the purpose of the system by disrupting the flow of goods.

Channel Captain *channel member who is most powerful in determining the roles and rewards of other members*

Channel Leadership

Usually one channel member—the **channel captain**—can determine the roles and rewards of the others. The channel captain is often a manufacturer or an originator of a service. Jewelry artisan Thomas Mann is in such demand that wholesalers and retailers wait years for the chance to distribute his Techno Romantic creations. Mann selects channel members, sets prices, and determines product availability. In other industries, an influential wholesaler or a large retailer such as Walmart may be a channel captain because of large sales volume.

Learning Objective 13-2

Describe the role of wholesalers and the functions performed by e-intermediaries.

Wholesaling

The roles differ among the various intermediaries in distribution channels. Wholesalers provide a variety of services to buyers of products for resale or business use. In addition to storing and providing an assortment of products, some wholesalers offer delivery, credit, and product information. The range of services depends on the type of intermediary: *merchant wholesaler, agent/broker*, or *e-intermediary*.

Merchant Wholesalers *independent wholesaler who takes legal possession of goods produced by a variety of manufacturers and then resells them to other organizations*

Full-Service Merchant Wholesalers *merchant wholesaler that provides credit, marketing, and merchandising services in addition to traditional buying and selling services*

Limited-Function Merchant Wholesaler *merchant wholesaler that provides a limited range of services*

Drop Shippers *limited-function merchant wholesaler that receives customer orders, negotiates with producers, takes title to goods, and arranges for shipment to customers*

Merchant Wholesalers

Most wholesalers are independent operations that sell various consumer or business goods produced by a variety of manufacturers. The largest group are the **merchant wholesalers**, who buy products from manufacturers and sell them to other businesses. They own the goods that they resell and usually provide storage and delivery.

Full-service merchant wholesalers (about 80 percent of all merchant wholesalers) provide value-adding services, including credit, marketing advice, and merchandising services. **Limited-function merchant wholesalers** provide fewer services, sometimes merely storage. Customers are normally small operations that pay cash and pick up their own goods. **Drop shippers** don't even carry inventory or handle products. They take orders from customers, negotiate with producers to supply goods, take title to them, and arrange for shipment. Rack jobbers market consumer goods (mostly nonfood items) directly to retail stores, marking prices and setting up displays in a variety of stores. Procter & Gamble (P&G) uses rack jobbers to distribute products such as its Pampers diapers.

Agents and Brokers

Agents and brokers, including online e-agents, serve as independent sales representatives for many companies' products. They work on commission, usually about 4 to 5 percent of net sales. Unlike wholesalers, agents and brokers do not own their merchandise. Rather, they serve as sales and merchandising arms for producers or sellers who do not have their own sales forces.

The value of agents and brokers lies in their knowledge of markets and their merchandising expertise. They show sale items to potential buyers and, for retail stores, they provide such services as shelf and display merchandising and advertising layout. They remove open, torn, or dirty packages, arrange products neatly, and generally keep goods attractively displayed. Many supermarket products are handled through brokers.

The E-Intermediary

The ability of e-commerce to bring together millions of widely dispersed consumers and businesses has changed the types and roles of intermediaries. **E-intermediaries** are online channel members—wholesalers—who perform one or both of two functions: (1) They collect information about sellers and present it to consumers (such as kayak.com, which deals with travel services) or (2) they help deliver online products to buyers (such as Amazon).

E-Intermediary *Internet distribution channel member that assists in delivering products to customers or that collects information about various sellers to be presented to consumers, or they help deliver online products to buyers*

Syndicated Sellers **Syndicated selling** occurs when one website offers another a commission for referring customers. Expedia.com and Dollar Car Rental illustrate syndicated selling perfectly. With millions of users each month, Expedia.com is a heavily visited travel-services website. Expedia has given Dollar Car Rental a special banner on its web page. When Expedia customers click on the banner for a car rental, they are transferred from the Expedia site to the Dollar site. Dollar pays Expedia a fee for each booking that comes through this channel. Although the Expedia intermediary increases the cost of Dollar's supply chain, it also adds value for customers. Travelers avoid time-consuming online searches and are efficiently guided to a car-rental agency.

Syndicated Selling *e-commerce practice whereby a website offers other websites commissions for referring customers*

Shopping Agents **Shopping agents (e-agents)** help online consumers by gathering and sorting information. Although they don't take possession of products, they know which websites and stores to visit, give accurate comparison prices, identify product features, and help consumers complete transactions by presenting information in a usable format—all in an instant. Hotwire.com is a well-known shopping agent for a variety of travel products. When you specify the product—hotels, flights, vacations, cars—Hotwire searches for vendors, does price comparisons, lists prices from low to high, and then transfers you to the websites of different e-stores.

Shopping Agent (E-Agent) *e-intermediary (middleman) in the Internet distribution channel that assists users in finding products and prices but does not take possession of products*

Business-to-Business Brokers E-commerce intermediaries provide online value-adding services for business customers. The pricing process between business-to-business (B2B) buyers and sellers of commodities and services can be outsourced, for example, to the online company MediaBids.com. As a pricing broker for advertising services, MediaBids links any large-volume buyer of advertising services with potential suppliers that bid to become the supplier for the industrial customer. Client companies (the buyers of advertising services), such as Biocentric Health Inc., Christian Science Monitor, and Simplicity Sofas, can pay a fixed annual subscription fee and receive networking into MediaBids's auction headquarters, where real-time bids come in from suppliers at remote locations. The website provides current information until the bidding ends with the low-price supplier. In brokering the auction transactions, MediaBids doesn't take possession of any products. As a broker, it brings together timely information and links businesses to one another.

entrepreneurship and new ventures

Dispensing Hope

Algramo

Though inexpensive compared to major American and European cities, the cost of living in and around Santiago, Chile, is more expensive than almost 65 percent of the rest of the country. The lack of population density and a multitude of low household incomes have resulted in very few supermarkets. Most residents shop at small stores with narrow product lines and prices up to 40 percent higher than those in more populated areas. In the hope of improving the lives of people living in these areas, Algramo, a Santiago-based company, has a unique distribution model. Algramo, whose name means "by the gram," buys products in bulk, keeping its costs low. The company installs high-tech vending machines in local stores and stocks them with beans, lentils, rice, sugar, and other products. Algramo doesn't charge the storeowner for installing the machine and shares the profits from all sales equally with the shopkeeper. By 2022, after nine years of operation, Algramo had expanded to more than 2,000 locations in Chile, Jakarta, and New York City.

The company is the brainchild of Chilean student Jose Manuel Moller. He and three friends moved to a small community outside Santiago in hopes of gaining a better understanding of the conditions for residents. While the neighborhood stores are essential meeting places for the communities, high food prices and low wages result in most residents struggling to meet their most basic needs. Moller began to see these high prices as a "poverty tax" imposed on the 70 percent of the Chilean population living outside the major cities, and he was determined to make a difference. The company estimates that its model has allowed buyers to save up to 40 percent per month on household products, allowing them to use the saved funds to obtain better health care or to provide quality educational opportunities for their children. The benefits of Algramo's business model are not limited to the consumer but also extend to shopkeepers. Algramo's vending machines generate profits for small stores that operate on narrow margins, allowing them to stay in business and improve the owners' quality of life.

Benefits of the model even extend to the environment—Algramo dispenses its products in reusable containers, reducing the waste associated with disposable packaging.[2] The performance of the company and its commitment to reducing waste have resulted in nods from various international environmental conservation organizations and over $11 million USD in venture capital funding.

Learning Objective 13-3

Describe the different types of retailing and explain how online retailers add value for consumers on the Internet.

Retailing

There are more than 5 million brick-and-mortar retail establishments in the United States. Many consist only of owners and part-time help. Indeed, more than one-half of the nation's retailers account for less than 10 percent of all retail sales. Retailers also include huge operations, such as Walmart, the world's largest corporate employer; Kroger; and Home Depot. Although many other countries have large retailers—Metro and Aldi in Germany, Carrefour in France, and AEON in Japan—most of the world's largest retailers are U.S. businesses.

Types of Brick-and-Mortar Retail Outlets

U.S. retail operations vary widely by type as well as size. They can be classified by their pricing strategies, locations, range of services, or range of product lines. Choosing the right types of retail outlets is a crucial aspect of distribution strategy. This section describes U.S. retail stores by using three classifications: (1) *product-line retailers*, (2) *bargain retailers*, and (3) *convenience stores*.

Product-Line Retailers Retailers featuring broad product lines include **department stores**, which are organized into specialized departments: shoes, furniture, women's petite sizes, and so on. Stores are usually large, handle a wide range of goods, and offer a variety of services, such as credit plans and delivery. Similarly, **supermarkets** are divided into departments of related products: fresh food products, frozen food products, household products, and so forth. They often stress low prices, self-service, and large selections.

In contrast, **specialty stores**, such as Lids, a retailer with more than 1,100 stores selling athletic fashion headwear, are small, serve specific market segments with full product lines in narrow product fields, and often feature especially knowledgeable sales associates.

Department Store *large product-line retailer characterized by organization into specialized departments*

Supermarket *large product-line retailer offering a variety of food and food-related items in specialized departments*

Specialty Store *retail store carrying one product line or category of related products*

Bargain Retailers **Bargain retailers** carry wide ranges of products at low prices. **Discount houses** began by selling large numbers of items at substantial price reductions to cash-only customers. As they became more established, they began moving to better locations, improving decor, selling better-quality merchandise at higher prices, and offering services such as credit plans and noncash sales. For example, T.J. Maxx buys clothing, personal care products, toys, and housewares from major brands, high-end designers, and other retailers, which it can offer to consumers at prices that are 20–60 percent lower than the full retail price. Many of their products were either overproduced or overbought, allowing T.J. Maxx to negotiate a low price when buying. As it's grown, T.J. Maxx has expanded to include online shopping, exclusive merchandise manufactured for their stores, and a credit card that provides rewards to frequent shoppers.[3]

Catalog showrooms mail catalogs and/or send online ads to attract customers into showrooms to view display samples, place orders, and wait briefly while clerks retrieve orders from attached warehouses. **Factory outlets** are manufacturer-owned stores that avoid wholesalers and retailers by selling merchandise directly from factory to consumer. **Wholesale clubs**, such as Costco, offer large discounts on a wide range of brand-name merchandise to customers who pay annual membership fees.

Bargain Retailer *retailer carrying a wide range of products at bargain prices*

Discount House *bargain retailer that generates large sales volume by offering goods at substantial price reductions*

Catalog Showroom *bargain retailer in which customers place orders for catalog items to be picked up at on-premises warehouses*

Factory Outlet *bargain retailer owned by the manufacturer whose products it sells*

Wholesale Club *bargain retailer offering large discounts on brand-name merchandise to customers who have paid annual membership fees*

Convenience Stores **Convenience store** chains, such as 7-Eleven and Circle K stores, stress easily accessible locations, extended store hours, and speedy service. They differ from most bargain retailers in that they carry fewer products and generally charge somewhat higher prices in exchange for the convenience they provide.

Convenience Store *retail store offering easy accessibility, extended hours, and fast service*

Nonstore Retailing

Some retailers sell products without brick-and-mortar stores. Certain types of products, such as snack foods, bottled water, and soft drinks, sell well from card- and coin-operated machines. The same can be said for some forms of entertainment (pinball, video games, and billiards) when placed in certain venues (such as movie theater lobbies, bowling alleys, and so forth). In 2019, Kylie Cosmetics began selling makeup via vending machines in the Las Vegas airport, and has since expanded this strategy to include airports across the United States.[4] Best Buy was an early adopter of this approach, targeting on-the-go travelers looking to buy headphones, chargers, electric razors, and GoPro cameras from its Best Buy Express machines.[5] For all products, global vending market size was valued at $51.91 billion in 2021 and is expected to see a compound annual growth rate of 10.7 percent from 2022 to 2030. Still, vending machine sales make up less than 1 percent of all U.S. retail sales.[6]

Nonstore retailing also includes **direct-response retailing**, in which firms contact customers directly to inform them about products and to solicit sales orders. **Mail order** (or **catalog marketing**) is a popular form of direct-response retailing practiced by Orvis, The J. Peterman Company, and Garnet Hill. While many catalog marketers do not have brick-and-mortar stores, almost all of them offer online shopping. Even e-commerce giants like Amazon and mall anchor stores like Cabela's mail catalogs to their customers. Less popular in recent years because of do-not-call registries, outbound

Direct-Response Retailing *form of nonstore retailing in which firms directly interact with customers to inform them of products and to receive sales orders*

Mail Order (Catalog Marketing) *form of nonstore retailing in which customers place orders for catalog merchandise received through the mail*

finding a better way

The Store of the Future May Be Coming to You

Alex Cimbal/Shutterstock

Experts have long predicted that retail shopping would inevitably involve no checkout, no cash, and no unwanted waiting, all for a better customer shopping experience. In 2019, most brick-and-mortar stores were still using some form of checkout counter and cash register. However, the pandemic of 2020 rapidly changed all that as stores across the country moved to curbside delivery and remote payment systems, taking advantage of the innovations developed by trendsetters like Amazon.

A few pioneers were early in challenging tradition. Amazon opened its first cashier-less store on December 5, 2016, branded as Amazon Go in Seattle for Amazon employees only as they tested the concept and the technology. The store opened to the general public on January 22, 2018, and by 2023, despite Amazon scaling back its physical presence in most cities, there were still 26 Amazon Go stores in four different states. The stores use computer vision and deep learning algorithms like the ones used in autonomous driving vehicles to watch what customers are putting into their shopping bags. Customers scan a QR code when they enter the store through an app, which is connected to their Amazon .com account. After shopping, customers can simply leave the store. Amazon automatically charges the customers' Amazon account, and the receipt is sent to the app.

Even the savviest small-business owners used to have some trouble taking credit cards. Fees were high, processing cumbersome, and payments slow to arrive. Now they have access to card readers and apps like Square, PayPal, Venmo, and a multitude of other online processing tools, many of which integrate with the company's accounting software, making it possible for even a single-person shop to take advantage of a much wider array of payment options. Further, an iPad that includes a credit card reader costs far less than a cash register, and the financial data are easily integrated with financial and customer management systems. For instance, a small restaurant can seamlessly place an order, send it to the kitchen for processing, and accept payment from a card reader, all on the same system.

Though the pandemic created a boom in contactless shopping, with an explosion of online ordering apps and other options, it also created obstacles for companies like Wheelys, which was developing an autonomous convenience store contained in a self-driving vehicle the size of a bus.[8] When funding for new projects dried up, so did its opportunity. Mega-retailers like Walmart and Amazon continue to lead innovations in contactless shopping, with smaller companies working to differentiate themselves. As technology and demand both drive continued and faster progress, we can expect to see more consumers taking advantage of and even demanding these developments.

Telemarketing *form of nonstore retailing in which the telephone is used to sell directly to consumers*

Direct Selling *form of nonstore retailing typified by door-to-door sales*

telemarketing uses phone calls to sell directly to consumers. However, telemarketing also includes inbound toll-free calls from customers, a service that most catalog and other retail stores make available. Finally, more than 600 U.S. companies, including Mary Kay cosmetics, use **direct selling** to sell door-to-door or through home-selling parties. Avon Products, one of the world's largest direct sellers, has approximately 6 million door-to-door sales representatives in more than 50 countries.[7]

Online Retailing

Online Retailing *nonstore retailing in which information about the seller's products and services is connected to consumers' computers, allowing consumers to receive the information and purchase the products in the home*

In 2021, global business-to-consumer (B2C) sales amounted to $3.67 trillion, and they are projected to exceed the $6.5 trillion level by 2030. More than 2.14 billion consumers have made online purchases. Apple's iTunes outsells brick-and-mortar music retailers, and Amazon is the world's largest online retailer, selling nationally and internationally, with total revenues in 2022 of $502.19. **Online retailing** allows sellers to inform, sell to, and distribute to consumers using online technology. Some of the largest U.S. "e-tailers" are shown in Table 13.1. In addition to large companies, millions of small businesses around the globe also have their own websites.[9]

Social Media Social media companies offer functionality so companies can sell directly to consumers within the platform. Instagram and Facebook offer

table 13.1 Leading Online Retailers in Selected Consumer Products Categories*

Consumer Product Category	Online Retailer
Mass merchandise	Amazon.com
Office supplies	Staples Inc.
Computers and electronics	Apple Inc.
Video and audio entertainment	Netflix Inc.
Home repair and improvement	Home Depot
Apparel and accessories	L.L. Bean Inc.
Home furnishings and housewares	Williams-Sonoma Inc.
Health and beauty	Bath & Body Works
Sporting goods	Cabela's Inc.

*Adapted from "Top 500 Guide," Internet Retailer (2021), https://www.internetretailer.com/top500/list/.

businesses and sellers a way to create a digital storefront and shop, group collections of merchandise, post photos of products, and offer a seamless checkout experience right from inside the apps. Sellers can also create searchable product tags, purchase reminders, and announcements about upcoming sales and promotions. TikTok's partnership with Shopify allows in-app shopping as well. In 2022, 28 percent of Millennial and Gen Z consumers reported buying products directly in a social media app in the past three months.[10]

Electronic Catalogs **E-catalogs** use online displays of products to give millions of retail and business customers instant access to product information. The seller avoids the costs of printing and mail distribution, and once an online catalog is in place, the costs of maintaining and updating it are lower. About 90 percent of all catalogs are now online, with digital sales accounting for more than 50 percent of all catalog sales. Even IKEA discontinued its iconic print catalog in 2020, but it continues to provide a range of e-catalogs and digital brochures on its website.[11]

E-Catalog *nonstore retailing in which the Internet is used to display products*

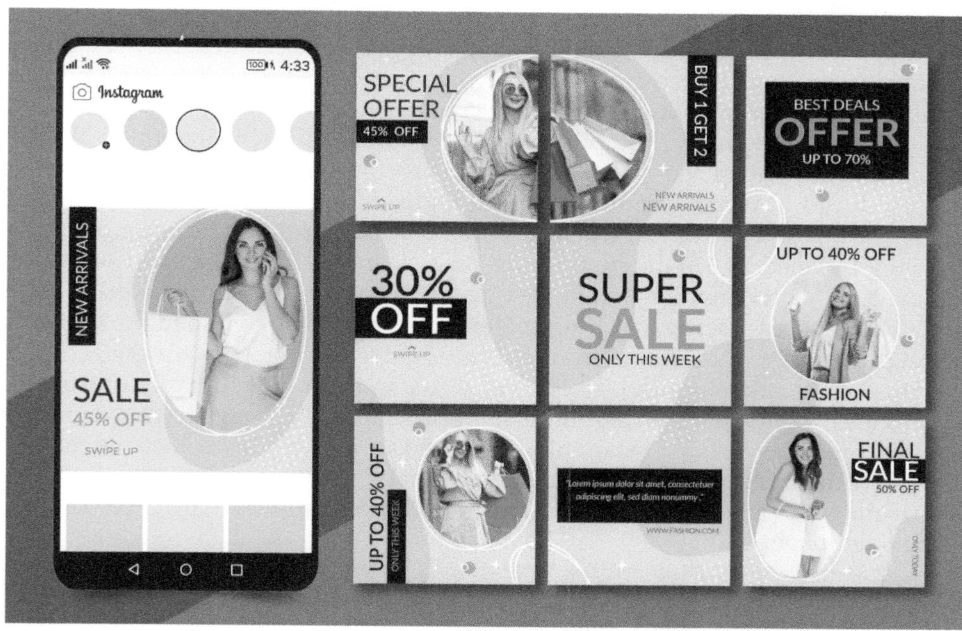

E-catalogs have become increasingly popular and are quickly replacing traditional paper catalogs. These are especially effective when combined with a strong social media strategy. This E-catalog, for instance, has been distributed through Instagram and can be accessed on smartphones and other connected devices.
Source: Free Vector | Creative instagram puzzle feed with 9 templates. (2020, September 22). Freepik. https://www.freepik.com/free-vector/creative-instagram-puzzle-feed-with-9-templates_10212968.htm

Electronic Storefront *commercial website at which customers gather information about products and buying opportunities, place orders, and pay for purchases*

Cybermall *collection of virtual storefronts (business websites) representing a variety of products and product lines on the Internet*

Electronic Storefronts and Cybermalls

Each seller's website is essentially an **electronic storefront** (or *virtual storefront*) from which shoppers collect information about products and buying opportunities, place orders, and pay for purchases. Producers of large product lines, such as Dell, dedicate storefronts to their own product lines. Other sites, such as Newegg.com, which offers computer and other electronics equipment, are category sellers whose storefronts feature products from many manufacturers.

Search engines such as Google Shopping and Dogpile serve as **cybermalls**, collections of virtual storefronts and links representing diverse products and offering speed, convenience, 24-hour access, easy price comparison, and efficient searching. After entering a cybermall, shoppers can navigate by choosing from a list of stores (L.L.Bean, Lids, or Macy's), product listings (sporting goods, women's fashion, or mobile devices), or departments (apparel or bath/beauty) or search for a specific product.

Video Retailing *nonstore retailing to consumers via home television*

Interactive and Video Retailing

Today, retailers and B2C customers interact with multimedia sites using voice, graphics, animation, video, and chat. Many e-tailers provide real-time sales and customer service that allow customers to enter a live chat room with a service operator who can answer their specific product questions.

Video retailing, a long-established form of interactive marketing, lets viewers shop at home from channels on their TVs or other digital devices. QVC, for example, displays and demonstrates products, allows viewers to phone in or e-mail orders, and is available on Facebook, YouTube, and Twitter. Current-generation televisions are available with online capabilities as well, allowing online networking. A television with Wi-Fi network access thus becomes a platform for comfortable at-home online shopping with a large-screen visual display.

Learning Objective 13-4

Define *physical distribution* and describe the major activities in the physical distribution process.

Physical Distribution

Physical Distribution *activities needed to move a product efficiently from manufacturer to consumer*

Physical distribution refers to the activities needed to move products from an intermediary or a manufacturer to customers and includes *warehousing* and *transportation operations*. Its purpose is to make goods available when and where customers want them, keep costs low, and provide services to satisfy customers. Because of its importance for customer satisfaction, some firms have adopted distribution as their marketing strategy of choice.

Consider, for example, the pioneering global distribution system of National Semiconductor, one of the world's largest microchip makers. Finished microchips were produced in plants around the world and shipped to hundreds of customers, such as IBM, Toshiba, and HP, which also operated factories around the globe. Chips originally traveled 20,000 different routes on as many as 12 airlines and sat waiting at one location after another—on factory floors, at customs, in distributors' facilities, and in warehouses—before reaching customers. National streamlined the system by air-freighting chips worldwide from a single center in Singapore. Every activity—storage, sorting, and shipping—was centralized and run by FedEx. By outsourcing the activities, National's distribution costs were reduced, delivery times were cut by half, and sales increased substantially. Acquired in 2011 by Texas Instruments (TI), National Semiconductor and its innovative global distribution system is TI's Silicon Valley Analog division that remains a world leader for producing high-performance analog components.

Warehousing *physical distribution operation concerned with the storage of goods*

Private Warehouse *warehouse owned by and providing storage for a single company*

Warehousing Operations

Storing, or **warehousing**, is a major part of distribution management. In selecting a strategy, managers must keep in mind both the different characteristics and costs of warehousing operations. **Private warehouses** are owned by a single manufacturer, wholesaler, or retailer that deals in mass quantities and needs regular storage. Most are run by large firms that deal in mass quantities and need regular storage. Walmart, for example, maintains its own warehouses (as well as its own trucking fleet) to facilitate the movement of products to its retail stores.

Independently owned and operated **public warehouses**, which rent to companies only the space they need, are popular with firms needing storage only during peak periods and with manufacturers who need multiple storage locations to get products to multiple markets.

Public Warehouse *independently owned and operated warehouse that stores goods for many firms*

The digital age has brought with it massive quantities of data that need to be safely stored, preserved, organized, and accessible to users. Many companies, to protect their valuable data resources, rely on remote off-site digital storage services such as ZipCloud for Business as a safety net. Home users, too, use daily online backup services, such as Carbonite and SOS Online Backup, to protect against losing data when their computers crash. In the event of any physical catastrophe—floods, fires, earthquakes—at the client's facility, data can be restored online from the backup system.

Transportation Operations

Physically moving a product creates the highest cost many companies face. In addition to transportation methods, firms must also consider the nature of the product, the distance it must travel, the speed with which it must be received, and customer wants and needs.

Differences in cost among the major transportation modes—trucks, railroads, planes, digital transmission, water carriers, and pipelines—are usually most directly related to delivery speed.

With 3.5 million professional truck drivers and a fleet of approximately 15 million vehicles, trucks haul more than two-thirds of all tonnage carried by all modes of U.S. freight transportation. The advantages of trucks include flexibility for any-distance distribution, fast service, and dependability. Increasing truck traffic, however, raises concerns about highway safety and traffic congestion.[12]

Air is the fastest but also the most expensive mode of transportation for physical goods. Air-freight customers benefit from lower inventory costs by eliminating the need to store items that might deteriorate. Shipments of fresh fish, for example, can be picked up by restaurants each day, avoiding the risk of spoilage from packaging, storing, and/or extended delivery times.

For downloads of music, software, books, movies, and other digital products, the transportation mode of choice, online transmission, is newer, faster, and less expensive than all other modes. Of course, it is also restricted to products that exist in digital form that can be transmitted over communication channels.

Aside from digital transmission, water is the least expensive mode but, unfortunately, also the slowest. Networks of waterways—oceans, rivers, and lakes—let water carriers reach many areas throughout the world. Boats and barges are used mostly for moving bulky products (such as oil, grain, and gravel). Railroads can economically transport high-volume, heavy, bulky items, such as cars, steel, and coal. However, their delivery routes are limited by fixed, immovable rail tracks. Pipelines are slow and lack flexibility and adaptability, but for specialized products, such as liquids and gases, they provide economical and reliable delivery.

Distribution Through Supply Chains as a Marketing Strategy

Instead of just offering advantages in product features, quality, price, and promotion, many firms have turned to supply chains that depend on distribution as a cornerstone of business strategy. This approach means assessing, improving, and integrating the entire sequence of activities—upstream suppliers, wholesaling, warehousing, transportation, delivery, and follow-up services—involved in getting products to customers.

Chris Salvo/Salvo Photography

Specializing in long-haul shipping, US Xpress employs over 3,000 drivers to operate a fleet of 6,400 trucks and 13,600 trailers. Trucks have satellite capabilities, anti-collision radar, vehicle-detection sensors, computers for shifting through 10 speeds, and roomy cabs with sleepers, refrigerators, and microwaves.

Since the 1960s, starting with Toyota in Japan, the industrial world has seen the rise of the just-in-time (JIT) inventory system, discussed in Chapter 7. Initially used for quality improvement and cost savings, it was primarily adopted by U.S. manufacturing firms coming by way of Ford Motor Company in the early 1980s. Along with JIT, the past few decades have seen dramatic improvements in supply chain technology and management, and its adoption by the retail sector. In the 1980s, Walmart decided to build its own distribution system using the best practices of both JIT and supply chain processes instead of the industry practice of relying on outside freight haulers and wholesalers. Let's look at how this has enabled Walmart to dominate its competition and made it the leading retailer in the world:

Suppose you are shopping at Walmart and decide to pick up a Mr. Coffee eight-cup coffee maker. When you check out, the scanner reads the barcode on the box, and Walmart's inventory system is updated instantly, showing that a replacement coffee maker is needed on the shelf. The replacement comes from "the back" of that store, where the remaining on-hand supply count is reduced in Walmart's information system. Once the back-room supply dwindles to *its* automatic triggering number, Walmart's distribution warehouse receives a digital signal notifying that this store needs more Mr. Coffee eight-cup coffee makers. At the same time, the computer system also notifies the manufacturer that Walmart's distribution warehouse needs a replenishment supply. The manufacturer's suppliers, too, are notified, and so on, continuing upstream with information that enables faster resupply coordination throughout the supply chain. Walmart's data mining system determines the reorder number for every product based on sales (daily, weekly, and even by time of the year). Because of Walmart's constant rapid restocking from upstream sources, its store shelves are resupplied without having to keep large inventories in its warehouses and retail stores, thus reducing inventory costs and providing lower prices.

Walmart's JIT system and supply chain efficiency have allowed it to achieve as low as a two-day turnaround from manufacturer to the store shelf, thus providing cost control and product availability. It maintains lower levels of inventory, meets customer demand, and keeps prices among the lowest in the retail industry. Another retailer that has been able to adopt this method on a similar scale and compete effectively with Walmart (but only in groceries) is the H-E-B Grocery Company's chain of stores in Texas. Its data mining software can evaluate what products are purchased when and with what other products (so, for example, it knows to have tamales available at Christmas with accompanying coupons for enchilada sauce) and uses this information for forecasting upcoming demand.

The Importance of Promotion

Learning Objective 13-5

Identify the objectives of promotion and the considerations in selecting a promotional mix and discuss the various kinds of advertising promotions.

Promotion refers to techniques for communicating information about products and is part of the *communication mix*, the total message any company sends to customers about its product. Promotional techniques, especially advertising, must communicate the uses, features, and benefits of products, and marketers use an array of tools for this purpose.

Promotion *aspect of the marketing mix concerned with the most effective techniques for communicating information about and selling a product*

Promotional Objectives

The ultimate objective of any promotion is to increase sales. In addition, marketers may use promotion to *communicate information, position products, add value*, and *control sales volume*.

As we saw in Chapter 11, **positioning** is the process of establishing an easily identifiable product image in the minds of consumers by fixing, adapting, and communicating the nature of the product itself. First, a firm must identify which market segments are likely to purchase its product and how its product measures up against competitors. Then, it can focus on promotional choices for differentiating its product and positioning it in the minds of the target audience. As an example, if someone says, "facial tissue," most people respond with . . . Kleenex. "The Ultimate Driving Machine" is . . . BMW. These ubiquitous associations are indicative of successful positioning.

Positioning *process of establishing an identifiable product image in the minds of consumers*

Promotional mixes are often designed to communicate a product's *value-added benefits* to distinguish it from the competition. Mercedes automobiles and Ritz-Carlton hotels, for example, promote their products as upscale goods and services featuring high quality, style, and performance, all at a higher price.

Promotional Strategies

Once its larger marketing objectives are clear, a firm must develop a promotional strategy to achieve them. Two prominent types of strategies are considered here:

- A **pull strategy** appeals directly to consumers who will demand the product from retailers. Pharmaceutical companies use *direct-to-consumer advertising* (DTC) to persuade consumers to aggressively request a product rather than to wait passively until the doctor suggests trying it. "Talk to your doctor about Allegra-D" is just one example of the vast number of television and online ads for prescription drugs, knee replacement systems, and other medical products. The resulting demand by end users stimulates demand for the product from wholesalers and producers.

Pull Strategy *promotional strategy designed to appeal directly to consumers who will demand a product from retailers*

- Using a **push strategy**, a firm markets its product to wholesalers and retailers, who then persuade customers to buy it. Brunswick Corp., for instance, uses a push strategy to promote Bayliner pleasure boats, directing its promotions at dealers and persuading them to order more inventory. Dealers are then responsible for stimulating demand among boaters at outdoor shows and through other promotions in their market districts.

Push Strategy *promotional strategy designed to encourage wholesalers or retailers to market products to consumers*

Many large firms combine pull and push strategies. General Mills, for example, advertises to create consumer demand (pull) for its breakfast cereals, including Lucky Charms, Cheerios, and Count Chocula. At the same time, it pushes wholesalers and retailers to stock and display them.

The Promotional Mix

Promotional Mix *combination of tools used to promote a product*

Five of marketing's most powerful promotional tools are advertising, personal selling, sales promotions, direct or interactive marketing, and publicity and public relations. The optimal combination of these tools—the best **promotional mix**—depends on many factors. The most important is the target audience. As an example, two generations from now, 25 percent of the U.S. workforce will be Latina/o/x. With an estimated 52 million American Latin/o/xs, the rise in this group's disposable income has made them a potent economic force, and marketers are working to redesign and promote products to appeal to them with Spanish-language commercials and ads. Several major cable networks such as HBO and ESPN offer separate Spanish-language channels.

In establishing a promotional mix, marketers match promotional tools with the five stages in the buyer decision process:

1 When consumers first recognize the need to make a purchase, marketers use advertising and publicity, which can reach many people quickly, to make sure buyers are aware of their products.

2 As consumers search for information about available products, advertising and personal selling are important methods to educate them.

3 Personal selling can become vital as consumers compare competing products. Sales representatives can demonstrate product quality, features, benefits, and performance in comparison with competitors' products.

4 When buyers are ready to purchase products, sales promotion can give consumers an incentive to buy. Personal selling can help by bringing products to convenient purchase locations.

5 After making purchases, consumers evaluate products and assess (and remember) their strengths and deficiencies. At this stage, advertising and personal selling can remind customers that they made wise purchases.

Figure 13.3 summarizes the effective promotional tools for each stage in the consumer buying process.

Advertising

Advertising *any form of paid nonpersonal communication used by an identified sponsor to persuade or inform potential buyers about a product*

Advertising is paid, nonpersonal communication by which an identified sponsor informs an audience about a product. In 2021, firms in the United States spent over $175 billion on advertising—almost $35 billion by just 10 companies.[13] Figure 13.4 shows U.S. advertising expenditures for the top-spending firms. Let's take a look at the different types of advertising media, noting some of the advantages and limitations of each.

Advertising Media Consumers tend to ignore the bulk of advertising messages that bombard them—they pay attention only to what interests them. Moreover, the advertising process is dynamic, reflecting the changing interests

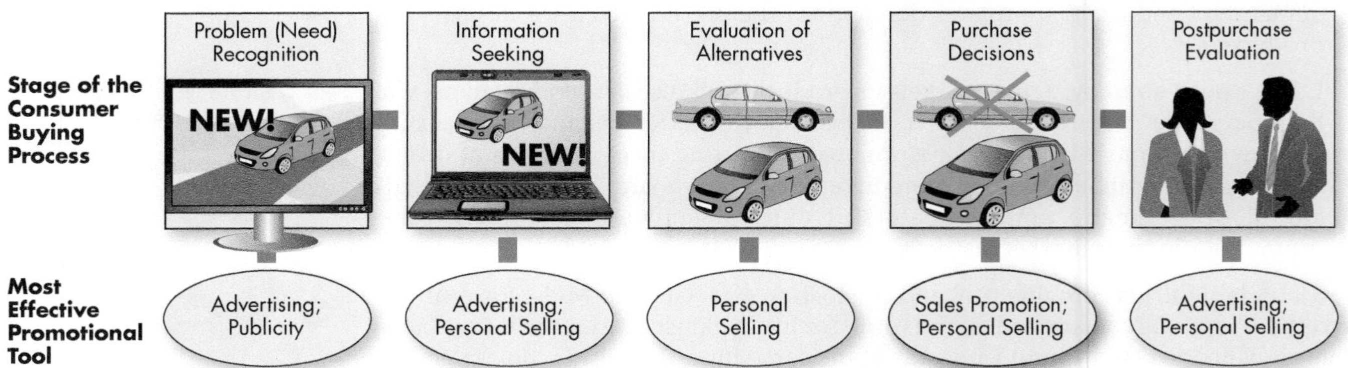

FIGURE 13.3 The Consumer Buying Process and the Promotional Mix

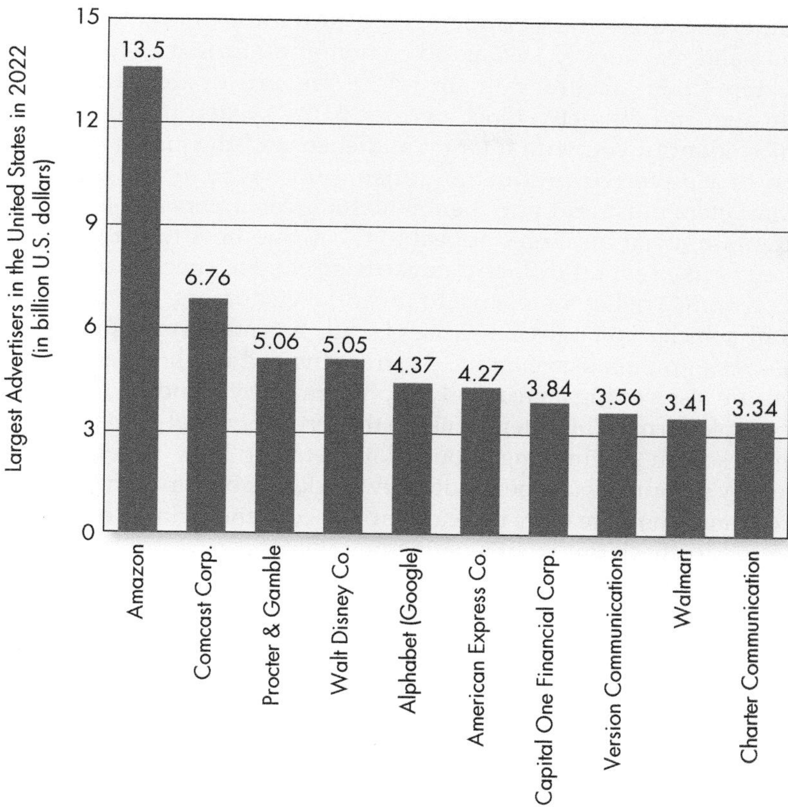

FIGURE 13.4 Top 10 U.S. National Advertisers
Source: https://www.statista.com/statistics/275446/ad-spending-of-leading-advertiser

and preferences of both customers and advertisers. One recent customer survey, for example, reports that mail ads are rated as most irritating and boring, and newspaper and magazine ads are least annoying. Yet, although newspaper ads are rated as more informative and useful than some other media, advertisers continue to shift away, using instead more online advertising because newsprint readership (the audience) is dwindling.[14] Of course, in a few instances, most prominently the Super Bowl, advertising has become an attraction in itself. Polls track the most popular ads, and some people even acknowledge that they watch the game only to see the commercials. Advertisers also create special ads and often use them to promote "big events." Not surprisingly, of course, ads during the Super Bowl are also very expensive—$6.5 million was the fee for a single 30-second commercial during the 2022 game.

During the 2020 COVID-19 pandemic, some advertisers developed new ads (TV, online, and print) to promote their products and services in the context of the pandemic. For instance, AT&T promoted itself as a way for people to stay in touch while social distancing. State Farm advertised that since driving was being reduced, so, too, were accidents, and therefore it was lowering insurance premiums. And many restaurant chains like Olive Garden advertised their new curbside and delivery options for people wanting their favorite food while social distancing.

Real-Time Ad Tracking Advertisers always want better information about who looks at ads and for how long. Which target audiences and demographics are more attracted to various ad contents? Accurate ad-watching behavior of shoppers in malls, theaters, and grocery stores is on the increase, with assistance from high-tech real-time surveillance. As passing consumers watch ads on video screens, cameras watch the shoppers, and software analyzes the viewers' demographics and reactions to various ad contents and formats. The makers of the tracking system claim accuracy of up to 90 percent for determining gender, approximate age, and ethnicity. Once perfected, the system might measure your demographics, identify you with a target audience, and then instantly change the presentation to a preferred product and visual format to attract and hold your attention. Marketers must find out, then, who their customers are, to which media they pay attention, what messages appeal to them, and how to get their attention. Thus, marketers use several different **advertising media**, specific communication devices for carrying a seller's message to potential customers. The combination of media through which a company advertises is called its **media mix**. Table 13.2 shows the relative sizes of media usage and their strengths and weaknesses.

Advertising Media *variety of communication devices for carrying a seller's message to potential customers*

Media Mix *combination of advertising media chosen to carry a message about a product*

Marketers are also getting increasingly sophisticated by blending their media mix across different platforms. This often comes in the form of marketing partnerships. For example, suppose you are thinking about taking a trip to New York City. As part of your preliminary planning, you check out a new backpack on Amazon, look at airfares on United.com, and compare hotel rates at Marriott.com and Hilton.com. A few hours later you decide to check out what's happening with your friends on Instagram or Facebook. Scattered among the posts from your friends you are likely to see ads for the same hotels, flights, and backpacks you were checking out earlier. That's because Amazon, United, Hilton, and Marriott each pay Meta Facebook a fee to link your shopping searches back to your Instagram or Facebook feed.

table 13.2 Total U.S. Media Usage, Strengths, and Weaknesses

Advertising Medium	Percentage* of Advertising Outlays	Strengths	Weaknesses
Television	35%	Program demographics allow for customized ads Large audience	Most expensive
Internet	20%	Targeted audience Measurable success	Nuisance to consumers Easy to ignore
Direct mail	10%	Targeted audience Personal messages Predictable results	Easily discarded Environmentally irresponsible
Newspapers	10%	Broad coverage Ads can be changed daily	Quickly discarded Broad readership limits ability to target specific audience
Radio	8%	Inexpensive Large audience Variety of ready market segmentation	Easy to ignore Message quickly disappears
Magazines	8%	Often reread and shared Variety of ready market segmentation	Require advanced planning Little control over ad placement
Outdoor	3%	Inexpensive Difficult to ignore Repeat exposure	Presents limited information Little control over audience

A combination of additional unmeasured media, such as yellow pages, catalogs, special events, sidewalk handouts, ads on transport vehicles, skywriting, movies, and door-to-door communications, are not included.

*Estimated.

Personal Selling

Learning Objective 13-6

Outline the tasks involved in personal selling and describe the various types of sales promotions.

In the oldest and most expensive form of sales, **personal selling**, a salesperson communicates one-on-one with potential customers to identify their needs and align them with products. Salespeople gain credibility by investing time getting acquainted with potential customers and answering their questions. This professional interaction is especially effective in relationship marketing. It gives the seller a clearer picture of the buyer's business and allows salespeople to provide buyers with value-adding services.

Personal Selling *person-to-person sales*

Salespeople must consider the ways in which personal sales activities are affected by the differences between consumer and industrial products:

- **Retail selling** is selling a consumer product for the buyer's personal or household use.
- **Industrial selling** is selling products to other businesses, either for the purpose of manufacturing or for resale. Levi's, for instance, sells jeans to Walmart (industrial selling). In turn, consumers purchase Levi's jeans at Walmart stores (retail selling).

Retail Selling *selling a consumer product for the buyer's personal or household use*

Industrial Selling *selling products to other businesses, either for the purpose of manufacturing or for resale*

Each of these situations has distinct characteristics. In retail selling, the buyer usually comes to the seller, whereas the industrial salesperson typically calls on the prospective buyer. An industrial decision usually takes longer than a retail decision because it involves more money, decision makers, and weighing of alternatives. As we saw in Chapter 11, organizational buyers are professional purchasing agents accustomed to dealing with salespeople. Consumers in retail stores, in contrast, may actually be intimidated or irritated by salespeople, especially if they are too aggressive.

Personal Selling Tasks

Salespeople must be adept at performing three basic tasks of personal selling. In **order processing**, a salesperson receives an order and sees to its handling and delivery. Route salespeople, who call on regular customers to check inventories, are often order processors. With the customer's consent, they may decide on the sizes of reorders, fill them directly from their trucks, and even stock shelves. Frito-Lay, Coca-Cola, and many beer distributorships use this approach.

Order Processing *personal-selling task in which salespeople receive orders and see to their handling and delivery*

In other situations, however, when potential customers may be less certain that they need or want a product, **creative selling** involves providing information and demonstrating product benefits to persuade buyers to complete a purchase. Creative selling is crucial for industrial products and high-priced consumer products, such as cars, for which buyers comparison shop. Finally, a salesperson may use **missionary selling** to promote a company and its products rather than simply to close a sale. Pharmaceutical companies often use this method to make doctors aware of the company and its products so they will recommend the company's products to others, or so the doctor will prescribe the products to patients. The sale of the product, then, is actually made at the pharmacy. In missionary selling, the goal may be to promote the company's long-term image as much as any given product. Another activity in missionary selling is after-sale technical assistance for complex products. IBM uses after-sale selling to ensure that industrial customers know how to use IBM equipment and services.

Creative Selling *personal-selling task in which salespeople try to persuade buyers to purchase products by providing information about their benefits*

Missionary Selling *personal-selling task in which salespeople promote their firms and products rather than try to close sales*

Depending on the product and company, sales jobs usually require individuals to perform all three tasks—order processing, creative selling, and missionary selling—to some degree.

managing in turbulent times

Finding the Right Balance

Advertising campaigns have been alive as long as there has been mass media. Today, however, the tried-and-true marketing formula of a celebrity or "expert" defining a problem and presenting the solution no longer holds sway with viewers. Younger generations, many of whom have never watched a show with ads or according to a broadcaster's schedule, are accustomed to clicking "Skip Ad" and have little patience with traditional advertising techniques. Instead, these consumers will look for personal testimony and the creative selling of influencers. Brands are increasingly eager to develop partnerships with not only celebrities from music, film, and television but also social media figures who amass hundreds of thousands of followers. Going into 2023, the influencer marketing industry was worth $16.4 billion.[15]

Occasionally, however, these relationships can backfire. Anheuser-Busch saw immediate backlash from anti-trans and right-wing customers over a Bud Light promotion with trans TikTok artist Dylan Mulvaney. In response, the brand distanced itself from Mulvaney, which resulted in a surge of criticism from the LGBTQIA+ community.

Teton Trade Cloth made a name for itself as a company that honored Indigenous artists. The textile company contracted with Indigenous artists to produce fabric designs, which would then be available for small-batch direct purchase by retailers, other artists, and the general public. Cast members of the Hulu show *Reservation Dogs* wore the firm's fabrics, and during one episode, the camera panned across a wall where viewers could see one of the company's stickers.

Teton's brand ambassador Devan Kicknosway, a longtime friend of cofounder Craig Jones, had long supported and represented the company. In the fall of 2022, Kicknosway, who had been hosting regular Facebook Live events with other Indigenous artists, was accused of sexual assault by a young Indigenous woman. Jones posted a simple comment amid the controversy in what he thought was a small show of support for Kicknosway and his family. A single hashtag—#teamkicknosway—created a backlash that resulted in a demand for accountability from the brand and personal attacks on Jones, whose identifying information, including his home address and photos of his home, was posted publicly. Six months later, though the brand had been sold to the Delaware Tribe of Oklahoma, it was still addressing the controversy.[16]

Torontonian/Alamy Stock Photo

Partnering with social media influencers can offer companies a way to promote their brands without creating a costly media campaign or hiring a celebrity spokesperson. But, like all advertising, it risks alienating the very customers they hope to attract. As social media platforms and influence grow, brands must weigh the pros and cons of these relationships.

The Personal Selling Process

Perhaps the most complex and challenging of these three sales tasks is creative selling. The creative salesperson is responsible for starting and following through on most of the steps in the personal selling process:

Prospecting *step in the personal selling process in which salespeople identify potential customers*

Qualifying *step in the personal selling process in which salespeople determine whether prospects have the authority to buy and ability to pay*

- ***Prospecting and qualifying.*** A salesperson must first have a potential customer, or prospect. **Prospecting** is the process of identifying potential customers. Salespeople find prospects through company personnel records, from social and professional networking on sites such as LinkedIn, and customers, friends, and business associates. In **qualifying**, prospects must be assessed to determine whether they have the authority to buy and the ability to pay.
- ***Approaching.*** The *approach* refers to the first few minutes of a salesperson's contact with a qualified prospect. Because it affects the salesperson's credibility, the success of later stages depends on the prospect's first impression. A salesperson must, therefore, present a professional appearance and greet prospects in a manner that instills confidence.
- ***Presenting and demonstrating.*** Next, the salesperson makes a presentation, a full explanation of the product, its features, and its uses. Most important, the

presentation links product benefits to the prospect's needs. A presentation may or may not include a demonstration. During the 2020 COVID-19 pandemic, much of this kind of work was quickly moved online using platforms like Zoom and Microsoft Teams.

- ***Handling objections.*** No matter what product is for sale, prospects will have some *objections*. At the very least, they may open the door to negotiate for discounts by objecting to price. Objections, however, not only indicate that the buyer is interested but also pinpoint the parts of the presentation that trouble the buyer.
- ***Closing.*** The most critical part of the selling process is the **closing**, in which the salesperson asks the prospect to buy the product. Successful salespeople recognize the signs that a customer is ready to buy. Prospects who start to figure out monthly payments are clearly indicating readiness to buy. Salespeople should then try to close the sale, either asking directly for the sale or implying a close indirectly. Questions such as "Could you take delivery Tuesday?" and "Why don't we start off with an initial order of 10 cases?" are implied closes. Indirect closes place the burden of rejecting the sale on the prospect, who may find it a little harder to say no.

Closing *step in the personal selling process in which salespeople ask prospective customers to buy products*

- ***Following up.*** Follow-up is a key activity, especially in relationship marketing. For lasting relationships with buyers, good salespeople don't end the sales process with the closing. They want sales to be so successful that customers will buy from them again. Thus, they supply additional services, such as after-sale support that provides convenience and added value. Follow-ups include quick processing of customer orders, on-time delivery, speedy repair service, and timely answers to user questions.

Sales Promotions

Sales promotions are short-term promotional activities designed to encourage consumer buying, industrial sales, or cooperation from distributors. They can increase the likelihood that buyers will try products, enhance product recognition, and increase purchase size and sales revenues.

Sales Promotion *direct inducements such as premiums, coupons, and package inserts to tempt consumers to buy products*

Successful sales promotions provide potential customers with convenience and accessibility when the decision to buy occurs. If Harley-Davidson holds a 1-week motorcycle promotion but you, an interested buyer, have no local dealer and no access to a test ride, the promotion may be useless to you and so you won't buy a motorcycle. In contrast, if Tide detergent offers a $1-off coupon that you can save and use on your next trip to the supermarket, the promotion is both convenient and accessible for you.

D. Hurst/Alamy Stock Photo

Personal selling is still very common, especially for expensive items such as automobiles and houses. This realtor, for example, is congratulating the buyers of a house that her firm had listed.

Coupon *sales-promotion technique in which a certificate is issued entitling the buyer to a reduced price*

Most consumers have taken part in a variety of sales promotions such as free *samples* (giveaways), which let customers try products without risk, and **coupon** promotions, which use certificates entitling buyers to discounts to encourage customers to try new products, lure them away from competitors, or induce them to repurchase (buy more of a product). Coupons are available from many sources, including in mailings and at checkout counters when shopping. For example, Kohl's department stores offer Kohl's Cash, which is a coupon that buyers receive upon checkout to encourage them to return within a certain time period to make an additional purchase. Online coupon sites such as Coupons.com, RetailMeNot.com, and Groupon provide access to printable cost-saving coupons and to some free coupons.

Premium *sales-promotion technique in which offers of free or reduced-price items are used to stimulate purchases*

Premiums are free or reduced-price items, such as pencils, coffee mugs, and six-month low-interest credit cards, given to consumers in return for buying a specified product. *Contests* can boost sales by rewarding high-producing distributors and sales representatives with vacation trips to Hawaii or Paris. Consumers, too, may win prizes by entering their pets in the IGA-Purina Pet Photo Contest, for example, by submitting pictures of their pets to win coupons.[17]

Loyalty Programs *sales promotion technique in which frequent customers are rewarded for making repeat purchases*

Loyalty programs reward frequent buyers for making repeat purchases. Oceania Cruises and Tauck (a tour company) offer vacation specials with significant price reductions to loyal customers. Online and mail promotions, for example, may announce two-for-one prices on upcoming cruises and reduced prices for upgrading to more luxurious accommodations. Tour specials may feature reduced airfares, along with free Wi-Fi and shore excursions for repeat customers. Bargain retailers also offer loyalty programs to frequent buyers. For example, discount chain Ollie's invites customers to join their loyalty program, Ollie's Army, which increases its rewards and surprise offers as customers spend more.[18]

Point-of-Sale (POS) Display *sales-promotion technique in which product displays are located in certain areas to stimulate purchase or to provide information on a product*

To grab customers' attention in stores, companies use **point-of-sale (POS) displays** at the ends of aisles or near checkout counters to ease finding products and to eliminate competitors from consideration. In addition to physical goods, POS pedestals also provide services, namely, information for consumers. Some bank lobbies and physicians' waiting rooms, for example, have interactive kiosks inviting clients to learn more about bank products and educational information about available treatments on consumer-friendly touch-screen displays. For B2B promotions, industries sponsor **trade shows** in which companies rent booths to display and demonstrate products to customers who have a special interest or who are ready to buy.

Trade Show *sales-promotion technique in which various members of an industry gather to display, demonstrate, and sell products*

Direct (or Interactive) Marketing

Direct (or Interactive) Marketing *one-on-one nonpersonal selling by nonstore retailers and B2B sellers using direct contact with prospective customers, especially via the Internet*

Direct (or interactive) marketing is one-on-one nonpersonal selling that tries to get consumers to make purchases away from retail stores and, instead, to purchase from home, at work, or using a mobile device. This fast-growing selling method includes nonstore retailers (catalogs, telemarketing, home video shopping); direct mail; direct response advertising (such as infomercials and direct response magazine and newspaper ads); and, most important, online connections. When used by B2B businesses, direct marketing is primarily lead generation so a salesperson can close the sale where interest has been shown. In B2C businesses, it has primarily a selling goal. The advantage of direct marketing is that you can target the message to the individual and you can measure the results. For example, Amazon knows when you sign in who you are and what you have purchased in the past and makes recommendations based on your purchase history. And when you select a certain book title or other product, it can suggest additional titles that other buyers of your selection have also purchased and in that way potentially increase sales to you.

The Internet has clearly enhanced traditional direct marketing methods, especially direct mail. By using *permission marketing*, a form of e-mail in which consumers give a company permission to contact them, a list of customers' e-mails is compiled and the customers are regularly contacted with special offers and deals based on their past purchases. The e-mail is coming from a company with which the consumer has experience and has agreed to receive the company's messages, and it contains a direct link to the company's website and the sale item. Companies such as Amazon, Dell, Gap, and Kate Spade are among those who have used this direct marketing method and technology successfully.

Publicity and Public Relations

Publicity is information about a company, a product, or an event transmitted by the general mass media to attract public attention. Although publicity is free, marketers have no control over the content media reporters and writers disseminate, and because it is presented in a news format, consumers often regard it as objective and credible. Online security breaches, airplane crashes, automobiles recalls, oil spills, and ethical scandals often tarnish the reputations of the businesses involved. Following two fatal airplane crashes involving the Boeing 737 Max, regulators grounded all planes of that model for 20 months. The 737 Max had been the company's best-selling plane, and having that model grounded during the FAA's investigation is estimated to have cost Boeing more than $20 billion.[19] During the high-profile investigation, e-mails from Boeing employees went public, revealing that many inside the company, including managers, knew that the 737 Max was flawed and dangerous.[20] Following the crashes, 80 percent of air travelers said they would avoid flying on a 737 Max in its first six months back in service; half said they would pay more to fly on a different plane.[21] However, a firm that engages in positive behaviors may also attract positive newsworthy attention. During the 2020 COVID-19 pandemic, Houston television stations reported how idled United Airlines employees were working in a nonessential repair facility to package food to distribute to homeless shelters and food banks.

Publicity *promotional tool in which information about a company, a product, or an event is transmitted by the general mass media to attract public attention*

In contrast to publicity, **public relations** is company-influenced information that seeks either to build good relations with the public by publicizing the company's charitable contributions, for example, or to deal with unfavorable events. In the Boeing case, many experts criticized the public relations response of then CEO Dennis Muilenburg, who called then President Donald Trump and asked him to intervene in the FAA's decision to ground the 737 Max, even after it was removed from service in nearly every other country. Muilenburg minimized the problem and predicted that the 737 Max would be back in service quickly, which made it impossible for Boeing and its airline clients to plan a reasonable solution. Finally, regulators, lawmakers, the public, and the victims' families believed that Muilenburg's apologies were insufficient, and he was fired not long after the second crash. Boeing is primarily a business-to-business company, so its public relations team was not prepared to deal with a long-term crisis that impacted consumers.[22]

Public Relations *communication efforts directed at building goodwill and favorable attitudes in the minds of the public toward the organization and its products*

summary of learning objectives

LEARNING OBJECTIVE 13-1

Explain the meaning of *distribution mix* and identify the different channels of distribution.

The success of any product depends on its distribution mix: the combination of distribution channels for getting products to end users—consumers and industrial buyers. *Intermediaries* help to distribute a producer's goods by moving them to customers: *Wholesalers* sell products to other businesses, which resell them to final users. *Retailers*, in contrast, sell products directly to end users. In the simplest of four distribution channels—the *direct channel*—the producer sells directly to the consumer or organizational buyer without intermediaries. In *retail distribution*, producers distribute products through retailers who, in turn, distribute to the consumer or industrial customer. *Wholesale distribution* involves both a wholesaler and then a retailer before the product reaches the end user. In the last type of distribution channel, a sales agent or a broker sells to the consumer or to the industrial customer. A disadvantage of channels with more intermediaries is higher prices because each intermediary charges a markup or commission. However, intermediaries can provide added value by supplying time-saving information and ensuring that products arrive at the right time and place.

In addition to selecting the distribution channel, marketers must select a *market coverage strategy*. *Intensive distribution* means distributing through as many channels and channel members as possible, and *exclusive distribution* occurs when the manufacturer grants the exclusive right to distribute or sell a product to a limited number of wholesalers or retailers, usually for a specific geographic area. Finally, *selective distribution* is a midpoint between intensive and exclusive; it is a strategy in which the producer selects a limited number of wholesalers and retailers to sell its product.

LEARNING OBJECTIVE 13-2

Describe the role of wholesalers and the functions performed by e-intermediaries.

Wholesalers provide a variety of services—delivery, credit arrangements, and product information—to buyers of products for resale or business use. In buying and reselling products, wholesalers provide storage and marketing advice, and they assist customers by marking prices and setting up displays. Most wholesalers are independent operations that sell goods produced by a variety of manufacturers. The largest group, *merchant wholesalers*, buys products from manufacturers and sells them to other businesses. They own the goods that they resell, store, and deliver. *Agents* and *brokers* work on commission and serve as independent sales representatives for many companies' products. Unlike wholesalers, agents and brokers do not own their merchandise. Rather, they serve as sales and merchandising arms for producers or sellers who do not have their own sales forces.

E-intermediaries are Internet-based channel members—wholesalers—who perform one or both of two functions: (1) They collect information about sellers and present it to consumers or (2) they help deliver online products to buyers. One type of e-intermediary, the *syndicated seller*, is a website that receives commissions for referring online customers to other companies' websites. *Shopping agents (e-agents)* help online customers—both industrial customers and consumers—by gathering and sorting information, identifying websites to visit, providing comparison prices, and identifying product features.

LEARNING OBJECTIVE 13-3

Describe the different types of retailing and explain how online retailers add value for consumers on the Internet.

Retail stores can be organized into three classifications: product-line retailers, bargain retailers, and convenience stores. Product-line retailers include department stores, supermarkets, and specialty stores. *Department stores* have specialized departments for different products. These stores offer a variety of services, such as credit plans and delivery. Similarly, *supermarkets* are divided into departments, and they stress low prices, self-service, and wide selection. In contrast, *specialty stores* are small, offering a full product line in narrow product fields, with knowledgeable sales personnel.

Bargain retailers include discount houses, catalog showrooms, factory outlets, and wholesale clubs. *Catalog showrooms* allow customers to view display samples, place orders, and receive purchases from attached warehouses. *Discount houses* offer a wide variety of products at low prices. *Factory outlets* are manufacturer-owned stores that avoid intermediaries by selling merchandise directly from factory to consumer. *Wholesale clubs* offer large discounts on a wide range of merchandise to customers who pay annual membership fees.

Convenience stores stress easily accessible locations, extended store hours, and speedy service. However, they generally do not feature low prices on most products.

Nonstore retailing includes *direct-response* firms that contact customers to receive sales orders. *Mail order* (or *catalog marketing*) is one form of direct-response retailing, as is outbound *telemarketing* that uses phone calls to sell directly to consumers. Finally, *direct selling* uses door-to-door sales and home-selling parties.

Online retailing provides the convenience of shopping anywhere using the Internet and social media, and includes *e-catalogs, electronic storefronts, cybermalls,* and *interactive and video* retailing. *E-catalogs* use online displays of products and product information, thus avoiding mail distribution and printing costs. Each seller's website is an *electronic storefront* where shoppers collect information about products, place orders, and pay for purchases. *Cybermalls* are collections of virtual storefronts where shoppers can navigate from a list of stores or product listings. *Video retailing* lets viewers shop at home from channels on their TVs. For TVs with Internet-ready capabilities, users can relax comfortably at home while shopping online with a large-screen visual display.

LEARNING OBJECTIVE 13-4

Define *physical distribution* and describe the major activities in the physical distribution process.

Physical distribution refers to the activities needed to move products from an intermediary or a manufacturer to customers and includes *warehousing* and *transportation operations.* Its purpose is to make goods available when and where customers want them, keep costs low, and provide services to satisfy customers.

Physical distribution activities include providing customer services, warehousing, and transportation of products. Storing, or *warehousing*, includes *private warehouses*, owned by a single firm that deals in mass quantities and needs regular storage. Independently owned *public warehouses* rent to companies only the space they need, often for storage needs during peak periods. To store digital assets, many companies and home users rely on remote off-site digital storage services to protect against losing data. In the event of physical catastrophe—floods, fires, earthquakes—at the client's facility, data can be restored online from the backup system.

Transportation operations physically move products from suppliers to customers. Differences in cost among the major transportation modes, trucks, railroads, planes, water carriers (boats and barges), digital transmission, and pipelines, are usually most directly related to delivery speed. *Trucks* are the most-used carriers of all modes of U.S. freight transportation. The advantages of trucks include flexibility for any-distance distribution, fast service, and dependability. *Planes* are the fastest and most expensive mode of transportation for physical goods. *Online transmission* of products in digital form is faster and less expensive than all other modes. Aside from digital transmission, transporting by *water carriers* is the least expensive mode, but also the slowest. *Railroads* can economically transport high-volume, heavy, bulky items, such as cars, steel, and coal. However, delivery routes are limited by fixed, immovable rail tracks. *Pipelines* are slow and lack flexibility and adaptability, but for specialized products, like liquids and gases, they provide economical and reliable delivery.

LEARNING OBJECTIVE 13-5

Identify the objectives of promotion and the considerations in selecting a promotional mix and discuss the various kinds of advertising promotions.

Promotion refers to techniques for communicating information about products and is part of the *communication mix*, the total message any company sends to customers about its products. Although the ultimate goal of any *promotion* is to increase sales, other goals include communicating information about the company and its products, positioning a product (establishing an identifiable image in the minds of consumers), adding value to distinguish a product from competing products, and controlling sales volume.

Once marketing objectives are clear, a firm must develop a promotional strategy to achieve them. A *pull strategy* appeals directly to consumers who will demand the product from retailers, whereas a *push strategy* occurs when a firm markets its products to wholesalers and retailers who then persuade customers to buy it. In deciding on the appropriate *promotional mix*—the best combination of promotional tools (e.g., advertising, personal selling, sales promotions, direct or interactive marketing, public relations)—marketers must consider the good or service being offered, characteristics of the target audience, the buyer's decision process, and the promotional mix budget. *Advertising* is paid, nonpersonal communication by which an identified sponsor informs an audience about a product. To better understand how consumers respond to ads, marketers use *real-time ad tracking* to find out who their customers are, to which media they pay attention, what messages appeal to them, and how to get their attention. Marketers use several different *advertising media*—specific communication devices for carrying a seller's message to potential customers—each having its advantages and drawbacks. TV is the most used and most expensive U.S. medium, with the largest audience. The Internet is the fastest-growing medium because it can target specific audiences and its ad success can be measured, but it is also easy to ignore. Outdoor advertising, one of the least-used of major media, is among the least expensive but is limited in the information it presents and exposure time is brief. Other often-used media include newspapers (broad readership), direct mail (for targeted audience), radio (low ad cost), and magazines (often shared and reread). The combination of media through which a company advertises is called its *media mix*.

LEARNING OBJECTIVE 13-6

Outline the tasks involved in personal selling and describe the various types of sales promotions.

Personal selling is the oldest and most expensive form of promotion. Personal selling tasks include *order processing* (receiving an order and seeing to its handling and delivery), *creative selling* (providing information and demonstrating product benefits to persuade buyers), and *missionary selling* (activities that promote a company and its products). The first step in the personal selling process includes *prospecting* (identify potential customers) and *qualifying* (determine authority to buy and pay). The next step is *approaching* (initial moments of contact with prospect), followed by *presenting* and *demonstrating* (displaying and explaining the product and its use), *handling objections* (overcoming buyer problems), *closing* (asking the prospect to buy the product), and *following up* (supplying after-sales services).

Sales promotions are short-term promotional activities to encourage consumer buying, industrial sales, or cooperation from distributors. They can increase the likelihood that buyers will try products, enhance product recognition, and increase purchase size and sales revenues. Sales promotions include *point-of-sale (POS) displays* to attract consumer attention; help them find products in stores, offices, lobbies, and waiting rooms; and provide product information. *Loyalty programs* reward frequent buyers for past repeat purchases by giving them reduced prices, upgraded products, or other special considerations. Other sales promotions give purchasing incentives, such as *samples* (customers can try products without having to buy them), *coupons* (a certificate for price reduction to encourage customers to try new products, lure them away from competitors, or induce them to buy more of a product), and *premiums* (free or reduced-price rewards for buying products). At *trade shows*, B2B sellers rent booths to display products to industrial customers. *Contests* intend to stimulate sales, with prizes to high-producing intermediaries and consumers who use the seller's products.

The final element of the promotional mix is publicity and public relations. *Publicity* is information about a company, product, or event transmitted by the general mass media to attract public attention. Although publicity is free, marketers have no control over the content media reports ad writers disseminate, and because it is presented in a news format, consumers often regard it as objective and credible. In contrast to publicity, *public relations* is company-influenced information that seeks to build good relations with the public by publicizing the company's charitable contributions or to deal with unfavorable events.

key terms

advertising **(p. 426)**
advertising media **(p. 428)**
bargain retailer **(p. 419)**
broker **(p. 414)**
catalog showroom **(p. 419)**
channel captain **(p. 416)**
channel conflict **(p. 416)**
closing **(p. 431)**
convenience store **(p. 419)**
coupon **(p. 432)**
creative selling **(p. 429)**
cybermall **(p. 422)**
department store **(p. 419)**
direct (or interactive) marketing **(p. 432)**
direct channel **(p. 414)**
direct selling **(p. 420)**
direct-response retailing **(p. 419)**
discount house **(p. 419)**
distribution channel **(p. 413)**
distribution mix **(p. 413)**
drop shippers **(p. 416)**
e-catalog **(p. 421)**
e-intermediary **(p. 417)**
electronic storefront **(p. 422)**

exclusive distribution **(p. 415)**
factory outlet **(p. 419)**
full-service merchant wholesaler **(p. 416)**
industrial selling **(p. 429)**
intensive distribution **(p. 415)**
intermediary **(p. 413)**
limited-function merchant wholesaler **(p. 416)**
loyalty program **(p. 432)**
mail order (catalog marketing) **(p. 419)**
media mix **(p. 428)**
merchant wholesaler **(p. 416)**
missionary selling **(p. 429)**
online retailing **(p. 420)**
order processing **(p. 429)**
personal selling **(p. 429)**
physical distribution **(p. 422)**
point-of-sale (POS) display **(p. 432)**
positioning **(p. 425)**
premium **(p. 432)**
private warehouse **(p. 422)**
promotion **(p. 425)**
promotional mix **(p. 426)**
prospecting **(p. 430)**
public relations **(p. 433)**
public warehouse **(p. 423)**
publicity **(p. 433)**
pull strategy **(p. 425)**
push strategy **(p. 425)**
qualifying **(p. 430)**
retail selling **(p. 429)**
retailer **(p. 413)**
sales agent **(p. 414)**
sales promotion **(p. 431)**
selective distribution **(p. 415)**
shopping agents (e-agents) **(p. 417)**
specialty store **(p. 419)**
supermarket **(p. 419)**
syndicated selling **(p. 417)**
telemarketing **(p. 420)**
trade show **(p. 432)**
video retailing **(p. 422)**
warehousing **(p. 422)**
wholesale club **(p. 419)**
wholesaler **(p. 413)**

questions & exercises

QUESTIONS FOR REVIEW

13-1. What are the types of distribution channels that sellers use to get products to end users? Give an example of each.

13-2. What are the three distribution strategies for market coverage? When is each most appropriate?

13-3. How do retailers add value to consumers? Why don't more manufacturers sell direct to consumers?

13-4. What are the major activities in the process of physically distributing goods?

13-5. What are the steps in the personal selling process?

QUESTIONS FOR ANALYSIS

13-6. Describe the four forms of nonstore retailing. Give examples of products that would be most appropriate for each, and discuss the reasons why that product would do well with that particular form.

13-7. What are the major types of product line and bargain retailers? Identify at least one example of each type.

13-8. Identify the major tools of sales promotion. At which stage of the consumer buying process is each most important? Why?

APPLICATION EXERCISES

13-9. In addition to being a major online retailer, Amazon acts as an e-intermediary for many small to medium-sized businesses. Imagine that you are interested in selling refurbished cell phones. Using the information on Amazon's website, how would you become a seller on Amazon? What costs are associated with selling your products through Amazon? If you decided to sell your products through your own website instead, what would be the pros and cons?

13-10. Search for some of the best viral marketing videos of all time and choose one to analyze. What is the product being marketed, and who is the target market? How does the advertisement appeal to the target market? Why do you think this particular video was effective?

building a business: continuing team exercise

ASSIGNMENT

Meet with your team members to consider your new business venture and how it relates to the marketing issues relating to distributing and promoting products, as discussed in this chapter. Develop specific responses to the following:

13-11. Consider once again the target market(s) for your business. For that target market, develop a "Statement of Promotional Objectives" for your company. What do you intend to accomplish with your chosen promotional objectives?

13-12. Considering your target market, discuss alternative promotional strategies that may be appropriate for your company. What are the pros and cons for each strategy you considered? Which strategy, at the present time, seems more favorable and why?

13-13. Outline the elements for your promotional mix, including specific promotional tools to be included at the onset (opening) of your company. Rank, in order, the relative importance of each tool in your promotional efforts. How might those rankings change, if at all, after your company is better established?

13-14. Develop a preliminary design of your company's start-up distribution mix, including the reasons for your choices on distribution channels and physical distribution. Explain why (how) your chosen distribution mix is appropriately matched to your target market.

13-15. Estimate the costs required to implement the distribution mix and promotional mix if those mixes are to be ready to go when your company opens for business.

team exercise

MAKING A DIFFERENCE

Team Activity

You and your team are students at Huge University, which has been hit with major budget cuts from state funding agencies as well as increased competition from state-supported "free" colleges. The university is interested in expanding the incoming student body to offset the decreases in revenues and cost increases, such as increasing expenses for technology and student services. One of the programs the administration has chosen to promote is the Summer Away program. Over the course of a 10-week summer semester, students will earn 10 to 12 college credits and will work to improve a community in need through partnerships with programs such as Habitat for Humanity and the United Nations World Food Programme. Your team has been assembled to develop a promotional plan for the program with the goal of attracting 150 new students from across the country.

ACTION STEPS

13-16. As a group, develop your promotional objectives. What are the initial objectives of your promotional campaign? Will these change over time?

13-17. What role will each element of the promotional mix play in your promotional plan?

13-18. Develop a one- to two-page recommendation that you could present to the university's leadership team. Remember to address the target audience (e.g., high school students, returning students, transfer students from community colleges).

13-19. Do you think that the promotional mix will change over time? How might it be different in three years? Be sure to address this in your proposal.

exercising your ethics

THE CHAIN OF RESPONSIBILITY

The Dilemma

A customer bought an expensive vase as a wedding gift at a local store and asked that it be shipped to the bride in another state. Several months after the wedding, the buyer became concerned when she had not received a thank-you note from the happy couple. She contacted the bride, who indicated that she never received the vase. Arguing that the merchandise had not been delivered, the customer requested a refund from the retailer.

The store manager gathered the following information:

- All shipments from the store were handled by a well-known national delivery firm.
- The delivery firm verified that the package had been delivered to the designated address two days after the sale.
- Normally, the delivery firm does not obtain recipient signatures; deliveries are made to the address of record, regardless of the name on the package.

The gift giver argued that even though the package had been delivered to the right address, it had not been delivered to the named recipient. It turns out that, unbeknownst to the gift giver, the bride and groom had moved. It stood to reason, then, that the gift was in the hands of the new occupant at the couple's former address. The manager informed the gift giver that the store had fulfilled its obligation. The cause of the problem, she explained, was the incorrect address given by the customer. She refused to refund the customer's money and suggested that the customer might want to recover the gift by contacting the stranger who received it at the couple's old address.

QUESTIONS TO ADDRESS

13-20. What are the responsibilities of each party—the customer, the store, and the delivery firm—in this situation?

13-21. From an ethical standpoint, in what ways is the store manager's action right? In what ways is it wrong?

13-22. If you were appointed to settle this matter, what actions would you take?

cases

CHAOS THEORY AT WORK

Continued from page 413

At the beginning of this chapter, you read about the unusual way Amazon organizes its warehouses to maximize efficiency. Using the information presented in this chapter, you should now be able to answer the following questions:

QUESTIONS FOR DISCUSSION

13-23. Why are online retailers taking so much market share from the traditional brick-and-mortar stores?

13-24. Do you think that legacy stores such as Macy's and even Walmart will be able to compete with online stores in the future? How would they have to change in order to be more competitive?

13-25. How have changes in physical distribution changed the marketplace? How has the marketplace changed the distribution networks?

13-26. If everything were available to purchase online, would there still be products and services you would want to buy in person? How can online retailers become more competitive against traditional stores for items that people still prefer to buy in person?

THE LONG TAIL, REVISITED

Back in 2005, the editor of *Wired* Magazine, Chris Anderson, wrote *The Long Tail: Why the Future of Business Is Selling Less of More*. He proposed that, because of the expansion of e-commerce, consumers now had access to an amazing array of products that traditional brick-and-mortar stores would never keep in stock. The term *long tail* refers to the extended tapering-off portion of the overall demand curve. Without the constraints of physical shelf space and with more access to distribution channels, narrowly targeted goods and services can be as economically attractive as mainstream fare.

Anderson argued that traditional retail economics dictates that stores stock only the most popular items because shelf space is expensive, but online retailers, like Amazon, can stock virtually everything in theory. Amazon's apparent success in generating profits from its endless aisles of products has spurred many competitors to adopt long-tail strategies. However, Amazon doesn't stock all the specialty items itself—instead, Amazon offers a marketplace for long-tail items. In other words, Amazon focuses on directly selling and fulfilling high-demand products and leaves long-tail merchandise for its independent sellers to fulfill. Next time you shop on Amazon, take a look for yourself. Search for clothing, electronics, household items, or anything else of interest to you and try to sort out Amazon the store from Amazon the intermediary.

For the consumer, there is a definite upside to the long tail. Products that were previously unavailable in the open market are now available. For instance, a how-to book on breeding and raising gerbils may have been impossible to find before the "endless aisles" of the Internet, but now niche marketers can provide extremely specific items to an audience that is scattered geographically. Even though they may be working out of a small office, niche sellers know their markets and have better access to and relationships with niche suppliers. For Amazon, though, allowing third-party sales on its website provides long-tail data. Amazon can then use that data to directly offer products that have begun to sell well. Essentially, Amazon crowdsources its market research using demographic and sales data provided by long-tail sellers.

QUESTIONS FOR DISCUSSION

13-27. What kinds of products do you think you would find in Anderson's "long tail"? Give examples.

13-28. Do you believe the long-tail theory is still applicable? Why or why not?

13-29. Would you start a niche marketing business? If so, why and how would you market your products or services? If not, why not?

13-30. Do you think it is ethical for companies like Amazon to collect third-party data? How would you feel and what would you do if your product suddenly became mainstream and Amazon started carrying it, selling it, and fulfilling those sales? What are the issues? What are the pros and cons?

endnotes

[1] Jeff Collins, "4.1 Million-Square-Foot Warehouse in California Will Be Amazon's Biggest Ever," *The Seattle Times*, June 6, 2022, https://www.seattletimes.com/business/4-1-million-square-foot-warehouse-in-california-will-be-amazons-biggest-ever/#:~:text=At%20almost%204.1%20million%20square,Amazon%20warehouse%20in%20the%20world.

[2] "For Filling an Ignored Food Gap," *Fast Company*, no. 193: 128, Business Source Premier, EBSCOhost, accessed May 20, 2015; "Jose Manuel, Founder and CEO of Algramo, Is the Venture Social Entrepreneur Contender from Chile," Venture.com, accessed June 12, 2015, https://www.theventure.com/global/en/finalists/.

[3] T.J. Maxx, "How We Do It," accessed August 2023, https://tjmaxx.tjx.com/store/jump/topic/how-we-do-it/2400087.

[4] Kaleigh Fasanella, "Kylie Cosmetics Is Not Sold in Vending Machines," *Allure*, November 15, 2019, https://www.allure.com/story/kylie-cosmetics-vending-machines-las-vegas-airport.

[5] Best Buy, "Best Buy Express Vending Machines Turn 10," August 30, 2018, https://corporate.bestbuy.com/best-buy-express-vending-machines-turn-10/.

[6] Grand View Research, "Retain Vending Machine Market Size & Trends Report, 2030," 2021, https://www.grandviewresearch.com/industry-analysis/global-vending-machine-market.

[7] Avon, 2022 Annual Report, http://investor.avoncompany.com/, accessed June 2, 2023.

[8] Ryan Lawler, "Wheelys Is Launching an Unmanned Convenience Store in Shanghai," *TechCrunch*, March 7, 2017, https://techcrunch.com/2017/03/07/wheelys-unmanned-convenience-store/.

[9] "Retail E-Commerce Sales Worldwide from 2014 to 2023 (in Billion U.S. Dollars)," Statista, accessed April 20, 2020, https://www.statista.com/statistics/379046/worldwide-retail-e-commerce-sales/; Don Davis, "Amazon's North America Sales Surge 29% in Q1 as Coronavirus Drives Demand," Digital Commerce 360, accessed June 2, 2023, https://www.digitalcommerce360.com/article/amazon-sales/.

[10] HubSpot, *2022 State of U.S. Consumer Trends Report*, 2023, https://blog.hubspot.com/marketing/how-each-generation-shops-differently.

[11] https://ikeamuseum.com/en/explore/the-story-of-ikea/an-icon-is-retired/.

[12] "Truck Drivers in the USA," AllTrucking.com, accessed June 3, 2023, http://www.alltrucking.com/faq/truck-drivers-in-the-usa/; Jennifer Cheeseman Day and Andrew W. Hait, "Number of Truckers at All-Time High," United States Census Bureau, June 6, 2019, https://www.census.gov/library/stories/2019/06/america-keeps-on-trucking.html; "Trucking Statistics," Truckinfo.net, accessed June 2, 2023, https://www.truckinfo.net/trucking/stats.htm.

[13] "Ad Age: 200 Leading National Advertisers 2018 Fact Pack," *Ad Age*, 2018, http://digitalgabe.com/wp-content/uploads/2018/06/Top-200-Media-Spenders.pdf.

[14] Nat Ives, "Consumers Are Bugged by Many Ads," *Advertising Age*, December 1, 2008, 6.

[15] Jacinda Santora, "17 Key Influencer Marketing Statistics Fuel Your Strategy," July 18, 2023, https://influencermarketinghub.com/influencer-marketing-statistics/.

[16] "Interview with Craig Jones of Teton Trade Cloth," by Joe Cooke, summer 2023.

[17] "Sweepstakes," IGA, accessed April 21, 2020, https://www.iga.com/sweepstakes.

[18] Ollie's, "Ollie's Army Recruitment Office," accessed August 2, 2023, https://www.ollies.us/ollies-army-office/.

[19] Chris Isidore, "Former Boeing Executive Indicted for Fraud in 737 Max Tragedy," October 15, 2021, https://www.cnn.com/2021/10/14/business/boeing-indictment-737-max/index.html.

[20] Mark Sweney and Gwyn Topham, "737 Max Scandal: The Internal Boeing Messages and Emails," *The Guardian*, January 10, 2020, https://www.theguardian.com/business/2020/jan/10/737-max-scandal-the-internal-boeing-messages-and-emails.

[21] David Schaper, "737 Max Scandal Cuts Boeing's Once Rock-Solid Image," NPR, November 26, 2019, https://www.npr.org/2019/11/26/783197253/737-max-scandal-cuts-boeings-once-rock-solid-image.

[22] Greg Beaubien, "Crisis Communication Lessons from Boeing's 737 MAX Tragedies," PRSA, January 2021, https://www.prsa.org/article/crisis-communication-lessons-from-boeing-s-737-max-tragedies.

[23] Howard Schultz and Dori Jones Yang, *Pour Your Heart into It: How Starbucks Built a Company One Cup at a Time*, New York, NY: Hachette, 2014. Kindle Edition page 242.

[24] Schultz and Jones Yang, *Pour Your Heart into It*. Kindle Edition page 249.

[25] Schultz and Jones Yang, *Pour Your Heart into It*. Kindle Edition page 276.

part 4

Integrative Learning Portfolio

crafting a business plan

Goal of the Exercise

So far, your business has an identity; you've described the factors that will affect your business; and you've examined your employees, the jobs they'll be performing, and the ways in which you can motivate them. Part 4 of the business plan project asks you to think about marketing's Four Ps—*product, price, place (distribution)*, and *promotion*—and how they apply to your business. You'll also examine how you might target your marketing toward a certain group of consumers.

Exercise Background: Part 4 of the Business Plan

In Part 1, you briefly described what your business will do. The first step in Part 4 of the plan is to more fully describe the product (good or service) you are planning to sell. Once you have a clear picture of the product, you'll need to describe how this product will "stand out" in the marketplace—that is, how will it differentiate itself from other products?

In Part 1, you also briefly described who your customers would be. The first step in Part 4 of the plan is to describe your ideal buyer, or target market, in more detail, listing their income level, educational level, lifestyle, age, and so forth. This part of the business plan project also asks you to discuss the price of your products as well as where the buyer can find your products.

Finally, you'll examine how your business will get the attention and interest of the buyer through its *promotional mix*—advertising, personal selling, sales promotions, and publicity and public relations.

This part of the business plan encourages you to be creative. Have fun! Provide as many details as you possibly can because this reflects an understanding of your product and your buyer. Marketing is all about finding a need and filling it. Does your product fill a need in the marketplace?

Your Assignment

STEP 1

Open the saved *Business Plan* file you began working on in Parts 1 and 3.

STEP 2

For the purposes of this assignment, you will answer the following questions in "Part 4: Principles of Marketing":

P4-1. Describe your target market in terms of age, education level, income, and other demographic variables.

Hint: Refer to Chapter 11 for more information on the aspects of target marketing and market segmentation that you may want to consider. Be as detailed as possible about who you think your customers will be.

P4-2. Describe the features and benefits of your product or service.

Hint: As you learned in Chapter 11, a product is a bundle of attributes—features and benefits. What features does your product have—what does it look like, and what does it do? How will the product benefit the buyer?

P4-3. How will you make your product stand out in the crowd?

Hint: There are many ways to stand out in the crowd, such as a unique product, an outstanding service, or a great location. What makes your great idea special? Does it fill an unmet need in the marketplace? How will you differentiate your product to make sure that it succeeds?

P4-4. What pricing strategy will you choose for your product, and what are the reasons for this strategy?

Hint: Refer to Chapter 12 for more information on pricing strategies and tactics. Because your business is new, so is the product. Therefore, you probably want to choose between price skimming and penetration pricing. Which will you choose, and why?

P4-5. Where will customers find your product or service? (That is, what issues of the distribution mix should you consider?)

Hint: If your business does not sell its product directly to consumers, what types of retail stores will sell your product? If your product will be sold to another business, which channel of distribution will you use? Refer to this chapter for more information on aspects of distribution you may want to consider.

P4-6. How will you advertise to your target market? Why have you chosen these forms of advertisement?

Hint: Marketers use several different advertising media—specific communication devices for carrying a seller's message to potential customers—each having its advantages and drawbacks. Refer to this chapter for a discussion of the types of advertising media you may wish to consider here.

P4-7. What other methods of promotion will you use and why?

Hint: There's more to promotion than simple advertising. Other methods include personal selling, sales promotions, and publicity and public relations. Refer to the discussion of promotion in this chapter for ideas on how to promote your product that go beyond just advertising.

Note: Once you have answered the questions, save your Word document. You'll be answering additional questions in later chapters.

case PART 4 STARBUCKS 1992–2007

"Every business has a memory. The memory of sacrificing quality for profit would have been fixed in the minds of Starbucks people forever. It would have been an impossible price to pay."[23]

— Howard Schultz

In 1992, its 21st year in business, Starbucks boasted 140 stores, all in North America. Starbucks went public that year with an initial public offering (IPO) on June 26 at a share price of $17, raising $29 million in additional capital. At the date of the IPO, with $10,000, you could have purchased roughly 588 shares of the coffee chain. The company's stock grew enough that management enacted six 2-for-1 stock splits between the IPO and mid-2023, multiplying the number of issued shares by a factor of 64. Your initial 588 shares would have grown to become 37,632 shares after the many rounds of splits. If you sold at $100 in 2023, you'd have $3,763,200 and a hefty tax bill.

Despite the appearance of steady growth over the long term, Starbucks's stock prices have not always gone up. For instance, in 1994, after several years of almost 50 percent growth, a late frost in Brazil doubled and then tripled the price of raw beans. Even though Starbucks didn't buy from Brazil, the South American country supplied a quarter of the world's coffee beans, and a shortage there affected prices across the board as the Brazil buyers turned to other markets. Even before that, in 1989, prices had been so low that many growers had left the market, turning their fields into more profitable crops, such as sugar.

The combined power of Nestlé, Kraft, and Procter & Gamble commanded 70 percent of the coffee market at that time, and those three raised their prices to cover the increased costs, but Starbucks chose to keep prices stable until it ran out of its lower-cost beans and then only raised prices a bit. Most importantly, the company opted to continue to buy the highest-quality beans rather than try to cut costs with cheaper products. When Starbucks finally did raise prices, the company was honest and open with customers.

The silver lining in the price crisis was that Orin Smith and his team were forced to examine all aspects of the company to determine where they could cut costs without sacrificing the quality of both products and services. Smith had just succeeded Schultz as president and chief operating officer of the company, but Schultz canceled his vacation with his family to come back and help the company through the crisis.

Brand loyalty carried Starbucks through the pricing crisis of 1994 and again in 1997. Schultz also notes that this brand loyalty was created one customer at a time by providing quality coffee first and foremost, prepared by competent, well-trained partners and served in a comfortable setting. As the president of international operations Howard Behar put it, "We're not in the coffee business serving people; we're in the people business serving coffee."[24]

dpa picture alliance archive/Alamy Stock Photo

Despite the shakeup, or even perhaps because of it, Starbucks stock began to climb again, and the company took on even more ambitious growth goals for the new millennium. By the time Orin Smith retired in 2005, Starbucks had expanded to more than 10,000 locations worldwide and reported more than $5 billion in sales.

In 2005, the board of directors named Jim Donald as the chief executive officer. Donald came from a retail background and had joined Starbucks in 2002 as president of the North American division. For the next few years, Starbucks enjoyed record growth, opening an average of 6 new stores every day. However, in 2007, with home values dropping and fuel prices soaring, store traffic dropped, and McDonalds and Dunkin' Donuts both began to offer gourmet coffee drinks. Because of these outside influences, the company's stock dropped by over 50 percent in just a few months. Investors, who demand a consistent and robust return on investment and who expect constant, measurable growth, were dumping Starbucks stock, driving the price down. It was another critical time at the company, and in order to try to salvage the situation, the board ousted Jim Donald, and Howard Schultz stepped back into the leadership role of CEO to right the faltering ship. Once again, he had his work cut out for him.

QUESTIONS FOR DISCUSSION

P4-8. Without the benefit of hindsight, do you think Starbucks did the right thing by resisting raising prices when the cost of raw materials increased dramatically?

P4-9. Schultz claims he was "trying to build a big business on a foundation of small business values."[25] In what ways do you see that legacy today?

P4-10. Starbucks was vertically integrated in the early days, meaning it bought and roasted its own beans rather than buying pre-roasted beans. What advantages and disadvantages are there to that kind of integration?

P4-11. How do you think Starbucks established its prices for drinks? What do you suppose would be the ramifications today of a significant price increase?

P4-12. What factors of the external marketing environment, both at home and abroad, worked in Starbucks's favor as it grew in the early years? Which factors worked against it? Explain your reasoning.

finding your path

CAREERS IN BUSINESS

Marketing is a popular major in most business programs. As a profession, marketing has a strong external focus. In Chapter 11, we defined marketing as "activities, a set of institutions, and processes for creating, communicating, delivering, and exchanging offerings that have value for customers, clients, partners, and society at large." Marketing managers are often generalists responsible for all marketing-related activities for a particular product or product group. Within this broad area, though, there are also specialized marketing jobs that focus on more particular areas like direct or personal selling, online sales, marketing research, packaging, advertising, industrial marketing, social media, and distribution. Retailing is also closely related to marketing. Performance of marketing managers is usually assessed in terms of such criteria as successful new products launched, market share growth, revenue growth, and similar indicators. The number of marketing-related jobs is expected to grow by 8 percent by 2028. In 2021, the average starting salary for marketing majors was $41,790.

MAKING YOURSELF EMPLOYABLE

Marketing can be an exciting and rewarding career. To increase your chances of getting a marketing job, you should understand and develop certain skills. It is also helpful to understand how best to market yourself.

Marketing Skills

A lot of the work of marketing managers involves interpersonal relationships, so human relations skills are obviously important. In addition, many recruiters suggest that when they are hiring people for marketing jobs they want people with insights into how to assess marketing trends, who understand key points in product development and pricing, and who can interpret marketing research data. They also stress communications skills because marketing managers need to be able to communicate effectively with several different audiences. Data analytics skills are also becoming increasingly important. And for many marketing jobs, proficiency with software such as Adobe Creative Suite is also beneficial. So, look for opportunities to learn, develop, refine, and apply these skills throughout your education.

Marketing Yourself

Some experts suggest that when you are looking for a new position you should approach the search process like a marketing problem. Think of it like this: As a customer choosing which product to buy, you are most likely to select the one that has the optimal set of features and benefits that will most closely satisfy your needs. With this in mind, frame your job search from the perspective that you, as a business professional, are one product among several and that potential employers are customers looking for the product that has the optimal set of features and benefits that will most closely satisfy their needs. With this in mind, do the following:

- Make a list of the "product *features*" (both tangible and intangible) that you possess (or intend to possess) as a business professional. For instance, potential features might include leadership in a club or other organization, the ability to speak a second language, good grades in quantitative courses, and the ability to juggle school and a part-time job.
- Make a list of the product *benefits* that your features provide (or will provide) for potential employers. The features noted above might translate into such benefits as leadership, analytical, and time management skills and the ability to interact with a diverse team.
- Identify an industry or organization(s) that you are interested in for your career. Think of this as your target market. List key *characteristics* of the customer(s) in this target market. What are some specific needs they expect employees to satisfy? For instance, let's assume you might want to work for Apple or Google. What do you think these firms look for in potential employees? You might assume they want people with good leadership and analytical skills and who can interact effectively with a diverse team. You might also, though, assume they want people who are creative and innovative.
- Compare your features and benefits lists from Steps 1 and 2 with your target market's needs. Do you detect any gaps that might indicate a mismatch? Comparing the lists, you might determine that for the most part you match up well. However, assuming you are correct in your prediction that potential employers will want people who are creative, you might also realize that while you think of yourself as being creative you have no real evidence to support this. To help address this potential mismatch, you might decide to use one of your course electives to take a course in general creativity, creative writing, art, or any other field in which creativity is important.
- What changes in your career plans might improve the match between you and your target customers? In addition to coursework, you might also look for a different part-time job, or perhaps an internship, in which creativity is especially important. For instance, you might spend time working in an advertising agency.

Your Image and Résumé

In many cases, the first impressions your potential employer will have of you will come from your résumé and, potentially, a photo you use on sites such as LinkedIn. For social media that might be available to an employer, select an image that shows you smiling, dressed appropriately, and in a neutral setting (e.g., not wearing a swimsuit while in a bar on the beach). Your résumé, of course, is especially important. Most colleges and universities have career centers where you can go for help in putting your résumé together. The résumé, along with a cover letter or e-mail, will most likely be your first point of contact with potential employers, so do not underestimate its importance!

PART 5 | MANAGING INFORMATION FOR BETTER BUSINESS DECISIONS

chapter 14

Information Technology (IT) for Business

Rawpixel.com/Shutterstock

learning objectives

After reading this chapter, you should be able to:

14-1 **Discuss** the impacts information technology is having on the business world.

14-2 **Identify** the IT resources businesses have at their disposal and how these resources are used.

14-3 **Describe** the role of information systems, the different types of information systems, and how businesses use such systems.

14-4 **Identify** the threats and risks information technology poses to businesses.

14-5 **Describe** the ways in which businesses protect themselves from the threats and risks information technology poses.

what's in it for me?

Information technologies are reshaping the business landscape. Even the most traditional businesses must change with the times, whether those times are defined by paper and pencil, telephone and fax machine, or digital language translators and smartphones and smartwatches. Indeed, it may seem like the times are changing more rapidly with each passing year, and it is in this context that our discussion of the various kinds of information technology, their functions, and the benefits and risks associated with each assumes particular importance. By understanding the material in this chapter, you'll have a clearer picture of how technology is used by and affects business and how you can use it to your best advantage—as an employee, investor, manager, or business owner.

But businesses and individuals alike face information technology-related risks. Text messages saying victims' credit cards have been deactivated lure bank customers into relaying account information to an unknown sender. Internet-based phone users receiving fake caller IDs of real hospitals, government agencies, banks, and other businesses fall prey to a now popular form of telephone phishing that talks victims into revealing personal information. Perhaps most impressive, cyberthieves are using marketing techniques—most notably "targeting"—to reach specific audiences. Also known as "spear phishing," with targeting, scammers do research to identify wealthy individuals, families, and professional money managers. Victims

Take A Pix Media/Shutterstock

receive friendly sounding e-mails and social networking contacts containing contaminated attachments that, once opened, infect their computers, exposing bank account and other identity information to scammers. Although computer security devices—spam filters, data encryption, firewalls, and antivirus software—catch a vast number of intrusions, the threat remains.[1] In 2021, a ransomware attack forced Colonial Pipeline to shut down a 5,500-mile stretch of pipeline for about a week, cutting off a major supply of the East Coast's gasoline, natural gas, and diesel fuel.[2] Darkside, a criminal hacker group, was responsible for the attack and demanded a $4.4 million ransom in bitcoin. Desperate to minimize the damage and get the pipeline running again, Colonial Pipeline paid it. Restoring the system's integrity required intervention by the U.S. Department of Energy and other federal agencies.[3] The U.S. Department of Justice was able to seize about $2.3 million of the ransom, but the attack made it clear how vulnerable companies are to digital extortion.[4]

Cyberinvasions are a related risk. Some governments, to save money, are actively scamming others, using hackers to steal technology secrets for leading-edge military equipment, including defense systems of other countries. Organizations of all kinds are finding cybersecurity more difficult as more and more employees use their personal phones and computers for conducting business. Organizational information, then, is more widely dispersed and increasingly susceptible to intrusion via mobile-phone malware, virus-contaminated applications, and links containing spyware sent from text messages.[5]

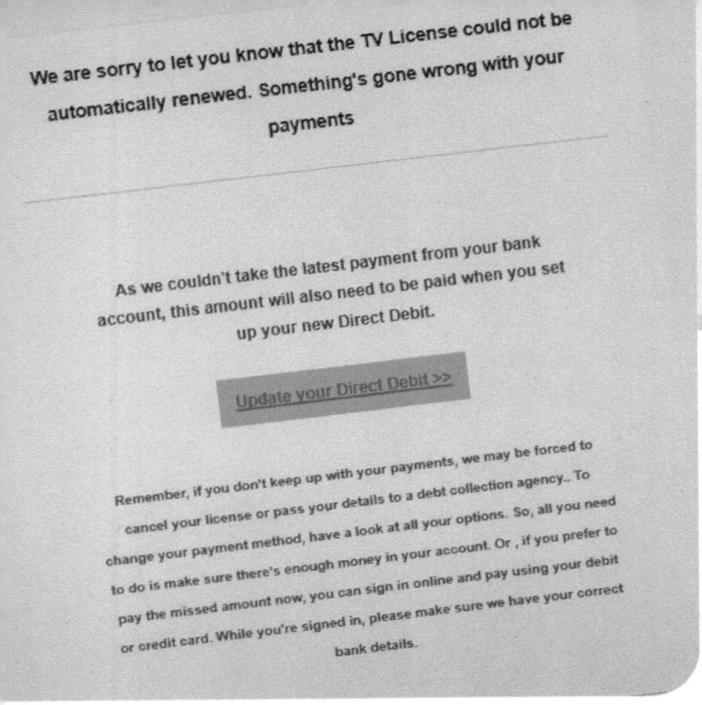

Sam Oaksey/Alamy Stock Photo

Think Before You Click

Kelly went into Memorial Day weekend with typical summer kickoff plans: She had tickets to a Phillies game and was expecting guests for a barbecue. She noticed a text message from a work colleague, but since it came in after working hours on Friday, she ignored it. Working remotely for a nonprofit gave Kelly the flexibility to do her job while also parenting two children under three years old, but it did come with some headaches. With a team largely composed of contractors in different time zones, it was sometimes difficult to make connections.

On Tuesday morning, she logged into her work accounts to find a message from the outsourced payroll officer asking her to call to confirm the change in her direct deposit details. Alarmed, she immediately checked her payroll account to find that the routing and checking account numbers did not match the details she'd previously provided. As she started reviewing e-mails, she was dismayed to find that the CEO and the accounting firm had fallen prey to a social engineering scam. Someone had created an e-mail with Kelly's name, and the scammer used just enough detail to lure the organization's officers to change sensitive information.

The scammer sent an e-mail to the CEO, asking for help changing their banking details. The CEO mentioned the name of the payroll platform and the name of the accountant she was including in the correspondence. As the correspondence progressed, the scammer was able to direct the accountant to change Kelly's direct deposit to their own account. Even though the e-mail address did not match any known addresses on file for Kelly, the accountant felt certain that she was corresponding with Kelly and skipped the crucial basic security step of confirming her identity. From publicly available information (Kelly's name and the CEO's name and e-mail address), the scammer was able to convince two otherwise savvy women that they were talking with their colleague and friend, counting on a level of informality in a small organization. Luckily, the organization was able to quickly stop the deposit and reroute it back to Kelly's bank account, but not all these stories end happily.

As remote work has become more common, these types of scams have become more common. Not only do businesses and workers rely more on technology to get things done, but they also spend less time together in the same place. When organizations like Kelly's do business in a variety of time zones and many people get e-mail and text messages around the clock, it can be even harder to stop scams before they are detected. Following clear procedures and processes and having strong cybersecurity systems in place can prevent security breaches and digital fraud, protecting all stakeholders. (After studying the content in this chapter, you should be able to answer a set of discussion questions found at the end of the chapter.)

Information Technology Impacts: A Driver of Changes for Business

Learning Objective 14-1

Discuss the impacts information technology is having on the business world.

The effect of **information technology (IT)** on business cannot be overstated. In fact, IT—the various appliances and devices for creating, storing, exchanging, and using information in diverse modes, including visual images, voice, multimedia, and business data—has altered the very foundations of all organizations, radically changing the way people inside and outside those organizations interact. We see ads everywhere for the latest smartphones, tablets, and laptops, and most of us go online daily without even thinking about what we are doing. E-mail has become a staple in business—and is now seen as a bit old fashioned among many younger people—and even such traditionally "low-tech" businesses as nail salons and garbage collection companies are dependent on online connectivity, computers, and networks. As consumers, we interact with databases of IT networks every time we move money between accounts, order food at McDonald's, make a purchase using a credit card, or check on the status of a package at UPS.com. Technology and its effects are evident everywhere.

Information Technology (IT) *various appliances and devices for creating, storing, exchanging, and using information in diverse modes, including visual images, voice, multimedia, and business data*

E-commerce (short for *electronic commerce*), the use of online networks and other electronic means for retailing and business-to-business transactions, has created new market relationships around the globe. In this section, we'll look at how businesses are using IT to bolster productivity, improve operations and processes, create new opportunities, and communicate and work in ways not possible until just a few years ago.

E-commerce *use of the Internet and other electronic means for retailing and business-to-business transactions*

Creating Portable Offices: Providing Remote Access to Instant Information

IT devices such as Samsung Galaxy phones and Apple iPhones, along with IBM wireless Internet access and PC-style office applications, save businesses time and travel expenses by enabling employees, customers, and suppliers to communicate from any location. IT's mobile messaging capabilities mean that geographic separation between the workplace and headquarters is no longer a barrier to getting things done. Employees no longer work only at the office or the factory, nor are all of a company's operations performed at one place—people take their offices with them. When using such devices, off-site employees have continuous access to information instead of being forced to be at a desk to access their work and work-related data and information. Client project folders, e-mail, and voice messaging are accessible from virtually any location. The 2020 pandemic tested these systems like never before, forcing workers around the world to rely on these systems simply to stay in business. The process stretched IT systems to the breaking point, and even monster systems like those used by Google were forced to evolve to deal with increased demand from users.

Enabling Better Service by Coordinating Remote Deliveries

With access to the Internet, company activities may be geographically scattered but still remain coordinated through a networked system that provides better service for customers. Many businesses, for example, coordinate activities from one centralized location, but their deliveries flow from several remote locations, often at lower cost. Consider Amazon and its Prime membership service. By becoming a Prime member, customers can receive next-day delivery on qualifying items. Without warehouses

Shutterstock

Participants in high-level meetings like this one often use digital technology like smartphones and laptops during the meetings. Encryption software and other advanced security measures are called for to help protect against unauthorized users knowing the details of the meetings.

located all over the country, this type of service would not be possible to facilitate. This also allows for companies to coordinate shipments when items are in multiple locations. When you order furniture—for example, a chair, a sofa, a table, and two lamps—the chair may come from a warehouse in Philadelphia and the lamps from a manufacturer in California; the sofa and table may be shipped direct from different suppliers in North Carolina. Beginning with the customer's order, activities are coordinated through the company's network, as if the whole order were being processed at one place. This avoids the expensive in-between step of first shipping all the items to a central location.

Creating Leaner, More Efficient Organizations

Networks and technology are also leading to leaner companies with fewer employees and simpler structures. Because networks enable firms to maintain information linkages among both employees and customers, more work and customer satisfaction can be accomplished with fewer people. Bank customers connect into a 24-hour information system and monitor their accounts without human assistance. Instructions that once were given to assembly workers by supervisors are now delivered to workstations electronically. IT communications provide better use of employee skills and greater efficiencies from physical resources. For example, truck drivers used to return to a shipping terminal to receive instructions from supervisors on reloading freight for the next delivery. Today, one dispatcher using IT has replaced several supervisors. Instructions to the fleet arrive on electronic screens in trucks on the road so drivers know in advance the next delivery schedule, and satellite navigation services, such as Waze, alert drivers of traffic incidents ahead and even reroute drivers automatically to avoid delivery delays.[6]

Enabling Increased Collaboration

Collaboration among internal units and with outside firms is greater when firms use software and other IT communications devices designed to support teamwork. Companies are learning that complex problems can be better solved through IT-supported collaboration, either with formal teams or with spontaneous interaction among people and departments. The design of new products, for example, was once an engineering responsibility; now it is a shared activity using information from customers, along with people in marketing, finance, production, engineering, and

TonyV3112/Shutterstock

This Boeing aircraft was the result of collaboration among Boeing engineers, suppliers, and customers.

purchasing, who collectively determine the best design. For example, the design of Boeing's 787 Dreamliner aircraft is the result of collaboration not just among engineers but also with passengers (who wanted in-seat electrical outlets to recharge personal digital devices), cabin crews (who wanted more bathrooms and wider aisles), and air-traffic controllers (who wanted larger, safer air brakes). Although the 787 suffered from some initial design flaws, solutions involved a worldwide network of technical collaboration among Boeing engineers, suppliers, customers, and the National Aeronautics and Space Administration (NASA), and now the 787 has become a major business success for Boeing.[7] Perhaps the greatest changes in how products are designed, though, is driven by customer interaction. Companies have instantaneous access to customer complaints and comments through the ratings systems employed by most e-commerce organizations, and can use that feedback to improve products and solve problems in real time. This process allows companies to be more attentive to customers and increase consumer satisfaction.

Enabling Global Exchange

The global reach of IT enables business collaboration on a scale that was once unheard of. Consider Lockheed Martin's contract for designing and supplying thousands of Joint Strike Fighters in different versions for the United States, Britain, Italy, Denmark, Canada, and Norway. Lockheed can't do the job alone—over the project's 20-year life, more than 1,500 firms will supply everything from radar systems to engines to bolts. In just the start-up phase, Lockheed collaborated with Britain's BAE Systems along with more than 70 U.S. and 18 international subcontractors at some 190 locations, including an Australian manufacturer of aviation communications and a Turkish electronics supplier. In all, 40,000 remote computers are collaborating on the project using Lockheed's online system. Digital collaboration on a massive scale is essential for coordinating design, testing, and construction at this level while avoiding delays, holding down costs, and maintaining quality.[8]

Providing Flexibility for Customization

IT advances also create new manufacturing and service capabilities that enable businesses to offer customers greater variety, customizable options, and faster delivery cycles. Whether it's an iPhone app or a Rawlings baseball glove, today's design-it-yourself world is possible through fast, flexible manufacturing using IT networks. A few years ago, Porsche had a problem. Customers of their famous 911 model became bored with their standard color offerings and reached out to the company to come up with something different. Porsche worked with an IT firm to develop a new system that allowed customers to order a car in any color they wanted . . . any color. Porsche used a scanning system to capture the color and then a separate paint mixture station to replicate it. The process makes it possible for Porsche customers to have their 911 in any color they would like: lobster orange, Pepto Bismol pink, or whatever. This system represents quite the change from 100 years ago, when Henry Ford said that customers could "have any color car that they wanted, so long as it was black." Similarly, at San Francisco–based Timbuk2's website, you can "build your own" custom messenger bag at different price levels with your choice of size, fabric, color combination, accessories, liner material, strap, and even left- or right-hand access.[9] This principle of **mass customization** allows companies to produce in large volumes, and IT allows each item to feature the unique options the customer prefers. With IT, the old standardized assembly line has become quickly adaptable because workers have instantaneous access to assembly instructions for all the product options, and equipment can be changed quickly for each customer's order.

Mass Customization *principle in which companies produce in large volumes, but each item features the unique options the customer prefers*

As shown in Figure 14.1, flexible production and speedy delivery depend on an integrated network of information to coordinate all the activities among customers, manufacturers, suppliers, and shippers.

Service industries, too, including health care, banking, and recreation, are emphasizing greater flexibility for meeting customers' needs. Grocery chains like Kroger, H-E-B, Publix, and Safeway now accept grocery orders from customers online,

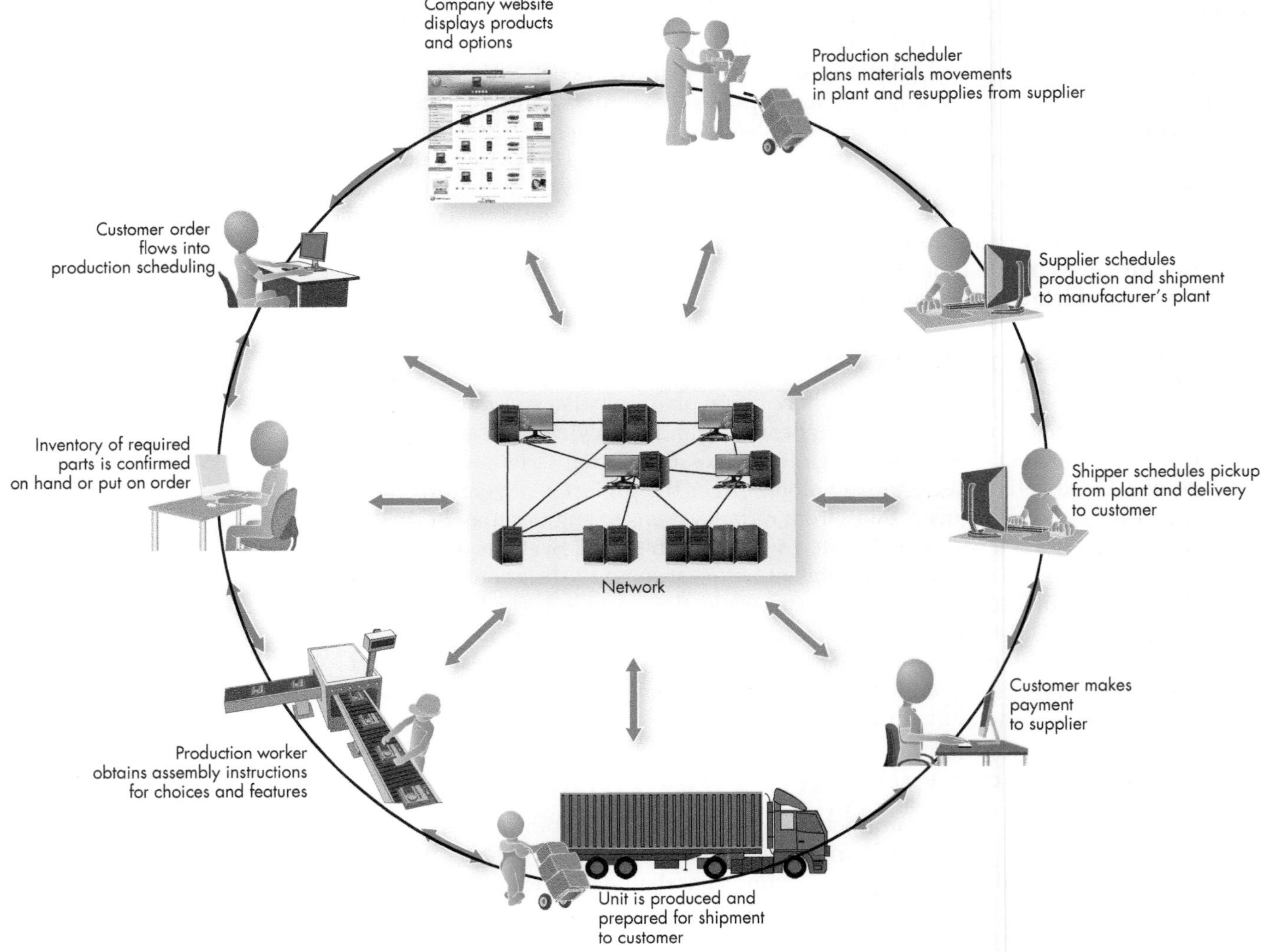

FIGURE 14.1 Networking for Mass Customization of a Physical Product

sending workers out to collect and package the various items and then delivering them to customer cars in the parking lot or directly to customers' homes. In tourism, at Sandals.com, customers have the flexibility of specifying personalized service experiences at the resort, personalizing meal plans during their stay, arranging day trip excursions, and even customizing the travel experience to and from the resort itself.

Providing New Business Opportunities

Not only is IT improving existing businesses, it also is creating entirely new businesses where none existed before. For big businesses, this means developing new products, offering new services, and reaching new clients. Only a few years ago, today's multibillion-dollar behemoth known as Google was a fledgling search engine. That company now boasts not just a search engine but hundreds of services, including virtual maps, YouTube video, Twitter accounts, Facebook pages, instant messaging, Gmail (Google's e-mail service), and online voicemail and software services such as photo editing, cloud storage, and document creation.

IT-based industries, including computer backup and identity-theft protection, offer valuable services for individuals and business customers. Online backup protects against data loss resulting from hard-drive crashes, fire, flood, and other causes. Carbonite.com, Google Cloud Storage, and iCloud, for example, provide automatic continuous backup so clients can recover lost data quickly. For guarding against identity theft, firms such as LifeLock.com and IdentityGuard.com protect personal information by alerting clients to various information-theft risks and sending advice on steps for avoiding identity theft.

The IT landscape has also presented home-based businesses with new e-business opportunities. Consider Ann Marie "Ree" Drummond, better known as "The Pioneer Woman." Drummond was taking a trip from California to New York to start a new life in the city when she stumbled upon a cowboy named Ladd in the small town of Pawhuska, Oklahoma. She fell in love with Ladd and married him, but what about her career? Enter the Internet. Drummond began blogging about food, cooking, and her new life on the ranch and soon developed a following of readers. Her unique style and approach to cooking became so popular that the Food Network approached her about doing her own cooking show. The show became such a success that Drummond soon published her own cookbooks, developed an entire line of cooking supplies, and even established her own online mercantile for fans to order her products. She has also partnered with Walmart, which sells exclusive housewares, clothing, furniture, and frozen food. Today Drummond is worth an estimated $50 million, and her food blog is the most popular on the Internet.[10]

Improving the World and Our Lives

Can advancements in IT really make the world a better place? Developments in smartphones, social networking, home entertainment, automobile safety, and other applications have certainly brought enjoyment and convenience to the everyday lives of millions of people around the globe. Extending technology beyond previous model cell phones and PCs, new technologies provide access to endless choices of *apps* (shorthand for *application software*), allowing you to "build it your way," depending on what you want your device to do and how and where you'll be using it. Apps for computers and smartphones include *programs* for learning languages, music, work, games, traveling, art, home design, business management, and almost any other area of interest. Just two years after its opening, Apple's App Store had supplied more than 40 billion app downloads worldwide to users of Macs, iPhones, iPads, and iPod touches. And that number has continued to grow steadily in the years since.

Social networking, a valuable service for individuals and organizations, is made possible by IT. The many forms of social media—blogs, chats, and networks such as LinkedIn, Twitter, and Facebook—are no longer just playthings for gossips and hobbyists. They're also active tools for getting a job. While many people began working from home during the 2020 pandemic, for some this was not an option they could pursue. For example, those involved in the service industry, such as servers at

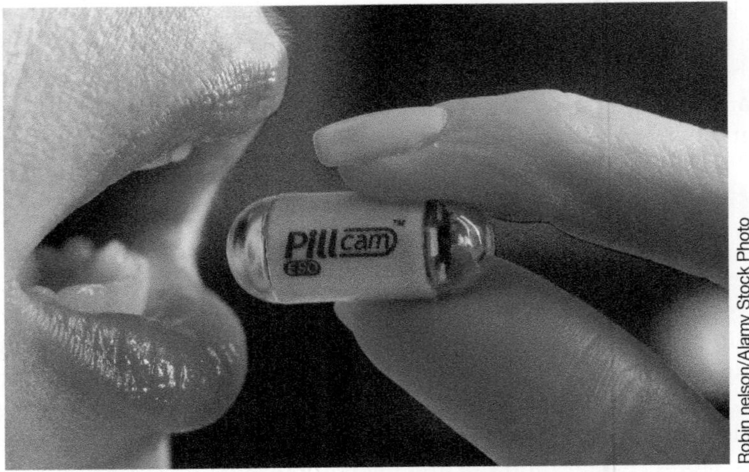

Robin nelson/Alamy Stock Photo

After this capsule is swallowed, the camera inside it can transmit almost 50,000 images during its eight-hour journey through the digestive tract.

restaurants, quickly found themselves out of a job. When the economic meltdown hit, millions of job seekers turned to online networking—tapping leads from friends, colleagues, and acquaintances—for contacts with companies that might be hiring. Peers and recruiters are networking using electronic discussion forums and bulletin boards at websites of professional associations and trade groups, technical schools, and alumni organizations. Some social sites provide occupation-specific career coaching and job tips. Scientists connect with Epernicus, top managers use Meet the Boss and ExecuNet, and graduate students are connecting with Graduate Junction.[11]

Organizations, too, including hospitals and medical equipment companies, have embraced IT advancements to provide better services. For example, when treating combat injuries, surgeons at Walter Reed National Military Medical Center in Bethesda, Maryland, rely on high-tech imaging systems that convert two-dimensional photographs of their patients' anatomies into three-dimensional (3D) physical models for presurgical planning. These 3D mockups of shoulders, femurs, and facial bones give doctors the opportunity to see and feel the anatomy as it will be seen in the operating room before they even use their scalpels. Meanwhile, pill-sized cameras that patients swallow are providing doctors with images of the insides of the human body, helping them make better diagnoses for such diseases as ulcers and cancer.[12]

IT Building Blocks: Business Resources

Learning Objective 14-2

Identify the IT resources businesses have at their disposal and how these resources are used.

Businesses today have a wide variety of IT resources at their disposal. In addition to the Internet and e-mail, these include communications technologies, networks, hardware devices, and software, as shown at technology media sites such as informationweek.com.

The Internet and Other Communication Resources

Internet *gigantic system of interconnected computer networks linked together by voice, electronic, and wireless technologies*

Hypertext Transfer Protocol (HTTP) *communications protocol used for the World Wide Web, in which related pieces of information on separate web pages are connected using hyperlinks*

The **Internet** is a gigantic global system of interconnected computer networks belonging to millions of collaborating organizations and agencies—government, business, academic, and public—linked together by voice, electronic, and wireless technologies.[13] Computers within the networks are connected by various communications protocols, or standardized coding systems, such as the **hypertext transfer protocol (HTTP)** and

hypertext transfer protocol secure (HTTPS), which is used for the **World Wide Web**, a branch of the Internet consisting of interlinked hypertext documents, or web pages. Other protocols serve a variety of purposes, such as sending and receiving e-mail. The World Wide Web and its protocols provide the common language that allows information sharing on the Internet. The Internet has also spawned a number of other business communications technologies, including *intranets, extranets, electronic conferencing*, and *VSAT satellite communications*.

Hypertext Transfer Protocol Secure (HTTPS) *a more secure communications protocol used for the World Wide Web to transmit and present more sensitive information*

World Wide Web *branch of the Internet consisting of interlinked hypertext documents, or web pages*

Intranets Many organizations have extended Internet technology by maintaining what are essentially internal websites linked throughout the business. These private networks, or **intranets**, are accessible only to employees (and others who may be granted access) and may contain confidential information on benefits programs, a learning library, production management tools, product design resources, HR information, and so forth. General Electric's intranet is accessible to 168,000 employees spread across six continents. With so many people working for the company, it is easy for employees to feel disconnected and alone. To combat this, GE redesigned its internal communication via its intranet. In particular, GE created a social media–like platform that allowed employees all over the world to take part in the firm's regular opinion surveys, in which employees get to weigh in on a variety of topics related to the company and its direction. The same platform is used to host regular "town halls" during which company leaders provide information, make announcements, and answer questions. This participation gave employees a voice in the mammoth company and allowed them to feel—rather than disconnected—as if they have a say in the decision-making process.

Intranet *organization's private network of internally linked websites accessible only to employees*

Extranets **Extranets** are similar to intranets but allow more outsiders limited access to a firm's internal information network. The most common application allows buyers to enter a system to see which products are available for sale and delivery, thus providing convenient product availability information. Industrial suppliers are often linked into customers' information networks so that they can see planned production schedules and prepare supplies for customers' upcoming operations. The extranet at Nucor Corporation, for example, lets customers shop electronically through its storage yards and gives them electronic access to Nucor's planned inventory of industrial steel products. Service industries, too, allow customers access to supplies of available services. For example, tour providers such as Tauck, Globus, and Viking River Cruises rely on major airlines such as Delta to provide flights for tour customers. By connecting into Delta's future flight schedules, tour companies can reserve blocks of flight seats to accommodate tourists.

Extranet *system that allows outsiders limited access to a firm's internal information network*

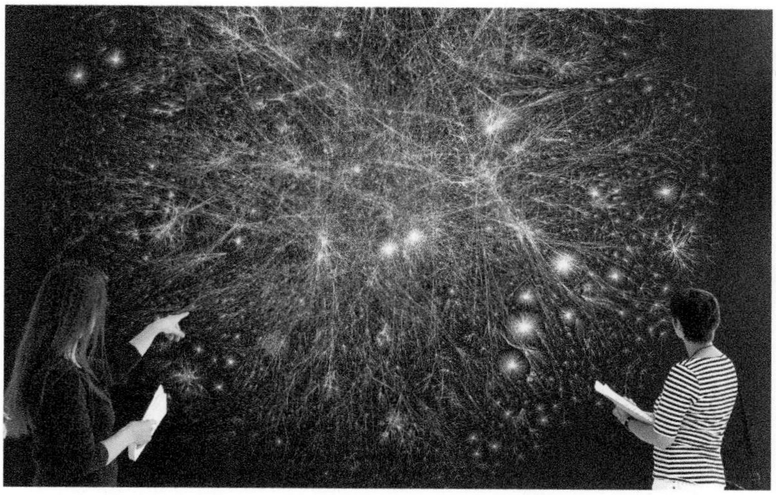

Carsten Rehder/dpa picture alliance/Alamy Stock Photo

The Internet, along with other communication technologies, have myriad uses, and those uses continue to expand at a rapid rate. This image, for instance, is a computer—generated representation of information flows around the world.

Electronic Conferencing *IT that allows groups of people to communicate simultaneously from various locations via e-mail, phone, or video*

Electronic Conferencing **Electronic conferencing** allows groups of people to communicate simultaneously from various locations via e-mail, phone, or video, thereby eliminating travel time and providing immediate contact. *Videoconferencing* allows participants to see one another on digital screens while the conference is in progress. For example, during the 2020 COVID-19 pandemic and the subsequent shelter in place orders, companies were forced to send their employees home in order to combat the spread of the disease. Companies immediately implemented protocols for videoconferencing, such as Zoom and Teams, to bring quarantined workers back into meeting environments. This allowed organizations to maintain function even when employees were, at times, many miles away from their normal workplace.

VSAT Satellite Communications *network of geographically dispersed transmitter-receivers (transceivers) that send signals to and receive signals from a satellite, exchanging voice, video, and data transmissions*

VSAT Satellite Communications Another Internet technology businesses use to communicate is **VSAT satellite communications**. VSAT (short for *very small aperture terminal*) systems have a transmitter-receiver (*transceiver*) that sits outdoors with a direct line of sight to a satellite. The hub, a ground-station computer at the company's headquarters, sends signals to and receives signals from the satellite, exchanging voice, video, and data transmissions. An advantage of VSAT is privacy. A company that operates its own VSAT system has total control over communications among its facilities, no matter their location, without dependence on other companies. A firm might use VSAT to exchange sales and inventory information, advertising messages, and visual presentations between headquarters and store managers at remote sites. For example, offices in Minneapolis, London, and Boston might communicate with headquarters in New York, sending and receiving information via a satellite, as shown in Figure 14.2. The technology surrounding VSAT is continuously improving and is close to eliminating the one

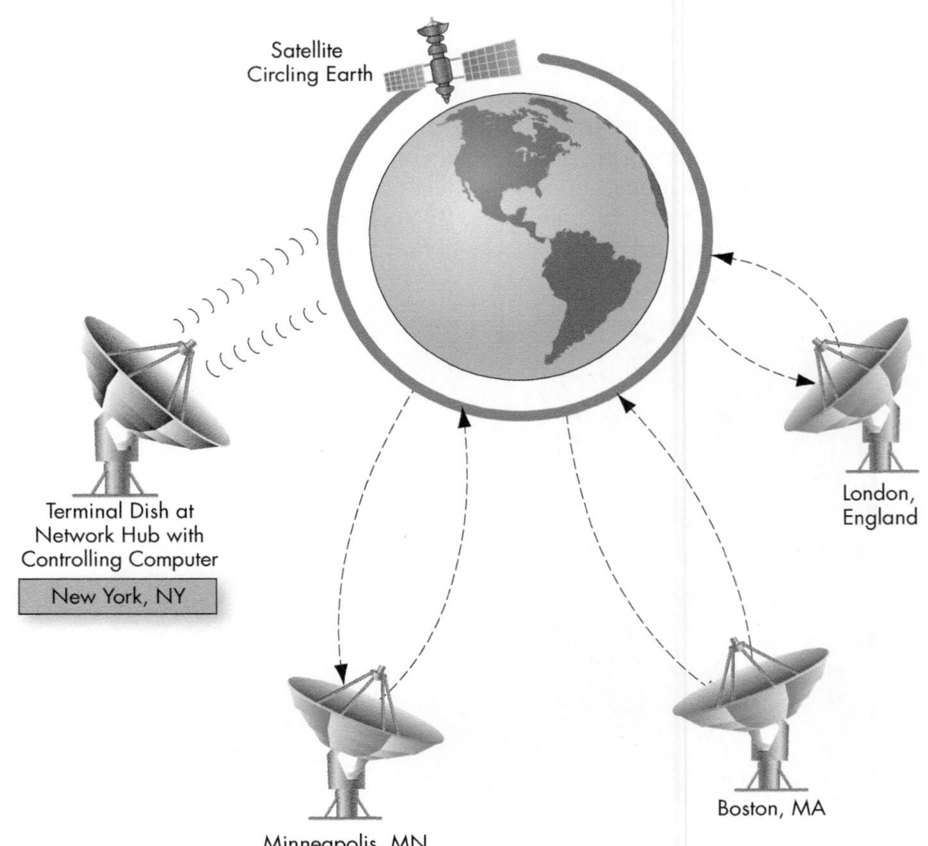

FIGURE 14.2 A VSAT Satellite Communication Network

major drawback of VSAT over the past decade, that it was somewhat slower than traditional networks. However, ongoing improvement of existing technology should find parity with ground-based Internet in the coming years.

Networks: System Architecture

A **computer network** is a group of two or more computers linked together, either hardwired or wirelessly, to share data or resources, such as a printer. The most common type of network used in businesses is a **client–server network**. In client-server networks, *clients* are usually the laptop or desktop computers through which users make requests for information or resources. *Servers* are the computers that provide the services shared by users. In big organizations, servers are usually assigned a specific task. For example, in large organizations it has become more cost efficient to make use of *application servers*, which store the word-processing, spreadsheet, and other programs used by all computers connected to the network. This saves space on individual users' computers and allows for cheaper software licensing for the company. A *print server* controls the printers, stores printing requests from client computers, and routes jobs as the printers become available. An *e-mail server* handles all incoming and outgoing e-mail. With a client–server system, users can share resources and Internet connections—and avoid costly duplication.

Computer Network *group of two or more computers linked together by some form of cabling or by wireless technology to share data or resources, such as a printer*

Client–Server Network *common business network in which clients make requests for information or resources and servers provide the services*

Cloud computing modifies traditional networks by adding an externally located component—the "cloud"—that replaces the functions previously performed by application servers. With a cloud, information resources are retrieved via the Internet from a remote storage service, instead of relying on network-connected user-shared servers for storing data and software packages in client–server systems. Data and software resources are accessible through Internet-based devices, including laptops, desktops, tablets, mobile phones, and other devices with access to the web. The cloud enhances user flexibility, especially for people working remotely, because users can access e-mails and data files from any online location rather than from one particular location.

Further, the storage capacity of the cloud for data is truly massive, allowing for secure storage of significant amounts of data and saving companies money. For example, Amazon's Simple Storage Service (S3) is an example of a *public* cloud that rents Internet storage space where users can store any amount of data and retrieve it anytime from anywhere on the Web. S3 services have become cost savers for companies by eliminating the need for buying, installing, and maintaining in-house server computers, many of which have excessive unused storage capacity "just in case it's needed in the future." S3 allows you to store and manage your application data, search files online, upgrade software quickly, and then download and share data. In contrast with public clouds, *private* cloud services such as JustCloud and ZipCloud provide an added layer of security by surrounding the user-company's storage with a firewall to ensure against intrusion. Private clouds provide added flexibility for creating customized data storage, automated data integration, and integrated software applications to better meet users' needs. Networks can be classified according to geographic scope and means of connection (either wired or wireless).

Wide Area Networks (WANs)

Computers that are linked over long distances—statewide or even nationwide—through long-distance telephone wires, microwave signals, or satellite communications make up what are called **wide area networks (WANs)**. Firms can lease lines from communications vendors or maintain private WANs. Walmart, for example, depends heavily on a private satellite network that links thousands of U.S. and international retail stores to its Bentonville, Arkansas, headquarters.

Wide Area Network (WAN) *computers that are linked over long distances through telephone lines, microwave signals, or satellite communications*

Local Area Networks (LANs)

In **local area networks (LANs)**, computers are linked in a smaller area, such as an office or a building, using fiber-optic or coaxial

Local Area Network (LAN) *computers that are linked in a small area, such as all of a firm's computers within a single building*

cables. For example, a LAN unites hundreds of operators who enter call-in orders at TV's Home Shopping Network facility. The arrangement requires only one computer system with one database and one software system.

Wireless Wide Area Network (WWAN) *network that uses airborne electronic signals instead of wires to link computers and electronic devices over long distances*

Wireless Networks Wireless networks use airborne electronic signals to link network computers and devices. Like wired networks, wireless networks can reach across long distances or exist within a single building or small area. For example, smartphone systems allow users to send and receive transmissions on the **wireless wide area networks (WWANs)** of hundreds of service providers—such as AT&T (United States), T-Mobile (United States), and Vodafone Italia (Italy)—in more than 90 countries throughout the world. A *firewall* provides privacy protection. We'll discuss firewalls in more detail later in the chapter.

Wi-Fi *technology using a wireless local area network*

Wireless Local Area Network (Wireless LAN or WLAN) *local area network with wireless access points*

Wi-Fi You probably use—or have at least heard of—"hotspots." Millions of locations worldwide, such as coffee shops, hotels, airports, and cities, use hotspots that provide wireless Internet connections for people on the go. Each hotspot, or **Wi-Fi** (a play on the audio recording term *Hi-Fi*) access point, uses its own small network, called a **wireless local area network (wireless LAN or WLAN)**. Although wireless service is free at some hotspots, others charge a fee—a daily or hourly rate—for the convenience of Wi-Fi service.

The benefit of Wi-Fi is that its millions of users are not tethered to a cable for accessing the Internet, which essentially allows users to take the Internet with them. Employees can wait for a delayed plane in the airport and still be online through their wireless-enabled laptops or other devices. However, as with every technology, Wi-Fi has limitations, including a short range of distance. This means that your laptop's Internet connection can be severed if you move farther than about 300 feet from the hotspot. In addition, thick walls, construction beams, and other obstacles can interfere with the signals sent out by the network. So, although a city may have hundreds of hotspots, your laptop must remain near one to stay connected. *WiMAX* (*Worldwide Interoperability for Microwave Access*), the next step in wireless advancements, improves this distance limitation with its wireless range of up to 30 miles. Additionally, *LTE (Long Term Evolution)* describes the cellular advancements of both 4G and 5G, which are challenging some of the fastest direct Internet and data connections.

"Super Wi-Fi" Network *a powerful Wi-Fi network with extensive reach and strong signals that flow freely through physical objects such as walls*

Suggesting a bolder approach for the future, a few years ago the U.S. Federal Communications Commission announced a proposed multiyear project for nationwide **"super Wi-Fi" networks** to be developed by the federal government. More powerful than today's networks, the super Wi-Fi would have further reach, stretching across major metropolitan areas and covering much of the rural countryside as well. Super Wi-Fi's stronger signals would flow more freely, without obstruction, through concrete walls, steel beams, forests, and hills. The proposal would enable users to surf the Internet and make mobile phone calls without paying a monthly cell phone bill or Internet bill.[14] Scientists have also encouraged the government to use the bandwidth from old television frequencies to support super Wi-Fi.

Airlines, too, are expanding Wi-Fi service beyond just domestic flights by providing satellite-based Internet service on long-haul international flights. Japan Airlines offers Wi-Fi on routes between New York and Tokyo, in addition to flights between Tokyo and Los Angeles, Chicago, and Jakarta, Indonesia. Other airlines gearing up for (or already providing) Wi-Fi on long-haul flights include Air France, Delta, and United. Indeed, by 2026 it is expected that Wi-Fi service will be provided by almost all airlines.

Finally, *groupware*—software that connects group members for message distribution, electronic meetings, message storing, appointments and schedules, and group writing—allows people to collaborate from their own desktop PCs, even if they're remotely located. It is especially useful when people work together regularly and rely heavily on information sharing. Groupware systems include EGroupware, Google's G Suite, and, on a more simplistic level, GroupMe.

Wearable Technology Wearable technology refers to electronic devices that can be worn on the body, typically as accessories or clothing items, and are designed to provide various functionalities and features. These devices are equipped with sensors, processors, and wireless connectivity, allowing them to collect data, perform computations, and interact with other devices or networks.

Examples of wearable technology include smartwatches, fitness trackers, smart glasses, smart clothing, smart jewelry, and head-mounted displays, including virtual reality (VR) headsets. These and other emerging forms of wearable technology can assist users to better monitor their health and wellness, be more productive, and establish connections with first responders in the event of an accident or other safety concerns.

entrepreneurship and new ventures

Beyond Contactless Payment

In 2007, the motion-tracking Fitbit introduced wearable technology to everyday consumers. The company's bracelet measured steps taken, distance traveled, target heart rate, and other exercise metrics. Since then, the market has seen countless wearable tech products, including the ubiquitous Apple Watch, which is worn on millions of arms worldwide. Wearable tech is increasingly popular thanks to increasing functionality and decreasing price and size.

Wearable tech is also gaining popularity in the workplace. Where employees might have had to stamp a timecard or swipe a badge to track time or enter a workplace, now a simple wave of the arm will get them what they need. Amazon employees can use smart glasses that allow for hands-free operation and real-time data updates, and many law enforcement agencies use body-mounted cameras for documentation and public safety.

Implantable technology has been around since cardiology patients started getting pacemakers. Devices that take blood sugar readings and deliver appropriate insulin dosages have freed people with diabetes from endless finger pricks and injections. Patients with chronic pain may be able to opt into a device—like Proclaim from Abbott—that takes biometric readings and interprets pain signals to receive real-time pain relief delivered automatically.[15]

The next advancement in biotech is already here. As of 2023, more than 50,000 people have opted for surgical implantation of a chip between their thumb and first finger, serving as a swipeable house key or payment method. Instead of holding their phone or card next to a reader, they simply wave their hand to complete the transaction.[16]

PopTika/Shutterstock

Swedish tech pioneer Jowan Österlund began implanting these tiny devices in 2019, and in 2023, the British firm BioTeq Limited introduced additional assistive capabilities with such a chip.[17] These chips help people with mobility or strength issues easily unlock and open doors, gain access to their cars without having to manage a key fob or door handle, and offer audible cues to vision-impaired customers to help with orientation and navigation.[18]

Ethical issues arise with these leaps in technology. From privacy and security concerns to governmental oversight, the answers are unclear. Some regions have already passed laws to prevent employers from requiring implantable tech, but ethicists warn that in other areas, these implantable chips could be used by an authoritarian government for control of a populace. Wearable and implantable technology—like other forms of artificial intelligence—is definitely developing faster than the rules and laws that regulate their use.

Learning Objective 14-3

Describe the role of information systems, the different types of information systems, and how businesses use such systems.

Information Systems: Harnessing the Competitive Power of IT

Information System (IS) *system that uses IT resources to convert data into information and to collect, process, and transmit that information for use in decision making*

Data *raw facts and figures that, by themselves, may not have much meaning*

Information *meaningful, useful interpretation of data*

Business today relies on information management in ways that no one could have foreseen a decade ago. Managers now treat IT as a basic organizational resource for conducting daily business. At major firms, every activity—designing services, ensuring product delivery and cash flow, and evaluating employee performance—is linked to *information systems*. An **information system (IS)** uses IT resources that enable managers to take **data**, raw facts and figures that, by themselves, may not have much meaning, and turn those data into **information**, the meaningful, useful interpretation of data. Information systems also enable managers to collect, process, and transmit that information for use in decision making.

Walmart is well known for its strategic use of information systems. The nerve center for company operations is a centralized IS in Bentonville, Arkansas. The IS drives costs down and raises efficiency because the same methods and systems are applied for all 10,500-plus stores in 27 countries. Data on the billions of sales transactions—time, date, and place—flow to Bentonville. The IS tracks millions of stock-keeping units (SKUs) weekly; enforces uniform reordering and delivery procedures on its more than 100,000 suppliers, including over 20,000 in China; and regulates the flow of merchandise through its distribution centers and stores.

Beyond the firm's daily operations, information systems are also crucial in planning. Managers routinely use the IS to decide on products and markets for the next 5 to 10 years. The company's vast database enables marketing managers to analyze customer demographics for better marketing, and it is also used for financial planning, materials handling, and electronic funds transfers with suppliers and customers.

Information Systems Managers *managers who are responsible for the systems used for gathering, organizing, and distributing information*

Walmart, like most businesses, regards its information as a private resource, an asset that's planned, developed, and protected. Therefore, it's not surprising that they have **information systems managers** who are responsible for the systems used for gathering, organizing, and distributing information, just as they have production, marketing, and finance managers. These managers use many of the IT resources we discussed previously—the Internet, communications technologies, networks, hardware, and software—to sift through information and apply it to their jobs.

Leveraging Information Resources: Data Warehousing and Data Mining

Almost everything you do leaves a trail of information about you. Your preferences in movie rentals, television viewing, online searches, and grocery buying; your phone calls, your credit card charges, your financial status; and personal information about your age, gender, marital status, and even your health are just a few of the items about each of us that are stored in scattered databases. The behavior patterns of millions of users can be traced by analyzing files of information gathered over time from their online activity and in-store purchases.

Data Warehousing *the collection, storage, and retrieval of data in electronic files*

The collection, storage, and retrieval of such data in electronic files is called **data warehousing**. For managers, the data warehouse can be a gold mine of information about their business. Indeed, Kroger Co., the Ohio-based grocery chain, collects data on customer shopping habits to find ways to gain greater customer loyalty. As part owner of a data-mining firm, Kroger accumulates information from its shopper cards, analyzes the data to uncover shopping patterns, and sends money-saving coupons to regular customers for the specific products they usually buy. Kroger's precision targeting pays off, especially in a sluggish economy. With a rate of coupon usage that is around 50 times the industry average, it's a money saver for Kroger customers and boosts the company's sales, too.[19] To help put this in context, coupons from Kroger's quarterly mailers, uniquely customized for each customer, have a 70 percent redemption rate within six weeks of delivery.

Data Warehousing and data mining have become increasingly important resources for businesses today. Meta for Business and Amazon Web Services are two of the largest firms that provide these resources today.

Data Mining After collecting information, managers use **data mining**, the application of advanced statistical analyses and electronic technologies for searching, sifting, and reorganizing pools of data to uncover useful information. Data mining helps managers plan for new products, set prices, and identify trends and shopping patterns. By analyzing what consumers actually do, businesses can determine what subsequent purchases they are likely to make and then send them tailor-made ads. And data mining is happening at every click within the Internet. Amazon, for example, realizes that to capture continuous business it needs to focus advertising as much as possible, yet this is extremely challenging when you deal in as many products as Amazon does. Data warehousing and data mining are used as a partial solution. With every click on the Amazon website, what you looked at is tracked and catalogued. Then, based on the patterns of your browsing, previous buying history, and so forth, Amazon determines which of the items viewed you are most likely to purchase. In the event that you do not end up buying anything, you are likely to find advertisements for those same items in your social media feeds the next day. This is targeted marketing at its best, and data warehousing gives Amazon the power to make it work.

Data Mining *the application of electronic technologies for searching, sifting, and reorganizing pools of data to uncover useful information*

Information Linkages with Suppliers The top priority for Walmart's IS—improving in-stock reliability—requires integration of Walmart and suppliers' activities with store sales. That's why Procter & Gamble (P&G), Johnson & Johnson, and other suppliers connect into Walmart's information system to observe up-to-the-minute sales data on individual items, at the individual store level. They can use the system's online tools—spreadsheets, sales forecasting, and even weather information—to forecast sales demand and plan delivery schedules. Coordinated planning avoids excessive inventories, speeds up deliveries, and holds down costs throughout the supply chain while keeping shelves stocked for retail customers.

Types of Information Systems

Employees have a variety of responsibilities and decision-making needs, and a firm's IS may actually be a set of multiple systems that share information while serving different levels of the organization, different departments, or different operations. Because they work on different kinds of problems, managers and their employees have access to the specialized information systems that satisfy their specific information needs.

In addition to different types of users, each business *function*—marketing, human resources, accounting, production, and finance—has special information needs, as do groups working on major projects. Each user group and department, therefore, may need a special information system.

managing in turbulent times

Protecting More Than Data

fizkes/123RF

In 2023, a series of ransomware attacks stopped business at a number of organizations. Dole Food Company, a giant in the industry, was forced to stop operations and temporarily shut down all its sites in the United States, halting everything from production lines to deliveries, because of a ransomware attack. Yum! Brands, owner of KFC, Pizza Hut, and Taco Bell, temporarily closed 300 of its restaurant locations in the United Kingdom to isolate and respond to an attack. The city of Oakland, California, had to take all its systems offline until it could secure its network. And the United Kingdom's mail delivery service, the Royal Mail, was hit by a ransomware attack that severely impacted both domestic and international deliveries.[20]

Ransomware attacks are malware designed to lock a user out of a system until they pay a ransom to regain access. Ransomware is so profitable that it's become its own industry, where hackers develop the malware and then sell it to users for an upfront fee plus a portion of the ransom. These are just a few of the most visible ransomware attacks in a single year. Statista reports that over 493 million ransomware attacks were reported worldwide in 2022. That number doesn't include small businesses or individuals who simply paid the ransom to regain access to their data.[21]

Cybersecurity expert Cherie Griffith-Dunn launched Cyproteck in 2000 to combat this kind of attack. In addition to helping its clients defend their organizations against attack, Cyproteck helps companies recover data and works with law enforcement agencies to help track down attackers. The company specializes in small businesses that may not see themselves as vulnerable, so a lot of Griffith-Dunn's job entails education and training.[22]

As a Black woman founder of a cybersecurity firm, Griffith-Dunn is something of a unicorn in the white male–dominated industry. In 2015, she founded CGD Government Solutions to offer a full suite of security audits, consulting, coaching, training, project management, and more. Cyproteck grew out of her work with various companies and governments.

Griffith-Dunn, who is an author, speaker, and podcaster, describes herself as "feminine and hardcore." She uses her experiences growing up in a mixed-race household and raising six sons to inform her coaching and speaking and acknowledges, "Living in a world where discrimination never shuts off, I found myself living by my parents' creed to keep up and stand out. 'Work ten times harder than the next to get ahead.'" Griffith-Dunn uses her experiences to teach others—especially women of color—how to operate in the technology sector and in other careers. Her work with Cyproteck combines with her coaching and education work to improve the landscape for other women while protecting vulnerable clients.

This type of knowledge segmentation is based on the general idea that workers function best when they have only the knowledge they need without being overburdened by information they do not need. However, as we will see in the sections below, modern business is beginning to challenge this notion. This is particularly true as we begin to consider the impact of knowledge workers in the modern work environment.

Knowledge Management System *information system that supports knowledge workers by providing resources to create, store, use, and transmit new knowledge for useful applications*

Computer-Aided Design (CAD) *IS with software that helps knowledge workers design products by simulating them and displaying them in three-dimensional graphics*

Information Systems for Knowledge Workers As we discussed in Chapter 10, *knowledge workers* are employees for whom information and knowledge constitute the core of their work, such as engineers, scientists, and IT specialists who rely on IT to design new products or create new processes. These workers require **knowledge management systems**, which provide resources to create, store, use, and transmit new knowledge for useful applications—for instance, databases to organize and retrieve information and computational power for data analysis.

Specialized support systems have also increased the productivity of knowledge workers. **Computer-aided design (CAD)** helps knowledge workers—and now many other kinds of people, too, as we saw with consumers designing customized

Mocart/Shutterstock

The 3D computer model of this dinosaur is constructed from digital scans of fossilized tissue.

products earlier in this chapter—design products ranging from cell phones to jewelry to auto parts by simulating them and displaying them in 3D graphics. In a more advanced version, known as *rapid prototyping*, the CAD system electronically transfers instructions to a computer-controlled machine that quickly builds a prototype—a physical model—of the newly designed product, such as a toy, an artificial limb for people with disabilities, or a solar panel. The older method—making handcrafted prototypes from wood, plastic, or clay—is replaced with faster, cheaper prototyping. The ultimate manifestation of this process is 3D printing, in which CAD is literally produced to actual specifications before our eyes.

CAD is helping archaeological scientists uncover secrets hidden in fossils using 3D computer models of skeletons, organs, and tissues constructed with digital data from computed tomography (CT) scans of dinosaur fossils. From these models, scientists have learned, for example, that the neck of the giant *Apatosaurus* curved downward instead of high in the air as once thought. By seeing how the animals' bones fit together with cartilage, ligaments, and vertebrae, scientists are discovering more about how these prehistoric creatures interacted with their environment.[23] The same technology helps archaeologists "see" underground without digging, helping them locate significant sites or buried objects.

Computer-Aided Manufacturing (CAM) *IS that uses computers to design and control equipment in a manufacturing process*

In a direct offshoot of computer-aided design, **computer-aided manufacturing (CAM)** uses computers to design and control the equipment needed in a manufacturing process. For example, CAM systems can produce digital instructions to control all the machines and robots on a production line, say, as an example, in making jewelry cases. CAM-guided machines cut the materials, move them through the stages of production, and then assemble each stylish case without human physical involvement in production activities. CAD and CAM coupled together (CAD/CAM) are useful to engineers in a manufacturing environment for designing and testing new products and then designing the machines and tools to manufacture those products.

It is interesting that with the dawn of the knowledge worker, the previous thinking concerning how information and knowledge should be segmented to employees—in other words, that employees needed to understand or think only about information that was directly pertinent to their job—is being challenged. This is because knowledge work crosses many areas of the company, and, as such, those involved need to know how other areas of the company function, what the requirements of those areas are, and what the limitations of those areas are. As knowledge work continues to advance, the need for a more systems-based approach to knowledge sharing is being felt every day.

Information Systems for Managers In contrast to the previous notion about knowledge workers, each manager's information activities and IS needs vary according to that manager's functional area (accounting or human resources and so forth) and management level. The following are some popular information systems used by managers for different purposes.

Enterprise Resource Planning (ERP) *information system for organizing and managing a firm's activities across product lines, departments, and geographical location*

Enterprise Resource Planning With digital processing of databases, specialized software, and interactive networks, instantaneous information is accessible and useful to all levels of management. For example, consider **enterprise resource planning (ERP)**, which is an information system for organizing and managing a firm's activities across product lines, departments, and geographic locations. The ERP stores real-time information on work status and upcoming transactions and notifies employees when action is required if certain schedules are to be met. It coordinates internal operations with activities of outside suppliers and notifies customers of upcoming deliveries and billings. Consequently, more managers routinely use it for planning and controlling company-wide operations. Today, a manager at Hershey Foods, for example, uses ERP to check on the current status of any customer order for Kisses or strawberry Twizzlers, inspect productivity statistics for each workstation, and analyze the delivery performance on any shipment. Managers can better coordinate company-wide performance. They can identify departments that are working well together and those that are lagging behind schedule and creating bottlenecks.

Management Information System (MIS) *computer system that supports managers by providing information—reports, schedules, plans, and budgets—that can be used for making decisions*

Management Information Systems **Management information systems (MIS)** support managers by providing reports, schedules, plans, and budgets that can then be used for making both short- and long-term decisions. For example, at Walsworth, which specializes in printing yearbooks and trade publications, managers rely on detailed information—current customer orders, staffing schedules, employee attendance, production schedules, equipment status, and materials availability—for moment-to-moment decisions during the day. They require similar information to plan such midrange activities as employee training, materials movements, and cash flows. They also need to anticipate the status of the jobs and projects assigned to their departments. Many management information systems—cash flow, sales, production scheduling, and shipping—are indispensable for helping managers complete these tasks.

For longer-range decisions involving business strategy, Walsworth managers need information to analyze trends in the publishing industry and overall company performance. They need both external and internal information, current and future, to compare current performance data to data from previous years and to analyze consumer trends and economic forecasts.

Decision Support System (DSS) *interactive system that creates virtual business models for a particular kind of decision and tests them with different data to see how they respond*

Decision Support Systems Managers who face a particular kind of decision repeatedly can get assistance from **decision support systems (DSS)**, interactive systems that create virtual business models and test them with different data to see how they respond. When faced with decisions on plant capacity, for example, Walsworth managers can use a capacity DSS. The manager inputs data on anticipated sales, working capital, and customer-delivery requirements. The data flow into the DSS processor, which then simulates the plant's performance under the proposed data conditions. A proposal to increase facility capacity by, say, 10 percent could be simulated to find costs of operation, percent of customer order fulfillments, and other performance measures that would result due to the expanded capacity. After experimenting with various data conditions, the DSS makes recommendations on the best levels of plant capacity—those that result in best performance—for each future time period.

Artificial Intelligence

Artificial Intelligence (AI) *computer systems and algorithms that are capable of performing tasks that typically require human intelligence*

Artificial intelligence (AI) refers to computer systems and algorithms that are capable of performing tasks that typically require human intelligence, including solving complex problems, analyzing data, uncovering relationships, and making decisions.

ChatGPT, an AI language model, identified five key concepts in artificial intelligence:

1 ***Machine learning (ML).*** Algorithms and statistical models allow machines to learn from data and improve their performance without additional programming. ML involves using large volumes of data to train models, which is the process of allowing ML programs to analyze inputs, make predictions, and test those predictions on new data sets. As this process repeats, ML models are able to recognize patterns, improve their predictions, and classify information based on what they have been trained on.

2 ***Neural networks.*** A fundamental component of AI is inspired by the human brain's structure and functioning. Neural networks consist of interconnected nodes that process and transmit information. Neural networks can learn from examples, adjust their internal parameters, and make predictions or decisions.

3 ***Natural language processing (NLP).*** In order for machines to effectively communicate with humans, they need to be able to synthesize and use language. NLP programs are trained on inputs that come from human speech and written language, analyze its meaning, and respond to questions. This is particularly useful in language translation, sentiment analysis, chatbots, and voice recognition.

4 ***Computer vision.*** Computer vision focuses on enabling machines to understand and interpret visual information from images or videos. It involves tasks such as object detection, image classification, facial recognition, and scene understanding. One application of computer vision is automatic braking systems in newer cars. For example, a car might be equipped with computers that are trained to analyze the backup camera's frame and automatically stop the car when it identifies a person, animal, or object.

5 ***Robotics.*** When AI is combined with mechanical engineering, the resulting machines can interact with the physical world, navigate environments, and execute complex actions based on algorithms.

AI in Action

AI is being used in a number of different areas. These applications of artificial intelligence include:

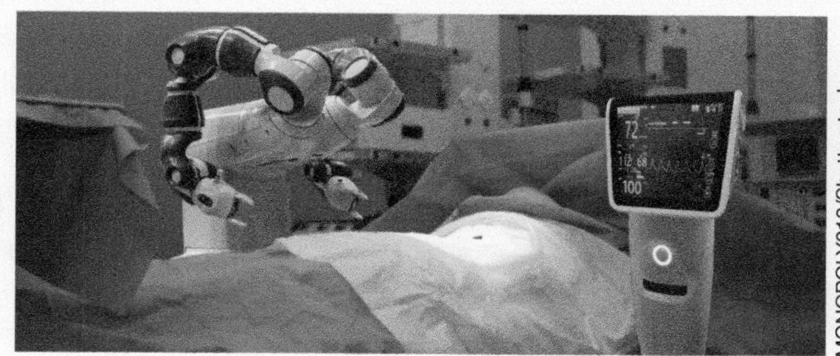

MONOPOLY919/Shutterstock

1 ***Health care.*** AI is applied in medical imaging analysis, disease diagnosis, drug discovery, personalized medicine, and patient monitoring. It can help in the early detection of diseases, improving treatment plans, and enhancing health care delivery.

2 ***Autonomous vehicles.*** AI is a key component in the development of self-driving cars and autonomous vehicles. It involves perception, decision-making, and control systems to navigate and interact with the environment.

3 ***Virtual assistants.*** AI powers virtual assistants like Siri, Alexa, or Google Assistant, which can understand voice commands, answer questions, perform tasks, and provide personalized recommendations.

4 ***Finance and trading.*** AI algorithms are used in financial institutions for tasks such as fraud detection, risk assessment, algorithmic trading, and credit scoring.

5 ***Manufacturing and automation.*** AI is used to optimize manufacturing processes, monitor equipment performance, predict maintenance needs, and automate repetitive tasks in industries.

6 ***Natural language processing.*** AI-based language processing systems are used for automated translation, sentiment analysis, chatbots, voice assistants, and content generation.

7 ***Gaming.*** AI techniques are employed in computer games to create intelligent virtual characters, enhance gameplay, and provide realistic simulations.

Source: This box was created by ChatGPT.

Predictive Analytics *the process of analyzing historical data, statistical models, and machine learning techniques to predict future outcomes or behaviors*

Predictive Analytics **Predictive analytics** involves using AI models to analyze historical data and use the findings to predict future outcomes. This can be useful in forecasting events or behaviors that are likely to occur under similar conditions as they did in the past. For example, Netflix uses predictive analytics to create recommender algorithms that can suggest other movies a customer might like based on what they previously watched and enjoyed. The same approach works in online retail, where customers are shown additional products after putting an item in their cart.

AI in Action

The key steps involved in predictive analytics are:

1. ***Data collection.*** Gathering relevant data from various sources, such as databases, sensors, or online platforms.
2. ***Data cleaning and preprocessing.*** Cleaning the data, handling missing values, removing outliers, and transforming the data into a suitable format for analysis.
3. ***Feature selection and engineering.*** Identifying the most relevant variables (features) that are likely to impact the prediction and creating new features based on domain knowledge or data transformations.
4. ***Model selection and training.*** Choosing an appropriate predictive model, such as regression, decision trees, or neural networks, and training it using historical data. The model learns the patterns and relationships in the data during the training process.
5. ***Model evaluation.*** Assessing the performance of the trained model using evaluation metrics, such as accuracy, precision, recall, or area under the curve (AUC), to determine how well it predicts the outcomes.
6. ***Prediction and deployment.*** Using the trained model to make predictions on new, unseen data and integrating the predictive model into business processes or applications.

Source: This box was created by ChatGPT.

Machine Learning *a subset of artificial intelligence (AI) that focuses on algorithms and statistical models that enable computers to learn from data and make predictions or decisions without explicit programming*

Machine Learning **Machine learning** is a subset of artificial intelligence (AI) that aims to develop algorithms that can change and adapt without additional programming as they find new patterns. ML programs can respond to changes in inputs to make better decisions and fine-tune their predictions over time.

ChatGPT identified the following uses for ML:

1. ***Training data.*** Providing a large, labeled data set for the algorithm to learn patterns and relationships between input features and corresponding output labels.
2. ***Feature extraction.*** Identifying relevant features from the input data that contribute to the desired prediction or decision.
3. ***Model selection and training.*** Choosing an appropriate machine learning algorithm (e.g., linear regression, decision trees, support vector machines, or neural networks) and training it using the labeled training data.
4. ***Model evaluation.*** Assessing the trained model's performance using evaluation metrics, cross-validation, or separate test data sets to ensure it generalizes well to unseen data.
5. ***Prediction and deployment.*** Using the trained model to make predictions or decisions on new, unseen data.

AI in Action

ChatGPT is a state-of-the-art language model developed by OpenAI. It is part of the GPT series, which stands for "Generative Pre-trained Transformer," and builds upon the success of previous iterations like GPT-2 and GPT-3. GPT-3.5, based on the GPT-3 architecture, is one of the most advanced versions.

ChatGPT is specifically designed for generating humanlike text responses in conversational settings. It has been trained on a massive amount of diverse text data from the Internet, enabling it to understand and generate coherent and contextually relevant responses across a wide range of topics.

Iryna Imago/Shutterstock

Key Features and Capabilities of ChatGPT

1 ***Natural language understanding.*** ChatGPT has a strong ability to understand and interpret human language. It can comprehend and respond to a wide array of questions, prompts, and statements, making it suitable for engaging in dynamic and interactive conversations.

2 ***Contextual understanding.*** ChatGPT maintains contextual understanding throughout a conversation, allowing it to generate responses that take into account the previous context and provide coherent and contextually appropriate replies.

3 ***Coherence and fluency.*** The model generates text that is generally fluent and coherent, making it capable of producing meaningful and contextually relevant responses. However, occasional errors or nonsensical outputs can still occur.

4 ***Open-ended dialogue.*** ChatGPT excels at engaging in open-ended conversations, where it can provide informative or creative responses, share opinions, suggest ideas, or even tell stories based on the given prompts or queries.

5 ***Topic versatility.*** It can discuss a wide range of subjects due to its training on a diverse corpus of text from various domains. While it strives to provide accurate and helpful information, it's important to verify the information it generates for critical or sensitive topics.

6 ***Limitations.*** While ChatGPT is a powerful language model, it has certain limitations. It may sometimes provide incorrect or incomplete information, generate responses that sound plausible but are factually inaccurate, exhibit sensitivity to phrasing, or respond to harmful or biased instructions if not explicitly guided to avoid such behavior.

Uses and Applications

1 ***Personal assistance.*** ChatGPT can provide quick answers to questions, assist with general information, help with task management, or engage in small talk.

2 ***Content generation.*** It can aid in content creation for writing, brainstorming ideas, generating storylines, or assisting in creative tasks like character development.

3 ***Customer support.*** ChatGPT can support customer interactions by providing initial assistance, answering frequently asked questions, or guiding users through basic troubleshooting.

4 ***Education and learning.*** It can act as an educational resource, providing explanations, clarifications, or answering queries on a wide range of topics.

5 ***Research and information retrieval.*** ChatGPT can assist researchers or professionals in retrieving information, suggesting relevant sources, or providing insights into various subjects.

Source: This box was created by ChatGPT.

Learning Objective 14-4

Identify the threats and risks information technology poses to businesses.

IT Risks and Threats

Unfortunately, the growth and increased sophistication of information technology have been accompanied by parallel growth in risks and threats to those who use it. These risks and threats range from mild nuisance to theft to outright destruction. Casual IT users everywhere are finding that even social networking and cell phones have a "dark side"—privacy invasion. Facebook postings of personal information about users have been intercepted and misused by intruders. Beacon, the former data-gathering service, caused a public uproar when it published peoples' online purchases publicly on their Facebook newsfeeds. And with cellular technology, some features of Bluetooth connections allow savvy intruders to access a victim's text messages, listen in on live conversations, and even view unwary users' photos.[24]

Additionally, some leakages of data flow from within the organization itself. For example, accidental data leakage occurs frequently in organizations. This type of leakage is truly unintentional, such as when an employee sends a text message to a client with confidential information enclosed in the text, only to discover that she or he sent it to the wrong client by mistake. At other times, the leakage is more malicious, as when an employee becomes angry and decides to take information outside the organization and leak it for spiteful reasons, a phenomenon known as *data exfiltration*.[25]

Businesses, too, are affected by IT's dark side. Hackers break into computers, stealing personal information about both customers and employees as well as confidential information. Meanwhile, the ease of online information sharing has proven costly for companies who are having an increasingly difficult time protecting their intellectual property, and viruses that crash computers have cost companies many billions annually. Over the years, the perception of hackers as being enterprising young people engaged in a game of cat-and-mouse with larger systems has changed to that of criminals who are intent on causing disruption or even financial ruin. In this section, we'll look at these and other IT risks. In the next section, we'll discuss ways in which businesses are protecting themselves from these risks.

Hackers

Hacker *cybercriminal who gains unauthorized access to a computer or network, either to steal information, money, or property or to tamper with data*

The term *breaking and entering* once referred to physical intrusion, but today it applies to IT intrusions as well. **Hackers** are cybercriminals who gain unauthorized access to a computer or network, either to steal information, money, or property or to tamper with data. Hackers once accessed Twitter's systems and may have intercepted information—names, passwords, e-mail addresses—of some 250,000 of the social media's users. With different motives than the Twitter intruders, Chinese-based hackers, including the Chinese government, are suspected of continuing cyberattacks into the computer systems of several newspapers, including the *New York Times*, the *Washington Post*, and the *Wall Street Journal*. China-based intruders have been accused of a multiyear campaign to illegally gain corporate secrets and confidential information that can be used to frighten critics from writing unfavorable articles, accusations that the Chinese government has denied.[26] And there were widespread charges that Russian hackers attempted to influence the outcome of the 2016 U.S. presidential election. North Korea also relies on state-sponsored hacking groups to penetrate banking systems and steal money. In 2016, North Korea's infamous Lazarus Group attempted to steal $1 billion from the Bangladesh Bank, the country's central bank. The U.S. Federal Reserve and the FBI flagged the activity as suspicious and managed to stop most of the transactions, but the cyberthieves managed to steal $81 million.[27] In 2022, the Lazarus Group targeted the blockchain project of Axie Infinity, an online game company, to steal $620 million in virtual currency.[28]

Another common hacker activity is to launch *denial of service (DoS) attacks*. DoS attacks flood networks or websites with bogus requests for information and resources, thereby overloading and shutting the networks or websites down. These shutdowns, in turn, prevent legitimate users from accessing them. The result is a reduction in profitability for the company and sunk costs of the manpower needed to get the system up and running again.

One need only walk into local businesses and look for open or "free" Wi-Fi on your phone to see how dangerously unprotected networks are. These open networks allow access from anyone but provide little or no security to the users who access them. These types of open networks are a fertile ground for hackers to access information on the users without their knowing. Once inside an unsecured wireless network, hackers (sometimes called wireless moochers in these cases) can use it to conduct illegal business, such as child pornography or money laundering. When law enforcement officers try to track down these criminals through their Internet usage, they are long gone. However, the innocent but naïve network host has now been potentially exposed to criminal prosecution. One of the best ways to protect yourself on an open Wi-Fi network is through using a virtual private network (VPN). We can think of a VPN as an encrypted pipeline between the user and the network. Information is the most accessible on its way from the user to the network, and a VPN provides total encryption, which prevents others from accessing information.

Hackers often break into company networks to steal company or trade secrets. But not only hackers are doing the stealing. Because the chances of getting caught seem slim, some home users continue, illegally, to download unpaid-for movies, music, and other resources from file-swapping networks. A recent study shows that video piracy costs U.S. businesses at least $29.2 billion annually and job losses of around 230,000 jobs annually.[29] However, these losses also showcase what can happen to businesses that fail to adapt to changes in technology. For example, for years the music recording industry was reluctant to embrace online distribution as a revenue path, preferring to prosecute pirates rather than offer them legal online alternatives. In contrast, Apple has benefited immensely from its online (download) distribution models, enabling it to become one of the world's most popular music vendors.[30]

Identity Theft

Once inside a computer network, hackers are able to commit **identity theft**, such as stealing personal information (for example, an individual's Social Security number and address) to get loans, credit cards, or other monetary benefits by impersonating the victim. Recent studies suggest that as many as 16.6 million victims fall prey to identify theft each year, and many fail to realize it until it is far too late and the criminals are long gone. Indeed, identity theft is among the fastest-growing crimes in the United States and the world.

Identity Theft *unauthorized use of personal information (such as Social Security number and address) to get loans, credit cards, or other monetary benefits by impersonating the victim*

Clever crooks get information on unsuspecting victims by digging in trash, stealing mail, or using *phishing* or *pharming* schemes to lure online users to bogus websites. For instance, in a recent ploy, criminals, posing as representatives of state government, send an e-mail to users. The users are notified that an old insurance policy overbilled them and that they are entitled to reimbursement. The users need only to visit a website and fill out some information. If the users click on the provided link, they are transferred to a spoofed (falsified) web page that looks very official and is, in fact, modeled after a given state's web page. The users then enter the requested information: Social Security number, address, credit card information, bank account numbers, and so forth. In the end, the users think that they are going to receive a check in the mail, but all they have really done is provide a thief with the information needed to apply for loans, establish bogus credit cards, and generally cause havoc. The accounts of the victims are emptied, and the victims can do little to recover their losses.

Intellectual Property Theft

Nearly every company faces the dilemma of protecting product plans, new inventions, industrial processes, and other **intellectual property**, something produced by the intellect or mind that has commercial value. Its ownership and right to its use may be protected by patent, copyright, trademark, and other means. But crooks may be able to steal information about intellectual property and create unauthorized duplications. This type of theft has become such a grave concern that the Federal Bureau of Investigation (FBI), in partnership with the Department of Justice, is now

Intellectual Property *something produced by the intellect or mind that has commercial value*

running the National Intellectual Property Rights Coordination Center (NIPRCC), an organization entirely dedicated to preventing the exploitation of intellectual property.

Computer Viruses, Worms, and Trojan Horses

Another IT risk facing businesses is rogue programmers who disrupt IT operations by contaminating and destroying software, hardware, or data files. *Viruses, worms,* and *Trojan horses* are three kinds of malicious programs that, once installed, can shut down any computer system. A *computer virus* exists in a file that attaches itself to a program and migrates from computer to computer as a shared program or as an e-mail attachment. It does not infect the system unless the user opens the contaminated file, and users typically are unaware they are spreading the virus by file sharing. It can, for example, quickly copy itself over and over again, using up all available memory and effectively shutting down a computer.

Worms are a particular kind of virus that travel from computer to computer within networked computer systems, without your needing to open any software to spread the contaminated file. In a matter of days, the notorious Blaster worm once infected some 400,000 computer networks, destroying files and even allowing outsiders to take over computers remotely. The worm replicates itself rapidly, sending out thousands of copies to other computers in the network. Traveling through Internet connections and e-mail address books in the network's computers, it absorbs system memory and shuts down network servers, web servers, and individual computers.

Unlike viruses, a *Trojan horse* does not replicate itself. Instead, it most often comes into the computer, at your request, masquerading as a harmless, legitimate software product or data file. Once installed, however, the damage begins. For instance, it may simply redesign desktop icons (as a "prank") or, more maliciously, delete files and destroy information.

Spyware

Spyware *program unknowingly downloaded by users that monitors their computer activities, gathering e-mail addresses, credit card numbers, and other information that it transmits to someone outside the host system*

As if forced intrusion isn't bad enough, Internet users can also unwittingly invite spies—masquerading as a friendly file available as a giveaway or shared among individual users on their PCs. This so-called **spyware** is downloaded by users who are lured by "free" software or phony updates. Once installed, it "crawls" around to monitor the host's computer activities, gathering e-mail addresses, credit card numbers, passwords, and other inside information that it transmits back to someone outside the host system. Spyware authors assemble incoming stolen information to create their own "intellectual property" that they then sell to other parties to use for marketing and advertising purposes or for identity theft. In contrast to viruses, worms, and Trojan horses, which often give clues to users that something is wrong, in the case of spyware the user is normally quite unaware that something is amiss. Thus, the spyware does its job without anyone being the wiser.[31]

Spam

Spam *junk e-mail sent to a mailing list or a newsgroup*

Spam, junk e-mail sent to a mailing list or a newsgroup (an online discussion group), is a greater nuisance than postal junk mail because the Internet is open to the public, e-mail costs are negligible, and massive mailing lists are accessible through file sharing or by theft. Spam operators send unwanted messages ranging from explicit pornography to hate mail to advertisements, and even destructive computer viruses. In addition to wasting users' time, spam also consumes a network's bandwidth, thereby reducing the amount of data that can be transmitted in a fixed amount of time for useful purposes. U.S. industry experts estimate spam's annual damage in lost time and productivity at between $28 and $66 billion in the United States alone and that it could be as high as $620 billion globally.[32]

Although spammers sometimes gain significant incomes, they also risk anti-spamming prosecution that can be extremely costly. The judge in a lawsuit against Sanford Wallace, who proclaimed himself the "Spam King," issued a judgment for

$711 million against Wallace, one of the largest fines ever in an anti-spamming case. He was accused of sending 27 million spam mailings to Facebook, using phishing to get passwords from thousands of Facebook users, and then entering their accounts to post fraudulent information. He was also charged with electronic mail fraud, damage to protected computers, and criminal contempt.[33]

IT Protection Measures

Learning Objective 14-5

Describe the ways in which businesses protect themselves from the threats and risks information technology poses.

Security measures against intrusion and viruses are a constant challenge. Most systems guard against unauthorized access by requiring users to provide confidential login credentials such as user IDs and passwords. Other measures include firewalls, special software, and encryption.

Preventing Unauthorized Access: Firewalls

Firewalls are security systems with special software and/or hardware devices designed to keep computers safe from hackers. A firewall is located where two networks—for example, the Internet and a company's internal network, or intranet—interface. It contains two components for filtering incoming data:

Firewall *security system with special software or hardware devices designed to keep computers safe from hackers*

- The company's *security policy*—Access rules that identify every type of data that the company doesn't want to pass through the firewall
- A *router*—A table of available routes or paths; a "traffic switch" that determines which route or path on the network to send each piece of data after it is tested against the security policy

Only the information that meets the conditions of the user's security policy is routed through the firewall and permitted to flow between the two networks. Data that fail the access test are blocked and cannot flow between the two networks.

Preventing Identity Theft

Although foolproof prevention is impossible, steps can be taken to avoid being victimized. A visit to the Identity Theft Resource Center (http://www.idtheftcenter.org) is a valuable first step to get information on everything from scam alerts to victim issues to legislation such as the Fair and Accurate Credit Transactions Act (FACTA). FACTA strengthens identity-theft protections by specifying how organizations must destroy information instead of dropping it in a dumpster. When a company disposes of hardcopy documents that contain credit or Social Security information, for instance, they must be shredded, pulverized, or burned, and all digital records (such as those stored in computers and databases) must be permanently removed to keep them out of the hands of intruders.[34]

Outside of the direct business environment, several companies such as LifeLock have emerged over the past decade. These organizations charge a fee for users and monitor data and interactions on the Internet. In the event that suspicious activities are noted concerning a covered user, the user is notified to determine if the activities are legitimate or fraudulent. In the event that fraud is determined, many of these organizations will help to investigate and even litigate in order for the user's assets to be recovered.

Preventing Infectious Intrusions: Antivirus Software

Combating viruses, worms, Trojan horses, and any other infectious software (collectively known as *malware*) has become a major industry for systems designers and software developers. Installation of any of hundreds of **antivirus software** products protects systems by searching incoming e-mail and data files for "signatures" of known viruses and virus-like characteristics. Contaminated files are discarded or

Antivirus Software *product that protects systems by searching incoming e-mails and data files for "signatures" of known viruses and virus-like characteristics*

placed in quarantine for safekeeping. Many viruses take advantage of weaknesses in operating systems, such as Microsoft Windows, to spread and propagate. Software distributors, for their part, are continuously monitoring their own products for potential weaknesses and updating them to thwart malware. Network administrators must make sure that the computers on their systems are using the most up-to-date operating system that includes the latest security protection.

Protecting Electronic Communications: Encryption Software

Security for electronic communications is another concern for businesses. Unprotected e-mail can be intercepted, diverted to unintended computers, and opened, revealing the contents to intruders. Protective software is available to guard against those intrusions, adding a layer of security by encoding e-mails so that only intended recipients can open them. An **encryption system** works by scrambling an e-mail message so that it looks like garbled nonsense to anyone who doesn't possess the "key," another part of the software that decodes encrypted e-mails.

Encryption System *software that assigns an e-mail message to a unique code number (digital fingerprint) for each computer so only that computer, not others, can open and read the message*

Avoiding Spam and Spyware

To help their employees avoid privacy invasion and to improve productivity, businesses often install antispyware and spam-filtering software on their systems. Although dozens of antispyware products provide protection—software such as Webroot Spy Sweeper and Microsoft Windows Defender—they must be continually updated to keep pace with new spyware techniques.

The federal CAN-SPAM Act of 2003 requires the Federal Trade Commission to shield the public from falsified header information, sexually explicit e-mails that are not so labeled, online spoofing (using trickery to make a message appear as if it came from a trusted source), and hijacking of computers through worms or Trojan horses. Although it cannot be prevented entirely, spam is abated by many Internet service providers (ISPs) that ban the spamming of ISP subscribers. In a now-classic punishment, an ISP in Iowa was awarded $1 billion in a lawsuit against 300 spammers that jammed the ISP system with an astounding 10 million e-mails a day. Anti-spam groups, too, promote the public's awareness of known spammers. The Spamhaus Project (http://www.spamhaus.org), for example, maintains a list of "The 10 Worst Spammers," career spammers that are responsible for most of the world's spam traffic.

Ethical Concerns in IT

It is obvious that IT developments and usage are progressing faster than society's appreciation for the potential consequences, including new ethical concerns. Along with IT's many benefits, its usage is creating previously unanticipated problems for which solutions are needed, yet they don't exist. Ease of access to computers, mobile devices, and the Internet, together with messaging capabilities and social networking, promote widespread public exposure of people's private lives, including personal information about how they think and feel. Just how this information should be used, by whom, under what conditions, and with what restrictions, if any, are issues teeming with ethical considerations. The issues of right and wrong, legal and illegal, have had concerns raised to the level of the Supreme Court, with the landmark 2018 case of *Carpenter v. United States*, in which the Court decided that law enforcement had to have a warrant to secure cell phone records. In this case, the Court found that there was an expectation of privacy during digital communication, a decision that could soon be applied to additional forms of digital communication such as online communication.[35] This finding has subsequently led to calls for an even more expansive view of what digital privacy means. This will likely lead to additional Supreme Court decisions in the future that will set the precedent for what our expectations of privacy should be in all forms of the digital environment. Several real-life episodes with ethical implications are shown in Table 14.1. See if you can identify significant ethical issues among the episodes in the table.

table 14.1 Areas for Ethical Concerns in Information Technology and Its Uses

- In a now-classic case of cyberbullying, a 13-year-old girl hanged herself after being taunted by a hoax message on her Myspace page.
- Secret webcasts of other people's behavior have resulted in embarrassment and even death: A university student, leaving a final message on his Facebook page, jumped from a bridge to his death after other students covertly webcast his sexual activities with another student.
- IT is used increasingly for sending out cries for help. Many college students have posted public messages requesting physical and emotional support. Others, having read those messages, are unsure whether they should respond.
- Employers and employees struggle about the extent of personal use of the company's IT. Many employees admit they use social networking and personal e-mailing at work, but should they? Many companies say "No," adding that employees should know that the company has access to all e-mails sent, received, and stored on its IT system.
- States are forming database pools, sharing information to check on suspicious prescription drug activities. Data are gathered on purchases at pharmacies, physicians' prescriptions, and police records to identify drug abuse by individuals and companies within states and are being shared across state lines.
- The Department of Homeland Security abandoned one of its major data mining tools for combating terrorism after questions about its compliance with privacy rules. It was discovered that DHS had tested the data mining program using information about real people, without ensuring the privacy of that information.
- To save money, IT users retrieve and share intellectual property—movies, articles, books, music, industrial information—with others, ignoring copyright, trademark, and patent protections. Written content is often taken from the Internet, inserted into the user's written work, and represented as the user's own original creation without citing its true source.
- Job seekers are being asked to answer unexpected questions by interviewers: "What are your Facebook username and password?" Some applicants are responding, "No, that's a terrible privacy invasion." Others are revealing the requested information to interviewers.

finding a better way

AI Gets Emotional

Companies around the globe are using conversational artificial intelligence like chatbots to simulate human conversation. Some of the biggest companies in the world use conversational AI to help with routine customer inquiries, direct customers to desirable products, and solve customer service problems. Conversational AI uses machine learning to essentially teach computers how to interact like humans. By teaching computers what appropriate responses look like based on context and how to classify a request, companies like Amazon are able to leverage AI successfully to make customers feel like they're talking to a person named Alexa, who magically knows exactly what they want to listen to, read, or buy.

Shutterstock

Some companies are going further with machine learning and using AI to teach computers to recognize feelings. Affective AI, also known as emotion AI or emotional intelligence AI, is a branch of artificial intelligence that focuses on understanding, interpreting, and responding to human emotions. A computer or machine using affective AI will theoretically be able to respond to requests with more than just information; affective AI aims to teach computers to appear empathetic.

The field of affective AI was pioneered by Dr. Rosalind Picard and aided by the study of autism. Early in her research and development of affective AI, she was giving a presentation on teaching computers how to recognize changes in facial expressions as emotions. An audience member noted the similarities between teaching computers and people with autism how to recognize and respond to emotion.[36]

Dr. Picard was joined by Dr. Rana el Kaliouby, and in 2009, they moved their research out of the MIT lab and into commerce when they founded Affectiva. Acquired by Smart Eye in 2021, Affectiva is an industry leader in driver monitoring systems (DMS), AI that can monitor things as urgent as object

(continued)

detection to avoid collisions and as minute as changes in the emotional state of the driver.[37]

From identifying authorized users of fleet vehicles to alerting emergency services in the event of driver health crises or collisions, DMS software used to be a premium feature available only in high-end luxury cars. Lawmakers and regulators, however, are increasingly recognizing the potential of these systems to reduce the staggering number of people injured or killed in vehicle-related collisions around the world.[38]

AI in Action

There are also numerous specific ethical issues related to the emerging use of AI, machine learning, and ChatGPT. Some of these include the following:

1 ***Privacy and data security.*** AI-powered chatbots often collect and process large amounts of user data. There is a risk of potential privacy breaches or unauthorized access to sensitive information. Proper data protection measures and user consent mechanisms should be in place to ensure privacy and data security.

2 ***Bias and discrimination.*** AI systems, including chatbots, can inherit and amplify biases present in the data they are trained on. If the training data contains biases based on factors such as race, gender, or ethnicity, the chatbot's responses may exhibit discriminatory behavior. Careful attention needs to be given to data selection and algorithmic design to mitigate biases and promote fairness.

3 ***Transparency and explainability.*** Many AI algorithms, such as deep learning models, can be complex and opaque, making it difficult to understand the reasoning behind their decisions. Lack of transparency can be problematic in situations where the chatbot's actions have significant consequences. Efforts are being made to develop methods for explaining AI decisions to users and ensuring transparency in their operations.

4 ***User manipulation and deception.*** Chatbots can be designed to simulate humanlike interactions, blurring the line between human and AI. This raises concerns about potential deception and manipulation of users. Developers should be transparent about the chatbot's AI nature and ensure that users are aware they are interacting with an automated system.

5 ***Accountability and liability.*** Determining responsibility and accountability when AI systems cause harm or make errors can be challenging. Establishing clear legal frameworks and guidelines for assigning liability in cases where chatbots cause harm or engage in unethical behavior is crucial.

6 ***Psychological impact.*** Chatbots that mimic human emotions and engage in empathetic interactions can have psychological effects on users. While this can be beneficial in some cases, it is important to consider the potential risks and responsibilities associated with emotionally engaging with AI systems.

7 ***Unemployment and socioeconomic impacts.*** As AI technology advances, there is a concern that automation, including chatbots, may lead to job displacement and socioeconomic inequality. The ethical implications of widespread deployment of chatbots should consider the potential impact on employment and ensure measures are taken to address the resulting societal challenges.

Addressing these ethical concerns requires collaboration between developers, policymakers, and the wider society. Ethical guidelines, regulations, and industry standards can help ensure responsible and beneficial deployment of AI and chatbot technologies. As just one example of these issues, the lead AI scientist at Google resigned in 2023 because he believed that the technology was moving too fast without oversight or governance.

Source: This box was created by ChatGPT.

summary of learning objectives

LEARNING OBJECTIVE 14-1

Discuss the impacts information technology is having on the business world.

The growth of IT—the various appliances and devices for creating, storing, exchanging, and using information in diverse modes, including visual images, voice, multimedia, and business data—has changed the very structure of business organizations. Its adoption provides new modes of communication, including portable offices using mobile messaging capabilities, resulting in the geographic separation of the workplace from headquarters for many employees. With access to the Internet, company activities may be geographically scattered but still remain coordinated through a networked system that provides better service for customers. Networks and technology are also leading to leaner companies with fewer employees and simpler structures. Because networks enable firms to maintain information linkages among employees and customers, more work and customer satisfaction can be accomplished with fewer people. IT also contributes to greater flexibility in serving customers and enables closer coordination with suppliers. Company activities may be geographically scattered but remain coordinated through a network system that provides better service for customers. Many businesses coordinate activities from one centralized location, but their deliveries flow from several remote locations, often at lower cost. IT's global reach facilitates project collaboration with remote business partners and the formation of new market relationships around the globe. Just as electronic collaboration has changed the way employees interact with each other, IT networks have created new manufacturing flexibility for mass customization, and Internet access has brought new opportunities for small businesses.

LEARNING OBJECTIVE 14-2

Identify the IT resources businesses have at their disposal and how these resources are used.

The Internet and the World Wide Web serve computers with information and provide communication flows among networks around the world. For many businesses, the Internet has replaced the telephone, fax machine, and standard mail as the primary communications tool. To support internal communications, many companies maintain internal websites—*intranets*—accessible only to employees. Some firms give limited network access to outsiders via *extranets*, allowing access to private information among businesses, customers, and suppliers for better planning and coordination of their activities. Electronic conferencing allows simultaneous communication globally among groups from various locations, saving travel time, time for information exchanges, and expenses. *VSAT satellite networks* provide private remote communications for voice, video, and data transmissions.

Computer networks, including wide area networks and local area networks, enable the sharing of information, hardware, software, and other resources over wired or wireless connections. *Wi-Fi* provides wireless Internet connections through laptops or other devices at "hotspots" or local access points. All computer networks or systems need hardware, the physical components such as keyboards, monitors, and printers. In addition, all systems require *software*, programs that tell the computer how to function. *Application software* includes programs to meet specific user needs, such as groupware with voice and video connections for remote collaboration.

LEARNING OBJECTIVE 14-3

Describe the role of information systems, the different types of information systems, and how businesses use such systems.

An *information system (IS)* uses IT resources that enable users to create, process, and transmit information for use in decision making. An IS often includes *data warehousing*, a vast collection, storage, and retrieval system, that provides the data resources needed for creating information. The IS also includes *data-mining* capabilities, the application of technologies for searching, sifting, and reorganizing data, to uncover useful information for planning new products, setting prices, and identifying trends.

The IS is often a set of several systems that share information while serving different levels of an organization, different departments, or different operations. *Knowledge information systems* support knowledge workers—engineers, scientists, and other specialists—by providing resources to create, store, use, and transmit new knowledge they use for specialty applications. Knowledge systems include *computer-aided design (CAD)*, software systems that receive engineering data and convert them into three-dimensional displays, for rapid development of new products. *Computer-aided manufacturing (CAM)* uses computers to design and control the equipment needed in a manufacturing process. *Management information systems (MIS)* support managers by providing reports, schedules, plans, and budgets that can then be used for making decisions at all levels, ranging from detailed daily activities to long-range business strategies. The many uses of information systems include experimenting with *decision support systems (DSS)*, interactive systems that create business models and test them with different data to see how the models respond under diverse business conditions, to test the effectiveness of potential decisions.

LEARNING OBJECTIVE 14-4

Identify the threats and risks information technology poses to businesses.

IT has attracted abusers that do mischief, with severity ranging from mere nuisance to outright destruction, costing companies millions. Everything from Facebook postings to Bluetooth usage to private computer systems is subject to break-ins and destruction. *Hackers* break into computers, steal personal information and company secrets, tamper with data, and launch attacks on other computers. *Wireless moochers* use victims' networks for illegal activities, exposing the host to criminal prosecution. Once inside a computer network, hackers are able to commit *identity theft*, the unauthorized stealing of personal information to get loans, credit cards, or other monetary benefits by impersonating the victim. Even the ease of information sharing on the Internet poses a threat. It has proven costly for companies who are having a difficult time protecting their *intellectual property*, such as software products, movies, and music. Hackers break into company networks to steal anything of commercial value, including trade secrets, new inventions, and other valuable information that is protected by patent, copyright, or trademark. Another IT risk facing businesses is system shutdown and destruction of software, hardware, or data files by *viruses, worms*, and *Trojan horses* that can shut down a computer system or otherwise disrupt IT operations by contaminating and destroying software, hardware, or data files. After invading a victim's computer, *spyware* gathers inside information and transmits it to outside spies. Masquerading as a friendly file available as a giveaway or shared among individual users on PCs and mobile devices, spyware is downloaded by unsuspecting users. Once installed, it monitors the host's electronic activities, gathers personal information, and transmits stolen information to an outside system. *Spam*, junk e-mail sent to a mailing list or news group, is costly in terms of lost time and productivity by overloading the network's capacity with massive mailings of unwanted messages.

LEARNING OBJECTIVE 14-5

Describe the ways in which businesses protect themselves from the threats and risks information technology poses.

Most systems guard against unauthorized access by requiring users to have protected passwords. In addition, many firms rely on *firewalls*, security systems with special software or hardware devices that intercept would-be intruders, so that only messages that meet the conditions of the company's security policy are permitted to flow through the network. Firms can protect against identity theft by using assistance from advisory sources, such as the Identity Theft Resource Center, and by implementing the identity-theft protection provisions of the federal FACTA rule for maintaining and destroying personal information records. To combat infectious intrusions by viruses, worms, and Trojan horses, *antivirus software* products search incoming e-mail and data files for "signatures" of known viruses and virus-like characteristics. Contaminated files are discarded or placed in quarantine for safekeeping. Additional intrusion protection is available by installing *antispyware* and *spam-filtering software*. *Encryption* adds security by encoding, scrambling messages so they look like garbled nonsense to anyone who doesn't possess the key, so that the message can be read only by intended recipients. The federal *CAN-SPAM Act* requires the Federal Trade Commission to shield the public from falsified header information, sexually explicit e-mails that are not so labeled, Internet spoofing (using trickery to make a message appear as if it came from a trusted source), and hijacking of computers through worms or Trojan horses. Although it cannot be prevented entirely, *spam* is abated by many Internet service providers (ISPs) that ban the spamming of ISP subscribers.

key terms

antivirus software **(p. 471)**
artificial intelligence (AI) **(p. 464)**
client–server network **(p. 457)**
computer-aided design (CAD) **(p. 462)**
computer-aided manufacturing (CAM) **(p. 463)**
computer network **(p. 457)**
data **(p. 460)**
data mining **(p. 461)**
data warehousing **(p. 460)**
decision support system (DSS) **(p. 464)**
e-commerce **(p. 449)**
electronic conferencing **(p. 456)**
encryption system **(p. 472)**
enterprise resource planning (ERP) **(p. 464)**
extranet **(p. 455)**
firewall **(p. 471)**
hacker **(p. 468)**
hypertext transfer protocol (HTTP) **(p. 454)**
hypertext transfer protocol secure (HTTPS) **(p. 455)**
identity theft **(p. 469)**
information **(p. 460)**
information system (IS) **(p. 460)**
information systems managers **(p. 460)**
information technology (IT) **(p. 449)**
intellectual property **(p. 469)**
Internet **(p. 454)**
intranet **(p. 455)**
knowledge management system **(p. 462)**
local area network (LAN) **(p. 457)**
machine learning **(p. 466)**
management information system (MIS) **(p. 464)**
mass customization **(p. 452)**
predictive analytics **(p. 466)**
spam **(p. 470)**
spyware **(p. 470)**
"super Wi-Fi" network **(p. 458)**
VSAT satellite communications **(p. 456)**
wide area network (WAN) **(p. 457)**
Wi-Fi **(p. 458)**
wireless local area network (wireless LAN or WLAN) **(p. 458)**
wireless wide area network (WWAN) **(p. 458)**
World Wide Web **(p. 455)**

questions & exercises

QUESTIONS FOR REVIEW

14-1. Compare and contrast an intranet with an extranet.

14-2. How does electronic conferencing increase a company's productivity and efficiency? In what ways does it hinder them?

14-3. What are the advantages and risks of cloud computing?

14-4. How can companies protect against hackers?

14-5. What is *intellectual property*? Provide at least three examples.

QUESTIONS FOR ANALYSIS

14-6. Describe how a company might use data warehousing and data mining in its information system to better plan for new products.

14-7. How could an airline use AI to enhance the customer experience?

14-8. How do your bank, employer, and e-mail provider protect your personal information from unauthorized use?

APPLICATION EXERCISES

14-9. Consider your daily activities—as a consumer, student, parent, friend, homeowner or renter, car driver, employee, and so forth—and think about the ways that you are involved with IT systems. Make a list of your recent IT encounters and then recall instances in those encounters in which you revealed personal information that could be used to steal your identity. Are some encounters on your list riskier than others? Why or why not?

14-10. After reading the first section of this chapter, consider how IT has changed the business of higher education. Identify at least three functions, services, or activities that would not have been available even 10 years ago. How do you think that colleges and universities will change in the future because of advances in IT?

building a business: continuing team exercise

ASSIGNMENT

Meet with your team members to consider your new business venture and how it relates to the information technology topics in this chapter. Develop specific responses to the following:

14-11. In what ways do you expect IT will enable collaboration among your employees? Identify examples of occasions where IT will be useful for providing remote access between employees, and remote access between employees and company data files.

14-12. In what ways will IT be used for collaboration with external stakeholders, such as customers, suppliers, and other constituents? What types of remote interactions do you expect, and what kinds of IT equipment and installations will be needed for those interactions? Discuss how your team is going to identify the IT equipment requirements at this stage of development of your business.

14-13. At what stage of your company's development will you begin planning for its information system(s), if any? Discuss the technical skills and information-management skills necessary for determining the kind(s) of information system(s) needed for your company's first two years of operation.

14-14. Based on your findings for Question 14-13, where will your company get the skills and resources for IS development and implementation? Have you included the anticipated costs for developing the information systems in your financial plan for year 1 or will you do so? Explain why, or why not.

14-15. What measures, if any, will you take for protecting against intrusions into your company's IT system? What actions will be taken to prevent unauthorized access to the information of customers, suppliers, and other external constituents? What security measures will be taken to protect non-IT information? Explain.

team exercise

NEW AGE HELP DESK

The Situation

You have been hired to develop and lead a technical support team for a rapidly growing start-up that provides data analysis, business consulting, and targeted marketing to auto dealers. For instance, customers who recently came in for service on an older car would receive trade-in offers suggesting a newer vehicle, as would customers who had purchased more than five years earlier. The company began several years ago when four recent college graduates in Portland, Oregon, spotted a need in the local market and combined their business and technical skills to meet that need. The company quickly grew, adding more than 80 employees in just five years. It now serves dealers in seven West Coast cities, and management is seeking to expand into 10 more cities within the next two years, with an ultimate goal of taking the company public within six years. While all of the employees are currently located in the Portland area, the corporate culture has been based on flexible work hours, and most of the employees work from home at least three days a week. Because the company has grown organically from that flexible culture, there hasn't been much of a technical support team at the company. An informal network of experts made decisions about which computers to buy, the software they purchased, and their high-speed Internet in the office, and employees depended on friends, family members, or coworkers if they had trouble with their hardware or software. However, the company's rapid growth has strained this informal network, and so management decided to budget three IT professionals for a technical support department. As the first hire and leader of this nascent department, your first task is to make recommendations for next steps.

QUESTIONS FOR DISCUSSION:

14-16. Many of the company's employees work from home. What benefits can the company and employee expect from allowing employees to do so? Are there some jobs in which working from home is not appropriate?

14-17. The company has not had a consistent policy about the technology for those working from home. Should the company provide employees with a computer to use in their home office, or is this a responsibility of the employee? What are the benefits and costs of each?

14-18. How will you provide technical support to employees working from home? Would this be easier if the company provided the employee with a computer? Why or why not?

14-19. Are there additional data security risks with employees working from home? Describe the potential risks or concerns and how they might be addressed.

14-20. Briefly outline the policies, procedures, and guidelines that your department should propose in your first year on the job.

exercising your ethics

TO READ OR NOT TO READ

The Situation

Companies can monitor how their employees use the company e-mail system and track a history of employees' Internet use while using company resources. This type of surveillance is often theoretically conducted to reduce workplace violence and injury and increase productivity. Although these represent legitimate concerns in the modern business world, it is increasingly unclear how companies can balance business interests with reasonable expectations of privacy for their employees. This exercise illustrates how ethical issues may arise in tracking and monitoring employee use of digital assets.

The Dilemma

You have been hired as a manager at a local biotechnology company. This is your dream job, and you are delighted to have been recognized for your hard work. As you are going through orientation, the human resource (HR) manager explains that the company maintains logs of employee e-mails and tracks all Internet usage on company computers. The HR director assures you this is entirely legal. The company is concerned that employees may be wasting time on YouTube and other websites while at work, so they believe this program of scanning Internet usage has a valid business purpose. Part of your job is to scan e-mail logs to ensure that employees are not sharing confidential information or trade secrets and to monitor suspicious computer activities.

QUESTIONS TO ADDRESS

14-21. Given the factors in this situation, what, if any, ethical issues exist?

14-22. Do you think the company is wise to monitor employees in this manner? Why or why not?

14-23. If you discovered that an employee was spending a lot of time on non-work-related searches, how would you address the issue with the employee?

cases

THINK BEFORE YOU CLICK

Continued from page 449

At the beginning of this chapter, you read about illicit activities of IT pirates and their methods for preying on victims, including both organizations and individuals around the globe. You saw that pirating aims to steal money and other resources by luring vulnerable potential victims with seemingly attractive offers of personal gain. Using the information presented in this chapter, you should now be able to answer the following questions.

QUESTIONS FOR DISCUSSION

14-24. Think about recent spam e-mails and text messages that you have received. What kinds of information were the intruders seeking?

14-25. Were you able to identify the e-mails and messages as "scams" before opening them, or did you discover their real contents after you opened them? What might have alerted you to the risks?

14-26. In what ways might the "opened" message from a scammer be harmful to you? To your IT devices and systems?

14-27. What steps can you take (or have you taken) to protect against such intrusions? What costs would be involved for gaining that protection?

14-28. Consider the various IT systems you use daily. What kinds of protection do they have against invasion by cyberpirates?

SELLING CUSTOMER SEARCH DATA

In late 2016, the Federal Communications Commission (FCC) passed regulations that required Internet service providers (ISPs) to get approval from their customers before they could sell information about what websites they visit to third parties. However, businesses like Amazon, Facebook, and Google fall under the jurisdiction of the Federal Trade Commission (FTC), not the FCC, and the FTC regulations are more lax than the ones passed by the FCC. Internet service providers successfully lobbied Congress to overturn the FCC regulations, and now ISPs can sell your browsing information.

The ISP lobby argued that ISPs should be subject to the same rules as other Internet-based businesses that collect, analyze, and disseminate consumer data and then use consumer profiles to target advertising. However, ISPs have an advantage in this market because they can see all of the websites their customers visit, not just the ones that happen to participate in a particular company's ad network. If you visit a lot of travel sites, for example, your ISP might have software that tells ad networks to show you more ads for airline flights or hotel rooms. Amazon gathers data only while you are logged on to Amazon.com, and even browsers like Google can collect data only while you are in the browser. The ISP has access to all of the browsing history, all of the time.

A 2021 FTC report revealed that ISPs are dealing in more than Internet traffic data. Providers made sensitive details available to third-party sellers: specific location data, race, gender, and even height and weight were collected and shared. Though the ISPs argue they weren't selling the information, other parties were not restricted from monetizing the data.[39]

Proponents of the now-repealed FCC regulations limiting ISP data sharing claim that greater access to customer browsing history comes with a correspondingly higher responsibility to keep that information private and that even if consumers can "opt out" to keep their data private, most people won't be able to find or understand that provision buried in the fine print of the user agreement.

QUESTIONS FOR DISCUSSION

14-29. How and where do you see your browsing data affecting the ads that you see?

14-30. Do you appreciate the targeted marketing that more and more companies use, or do you feel that it is limiting your options? If so, how?

14-31. As a consumer, how do you feel about your Internet service provider selling your browsing data? How do you feel about that as a business owner, marketing manager, or entrepreneur? What arguments could you make to Congress either for or against enacting tougher restrictions on data like purchasing patterns, search history, and page visits?

14-32. As part of the marketing department of a consumer products company, how would you use browsing history to help market your products?

14-33. What kinds of measures could you implement to protect your privacy? Would you do those things, or do you feel that Internet privacy is an oxymoron?

endnotes

[1] M. P. McQueen, "Cyber-Scams on the Uptick in Downturn," *Wall Street Journal*, January 29, 2009, D1, D4; Joseph De Avila, "Beware of Facebook 'Friends' Who May Trash Your Laptop," *Wall Street Journal*, January 29, 2009, D1, D4; Byron Acohido and Jon Swartz, "Data Scams Have Kicked into High Gear as Markets Tumble," *USA Today*, January 28, 2009, http://www.usatoday.com/tech/news/computersecurity/2009-01-28-hackers-data-scams_N.htm; Chris Wragge, "FBI Warns of High-Tech Cyber ID Theft," wcbstv.com, April 8, 2009, http://wcbstv.com/local/cyber.criminals.fbi.2.980245.html; Jordan Robertson, "Bad Economy Helps Web Scammers Recruit 'Mules,'" ABC News, December 9, 2008, http://abcnews.go.com/print?id=6422327.

[2] https://www.wired.com/story/colonial-pipeline-ransomware-attack/.

[3] https://www.cisa.gov/news-events/news/attack-colonial-pipeline-what-weve-learned-what-weve-done-over-past-two-years.

[4] https://www.cnn.com/2021/06/07/politics/colonial-pipeline-ransomware-recovered/index.html.

[5] "Hackers in China Blamed for Cyber-Attacks," *Columbia Daily Tribune*, February 10, 2011, 5B, http://www.columbiatribune.com/news/2011/feb/10/hackers-in-china-blamed-for-cyber-attacks/?news; Mary Ann Milbourn, "Beware of Fake Job Offers," *Orange County Register*, October 12, 2010, http://economy.ocregister.com/2010/10/12/beware-of-fake-job-offers/42194/; Richard Eppstein, "Scammers Pop Up During Economic Downturns," *Toledo Biz Insider*, March 4, 2010, http://www.toledoblade.com/article/20100304/BUSINESS11/100309863/-1/BUSINESS; Matt Warman, "Viruses on Smartphones: Security's New Frontier," *The Telegraph*, February 8, 2011, http://www.telegraph.co.uk/technology/news/8311214/Viruses-on-smartphones-securitys-new-frontier.html.

[6] See SiriusXM, http://www.siriusxm.com/navtraffic/, accessed on October 2, 2023.

[7] "Appropriator Asks NASA to Help Boeing Fix Dreamliner Problems," January 13, 2013, http://fattah.house.gov/latest-news/appropriator-asks-nasa-to-help-boeing-fix-dreamliner-problems/.

[8] "Lockheed Martin Aeronautics: Siemens' PLM Software," Siemens, accessed May 4, 2020, http://www.plm.automation.siemans.com/en_us/about-us/success/case_s.

[9] Laura Northrup, "Timbuk2 Really, Really Wants You to Be Happy with Their Bags," *The Consumerist*, June 5, 2009, http://www.consumerist.com/2009/06/timbuk2really-really-wants-you-to-be-happy-with-their-bags.html.

[10] Ree Drummond, *The Pioneer Woman*, accessed May 4, 2020, https://thepioneerwoman.com.

[11] David LaGesse, "How to Turn Social Networking into a Job Offer," *U.S. News & World Report*, May 11, 2009, http://www.usnews.com/money/careers/articles/2009/05/11/how-to-turn-social-networking-into-a-job-offer.html.

[12] "3D Systems Helps Walter Reed Army Medical Center Rebuild Lives," 3D Systems, accessed June 15, 2009, http://www.3dsystems.com/appsolutions/casestudies/walter_reed.asp; Hannah Hickey, "Camera in a Pill Offers Cheaper, Easier Window on Your Insides," UWNews.org, January 24, 2008, http://uwnews.org/article.asp?articleid=39292. See also https://tricare.mil/mtf/Walterreed.

[13] See Internet World Stats, May 4, 2020, http://www.Internetworldstats.com/stats.htm.

[14] "Companies Take Sides on Super Wi-Fi," *Columbia Daily Tribune*, February 4, 2013, 6B.

[15] "For Chronic Pain Relief," Bold New Spinal Cord Stimulation—Proclaim XR SCS System, accessed July 2, 2023, https://proclaimxr.com/.

[16] Zhanna L. Malekos Smith, "Human Microchip Implants Take Center Stage," *The Hill*, January 23, 2023. https://thehill.com/opinion/technology/3817029-human-microchip-implants-take-center-stage/.

[17] Vivienne Walt, "Is 'Biochipping' a Good Idea?," *Fortune*, June 7, 2021, https://fortune.com/longform/biochipping-biohax-microchip/.

[18] BioTeq, "Assistive Technology," accessed July 2, 2023, https://www.bioteq.co.uk/index.php/assistive-technology.

[19] "Kroger Tailors Ads to Its Customers," *Columbia Daily Tribune*, January 12, 2009, 7B; Josh Pichler, "dunnhumby: Retailer's Secret Weapon," Cincinnati.com, January 31, 2013, news.cincinnati.com/article/20130130/BIZ/301190100/dunnhumby-Retailers-secret-weapon?nclick_check=1.

[20] Antonia Din, "Companies Affected by Ransomware [Updated 2023]," Heimdal Security Blog, June 7, 2023, https://heimdalsecurity.com/blog/companies-affected-by-ransomware/.

[21] Ani Petrosyan, "Number of Ransomware Attacks per Year 2022," Statista, June 23, 2023, https://www.statista.com/statistics/494947/ransomware-attacks-per-year-worldwide/#:~:text=In%202022%2C%20organizations%20all%20around,nearly%20155%20million%20cases%2C%20respectively.

[22] "Cyproteck®—Cybersecurity Defense—About." CYPROTECK®—Cybersecurity Defense—AI-Driven Cybersecurity Solutions, May 23, 2023, https://cyproteck.com/about/.

[23] Jo Marchant, "Virtual Fossils Reveal How Ancient Creatures Lived," *New Scientist*, May 27, 2009, http://www.newscientist.com/article/mg20227103.500-virtual-fossils-reveal-how-ancient-creatures-lived.html.

[24] Warman, "Viruses on Smartphones: Security's New Frontier"; Jacqui Cheng, "Canadian Group: Facebook 'A Minefield of Privacy Invasion,'" May 30, 2008, http://arstechnica.com/tech-policy/news/2008/05/canadian-group-files-complaint-over-facebook-privacy.ars; "Cell Phones a Much Bigger Privacy Risk Than Facebook," Fox News, February 20, 2009, http://www.foxnews.com/printer_friendly_story/0,3566,497544,00.html.

[25] "What Is Data Leakage?," Forcepoint, 2020, https://www.forcepoint.com/cyber-edu/data-leakage.

[26] Siobhan Gorman, Devlin Barrett, and Danny Yadron, "China Hackers Hit U.S. Media," *Wall Street Journal*, February 1, 2013, B1, B2; "Hackers Hit Twitter, Washington Post," *Columbia Daily Tribune*, February 4, 2013, 6B.

[27] https://www.bbc.com/news/stories-57520169.

[28] https://home.treasury.gov/news/press-releases/jy0768.

[29] https://cybernews.com/news/piracy-costs-entertainment-industry-billions-says-report/#:~:text=Online%20TV%20and%20film%20piracy,hundreds%20of%20thousands%20of%20jobs; Oscar Gonzalez, "Digital Video Piracy Costs Movie and TV Industry at Least $29 Billion a Year, Study Says," Cnet, June 18, 2019, https://www.cnet.com/news/digital-video-piracy-costs-the-movie-and-tv-industry-at-least-29-billion-study-says/.

[30] Donald Melanson, "Apple: 16 Billion iTunes Songs Downloaded, 300 Million iPods Sold," Engadget, October 4, 2011, https://www.engadget.com/2011/10/04/apple-16-billion-itunes-songs-downloaded-300-million-ipods-sol/; Christopher Burgess and Richard Power, "How to Avoid Intellectual Property Theft," CIO, July 10, 2006, http://www.cio.com/article/22837; "For Students Doing Reports," RIAA, accessed February 4, 2013, www.riaa.com/faq.php; Ben Sisario, "AC/DC Joins iTunes, as Spotify Emerges as Music's New Disrupter," *New York Times*, November 19, 2012, https://mediadecoder.blogs.nytimes.com/2012/11/19/acdc-joins-itunes-as-spotify-emerges-as-musics-new-disrupter/.

[31] See Vangie Beal, "Spyware," Webopedia, http://www.webopedia.com/TERM/S/spyware.html, accessed on October 2, 2023.

[32] Donald A. Norman, "Got Spam?," MAPI: Manufacturers Alliance for Productivity and Innovation, October 20, 2016, http://www.mapi.net/blog/2016/10/got-spam.

[33] "'Spam King' Faces Federal Fraud Charges," *Columbia Daily Tribune*, January 21, 2013, http://www.columbiatribune.com/wire/spam-king-faces-federal-fraud-charges/article_042ac575-7820-5bb4-bb17-3e425f2f24c0.html#.URE7hPKmFcI.

[34] Brad Carlson, "Organizations Face New Records-Destruction Rule," *Idaho Business Review*, July 25, 2005, http://www.idahobusiness.net/archive.htm/2005/07/25/Organizations-face-new-recordsdestruction-rule.

[35] Carpenter v. United States, 585 U.S.___(2018) (U.S. Supreme Court, June 22, 2018), https://www.supremecourt.gov/opinions/17pdf/16-402_h315.pdf; Daniel Woislaw, "With 5G Arriving, the Supreme Court Needs to Rule on What Digital Privacy Means," Pacific Legal Foundation, January 1, 2020, https://pacificlegal.org/with-5g-arriving-the-supreme-court-needs-to-rule-on-what-digital-privacy-means/.

[36] Adam Higginbotham, "Welcome to Rosalind Picard's Touchy-Feely World of Empathic Tech," *Wired UK*, November 27, 2012, https://www.wired.co.uk/article/emotion-machines.

[37] Affectiva, "Our Origins—About Affectiva," March 6, 2023, https://www.affectiva.com/about-affectiva/.

[38] Smart Eye, "Driver Monitoring System (DMS)," May 23, 2023, https://smarteye.se/solutions/automotive/driver-monitoring-system/.

[39] Federal Trade Commission, "FTC Staff Report Finds Many Internet Service Providers Collect Troves of Personal Data, Users Have Few Options to Restrict Use." Federal Trade Commission, March 4, 2022. https://www.ftc.gov/news-events/news/press-releases/2021/10/ftc-staff-report-finds-many-internet-service-providers-collect-troves-personal-data-users-have-few.

chapter 15

The Role of Accountants and Accounting Information

Skorzewiak/Alamy Stock Photo

learning objectives

After reading this chapter, you should be able to:

15-1 **Explain** the role of accountants in business and distinguish among the kinds of work done by public accountants, private accountants, management accountants, and forensic accountants.

15-2 **Explain** the accounting equation and how it is used.

15-3 **Describe** the three basic financial statements and show how they reflect the activity and financial condition of a business.

15-4 **Explain** the key standards and principles for compiling and reporting financial statements.

15-5 **Describe** how computing financial ratios can help investors and other stakeholders get more information from financial statements to determine the financial strengths of a business.

15-6 **Discuss** the role of ethics in accounting.

15-7 **Describe** the purpose of the International Accounting Standards Board and explain why it exists.

what's in it for me?

For many of us, the words and ideas used in accounting can seem like a foreign language, and for that very reason, the specialized terminology can be used to mask fraud and corruption. However, accounting terminology is a necessary tool that allows professionals in every industry to analyze growth, understand risk, and communicate detailed ideas about a firm's financial health. This chapter will cover the fundamental concepts of accounting and apply them to familiar business situations. By grasping the basic accounting vocabulary, you—as an employee, taxpayer, investor, or owner—will be better able to participate when the conversation turns to the financial matters that constitute so much of a firm's daily operations. As a manager, you will also better understand how to use financial data to make better decisions.

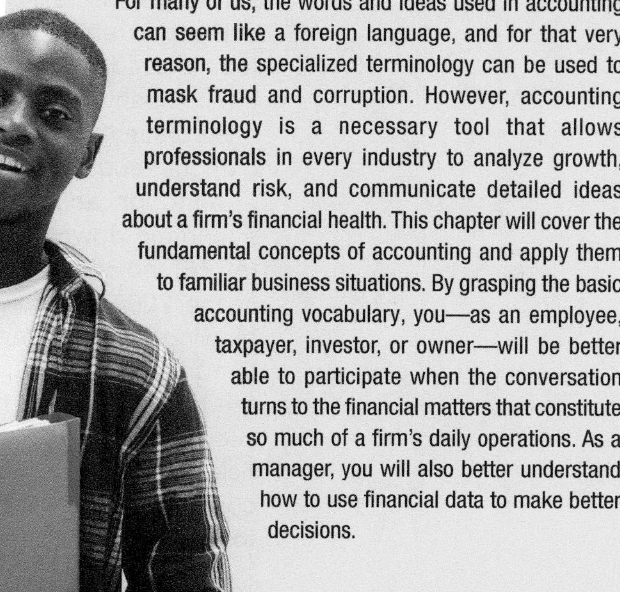

Shutterstock

Feifei Cui-Paoluzzo/Getty Images

CSI: Wall Street

In 2023, after several years of litigation, Evoqua Water Technologies Corp (AQUA) agreed to pay an $8.5 million fine to settle U.S. Securities and Exchange Commission (SEC) charges that the water treatment company used improper accounting to fraudulently inflate revenue in 2017 and 2018, as the company prepared for its initial public offering (IPO). Evoqua was charged with recording revenue from the sale of filtration products by billing for products that would be delivered on a later date. The basic rule for financial accounting is that the revenue should be recorded when the product is delivered. According to the SEC, the company reported nearly $12 million of extra expected revenue in filings related to its November 2017 IPO.[1]

According to Al Vondra, partner in Forensic Services and a Certified Fraud Examiner at PricewaterhouseCoopers, some of the most common fraudulent practices involve overstating revenues, as Evoqua did, and hiding expenses under incorrect categories, such as "Other Current Liabilities." The SEC and the Financial Accounting Standards Board (FASB) try to stay ahead of the game, but perpetrators of fraud are inventive, and sometimes companies find loopholes or bend the rules. For instance, in 2023, the FASB came out with a new set of rules to disclose supply-chain financing arrangements that allow companies to pay bills early in order to take advantage of discounts by using a third party. This is a perfectly legal arrangement, but companies were using it to make their financial situations look better than they actually were. They did this by listing the bank loans as long-term financing, which increased short-term cash flows on financial reports.

In 2023, the International Accounting Standards Board (IASB), which sets the financial reporting guidelines used by most countries, was still considering requiring similar disclosures. One of the precipitating events was the unexpected bankruptcy of Brazilian retailer Americanas SA, which reported its supply-chain financing as long-term instead of short-term debt. Changing the way the debt was reported subjected the company to $8 billion in early debt extinguishment. Management classified the misrepresentation as an inconsistency, but shareholders and analysts saw it as outright fraud.[2]

Although accounting scandals have always existed, they spike upward in economic downturns. Data from the Association of Certified Fraud Examiners (ACFE) indicates that corporate fraud cases began increasing significantly early in the 2008 recession, as more than 3,000 fraud-related reports and whistle-blowing tips were reported from within U.S. firms. A 2023 study indicated that up to 10 percent of U.S. companies commit fraud each year.[3] ACFE members believe the increase stems from heavier financial pressures: When employees feel less secure, they may falsify data to show better performance, or they may take greater risks that need to be covered up to show financial success.[4] (After studying the content in this chapter, you should be able to answer a set of discussion questions found at the end of the chapter.)

What Is Accounting, and Who Uses Accounting Information?

Learning Objective 15-1

Explain the role of accountants in business and distinguish among the kinds of work done by public accountants, private accountants, management accountants, and forensic accountants.

Accounting is a comprehensive system for collecting, analyzing, and communicating financial information to a firm's owners and employees, to the public, and to various regulatory agencies. To perform these functions, accountants keep records of taxes paid, income received, and expenses incurred, a process historically called **bookkeeping**, and they assess the effects of these transactions on business activities. By sorting and analyzing such transactions, accountants can determine how well a business is being managed and assess its overall financial strength.

Because businesses engage in thousands of transactions, ensuring consistent, dependable financial information is a necessity. This is the job of the **accounting information system (AIS)**, an organized procedure for identifying, measuring, recording, and retaining financial information so that it can be used in accounting statements and management reports. The system includes all of the people, reports, computers, procedures, and resources that are needed to compile financial transactions.[5]

Accounting *comprehensive system for collecting, analyzing, and communicating financial information*

Bookkeeping *recording of accounting transactions*

Accounting Information System (AIS) *organized procedure for identifying, measuring, recording, and retaining financial information for use in accounting statements and management reports*

Many different individuals, groups, and other entities use accounting information:

- *Managers* use it to develop goals and plans, set budgets, and make decisions about market opportunities.
- *Employees and unions* use it to plan for and receive compensation and such benefits as health care, vacation time, and retirement pay.
- *Investors and creditors* use it to estimate returns to shareholders, determine growth prospects, and decide whether a firm is a good credit risk.
- *Tax authorities* use it to plan for tax inflows (revenues), determine the tax liabilities of individuals and businesses, and ensure that correct amounts are paid on time.
- *Government regulatory agencies* rely on it to fulfill their duties toward the public. The Securities and Exchange Commission (SEC), for example, requires firms to file financial disclosures so that potential investors have valid information about their financial status.

The **controller**, or chief accounting officer, manages a firm's accounting activities by ensuring that the AIS provides the reports and statements needed for planning, decision making, and other management activities. This range of activities requires different types of accounting specialists. In this section, we begin by distinguishing between the two main fields of accounting: *financial* and *managerial*. Then, we discuss the different functions and activities of *certified public accountants, private accountants, management accountants*, and *forensic accountants*.

Controller *person who manages all of a firm's accounting activities (chief accounting officer)*

Financial Versus Managerial Accounting

In any company, two forms of accounting—financial and managerial—can be distinguished by the users they serve: those outside the company and those within.[6]

Financial Accounting A firm's **financial accounting** system is concerned with external information users: consumer groups, unions, shareholders, suppliers, creditors, and government agencies. It prepares reports such as income statements and balance sheets that focus on the activities of the company as a whole rather than on individual departments or divisions or internal projects and operations.[7]

Financial Accounting *field of accounting concerned with external users of a company's financial information*

Managerial Accounting **Managerial accounting**, on the other hand, serves internal users. Managers at all levels need information to make departmental decisions, monitor projects, and plan future activities. Other employees also need accounting information. Engineers must know certain costs, for example, before making product or operations improvements, purchasing agents use information on materials costs

Managerial (Management) Accounting *field of accounting that serves internal users of a company's financial information*

to negotiate terms with suppliers and to set performance goals, and salespeople need historical sales data for each geographic region and for each of its products.

Certified Public Accountants

Certified Public Accountant (CPA) *accountant licensed by the state and offering services to the public*

Public accountants offer accounting services to the public and are distinguished by their independence from the clients they serve. That is to say, they typically work for an accounting firm providing services for outside client firms in which the public accountant has no vested interest, thus avoiding any potential biases in conducting their professional services. Among public accountants, **certified public accountants (CPAs)** are licensed by a state after passing an exam prepared by the American Institute of Certified Public Accountants (AICPA). Preparation for certification begins with majoring in a college program studying the theory, practices, and legal aspects of accounting. In addition to the CPA exam, certification in most states requires some practice (experience), varying up to two years, in a private company or government entity under the direction of a CPA. Once certified, the CPA can perform services beyond those allowed by non-CPAs.[8] Whereas some CPAs work as individual practitioners, many form or join existing partnerships or professional corporations.

The "Big Four" Public Accounting Firms Although thousands of CPA companies of various sizes, ranging from small one-person local operations to large multinationals, operate in the United States, about one-half of total revenues for public accounting services are generated by the four biggest CPA firms (listed with their headquarters):

- Deloitte (United Kingdom)
- Ernst & Young (United Kingdom)
- PricewaterhouseCoopers, PwC (United Kingdom)
- KPMG (Netherlands)

In addition to prominence in the United States, international operations are important for all four of these companies. For instance, they have experienced especially rapid growth in recent years for CPA services in Asia and Latin America. Each of the Big Four firms has more than 200,000 employees worldwide.[9]

Hannah McKay/PA Images/Alamy Stock Photo

Accountants help monitor and analyze a firm's financial information to make sure that it is accurate and that proper reporting procedures are being followed. In 2017, accountants uncovered fraudulent activities at Tesco, a large British retailer, resulting in jail time for these three former Tesco executives. All told, accountants discovered that they had inaccurately reported over $400 million in revenues and expenses in order to falsely boost Tesco stock prices.

CPA Services Virtually all CPA firms, whether large or small, provide auditing (sometimes called *assurance*), tax, and management services. Larger firms such as Deloitte Touche Tohmatsu and Ernst & Young earn much of their revenue from auditing and tax services and consulting (management advisory) services. For instance, in 2022 Ernst & Young earned $4.4 billion in revenues, with 31.7 percent from auditing/assurance, 24.9 percent from tax services, and 30.5 percent from consulting services.[10] Smaller firms earn most of their income from tax and management services.

Auditing An **audit** examines a company's AIS to determine whether financial reports reliably represent its operations.[11] Organizations must provide audit reports when applying for loans, selling stock, or going through a major restructuring. Independent auditors who do not work for the company must ensure that clients' accounting systems follow **generally accepted accounting principles (GAAP)**, which are formulated by the Financial Accounting Standards Board (FASB) of the AICPA and govern the content and form of financial reports.[12] The auditing of a firm's financial statements is one of the services that can be performed only by a CPA. The Securities and Exchange Commission (SEC) is the U.S. government agency that legally enforces accounting and auditing rules and procedures. Ultimately, the CPA performing the audit is expected to certify whether or not the client's reports comply with GAAP.

Audit *systematic examination of a company's accounting system to determine whether its financial reports reliably represent its operations*

Generally Accepted Accounting Principles (GAAP) *accounting guidelines that govern the content and form of financial reports*

Tax Services **Tax services** include assistance not only with tax-return preparation but also with tax planning. A CPA's advice can help a business structure (or restructure) operations and investments and perhaps save millions of dollars in taxes. Staying abreast of tax-law changes is no simple matter. Some critics charge that the changing of tax regulations has become a full-time vocation among some state and federal legislators, who add increasingly complicated laws and technical corrections on taxation each year.

Tax Services *assistance provided by CPAs for tax preparation and tax planning*

Management Advisory Services As consultants, some accounting firms also provide **management advisory services** ranging from personal financial planning to planning corporate mergers. Other services include production scheduling, information systems studies, AIS design, and even executive recruitment. The staffs of the largest CPA firms sometimes include engineers, architects, mathematicians, and psychologists, all of whom are available for consulting on relevant issues, challenges, and initiatives.

Management Advisory Services *assistance provided by CPA firms in areas such as financial planning, information systems design, and other areas of concern for client firms*

Noncertified Public Accountants Many accountants don't take the CPA exam; others work in the field while getting ready for it or while meeting requirements for state certification. Many small businesses, individuals, and even larger firms rely on these non-CPAs for basic income-tax preparation, payroll accounting, and financial-planning services so long as they abide by local and state laws. Non-CPAs often put together financial statements that are used in the firm for internal purposes, based on information provided by management. These statements may include a notification that auditing methods were not used in their preparation.

The CPA Vision Project A continuing talent shortage in accounting has led the profession to rethink its culture and lifestyle.[13] With grassroots participation from CPAs, educators, and industry leaders, the AICPA, through its CPA Vision Project, is redefining the role of the accountant for today's world economy. The Vision Project identifies a unique combination of skills, technology, and knowledge, called **core competencies for accounting**, that will be necessary for future CPAs. The AICPA summarizes the project's core purpose as follows: "CPAs . . . Making sense of a changing and complex world."[14] As Table 15.1 shows, those skills, which include communication, critical thinking, and leadership, go far beyond the ability to "crunch numbers." They include certain communications skills, along with skills in critical thinking and leadership. Indeed, the CPA Vision Project foresees CPAs who combine specialty skills with a broad-based orientation to communicate more effectively with people in a wide range of business activities.

Core Competencies for Accounting *the combination of skills, technology, and knowledge that will be necessary for the future CPA*

table 15.1 AICPA's Competencies for Success in Accounting

Skills in Strategic Thinking and Critical Problem Solving	The accountant can combine data with reasoning and professional knowledge to recognize and help solve critical problems for better strategic action.
Communications, Interpersonal Skills, and Effective Leadership	The accountant can communicate effectively in various business situations using meaningful communications skills that provide interpersonal effectiveness and leadership.
Dedication to Meeting Customer Needs	The accountant surpasses the competition in understanding each client's unique needs, in meeting those needs, and in visualizing the client's future needs.
Ability to Integrate Diverse Information	The accountant can combine financial and other kinds of information to gain new meaning that provides clients with useful insights and understanding for solving problems.
Proficiency with Information Technology	The accountant can use information technology (IT) in performing services for clients and can identify IT applications that the client can adopt for added value to the business.

Source: Based on "The CPA Vision Project," The American Institute of Certified Public Accountants, accessed July 25, 2023, https://us.aicpa.org/content/dam/aicpa/research/cpahorizons2025/cpavisionproject/downloadabledocuments/cpavisionproject-finalreport.pdf.

Private Accountants and Management Accountants

Private Accountant *salaried accountant hired by a business to carry out its day-to-day financial activities*

To ensure integrity in reporting, CPAs engaged in auditing activities are always independent of the firms they audit. However, many businesses also hire their own **private accountants** as salaried employees to perform day-to-day activities. These accountants may also be CPAs but cannot engage in the external audit process.

Private accountants perform numerous jobs. An internal auditor at ConocoPhillips, for example, might fly to the North Sea to confirm the accuracy of oil-flow meters on offshore petroleum drilling platforms. A supervisor responsible for $2 billion in monthly payouts to vendors and employees may never leave the executive suite, with duties such as hiring and training, assigning projects, and evaluating performance of accounting personnel. Large businesses employ specialized accountants in such areas as budgeting, financial planning, internal auditing, payroll, and taxation. In small businesses, a single person may handle all accounting tasks.

Management Accountant *private accountant who provides financial services to support managers in various business activities within a firm*

Certified Management Accountant (CMA) *professional designation awarded by the Institute of Management Accountants (IMA) in recognition of management accounting qualifications*

Although private accountants may be either CPAs or non-CPAs, most are what are called **management accountants**, who provide services to support managers in various activities (marketing, production, engineering, and so forth). Many hold the **certified management accountant (CMA)** designation, awarded by the Institute of Management Accountants (IMA), recognizing qualifications of professionals who have passed IMA's experience and examination requirements. With more than 150,000 members in 150 countries, IMA is dedicated to supporting accounting professionals to create quality internal controls and financial practices in their companies.[15]

Forensic Accountants

Forensic Accounting *the practice of accounting for legal purposes*

One of the fastest-growing areas in accounting is **forensic accounting**, the use of accounting for legal purposes.[16] Sometimes known as "the private eyes of the corporate culture," forensic accountants must be good detectives. They look behind the corporate façade instead of accepting financial records at face value.

In combining investigative skills with accounting, auditing, and the instincts of a detective, they assist in the investigation of business and financial issues that may have application to a court of law. Forensic accountants may be called on by law enforcement agencies, insurance companies, law firms, private individuals, and business firms for both investigative accounting and litigation support in crimes against companies, crimes by companies, and civil disagreements. They may conduct criminal investigations of online scams and misuse of government funds. Civil cases often require investigating and quantifying claims of personal injury loss as a result of negligence and analyzing financial issues in divorce proceedings. Forensic accountants also assist business firms in tracing and recovering lost assets from employee business fraud or theft.

Investigative Accounting Law enforcement officials may ask a forensic accountant to investigate a trail of financial transactions behind a suspected crime, as in a money-laundering scheme or an investment swindle. The forensic accountant, being familiar with the legal concepts and procedures of the case, would then identify and analyze pertinent financial evidence—documents, bank accounts, phone calls, computer records, and people—and present accounting conclusions and their legal implications. They also develop reports, exhibits, and documents to communicate their findings.

Litigation Support Forensic accountants assist in the application of accounting evidence for judicial proceedings by preparing and preserving evidence for these proceedings. They also assist by presenting visual aids to support trial evidence, by testifying as expert witnesses, and, especially, by determining economic damages in any case before the court. A divorce attorney, for example, may suspect that the assets of one party are being understated and request financial analysis by a forensic accountant. A movie producer may need help in determining damages for breach of contract by an actor who quits before a film is completed.

Certified Fraud Examiners One specific area within forensic accounting, the **Certified Fraud Examiner (CFE)** designation, is administered by the ACFE. The CFE's activities focus specifically on fraud-related issues, such as fraud detection, evaluating accounting systems for weaknesses and fraud risks, investigating white-collar crime on behalf of law enforcement agencies, evaluating internal organizational controls for fraud prevention, and expert witnessing. Many CFEs find employment in corporations seeking to prevent fraud from within. The CFE examination covers four areas:

Certified Fraud Examiner (CFE) *professional designation administered by the ACFE in recognition of qualifications for a specialty area within forensic accounting*

1 ***Fraud prevention and deterrence.*** Includes why people commit fraud, theories of fraud prevention, and professional code of ethics
2 ***Financial transactions.*** Examines types of fraudulent financial transactions incurred in accounting records
3 ***Fraud investigation.*** Pertains to tracing illicit transactions, evaluating deception, and interviewing and taking statements
4 ***Legal elements of fraud.*** Includes rules of evidence, criminal and civil law, and rights of the accused and accuser

Eligibility to take the exam includes both educational and experience requirements. Although a minimum of a bachelor's degree is required, it does not have to be in accounting or any other specific field of study. Candidates without a bachelor's degree, but with fraud-related professional experience, may substitute two years of experience for each year of academic study. Experience requirements for certification include at least two years in any of several fraud-related areas, such as auditing, criminology, fraud investigation, or law.

entrepreneurship and new ventures

Skimming Off the Top

Jennifer Mayberry runs a respectable coffee shop in a small Pacific Northwest town. For years she's dropped her daily receipts off in the night deposit slot at the local Chase bank, where her friend works, but Jennifer, trusting the banking system, never reconciled her deposit slips to her accounting records. In fact, she never reconciled her checking account to the bank statement. But when her accountants started tallying up revenues for tax reporting, they found a $1,000 discrepancy in the November deposit. That led to the hiring of a forensic accountant, who discovered that, despite internal controls at the bank, Jennifer's friend had been skimming the cash from the deposits, changing the deposit slips, and then making the smaller deposit into the account. Over the course of 18 months, the friend skimmed $42,828.96. Jennifer could have prevented this had the coffee shop had some simple accounting procedures in place.[17]

Meanwhile, down in Texas at the Collin Street Bakery, world famous for its delectable fruitcakes, owner Bob McNutt was unraveling a decade of embezzlement. It had started when the head accountant, feeling underpaid, bought himself a new Lexus and paid for it with a company check, covering his tracks by voiding that check in the system and writing another check to a legitimate vendor, which he then never sent. In the bank account, a check cleared for $20,000, and the accounting records showed a payment of $20,000. Since there were no other accountants and the business owner didn't audit the records, no one caught the theft. Soon, the accountant was taking up to $98,000 a month from the bakery and he and his wife were living a lavish lifestyle, explaining it away as the result of an inheritance. No one much questioned the fine cars, vacations, jewelry, country club membership, home remodeling, and other obviously expensive purchases. Eventually McNutt, who had been scratching his head now for years trying to figure out how his business, which seemed so outwardly successful, was cash poor and struggling year after year, examined labor expenses, product expenses, prices, and everything he could think of but found nothing helpful. But one day, a new hire in the accounting department found a curious voided check in the system. That was the beginning of the end for the thief. As the story unfolded, McNutt found that this one accountant had managed to skim over $17 million from Collin Street Bakery, using an unsophisticated scheme that could have been prevented by a few simple internal control procedures.[18]

The Fort Worth Star-Telegram/Ron Jenkins/AP Images

Small and medium-sized businesses aren't the only ones who get hit by embezzlers. Cargill Inc. is a global agribusiness corporation based in Minnesota, and although it's privately held, on the Fortune 500 list it would rank ahead of AT&T. In 2016, one of the accounting managers pled guilty to skimming over $3 million from the company by depositing customer payments into her personal account.[19] In 2021, Cargill lost $45 million when two employees conspired with a vendor, Women's Distribution Services, or WDS, of South Carolina, to overcharge Cargill for their own benefit.[20]

It's not just high-tech scams that these businesses need to watch out for. All three of these instances occurred because the business owners took a relaxed view of the kinds of accounting policies and procedures that protect one of the most valuable and easily lifted assets—cash. That's why it pays to become educated in basic financial accounting and human resource management as you move your way up in business.

Federal Restrictions on CPA Services and Financial Reporting: Sarbox

Sarbanes-Oxley Act of 2002 (Sarbox or **SOX)** *enactment of federal regulations to restore public trust in accounting practices by imposing new requirements on financial activities in publicly traded corporations*

The financial wrongdoings associated with firms such as ImClone Systems, Tesco, Tyco, WorldCom, Enron, Arthur Andersen, and others have not gone unnoticed in legislative circles. Federal regulations, primarily the **Sarbanes-Oxley Act of 2002 (Sarbox** or **SOX)**, have been enacted to restore and maintain public trust in corporate accounting practices.

Sarbox restricts the kinds of nonaudit services that CPAs can provide. Under the Sarbox law, for example, a CPA firm can help design a client's financial information system, but not if it also does the client's auditing. Hypothetically, an unscrupulous accounting firm's audit might intentionally overlook a client's false financial statements if, in return, the client rewards the accounting firm with a contract for lucrative

table 15.2 Selected Provisions of the Sarbanes-Oxley Act[21]

- Creates a national Accounting Oversight Board that, among other activities, must establish the ethics standards used by CPA firms in preparing audits
- Requires that auditors retain audit working papers for specified periods of time
- Requires auditor rotation by prohibiting the same person from being the lead auditor for more than five consecutive years
- Requires that the CEO and CFO certify that the company's financial statements are true, fair, and accurate
- Prohibits corporations from extending personal loans to executives and directors
- Requires that the audited company disclose whether it has adopted a code of ethics for its senior financial officers
- Requires that the SEC regularly review each corporation's financial statements
- Prevents employers from retaliating against research analysts who write negative reports
- Imposes criminal penalties on auditors and clients for falsifying, destroying, altering, or concealing records (10 years in prison)
- Imposes a fine or imprisonment (up to 25 years) on any person who defrauds shareholders
- Increases penalties for mail and wire fraud from 5 to 20 years in prison
- Establishes criminal liability for failure of corporate officers to certify financial reports

nonaccounting services, such as management consulting. This was a core allegation in the Enron–Arthur Andersen scandal several years ago. Arthur Andersen, one of the world's largest accounting firms at the time, filed audits that failed to disclose Enron's shaky financial condition, which eventually led to the massive energy company's bankruptcy and to Andersen's dissolution. Andersen's auditors gained more money from consulting at Enron than from the actual auditing work.[22] By prohibiting auditing and nonauditing services to the same client, Sarbox encourages audits that are independent and unbiased.

Sarbox imposes requirements on virtually every financial activity in publicly traded corporations, as well as severe criminal penalties for persons committing or concealing fraud or destroying financial records. CFOs and CEOs, for example, have to pledge that the company's finances are correct and must personally vouch for the methods and internal controls used to get those numbers. Companies have to provide a system that is safe for all employees to anonymously report unethical accounting practices and illegal activities without fear of retaliation. Table 15.2 provides brief descriptions of several of Sarbox's many provisions.

The Accounting Equation

Learning Objective 15-2

Explain the accounting equation and how it is used.

All accountants rely on record keeping to enter and track transactions. Underlying all record-keeping procedures is the most basic tool of accounting, the **accounting equation**:

$$\text{Assets} = \text{Liabilities} + \text{Owner's Equity}$$

Accounting Equation *Assets = Liabilities + Owners' Equity; used by accountants to balance data for the firm's financial transactions at various points in the year*

After each financial transaction (e.g., payments to suppliers, sales to customers, wages to employees), the accounting equation must be in balance. If it isn't, then an accounting error has occurred. To better understand the importance of this equation, we must understand the terms *assets, liabilities*, and *owners' equity*.

Assets and Liabilities

An **asset** is any economic resource that is expected to benefit a firm, its owner(s), or both. Assets for accounting purposes include land, buildings, equipment, inventories, and payments due the company (accounts receivable). Apple, for example, held total assets amounting to $352,755 million at year end 2022.[23] A **liability**, in contrast, is a debt that a firm owes to an outside party. The total of Apple's liabilities—all the debt owed to others—was $302,083 million at the end of 2022.

Asset *any economic resource expected to benefit a firm or an individual who owns it*

Liability *debt owed by a firm to an outside organization or individual*

Peregrine/Alamy Stock Photo

An asset is an economic resource that benefits the firm. Apple's assets include retail outlets and the inventories of Apple products that the stores keep on hand to sell to customers.

Owners' Equity

Owners' Equity *amount of money that owners would receive if they sold all of a firm's assets and paid all of its liabilities*

You may be familiar with the concept of *equity* that a homeowner has in a house—the amount of money that could be made (or lost) by selling the house and paying off the mortgage. Similarly, **owners' equity** in a business is the amount of money that owners would theoretically receive if they sold all of a company's assets at their presumed value and paid all of its liabilities. Apple's financial reports for 2022 declared shareholders' equity of $50,672 million. At Apple, then, we see that the accounting equation is in balance, as it should be.

$$\text{Assets} = \text{Liabilities} + \text{Owner's Equity}$$
$$\$352,755 = \$302,083 + \$50,672 \text{ million}$$

We can also rewrite the equation to highlight how owners' equity relates to assets and liabilities.

$$\text{Assets} - \text{Liabilities} = \text{Owner's Equity}$$

Another term for this is *net worth*: The difference between what a firm owns (assets) minus what it owes (liabilities) is its net worth, or owners' equity. If a company's assets exceed its liabilities, owners' equity is *positive*. At Apple, owners' equity is $50,672 million ($= \$362,755$ million $- \$302,083$ million). If the company goes out of business, the owners may receive some cash (a gain) after selling assets and paying off liabilities. However, if liabilities outweigh assets, owners' equity is *negative*; assets are insufficient to pay off all debts, and the firm is insolvent. If the company goes out of business, the owners will get no cash, and some creditors won't be paid.

Owners' equity is meaningful for both investors and lenders. Before lending money to owners, for example, lenders want to know the amount of owners' equity in a business. A larger owners' equity indicates greater security for lenders. Owners' equity consists of two sources of capital:

1 The amount that the owners originally invested (this is also referred to as *contributed capital*)

2 Profits (also owned by the owners) earned by and then reinvested in the company (legally called *retained earnings*)

When a company operates profitably, its assets increase faster than its liabilities. Owners' equity, therefore, will increase if profits are retained in the business instead of paid out as dividends to stockholders. Owners' equity also increases if owners invest more of their own money to increase assets. However, owners' equity can shrink if the company operates at a loss or if owners withdraw assets.

managing in turbulent times

United States Versus the World

The International Financial Reporting Standards (IFRS) set of accounting rules is used in more than 168 countries around the world, including the European Union and many Asian and South American countries. The generally accepted accounting standards (GAAP) set of guidelines, set by the Financial Accounting Standards Board (FASB), is used only in the United States.

Differences between the two standards can be significant. Samsung, maker of the Galaxy phones, is a Korean company, and its financial statements are prepared according to Korea's version of IFRS and stated in won, the Korean currency. Apple is a U.S. company with GAAP-based financials. GAAP requires companies to report research and development (R&D) costs as expenses as they are incurred, under the theory that most R&D doesn't result in a viable product, but IFRS allows companies to record R&D as an asset on the balance sheet and to then spread the costs out over subsequent years. For two hypothetically identical companies, this would mean that the U.S. financials would show less profit in the current year but slightly more in subsequent years, as the international company spread the costs out. And that's only one of the many divergent practices.

Although the FASB and the London-based International Accounting Standards Board (IASB) have agreed in principle to work together toward a more unified set of standards, progress on this "convergence" has been slow for several reasons. First, IFRS are principle based, offering more philosophical guidance rather than the more definitive rule-based provisions of GAAP. Regulators and professionals in the United States argue that in our litigious society, we need stricter guidance, not looser.

Lukmanazis/Shutterstock

Even though Samsung and Apple compete in the smartphone market, they use different accounting standards.

In addition, the FASB and the SEC are unlikely to concede their long-established standard-setting authority to the relatively new IASB. Third, U.S. companies and investors alike have a long-standing investment of both time and money in GAAP, and changing could be disruptive and expensive.

Even though the U.S. accounting profession shows no sign of adopting IFRS in the near future, recent work around a conceptual framework for GAAP, an overall trend toward more and more globalization, and the flexibility and adaptability of a more principle-based system of accounting are just some of the forces pushing the convergence process onward. In the meantime, savvy investors understand the differences between various systems and rely on the disclosures to the audited financial statement to explain accounting practices and choices.

Financial Statements

Learning Objective 15-3

Describe the three basic financial statements and show how they reflect the activity and financial condition of a business.

As noted previously, accountants summarize the results of a firm's transactions and compile reports to help managers make informed decisions. Among the most important reports are **financial statements**, which fall into three broad categories: *balance sheets, income statements*, and *statements of cash flows*. Together, these reports indicate the firm's financial health and what affected it. In this section, we discuss these three financial statements as well as the function of the budget as an internal financial statement.

Financial Statement *any of several types of reports summarizing a company's financial status to stakeholders and to aid in managerial decision making*

Balance Sheets

Balance sheets supply detailed information about the items that constitute the accounting equation: *assets, liabilities*, and *owners' equity*. Because they also show a firm's financial condition at one specific point in time, they are sometimes called *statements of financial position*. Figure 15.1 is a simplified presentation of the balance sheet for Apple, Inc. on the last day of its 2022 fiscal year.

Balance Sheet *financial statement that supplies detailed information about a firm's assets, liabilities, and owners' equity*

Assets From an accounting standpoint, most companies have major three types of assets: *current, fixed*, and *intangible*.

Balance sheet for 2022 fiscal year

Current assets:	
Cash and cash equivalents	$ 23,646
Marketable securities	24,658
Accounts receivable	28,184
Inventories	4,946
Vendor non-trade receivables	32,748
Other current assets	21,223
Total current assets	$ 135,405
Non-current assets:	
Marketable securities	$ 120,805
Property, plant, and equipment	42,117
Other non-current assets	54,428
Total non-current assets	$ 217,350
Total assets	$ 352,755

Current liabilities:	
Accounts payable	$ 64,115
Other current liabilities	60,845
Deferred revenue	7,912
Commercial paper	9,982
Term debt	11,128
Total current liabilities	$ 153,982
Non-current liabilities:	
Term debt	$ 98,959
Other non-current liabilities	49,142
Total non-current liabilities	$ 148,101
Total liabilities	$ 302,083
Stockholders' equity:	
Common stock & APIC	$ 64,849
RE/accumulated deficit	(3,068)
Other	(11,109)
Total stockholders' equity	$ 50,672
Liabilities and SHE	$ 352,755

FIGURE 15.1 Apple's Balance Sheet
Source: Apple, Inc., Fourth-Quarter 2022 10-K.

Current Asset *asset that can or will be converted into cash within a year*

Liquidity *ease with which an asset can be converted into cash*

CURRENT ASSETS **Current assets** include cash and assets that can be converted into cash within a year. The act of converting something into cash is called *liquidating*. Assets are normally listed in order of **liquidity**, the ease of converting them into cash. Debts, for example, are usually paid in cash. A company that needs but cannot generate cash—a company that's not "liquid"—may be forced to sell assets at reduced prices or even to go out of business.

By definition, cash is completely liquid. *Marketable securities* purchased as short-term investments are slightly less liquid but can be sold quickly. These include stocks or bonds of other companies, government securities, and money market certificates. Many companies hold other nonliquid assets such as *merchandise inventory*, the cost of merchandise that's been acquired for sale to customers and is still on hand. Apple keeps very little inventory on hand. For instance, as new iPhones are manufactured, they are shipped directly to retailers like AT&T or Verizon and are then carried as inventory on the balance sheets of those companies. However, because Apple generates so much cash, it does maintain robust investments in long-term marketable assets.

fixed asset *asset with long-term use or value, such as land, buildings, and equipment*

depreciation *accounting method for distributing the cost of an asset over its useful life*

FIXED ASSETS **Fixed assets** (such as land, buildings, and equipment) have long-term use or value, but as buildings and equipment wear out or become obsolete, their value decreases. Accountants use **depreciation** to spread the cost of an asset over the years of its useful life. To reflect decreasing value, accountants calculate an asset's expected useful life in years, divide its worth by that many years, and subtract the resulting amount each year. Every year, therefore, the remaining value (or net value) decreases on the firm's records. In Figure 15.1, Apple shows fixed assets of $42,117 million after depreciation.

INTANGIBLE ASSETS Although their worth is hard to calculate, **intangible assets** have monetary value in the form of expected benefits, which may include fees paid by others for obtaining rights or privileges—such as patents, trademarks, copyrights, and franchises—to your products. **Goodwill** is the amount that a buyer would be expected to pay for an existing business beyond the value of its other assets. A purchased firm, for example, may have a particularly good reputation or location. Apple declares both intangible assets and goodwill in its expanded balance sheet.

Intangible asset *nonphysical asset, such as a patent or trademark, that has economic value in the form of expected benefit*

Goodwill *amount paid for an existing business above the value of its other assets*

Liabilities Like assets, liabilities are often separated into different categories. **Current liabilities** are debts that must be paid within 1 year. These include **accounts payable (payables)**, unpaid bills to suppliers for materials as well as wages and taxes that must be paid in the coming year. Apple has current liabilities of $153,982 million. **Long-term liabilities** are debts that are not due for at least a year. These normally represent borrowed funds on which the company must pay interest. The long-term liabilities of Apple are $148,101 million.

Current Liability *debt that must be paid within one year*

Accounts Payable (Payables) *current liability consisting of bills owed to suppliers, plus wages and taxes due within the coming year*

Long-Term Liability *debt that is not due for at least one year*

Owners' Equity The final section of the balance sheet in Figure 15.1 shows owners' equity (shareholders' equity) broken down into *paid-in capital* and *retained earnings*. When Apple was first formed, it sold a small amount of common stock that provided its first *paid-in capital*. **Paid-in capital** is money invested by owners. This includes both the original infusion of capital as well as additional capital raised when a firm issues additional stock as it grows.

Retained earnings are net profits kept by a firm rather than paid out as dividend payments to stockholders. As businesses earn profits, they can divide those profits to shareholders in the form of dividends (discussed in Chapter 17) or retain them to finance future growth.

The balance sheet for any company, then, is a barometer for its financial condition at one point in time. By comparing the current balance sheet with those of previous years, creditors and owners can better interpret the firm's financial progress and future prospects in terms of changes in its assets, liabilities, and owners' equity.

Paid-In Capital *money that is invested in a company by its owners*

Retained Earnings *earnings retained by a firm for its use rather than paid out as dividends*

Income Statements

The **income statement** is sometimes called a **profit-and-loss statement** because its description of revenues and expenses results in a figure showing the firm's annual profit or loss. In other words,

$$\text{Profit (or Loss)} = \text{Revenues} - \text{Expenses}$$

Income Statement (Profit-and-Loss Statement) *financial statement listing a firm's annual revenues and expenses so that a bottom line shows annual profit or loss*

Commonly known as the *bottom line*, profit or loss is probably the most important figure in any business enterprise. Figure 15.2 shows the 2022 income statement for Apple, whose bottom line was $99,803 million in profit. The income statement includes four major categories: (1) *revenues*, (2) *cost of revenues*, (3) *operating expenses*, and (4) *net income*. Unlike a balance sheet, which shows the financial condition at a specific *point in time*, an income statement shows the financial results that occurred across a *period of time*, such as a month, quarter, or year.

Revenues When a law firm receives $250 for preparing a will or a supermarket collects $65 from a grocery shopper, both are receiving **revenues**, the funds that flow into a business from the sale of goods or services. In 2022, Apple reported revenues of $394,328 million from the sale of iPhones, iPads, computers, digital music, watches, and other products.

Revenues *funds that flow into a business from the sale of goods or services*

Cost of Revenues (Cost of Goods Sold) In the Apple income statement, the **cost of revenues** section shows the costs of obtaining the revenues from other companies during the year. These are the costs that Apple pays manufacturers

Cost of Revenues *costs that a company incurs to obtain revenues from other companies*

Income statement for 2022 fiscal year

Revenues (Total Net Sales)	**$**	**394,328**
Total Cost of Sales		**223,546**
Gross Margin	**$**	**170,782**
Operating Expenses:		
Research & development		26,251
Selling, general & administrative		25,094
Total operating expenses		(51,345)
Operating income	**$**	**119,437**
Other income/expenses, net		(334)
Income before provision for income taxes		119,103
Provision for income taxes		19,300
Net Income	**$**	**99,803**

FIGURE 15.2 Apple's Income Statement
Source: Apple, Inc., *2022 Annual Report* (Mountain View, CA: Author, 2022.)

for producing its hardware products like phones, tablets, and computers and the licensing fees it pays for the right to distribute music, movies, and so forth. Other costs include expenses arising from the operation of Apple's data centers, including labor, energy, and costs of processing customer transactions. The cost of revenues for Apple in 2022 was $223,546 million.

We should also note that Apple does very little of its own manufacturing—most of its manufacturing is outsourced to low-cost producers in Asia. Traditional manufacturing companies, however, like Ford and Procter & Gamble, use a different reporting category, **cost of goods sold**, which are the costs of obtaining and transforming materials to make physical products sold during the year.

Cost of Goods Sold *costs of obtaining materials for making the products sold by a firm during the year*

Gross Profit Managers are often interested in **gross profit**, a preliminary, quick-to-calculate profit figure that considers just two pieces of data—revenues and cost of revenues (the direct costs of getting those revenues)—from the income statement. To calculate gross profit, simply subtract cost of revenues from revenues obtained by selling the firm's products.

Gross Profit *preliminary, quick-to-calculate profit figure calculated from the firm's revenues minus its cost of revenues (the direct costs of getting the revenues)*

Operating Expenses In addition to costs directly related to generating revenues, every company has general expenses ranging from office supplies to the CEO's salary. Like cost of revenues and cost of goods sold, **operating expenses** are resources that must flow out of a company if it is to earn revenues. As shown in Figure 15.2, Apple had operating expenses of $51,345 million in 2022.

Operating Expenses *costs, other than the cost of revenues, incurred in producing a good or service*

Research development expenses are associated with exploring new services and technologies that might be introduced in the future. *Selling expenses* result from activities related to selling goods or services, such as sales-force salaries and advertising expenses. *Administrative and general expenses,* such as management salaries and maintenance costs, are related to the overall management of the company.

Operating and Net Income **Operating income** compares the gross profit from operations against operating expenses. This calculation for Apple ($170,782 million – $51,345) yields an operating income, or income before taxes, of $119,437 million. Apple also earned $2,825 million from interest on investments (this is not considered to be operating income) and incurred tax liabilities of $19,300 million. Adding the interest revenue and subtracting estimated income taxes from operating income ($119, 437 million + $2, 825 million − $19, 300 million) yields **net income (net profit or net earnings)**. Apple's net income for 2022 was $99.803 million. The step-by-step detail in an income statement shows how a company obtained its net income for the period, making it easier for shareholders and other stakeholders to evaluate the firm's financial performance.

Operating Income *gross profit minus operating expenses*

Net Income (Net Profit or Net Earnings) *gross profit minus operating expenses and income taxes*

Statements of Cash Flows

Some companies prepare only balance sheets and income statements. However, the SEC requires all firms whose stock is publicly traded to issue a third report, the **statement of cash flows**. This statement summarizes yearly cash receipts and cash payments. Because it provides the most detail about how the company generates and uses cash, some investors and creditors consider it one of the most important statements of all. It shows the effects on cash of three aspects of a business: *operating activities, investing activities*, and *financing activities*. Apple's (simplified) 2022 statement of cash flows is shown in Figure 15.3.

Statement of Cash Flows *financial statement describing a firm's yearly cash receipts and cash payments*

- ***Cash flows from operations.*** The first set of information presented in the statement concerns primary operating activities: cash transactions involved in buying and selling goods and services. For Apple, it reveals how much of the year's cash balance results from the firm's primary business, sales of iPhones, iPads, computers, watches, and music. At the beginning of 2022, Apple had $35,929 million in cash on hand. During the year, it generated an additional $99,803 million in cash from the sales of its primary product lines.
- ***Cash flows from investing.*** A second set of information in the statement reports net cash used in or provided by investing. It includes cash receipts and payments from buying and selling stocks, bonds, property, equipment, and other productive assets. These sources of cash are not the company's main business. Apple generated $37,446 million from sales of marketable securities but also spent $76,923 million on other marketable securities.
- ***Cash flows from financing.*** The third set of information reports net cash from all financing activities. It includes cash inflows from borrowing or issuing stock, as well as outflows for payment of dividends and repayment of borrowed money. Apple's financing activities included $1,175 million in proceeds from the issuance of common stock but also $89,402 million spent on the repurchase of common stock at different times during the year.
- The overall change in cash from all of these sources, as well as a few other minor sources, was a decrease in cash from $35,929 million at the beginning of 2022 to $24,977 million at the end of 2022. When creditors and stockholders know how a firm obtained and used funds during the course of a year, it's easier for them to interpret year-to-year changes in the balance sheet and income statement.

The Budget: An Internal Financial Statement

For planning, controlling, and decision making, the most important internal financial statement is the **budget**, a detailed report on estimated receipts and expenditures for a future period of time. Although that period is usually 1 year, some companies also prepare longer-term projections, most commonly three- or five-year budgets,

Budget *detailed statement of estimated receipts and expenditures for a future period of time*

Statement of Cash Flows for 2022 fiscal year

Cash beginning balance	$ 35,929
Operating Activities (NI)	99,803
Adjustments (total)	21,148
Changes in operating A and L:	
Accounts receivable (net)	(1,823)
Inventories	1,484
Vendor non-trade receivables	(7,520)
Other current/noncurrent assets	(6,499)
Accounts payable	9,448
Deferred revenue	478
Other current/noncurrent liabilities	5,832
Cash generated by operating activities	122,151
Investing activities:	
Marketable securities	(76,923)
Proceeds from maturities	29,917
Proceeds from sales	37,446
Payments for PPE	(10,708)
Payments for business acquisitions	(306)
Other	(1,780)
Cash used in investing activities	(22,354)
Financing activities:	
Payments for taxes	(6,223)
Payments for dividends	(14,841)
Repurchases of common stock	(89,402)
Proceeds from issuance of term debt	5,465
Repayments of term debt	(9,543)
Proceeds from commercial paper	3,955
Other	(160)
Cash used in financing activities	(110,749)
Decrease in cash & equivalents	(10,952)
Cash & equivalents ending balance	$ 24,977

FIGURE 15.3 Apple's Statement of Cash Flows
Source: Apple, Inc., *2022 Annual Report* (Mountain View, CA: Author, 2022.)

especially when considering major capital expenditures. The budget differs from the other statements we have discussed in that it is not shared outside the company (hence the "internal financial statement" term). During the 2020 COVID-19 pandemic, many firms found it necessary to revise their existing budgets due to dramatic and unexpected declines in revenue.

Although the accounting team coordinates the budget process, it needs input from many other managers in the organization about proposed activities and required resources. Figure 15.4 is a sales budget for a hypothetical wholesaler, Perfect Posters. In preparing next year's budget, accounting must obtain from the sales group projections for units to be sold and expected expenses for the coming year. Then, accounting draws up the final budget and, throughout the year, compares the budget to actual expenditures and revenues. Discrepancies signal potential problems and spur action to improve financial performance.

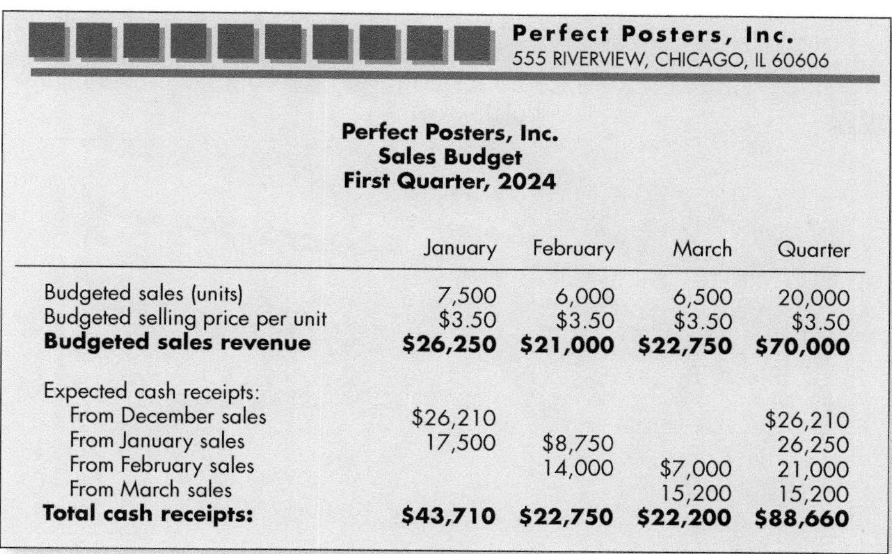
Perfect Posters, Inc.
555 RIVERVIEW, CHICAGO, IL 60606

Perfect Posters, Inc.
Sales Budget
First Quarter, 2024

	January	February	March	Quarter
Budgeted sales (units)	7,500	6,000	6,500	20,000
Budgeted selling price per unit	$3.50	$3.50	$3.50	$3.50
Budgeted sales revenue	**$26,250**	**$21,000**	**$22,750**	**$70,000**
Expected cash receipts:				
From December sales	$26,210			$26,210
From January sales	17,500	$8,750		26,250
From February sales		14,000	$7,000	21,000
From March sales			15,200	15,200
Total cash receipts:	**$43,710**	**$22,750**	**$22,200**	**$88,660**

FIGURE 15.4 Perfect Posters' Sales Budget

Reporting Standards and Practices

Learning Objective 15-4

Explain the key standards and principles for compiling and reporting financial statements.

Accountants follow standard reporting practices and principles when they prepare external reports. The common language dictated by standard practices and spelled out in GAAP is designed to give external users confidence in the accuracy and meaning of financial information. GAAP cover a range of issues, such as when to recognize revenues from operations and how to make full public disclosure of financial information. Without such standards, users of financial statements wouldn't be able to compare information from different companies and would misunderstand—or be led to misconstrue—a company's true financial status. Forensic accountants, such as Al Vondra from the opening case, watch for deviations from GAAP as indicators of possible fraudulent practices.

Revenue Recognition and Activity Timing

The reporting of revenue inflows, and the timing of other transactions, must abide by accounting principles that govern financial statements. **Revenue recognition**, for example, is the formal recording and reporting of revenues at the appropriate time. Although a firm earns revenues continuously as it makes sales, earnings are not reported until the *earnings cycle* is completed. This cycle is complete under two conditions:

Revenue Recognition *formal recording and reporting of revenues at the appropriate time*

1. The sale is complete and the product delivered.
2. The sale price has been collected or is collectible (accounts receivable).

The end of the earnings cycle determines the timing for revenue recognition in a firm's financial statements. Suppose a toy company signs a sales contract in January to supply $1,000 of toys to a retail store with delivery scheduled in February. Although the sale is completed in January, the $1,000 revenue should not then be recognized (that is, not be reported in the firm's financial statements) because the toys have not been delivered and the sale price is not yet collectible, so the earnings cycle is incomplete. Revenues are recorded in the accounting period—February—in which the product is delivered and collectible (or collected). This practice ensures that the statement gives a fair comparison of what was gained (revenues) in return for the resources that were given up (cost of materials, labor, and other production and delivery expenses) for the transaction.

Toys R Us was once the largest toy retailer in the world. However, the firm filed for bankruptcy in 2018 and closed all of its stores in 2021. Macy's recently acquired the firm's remaing assets and plan to open Toys R Us branded departments in over 400 of its stores. Investors in the original firm received mild warnings about the firm's financial health before the 2018 bankruptcy.

Full Disclosure

Full Disclosure *guideline that financial statements should not include just numbers but should also furnish management's interpretations and explanations of those numbers*

To help users better understand the numbers in a firm's financial statements, GAAP requires that financial statements also include management's interpretations and explanations of those numbers. The idea of requiring input from the manager is known as the **full disclosure** principle. Because they know about events inside the company, managers prepare additional information to explain certain events or transactions or to disclose the circumstances behind certain results.

For example, a chain called Borders was once the second-largest brick-and-mortar bookseller in the United States (behind Barnes & Noble). However, the firm filed for bankruptcy in early 2011 and closed its last store in September of that same year. In its annual reports and financial statements beginning as early as 2008, the management of Borders had discussed the competitive and economic risks facing the company. These disclosures noted that consumer spending trends were shifting to online retailers and e-books and away from in-store purchasing, thus posing growing risks for Borders's cash flows and overall financial condition. Management's discussion noted there could be *no assurance that Borders would muster adequate financial resources to remain competitive*, and, indeed, it soon happened. On filing for bankruptcy, Borders's liabilities of $1.29 billion had surpassed its assets of $1.28 billion.[24] The previous disclosure information helped investors and other stakeholders make informed decisions about the risks associated with investing in or doing business with Borders. Therefore, they could not claim that they had no idea the firm was struggling. It would have been a far different story, however, had Borders's managers been offering deceptively optimistic assessments of the business's future.

Learning Objective 15-5

Describe how computing financial ratios can help investors and other stakeholders get more information from financial statements to determine the financial strengths of a business.

Analyzing Financial Statements

Financial statements present a lot of information, but how can it be used? How, for example, can statements help investors decide what stock to buy or help lenders decide whether to extend credit? Answers to such questions for various stakeholders—employees, managers, unions, suppliers, the government, customers—can be answered this way: Statements provide data, which can, in turn, reveal trends and be applied to create various *ratios* (comparative numbers). We can then use these trends and ratios to evaluate a firm's financial health, its progress, and its prospects for the future.

Ratios are normally grouped into three major classifications:

1 **Solvency ratios** for estimating short-term and long-term risk
2 **Profitability ratios** for measuring potential earnings
3 **Activity ratios** for evaluating management's use of assets

Solvency Ratio *financial ratio, either short or long term, for estimating the borrower's ability to repay debt*

Profitability Ratio *financial ratio for measuring a firm's potential earnings*

Activity Ratio *financial ratio for evaluating management's efficiency in using a firm's assets*

Depending on the decisions to be made, a user may apply none, some, or all of these ratios.

Solvency Ratios: Borrower's Ability to Repay Debt

What are the chances that a borrower will be able to repay a loan and the interest due? This question is first and foremost in the minds of bank lending officers, managers of pension funds and other investors, suppliers, and the borrowing company's own financial managers. Solvency ratios provide measures of a firm's ability to meet its debt obligations.

The Current Ratio and Short-Term Solvency **Short-term solvency ratios** measure a company's liquidity and its ability to pay immediate debts. The most commonly used of these is the **current ratio** or "banker's ratio." This ratio measures a firm's ability to generate cash to meet current obligations through the normal, orderly process of selling products and services and collecting revenues from customers. It is calculated by dividing current assets by current liabilities. The higher a firm's current ratio, the lower the risk to investors. As a general rule, a current ratio is satisfactory at 2:1 or higher—that is, if current assets more than double current liabilities. A smaller ratio may indicate that a firm will have trouble paying its bills. Of course, a large, successful firm may be able to maintain a lower current ratio. By contrast, if the current ratio is too large, it suggests that the firm has a surplus of cash. This surplus, in turn, may prompt investors to question why the firm is not making investments for future growth (e.g., through research and development) or, alternatively, not paying case dividends.

Short-Term Solvency Ratio *financial ratio for measuring a company's ability to pay immediate debts*

Current Ratio *financial ratio for measuring a company's ability to pay current debts out of current assets*

Long-Term Solvency Stakeholders are also concerned about **long-term solvency**. Has the company been overextended by borrowing so much that it will be unable to repay debts in future years? A firm that can't meet its long-term debt obligations is in danger of collapse or takeover, a risk that makes creditors and investors quite cautious. To evaluate a company's risk of running into this problem, creditors turn to the balance sheet to see the extent to which a firm is financed through borrowed money. Long-term solvency is calculated by dividing **debt** (total liabilities) by owners' equity. The lower a firm's debt, the lower the risk to investors and creditors. Companies with more debt may find themselves owing so much that they lack the income needed to meet interest payments or to repay borrowed money.

Long-Term Solvency *financial ratio for measuring a company's ability to pay its long-term debt*

Debt *company's total liabilities*

Sometimes, manageably high debt can be not only acceptable but also desirable. Borrowing funds gives a firm **leverage**, the ability to make otherwise unaffordable investments. In *leveraged buyouts*, firms have willingly taken on sometimes huge debts to buy out other companies. If owning the purchased company generates profits above the cost of borrowing the purchase price, leveraging often makes sense. Unfortunately, many buyouts have caused problems because profits fell short of expected levels or because rising interest rates increased payments on the buyer's debt. For instance, Elon Musk bought Twitter, starting firing people and cuttings costs, and quickly saw his investment decline in value by more than $10 billion.

Leverage *ability to finance an investment through borrowed funds*

Profitability Ratios: Earnings Power for Owners

It's important to know whether a company is solvent in both the long and the short term, but risk alone is not an adequate basis for investment decisions. Investors also want some indication of the returns they can expect. Evidence of earnings power is available from profitability ratios, such as earnings per share and the price earnings ratio.

Earnings Per Share *profitability ratio measuring the net profit that the company earns for each share of outstanding stock*

Price Earnings Ratio *most commonly known as the P/E ratio, this ratio is the comparison of a firm's current share price to its current earnings per share*

Defined as net income divided by the number of shares of common stock outstanding (that is, shares in the hands of investors), **earnings per share** determines the size of the dividend that a firm can theoretically pay shareholders. As an indicator of a company's wealth potential, investors might use this ratio to decide whether to buy or sell the firm's stock. As the ratio goes up, stock value increases because investors know that the firm can better afford to pay dividends. Naturally, stock loses market value if financial statements report a decline in earnings per share. Another useful profitability ratio is the **price earnings ratio**, most commonly known as the P/E ratio. This ratio is the comparison of a firm's current share price to its current earnings per share.

Activity Ratios: How Efficiently Is the Firm Using Its Resources?

The efficiency with which a firm uses resources is linked to profitability. As a potential investor, you want to know which company gets more mileage from its resources. Information obtained from financial statements can be used for *activity ratios* to measure this efficiency. For example, two firms use the same amount of resources or assets to perform a particular activity. If Firm A generates greater profits or sales, it has used its resources more efficiently and so enjoys a better activity ratio. This may apply to any important activity, such as advertising, sales, or inventory management.

Retailers, for example, often focus on inventory turnover ratios. Suppose an appliance retailer expects to sell an average of 30 refrigerators per month over the next year. One strategy would be to order 360 refrigerators to arrive on January 1. This would be an ill-advised strategy, however, for many different reasons: The retailer would need to maintain and pay for a huge warehouse space, there would be increased risk of damage to the refrigerators that will not be sold for several months, and the retailer will have to pay for refrigerators now that will not generate revenue for several months. A better option would be to order fewer refrigerators so that they arrive in smaller quantities but more frequent intervals.

Learning Objective 15-6

Discuss the role of ethics in accounting.

Bringing Ethics into the Accounting Equation

Ethics plays a critical role in accounting. While ethical conduct should be expected of all managers and employees regardless of their roles, ethics is particularly important in accounting as a basis to maintain public confidence in business institutions, financial markets, and the products and services of the accounting profession. Without ethics, all of accounting's tools and methods would be meaningless because their usefulness depends, ultimately, on veracity in their application.

In addition to the business world's many favorable opportunities and outcomes, there have also been instances of misconduct. Amid public reports of unscrupulous activity, ethics remains an area in which one person who is willing to "do the right thing" can make a difference—and people do, every day. The role of ethics in the ground-breaking scandal from several years ago remains a classic example: Refusing to ignore unethical accounting around her at Enron, the now-failed giant energy corporation, Lynn Brewer tried to alert people inside about misstatements of the company's assets. When that failed, she, along with colleagues Sherron Watkins and Margaret Ceconi, talked with the U.S. Committee on Energy and Commerce to voice concerns about Enron's condition. To Brewer, maintaining personal and professional integrity was an overriding concern, and she acted accordingly.

table 15.3 Highlights from the Code of Ethics for CPAs

By voluntarily accepting Certified Public Accountant membership, the accountant also accepts self-enforced obligations, listed here, beyond written regulations and laws.	
Responsibilities as a Professional	The CPA should exercise duties with a high level of morality and in a manner that is sensitive to bringing credit to the profession.
Serving the Public Interest	The CPA should demonstrate commitment to the profession by respecting and maintaining the public trust and serving the public honorably.
Maintaining Integrity	The CPA should perform all professional activities with highest regard for integrity, including sincerity and honesty, so as to promote the public's confidence in the profession.
Being Objective and Independent	The CPA should avoid conflicts of interest, and the appearance of conflicts of interest, in performing professional responsibilities. The CPA should be independent from the client when certifying to the public that the client's statements are true and genuine.
Maintaining Technical and Ethical Standards Through Due Care	The CPA should exercise "due care," through professional improvement, abiding by ethical standards, updating personal competence through continuing accounting education, and improving the quality of services.
Professional Conduct in Providing Services	The CPA in public practice should abide by the meaning and intent of the Code of Professional Conduct when deciding on the kinds of services and the range of actions to be supplied competently and diligently for clients.

Source: Based on "Code of Professional Conduct," AICPA, accessed April 19, 2020, www.aicpa.org/Research/Standards/CodeofConduct/Pages/sec50.aspx.

AICPA's Code of Professional Conduct

The **code of professional conduct** for public accountants in the United States is maintained and enforced by the AICPA. The institute identifies six ethics-related areas—listed in Table 15.3—with which accountants must comply to maintain certification. Comprehensive details for compliance in each area are spelled out in the AICPA Code of Professional Conduct. The IMA maintains a similar code to provide ethical guidelines for the management accounting profession.

Code of Professional Conduct *code of ethics for CPAs as maintained and enforced by the AICPA*

In reading the AICPA's code, you can see that it forbids misrepresentation and fraud in financial statements. Deception certainly violates the call for exercising moral judgments (in "Responsibilities"), is contrary to the public interest (by deceiving investors), and does not honor the public trust (in "The Public Interest"). Misleading statements destroy the public's confidence in the accounting profession and in business in general. Although the code prohibits such abuses, its success depends, ultimately, on its acceptance and use by the professionals it governs.

Violations of Accounting Ethics and GAAP

Unethical and illegal accounting violations have dominated the popular press in recent years. Some of the more notorious cases, listed in Table 15.4, violated the public's trust, ruined retirement plans for tens of thousands of employees, and caused business shutdowns and significant job loss.[25] As you read each case, you should be able to see how its violation relates to the presentation of balance sheets and income statements in this chapter. In each case, adversity would have been prevented if employees had followed the code of professional conduct. In each case, nearly all of the code's six ethics-related areas were violated, and "professionals" willingly participated in unethical behavior. Such unscrupulous behavior was the impetus for passage of the Sarbanes-Oxley (Sarbox) Act.

table 15.4 Examples of Unethical and Illegal Accounting Actions

Corporation	Accounting Violation
Kraft Foods Inc.	In 2019, Kraft Foods had to pay a fine of $16 million in settlement after the CFTC (Commodities Futures Trading Commission) accused Kraft of using manipulative market strategies to force the market to sell wheat to the company at lower prices in order to earn Kraft an illicit profit.
Steinhoff	In 2019, PwC found that Steinhoff, a South African retailer, recorded fictitious transactions that totaled $7.4 billion over a 10-year period.
Huawei	Huawei's Chief Financial Officer Meng Wanzhou was arrested in December 2018 after the United States charged Meng and Huawei with bank and wire fraud in violation of American sanctions on Iran.
Wells Fargo	Wells Fargo admitted having opened over 2 million fraudulent customer accounts to meet cross-selling target goals over the course of five years. A settlement of $185 million was paid in September 2016.
Theranos	Theranos was charged with civil securities fraud after it made fraudulent and misleading statements about revenue projection and technology, among other things, while raising over $700 million from private investors. It is estimated that investors lost nearly $1 billion when the company dissolved in 2018. The firm's founder began a 13-year prison sentence in 2023.
Caldwell & Smith	In 2018, the SEC charged Caldwell, pastor at the largest Methodist church in Houston, and Smith, a self-proclaimed financial planner, with fraud after they collected $3.4 million from elderly investors and promised a huge return on fraudulent bonds.
Wirecard AG	In 2020, investigative journalists and short sellers alleged that the German fintech company had inflated the value of its cash assets by $2.1 billion. The scandal led to Wirecard's bankruptcy and the arrest of several executives, including its CEO, who had previously been a consultant with KPMG. (One executive fled the country and remained on the run until 2023.)
Nikola	In 2021, Nikola, an electric truck company, was charged with securities fraud after it made false claims about its products to raise more than $500 million from investors. The company released a video of the Nikola One truck, which it claimed was close to release. But the vehicle was not nearly functional, and the video had been created by towing it up a hill and letting it roll back down.

Sources: Matthew Heller, "Kraft Settles Futures Market Manipulation Case," *CFO*, https://www.cfo.com/fraud/2019/08/kraft-settles-futures-market-manipulation-case/, accessed November 4, 2019; Tiisetso Motsoeneng, "PwC Investigation Finds $7.4 Billion Accounting Fraud at Steinhoff, Company Says," Reuters, March 15, 2019, https://www.reuters.com/article/us-steinhoff-intln-accounts/pwc-investigation-finds-74-billion-accounting-fraud-at-steinhoff-company-says-idUSKCN1QW2C2; BBC News, "Huawei Faces US Charges: The Short, Medium and Long Story," May 7, 2019, https://www.bbc.com/news/world-us-canada-47046264; Arjun Kharpal, "The Extradition Trial of Huawei's CFO Starts This Month—Here's What to Watch," January 9, 2020, https://www.cnbc.com/2020/01/10/huawei-cfo-meng-wanzhou-extradition-trial-explained.html; Brian Tayan, "The Wells Fargo Cross-Selling Scandal," https://corpgov.law.harvard.edu/2019/02/06/the-wells-fargo-cross-selling_scandal-2/; "Theranos Founder Elizabeth Holmes Charged with Massive Fraud," press release, https://www.sec.gov/news/press-release/2018-51; "Houston, Texas Pastor Pleads Guilty to His Role in a Multimillion-Dollar Investment Scheme," March 11, 2020, https://www.justice.gov/usao-wdla/pr/houston-texas-pastor-pleads-guilty-his-role-multimillion-dollar-investment-scheme; https://www.reuters.com/article/us-germany-wirecard-inquiry-timeline-idUSKBN2B811J; https://www.theverge.com/2021/7/29/22599726/nikola-founder-securities-fraud-charge-milton.

finding a better way

Integrated Profit and Loss

T. Schneider/Shutterstock

Natura&Co is a cosmetics company headquartered in São Paolo, Brazil. The company's mission statement reads: "Since 1969, Natura's reason for being has been to create and sell products and services that promote the harmonious relationship of the individual with oneself, with others and with nature."[26] Like many multinational businesses, Natura started out as a small shop that grew gradually in the early years. By 2023, it had grown to operate more than 3,200 stores and locations and include subsidiaries such as Avon and The Body Shop.

In 2021, the company adopted an integrated profit and loss (IP&L) approach to reporting the results of operations and quickly became a leader in impact accounting, using its IP&L and underlying methodology to quantify the impacts and net value of its corporate performance on environmental, social, and human capital.[27] As part of the IP&L initiative, the company established a cross-functional committee responsible for the development and strategy of the IP&L methodology, which includes the controllership and technical accounting team as well as members of the financial planning and analysis (FP&A) team.[28]

Natura promotes itself as eco-friendly and sustainable, and the IP&L model provides quantitative information about all business activities, not just financial results. For instance, the IP&L takes into account the impact of corporate performance in the environmental, social, and human dimensions. In addition to traditional financial results, the IP&L work considers several other fronts of the company's performance, such as carbon emission and offsetting, circularity, regeneration and conservation of biomes, income generation for the network (and its impacts on health and welfare). According to the model's application, based on 2021 results, for every $1 of Natura revenue, the brand generated a net return of $1.5 in benefits for society.[29] In essence, the IP&L connects what the business sells with what it accomplishes and the impacts it has on people and communities.

Internationalizing Accounting

Learning Objective 15-7

Describe the purpose of the International Accounting Standards Board and explain why it exists.

Accounting in its earliest forms is known to have existed more than 7,000 years ago in Mesopotamia and Egypt for recording trade transactions and keeping track of resources. With the passage of time, each country's or region's accounting practices were refined to meet its needs in commerce while also accommodating local cultural traditions and developments in the region's laws. Although unique practices served each region well, they later posed problems as international business became prominent. By the late twentieth century, it was apparent that the upsurge in multinational organizations and the global economy demanded more uniformity among accounting practices. The development of "universal" procedures would allow governments and investors in, say, China, Brazil, and Italy to read, interpret, and compare financial statements from all those countries, whereas such comparisons even today are difficult if not sometimes impossible.

International Accounting Standards Board

Established in 2001 and housed in London, England, the **International Accounting Standards Board (IASB)** is an independent, nonprofit organization responsible for developing a set of global accounting standards and for gaining the support and cooperation of the world's various accounting organizations to implement those standards.

International Accounting Standards Board (IASB) *organization responsible for developing a set of global accounting standards and for gaining implementation of those standards*

IASB's 14 board members from various countries are full-time accounting experts with technical and international business experience.[30] Because the board cannot command sovereign nations to accept its recommended standards, its commitment to gaining cooperation around the world is a continuing task. Yet international acceptance is essential for success. Accordingly, the board's task is a long-term process that requires working with various countries to design proposed standards. As an example, for any IASB proposal to be accepted in the United States, it must first be approved by the U.S.-based FASB and by the U.S. SEC. However, IASB's efforts extend beyond the United States, to all nations. For years IASB has been working toward convergence in consistent accounting practices across many local GAAPs into one global set of practices.

Why One Set of Global Practices?

Although more than 138 countries have adopted IASB's accounting practices, over 50 others continue to use their national GAAP.[31] U.S.-based global companies such as Google, Caterpillar, and Microsoft may prepare different financial reports using local accounting practices for each country in which they conduct business. They also report the company's overall performance in a set of consolidated statements that combines the financial results of all its global affiliates, using U.S. GAAP. Using different accounting standards, however, can result in very different pictures of a firm's financial health. Income statements, balance sheets, and statements of cash flows using local GAAPs versus IASB practices, for example, may contain conflicting information with inconsistencies leading to confusion and misunderstandings among investors and other constituents. To emphasize this point, Hans Hoogervorst, chairman of the IASB, notes that a company using IASB standards can report balance sheet figures that are twice the size of those using U.S. GAAP accounting standards.[32] Which of the reports tells how well the company is doing? Such inconsistencies in reporting are unacceptable in a global economy, and accordingly, protection against them is a goal of IASB.

Example Areas Targeted for Aligning U.S. GAAP and IASB Among the many differences between the practices of U.S. GAAP and IASB—some reports identify more than 400 such discrepancies—the following examples illustrate some discrepancies and proposals for convergence toward universal standards in financial reporting.

- *In valuing assets* (reported on the balance sheet), U.S. GAAP allows an asset to be written down if for some reason its value decreases. However, the value cannot later be rewritten up, even if its actual value has increased. IASB standards, in contrast, do allow such write-ups reflecting increased market value, so the reported value of a company's assets can be quite different, depending on the chosen accounting system.[33] For instance, suppose a firm buys land for future expansion. The price paid for that land is initially used on the balance sheet to reflect its value. Suppose, though, that in five years the firm has still not expanded but the land value has dropped by half. Both IASB and U.S. GAAP allow the firm to lower its value on the balance sheet. But what happens if the value of the undeveloped land doubles? IASB allows firms to reflect this increase on the balance sheet, but U.S. GAAP does not.
- *In revenue recognition*, when revenues from customers should be recognized (reported), and in what amounts on the income statement, the U.S. GAAP and IASB procedures differ from each other. A current joint proposal, if approved, would remove existing inconsistencies and provide a single standard that recognizes revenue at the time the goods and services are transferred to the customer, and in the amounts that are expected to be received (or are received) from the customer.[34]
- *In devaluing of financial assets*, such as writing down bad loans in the financial crisis, both U.S. GAAP and IASB currently use the same procedure: After a loss occurs (but not until after the fact), the loan's value can be written down in the firm's financial statements, reflecting its lower value. Both groups, however,

believe an "expected loss model" that recognizes (and reports) likely loan losses *ahead of time* will provide more timely information for investors and financial planners. A joint proposal for such a procedure has been presented but is still being discussed.[35]

- *In fair value disclosure*, the FASB and IASB jointly propose new standards for improving the comparability of fair value disclosures in financial statements. Unlike dissimilar disclosure practices among many local GAAPs, both groups want the reported "fair value" for an asset, a liability, and an item in shareholders' equity to have the same meaning under both FASB and IASB procedures. The disclosure should identify the techniques and inputs used to measure fair value so that users can more clearly assess and compare financial statements.[36]

Timetable for Implementation The U.S. SEC originally targeted 2015 as the earliest date that U.S. companies would be required to use IASB procedures for financial reporting, and some procedures were indeed implemented that year. However, others were deferred or set to be phased in over a period of several years. But, as of 2020, the United States did not have an IFRS mandate.[37] To fully implement any given procedure, IASB must first demonstrate that its standards are developed adequately for use in the U.S. financial reporting system. Doing so includes ensuring that investors have developed an understanding of and education in using IASB standards. Accounting education, too, is being updated to prepare U.S. accounting students for IASB as well as updating practitioners in CPA firms. The AICPA has begun a process of introducing international standards in the CPA examinations. A number of the exam's questions now address some areas of difference between U.S. GAAP and International Financial Reporting Standards.

summary of learning objectives

LEARNING OBJECTIVE 15-1

Explain the role of accountants in business and distinguish among the kinds of work done by public accountants, private accountants, management accountants, and forensic accountants.

The role of accountants is to maintain a comprehensive system for collecting, analyzing, and communicating financial information for use by external constituents and within firms for planning, controlling, and decision making. It measures business performance and translates the results into information for management decisions. The users of accounting information include business managers, employees and unions, investors and creditors, tax authorities, and government regulatory agencies.

The *controller*, or chief accounting officer, manages a firm's accounting activities by ensuring that the *accounting information system* provides the reports and statements needed for planning, decision making, and other management activities. Accounting activities may be either financial or managerial. *Financial accounting* is concerned with external users of information, such as consumer groups, unions, stockholders, and government agencies, and focuses on the entity as a whole. *Managerial accounting*'s focus is internal users, such as managers, engineers, purchasing agents, and salespeople. Managerial accounting focuses on the detailed information needed to make decisions within the organization.

Public accountants offer accounting services to individuals and businesses outside their organization and are distinguished by their independence from the clients they serve. *Certified public accountants (CPAs)* are licensed professionals who provide auditing, tax, and management advisory services for other firms and individuals. Only CPAs can audit a firm's financial statements, and CPAs are always independent of the firms they audit. Many businesses hire their own salaried employees—*private accountants*—to perform internal accounting activities, such as internal auditing, taxation, cost analysis, and budgeting. Among private accountants, *certified management accountants* have passed the profession's experience and examination requirements for proficiency to provide internal accounting services that support managers in various activities (such as marketing, production, and engineering). *Forensic accountants* use accounting for legal purposes by providing investigative and litigation support in crimes against companies, crimes by companies, and civil cases.

LEARNING OBJECTIVE 15-2

Explain the accounting equation and how it is used.

Accountants use the following equation to balance the data pertaining to financial transactions:

$$\text{Assets} - \text{Liabilities} = \text{Owner's Equity}$$

After each financial transaction (e.g., payments to suppliers, sales to customers, wages to employees), the *accounting equation* must be in balance. If it isn't, then an accounting error has occurred. An *asset* is any economic resource that is expected to benefit a firm or an individual who owns it. Assets include land, buildings, equipment, inventory, and payments due the company (accounts receivable). A *liability* is a debt that the firm owes to an outside party. *Owners' equity* consists of capital from two sources: (1) the amount that the owners originally invested; and (2) profits (also owned by the owners) earned by and reinvested in the company. Owners' equity is meaningful for both investors and lenders. Before lending money to owners, lenders want to know the amount of owners' equity in a business. A larger owners' equity indicates greater security for lenders. As shown from the accounting equation, if assets exceed liabilities, owners' equity is positive; if the firm goes out of business, owners will receive some cash (a gain) after selling assets and paying off liabilities. If liabilities outweigh assets, owners' equity is negative; assets aren't enough to pay off debts. If the company goes under, owners will get no cash and some creditors won't be paid, thus losing their remaining investments in the company.

LEARNING OBJECTIVE 15-3

Describe the three basic financial statements and show how they reflect the activity and financial condition of a business.

Accounting summarizes the results of a firm's transactions and issues reports—including *financial statements*—to help managers and other stakeholders make informed decisions. The *balance sheet* (sometimes called the *statement of financial position*) supplies detailed information about the accounting equation items—assets, liabilities, and owners' equity—that together are a barometer of the firm's financial condition at a point in time. By comparing the current balance sheet with those of previous years, creditors and owners can better interpret the firm's financial progress and future prospects in terms of changes in assets, liabilities, and owners' equity.

The *income statement* (sometimes called a *profit-and-loss statement*) describes revenues and expenses to show a firm's annual profit or loss during a period of time, such as a year. The information in an income statement shows how a company obtained its net income for the accounting period, making it easier for shareholders and other stakeholders to evaluate the firm's financial health.

A publicly traded firm must issue a *statement of cash flows*, which describes its yearly cash receipts (inflows) and payments (outflows). It shows the effects on cash during the year from three kinds of business activities: (a) cash flows from operations, (b) cash flows from investing, and (c) cash flows from financing. The statement of cash flows then reports the overall change in the company's cash position at the end of the accounting period. When creditors and stockholders know how a firm obtained and used funds during the course of a year, it's easier for them to interpret year-to-year changes in the balance sheet and income statement.

For planning, controlling, and decision making, the most important internal financial statement is the *budget*, a detailed report on estimated receipts and expenditures for a future period of time. Budgets are internal documents and not usually shared outside the company.

LEARNING OBJECTIVE 15-4

Explain the key standards and principles for compiling and reporting financial statements.

Accountants follow standard reporting practices and principles when they prepare financial statements. The common language dictated by standard practices and spelled out in generally accepted accounting principles (GAAP) is designed to give external users confidence in the accuracy and meaning of financial information. Without these standards, users wouldn't be able to compare information from different companies, and they might misunderstand—or be led to misconstrue—a company's true financial status.

Two of the most important standard reporting practices and principles are revenue recognition and full disclosure. *Revenue recognition* refers to the rules associated with the recording and reporting of revenues in financial statements. All firms earn revenues continuously as they make sales, but earnings are not reported until the earnings cycle is completed. This cycle is complete under two conditions: (a) The sale is complete and the product delivered; (b) the sale price has been collected or is collectible (accounts receivable). This practice assures interested parties that the statement gives a fair comparison of what was gained (revenues) for the resources that were given up (cost of materials, labor, and other expenses) for the transaction.

Full disclosure recognizes that a firm's managers have inside knowledge—beyond just the numbers reported in its financial statements—that can explain certain events, transactions, or otherwise disclose the circumstances behind certain results. Full disclosure means that financial statements include management interpretations and explanations to help external users understand the financial information contained in statements.

LEARNING OBJECTIVE 15-5

Describe how computing financial ratios can help investors and other stakeholders get more information from financial statements to determine the financial strengths of a business.

Financial statements contain data that can be used in *ratios* (comparative numbers) to analyze the financial health of a company in terms of solvency, profitability, and efficiency in performing activities. Ratios can help creditors, investors, and managers assess a firm's current status and check its progress by comparing current with past statements. *Solvency ratios* use balance sheet data to measure the firm's ability to meet (repay) its debts. The most commonly used solvency ratio is known as the current ratio. The *current ratio* measures the ability to meet current (short-term) liabilities out of current assets. It is calculated by dividing current assets by current liabilities. The higher a firm's current ratio, the lower the risk to investors. A smaller ratio may indicate that a firm will have trouble paying its bills. Stakeholders are also concerned about long-term solvency. *Long-term solvency ratios* compare the firm's total liabilities (including long-term debt) against the owners' equity. High indebtedness (a high ratio) can be risky because it requires payment of interest and repayment of borrowed funds that may not be available.

Profitability ratios, such as earnings per share, measure current and potential earnings. Investors are interested in this ratio because it indicates the firm's earnings power and the returns they can expect from their investments. *Activity ratios* reflect management's use of assets by measuring the efficiency with which a firm uses its resources for a particular activity, such as sales, advertising, or inventory management. Sales efficiency, for example, can be measured from income statement data for annual sales revenues as compared with sales expenses. Sales efficiency has increased if the year-to-year growth in sales revenues is larger than the growth in sales expenses.

LEARNING OBJECTIVE 15-6

Discuss the role of ethics in accounting.

The purpose of ethics in accounting is to maintain public confidence in business institutions, financial markets, and the products and services of the accounting profession. Without ethics, all of accounting's tools and methods would be meaningless because their usefulness depends, ultimately, on truthfulness in their application. Accordingly, professional accounting associations such as the AICPA and IMA enforce codes of professional conduct that include ethics-related areas, such as the accountant's responsibilities, the public interest, integrity, and due care. The codes prohibit, among other things, misrepresentation and fraud in financial statements because misleading statements destroy the public's confidence in the accounting profession and in business in general. Although the code prohibits such abuses, its success depends ultimately on its acceptance and use by the professionals it governs.

LEARNING OBJECTIVE 15-7

Describe the purpose of the International Accounting Standards Board and explain why it exists.

The *International Accounting Standards Board (IASB)* is an independent, nonprofit organization established for the purposes of developing a set of global accounting standards and for gaining the support and cooperation of the world's various accounting organizations to implement those standards. It exists because the upsurge in multinational organizations and the global economy demand more uniformity among accounting practices, so that accounting reports become more understandable across nations and regions. Because the board cannot command sovereign nations to accept its recommended standards, its commitment to gaining cooperation around the world is a continuing task that requires working with various countries to design proposed international standards. Although more than 100 countries have adopted IASB's accounting practices, nearly 40 others, including China, India, and the United States, continue to use their national accounting standards that are often not comparable and can result in vastly different pictures of a firm's financial health. The development of "universal" procedures would allow governments and investors everywhere to read, interpret, and compare financial statements from every country, whereas such comparisons even today are difficult, if not sometimes impossible. Different accounting standards, such as how assets are valued and how revenues should be recognized, can provide quite different perspectives on the financial health of an organization. Income statements, balance sheets, and statements of cash flows using U.S. GAAP versus IASB practices may contain conflicting information with inconsistencies leading to confusion and misunderstandings among investors and other constituents. The U.S. SEC targeted 2015 as the earliest date that U.S. companies would be required to use IASB procedures for financial reporting. However, some procedures have been deferred and others are being implemented in phases.

key terms

profitability ratio (p. 501)
retained earnings (p. 495)
revenue recognition (p. 499)
revenues (p. 495)
Sarbanes-Oxley Act of 2002 (Sarbox or SOX) (p. 490)
short-term solvency ratio (p. 501)
solvency ratio (p. 501)
statement of cash flows (p. 497)
tax services (p. 487)

questions & exercises

QUESTIONS FOR REVIEW

15-1. Who are the users of financial accounting information, and for what purposes do they use it?

15-2. What are the three types of services performed by CPAs?

15-3. How does financial accounting differ from managerial accounting?

15-4. What are the activities and services performed by forensic accountants?

15-5. What are the three basic financial statements, and what major information does each contain?

QUESTIONS FOR ANALYSIS

15-6. If you were planning to invest in a company, from what source would you obtain financial information, and what financial information would you focus on?

15-7. What are the basic financial statements and how are they related to each other? Also, how are they different?

15-8. What are three or more barriers to the United States adopting IFRS?

APPLICATION EXERCISES

15-9. Create a personal budget that includes a way to monitor actual monthly expenditures against budget and a way to forecast future cash balances. How could you use this budget to increase your personal net worth?

15-10. Identify your accounting assets and liabilities. Use the accounting equation to determine your own net worth (equity). Using this information, how would you go about increasing your net worth in the future?

building a business: continuing team exercise

ASSIGNMENT

Meet with your team members to consider your new business venture and how it relates to the accounting topics in this chapter. Develop specific responses to the following:

15-11. In your first year of operation, who will perform accounting functions inside your company? Will you contract some or all of the work to a public accounting firm?

15-12. Create a list of the types of transactions that your accountant will record, including the purchase and sale of assets as well as revenues and expenses.

15-13. Based on the development of your business to date, create a preliminary or pro forma income statement for your firm's first year of operation. Be sure it includes listings of relevant terms from the accounting equation. See if you can estimate anticipated data for each element in the income statement.

15-14. Based on the development of your business to date, create a preliminary or pro forma balance sheet for your firm's first year of operation. Be sure it includes listings of relevant terms from the accounting equation. See if you can estimate anticipated data for each element in the balance sheet.

15-15. Consider the sources for start-up funds you will need to finance your business. What financial ratios (ratio analysis), if any, are likely to be of interest to lending institutions, personal investors (including yourselves), or other providers of funds? Explain why ratio analysis will be of interest to them or why it will not be of interest.

team exercise

AN AMERICAN LEGEND

Kohl's is an iconic American company, but like many brick-and-mortar retailers, it has been struggling to maintain market share against stores like Macy's, Target, and Nordstrom. For this exercise, you and your team need to find the company's most recent financial statements, including the income statement and balance sheet. There are many sources of these data, but one quick source is Morningstar.com. If you enter the company's ticker symbol, "KSS," in the quote box, you will find a report on the company's stock price as well as a host of other information, such as performance, key ratios, and financials. On the financial tab, you can find the income statement and balance sheet for the past five years.

QUESTIONS FOR DISCUSSION

15-16. According to Kohl's most recent income statement, what has been the trend in sales (total revenue) as well as net income over the past three years? How is Kohl's faring compared to its competitors?

15-17. As you have learned, gross profit is the difference between sales (or total revenues) and cost of sales (or cost of revenues). Gross profit percentage is calculated by dividing gross profit by sales (or total revenues). What is Kohl's gross profit percentage for the past three years? What do these data tell you about Kohl's pricing strategy and costs?

15-18. According to the balance sheet, what is Kohl's current ratio for the three most recent years? What is the significance of these numbers? Have they been improving or getting worse?

15-19. What is the relationship between the price of Kohl's stock and earnings? What are the earnings per share for each of the past three years, and what does that number mean to investors?

exercising your ethics

GIVE AND TAKE WITH ACCOUNTING CLIENTS

The Situation

Aaron Ault is the owner of a bottling business. In late January, he sent his QuickBooks files to Katrina Belinski, CPA, so she could prepare the prior fiscal year's financial statements and tax returns for Ault's company. Several weeks later, Katrina delivered the completed financial statements and tax return to Ault just before the March 15 filing deadline for federal corporate income tax returns. In addition to corporate financial accounting and consulting services, Belinski provides personal income tax and financial planning to Ault, several of his top-level employees, and several of his family members, making him one of her most valuable clients.

The Dilemma

Aaron was pleased with the financial statements because they showed a large profit, but then he realized that he was going to owe $300,000 in taxes. His business is just recovering from tough times and he had reinvested all his profits in his business, so he can't afford to pay such a large tax bill. One particularly large job was completed in December of the prior year but billed in January, and the money was not received until late February. Ault argues that this should be current year revenue since it was received in January, which would result in a much lower taxable income for the prior year. However, Belinski informs him that according to GAAP, the revenue has to be reported in the period it is earned. Ault insists that she change the tax returns, reminds her that his company is privately held and not subject to GAAP, and also tells her that if she doesn't change it, he will find an accounting firm that will.

QUESTIONS TO ADDRESS

15-20. What are the ethical issues in this situation?

15-21. What are the basic arguments for and against Aaron Ault's position in this situation? For and against Katrina Belinski's position?

15-22. What do you think that Ault and Belinski should do in this situation?

cases

CSI: WALL STREET

Continued from page 484

At the beginning of this chapter, you read about forensic accountants and their role in fighting various kinds of fraudulent accounting practices, especially during troubled economic times. Using the information presented in this chapter, you should now be able to answer the following questions.

QUESTIONS FOR DISCUSSION

15-23. What factors do you think are most important in choosing among various methods to protect against fraud in a firm?

15-24. Suppose you are hoping for a career as a Certified Fraud Examiner (CFE). How do recent trends in fraud provide new opportunities for such a career?

15-25. An external auditor, such as a CPA firm's accountant, may suspect some irregularities in a client firm's accounting practices. In what ways might a CFE be of assistance?

15-26. Consider the antifraud training for a company's employees and create an agenda that includes four (or more) topics that should be incorporated into that training, along with descriptions of each.

15-27. What ethical issues, if any, are involved in a decision to investigate a suspected case of fraud in a firm's accounting activities?

IN THE DARK

You are an accountant for small businesses and have recently taken on a new client. Amelia Penny is a photographer using QuickBooks connected to Studio Ninja, her customer relationship manager. She uses a bookkeeper for day-to-day financial management, like paying bills and overseeing QuickBooks. Amelia hired a business consultant because she feels like she's working harder and bringing in more revenue than ever, but she still feels broke at the end of the month.

The consultant has taken over client management and has been asking questions about discrepancies between Studio Ninja's revenue statements and the QuickBooks records. Specifically, the consultant asks about accurate reconciliation, outstanding accounts, and unapplied payments. The bookkeeper has told Amelia that it's complicated, that her checking account balance is up to date and accurate, and that she should not worry about it.

When the consultant pressed for more information, the bookkeeper didn't answer phone calls, sent vague responses to emails, and then went out of town for an unexpected trip. Amelia trusts her bookkeeper and considers her a friend, but her business consultant insisted she contact you immediately.

QUESTIONS FOR DISCUSSION

15-28. If this client approached you, what would you do?

15-29. What red flags do you see in this scenario?

15-30. Why is it essential for business owners and managers to have a basic understanding of accounting? How would you advise this client?

15-31. What are the risks to your client if she does nothing? What are the benefits if she takes your advice?

endnotes

1 "Evoqua Water Technologies Corp. and Imran Parekh (Release No. LR-25662; Mar. 13, 2023)," March 13, 2023, https://www.sec.gov/litigation/litreleases/2023/lr25662.htm.

2 Nicola M. White and Lucca de Paoli, "$4 Billion Accounting Scandal Exposes Supplier Finance Risks (1)," Bloomberg Law, January 25, 2023, https://news.bloomberglaw.com/bankruptcy-law/a-4-billion-accounting-bombshell-exposes-supplier-finance-risks.

3 A. Dyck, A. Morse, and L. Zingales, "How Pervasive Is Corporate Fraud?," *Review of Accounting Studies* (2023), https://doi.org/10.1007/s11142-022-09738-5.

4 ACFE, "ACFE Releases 2018 Report to the Nations," May/June 2018, https://www.acfe.com/article.aspx?id=4295001895.

5 See Marshall B. Romney and Paul John Steinbart, *Accounting Information Systems*, 14th ed. (Upper Saddle River, NJ: Prentice Hall, 2019), Chapter 1.

6 See Anthony A. Atkinson, Robert S. Kaplan, Ella Mae Matsumura, and S. Mark Young, *Management Accounting*, 8th ed. (Upper Saddle River, NJ: Prentice Hall, 2018), Chapter 1.

7 See Walter T. Harrison and Charles T. Horngren, *Financial Accounting and Financial Tips*, 10th ed. (Upper Saddle River, NJ: Prentice Hall, 2018), Chapter 1.

8 "Public Accounting Tips," LifeTips.com, accessed September 13, 2010, http://accountingjobs.lifetips.com/cat/64430/public-accounting/index.html; "Business Glossary," AllBusiness.com, accessed April 15, 2020, http://www.allbusiness.com/glossaries/review/4954577-1.html.

9 E. Mazareanu, "Number of Employees of the Big Four Accounting / Audit Firms Worldwide 2018," Statista, December 12, 2019, accessed April 30, 2020, https://www.statista.com/statistics/250503/big-four-accounting-firms-number-of-employees/.

10 https://www.ey.com/en_gl/news/2022/09/ey-achieves-highest-growth-in-nearly-two-decades-reports-record-global-revenue-of-us45-4b.

11 See Alvin A. Arens, Randal J. Elder, and Mark S. Beasley, *Auditing and Assurance Services: An Integrated Approach*, 15th ed. (Upper Saddle River, NJ: Prentice Hall, 2018), Chapter 1.

12 See Meg Pollard, Sherry T. Mills, and Walter T. Harrison, *Financial and Managerial Accounting* (Upper Saddle River, NJ: Prentice Hall, 2018), Chapter 1.

13 "Talent Shortage Survey," ManpowerGroup, accessed April 25, 2020, http://www.manpowergroup.us/campaigns/talent-shortage-2018/.

14 The American Institute of Certified Public Accountants, "The CPA Vision Project and Beyond," accessed April 15, 2020, http://www.aicpa.org/RESEARCH/CPAHORIZONS2025/CPAVISIONPROJECT/Pages/CPAVisionProject.aspx.

15 https://www.investopedia.com/terms/i/institute-of-management-accountants.asp#:~:text=Understanding%20the%20IMA&text=3%20It%20has%, Accessed June 3, 2023.

16 D. Larry Crumbley, Lester E. Heitger, and G. Stevenson Smith, *Forensic and Investigative Accounting*, 8th ed. (Chicago: CCH, 2022), Chapter 1.

17 See Terry McConn, "Ex-Chase Bank Teller Charged with Stealing from Walla Walla Business," *Walla Walla Union Bulletin*, September 2016, http://www.union-bulletin.com/news/courts_and_crime/ex-chase-bank-teller-charged-with-stealing-from-walla-walla/article_0eca4f2e-859b-11e6-baad-c75a9d6d7c00.html.

18 Katy Vine, "Just Desserts," *Texas Monthly*, January 2016, http://www.texasmonthly.com/articles/just-desserts/.

19 United States Department of Justice, Press Release, November 28, 2016, https://www.justice.gov/opa/pr/upstate-new-york-woman-admits-stealing-31-million-cargill-inc.

20 Jeff Beach, "After Losing $45 million in Employee Fraud, Cargill Sues Insurance Company That Offered Crime Coverage," *Agweek*, November 29, 2021, https://www.agweek.com/after-losing-45-million-in-employee-fraud-cargill-sues-insurance-company-that-offered-crime-coverage.

21 Conference of State Bank Supervisors, "Executive Summary of the Sarbanes-Oxley Act of 2002 P.L. 107–204," accessed April 15, 2020, http://www.csbs.org/legislative/leg-updates/Documents/ExecSummary-SarbanesOxley-2002.pdf; "Sarbanes-Oxley Executive Summary," *Securities Law Update* (Orrick, Herrington & Sutcliffe LLP), August 2002, http://www.orrick.com/fileupload/144.pdf.

[22] Michael Rapoport, "Eyebrows Go Up as Auditors Branch Out," *Wall Street Journal*, December 7, 2012, C1, C2.

[23] Apple's financial records, accessed on June 5, 2023, https://www.apple.com/newsroom/pdfs/FY22%20Consolidated%20Financial%20Statements.pdf.

[24] "Borders Files for Bankruptcy, to Close 200 Stores," Reuters, February 16, 2011, http://www.reuters.com/article/2011/02/17/us-borders-idUSTRE71F2P220110217.

[25] Matthew Heller, "Kraft Settles Futures Market Manipulation Case," CFO, August 16, 2019, https://www.cfo.com/fraud/2019/08/kraft-settles-futures-market-manipulation-case/; Tiisetso Motsoeneng and Emma Rumney, "PwC Investigation Finds $7.4 Billion Accounting Fraud at Steinhoff, Company Says," Reuters, March 15, 2019, https://www.reuters.com/article/us-steinhoff-intln-accounts/pwc-investigation-finds-74-billion-accounting-fraud-at-steinhoff-company-says-idUSKCN1QW2C2; "Huawei Faces US Charges: The Short, Medium and Long Story," BBC News, May 7, 2019, https://www.bbc.com/news/world-us-canada-47046264; Arjun Kharpal, "The Extradition Trial of Huawei's CFO Starts This Month—Here's What to Watch," CNBC, January 9, 2020, https://www.cnbc.com/2020/01/10/huawei-cfo-meng-wanzhou-extradition-trial-explained.html; Sara Ashley O'Brien, "Theranos Founder Elizabeth Holmes Charged with Massive Fraud," CNN Business, March 14, 2018, https://money.cnn.com/2018/03/14/technology/theranos-fraud-scandal/index.html; "SEC Charges Prominent Pastor, Financial Planner in Scheme to Defraud Elderly Investors," Press Release, U.S. Securities and Exchange Commission, March 30, 2018, https://www.sec.gov/news/press-release/2018-51.

[26] Natura, "About Us," accessed June 25, 2023, https://www.naturabrasil.com/pages/about-us.

[27] IFAC, "Case Study: Integrated Profit and Loss Accounting at Natura&Co.," accessed June 25, 2023, https://www.ifac.org/knowledge-gateway/supporting-international-standards/discussion/case-study-integrated-profit-and-loss-accounting-natura-co.

[28] IFAC, "Case Study."

[29] Natura RI, "Management by Impact—IP&L," June 1, 2022, https://ri.naturaeco.com/en/gestao-por-impacto-ipl/.

[30] Financial Accounting Standards Board, "IASB and FASB Propose a New Joint Standard for Revenue Recognition," June 24, 2010, http://www.fasb.org/cs/ContentServer?c=FASBContent_C&pagename=FASB%2FFASBContent_C%2FNewsPage&cid=1176156953088.

[31] "IFRS Overview," NYSSCPA.ORG, accessed April 19, 2020, http://www.nysscpa.org/ifrs/overview.htm.

[32] Financial Accounting Standards Board, "IASB and FASB Propose to Align Balance Sheet Netting Requirements Differences in IFRS and US GAAP Offsetting Requirements to Be Eliminated," News Release, January 28, 2011, http://www.fasb.org/cs/ContentServer?c=FASBContent_C&pagename=FASB/FASBContent_C/NewsPage&cid=1176158186333.

[33] John Briginshaw, "What Will the International Financial Reporting Standards (IFRS) Mean to Businesses and Investors?" *Graziadio Business Review* 11, no. 4 (2008), http://gbr.pepperdine.edu/2010/08/what-will-the-international-financial-reporting-standards-ifrs-mean-to-businesses-and-investors/.

[34] Financial Accounting Standards Board, "IASB and FASB Propose a New Joint Standard for Revenue Recognition."

[35] Financial Accounting Standards Board, "IASB and FASB Propose Common Solution for Impairment Accounting," News Release, January 31, 2011, http://www.fasb.org/cs/ContentServer?c=FASBContent_C&pagename=FASB/FASBContent_C/NewsPage&cid=1176158192211.

[36] Insurance Networking News, "FASB, IASB Propose Changes in Fair Value Standards," June 29, 2010, http://www.insurancenetworking.com/news/insurance_fair_value_standards_accounting_IASB_FASB_GAAP_IFRS-25136-1.html; International Accounting Standards Board, "Measurement Uncertainty Analysis Disclosure for Fair Value Measurements," June 2010, http://www.iasb.org/NR/rdonlyres/07855A41-D0A9-4197-ADF9-15A1088E466A/0/EDMeasurementUncertaintyAnalysis0610.pdf.

[37] Will Kenton, "International Accounting Standards (IAS)," *Investopedia*, January 22, 2020, https://www.investopedia.com/terms/i/ias.asp.

[38] Rodd Wagner, "Happy Employees Equal Happy Customers? Well, Yes, but It's Complicated," *Forbes*, February 27, 2017, https://www.forbes.com/sites/roddwagner/2017/02/27/happy-employees-equal-happy-customers-well-yes-but-its-complicated/?sh=29b702f37c6e.

[39] Leslie Wayne, "Starbucks Chairman Fears Tradition Is Fading," *The New York Times*, February 24, 2007, https://www.nytimes.com/2007/02/24/business/24coffee.html.

[40] Husain et al., "How Starbucks Pulled Itself out of the 2008 Financial Meltdown," *Business Today*, May 4, 2015.

[41] Nathanial Meyersohn, "3 Times Howard Schultz Saved Starbucks," *CNN Money*, June 5, 2018, https://money.cnn.com/2018/06/05/news/companies/starbucks-howard-schultz-coffee/index.html.

[42] Heidi Peiper, "A Look Back at 20 Years of Starbucks Cards," Starbucks Stories, accessed July 9, 2023, https://stories.starbucks.com/stories/2020/a-look-back-at-20-years-of-starbucks-cards/.

[43] Everett Rosenfeld, "Howard Schultz Stepping Down as Starbucks CEO; Current COO to Replace Him," CNBC, December 2, 2016, https://www.cnbc.com/2016/12/01/howard-schultz-stepping-down-as-starbucks-ceo.html.

[44] Andrew Edgecliffe-Johnson, "Starbucks' Kevin Johnson: Taking on a Founder's Brand," *Financial Times*, December 10, 2018, https://www.bizjournals.com/bizjournals/news/2018/12/10/starbucks-kevin-johnson-taking-on-a-founder-s.html.

part 5
Integrative Learning Portfolio

crafting a business plan

Goal of the Exercise

This part of the business plan asks you to think about your business in terms of *information technology needs* and *costs*.

Exercise Background: Part 5 of the Business Plan

In Chapter 14, we discussed the major impact that IT—computers, the Internet, software, and so on—has had on businesses today. This part of the business plan asks you to assess how you will use technology to improve your business. Will you, for example, use a database to keep track of your customers? How will you protect your business from hackers and other IT security risks?

This part of the business plan also asks you to consider the costs of doing business, such as salaries, rent, and utilities. You'll also be asked to complete the following financial statements:

- ***Balance sheet.*** The balance sheet is a foundation for financial reporting. This report identifies the valued items of the business (its *assets*) as well as the debts that it owes (its *liabilities*). This information gives the owner and potential investors a "snapshot" into the health of the business.
- ***Income statement (or profit-and-loss statement).*** This is the focus of the financial plan. This document will show you what it takes to be profitable and successful as a business owner for your first year.

Your Assignment

STEP 1

Open the saved *Business Plan* file you began working on in Parts 1 to 4.

STEP 2

For the purposes of this assignment, you will answer the following questions in "Part 5: Managing Information":

P5-1. What kinds of IT resources will your business require?

Hint: Think about the employees in your business and what they will need to do their jobs. What computer hardware and software will they need? Will your business need a network and an Internet connection? What type of network? Refer to Chapter 14 for a discussion on IT resources you may want to consider.

P5-2. How will you use IT to keep track of your customers and potential customers?

Hint: Many businesses—even small businesses—use databases to keep track of their customers. Will your business require a database? What about other information systems? Refer to Chapter 14 for more information on these topics.

P5-3. What are the *costs* of doing business? Equipment, supplies, salaries, rent, utilities, and insurance are just some of these expenses. Estimate what it will cost to do business for one year.

Hint: The *Business Plan Student Template* provides a table for you to insert the costs associated with doing business. Note that these are only estimates—just try your best to include accurate costs for the expenses you think will be a part of doing business.

P5-4. How much will you charge for your product? How many products do you believe that you can sell in one year (or how many customers do you think your business can attract)? Multiply the price that you will charge by the number of products that you hope to sell or the amount you hope each customer will spend. This will give you an estimate of your *revenues* for one year.

Hint: You will use the amounts you calculate in the costs and revenues questions in this part of the plan in the accounting statements in the next part, so be as realistic as you can.

P5-5. Create a balance sheet and an income statement (profit-and-loss statement) for your business.

Hint: You will have two options for creating these reports. The first option is to use the Microsoft Word versions that are found within the *Business Plan Student Template* itself. The second option is to use the specific Microsoft Excel templates created for each statement, which are found on the book's companion website at www.pearsonhighered.com/ebert. These Excel files are handy to use because they already have the worksheet calculations preset—all you have to do is "plug in" the numbers and the calculations will be performed automatically for you. If you make adjustments to the different values in the Excel worksheets, you'll automatically see how changes to expenses, for example, can improve the bottom line.

Note: Once you have answered the questions, save your Word document. You'll be answering additional questions in later chapters.

case PART 5 STARBUCKS 2008–2016

"We built the Starbucks brand first with our people, not with the consumers. Because we believed that the best way to meet and exceed the expectations of our customers was to hire and train great people, we invested in employees."[38]

—Howard Schultz

Sorbis/Shutterstock

For reporting purposes, Starbucks has designated a fiscal year, which ends on the Sunday closest to September 30 of each year. This means that every four years the fiscal year is 53 weeks instead of 52. The fiscal year is identified by what year it ends, so the fiscal year that ended on September 30, 2007, would be the company's 2007 fiscal year. After the departure of Jim Donald in January 2008, Schultz shuffled around leadership and made plans to refocus the company on customer service and great coffee. In a leaked internal memo in 2007, Schultz lamented that the aggressive growth had led to "a watering down of the Starbucks experience."[39]

Schultz regained the helm during the second quarter of the 2008 fiscal year and inherited the results of both rapid growth and a recession. People weren't splurging as much on luxury items like gourmet coffee. In addition, McDonald's began serving McCafé espresso drinks and setting up coffee bars. Even so, in the fiscal year 2008 annual report, Schultz stated that the company boasted 160,000 partners (frontline employees) in almost 17,000 stores in 49 countries, processing 50 million transactions a week. Even so, the company's operating income dropped. Operating income is revenues from the normal course of business minus expenses (the costs of doing business). For Starbucks, operating income had been on a steady climb for many years, topping $1 billion in 2007, but in 2008, it dropped to $504 million (Figure 15.5).

In addition to declining revenues, increasing expenses, and a less-than-spectacular bottom line, the debt-to-equity ratio, a measure of the overall viability of the company, had dropped from 1:1 to 3:2 due to heavy debt financing for the company's expansion. In other words, the company was holding $3 in debt for every $2 in shareholders' equity.

Schultz announced the closing of 600 underperforming stores and a revival of the Starbucks experience. Jim Donald had pointed to the collapsing economy and high cost of dairy products as causing the slump in sales, along with heightened competition, but Schultz told the employees, "The company shouldn't just blame the economy; Starbucks's heavy spending to accommodate its expansion has created a bureaucracy that masked its problems."[40]

In Schultz's opinion, Starbucks coffee had become a commodity and had lost its competitive advantage. No one particular thing had caused the watering down, but Schultz could point to things like food offerings and pre-ground coffee that eliminated the coffee aroma that the company was famous for and even the taller espresso machines that hid the artistry of the baristas. The company had also experimented with

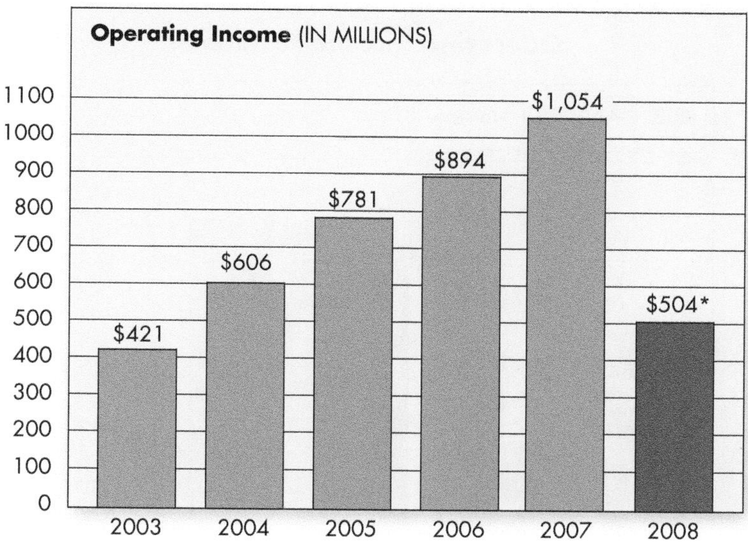

FIGURE 15.5
Source: https://s22.q4cdn.com/869488222/files/doc_financials/annual/2008/SBUX2008ARv5_2008.pdf

SUJIN SAENSING/Shutterstock

expanding into the entertainment business, which turned out to be another distraction from the core business of coffee.[41]

One of Schultz's initiatives to help get the company back on course was technological. Starbucks was among the first major retailers to offer a reloadable gift card, which it had debuted in 2001. It became one of the most popular holiday gifts of the season, selling nearly 200,000 in the first week alone. In 2008, Starbucks and Schultz launched the Starbucks Rewards program, which built on the company's success with its gift cards. Any reloadable gift card included the new loyalty program's benefits. In January 2011, the company took another leap forward when it launched mobile payments through the Starbucks Card Mobile App, turning smartphones into Starbucks cards. By Valentine's Day that same year, Starbucks rolled out eGift, allowing customers to send the gift of Starbucks by email.[42]

Schultz was also on a mission to stay out front on issues related to sustainability and fair trade. By 2015, the company achieved 99 percent ethically sourced coffee, a goal it had set back in 2008. In addition, the company increased purchases of renewable energy from 20 percent in 2008 to 100 percent in 2015. In 2008, the company had one LEED-certified store, and by 2015, there were more than 800.

By focusing on the core business and being socially and environmentally active, the giant was able to right itself. With just half a million dollars of profit in 2008, Starbucks grew to almost $2 billion in fiscal year 2012, and by the end of 2016, the company had 23,000 stores generating $21 billion in sales and over $4 billion in operating income (Figure 15.6).

At the end of calendar year 2016, the stock was trading at a record high near $60 per share. The shares had split six times. One Starbucks share issued during the 1992 IPO at $21.76 was now 64 shares with a total cost of $1,392.64, which would be $0.34 per share, an annual rate of return of about 22 percent.

On a Thursday afternoon in December 2016, in a surprise announcement, Schultz once again announced he was stepping down as CEO. He picked as his replacement Kevin Johnson, the current president and chief operating officer (COO), whom he credited for helping make 2016 a banner year. Since joining Starbucks in 2015, Johnson had led the company's global operating businesses and the core support functions of Starbucks's supply chain, marketing, human resources, technology, and mobile and digital platforms.[43]

Johnson said he hoped to bring to the job "the wisdom to know what to honor from the past and the courage to reimagine the future." Meanwhile, Schultz announced that he would remain involved with Starbucks as executive chairman, focusing on strategic initiatives such as Starbucks Reserve Roasteries and retail stores as well as social issues and initiatives.[44]

QUESTIONS FOR DISCUSSION

P5-6. Some economists posit that the only legal duty a corporation owes its shareholders is to make a profit and therefore maximize the share price. Others say that corporations have a social responsibility to the public that goes beyond just making a profit. Which position do you support, and why?

P5-7. How much of Starbucks's success do you think is directly attributable to one person? Do you think that is true for all successful corporations?

P5-8. Why would a company "go public"? What does that mean? What is involved in that process?

P5-9. What are the roles of accountants in providing outside users with financial information? What are the roles of accountants in providing internal users (management) with information? How are those two different types of accounting similar, and how are they different?

P5-10. What are a few innovative ways that information technology is being used in retailing today?

Operating Income (in Millions)

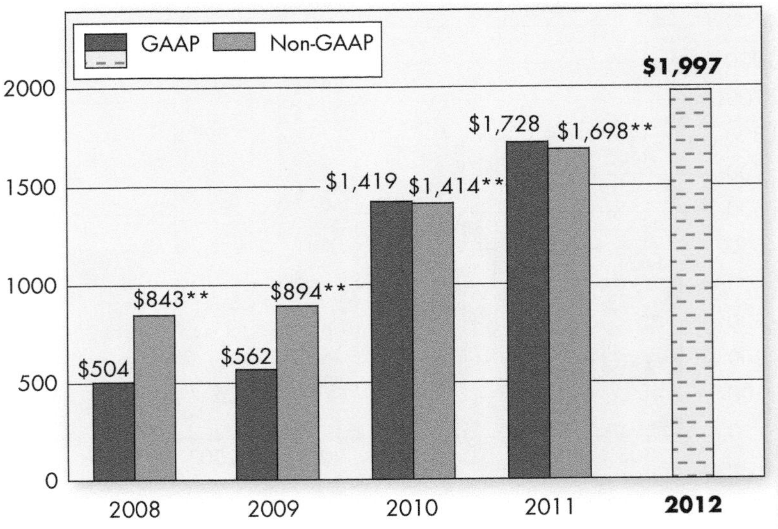

FIGURE 15.6

finding your path

CAREERS IN BUSINESS

Accounting and information technology (IT) are two of the more popular majors or career tracks in business programs today. Future job growth prospects for accounting graduates is around 6 percent overall growth by 2028. However, it's helpful to look at this number in a bit more detail. Two common tracks for accounting are auditing-related services and taxation. In recent years, the number of jobs in auditing-related services has been increasing at a rate higher than the overall growth rate, while the number of jobs in taxation has been growing at a much lower rate. In 2022, the average starting salary for an accounting graduate was $67,945. Most accounting degree programs are fairly similar (for reasons outlined below) and generally are more structured than most other business degree programs.

IT graduates, meanwhile, are experiencing the highest demand of all business school majors, with job growth expected to exceed 11 percent by 2028. Average starting salaries for graduates in 2022 were over $80,000. However, more than most other common business majors, IT graduates face job competition from non-business majors. For example, many engineering colleges and computer science departments offer coursework that helps prepare students for IT jobs.

MAKING YOURSELF EMPLOYABLE

People who major in accounting or IT will most likely have academic profiles very similar to the profiles of other graduates in those same programs. That doesn't mean, however, that you cannot distinguish yourself from other job seekers.

Accounting

More than other business majors, accounting has a clear and universally understood competency standard—obtaining the credential of being a certified public accountant, or CPA. Becoming a CPA, in turn, requires passing a standardized exam that is administered in multiple parts. The four parts of the exam are (1) Auditing and Attestation, (2) Financial Accounting and Reporting, (3) Regulation, and (4) Business Environment and Concepts. Before a person can even sit for the exam, they must meet certain standards. For instance, the individual must have been awarded a bachelor's degree in accounting that includes a specified set of courses. Some states require additional coursework that typically calls for another year of education. An individual need not pass all four parts in one sitting. For instance, if a person passes three parts but fails the fourth, they have to re-take only the fourth part. However, all four parts must be passed within an 18-month period to pass the overall exam. (Only around 50 percent of all exam takers pass all four parts on the first try.) Individuals working for large accounting firms usually get a salary increase after successfully passing the CPA exam. Some firms have a policy that an individual who does not pass the exam within a defined period may even be terminated.

Many people also have successful careers without taking or passing the CPA exam. However, in most cases these individuals earn lower salaries and also have less upward mobility. For example, they may join local or regional public accounting firms. These firms are often structured as partnerships, with the partners all being CPAs. The firm may also employ other CPAs who are not partners and other non-CPAs to assist with the firm's accounting work. For example, a firm might assign standard tax return preparation to a non-CPA, with the finalized return being reviewed by a CPA before it is returned to the client. A non-partner CPA may hope to one day become a partner in the firm. It is much less likely, though, that a non-CPA would be offered a partnership.

Beyond the core accounting skills and competencies, accounting graduates may be more employable if they have a clear and demonstrable understanding of financial reporting processes and standards. Forecasting is also an important competency to develop. In addition, many accounting tasks, functions, and activities are becoming automated and/or being handled digitally. Therefore, IT skills are also becoming more important for accounting graduates.

Information Technology (IT)

As noted previously, information technology is a growing field. It tends to be highly technical, which, unfortunately, may limit some people's capabilities in pursuing a career in this area. Individuals who want to enter the field of IT need to understand systems analysis and database management, digital forensics, and issues associated with IT governance. One key thing you can do to distinguish yourself from non-business IT majors (such as some engineering or computer science majors) is to focus on IT as a business function. That is, while other majors may have strong competencies in the technical details of IT, they may be less likely to also have training in such business functions as accounting, management, marketing, or finance. As a result, you can have a competitive advantage if you can clearly relate the IT function to other areas of business.

Finally, while accounting and IT degree programs may be very similar, you can also distinguish yourself in other ways. Get involved in community service work, do a study abroad trip, volunteer with a local theater group, or serve on the board of a non-business-related group. Unfortunately (and inaccurately), accounting and IT students are sometimes stereotyped as being "nerdy" and uninteresting. So demonstrate that your interests extend beyond your academic focus. Suppose a recruiter asks you to name the last book you read and the answer is your accounting textbook. This may demonstrate your commitment to accounting but will also not be particularly interesting. But if your answer is a serious literary work or a book devoted to cutting-edge social commentary, you will be setting yourself apart.

PART 6 | THE FINANCIAL SYSTEM AND ISSUES IN FINANCIAL MANAGEMENT

chapter 16 Understanding Money and the Role of Banking

Adam Parent/Shutterstock

learning objectives

After reading this chapter, you should be able to:

16-1 **Define** *money* and identify the different forms that it takes in the nation's money supply.

16-2 **Describe** the different kinds of financial institutions that compose the U.S. financial system and explain the services they offer.

16-3 **Explain** how financial institutions create money and describe the means by which they are regulated.

16-4 **Discuss** the functions of the Federal Reserve System and describe the tools that it uses to control the money supply.

16-5 **Identify** three important ways in which the money and banking system is changing.

16-6 **Discuss** some of the institutions and activities in international banking and finance.

what's in it for me?

Dealing in matters of money is vastly more complicated than counting the cash and coins in your pocket or using your smartphone to check your bank balance, especially when technology and globalization come into play. At its core are questions about where money comes from, how national economies depend on it, and the public's trust in its value. This chapter will give you a solid understanding of the different forms of money and how it is created and controlled by different kinds of financial institutions and government regulations.

Here's where things get tricky. Open-market operations are the equivalent of printing new money. When times get tough, the Fed can repurchase debt from the public, which results in cash in the banks. The bank only has to keep 10 percent of that cash on hand. As it lends out the rest, it creates more and more money. Imagine that someone borrows the $900 in excess of the required reserves on your deposit, buys a boat, and the boat dealer puts that $900 into a checking account. The bank only needs to keep $90 on hand and can relend the other $810. This is called the money multiplier.

Enter *economist* and past Federal Reserve Chair Ben Bernanke. In the aftermath of the fiscal crisis of 2008–2009, Bernanke believed that the fiscal stimulus enacted by Congress wasn't enough and that the country would fall into a further recession without additional intervention. Congress, being a large political body, could only do so much, but the Fed, insulated as it was from political pressure and composed of economists and bankers, had a mandate to stabilize the economy and the tools to do it. First of all, the Fed lowered the federal funds rate to zero, allowing banks to borrow money interest free. In addition, between 2010 and 2014, the Fed bought over $4.5 trillion in debt from the public, a strategy economists call "quantitative easing," which then increased spendable funds, known as M-1, from $1.4 trillion to $3.4 trillion in just 10 years. Even so, this influx of money didn't drive hyperinflation as some critics thought it would. In fact, inflation, which is a leading indicator of economic growth, never reached the Fed's target rate of 2 percent. In retrospect, analysts reason that the hyperinflation experienced by other countries was due more to printing paper money while

Portrait Images Asia By Nonwarit/Shutterstock

UPI/Alamy Stock Photo

Monetary Policy Hits Home

The Federal Reserve System is the central bank of the United States. According to the Federal Reserve's website, "The Fed," as it is often referred to, is tasked with five main functions: conducting monetary policy, supervising and regulating financial institutions and activities, promoting consumer protection and community development, promoting financial system stability, and fostering payment and settlement system safety and efficiency. But what does that mean in real life? The Fed's monetary policy and oversight may seem to have little to do with your everyday life, but the truth is more complicated.[1]

The Fed manages monetary policy to keep the economy running smoothly. If the economy is booming—"running hot"—inflation can escalate quickly, raising consumer prices of everything from luxury cars to diapers. To prevent that, the Fed steps in and raises the federal funds rate, which is the rate at which banks and other financial institutions lend money to each other. The Federal Open Market Committee sets a target rate, which lending institutions use to determine their own lending rates. An index of interest rates that banks and others charge is called the *prime rate*, which is generally about 3 percentage points higher than the federal rate. For example, in August 2023, the federal rate was 5.33 percent and the prime rate was 8.5 percent.

This explanation may make it seem *less* likely that the Fed has anything to do with your daily life, but if borrowing is more expensive for banks, it's more expensive for bank customers as well. That means if you're shopping for a mortgage and the federal rate goes up, followed by the prime rate, your borrowing power is reduced. If you have an adjustable-rate loan, like a line of credit or a home equity loan, your payments may go up, or your monthly payments won't reduce the principal—the amount of money you still owe—as quickly. Instead, a higher interest rate means a larger portion of your regular payment will be needed to pay interest on the loan.[2]

Though the Fed is tasked with promoting consumer protection, some people feel the interests of powerful financial institutions are prioritized over their customers. Elizabeth Warren, Democratic senator from Massachusetts, has long been a critic of the Federal Reserve's distance from the American public, and she has been particularly vocal about consumer protection. In 2010, thanks in part to Warren's work to increase regulation and transparency in consumer lending, the Obama administration formed the Consumer Financial Protection Bureau (CFPB). Among other things, the CFPB is responsible for monitoring fees

at the same time experiencing severe limitations in the supply of goods and services, as in the case of Germany in the aftermath of World War II. In the United States, banks did not lend out all the excess reserves, instead choosing to hoard the newly minted electronic currency, investing it but not putting it into general circulation.

In 2014, then President Barack Obama appointed Janet Yellen to lead the Federal Reserve Board, succeeding Ben Bernanke. In 2017, the Fed raised the federal funds rate slightly and finally, after almost 10 years, began to reverse the quantitative easing policy. Unemployment dropped to 4.5 percent, and by early 2017, the stock market was seeing healthy increases after years of relative stagnation. At the end of 2017, President Donald Trump nominated Jerome Powell to the Fed chair position, Congress approved a significant tax cut, and in early 2018, as Powell took office, President Trump gave the green light to an increase in public expenditures, basically pouring new money into an already recovering economy. The stock market was climbing, and the biggest economic challenge on the horizon seemed to be the escalating trade war with China. But everything can change in a single moment. As COVID-19 spread throughout the world, devastating the global economy, including that of the United States, sending financial markets into a tailspin and putting millions of people out of work, the Fed once again cut rates, resumed quantitative easing, and started lending money to businesses and state and local governments. In addition to these monetary interventions, Congress initiated a multitrillion-dollar stimulus package (fiscal policy). This resulted in a temporary stabilization of the country's financial woes, but in 2022 and 2023, inflation increased dramatically. In response, the Fed began to gradually raise interest rates to curb inflation while trying to avoid a recession. In 2022, Jerome Powell was reappointed as Fed chair; his term will expire in 2026.

in lending, receiving and resolving consumer complaints, and promoting diversity, equity, and inclusion within the borrowing industry.[3]

Warren continues to champion the rights of individual consumers and remains an outspoken critic of fiscal policies with negative impacts on consumers. In March 2023, after the Fed announced another rate hike, she questioned Federal Reserve Chair Jerome Powell about the consequences of the hike. The higher interest rate was projected to raise the unemployment rate to 4.6 percent—a full percentage point increase—by the end of the year. That increase translated to 1.7 million jobs. Warren insisted that the Fed has a responsibility not just to the system overall but to individual citizens and their families and that the Fed had historically not been able to balance slowing inflation and rising unemployment. As Senator Warren asserted in a public hearing, "We need a Fed that will fight for families."[4]

Federal monetary policy may seem far removed from the everyday life of average Americans, but its impacts—both positive and negative—are very real. Understanding the way fiscal policies are set and being aware of current federal policy will help you make better borrowing decisions, saving you money in both the short and long term. (After studying the content in this chapter, you should be able to answer a set of discussion questions found at the end of the chapter.)

What Is Money?

Learning Objective 16-1

Define *money* and identify the different forms that it takes in the nation's money supply.

If someone asks you how much money you have, do you count the dollar bills and coins in your pockets? Do you include your checking and savings accounts? Do you check your balance in Apple Pay or a similar digital payment option? What about stocks and bonds? Do you count the value of your house or car? Your retirement savings? Taken together, the value of all these combined is your personal wealth. Not all of it, however, is "money." This section considers more precisely what *money* is and what it does.

The Characteristics of Money

Modern money generally takes the forms of stamped metal or printed paper issued by governments as well digital representations of these. Theoretically, however, just about anything *portable*, *divisible*, *durable*, and *stable* can serve as **money**. To appreciate these qualities, imagine using something that lacks them—for example, a 1,000-pound cow used as a unit of exchange in ancient agrarian economies:

Money *object that is portable, divisible, durable, and stable, and that serves as a medium of exchange, a store of value, and a measure of worth*

- ***Portability.*** Try lugging 1,000 pounds of cow from shop to shop. In contrast, modern currency is light and easy to handle.
- ***Divisibility.*** How would you divide your cow if you wanted to buy a hat, a book, and a new phone case from three different stores? Is a pound of cow head worth as much as a pound of cow leg? Modern currency is easily divisible into smaller parts with fixed values—for example, a dollar for four quarters or ten dimes, but a cow is much harder to divide.
- ***Durability.*** Your cow will lose value every day (and eventually die). Modern currency, however, neither dies nor spoils, and if it wears out, it can be replaced. It is also hard to counterfeit—certainly harder than cattle breeding.
- ***Stability.*** If cows were in short supply, you might be able to make quite a deal for yourself. In the middle of an abundant cow year, however, the market would be flooded with cows, so their value would fall. The value of our paper money also fluctuates, but it is considerably more stable and predictable.

The Functions of Money

Imagine a successful cow rancher who needs a new fence. In a *barter economy*, one in which goods are exchanged directly for another, they would have to find someone who is willing to exchange a fence for a cow (or parts of it). If no fence maker wants

Thinkstock Images/Getty Images

Cattle are not portable, divisible, durable, or stable, making them an unsuitable medium of exchange in the modern monetized economy.

a cow, the rancher must find someone else—for example, a wagon maker—who does want a cow. Then, the rancher must hope that the fence maker will trade for a new wagon. In a money economy, though, the rancher would sell their cow, receive money, and exchange the money for such goods as a new fence.

Money serves three essential functions:

1 ***Money is a medium of exchange.*** Like the rancher "trading" money for a new fence, money is used to buy and sell things. Without money, we would be bogged down in a system of constant barter.
2 ***Money is a store of value.*** Pity the rancher whose cow gets sick on Monday and who wants to buy some clothes on the following Saturday, by which time the cow may have died and lost its value. In the form of currency, however, money can be used for future purchases and therefore "stores" its value.
3 ***Money is a measure of worth.*** Money lets us measure the relative values of goods and services. It acts as a measure of worth because all products can be valued and accounted for in terms of money. For example, the concepts of $1,000 worth of clothes or $500 in labor costs have universal meaning.

We see, then, that money adds convenience and simplicity to our everyday lives, for consumers and businesses alike. Employees, consumers, and businesses use money as the measure of worth for determining wages and for buying and selling products—everything from ice cream to housing rentals. Consumers with cash can make purchases wherever they go because businesses everywhere accept money as a medium for exchange. And because money is stable, businesses and individuals save their money, trusting that its value will be available for future use.

M-1: The Spendable Money Supply

Of course, for money to serve its basic functions, both buyers and sellers must agree on its value. The value of money, in turn, depends in part on its *supply*—how much money is in circulation. All else equal, when the supply of money is high, its value drops, and when the supply of money is low, its value increases. (Note that this pattern is consistent with the principles of supply and demand as discussed in Chapter 1.)

Unfortunately, there is no single measure of the supply of money that all experts accept. The oldest and most basic measure, **M-1**, counts only the most liquid, or spendable, forms of money—cash, checks, and funds in checking accounts.

M-1 *measure of the money supply that includes only the most liquid (spendable) forms of money*

Currency (Cash) *government-issued paper money and metal coins*

- Paper money and metal coins are **currency (cash)** issued by the government and widely used for small exchanges. U.S. law requires creditors to accept it in payment of debts.

Hawala, which means "trust" in Arabic, is an ancient system of moving money and is still in use today. Many people who work as traders, like Muhammed Essa in Quetta, Pakistan, transfer funds through handshakes and code words. Although illegal in most countries, the worldwide hawala system moves billions of dollars past regulators annually and leaves no paper trail.

- A **check** is essentially an order instructing a bank to pay a given sum to a payee. Checks are usually, but not always, accepted because they are valuable only to specified payees and can be exchanged for cash.

Check *demand deposit order instructing a bank to pay a given sum to a specified payee*

- **Checking accounts**, or **demand deposits**, are money because their funds may be withdrawn or transferred at any time on demand (including through digital platforms like Venmo).

Checking Account (Demand Deposit) *bank account funds, owned by the depositor, that may be withdrawn at any time by check or cash*

These are all non-interest-bearing or low-interest-bearing forms of money. As of December 2022, M-1 in the United States totaled $19,686 trillion.[5]

M-2: M-1 Plus the Convertible Money Supply

M-2, a second measure of the money supply, is often used for economic planning by businesses and government agencies. **M-2** includes everything in M-1 plus other forms of money that are not quite as liquid, for example, short-term investments that are easily converted to spendable forms, including *time deposits*, *money market mutual funds*, and *savings accounts*. Totaling $21,207 trillion in December 2023, M-2 accounts for most of the nation's money supply.[6] It measures the store of monetary value available for financial transactions by individuals and small businesses. As this overall level increases, more money is available for consumer purchases and business investments. When the supply is tightened, less money is available—financial transactions, spending, and business activity slow down.

M-2 *measure of the money supply that includes all the components of M-1 plus the forms of money that can be easily converted into spendable forms*

Unlike demand deposits, **time deposits**, such as certificates of deposit (CDs), have a fixed term, are intended to be held to maturity, cannot be transferred by check, and pay higher interest rates than checking accounts. Time deposits in M-2 include only accounts of less than $100,000 that can be redeemed on demand, with penalties for early withdrawal. With **money market mutual funds**, investment companies buy a collection of short-term, low-risk financial securities. Ownership of and profits (or losses) from the sale of these securities are shared among the fund's investors.

Time Deposit *bank funds that have a fixed term of time to maturity and cannot be withdrawn earlier or transferred by check*

Money Market Mutual Fund *fund of short-term, low-risk financial securities purchased with the pooled assets of investor-owners*

Figure 16.1 shows how M-1 and M-2 have grown since 1993. For many years, M-1 was the traditional measure of liquid money. Because it was closely related to gross domestic product, it served as a reliable predictor of the nation's real money supply. This situation changed in the early 1980s, with the introduction of new types

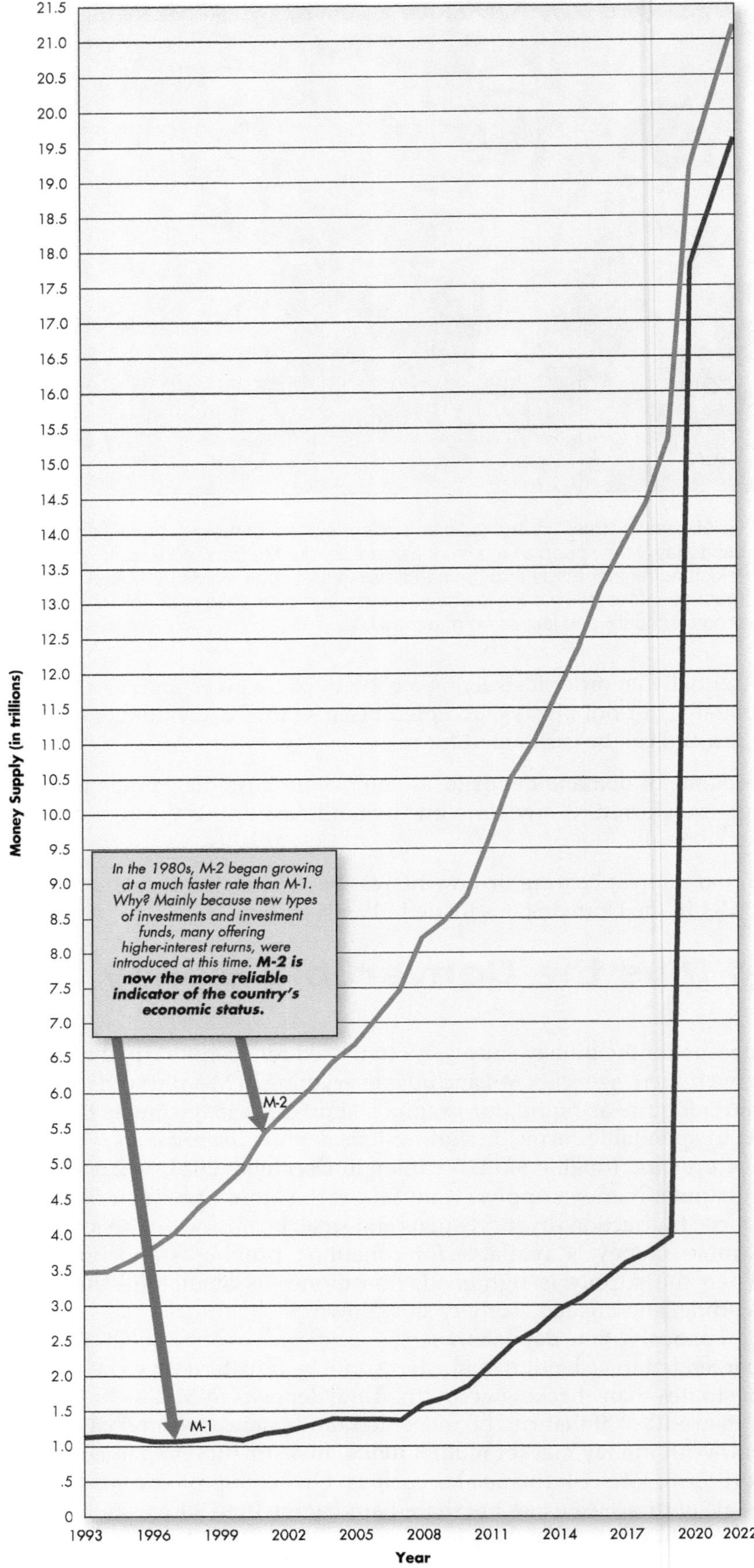

FIGURE 16.1 Money Supply Growth
Source: Federal Reserve, "Money Stock Measures," accessed May 15, 2023, http://www.federalreserve.gov/releases/h6/current/.

of investments and the easier transfer of money among investment funds to gain higher interest returns. As a result, most experts today view M-2 as a more reliable measure than M-1.

Credit Cards and Debit Cards: Plastic Money?

The use of credit and debit cards (both physical cards and online apps such as Apple Pay and Venmo that function in the same way) has become so widespread that some people refer to them as "plastic money." Credit cards, however, are not money and, therefore, are not included in M-1 or M-2 when measuring the nation's money supply. Why? Because spending with a credit card creates a debt, but does not move money until later when the debt is paid by cash or check. Debit card transactions, in contrast, transfer money immediately from the consumer's bank account, so they affect the money supply the same way as spending with a check or cash, and are included in M-1. Although consumers enjoy the convenience of credit cards, they may also find that irresponsible use of these cards can be hazardous to their financial health. A discussion of managing the use of credit cards is found in Appendix III: Managing Your Personal Finances.

The U.S. Financial System

Learning Objective 16-2

Describe the different kinds of financial institutions that compose the U.S. financial system and explain the services they offer.

Many forms of money depend on the existence of financial institutions that provide money-related services to both individuals and businesses. Just how important are these financial institutions, how do they work, and what are some of the services that they offer? We will explore the answers to these questions in the sections that follow as we explain their role as creators of money and discuss the services they offer in the U.S. banking system.

Financial Institutions

The main function of financial institutions is to facilitate the flow of money from users with surpluses to those with deficits by attracting funds into checking and savings accounts. Incoming funds can be lent to individuals and businesses and perhaps invested in government securities. U.S. consumers have access to more than 90,000 U.S. branches and offices of *commercial banks*, *savings institutions*, *credit unions*, and various *nondeposit institutions*.

Commercial Bank *company that accepts deposits that it uses to make loans, earn profits, pay interest to depositors, and pay dividends to owners*

Commercial Banks Federally insured **commercial banks** accept deposits, make loans, earn profits, and pay interest and dividends. Some 4,200 commercial banks range from the largest institutions headquartered in New York, such as Citigroup, Bank of America, and JPMorgan Chase, to small local banks dotting the rural landscape. Bank liabilities, or holdings owed to others, include checking accounts and savings accounts. U.S. banks hold assets totaling more than $20 trillion, consisting of a wide variety of loans to individuals, businesses, farms and ranches, and government entities.[7]

Every bank receives a major portion of its income from interest paid on loans by borrowers. As long as terms and conditions are clearly revealed to borrowers, banks may set their own interest rates, within limits set by each state. Traditionally, banks only offered the lowest rate, or **prime rate**, to their most creditworthy commercial customers. Most commercial loans are set at markups over prime, such as prime +1, which means 1 percent over the prime rate. To remain competitive with lower-interest foreign banks, U.S. banks offer some commercial loans at rates below prime. Figure 16.2 shows the changes in the prime rate since 2000. Lower rates in 2008–2013 encouraged banks to continue lending in the economic downturn. Indeed, the prime rate stayed around 3.25 percent for several years, edged closer to 4.00 percent in 2017,

Prime Rate *interest rate available to a bank's most creditworthy customers*

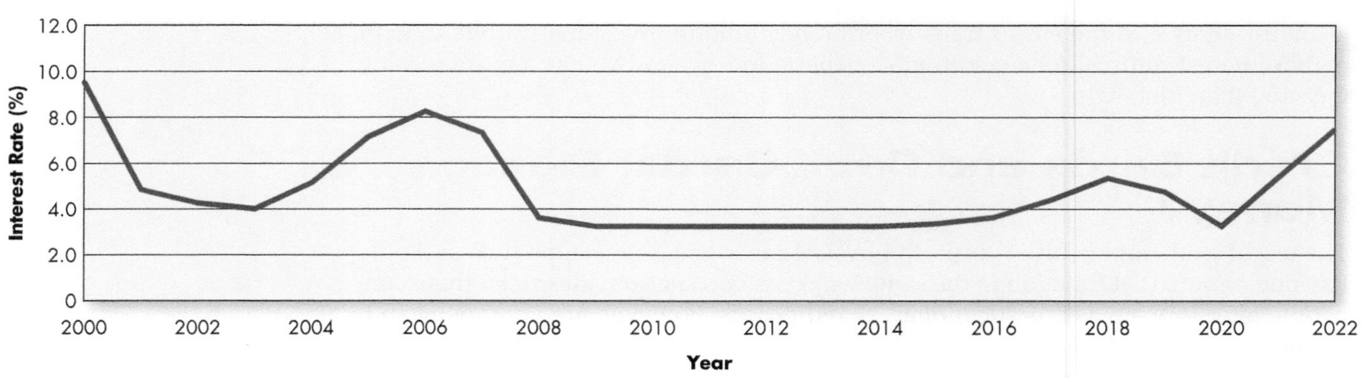

FIGURE 16.2 The Prime Rate
Source: "Prime Interest Rate History," accessed May 15, 2023, http://www.fedprimerate.com/prime_rate_history-monthly.htm#current-monthly-prime-rate.

reached 5.50 percent in December 2018, and then went back down to 3.25 percent in 2020. Since then, though, rates have gradually climbed, reaching 7.50 percent in December 2022 and 8.25 percent in June 2023.

Savings Institutions Savings institutions include mutual savings banks and savings and loan associations. They were once called *thrift institutions* because they were established decades ago to promote the idea of saving among the general population and are still referred to by this label by some older Americans.

Savings and Loan Association (S&L) *financial institution accepting deposits and making loans primarily for home mortgages*

Savings and Loan Associations Like commercial banks, **savings and loan associations (S&Ls)** accept deposits, make loans, and are owned by investors. Most S&Ls were created to encourage savings habits and provide financing for homes; they did not originally offer checking services. Today, they have ventured into a variety of other loans and services, including checking accounts.

Mutual Savings Bank *financial institution whose depositors are owners sharing in its profits*

Mutual Savings Banks In a **mutual savings bank**, all depositors are considered owners of the bank. All profits are divided proportionately among depositors, who receive dividends. About 600 U.S. mutual savings banks attract most of their funds in the form of savings deposits, and funds are lent out in the form of mortgages.

Credit Union *nonprofit, cooperative financial institution owned and run by its members, usually employees of a particular organization*

Credit Unions A **credit union** is a nonprofit, cooperative financial institution owned and run by its members. Its purpose is to promote *thrift*, careful management of one's money or resources, and to provide members with a safe place to save and borrow at reasonable rates. Members pool their funds to make loans to one another. Each credit union decides whom it will serve, such as a group of employees of a given organization or from a defined industry, people in a particular community, or members of an association. The credit unions of some universities and the U.S. Navy, for example, are among the nation's 5,288 credit unions.

Nondeposit Institutions A variety of other organizations take in money, provide interest or other services, and make loans. Unlike commercial banks, these *nondeposit institutions* use inflowing funds for purposes other than earning interest for depositors. Four of the most important are (1) *pension funds*, (2) *insurance companies*, (3) *finance companies*, and (4) *securities investment dealers*.

Pension Fund *nondeposit pool of funds managed to provide retirement income for its members*

1. A **pension fund** is a pool of funds that is managed to provide retirement income for its members. *Public pension funds* in the United States include Social Security and the more than $4 trillion in retirement programs for state and local government employees. *Private pension funds*, operated by employers, unions, and other private groups, cover about 36 million people and have total assets of around $35.5 trillion.

2 **Insurance companies** accumulate money from premiums charged for coverage. They invest these funds in stocks, real estate, and other assets. Earnings pay for insured losses, such as death benefits, automobile damage, and health care expenses.

Insurance Company *nondeposit institution that invests funds collected as premiums charged for insurance coverage*

3 **Finance companies** specialize in making loans to businesses and consumers. HSBC Finance, for example, offers mortgage refinancing and personal loans. *Commercial finance companies* lend to businesses needing capital or long-term funds. *Consumer finance companies* devote most of their resources to providing small noncommercial loans to individuals. Some of these lenders are willing to take on higher-risk borrowers but, in return, charge higher interest rates on their loans.

Finance Company *nondeposit institution that specializes in making loans to businesses and consumers*

4 **Securities investment dealers (brokers)**, such as Merrill Lynch and A. G. Edwards Inc., buy and sell stocks and bonds for client investors. They also invest in securities by buying stocks and bonds for their own accounts in hopes of reselling them later at a profit. These companies hold large sums of money for transfer between buyers and sellers. (We discuss the activities of brokers and investment banking more fully in Chapter 17.)

Securities Investment Dealer (Broker) *financial institution that buys and sells stocks and bonds both for investors and for its own accounts*

Many of us know how much money we have and owe, but otherwise don't realize where much of the nation's money resides. The various financial institutions discussed in this section are "money businesses"—they accept money, hold it for savers, lend it to borrowers, and otherwise use it to earn profits for their constituents. As individuals, many of us at one time or another seek out and benefit from the services of these companies. These same institutions provide jobs and careers for millions of people in the financial industry.

The Growth of Financial Services

The finance business today is highly competitive. No longer is it enough for commercial banks to accept deposits and make loans. Most, for example, also offer bank-issued credit and debit cards, safe-deposit boxes, ATMs, electronic money transfer, online banking, and foreign currency exchange. In addition, many offer pension, trust, international, and brokerage services and financial advice.

Pension and Trust Services

Individual retirement accounts (IRAs) are (typically) tax-deferred pension funds that wage earners and their spouses can set up to supplement other retirement funds. Advantages and drawbacks to various kinds of IRAs—*traditional*, *Roth*, and *education*—are discussed in Appendix III.

Individual Retirement Account (IRA) *tax-deferred pension fund that wage earners set up to supplement retirement funds*

Many commercial banks offer **trust services**, the management of funds left in the bank's trust. In return for a fee, the trust department will perform such tasks as making your monthly bill payments and managing your investment portfolio. Trust departments also manage the estates of deceased persons.

Trust Services *management by a bank of an estate, investments, or other assets on behalf of an individual*

International Services

Suppose a U.S. company wants to buy a product from a Chinese supplier. For a fee, it can use one or more of three services offered by its bank:

1 ***Currency exchange.*** It can exchange U.S. dollars for Chinese yuan to pay the supplier.

2 ***Letters of credit.*** It can pay its bank to issue a **letter of credit**, a promise by the bank to pay the Chinese firm a certain amount if specified conditions are met.

3 ***Banker's acceptances.*** It can pay its bank to draw up a **banker's acceptance**, which promises that the bank will pay some specified amount at a future date.

Letter of Credit *bank promise, issued for a buyer, to pay a designated firm a certain amount of money if specified conditions are met*

A banker's acceptance requires payment by a particular date. Letters of credit are payable only after certain conditions are met. The Chinese supplier, for example, may not be paid until shipping documents prove that the merchandise has been shipped from China.

Banker's Acceptance *bank promise, issued for a buyer, to pay a designated firm a specified amount at a future date*

Financial Advice and Brokerage Services Many banks, both large and small, help their customers manage their money. Depending on the customer's situation, the bank, in its role as financial advisor, may recommend different investment opportunities. The recommended mix might include CDs, mutual funds, stocks, and bonds. Many banks also serve as securities intermediaries, using their own stockbrokers to buy and sell securities and their own facilities to hold them.

Electronic Funds Transfer (EFT) *communication of fund-transfer information over wire, cable, or microwave*

Electronic Funds Transfer **Electronic funds transfer (EFT)** provides for payments and collections by transferring financial information electronically. PayPal, Venmo, Zelle, and similar services offer online payments and money transfers among businesses and individuals, nationally and internationally, in various currencies, requiring only that recipients have an e-mail address. Consumers using debit cards and mobile devices instead of writing personal checks enjoy EFT's convenience and speed at the checkout. In addition, EFT systems provide automatic payroll deposit, ATM transactions, bill payment, and automatic funds transfer. Such systems can help a businessperson close an important business deal by transferring money from San Francisco to Miami within a few seconds. The U.S. Treasury reports that it costs around $1.03 to issue a check payment, but only $0.105 to issue an EFT payment. The U.S. Social Security system estimates that it has saved more than $1 billion since it began phasing out paper check payments in 2013 and instead started using paperless payments for federal benefits.[8]

Automated Teller Machine (ATM) *electronic machine that allows bank customers to conduct account-related activities 24 hours a day, 7 days a week*

Automated teller machines (ATMs) allow customers to withdraw money, make deposits, transfer funds between accounts, and access information on their accounts. There are around 470,000 machines at U.S. locations. Increasingly, ATMs have become multilingual global fixtures. As Figure 16.3 shows, among the world's more than

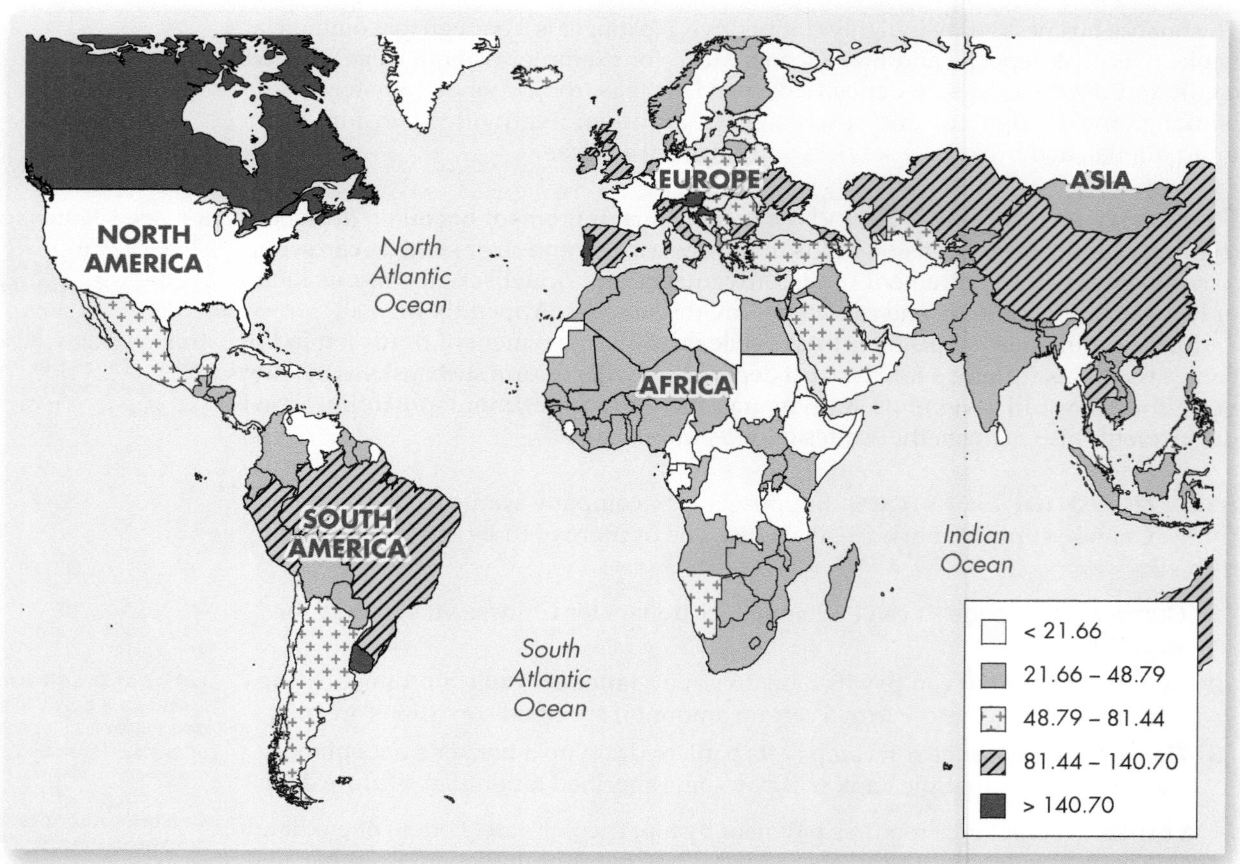

FIGURE 16.3 Global Dispersion of ATMs

Source: Automated Teller Machines (atms) (per 100,000 adults). World Bank Open Data. (n.d.). https://data.worldbank.org/indicator/FB.ATM.TOTL.P5?end=2021&start=2021&view=map

managing in turbulent times

Bailing Out the Banks

Xinhua/Alamy Stock Photo

The 1946 film *It's a Wonderful Life* centers around George Bailey, a man who has given up his dreams of world travel to settle down and run Bailey Bros.'s Building and Loan, a small community bank. When the greedy Mr. Potter buys the bank's competition and demands that all outstanding debts be paid immediately, the community panics, and customers rush to the bank to withdraw all their money. In the movie, the kindhearted George Bailey calms the customers and prevents a collapse, finally using the money set aside for his honeymoon to bail out the bank.

Bailey stands in front of a mob of panicked depositors, trying to educate them about banking, crying, "You're thinking of this place all wrong! As if I had the money back in a safe. The money's not here." Financial institutions don't accept stacks of cash and stock it in a massive vault despite what every clever bank heist movie would have you believe. Instead, banks keep a very small fraction of that amount of cash on hand, investing or lending the rest, counting on investment returns to show a profit. But those investments have to be sound.

In 2010, in response to predatory lending practices and other unethical actions, Congress passed an extensive piece of legislation named the Dodd-Frank Wall Street Reform and Consumer Protection Act. The act changed the regulatory structure, added new restrictions on lending, required the SEC to implement new rules, and even amended the Federal Reserve Act. In addition, the industry tightened credit standards and lending practices.

The act had a positive impact, and the delinquency rate of mortgages fell from a high of nearly 30 percent during the 2008 Global Financial Crisis to an average of 2.52 percent in 2019, offering better protection for investments and depositors. In 2018, however, with strong support from Silicon Valley Bank Chief Executive Greg Becker, then President Donald Trump signed a bill into law that, among other things, lessened regulatory oversight and reporting requirements for midsize lenders and banks.

In early 2023, Silicon Valley Bank, a prominent tech start-up lender, revealed that it had been trying to find a buyer but had not yet been successful and that its failing investments had prompted drastic actions. The bank had sold off most of its liquid assets, borrowed more cash, and organized an emergency stock sale. Banks are extremely reluctant to do any one of those things and signal instability to investors, but Silicon Valley had done all three at once, prompting rumors of a bank run. In the 1946 film, news of a potential bank failure traveled by word of mouth, but in 2023, the run on SVB was spread like wildfire on Twitter(X).

While the Federal Deposit Insurance Corporation (FDIC) insures deposits up to $250,000, meaning that depositors will get all of their money back in the event of a failure, almost 98 percent of Silicon Valley's deposits were over that limit and thus uninsured. When the FDIC stepped in to take over the bank, it announced that it would be issuing certificates to investors, meaning they'd be first in line to see their investments repaid as funds are recovered. There's no guarantee that these investors will recover any of their funds.

The bailout of Silicon Valley Bank prompted fears of other bank failures, and indeed several other similar lenders announced dire circumstances in the following weeks. Questions remain about how the bank ended up in this situation, whether the FDIC should be doing more to protect investors, how to balance bank customers' due diligence with bank's self-regulation, and how far the government should go to protect uninsured deposits.

3.24 million ATMs, most are located outside North America, and many U.S. banks offer international ATM services. China became the world's largest ATM market in 2015 and still holds the title today.[9]

How Financial Institutions Create Money and Are Regulated

Learning Objective 16-3

Explain how financial institutions create money and describe the means by which they are regulated.

When individuals make decisions about spending and saving money, they often don't realize they are taking a financial risk. Getting more value for your money requires an awareness of how the value of your money, including savings, changes—and it does change. As the value of money goes down, your purchasing power goes down. Conversely, purchasing power goes up as the value of your money increases. By predicting changes in value, you can time your spending and savings decisions to get the most for your money. Predictions of future values become possible by (1) understanding how money is created and (2) understanding how the Federal Reserve controls the supply of money. We explore these issues in the following sections.

How Money Is Created

Financial institutions provide a special service to the economy: They create money. They don't actually print bills and mint coins, but by taking in deposits and making loans, they expand the money supply. As Figure 16.4 shows, the money supply expands because banks are allowed to lend most (although not all) of the money they take in from deposits. If you deposit $100 in your bank and banks are allowed to lend 90 percent of all their deposits, then your bank will hold $10 in reserve and lend $90 of your money to borrowers. (You still have $100 on deposit.) Meanwhile, a borrower—or the people paid by the borrower—will deposit the $90 loan money in a bank (or banks). The bank will then have another $81 (90 percent of $90) available for new loans. The banks, therefore, have turned your original $100 into $271($100 + $90 + $81). The chain continues, with borrowings from one bank becoming deposits in the next.

How Banks Are Regulated

Because commercial banks are essential to the creation of money, the government regulates them to ensure a sound and competitive financial system. Federal and state agencies regulate banks to ensure that the failure of some will not cause the public to lose faith in the banking system itself.

Federal Deposit Insurance Corporation (FDIC) *federal agency that guarantees the safety of deposits up to $250,000 in the financial institutions that it insures*

The **Federal Deposit Insurance Corporation (FDIC)** supervises banks and insures deposits in banks and thrift institutions. The FDIC is a government agency created by President Franklin D. Roosevelt in 1933 to restore public confidence in banks during the Depression era. More than 99 percent of the nation's commercial banks and savings institutions pay fees for membership in the FDIC. In return, the FDIC guarantees the safety of all accounts—checking, savings, and CDs—of every account owner up to the maximum of $250,000. If a bank collapses, or fails, the FDIC promises to pay each depositor for losses up to $250,000 per account. A person with more money can establish accounts in more than one bank to protect sums in excess of $250,000. (A handful of the nation's approximately 5,000 commercial banks are insured by states rather than by the FDIC.) To ensure against multiple bank failures, the FDIC maintains the right to examine the activities and accounts of all member banks.

Deposit	Money Held in Reserve by Bank	Money to Lend	Total Supply
$100.00	$10.00	$90.00	**$190.00**
90.00	9.00	81.00	**271.00**
81.00	8.10	72.90	**343.90**
72.90	7.29	65.61	**409.51**
65.61	6.56	59.05	**468.56**

FIGURE 16.4 How Banks Create Money

The Federal Deposit Insurance Corporation, or FDIC, protects deposits placed in member banks. Those member banks, in turn, promote the fact that they belong to the FDIC to instill confidence among customers that funds they place on deposit there are safe in the event of a bank failure or other loss. When First Republic Bank, shown here, failed in 2023, the FDIC's agreement with JPMorgan Chase Bank ensured First Republic's customers did not lose any money.

What happens with banks that fail, such as the nearly 300 U.S. banks that failed in 2009 and 2010? The FDIC becomes responsible for disposing of failed banks. One option is to sell them to other banks that are then responsible for the liabilities of the failed banks. Alternatively, the FDIC can seize the assets of the failed banks and undertake two activities: (1) pay insurance to depositors and (2) dispose of the banks' assets and settle their debts, all at the lowest cost to the FDIC's insurance deposit fund. The resulting net gain (or loss) is put into (or paid from) the insurance deposit fund. Many banks failed during the recession, costing the FDIC a great deal of money. For example, the fund dwindled from $45 billion in 2008 to $13 billion by the end of 2009. Fortunately, the fund had grown back to $125 billion by the end of 2022. All told, the FDIC now insures around $9.9 trillion in over 600 million accounts at approximately 4,746 institutions. Many other banking activities are regulated by the Federal Reserve System, which is discussed next.

The Federal Reserve System

Learning Objective 16-4

Discuss the functions of the Federal Reserve System and describe the tools that it uses to control the money supply.

Perched atop the U.S. financial system and regulating many aspects of its operation is the **Federal Reserve System (the Fed)**, the nation's central bank, established by Congress in 1913. This section describes the structure of the Fed, its functions, and the tools it uses to control the nation's money supply.

Federal Reserve System (the Fed) *central bank of the United States, which acts as the government's bank, serves member commercial banks, and controls the nation's money supply*

The Structure of the Fed

The Fed consists of a board of governors, a group of reserve banks, and member banks. As originally established by the Federal Reserve Act of 1913, the system consisted of 12 relatively autonomous banks and a seven-member committee whose powers were limited to coordinating the activities of those banks. By the 1930s, however, both the structure and function of the Fed had changed dramatically.

finding a better way

A Better Way to Pay?

The U.S. money supply is centralized and regulated by the Federal Reserve Bank, but who oversees the supply of cryptocurrencies like Bitcoin?

The term "cryptocurrency" is a combination of the terms "cryptography" and "currency." Cryptography provides a secure way to communicate and dates back to ancient times. Currency is something tangible in circulation as a medium of exchange.

Bitcoin is a worldwide cryptocurrency that was created by a group of users in 2009 as a response to the market crash of 2008. Using cryptocurrency, someone in the United States who buys something from a seller in Brazil using Bitcoin doesn't have to worry about conversion rates. It's a decentralized currency validated by a peer-to-peer network where all transactions are public and transaction data is almost impossible to manipulate. Every Bitcoin transaction is logged and recorded in a public ledger of all Bitcoin transactions. Each virtual page of that ledger is linked to the one before it, creating a chain of blocks. Each Bitcoin user has a public identity and a private identity for each transaction, keeping transactions public and verified but leaving the parties to the transaction anonymous.

By spreading its operations across a network of computers, blockchain allows cryptocurrencies like Bitcoin to operate without the need for a central authority. Cryptocurrency advocates argue that this reduces not only risk but also processing and transaction fees and creates a truly global currency. Proponents of cryptocurrencies claim that they are making currency more democratic by eliminating intermediary banks. Critics, however, say because there is no central controlling entity, standard monetary policy tools like changing interest rates do not apply. They also argue that cryptocurrencies are subject to greater risk of theft and fraud because the exchanges required to access them are unregulated and have a low barrier to entry.

Some investors hold cryptocurrencies as investments rather than using them as money. Volatility in cryptocurrency markets has led many people to debate about how bitcoins can be valued since they do not have any underlying assets. Regulations around cryptocurrencies vary, with some governments embracing cryptocurrencies and others banning or limiting their use. As of February 2023, 114 countries, including the United States, were considering introducing their own central bank digital currencies (CBDCs) to compete with the cryptocurrency boom.[10] Other governments are considering using Bitcoin's blockchain technology to maintain secure records related to fiat currency.

Senior Fellow Sebastian Mallaby of the Council on Foreign Relations posits, "You can imagine a new kind of financial system being constructed out of blockchain-based tokens that have advantages over the old, centralized kinds of money. You trust the code, and you trust the blockchain and the decentralized ledger, and it's a new way of organizing finance."[11]

The Board of Governors The Fed's board of governors consists of seven members appointed by the U.S. president for overlapping terms of 14 years. The chair of the board serves on major economic advisory committees and works actively with the administration to formulate economic policy. The board plays a large role in controlling the money supply. It alone determines the reserve requirements, within statutory limits, for depository institutions. It also works with other members of the Fed to set discount rates and handle the Fed's sale and purchase of government securities.

Reserve Banks The Fed consists of 12 districts, as shown in Figure 16.5. Each Federal Reserve Bank holds reserve deposits from and sets the discount rate for commercial banks in its geographic region. Reserve banks also play a major role in the nation's check-clearing process.

Open Market Committee The Federal Open Market Committee is responsible for formulating the Fed's monetary policies to promote economic stability and growth by managing the nation's money supply. Its members include the Board of Governors, the president of the Federal Reserve Bank of New York, and the presidents of four other Reserve Banks, who serve on a rotating basis.

Member Banks All nationally chartered commercial banks and some state-chartered banks are members of the Fed. The accounts of all member bank depositors are automatically covered by the FDIC (as discussed earlier).

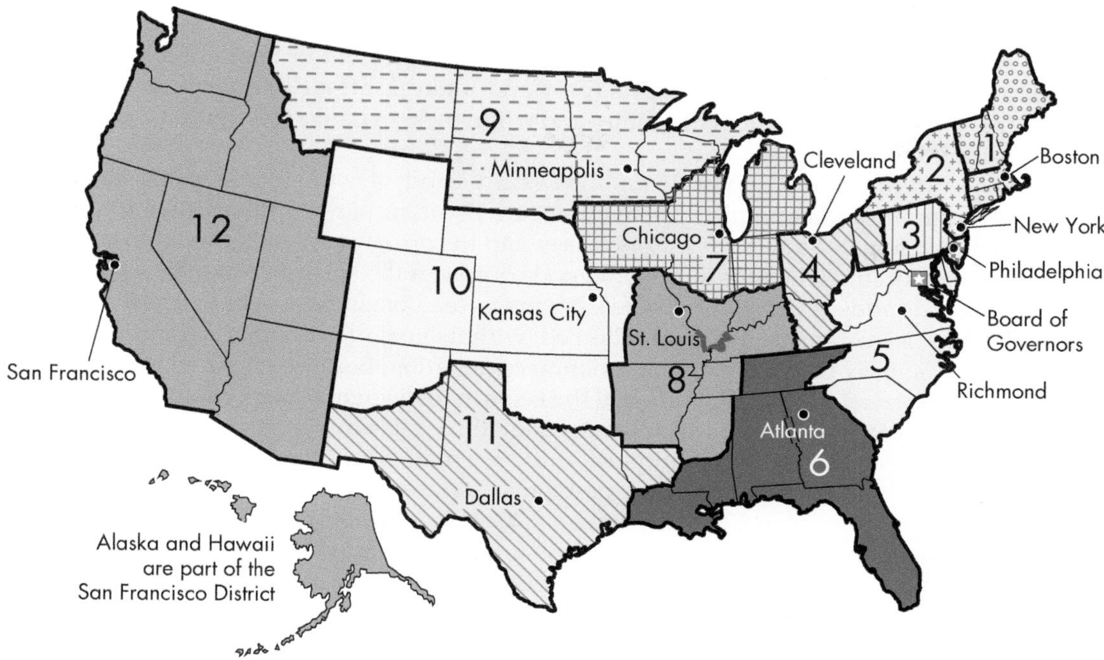

FIGURE 16.5 The Twelve Federal Reserve Districts
Source: Board of Governors of the Federal Reserve System, accessed August 11, 2023, https://www.federalreserve.gov/aboutthefed/federal-reserve-system.htm.

Other Depository Institutions Although many state-chartered banks, credit unions, and S&Ls do not belong to the Fed, they are subject to its regulations, pay deposit insurance premiums, and are covered by the FDIC or the National Credit Union Administration (NCUA), an independent federal agency that supervises and insures federal credit unions.

The Functions of the Fed

In addition to chartering national banks, the Fed serves as the federal government's bank and the "bankers' bank," regulating a number of banking activities. Most importantly, it controls the money supply.

The Government's Bank The Fed produces the nation's paper currency and decides how many bills to produce and destroy. It also lends money to the government by buying bonds issued by the Treasury Department to help finance the national deficit.

The Bankers' Bank Individual banks that need money can borrow from the Fed and pay interest on the loans. In addition, the Fed provides storage for commercial banks, which are required to keep funds on reserve at a Federal Reserve Bank.

Check Clearing The Fed also clears checks for commercial banks to ensure that cash is deducted from the check writer's bank account and deposited into the check receiver's account. With electronic payments, however, the number of paper checks processed is steadily declining. In 2000, the Fed cleared 60 billion paper checks. By 2022, though, this number had dropped to 14.7 billion paper checks and another 4.1 billion checks cleared as images from mobile apps. Consumers prefer the convenience of debit and credit cards and electronic transactions such as direct deposits and online payments. Even with paper checks, however, the clearing is faster because banks now send the Fed electronic images for presentment, payment, and record keeping (instead of shipping the checks). As a result, the Fed now has just one full-service check-processing site, instead of the 45 locations needed as recently as 2003.[12]

Monetary Policy *management of the nation's economic growth by managing the money supply and interest rates*

Controlling the Money Supply The Fed is responsible for the implementation of U.S. **monetary policy**, the management of the nation's economic growth by managing the money supply and interest rates. By controlling these two factors, the Fed influences the ability and willingness of banks throughout the country to lend money.

As defined in Chapter 1, *inflation* is a period of widespread price increases throughout an economic system. It occurs if the money supply grows too large. Demand for goods and services increases, and the prices of everything rise. In contrast, *deflation* occurs when the supply of goods outpaces the supply of money, so demand for goods and services falls. Decreasing prices lead businesses to cut output and also lead to rises in unemployment. The Fed, with its goal of economic stability, uses the money supply to avoid extreme inflation or deflation. Because commercial banks are the main creators of money, much of the Fed's management of the money supply takes the form of regulating the supply of money through commercial banks. In a healthy economy, small annual inflation rates are normal. However, beginning in 2021, as the world was coming out of the pandemic, inflation in the United States started to increase—7 percent in 2021, 6.5 percent in 2022, and 4.9 percent in the first half of 2023. If responses by the Fed to limit inflation are too extreme, however, there is a risk of causing a recession. So, during this period, the Fed very carefully manipulated the money supply in an effort to both reduce inflation and avoid a recession.

The Tools of the Fed

According to the Fed's original charter, its primary duties were to supervise banking and to manage the nation's currency. The duties of the Fed have evolved to include an emphasis on broad economic goals as discussed in Chapter 1, especially growth and stability. The Fed's role in controlling the nation's money supply stems from its role in setting policies to help reach these goals. To control the money supply, the Fed uses *reserve requirements*, *interest rate controls*, and *open-market operations*.

Reserve Requirement *percentage of its deposits that a bank must hold in cash or on deposit with the Fed*

Reserve Requirements The **reserve requirement** is the percentage of its deposits that a bank must hold, in cash or on deposit, with a Federal Reserve Bank. High requirements mean that banks have less money to lend and the money supply is reduced. Conversely, low requirements permit the supply to expand. Because the Fed sets requirements for all depository institutions, it can adjust them to make changes to the overall supply of money in the economy. The Fed's reserve requirements for 2023 depend on the sizes of depositors' accounts. The smallest accounts are exempt (0 percent reserve), for account transactions more than $21.1 million the reserve is 3 percent, and the rate is 10 percent for account transactions greater than $182.9 million.

Discount Rate *interest rate at which member banks can borrow money from the Fed*

Federal Funds Rate (Key Rate) *interest rate at which commercial banks lend reserves to each other, usually overnight*

Interest Rate Controls As the bankers' bank, the Fed loans money to banks. The interest rate on these loans is known as the **discount rate**. If the Fed wants to reduce the money supply, it increases the discount rate, making it more expensive for banks to borrow money and less attractive for them to lend it. Conversely, low rates encourage borrowing and lending and expand the money supply.

More familiar to consumers, the **federal funds rate (key rate)** reflects the rate at which commercial banks lend reserves overnight to each other. Although the Fed can't actually control this rate, which is determined by the supply and demand of bank reserves, it can control the supply of those reserves to create the desired rate. By instructing its bond traders to buy fewer government bonds, the supply of reserves was decreased, resulting in a series of key rate increases—from a then-historic low of 1 percent in 2004 up to 5.25 percent in 2006—to slow a booming U.S. economy. The Fed then reversed its policy as the economy lost momentum, cutting the target rate gradually down to 0.25 percent in 2008 (to boost the economy during the recession), followed by 0.00–0.25 percent in 2009, and then continuing at 0.00–0.25 percent into 2016 to encourage the economic recovery.[13] And as noted earlier, the Fed has continued to work to control inflation while working toward economic stability.

Open-Market Operations **Open-market operations** refer to the Fed's sale and purchase of securities (usually U.S. Treasury notes and short-term bonds) in the open market, as directed by the Fed's Open-Market Committee. Open-market operations are particularly effective because they act quickly and predictably on the money supply. The Fed buys government securities from a commercial dealer, whose bank account is credited for the transaction, thus giving that bank more money to lend, so this transaction expands the money supply.

Open-Market Operations *the Fed's sale and purchase of securities in the open market*

The opposite happens when the Fed sells securities. Selling Treasury securities to investors allows the U.S. government to raise money and contract the money supply. These securities may include Treasury bills (T-bills), T-notes, and T-bonds with maturity dates ranging from short term (a few weeks) to long term (up to 30 years). Treasury securities are highly liquid because they are actively traded on national securities markets, and traditionally have been considered a risk-free investment because they are backed by the U.S. government.

The Changing Money and Banking System

Learning Objective 16-5

Identify three important ways in which the money and banking system is changing.

The U.S. money and banking system continues to change today. Government emergency intervention aims to stabilize a troubled financial system. Enforcement of antiterrorism regulations deters criminal misuse of the financial system. And with the expansion of banking services, electronic technologies affect how you obtain money and how much interest you pay for it.

Government Intervention for Stabilizing the U.S. Financial System

The financial world was shaken with the 2008 collapse of Lehman Brothers, the leading U.S. investment bank. Lehman's bankruptcy was soon followed by the threat of another giant's demise, as Bear Stearns almost collapsed but was then bought by JPMorgan Chase. But JPMorgan Chase's purchase of Bear Stearns became possible only when the Federal Reserve stepped forward with $26 billion to guarantee potential losses on Bear Stearns's assets. With a goal of stabilizing the fractured financial system, the government continues its unprecedented infusion of funding for U.S. financial institutions.

Government Emergency Investment By mid-2009, the Fed's investments reached nearly $300 billion, mostly in lending programs to commercial banks. Banks used the loans to write off or sell bad mortgages and other hard-to-sell assets, thereby gaining cash for lending to bank customers. Another source of funds, the Troubled Asset Relief Program (TARP), a temporary program under the U.S. Treasury, was included in the government's bailout efforts. TARP support included $15 billion to auto-financing companies at risk of failure and $235 billion in direct investments to some 600 banks to encourage lending. Other government sources provided more than $130 billion to rescue Freddie Mac and Fannie Mae, two government-sponsored enterprises on the verge of financial failure. Freddie Mac and Fannie Mae (also known as FM2) buy home mortgages from the original lenders—for example, from banks—and hold them or resell them. In 2008, FM2 held 80 percent of U.S. home mortgages, many of which turned bad in the collapsed housing market, and many more that continue to default today. FM2 still held some $5 trillion in mortgage assets as of 2013. As a result, critics questioned whether the government should be involved in the mortgage loan business.[14] During the economic collapse associated with the 2020 COVID-19 pandemic, the U.S. government injected over a trillion dollars into the economy in the form of both grants and loans to businesses and direct payments to individual citizens.

Assurances of Repayment In return for its investments, the government imposes various kinds of assurances. The Fed's loans to banks, for example, are secured by the banks' assets. That is, the Fed holds some of the banks' assets, such as commercial loans, residential mortgages, and asset-backed securities, as collateral until the banks repay the Fed. In return for TARP funds, the U.S. Treasury holds preferred stock (dividend-paying ownership shares) of the banks. The Treasury also holds *warrants*, which give the right to buy shares of the banks' stock in the future at a preset price. In addition to creating the government's precedent-setting part ownership, TARP also imposes stricter executive compensation requirements. In the bailout of FM2, both firms were taken over by the Federal Housing Finance Agency (FHFA) because the failure of either would severely damage global financial markets along with the U.S. economy. FHFA took full control over the two firms' assets and operations.[15]

Anticrime and Antiterrorism Regulations

Enforcement of antiterrorism regulations deters criminal misuse of the financial system. Under provisions of the *Bank Secrecy Act (BSA)*, the U.S. Department of the Treasury imposed a $15 million fine on the Shinhan Bank of America (SHBA). SHBA is a South Korean banking corporation with branches in many major U.S. cities. The fine was due to the bank knowingly not following BS rules that safeguard against money laundering.[16] In recent year fines have also been levied against Danske Bank, LaFarge, USAA, National Bank of Pakistan, Robinhood, BitMEX, Wells Fargo, CHS Hedging, and Sterling Bank and Trust.[17]

The *USA PATRIOT Act*, passed in 2001 and designed to reduce terrorism risks, requires banks to have more information about a customer's true identity than was true previously by obtaining and verifying their name, address, date of birth, and Social Security (or tax identification) number. They must also implement a *customer identification program (CIP)* to verify identities, keep records of customer activities, and compare identities of new customers with government terrorist lists. Enforcement resides with examiners from the Department of the Treasury.

The Impact of Electronic Technologies

Banks are among the most enthusiastic adopters of technology to improve efficiency and customer service. Customers of JPMorgan Chase include more than 33 million mobile users, and at Bank of America, more than 100,000 checks each day are deposited remotely by mobile devices.[18] In addition to EFT systems and mobile devices, banks offer access via telephone, TV, and online banking, which allow customers to make around-the-clock transactions. Each business day, trillions of dollars exist in and among banks and other financial institutions in purely electronic form. Each day, the Fed's Fedwire funds transfer system, the world's largest electronic payments system, processes about $5 trillion in transactions for nearly 10,000 financial institutions.

Automated Clearing House (ACH) Network ACH is an electronic funds transfer system that provides interbank clearing of electronic payments for the nation's financial institutions. The ACH network allows businesses, government, and consumers to choose an electronic-over-paper alternative for payments (instead of written checks). The system is green, safe, and efficient.

ACH payments include the following:

- Internet-initiated debit and credit payments by businesses and consumers
- Business-to-business (B2B) electronic payments
- Direct deposit of payroll, Social Security benefits, and tax refunds
- Federal, state, and local tax payments

- E-checks
- Direct payment of consumer bills: mortgages, loans, utility bills, and insurance premiums
- E-commerce payments

In 2022, the ACH system processed over 30 billion payments that were initiated or received by customers at more than 15,000 U.S. businesses and financial institutions. Those payments totaled more than $76.7 trillion. With the federal government's use of ACH, each direct deposit that replaces a check saves $0.925. With each $1 billion of direct deposits, the federal savings is nearly $1 billion.

The ACH system is governed by NACHA, the Electronic Payments Association, which administers and enforces the association's strict *NACHA Operating Rules* for sound risk management practices. Although NACHA was formed within the American Bankers Association, it later became an independent not-for-profit association that launched the Accredited ACH Professional program and established the system's operating rules.[19]

Check 21: Making the Paper Check Go Away The *Check Clearing for the 21st Century Act (Check 21)*, which became federal law in 2004, allows a receiving bank to make an electronic image of a paper check and electronically send the image to the paying bank for instant payment instead of waiting days for the paper check to wind its way back to the sender. More banks are adopting check image processing (Check 21) and benefiting from its speed and cost efficiency: less paper handling, reduced reliance on physical transportation, faster collection times, and elimination of expensive float. Today, almost 99 percent of the items processed by the Fed are images instead of in paper form. The days of writing a check, mailing it, and having several days to put money in the account to cover it are numbered as a result of faster check clearing.[20]

Blink Credit Card "Blink" technology uses a computer chip that sends radio-frequency signals in place of the magnetic strips that have been embedded in credit cards for the past 30 years. The "contactless" payment system lets consumers wave the card in front of a merchant's terminal at a gas pump or retailer without waiting to swipe and sign. Radio-frequency identification, although relatively new to credit cards, is familiar on toll roads with electronic passes that allow drivers to avoid waiting in line to pay.

Debit Cards Unlike credit cards, **debit cards** do not increase the funds at an individual's disposal but allow users only to transfer money between accounts to make retail purchases. Debit cards are used more than credit cards as payment for U.S. consumer transactions. However, the risk of financial loss is greater for debit cards. Federal law limits the credit card holder's liability to $50 for stolen or fraudulent use. However, a debit card holder's liability for fraudulent card losses can be higher—ranging up to $500—depending on how quickly the lost card is reported.[21] Many retailers that accept debit cards use **point-of-sale (POS) terminals** to communicate relevant purchase information with a customer's bank. A customer inserts a card, and the bank automatically transfers funds from the customer's account to the store's account.

Debit Card *plastic card that allows an individual to transfer money between accounts*

Point-of-Sale (POS) Terminal *electronic device that transfers funds from the customer's bank account to pay for retail purchases*

Smart Cards A **smart card** has an embedded computer chip that can be programmed with "electronic money." Also known as *electronic purses* or *stored-value cards*, smart cards have existed for more than a decade. They are most popular in gas-pump payments, followed by prepaid phone service, ATMs, self-operated checkouts, vending machines, and automated banking services.[24] Embedded chip technology is also replacing the standard magnetic strips on traditional credit cards and debit cards. This technology provides greater security for both parties during financial transactions.

Smart Card *credit-card-sized plastic card with an embedded computer chip that can be programmed with electronic money*

entrepreneurship and new ventures

Managing a Risky Business

Samuel S/Nchez El Pais Photos/Newscom

When Larry Fink graduated from UCLA's business school in 1976, he went straight to Wall Street and took a job at First Boston as a bond trader. He put in his time, proved himself, and within three years was in charge of what was then a fairly new business segment for First Boston—structuring and trading mortgage-backed securities. Over the years, his hard work and talent led him to fame as one of the architects of the multitrillion-dollar innovative debt-securitization market. But then, in 1986, predicting that interest rates would rise, Fink took a risky position in the market. Interest rates defied his predictions, and his department lost $100 million. Once First Boston's golden boy, overnight he became a pariah.

Being forced out of First Boston was a turning point for Larry Fink. He was tired of the way Wall Street treated its clients and its traders. Realizing that he'd failed because he wasn't aware of the risks involved, he vowed never to be in that kind of situation again. Coming from that paradigm, he decided to build a company that would invest money for clients and offer sophisticated risk management. From a humble beginning renting a corner office on the Bear Stearns trading floor, Larry Fink has taken BlackRock from its initial $5 million line of credit to nearly $9 trillion in clients' money, more than any asset manager on Earth—even more than Vanguard.

BlackRock's success even led to the Federal Reserve tapping the company for help in the COVID-19 2020 market response. The Fed hired BlackRock to manage a trio of programs aimed at stabilizing the corporate bond market. Unlike a similar situation in 2008, in which BlackRock also helped stabilize a rocky market, the terms of the 2020 deal were made public early, with a fee and total cap on profits.

BlackRock is also a leader in investing in "green" stocks despite Fink's stance against using the popular term "ESG" (environmental, social, and corporate governance). ESG is a broad category that includes a range of socially responsible business practices such as cutting carbon emissions and addressing discrimination in the workplace. Fink says, "I don't use the word ESG anymore because it's been entirely weaponized . . . by the far left and weaponized by the far right."[22]

Fink, who turned 70 in 2023, has no plans to retire, but the company is still planning for his succession. "I have no higher priority than developing the next generational leaders for BlackRock," he said to a group of investors.[23]

Learning Objective 16-6

Discuss some of the institutions and activities in international banking and finance.

International Banking and Finance

Electronic technologies permit nearly instantaneous financial transactions around the globe. These business exchanges—the prices asked and paid—are affected by *values of the currencies* among the various nations involved in the transactions. Once agreements are reached, the *international payments process* that moves money between buyers and sellers on different continents is not subject to any worldwide policy system beyond loosely structured agreements among countries.

Currency Values and Exchange Rates

Euros, pesos, yuans, pounds, dollars, and yen—money comes in all sizes and stripes. With today's global activities, travelers, shoppers, investors, and businesses often rely on banks to convert their dollars into other currencies. When it comes to choosing one currency over others, the best choice literally changes from day to day. Why? Because every currency's value changes, reflecting global supply and demand—what traders are willing to pay—for one currency relative to others. One index for the value of the U.S. dollar, for example, is the average of its foreign exchange values against the currencies of a large group of major U.S. trading partners. The resulting **exchange rate**, the value of one currency compared to the value of another, reveals how much of one currency must be exchanged for another. At any one time, then, some currencies are "strong"—selling at a higher price and worth more—whereas others are "weak."

Exchange Rate *the value of one currency compared to the value of another*

Rates of exchange among currencies are published daily in financial media around the world and at online foreign currency exchange (forex) markets.[25]

Strong Currency or Weak: Which Is Better? Intuitively, it would seem logical to prefer a "strong" currency, right? But in reality, the answer is not so simple and actually depends on how it will be used. Using money for international activities, such as taking a vacation, is really one of those "good news–bad news" situations.

Consider the value of the euro versus the U.S. dollar, as exchange rates fluctuated for those currencies between the 20-year period 2002 and 2022. As a citizen in one of the euro-area countries—for example, France—suppose you were going to take a vacation to the United States in 2002 but, instead, you chose to delay that vacation until 2012; later, in 2022 you decided to visit again. Now, compare your vacation costs if you had gone in 2002 versus 2012, based on currency exchange rates at those times. Each euro in 2012 paid for about $1.45 of the trip (based on currency exchange rates at that time). However, each euro would have covered only $0.87 in 2002 (based on prevailing exchange rates). That's the good news: The stronger euro in 2012 meant more purchasing power against the weaker dollar for French vacationers. It's bad news, though, for French innkeepers because Americans could go elsewhere to avoid expensive European travel that requires $1.45 to pay for each euro of vacation cost, up from only $0.83 to pay per euro 10 years previously. Simply put, that $0.83 cup of coffee at a French sidewalk café in 2002 cost $1.45 in 2012. Since 2012, though, the euro has declined in value relative to the dollar, and in 2017, its value was about the same level as in 2002. As a result, it was again less expensive for the French to travel to the United States in 2012. By 2022, the exchange rate had continued to decline and hovered around 1.08, so one euro was worth only 8 cents more than one dollar.

Milkovasa/Shutterstock

Exchanges describe the relative value of one currency to another. For instance, if the exchange rate between U.S. dollars and British pounds was 2:1, this would mean that you would need two dollars to "buy" (or exchange for) one pound, or one pound could be exchanged for two dollars. Businesses that handle money exchanges charge a commission on each exchange to generate profits for themselves. Alternatively, they may advertise "no commission" but offer less attractive exchange rates. This sign in the Mexico City airport is quoting exchange rates for buying and selling U.S. dollars, euros, pounds, and Canadian dollars relative to the Mexican peso.

In terms of trade, the strong euro in 2012 proved to be a stumbling block for Europe's economy, especially for industries that export to non-euro countries with weaker currencies. Prices (in U.S. dollars) had to be increased, for example, on German-made Mercedes and BMW auto exports to the United States to cover the higher euro-based manufacturing costs, causing weaker U.S. demand and sales. Although the weaker dollar hurt many European firms that export products to the United States, others gained by increasing their U.S. investments. When Mercedes-Benz, for example, produces Mercedes M-class autos in Alabama, it pays in weaker dollars for manufacturing them, exports cars to Europe, and sells in euros for windfall profits. On balance, however, many euro-based firms faced sagging sales, with slower revenue growth the result of a strong euro. Again, though, as the euro weakened, those same firms have seen their foreign revenues begin to grow.

Bank Policies Influence Currency Values In managing the money supply and interest rates, as discussed earlier, the Fed strongly influences the dollar's strength against other currencies. The European Central Bank (ECB) has the same role in the euro zone. The raising of interest rates tends to increase an economic system's currency value, whereas lowering the rate has the opposite effect. However, the impact of ECB policies is often slower to reach its intended goals than is the case of the Fed in the U.S. This is because the ECB and the Euro itself span multiple countries, and local government policies may serve to at least moderately influence how ECB actions are felt internally.

Compounding the uncertainties facing foreign exchange has been Britain's exit from the European Union. Unlike other EU members, Britain never dropped its traditional currency in favor of the euro. But economists, government officials, and business leaders are all working to disentangle the effects of Brexit on Britain's international trade, international trade of the EU, and the ripple effects of the major trading partners of both Britain and the EU member nations. Consequently, foreign exchange rates for both the British pound and the euro are likely to fluctuate more than usual over the next few years.

Why care, then, about currency exchange rates? Currencies matter greatly to companies when they buy, sell, and invest with other companies around the globe. Individuals, too, have similar concerns, as when farmers buy grain from Brazil and tractors made in Japan or India, sometimes at higher prices and other times at lower prices, depending on the currency exchange rates of the countries involved. Those exchange rates can be the difference between making a living and losing money during any year. Prices for consumer products, such as electronics by Samsung and autos made in Sweden or Germany, depend on currency exchange rates, too. As an investor looking toward retirement, you may buy an individual retirement account (IRA) in the T. Rowe Price European Stock Fund or, alternatively, invest in any of the many other global opportunities for accumulating wealth to meet future needs and dreams. In all of these endeavors, the success or disappointments in your decisions—if and when to buy and to not buy—will be influenced by changes in currency exchange rates. Likewise, as a potential entrepreneur, your business success will be determined, in part, by changes in currency exchange rates.

The International Payments Process

Financial settlements between buyers and sellers in different countries are simplified through services provided by banks. For example, payments from U.S. buyers start at a local bank that converts them from dollars into the seller's currency, such as into euros to be sent to a seller in France. At the same time, payments and currency conversions from separate transactions also are flowing between French businesses and U.S. sellers in the other direction.

If trade between the two countries is in balance—if money inflows and outflows are equal for both countries—then *money does not actually have to flow between the two countries*. If inflows and outflows are not in balance at the U.S. bank (or at the

French bank), then a flow of money—either to France or to the United States—is made to cover the difference.

International Bank Structure

There is no worldwide banking system comparable, in terms of policy making and regulatory power, to the system of any industrialized nation. Worldwide banking stability relies on a loose structure of agreements among individual countries or groups of countries.

Two United Nations agencies, the *World Bank* and the *International Monetary Fund*, help to finance international trade. Unlike true banks, the **World Bank** (technically, the International Bank for Reconstruction and Development) provides only a limited scope of services. For instance, it funds national improvements by making loans to build roads, schools, power plants, and hospitals. The resulting improvements eventually enable borrowing countries to increase productive capacity and international trade.

World Bank *UN agency that provides a limited scope of financial services, such as funding improvements in underdeveloped countries*

Another U.N. agency, the **International Monetary Fund (IMF)**, is a group of 190 nations that have combined resources for the following purposes:

International Monetary Fund (IMF) *UN agency consisting of about 150 nations that have combined resources to promote stable exchange rates, provide temporary short-term loans, and serve other purposes*

- To promote the stability of exchange rates
- To provide temporary, short-term loans to member countries
- To encourage members to cooperate on international monetary issues
- To encourage development of a system for international payments

The IMF makes loans to nations suffering from temporary negative trade balances. By making it possible for these countries to continue buying products from other countries, the IMF facilitates international trade. On some occasions the assistance is targeted to specific problem areas. For example, the IMF made loans to Greece in 2016 to help support that country's struggling economy. However, some nations have declined IMF funds rather than accept the economic changes that the IMF demands. For instance, some developing countries reject the IMF's requirement that they cut back on social programs and spending to bring inflation under control. In other situations, financial assistance from the IMF may be more widespread and in the form of grants or loans. In 2020, for example, the IMF provided assistance to literally dozens of struggling economies around the world.

summary of learning objectives

LEARNING OBJECTIVE 16-1

Define *money* and identify the different forms that it takes in the nation's money supply.

Modern money takes the form of stamped metal or printed paper issued by governments. However, any item that's *portable*, *divisible*, *durable*, and *stable* satisfies the basic characteristics of money. Money also serves as a *medium of exchange* (it is generally accepted as payment for buying and selling things), a *store of value* (it can be saved and used for future purchases), and a *measure of worth* (it acts as a measure of worth because all products can be valued in terms of money).

A nation's money supply is usually measured in two ways. *M-1*, the spendable money supply, includes the most liquid (or spendable) forms of money: currency (cash), checks, and checking accounts (demand deposits). *M-2* includes M-1 plus other forms of money that are not quite as liquid but are converted easily to spendable forms: time deposits, money market funds, and savings accounts. M-2 is often used for economic planning by businesses and government agencies because it accounts for most of the nation's money supply. M-2 measures the store of monetary value available for consumer purchases and business investments.

LEARNING OBJECTIVE 16-2

Describe the different kinds of financial institutions that compose the U.S. financial system and explain the services they offer.

Federally insured commercial banks offer checking accounts and accept deposits that they use to make loans and earn profits for shareholders. Every bank receives a major portion of its income from interest paid on loans by borrowers. As long as terms and conditions are clearly revealed to borrowers, banks may set their own interest rates, within limits set by each state. Traditionally, banks only offered the lowest rate, or *prime rate*, to their most creditworthy commercial customers.

Banks also offer (1) pension services, such as IRAs or other pension options, and trust services in which the bank manages funds on behalf of and in accordance with the wishes of the client that entrusts funds to the bank; (2) international services, including currency exchanges, letters of credit, and banker's acceptances; (3) financial advice by recommending various investment opportunities, and brokerage services in which the bank's stockbrokers can buy and sell securities and hold them in the bank for the client; (4) *electronic funds transfer (EFT)*, payments and collections by transferring financial information electronically; and (5) ATMs for conveniently accessible financial transactions.

Savings institutions, also called thrift institutions, include mutual savings banks and savings and loan associations. *Savings and loan associations (S&Ls)* are owned by shareholders. Most S&Ls were created to encourage savings habits and provide financing for homes. Today, S&Ls accept deposits and make loans and offer many of the same services as commercial banks. In *mutual savings banks*, all depositors are owners of the bank, and all profits are divided among them. *Credit unions* are nonprofit cooperative financial institutions, owned and run by their members, who pool their funds to make loans to one another at reasonable rates. Other organizations called *nondeposit institutions*—pension funds, insurance companies, finance companies, and securities investment dealers—take in money, provide interest or other services, and make loans.

LEARNING OBJECTIVE 16-3

Explain how financial institutions create money and describe the means by which they are regulated.

The nation's money supply—the amount of money in circulation—expands because banks and other financial institutions can lend most of the money they take in from deposits. The loans create additional deposits as follows: Out of a deposit of $100, the bank may hold $10 in reserve and lend 90 percent—$90—to borrowers. There will still be the original $100 on deposit, and borrowers (of the $90) will also deposit the $90 loans in their banks. Now, the borrowers' banks have $81 of new deposits available for new loans (90 percent of $90). Banks, therefore, have turned the original $100 deposit into $271($100 + $90 + $81) of deposits. The chain continues, with borrowings from one bank becoming deposits in the next.

The government regulates all nationally charted commercial banks and most state-chartered banks to ensure a sound financial system. Federal and state agencies regulate banks to ensure that the failure of some will not cause the public to lose faith in the banking system. The *Federal Deposit Insurance Corporation (FDIC)* insures deposits and guarantees the safety of all deposits up to $250,000 per account in each bank. To ensure against failures, the FDIC examines the activities and accounts of all member banks and thrift institutions. The FDIC becomes responsible for disposing of failed banks by selling them to other banks or by seizing the assets of failed banks and then (1) paying insurance to depositors and (2) disposing of the failed banks' assets and settling their debts.

LEARNING OBJECTIVE 16-4

Discuss the functions of the Federal Reserve System and describe the tools that it uses to control the money supply.

The *Federal Reserve System (the Fed)* is the nation's central bank that regulates many aspects of the United States financial system. Although some state-chartered banks, credit unions, and S&Ls do not belong to the Fed, they are subject to its regulations and pay deposit insurance premiums. The Fed consists of a board of governors, a group of reserve banks, and member banks. The Fed's board of governors consists of seven members appointed by the U.S. president for overlapping terms of 14 years. The Fed consists of 12 districts, each with a Federal Reserve Bank. The Fed's Open Market Committee is responsible for formulating the monetary policies to promote economic stability and growth by managing the nation's money supply and interest rates. As the government's bank, the Fed produces currency and lends money to the government by buying bonds issued by the Treasury Department to help finance the national debt. As the bankers' bank, it lends money to member banks, provides storage for funds that commercial banks are required to keep on reserve at a Federal Reserve Bank, and clears checks for commercial banks.

The Fed is responsible for the conduct of U.S. *monetary policy*, the management of the nation's economic growth by managing the money supply and interest rates. Among its tools for controlling the money supply, the Fed specifies *reserve requirements* (the percentage of its deposits that a commercial bank must hold), it sets the *discount rate* at which the Fed lends money to banks, and it conducts *open-market operations* to buy and sell securities in the open market. When the Fed buys securities from a commercial dealer, the dealer's bank account is immediately credited, so that bank has more money to lend and thus the money supply expands and interest rates fall. The opposite happens when the Fed sells securities to investors. Money in the buyer's bank account is reduced, decreasing the money supply and increasing interest rates.

LEARNING OBJECTIVE 16-5

Identify three important ways in which the money and banking system is changing.

The U.S. money and banking system continues to change today. Government emergency intervention aims to stabilize a troubled financial system. Enforcement of antiterrorism regulations deters criminal misuse of the financial system. The Federal Reserve took unprecedented investment actions to stabilize the U.S. financial system following the collapse of major banks in 2008. Commercial banks received massive loans to cover bad mortgages and other toxic assets and to encourage lending to stimulate the sagging economy. The Troubled Asset Relief Program (TARP), a temporary program under the U.S. Treasury, was included in the government's bailout effort, providing billions of dollars to auto-financing companies at risk of failure and billions more to over 600 banks to encourage lending. Other government sources provided funds to rescue Freddie Mac and Fannie Mae, which held vast numbers of defaulted mortgages in the collapsed housing market.

Anticrime and antiterrorism regulations have been enacted to detect and abate use of the financial system for illegal purposes. The Bank Secrecy Act requires financial institutions to deter funding of crimes by tracking and reporting suspicious transactions. The USA PATRIOT Act requires banks to implement a customer identification program to verify identities and compare them with government lists of terrorists.

Banks have adopted new technologies to improve efficiency and customer service. ACH is an electronic funds transfer system that provides interbank clearing of electronic payments for the nation's financial institutions. The ACH network allows businesses, government, and consumers to choose an electronic-over-paper alternative for payments (instead of written checks). In addition to EFT systems and mobile devices, banks offer access through telephone, TV, and Internet banking. *Electronic check clearing* speeds up the check-clearing process, and the "blink" credit card speeds up consumer checkout by replacing magnetic strip cards with contactless cards. *Debit cards* allow the transfer of money from the cardholder's account directly to others' accounts.

LEARNING OBJECTIVE 16-6

Discuss some of the institutions and activities in international banking and finance.

Changes in currency values and exchange rates reflect global supply and demand—what traders are willing to pay for various currencies. The resulting exchange rate—the value of one currency compared to the value of another—reveals how much of one currency must be exchanged for another. At any one time, then, some currencies are "strong"—selling at a higher price and worth more—whereas others are "weak." In managing the money supply and interest rates, the Fed strongly influences the dollar's strength against other currencies. The European

Central Bank (ECB) has the same role in the euro zone. The raising of interest rates tends to increase an economic system's currency value, whereas lowering the rate has the opposite effect.

Country-to-country transactions rely on an international payments process that moves money between buyers and sellers in different nations. If trade between two countries is in balance—if money inflows and outflows are equal for both countries—money does not have to flow between the two countries. If inflows and outflows are not in balance, then a flow of money between them is made to cover the difference.

Because there is no worldwide banking system, global banking stability relies on agreements among countries. Two United Nations agencies help to finance international trade: (1) The *World Bank* funds loans for national improvements so borrowers can increase productive capacity and international trade. (2) The *International Monetary Fund* makes loans to nations suffering from temporary negative trade balances and to provide economic and monetary stability for the borrowing country.

key terms

automated teller machine (ATM) **(p. 530)**
banker's acceptance **(p. 529)**
check **(p. 525)**
checking account (demand deposit) **(p. 525)**
commercial bank **(p. 527)**
credit union **(p. 528)**
currency (cash) **(p. 524)**
debit card **(p. 539)**
discount rate **(p. 536)**
electronic funds transfer (EFT) **(p. 530)**
exchange rate **(p. 540)**
Federal Deposit Insurance Corporation (FDIC) **(p. 532)**
federal funds rate (key rate) **(p. 536)**
Federal Reserve System (the Fed) **(p. 533)**
finance company **(p. 529)**
individual retirement account (IRA) **(p. 529)**
insurance company **(p. 529)**
International Monetary Fund (IMF) **(p. 543)**
letter of credit **(p. 529)**
M-1 **(p. 524)**
M-2 **(p. 525)**
monetary policy **(p. 536)**
money **(p. 523)**
money market mutual fund **(p. 525)**
mutual savings bank **(p. 528)**
open-market operations **(p. 537)**
pension fund **(p. 528)**
point-of-sale (POS) terminal **(p. 539)**
prime rate **(p. 527)**
reserve requirement **(p. 536)**
savings and loan association (S&L) **(p. 528)**
securities investment dealer (broker) **(p. 529)**
smart card **(p. 539)**
time deposit **(p. 525)**
trust services **(p. 529)**
World Bank **(p. 543)**

questions & exercises

QUESTIONS FOR REVIEW

16-1. What are the four characteristics of money?

16-2. What are the components of M-1 and M-2?

16-3. What is the role of banking, and do you think cryptocurrencies will make banks obsolete? Why or why not?

16-4. How and why does the federal government try to control the money supply?

QUESTIONS FOR ANALYSIS

16-5. As a consumer, when would you favor a strong dollar? What about a weak dollar? Would you consider these factors differently as an employee or employer?

16-6. Should commercial banks be regulated, or should market forces be allowed to determine the kinds of loans and the interest rates for loans and savings deposits? Why?

16-7. If you were choosing a new bank, would you prefer a completely online bank or a more traditional bank with physical locations in the community? Explain your reasoning.

16-8. Start with a $1,000 deposit and assume a reserve requirement of 10 percent. How much would the money supply increase after five lending cycles?

APPLICATION EXERCISES

16-9. The Federal Reserve Bank maintains historical and current data on exchange rates. You can find detailed historical rates by going to http://www.federalreserve.gov/releases/h10/Hist/. If you used $5,000 to purchase Chinese yuan 5 years ago, how many yuan would you have received? What would those yuan be worth today? (Use the data on the Fed site to calculate these values and explain your calculations.)

16-10. Interview the manager of a local commercial bank. Identify and list some of the regulations that the bank has to comply with. Does the manager feel that these regulations are just a burden, or do they provide value? How do you feel about the regulations?

building a business: continuing team exercise

ASSIGNMENT

Meet with your team members to consider your new business venture and how it relates to the money and banking topics in this chapter. Develop specific responses to the following:

16-11. How will your business venture be connected with banks and other financial institutions? In what ways, if any, are such institutions important to your business? Of these relationships, which will be most critical?

16-12. Sales of the product(s) your business offers to customers will depend, in part, on their ability to pay for those products. In what ways, if any, will customers rely on financial institutions for such purchases? Will your company assist customers in connecting with financial institutions to finance their purchases?

16-13. Consider the ways that currency exchange rates will affect your company. Consider also how those rates will affect your customers and their willingness to buy your product(s). Discuss how your team will adjust pricing of your product(s) when the U.S. dollar is strong and when the dollar is weak versus other currencies.

16-14. In what ways will your plans and methods for marketing change, if at all, when the currency values of the U.S. dollar change significantly? Explain.

16-15. Discuss how your team will determine if, and in what ways, your company must comply with the Bank Secrecy Act and the USA PATRIOT Act in conducting your company's business. Will these acts be a serious concern for your firm? Discuss why or why not.

team exercise

THE WEAKENING DOLLAR

The Situation

RK Industries sells a variety of health and fitness beverages. Raw materials come from overseas, but all the mixing and packaging is done in the United States. The company has a loyal customer base and differentiates its product based on high-quality ingredients rather than competing on price alone. Currently the price of the company's product is about 20 percent higher than similar products on the shelf.

The Dilemma

The company is facing a weakening dollar and rising prices of raw materials. The chief financial officer (CFO) insists that the only way to protect the bottom line is to reduce costs or increase prices. The president is concerned about customer loyalty since about 80 percent of sales are to repeat customers and there is a lot of competition in the industry. The production supervisor insists that costs of production are as low as possible and the only way to reduce costs would be to buy cheaper raw materials.

Team Activity

Assemble a group of four students and assign each group member to one of the following roles:

- Bill Decker (president and CEO)
- Gloria Liu (CFO)
- Carolyn Kleen (production supervisor)
- Karl Marcks (chair of the board of directors)

Action Steps

16-16. Based on the perspective of your assigned role, what are the advantages and disadvantages of raising prices?

16-17. Draft a quick memo to the board justifying your position.

16-18. Why would a weakening dollar push prices upward?

16-19. If you were called on to testify in front of the Federal Reserve Bank directors, what course of action would you recommend, if any?

16-20. Discuss as a group the effect that monetary policy in the United States has on consumers and businesses.

exercising your ethics

TELLING THE ETHICAL FROM THE STRICTLY LEGAL

The Situation

A regional commercial bank in the western United States has more than 300 ATMs serving the nearly 400,000 checking and savings accounts of its customers. Bank customers are not charged a fee when they make deposits or withdrawals, just as completing these transactions with a teller in the bank or at a drive-through window is free of charge. In fact, the bank has analyzed the costs associated with each option and has found that deposits and withdrawals are the least expensive option per transaction to the bank. The regional bank is considering charging ATM access fees to all customers in the amount of $3 for in-network transactions and $5 for out-of-network transactions. The bank's officers are hesitating to implement ATM surcharges because of public protests against other banks with similar surcharges in Santa Monica, New York City, and Chicago. To date, the courts have ruled that the access fees are legal, but some organizations—such as the U.S. Public Interest Research Group (PIRG)—continue to fight publicly against them.

The Dilemma

In considering its current policies, the western bank's vice president for community relations is concerned about more than mere legalities. She wants to ensure that her company is "being a good citizen and doing the right thing." Any decision on ATM fees will ultimately affect the bank's customers, its image in the community and industry, and its profitability for its owners. She's been asked to make a presentation to the board of directors on the pros and cons of ATM fees.

QUESTIONS TO ADDRESS

16-21. From the standpoint of a commercial bank, can you find any economic justification for ATM access fees?

16-22. Based on the scenario described for our bank, do you find any ethical issues in this situation? Or do you find the main issues legal and economic rather than ethical?

16-23. As an officer for this bank, how would you handle this situation?

cases

MONETARY POLICY HITS HOME

Continued from page 523

At the beginning of this chapter, you read about the Fed's role in stabilizing the economy through monetary policy. Using the information presented in this chapter, you should be able to answer the following questions:

16-24. Describe the differences between fiscal policy and monetary policy. What effects do you think each has on the day-to-day operations of a business? Should a business owner be concerned with these kinds of macroeconomic issues? If so, why?

16-25. The Fed is supposedly a nonpolitical body. Do you agree with this observation? Do you think it should be or shouldn't be? Why?

16-26. In 2017, the U.S. government was $20 trillion in debt, and by mid-2023, that had ballooned to over $30 trillion. Should the government try to pay off that debt? If so, how, and what effect would such a strategy have on consumers and business?

16-27. Why do economically stressed countries with massive debt have difficulty borrowing outside money needed for economic recovery? What solutions could you propose?

16-28. What are the functions of the Federal Reserve Bank, and how do they affect the average worker and consumer?

GLOBAL TRADING PARTNER RESETS ITS ECONOMIC COMPASS

Although Japan may be a small nation, with a 2023 population of just over 125 million people and relatively limited natural resources, it remains one of the world's economic powers. In the current era of global interdependence, there is no better example of continuing economic relationships—in terms of both trade and capital flows—than that between Japan and the United States. The two countries are both strong industrialized economies that enjoy high standards of living. Per capita GDP, or GDP per person, is a better measure of the standard of living than overall GDP, and Japan ranks high on that measure. For example, even though Japan ranked a distant third in the world's gross domestic product (GDP) in 2017 at 5 trillion in U.S. dollars, behind the United States ($20.5 trillion) and China ($13.4 trillion), its per capita GDP of $39,313 USD in 2017 is closer to that of the United States ($70,249) than that of China ($12,556). One reason for these rather strange numbers is the fact that the U.S. population in 2023 of roughly 332 million people is more than double that of Japan, and the geographic area of 3.8 million square miles is roughly 26 times that of Japan. In addition, even though the United States has only 5 percent of the world's population, it consumes almost 50 percent of the world's goods and services.

However, while people in the United States tend to spend more and save less, the Japanese population has a long-standing devotion to saving, resulting at times in a deflationary economy and slow economic growth.

Japan was once the largest source of U.S. imports, but that status has been gradually changing. In 2016, Japan was the fourth-largest supplier (behind Canada, Mexico, and China) of goods imported to the United States—electrical machinery, vehicles, organic chemicals, optic and medical instruments, and agricultural products—amounting to $163 billion. As a trading partner, Japan was the United States' fourth-largest goods export market—including medical instruments, cereals, aircraft, and machinery—amounting to $107 billion. The resulting U.S. trade deficit with Japan was $56 billion.[26]

Its decreasing role in trade with the United States is attributed, among other factors, to Japan's past problems with deflation and the relatively high value of its currency—the yen. Deflationary pressures since the early 1990s stem from the Japanese penchant for saving, rather than spending, together with the Bank of Japan's long-standing monetary policy that limits the supply of money. With limited availability of credit and personal spending, prices tended downward (the opposite of inflation) and purchases were delayed in anticipation of even lower future prices. Along with diminished profits, employment and incomes suffered, as did the economic expectations of the Japanese people. Meanwhile, the price of the yen in U.S. dollars hit a low of 80 yen per dollar in 2011, down from a range between 200 and 250 in the early 1980s. This sounds at first like a favorable trend, but in reality, it deterred other countries from purchasing Japan's products—as one dollar buys fewer and fewer yen, it also buys fewer and fewer products. All of these factors resulted in years of sluggish, and even recessionary, economic performance.

In 2012, the Bank of Japan launched a new anti-deflation program using a more aggressive monetary policy in which the boosting of consumer confidence is a key component for overcoming the deflationary mindset. The new policy was expected to double the amount of yen held by individuals during the next two years, seeking to increase spending and raise Japan's annual inflation rate to 2 percent. The Japanese central bank injected large amounts of money into the economy using methods similar to those of the U.S. Federal Reserve's "quantitative easing" in an attempt to boost the economy, drive interest rates down to near zero, weaken the yen, and promote Japan's entrepreneurship and competition. By 2023, annual inflation was at 3.2 percent, well above the target rate of 2 percent, the highest in 40 years, and the Fed rate in Japan was –0.1 percent.

While the Bank of Japan continued monetary policies to keep interest rates low, the U.S. was tightening monetary policy to curb historically high inflation, pushing interest rates higher. As a result, investors were selling yen to buy dollars in order to invest their money in dollars with higher interest rates, thus weakening the yen against the dollar.

QUESTIONS FOR DISCUSSION

16-29. Why would a national tendency toward saving cause deflation?

16-30. Why would the Bank of Japan pump money into the Japanese economy using tactics similar to the Federal Reserve Bank in the United States?

16-31. What does it mean for Japan to be "weakening" the yen, and how would that happen? Compare and discuss the positive implications and the negative implications for both a strong and a weak yen.

16-32. Why would a country want to encourage inflation (increasing consumer prices) rather than deflation (decreasing consumer prices)?

16-33. Consider Japan's trading status as the fourth-largest source of U.S. imports and the fourth-largest market for U.S. goods exports. Would you expect that status to change soon relative to other U.S. trading partners such as Canada, China, Germany, Mexico, and others? Explain.

endnotes

[1] Federal Reserve Board, "The Fed Explained," accessed July 5, 2023, https://www.federalreserve.gov/aboutthefed/the-fed-explained.htm.

[2] Benjamin Curry, "What Happens When the Fed Raises Interest Rates?," *Forbes*, June 21, 2023, https://www.forbes.com/advisor/investing/fed-raises-interest-rates.

[3] Consumer Financial Protection Bureau, "About Us," accessed July 5, 2023, https://www.consumerfinance.gov/about-us/.

[4] ICYMI: At Hearing, Senator Warren Calls out Chair Powell for Fed's Plan to Throw At Least 2 Million People Out of Work." *Newsroom | U.S. Senator Elizabeth Warren of Massachusetts*, March 7, 2023. U.S. Senator Elizabeth Warren of Massachusetts. https://www.warren.senate.gov/newsroom/press-releases/icymi-at-hearing-senator-warren-calls-out-chair-powell-for-feds-plan-to-throw-at-least-2-million-people-out-of-work.

[5] https://www.federalreserve.gov/releases/h6/20230124/. Accessed June 1, 2023.

[6] https://www.federalreserve.gov/releases/h6/20230124/. Accessed June 1, 2023.

[7] Federal Reserve Bank of St. Louis, "Economic Research," accessed April 1, 2020, https://fred.stlouisfed.org/series/TLAACBW027SBOG.

[8] Financial Management Service, "Electronic Funds Transfer," accessed April 30, 2020, http://fms.treas.gov/eft/index.html.

[9] Accessed June 1, 2023, https://www.atmia.com/regions/asia/china-corner/.

[10] Built In, "33 Blockchain Applications and Real-World Use Cases," accessed July 16, 2023, https://builtin.com/blockchain/blockchain-applications.

[11] Council on Foreign Relations, "Cryptocurrencies, Digital Dollars, and the Future of Money," accessed July 16, 2023, https://www.cfr.org/backgrounder/cryptocurrencies-digital-dollars-and-future-money.

[12] Federal Reserve Bank of San Francisco, "Ask Dr. Econ: Is the Fed Still in the Business of Processing Checks?" 1st Quarter, 2012, accessed May 1, 2020, http://www.frbsf.org/education/activities/drecon/2012/Dr-Econ-q1.html; Katy Jacob, Daniel Littman, Richard D. Porter, and Wade Rousse, "Two Cheers for the Monetary Control Act," *Chicago Fed Letter* (June 2010, Number 275), The Federal Reserve Bank of Chicago, http://www.chicagofed.org/digital_assets/publications/chicago_fed_letter/2010/cfljune2010_275.pdf; Paul W. Bauer and Geoffrey R. Gerdes, "The Check Is Dead! Long Live the Check! A Check 21 Update," Federal Reserve Bank of Cleveland, September 21, 2009, http://www.clevelandfed.org/research/commentary/; Jim Savage, "Federal Reserve Banks Complete Check Processing Infrastructure Changes," Board of Governors of the Federal Reserve System, March 2, 2010, http://www.federalreserve.gov/newsevents/press/other/20100302a.htm. https://www.federalreserve.gov/paymentsystems/regcc-faq-check21.htm

[13] Board of Governors of the Federal Reserve System, "Open Market Operations," February 6, 2013, http://www.federalreserve.gov/monetarypolicy/openmarket.htm#2006.

[14] David Goldman, "CNNMoney.com's Bailout Tracker," CNNMoney.com, accessed April 21, 2011, http://money.cnn.com/news/storysupplement/economy/bailouttracker/; John Griffith, "7 Things You Need to Know About Fannie Mae and Freddie Mac," Center for American Progress, September 6, 2012, http://www.americanprogress.org/issues/housing/report/2012/09/06/36736/7-things-you-need-to-know-about-fannie-mae-and-freddie-mac/.

[15] Michael R. Crittenden, "Regulators See Risk in U.S. Bank Stakes," *Wall Street Journal*, April 24, 2009, http://online.wsj.com/article/SB124051525463449225.html; Rebecca Christie, "Treasury May Keep U.S. Bank Stakes After Buyback (Update 3)," Bloomberg.com, April 17, 2009, http://www.bloomberg.com/apps/news; Goldman, "CNNMoney.com's Bailout Tracker,"

CNNMoney.com; Mark Jickling, "Fannie Mae and Freddie Mac in Conservatorship," *CRS Report for Congress*, September 15, 2008, http://fpc.state.gov/documents/organization/110097.pdf.

[16] https://www.fincen.gov/news/news-releases/fincen-announces-15-million-civil-money-penalty-against-shinhan-bank-america, accessed on October 10, 2023.

[17] https://constantinecannon.com/whistleblower/top-ten-money-laundering-enforcement-actions-2022/, accessed on October 13, 2023.

[18] Robin Sidel, "Banks Make Smartphone Connection," *Wall Street Journal*, February 12, 2013, C1, C2; "Letter to Shareholders," JPMorgan Chase, accessed April 30, 2020, https://www.jpmorganchase.com/corporate/investor-relations/document/line-of-business-ceo-letters-to-shareholders-2018.pdf.

[19] https://plaid.com/resources/ach/ach-processing/, Accessed on October 13, 2023. The Federal Reserve Bank of Philadelphia, "Supporting the Nation's Payment System," April 22, 2011, http://www.philadelphiafed.org/about-the-fed/who-we-are/payment-system.cfm; NACHA: The Electronic Payments Association, "Intro to the ACH Network," accessed April 22, 2011, http://nacha.org/c/intro2ach.cfm.

[20] Jacob, Littman, Porter, and Rousse, "Two Cheers for the Monetary Control Act"; Bauer and Gerdes, "The Check Is Dead! Long Live the Check! A Check 21 Update"; Savage, "Federal Reserve Banks Complete Check Processing Infrastructure Changes."

[21] https://www.spglobal.com/marketintelligence/en/news-insights/research/debit-surpasses-credit-as-consumers-preferred-payment-card, accessed on June 23, 2023.

[22] I. Binnie, "Blackrock's Fink Says He's Stopped Using 'Weaponised' Term ESG," Reuters, June 26, 2023, https://www.reuters.com/business/environment/blackrocks-fink-says-hes-stopped-using-weaponised-term-esg-2023-06-26/.

[23] Carolina Mandl and Davide Barbuscia, "Blackrock CEO Fink Says He Does Not Plan to Leave the Firm 'Any Time Soon,'" Reuters, June 14, 2023, https://www.reuters.com/business/finance/blackrock-ceo-fink-says-he-does-not-plan-leave-firm-any-time-soon-2023-06-14/.

[24] Smart Card Alliance, "Smart Card Primer," accessed July 25, 2023, https://www.securetechalliance.org/smart-cards-intro-primer/.

[25] "Summary Measures of the Foreign Exchange Value of the Dollar," Federal Reserve Statistical Release H:10, accessed June 2, 2023, http://www.federalreserve.gov/releases/H10/Summary/.

[26] Trade Memo, Office of the United States Trade Representative, accessed May 1, 2020, https://ustr.gov/countries-regions/japan-korea-apec/japan.

chapter 17

Managing Business Finances

Natee Meepian/Shutterstock

learning objectives

After reading this chapter, you should be able to:

17-1 **Explain** the concept of the time value of money and the principle of compound growth and discuss the characteristics of common stock.

17-2 **Identify** reasons for investing and the investment opportunities offered by mutual funds and exchange-traded funds.

17-3 **Describe** the role of securities markets and identify the major stock exchanges and stock markets.

17-4 **Describe** the risk–return relationship and discuss the use of diversification and asset allocation for investments.

17-5 **Describe** the various ways that firms raise capital and identify the pros and cons of each method.

17-6 **Identify** the reasons a company might make an initial public offering of its stock, explain how stock value is determined, and discuss the significance of market capitalization.

17-7 **Explain** how securities markets are regulated.

what's in it for me?

Businesses from all over the world, representing every industry, converge in global financial markets every day, seeking funds that can be used to finance their activities and pay their debts. Individual investors gather as well, in person or—more often—online, looking to make their money "work" for them by buying and selling commodities, stocks, and bonds. The history of Fogo de Chão, discussed on the next page, illustrates each of these activities. This chapter will help you understand the various ways this is possible, whether your goals are short or long term, whether you are motivated by the desire for profit or security, or simply because you enjoy the challenges inherent in successfully raising and investing capital.

With dinner plates ranging from $50 to $60, Fogo de Chão competes with the more upscale steakhouses such as Ruth's Chris Steakhouse, Del Frisco's, and The Capital Grille. According to SEC documents (the annual 10-K) the company generated $314.4 million in revenues in 2017 and a net income of $28.4 million, which seems respectable, but in reality, 2016 and 2017 were rough on the restaurant industry overall, and even with a positive earnings report, Fogo de Chão was no exception. By early 2017, the stock that had hit the market at a sizzling $20 per share was down to $15,

Prostock-studio/Shutterstock

Tada Images/Shutterstock

Fire on the Ground

In 1979, two sets of brothers, Jair and Arri Coser and Jorge and Aleixo Ongaratto, opened a churrascaria (Brazilian-style steakhouse) in a shed with a grass roof in Porto Alegre, Brazil, and called it Fogo de Chão (for *fire on the ground*). Roving gaucho chefs served a variety of fire-roasted meats, carved at the table. Diners could also visit the all-you-can-discover Churrasco experience that includes Fogo's Market Table (fresh salads, seasonal vegetables, imported charcuterie, etc.) and a continuous rotation of fire-roasted meats carved tableside.

Over the next six years, the company prospered, and the brothers opened two additional locations up the coast to the north in São Paulo. Then, in 1995, former U.S. President George H. W. Bush, after marveling at the dining experience, encouraged the brothers to expand their operations to the United States. Two weeks later, two of the brothers headed to Texas. The rest, as they say, is history. "I think about why I came to the United States all the time," says Jair Coser. "I cannot explain it. I had a good life at that time in Brazil. I have my house. I have my family. I have my business. And it was, 'Let's go.'"

In 2005, the Ongaratto brothers cashed out, selling their part of the company to the Cosers. To obtain money for continued expansion, the Cosers sold a partial interest in the company to GP Investments, one of the largest investment funds in Brazil. In 2012, the Coser brothers also decided to cash out, selling their controlling interest in the company to Thomas H. Lee Partners L. P. for $426 million. At that time, the chain was up to 16 U.S. restaurants and seven locations in Brazil.

The new ownership team successfully continued the restaurant chain's expansion, retaining many upper-level managers and bringing in new talent and expertise to shore up accounting and management practices. In 2015, the company went public with an initial public offering (IPO) of just over 4.4 million shares of stock, raising $88.2 million at a price per share of $20, well above the projected selling price range of $16 to $18 per share. Despite the number of shares sold to the public, Thomas H. Lee Partners L. P. kept an 80 percent controlling interest. Fogo de Chão Brazilian Steakhouse (listed on NASDAQ as FOGO) used the IPO money to pay down debt and pursue expansion plans.

By 2023, the chain had 74 locations worldwide, with expansion plans for 10 more that year. On the Fogo de Chão website, investors can explore franchise opportunities at a glance. This strategic growth plan has been paying off for Fogo. With nine straight years of growth—even through a global pandemic—the restaurant chain reported $10 million in volume by November 2022. The chain's latest plans include dropping "Brazilian Steakhouse" from its name to emphasize non-meat options for a younger clientele interested in upscale vegetarian dining. Fogo aims to positively contribute

and it spent the rest of the year bouncing between that ceiling and a floor of about $10, and after paying down debt incurred during expansion with the proceeds from the IPO, the company was strapped for cash. In late 2017, an unidentified restaurant chain tendered an offer of $17 per share to buy the entire company, but in the interest of the future of the Fogo de Chão brand, the board of directors instead accepted an offer from a "preferred buyer" in the form of Rhône Capital. So, in 2018, the company once again changed hands, falling off the public stock exchange and becoming part of Rhône's ever-increasing stable of investments that includes Nestlé's U.S. confectionery business, Elizabeth Arden cosmetics, and Quicksilver surfer apparel. At the end of 2019, Fogo was operating in nearly 50 separate locations across the globe, including the United States, Mexico, Brazil, the UAE, and Saudi Arabia, with plans to double that within a few years.

to local communities, offering employee benefits and sustainability efforts in addition to programs to reduce food insecurity.[1] (After studying the content in this chapter, you should be able to answer a set of discussion questions found at the end of the chapter.)

Maximizing Capital Growth

Learning Objective 17-1

Explain the concept of the time value of money and the principle of compound growth and discuss the characteristics of common stock.

Wise investments are the key to growing your money, especially if you are seeking to accumulate capital to start (or grow) your own business or simply as a cushion for a sound financial future. In searching for investment opportunities, a number of concepts come into play for evaluating alternative investments and sorting out the good from the bad. (As we will discuss more fully later in the chapter, a key element to consider is the relationship between potential returns on investments and investment risk.)

The Time Value of Money and Compound Growth

The most-proven "road to wealth" lies in a strategy of saving and investing over a period of years. Only rarely does a "one-in-a-million" opportunity provide a quick fortune. Although the popular "I want it all, and I want it now!" mentality sounds good, it becomes a reality for very few wealth seekers.

The **time value of money**, perhaps the single most important concept in business finance, recognizes the basic fact that, when it's invested over time, money grows by earning interest or yielding some other form of return. Time value, in turn, stems from the principle of **compound growth**, the cumulative growth from interest paid to the investor over given time periods. With each additional time period, an investment grows as interest payments accumulate and earn even more interest, thus multiplying the earning capacity of the initial investment.

Time Value of Money *principle that invested money grows, over time, by earning interest or some other form of return*

Compound Growth *compounding of interest over time—with each additional time period, interest returns accumulate and earn more interest*

The Rule of 72 We can better appreciate the concept of the "time value of money" with a practical example based on this question: How long does it take to double an investment? A handy rule of thumb to answer this question is called the "Rule of 72." You can find the number of years needed to double your money by dividing the annual interest rate (in percent) into 72. If, for example, you can reinvest annually at 8 percent, you'll double your money in about 9 years:

$$\frac{72}{8} = 9 \text{ years to double the money}$$

By the same reasoning, if you reinvest annually at 4 percent, your money will double in about 18 years.

The Rule of 72 can also calculate how much interest you must get if you want to double your money in a given number of years: Simply divide 72 by the desired number of years. If you have a goal of doubling your money in 10 years, you will need to get 7.2 percent:

$$\frac{72}{10} = 7.2 \text{ percent interest needed to double the money}$$

The lesson for the investor is clear (and obvious): seek *higher* interest rates because money will grow faster. (Of course, the investor must also consider the risk involved in various alternative investment options. We discuss risk later.)

Making Better Use of Your Time Value What if you invested \$10,000 at 7 percent interest for one year? You would earn \$700 on your \$10,000 investment. If you reinvested the principal amount plus the interest you earned during the first year,

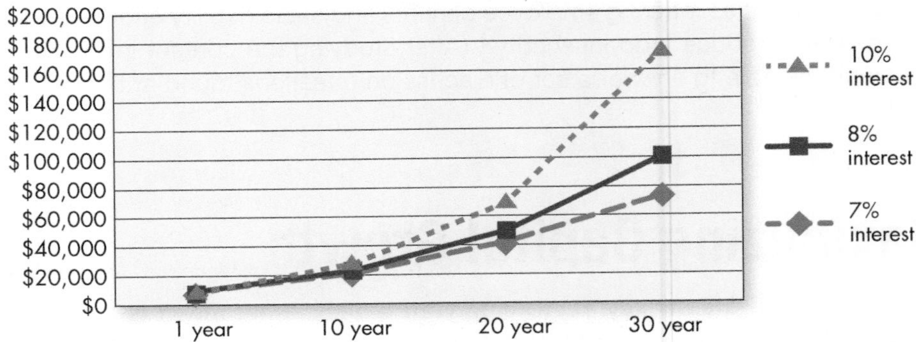

FIGURE 17.1 Amount to Which an Initial $10,000 Investment Grows

and then continued to reinvest both the original principal and all interest earned each year for another four years, you'd end up with $14,025. Now, if you were planning for retirement and reinvested that money at the same interest rate for another 25 years, you could retire with $76,122—almost eight times the amount you started with!

Figure 17.1 illustrates how the returns from an initial investment of $10,000 accumulate substantially over longer periods of time. Notice that the gains for the last 10 years are much greater than for the first 10 years, illustrating the power of compound growth. This is because each year the interest is applied to a larger sum. The figure also illustrates that the accumulations grow even faster at higher interest rates. Even a seemingly small increase in interest rates, from 7 to 8 percent, results in much larger accumulations.

As you can see from Figure 17.1, the best way to take advantage of the time value of money is to obtain a high rate of return on your investment. However, various kinds of investments offer opportunities for fulfilling different financial objectives, such as aggressive growth, financial safety, and others, which we discuss later.

Common Stock Investments

Stock *portion of ownership of a corporation*

Common Stock *most basic form of ownership, including voting rights on major issues, in a company*

History has shown that one way to achieve a high rate of return, compared with many other ways, is to invest in the stock market. Consider the average rate of return on the U.S. stock market, as of the beginning of 2023. The 100-year average (1922–2022) was more than 9.74 percent annually (assuming dividends are reinvested), and the most recent 25-year average return was more than 12.5 percent.[2] A **stock** is a portion of the ownership of a corporation. The corporation's total ownership is divided into small parts called *shares* that can be bought and sold to determine how much of the company (how many shares of stock) is owned by each shareholder. This widespread ownership has become possible because of the availability of different types of stocks and because markets have been established that enable individuals to conveniently buy and sell them.

Although several types of stock exist, so-called "common stock" is the most prominent. A share of **common stock** is the most basic form of ownership in a company. Individuals and other companies purchase a firm's common stock in the hope that it will increase in value and/or provide dividend income. In addition, each individual common share has one vote on major issues that are brought before the shareholders. (So, for instance, if you own 100 shares of a firm's common stock, then you also have 100 votes.)

Stock values are usually expressed in two different ways: as (1) *market value* and (2) *book value*.

Market Value *current price of a share of stock in the stock market*

Book Value *value of a common stock expressed as the firm's owners' equity divided by the number of common shares*

1 A stock's real value is its **market value**, the current price of a share in the stock market. Market value reflects the amount that buyers are willing to pay for a share of the company's stock.

2 The **book value** for a share of common stock is determined as the firm's owners' equity (from the balance sheet) divided by the number of common shares owned by all shareholders. Book value is used as a comparison indicator

because the market value for successful companies like Apple, Amazon, and Walmart is usually greater than their book value. Thus, when market price falls to near book value, some profit-seeking investors buy the stock based on the assumption that it is underpriced and will increase in the future.

Investment Traits of Common Stock Unfortunately, common stocks are also among the riskiest of all investments. Uncertainties about the stock market itself can quickly change a given stock's value. Furthermore, when companies have unprofitable years, or when industry or general economic conditions stagnate, they often cannot pay dividends, and potential investors become wary of future stock values, so share price drops. U.S. stocks, for example, lost more than half their value in the recession years 2008 and early 2009. More recently, when energy prices plummeted in 2015 most stock prices remained high but the stock prices of oil-related companies dropped. On the positive side, however, common stocks offer high growth potential; when a company's performance improves (because of the introduction of a hot new product, for example) share price can sharply increase. Historically, stock values generally rise with the passage of time. By mid-2013, most U.S. common stocks had recovered the values they lost in 2008–2009, and many had moved on to new record levels. Similarly, as energy prices began to climb in 2017 so, too, did the stock prices of oil companies. Then, prices plummeted again in 2020 during the COVID-19 pandemic. The price of a barrel of oil, for example, dropped to nearly zero, and, for a few hours one day, even went negative. As a result, stocks for firms involved in energy production, such as Chevron, ExxonMobil, Halliburton, and others, were all hurt. Similarly, stock prices of firms most directly affected by the pandemic—airlines, cruise lines, Disney, and many others—all experienced significant drops. As the effects of the pandemic wane, stock prices have again increased in value and in early 2023 were almost back to pre-pandemic levels.

Dividends A **dividend** is a payment to shareholders, on a per-share basis, from the company's earnings. Dividend payments are optional and variable. The corporation's board of directors decides whether and when a dividend will be paid, as well as the amount that is best for the future of the company and its shareholders. Many companies distribute between 30 and 70 percent of their profits to shareholders. The so-called **blue-chip stocks**, those issued by the strongest, well-established, financially sound and respected firms, such as Coca-Cola and ExxonMobil, have historically provided investors steady income through consistent dividend payouts. However, some firms, especially fast-growing companies, do not pay dividends. Instead, they use cash earnings for expanding the company so that future earnings can grow even faster. What's more, any company can have a bad year and decide to reduce or omit dividend payments to stockholders. For instance, during the 2020 COVID-19 pandemic, Disney canceled its July dividend payment due to its sharply declining revenues and accumulating losses. At times, though, managers face complex decisions about dividends. In December 2022, for example, the flight management systems for Southwest Airlines crashed, affecting over 16,000 flights and tens of thousands of travelers. In the aftermath of the system crash, clear evidence emerged that Southwest's system was out-of-date and had been in need of an upgrade for years. In early 2023, the airline announced that it would pay its normal dividends to shareholders. The chair of a U.S. Senate Committee criticized this move, indicating that the committee thought Southwest should have invested these funds into upgrading its technology rather than paying dividends.[3]

Dividend *payment to shareholders, on a per-share basis, out of the company's earnings*

Blue-Chip Stock *common stock issued by a well-established and respected company with a sound financial history and a stable pattern of dividend payouts*

We see, then, that success in accumulating capital depends significantly on exploiting the time value of money because compound growth from interest payments across several time periods multiplies the earning capacity of the firm's investments. Investments in common stocks, too, offer the potential for increasing capital growth, but only if the stock provides dividend income and its market value increases.

Learning Objective 17-2

Identify reasons for investing and the investment opportunities offered by mutual funds and exchange-traded funds.

Investing to Fulfill Financial Objectives

Mutual funds and exchange-traded funds are popular alternatives to stocks because they offer attractive investment opportunities for various financial objectives and often do not require large sums of money for entry. In addition, the simple and easy transaction process makes them very accessible to individual investors.

Mutual Fund *company that pools cash investments from individuals and organizations to purchase a portfolio of stocks, bonds, and other securities*

Mutual funds are created by investment firms such as T. Rowe Price and Vanguard. These firms essentially pool cash investments from individuals and organizations to purchase bundles of stocks, bonds, and other securities. The bundles are expected to appreciate in market value and otherwise produce income for the mutual fund and its investors. Thus, investors, as part owners, expect to receive financial gains as the fund's assets become increasingly valuable. For example, if you invest $1,000 in a mutual fund with assets worth $100,000, you own 1 percent of that fund. Investors in **no-load funds** are not charged sales commissions when they buy into or sell out of funds. Investors in **load funds** generally pay commissions of 2 percent to 8 percent.

No-Load Fund *mutual fund in which investors pay no commissions when they buy in or sell out*

Load Fund *mutual fund in which investors are charged sales commissions when they buy in or sell out*

Reasons for Investing

It's relatively easy to open a mutual fund account online or by phone. There are numerous funds that meet any chosen financial objective. The funds vary in their investment goals—different funds are designed to appeal to the different motives and goals of investors. Three of the most common objectives are (1) financial stability, (2) conservative growth, and (3) aggressive growth.

- *Stability and safety.* Funds stressing safety (i.e., the lowest risk) accept only modest growth with little fluctuation in principal value regardless of economic conditions. They include *money market mutual funds* and other funds that preserve the fund holders' capital and reliably pay current income. Typical assets of these funds include lower-risk U.S. corporate bonds, U.S. government bonds, and other similarly safe short-term securities that provide stable income from interest and dividends. These funds often appeal to older investors who may be approaching retirement and who place the highest priority on safeguarding their financial future.
- *Conservative capital growth.* Mutual funds that stress preservation of capital and current income but also seek some capital appreciation are called *balanced funds.* Typically, these funds hold a mixture of long-term municipal bonds, corporate bonds, and common stocks with good dividend-paying records for steady income. The common stocks offer potential for market appreciation (higher market value), though there is always the risk of price declines if the general stock market falls.
- *Aggressive growth. Aggressive growth funds* seek maximum long-term capital growth. They sacrifice current income and safety by investing in stocks of new (and even troubled) companies, firms developing new products and technologies, and other higher-risk securities. They are designed for investors who can accept the risk of loss inherent in common stock investing with severe price fluctuations but also the potential for superior returns over time.

Most Mutual Funds Don't Match the Market

Many, but not all, mutual funds are managed by "experts" who select the fund's stocks and other securities that provide the fund's income. Unfortunately, some estimates indicate that up to 80 percent of these managed funds do not perform as well as the average return of the overall stock market as a result of costly management expenses and underperforming stocks.[4] This underperformance disadvantage has resulted in the emergence of passively managed funds, in which the fund manager invests by using a fixed, predetermined strategy that replaces judgmental choices for buying and selling its stock holdings. Those choices are predefined by the strategy, not by the fund manager. The most widespread use of passively managed funds is with index mutual funds, which seek to mimic the holdings and performance of a particular market index. As an example, the widely watched Standard and Poor's 500 Index (S&P 500), which is discussed later, consists of 500 specific common stocks. Any mutual fund company can establish its own index fund by purchasing shares of those same 500 companies, thus matching the market performance of the S&P 500. The selection of which stocks to purchase in an index fund is relatively automatic—it holds many of the same stocks as the market it tracks—and requires little human input, thus reducing management expenses.

Exchange-Traded Funds

As with an index mutual fund, an **exchange-traded fund (ETF)** is a bundle of stocks (or bonds) that are in an index that tracks the overall movement of a market. Unlike a mutual fund, however, an ETF can be traded like a stock. Each share of an ETF rises and falls as market prices change continuously for the market being tracked.

Exchange-Traded Fund (ETF) *bundle of stocks or bonds that are in an index that tracks the overall movement of a market, but unlike a mutual fund can be traded like a stock*

ETFs offer three areas of advantage over mutual funds. First, they can be traded throughout the day like a stock, they have low operating expenses, and they do not require high initial investments. Because they are traded on stock exchanges (hence, "exchange traded"), ETFs can be bought and sold—priced continuously—anytime throughout the day. This *intraday trading* means you can time your transaction during the day to buy or sell when (or if) the market reaches a desired price. Mutual fund shares, in contrast, are priced once daily, at the end of the day. Thus, when you buy or sell during the day, you don't find out the share price until after the day has ended.

Second, whereas many mutual funds pass the costs of expensive active management on to shareholders, an ETF is bound by a rule that specifies what stocks will be purchased and when; once the rule is established, little or no active human decisions are involved. The *lower annual operating expenses* mean that, for the buy-and-hold investor, annual fees for ETFs are as low as 0.04 percent of assets; annual fees for mutual funds average 1.4 percent.[5]

Finally, unlike mutual funds, ETFs require no minimum investment, meaning they offer *ease of entry* for investors getting started without much money.[6] However, because ETFs must be bought and sold through a broker, they require payment of a brokerage commission (transaction fees). Traders who buy and sell frequently can end up paying more in transaction fees, even surpassing a mutual fund's high management expenses.[7]

We see, then, because firms have different financial objectives for investing, they often consider other alternatives, in addition to common stocks, such as mutual funds with varying degrees of safety and stability, funds that seek conservative capital growth, and riskier aggressive growth funds. ETFs are available to those firms that have the time to track moment-to-moment stock market movements for intraday trading. By allowing low minimum investments, ETFs offer ease of entry in addition to low annual operating expenses.

entrepreneurship and new ventures

Social Capital Is Making the World a Better Place

While big banks strive for profitability, sometimes through seemingly questionable lending practices, smaller companies, like the nonprofit organization Kiva, strive to reduce poverty by connecting people through microlending. It also now supports entrepreneurs across the world, including in the United States, by connecting individual lenders with borrowers traditional banks consider to be too risky. The loans are crowdfunded by accumulating donations as small as $25. Since 2005, Kiva's microlending platform has helped entrepreneurs in emerging markets in 82 countries borrow $1.6 billion with a 96 percent repayment rate, and 81 percent of the borrowers identify as female.[8] In addition, organizations such as the International Rescue Committee (IRC) are making microloans and providing training and support for refugees to help them get a fresh start, and Microfinancing Partners in Africa is making microloans

(continued)

to help lift women from poverty.[9] One commonality these organizations share is a reliance on character, trust, and potential community benefits to determine who gets a loan, rather than credit reports and financial statements.

Microlending isn't limited to crowdfunded sources. There are small, community-based microlenders who receive their funding from state and local governments and are monitored by the Small Business Administration. However, crowdfunded microlenders rely on social capital to determine the borrower's creditworthiness, whereas traditional lenders rely on a stringent underwriting process. Even so, with small loan amounts and short payback periods, these microloans are designed for entrepreneurs who have limited credit history and personal funds.

Crowdfunding sites such as Kickstarter and GoFundMe can also help start-ups get their products to market, but they tend to favor more commercial products rather than the smaller entrepreneurial ventures that the microlenders target. Direct crowdfunding carries unique risks; crowdfunding efforts that don't meet their stated goals do not receive any of the money generated by the campaign, and there are fees associated with crowdfunding sites that may outweigh microloan fees. Even so, some evidence indicates that crowdfunding sites favor women entrepreneurs over men, and these campaigns may offer opportunities unavailable to marginalized groups.

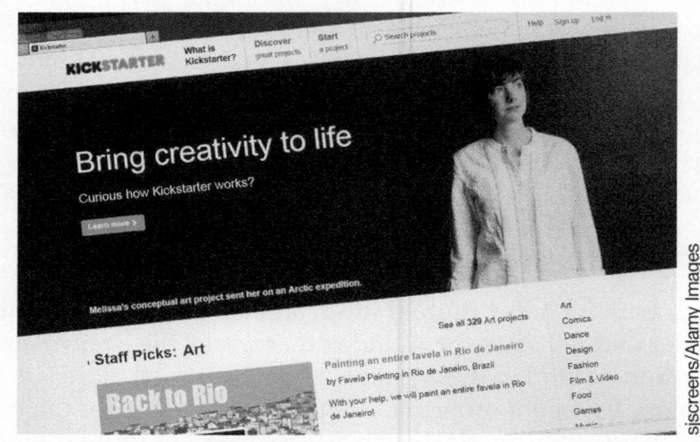

sjscreens/Alamy Images

[Photo caption TK]

Learning Objective 17-3

Describe the role of securities markets and identify the major stock exchanges and stock markets.

The Business of Trading Securities

Stocks, bonds, and mutual funds are known as **securities** because they represent *secured*, or financially valuable, claims on the part of investors. The markets in which stocks and bonds are sold are called **securities markets**. By facilitating the buying and selling of securities, the securities markets provide the capital that companies rely on for survival. Mutual funds, in contrast, are not bought and sold on securities markets but are managed by financial professionals in the investment companies that create, buy, and sell the funds.

Securities *stocks, bonds, and mutual funds representing secured, or asset-based, claims by investors against issuers*

Securities Markets *markets in which stocks and bonds are sold*

Primary and Secondary Securities Markets

In **primary securities markets**, new stocks and bonds are bought and sold by firms and governments. New securities are sometimes sold to single buyers or small groups of buyers. These *private placements* are desirable because they allow issuers to keep their plans confidential.

Primary Securities Market *market in which new stocks and bonds are bought and sold by firms and governments*

Most new stocks, however, and some bonds are sold on the wider public market. To bring a new security to market, the issuing firm must get approval from the U.S. **Securities and Exchange Commission (SEC)**, the government agency that regulates U.S. securities markets. The firm also relied, traditionally, on the services of an **investment bank**, a financial institution that specialized in issuing and reselling new securities. All that changed, however, in the financial collapse of 2008, when the fall of Lehman Brothers became the largest bankruptcy in U.S. history, Bear Stearns was purchased by JPMorgan Chase, and the two remaining large U.S. investment banks—Morgan Stanley and Goldman Sachs—were allowed to become bank holding companies (much like a commercial bank).[10] Although the companies' structures have changed, they still provide three important investment banking services:

Securities and Exchange Commission (SEC) *government agency that regulates U.S. securities markets*

Investment Bank *financial institution that specializes in issuing and reselling new securities*

1. *Advise* companies on the timing and financial terms of new issues.
2. *Underwrite*—buy and assume liability for—new securities, thus providing the issuing firms with 100 percent of the money (less commission). The inability to resell the securities is a risk that the banks must bear.

3 *Create* distribution networks for moving new securities through groups of other banks and brokers into the hands of individual investors.

New securities, however, represent only a small portion of traded securities. *Existing* stocks and bonds are sold in the much larger **secondary securities market**, which is handled by such familiar entities as the New York Stock Exchange and by online trading with electronic communication networks.

Secondary Securities Market *market in which existing (not new) stocks and bonds are sold to the public*

Stock Exchanges

Most of the buying and selling of stocks has historically been handled by organized *stock exchanges*. A **stock exchange** is an organization of individuals coordinated to provide an institutional auction setting in which stocks can be bought and sold.

Stock Exchange *an organization of individuals to provide an institutional auction setting in which stocks can be bought and sold*

The Trading Floor Each exchange regulates the places and times at which trading may occur. The most important difference between traditional exchanges and the electronic market is the geographic location of the trading activity. Brokers at an exchange trade face-to-face on the *trading floor* (also referred to as an *outcry market*). The electronic market, in contrast, conducts trades electronically among thousands of dealers in remote locations around the world.

Trading floors today are equipped with vast arrays of electronic communications equipment for displaying buy and sell orders or confirming completed trades. A variety of news services furnish up-to-the-minute information about world events and business developments. Any change in these factors, then, may be swiftly reflected in share prices.

The Major Stock Exchanges Among the stock exchanges that operate on trading floors in the United States, the New York Stock Exchange is the largest. Today, it faces stiff competition from both the electronic market in the United States and large foreign exchanges, such as those in London and Tokyo.

The New York Stock Exchange For many people, "the stock market" means the *New York Stock Exchange (NYSE)*. Founded in 1792, the NYSE is the model for exchanges worldwide. The merger with Euronext in 2007 formed NYSE Euronext, bringing together marketplaces across Europe and the United States, representing one-third of stock trading worldwide. Only firms meeting certain minimum

xPACIFICA/Alamy Stock Photo

Founded in 1792 and physically located at the corner of Wall and Broad Streets in New York City, the New York Stock Exchange sees billions of shares change hands each day.

requirements—earning power, total value of outstanding stock, and number of shareholders—are eligible for listing on the NYSE.[11]

Today's NYSE is a *hybrid market* that uses both floor and electronic trading. When a client places an order through a brokerage house or online, it is transmitted to a broker on the NYSE floor. Floor brokers who want to trade that stock meet together to agree on a trading price based on supply and demand, and the order is executed. Alternatively, buyers can use the NYSE's Direct+ service to automatically execute trades electronically.

Global Stock Exchanges As recently as 1980, the U.S. market accounted for more than half the value of the world market in traded stocks. Market activities, however, have shifted as the value of shares listed on foreign exchanges continues to grow. Table 17.1 identifies the 10 largest exchanges in 2019, the trading volume, which is the dollar volume of shares traded that year, and the number of firms listed for trade. While new exchanges are emerging in such diverse settings as Vietnam, Laos, and Rwanda, earlier start-ups are flourishing in cities from Shanghai to Warsaw, and others are merging or partnering in other regions. NYSE Euronext, for example, gained an important presence in the Middle East by joining with Qatar Stock Exchange, which also enabled Qatar to become a stronger international exchange.[12]

National Association of Securities Dealers Automated Quotation (NASDAQ) System *world's oldest electronic stock market consisting of dealers who buy and sell securities over a network of electronic communications*

The NASDAQ Market The **National Association of Securities Dealers Automated Quotation (NASDAQ) System**, the world's oldest electronic stock market, was established in 1971. Whereas buy and sell orders to the NYSE are gathered on the trading floor, NASDAQ orders are gathered and executed on a digital network connecting 500,000 terminals worldwide. NASDAQ has also been working with officials in an increasing number of countries to replace the physical trading floors of traditional exchanges with electronic networks like NASDAQ's.

The stocks of some 3,300 companies, both established and well-known companies as well as newer firms, are traded by NASDAQ. Examples include Marvell, Apple, Microsoft, Intel, and Staples. Although the volume of shares traded surpasses that of the NYSE, the total market value of NASDAQ's U.S. stocks is less than that of the NYSE.

International Consolidation and Cross-Border Ownership

A wave of technological advances, along with regulatory and competitive factors, has propelled the consolidation of stock exchanges and the changeover from physical to digital trading floors across international borders. Electronic communication networks

table 17.1 Selected Global Stock Exchanges and Markets

Exchange	Trade Volume (2019) (billions $)	Listings
New York Stock Exchange	$30.1	2,400
NASDAQ	$10.9	3,500
Japan Exchange Group	$5.7	3,687
Shanghai Stock Exchange	$5.5	1,000
Hong Kong Stock Exchanges and Clearing Limited (HKEX)	$4.6	2,315
Euronext	$4.5	1,500
London Stock Exchange Group	$4.5	2,483
Shenzhen Stock Exchange	$3.5	1,420
TMX Group	$2.9	1,500
Bombay Stock Exchange	$2.1	5,439

Sources: https://www.tradinghours.com/exchanges/, https://therobusttrader.com/top-20-biggest-stock-exchanges-in-the-world-largest-stock-exchanges-by-market-capitalization/, accessed May 5, 2020.

have opened the door to around-the-clock and around-the-globe trading. Every major European stock exchange had gone electronic by the end of the twentieth century, and by 2010 the United States had caught up. Stock exchanges that didn't have a strong enough digital presence have merged or partnered with those having more advanced trading systems. The intensified competition among stock exchanges has brought faster transactions and lower transaction fees for investors.

Nonexchange Trading: Electronic Communication Networks

The SEC authorized the creation of **electronic communication networks (ECNs)** in 1998. These networks are electronic trading systems that bring buyers and sellers together outside traditional stock exchanges by automatically matching buy and sell orders at specified prices. ECNs gained rapid popularity because the trading procedures are fast and efficient, often lowering transaction costs per share to mere pennies. They also allow after-hours trading (after traditional markets have closed for the day) and protect traders' anonymity.[13]

Electronic Communication Network (ECN) *electronic trading system that brings buyers and sellers together outside traditional stock exchanges*

ECNs must register with the SEC as broker-dealers. The ECN then provides service to subscribers—that is, other broker-dealers and institutional investors. Subscribers can view all orders at any time on the system's website to see information on what trades have taken place and at what times. Individual investors must open an account with a subscriber (a broker-dealer) before they can send buy and sell orders to the ECN system.

Individual Investor Trading

More than half of all U.S. citizens have some form of ownership in stocks, bonds, or mutual funds.[14] On the one hand, many of these individual investors rely on the advice of experienced professionals or brokers. On the other hand, individual investors who are well informed and experienced often prefer to invest independently without outside guidance.

Stock Brokers Some of the people on the trading floor of stock exchanges are employed by the stock exchange itself. Others are trading stocks for themselves. Many, however, are **stock brokers** who earn commissions by executing buy and sell orders for outside customers. Although they match buyers with sellers, brokers do not own the securities. They earn commissions from the individuals and organizations for whom they place orders.

Stock Broker *individual or organization that receives and executes buy and sell orders on behalf of outside customers in return for commissions*

Discount Brokers As with many other products, brokerage assistance can be purchased either at discount or at full-service prices. Discount brokers, such as E*TRADE and Scottrade, offer well-informed individual investors who know what they want to buy or sell a fast, low-cost way to participate in the market. Some discount brokers charge no fees to buy or sell a U.S. stock listed on a major exchange. In other cases, though, fees may vary based on the number of trades executed and the value of those trades. Further, fees vary across different kinds of investment vehicles—stocks, bonds, and so forth. Price differences are obvious even among the discount brokers, but the highest discount price is well below the price of a full-service broker. Sales agents receive fees or salaries, not commissions. Unlike many full-service brokers, many discount brokers do not offer in-depth investment advice or person-to-person sales consultations. They do, however, offer automated online services, such as stock research, industry analysis, and screening for specific types of stocks.

Full-Service Brokers Despite the growth in online investing, full-service brokers remain an important resource, both for new, uninformed investors and for experienced investors who don't have time to keep up with all the latest developments. Full-service brokers, such as Merrill Lynch Wealth Management, offer clients consulting advice in personal financial planning, estate planning, and tax strategies, along with a wider range of investment products. In addition to delivering and interpreting information, financial advisors can point clients toward investments that might otherwise be lost in an avalanche of online financial data.

Online Investing The popularity of digital trading stems from convenient access to online information; fast, no-nonsense transactions; and the opportunity for self-directed investors to manage their own investments while paying low fees for trading.

Online investors buy and sell the stocks of thousands of companies daily. Consequently, keeping track of who owns what at any given time has become extremely complex. As a result, most ownership records are now maintained through what is referred to as **book-entry ownership**. Shares of stock were historically issued as physical paper certificates. But now, though, they are simply recorded in the companies' records (or "books"), thereby eliminating the costs of printing, storing, exchanging, and replacing paper certificates. (Of course, these ownership records now are primarily stored digitally with both strong offsite and cloud backup.)

Book-Entry Ownership *procedure that holds investors' shares in book-entry form, rather than issuing a physical paper certificate of ownership*

Tracking the Market Using Stock Indexes

For decades, investors have used stock indexes to measure market performance and to predict future movements of stock markets. Although not indicative of the status of individual securities, **market indexes** provide useful summaries of overall price trends, both in specific industries and in the stock market as a whole. Market indexes, for example, reveal *bull* and *bear market* trends. **Bull markets** are periods of rising stock prices, generally lasting 12 months or longer. During bull markets, investors are motivated to buy, confident they will realize capital gains. Periods of falling stock prices, usually 20 percent off peak prices, are called **bear markets**. During bear markets, investors are motivated to sell, anticipating further falling prices.

Market Index *statistical indicator designed to measure the performance of a large group of stocks or track the price changes of a stock market*

Bull Market *period of rising stock prices, lasting 12 months or longer, featuring investor confidence for future gains and motivation to buy*

Bear Market *period of falling stock prices marked by negative investor sentiments with motivation to sell ahead of anticipated losses*

As Figure 17.2 shows, the past 40 years have been characterized primarily by bull markets, including the longest in history, from 1981 to the beginning of 2000. In contrast, the period 2000–2003 was characterized by a bear market. The period 2007–2009 was the second-worst bear market of all time, exceeded only by that of 1929–1932.[15] The data that characterize such periods are drawn from four leading market indexes: the Dow Jones, Standard & Poor's, NASDAQ Composite, and the Russell 2000 (not shown in Figure 17.2). In early 2020, plunging stock prices amid economic turmoil attributable to the COVID-19 pandemic also seemed to predict the onset of a bear market. However, after a brief decline, stocks rebounded through the end of 2020. In 2022, stocks generally dropped due to concerns about rising interest rates and inflation and fears of an impending recession. But stocks again generally moved up in the first months of 2023, quelling fears of a bear market.

The Dow The **Dow Jones Industrial Average (DJIA)** is the oldest and most widely cited U.S. market index. It measures the performance of the industrial sector of the U.S. stock markets by focusing on just 30 blue-chip, large-cap companies as reflectors of the economic health of the many similar U.S. firms. The Dow is an average of the stock prices for these 30 large firms, and traders and investors use it as a traditional barometer of the market's overall movement. Because it includes only 30 of the thousands of companies on the market, the Dow is only an approximation of the overall market's price movements.

Dow Jones Industrial Average (DJIA) *oldest and most widely cited market index based on the prices of 30 blue-chip, large-cap industrial firms on the NYSE*

Over the past several decades, the Dow has been revised and updated to reflect the changing composition of U.S. companies and industries. Recent modifications occurred in 2008–2009, when three companies were added—Kraft Foods, insurance giant Travelers Companies, and technology titan Cisco Systems—replacing insurance company

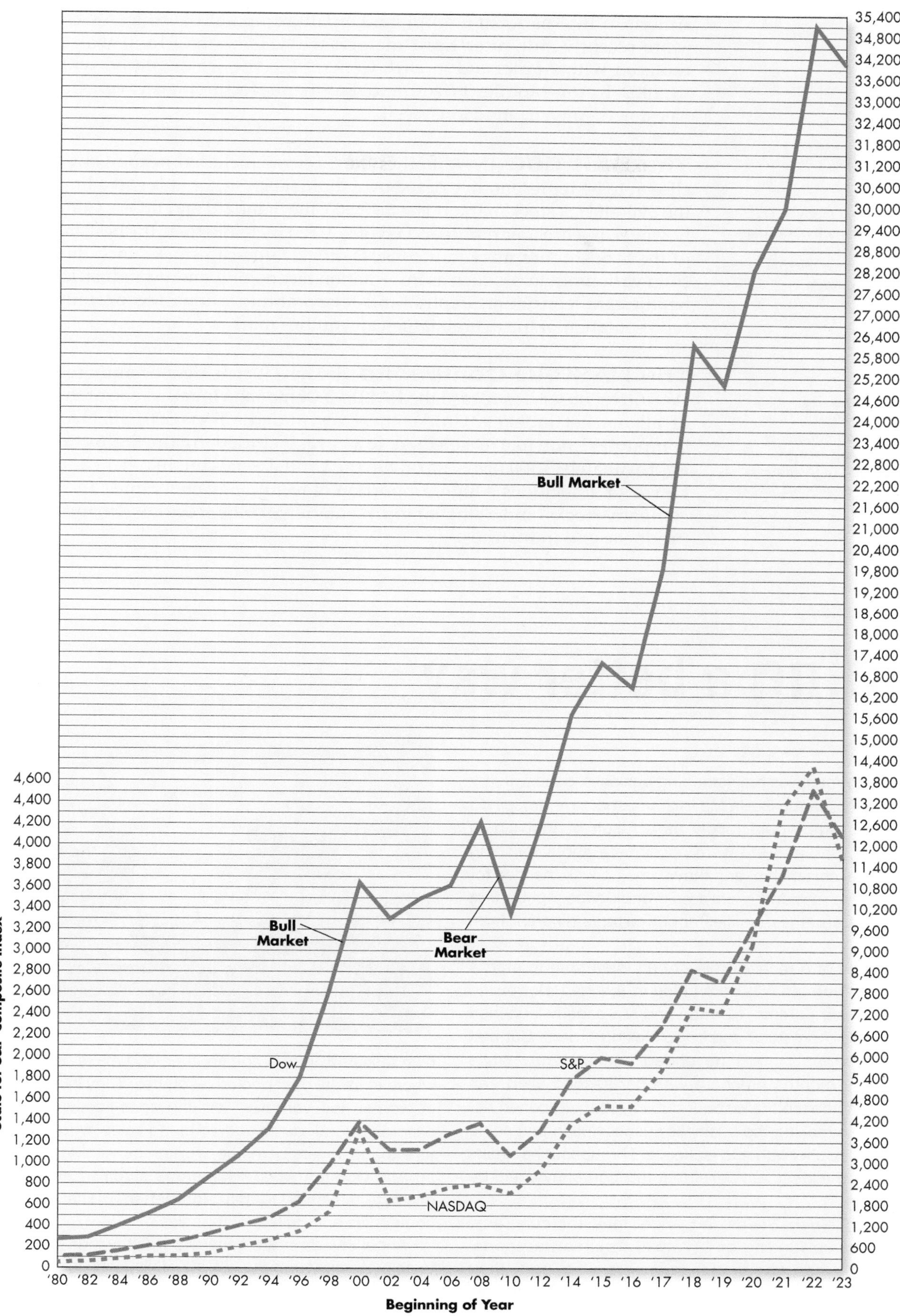

FIGURE 17.2 Bull and Bear Markets
Source: Yahoo! Finance, at http://finance.yahoo.com, accessed on October 16, 2023.

American International Group, banker Citigroup, and auto icon General Motors. More recently still, after Kraft merged with Heinz in 2015, it was dropped and replaced with Apple, and in 2018 General Electric was replaced with Walgreens. In 2022 Exxon-Mobile, Pfizer, and Raytheon Technologies were replaced with Salesforce, Amgen, and Honeywell.

S&P 500 *market index of U.S. equities based on the performance of 500 large-cap stocks representing various sectors of the overall equities market*

The S&P 500 Even though the 30 firms included in the Dow are carefully chosen to be representative of the overall financial sector, it is still a limited gauge of the overall U.S. stock market. The **S&P 500**, the Standard and Poor's Composite Index, however, is a broader report and is considered by many to be the best single indicator of the U.S. equities market. It consists of 500 large-cap stocks, including companies from various sectors—such as information technology, energy, industrials, financials, health care, consumer staples, and telecommunications—to provide a balanced representation of the overall large-cap equities market.

NASDAQ Composite Index *market index that includes all NASDAQ-listed companies, both domestic and foreign, with a high proportion of technology companies and small-cap stocks*

The NASDAQ Composite Because it considers even more stocks, some Wall Street observers regard the **NASDAQ Composite Index** as one of the most useful of all market indexes. Unlike the Dow and the S&P 500, all NASDAQ-listed companies, not just a selected few, are included in the index for a total of approximately 3,300 firms, mostly in the United States but in other countries as well. However, it includes a high proportion of technology companies, including small-company stocks, and a smaller representation of other sectors—financial, consumer products, and industrials.

finding a better way

Angel Investors

When Amy Norman was brainstorming business ideas with her former eBay colleague Stella Ma in 2009, she never imagined the road that she would follow as a result of that single conversation. She and Ma were passionate about teaching children global citizenship, and they came up with the idea for Little Passports, a monthly children's book subscription that educates kids and their families about cultures different from their own.

The middle of a recession is not an ideal time to start a business, but Norman was committed to the idea. Borrowing $25,000 from her parents, Norman and Ma eagerly launched their website in April 2009 and began taking orders. But that weekend, Norman's marriage ended unexpectedly while she was eight months pregnant with her second child—an experience she doesn't talk about publicly that deepened her commitment to making the business successful. In that same year, Norman lost her father to leukemia. Throughout her trials, she maintained a steadfast belief that this company could be something big.[16]

In 2010, Golden Seeds, an angel investor company, provided start-up funding of $175,000 to Little Passports. Golden Seeds has about 350 members who pool their individual wealth to fund business ideas. The members do their

Chris Goodney/Bloomberg/Getty Images

own research, inform one another, and make decisions about where to invest their pooled resources. They invest exclusively in women-led ventures, looking specifically for women in executive leadership and in hiring roles who will continue to expand diversity in the workplace. Golden Seeds CEO Jo Ann Corkran says, "Numerous studies have shown that diversity makes every decision better. That's true for public companies and private companies."[17]

Angel investors are generally wealthy individuals, referred to as *high-net-worth individuals* (HNIs), who look for start-ups or early-stage businesses to invest in. These investors usually aren't in the business of making loans but look instead to realize a return on their investment through partial ownership or shares in the company. Angel investing is a long game, with most investments requiring seven to 10 years before investors exit with a return. Angel investing is also a risky bet, with an average of 50 percent of businesses either folding or offering only a partial return. As a result, angels usually invest no more than 10 percent of their portfolio this way. The most famous example of angel investors may be the television show *Shark Tank*, where contestants vie for the attention and investment of a few wealthy individuals.

Venture capitalists are also looking to invest in a business on the idea that partial ownership will eventually return a large profit. Venture capitalists, however, look for successful businesses that can be scaled up quickly or sold after the initial investment. These investors are usually a company and operate in a hands-off way, whereas angel investors may be deeply involved in the strategic planning or even day-to-day running of their investments.

In the case of Little Passports, Amy Norman was a good bet for Golden Seeds. The children's educational company BEGIN acquired Little Passports in December 2021, with Amy Norman at the helm as CEO. In 2022, Little Passports posted $27.5 million in revenue. Norman is grateful every day that she clung to the dream of one day telling her story as a successful entrepreneur. "Now my son sees that I'm a CEO, and we have around 50 employees, and he sees his mom as successful," she says. "I do like the idea that my children think I'm strong and independent. I'm proud of being that role model. I think they're proud of Little Passports. And my son wants to do an internship here as soon as he's old enough."[18]

The Russell 2000 Investors in the U.S. small-cap market are interested in the **Russell 2000 Index**, a specialty index that measures the performance of the smallest publicly traded U.S. companies based on market capitalization. As the most quoted index focusing on the small-cap portion of the U.S. economy, its stocks represent a range of sectors such as financials, consumer discretionary, health care, technology, materials, and utilities.

Russell 2000 Index *specialty index that uses 2,000 stocks to measure the performance of the smallest U.S. companies*

Index-Matching ETFs Countless other specialty indexes exist for specific industries, countries, and economic sectors to meet investors' diverse needs. In addition, many ETFs are available to investors for duplicating (or nearly duplicating) the market performance of popular stock-market indexes. For example, one ETF, Standard & Poor's Depositary Receipts (SPDRS, known as *Spiders*), owns a portfolio of stocks that matches the composition of the S&P 500 index. Similarly, the Fidelity® NASDAQ Composite Index® Tracking Stock holds a portfolio of equities for tracking the NASDAQ Composite Index.

We have now seen that the securities markets, the markets in which stocks and bonds are bought and sold, provide the capital that companies rely on for survival. These markets also provide investment opportunities by which companies trade securities to increase a firm's wealth. Firms issuing new securities raise capital with the assistance of investment banking services. Existing securities are traded throughout the day in the secondary securities market (where buyers and sellers make transactions at the major stock exchanges) and through ECNs. For trading securities, many individuals and companies rely on the services of securities brokers, and other self-directed traders use online trading to self-manage their investments. Investors often use stock indexes to measure market performance and to predict future market movements of stock markets. Market indexes reveal bull and bear markets, showing the risks and opportunities for gaining and losing wealth that are inherent in securities investments.

The Risk–Return Relationship

Learning Objective 17-4

Describe the risk–return relationship and discuss the use of diversification and asset allocation for investments.

Individual investors have different motivations and personal preferences for safety versus risk. That is why, for example, some individuals and firms invest in stocks, while others invest only in bonds. Although all investors anticipate receiving future cash flows, some cash flows are more certain than others. Investors generally expect to receive higher returns for higher uncertainty. They do not generally expect large returns for secure, stable investments such as government-insured bonds. The investment's time commitment, too, contains an element of risk. While short-term investments are generally considered to be less risky, longer-term investments are subject to future uncertainties in the economy and financial markets. The one-year treasury yield as of March 2023 was 4.9 percent, 3.96 percent on a five-year bill, and 3.7 percent on a 10-year bill. Each type of investment, then, has a **risk–return (risk–reward) relationship**: Safer investments tend to offer lower returns, and riskier investments tend to offer higher returns (rewards).

Risk–Return (Risk–Reward) Relationship *principle that safer investments tend to offer lower returns, whereas riskier investments tend to offer higher returns (rewards)*

Figure 17.3 shows the general risk–return relationship for various financial instruments, along with the types of investors they attract. Thus, conservative investors, who have a low tolerance for risk, will opt for no-risk U.S. Treasury Bills (fully insured by the U.S. government), or even intermediate-term high-grade corporate bonds that rate low in terms of risk on future returns, but also low on the size of expected returns. The reverse is true of aggressive investors who prefer the higher risks and potential returns from long-term junk bonds and common stocks.[19]

Investment Dividends (or Interest), Appreciation, and Total Return

In evaluating potential investments, investors look at returns from dividends (or from interest), returns from price appreciation, and total return.

Dividends The rate of return from dividends paid to shareholders is commonly referred to as the **current dividend yield** (or, in the case of interest from a loan, the **current interest yield**) and is calculated by dividing the yearly dollar amount of dividend income by the investment's current market value. For example, during one recent time period, each share of AT&T stock was receiving annual dividend payments

Current Dividend Yield and Current Interest Yield *yearly dollar amount of income divided by the investment's current market value, expressed as a percentage*

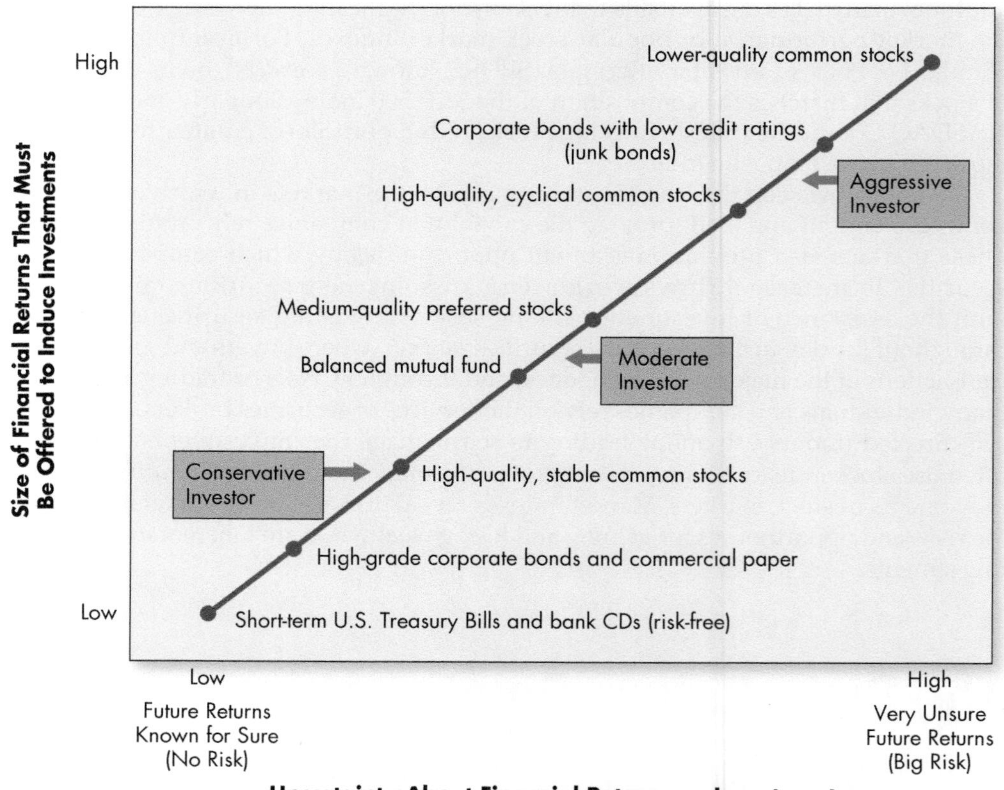

FIGURE 17.3 Potential Financial Returns Rise with Riskier Investments

of $1.80. Now, if the share price was $35.67 on a particular day, the current yield would be 5.05 percent or ($1.80/$35.67 × 100). This dividend can then be compared against current yields from other investments. Larger dividend yields, of course, are preferred to smaller returns.

Price Appreciation Another source of returns depends on whether the investment is increasing or decreasing in dollar value. **Price appreciation** is an increase in the dollar value of an investment. Suppose, for example, you purchased a share of AT&T stock for $35.67 and then sold it one year later for $37.45. The price appreciation is $1.78 or ($37.45 − 35.67). This profit, realized from the increased market value of an investment, is known as a **capital gain**.

Price Appreciation *increase in the dollar value of an investment at two points in time (the amount by which the price of a security increases)*

Capital Gain *profit realized from the increased value of an investment*

Total Return The sum of an investment's current dividend (interest) yield and capital gain is referred to as its *total return*. Total return cannot be accurately evaluated until it is compared to the investment that was required to get that return. Total return as a percentage of investment is calculated as follows:

Total return (%) = (Current dividend payment + Capital gain)/ Original investment × 100.

To complete our AT&T example, the total return as a percentage of our one-year investment would be 10.04 percent or [($1.80 + $1.78)/$35.67 × 100]. Again, obviously, larger total returns are preferred to smaller ones.

Fantasy Stock Markets

Enthusiasts of fantasy baseball, football, hockey, and other "hypothetical" games aren't the only people who enjoy competing in fantasy realms. Fantasy stock markets are also popular venues for learning how securities markets work, for trying your hand at various investment strategies, and for earning a fantasy fortune (or going broke!). Online games, including free ones such as *Wall Street Survivor* and *How the Market Works*, provide an investment experience that is educational, challenging, and entertaining. Starting with an initial sum of virtual cash with which to manage their own fantasy portfolio of real companies, participants must live with real market results. It's a learn-by-doing experience—using online symbol lookups to enter stock ticker symbols, searching various information sources for research on companies of interest, making buy and sell decisions, and then discovering the financial results as real market prices change for the portfolio holdings. Many students and business practitioners are finding these games to be a valuable resource for learning the "how to" of online investing.

Managing Risk with Diversification and Asset Allocation

Investors seldom take an extreme approach—total risk or total risk avoidance—in selecting their investments. Extreme positions tend to lead to extreme results. Instead, most investors select a mixed portfolio of investments—some riskier and some more conservative—that, collectively, provides the overall level of risk and financial returns that feels comfortable. After determining the desired *risk–return* balance, they then achieve it in two ways: through (1) *diversification* and (2) *asset allocation*.

Diversification **Diversification** (as applied to investment options) means buying several different kinds of investments rather than just one. For example, diversification as applied to common stocks means that you invest in stocks of several different companies, companies in different industries, and companies in various countries. The risk of loss is reduced by spreading the total investment across different kinds of stocks because although any one stock price may decline the chances are less that all of them will decline at the same time. For instance, in 2020 stock prices for oil and gas

Diversification *purchase of several different kinds of investments rather than just one*

companies like Shell and Chevron fell, as did stock prices for travel-related companies like Delta Airlines and Princess Cruises. However, stock prices for companies that made cleaning products, like Clorox's parent company Procter & Gamble, and online retailers like Amazon saw their stock prices increase.

Even more diversification is gained when assets are spread across a variety of investment alternatives—stocks, bonds, mutual funds, precious metals, real estate, and so on. However, employees who do not have diversified investments and instead have all their retirement funds invested in their firm's stock can lose everything if their company goes bankrupt or invests poorly. The collapse of Enron Corporation in 2001, one of the 10 largest U.S. firms at the time, was a financial disaster for its thousands of its employees because Enron's retirement program was invested solely in Enron common stock. Enron's stock price dropped from near $90 per share to nearly $5, effectively wiping out employees' retirement savings. Putting all their eggs in one basket was an extremely risky position, as they learned the hard way. When their firm's stock took a free fall as a result of a market collapse and resulting scandal, the retirement funds disappeared.

Asset Allocation *relative amount of funds invested in (or allocated to) each of several investment alternatives*

Asset Allocation **Asset allocation** is the proportion (the relative amounts) of funds invested in (or allocated to) each of the investment alternatives. You may decide, for example, to allocate 50 percent of your funds to common stocks, 25 percent to a money market mutual fund, and 25 percent to a U.S. Treasury bond mutual fund. Ten years later, with more concern for financial safety as you get closer to retirement, you may decide on a less risky asset allocation of 20 percent, 40 percent, and 40 percent in the same investment categories, respectively. In this example and in Figure 17.4, the portfolio has been changed from moderate-risk to lower-risk investments for the purpose of preserving the investor's accumulated capital. That is, the asset allocation was changed accordingly.

Portfolio *combined holdings of all the financial investments of any company or individual*

Performance Differences for Different Portfolios Once an investor has chosen an investment objective with an acceptable risk level, the investor can put the tools of diversification and asset allocation to use in their investor's *portfolio*. A **portfolio** is the combined holdings of all the financial investments—stocks, bonds, mutual funds, real estate—of any company or individual.

Just like investors, investment funds have different investment objectives—ranging from aggressive growth/high risk to stable income/low volatility—and their holdings are diversified accordingly among hundreds of company stocks, corporate bonds, or

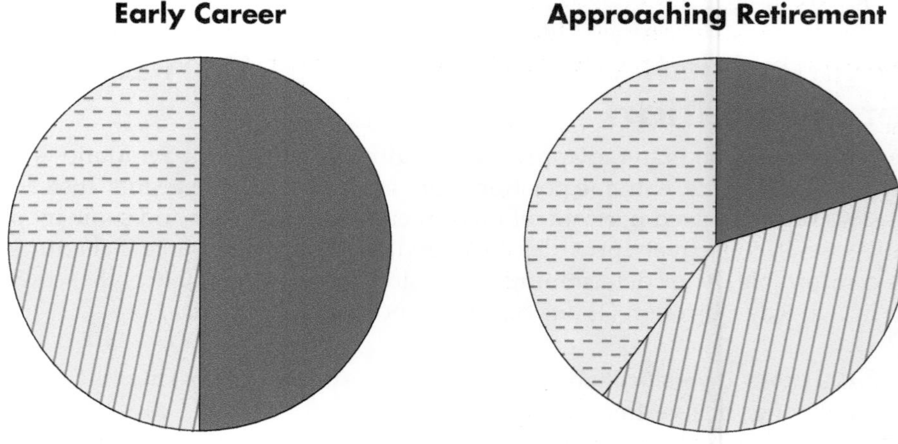

FIGURE 17.4 People's asset allocation is likely to change to minimize risk as they approach retirement

government bonds that provide the desired orientation. The money in a diversified portfolio is allocated in different proportions among a variety of funds. If all goes according to plan, most of these funds will meet their desired investment objectives, while a few may not, but the overall portfolio will increase in value.

A risk–return relationship is inherent in every business investment. Whereas safer investments tend to offer lower returns, riskier investments tend to offer higher returns (rewards). Different types of investments vary along the risk–reward continuum, and most firms strive for a mixture of investments that, overall, provide that firm's desired risk–return posture. Each investment's total financial return is the sum of its capital gain and dividend (interest) yield. After determining the desired risk–return balance, investors use two methods for achieving it: (1) diversification and (2) asset allocation. Diversification means buying several different kinds of investments rather than just one. Asset allocation is the proportion of funds invested in each of the investment alternatives. Diversification and asset allocation, together, are essential to protect against the uncertainties (risks) inherent in any single investment.

Financing the Business Firm

Learning Objective 17-5

Describe the various ways that firms raise capital and identify the pros and cons of each method.

If you invest wisely and your goal is to start your own firm, you may find yourself in a position to do so. However, that's only the first step in the complicated process of financing a business. Every company needs cash to function. Although a business owner's savings may be enough to get a new venture up and running, ongoing businesses depend on sales revenues to survive. When current sales revenues are insufficient to pay for expenses, firms tap into various other sources of funds, typically starting with the owners' savings (as discussed in Chapter 15, owners usually contribute funds, or paid-in capital, from their own pockets). If a firm needs more money, it can turn to borrowing from banks, soliciting cash from private outside investors, or selling bonds to the public.

Secured Loans for Equipment

Money to purchase new equipment often comes in the form of loans from commercial banks. In a **secured loan (asset-backed loan)**, the borrower guarantees repayment of the loan by pledging the asset as **collateral** to the lender. Suppose a local trucking company needs a $400,000 bank loan to purchase five dump trucks. The borrower may be required to pledge the trucks plus the company's office building as collateral to the bank. That is, if the borrower defaults, or fails to repay the loan, the bank can take possession of the borrower's pledged assets and sell them to recover the outstanding debt. However, as lenders learned in the 2008 recession, assets from loans defaulted by businesses (and home buyers) may have little or no value.

Secured Loan (Asset-Backed Loan) *loan to finance an asset, backed by the borrower pledging the asset as collateral to the lender*

Collateral *asset pledged for the fulfillment of repaying a loan*

The amount of money that is loaned and must be repaid is the **loan principal**. However, borrowers must also pay the lender an additional fee, **interest**, for the use of the borrowed funds. The amount of interest owed depends on an **annual percentage rate (APR)** that is agreed on between the lender and borrower. The interest amount is found by multiplying the APR by the loan principal.

Loan Principal *amount of money that is loaned and must be repaid*

Interest *fee paid to a lender for the use of borrowed funds; like a rental fee*

Annual Percentage Rate (APR) *one-year rate that is charged for borrowing, expressed as a percentage of the borrowed principal*

Working Capital and Unsecured Loans from Banks

Firms need more than just fixed assets for daily operations. They also need current, liquid assets available to meet short-term operating expenses such as employee wages, utility costs, rent, and marketing expenses. The firm's ability to meet these expenses is measured by its working capital:

$$\text{Working capital} = \text{Current assets} - \text{Current liabilities}$$

Unsecured Loan *loan for which collateral is not required*

Positive working capital means the firm's current assets are large enough to pay off current liabilities (see Chapter 15). Negative working capital means the firm's current liabilities are greater than current assets, so it may need to borrow money from a commercial bank. With an **unsecured loan**, the borrower does not have to put up collateral. In many cases, however, the bank requires the borrower to maintain a *compensating balance*—the borrower must keep a portion of the loan amount on deposit with the bank in a non-interest-bearing account.

Firms with low credit scores typically cannot get unsecured loans. Because access to such loans requires a good credit history, many firms establish a relationship with a commercial bank and, over time, build a good credit record by consistently repaying loan principal and interest on time. In extreme conditions, however, even a good credit history may not be enough. During the deepening recession back in 2008, the cash shortages at many banks prevented loans to nearly any kind of business customers, thereby slowing down the economy even more. Even after vast injections of cash from TARP and other government sources, banks lagged far behind in supplying loans to meet the working-capital needs of cash-strapped business borrowers.

Even worse, during extreme conditions businesses in good financial standing may still suffer. One Houston-area home builder, for instance, had a $20 million credit line with a consortium of local banks and an outstanding balance of $16 million. On paper, then, the builder was in good standing and still had available credit of $4 million. However, during the 2008 recession and housing market collapse, the bankers reduced the builder's credit line to $10 million as part of an overall credit reduction and informed the builder that he had 60 days to cover the $6 million that he was now "overdrawn." When he was unable to do so, he was forced to declare bankruptcy and eventually went out of business.

Small business entrepreneurs, especially, often underestimate the value of establishing bank credit as a source of funds. Some banks offer financial analysis, cash flow planning, and suggestions based on experiences with other local firms. Some provide loans to small businesses in bad times and work to keep them going. Obtaining credit, therefore, begins with finding a bank that can—and will—support a small firm's financial needs. Once a line of credit is obtained, the small business can seek more liberal credit policies from other businesses. Sometimes, for instance, suppliers give customers longer credit periods—say, 45 or 60 days rather than 30 days—to make payments. Liberal trade credit terms with their suppliers let firms increase short-term funds and avoid additional borrowing from banks.

Obtaining longer-term loans is more difficult for new businesses than for established companies. With unproven repayment ability, start-up firms can expect to pay higher interest rates than older firms. If a new enterprise displays evidence of sound financial planning, however, the U.S. Small Business Administration (SBA; see Chapter 3) may support a guaranteed loan. The presentation of a sound business plan demonstrates to potential lenders that the borrower may be a good credit risk. The business plan is a document that tells potential lenders why the money is needed, the amount, how the money will be used to improve the company, and when it will be paid back.

Planning for *cash flow requirements* is especially valuable for meeting the small business's financial needs. It also demonstrates to lenders the borrower's prudent use of financial resources. The firm's success or failure may hinge on anticipating those times when either cash will be short or excess cash can be expected. Consider how the owner would compare the expected cash inflows, cash outflows, and net cash position (inflows minus outflows) month by month for Slippery Fish Bait Supply Co., a highly seasonal business. Bait stores (Slippery's customers) buy heavily from Slippery during the spring and summer months. Revenues outpace expenses, leaving surplus funds that can be invested. During the fall and winter, however, expenses exceed revenues. Slippery must borrow funds to keep going until revenues pick up again in the spring. Comparing predicted cash inflows from sales with outflows for expenses will show the firm's expected monthly cash-flow position. Such information can be invaluable for the small-business manager. By anticipating shortfalls, managers can seek funds in advance and minimize their costs. By anticipating excess cash, a manager can plan to put the funds to work in short-term, interest-earning investments.

Angel Investors and Venture Capital

Once a business has been successfully launched, it most likely needs additional capital for growth. Outside individuals who provide such capital are often called **angel investors.** Angel investors help many firms grow rapidly by providing what is known as **venture capital**, private funds from wealthy individuals or companies (see Chapter 3) that seek investment opportunities in new growth companies. In most cases, the growing firm turns to venture capital sources because it has not yet built enough credit history to get a loan from commercial banks or other lending institutions. Peter Thiel supplied an initial $500,000 angel investment in Facebook's early years.

Angel Investors *outside investors who provide new capital for firms in return for a share of equity ownership*

Venture Capital *private funds from wealthy individuals seeking investment opportunities in new growth companies*

In 2022, experts estimated that $29.1 billion was invested in around 69,000 entrepreneurial ventures. Estimates also suggest that there are about 300,000 such investors in the United States. In return for their investment, angel investors typically expect a sizable portion of ownership in the company (up to 50 percent of its equity). They may also want a formal say in how the company is run. If the firm is bought by a larger company or if it sells its stock in a public offering, the angel may receive additional payments.

Sale of Corporate Bonds

Corporations can also raise capital by issuing bonds. A **corporate bond** is a formal pledge (essentially an IOU) obligating the issuer to pay interest periodically and then repay the principal at maturity (a preset future date) to the lender. The federal government also issues bonds to finance projects and meet obligations, as do state and local governments (called *municipal bonds*) for financing the building of schools, roads, sewage disposal systems, and similar projects.

Corporate Bond *formal pledge obligating the issuer (the company) to pay interest periodically and repay the principal at maturity*

Characteristics of Corporate Bonds

The bondholder (the lender) has no claim to ownership of the company and does not receive dividends. However, interest payments and repayment of principal are financial obligations. Payments to bondholders have priority over dividend payments to stockholders in cases of financial distress.

Each new bond issue has specific terms and conditions spelled out in a **bond indenture**, a legal document identifying the borrower's obligations and the financial returns to lenders. One of the most important details is the **maturity date** (or due date), when the firm must repay the bond's **face value** (also called **par value**, or the amount purchased) to the lender.

Bond Indenture *legal document containing complete details of a bond issue*

Maturity Date (Due Date) *future date when repayment of a bond is due from the bond issuer (borrower)*

Face Value (Par Value) *amount of money that the bond buyer (lender) lent the issuer and that the lender will receive on repayment*

Corporate bonds have been traditionally issued to fund outstanding debts and major projects for various lengths of time. Short-term bonds mature less than five years after they are issued. Bonds with five- to 10-year lives are considered intermediate term, and anything longer than 10 years is considered long term. Longer-term corporate bonds are somewhat riskier than shorter-term bonds because they are exposed to greater unforeseen economic conditions that may potentially lead to default. In general, of course, large companies that have been in existence for decades, such as Ford or General Electric, are not likely to default. At the same time, though, similar firms like Eastman Kodak and Bethlehem Steel failed and subsequently defaulted on outstanding long-term corporate bonds in the process.

Default *failure of a borrower to make payment when due to a lender*

Default and Bondholders' Claim

A bond is said to be in **default** if the borrower fails to make payment when due to lenders. Bondholders may then file a **bondholders' claim**, a request for court enforcement of the bond's terms of payment. When a financially distressed company cannot pay bondholders, it may seek relief by filing for **bankruptcy**, the court-granted permission not to pay some or all debts. After a restructured General Motors emerged from bankruptcy in 2009, the holders

Bondholders' Claim *request for court enforcement of a bond's terms of payment*

Bankruptcy *court-granted permission for a company to not pay some or all debts*

of the "old" General Motors Corporation's $24 billion in bonds wondered how much payment, if any, they would recover from the financially strapped company. In the 2011 settlement, investors holding bonds in the "old" GM received stock shares in the "new" GM that provided a recovery rate of about 40 cents on the dollar of the original bond investment.[20] More recently, both Carvana and Bed Bath & Beyond went through debt restructuring in attempts to survive. In both cases, their proposals to bankruptcy court called for current bond holders to accept payments lower than the original bond purchase prices. In the case of Bed Bath & Beyond the firm closed its brick-and-mortar stores and part of its inventory, and then on August 1, 2023 emerged from bankruptcy as an online retailer with expanded inventory.

Risk Ratings To aid investors in making purchase decisions, several services measure the default risk of bonds. Table 17.2, for example, shows the rating systems of two well-known services, Moody's and Standard & Poor's. The highest (safest) grades are Aaa and AAA, and the lowest are C and D, representing speculative and highly risky bonds. Low-grade bonds are usually called *junk bonds*. Negative ratings do not necessarily keep issues from being successful. Rather, they raise the interest rates that issuers must offer to attract lenders.

Flawed Ratings Misread Recession Risks The financial meltdown of 2008 raised questions about whether any good purpose is being served by credit-rating agencies. Among many other investors, California Public Employees Retirement Fund (CalPERS), the nation's largest public pension fund, filed a suit against the three top agencies—Moody's, Standard & Poor's, and Fitch—charging losses caused by "wildly inaccurate and unreasonably high" credit ratings. CalPERS officials relied on ratings for investments that proved to be wrong—many failing altogether. Skepticism of agencies' ratings has also increased following the collapse or near-collapse of highly rated giants such as Lehman Brothers, Goldman Sachs, and Citigroup, along with high ratings on billions of dollars of mortgage-backed securities that eventually became toxic. Various lawsuits, including those by the states of Ohio and Connecticut, accused credit-rating agencies of reckless assessments that misled investors.[21] These issues continue to persist today. For instance, credit-rating agencies often do not know how to accurately account for a firm's investments in environmental, social, and governance (ESG) activities. Some agencies reward firms for these kinds of investments, while others penalize them.

Mortgage-Backed Security (MBS) *mortgages pooled together to form a debt obligation—a bond—that entitles the holder (investor) to cash that flows in from the bundled mortgages*

Mortgage-backed securities (MBS) became a trillion-dollar investment industry during the pre-2007 housing market boom. Financial institutions bundled home mortgages into packages and resold them as securities to investors who trusted in the securities' risk ratings given by Moody's, Standard & Poor's, and Fitch. Each MBS is a group of mortgages bundled together to form a debt obligation (a bond) that entitles the holder (the investor) to the cash that flows in from the mortgages. Unknown to investors, some $3 trillion of MBSs contained subprime mortgages—high-risk loans to applicants with bad credit, low income, and low down payments—most of which had received high ratings (AAA) by credit-rating agencies. Misled by flawed risk assessments, investors were left with little or nothing when the highly rated securities turned toxic, causing the collapse of the housing and financial markets.[22]

table 17.2 Bond Rating Systems

Rating System	High Grades	Medium Grades (Investment Grades)	Speculative	Poor Grades
Moody's	Aaa, Aa	A, Baa	Ba, B	Caa to C
Standard & Poor's	AAA, AA	A, BBB	BB, B	CCC to D

Becoming a Public Corporation

Learning Objective 17-6

Identify the reasons a company might make an initial public offering of its stock, explain how stock value is determined, and discuss the significance of market capitalization.

Initial public offerings (IPOs), the first sale of a company's stock to the general public, are a major source of funds that fuel continued growth for many firms and introduce numerous considerations inherent in running a public company. In one of the biggest IPOs in history, Facebook's public offering of common stock in 2012, with an opening price of $38 per share, raised more than $100 billion. In this section, we discuss many of the issues public companies face, such as potential loss of control, fluctuating share prices, how businesses use market capitalization, and how they choose capital sources.

Initial Public Offering (IPO) *first sale of a company's stock to the general public*

Going Public Means Selling Part Ownership of the Company

Private owners lose some control of the company when shares are sold to the public. Common shareholders usually have voting rights in corporate governance, so they elect the board of directors and vote on major issues put forth at the company's annual shareholders' stock meeting. Anyone owning a large proportion of the company's shares, therefore, gains a powerful position in determining who runs the corporation and how.

At an extreme, a **corporate raider**, an investor conducting a type of hostile (unwanted) takeover, buys shares on the open market, attempting to seize control of the company and its assets. The raider then sells off those assets at a profit, perhaps even resulting in the company's dissolution. A company is a prime target for raiding when its stock price falls so shares can be cheaply bought, although its assets still have high value.

Corporate Raider *investor conducting a type of hostile corporate takeover against the wishes of the company*

Stock Valuation

What determines a stock's value after it is offered to the general public? Investors' assessments of the company's management record in past ventures, expectations for competing in the industry, and belief in the public's acceptance of the company's products are among many factors that affect a stock's value, which in turn affects the value of the business. In addition, different investors measure value differently, and their measurements may change according to circumstances. Because of the

Cosmo Condina/Alamy Stock Photo

When firms go public, they sell part of their ownership to other investors through a public offering of stock. Monitors such as this one show current prices and overall stock price indicators such as the Dow, S&P, and NASDAQ. Investors then use this information to decide when to buy or sell stock.

managing in turbulent times

Backing a Unicorn

Jackal Pan/Visual China Group/Getty Images

When Adam Neumann founded the office-sharing start-up WeWork, he did so with the guiding start-up philosophy coined by Meta's Mark Zuckerberg: Move fast and break things. After a 2017 investment of $4 billion by the Japanese conglomerate SoftBank, Neumann's own lifestyle began to look like he was a billionaire himself. Reports of a $60 million dollar jet to take his family on surfing vacations, six homes to his name, and traveling around the world with his hairdresser raised eyebrows. SoftBank would ultimately invest $18.5 billion in WeWork. The company's IPO garnered over $10 per share at the opening bell in September 2020. That IPO was boosted by investors valuing the company at a staggering $47 billion. Three years later, the company was valued at less than 30 cents a share and had a debt-to-equity ratio of nearly negative 92 percent.[23]

Neumann's start-up reached "unicorn" status, with a private market valuation of over $1 billion. When a start-up looks that good, investors will swarm, trying to get a piece of a potentially huge return on their investment. Investing becomes something of a self-sustaining cyclone, where initial investors want to attract more investors, so they soften due diligence requirements or push aside any concerns. The results are inflated valuations, reduced oversight, and little public scrutiny. With massive financing pouring in, founders can justify huge salaries with balance sheets that are optimistic at best and sometimes downright fraudulent. Since WeWork was a private company, Neumann was able to avoid accountability almost entirely.

One proposal to reduce these risks is authored by Matthew Wansley, an assistant professor at Yeshiva University's Cardozo School of Law in New York. In his academic paper "Taming Unicorns," Wansley argues for changing securities laws to allow for limited trading of start-up shares, increasing public disclosure requirements, and allowing venture capitalists to sell off shares if an investment starts to sour. He acknowledges that's a heavy lift in a market where 2021 investments set a record of $330 billion., almost twice the amount of the previous record-setting year.[24]

Though there's no evidence that Neumann paid for his extravagances with WeWork funds, the optics were bad enough to sink his personal brand and damage WeWork beyond repair so far. A charismatic and beloved founder takes a great deal of credit for a successful start-up, and personal status can go a long way to securing investments. The problem with being such a visible leader of a unicorn start-up is that when it goes south, the leader is also positioned to take all the blame.

uncertainties involved in stock prices, investment professionals believe day-to-day prices to be a generally poor indicator of any stock's real value. Instead, a long-run perspective considers the company's overall financial health, past history of results and future forecasts, record for managerial performance, and overall prospects for competing successfully in the coming years. Accordingly, any stock's value today looks beyond the current price and is based on expectations of the financial returns it will provide to shareholders during the long run.

Why Shares Are Different Prices On August 1, 2023, the price of Google Inc. was about $131.89 per share on the NYSE, GE shares traded at about $113.22, Delta Airlines shares were priced at about $45.40, and Berkshire Hathaway shares traded for $534,400.

Why such differences? One reason is supply and demand for each company's shares; another is because some corporations want the shares to sell within a particular price range, say, between $20 and $80, believing it will attract a larger pool of investors. If the price gets too high, many investors can't afford to buy shares. A company can restore shares to the desired lower range by a **stock split,** a stock dividend paid in additional shares to shareholders. Here's how it works. Suppose company *X* has 100,000 common shares outstanding that are trading at $100 per share, but the company wants them priced in the $20 to $80 range. *X* can declare a 2-for-1 stock

Stock Split *stock dividend paid in additional shares to shareholders, thus increasing the number of outstanding shares*

table 17.3 Financial Comparison: Coca-Cola and PepsiCo

	Coca-Cola	PepsiCo
Recent price	$61.77	$186.82
EPS	$2.27	$5.72
Dividend yield	2.97%	2.58%

split, meaning the company gives shareholders one additional share for each share they own. Now *X* has 200,000 shares outstanding but its financial performance has not changed, so the stock price immediately adjusts to $50 per share on the open market. Every shareholder's investment value, however, is unchanged: they previously owned one share at $100, and now they own two shares at $50 each.

Comparing Prices of Different Stocks Consider a random trading day when PepsiCo's share price was $186.82 and Coca-Cola was $61.77 per share. Does the price difference mean that PepsiCo is a better company than Coca-Cola because its shares are more expensive? Or does it mean that Coke shares are a better value because they can be bought at a lower price than PepsiCo's? In fact, neither of these two reasons is correct. Share prices alone do not provide enough information to determine which is the better investment. Table 17.3 can help us make a better comparison with further information.

First, earnings per share (EPS) are greater for PepsiCo ($5.72 versus $2.27 per share). But since you pay more, you also have reason to expect more return. In reality, at the time these data were collected, the return for PepsiCo was actually slightly lower than for Coke ($5.72 earnings/$186.82 = $0.03 for Pepsi versus $2.27 earnings/ $61.77 investment = $0.4 for Coke). Both companies generated about the same earnings power for each dollar of shareholder investment.

Now consider annual dividends paid to shareholders. The dividend yield from Coca-Cola was 2.97 percent. That is, the dividend payment amounted to a 2.97 percent return on the shareholder's $61.77 investment, or $1.83 = ($61.77 × 2.97%). PepsiCo's dividend yield was 2.58 percent, so the dividend payment was about $4.82 ($186.82 × 2.58%). From these limited data it would appear that Pepsi might be a better investment than Coke. However, over the past 14 years, each firm outperformed the other exactly seven times each but never by a very wide margin! Therefore, it is really not clear which of the two companies is the better investment. A more complete evaluation would compare historical performance consistency over a longer period of time, along with a detailed analysis of each firm's prospects for the future.

Market Capitalization

A widely used measure of corporate size and value is known as **market capitalization (market cap)**, the total dollar value of all the company's outstanding shares, calculated as the current stock price multiplied by the number of shares outstanding. As indicated in Table 17.4, the investment industry categorizes firms according to size of capitalization. Investors typically regard larger market caps as less risky, and firms

Market Capitalization (Market Cap) *total dollar value of all the company's outstanding shares*

table 17.4 Corporation Sizes Based on Capitalization

Capitalization Category	Range of Capitalization
Micro-Cap	Below $300 million
Small-Cap	$300 million–$2 billion
Mid-Cap	$2 billion–$10 billion
Large-Cap	Over $10 billion

with small market caps (small-cap firms) as being particularly risky investments. In early 2020, Apple had a market cap of approximately $1.29 trillion, making it the most valuable U.S. company at that time.

Choosing Equity Versus Debt Capital

Firms can meet their capital needs through two sources: (1) *debt financing* (from outside the firm) or (2) *equity financing* (putting the owners' capital to work).

Debt Financing *long-term borrowing from sources outside a company*

Pros and Cons of Debt Financing

Long-term borrowing from sources outside the company, **debt financing**, via loans or the sale of corporate bonds is a major component in most U.S. firms' financial planning.

Long-Term Loans Long-term loans are attractive for several reasons:

- Because the number of parties involved is limited, loans can often be arranged quickly.
- The firm need not make public disclosure of its business plans or the purpose for which it is acquiring the loan. (In contrast, the issuance of corporate bonds requires such disclosure.)

Long-term loans also have some disadvantages. Borrowers, for example, may have trouble finding lenders to supply large sums. Long-term borrowers may also face restrictions as conditions of the loan. For example, they may have to pledge long-term assets as collateral or agree to take on no more debt until the loan is paid.

Corporate Bonds Bonds are attractive when firms need large amounts for long periods of time. The issuing company gains access to large numbers of lenders through nationwide bond markets. However, bonds entail high administrative and selling costs. They may also require stiff interest payments, especially if the issuing company has a poor credit rating. Bonds also impose binding obligations on the firm, in many cases for up to 30 years, to pay bondholders a stipulated sum of annual or semiannual interest, even in times of financial distress. If the company

Sundry Photography/Shutterstock

A firm's market capitalization (or market cap) is the number of its outstanding shares of stock multiplied by the current price of that stock. Amazon has become one of the world's most valuable businesses (that is, it has one of the largest market caps). In 2020, its market cap was around $1.5 trillion. But in 2022, its cap value had dropped to $856.94 billion—a drop of 49.32 percent. In mid-2023, this cap had surged again to $1.25 trillion.

fails to make a bond payment, it goes into default. A classic example is WorldCom (now MCI), which filed for bankruptcy in 2002 when it was the nation's number-two long-distance phone company. With $102 billion in assets, WorldCom's bankruptcy at the time was the largest in U.S. history. Even with those massive assets, however, the firm was crushed by its $41 billion debt, $24 billion of which was in bonds. Facing prospects that the firm would default on upcoming interest payments, many of its creditors began withholding additional money unless loans were secured with WorldCom assets. With more than 1,000 creditors—including Citibank, JPMorgan Chase, and Credit Suisse First Boston—the firm was allowed to operate while in bankruptcy. In 2003, WorldCom changed its name to MCI, before emerging from bankruptcy status in 2004. More recently, in 2019, oil field services company Weatherford International declared bankruptcy and defaulted on $7.4 billion in bond debt. Moody's Investment Services indicated that Weatherford bondholders should expect to eventually receive somewhere between 35 and 65 percent on the value of their investments.[25]

Pros and Cons for Equity Financing Although debt financing often has strong appeal, **equity financing**, looking inside the company for long-term funding, is sometimes preferable. Equity financing includes either issuing common stock or retaining the firm's earnings.

Equity Financing *using the owners' funds from inside the company as the source for long-term funding*

The Expense of Common Stock The use of equity financing by means of common stock can be expensive because paying dividends is more expensive than paying bond interest. Interest paid to bondholders is a business expense and therefore a tax deduction for the firm. Payments of cash dividends to shareholders are not tax deductible.

Retained Earnings as a Source of Capital As discussed in Chapter 15, *retained earnings* are net profits retained for the firm's use rather than paid out in dividends to stockholders. If a company uses retained earnings as capital, it will not have to borrow money and pay interest. If a firm has a history of reaping profits by reinvesting retained earnings, it may be attractive to some investors. Retaining earnings, however, means smaller dividends for shareholders. This practice may decrease the demand for—and therefore the price of—the company's stock.

We have seen, then, that becoming a public corporation means selling part of the ownership of the business through an initial public offering of stock. Several factors determine the stock's value after that stock is available to the general public. The day-to-day price is a weak indicator of the stock's value, whereas prospects for the firm's future financial health, the performance record of its management, and prospects for competing in the future are considerations that determine the stock's value. Market capitalization, the current stock price multiplied by the number of shares outstanding, is a widely used measure of company size and overall value. A public corporation's continued growth is accompanied by the need for more capital that can be met through two sources: debt financing or equity financing. Borrowing via long-term loans and the issuance of corporate bonds can provide a large supply of funds but also imposes binding obligations on the firm. Likewise, funds can be raised by issuing additional common stock or by increasing retained earnings, but doing so means smaller dividends for shareholders.

Regulating Securities Markets

Learning Objective 17-7

Explain how securities markets are regulated.

The U.S. government, along with various state agencies, plays a key role in monitoring and regulating the securities industry. Businesses cannot exist in the United States without the public's trust and the public's willingness to participate in business ownership and everyday transactions with companies. Regulation of the U.S. securities markets plays a vital role in maintaining the public's trust in fair and open business ownership.

The Securities and Exchange Commission

The U.S. SEC is the regulation and enforcement agency that oversees the markets' activities, including the ways securities are issued. The SEC was created in 1934 to prevent numerous abuses and questionable practices that contributed to the stock market crash of 1929. The SEC regulates the public offering of new securities by requiring that all companies file a prospectus before proposed offerings commence. To protect investors from fraudulent issues, a **prospectus** contains pertinent information about both the offered security and the issuing company. False statements in a prospectus are subject to criminal penalties.

Prospectus *registration statement filed with the SEC containing information for prospective investors about a security to be offered and the issuing company*

Insider Trading *illegal practice of using special knowledge about a firm for profit or gain*

The SEC also enforces laws against **insider trading**, the use of special knowledge about a firm for profit or gain. Suppose, for example, that you work for a pharmaceutical company that is developing a major new drug that, if approved for use, will lead to the stock in your company doubling or even tripling in value. You have just seen test results that prove the value of the drug and know that it will now be approved for general use in the next 6 months. You could tell your friends and family members to buy your company's stock now so they can make large sums of money after the drug is introduced and the stock value increases. Doing so, however, would be against the law. In general, it is illegal for an employee of a firm to tell others about an anticipated event that may affect the value of that firm's stock, such as an impending acquisition or a merger, before news of that event is made public. Those in possession of such insider knowledge would have an unfair advantage over other investors.

Regulations Against Insider Trading

In March 2011, the U.S. Attorney began a criminal trial in New York against Raj Rajaratnam, founder of Galleon Group, on charges that the billionaire fund manager profited from illegal stock tips with a network of financial insiders. Reports indicate the accused gained profits of up to $60 million by using illicit information, confidential company information not available to the public, revealing that stock prices of various companies would be increasing or falling. In conjunction with his arrest in 2009, charges were leveled against 26 others in the case—executives and securities traders—19 of whom pleaded guilty. In May 2011, Rajaratnam was convicted on 14 charges and faced possible maximum prison sentences totaling up to 205 years. He was finally sentenced to serve 11 years in prison, the longest ever for an insider-trading violation. In addition to the criminal trial, he faced civil charges brought by the SEC. As a U.S. Attorney stated some years previously, "Insider trading is a crime. Corporate executives are prohibited from enriching themselves while the public remains in the dark about the true financial condition of their companies."[26] In a more recent but much smaller case, a former tax partner at KPMG who worked on upcoming mergers and acquisitions was accused of passing information about those mergers and acquisitions to his stock broker and friends. In 2019, he agreed to pay a penalty of $125,000 but neither admitted nor denied the charges.[27]

The SEC offers a reward to any person who provides information leading to a civil penalty for illegal insider trading. The courts can render a penalty of up to three times the illegal profit that was gained, and the reward can be between 10 and 30 percent of that penalty.

ZUMA Press, Inc./Alamy Stock Photo

Raj Rajaratnam, founder of the Galleon Group, was sentenced to 11 years in federal prison after being convicted for insider trading.

Along with the SEC's enforcement efforts, the stock exchanges and securities firms have adopted self-regulation by participating with the Financial Industry Regulatory Authority (FINRA) in detecting and stopping insider action and violations of other industry regulations. Established in 2003, FINRA's mission is to protect U.S. investors by overseeing the nation's brokerage firms and securities representatives. The major U.S. stock markets are under a contract that allows FINRA to regulate those markets by writing rules, examining securities firms, enforcing the rules, and enforcing federal securities laws as well.

summary of learning objectives

LEARNING OBJECTIVE 17-1

Explain the concept of the time value of money and the principle of compound growth and discuss the characteristics of common stock.

The time value of money, perhaps the single most important concept in business finance, recognizes the basic fact that, when it's invested over time, money grows by earning interest or yielding some other form of return. Time value stems from the principle of *compound growth*—the cumulative growth from interest paid to the investor over given time periods. With each additional time period, the investment grows as interest payments accumulate and earn more interest, thus multiplying the earning capacity of the investment.

The "Rule of 72" is a practical example that illustrates the concept of the time value of money. The rule shows the number of years required for an initial investment to double in value, depending on the interest rate received in return for the investment. The rule demonstrates that higher rates of return (interest) result in fewer years required to double the original investment.

A share of *common stock* is the most basic form of ownership in a company. Individuals and organizations purchase a firm's common stock in the hope that it will increase in value and provide dividend income. Each common share has a vote on major issues that are brought before the shareholders. A stock's real value is its *market value*—the current price of a share in the stock market—reflecting the amount buyers are willing to pay for a share of the company's stock. Common stocks are among the riskiest of all investments because uncertainties about the stock market can quickly change the stock's value. *Blue-chip stocks* are issued by the strongest and most well established, financially sound, and respected firms. They have historically provided investors steady income through consistent dividend payouts.

LEARNING OBJECTIVE 17-2

Identify reasons for investing and the investment opportunities offered by mutual funds and exchange-traded funds.

Mutual funds are attractive investments because different funds are designed to appeal to different financial motives and goals of investors. Three of the most common alternative objectives for investing in mutual funds are stability and safety, conservative capital growth, and aggressive growth. Funds stressing stability and safety seek only modest growth while preserving the fund holders' capital and reliably paying modest current income. Conservative capital growth funds stress preservation of capital and current income but also seek some capital appreciation. Aggressive growth funds seek maximum long-term capital growth.

Unfortunately, many mutual funds do not perform as well as the average return of the overall stock market as a result of costly management expense and underperforming stocks. Index mutual funds, however, closely match the performance of a particular market. An *exchange-traded fund (ETF)*, as with an index mutual fund, is a bundle of stocks (or bonds) that are an index that tracks the overall movement of a market. However, ETFs offer three areas of advantage over mutual funds: They can be traded throughout the day like a stock (whereas a mutual fund cannot be traded like a stock), they have low operating expenses, and they require low initial investments resulting in ease of entry for investors getting started without much money. Because they are traded on stock exchanges (hence, "exchange traded"), ETFs can be bought and sold—priced continuously—any time throughout the day. Mutual fund shares, in contrast, are priced once daily, at the end of the day.

LEARNING OBJECTIVE 17-3

Describe the role of securities markets and identify the major stock exchanges and stock markets.

The markets in which stocks and bonds are sold are called *securities markets*. By facilitating the buying and selling of securities, the securities markets provide the capital that companies rely on for survival. In *primary securities markets*, new stocks and bonds are bought and sold by firms and governments. Sometimes, new securities are sold to single buyers or small groups of buyers. These private placements are desirable because they allow issuers to keep their business plans confidential. Firms issuing new securities must get approval from the SEC. Issuing firms also usually rely on investment banking services to issue and resell new securities. Investment banks provide several important services. (1) They advise companies on the timing and financial terms of the new issue. (2) The investment bank buys and assumes liability for the new securities, a process referred to as *underwriting*. (3) Investment banks create distribution networks for moving new securities through groups of other financial institutions into the hands of individual investors. In contrast with new securities issues, *existing* stocks and bonds are sold in the much larger *secondary securities market*, consisting largely of *stock exchanges*. A stock exchange is an organization of individuals coordinated to provide an institutional auction setting in which stocks can be bought and sold. Major stock exchanges include the New York Stock Exchange, the NASDAQ market in the United States, and NYSE Euronext, along with various other foreign exchanges such as the London Stock Exchange and the Tokyo Exchange, and online trading with other stock exchanges around the globe.

In 1998, the SEC authorized the creation of *electronic communication networks (ECNs)*, electronic trading systems that bring buyers and sellers together outside traditional stock exchanges by automatically matching buy and sell orders at specified prices. ECNs gained rapid popularity because the trading procedures are fast and efficient, often lowering transaction costs per share to mere pennies. They also allow after-hours trading (after traditional markets have closed for the day) and protect traders' anonymity.

Stock brokers are financial services professionals who earn commissions by executing buy and sell orders for outside customers. As with many other products, brokerage assistance can be purchased at either discount or full-service prices. Discount brokers, such as E*TRADE and Scottrade, offer well-informed individual investors who know what they want to buy or sell a fast, low-cost way to participate in the market. Full-service brokers, such as Merrill Lynch Wealth Management, offer clients consulting advice in personal financial planning, estate planning, and tax strategies, along with a wider range of investment products.

Although not indicative of the status of individual securities, *market indexes*, such as the Dow Jones Industrial Average and S&P 500, provide useful summaries of overall price trends, both in specific industries and in the stock market as a whole. Market indexes, for example, reveal *bull* and *bear market* trends. *Bull markets* are periods of rising stock prices, generally lasting 12 months or longer; investors are motivated to buy, confident they will realize capital gains. Periods of falling stock prices, usually 20 percent off peak prices, are called *bear markets*; investors are motivated to sell, anticipating further falling prices.

LEARNING OBJECTIVE 17-4

Describe the risk–return relationship and discuss the use of diversification and asset allocation for investments.

Individual investors have different motivations and personal preferences for safety versus risk. While all investors anticipate receiving future cash flows, some cash flows are more certain than other riskier returns. Investors generally expect to receive higher financial returns for investments having higher uncertainty. They do not expect large returns from secure, stable investments. Each type of investment, then, has a risk–return (risk–reward) relationship. The risk–return relationship is the principle that investors expect to receive higher returns for riskier investments and lower returns for safer investments. Conservative investors who have a low tolerance for risk will seek safer investments with low expected returns. The reverse is true for aggressive investors who prefer taking higher risks with the potential for higher returns.

When evaluating potential investments, investors look at returns from dividends or interest, returns from price appreciation, and total return. The rate of return from dividends paid to shareholders is commonly referred to as the *current dividend* yield. In the case of interest from a loan, the term *interest yield* is used. *Price appreciation* is an increase in the value of an investment over time. *Total* return is the sum of the investment's dividend or interest yields and the *capital gain* from price appreciation.

Diversification and asset allocation are tools for helping investors achieve the desired risk–return balance for an investment portfolio. *Diversification* means buying several different kinds of investments—stocks of different companies, securities of companies in different industries, investments in different countries, combinations of stocks/bonds/real estate/precious metals—to reduce the risk of loss if the value of any one investment should fall. *Asset allocation* is the proportion of overall money invested in each of various investment alternatives so that the overall risks for the portfolio are low, moderate, or high, depending on the investor's objectives and preferences.

LEARNING OBJECTIVE 17-5

Describe the various ways that firms raise capital and identify the pros and cons of each method.

Every company needs cash to function. Firms often begin with the owner's personal savings. As more money is needed, it is obtained from sales revenues, borrowing from banks, cash from private investors, issuing bonds, or selling stock. Money to purchase new equipment often comes in the form of loans from commercial banks. In a *secured loan (asset-backed loan)* the borrower guarantees repayment of the loan by pledging the asset as *collateral* to the lender. The amount of money that is loaned and must be repaid is the *loan principal*. However, borrowers also pay the lender an additional fee, *interest*, for the use of the borrowed funds. The amount of interest owed depends on an *annual percentage rate (APR)* that is agreed on between the lender and borrower. The interest amount is found by multiplying the APR by the loan principal. With an *unsecured loan*, the borrower does not have to put up collateral. In many cases, however, the bank requires the borrower to maintain a *compensating balance*; the borrower must keep a portion of the loan amount on deposit with the bank in a non-interest-bearing account.

Once a business has been successfully launched, it needs additional capital for growth. Outside individuals who provide such capital are called *angel investors*. Angel investors help many firms grow rapidly by providing what is known as *venture capital*, private funds from wealthy individuals or companies that seek investment opportunities in new growth companies. In most cases, the growth firm turns to venture capital sources because they have not yet built enough credit history to get a loan from commercial banks or other lending institutions.

Corporations can raise capital by issuing bonds. A *corporate bond* is a formal pledge (an IOU) obligating the issuer to pay interest periodically and repay the principal at maturity (a preset future date) to the lender. The federal government also issues bonds to finance projects and meet obligations, as do state and local governments (called *municipal bonds*) for financing the building of schools, roads, and sewage disposal systems.

LEARNING OBJECTIVE 17-6

Identify the reasons a company might make an initial public offering of its stock, explain how stock value is determined, and discuss the significance of market capitalization.

The *initial public offering (IPO)*—the first sale of a company's stock to the general public—is a major source of funds for fueling the growth of many firms. IPOs reach far more potential investors, thereby providing access to a larger pool of funds than is available from the owner's personal funds and other private sources. A stock's real value is its market value—the current price of a share in the stock market. Market value reflects the amount that buyers are willing to pay for a share of the company's stock at any given time. However, the valuing of any stock today looks beyond the current price and is based on expectations of the financial returns it will provide to shareholders during the long run. A long-run perspective considers the company's financial health, past history of results and future forecasts, its record for managerial performance, and overall prospects for competing successfully in the coming years. Although supply and demand are a major determiner of a stock's price, another factor is a company's desire that its shares sell within a particular price range, believing it will attract a larger pool of investors. If the stock's market price gets too high, many investors cannot afford to buy shares. A company can restore shares to the desired lower price range by using a *stock split* in which the company gives shareholders an additional stock holding for each share they own. The market price per share falls immediately after the split, but with a larger number of shares, every shareholder's investment value is unchanged.

Market capitalization, the total market value of all the company's outstanding shares, is a widely used measure of corporate size and value. Investors leaning toward risk avoidance typically regard larger market-cap firms as less risky, and firms with small market-caps (small-cap firms) as being particularly risky investments. Thus, the persistent demand for large-cap stocks tends to sustain or increase their market values.

Although debt financing often has strong appeal, *equity financing*, looking inside the company for long-term funding, is sometimes preferable. Equity financing includes either issuing common stock or retaining the firm's earnings. The use of equity financing by means of common stock can be expensive because paying dividends is more expensive than paying bond interest. Interest paid to bondholders is a business expense and therefore a tax deduction for the firm. Payments of cash dividends to shareholders are not tax deductible. *Retained earnings* are net profits retained for the firm's use rather than paid out in dividends to stockholders. If a company uses retained earnings as capital, it will not have to borrow money and pay interest. If a firm has a history of reaping profits by reinvesting retained earnings, it may be attractive to some investors. Retained earnings, however, mean smaller dividends for shareholders. This practice may decrease the demand for—and the price of—the company's stock.

LEARNING OBJECTIVE 17-7

Explain how securities markets are regulated.

The U.S. government, along with various state agencies, plays a key role in monitoring and regulating the securities industry. The U.S. Securities and Exchange Commission (SEC) is the regulation and enforcement agency that oversees the markets' activities. The SEC regulates the public offering of new securities by requiring companies to file *prospectuses* before proposed offerings commence. To protect investors from fraudulent securities issues, the prospectus contains information about the offered security and the issuing company. False statements are subject to criminal penalties.

The SEC also enforces laws against *insider trading*—the use of special knowledge about a firm for profit or gain. An example of illegal insider trading includes an employee of a firm telling others about an anticipated event that may affect the value of that firm's stock, such as an acquisition or a merger, before news of that event is made public. Those in possession of such insider knowledge would have an unfair advantage over other investors. The SEC offers a reward to any person who provides information leading to a civil penalty for illegal insider trading.

Along with the SEC's enforcement, the stock exchanges and securities firms have adopted self-regulation by participating with the Financial Industry Regulatory Authority (FINRA) in detecting and stopping violations of industry regulations. FINRA's mission is to protect U.S. investors by overseeing the nation's brokerage firms and securities representatives. FINRA regulates the U.S. stock markets by writing rules, examining securities firms, enforcing the rules, and enforcing federal securities laws.

key terms

questions & exercises

QUESTIONS FOR REVIEW

17-1. What is the *time value of money*?

17-2. What are the major securities markets and how are they regulated?

17-3. What is the relationship between risk and return on investment, and how would you explain that relationship?

17-4. How is the market value (price) of a stock determined?

17-5. What is the difference between debt financing and equity financing?

QUESTIONS FOR ANALYSIS

17-6. Research several stocks online. You will notice that they continually fluctuate in price. What might be the reason for this? Is a higher-priced stock a better investment than a lower-priced stock? What factors would you consider in purchasing stocks?

17-7. Suppose that you are a business owner and you need new equipment and immediate funds to meet short-term operating expenses. From what sources could you gain the capital you need, and what are some of the characteristics of these sources? Are you limited by your form of doing business, and if so, how?

17-8. Suppose that you are a business owner and you are seeking funds for long-term expansion. From what sources could you gain the capital you need, and what are some of the characteristics of these sources? Are you limited by your form of doing business, and if so, how? How do these kinds of funding sources differ from funding sources for new equipment and short-term operating expenses?

APPLICATION EXERCISES

17-9. Research several mutual funds. What are the investment goals of each fund? What do they invest in? How are they similar, and how are they different? Which ones would you invest in, if any, and why?

17-10. Many venture capitalists structure the initial investment in a company using Series A Preferred Stock. What is that, and what are the attributes of such an investment structure that make it useful? Could you, as an individual, buy Series A Preferred Stock? Why or why not?

building a business: continuing team exercise

ASSIGNMENT

Meet with your team members to consider your new business venture and how it relates to the finance topics in this chapter. Develop specific responses to the following:

17-11. What role will debt financing play in your business's financial plan? What types of debt financing will you use? Why?

17-12. As your business grows, will you consider bringing in angel investors or venture capital? Why or why not? How would you structure such a transaction?

17-13. Would you consider selling stock to the general public? What advantages would a public sale of stock bring? Are there any downsides to this decision?

17-14. If you decide to sell stock through an initial public offering, what factors will be most important in the valuation of your stock?

17-15. How will the financing of your business change over time?

team exercise

MARKET UPS AND DOWNS

Background Information

Investing in stocks requires an understanding of the various factors that affect stock prices. These factors may be intrinsic to the company itself or part of the external environment.

- Internal factors relate to the company itself, such as an announcement of poor or favorable earnings, earnings that are more or less than expected, major layoffs, labor problems, new products, management issues, and mergers.
- External factors relate to world or national events, such as wars, recessions, weather conditions that affect sales, the Fed's adjustment of interest rates, and employment figures that are higher or lower than expected.

By analyzing these factors, you will often learn a lot about why a stock did well or why it did poorly. Being aware of these influences will help you anticipate future stock movements.

QUESTIONS FOR ANALYSIS

17-16. Choose a company with publicly traded stock, such as IBM, JPMorgan Chase, AT&T, Amazon.com, United Healthcare, and Apple. Research the stock price for the past 5 or 10 years, at least. What has been the overall trend?

17-17. If you had invested $50,000 in your selected company 10 years ago, how many shares would you have purchased? What would your investment be worth today?

17-18. Identify dates associated with sharp peaks or valleys in the stock price. Use a search engine or your library's online databases to search for articles that might discuss internal or external factors that explain the change in stock price. Write a brief summary explaining why the stock increased or decreased in price during the periods that you have identified.

17-19. Based on your research, what internal and external factors will have the most significant impact on the price of your selected company's stock in the future?

exercising your ethics

ARE YOU ENDOWED WITH GOOD JUDGMENT?

The Situation

Youth Dreams Charities (YDC) is a not-for-profit, 501(c)(3) organization that assists low-income families in gaining access to educational opportunities. Governance and policymaking reside with a board of directors—10 part-time, community-minded volunteers who are entrusted with carrying out YDC's mission—but daily operating decisions are entrusted to a full-time professional manager (the executive officer).

Tuition comes from annual fund-raising activities (a white-tie dance and a seafood carnival) and from financial returns from YDC's $2.1 million endowment, amassed from charitable donations during the past 12 years. For the current year, 23 students received tuition totaling $92,000 paid by YDC. The board's goal is to raise the endowment to $4 million in five years, in the hope of increasing the amount of scholarships that the organization can provide.

The Dilemma

Based on the finance committee's suggestions, the board is considering a change in YDC's investment policies. The current conservative approach invests the endowment in bonds and public utility stocks, which have consistently yielded a 5 percent annual return. This practice has allowed the endowment to grow modestly (less than 1 percent per year), with the remaining investment proceeds (4 percent) flowing out for tuition. The proposed plan is to move the organization's investment into stocks or mutual funds with a higher rate of return. If the organization is able to generate at least 17.5 percent on its investment over the next five years, as well as maintain the current level of financial assistance, the endowment will reach its $4 million goal. Due to a vacancy on the board, there are an even number of board members and they are evenly split, philosophically, between the risk averse and the proponents of faster growth. You have been asked to advise the executive director and the board on this issue at their next meeting.

QUESTIONS TO ADDRESS

17-20. Why might a conservative versus risky choice be different at a not-for-profit organization than at a for-profit organization?

17-21. What are the ethical issues in this situation?

17-22. What options/alternatives/actions would you recommend to the board?

cases

FIRE ON THE GROUND

Continued from page 555

At the beginning of this chapter, you read about Fogo de Chão, how it changed hands multiple times, and how the restaurant chain grew from a single location in Brazil to an international operation. Using the information presented in this chapter, you should be able to answer the following questions:

17-23. When the Coser and Ongaratto brothers started Fogo de Chão, what do you suppose were their primary sources of financing?

17-24. After the Coser brothers acquired the Ongaratto brothers' shares of the company, they brought in GP Investments, a Brazilian venture capital firm. What are the advantages and disadvantages of using venture capital to build a business venture?

17-25. After the sale of Fogo de Chão to Thomas H. Lee Partners, the board and management team decided to issue an IPO of common stock. What were the goals of the IPO?

17-26. What are the benefits of an IPO as a source of financing? What other options did the company have?

17-27. Would you have considered investing in Fogo de Chão in June 2015 when it went public? Why or why not?

17-28. If an investor had bought $1,000,000 of stock during the IPO, what would that investment have been worth when Rhone bought the company for $15.75 per share?

TIME TO GOGO?

The roots of Gogo Inflight Internet services go back to 1991, when the company, then called Aircell, developed technology for in-flight phone services. In 2006, the company made a major change in strategy when it secured a 10-year license through the Federal Communications Commission for in-flight Internet services.

Though Gogo offered airline passengers in-flight Internet options, the planes using air-to-ground technology still experienced significant lags and were unable to support the streaming of movies and other data-heavy applications. In 2016, Gogo announced the installation of 2Ku in an Aeromexico Boeing 737-800. Gogo's newest technology dramatically increased speed and coverage, enabling not only streaming but also "gate-to-gate" coverage, allowing passengers to maintain seamless Internet coverage in airports and within connecting flights. As of 2019, 2Ku had been installed in over 1300 aircraft belonging to 17 different airlines.

After raising $187 million in a June 2013 IPO, underwritten by Wall Street heavy hitters such as Morgan Stanley, JPMorgan, and UBS, Gogo hit the market at $17 per share. The price of the stock fell quickly over the following months, bottoming out at just over $10. Though Gogo saw a surge in sales with the expansion of its 2Ku network, it saw sales decline in a critical period when even the most robust travel-related industries are experiencing major contraction. At the end of 2019, Gogo was already running short of cash, having used up the proceeds from its 2013 public offering to invest in the 2Ku initiative and further endangering its already precarious market position. The stock continued to experience a rocky journey and was hammered by the enormous impact of the 2020 COVID-19 pandemic on the travel industry. In mid-2020, its shares were trading at an anemic $2.21, but aided by a $400 million cash purchase by Intelsat in December 2020, Gogo Inflight shares were trading at almost $18 by mid-2023.

QUESTIONS FOR DISCUSSION

17-29. Given the risk, what would motivate an investor to purchase stock in Gogo?

17-30. Why would Gogo sell stock rather than taking on additional debt financing? Do you think this was a good decision?

17-31. What role did underwriters, such as Morgan Stanley, JPMorgan, and UBS, play in the Gogo IPO?

17-32. Using a web source, such as Yahoo! Finance or www.nasdaq.com, obtain the current price of Gogo stock. What has happened to the price of the stock over the past six months? What about the past two years? What do you predict will happen in the future, and why?

17-33. Would you invest in Gogo right now? Why or why not?

endnotes

[1] Fogo de Chão—US, "Fogo de Chao: Global Development," March 20, 2022, https://fogodechao.com/global-development/.

[2] Macrotrends, "S&P 500 Historical Annual Returns," June 1, 2023, https://www.macrotrends.net/2526/sp-500-historical-annual-returns.

[3] https://www.reuters.com/business/aerospace-defense/us-senator-seeks-full-accounting-southwest-airlines-meltdown-refunds-2023-02-16/

[4] "Advantages and Disadvantages of Mutual Funds," accessed June 18, 2020, https://finance.zacks.com/advantages-disadvantages-stock-mutual-funds-4052.html; http://www.fool.com; "Who Pays for Cap and Trade?" *Wall Street Journal*, March 9, 2009, http://online.wsj.com/article/SB123655590609066021.html.

[5] "Here's Why Investors Are Pouring Trillions into Exchange-Traded Funds," May 29, 2020, https://www.cnbc.com/2020/05/29/why-investors-are-pouring-trillions-into-exchange-traded-funds.html; Andrea Coombes, "Calculating the Costs of an ETF," *Wall Street Journal*, October 23, 2012, http://online.wsj.com/article/SB10000872396390444024204578044293008576204.html.

[6] Andrew Bary, "Embracing ETFs," *Barron's*, November 15, 2010, 29–34.

[7] Bary, "Embracing ETFs."

[8] Kiva, "Kiva US 2022 Highlights: Advancing Kiva's Mission and Improving the US Borrower Experience," accessed July 23, 2023, https://www.kiva.org/blog/kiva-us-2022-highlights-advancing-kivas-mission-and-improving-the-us-borrower-experience.

[9] "About Microfinancing Partners in Africa." Microfinancing Partners in Africa," May 10, 2023. https://microfinancingafrica.org/about/.

[10] UPI.com, "U.S. Investment Banking Era Ends," September 22, 2008, http://www.upi.com/Business_News/2008/09/22/US-Investment-banking-era-ends/UPI-96221222086983/.

[11] New York Stock Exchange, accessed June 1, 2023, http://www.nyse.com.

[12] "The State of Qatar Launches 'Qatar Exchange' as It Signs Today Formal Terms of Strategic Partnership with NYSE Euronext," NYSE News Release, June 19, 2009, http://www.nyse.com/press/1245406656784.html.

[13] InvestingAnswers, "Electronic Communication Network (ECN)," accessed May 5, 2020, http://www.investinganswers.com/financial-dictionary/stock-market/electronic-communication-network-ecn-757.

[14] Rasmussen Reports, "Just 25% Recognize That Most Americans Are Investors," February 11, 2011, http://www.rasmussenreports.com/public_content/business/general_business/february_2011/just_25_recognize_that_most_americans_are_investors.

[15] Steven Norwitz, ed., "A Bear Market of Historic Proportions," *T. Rowe Price Report*, Spring 2009, 1.

[16] Guadalupe Gonzalez, "This Founder's Launch Story Was a Nightmare. Here's How She Persevered and Pulled Off Her Dream," *Inc.*, May 9, 2019, https://www.inc.com/guadalupe-gonzalez/little-passports-amy-norman-pregnancy-divorce-startup.html.

[17] Barron's, "Future Returns: Angel Investing in Women-Led Companies," February 21, 2023, https://www.barrons.com/articles/future-returns-angel-investing-in-women-led-companies-fc19a355.

[18] Zippia, "Little Passports Revenue," April 6, 2023, https://www.zippia.com/little-passports-careers-1396147/revenue/#investors.

[19] Carl R. Beidleman, *The Handbook of International Investing* (Chicago: Probus Pub. Co., 1987), 133.

[20] David Welch, "Old GM Bondholders Getting Shares in New General Motors May Depress Price," Bloomberg.com, April 6, 2011, http://www.bloomberg.com/news/2011-04-06/old-gm-bondholders-getting-shares-in-new-general-motors-may-depress-price.html.

[21] Ajay Kumar, "Can We Trust Moody's, Fitch, Standard & Poor?" CommodityOnline, accessed July 22, 2009, http://www.commodityonline.com/printnews.php?news_id=15888; David Evans and Caroline Salas, "Flawed Credit Ratings Reap Profits as Regulators Fail (Update 1)," Bloomberg.com, April 29, 2009, http://www.bloomberg.com/apps/news?pid=20670001&sid=au4oIx.judz4; Leslie Wayne, "Calpers Sues Over Ratings of Securities," *New York Times*, July 15, 2009, http://www.nytimes.com/2009/07/15/business/15calpers.html; David Segal, "Ohio Sues Rating Firms for Losses in Funds," *New York Times*, November 20, 2009, http://www.nytimes.com/2009/11/21/business/21ratings.html; Lynn Hume, "Connecticut AG Sues All Three Rating Agencies," *The Bond Buyer*, July 31, 2008, http://www.bondbuyer.com/issues/117_145/-292250-1.html.

[22] U.S. Securities and Exchange Commission, "Mortgage-Backed Securities and Collateralized Mortgage Obligations," accessed July 31, 2023, http://www.sec.gov/answers/mortgagesecurities.htm; Bankrate.com, "What Are Mortgage-Backed Securities?," June 6, 2023, https://www.bankrate.com/mortgages/what-are-mortgage-backed-securities/.

[23] Scott Cohn, "Founders Get Blamed for Start-Up Scandals, but Where Were the Investors?" CNBC, January 14, 2022, https://www.cnbc.com/2022/01/14/founders-get-blamed-for-start-up-scandals-but-where-were-investors.html

[24] https://papers.ssrn.com/sol3/papers.cfm?abstract_id=3801131

[25] Joy Wiltermuth, "Rising Defaults in High-Yield Bonds Puts This Year on Track for Postcrisis Record, Warns Goldman Sachs," MarketWatch, August 18, 2019, https://www.marketwatch.com/story/rising-defaults-in-high-yield-bonds-puts-this-year-on-track-for-post-2008-crisis-record-warns-goldman-sachs-2019-08-17, accessed May 8, 2020.

[26] "Rajaratnam Insider Trading Trial Begins," *Huffington Post*, March 9, 2011, http://www.huffingtonpost.com/2011/03/09/rajaratnam-trial_n_833326.html; U.S. Department of Justice, "Joseph P. Nacchio Indicted by Federal Grand Jury: Former Chief Executive Officer of Qwest Communications Charged with Insider Trading, Selling Over $100 Million Stock," December 20, 2005, http://lawprofessors.typepad.com/whitecollarcrime_blog/files/nacchio_indictment.pdf.

[27] Jaclyn Jaeger, "Ex-KPMG Partner to Pay $125K in Insider Trading Case," Compliance Week, August 9, 2019, https://www.complianceweek.com/regulatory-enforcement/ex-kpmg-partner-to-pay-125k-in-insider-trading-case/27544.article.

[28] Nathaniel Meyersohn, "3 Times Howard Schultz Saved Starbucks," *CNNMoney*, June 5, 2018, https://money.cnn.com/2018/06/05/news/companies/starbucks-howard-schultz-coffee/index.html.

[29] Starbucks, "Starbucks Reports Q4 and Full Year Fiscal 2017 Results." Starbucks Corporation, accessed July 20, 2023, https://investor.starbucks.com/press-releases/financial-releases/press-release-details/2017/Starbucks-Reports-Q4-and-Full-Year-Fiscal-2017-Results/default.aspx.

[30] Adi Ignatius, "Starbucks CEO Kevin Johnson on Work, Joy, and, Yes, Coffee," *Harvard Business Review*, September 27, 2019, https://hbr.org/2019/09/starbucks-ceo-kevin-johnson-on-work-joy-and-yes-coffee.

[31] Starbucks, "Starbucks Strengthens Its Support for the U.S. Military Community," press release, July 31, 2023, https://www.businesswire.com/news/home/20230731567034/en/Starbucks-Strengthens-its-Support-for-the-U.S.-Military-Community/.

[32] Kaitlin Lyle, "Danbury Starbucks Becomes Third in CT to Vote to Unionize," *NewsTimes*, July 8, 2023, https://www.newstimes.com/news/article/danbury-ct-starbucks-union-vote-18189748.php#photo-24011395.

[33] Grace Dean, "Howard Schultz to Return as Interim Starbucks CEO After Kevin Johnson Announces Retirement," *Business Insider*, March 16, 2022, https://www.businessinsider.com/starbucks-ceo-kevin-johnson-retire-howard-schultz-interim-ceo-coffee-2022-3.

[34] Starbucks, "Laxman Narasimhan Assumes Role of Starbucks Chief Executive Officer," Starbucks Stories & News, March 20, 2023, https://stories.starbucks.com/press/2023/laxman-narasimhan-assumes-role-of-starbucks-chief-executive-officer/.

part 6

Integrative Learning Portfolio

crafting a business plan

Goal of the Exercise

In this final part of the business plan project, you'll consider how you'll finance your business as well as create an executive summary for your plan.

Exercise Background: Part 6 of the Business Plan

In the previous part of the business plan, you discussed the costs of doing business as well as how much revenue you expect to earn in one year. It's now time to think about how to finance the business. To get a "great idea" off the ground requires money. But how will you get these funds?

You'll then conclude this project by creating an *executive summary*. The purpose of the executive summary is to give the reader a quick snapshot of your proposed business. Although this exercise comes at the end of the project, once you're done writing it, you'll end up placing the executive summary at the *beginning* of your completed business plan.

Your Assignment

STEP 1

Open the saved *Business Plan* file you began working on in Parts 1 to 5.

STEP 2

For the purposes of this assignment, you will answer the following questions, shown in "Part 6: Financial Issues":

P6-1. How much money will you need to get your business started?

Hint: Refer back to Part 5 of the plan, where you analyzed the costs involved in running your business. Approximately how much will you need to get your business started?

P6-2. How will you finance your business? For example, will you seek out a bank loan? Borrow from friends? Sell stocks or bonds initially or as your business grows?

Hint: Refer to Chapter 17 for information on securities, such as stocks and bonds. Refer also to Appendix I: Financial Risk and Risk Management and Chapter 3 for more information on sources of short-term and long-term funds.

P6-3. Now, create an executive summary for your business plan. The executive summary should be brief—no more than two pages long—and should cover the following points:

- The name of your business
- Where your business will be located
- The mission of your business
- The product or service you are selling
- Who your ideal customers are
- How your product or business will stand out from the crowd
- Who the owners of the business are and what experience they have
- An overview of the future prospects for your business and industry

Hint: At this point, you've already answered all of these questions, so what you need to do here is put the ideas together into a "snapshot" format. The executive summary is really a sales pitch—it's the investor's first impression of your idea. Therefore, as with all parts of the plan, write in a clear and professional way.

Congratulations on completing the business plan project!

case PART 6 STARBUCKS, 2017–2023

"To establish Starbucks as the premier purveyor of the finest coffee in the world while maintaining our uncompromising principles as we grow."

– Starbucks mission circa 1991

Steve Heap/Shutterstock

From the very beginning, Howard Schultz established a vision and culture for the company based on his experience in Milan. He embodied the belief that people were looking for connection and, therefore, a place to connect and that Starbucks could be that place. He also placed a high value on the employee experience and insisted that unionization was not necessary if you treated the employees exceptionally well. However, by the time Schultz became CEO for the second time in 2008, his focus had shifted to replication and continuous growth rather than putting people before profits. This was something that Jim Donald, who had been CEO in 2007, had identified as the reason for a "watering down of the Starbucks experience" and a "commoditization of the brand." Indeed, it did seem like there was no immediate limit to the number of stores since the company had barely tapped into China at that point and had yet to make progress in India, two of the largest markets in the world.

As Starbucks, the unstoppable leviathan, cut through the sea of emerging markets and focused on growth, it left its developed customer base longing for the "third place" (i.e., not home or work). Meanwhile, Starbucks sold CDs and food and stopped roasting beans in the stores. Its employees were spread thin, and new hires trained one another. All of this created room in the industry for locally owned shops that often resembled the Starbucks in its early days, with a full view of the baristas who would know the customers' names and favorite drinks, a few cozy tables, the aroma of roasting coffee, and the allure of sitting alone and sipping a drink while still being in a small cohort of other aficionados.

As Schultz developed his battle plan to bring Starbucks back, he unveiled a new mission statement: "To nurture and inspire the human spirit—one person, one cup, one neighborhood at a time." In a 2007 memo to the Starbucks executive team, Schultz said, "Some people even call our stores sterile, cookie cutter, no longer reflecting the passion our partners feel about our coffee."[28]

Schultz shuttered underperforming stores and reinstalled his former leadership team. The company shut down all stores for an afternoon to retrain employees to reestablish a "third place" experience. It discontinued breakfast sandwiches so the stores would smell more like coffee. Schultz's driving force during that time was to get back to the mission.

Schultz stayed on to guide the company through technological changes, loyalty programs, and the rise of mobile payments, and by the time Kevin Johnson took over as CEO on April 3, 2017, Starbucks was a thriving organization again, and the numbers looked good. For the fiscal year 2017 (the 52-week period ended October 1, 2017), the company reported a 3 percent increase in same-store sales in the United States and 7 percent in China. Overall revenues grew 5 percent to $22.4 billion with operating income of $4.1 billion. The company opened 603 net new stores globally during the fiscal year, bringing the total store count to 27,339 across 75 countries. Membership in Starbucks Rewards grew 11 percent year-over-year to 13.3 million active members in the United States, with member spending representing 36 percent of U.S. company-operated sales, and Mobile Order and Pay reached 10 percent of transactions in U.S. company-operated stores. The board of directors declared a cash dividend of $0.30 per share on the 1.4 billion shares outstanding, and the price of the stock was hovering around $54 compared to a split-adjusted IPO price of $0.34, an increase of almost 16,000 percent. In addition, the company announced a new commitment to returning $15 billion to shareholders over the next three years through dividends and share repurchases.[29]

Johnson inherited Schultz's legacy but brought a different philosophy to running the company. In a 2019 interview, he reflected on the differences between his analytical leadership style and Schultz's more informal style of leading from the gut: "I'm probably more analytical, and I acknowledge it. I don't have three and a half decades of institutional knowledge the way Howard has, and I don't try to pretend that I do. I leverage data to help inform decisions, but I also believe in a distributed leadership model...with clear accountability, leveraging analytics and data to help inform the decisions we make."[30]

Since 1988, Starbucks has offered health care to all full-time and part-time employees. The company offers a stock plan, free college tuition, and paid parental and sick leave for its workers. It pays above minimum wage and achieved race and gender pay equity in early 2018. Starbucks has also taken proactive stances on sensitive issues, including immigration, same-sex marriage, guns, and racism. It is also a leading employer of military veterans and their families through the Starbucks Armed Forces Network and Military Family Stores.[31]

Gene J. Puskar/AP Images

Danbury Starbucks becomes third in CT to vote to unionize (newstimes.com)

Still, there were underlying issues that indicated that the company was not yet fulfilling its stated values of nurturing and inspiring the human spirit. For instance, although Schultz had been anti-union from the very beginning and believed that sentiment was baked into the DNA of the company, in 2021, the Buffalo, New York, location paved the way for unionization of the baristas. In 2023, staff at the Starbucks shop in Danbury's Berkshire Shopping Center in Connecticut voted 18–1 to form a union, joining more than 300 stores that had unionized by early 2023.[32]

On March 16, 2022, Kevin Johnson announced his retirement, and on April 4, Howard Schultz took over once again as interim CEO, saying, "Although I did not plan to return to Starbucks [as CEO for the third time], I know the company must transform once again to meet a new and exciting future where all of our stakeholders mutually flourish."[33]

Schultz's third stint was a short one. In March 2023, he turned the helm over to Laxman Narasimhan. In the months leading up to his official start date, the new CEO had immersed himself in the culture of the company, traveling and learning the ropes from the ground up.

In a press release, Narasimhan said, "I am humbled to officially step into my role as Starbucks chief executive officer, leading our incredible team of more than 450,000 green apron partners around the world. The foundation Howard has laid—building from scratch an iconic global brand fueled by a lasting passion to uplift humanity—is truly remarkable, and I am honored to have the opportunity to build on this deep heritage. As a human connection business, we have limitless possibilities to deliver for our partners, our customers, our investors, and our communities through every cup and every connection. I am excited to work alongside our partners worldwide to unlock the limitless future of Starbucks."[34]

With the change in leadership, the company announced a new guiding mission: "With every cup, with every conversation, with every community—we nurture the limitless possibilities of human connection."

P6-1. Compare and contrast Schultz's leadership style with Johnson's. Which do you think is better for a mature organization like Starbucks? Which do you think would be better for a start-up company, and why?

P6-2. Do some research on your own and prepare a brief memo on why you do or do not see Starbucks as a socially responsible corporation.

P6-3. Do you think opening more stores in more countries is mission-driven? Is the company's actual mission different than the one presented to the public? Do you think it's appropriate for a company to include financial profits, growth objectives, and even profits and the role of shareholders in the mission? Craft a mission statement based on your objective external opinion of the business.

P6-4. Research Starbucks on the web and determine the current share price and the price/earnings ratio. How many shares are outstanding, and what is the market capitalization (share price times number of shares outstanding)?

P6-5. Many companies borrow money to fund their ventures. Just before Howard Schultz bought Starbucks from the three original founders, the company had gone seriously into debt to purchase Peet's coffee and was struggling financially. Howard hit the streets and talked to every mover and shaker he could get an audience with so that he could raise enough capital to fund the purchase. Which do you think is the better options, debt or equity financing, and why?

P6-6. Starbucks has posted an annual return without regard to dividends (which is significant) of 22 percent. If risk and return are correlated, why do you think the return on investment (ROI) is so robust?

finding your path

CAREERS IN BUSINESS

Finance is a very popular major in most business programs. It does, however, require especially strong technical and quantitative abilities, and this serves as a deterrent for some people. A strong background in economics is also expected. Jobs within the finance field include investment banking, commercial banking, real estate, insurance, and financial planning. Job growth for finance majors is projected to be around 7 percent by 2028, and the average starting salary for finance graduates in 2022 was $64,825. However, there is a large range around this average. For example, finance graduates who are able to secure a position with a top investment company on Wall Street (these positions are generally available only to top graduates from leading schools, by the way) can expect salaries of $95,000 or even higher. In contrast, entry level jobs in the insurance and real estate fields are likely to be somewhat below the average.

MAKING YOURSELF EMPLOYABLE

If you want a career in finance, you can do certain things to make yourself more employable. And regardless of your initial career path, you will likely have times in your career when you consider looking for a new job.

Getting a Job in Finance

If you want to pursue a job in the finance field, the obvious starting point is your major. Most business schools offer majors in finance. Some also offer more specialized majors (or minors) in related fields such as real estate and/or insurance. Moreover, in some universities the economics department resides within the business school, while in others economics is in a different college. Any of these options—finance, real estate, insurance, or economics—can serve as a foundation for a career in the field of finance.

One important path to enhancing your employability in the field of finance is through internships. Perhaps even more than for other business fields, internships play a major role in finance. Ideally, you should try to secure more than one internship, say, between your sophomore and junior years and then again between your junior and senior years. Further, it might also be useful to secure these internships in different areas of finance. For a career in banking, for example, internships in both investments and commercial banking can be useful. Similarly, for real estate, internships in commercial and residential real estate might be a good idea. Why? Suppose you are interviewing for your first job and the recruiter asks you, "Why are you interested in investment banking?" You can reply along these lines: "I've always been interested in banking but wasn't sure which path was best for me. So, I did an internship in each area. I enjoyed the commercial banking work but found the investments work to be more interesting, fulfilling, and challenging. And those things are really important to me."

Looking for a New Job

Regardless of your field of study and your first job, it is likely that at some point in your career (and also likely this will happen more than once) you will consider looking for a new job. Here are some reasons why changing jobs may make sense:

1. Your job or industry is becoming obsolete because of changes in technology.
2. The personal costs of your job—long hours, too much travel, excessive stress and pressure—outweigh its benefits.
3. You've been fired, laid off, or furloughed and you suspect a big reason is that you are not well suited for the job.
4. Your financial needs have changed.
5. You feel bored or burned out.
6. You don't fit in.

In contrast, here are some reasons why changing jobs may not make as much sense as you think:

1. You see a friend with a job that seems better than yours but you do not really know all the details.
2. You are considering a new job in which extra money or job security is the only plus.
3. You are considering a new job because a parent, sibling, or close friend works in that field.
4. You hear anecdotal evidence that a certain field is growing but you have not really looked at the evidence.

So now you have assessed your motivation and decide to proceed. A great starting point is to revisit the marketing exercise in the *Finding Your Path* feature at the end of Part 5. Of course, this time you'll have more "features" to add to your "product description"—more experience, more accomplishments, and so forth. As you are doing this, you might also ask yourself this question: "Am I unhappy with my employer, or just my job?" It might well be the case that even if you are bored or tired of your current job, your employer might have more exciting and fulfilling jobs. If this is the case, you could explore the possibility of requesting a transfer or applying for a different job within your current organization.

If you still want to look for a new job or perhaps even change fields, do your homework and make yourself as prepared as possible. And when you get an interview with a potential new employer, know in advance that you will be asked (perhaps more than once), "Why do you want to leave your current job?" Knowing this question is coming, be prepared! And as part of this preparation, know that you should not place all the blame on your current employer. You do not want to come across as a complainer or malcontent. Be honest about issues on both sides.

Finally, do not burn bridges with your current employer. At the appropriate time, inform your employer of your interest in leaving or your intent to do so. Be sure to give plenty of advance notice and continue to fulfill your work responsibilities right up until your last hour on the job. It is increasingly common for people to return to a former employer, so make sure you exit in a respectful and professional manner.

appendix I

Risk Management

In Chapters 3, 9, and 17, as well as other places, we discussed risk from various perspectives. In this appendix, we describe other types of risks that businesses face and discuss some of the ways in which they typically manage them.

Coping with Risk

Businesses constantly face two basic types of **risk**—uncertainty about future events. **Speculative risks**, such as financial investments, involve the possibility of gain or loss. **Pure risks** involve only the possibility of loss or no loss. Designing and distributing a new product, for example, is a speculative risk—the product may fail or it may succeed and earn small or large profits. In contrast, the chance of a warehouse fire is a pure risk.

Risk *uncertainty about future events*

Speculative Risk *risk involving the possibility of gain or loss*

Pure Risk *risk involving only the possibility of loss or no loss*

For a company to survive and prosper, it must manage both types of risk in a cost-effective manner. We can define the process of **risk management** as conserving the firm's earning power and assets by reducing the threat of losses as a result of uncontrollable events. In every company, each manager must be alert for risks to the firm and their impact on profits.

Risk Management *process of conserving the firm's earning power and assets by reducing the threat of losses as a result of uncontrollable events*

The risk-management process usually involves five steps:

Step 1: Identify Risks and Potential Losses Managers analyze a firm's risks to identify potential losses. Unfortunately, though, some risks are simply too unpredictable to account for. The 2020 COVID-19 pandemic provides a vivid example. Even though various indicators have suggested for years that businesses should prepare for a pandemic, few actually did. Further, even though a few businesses thought they were prepared, even most of those firms could not have anticipated exactly how and in what form COVID-19 would affect them. Another example might be potential hurricane damage for a business operating near a coastline.

Step 2: Measure the Frequency and Severity of Losses and Their Impact To measure the frequency and severity of losses, managers must consider both history and current activities. How often can the firm expect the loss to occur? What is the likely size of the loss in dollars? Again, as managers were dealing with the COVID-19 pandemic in 2020, they were also trying to understand how long the effects would last, if the effects would increase or decrease in the future, what changes (if any) the managers would need to apply to their business practices, and so forth. Hurricanes have a greater frequency of occurrence but with varying degrees of impact.

Step 3: Evaluate Alternatives and Choose the Techniques That Will Best Handle the Losses Having identified and measured potential losses, managers are in a better position to decide how to handle them. They generally have four choices:

- A firm opts for **risk avoidance** by declining to enter or by ceasing to participate in a risky activity. In 2020, some businesses were very aggressive in reopening as soon as they were allowed to do so, while others were more cautious. In the days

Risk Avoidance *practice of avoiding risk by declining or ceasing to participate in an activity*

preceding a hurricane, some businesses close quickly and urge their employees to evacuate the area while others remain open for longer times.

Risk Control *practice of minimizing the frequency or severity of losses from risky activities*

- When avoidance is not practical or desirable, firms can practice **risk control**—the use of loss-prevention techniques to minimize the frequency or severity of losses. Some businesses in hurricane-prone areas have strengthened their facilities and reinforced especially vulnerable areas so as to better withstand high winds and water.
- When losses cannot be avoided or controlled, firms must cope with the consequences. When such losses are manageable and predictable, the firm may decide to cover them out of company funds. The firm is said to assume or retain the financial consequences of the loss; hence, the practice is known as **risk retention**.

Risk Retention *practice of covering a firm's losses with its own funds*

Risk Transfer *practice of transferring a firm's risk to another firm*

- When the potential for large risks cannot be avoided or controlled, managers often opt for **risk transfer** to another firm—namely, an insurance company—to protect itself.

Step 4: Implement the Risk-Management Program The means of implementing risk-management decisions depend on both the technique chosen and the activity being managed.

- Risk avoidance for certain activities can be implemented by purchasing those activities from outside providers.
- Risk control might be implemented by training employees and designing new work methods and equipment for on-the-job safety. Hand sanitizers, face masks, social distancing protocols, and other safeguards were implemented by some businesses in 2020.
- For situations in which risk retention is preferred, reserve funds can be set aside from revenues.
- When risk transfer is needed, implementation means selecting an insurance company and buying the appropriate coverage.

Step 5: Monitor Results New types of risks emerge with changes in customers, facilities, employees, and products. Insurance regulations change, and new types of insurance become available. Consequently, managers must continuously monitor a company's risks, reevaluate the methods used for handling them, and revise them as necessary.

Insurance as Risk Management

Insurance Premium *fee paid to an insurance company by a policyholder for insurance coverage*

Insurance Policy *formal agreement to pay the policyholder a specified amount in the event of certain losses*

Deductible *amount of the loss that the insured must absorb before reimbursement is made*

To deal with some risks, both businesses and individuals may choose to purchase insurance. Insurance is purchased by paying **insurance premiums**—payments to an insurance company to buy a policy and keep it active. In return, the insurance company issues an **insurance policy**—a formal agreement to pay the policyholder a specified amount in the event of certain losses. In some cases, the insured party must also pay a **deductible**, an agreed-on amount of the loss that the insured must absorb before reimbursement is made. Buyers find insurance appealing because they are protected against large, potentially devastating losses in return for a relatively small sum of money.

With insurance, individuals and businesses share risks by contributing to a fund from which those who suffer losses are paid. Insurance companies are willing to accept these risks because they make profits by taking in more premiums than they pay out to cover policyholders' losses. Although many policyholders are paying for protection against the same type of loss, by no means will all of them suffer such a loss.

Insurable Versus Uninsurable Risks Like every business, insurance companies must avoid certain risks. Insurers divide potential sources of loss into *insurable risks* and *uninsurable risks*. They issue policies only for insurable risks. Although some exceptions are possible, an insurable risk must meet the following four criteria:

1. *Predictability.* The insurer must be able to use statistical tools to forecast the likelihood of a loss. This forecast also helps insurers determine premiums charged to policyholders.
2. *Casualty.* A loss must result from an *accident*, not from an intentional act by the policyholder. To avoid paying in cases of fraud, insurers may refuse to cover losses when they cannot determine whether policyholders' actions contributed to them.
3. *Unconnectedness.* Potential losses must be random and must occur independently of other losses. No insurer can afford to write insurance when a large percentage of those who are exposed to a particular kind of loss are likely to suffer such a loss. By carefully choosing the risks that it will insure, an insurance company can reduce its chances of a large loss or insolvency.
4. *Verifiability.* Insured losses must be verifiable as to cause, time, place, and amount.

Some insurers have stopped issuing new policies for home insurance in California. This is due to a combination of increased risk from wildfires and the high cost of replacement construction in that state.

Special Forms of Insurance for Business

Businesses have special insurable concerns—*liability*, *property*, *business interruption*, *key person insurance*, and *business continuation agreements*.

LIABILITY INSURANCE *Liability* means responsibility for damages in case of accidental or deliberate harm to individuals or property. **Liability insurance** covers losses resulting from damage to people or property when the insured party is judged liable.

Liability Insurance *insurance covering losses resulting from damage to people or property when the insured party is judged liable*

A business is liable for any injury to an employee when the injury arises from activities related to the occupation. When workers are permanently or temporarily disabled by job-related accidents or disease, employers are required by law to provide **workers' compensation coverage** for medical expenses, loss of wages, and rehabilitation services.

Workers' Compensation Coverage *coverage provided by a firm to employees for medical expenses, loss of wages, and rehabilitation costs resulting from job-related injuries or disease*

PROPERTY INSURANCE A firm purchases **property insurance** to cover injuries to itself resulting from physical damage to or loss of real estate or personal property. Property losses may result from fire, lightning, wind, hail, explosion, theft, vandalism, or other destructive forces.

Property Insurance *insurance covering losses resulting from physical damage to or loss of the insured's real estate or personal property*

BUSINESS INTERRUPTION INSURANCE In some cases, loss to property is minimal in comparison to loss of income. If a firm is forced to close down for an extended time, it will not be able to generate income. During this time, however, certain expenses—such as taxes, insurance premiums, and salaries for key employees and managers—may continue. To cover such losses, a firm may buy **business interruption insurance**. There was considerable debate about business interruption coverage during the COVID-19 pandemic. Most insurers, for instance, argued that their policies either expressly excluded interruptions related to viral contamination or that their coverage applied only to physical damage to business facilities.

Business Interruption Insurance *insurance covering income lost during times when a company is unable to conduct business*

KEY PERSON INSURANCE Many businesses choose to protect themselves against loss of the talents and skills of key employees, as well as the recruitment costs to find a replacement and training expenses once a replacement is hired. **Key person insurance** is designed to offset both lost income and additional expenses.

Key Person Insurance *special form of business insurance designed to offset expenses entailed by the loss of key employees*

BUSINESS CONTINUATION AGREEMENTS Who takes control of a business when a partner or associate dies? Surviving partners are often faced with the possibility of

Business Continuation Agreement *special form of business insurance whereby owners arrange to buy the interests of deceased associates from their heirs*

having to accept an inexperienced heir as a management partner. This contingency can be handled in **business continuation agreements**, whereby owners make plans to buy the ownership interest of a deceased associate from their heirs. The value of the ownership interest is determined when the agreement is made. Special policies can also provide survivors with the funds needed to make the purchase.

appendix II

The Legal Context of Business

In this appendix, we describe the basic tenets of U.S. law and show how these principles work through the court system. We'll also survey a few major areas of business-related law.

The U.S. Legal and Judicial Systems

Laws are the codified rules of behavior enforced by a society. In the United States, Constitutional Law, sometimes referred to as the "law of the land," is the highest form of law and is derived from the U.S. Constitution. Interpretation of this form of law may have to be determined by the Supreme Court. Within this very broad context, most laws fall into three broad categories according to their origins: *common, statutory,* and *regulatory*.

Laws *codified rules of behavior enforced by a society*

Types of Law

Law in the United States originated primarily with English common law. U.S. law includes the U.S. Constitution, state constitutions, federal and state statutes, municipal ordinances, administrative agency rules and regulations, executive orders, and court decisions.

Common Law Court decisions follow *precedents*, or the decisions of previous cases. Following precedent lends stability to the law by basing judicial decisions on cases anchored in similar facts. This principle is the keystone of **common law**—the body of decisions handed down by courts ruling on individual cases.

Common Law *body of decisions handed down by courts ruling on individual cases*

Statutory Law Laws created by constitutions or by federal, state, or local legislative acts constitute **statutory law**. Under the U.S. Constitution, federal statutes take precedence over state and local statutes.

Statutory Law *law created by constitution(s) or by federal, state, or local legislative acts*

Regulatory Law Statutory law and common law have long histories. Relatively new is **regulatory (or administrative) law**—law made by the authority of administrative agencies.

Regulatory (Administrative) Law *law made by the authority of administrative agencies*

Although Congress retains control over the scope of agency action, regulations have the force of statutory law once passed. Government regulatory agencies act as a secondary judicial system, determining whether regulations have been violated and then imposing penalties. Much agency activity consists of setting standards for safety or quality and monitoring the compliance of businesses.

Congress has created numerous agencies in response to pressure to address social issues. In some cases, agencies were established in response to public concern about corporate behavior. The activities of these agencies have sometimes forced U.S. firms to consider the public interest almost as routinely as they consider their own financial performance.

Keeping an Eye on Business Today a host of agencies regulate U.S. business practices. Among the most significant are the following:

- Equal Employment Opportunity Commission (EEOC)
- Environmental Protection Agency (EPA)
- Food and Drug Administration (FDA)
- Federal Trade Commission (FTC)
- Occupational Safety and Health Administration (OSHA)
- Securities and Exchange Commission (SEC)

Deregulation *elimination of rules that restrict business activity*

Trends in Deregulation and Regulation Although government regulation has benefited U.S. business in many ways, it is not without its drawbacks. Managers and business owners complain—with some justification—that government regulations require too much costly paperwork. Many people in both business and government support broader **deregulation**—the elimination of rules that restrict business activity. Deregulation, they argue, is a primary incentive to innovation. Deregulated industries are incentivized to innovate to survive in competitive industries. Those firms that are already conditioned to compete by being more creative will outperform firms that have been protected by regulatory climates in their home countries.

Over time there are swings between deregulation and then back toward regulation, depending on which political party is in control in Washington as well as prevailing public opinion. Many critics blamed the financial crisis and economic recession of 2008 on the uncontrolled actions of major U.S. banks and called for more regulation to help prevent a future recurrence of the same mistakes. President Barack Obama responded by increasing regulation of the banking and financial sector. He also increased regulation related to environmental protection in response to concerns about global warming. During President Donald Trump's administration beginning in 2017, however, many of these regulations were reduced or eliminated altogether. However, after President Joe Biden assumed office, there was a swing back toward more regulation. In general, the Democratic Party tends to prefer more regulation of business while the Republican Party tends to prefer less.

The U.S. Judicial System

Much of the responsibility for law enforcement falls to the courts. Litigation is a significant part of contemporary life, and we have given our courts a voice in a wide range of issues, some touching personal concerns, some ruling on matters of public policy that affect all our lives.

The Court System The U.S. judicial system has three levels—*federal*, *state*, and *local*. Federal courts hear cases on questions of constitutional law, disputes relating to maritime laws, and violations of federal statutes. They also rule on regulatory actions and on such issues as bankruptcy, postal law, and copyright or patent violation. Both the federal and most state systems embody a three-tiered system of *trial*, *appellate*, and *supreme courts*.

Trial Court *general court that hears cases not specifically assigned to another court*

TRIAL COURTS At the lowest level of the federal court system are the **trial courts**, the general courts that hear cases not specifically assigned to another court. Every state has at least one federal trial court, called a *district court*.

Trial courts also include special courts and administrative agencies. Special courts hear specific types of cases, such as cases involving tax evasion, fraud, international disputes, or claims against the U.S. government. Within their areas of jurisdiction, administrative agencies also make judgments much like those of courts.

Courts in each state deal with the same issues as their federal counterparts. However, they may rule only in areas governed by state law. For example, a state special court would hear a case involving state income tax laws. Local courts in each state system also hear cases on municipal ordinances, local traffic violations, and similar issues.

Appellate Courts A losing party in a trial court may disagree with the court ruling. If that party can show grounds for review, the case may go before a federal or state **appellate court**. These courts consider questions of law, such as possible errors of legal interpretation made by lower courts. They do not examine questions of fact, however.

Appellate Court *court that reviews case records of trials whose findings have been appealed*

Supreme Courts Cases still not resolved at the appellate level can be appealed to the appropriate state supreme courts or to the U.S. Supreme Court. If it believes that an appeal is warranted or that the outcome will set an important precedent, the U.S. Supreme Court also hears cases appealed from state supreme courts.

Business Law

Most legal issues confronted by businesses fall into one of six basic areas: *contract, tort, property, agency, commercial*, or *bankruptcy law*. These areas cover a wide range of business activity.

Contract Law

A **contract** is any agreement between two or more parties that is enforceable in court. As such, it must meet six conditions. If all these conditions are met, one party can seek legal recourse from another if the other party breaches, or violates, the terms of the agreement.

Contract *agreement between two or more parties enforceable in court*

1 *Agreement.* Agreement is the serious, definite, and communicated offer and acceptance of the same terms.
2 *Consent.* A contract is not enforceable if any of the parties have been affected by an honest mistake, fraud, or pressure.
3 *Capacity.* To give real consent, both parties must demonstrate legal **capacity** (competence). A person under legal age (usually 18 or 21) cannot enter into a binding contract.
4 *Consideration.* An agreement is binding only if it exchanges **considerations**—items of value. Note that items of value do not necessarily entail money. Contracts need not be rational, nor must they provide the best possible bargain for both sides. They need only include legally sufficient consideration. The terms are met if both parties receive what the contract details.
5 *Legality.* A contract must be for a lawful purpose and must comply with federal, state, and local laws and regulations.
6 *Proper form.* A contract may be written, oral, or implied from conduct. It must be written, however, if it involves the sale of land or goods worth more than $500. It must also be written if the agreement requires more than a year to fulfill. All changes to written contracts must also be in writing.

Capacity *competence required of individual entering into a binding contract*

Consideration *item of value exchanged between parties to create a valid contract*

Breach of Contract

Contract law offers a variety of remedies designed to protect the reasonable expectations of the parties and, in some cases, to compensate them for actions taken to enforce the agreement. As the injured party to a breached contract, any of the following actions might occur:

- You might cancel the contract and refuse to comply with your part of the agreement.
- You might sue for damages up to the amount that you lost as a result of the breach.
- If money cannot repay the damage you suffered, you might demand specific performance, or require the other party to fulfill the original contract.

Tort Law

Tort *civil injury to people, property, or reputation for which compensation must be paid*

Tort law applies to most business relationships *not* governed by contracts. A **tort** is a *civil*—that is, noncriminal—injury to people, property, or reputation for which compensation must be paid. Trespass, fraud, defamation, invasion of privacy, and even assault can be torts, as can interference with contractual relations and wrongful use of trade secrets. There are three classifications of torts: *intentional*, *negligence*, and *product liability*.

Intentional Tort *tort resulting from the deliberate actions of a party*

Compensatory Damages *monetary payments intended to redress injury actually suffered because of a tort*

Punitive Damages *fines imposed over and above any actual losses suffered by a plaintiff*

Negligence *conduct that falls below legal standards for protecting others against unreasonable risk*

Product Liability *tort in which a company is responsible for injuries caused by its products*

Strict Product Liability *principle that liability can result not from a producer's negligence but from a defect in the product itself*

Intentional Torts

Intentional torts result from the deliberate actions of another person or organization. To remedy torts, courts will usually impose **compensatory damages**—payments intended to redress an injury actually suffered. They may also impose **punitive damages**—fines that exceed actual losses suffered by plaintiffs and are intended to punish defendants.

Negligence Torts

Most suits involve charges of **negligence**—conduct that falls below legal standards for protecting others against unreasonable risk.

Product Liability Torts

In cases of **product liability**, a company may be held responsible for injuries caused by its products.

Strict Product Liability Since the early 1960s, businesses have faced a number of legal actions based on the relatively new principle of **strict product liability**—the principle that liability can result not from a producer's negligence but from a defect in the product itself. An injured party need only show the following:

1 The product was defective when it was sold.
2 The defect was the cause of injury or loss.
3 The defect caused the product to be unreasonably dangerous.

Because plaintiffs need not demonstrate negligence or fault, these suits often have a good chance of success.

Property Law

Property *anything of value to which a person or business has sole right of ownership*

Tangible Real Property *land and anything attached to it*

Tangible Personal Property *any movable item that can be owned, bought, sold, or leased*

Intangible Personal Property *property that cannot be seen but that exists by virtue of written documentation*

Intellectual Property *something produced by the intellect or mind that has commercial value*

Property is anything of value to which a person or business has sole right of ownership. Legally speaking, the right of ownership is itself property.

Within this broad general definition, we can divide property into four categories:

1 **Tangible real property** is land and anything attached to it.
2 **Tangible personal property** is any movable item that can be owned, bought, sold, or leased.
3 **Intangible personal property** cannot be seen but exists by virtue of written documentation.
4 **Intellectual property** is created through a person's creative activities.

Protection of Intellectual Rights

The U.S. Constitution grants protection to intellectual property by means of copyrights, trademarks, and patents. Copyrights and patents apply to the tangible expressions of an idea, not to the ideas themselves.

Copyright *exclusive ownership right belonging to the creator of a book, article, design, illustration, photo, film, or musical work*

Copyrights **Copyrights** give creators exclusive ownership rights to their intellectual property. Copyrights extend to creators for their entire lives and to their estates for 70 years thereafter.

Trademarks Because the development of products is expensive, companies seek to prevent other firms from using their brand names. Often, they must act to keep competitors from confusing consumers with similar or substitute products. A producer can apply to the U.S. government for a **trademark**—the exclusive legal right to use a brand name.

Trademark *exclusive legal right to use a brand name or symbol*

Trademarks are granted for 20 years and may be renewed indefinitely if a firm continues to protect its brand name. If a firm allows the brand name to lapse into common usage, it may lose protection. Common usage takes effect when a company fails to use the ® symbol to indicate that its brand name is a registered trademark. It also takes effect if a company seeks no action against those who fail to acknowledge its trademark.

PATENTS **Patents** provide legal monopolies for the use and licensing of manufactured items, manufacturing processes, substances, and designs for objects. A patentable invention must be *novel*, *useful*, and *nonobvious*. Patents on new products and on business process are valid for 20 years, with the term running from the date on which the application was *filed*, not the date on which the patent itself was *issued*. Patents on *designs* extend for 14 years.

Patent *exclusive legal right to use and license a manufactured item or substance, manufacturing process, or object design*

Restrictions on Property Rights

Property rights are not always absolute. For example, rights may be compromised under the following circumstances:

- Utility companies typically have rights called *easements*, such as the right to run power lines over private property or to lay cable or pipe under it.
- Under the principle of **eminent domain**, the government may, on paying owners fair prices, claim private land to expand roads, erect public buildings, and similar infrastructure projects.

Eminent Domain *principle that the government may claim private land for public use by buying it at a fair price*

Agency Law

The transfer of property often involves agents. An **agent** is a person who acts for and in the name of another party, called the **principal**. Courts have ruled that both a firm's employees and its outside contractors may be regarded as its agents.

Agent *individual or organization acting for and in the name of another party*

Principal *individual or organization authorizing an agent to act on its behalf*

Authority of Agents

Agents have the authority to bind principals to agreements. They receive that authority, however, from the principals themselves; they cannot create their own authority. An agent's authority to bind a principal can be **express**, **implied**, or **apparent**.

Express Authority *agent's authority, derived from written agreement, to bind a principal to a certain course of action*

Implied Authority *agent's authority, derived from business custom, to bind a principal to a certain course of action*

Apparent Authority *agent's authority, based on the principal's compliance, to bind a principal to a certain course of action*

Responsibilities of Principals

Principals have several responsibilities to their agents. They owe agents reasonable compensation, must reimburse them for related business expenses, and should inform them of risks associated with their business activities. Principals are liable for actions performed by agents *within the scope of their employment*. If agents make untrue claims about products or services, the principal is liable for making amends. Employers are similarly responsible for the actions of employees. Firms are often liable in tort suits because the courts treat employees as agents. Businesses are also increasingly being held accountable for *criminal* acts by employees. Court findings have argued that firms are expected to be aware of workers' negative propensities, to check their employees' backgrounds, and to train and supervise employees properly.

Commercial Law

Managers must be well acquainted with the most general laws affecting commerce. Specifically, they need to be familiar with the provisions of the **Uniform Commercial Code (UCC)**, which describes the rights of buyers and sellers in transactions. One key area of coverage by the UCC, contracts, was discussed previously. Another key area is warranties.

Uniform Commercial Code (UCC) *body of standardized laws governing the rights of buyers and sellers in transactions*

Warranty *seller's promise to stand by its products or services if a problem occurs after the sale*

Express Warranty *a warranty whose terms are specifically stated by the seller*

Implied Warranty *a warranty, dictated by law, based on the principle that products should fulfill advertised promises and serve the purposes for which they are manufactured and sold*

A **warranty** is a seller's promise to stand by its products or services if a problem occurs after the sale. Warranties may be express or implied. The seller specifically states the terms of an **express warranty**, whereas an **implied warranty** is dictated by law. Implied warranties embody the principle that a product should (1) fulfill the promises made by advertisements and (2) serve the purpose for which it was manufactured and sold. It is important to note, however, that warranties, unlike most contracts, are easily limited, waived, or disclaimed. Consequently, they are the source of tort action more often, as dissatisfied customers seek redress from producers.

Bankruptcy Law

Both organizations and individuals can seek debt relief by filing for bankruptcy—the court-granted permission not to pay some or all incurred debts. Many individuals and businesses file for bankruptcy each year, and their numbers continue to increase. Three main factors account for the increase in bankruptcy filings:

1. The increased availability of credit
2. The "fresh-start" provisions in current bankruptcy laws
3. The growing acceptance of bankruptcy as a financial tactic

Involuntary Bankruptcy *bankruptcy proceedings initiated by the creditors of an indebted individual or organization*

Voluntary Bankruptcy *bankruptcy proceedings initiated by an indebted individual or organization*

In some cases, creditors may force an individual or firm into **involuntary bankruptcy** and press the courts to award them payment of at least part of what they are owed. Far more often, however, a person or business chooses to file for court protection against creditors. In general, individuals and firms whose debts exceed total assets by at least $1,000 may file for **voluntary bankruptcy**.

Business Bankruptcy

One of three plans resolves a business bankruptcy:

1. Under a *liquidation plan*, the business ceases to exist. Its assets are sold and the proceeds are used to pay creditors.
2. Under a *repayment plan*, the bankrupt company simply works out a new payment schedule to meet its obligations. The time frame is usually extended, and payments are collected and distributed by a court-appointed trustee.
3. *Reorganization* is the most complex form of business bankruptcy. The company must explain the sources of its financial difficulties and propose a new plan for remaining in business. Reorganization may include a new team of managers and a new financial strategy. A judge may also reduce the firm's debts to ensure its survival.

Legislation passed since 1994 restricts how long a company can protect itself in bankruptcy while continuing to do business. Critics have charged that many firms have succeeded in operating for long periods of time under bankruptcy protection. During that time, they were able to cut costs and prices, not only competing with an unfair advantage but also dragging down overall industry profits. The new laws place time limits on various steps in the filing process. The intended effect is to speed the process and prevent assets from being lost to legal fees. Several firms, including Neiman Marcus, J.Crew, Gold's Gym, and Diamond Offshore Drilling, filed for bankruptcy as a result of the COVID-19 pandemic in 2020.

The International Framework of Business Law

Laws vary from country to country, and many businesses today have international markets, suppliers, and competitors. As a result, managers need a basic understanding of the international framework of business law that affects the ways in which they can do business. Issues such as pollution across borders are matters of **international law**—the general set of cooperative agreements and guidelines established by countries to govern the actions of individuals, businesses, and nations themselves.

International Law *general set of cooperative agreements and guidelines established by countries to govern the actions of individuals, businesses, and nations*

International law has several sources. One source is custom and tradition. Among countries that have been trading with one another for centuries, many customs and traditions governing exchanges have gradually evolved into practice. Although some trading practices still follow ancient unwritten agreements, there has been a clear trend in more recent times to approach international trade within a more formal legal framework. Key features of that framework include a variety of formal trade agreements.

Another important source of international law is the formal trade treaties that nations negotiate with one another. Governing entities such as the World Trade Organization and the European Union, for instance, also provide legal frameworks within which participating nations agree to abide.

appendix III

Managing Your Personal Finances

Dealing with personal finances is a lifelong job involving a crucial choice between two extremes:

1 Committing to the rational management of your personal finances by controlling them, helping them grow, and therefore enjoying greater personal satisfaction and financial stability

2 Letting the financial chips fall where they may and hoping for the best (which seldom happens) and therefore inviting frustration, disappointment, and financial distress

Personal finance management requires consideration of cash management, financial planning and control, investment alternatives, and risk. Let's start by looking at one key factor in success: the personal financial plan. We'll then discuss the steps in the planning process and show how you can make better decisions to manage your personal finances.

Building Your Financial Plan

Financial planning is the process of looking at your current financial condition, identifying your goals, and anticipating steps toward meeting those goals. Because your goals and finances will change as you get older and as your income changes, your plan should always allow for revision. Figure AIII.1 summarizes a step-by-step approach to personal financial planning.

Financial Planning *process of looking at one's current financial condition, identifying one's goals, and anticipating requirements for meeting those goals*

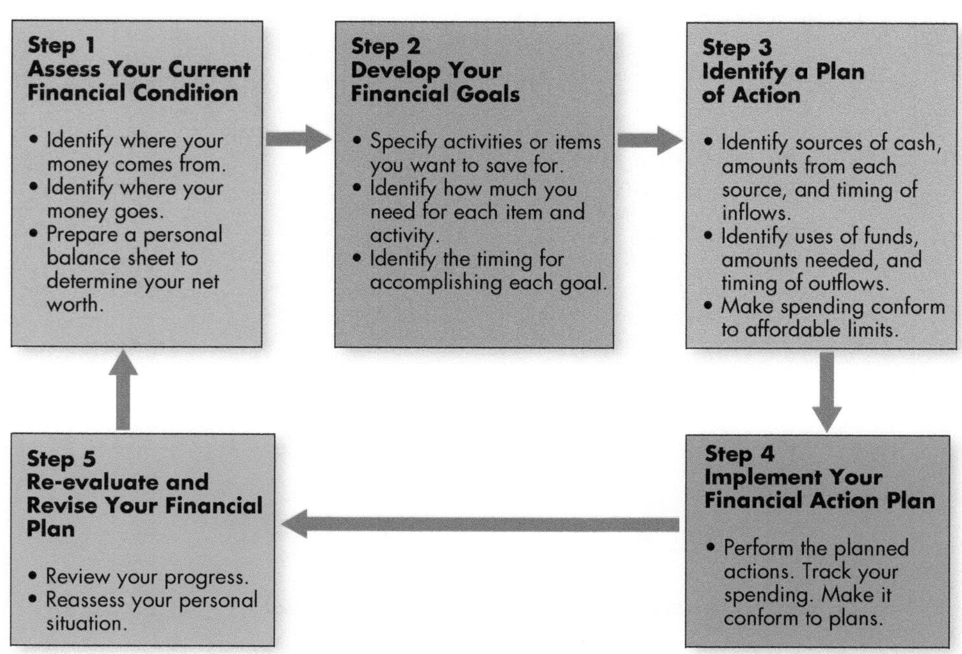

FIGURE AIII.1 Developing a Personal Financial Plan

Assessing Your Current Financial Condition

Personal Net Worth *value of one's total assets minus one's total liabilities (debts)*

The first step in developing a personal financial plan is assessing your current financial position. Your **personal net worth** is the value of all your assets minus all your liabilities (debts) *at the present time*. The worksheet in Figure AIII.2 provides some sample calculations for developing your own personal "balance sheet." Because assets and liabilities change over time, updating your balance sheet not only allows you to monitor changes but also provides more accurate information for realistic budgeting and planning.

Developing Your Financial Goals

Step 2 involves setting three different types of future goals: *immediate* (within one year), *intermediate* (within five years), and *long term* (more than five years). The worksheet in Figure AIII.3 will help you establish these goals. By thinking about your

Assets: What You Own		Example Numbers	Your Numbers
LIQUID ASSETS:			
1. Cash	$	300	______
2. Savings	+	3,700	______
3. Checking	+	1,200	______
INVESTMENTS:			
4. IRAs	+	12,400	______
5. Securities	+	500	______
6. Retirement Plan	+	—	______
7. Real Estate (other than primary residence)	+	—	______
HOUSEHOLD:			
8. Cars (market value)	+	18,000	______
9. House (market value)	+	—	______
10. Furniture	+	3,400	______
11. Personal Property	+	6,600	______
12. Other assets		—	______
13. Total Assets (add lines 1–12)	**=**	**$46,100**	______
Liabilities (Debt): What You Owe			
CURRENT LIABILITIES:			
14. Credit card balance	$	1,300	______
15. Unpaid bills due	+	1,800	______
16. Alimony and child support	+	—	______
LONG-TERM LIABILITIES:			
17. Home mortgage	+	—	______
18. Home equity loan	+	—	______
19. Car loan	+	4,100	______
20. Student loan	+	3,600	______
21. Other liabilities	+	2,400	______
22. Total Liabilities (add lines 14–21)	**=**	**$13,200**	______
Net Worth			
23. Total Assets (line 13)		$ 46,100	______
24. Less: Total Debt (line 22)	–	13,200	______
25. Results: Net Worth	**=**	**$32,900**	______

FIGURE AIII.2 Worksheet for Calculating Net Worth

Name the Goal	Financial Requirement (Amount) for This Goal	Time Frame for Accomplishing Goal	Importance (1= Highest, 5 = Lowest)
Immediate Goals:			
Live in a better apartment	______	______	______
Establish an emergency cash fund	______	______	______
Pay off credit card debt	______	______	______
Other	______	______	______
Intermediate Goals:			
Obtain adequate health, life, disability, liability, property insurance	______	______	______
Save for wedding	______	______	______
Save to buy new car	______	______	______
Establish regular savings program (5% of gross income)	______	______	______
Save for college for self	______	______	______
Pay off major outstanding debt	______	______	______
Make major purchase	______	______	______
Save for home remodeling	______	______	______
Save for down payment on a home	______	______	______
Other	______	______	______
Long-Term Goals:			
Pay off home mortgage	______	______	______
Save for college for children	______	______	______
Save for vacation home	______	______	______
Increase personal net worth to $___ in ___ years.	______	______	______
Achieve retirement nest egg of $ __ in ___ years.	______	______	______
Accumulate fund for travel in retirement	______	______	______
Save for long-term care needs	______	______	______
Other	______	______	______

FIGURE AIII.3 Worksheet for Setting Financial Goals

finances in three different time frames, you'll be better able to set measurable goals and completion times, or to set priorities for rationing your resources if, at some point, you're not able to pursue all your goals.

Because Step 3 (identifying a plan of action) and Step 4 (implementing your plan) will affect your assets and liabilities, your personal balance sheet will change over time (in the same way that a business balance sheet changes). As a result, Step 5 (reevaluating and revising your plan) needs periodic updating.

Making Better Use of the Time Value of Money

As discussed in Chapter 17, the value of time with any investment stems from the concept of compound growth, the compounding of interest received over several time periods. With each additional time period, interest receipts accumulate and earn even more interest, thus multiplying the earning capacity of the investment. Whenever you make everyday purchases, you're giving up interest that you could have earned with the same money if you'd invested it instead. From a financial standpoint, "idle" or uninvested money, which could be put to work earning more money, is a wasted resource.

Planning for the "Golden Years"

The sooner you start saving, the greater your financial power will be in the future. This is determined by the fact that you will have taken advantage of the time value of money for a longer period of time. Consider coworkers Juanita and Barbara, who are both planning to retire in 25 years, as can be seen in Figure AIII.4.

Over that period, assume that each can expect a 10 percent annual return on investment. (Note: The U.S. stock market averaged more than 10 percent returns for the 75 years before the 2008 recession. However, since the recession ended, average returns have not regained the 10 percent level for a sustained period so a more conservative approach may be called for in the future.) Their savings strategies, however, are different: Barbara begins saving immediately, whereas Juanita plans to start later but invest larger sums. Barbara will invest $2,000 annually for each of the next five years (years 1 through 5), for a total investment of $10,000. Juanita, meanwhile, wants to live a little larger by spending rather than saving for the next 10 years. Then, for years 11 through 20, she'll start saving $2,000 annually, for a total investment of $20,000. They will both allow annual returns to accumulate until they retire in year 25. Juanita expects to have a larger retirement fund than Barbara because she has contributed twice as much, but she is in for a surprise. Barbara's retirement

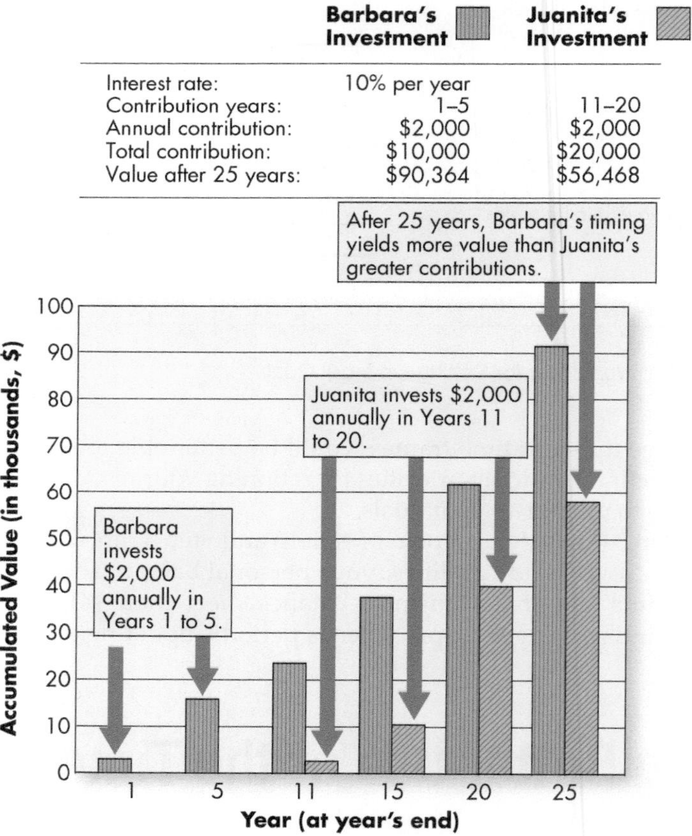

FIGURE AIII.4 Compounding Money over Time

fund will be much larger—$90,364 versus Juanita's $56,468—even though she invested only half as much. Barbara's advantage lies in the length of her savings program. Her money is invested longer—over a period of 21 to 25 years—with interest compounding over that range of time. Juanita's earnings are compounded over a shorter period—6 to 15 years. Granted, Juanita may have had more fun in years 1 to 10, but Barbara's retirement prospects look brighter.

Other factors that have to be considered are anticipated retirement age and life expectancy. Not that long ago most people considered age 65 to be the "official" retirement age, and many people actually retired earlier than that, some as early as 58. Similarly, the average life expectancy for people born in 1950 was around 65 years at the time of their birth. Now, however, due to healthier lifestyles and better health care, life expectancies have been extended to around 78 years and many people work well into their 70s before retiring. As a result of these trends, if a person wants to retire at a relatively early age they will need even more retirement savings in anticipation of a longer life. Numerous online financial planning tools are available to help determine projected financial needs based on different retirement periods.

Time Value as a Financial-Planning Tool

A good financial plan takes into account future needs, the sources of funds for meeting those needs, and the time needed to develop those funds. When you begin your financial plan, you can use various time-based tables to take into account the time value of money. Figure AIII.5 shows how much a $1.00 investment will grow over different lengths of time and at different interest rates.

A timetable like this can determine the factor at which your money will multiply over a given period of time and at a given interest rate. It can also help you determine how long and at what interest rate you will need to invest to meet your financial goals. For example, if you wanted to double your money in less than 10 years, you would have to find an interest rate of return of at least 8 percent. The catch is that to obtain a high interest rate, you will have to make riskier investments, such as buying stocks. Because higher interest rates carry greater risks, it is unwise to "put all your eggs in one basket." A sound financial plan will include more conservative investments, such as a highly rated money market account or a bank certificate of deposit (CD), to mitigate the risks of more speculative investments.

n	1%	2%	4%	6%	8%	10%
1	1.010	1.020	1.040	1.060	1.080	1.100
2	1.020	1.040	1.082	1.124	1.166	1.210
3	1.030	1.061	1.125	1.191	1.260	1.331
4	1.041	1.082	1.170	1.262	1.360	1.464
5	1.051	1.104	1.217	1.338	1.469	1.611
6	1.062	1.126	1.265	1.419	1.587	1.772
7	1.072	1.149	1.316	1.504	1.714	1.949
8	1.083	1.172	1.369	1.594	1.851	2.144
9	1.094	1.195	1.423	1.689	1.999	2.358
10	1.105	1.219	1.480	1.791	2.159	2.594
15	1.161	1.346	1.801	2.397	3.172	4.177
20	1.220	1.486	2.191	3.207	4.661	6.727
25	1.282	1.641	2.666	4.292	6.848	10.834
30	1.348	1.811	3.243	5.743	10.062	17.449

Note: n = number of time periods; % = various interest rates

FIGURE AIII.5 Timetable for Growing $1.00

Conserving Money by Controlling It

A major pitfall in any financial plan is the temptation to spend more than you can afford, especially when credit is usually very easy to get. Because many credit card issuers target college students and recent graduates with tempting offers appealing to the desire for financial independence, it is important that you arm yourself with a solid understanding of the financial costs entailed by credit cards. The same lessons apply equally to other loans, such as home mortgages, car loans, and student financial aid.

Credit Cards: Keys to Satisfaction or Financial Handcuffs?

Although some credit cards don't charge annual fees, all of them charge interest on unpaid (outstanding) balances. Figure AIII.6 reprints part of a page from Bankrate.com's credit card calculator at www.bankrate.com/brm/calc/MinPayment.asp. Using the table as a guide, suppose you owe $5,000 for credit card purchases, and your card company requires a minimum monthly payment (minimum payment due [MPD]) of 5 percent of the unpaid balance. The interest rate is 18 percent APR (annual percentage rate) on the outstanding balance.

If you pay only the monthly minimum and don't make new charges on the card, it will take you 115 months—more than $9\frac{1}{2}$ years—to pay off your credit card debt. During this time you will pay $2,096.70 in interest, almost half again the principal balance! Repayment takes so long because you are making only the MPD, which decreases with each monthly payment.

Save Your Money: Lower Interest Rates and Faster Payments

Figure AIII.6 confirms two principles for saving money that you can apply when borrowing from any source, not just credit cards: Look for lower interest rates and make faster repayments.

Seeking Lower Interest Rates Look again at Figure AIII.6 and compare the cost of borrowing $5,000 at 18 percent with the cost of borrowing it at 9 percent. If you assume the same 5 percent minimum monthly payment, a 9 percent APR will save you $1,232.14 in interest during the repayment period—a nearly 59 percent savings.

Making Faster Payments Because money has a time value, lenders charge borrowers according to the length of time for which they borrow it. In general, longer lending periods increase the cost, and shorter periods are cheaper. Using Figure AIII.6, compare the costs of the 5 percent MPD with the faster 10 percent MPD. The faster

Balance = $5,000	MPD 3%		MPD 5%		MPD 10%	
APR	Months	Costs	Months	Costs	Months	Costs
6%	144	$5,965.56	92	$5,544.58	50	$5,260.74
9%	158	$6,607.24	96	$5,864.56	51	$5,401.63
12%	175	$7,407.50	102	$6,224.26	53	$5,550.32
18%	226	$9,798.89	115	$7,096.70	55	$5,873.86
21%	266	$11,704.63	123	$7,632.92	57	$6,050.28

Note: APR, annual percentage rate; MPD, minimum payment due

FIGURE AIII.6 Paying Off Credit Card Debt

schedule cuts the repayment period from 115 to 55 months and, at 18 percent APR, reduces interest costs by $1,222.84. Combining both faster repayment and the lower interest rate cuts your total interest cost to $450.30—a savings of $1,695.07 over the amount you'd pay if you made slower repayments at the higher rate.

Declining Asset Value: A Borrower's Regret Financially speaking, nothing's more disappointing than buying an expensive item and then discovering that it's not worth what you paid. For example, if you buy a $5,000 used car with a credit card at 18 percent APR and make only the MPD, as in the preceding example, you'll end up spending a total of $7,407.50 over $9\frac{1}{2}$ years. By that time, however, the car you bought will be worth less than $1,000. Some of this loss in asset value can be avoided through realistic planning and spending—by knowing and staying within your financial means.

Financial Commitments of Home Ownership

Deciding whether to rent or buy a home involves a variety of considerations, including life stage, family needs, career, financial situation, and preferred lifestyle. If you decide to buy, you have to ask yourself what you can afford, and that requires asking yourself questions about your personal financial condition and your capacity for borrowing. Figure AIII.7 summarizes the key considerations in deciding whether to rent or buy.

How Much House Can You Afford?

Buying a home is the biggest investment that most people make. Unfortunately, many make the mistake of buying a house that they can't afford, resulting in unnecessary stress and even significant financial loss. This happened on a massive scale in the housing downfall that began in 2007 and has still not fully ended. The seeds for destruction sprouted during the years 2000–2007, when millions of optimistic home buyers borrowed beyond their means by getting larger loans than they could realistically afford. With the rising demand for home ownership, housing prices became inflated and borrowers responded by seeking larger and larger loans. They implicitly assumed that market prices would continue to rise indefinitely, thereby providing a profitable investment. Borrowers were aided by lenders using reduced credit standards, unlike the more conservative time-proven standards that will be presented here, leading to unrealistic repayment requirements. By 2007 the housing market was oversold and the U.S. economy entered a severe recession. With rising unemployment, borrowers were unable to meet monthly payments, especially

Renting	Buying
• No down payment to get started	• Must make payments for mortgage, property taxes, and insurance
• Flexibility to leave	• Equity builds up over time
• No obligation for upkeep or improvements	• More privacy
• No groundskeeping	• Value of property may increase
• Easy cash-flow planning (a single monthly payment)	• Lower income taxes: mortgage-interest and property tax payments reduce taxable income
• May provide access to recreation and social facilities	• Financial gains from selling house can be exempt from taxes
• Rental conditions may be changed by owner	• Greater control over use of property and improvements
• Timing for repairs controlled by owner	• The home can become a source of cash by refinancing with another mortgage loan or a home-equity loan

FIGURE AIII.7 To Buy or Not to Buy

when interest rates (and thus payments) on loans increased. Consequently, housing vacancies increased and property values plummeted. Borrowers lost their homes and the equity they had built up in them. The depressed housing market did not begin to revive until 2014. In the years since there have been times when property values surged and other times when values remained flat or even decreased. There are also, of course, variations across regions and cities.

In addition to loan payments, the typical demands of ownership, time, and other resources for maintaining and improving a home tend to reduce the money otherwise available for recreation, eating out, taking vacations, and so on. You can reduce the financial pressure by calculating in advance a realistic price range—one that not only lets you buy a house but also lets you live a reasonably pleasant life once you're in it.

Mortgage Loan *loan secured by property (the home) being purchased*

Most people need a loan to buy a house, apartment, or condominium. A **mortgage loan** is secured by the property—the home—being purchased. Because the size of a loan depends on the cost of the property, both borrowers and lenders want to know whether the buyer can afford the house they want. To determine how much you can afford, one time-tested (though somewhat conservative) rule recommends keeping the price below $2\frac{1}{2}$ times your annual income. If your income is $60,000, look for a house priced below $150,000.

Any such calculation, however, will give you only a rough estimate of what you can afford. You should also consider how much money you have for a down payment and how much you can borrow. Lending institutions want to determine a buyer's borrowing capacity, the borrower's ability to meet the *recurring costs* of buying and owning.

PITI Every month, the homeowner must pay **p**rincipal (pay back some of the borrowed money), along with **i**nterest, **t**axes, and homeowner's **i**nsurance, or PITI, for short. As Figure AIII.8 shows, the size of principal and interest payments depends on (1) the mortgage amount, (2) the length of the mortgage loan, and (3) the interest rate.

In evaluating loan applications, lenders use PITI calculations to estimate the buyer's ability to meet monthly payments. To determine how much someone is likely to lend you, calculate 28 percent of your gross monthly income (that is, before taxes and other deductions). If your PITI costs don't exceed that figure, your loan application probably will receive favorable consideration. With a monthly gross income of $4,000, for example, your PITI costs shouldn't exceed $1,120 (28 percent of $4,000). Additional calculations show a house price of $162,382 is the most this borrower can afford. Figure AIII.9 gives a sample calculation, and you should be able to make step-by-step computations by plugging your own numbers into the worksheet.

	Length of Loan				
Interest Rate (%)	3 Years	5 Years	10 Years	20 Years	30 Years
5.0	$299.71	$188.71	$106.07	$66.00	$53.68
6.0	304.22	193.33	111.02	71.64	59.96
6.5	306.49	195.66	113.55	74.56	63.21
7.0	308.77	198.01	116.11	77.53	66.53
8.0	313.36	202.76	121.33	83.65	73.38
9.0	318.00	207.58	126.68	89.98	80.47
10.0	322.67	212.47	132.16	96.51	87.76
11.0	327.39	217.42	137.76	103.22	95.24
12.0	332.14	222.44	143.48	110.11	102.86

FIGURE AIII.8 Monthly Payments on a $10,000 Loan

ASSUMPTIONS:

30-year mortgage
Closing costs (fees for property, survey, credit report, title search, title insurance, attorney, interest advance, loan origination) = $5,000
Funds available for closing costs and down payment = $25,000
Interest rate on mortgage = 6½% per year
Estimated real estate taxes = $200 per month
Estimated homeowner's insurance = $20 month

Example Numbers		Your Numbers
1. Monthly income, gross (before taxes or deductions)........	$4,000	______
2. Apply PITI ratio (0.28 x amount on line 1) to determine borrower's payment capacity: 0.28 x $4,000 = ...	$1,120	______
3. Determine mortgage payment (principal and interest) by subtracting taxes and insurance from PITI (line 2)........	–$ 220	______
4. Result: Maximum mortgage payment (principal and interest)........	**$900**	______
5. Using Figure AIII.8, find the monthly mortgage payment on a $10,000 loan at 6½% interest for 30 years........	$63.21	______
6. Since each $10,000 loan requires a $63.21 monthly payment, how many $10,000 loans can the borrower afford with the $900 payment capacity? The answer is determined as follows: $900.00/$63.21 = 14.2382 loans of $10,000 each		______
7. Result: Maximum allowable mortgage loan [calculated as follows]: 14.2382 loans (from line 6 above) x $10,000 per loan = ...	**$142,382**	______
8. Result: Maximum house price borrower can afford using PITI (amount of house that can be bought with available funds):		
From loan........	$142,382	______
From down payment........	$ 25,000	______
Less closing cost........	–$ 5,000	______
....	**$162,382**	______

FIGURE AIII.9 Worksheet for PITI Calculations

Other Debt In evaluating financial capacity, lenders also look at any additional outstanding debt, such as loans and credit card bills. They will generally accept indebtedness (including PITI) up to 36 percent of gross income. Because PITI itself can be up to 28 percent, you might be allowed as little as 8 percent in other long-term debt. With your $4,000 monthly gross income, your total debt should be less than $1,440 ($1,120 for PITI and $320 for other debt). If your total debt exceeds $1,440, you may have to settle for a smaller loan than the one you calculated with the PITI method.

Finally, lenders will also take into account the "quality" of the debt. For instance, suppose you have purchased a car that seems appropriate for your income level and you have a monthly payment of $300 for another three years on your car loan. A mortgage lender might not weight that as negatively as multiple high-interest credit card accounts with the same combined monthly payments. Why? The car loan would generally be considered a reasonable financial decision, whereas the credit card debt would reflect poor financial decisions. Websites such as http://mortgages.interest.com provide mortgage calculators for testing interest rates, lengths of loans, and other personal financial information.

Cashing Out from Tax Avoidance (Legally)

Personal expenditures always require cash outflows. Some also reduce your tax bill and save you some cash. Individual retirement accounts (IRAs) and some education savings accounts have this effect. (Before you commit any money to these instruments or activities, check with an expert on tax regulations. Regulations affecting these items change from time to time.)

The IRA Tax Break

Traditional Individual Retirement Account (IRA) *provision allowing individual tax-deferred retirement savings*

With a **traditional individual retirement account (IRA)**, you can make an annual tax-deductible savings deposit of up to \$5,500, depending on your income level. IRAs are long-term investments, intended to provide income after age $59\frac{1}{2}$. For distant future savings, an IRA boasts immediate cash advantages over a typical savings account because it reduces your current taxable income by the amount of your contribution.

Here's how it works: Assume that you're a qualified employee with a federal income tax rate of 20 percent in year 2023. If you contribute \$4,000 to an IRA, you avoid \$800 in income taxes $(0.20 \times \$4,000 = \$800)$. Your untaxed contributions and their accumulated earnings will only be taxed later when you withdraw money from your IRA. The tax break is based on the assumption that, after you retire, you're likely to have less total income than you do now and will have to pay less tax on the money withdrawn as income from your IRA.

IRA Risks If you underestimate your future cash requirements and have to withdraw money before you reach $59\frac{1}{2}$, however, you'll probably have to pay a 10 percent penalty. You can, however, make penalty-free withdrawals under certain circumstances—buying a first home, paying college expenses, and paying large medical bills, for example.

The unpredictability of future income tax rates also poses a financial risk. If tax rates increase substantially, future IRA withdrawals could actually be taxed at higher rates, which may offset your original tax savings.

Roth IRA *provision allowing individual retirement savings with tax-free accumulated earnings*

Roth IRA Versus Traditional IRA The **Roth IRA** is the reverse of the traditional IRA in that contributions are not tax deductible (you pay taxes on the money before it is placed into the account), withdrawals on initial contribution are not penalized, and withdrawals on both the original contributions and accumulated earnings after the age of $59\frac{1}{2}$ are not taxed.

Figure AIII.10 shows the significant advantage of this last feature. Accumulated earnings typically far outweigh the initial contribution, so although you pay an extra \$1,285 in front-end taxes, you get \$40,732 in additional cash at retirement—and even more if income tax rates have increased.

IRAs and Education Depending on your income level, you can contribute up to \$2,000 annually to a Coverdell Education Savings Account (also known as an *Education IRA*) for each child under age 18. As with the Roth IRA, your initial contribution is not tax deductible, your earnings are tax free, and you pay no tax on withdrawals to pay for qualified education expenses. However, the Education IRA

Assumptions: Initial contribution and earnings average 10 percent growth annually. Initial contribution and earnings remain invested for 40 years. Income tax rate is 30 percent.	Traditional IRA	Roth IRA
Initial cash contribution to IRA	$3,000	$3,000
Income tax paid initially: $4,285 income x 30% tax rate = $1,285 tax	0	1,285
Total initial cash outlay	**$3,000**	**$4,285**
Accumulated earnings (40 years)	$132,774	$132,774
Initial contribution	+ 3,000	+ 3,000
Total available for distribution after 40 years	= $135,774	= $135,774
Income tax at time of distribution	− $40,732	0
After-tax distribution (cash)	= **$95,042**	= **$135,774**

FIGURE AIII.10 Cash Flows: Roth IRA Versus Traditional IRA

requires you to use the money by the time your child reaches age 30. Funds that you withdraw but don't use for stipulated education expense are subject to taxation plus a 10 percent penalty.

Protecting Your Net Worth

With careful attention, thoughtful saving and spending, and skillful financial planning (and a little luck), you can consistently increase your net worth over time. Every financial plan should also consider steps for preserving it. One approach involves the risk–return relationship discussed in Chapter 17. Do you prefer to protect your current assets, or are you willing to risk them in return for greater financial growth? At various life stages and levels of wealth, you should adjust your asset portfolio to conform to your risk and return preferences: conservative, moderate, or aggressive.

Why Buy Life Insurance?

You can think of life insurance as a tool for financial preservation. As explained in Appendix I, a life insurance policy is a promise to pay beneficiaries after the death of the insured party who paid the insurance company premiums during their lifetime.

What Does Life Insurance Do?

Upon the death of the policyholder, life insurance replaces income on which someone else is dependent. The amount of insurance you need depends on how many other people rely on your income. For example, while insurance makes sense for a married parent who is a family's sole source of income, a single college student with no financial dependents needs little or no insurance.

How Much Should I Buy?

The more insurance you buy, the more it's going to cost you. To estimate the amount of coverage you need, begin by adding up all your annual expenses—rent, food, clothing, transportation, education, outstanding debts—that you pay for the dependents who'd survive you. Then multiply the total by the number of years that you want the insurance to cover them. Typically, this sum will amount to several times—even 10 to 20 times—your current annual income.

Why Consider Term Insurance?

Term insurance pays a predetermined benefit when death occurs during the stipulated policy term. If the insured outlives the term, the policy loses its value and simply ceases. Term-life premiums are significantly lower than premiums for whole-life insurance.

Unlike term life, *whole-life insurance*, also known as *cash-value insurance*, remains in force as long as premiums are paid. In addition to paying a death benefit, whole life accumulates cash value over time—a form of savings. Paid-in money can be withdrawn; however, whole-life savings generally earn less interest than most alternative forms of investment.

How Much Does It Cost?

The cost of insurance depends on how much you buy, your life expectancy, and other statistical risk factors. To get the best match between your policy and your personal situation, you should evaluate the terms and conditions of a variety of policies. You can get convenient comparisons on websites such as www.intelliquote.com.

appendix IV

Unions and Labor Management

This appendix is an expansion of material covered in the last section of Chapter 10. After reading it, you should better understand how and why workers organize into labor unions, how unions and businesses relate to each other, and how the collective bargaining process works.

Why Do Workers Unionize?

A **labor union** is a group of individuals working together to achieve shared job-related goals, such as higher pay, shorter working hours, more job security, greater benefits, or better working conditions.[1] **Labor relations** is the process of dealing with employees who are represented by a union.

Labor Union *a group of individuals working together to achieve shared job-related goals, such as higher pay, shorter working hours, more job security, greater benefits, or better working conditions*

Labor Relations *process of dealing with employees who are represented by a union*

Labor unions grew in popularity in the United States in the nineteenth and early twentieth centuries. The labor movement was born with the Industrial Revolution, which also gave birth to a factory-based production system that carried with it enormous economic benefits. Job specialization and mass production had allowed businesses to create ever greater quantities of goods at ever lower costs.

But there was also a dark side to this era. Workers became more dependent on their factory jobs. Eager for greater profits, some owners treated their workers like other raw materials, as resources to be deployed with little or no regard for the individual worker's well-being. Many businesses forced employees to work long hours—60-hour weeks were common, and some workers were routinely forced to work 12 to 16 hours a day. With no minimum-wage laws or other controls, pay was also minimal and safety standards virtually nonexistent. Workers had no job security and received few (if any) benefits. Many companies, especially textile mills, employed large numbers of children at poverty wages. If people complained, nothing prevented employers from firing and replacing them at will.

Unions appeared and ultimately prospered because they constituted a solution to the worker's most serious problem. By uniting the workers, unions forced management to listen to the complaints of all their workers rather than to just the few who were brave (or foolish) enough to speak out. The power of unions, then, comes from collective action. **Collective bargaining** is the process by which union leaders and managers negotiate common terms and conditions of employment for the workers represented by unions. Although collective bargaining does not often occur in small businesses, many midsize and larger businesses must engage in the process.

Collective Bargaining *process by which labor and management negotiate conditions of employment for union-represented workers*

The Evolution of Unionism in the United States

As we discuss the growth—and the more recent decline—of unionism in this section, it is important to remember that the influence of labor unions goes far beyond their membership. For example, many nonunion members have benefited from the improved working conditions won by unions. Union gains often set standards for entire industries, and some organizations make workplace improvements just to discourage their employees from unionizing.

Early Unions

Labor unions grew up with the United States. The earliest formal organizations of U.S. workers appeared during the Revolutionary War. These early organizations were craft unions; each limited itself to representing workers whose common interest was a specific skilled job, and each sought to promote the economic welfare of the skilled craftspeople who made up its membership.

For example, the Federal Society of Journeymen Cordwainers, formed in Philadelphia in 1794, worked to better the pay and working conditions of shoemakers. The Cordwainers was also one of the first unions to encounter legal roadblocks to collective action. When the union struck for higher wages in 1806, the court ruled in favor of employers, who claimed that unions were illegal "combinations" conspiring to restrain trade. The court's ruling applied the *common law conspiracy doctrine*, the principle that the public interest was harmed when two or more people conspired to do something jointly. Unions continued to organize, but for the next four decades, they found it extremely difficult to take action in the face of the conspiracy doctrine.

A milestone in the history of U.S. labor occurred with the formation of the Knights of Labor in 1869. Like previous unions, the Knights began as a craft union. Soon, however, the organization set larger goals for itself. In a drive to organize any workers who were interested in its representation, the Knights expanded to encompass workers in numerous fields (noteworthy exceptions were lawyers, bankers, and bartenders). The Knights was also the first union that actively sought women and Black workers as members and was one of the few unions that has ever focused on political lobbying rather than collective bargaining as a means of reaching its goals.

The Knights championed such traditional union issues as better working conditions, campaigning especially for the 8-hour day and the abolition of child labor. At the same time, the union also hoped to achieve a broad range of social goals. Chief among these were such liberal, or reformist, objectives as worker ownership of factories and free public land for those who wished to farm.

These same goals also attracted to the labor movement a variety of radicals and other political reformers, many of whom came in the waves of European immigrants who had begun arriving a few decades previously. Their activities were directed against what they saw as the oppressive nature of the industrial capitalist system, and their tactics did not necessarily reflect the typical strategies of the labor unions. Spurred by a severe depression in 1873, for example, a series of violent labor actions characterized labor-management relations from the mid to late 1870s. Demonstrators and locked-out strikers blockaded factories, battled strikebreakers in the streets of major cities, and exchanged fire with municipal police, state militia, and armed private agents. Assassinations and bombings led to the trial and execution of anarchists and labor agitators.

However, much of the violence in this period came in direct response to the extraordinary pressures of the depression. Most U.S. laborers were conservative by nature and sought the stability of organizations such as the Knights of Labor. Under the leadership of Terence V. Powderly, the Knights grew to include roughly 700,000 members by the mid-1880s. The union was never successful, however, at increasing the number of skilled workers among its members. In addition, it was weakened by internal disagreements about social goals and outside charges of union violence. By the turn of the twentieth century, the Knights had disbanded.

The Emergence of the Major Unions

With its focus on the social welfare of unskilled workers, the Knights of Labor tended to forget that its economic strength lay with its skilled craft workers. As a result of this oversight, many of these workers soon began to look for organizations that would better represent their interests, namely, unions whose primary concern was to improve wages, hours, and working conditions for their members.

The American Federation of Labor Many workers disenchanted with the social agenda of the Knights of Labor found a home in the **American Federation of Labor (AFL)**. Made up of craft unions, the AFL was formed in 1886 by Samuel Gompers and other veteran organizers. Unlike the Knights of Labor, the AFL stressed no broad, idealistic legislative or political program. Gompers himself saw the labor union as an integral component, not the inherent enemy, of the capitalist system: "As we get a 25-cents-a-day wage increase," he argued, the process "brings us nearer the time when a greater degree of social justice and fair dealing will obtain among men." The enduring importance of the AFL lies in the fact that it established a solid organizational basis for collective bargaining, economic action, and a pragmatic approach to union–management relations.

American Federation of Labor (AFL) *an association of craft unions formed in 1886 by Samuel Gompers and others; the AFL had no political or social agenda but simply sought to improve working conditions and pay for its members*

The AFL grew rapidly in the early decades of the twentieth century, and by the end of World War I, membership had reached more than 5 million. The 1920s proved difficult for the AFL because increased employer resistance to unions contributed to a steady decline in membership. By 1929, membership had dropped to 3.4 million.

The Great Depression of the 1930s witnessed further membership decline. By 1933, membership stood at just 2.9 million. In the same year, however, newly elected President Franklin D. Roosevelt introduced the nation to the New Deal, a far-reaching program aimed at stimulating the U.S. economy and creating jobs. The New Deal inspired an era of recovery for organized labor. Moreover, as we will see later in this appendix, the New Deal Congress passed a series of laws that made it easier for workers to organize.

The Congress of Industrial Organizations By the mid-1930s, the advent of mass production had significantly increased the demand for semi-skilled workers in the automobile, steel, and mining industries. The AFL, while continuing to grow throughout the 1930s, remained open only to skilled craftspeople. In fact, most AFL leaders opposed **industrial unionism**, the organizing of employees by industry rather than by skill or occupation. When a 1935 convention of AFL unions confirmed this stance, dissident leaders, including John F. Lewis of the United Mine Workers, objected bitterly. Ultimately, the AFL expelled 32 national unions, which in 1938 banded together to form the **Congress of Industrial Organizations (CIO)**.

Industrial Unionism *the organizing of employees by industry rather than by skill or occupation*

Congress of Industrial Organizations (CIO) *an association of industrial unions formed in 1938 after being expelled from the American Federation of Labor (AFL)*

Soon, the CIO had organized the auto, steel, mining, meatpacking, paper, textile, and electrical industries. By the early 1940s, CIO unions claimed close to 5 million of the slightly more than 10 million unionized U.S. workers. Not surprisingly, the AFL soon abandoned rigid craft unionism and also began to charter industrial unions.

The AFL-CIO Union membership continued to increase during World War II, reaching more than 14 million by the end of the war. However, a series of postwar strikes led Congress to curtail the power of unions. Partly in response to this change, and partly in response to growing conflicts within their ranks, leaders of the AFL and the CIO began merger negotiations. These meetings culminated in the 1955 formation of the AFL-CIO, with a total membership of 15 million. At the same time, organized labor reached its membership zenith, claiming almost 35 percent of the nonfarm workforce.

Today, in addition to lobbying for pro-union issues, the AFL-CIO settles jurisdictional disputes between unions. Remember, however, that the AFL-CIO is not a union itself. Rather, it is a federation of 60 individual unions with about 12.5 million individual members who belong to various trade or industrial departments (such as building trades, maritime trades, and public employees).[2] The United Food and Commercial Workers is a union, as are the International Brotherhood of Teamsters and the National Education Association.

Unionism Today

While understanding the historical context of labor unions is important, so, too, is appreciating the role of unionism today, especially trends in union membership, union–management relations, and bargaining perspectives. We discuss these topics in the sections that follow.

Trends in Union Membership

Since the mid-1950s, U.S. labor unions have experienced increasing difficulties in attracting new members. Although millions of workers still belong to labor unions, union membership *as a percentage of the total workforce* has continued to decline at a steady rate. In 1977, for example, more than 26 percent of U.S. wage and salary employees belonged to labor unions. Today, that figure is about 10.1 percent. Moreover, if public employees are excluded from consideration, then only around 6 percent of all private industry wage and salary employees currently belong to labor unions.[3]

Furthermore, just as union membership has continued to decline, so has the percentage of successful union-organizing campaigns. In the years immediately following World War II and continuing through the mid-1960s, most unions routinely won certification elections. In recent years, however, labor unions have been winning certification fewer than 50 percent of the time when workers are called on to vote. By the same token, of course, unions still do win. Meat cutters at a Florida Walmart store recently voted to unionize, the first-ever successful organizing campaign against the retailing giant. "You'll see a lot more attention to Walmart now," exulted one AFL-CIO official. "It's not like Walmart stands out as some unattainable goal."[4] More recently, there have been successful union organizing campaigns at Amazon and Starbucks.

From most indications, then, the power and significance of U.S. labor unions, although still quite formidable, are also measurably lower than they were just a few decades ago. A number of factors help to explain the decline in union membership.

Composition of the Workforce Union membership was once composed predominantly of white males in blue-collar jobs. But as most of us know, today's workforce is increasingly composed of women, people of color, and indigenous people. Because these groups have much weaker traditions of union affiliation, their members are less likely to join unions when they enter the workforce. In a related trend, much of the workforce has shifted toward geographic areas in the South and toward occupations in the service sector that have traditionally been less heavily unionized. For instance, Nucor Steel locates its facilities in smaller communities in the southern United States in part because it knows these workers are not prone to unionization.

Anti-Unionization Activities A second reason is more aggressive anti-unionization activity on the part of employers. Although the National Labor Relations Act and other laws specify strict management practices with regard to labor unions, companies are still free to pursue certain strategies that by their very nature tend to minimize employee interest in unionization. Both PepsiCo and Procter & Gamble, for example, now offer no-layoff guarantees for most of their employees, provide competitive wage and benefit packages, and maintain formal grievance systems for all workers. These arrangements were once available only through unions. But because these and other firms offer them independently of any union contract, employees have fewer reasons for unionizing.

Some companies have also worked to create much more employee-friendly work environments and to purposefully treat all employees with respect and dignity. One goal of this approach is to minimize the attractiveness of labor unions for employees. Many Japanese and German automobile manufacturers who have set up shop in the United States have successfully avoided unionization efforts by the United Auto Workers (UAW) by providing job security, higher wages, and a work environment in which employees are allowed to participate and be actively involved in plant management.

Trends in Union–Management Relations

The gradual decline in unionization in the United States has been accompanied by some significant trends in union–management relations. In some sectors of the economy, perhaps most notably the automobile, steel, and shipping industries, labor unions still remain quite strong. In these areas, unions have large memberships and considerable power in negotiating with management. The UAW, for example, is still one of the strongest unions in the United States.

In most sectors, however, unions are clearly in a weakened position, and as a result, many have taken much more conciliatory stances in their relations with management. This situation contrasts sharply with the more adversarial relationship that once dominated labor relations in this country. Increasingly, for instance, unions recognize that they don't have as much power as they once held and that it is in their own best interests, as well as in those of the workers who they represent, to work with management instead of working against it. Ironically, then, union–management relations are in many ways better today than they have been in many years. Admittedly, the improvement is attributable in large part to the weakened power of unions. Even so, however, most experts agree that improved union–management relations have benefited both sides.

Trends in Bargaining Perspectives

Given the trends described in the two previous sections (declining membership and shifts in union–management relationships), we should not be surprised to find changes in bargaining perspectives as well. In the past, most union–management bargaining situations were characterized by union demands for dramatic increases in wages and salaries. A secondary issue was usually increased benefits for members. Now, however, unions often bargain for different benefits, such as job security. Of particular interest in this area is the trend toward relocating jobs to take advantage of lower labor costs in other countries. Unions, of course, want to restrict job movement, whereas companies want to save money by moving facilities—and jobs—to other countries.

As a result of organizational downsizing and several years of relatively low inflation in this country, many unions today find themselves, rather than striving for wage increases, fighting against wage cuts. Similarly, as organizations are more likely to seek lower health care and other benefits, a common goal of union strategy is preserving what's already been won. Unions also place greater emphasis on improved job security. A trend that has become especially important in recent years is toward improved pension programs for employees.

Unions have also begun increasingly to set their sights on preserving jobs for workers in the United States in the face of business efforts to relocate production in some sectors to countries where labor costs are lower. For example, the AFL-CIO has been an outspoken opponent of efforts to normalize trade relations with China, fearing that more businesses might be tempted to move jobs there. General Electric has been targeted for union protests recently because of its strategy to move many of its own jobs—and those of key suppliers—to Mexico. Issues associated with temporary workers are also becoming more widely discussed during labor negotiations.

The Future of Unions

Despite declining membership and some loss of power, labor unions remain a major factor in the U.S. business world. The 60 labor organizations in the AFL-CIO, as well as independent major unions (such as the Teamsters and the National Education Association), still play a major role in U.S. business. Moreover, some unions still wield considerable power, especially in the traditional strongholds of goods-producing industries. Labor and management in some industries, notably airlines and steel, are beginning to favor contracts that establish formal mechanisms for greater worker input into management decisions. Inland Steel (now a part of ArcelorMittal), for instance, once granted its major union the right to name a member to the board of directors. Union officers could also attend executive meetings.

The big question still remains: Will unions dwindle in power and perhaps disappear, or can they evolve, survive to face new challenges, and play a new role in U.S. business? They will probably evolve to take on new roles and responsibilities. More and more unions are asking for—and often getting—voices in management. In 1980, for example, as part of a government-backed and union-supported Chrysler bailout, UAW president Douglas Fraser became the first labor official appointed to the board of directors of a major U.S. corporation. Several other companies have since followed suit.

By the same token, unions are increasingly aware that they must cooperate with employers if both are to survive. Critics of unions contend that excessive wage rates won through years of strikes and hard-nosed negotiation are partly to blame for the demise of large employers such as Eastern Airlines and Bethlehem Steel. Others argue that excessively tight work rules limit the productivity of businesses in many industries. More often, however, unions are working with organizations to create effective partnerships in which managers and workers share the same goals: profitability, growth, and effectiveness with equitable rewards for everyone.

Contemporary Union Structure

Just as each organization has its own unique structure, each union creates a structure that best serves its own needs. As Figure AIV.1 shows, a general structure characterizes most national and international unions. A major function of unions is to provide service and support to both members and local affiliates. Most of these services are carried out by the types of specialized departments shown in Figure AIV.1. In other unions, departments serve specific employment groups. The Machinists Union—the International Association of Machinists and Aerospace Workers—has departments for automotive, railroad, and airline workers.

Locals

Local Unions (Locals) *organized at the level of a single company, plant, or small geographic region*

At the same time, most national unions are composed of **local unions (locals)**, which are organized at the level of a single company, plant, or small defined geographic region. The functions of these locals vary, depending not only on governance arrangements but also on bargaining patterns in particular industries. Some local unions bargain directly with management regarding wages, hours, and other terms of employment. Many local unions are also active in disciplining members for violations of contract standards and in pressing management to respond to worker complaints. Local unions also serve as grassroots bases for union political activities, registering voters and getting them out to vote on election day.

Shop Steward *a regular employee who acts as a liaison between union members and supervisors*

Each department or unit represented at the local level elects a **shop steward**, a regular employee who acts as a liaison between union members and supervisors. For example, if workers have a grievance, they take it to the steward, who tries to resolve

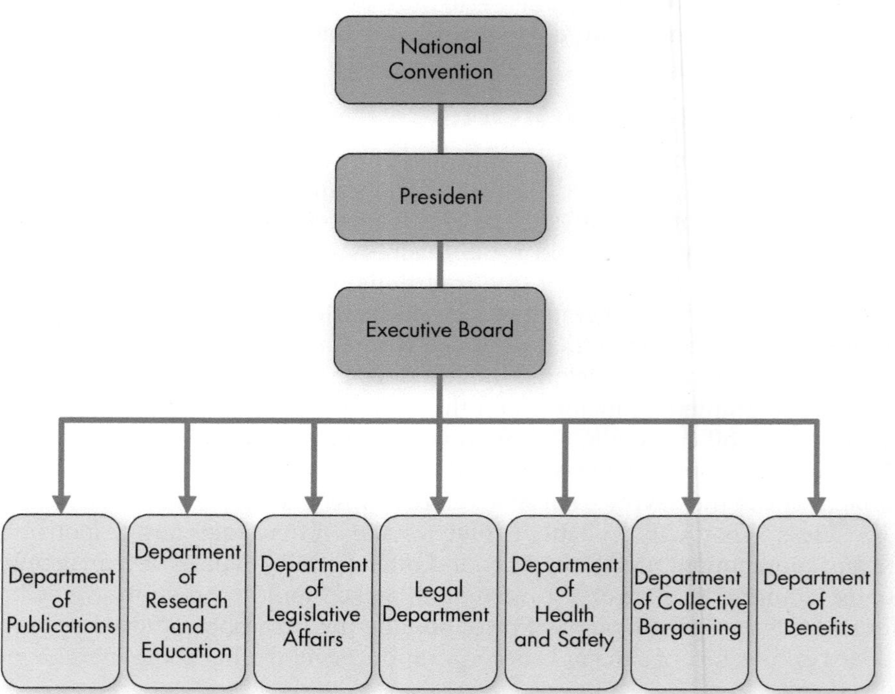

FIGURE AIV.1 Organization of a Large National Union

the problem with the supervisor. If the local is large, the union might hire a full-time **business agent** (or business representative) to play the same role.

Business Agent or **Business Representative** *a full-time employee hired to act as a liaison between union members and supervisors if a local union is large*

Within a given union, the main governing bodies are the national union (or international union when members come from more than one country) and its officers. Among their other duties, national and international unions charter local affiliates and establish general standards of conduct and procedures for local operations. For example, they set dues assessments, arrange for the election of local officers, sanction strikes, and provide guidance in the collective bargaining process. Many national unions also engage in a variety of political activities, such as lobbying. They may also help coordinate organizing efforts and establish education programs.

Given the magnitude of their efforts, it is little wonder that unions often take on many of the same characteristics as the companies for which their members work. For example, almost all large unions have full-time administrators, formal organizational structures (see Figure AIV.1), goals and strategic plans, and so forth. Sean M. O'Brien, current president of the International Brotherhood of Teamsters, oversees a large full-time staff.[5] His salary has not been reported, but in his previous position as a vice president with the Teamsters, he earned a total compensation package of $327,326.[6] A Teamsters representative told CNBC that O'Brien took a pay cut upon becoming president and "now has a constitutionally mandated salary that tops out at $225,000 per year and is tied to inflation."[7] (His predecessor, James P. Hoffa, earned an annual salary of $328,972.)[8] Because of their size, power, and importance, Congress has passed numerous laws to govern union activities. It is to these laws that we now turn our attention.

Laws Governing Labor-Management Relations

Like almost every other aspect of labor-management relations today, the process of unionizing workers is governed by numerous laws, administrative interpretations, and judicial decisions. In fact, the growth and decline of unionism in the United States can be traced by following the history of labor laws.

For the first 150 years of U.S. independence, workers were judged to have little legal right to organize. Indeed, interpretation of the 1890 Sherman Antitrust Act classified labor unions as monopolies, thus making them illegal. During the first 30 years of the twentieth century, however, social activism and turmoil in the labor force changed the landscape of U.S. labor relations.

The Major Labor Laws

Five major federal laws, all enacted between 1932 and 1959, laid the groundwork for all the rules, regulations, and judicial decisions governing union activity in the United States. A number of more recent laws have dealt with specific groups and specific issues. In general, these laws have been passed with a goal of maintaining a reasonable balance of power between business and labor such that neither side gains an unreasonable advantage over the other.

Norris-LaGuardia Act *act that imposed severe limitations on the ability of the courts to issue injunctions prohibiting certain union activities, including strikes*

Yellow-Dog Contracts *requirements that workers state that they did not belong to and would not join a union*

National Labor Relations Act or Wagner Act *act that put labor unions on a more equal footing with management in terms of the rights of employees to organize and bargain*

Norris-LaGuardia Act

During the 1930s, labor leaders finally persuaded lawmakers that the legal environment discriminated against the collective efforts of workers to improve working conditions. Legislators responded with the **Norris-LaGuardia Act** in 1932. This act imposed severe limitations on the ability of the courts to issue injunctions prohibiting certain union activities, including strikes. Norris-LaGuardia also outlawed **yellow-dog contracts**, requirements that workers state that they did not belong to and would not join a union.

National Labor Relations (Wagner) Act

In 1935 Congress passed the **National Labor Relations Act** (also called the **Wagner Act**), which is the cornerstone of contemporary labor relations law. This act put labor unions on a more equal footing with management in terms of the rights of employees to organize and bargain:

- It gave most workers the right to form unions, bargain collectively, and engage in group activities (such as strikes) to reach their goals.
- It forced employers to bargain with duly elected union leaders and prohibited employer practices that unjustly restrict employees' rights (e.g., discriminating against union members in hiring, promoting, and firing).

National Labor Relations Board (NLRB) *established by the Wagner Act to administer its provisions*

The Wagner Act also established the **National Labor Relations Board (NLRB)** to administer its provisions. Today, the NLRB administers virtually all labor law in this country. For example, it determines the appropriate unit for conducting bargaining at any workplace. The NLRB also oversees most of the elections held by employees to determine whether they will be represented by particular unions. It decides who is eligible to vote and who will be covered by bargaining agreements once they have been reached.

Fair Labor Standards Act *sets a minimum wage and requires the payment of overtime rates for work in excess of 40 hours per week*

Fair Labor Standards Act Enacted in 1938, the **Fair Labor Standards Act** addressed issues of minimum wages and maximum work hours:

- It set a minimum wage (originally $.25 an hour) to be paid to workers. The federal minimum wage has been increased many times since 1938 and now stands at $7.25 per hour. Several states have higher minimum wages. For instance, the minimum wage in Florida in 2022 was $11 an hour, and increased to $12 an hour in late 2023. By 2026, the state's minimum wage will reach $15 per hour.
- It set a maximum number of hours for the workweek, initially 44 hours per week, later 40 hours.
- It mandated time-and-a-half pay for those who worked beyond the legally stipulated number of hours.
- It outlawed child labor.

Taft-Hartley Act Supported by the Norris-LaGuardia, Wagner, and Fair Labor Standards Acts, organized labor eventually grew into a powerful political and economic force. But a series of disruptive strikes in the immediate post–World War II years began to turn public opinion against unions. Inconvenienced by strikes and the resulting shortages of goods and services, the public became openly critical of unions and pressured the government to take action. Congress responded by passing the Labor-Management Relations Act (more commonly known as the Taft-Hartley Act) in 1947.

Closed Shop *a workplace in which only workers already belonging to a union may be hired by an employer*

Right-to-Work Laws *such laws prohibit both union shops and agency shops, thus making it illegal to require union membership as a condition of employment*

Union Shop *requires employees to join a union within a specified period after being hired*

Agency Shop *requires employees to pay union fees even if they choose not to join*

Unfair and Illegal Union Practices The Taft-Hartley Act defined certain union practices as unfair and illegal. For example, it prohibited such practices as featherbedding (requiring extra workers solely to provide more jobs) and refusing to bargain in good faith. It also generally forbade the **closed shop**, a workplace in which only workers already belonging to a union may be hired by an employer. Instead, Taft-Hartley promoted open shops by allowing states to enact **right-to-work laws**. Such laws prohibit both union shops and agency shops, thus making it illegal to require union membership as a condition of employment. A **union shop** requires employees to join a union within a specified period after being hired. An **agency shop** requires employees to pay union fees even if they choose not to join. To date, 27 states have enacted right-to-work laws (West Virginia has also passed right-to-work legislation, but it is currently being appealed in court). These states are shown in Figure AIV.2.

Injunctions and Cooling-Off Periods Passed in the wake of crippling strikes in the steel industry, the Taft-Hartley Act also established procedures for resolving

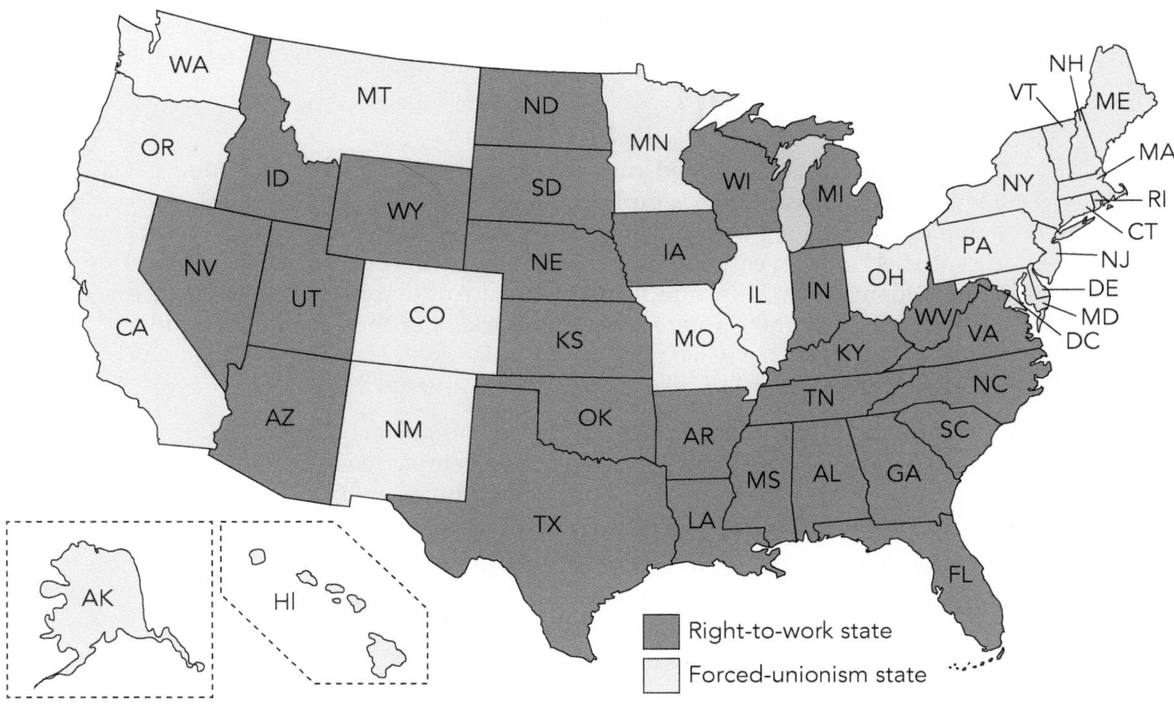

FIGURE AIV.2 Right-to-Work States

any strike deemed to pose a national emergency. Initially, the concept of national emergency was broadly interpreted. For example, virtually any large company could claim that a strike was doing irreparable harm to its financial base and that the nation's economy would be harmed if workers were not forced back to their jobs.

Today, however, the courts use a more precise definition of national emergency. For example, a strike must affect a whole industry or most of it. Similarly, the use of Taft-Hartley is more restrictive. Now the president may request an injunction requiring that workers restrain from striking for 60 days. During this cooling-off period, labor and management must try to resolve their differences.

Enforced Resolution If differences are not resolved during the cooling-off period, the injunction may be extended for another 20 days. During this period, employees must vote, in a secret ballot election, on whether to accept or reject the employer's latest offer. If they accept the offer, the threat of strike is ended and the contract signed. If they do not accept the offer, the president reports to Congress and the workers may either be forced back to work under threat of criminal action or fired and replaced by nonunion employees. Presidential intervention has been invoked only 35 times since Taft-Hartley was passed.

Landrum-Griffin Act The National Labor Relations Act was further amended by the **Landrum-Griffin Act** in 1959. Officially titled the **Labor-Management Reporting and Disclosure Act**, this law resulted from congressional hearings that revealed unethical, illegal, and undemocratic union practices. The act thus imposed regulations on internal union procedures:

- It required the election of national union leaders at least once every five years.
- It gave union members the right to participate in various union affairs.
- It required unions to file annual financial disclosure statements with the Department of Labor.

Landrum-Griffin Act or **Labor-Management Reporting and Disclosure Act** *amendment to the National Labor Relations Act that imposed regulations on internal union procedures*

How Unions Are Organized and Certified

Many of the laws described previously address the issue of union certification. Figure AIV.3 illustrates a simplified version of this process. First, there must be some interest among workers in having a union. Sometimes this interest comes from dissatisfied employees; sometimes it is stirred by professional organizers sent by unions themselves. For example, the United Auto Workers has for years dispatched organizers to promote interest among workers at the Honda plant in Marysville, Ohio. To date, they have had no success in Marysville or in Smyrna, Tennessee, where Nissan built its major U.S. plant. The process unfolds as follows:

1. ***Defining the bargaining unit.*** Interested organizers start by asking the NLRB to define the *bargaining unit*, the group of employees who will be represented by the union. For instance, a bargaining unit might be all nonmanagement employees in an organization or all electrical workers at a certain plant.
2. ***Gaining authorization.*** Organizers must then get 30 percent of the eligible workers within the bargaining unit to sign authorization cards requesting a certification election. If less than 30 percent of the workers want an election, the process ends and no election is held.
3. ***Conducting an election.*** If the required number of signatures is obtained, however, the organizers petition the NLRB to conduct the election. The NLRB then holds a secret ballot election. If a simple majority of those voting approves the certification, the union becomes the official bargaining agent of eligible employees. If a majority fails to approve certification, the process ends and an election cannot be called again for at least one year.

Unions are not necessarily permanent fixtures in a workplace, and if conditions warrant, a union may be *decertified*. For example, workers may become disenchanted with a union and may even feel that they are being hurt by its presence. They may believe that management is trying to be cooperative, while the union is refusing to negotiate in good faith.

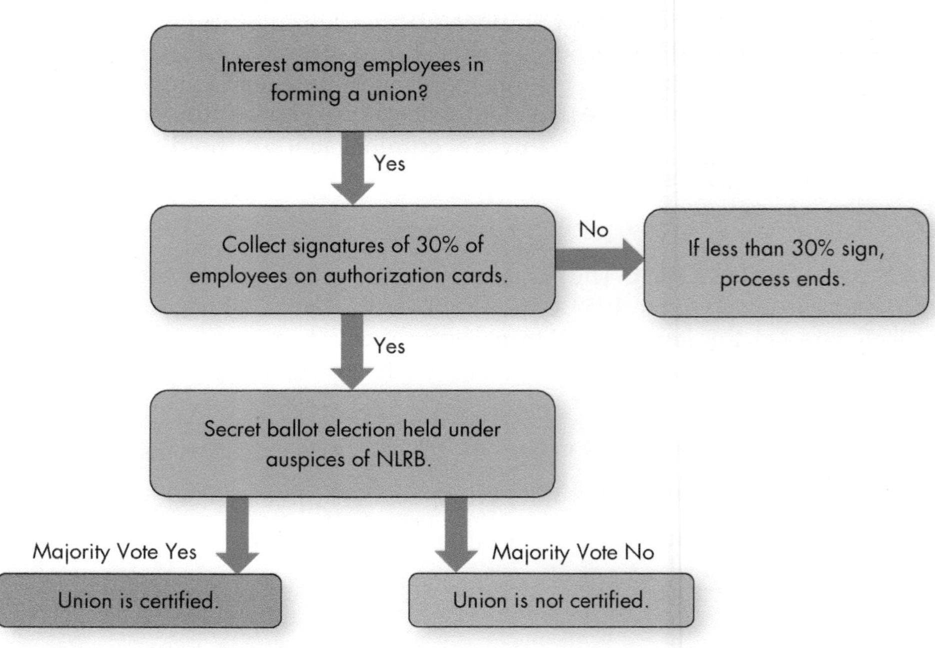

FIGURE AIV.3 Certifying a Labor Union

Decertification requires two conditions:

1 The union must have served the unit as its official bargaining agent for at least one year.
2 There must be no labor contract currently in effect.

If these conditions are met, employees or their representatives can solicit signatures on decertification cards. If 30 percent of the employees in the unit sign, the NLRB conducts a decertification election. If a majority of those voting favor decertification, the union is removed as the unit's official bargaining agent. Following decertification, a new election cannot be requested for at least one year.

Collective Bargaining

When a union has been legally certified, it assumes the role of official bargaining agent for the workers whom it represents. Collective bargaining is an ongoing process involving both the drafting and the administering of the terms of a labor contract.

Reaching Agreement on Contract Terms

The collective bargaining process begins when the union is recognized as the exclusive negotiator for its members. The bargaining cycle itself begins when union leaders meet with management representatives to agree on a contract. By law, both parties must sit down at the bargaining table and negotiate in good faith.

When each side has presented its demands, sessions focus on identifying the *bargaining zone*. The process is shown in Figure AIV.4. For example, although an employer may initially offer no pay raise, it may expect to grant a raise of up to 6 percent. Likewise, the union may initially *demand* a 10 percent pay raise while *expecting* to accept a raise as low as 4 percent. The bargaining zone, then, is a raise between 4 and 6 percent. Ideally, some compromise is reached between these levels and the new agreement submitted for a ratification vote by union membership.

Sometimes, this process goes quite smoothly. At other times, however, the two sides cannot—or will not—agree. The speed and ease with which such an impasse is resolved depend in part on the nature of the contract issues, the willingness of each side to use certain tactics, and the prospects for mediation or arbitration.

Contract Issues

The labor contract itself can address an array of different issues. Most of these concern demands that unions make on behalf of their members. In this section, we will

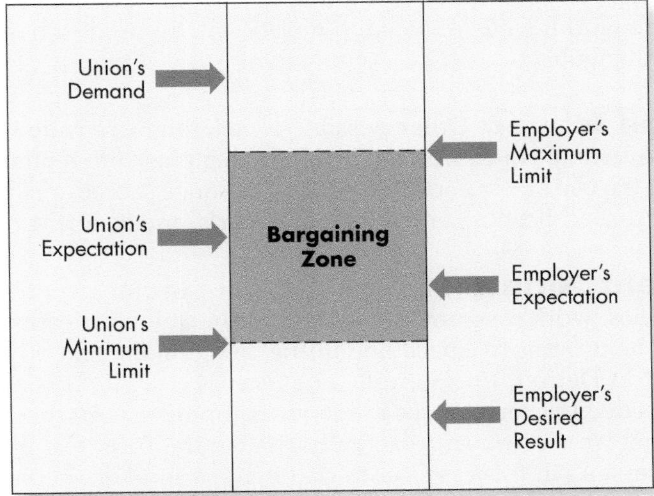

FIGURE AIV.4 The Bargaining Zone

survey the categories of issues that are typically most important to union negotiators: *compensation*, *benefits*, and *job security*. Although few issues covered in a labor contract are company sponsored, we will also describe the kinds of *management rights* that are negotiated in most bargaining agreements.

First, note that bargaining items generally fall into two categories:

- *Mandatory items* are matters over which both parties must negotiate if either wants to. This category includes wages, working hours, and benefits.
- *Permissive items* may be negotiated if both parties agree. A union demand for veto power over the promotion of managerial personnel would be a permissive bargaining item.

Illegal items may not be brought to the table by either party. A management demand for a nonstrike clause, for example, would be an illegal item.

Compensation The most common issue is compensation. One aspect of compensation is current wages. Obviously, unions generally want their employees to earn higher wages and try to convince management to raise hourly wages for all or some employees.

Of equal concern to unions is future compensation, wage rates to be paid during subsequent years of the contract. One common tool for securing wage increases is a **cost-of-living adjustment (COLA)**. Most COLA clauses tie future raises to the *consumer price index (CPI)*, a government statistic that reflects changes in consumer purchasing power. The premise is that as the CPI increases by a specified amount during a given period of time, wages will automatically be increased. Almost half of all labor contracts today include COLA clauses.

Cost-of-Living Adjustment (COLA) *labor contract clause tying future raises to changes in consumer purchasing power*

Wage reopener clauses are now included in almost 10 percent of all labor contracts. Such a clause allows wage rates to be negotiated at preset times during the life of the contract. For example, a union might be uncomfortable with a long-term contract based solely on COLA wage increases. A long-term agreement might be more acceptable, however, if management agrees to renegotiate wages every two years.

Wage Reopener Clause *clause allowing wage rates to be renegotiated during the life of the contract*

Benefits Employee benefits are also an important component in most labor contracts. Unions typically want employers to pay all or most of the costs of insurance for employees. Other benefits commonly addressed during negotiations include retirement benefits, paid holidays, and working conditions.

Job Security Nevertheless, the UAW's top priority in its most recent negotiations with U.S. automakers has been job security, an increasingly important agenda item in many bargaining sessions today. In some cases, demands for job security entail the promise that a company not move to another location. In others, the contract may dictate that if the workforce is reduced, seniority will be used to determine which employees lose their jobs.

Other Union Issues Other possible issues might include such things as working hours, overtime policies, rest period arrangements, differential pay plans for shift employees, the use of temporary workers, grievance procedures, and allowable union activities (dues collection, union bulletin boards, and so forth).

Management Rights Management wants as much control as possible over hiring policies, work assignments, and so forth. Unions, meanwhile, often try to limit management rights by specifying hiring, assignment, and other policies. At a Chrysler plant in Detroit, for example, one recent contract stipulated that three workers were needed to change fuses in robotic equipment, a machinist to open the robotic fuse panel, an electrician to actually change the fuse, and a supervisor to oversee the process. As in this case, contracts often bar workers in one job category from performing work that falls in the domain of another. Unions try to secure jobs by defining as many different categories as possible (the Chrysler plant had more than 100).

Of course, management resists the practice, which limits flexibility and makes it difficult to reassign workers.

When Bargaining Fails

An impasse occurs when, after a series of bargaining sessions, management and labor have failed to agree on a new contract or a contract to replace an agreement that is about to expire. Although it is generally agreed that both parties suffer when an impasse is reached and action is taken, each side can use several tactics to support its cause until the impasse is resolved.

Union Tactics When their demands are not met, unions may bring a variety of tactics to the bargaining table. Chief among these is the strike, which may be supported by *pickets*, *boycotts*, or both.

THE STRIKE A **strike** occurs when employees temporarily walk off the job and refuse to work. Most strikes in the United States are **economic strikes**, triggered by stalemates over mandatory bargaining items, including such noneconomic issues as working hours. For example, the Teamsters union struck United Parcel Service (UPS) a few years ago over several noneconomic issues. Specifically, the union wanted the firm to transform many of its temporary and part-time jobs into permanent and full-time jobs. Strikers returned to work only when UPS agreed to create 10,000 new jobs. The Teamsters also struck Union Pacific Corp. in 2013. And union members at the Lockheed-Martin plant in Fort Worth, Texas, staged a 2-week strike in 2014. Reflected the president of the union local: "I think our people gained a lot of respect for taking a stand. We had a good strike."

Strike *labor action in which employees temporarily walk off the job and refuse to work*

Economic Strikes *strikes triggered by stalemates over mandatory bargaining items, including such noneconomic issues as working hours*

Still, far fewer strikes take place today than in previous years. For example, there were 222 strikes in the United States in 1960 involving a total of 896,000 workers. In 1970, 2,468,000 workers took part in 381 strikes. But in 1990, there were only 44 strikes involving 185,000 workers. Since 1990, the largest number of major strikes in one year was 45 in 1994. Only 23 major strikes took place in 2022.[9] The largest of these occurred when 46,000 General Motors workers walked off their jobs for 29 days until new contract terms were reached. The Writers Guild of America went on strike in 2023, impacting the production of many movies and television programs. The primary issue was royalties for streaming content. The UAW also struck all three major U.S. automakers in 2023 seeking both higher wages and shorter workweeks, among other things.

Not all strikes are legal. Sympathy strikes (also called secondary strikes), which occur when one union strikes in sympathy with action initiated by another, may violate the sympathetic union's contract. Wildcat strikes, strikes unauthorized by the union that occur during the life of a contract, deprive strikers of their status as employees and thus of the protection of the national labor law.

OTHER LABOR ACTIONS To support a strike, a union faced with an impasse has recourse to additional legal activities:

- In *picketing*, workers stand or march at the entrance to the employer's facility with signs explaining their reasons for striking.
- A *boycott* occurs when union members agree not to buy the products of a targeted employer. Workers may also urge consumers to boycott the firm's products.
- Another alternative to striking is a work *slowdown*. Instead of striking, workers perform their jobs but at a much slower pace than normal. A variation is the sickout, during which large numbers of workers call in sick. Pilots at American Airlines engaged in a massive "sickout," causing the airline to cancel thousands of flights before a judge ordered them back to work.[10]

During the COVID-19 pandemic in 2020, some unions felt their employers were not taking sufficient steps to protect workers from infection. As a result, they threatened to walk off the job, and several filed labor grievances with the NLRB.

Unions representing workers at Sanderson Farms (a large poultry processor) and McDonald's were among these.

Management Tactics Like workers, management can respond forcefully to an impasse:

Lockout *management tactic whereby workers are denied access to the employer's workplace*

- **Lockouts** occur when employers deny employees access to the workplace. Lockouts are illegal if they are used as offensive weapons to give management a bargaining advantage. However, they are legal if management has a legitimate business need (for instance, avoiding a buildup of perishable inventory). Although rare today, ABC once locked out its off-camera employees because they staged an unannounced one-day strike during a critical broadcasting period.[11] Likewise, Major League Baseball players were locked out during contract negotiations in 2022.

Strikebreaker *worker hired as a permanent or temporary replacement for a striking employee*

A firm can also hire temporary or permanent replacements called **strikebreakers**. (The NFL employed temporary referees during the 2012 lockout.) However, the law forbids the permanent replacement of workers who strike because of unfair practices. In some cases, an employer can also obtain legal injunctions that either prohibit workers from striking or prohibit a union from interfering with its efforts to use replacement workers.

Mediation and Arbitration Rather than wield these often unpleasant weapons against one another, labor and management can agree to call in a third party to help resolve the dispute:

Mediation *method of resolving a labor dispute in which a third party suggests, but does not impose, a settlement*

Voluntary Arbitration *a neutral third party (the arbitrator) dictates a settlement between the two sides, who have agreed to submit to outside judgment*

Compulsory Arbitration *used to settle disputes between the government and public employees such as firefighters and police officers*

- In **mediation**, the neutral third party (the mediator) can advise, but cannot impose a settlement on the other parties.
- In **voluntary arbitration**, the neutral third party (the arbitrator) dictates a settlement between the two sides, who have agreed to submit to outside judgment.
- In some cases, arbitration is legally required to settle bargaining disputes. **Compulsory arbitration** is used to settle disputes between the government and public employees such as firefighters and police officers.

Administering a Labor Agreement

Once a labor agreement has been reached, its details are written into the form of a contract legally enforceable in the courts. Labor contracts almost always have precise agreements as to how the agreement will be enforced. In some cases, of course, enforcement is quite clear. If the two sides agree that the company will increase wages by 2 percent per year over the next three years according to a prescribed schedule, then there is little opportunity for disagreement. Wage increases can be mathematically calculated and union members will see the effects in their paychecks. But other provisions may be much more prone to misinterpretation and different perceptions.

Suppose, for example, that a labor contract specifies the process for allocating overtime assignments. Such strategies are often complex, and the employer may have to take into account a variety of factors, such as seniority, previous overtime allocations, the hours or days in which the overtime work is needed, and so forth. Now suppose that a factory supervisor is trying to follow the labor contract and offers overtime to a specific employee. This employee, however, indicates that before accepting, it may be necessary to check with their spouse to make sure that child care responsibilities can be rearranged. The supervisor, however, may feel the pressure of a deadline and award the overtime opportunity to a second employee. If the first employee objects to this course of action, then they may file a complaint with the union.

When such differences of opinion arise, the union member takes the complaint to the shop steward. The shop steward may advise the employee that the supervisor handled things properly, but other appeal mechanisms are available, and the employee, even if refuted by the shop steward, still has channels for appeal.

Of course, if the shop steward agrees with the employee, the shop steward may follow prescribed methods for pursuing the complaint. The prescribed methods might include talking with the supervisor to get the other side of the story and then provide for lines of appeal on up the hierarchy of both the union and the company. In some cases, mediation or arbitration may be called into play, as may other efforts to resolve the dispute. The overtime, for example, may be reassigned to the first employee. Or the overtime may remain with the second employee while the first employee is also paid.

Let's return for a moment to the agreement reached by the Teamsters and United Parcel Service that we described previously. After the agreement was reached, the union became concerned that UPS was not moving quickly enough to create the new jobs to which it had agreed two years earlier. The union submitted its complaint to arbitration and won. UPS was given a specific timetable for adding the new jobs as agreed.[12]

endnotes

1 David Lipsky and Clifford Donn, *Collective Bargaining in American Industry* (Lexington, MA: Lexington Books, 1981). See also John Fossum, *Labor Relations: Development, Structure, Process*, 13th ed. (Homewood, IL: Irwin Management, 2020).

2 AFL-CIO, "Our Unions and Allies," AFLCIO.org, accessed June 10, 2023, https://aflcio.org/about-us/our-unions-and-allies.

3 U.S. Bureau of Labor Statistics, U.S. Department of Labor, "Union Members–2022," news release, January 19, 2023, https://www.bls.gov/news.release/pdf/union2.pdf.

4 David Koenig, "Labor Unions Say Recent Victories Signal a Comeback," Associated Press news release published in *The Bryan-College Station Eagle*, June 11, 2013, E1, E6.

5 Noam Scheiber, "A Hoffa Ally, Then a Foe, and Soon the Teamsters President," *The New York Times*, November 19, 2021, https://www.nytimes.com/2021/11/19/business/economy/teamsters-sean-obrien-hoffa.html.

6 Teamsters for a Democratic Union (TDU), "Teamster Officers Salary Report," TDU.org, April 19, 2021, https://www.tdu.org/teamster_officers_salary_report_2021.

7 Chelsey Cox, "Oklahoma Republican Tells Teamsters President 'Shut Your Mouth' in Terse Exchange at Senate Hearing," CNBC.com, March 8, 2023, https://www.cnbc.com/2023/03/08/oklahoma-republican-tells-teamsters-president-shut-your-mouth-in-terse-exchange-at-senate-hearing.html.

8 Teamsters for a Democratic Union (TDU), "How Teamster Officer Salaries Dramatically Changed—and Why," TDU.org, April 19, 2021, https://www.tdu.org/how_teamster_salaries_dramatically_changed_and_why.

9 U.S. Bureau of Labor Statistics, "Work Stoppages," BLS.gov, accessed on June 15, 2023, https://www.bls.gov/wsp/.

10 Stephanie Amour, "Will Fine Divide or Solidify Pilots?" *USA Today*, February 15, 1999, 1B.

11 Stephanie Amour, "ABC Locks Out Striking Employees," *USA Today*, November 3, 1998, B1.

12 Kerry Flynn, "MLB Lockout: What Is It? Why Is It Happening? When Is It Over?," CNN.com, March 5, 2022, https://www.cnn.com/2022/03/05/sport/mlb-lockout-explainer-baseball-spt-intl/index.html.

glossary

A

Absenteeism when an employee does not show up for work

Absolute Advantage the ability to produce something more efficiently than any other country can

Accommodative Stance approach to social responsibility by which a company, if specifically asked to do so, exceeds legal minimums in its commitments to groups and individuals in its social environment

Accountability obligation employees have to their manager for the successful completion of an assigned task

Accounting comprehensive system for collecting, analyzing, and communicating financial information

Accounting Equation Assets = Liabilities + Owners' Equity; used by accountants to balance data for the firm's financial transactions at various points in the year

Accounting Information System (AIS) organized procedure for identifying, measuring, recording, and retaining financial information for use in accounting statements and management reports

Accounts Payable (Payables) current liability consisting of bills owed to suppliers, plus wages and taxes due within the coming year

Acquisition the purchase of one company by another

Activity Ratio financial ratio for evaluating management's efficiency in using a firm's assets

Adverse Impact when people of color and women meet or pass the requirement for a job at a rate less than 80 percent of the rate of non-Hispanic, white, male group members (in the United States)

Advertising Media variety of communication devices for carrying a seller's message to potential customers

Advertising any form of paid nonpersonal communication used by an identified sponsor to persuade or inform potential buyers about a product

Affect a person's feelings toward something

Affirmative Action intentionally seeking and hiring employees from groups that are underrepresented in the organization

Affirmative Action Plan written statement of how the organization intends to actively recruit, hire, and develop members of relevant protected classes

Age Discrimination in Employment Act outlaws discrimination against people older than 40 years

Agency Shop requires employees to pay union fees even if they choose not to join

Agent individual or organization acting for and in the name of another party

Aggregate Output the total quantity of goods and services produced by an economic system during a given period

American Federation of Labor (AFL) an association of craft unions formed in 1886 by Samuel Gompers and others; the AFL had no political or social agenda but simply sought to improve working conditions and pay for its members

Americans with Disabilities Act forbids discrimination on the basis of disabilities and requires employers to provide reasonable accommodations for disabled employees

Angel Investors outside investors who provide new capital for firms in return for a share of equity ownership

Annual Percentage Rate (APR) one-year rate that is charged for borrowing, expressed as a percentage of the borrowed principal

Antivirus Software product that protects systems by searching incoming e-mails and data files for "signatures" of known viruses and virus-like characteristics

Apparent Authority agent's authority, based on the principal's compliance, to bind a principal to a certain course of action

Appellate Court court that reviews case records of trials whose findings have been appealed

Arbitration method of resolving a labor dispute in which both parties agree to submit to the judgment of a neutral party

Artificial Intelligence computer systems and algorithms that are capable of performing tasks that typically require human intelligence

Assembly Line Layout a same-steps layout in which a product moves step by step through a plant on conveyor belts or other equipment until it is completed

Asset any economic resource expected to benefit a firm or an individual who owns it

Asset Allocation relative amount of funds invested in (or allocated to) each of several investment alternatives

Association of Southeast Asian Nations (ASEAN) organization for economic, political, social, and cultural cooperation among Southeast Asian nations

Attitudes a person's beliefs and feelings about specific ideas, situations, or people

Audit systematic examination of a company's accounting system to determine whether its financial reports reliably represent its operations

Authoritarianism the extent to which a person believes that power and status differences are appropriate within hierarchical social systems such as organizations

Authority power to make the decisions necessary to complete a task

Automated Teller Machine (ATM) electronic machine that allows bank customers to conduct account-related activities 24 hours a day, 7 days a week

B

Balance of Payments flow of all money into or out of a country

Balance of Trade economic value of all products a country exports minus the economic value of all products it imports

Balance Sheet financial statement that supplies detailed information about a firm's assets, liabilities, and owners' equity

Banker's Acceptance bank promise, issued for a buyer, to pay a designated firm a specified amount at a future date

Bankruptcy court-granted permission for a company to not pay some or all debts

Bargain Retailer retailer carrying a wide range of products at bargain prices

Bear Market period of falling stock prices marked by negative investor sentiments with motivation to sell ahead of anticipated losses

Behavioral Approach to Leadership focused on determining what behaviors are employed by leaders

Behavioral Segmentation a segmentation strategy that uses behavioral variables to identify different market segments

Behavioral Variables behavioral patterns displayed by groups of consumers and that are used in developing a segmentation strategy

Benefits compensation other than wages and salaries

"Big Five" Personality Traits five fundamental personality traits especially relevant to organizations

Blue-Chip Stock common stock issued by a well-established and respected company with a sound financial history and a stable pattern of dividend payouts

Board of Directors governing body of a corporation that reports to its shareholders and delegates power to run its day-to-day operations while remaining responsible for sustaining its assets

Bond Indenture legal document containing complete details of a bond issue

Bondholders' Claim request for court enforcement of a bond's terms of payment

Bonus individual performance incentive in the form of a special payment made over and above the employee's salary

Book Value value of a common stock expressed as the firm's owners' equity divided by the number of common shares

Book-Entry Ownership procedure that holds investors' shares in book-entry form, rather than issuing a physical paper certificate of ownership

Bookkeeping recording of accounting transactions

Boycott labor action in which workers refuse to buy the products of a targeted employer

Branch Office foreign office set up by an international or multinational firm

Brand Awareness extent to which a brand name comes to mind when a consumer considers a particular product category

Brand Competition competitive marketing that appeals to consumer perceptions of benefits of products offered by particular companies

Brand Loyalty pattern of repeated consumer purchasing based on satisfaction with a product's performance

Branding process of using symbols to communicate the qualities of a product made by a particular producer

Breakeven Analysis identifies the sales volume where total costs equal total revenues by assessing costs versus revenues at various sales volumes and showing, at any particular selling price, the amount of loss or profit for each volume of sales

Breakeven Point sales volume at which the seller's total revenue from sales equals total costs (variable and fixed) with neither profit nor loss

Broker independent intermediary who matches numerous sellers and buyers as needed, often without knowing in advance who they will be

Budget detailed statement of estimated receipts and expenditures for a future period of time

Bull Market period of rising stock prices, lasting 12 months or longer, featuring investor confidence for future gains and motivation to buy

Bundling Strategy grouping several products together to be sold as a single unit at a reduced price, rather than individually

Business organization that provides goods or services to earn profits

Business (or Competitive) Strategy strategy, at the business-unit or product-line level, focusing on improving a firm's competitive position

Business Agent or **Business Representative** a full-time employee hired to act as a liaison between union members and supervisors if a local union is large

Business Continuation Agreement special form of business insurance whereby owners arrange to buy the interests of deceased associates from their heirs

Business Cycle short-term pattern of economic expansions and contractions

Business Ethics ethical or unethical behaviors by employees in the context of their jobs

Business Interruption Insurance insurance covering income lost during times when a company is unable to conduct business

Business Plan document in which the entrepreneur summarizes the business strategy for the proposed new venture and how that strategy will be implemented

Business Practice Law law or regulation governing business practices in given countries

Business Process Reengineering rethinking and radical redesign of business processes to improve performance, quality, and productivity

C

Cafeteria Benefits Plan benefit plan that sets limits on benefits per employee, each of whom may choose from a variety of alternative benefits

Capacity amount of a product that a company can produce under normal conditions

Capacity competence required of individual entering into a binding contract

Capital funds needed to create and operate a business enterprise

Capital Gain profit realized from the increased value of an investment

Capital Items expensive, long-lasting, infrequently purchased industrial products, such as a building, or industrial services, such as a long-term agreement for data warehousing services

Capitalism system that sanctions the private ownership of the factors of production and encourages entrepreneurship by offering profits as an incentive

Cartel association of producers whose purpose is to control supply and prices

Catalog Showroom bargain retailer in which customers place orders for catalog items to be picked up at on-premises warehouses

Centralized Organization organization in which most decision-making authority is held by upper-level management

Certified Fraud Examiner (CFE) professional designation administered by the ACFE in recognition of qualifications for a specialty area within forensic accounting

Certified Management Accountant (CMA) professional designation awarded by the Institute of Management Accountants (IMA) in recognition of management accounting qualifications

Certified Public Accountant (CPA) accountant licensed by the state and offering services to the public

Chain of Command reporting relationships within a company

Channel Captain channel member who is most powerful in determining the roles and rewards of other members

Channel Conflict conflict arising when the members of a distribution channel disagree over the roles they should play or the rewards they should receive

Charismatic Leadership type of influence based on the leader's personal charisma

Check demand deposit order instructing a bank to pay a given sum to a specified payee

Checking Account (Demand Deposit) bank account funds, owned by the depositor, that may be withdrawn at any time by check or cash

Chief Executive Officer (CEO) the top manager of an organization

Civil Rights Act of 1991 amended the original Civil Rights Act

Classical Theory of Motivation theory holding that workers are motivated solely by money

Client-Server Network common business network in which clients make requests for information or resources and servers provide the services

Closely Held (or Private) Corporation corporation whose stock is held by only a few people and is not available for sale to the general public

Closed Shop a workplace in which only workers already belonging to a union may be hired by an employer

Closing step in the personal selling process in which salespeople ask prospective customers to buy products

Coalition an informal alliance of individuals or groups formed to achieve a common goal

Code of Professional Conduct code of ethics for CPAs as maintained and enforced by the AICPA

Coercive Power the power to force compliance by means of psychological, emotional, or physical threat

Cognition the knowledge a person presumes to have about something

Cognitive Dissonance when two sets of cognitions or perceptions are contradictory or incongruent

Collateral asset pledged for the fulfillment of repaying a loan

Collective Bargaining process by which labor and management negotiate conditions of employment for union-represented workers

Collusion illegal agreement between two or more companies to commit a wrongful act

Commercial Bank company that accepts deposits that it uses to make loans, earn profits, pay interest to depositors, and pay dividends to owners

Committee and Team Authority authority granted to committees or teams involved in a firm's daily operations

Common Stock most basic form of ownership, including voting rights on major issues, in a company

Common Law body of decisions handed down by courts ruling on individual cases

Communism political system in which the government owns and operates all factors of production

Comparative Advantage the ability to produce some products more efficiently than others

Compensation System total package of rewards that organizations provide to individuals in return for their labor

Compensatory Damages monetary payments intended to redress injury actually suffered because of a tort

Competition vying among businesses for the same resources or customers

Competitive Environment the competitive system in which businesses compete

Competitive Product Analysis process by which a company analyzes a competitor's products to identify desirable improvements

Compound Growth compounding of interest over time—with each additional time period, interest returns accumulate and earn more interest

Compulsory Arbitration used to settle disputes between the government and public employees such as firefighters and police officers

Computer Network group of two or more computers linked together by some form of cabling or by wireless technology to share data or resources, such as a printer

Computer-Aided Design (CAD) IS with software that helps knowledge workers design products by simulating them and displaying them in three-dimensional graphics

Computer-Aided Manufacturing (CAM) IS that uses computers to design and control equipment in a manufacturing process

Conceptual Skills abilities to think in the abstract, diagnose and analyze different situations, and see beyond the present situation

Congress of Industrial Organizations (CIO) an association of industrial unions formed in 1938 after being expelled from the American Federation of Labor (AFL)

Consistency dimension of quality that refers to sameness of product quality from unit to unit

Consideration item of value exchanged between parties to create a valid contract

Consumer person who purchases products for personal use

Consumer Behavior study of the decision process by which people buy and consume products

Consumer Goods physical products purchased by consumers for personal use

Consumer Price Index (CPI) a measure of the prices of typical products purchased by consumers living in urban areas

Consumerism form of social activism dedicated to protecting the rights of consumers in their dealings with businesses

Contract agreement between two or more parties enforceable in court

Contingency Planning identifying aspects of a business or its environment that might entail changes in strategy

Contingent Worker employee hired on something other than a full-time basis to supplement an organization's permanent workforce

Controller person who manages all of a firm's accounting activities (chief accounting officer)

Controlling management process of monitoring an organization's performance to ensure that it is meeting its goals

Convenience Goods inexpensive physical goods that are consumed rapidly and regularly

Convenience Services inexpensive services that are consumed rapidly and regularly

Convenience Store retail store offering easy accessibility, extended hours, and fast service

Cooperatives form of ownership in which a group of sole proprietorships or partnerships agree to work together for common benefits

Copyright exclusive ownership right belonging to the creator of a book, article, design, illustration, photo, film, or musical work

Core Competencies for Accounting the combination of skills, technology, and knowledge that will be necessary for the future CPA

Corporate Blogs comments and opinions published on the web by or for an organization to promote its activities

Corporate Bond formal pledge obligating the issuer (the company) to pay interest periodically and repay the principal at maturity

Corporate Culture the shared experiences, stories, beliefs, and norms that characterize an organization

Corporate Governance roles of shareholders, directors, and other managers in corporate decision making and accountability

Corporate Raider investor conducting a type of hostile corporate takeover against the wishes of the company

Corporate Social Audit systematic analysis of a firm's success in using funds earmarked for meeting its social responsibility goals

Corporate Strategy strategy for determining the firm's overall attitude toward growth and the way it will manage its businesses or product lines

Corporation business that is legally considered an entity separate from its owners and is liable for its own debts; owners' liability extends to the limits of their investments

Cost-of-Living Adjustment (COLA) labor contract clause tying future raises to changes in consumer purchasing power

Cost of Goods Sold costs of obtaining materials for making the products sold by a firm during the year

Cost of Revenues costs that a company incurs to obtain revenues from other companies

Cost-of-Living Adjustment (COLA) labor contract clause tying future raises to changes in consumer purchasing power

Cost-Oriented Pricing pricing that considers the firm's desire to make a profit and its need to cover operating costs

Counterproductive Behaviors behaviors that detract from organizational performance

Coupon sales-promotion technique in which a certificate is issued entitling the buyer to a reduced price

Creative Selling personal-selling task in which salespeople try to persuade buyers to purchase products by providing information about their benefits

Credit Union nonprofit, cooperative financial institution owned and run by its members, usually employees of a particular organization

Crisis Management organization's methods for dealing with emergencies

Cultural Influences include culture, subculture, and social class influences that marketers use to study buying behavior

Currency (Cash) government-issued paper money and metal coins

Current Asset asset that can or will be converted into cash within a year

Current Dividend Yield and Current Interest Yield yearly dollar amount of income divided by the investment's current market value, expressed as a percentage

Current Liability debt that must be paid within one year

Current Ratio financial ratio for measuring a company's ability to pay current debts out of current assets

Customer Departmentalization dividing an organization to offer products and meet needs for identifiable customer groups

Customer Relationship Management (CRM) organized methods that a firm uses to build better information connections with clients, so that stronger company–client relationships are developed

Cybermall collection of virtual storefronts (business websites) representing a variety of products and product lines on the Internet

D

Data Mining the application of electronic technologies for searching, sifting, and reorganizing pools of data to uncover useful information

Data Warehousing the collection, storage, and retrieval of data in electronic files

Data raw facts and figures that, by themselves, may not have much meaning

Debit Card plastic card that allows an individual to transfer money between accounts

Debt company's total liabilities

Debt Financing long-term borrowing from sources outside a company

Decentralized Organization organization in which a great deal of decision-making authority is delegated to levels of management at points below the top

Decision Making choosing one alternative from among several options

Decision Support System (DSS) interactive system that creates virtual business models for a particular kind of decision and tests them with different data to see how they respond

Decision Tree Approach approach to leadership that provides decision rules for deciding how much participation to allow

Decision-Making Process recognizing and defining the nature of a decision situation, identifying alternatives, choosing the "best" alternative, and putting it into practice

Decision-Making Skills skills in defining problems and selecting the best courses of action

Decisional Roles a category of managerial roles, including entrepreneur, disturbance handler, resource allocator, and negotiator

Deductible amount of the loss that the insured must absorb before reimbursement is made

Default failure of a borrower to make payment when due to a lender

Defensive Stance approach to social responsibility by which a company meets only minimum legal requirements in its commitments to groups and individuals in its social environment

Delegation process through which a manager allocates work to subordinates

Demand the willingness and ability of buyers to purchase a good or service

Demand and Supply Schedule assessment of the relationships among different levels of demand and supply at different price levels

Demand Curve graph showing how many units of a product will be demanded (bought) at different prices

Demographic Segmentation a segmentation strategy that uses demographic characteristics to identify different market segments

Demographic Variables characteristics of populations that may be considered in developing a segmentation strategy

Department Store large product-line retailer characterized by organization into specialized departments

Departmentalization process of grouping jobs into logical units

Depreciation accounting method for distributing the cost of an asset over its useful life

Depression a prolonged and deep recession

Deregulation elimination of rules that restrict business activity

Detailed Schedule schedule showing daily work assignments with start and stop times for assigned jobs

Development usually refers to teaching managers and professionals the skills needed for both present and future jobs

Direct (or **Interactive) Marketing** one-on-one nonpersonal selling by nonstore retailers and B2B sellers using direct contact with prospective customers, especially via the Internet

Direct Channel distribution channel in which a product travels from producer to consumer without intermediaries

Direct Selling form of nonstore retailing typified by door-to-door sales

Direct-Response Retailing form of nonstore retailing in which firms directly interact with customers to inform them of products and to receive sales orders

Discount price reduction offered as an incentive to purchase

Discount House bargain retailer that generates large sales volume by offering goods at substantial price reductions

Discount Rate interest rate at which member banks can borrow money from the Fed

Distribution Channel network of interdependent companies through which a product passes from producer to end user

Distribution Mix combination of distribution channels by which a firm gets its products to end users

Diversification purchase of several different kinds of investments rather than just one

Divestiture strategy whereby a firm sells one or more of its business units

Dividend payment to shareholders, on a per-share basis, out of the company's earnings

Division department that resembles a separate business in that it produces and markets its own products

Divisional Structure organizational structure in which corporate divisions operate as autonomous businesses under the larger corporate umbrella

Domestic Business Environment the environment in which a firm conducts its operations and derives its revenues

Double Taxation situation in which taxes may be payable both by a corporation on its profits and by shareholders on dividend incomes

Dow Jones Industrial Average (DJIA) oldest and most widely cited market index based on the prices of 30 blue-chip, large-cap industrial firms on the NYSE

Drop Shippers limited-function merchant wholesaler that receives customer orders, negotiates with producers, takes title to goods, and arranges for shipment to customers

Dumping practice of selling a product abroad for less than the cost of production

E

Earnings Per Share profitability ratio measuring the net profit that the company earns for each share of outstanding stock

E-Catalog nonstore retailing in which the Internet is used to display products

E-commerce use of the Internet and other electronic means for retailing and business-to-business transactions

Economic Environment relevant conditions that exist in the economic system in which a company operates

Economic Indicators statistics that help assess the performance of an economy

Economic System a nation's system for allocating its resources among its citizens

Economic Strikes strikes triggered by stalemates over mandatory bargaining items, including such noneconomic issues as working hours

E-Intermediary Internet distribution channel member that assists in delivering products to customers or that collects information about various sellers to be presented to consumers, or they help deliver online products to buyers

Electronic Communication Network (ECN) electronic trading system that brings buyers and sellers together outside traditional stock exchanges

Electronic Conferencing IT that allows groups of people to communicate simultaneously from various locations via e-mail, phone, or video

Electronic Funds Transfer (EFT) communication of fund-transfer information over wire, cable, or microwave

Electronic Storefront commercial website at which customers gather information about products and buying opportunities, place orders, and pay for purchases

Embargo government order banning exportation or importation of a particular product or all products from a particular country

Eminent Domain principle that the government may claim private land for public use by buying it at a fair price

Emotional Intelligence (Emotional Quotient, EQ) the extent to which people are self-aware, can manage their emotions, can motivate themselves, express empathy for others, and possess social skills

Emotional Motives reasons for purchasing a product that are based on nonobjective factors

Employee Behavior the pattern of actions by the members of an organization that directly or indirectly influences the organization's effectiveness

Employee Information System (Skills Inventory) computerized system containing information on each employee's education, skills, work experiences, and career aspirations

Employee Retirement Income Security Act (ERISA) of 1974 ensures the financial security of pension funds by regulating how they can be invested

Employee Stock Ownership Plan (ESOP) arrangement in which a corporation holds its own stock in trust for its employees, who gradually receive ownership of the stock and control its voting rights

Employee-Focused Leader Behavior leader behavior focusing on satisfaction, motivation, and well-being of employees

Employment at Will principle, increasingly modified by legislation and judicial decision, that organizations should be able to retain or dismiss employees at their discretion

Encryption System software that assigns an e-mail message to a unique code number (digital fingerprint) for each computer so only that computer, not others, can open and read the message

Enterprise Resource Planning (ERP) information system for organizing and managing a firm's activities across product lines, departments, and geographical location

Entrepreneur businessperson or individual who accepts the risks and opportunities involved in creating and operating a new business venture

Entrepreneur businessperson or individual who accepts the risks and opportunities involved in creating and operating a new business venture

Entrepreneurship the process of seeking business opportunities under conditions of risk

Environmental Analysis process of scanning the business environment for threats and opportunities

Equal Employment Opportunity legally mandated nondiscrimination in employment on the basis of race, creed, sex, or national origin

Equal Employment Opportunity Commission (EEOC) federal agency enforcing several discrimination-related laws

Equal Pay Act of 1963 requires that men and women be paid the same amount for doing the same job

Equity Financing using the owners' funds from inside the company as the source for long-term funding

Equity Theory theory of motivation holding that people evaluate their treatment by the organization relative to the treatment of others

Escalation of Commitment condition in which a decision maker becomes so committed to a course of action that they stay with it even when it appears to have been wrong

Established Market one in which many firms compete according to relatively well-defined criteria

Ethical Behavior behavior conforming to generally accepted social norms concerning beneficial and harmful actions

Ethical Compliance the extent to which the members of the organization follow basic ethical (and legal) standards of behavior

Ethical Leadership leader behaviors that reflect high ethical standards

Ethics beliefs about what is right and wrong or good and bad in actions that affect others

Euro a common currency shared among most of the members of the EU (excluding Denmark, Sweden, and the United Kingdom)

European Union (EU) agreement among major European nations to eliminate or make uniform most trade barriers affecting group members

Evoked Set (or Consideration Set) group of products consumers will consider buying as a result of information search

Exchange Rate rate at which the currency of one nation can be exchanged for the currency of another nation

Exchange-Traded Fund (ETF) bundle of stocks or bonds that are in an index that tracks the overall movement of a market, but unlike a mutual fund can be traded like a stock

Exclusive Distribution strategy by which a manufacturer grants exclusive rights to distribute or sell a product to a limited number of wholesalers or retailers in a given geographic area

Express Authority agent's authority, derived from written agreement, to bind a principal to a certain course of action

Express Warranty a warranty whose terms are specifically stated by the seller

Expectancy Theory theory of motivation holding that people are motivated to work toward rewards that they want and that they believe they have a reasonable chance of obtaining

Expense Items industrial products purchased and consumed within a year by firms producing other products

Experimentation research method using a sample of potential consumers to obtain reactions to test versions of new products or variations of existing products

Expert Power power derived from information or expertise

Export product made or grown domestically but shipped and sold abroad

Exporter firm that distributes and sells products to one or more foreign countries

Extranet system that allows outsiders limited access to a firm's internal information network

External Environment everything outside an organization's boundaries that might affect it

External Recruiting attracting persons outside the organization to apply for jobs

F

Face Value (Par Value) amount of money that the bond buyer (lender) lent the issuer and that the lender will receive on repayment

Factors of Production resources used in the production of goods and services—labor, capital, entrepreneurs, physical resources, and information resources

Factory Outlet bargain retailer owned by the manufacturer whose products it sells

Fair Labor Standards Act sets a minimum wage and requires the payment of overtime rates for work in excess of 40 hours per week

Family and Medical Leave Act (FMLA) of 1993 requires employers to provide up to 12 weeks of unpaid leave for family and medical emergencies

Federal Deposit Insurance Corporation (FDIC) federal agency that guarantees the safety of deposits up to $250,000 in the financial institutions that it insures

Federal Funds Rate (Key Rate) interest rate at which commercial banks lend reserves to each other, usually overnight

Federal Reserve System (the Fed) central bank of the United States, which acts as the government's bank, serves member commercial banks, and controls the nation's money supply

Finance Company nondeposit institution that specializes in making loans to businesses and consumers

Financial Accounting field of accounting concerned with external users of a company's financial information

Financial Planning process of looking at one's current financial condition, identifying one's goals, and anticipating requirements for meeting those goals

Financial Statement any of several types of reports summarizing a company's financial status to stakeholders and to aid in managerial decision making

Firewall security system with special software or hardware devices designed to keep computers safe from hackers

First-Line Manager manager responsible for supervising the work of employees

First-Mover Advantage any advantage that comes to a firm because it exploits an opportunity before any other firm does

Fiscal Policies policies used by a government regarding how it collects and spends revenue

Fixed asset asset with long-term use or value, such as land, buildings, and equipment

Fixed Cost cost that is incurred regardless of the quantity of a product produced and sold

Fixed-Position Layout labor, equipment, materials, and other resources are brought to the geographic location where all production work is done

Flat Organizational Structure characteristic of decentralized companies with relatively few layers of management

Flextime Programs method of increasing job satisfaction by allowing workers to adjust work schedules on a daily or weekly basis

Focus Group research method using a group of people from a larger population who are asked their attitudes, opinions, and beliefs about a product in an open discussion

Follow-Up operations control activity for ensuring that production decisions are being implemented

Foreign Direct Investment (FDI) arrangement in which a firm buys or establishes tangible assets in another country

Forensic Accounting the practice of accounting for legal purposes

Form Utility providing products with features that customers want

Franchise arrangement in which a buyer (franchisee) purchases the right to sell the good or service of the seller (franchiser)

Full Disclosure guideline that financial statements should not include just numbers but should also furnish management's interpretations and explanations of those numbers

Full-Service Merchant Wholesalers merchant wholesaler that provides credit, marketing, and merchandising services in addition to traditional buying and selling services

Functional Departmentalization dividing an organization according to groups' functions or activities

Functional Strategy strategy by which managers in specific areas decide how best to achieve corporate goals through productivity

Functional Structure organization structure in which authority is determined by the relationships between group functions and activities

G

Gainsharing Plan incentive plan that rewards groups for productivity improvements

Gantt Chart production schedule that breaks down large projects into steps to be performed and specifies the time required to perform each step

GDP Per Capita gross domestic product divided by total population

General (or Active) Partner partner who actively manages a firm and who has unlimited liability for its debts

General Agreement on Tariffs and Trade (GATT) international trade agreement to encourage the multilateral reduction or elimination of trade barriers

General Partnership business with two or more owners who share in both the operation of the firm and the financial responsibility for its debts

Generally Accepted Accounting Principles (GAAP) accounting guidelines that govern the content and form of financial reports

Geo-Demographic Segmentation using a combination of geographic and demographic traits for identifying different market segments in a segmentation strategy

Geo-Demographic Variables combination of geographic and demographic traits used in developing a segmentation strategy

Geographic Departmentalization dividing an organization according to the areas of the country or the world served by a business

Geographic Segmentation geographic units, from countries to neighborhoods, that may be considered in identifying different market segments in a segmentation strategy

Geographic Variables geographic units that may be considered in developing a segmentation strategy

Global Business Environment the international forces that affect a business

Globalization process by which the world economy is becoming a single interdependent system

Goal objective that a business hopes and plans to achieve

Goal Orientation the manner in which people are motivated to work toward different kinds of goals

Goods Operations (or Goods Production) activities producing tangible products, such as smartphones, coffee, clothing, buses, and textbooks

Goodwill amount paid for an existing business above the value of its other assets

Grapevine informal communication network that runs through an organization

Gross Domestic Product (GDP) total value of all goods and services produced within a given period by a national economy through domestic factors of production

Gross National Product (GNP) total value of all goods and services produced by a national economy within a given period regardless of where the factors of production are located

Gross Profit preliminary, quick-to-calculate profit figure calculated from the firm's revenues minus its cost of revenues (the direct costs of getting the revenues)

H

Hacker cybercriminal who gains unauthorized access to a computer or network, either to steal information, money, or property or to tamper with data

Hawthorne Effect tendency for productivity to increase when workers believe they are receiving special attention from management

Hierarchy of Human Needs Model theory of motivation describing five levels of human needs and arguing that basic needs must be fulfilled before people work to satisfy higher-level needs

High-Contact System level of customer contact in which the customer is part of the system during service delivery

Hostile Work Environment form of sexual harassment deriving from off-color jokes, lewd comments, and so forth

Human Capital reflects the organization's investment in attracting, retaining, and motivating an effective workforce

Human Relations Skills skills in understanding and getting along with people

Human Resources (HR) the people comprising an organization's workforce

Human Resource Management (HRM) set of organizational activities directed at attracting, developing, and maintaining an effective workforce

Hypertext Transfer Protocol (HTTP) communications protocol used for the World Wide Web, in which related pieces of information on separate web pages are connected using hyperlinks

Hypertext Transfer Protocol Secure (HTTPS) a more secure communications protocol used for the World Wide Web to transmit and present more sensitive information

I

Identity Theft unauthorized use of personal information (such as Social Security number and address) to get loans, credit cards, or other monetary benefits by impersonating the victim

Implied Authority agent's authority, derived from business custom, to bind a principal to a certain course of action

Implied Warranty a warranty, dictated by law, based on the principle that products should fulfill advertised promises and serve the purposes for which they are manufactured and sold

Import product made or grown abroad but sold domestically

Importer firm that buys products in foreign markets and then imports them for resale in its home country

Incentive Program special compensation program designed to motivate high performance

Income Statement (Profit-and-Loss Statement) financial statement listing a firm's annual revenues and expenses so that a bottom line shows annual profit or loss

Independent Agent individual or organization that agrees to represent an exporter's interests

Individual Differences personal attributes that vary from one person to another

Individual Retirement Account (IRA) tax-deferred pension fund that wage earners set up to supplement retirement funds

Industrial Buyer a company or other organization that buys products for use in producing other products (goods or services)

Industrial Goods physical products purchased by companies to produce other products

Industrial Market organizational market consisting of firms that buy goods that are either converted into products or used during production

Industrial Unionism the organizing of employees by industry rather than by skill or occupation

Industrial Selling selling products to other businesses, either for the purpose of manufacturing or for resale

Inflation occurs when widespread price increases occur throughout an economic system

Informal Organization network, unrelated to the firm's formal authority structure, of everyday social interactions among company employees

Information Resources data and other information used by businesses

Information System (IS) system that uses IT resources to convert data into information and to collect, process, and transmit that information for use in decision making

Information Systems Managers managers who are responsible for the systems used for gathering, organizing, and distributing information

Information Technology (IT) various appliances and devices for creating, storing, exchanging, and using information in diverse modes, including visual images, voice, multimedia, and business data

Information meaningful, useful interpretation of data

Informational Roles a category of managerial roles, including monitor, disseminator, and spokesperson

Initial Public Offering (IPO) first sale of a company's stock to the general public

Insider Trading illegal practice of using special knowledge about a firm for profit or gain

Institutional Investor large investor, such as a mutual fund or a pension fund, that purchases large blocks of corporate stock

Institutional Market organizational market consisting of such nongovernmental buyers of goods and services as hospitals, churches, museums, and charitable organizations

Insurance Company nondeposit institution that invests funds collected as premiums charged for insurance coverage

Insurance Policy formal agreement to pay the policyholder a specified amount in the event of certain losses

Insurance Premium fee paid to an insurance company by a policyholder for insurance coverage

Intangible asset nonphysical asset, such as a patent or trademark, that has economic value in the form of expected benefit

Intangible Personal Property property that cannot be seen but that exists by virtue of written documentation

Integrated Marketing Strategy strategy that blends together the Four Ps of marketing to ensure their compatibility with one another and with the company's nonmarketing activities

Intellectual Property something produced by the intellect or mind that has commercial value

Intensive Distribution strategy by which a product is distributed through as many channels as possible

Intention part of an attitude that guides a person's behavior

Intentional Tort tort resulting from the deliberate actions of a party

International Law general set of cooperative agreements and guidelines established by countries to govern the actions of individuals, businesses, and nations

Interest fee paid to a lender for the use of borrowed funds; like a rental fee

Intermediary individual or firm that helps to distribute a product

Intermediate Goal goal set for a period of 1 to 5 years into the future

Internal Recruiting considering present employees as candidates for openings

International Accounting Standards Board (IASB) organization responsible for developing a set of global accounting standards and for gaining implementation of those standards

International Competition competitive marketing of domestic products against foreign products

International Firm firm that conducts a significant portion of its business in foreign countries

International Monetary Fund (IMF) UN agency consisting of about 150 nations that have combined resources to promote stable exchange rates, provide temporary short-term loans, and serve other purposes

International Organizational Structures approaches to organizational structure developed in response to the need to manufacture, purchase, and sell in global markets

Internet gigantic system of interconnected computer networks linked together by voice, electronic, and wireless technologies

Interpersonal Roles a category of managerial roles, including figurehead, leader, and liaison

Intranet organization's private network of internally linked websites accessible only to employees

Intrapreneuring process of creating and maintaining the innovation and flexibility of a small-business environment within the confines of a large organization

Intuition an innate belief about something, often without conscious consideration

Inventory Control process of receiving, storing, handling, and counting of all raw materials, partly finished goods, and finished goods

Investment Bank financial institution that specializes in issuing and reselling new securities

Involuntary Bankruptcy bankruptcy proceedings initiated by the creditors of an indebted individual or organization

ISO 14000 certification program attesting to the fact that a factory, laboratory, or office has improved its environmental performance

ISO 9000 program certifying that a factory, laboratory, or office has met the quality management standards set by the International Organization for Standardization

J

Job Analysis systematic analysis of jobs within an organization

Job Description description of the duties and responsibilities of a job; its working conditions; and the tools, materials, equipment, and information used to perform it

Job Enrichment method of increasing job satisfaction by adding one or more motivating factors to job activities

Job Redesign method of increasing job satisfaction by designing a more satisfactory fit between workers and their jobs

Job Satisfaction degree of enjoyment that people derive from performing their jobs

Job Specialization the process of identifying the specific jobs that need to be done and designating the people who will perform them

Job Specification description of the skills, abilities, and other credentials and qualifications required by a job

Joint Venture strategic alliance in which the collaboration involves joint ownership of the new venture

Just-In-Time (JIT) Production type of lean production system that brings together all materials at the precise time they are required at each production stage

K

Key Person Insurance special form of business insurance designed to offset expenses entailed by the loss of key employees

Knowledge Management System information system that supports knowledge workers by providing resources to create, store, use, and transmit new knowledge for useful applications

Knowledge Workers employees who are of value because of the knowledge they possess

L

Labor (Human Resources) physical and mental capabilities of people as they contribute to economic production

Labor Relations process of dealing with employees who are represented by a union

Labor Union group of individuals working together to achieve shared job-related goals, such as higher pay, shorter working hours, more job security, greater benefits, or better working conditions

Labor-Management Relations Act (also known as the **Taft-Hartley Act**) passed to limit union power

Landrum-Griffin Act or Labor-Management Reporting and Disclosure Act amendment to the National Labor Relations Act that imposed regulations on internal union procedures

Laws codified rules of behavior enforced by a society

Law of Demand principle that buyers will purchase (demand) more of a product as its price drops and less as its price increases

Law of Supply principle that producers will offer (supply) more of a product for sale as its price rises and less as its price drops

Leader–Member Exchange (LMX) Model approach to leadership that stresses the importance of variable relationships between supervisors and each of their subordinates

Leadership the processes and behaviors used by someone, such as a manager, to motivate, inspire, and influence the behaviors of others

Leadership Neutralizers factors that may render leader behaviors ineffective

Leadership Substitutes individual, task, and organizational characteristics that tend to outweigh the need for a leader to initiate or direct employee performance

Leading management process of guiding and motivating employees to meet an organization's objectives

Lean Production System production system designed for smooth production flows that avoid inefficiencies, eliminate unnecessary inventories, and continuously improve production processes

Legal Compliance the extent to which the organization conforms to local, state, federal, and international laws

Legitimate Power power granted through the organizational hierarchy

Letter of Credit bank promise, issued for a buyer, to pay a designated firm a certain amount of money if specified conditions are met

Leverage ability to finance an investment through borrowed funds

Liability debt owed by a firm to an outside organization or individual

Liability Insurance insurance covering losses resulting from damage to people or property when the insured party is judged liable

Licensed Brands brand-name product for whose name the seller has purchased the right from an organization or individual

Licensing Arrangement arrangement in which firms choose individuals or organizations to manufacture or market their products in another country

Limited Liability Corporation (LLC) hybrid of a publicly held corporation and a partnership in which owners are taxed as partners but enjoy the benefits of limited liability

Limited Liability legal principle holding investors liable for a firm's debts only to the limits of their personal investments in it

Limited Partner partner who does not share in a firm's management and is liable for its debts only to the limits of said partner's investment

Limited Partnership type of partnership consisting of limited partners and a general (or managing) partner

Limited-Function Merchant Wholesaler merchant wholesaler that provides a limited range of services

Line Authority organizational structure in which authority flows in a direct chain of command from the top of the company to the bottom

Line Department department directly linked to the production and sales of a specific product

Liquidity ease with which an asset can be converted into cash

Load Fund mutual fund in which investors are charged sales commissions when they buy in or sell out

Loan Principal amount of money that is loaned and must be repaid

Lobbying the use of persons or groups to formally represent an organization or group of organizations before political bodies

Local Area Network (LAN) computers that are linked in a small area, such as all of a firm's computers within a single building

Local Content Law law requiring that products sold in a particular country be at least partly made there

Local Unions (Locals) organized at the level of a single company, plant, or small geographic region

Lockout management tactic whereby workers are denied access to the employer's workplace

Locus of Control the extent to which people believe that their behavior has a real effect on what happens to them

Long-Term Goal goal set for an extended time, typically 5 years or more into the future

Long-Term Liability debt that is not due for at least one year

Long-Term Solvency financial ratio for measuring a company's ability to pay its long-term debt

Low-Contact System level of customer contact in which the customer need not be part of the system to receive the service

Loyalty Programs sales promotion technique in which frequent customers are rewarded for making repeat purchases

M

M-1 measure of the money supply that includes only the most liquid (spendable) forms of money

M-2 measure of the money supply that includes all the components of M-1 plus the forms of money that can be easily converted into spendable forms

Machiavellianism used to describe behavior directed at gaining power and controlling the behavior of others

Machine Learning a subset of artificial intelligence (AI) that focuses on algorithms and statistical models that enable computers to learn from data and make predictions or decisions without explicit programming

Mail Order (Catalog Marketing) form of nonstore retailing in which customers place orders for catalog merchandise received through the mail

Make-to-Order Operations activities for one-of-a-kind or custom-made production

Make-to-Stock Operations activities for producing standardized products for mass consumption

Management process of planning, organizing, leading, and controlling an organization's resources to achieve its goals

Management Accountant private accountant who provides financial services to support managers in various business activities within a firm

Management Advisory Services assistance provided by CPA firms in areas such as financial planning, information systems design, and other areas of concern for client firms

Management by Objectives (MBO) set of procedures involving both managers and subordinates in setting goals and evaluating progress

Management Information System (MIS) computer system that supports managers by providing information—reports, schedules, plans, and budgets—that can be used for making decisions

Manager someone whose primary work responsibilities are a part of the management process

Managerial (Management) Accounting field of accounting that serves internal users of a company's financial information

Managerial Ethics standards of behavior that guide individual managers in their work

Market mechanism for exchange between buyers and sellers of a particular good or service

Market Capitalization (Market Cap) total dollar value of all the company's outstanding shares

Market Economy economy in which individuals control production and allocation decisions through supply and demand

Market Index statistical indicator designed to measure the performance of a large group of stocks or track the price changes of a stock market

Market Price (Equilibrium Price) profit-maximizing price at which the quantity of goods demanded and the quantity of goods supplied are equal

Market Segmentation process of dividing a market into categories of customer types, or "segments," having similar wants and needs and who can be expected to show interest in the same products

Market Share (or Market Penetration) company's percentage of the total industry sales for a specific product type

Market Value current price of a share of stock in the stock market

Marketing activities, a set of institutions, and processes for creating, communicating, delivering, and exchanging offerings that have value for customers, clients, partners, and society at large

Marketing Manager manager who plans and implements the marketing activities that result in the transfer of products from producer to consumer

Marketing Mix combination of product, pricing, promotion, and place (distribution) strategies used to market products

Marketing Objectives the things marketing intends to accomplish in its marketing plan

Marketing Plan detailed strategy for focusing marketing efforts on consumers' needs and wants

Marketing Research the study of what customers need and want and how best to meet those needs and wants

Marketing Strategy all the marketing programs and activities that will be used to achieve the marketing goals

Markup amount added to an item's purchase cost to sell it at a profit

Mass Customization principle in which companies produce in large volumes, but each item features the unique options the customer prefers

Master Limited Partnership form of ownership that sells shares to investors who receive profits and that pays taxes on income from profits

Master Operations Schedule schedule showing which products will be produced and when in upcoming time periods

Materials Management process of planning, organizing, and controlling the flow of materials from sources of supply through distribution of finished goods

Matrix Structure organizational structure created by superimposing one form of structure onto another

Maturity Date (Due Date) future date when repayment of a bond is due from the bond issuer (borrower)

Media Mix combination of advertising media chosen to carry a message about a product

Mediation method of resolving a labor dispute in which a third party suggests but does not impose a settlement

Merchant Wholesalers independent wholesaler who takes legal possession of goods produced by a variety of manufacturers and then resells them to other organizations

Merger the union of two corporations to form a new corporation

Merit Salary System individual incentive linking compensation to performance in nonsales jobs

Middle Manager manager responsible for implementing the strategies and working toward the goals set by top managers

Mission Statement organization's statement of how it will achieve its purpose in the environment in which it conducts its business

Missionary Selling personal-selling task in which salespeople promote their firms and products rather than try to close sales

Mixed Market Economy economic system featuring characteristics of both planned and market economies

Monetary Policy management of the nation's economic growth by managing the money supply and interest rates

Money object that is portable, divisible, durable, and stable, and that serves as a medium of exchange, a store of value, and a measure of worth

Money Market Mutual Fund fund of short-term, low-risk financial securities purchased with the pooled assets of investor-owners

Monopolistic Competition market or industry characterized by numerous buyers and relatively numerous sellers trying to differentiate their products from those of competitors

Monopoly market or industry in which there is only one producer that can therefore set the prices of its products

Mortgage-Backed Security (MBS) mortgages pooled together to form a debt obligation—a bond—that entitles the holder (investor) to cash that flows in from the bundled mortgages

Mortgage Loan loan secured by property (the home) being purchased

Motivation the set of forces that cause people to behave in certain ways

Multinational (or Transnational) Corporation form of corporation spanning national boundaries

Multinational Firm firm that designs, produces, and markets products in many nations

Mutual Fund company that pools cash investments from individuals and organizations to purchase a portfolio of stocks, bonds, and other securities

Mutual Savings Bank financial institution whose depositors are owners sharing in its profits

Myers-Briggs Type Indicator (MBTI) a popular questionnaire that some organizations use to assess personality types

N

NASDAQ Composite Index market index that includes all NASDAQ-listed companies, both domestic and foreign, with a high proportion of technology companies and small-cap stocks

National Association of Securities Dealers Automated Quotation (NASDAQ) System world's oldest electronic stock market consisting of dealers who buy and sell securities over a network of electronic communications

National Brands brand-name product produced by, widely distributed by, and carrying the name of a manufacturer

National Competitive Advantage international competitive advantage stemming from a combination of factor conditions, demand conditions, related and supporting industries, and firm strategies, structures, and rivalries

National Debt the amount of money the government owes its creditors

National Labor Relations Act (also known as the **Wagner Act**) sets up a procedure for employees to vote on whether to have a union

National Labor Relations Act or Wagner Act act that put labor unions on a more equal footing with management in terms of the rights of employees to organize and bargain

National Labor Relations Board (NLRB) established by the Wagner Act to enforce its provisions

Natural Monopoly industry in which one company can most efficiently supply all needed goods or services

Need for Achievement an individual's desire to accomplish a goal or task as effectively as possible

Need for Affiliation an individual's desire for human companionship

Need for Power the desire to control one's environment, including financial, material, informational, and human resources

Negligence conduct that falls below legal standards for protecting others against unreasonable risk

Net Income (Net Profit or Net Earnings) gross profit minus operating expenses and income taxes

Niche a segment of a market that is not currently being exploited

No-Load Fund mutual fund in which investors pay no commissions when they buy in or sell out

Nominal GDP GDP measured in current dollars or with all components valued at current prices

Nonprogrammed Decision decision that is relatively unstructured and that occurs with low frequency

Norris-LaGuardia Act act that imposed severe limitations on the ability of the courts to issue injunctions prohibiting certain union activities, including strikes

North American Free Trade Agreement (NAFTA) agreement to gradually eliminate tariffs and other trade barriers among the United States, Canada, and Mexico

O

Observation research method that obtains data by watching and recording consumer behavior

Obstructionist Stance approach to social responsibility that involves doing as little as possible and may involve attempts to deny or cover up violations

Occupational Safety and Health Act (OSHA) of 1970 federal law setting and enforcing guidelines for protecting workers from unsafe conditions and potential health hazards in the workplace

Odd-Even Pricing psychological pricing tactic based on the premise that customers prefer prices not stated in even dollar amounts

Officers top management team of a corporation

Offshoring the practice of outsourcing to foreign countries

Oligopoly market or industry characterized by a handful of (generally large) sellers with the power to influence the prices of their products

On-the-Job Training training, sometimes informal, conducted while an employee is at work

Online Retailing nonstore retailing in which information about the seller's products and services is connected to consumers' computers, allowing consumers to receive the information and purchase the products in the home

Open-Market Operations the Fed's sale and purchase of securities in the open market

Operating Expenses costs, other than the cost of revenues, incurred in producing a good or service

Operating Income gross profit minus operating expenses

Operational Plan plan setting short-term targets for daily, weekly, or monthly performance

Operations (or Production) activities involved in making products—goods and services—for customers

Operations (Production) Management systematic direction and control of the activities that transform resources into finished products that create value for and provide benefits to customers

Operations (Production) Managers managers responsible for ensuring that operations activities create value and provide benefits to customers

Operations Capability (Production Capability) special ability that production does especially well to outperform the competition

Operations Control process of monitoring production performance by comparing results with plans and taking corrective action when needed

Operations Process set of methods and technologies used to produce a good or a service

Order Processing personal-selling task in which salespeople receive orders and see to their handling and delivery

Organization Chart diagram depicting a company's structure and showing employees where they fit into its operations

Organizational Analysis process of analyzing a firm's strengths and weaknesses

Organizational Citizenship positive behaviors that do not directly contribute to the bottom line

Organizational Commitment an individual's identification with the organization and its mission

Organizational Stakeholders those groups, individuals, and organizations that are directly affected by the practices of an organization and who therefore have a stake in its performance

Organizational Structure specification of the jobs to be done within an organization and the ways in which they relate to one another

Organizing management process of determining how best to arrange an organization's resources and activities into a coherent structure

Outsourcing the practice of paying suppliers and distributors to perform business processes or to provide needed materials or services

Owners' Equity amount of money that owners would receive if they sold all of a firm's assets and paid all of its liabilities

P

Packaging physical container in which a product is sold, advertised, or protected

Paid-In Capital money that is invested in a company by its owners

Participative Management and Empowerment method of increasing job satisfaction by giving employees a voice in the management of their jobs and the company

Patent exclusive legal right to use and license a manufactured item or substance, manufacturing process, or object design

Path–Goal Theory theory of leadership that is a direct extension of the expectancy theory of motivation

Patriot Act legislation that increased U.S. government's power to investigate and prosecute suspected terrorists

Pay for Performance (or Variable Pay) individual incentive that rewards a manager for especially productive output

Pay-for-Knowledge Plan incentive plan to encourage employees to learn new skills or become proficient at different jobs

Penetration Pricing setting an initially low price to establish a new product in the market

Pension Fund nondeposit pool of funds managed to provide retirement income for its members

Perfect Competition market or industry characterized by numerous small firms producing an identical product

Performance Appraisal evaluation of an employee's job performance to determine the degree to which the employee is performing effectively

Performance Behaviors the total set of work-related behaviors that the organization expects employees to display

Performance dimension of quality that refers to how well a product does what it is supposed to do

Person–Job Fit the extent to which a person's contributions and the organization's inducements match one another

Personal Influences include lifestyle, personality, and economic status that marketers use to study buying behavior

Personal Net Worth value of one's total assets minus one's total liabilities (debts)

Personal Selling person-to person sales

Personality the relatively stable set of psychological attributes that distinguish one person from another

PERT Chart production schedule specifying the sequence of activities, time requirements, and critical path for performing the steps in a project

Philanthropic Giving the awarding of funds or gifts to charities or other worthy causes

Physical Distribution activities needed to move a product efficiently from manufacturer to consumer

Physical Resources tangible items that organizations use in the conduct of their businesses

Picketing labor action in which workers publicize their grievances at the entrance to an employer's facility

Place (Distribution) part of the marketing mix concerned with getting products from producers to consumers

Place Utility providing products where customers will want them

Planned Economy economy that relies on a centralized government to control all or most factors of production and to make all or most production and allocation decisions

Planning management process of determining what an organization needs to do and how best to get it done

Point-of-Sale (POS) Display sales-promotion technique in which product displays are located in certain areas to stimulate purchase or to provide information on a product

Point-of-Sale (POS) Terminal electronic device that transfers funds from the customer's bank account to pay for retail purchases

Political Action Committees (PACs) special organizations created to solicit money and then distribute it to political candidates

Political–Legal Environment the relationship between business and government

Portfolio combined holdings of all the financial investments of any company or individual

Positioning process of establishing an identifiable product image in the minds of consumers

Positive Reinforcement reward that follows desired behaviors

Possession Utility transferring product ownership to customers by setting selling prices, setting terms for customer credit payments, and providing ownership documents

Power the ability to affect the behavior of others

Power Orientation the beliefs that people in a culture hold about the appropriateness of power and authority differences in hierarchies such as business organizations

Predictive Analytics the process of analyzing historical data, statistical models, and machine learning techniques to predict future outcomes or behaviors

Premium sales-promotion technique in which offers of free or reduced-price items are used to stimulate purchases

Price Appreciation increase in the dollar value of an investment at two points in time (the amount by which the price of a security increases)

Price Earnings Ratio most commonly known as the P/E ratio, this ratio is the comparison of a firm's current share price to its current earnings per share

Price Lining setting a limited number of prices for certain categories of products

Price Skimming setting an initially high price to cover new product costs and generate a profit

Pricing process of determining the best price at which to sell a product

Pricing Objectives the goals that sellers hope to achieve in pricing products for sale

Primary Data new data that are collected from newly performed research

Primary Securities Market market in which new stocks and bonds are bought and sold by firms and governments

Prime Rate interest rate available to a bank's most creditworthy customers

Principal individual or organization authorizing an agent to act on its behalf

Private Accountant salaried accountant hired by a business to carry out its day-to-day financial activities

Private Brand (or Private Label) brand-name product that a wholesaler or retailer has commissioned from a manufacturer

Private Enterprise economic system that allows individuals to pursue their own interests without undue governmental restriction

Private Warehouse warehouse owned by and providing storage for a single company

Privatization process of converting government enterprises into privately owned companies

Proactive Stance approach to social responsibility by which a company actively seeks opportunities to contribute to the well-being of groups and individuals in its social environment

Process Departmentalization dividing an organization according to production processes used to create a good or service

Process Layout (Custom-Product Layout) physical arrangement of production activities that groups equipment and people according to function

Product good, service, or idea that is marketed to fill consumers' needs and wants

Product Adaptation modifying an existing product for greater appeal in different countries

Product Departmentalization dividing an organization according to specific products or services being created

Product Differentiation creation of a product feature or product image that differs enough from existing products to attract customers

Product Extension marketing an existing product globally instead of just domestically

Product Features tangible and intangible qualities that a company builds into its products

Product Layout (Same-Steps Layout) physical arrangement of production steps designed to make one type of product in a fixed sequence of activities according to its production requirements

Product Liability tort in which a company is responsible for injuries caused by its products

Product Life Cycle (PLC) series of stages in a product's commercial life

Product Line group of products that are closely related because they function in a similar manner or are sold to the same customer group who will use them in similar ways

Product Mix the group of products that a firm makes available for sale

Product Placement promotional tactic for brand exposure in which characters in television, film, music, magazines, or video games use a real product with its brand visible to viewers

Product Positioning process of fixing, adapting, and communicating the nature of a product

Production Items goods or services that are used in the conversion (production) process to make other products

Productivity a measure of economic growth that compares how much a system produces with the resources needed to produce it

Professional Corporation form of ownership allowing professionals to take advantage of corporate benefits while granting them limited business liability and unlimited professional liability

Profit Center separate company unit responsible for its own costs and profits

Profit-Sharing Plan incentive plan for distributing bonuses to employees when company profits rise above a certain level

Profitability Ratio financial ratio for measuring a firm's potential earnings

Profits difference between a business's revenues and its expenses

Programmed Decision decision that is relatively structured or recurs with some frequency (or both)

Promotion aspect of the marketing mix concerned with the most effective techniques for communicating information about and selling a product

Promotional Mix combination of tools used to promote a product

Property anything of value to which a person or business has sole right of ownership

Property Insurance insurance covering losses resulting from physical damage to or loss of the insured's real estate or personal property

Prospecting step in the personal selling process in which salespeople identify potential customers

Prospectus registration statement filed with the SEC containing information for prospective investors about a security to be offered and the issuing company

Protectionism practice of protecting domestic business against foreign competition

Psychographic Segmentation a segmentation strategy that uses psychographic characteristics to identify different market segments

Psychographic Variables consumer characteristics, such as lifestyles, opinions, interests, and attitudes, that may be considered in developing a segmentation strategy

Psychological Contract set of expectations held by an employee concerning what they will contribute to an organization (referred to as contributions) and what the organization will in return provide the employee (referred to as inducements)

Psychological Influences include an individual's motivations, perceptions, ability to learn, and attitudes that marketers use to study buying behavior

Psychological Pricing pricing tactic that takes advantage of the fact that consumers do not always respond rationally to stated prices

Public Relations communication efforts directed at building goodwill and favorable attitudes in the minds of the public toward the organization and its products

Public Warehouse independently owned and operated warehouse that stores goods for many firms

Publicity promotional tool in which information about a company, a product, or an event is transmitted by the general mass media to attract public attention

Publicly Held (or Public) Corporation corporation whose stock is widely held and available for sale to the general public

Pull Strategy promotional strategy designed to appeal directly to consumers who will demand a product from retailers

Punishment unpleasant consequences of an undesirable behavior

Punitive Damages fines imposed over and above any actual losses suffered by a plaintiff

Purchasing Power Parity the principle that exchange rates are set so that the prices of similar products in different countries are about the same

Purchasing acquisition of the materials and services that a firm needs to produce its products

Pure Risk risk involving only the possibility of loss or no loss

Push Strategy promotional strategy designed to encourage wholesalers or retailers to market products to consumers

Q

Qualifying step in the personal selling process in which salespeople determine whether prospects have the authority to buy and ability to pay

Quality combination of "characteristics of a product or service that bear on its ability to satisfy stated or implied needs"

Quality Control action of ensuring that operations produce products that meet specific quality standards

Quality Improvement Team total quality management tool in which collaborative groups of employees from various work areas work together to improve quality by solving common shared production problems

Quality Ownership principle of total quality management that holds that quality belongs to each person who creates it while performing a job

Quid Pro Quo Harassment form of sexual harassment in which sexual favors are requested in return for job-related benefits

Quota restriction on the number of products of a certain type that can be imported into a country

R

Rational Motives reasons for purchasing a product that are based on a logical evaluation of product attributes

Real GDP GDP adjusted to account for changes in currency values and price changes

Realistic Job Preview (RJP) providing the applicant with a real picture of what it would be like performing the job the organization is trying to fill

Recession a period during which aggregate output, as measured by GDP, declines

Recruiting process of attracting qualified persons to apply for jobs an organization is seeking to fill

Referent Power power based on identification, imitation, loyalty, or charisma

Regulation the establishment of laws and rules that dictate what organizations can and cannot do

Regulatory (Administrative) Law law made by the authority of administrative agencies

Reintroduction reviving obsolete or older products for new markets

Relationship Marketing marketing strategy that emphasizes building lasting relationships with customers and suppliers

Replacement Chart list of each management position, who occupies it, how long that person will likely stay in the job, and who is qualified as a replacement

Reseller Market organizational market consisting of intermediaries that buy and resell finished goods

Reserve Requirement percentage of its deposits that a bank must hold in cash or on deposit with the Fed

Responsibility duty to perform an assigned task

Retail Selling selling a consumer product for the buyer's personal or household use

Retailer intermediary who sells products directly to consumers

Retained Earnings earnings retained by a firm for its use rather than paid out as dividends

Revenue Recognition formal recording and reporting of revenues at the appropriate time

Revenues funds that flow into a business from the sale of goods or services

Reward Power the power to give or withhold rewards

Right-to-Work Laws such laws prohibit both union shops and agency shops, thus making it illegal to require union membership as a condition of employment

Risk uncertainty about future events

Risk Avoidance practice of avoiding risk by declining or ceasing to participate in an activity

Risk Control practice of minimizing the frequency or severity of losses from risky activities

Risk Management process of conserving the firm's earning power and assets by reducing the threat of losses as a result of uncontrollable events

Risk Propensity the degree to which a person is willing to take chances and make risky decisions

Risk Retention practice of covering a firm's losses with its own funds

Risk–Return (Risk–Reward) Relationship principle that safer investments tend to offer lower returns, whereas riskier investments tend to offer higher returns (rewards)

Risk Transfer practice of transferring a firm's risk to another firm

Russell 2000 Index specialty index that uses 2,000 stocks to measure the performance of the smallest U.S. companies

Roth IRA provision allowing individual retirement savings with tax-free accumulated earnings

S

S Corporation hybrid of a closely held corporation and a partnership, organized and operated like a corporation but treated as a partnership for tax purposes

S&P 500 market index of U.S. equities based on the performance of 500 large-cap stocks representing various sectors of the overall equities market

Salary compensation in the form of money paid for discharging the responsibilities of a job

Sales Agent independent intermediary who generally deals in the related product lines of a few producers and forms long-term relationships to represent those producers and meet the needs of many customers

Sales Promotion direct inducements such as premiums, coupons, and package inserts to tempt consumers to buy products

Sarbanes-Oxley Act of 2002 (Sarbox or SOX) enactment of federal regulations to restore public trust in accounting practices by imposing new requirements on financial activities in publicly traded corporations

Savings and Loan Association (S&L) financial institution accepting deposits and making loans primarily for home mortgages

Secondary Data data that are already available from previous research

Secondary Securities Market market in which existing (not new) stocks and bonds are sold to the public

Secured Loan (Asset-Backed Loan) loan to finance an asset, backed by the borrower pledging the asset as collateral to the lender

Securities stocks, bonds, and mutual funds representing secured, or asset-based, claims by investors against issuers

Securities and Exchange Commission (SEC) government agency that regulates U.S. securities markets

Securities Investment Dealer (Broker) financial institution that buys and sells stocks and bonds both for investors and for its own accounts

Securities Markets markets in which stocks and bonds are sold

Selective Distribution strategy by which a company uses only wholesalers and retailers who give special attention to specific products in its sales efforts

Self-Efficacy a person's belief about their capabilities to perform a task

Self-Esteem the extent to which a person believes that they are a worthwhile and deserving individual

Services products having nonphysical features, such as information, expertise, or an activity that can be purchased

Service Operations (or Service Production) activities producing intangible and tangible products, such as entertainment, transportation, and education

Services Companies Market firms engaged in the business of providing services to the purchasing public

Sexual Harassment making unwelcome sexual advances in the workplace

Shop Steward a regular employee who acts as a liaison between union members and supervisors

Shopping Agent (E-Agent) e-intermediary (middleman) in the Internet distribution channel that assists users in finding products and prices but does not take possession of products

Shopping Goods moderately expensive, infrequently purchased physical goods

Shopping Services moderately expensive, infrequently purchased services

Short-Term Goal goal set for the near future

Short-Term Solvency Ratio financial ratio for measuring a company's ability to pay immediate debts

Shortage situation in which quantity demanded exceeds quantity supplied

Situational Approach to Leadership assumes that appropriate leader behavior varies from one situation to another

Small Business independently owned business that has relatively little influence in its market

Small Business Administration (SBA) government agency charged with assisting small businesses

Small Business Development Center (SBDC) SBA program designed to consolidate information from various disciplines and make it available to small businesses

Small Business Investment Company (SBIC) government-regulated investment company that borrows money from the SBA to invest in or lend to a small business

Smart Card credit-card-sized plastic card with an embedded computer chip that can be programmed with electronic money

Social Influences include family, opinion leaders (people whose opinions are sought by others), and such reference groups as friends, coworkers, and professional associates that marketers use to study buying behavior

Social Learning learning that occurs when people observe the behaviors of others, recognize their consequences, and alter their own behavior as a result

Social Networking network of communications that flow among people and organizations interacting through an online platform

Social Networking Media websites or access channels, such as Facebook, Twitter, LinkedIn, and YouTube, to which consumers go for information and discussions

Social Orientation a person's beliefs about the relative importance of the individual versus groups to which that person belongs

Social Responsibility the attempt of a business to balance its commitments to groups and individuals in its environment, including customers, other businesses, employees, investors, and local communities

Socialism planned economic system in which the government owns and operates only selected major sources of production

Sociocultural Environment the customs, mores, values, and demographic characteristics of the society in which an organization functions

Sole Proprietorship business owned and usually operated by one person who is responsible for all of its debts

Solvency Ratio financial ratio, either short or long term, for estimating the borrower's ability to repay debt

Spam junk e-mail sent to a mailing list or a newsgroup

Span of Control number of people supervised by one manager

Specialty Goods expensive, rarely purchased physical goods

Specialty Services expensive, rarely purchased services

Specialty Store retail store carrying one product line or category of related products

Speculative Risk risk involving the possibility of gain or loss

Speed to Market strategy of introducing new products to respond quickly to customer or market changes

Spin-Off strategy of setting up one or more corporate units as new, independent corporations

Spyware program unknowingly downloaded by users that monitors their computer activities, gathering e-mail addresses, credit card numbers, and other information that it transmits to someone outside the host system

Stability condition in which the amount of money available in an economic system and the quantity of goods and services produced in it are growing at about the same rate

Stabilization Policy government economic policy intended to smooth out fluctuations in output and unemployment and to stabilize prices

Staff Authority authority based on expertise that usually involves counseling and advising line managers

Staff Members advisers and counselors who help line departments in making decisions but who do not have the authority to make final decisions

Staff Schedule assigned working times in upcoming days for each employee on each work shift

Standard of Living the total quantity and quality of goods and services people can purchase with the currency used in their economic system

State of Certainty when the decision maker knows with reasonable certainty what the alternatives are and what conditions are associated with each alternative

State of Risk when the availability of each alternative and its potential payoffs and costs are all associated with probability estimates

State of Uncertainty when the decision maker does not know all the alternatives, the risks associated with each, or the likely consequences of each alternative

Statement of Cash Flows financial statement describing a firm's yearly cash receipts and cash payments

Statutory Law law created by constitution(s) or by federal, state, or local legislative acts

Stock portion of ownership of a corporation

Stock Broker individual or organization that receives and executes buy and sell orders on behalf of outside customers in return for commissions

Stock Exchange an organization of individuals to provide an institutional auction setting in which stocks can be bought and sold

Stock Split stock dividend paid in additional shares to shareholders, thus increasing the number of outstanding shares

Stockholder (or Shareholder) owner of shares of stock in a corporation

Strategic Alliance arrangement (also called joint venture) in which a company finds a foreign partner to contribute approximately half of the resources needed to establish and operate a new business in the partner's country

Strategic Alliance strategy in which two or more organizations collaborate on a project for mutual gain

Strategic Goal goal derived directly from a firm's mission statement

Strategic Leadership leader's ability to understand the complexities of both the organization and its environment and to lead change in the organization so as to enhance its competitiveness

Strategic Management process of helping an organization maintain an effective alignment with its environment

Strategic Plan plan reflecting decisions about resource allocations, company priorities, and steps needed to meet strategic goals

Strategy broad set of organizational plans for implementing the decisions made for achieving organizational goals

Strategy Formulation creation of a broad program for defining and meeting an organization's goals

Strict Product Liability principle that liability can result not from a producer's negligence but from a defect in the product itself

Strike labor action in which employees temporarily walk off the job and refuse to work

Strikebreaker worker hired as a permanent or temporary replacement for a striking employee

Subsidy government payment to help a domestic business compete with foreign firms

Substitute Product product that is dissimilar from those of competitors but that can fulfill the same need

"Super Wi-Fi" Network a powerful Wi-Fi network with extensive reach and strong signals that flow freely through physical objects such as walls

Supermarket large product-line retailer offering a variety of food and food-related items in specialized departments

Supplier Selection process of finding and choosing suppliers from whom to buy

Supply the willingness and ability of producers to offer a good or service for sale

Supply Chain (or Value Chain) flow of information, materials, and services that starts with raw-materials suppliers and continues adding value through other stages in the network of firms until the product reaches the end customer

Supply Chain Management (SCM) principle of looking at the supply chain as a whole to improve the overall flow through the system

Supply Curve graph showing how many units of a product will be supplied (offered for sale) at different prices

Surplus situation in which quantity supplied exceeds quantity demanded

Survey research method of collecting consumer data using questionnaires, telephone calls, and face-to-face interviews

SWOT Analysis identification and analysis of organizational strengths and weaknesses and environmental opportunities and threats as part of strategy formulation

Syndicated Selling e-commerce practice whereby a website offers other websites commissions for referring customers

T

Tactical Plan generally short-term plan concerned with implementing specific aspects of a company's strategic plans

Talent Management the view that the people in an organization represent a portfolio of valuable talents that can be effectively managed and tapped in ways best targeted to organizational success

Tall Organizational Structure characteristic of centralized companies with multiple layers of management

Tangible Personal Property any movable item that can be owned, bought, sold, or leased

Tangible Real Property land and anything attached to it

Target Market the particular group of people or organizations on which a firm's marketing efforts are focused

Tariff tax levied on imported products

Task-Focused Leader Behavior leader behavior focusing on how tasks should be performed to meet certain goals and to achieve certain performance standards

Tax Services assistance provided by CPAs for tax preparation and tax planning

Technical Skills skills needed to perform specialized tasks

Technological Environment all the ways by which firms create value for their constituents

Telecommuting (or Teleworking) form of flextime that allows people to perform some or all of a job away from standard office settings

Telemarketing form of nonstore retailing in which the telephone is used to sell directly to consumers

Tender Offer offer to buy shares made by a prospective buyer directly to a target corporation's shareholders, who then make individual decisions about whether to sell

Theory X theory of motivation holding that people are naturally lazy and uncooperative

Theory Y theory of motivation holding that people are naturally energetic, growth-oriented, self-motivated, and interested in being productive

360-Degree Feedback performance appraisal technique in which managers are evaluated by everyone around them—their boss, their peers, and their subordinates

Time Deposit bank funds that have a fixed term of time to maturity and cannot be withdrawn earlier or transferred by check

Time Management Skills skills associated with the productive use of time

Time Orientation the extent to which members of a culture adopt a long-term versus a short-term outlook on work, life, and other elements of society

Time Utility providing products when customers will want them

Time Value of Money principle that invested money grows, over time, by earning interest or some other form of return

Title VII of the Civil Rights Act of 1964 forbids discrimination in all areas of the employment relationship

Top Manager manager responsible for a firm's overall performance and effectiveness

Total Quality Management (TQM) all activities involved in getting high-quality goods and services into the marketplace

Tort civil injury to people, property, or reputation for which compensation must be paid

Trade Deficit situation in which a country's imports exceed its exports, creating a negative balance of trade

Trade Show sales-promotion technique in which various members of an industry gather to display, demonstrate, and sell products

Trade Surplus situation in which a country's exports exceed its imports, creating a positive balance of trade

Training usually refers to teaching operational or technical employees how to do the job for which they were hired

Trait Approach to Leadership focused on identifying the essential traits that distinguished leaders

Trademark exclusive legal right to use a brand name or symbol

Traditional Individual Retirement Account (IRA) provision allowing individual tax-deferred retirement savings

Transactional Leadership comparable to management, it involves routine, regimented activities

Transformational Leadership the set of abilities that allows a leader to recognize the need for change, to create a vision to guide that change, and to execute the change effectively

Transportation activities in transporting resources to the producer and finished goods to customers

Trial Court general court that hears cases not specifically assigned to another court

Trust Services management by a bank of an estate, investments, or other assets on behalf of an individual

Turnover annual percentage of an organization's workforce that leaves and must be replaced

Two-Factor Theory theory of motivation holding that job satisfaction depends on two factors, hygiene and motivation

U

Uncertainty Orientation the feeling individuals have regarding uncertain and ambiguous situations

Unemployment the level of joblessness among people actively seeking work in an economic system

Unethical Behavior behavior that does not conform to generally accepted social norms concerning beneficial and harmful actions

United States–Mexico–Canada Agreement (USMCA) trade agreement signed by Canada, Mexico, and the United States in 2018 intended to promote trade among the three nations

Uniform Commercial Code (UCC) body of standardized laws governing the rights of buyers and sellers in transactions

Union Shop requires employees to join a union within a specified period after being hired

Unlimited Liability legal principle holding owners responsible for paying off all debts of a business

Unsecured Loan loan for which collateral is not required

Utility product's ability to satisfy a human want or need

V

Value relative comparison of a product's benefits versus its costs

Value Package a product that is marketed as a bundle of value-adding attributes, including reasonable cost

Value-Added Analysis process of evaluating all work activities, materials flows, and paperwork to determine the value that they add for customers

Variable Cost cost that changes with the quantity of a product produced and sold

Venture Capital private funds from wealthy individuals seeking investment opportunities in new growth companies

Venture Capital Company group of small investors who invest money in companies with rapid growth potential

Vestibule Training off-the-job training conducted in a simulated environment

Video Retailing nonstore retailing to consumers via home television

Viral Marketing type of marketing that relies on the Internet to spread information like a "virus" from person to person about products and ideas

Virtual Leadership leadership in settings where leaders and followers interact electronically rather than in face-to-face settings

Voluntary Arbitration a neutral third party (the arbitrator) dictates a settlement between the two sides, who have agreed to submit to outside judgment

Voluntary Bankruptcy bankruptcy proceedings initiated by an indebted individual or organization

VSAT Satellite Communications network of geographically dispersed transmitter-receivers (transceivers) that send signals to and receive signals from a satellite, exchanging voice, video, and data transmissions

W

Wage Reopener Clause clause allowing wage rates to be renegotiated during the life of the contract

Wages compensation in the form of money paid for time worked

Warranty seller's promise to stand by its products or services if a problem occurs after the sale

Warehousing physical distribution operation concerned with the storage of goods

Whistle-Blower employee who detects and tries to put an end to a company's unethical, illegal, or socially irresponsible actions by publicizing them

Wholesale Club bargain retailer offering large discounts on brand-name merchandise to customers who have paid annual membership fees

Wholesaler intermediary who sells products to other businesses for resale to final consumers

Wi-Fi technology using a wireless local area network

Wide Area Network (WAN) computers that are linked over long distances through telephone lines, microwave signals, or satellite communications

Wireless Local Area Network (Wireless LAN or WLAN) local area network with wireless access points

Wireless Wide Area Network (WWAN) network that uses airborne electronic signals instead of wires to link computers and electronic devices over long distances

Work Sharing (or Job Sharing) method of increasing job satisfaction by allowing two or more people to share a single full-time job

Work Slowdown labor action in which workers perform jobs at a slower than normal pace

Work Team groups of operating employees who are empowered to plan and organize their own work and to perform that work with a minimum of supervision

Workers' Compensation Insurance legally required insurance for compensating workers injured on the job

Workers' Compensation Coverage coverage provided by a firm to employees for medical expenses, loss of wages, and rehabilitation costs resulting from job-related injuries or disease

Workforce Diversity the range of workers' attitudes, values, beliefs, and behaviors that differ by gender, race, age, ethnicity, physical ability, and other relevant characteristics

World Bank UN agency that provides a limited scope of financial services, such as funding improvements in underdeveloped countries

World Trade Organization (WTO) organization through which member nations negotiate trading agreements and resolve disputes about trade policies and practices

World Wide Web branch of the Internet consisting of interlinked hypertext documents, or web pages

Y

Yellow-Dog Contracts requirements that workers state that they did not belong to and would not join a union

index

A

B

C

D

F

G

H

I

M

N

S

T

U

X

Y

Z